Social Work Practice

Social Work Practice

A Critical Thinker's Guide

Eileen Gambrill

Third Edition

OXFORD
UNIVERSITY PRESS

Oxford University Press is a department of the University of Oxford.
It furthers the University's objective of excellence in research, scholarship,
and education by publishing worldwide.

Oxford   New York
Auckland   Cape Town   Dar es Salaam   Hong Kong   Karachi
Kuala Lumpur   Madrid   Melbourne   Mexico City   Nairobi
New Delhi   Shanghai   Taipei   Toronto

With offices in
Argentina   Austria   Brazil   Chile   Czech Republic   France   Greece
Guatemala   Hungary   Italy   Japan   Poland   Portugal   Singapore
South Korea   Switzerland   Thailand   Turkey   Ukraine   Vietnam

Oxford is a registered trademark of Oxford University Press in the UK and certain other
countries.

Published in the United States of America by
Oxford University Press
198 Madison Avenue, New York, NY 10016

© Oxford University Press 2013

Library of Congress Cataloging-in-Publication Data
Gambrill, Eileen D., 1934-
   Social work practice : a critical thinker's guide / Eileen Gambrill. — 3rd ed.
      p. cm.
   Includes bibliographical references and index.
   ISBN 978-0-19-975725-1 (hardcover : alk. paper)
   1. Social service—United States.   2. Social case work—United States.   3. Social workers—United States.   I. Title.
   HV91.G325 2012
   361.3′20973—dc23
   2011041977

9 8 7 6 5 4 3 2 1
Printed in the United States of America
on acid-free paper

Contents

Preface vii
Acknowledgments xi

Part 1 Getting oriented

1. Social work: An introduction   3

2. Clients and services   22

3. Values, ethics, and obligations   41

Part 2 Thinking about knowledge and how to get it

4. Different views of knowledge   69

5. Critical thinking: Integral to evidence-based practice   94

Part 3 Thinking about problems and causes

6. Competing views of personal and social problems and their causes   117

7. Taking advantage of research findings about behavior and how it is influenced by the environment   141

Part 4 A decision-focused practice model

8. Problem solving and decision making: Integral to helping clients   165

9. Evidence-based practice: A decision-making process and philosophy   186

10. Posing questions and searching for answers   201

11. Critically appraising research: Thinking for yourself   221

Part 5 Getting started

12. A contextual assessment framework   247

13. Beginning: A practice guide   280

14. Engaging clients   317

Part 6 Relationship skills

15. Interpersonal helping skills   341

16. Handling challenging social situations   362

Part 7 Gathering and organizing information

17. Where to look: Deciding how to gather needed information   385

18. Observation: Learning to see   409

19. Reviewing resources and obstacles   425

20. Putting it all together   442

Part 8 Selecting plans and assessing progress

21. Selecting and implementing plans   465

22. Evaluating outcomes as integral to problem solving   489

23. Planning for endings   516

Part 9 Intervention options

24. Empowering clients: Providing information and skill building   529

25. Helping clients learn positive behavior change skills   548

26. Working with groups and families   566

27. Organizations and communities   583

Part 10 The long run

28. Maintaining skills and staying happy in your work   617

References   625
Index   669

Preface

Thinking critically about decisions that have life affecting consequences for clients is at the heart of this text. This book is for social workers who want to think critically about what they do, why they do it, and what outcomes result from services offered, and who wish to draw on practice and policy-related research in helping clients. It is for those who value thinking for themselves—those who want to dig beneath the surface of popular views of personal and social problems and beliefs about how to address them. Although some texts emphasize the importance of reflection, this text emphasizes the importance of critical reflection—a critical appraisal of points of view no matter what their source. History shows that basing practice and policy decisions on questionable criteria such as tradition (what's usually done), popularity (what most people do), or newness (what's the latest method), may harm rather than help clients and victimize rather than empower them.

Concern about decreasing avoidable suffering and helping clients to enhance the quality of their lives has been key in the core literature in social work. Clients deserve the best we have to offer. This text will help you to fulfill this obligation. It will do this in six main ways: 1. by highlighting important decisions and related uncertainties in making them, 2. by attending to key ethical issues such as involving clients as informed participants, 3. by integrating the personal and the political in emphasizing the importance of context, including public policies, 4. by taking advantage of theory and research in related areas including the helping process, human behavior and the environment, decision making and problem solving, and cultural differences, 5. by emphasizing the vital role of critical thinking in making sound decisions, and 6. by highlighting the importance of advocacy in recognizing and decreasing gaps between what is offered to clients and what is needed to attain outcomes clients value.

What Is New and What Is Not

This book updates content from the prior edition however the aims remain the same: to help social workers and their clients to make decisions that enhance the quality of clients' lives. Critical thinking skills are integral to evidence-informed practice.

In depth attention to critical thinking in social work and related venues is ever more important as resources shrink and propaganda in the helping professions grows, although it has grown so much and there has been so much exposure of conflicts of interests between pharmaceutical companies and academic researchers, that there is now a vigorous counterreaction as illustrated by websites such as Pharmedout.org. Propaganda is defined as encouraging beliefs and actions with the least thought possible (Ellul, 1965). Unique features of *Social Work Practice: A Critical Thinker's Guide* are maintained including chapters on knowledge (what it is and how to get it), on the origins and hallmarks of evidence-based practice, on critical thinking and its relationship to evidence-informed practice, and on guidelines for handling challenging social situations such as asking fellow staff: "Is there any evidence that this practice does more good than harm?" The deep interweaving of critical thinking throughout the text is one of its unique characteristics as it was in the first two editions.

As in the first two editions, a contextual, evidence-informed practice model built around the everyday decisions social workers make is described. Material is organized around key decisions such as deciding how to frame client concerns, what outcomes to focus on, what data to gather, how to integrate material from different sources, what criteria to consider when selecting practice methods, and how to evaluate progress. This text includes detailed assessment, intervention, and evaluation guidelines as well as a discussion of underlying assumptions and related controversies that should help you to use a planful approach in your work and to take advantage of corrective feedback regarding outcomes. The interrelationship among assessment, intervention, and evaluation is highlighted. Detailed guidance is provided in how to carry out important practice tasks, including involving clients as informed participants and choosing relevant, accurate assessment methods.

This third edition continues to draw heavily on social science knowledge related to social work and integrates this knowledge in relation to helping phases such as assessment and intervention so that both clients and social workers gain the benefits of available knowledge: clients by receiving effective methods (those likely to succeed in attaining outcomes they value) and avoiding ineffective or harmful ones, and social workers in having the satisfaction of helping them to do so. Examples of promising new directions and evidence-informed methods are included in this updated version as well as a description of the steps involved in the process of evidence-based practice. Common errors in making different kinds of decisions are described, drawing on literature in social psychology, problem solving, and decision making. Ethical issues are emphasized throughout the text including issues related to gaps between client needs and resources available. Chapters unique to this book, including attention to how problems are framed (what is a problem? who says it is a problem?), are updated. *Social work practice: A critical thinker's guide* is the only text that provides an in-depth description of basic behavioral principles that undergird the use of cognitive-behavioral methods and applied behavior analysis. As in earlier editions, a constructional practice model is

emphasized in which building on and enhancing client assets is emphasized.

The personal continues to be related to the political throughout, including the very definition of problems. This text describes a contextual practice model in which the reciprocal interactions between individuals and their environments are emphasized in accord with related research findings. Currently, psychiatric framing of problems-in-living is pervasive. Does such a framing maximize options for clients to enhance the quality of their lives? Does it reflect research findings regarding environmental challenges clients confront and options for addressing them including changes in policies, for example concerning housing and health care? In this book, you will find another narrative—one that focuses on the intersection of people and their environments and related research—one that guides the reader in constructing repertoires rather than eliminating them. The environments in which we live influence the risks we confront and the resiliencies we draw on. Advantages of a contextual practice model include its relationship to research findings, creatively searching for resources including client assets, and an emphasis on *functional* knowledge—information that decreases or reveals uncertainty about how to help clients. Major emphases include considering individual differences (including cultural ones), recognizing the role of environmental factors in contributing to client concerns and related circumstances, empowering clients by enhancing their influence over the quality of their lives, and evaluating outcomes in an ongoing manner so that timely changes in practices, programs, and policies can be made. You will find step-by-step assessment, intervention, and evaluation guidelines as well as description of valuable interpersonal skills.

Sources of information on the Internet including user-friendly web sites that organize and critically appraise information are drawn on in this third edition and readers are guided to useful sources. The Cochrane and Campbell Databases of Systematic Reviews continue to expand providing professionals with critical reviews of research related to specific clinical and policy questions. Even though these enterprises have been available for many years (the Cochrane Collaboration was initiated in 1992), I still find that master's degree students who have taken courses on evidence-based practice at well regarded social work programs have never heard of either of these invaluable sources. It is, and always has been, a struggle to "get the straight scoop." Indeed this challenge is related to another feature of this third edition—greater attention to conflicts of interest in the helping professions, including social work.

This third edition devotes greater attention to helping clients to become successful advocates by using social media and other technologies in pursuit of shared goals. In many ways it is a new world and we should offer clients the benefits of new options. New technology allows greater transparency of what is done to what effect. Greater attention has been given to propaganda in the helping professions. This includes helping clients to escape misleading definitions of problems-in-living as psychiatric disorders obscuring environmental circumstances such as disparities in health resources and educational opportunities. Such classification schemes obscure, rather than open, possibilities for growth and quality of life. Even though there is greater evidence for the interaction between genes and the environment and greater evidence for the influence of the environment on our health and psychological and existential well-being (including environmental pollutants imposed unjustly on the poor), there has been a growing biomedicalization of human miseries which is antithetical to the social reform history of social work; individual remedies are offered for systemic inequities.

This edition gives greater attention to avoidable ignorance, encouraged by the developing field of agnatology—the study of ignorance. One kind of avoidable ignorance consists of research reports describing the benefits of policies, programs, and practices on clients' quality of life that lie unused. Examples include showing low power people (such as children) how to change the behavior of high power people(such as teachers) and serving food family style rather than on individual plates to increase social exchanges of elderly residents of a retirement home. Appreciation of the role of avoidable ignorance in the helping professions illustrates the importance of drawing on literature in the past that has the potential to help clients. Thus readers will find not only current references in this text, but some that appeared many years ago that illustrate unused and underused knowledge. I have also included older references that describe the origin of ideas/programs.

As in earlier editions, controversial issues such as framing problems-in-living as psychiatric problems of individuals are highlighted. Other controversial issues include questions about "what is evidence?"and "what criteria should be relied on to promote practices and policies?" Problems discussed include ignoring research that could be of value to clients, overlooking uncertainty in decision making, ignoring outcomes clients value, not involving clients as informed participants, forcing unwanted "services" on clients, and overlooking harming done in the name of helping. Topics often ignored are discussed including coercion cloaked in professional jargon.

Changes Over The Past Years

Managed care has become more entrenched. The influence of the biomedical industrial complex on the framing of problems as biochemical disorders in need of treatment by medication has increased. Changes in social work include greater attention to diversity and international social work and the effects of globalization. Services for gay and lesbian clients and victims of domestic violence have received more attention. There has been greater attention to community influences reflected in concepts such as social capital and social exclusion and measures such as geographic information systems. Programs providing a safety net for struggling individuals and families have decreased in a long economic downturn and income disparities have grown. Devolution has increased—turning over responsibility for social service programs to the states from the federal level, as has the privatization of services. The diversity of the population continues to increase. There has been an expansion of the Internet and information that can be attained from this source to make informed decisions, including recognizing the uncertainty surrounding decisions. The Internet also provides a way to organize others with similar interests to seek desired changes, decrease inequities and reveal discrimination and abuses of power. Changes in access to information about the evidentiary status of claims encourage a rebalancing of power between professionals and clients in relation to knowledge shared—a rebalancing toward more democratic, participatory, transparent exchanges.

There has been greater attention to the gap between what is offered to clients and what could (and should) be provided and increased attention to harming in the name of helping and to candid recognition of errors and their causes. Little attention has been given to errors in social work, unlike medicine where it takes an entire book to review related research. Greater attention has been given to propaganda in the helping professions which is of key concern to social workers because they are the main providers of mental health services in the United States. It is important that they think for themselves in order to meet their ethical obligations to clients. All these developments highlight the importance of critically appraising claims about what is true and what is not. Evidence-informed practice requires this. The bottom line is how can social workers and clients make informed decisions? How can we protect ourselves and our clients from bogus claims that may result in the use of ineffective or harmful methods?

Key Assumptions

Being clear about assumptions helps readers to consider their advantages and limitations. And, it gives the writer a chance to emphasize themes in a text. In addition to the contextual focus and vital role of critical thinking skills, other assumptions include the following:

Ethical Obligations To Clients Should Be Placed Front And Center

Obligations described in our code of ethics provide a guide in difficult circumstances, as when needed resources are not available, for example to work together with others to try to increase needed resources. Informed consent requirements provide the grounding for questioning authorities who promote dubious claims and for being honest about what is done to what effect. Only if we know what we did and what effect it had can we improve future decisions. There is much more talk than action about social justice and offering clients the benefits of accurate assessment methods and effective interventions and involving clients as informed participants.

Uncertainty In Decision Making Is Inevitable

Acknowledging uncertainty allows us to take what steps we can to decrease it. Social work is a deeply interpersonal process with all the false paths that are possible in trying to understand other points of view. There are many ways communication can go wrong in spite of our best intentions. Recognizing this is vital for avoiding premature assumptions about what people mean, for example not checking out whether your understanding is accurate or not. Overlooking the uncertainty associated with decisions may have a number of unfortunate effects, such as encouraging overconfidence that may result in avoidable harm. It may result in misleading clients about how much change is possible via services at the individual or family level in contrast to seeking system-wide changes, for example in legislation.

We Can Reveal and Decrease Uncertainty by Drawing on Relevant Theories and Research Findings

We can decrease (or reveal) uncertainty by drawing on well-argued theories and related research as well as research concerning decision making, problem solving, and critical thinking. We can choose to really "see" clients and their circumstances.

Awareness of Our Personal Epistemology Is Important

Only if you reflect on your beliefs about what knowledge is and how we can get it can you examine your views about this important topic. Only if you are aware of the differences between science and pseudoscience are you likely to avoid quackery and fraud that can harm clients. Only by asking questions such as "Is this claim true?" will dubious claims be avoided. Mistakes provide important feedback about how to do better in the future. Identifying them and taking steps to decrease avoidable ones is vital. We can draw on the literature on errors and their systemic causes.

Courage is Needed to Question the "Obvious" and the Accepted

As you become immersed in your work with clients it is easy to become accustomed to making decisions that may not be best for clients. It is important to step back occasionally to see the big picture. Helping clients requires asking hard questions of professors and alleged "experts." Those who raise questions are not necessarily popular. It will take courage to raise questions others prefer to ignore; it will take caring about clients. Understanding the relationships between the personal and the political will contribute to your courage as will inspiration drawn from others including clients who acted rather than remained passive in the face of injustice.

Self-Awareness Is Vital

Only if we recognize our ignorance (for example, what we do not know) and our biases, are we likely to search for research findings that allow us to accurately inform clients about the uncertainty associated with decisions. Only if we are aware of our biases can we challenge them.

Compassion and Empathy for Others is Needed

Perhaps the greatest challenge as a social worker will be whether to see the difficult situations many people confront and to care enough to question current practices and policies and their effects and then act to try to improve client options. Some turn away from suffering. Others are overwhelmed by seeing too much and doing too little about it. But we can choose to see and ask questions that will encourage us to take what steps we can to help others. It is in this spirit that this book is written. It is written in the hope that readers will take what steps are possible to help clients make a better life for themselves, their family members, and their community and to have an even wider effect if possible. We can gain inspiration from the resiliency and creativity of clients themselves and work together with them to find solutions.

Being a Professional Calls for Lifelong Learning Skills

One of the joys and challenges of being a professional is continuing to learn. Social workers address a wide variety of problems in a wide variety of contexts. Taking advantage of related research findings requires learning-how-to-learn skills as well as information retrieval skills (getting needed information when you need it).

Approaches to this book

There are two ways to approach this book. Which is better depends on how soon you begin working with clients. One of the odd characteristics of social work education is that students often start working with clients before they are prepared to do so. If this applies to you, you could start with Chapter 12 and work back over the background chapters when you have time. The questions at the end of each chapter are included to help you to review related content knowledge, skills, and outcomes. You may find it helpful to review these sections before reading the chapters. Instructors may decide to use some chapters as required reading in other courses. For example Chapters 4 and 11 could be used in a research course and Chapters 6 and 7 in a course on Human Behavior and the Social Environment.

Social work offers an opportunity for lifelong learning used to help others—it is an opportunity worth pursuing.

Acknowledgments

I owe a debt to all those who have cared enough and have had the courage to question popular views of problems and claims of effectiveness about what helps people and what does not. We share an appreciation of criticism as the route to knowledge and avoidable ignorance. I have drawn liberally on practice and policy related research findings from varied sources as well as the questions, frustrations, and occasions for celebration of clients, practitioners, and students. I gratefully acknowledge the help of the University of California library system. In particular I want to thank Cris Guerrero and Craig Alderson at the School of Social Welfare Library. Thanks also to our computer support team Claudia Waters and Roger Edmond. I thank all those who have provided encouragement while the first edition of this book was in preparation, including Richard Dangel and Charles Cowger who provided valuable feedback on chapter drafts. I thank Maura Roessner and Nicholas Liu of Oxford University Press for their support in preparing this third edition. The resources provided by the Hutto Patterson chair contributed significantly to the completion of this new edition and I gratefully acknowledge this help. I thank those instructors who provided feedback about how to make material more useful. My grateful thanks to Sharon Ikami for her patience, good will, and word processing skills and to Gail Bigelow for her support, editorial skills, and caring about the world.

Part 1

Getting Oriented

1

Social Work: An Introduction

OVERVIEW This chapter offers a bird's-eye view of the profession of social work and suggests a philosophy of practice for providing services that clients value. The suggested philosophy is reflected in evidence-based practice and policy as described by their originators (e.g., Sackett, Richardson, Rosenberg, & Haynes, 1997). (See also Gray, 2001a; Straus et al., 2005.) The context of social work and its major functions are described, recurrent themes and controversies are highlighted, and current trends are discussed.

YOU WILL LEARN ABOUT

- Social work and social welfare

- The advantages and disadvantages of being a social worker

- The functions of social work and social welfare

- Social work as a profession

- The importance of a historical perspective

- The value of a global perspective

- A philosophy of practice

Social Work and Social Welfare

Some people have always needed help and some have always offered it. We all need help at times and, if we are fortunate and live in a society that is concerned about avoidable miseries, we may receive it. The institutions of social welfare are designed to fill vital gaps. However people differ in what they view as obligations of the state to minimize miseries and maximize opportunities for residents to thrive. These different values are reflected in public policies and legislation. Social welfare refers to the laws, programs, and services designed to provide benefits to people who require assistance in meeting their basic needs (Karger & Stoesz, 2009). Universal welfare programs such as Medicare and social security offer benefits to people in all income classes, whereas selective programs are designed solely for certain groups of people such as individuals falling below a certain income level. Popple and Leighninger (2002) organize social welfare services under three kinds of dependency, which they define as the inability to carry out expected social roles such as that of parent or employee.

1. Benefits for people who are economically dependent, including cash support programs and in-kind programs such as Medicaid and Medicare, subsidized housing, and food stamps.

2. Services for people who are dependent because they are unable to fulfill roles as perceived by themselves. Such assistance includes mental health services, family counseling, employment services, socialization services, and information and referral services.

3. Services for people who are dependent because they have not fulfilled roles as defined by others. These include probation and parole, child and adult protective services, and involuntary mental health services.

The term *welfare* is often associated with benefits for the poor. However, if it includes not paying full value for services/products and governmental aid, it provides benefits for the nonpoor as well. Examples of corporate welfare include subsidies and tax breaks for mining, aerospace, agricultural, high-tech, and finance industries (e.g., see Domhoff, 2007). Corporate welfare also includes supporting tobacco farmers and spending taxpayers' money to build roads in national forests that ease the way for private firms to gather timber. The United States has the third highest level of income inequality among "advanced economy" countries (Blow, 2011c, Feb. 18). Income inequality has increased greatly in the United States in the last decades. The top 1 percent of individuals control 42% of financial assets. One out of every three people in the United States lives very close to or in poverty; 49.1 million Americans are below the poverty line—$24,343 for a family of four (e.g., see DeParle, Gebeloff, & Tavernise, 2011; Tavernise & Gebeloff, 2011). Nearly one out of three children are poor in financial assets, which has repercussions for other assets such as access to health care and a good education. Immigrant children often face serious problems including poor education (The Future of Children, 2011). The top one-hundredth of 1 percent make an average of $27 million per household (http://www.motherjones.com, March–April 2011). (See also Krugman, 2011.)

Social work practice is carried out in public, nonprofit, and for profit agencies and includes direct services to individuals, families, groups, and communities, as well as supervision, management, and policy analysis (see Exhibit 1.1). Local, state, and federal governments fund public agencies that offer services mandated by legislation. Public agencies purchase services from nonprofit agencies, many of which are designed for particular groups such as children in foster care or the elderly. Public policies and related legislation are concerned with decisions about how resources should be distributed—how much money should be spent on which programs. Choices are influenced by values

EXHIBIT 1.1

Examples of Public and Nonprofit Organizations

AIDS Help & Prevention Plan
AIDS Legal Referral Panel
Alameda County Department of Social Services
Alameda County Probation Department
Asian Women's Shelter
Bay Area Information Referral System
Bayview Hunters Point Adult Day Health Center
Big Brothers/Big Sisters
Catholic Social Services
Center for Families in Transition
Center for Southeast Asian Refugee Resettlement
Children's Hospital, Social Service Dept.
Chinatown Youth Center
Coming Home Hospice
Community Board
Deaf Counseling, Advocacy & Referral Agency
East Bay Elder Abuse Consortium
Easter Seal Society
Eden Psychiatric Day Treatment Center
Emergency Services Network
Family Service Agency
Gay Rescue Mission
Gay Youth Community Coalition of the Bay Area
Health Care for the Homeless
Independent Living Resources
Japanese American Senior Center
Jewish Family and Children's Services
Korean Community Service Center
La Clinica de la Raza
Legal Aid Society
Marin Community Mental Health Services
On Lok Senior Health Services
Parent–Infant Neighborhood Center
Refugee Women's Programs
Suicide Prevention & Crisis Intervention
Teenage Pregnancy & Parenting Project
Travelers Aid Society
United Way of the Bay Area
Urban Indian Child Resource Center
Volunteers of America

and beliefs regarding individual responsibility, how free people are to influence the quality of their lives, and the obligation of the state to its citizens. Decisions about how resources should be distributed reflect differences of opinion about personal and social problems and their causes. Limited funding for welfare programs requires difficult decisions about service priorities. Recent budget deficits have resulted in calls to drastically cut many social programs including Head Start, housing for the elderly, in-home aid, planned parenthood, and aid to low-income mothers, babies, and children.

Social workers offer services for a broad range of circumstances, such as crises (e.g., sudden illness or death); alcohol or drug abuse; lack of housing, money, food, or medical care; transitions, such as retirement; and interpersonal problems, such as parent–child or marital conflict and child and elder abuse. Personal problems may require attention because they disrupt role performance (like that of parent). Examples include depression, anxiety, and stress from chronic poverty, illness, or disability. Conflicts with or a lack of responsiveness from agency personnel may be a problem. Immigrants and refugees may need assistance in establishing a new life in a new country. The goals of social work identified by the National Association of Social Workers in 1981 are still relevant today (see Exhibit 1.2). Social workers work with both poor and middle-class people. They offer services to both the homeless and families who abuse or neglect their children. They work in medical and psychiatric hospitals, old age homes, community mental health centers, employee assistance programs, probation departments, and group homes for troubled (or troubling) adolescents. Social workers can even be found in veterinary clinics (e.g., helping people who have recently lost a pet). Here are some examples.

Examples of Social Workers at Work

Joe is employed by a local outreach program for the homeless. Clients do not come to him; he goes to them. He spends much of his time talking and offering help to people who live on the streets. Lilly, a 28-year-old homeless woman, is typical of the people he sees. She has used cocaine for many years, supports herself through prostitution, and has been HIV positive for the past two years. He and his fellow staff often discuss different strategies for helping the homeless. Is outreach the best way? Joe

often wonders whether he is really helping anyone. As one of my students said to me, "No one prepared me for the clients I met in my work with the homeless." Joe works together with others in an advocacy group to increase the availability of low-cost housing for homeless families. He and his colleagues encounter many different beliefs about the homeless and related causes. They compete with many other groups that advocate for funds on behalf of their clients. The needs are great and the resources scant. Housing regulations and policies greatly affect his clients.

Jennifer works for a local community advocacy group, helping people with common concerns form coalitions. She spends time getting to know both community residents and staff in public and private community agencies. She finds that different people have different views of problems that are often held with great emotion. Jennifer helps the residents plan how to achieve their goals including attaining needed resources (usually more money) and, then, helps them to implement and evaluate the results. She keeps in touch with politicians and other advocacy groups. Her work requires her to make many decisions, such as which people to approach, how to approach them, how to win over reluctant participants, how persistent she should be, and how to keep up people's spirits when success is limited.

Tanya is employed in the emergency response unit of her city's child protective services. She investigates claims of child abuse and neglect and decides what action to take. Her decisions are typically based on one or two interviews. She is required to use her agency's risk assessment measure in making decisions. Tanya's caseload is large, and she has little time to linger over details before making a decision. She confronts limited resources including those in her own agency that would facilitate her work, such as access to computerized databases that would allow her to keep up with the latest research findings regarding decisions she and her clients must make. She receives little supervision and yearns for more detailed feedback that would help her to

---

EXHIBIT 1.2

Goals of Social Work

Goal	Goal	Goal	Goal
To enhance problem-solving, coping, and development	To link people with resources, services, and opportunities	To promote effective and humane service systems	To develop and improve social policy
Functions	**Functions**	**Functions**	**Functions**
Assessing Detecting/identifying Supporting/assisting Advising/counseling Advocating/enabling Evaluating	Referring Organizing Mobilizing Negotiating Exchanging Brokering Advocating	Administration and management development Supervision Coordination Consultation Evaluation Staff development	Policy analysis and development Policy advocacy

enhance her skills. Tanya is thinking of requesting a change to a unit that provides ongoing services to families. She is currently working with a group interested in establishing neighborhood service centers in low-income areas. The goal of these centers would be to increase client access to needed resources.

Barbara is the administrator of an inner-city homeless shelter for families in New York City, which houses about 60 families. She supervises a large staff and is responsible for the day-to-day running of the center. She and her staff have to decide when to enforce the rules and when not to. Running this center requires balancing the rights of people to do whatever they feel like doing and the rights of others to be protected from harm and abuse, not always an easy task. As in so many social work jobs, resources are scarce. In Barbara's case, this means that there are always more people who need housing than can be accommodated, requiring her staff to choose who will receive shelter and who will not. Limited counseling and material aid are provided by a community support program that is run by a local hospital. Barbara spends some of her free time writing proposals to the city's board of supervisors to fund more low-cost housing.

Ahnan works in a day care center for emotionally disturbed boys and girls between the ages of 12 and 18. His responsibilities include planning and carrying out treatment programs for each resident. He must decide when to use observation to gather information, when and how to observe relevant exchanges, what services to recommend, and how to evaluate his effectiveness. He and the other staff work closely together, holding weekly meetings during which they review each resident's progress in all areas (e.g., school, peer relationships, family relationships). Ahnan also helps run the weekly family counseling groups with the residents' parents and provides an anger management group for the residents. Ahnan enjoys these groups the most. He worries about some of the parents' lack of involvement and lack of follow-up services for youth.

Maria works at a clinic in San Francisco that provides medical services to the homeless. Many people do not keep their appointments, and she has no way of getting in touch with them, since most have no telephones. Many of her clients are IV-drug users and have AIDS. One night a week she visits a homeless shelter for families where she and a nurse offer help with medical and other concerns. A major part of Maria's job is to help clients obtain practical services they need. There are always more needs than resources to meet them.

Gail works in a hospice and visiting nurses agency that offers in-home help to clients who are terminally ill with cancer or other illnesses. She visits them at home, assesses their needs, and provides whatever help she can to address them, including helping them understand and meet their financial obligations. She also offers help to her clients' caregivers. Every day, Gail sees what happens to people with no health care insurance—some of whom spend their last days worrying about how they will pay their medical bills. She must make many decisions each day including choices about time scheduling (how to plan her day), what information to gather, and what service methods to use. Should Mr. Vincent be referred to a support group for HIV-positive clients? Should she suggest to Mrs. Martin that she attend a bereavement group? Does Mr. Kander need a home health aide and, if so, how many hours? Should she tell parents that their son is dying of AIDS? What is a good way to approach a potential service provider who has refused to offer needed resources? What can she do when needed services are not available? Gail struggles with many ethical decisions. Should she report a client's income that has not been declared? What should she do about a colleague who fails to visit clients as promised? What should she do about a client's intention to commit suicide?

Gloria works in an old-age home. Her responsibilities include helping the residents communicate more effectively with their relatives and the staff. For example, she may help residents get in touch with their relatives and plan how to enhance the quality of their exchanges. The residents usually do not come to her with concerns; rather, Gloria usually has to take initiative and discover what they would like, such as more frequent social contacts, answers to medical questions, and financial planning. Observing who does what, when, and to whom gives her opportunities to improve the quality of residents' lives. For example, when she first arrived at the center, she noticed that many residents looked bored, lonely, and depressed. She checked this out by talking to residents and staff. They confirmed her observations. She involved residents in planning recreational activities and group meetings. Gloria makes scores of decisions each day. Some involve ethical dilemmas. For example, should she contact the only living child of an elderly resident who is dying even though this resident has asked her not to do so? Does she have a right (or obligation) to try to involve bored, depressed residents in social and recreational activities, even though they have not asked to be included? What should she do about a staff member who makes nasty remarks about and patronizes the residents? How can she determine whether she is helping her clients? Gloria enjoys her work. She likes the freedom to choose what she does every day and gets pleasure from enhancing the quality of residents' lives. Her biggest worry is lack of resources. Additional staff are needed; little money is available for programs. She is working together with the residents and administrators to establish an ombudsperson program to mediate conflicts between staff and residents.

Joel is employed in program development and planning in a large social service agency. He and his fellow social workers make decisions about what programs to offer to fulfill their mandate to provide comprehensive services to those with mental health problems in the community. They must select criteria to use to guide selection in a context of competing bids for services, different views of personal and social problems and their causes, and scarce resources.

Ron is a social worker in an elementary school. Teachers refer students to him for "out-of-control" behavior and for concerns about child maltreatment and needed medical attention. He offers an anger management class for children who have difficulty controlling their aggressive behavior. He loves his job but often feels overburdened by the needs he sees and becomes angry at times when teachers do not seem to care about children. But he reminds himself that they too are overburdened.

Robert works in the employee assistance program of a large metropolitan hospital. He offers services to staff who seek his help with problems like depression, concerns about needle sticks (being stuck by a needle with blood from a patient), marital problems, problems between employees and supervisors, and substance abuse problems. Confidentiality is a key concern. Not even the supervisors of staff members who seek his help are informed about their visits, and his office is off-site to protect confidentiality. He makes decisions about what assessment methods to use, whether to involve significant others such as a partner of a patient who worries about contracting HIV, and what methods to use to help clients. Robert tries to keep up with practice-related research by attending workshops in areas of special interest to his clients, such as substance abuse and stress management. He enjoys the varied nature of his job and has improved the reputation of the social worker's role among staff in this large hospital. His main complaint is that there are not enough staff to provide services, which puts extra pressure on Robert and his fellow social workers.

In each of these examples, social policies and related legislation influence options. In each, inequities in access to resources may be directly related to problems clients confront such as poor quality schools, lack of affordable housing, lack of health care, limited recreational opportunities, and lack of protection from abuse or neglect. There is an intimate connection between personal and social problems and public policies and related legislation and the values they reflect (Mills, 1959). In each example we can ask, "Will resources available meet clients' needs?" All too often the answer may be "No." Group homes for troubled or troubling teenagers may provide neither promised treatment nor a safe environment in spite of repeated warnings of violations (Sontag, 2011a, b). Health services to gay/lesbian/bisexual/transgender youth may be insensitive to their needs. Our schools remain separate and unequal (Herbert, 2011). Agencies that purport to offer counseling regarding options for unplanned pregnancies may instead promote only one option.

The Advantages and Disadvantages of Being a Social Worker

Being a social worker has many advantages. One is that you get paid to help people. The Educational Policy and Accreditation Standards (2008) of the Council on Social Work Education describe the purpose of social work practice as follows:

> The purpose of the social work profession is to promote human and community well-being. Guided by a person and environment construct, a global perspective, respect for human diversity, and knowledge based on scientific inquiry, social work's purpose is actualized through its quest for social and economic justice, the prevention of conditions that limit human rights, the elimination of poverty, and the enhancement of the quality of life for all persons. (p. 1)

An interest in helping others draws many to social work. The benefits of helping are suggested in the quotes below from hospice staff and volunteers:

> One day my young patient with AIDS greeted me at the door with "I've been waiting for you to get here. I need the ray of sunshine and good cheer you always impart when you come to see me. I look forward to each of your visits." And with that he gave me a big hug. It made my day, and I felt good about everyone all day long—good and bad.

> One special note from a family read: "You made a difference to all of us. What could have been a terrible time for our family turned into something special. We have never been so close. Thank you." (Larson, 1993, p. 21)

Social reform functions of social work reflect an interest in minimizing injustices and avoidable suffering and related discriminatory and oppressive practices and policies including institutional racism, for example, providing higher quality services to white than to African American clients. Another advantage of social work is that you can continue to learn throughout your career. You may, for example, improve your skills in identifying client assets and tracking down research related to important decisions you and your clients make. A third advantage is flexibility in moving from one social work job to another. Many social workers who start out offering direct services move on to supervisory and administrative positions. Some transfer from one area of practice (working with the homeless) to another (working in a hospital emergency room). Other social workers combine a private practice with employment in a public or private agency.

One disadvantage of being a social worker is that you will probably not get rich. Some social workers supplement their salaries through private practice and consultation. Another disadvantage is that social workers sometimes are associated in the mind of the public with the poor and disenfranchised and, in their clients' minds, with the power of the state. You can counter this possible stigma by developing pride as a social worker based on helping people enhance the quality of their lives. A third and common disadvantage is that you may not have the resources needed to help clients, resulting in stress and disappointment.

The Functions of Social Work and Social Welfare

A historical and contextual view of social work and social welfare suggests three major functions: (1) relief of psychological distress and material need; (2) social control (e.g., maintaining social order and regulating the labor market); and (3) social reform (altering conditions related to psychological distress and material need). (See, for example, Trattner, 1999.) Recognizing these different, often conflicting functions will help you to understand the paradoxes in the field (such as statements of good intent not accompanied by action) and to identify resources and obstacles to helping clients. The ideas of Charity Organization Societies (COSs) and settlement houses that were imported from England to the United States emphasized these three functions to different degrees. Although there was a concern with eliminating poverty in both, they embodied quite different views of its causes. Staff in the COSs stressed individual responsibility. Friendly visitors visited the poor in their homes and listened and offered advice. The distribution of cash payments was discouraged. Mary Richmond, who was in charge of a COS, believed that it was important to identify the specific skills involved in providing charity to the poor. Her book, *Social Diagnosis,* was published in 1917. Those who worked in settlement houses pointed to environmental factors as the causes of poverty, such as unemployment, lack of health services, and poor quality housing. Religious ideas such as the Christian tradition influenced the development of charity and correction institutions (Leiby, 1978).

Relief of Psychological Distress and Material Need

In a broad sense, social welfare is designed to help people to function effectively in their social environment. This includes providing for basic survival needs (adequate nutrition, clothing, shelter, and medical care), and creating opportunities that enhance psychological well-being and social productivity (Federico, 1990, p. 25). The preamble of the NASW Code of Ethics states that "the primary mission of the social work profession is to enhance human wellbeing and help meet the basic human needs of all people, with particular attention to the needs and empowerment of people who are vulnerable, oppressed, and living in poverty. A historic and defining feature of social work is the profession's focus on individual wellbeing in a social context and the wellbeing of society" (NASW, 2008, p. 1). Helping may involve enhancing clients' knowledge and skills, as well as helping them obtain needed resources. It may require preventive efforts (e.g., school-wide anti-bullying programs), as well as altering agency practices that harm clients.

Societies throughout history have offered aid for practical problems such as lack of money, need for medical attention, shelter, food, and clothing (Morris, 1986). The expansion of social welfare in the United States from the early 1900s until recent cutbacks brought a change from volunteer to paid staff and use of social services by the middle class both to provide material aid and to relieve psychological distress. In 1965, Cloward and Epstein argued that expansion of entitlements and the increased demand for services by the middle class resulted in neglect of those who most need help and to a corresponding disinterest in environmental change. There have been dramatic changes over the past decades in American social policy. These include increased privatization and commercialization, retrenchment of services, and devolution (shifting programs from the federal to state governments). Income disparities continue to rise as does the percentage of families living in poverty. We live in an increasingly diverse society.

Social Reform

From the earliest days of social work, many social workers have stressed the need for social reform, believing that the lack of food, housing, health care, employment, and educational and recreational opportunities—not the unworthiness of individual persons—was responsible for social problems. "Fundamental to social work is attention to the environmental forces that create, contribute to, and address problems in living" (NASW, 2008). Jane Addams founded Hull House in Chicago in 1889. By 1911 there were hundreds of settlement houses in the United States. Settlement workers, who daily encountered environmental deprivation, emphasized reform. They also had a social control function. For example, settlement house staff socialized new immigrants into American customs, including ways of dressing (e.g., not wearing a "babushka"). Charity organizations also have been interested in pursuing social change:

> And especially in the way of social reform can such a society exercise its greatest influence. It can insist on open spaces in the city for the recreation of the poor.... It can prevent cruelty to children; preserve the dependent and neglected children from evil surroundings; it can institute "country weeks," and insure the prompt payment of wages. (McCulloch, 1879, speaking for the Associated Charities)

Gradually, private channels for relief to the poor, such as charity organizations, were replaced by public channels, such as departments of public welfare, which offered a range of services. For example, the Public Welfare Department of Dayton, Ohio, took responsibility for recreation, charity, correctional and reformatory institutions, disease control, and health needs. Individual distress was viewed as the concern of all people. D. Frank Garland (1916), the director of public welfare in Dayton, described the purpose of his department as "based on the principle that the welfare of all is the ultimate goal of the community.... For example,... [l]oss of employment is frequently due, not to the indifference of the individual workman, but to great industrial crises, or combinations and conditions in which workmen are allowed no vote" (Garland, 1916, p. 310). A key change was an increase in state-run mothers' aid programs. The Depression of the 1930s greatly increased the number and range of social workers' clients and emphasized the close connection between economic conditions and personal problems and the need for legislation on a broad level. President Franklin D. Roosevelt's New Deal legislation transferred the funding of social services from state to federal auspices. The Social Security Act was passed in 1935.

Some people believed that the new services were offered because of political reasons, as well as humanitarian purposes, to reduce discontent, win elections, and maintain the social system substantially unchanged. Social reform served many functions, including gaining political advantage over opponents (Katz, 1989). Some of these reform efforts served the needs of businesses (to protect and expand markets) and professional groups more effectively than the needs of those groups for which they were supposedly designed. Katz suggested that in order to secure low-paid workers, fast-food chains lobby legislators to pass bills requiring women on welfare to work. History shows that social reform has always been a struggle:

> If there is no struggle there is no progress. Those who profess to favor freedom and yet depreciate agitation, are men who want crops without plowing up the ground. They want rain without thunder and lightening. They want the ocean without the awful roar of its many waters.
>
> This struggle may be a moral one, and it may be a physical one, and it may be both moral and physical, but it must be a struggle. Power concedes nothing without a demand. It never did and it never will. Find out just what people will quietly submit to and you have found out the exact measure of injustice and wrong which will be imposed upon them, and these will continue till they are resisted with either words or blows, or with both. The limits of tyrants are prescribed by the endurance of those whom they oppress. (Frederick Douglass, West India Emancipation speech delivered at Canandaigua, New York, August 4, 1857, in *The Life and Writings of Frederick Douglass*, ed. P. S. Foner, Vol. 2, p. 437 [1950])

Social workers and many others advocated working to remedy inequities and to create a more just environment for all citizens. Unions sought equality of opportunity and tried to improve working conditions. Their efforts were often followed by violent attacks on union members (Boyer & Morais, 1994). Social work clients changed from supplicants to demonstrators and lobbyists, demanding help as a right. The lobbying efforts of elderly citizens brought about the indexing of Social Security under the Nixon administration. In the late 1960s, students in many schools of social work protested social service agencies' lack of commitment to their clients. During the 1980s, the individual change model and calls for professionalism rose to the fore, and the student protests and interest in courses on community organization ebbed. Recently there has been increased interest in such courses among students. However, related jobs are scarce. The NASW Code of Ethics calls on social workers to take action to forward social justice aims: "Social workers should promote the general welfare of society, from local to global levels, and the development of people, their communities, and their environments. Social workers should advocate for living conditions conducive to the fulfillment of basic human needs and should promote social, economic, political, and cultural values and institutions that are compatible with the realization of social justice" (NASW, 2008, Standard 6.01). So too, do Educational Standards emphasize this role.

"The purpose of social work is to 'promote human and community well being'" (EPAS, 2008, p. 1). The purpose "is actualized through its quest for social and economic justice, the prevention of conditions that limit human rights, the elimination of poverty, and the enhancement of the quality of life for all persons" (EPAS, 2008, p. 1). (See chapter 3, section on Social Justice for a discussion.)

Social Control

Social control is another function of social work and social welfare (Handler, 1973). It refers to encouraging adherence to social norms and minimizing, eliminating, or normalizing deviant behavior. Functions include protecting citizens from harm and reaffirming standards of morality (Conrad & Schneider, 1992, p. 7) (See also Foucault, 1973; Illich et al., 1978). Examples of formal social controls include laws, regulations, and actions by governmental representatives such as police and social workers. Foucault's (1979) notion of governmentality includes not only state politics, but the assumption of power over our very bodies as reflected in the ever-growing biomedical and wellness industries (e.g., biopower reflected in biomedicalization, Clarke et al., 2010). Public health regulations are designed to protect others from the spread of disease and, in so doing, often limit discretion. Institutions concerned with social control include the educational, social welfare, criminal justice, public health, and medical systems and the mass media. Moral values are reflected in the design, practices, and policies of these institutions and related legislation. For example, Handler and Hasenfeld (1991) argue that moral assumptions about clients are reflected in the classification system designed to distinguish between clients who are required to participate in work activities and those who are not. Examples of informal social control include internalized beliefs and norms and influence in face-to-face exchanges such as ridicule, praise, and ostracism.

Mimi Abramovitz argues that since colonial times, social welfare policies have treated women differently based on the extent to which their lives conformed to certain family ethics (1988, pp. 3–4). (See also the discussion of the "feminization of poverty," in DiNitto, 2000.) Based on his review of case records, Leslie Margolin (1997) contends that social work in public agencies is engaged mainly in political surveillance—keeping track of marginal and common people in their homes. (For a critique, see Wakefield, 1998.) Social workers are integrally involved in defining problems and deciding what should be done about them: what is healthy (good) or unhealthy (bad). It is they who investigate and keep records, which clients typically do not see and thus cannot correct. An ever-lengthening list of behaviors are defined as "mental illnesses" requiring the help of "experts" (see chapters 6 and 12). Women are the main recipients of such labels. Social workers provide most of the mental health services in the United States, and in this role, use the psychiatric classification system (*American Psychiatric Association (2000)*), which classifies hundreds of (mis)behaviors as mental illnesses. (See discussion in chapter 12.) The social control functions of social workers can be seen in their roles as probation and parole officers and as child protection workers when they remove children from neglectful or abusive parents, in protective services for the elderly when they arrange for conservatorship, and in mental health agencies when they recommend hospitalization or outpatient commitment. An interest in social control is reflected in concerns on the part of "friendly visitors" in the Charity Organization Societies to distinguish between those who deserve aid and those who do not.

> [A] discrimination must be made between those who are helpless from misfortune and those whose misery arises from their own default; and that to aid the willingly idle man or woman, or anyone who can help himself, is in the highest degree hurtful to the person aided and to society at large. Its [charity's] more immediate duty has been to extend aid to that class of worthy and industrious poor, who, by reason of sickness, accident, loss of employment or of property, have fallen temporarily behind, and to rescue them from permanent pauperism by timely assistance; to extend a helping hand to widows with dependent children, to aged and infirm people partly able to help themselves, to single women when work suddenly ceases; and, above all, to so do this [in a way] to prevent the injurious and wasteful results of indiscriminate giving. (McCagg, 1879, p. 147)

Katz argues that welfare has often been designed "to promote social order by appeasing protest or disciplining the poor" (1989, p. 33). (See also Katz, 1996.) A policy's social control function is not necessarily obvious. In *Punishing the Poor*, Wacquant (2009) argues that both social services and the criminal justice system have a key role in the "behavioral control of the marginal," including African American youth who grow up in ghettoes providing limited opportunities for pursuit of approved activities. The language of caring and nurturance may obscure manipulative and coercive practices (Margolin, 1997; Szasz, 1994; see also Handler, 1973).

The argument that social work helps to maintain a capitalistic economic system that benefits a few to the detriment of many by containing dissatisfaction of disadvantaged and oppressed groups such as poor inner-city residents has long been made. For example, Galper (1975) suggests that a major function of social work is to keep the economy working smoothly by controlling those with limited access to resources and providing a labor force. George and Wilding (1984) suggest that social services contribute to political stability in five ways:

1. Through apparent efforts to alleviate problems that might result in serious discontent and that could be used to criticize the current economic and political structure.

2. By defining social problems as caused by individual, family, or group factors rather than by structural and economic factors. A case approach to problems obscures political and economic causes and encourages a fragmented view. Clients' problems are dealt with one at a time (education, health, housing) and are delegated to a different group of professionals.

3. By promoting values and behaviors that support political stability. Schools reward conformity, effort, and achievement and downplay sources of inequity and conflict in economic and social life (Merelman, 1975).

4. By supporting authority and related hierarchical systems (e.g., keeping clients waiting for long periods in drab waiting rooms). The educational system helps legitimate inequality (hierarchy) by claiming to provide equal opportunity. Then if someone is not successful, the fault is with the individual (Tapper & Salter, 1978).

5. By replacing class conflict with group conflict. Funds for services are allotted by group (elderly, at-risk infants, the homeless), thereby obscuring the shared underclass status of many clients and the political and economic conditions contributing to this status. (See Webster, 1992.)

All five factors decrease the likelihood of political protest. This analysis from 35 years ago is, if anything, even more sound today as reflected in the ever greater inequality of income in the United States (Carlson & England, 2011) and the ever greater framing of problems-in-living as "mental illnesses" requiring the help of experts (often medication). (See chapter 6.)

Controversial Issues

A moment's reflection on the different functions of social work highlights the potential for conflicts and contradictions, deliberate mystification regarding the causes of personal and social problems, and paternalistic approaches to clients. The goal of social control competes with that of helping clients. This is a common dilemma in child welfare settings in which workers are mandated both to protect children and to help parents who have harmed (and may continue to harm) their children. They serve as double agents (i.e., of the state and of the client). The examples of social workers' everyday work given earlier in this chapter illustrate the variety of clients social workers see, the different venues in which they see them, and the different functions of social work: helping, social reform, and social control. These three functions often conflict, as in child protective services. Social control aims are often disguised as concerns about helping clients as can be seen in the history of institutionalized psychiatry (e.g., Szasz, 1994; Valenstein, 1986). Medical sociologists and anthropologists describe ways in which health care systems support prevailing cultural values (e.g., Loeske, 1999; Lock, 1993). Negotiating the optimal balance between individual freedom and the protection of others has been the subject of treatises both small and large.

Conflicting interests and related goals lead to different views of personal and social problems and how they should be addressed. The biomedical industrial complex encourages viewing personal problems such as anxiety and depression as "mental illnesses" requiring medication (e.g., Clarke et al., 2010; Conrad, 2007). Exposure of related conflicts of interests between academic researchers and this industry are common (Lo & Field, 2009). For example, Dr. Joseph Biederman of Harvard University Psychiatry Department, promoted the labeling of preschool age children as having "pediatric bipolar disorder" and recommended prescription of risperidone, an antipsychotic. He said that his ties to the company producing the medication had no influence on his work. He failed to report 1.6 million dollars he obtained from the company to his university (e.g., see Angell, 2009). Social workers provide most of the mental health services in the United States. They are influenced by aggressive advocacy of biomedical solutions to personal and social problems. Some people believe that welfare programs are too extensive, that they encourage dependence on government aid and diminish individual responsibility. Some believe that the programs developed during President Lyndon Johnson's War on Poverty were misguided. In his controversial book *Losing Ground* (1984), Charles Murray argues that the social policies of the 1960s and 1970s principally involved the transfer of funds from some groups of poor people to other groups of poor people and harmed the very people they were designed to help.

Some scholars argue that American welfare has always been inadequate, cruel, and irrational, pointing out that public social welfare expenses make up a smaller percentage of the United States' gross domestic product than they do in other wealthy nations and that resistance to social welfare programs is greater in this country (e.g., Katz, 1989). Handler and Hasenfeld (2007) argue that the focus on work for welfare clients continues "the age old themes of deterrence and reformation"—the assumption that clients have a "poor work ethic" (p. 3). Both changing political climates and budget deficits have resulted in less generous welfare provisions in many countries eroding safety nets. America is still the only Western democracy that does not have national health insurance. Many scholars see social welfare programs as focusing on the symptoms of inadequate social conditions rather than the conditions that create the problems (e.g., Piven & Cloward, 1993). For example, if the unemployment rate among urban inner-city black youth were not so high, urban crime and drug use might not be so prevalent in this population (Wacquant, 2009). The Bertelsmann Stiftung Foundation of Germany reported selected measures regarding social justice in the Organization for Economic Cooperation and Development (OECD). This indicated that the United States is fifth from the bottom. Measures used in this index include overall poverty

prevention, overall poverty rate, child poverty rate, senior citizen poverty rate, income and equality, pre-primary education, and health rating. The only countries below the United States were Greece, Chile, Mexico, and Turkey (Social Justice in the OECD: How member states compare. Governance Indicators, 2011, http://bertelsmann-stiftung.de)

Some people believe that social workers have no business doing psychotherapy, that it distracts them from helping clients build communities (Specht & Courtney, 1994). Others contend that psychotherapy is a legitimate role of social work (Wakefield, 1992). Whether it is or is not depends on how psychotherapy is defined, what other levels of change are pursued (e.g., in policy), and on beliefs about the purpose of social work and social welfare. As always, a key question is: "Who profits and who loses from a particular point-of-view?" Exploring who profits and who loses from a belief, policy, or procedure often reveals mismatches between words (intent) and outcome. Leroy Pelton (1989) sees the child welfare system's focus on investigation, blame, and subsequent child removal as diverting attention from the problems of poverty and its effects on children and from making fundamental changes in our social, economic, and public welfare system. (See also Pelton, 2008.) (Many others emphasize similar points, e.g., see Allan, Pease, & Briskman, 2010.)

Yet another controversy concerns what criteria to use to choose practices and policies. Should we rely on popularity or tradition (what is usually done)? Do these provide sound guides for decisions? Or should we follow ethical guidelines described in professional codes of ethics and Educational Policy and Accreditation Standards (EPAS, 2008) requiring an integration of research and practice—practice-informed research and research-informed practice (EP 2.1.6)? Other controversies include how honest to be with ourselves and with clients about harming in the name of helping and the lack of information about the effectiveness of most practices and policies. Here too, ethical codes provide direction. (See section on Informed Consent in chapter 3.) Lack of informed consent in everyday practice shows this to be a controversial issue. Also, how honest should we be with clients about controversies regarding how problems are framed (e.g., labeling (mis)behaviors of children as indicating a mental illness). (See chapter 6.)

Social Work as a Profession

Certain occupations—such as social work—have been transformed into professions, which Abbott defines as "exclusive occupational groups applying somewhat abstract knowledge to particular cases" (1988, p. 8). Professionals are expected to offer certain services in a competent manner. All professions claim special knowledge and skills to help clients achieve certain ends. This knowledge supposedly makes those with certain degrees "experts" in solving certain kinds of problems. The Council on

Social Work Education, formed in 1952, serves as an accrediting body for schools of social work. Degrees in social work include the bachelor's (BSW), master's (MSW), and doctorate (Ph.D.). As of 2009, there were 442 BSW and 168 MSW and 71 Ph.D. programs in the United States (http://www.cswe.org). Although the bachelor's degree is the entry-level social work degree, many positions require a master's degree, as well as a state license. Master's degree programs often are divided into problem-area specializations (e.g., mental health, aging, children and families, and health) and service-level specializations (e.g., direct practice with individuals, families, or groups and management and administration). Social work doctoral programs are for students who wish to do research or to teach or who want advanced practice knowledge and skills.

The National Association of Social Workers (NASW) was founded in 1955. It holds conferences and publishes a monthly periodical (*NASW News*), as well as journals including *Social Work,* which is distributed to all members. In 1970 social workers with a BSW degree were permitted to become full members of NASW. Other social work organizations include the National Association of Black Social Workers (NABSW), National Association of Puerto Rican Social Service Providers (NAPRSSP), and National Indian Social Worker Association (NISWA). NASW has 145,000 members (NASW web page). Its functions include "promoting the professional development of its members, establishing and maintaining professional standards of practice, advancing sound social policies for the betterment of the nation, and providing other services that protect its members and enhance their professional stature" (Barker, 2003, p. 287). NASW established the Academy of Certified Social Workers (ACSW) in 1962, whose members must have an MSW or doctorate from an accredited school, two years of supervised field time, or 3,000 hours of part-time practice experience. NASW maintains a National Register of Clinical Social Workers and offers a diplomate in clinical social work to eligible applicants. Do social workers with this credential offer better services compared to those without them?

The Role of Professions in a Society

In addition to providing help with certain kinds of problems, professions also have political and economic functions and interests. "No matter how disinterested its concern for knowledge, humanity, art, or whatever, the profession must become an interest group to at once advance its aims and to protect itself from those with competing aims. On the formal associational level, professions are inextricably and deeply involved in politics" (Friedson, 1973, pp. 29–30). The public mental health system is a huge industry consuming billions of dollars of taxpayers' money. Recognizing the political and economic functions of the profession helps to account for their vague codes of ethics (e.g., they serve both a public relations and an ideological role) and exaggerated claims of expertise and success (to gain public and legislative support), which can be seen in the ongoing battles to protect and expand "turf" (e.g., between psychologists and psychiatrists).

Professional status is not necessarily based on demonstrations of effectiveness (Goode, 1960). This is true of social work, as well as other professions, such as medicine. For example, midwifery was officially discredited at the beginning of the twentieth century when it was replaced by obstetric care, even though midwives had lower rates of stillbirths and puerperal sepsis than did the (male) physicians (Ehrenreich & English, 1973). The evolution of professions is a result of their interrelationships, and these interrelationships are influenced by the manner in which different occupational groups control their knowledge and skills. Abbott (1988) describes how different professions redefine problems and tasks in order to ward off "interlopers" and enlarge their jurisdiction to new problems. For example, "psychiatrists in the twenties tried to seize control over juvenile delinquency, alcoholism, industrial unrest, marital strife, and numerous other areas" (p. 23). (See also Larson, 1977.)

Understanding how professions develop and influences on them will help you to work toward changes that will improve services within your professional organization.

Controversial Issues

Not all social workers thought professionalization was a good idea. Many staff in the newly developed public agencies "saw in professionalism a defense of status, not of skills and proficiency" (Ehrenreich, 1985, p. 113). They attempted to develop a practice model that gave the environment a central role and contended that the concern with professionalism distracted social workers from community organizing and client advocacy, and directed them toward individual treatment approaches. Another controversy is whether credentials (e.g., licenses, degrees) protect clients. In *House of Cards: Psychology and Psychotherapy Built on Myth* (1994a), Dawes argues that licensing gives the public only the illusion of protection, but does serve the economic interests of professionals. Based on research showing that nonprofessionals are as successful as professionals in helping clients with a variety of problems, he argues that possession of a degree or "experience" does not ensure a unique domain of knowledge or a unique degree of success in helping people. That is, credentials may not be accompanied by a track record of success in resolving certain kinds of problems (see also Christensen & Jacobson, 1994). Authors such as Peter Breggin (1997) and Thomas Szasz (1987) argue that professional helpers often harm rather than help by unnecessarily depriving people of their freedom (e.g., locking them up in mental hospitals), undermining their ability to help themselves (e.g., only an expert can help), and injuring them in the name of helping (e.g., causing irreversible damage by using neuroleptics). (See also Cohen & Timimi, 2008; Whitaker, 2010; and the website of the Citizens Commission on Human Rights International).

Indeed, as a result of professional intervention, complaints may get worse or losses may occur that otherwise would not. For example, in a comparison of intensive services provided by social workers to frail elderly clients and the usual agency procedures, it was found that mortality was higher in the group receiving the former (Blenkner, Bloom, & Nielsen, 1971). Studies of decision making in professional contexts reveal a variety of avoidable errors including ratcheting (adhering to a particular point of view despite evidence that it is wrong) and templating (inappropriately applying correlational data to individual clients) (Howitt, 1992). Peter Breggin suggests that "mental health problems, led by psychiatry, have rushed into the void left by the default of the family, the schools, the society, and the environment" (1991, p. 275). He notes that blaming child victims of neglectful or abusive histories by diagnosing, drugging, and hospitalizing them takes "the pressure off the parents, the family, the school, and the society" (p. 275). (See also Timimi, 2008.)

Other ongoing controversies concern the balance between client rights and those of professionals, for example, concerning being accurately informed about the evidentiary status of recommended practices and policies. This concern is related to differences of opinion about the degree to which transparency is important, for example, are social workers obligated to be candid with clients about the uncertainty involved in making life-affecting decisions and views about the causes of behavior. Other ongoing controversies concern funding; Who should fund what services and to what extent? How should scarce resources be distributed? What should the balance be between managerial control over resource distribution and influence by clients and professionals? Trends that have contributed to the interest in evidence-based practice and policy include increased availability of information revealing avoidable harming in the name of helping and increased emphasis on rights of clients to be accurately informed. Decreased deference to authority may both contribute to and result from these trends.

The Importance of a Historical Perspective

A historical view, whether of a profession, policy, agency, community, problem, group, family, or individual, lends a depth of understanding that may otherwise not be possible. It reveals misguided beliefs and actions (e.g., *The March of Folly* by Barbara Tuchman, 1985) and hidden knowledge (avoidable ignorance). It illustrates the power of words and ideas to sway others and to wield influence in ways that may limit freedom and inflict harm. Consider the successful use of propaganda in pre–World War II Germany. Consider also propaganda distributed to consumers and practitioners by pharmaceutical companies and academic researchers paid by them. Until recently, these concerning conflicting interests were mostly hidden (Gambrill, 2012a). It shows the relentless redefinition of more and more common moods and behaviors as mental illness, which benefits the pharmaceutical industry, the *DSM* industry, and the mental health professions. It is important to remember that the General Assembly of the state of North Carolina at the session of 1830–1831 passed an act prohibiting the teaching of slaves to read. This act asserted that "the teaching of a slave to read and write has a tendency to excite dissatisfaction in their minds, and to produce insurrection

and rebellion to the manifest injury of the citizens of the state." History reveals patterns of discrimination including racism, classism, and sexism, as well as the ideologies that mask them (See for example Hook & Eagle, 2002; Kuno & Rothbard, 2002; Ponce et al., 2010; Wasserman et al., 2007).

History reveals that patterns of discrimination against many groups continue as shown, for example, in the recent report by the United Nations General Assembly on Discriminatory laws and practices and acts of violence against individuals based on their sexual orientation and gender identity (Human Rights Council, November 11, 2011). Studies of the history of housework highlight the role of economic profit in influencing even household work (Oakley, 1976). A historical perspective can help us to avoid false paths and be wary of potential harmful consequences and coercion involved in pursuing grand untested proposals for social change (utopias) rather than pursuing small-scale changes (Popper, 1961). Without "the long view," you may mistakenly assume there has been (and is) agreement about what is best, what is true. You may discover that ideas that you now accept as self-evident were rejected as misguided in other times. Concepts you may view as central may not be present in other cultures. A historical perspective combined with valuing critical discussion can help us to free ourselves from prejudice and error and to view our ideas not as inherent or self-created, but as influenced by the particular culture that surrounds us.

A historical view allows us to judge how far a field has advanced, stayed the same, or regressed. Do we know more today than we did a decade ago about how to help the unemployed, the homeless, families that abuse and neglect children, or people who drink too much? In his provocative essay "The End of Social Work" (1997), David Stoesz argues that social work as a profession has failed to make the transition to the postindustrial era. He and his colleagues published a withering critique of social work education documenting concerning problems such as open enrollment (admitting all students who apply to a program) (Stoesz, Karger, & Carrilio, 2010). History highlights the shifting balances in the profession regarding reform and control goals. A historical perspective will help us to recognize old functions in new guises, such as the traditional role of the social worker as the middle person between the rich and the poor, reflected in the competing interests between control and reform. Being familiar with the history of a profession will help you to recognize recurrent debates (e.g., how to classify people, the effects of welfare on the work ethic, and government's obligation to those in need). It will help you to recognize continuities between current approaches and past trends. For example, the emphasis on the role of the environment in creating and maintaining problems reflects a long-term theme in social work that has ebbed and flowed over the years. It may help us to avoid mistakes (e.g., Costello, 2003). A historical perspective will remind you that the struggle for human rights is ongoing and requires constant attention and advocacy (e.g., Farmer, Nizeye, Stulac, & Keshavjee, 2006). Key ideas in the declaration of human rights include human dignity, nondiscrimination, civil, economic, social, and cultural rights, and solidarity rights (Wronka, 2012).

The Value of a Global Perspective

A global perspective reveals how events in one part of the world such as free trade agreements and economic turmoil (reflected in the financial meltdown of 2008 in the United States), affect what happens in other locales. (See Healy & Link, 2012.) Violations of human rights in one part of the world such as buying young girls from poor families to serve as prostitutes in other countries create injustices in other countries. (See EPAS, 2008, 2.1.5 in Appendix A.) In "The Little Slaves of the Harp," Zucchi (1992) describes how poor families in Italy sold their children to "padrones" who took these children to large cities such as London and made them beg for money, using their little harps. State crimes in some countries affect residents of other countries (Chambliss, Michalowski, & Kramer, 2010). A global perspective often reveals that what we assume to be universally true is not, that what we take for granted as moral and ethical ways of behaving are not similarly viewed in other cultures and countries, and that what is viewed as a problem differs in different societies.

Service systems differ in various countries; for example, Canada and the United Kingdom have had national health insurance for decades. Portugal decriminalized all drugs including cocaine, heroin, and marijuana in 2001 (Greenwald, 2009). As a result, there was a decrease in problematic use, drug-related harms, and entry into the criminal justice system (Hughes & Stevens, 2010). Programs developed in one part of the world are increasingly used in other parts of the world such as microlending (Tice & Long, 2009). Karl Popper (1994) views cultural clashes as essential to knowledge development. More developed countries can learn from developing countries. (To explore the global context, see, for example, Gray et al., 2008, Social Workers across Nations (SWAN) and *Social Development Issues,* a journal sponsored by the International Consortium for Social Development.)

A Philosophy of Practice

Is a professional someone who applies special knowledge in a framework that honors the ethical codes of that profession? Is it someone who helps clients achieve outcomes they value and/ or someone who has successfully completed an MSW degree in social work and is licensed? Is it someone with all these characteristics? Different beliefs about what it means to be a professional influence how helpers act in their exchanges with clients. Some characteristics are more likely than others to avoid harm and increase the likelihood of helping. This is why a philosophy of practice is important. Philosophy is the study of what is right to do and believe and on what basis beliefs and actions should be selected. *Webster's New World Dictionary* (1988) defines philosophy as "a particular system of principles for the conduct of life." Philosophy is relevant to everyone because life requires making decisions that involve moral and ethical issues.

All men and all women are philosophers. If they are not conscious of having philosophical problems, they have, at any rate, philosophical prejudices. Most of these are theories which they take for granted: they have absorbed them from their intellectual environment or from tradition. Since few of these theories are consciously held, they are prejudiced in the sense that they are held without critical examination, even though they may be of great importance for the practical actions of people, and for their whole life. (Popper, 1992, p. 179)

John Dewey (1933) emphasized philosophy as criticism, as thinking reflectively and carefully about questions and issues.

The Importance of a Philosophy of Practice

A philosophy of practice involves three interrelated areas: ethics (e.g., How should I act?), epistemology (What is knowledge and how can I get it?), and technology (What tools should I use and how should I evaluate the results?). The purpose of a philosophy of practice is to increase the likelihood that clients receive effective service and are not harmed. It will help you to act consistently in accord with goals you value and can provide a source of renewal from the challenges of practice in a time of scarce resources. It will help you to review to quality of the education in social work you receive. (For a critique see Stoesz, Karger & Carrilio, 2010). The hallmarks suggested here guided selection of content in this book and complement the philosophy of evidence-based practice as described by its originators (see chapter 9). Ethical obligations to clients, as well as a vision of a better world, provide invaluable guides especially in challenging circumstances. The first three (being responsible for decisions made, helping clients, and avoiding harm) are key ones from which the others follow. These others have three interrelated sources: (1) what logically follows from the first three, such as making informed decisions; (2) research findings about problem solving and decision making, for example, corrective feedback is needed; and (3) research describing common errors in decision making such as ignoring relevant data (e.g., ignoring gaps between personal beliefs and available problem-related knowledge). The philosophy described complements Educational Policy and Accreditation Standards (2008) of the Council on Social Work Education (shown in the Appendix to this chapter).

1. *Professionals are responsible for the decisions they make.* The examples given earlier highlight the central role of decision making in social work. This includes deciding how to frame problems, what interventions to use, what criteria to use to select them (e.g., popularity, practice-related research findings), and how to evaluate progress. Taking responsibility for decisions is basic to accountability to clients. This guideline requires you to examine excuses used for mistakes and poor quality services. Some are justified and some are not (McDowell, 2000). Some social workers I talk to, students as well as experienced social workers, tell me they do not make

decisions. But they do, and only by accepting responsibility for them are they likely to honor ethical obligations to clients. Part of this responsibility is gathering needed information regarding the evidentiary status of different practices and policies. Do they do more good than harm?

2. *Services help clients and their significant others attain outcomes they value and enhance client assets.* Possible outcomes include: (a) clients acquire valued outcomes; (b) they are worse off than before; and (c) there is no change. It is important to distinguish between a feeling of helping and actually helping clients (e.g., feeling empowered and actually being empowered). This highlights the importance of achieving both aims. This also emphasizes the vital role of respect for clients and use of effective relationship skills, without which, helping is less likely to take place. Clients should leave having more rather than less and this includes valuable assets that they can draw on. The contextual perspective described in this book emphasizes the importance of identifying and building on client strengths, including useful problem-solving skills and loving social relationships. (See, for example, chapters 12 and 24.) The resilience and courage clients show in the face of adversity and related suffering is often striking and should be acknowledged.

The NASW Code of Ethics lists service as its first value: "Social workers' primary goal is to help people in need and to address social problems." Focusing on helping clients attain outcomes they value will help you to avoid getting sidetracked into pursuit of outcomes they do not value or pursuit of fine-sounding but impossible aims. "I stress a practical approach: the combating of evils, of avoidable suffering and of avoidable lack of freedom (by contrast with promises of a heaven on earth)" (Popper, 1992, p. 90). And, clients' interests must be balanced against the rights of others to be protected from harm and to pursue goals they value. Protecting some clients may require removing opportunities from others, such as the opportunity to abuse or neglect children or adults. Clients make decisions about how hard to work to achieve their goals. Barbara Simon (1994) argues that paternalism slips in when practitioners work harder than their clients to remedy troubling situations.

3. *Clients are not harmed.* Enhancing the welfare of clients entails avoiding harm. Not harming also emphasizes the vital role of positive regard for clients and effective relationship skills (e.g., avoiding negativity). Professionals often assume that they must act, and clients often expect action. It is easy to assume that taking some action may be best when it may not be. The history of the helping professions is partly a history of harm done in the name of helping (e.g., Sharpe & Faden, 1998; Szasz, 1994). For example, adolescents have been institutionalized for the treatment of substance abuse even though there was no evidence that institutionalization was effective (Schwartz, 1989). Caring is not enough to protect people from harm and to maximize the likelihood that they

will receive help. Rather than creating an environment in which residents can acquire skills that improve the quality of life, residential settings may create counter-habilitative conditions, such as increased dependency and isolation (Favell & McGimsey, 1993; Meinhold & Mulick, 1990; "The Shame of New York's Group Homes," *New York Times*, March 25, 2011, p. A20). Intent to "do good" focuses on the values and beliefs of the "helper" rather than the freedom, values, and rights of the clients. Decisions made involve balancing the risks and benefits of doing something (offering a "service") against the risks and benefits of doing nothing (e.g., "watchful waiting"). Avoidance of harm and provision of help require attention to the restrictiveness of methods. Restrictiveness refers to the removal of freedom and the use of aversive methods. Institutionalizing clients is more restrictive than working with them in their communities. Future, as well as current, outcomes of different courses of action should be considered when estimating restrictiveness. For example, not using a temporary restrictive plan may result in much more restrictiveness in the future, such as continued institutionalization.

4. *Clients (or their representatives) are involved as informed participants.* Clients have a right to be involved in decisions that affect their lives. This highlights the importance of accurately informing clients about the evidentiary status of recommended methods and alternatives, their risks, benefits, and costs. Has a service been critically tested and found to help clients achieve hoped-for outcomes? Are there negative side effects? If so, how likely are they? "Scared straight" programs designed to decrease delinquent behavior have been found to increase it (Petrosino, Turpin-Petrosino, & Buehler, 2003). Is this information shared with families? Professionals have an obligation to be candid about the evidentiary status of recommended services and alternatives. They have an obligation to share uncertainties and ignorance, as well as knowledge with clients in a supportive manner informed by practice theory and to clearly describe any coercive elements of contact such as investigatory aims. They have an obligation not to mislead clients.

Gathering data about degree of progress involves clients as informed participants in decisions about what to do next. This allows clients to find out whether the quality of their lives has improved, remained the same, or diminished. Anthony Flew (1985) contends that the sincerity of our interest in helping clients is reflected in the efforts we make to find out whether we do help them; compassion for the trouble of others requires caring enough to find out if we did help. Clients have a right to refuse to take part in services offered or forced on them. However, if they are harming others, refusal has certain consequences about which clients should be fully informed such as removal of neglected children from their care.

5. *Professionals are competent. They possess relevant available knowledge and skills, including learning skills to keep up-to-date.* Professionals claim certain rights not extended

to others based on the assumed possession of specialized knowledge and skills. They thus have an ethical obligation to be informed about the evidentiary status of practices and policies. Which services can you offer with required competence? The NASW Code of Ethics calls on social workers to base their practice on "recognized knowledge, including empirically based knowledge, relevant to social work and social work ethics" (2008, 4.01). (Use of the adjective "recognized" connotes reliance on consensus and authority rather than critical testing.) The importance of background knowledge in making decisions is highlighted in the literature on problem solving and professional decision making.

6. *Decisions are well reasoned.* Social workers' obligation to help and not to harm obligates them to critically appraise claims about what is true and what is not and to make well-reasoned decisions informed by related research findings. Well-reasoned decisions are those for which sound arguments can be made. Valuing truth over prejudice and ignorance entails critically testing claims and thinking critically about decisions that have life-affecting consequences. Popper (1994) argues that relying on unexamined claims reflects an arrogance that is at odds with a compassion for others. Avoidable errors often occur because of reliance on questionable criteria, such as anecdotal experience to evaluate the accuracy of claims. Making well-reasoned decisions requires valuing truth over ignorance and prejudice. This requires recognizing the uncertainty related to decisions. It requires valuing "truth, the search for truth, the approximation to truth through the critical elimination of error, and clarity" (Popper, 1994, p. 70).

Popper (1994) defines truth as the correspondence of statements with facts. If a community organizer says, "I helped this community" this statement should correspond with the facts (e.g., residents report that they have been helped because there is a new park, a new recreation center, a new citizens' advisory center, and a day care center for toddlers). Guesses about the causes of client concerns should be checked against related research findings, as well as data gathered in real-life settings, when this is necessary to help clients and evaluate outcomes. Only by collecting data in real-life settings may the unique circumstances and characteristics of clients be understood, including client assets (see chapter 18). Only by attending to individual life circumstances may we clarify clients' concerns and make informed decisions about whether we can be of help, and, if so, how. Attending to a client's unique circumstances and characteristics is a key component of evidence-based practice as described in chapter 9. Collecting data concerning degree of progress provides a guide for decisions; plans can be changed as necessary.

7. *There are no authorities.* In "Social Work: An Authority-Based Profession" (Gambrill, 2001), I argued that social workers (including academics) often rely on authority-based criteria such as tradition when making claims about what is

true and what is not. They may assume that a claim is true because some "expert" said so. In the Popperian philosophy described here, there are no authorities; all claims are (and should be) open to question. (See also Walton's (2008) pragmatic view of fallacies.) Only in this way can we discover our mistakes (including flawed theories) and perhaps understand how to help clients a bit more in the future. Karl Popper highlights the following principles of rational discussion:

1. The principle of fallibility: perhaps I am wrong and perhaps you are right. But we could easily both be wrong.
2. The principle of rational discussion: we want to try, as impersonally as possible, to weigh up our reasons for and against a theory: a theory that is definite and criticizable.
3. The principle of approximation to the truth: we can nearly always come closer to the truth in a discussion which avoids personal attacks. It can help us to achieve a better understanding; even in those cases where we do not reach an agreement. (Popper, 1992, p. 199)

Popper suggests that appeals to authority encourage a tendency to cover up mistakes for the sake of authority (closing ranks) (p. 63). Valuing truth highlights the vast extent of our ignorance about the world and the uncertainty in making decisions. As Popper notes, we are all equal in our vast ignorance. "It is important never to forget our ignorance. We should therefore never pre.tend to know anything, and we should never use big words. What I call the cardinal sin…is simply talking hot air, professing a wisdom we do not possess" (Popper, 1992, p. 86). We have "the obligation never to pose as a prophet" (p. 206). But the "prophet motive" (Jarvis, 1990) is difficult to resist, given the rewards thereof (e.g., power and money) and the public's interest in soothsayers.

8. *Self-knowledge (awareness) that contributes to well-reasoned decisions and needed advocacy is sought and used.* Nickerson (1986) views self-knowledge as one of three kinds of knowledge required for sound reasoning. Others include domain-specific knowledge and performance skills. Self-knowledge includes accurate description of gaps between personal knowledge (e.g., our current assumptions about a social problem such as poverty) and available domain-specific knowledge. It includes accurate appraisal of our knowledge, skills, and beliefs. Popper (1998) argues that "a *self-critical attitude*, frankness and openness towards oneself [is a] part of everyone's duty" (p. 64). Feedback regarding our beliefs and decisions is essential for discovering if they are correct (or incorrect).

Only if we critically examine our decision-making styles and influences on them can we take corrective steps to enhance our success in helping clients and avoiding harm. Only if we are aware of our ignorance and biases can we change them. Given that both may compromise the quality of services clients receive, such awareness is an ethical obligation of professionals. It is an ethical obligation that is often ignored to the detriment of clients as shown by the history of the helping professions, including social work. Consider promotion of dubious methods that do more harm than good by social workers (Pignotti & Thyer, 2009).

The vital role of self-awareness and continued learning highlights the importance of seeking corrective feedback regarding your knowledge, skills, and values. Criticism, both from ourselves as well as from others, is needed to help clients and avoid harm. And, this should be specific, otherwise it will not contribute to problem solving. Popper (1998) suggests that "since we must learn from our mistakes, we must learn to accept, indeed accept with thanks their being pointed out to us by others" (p. 64). Only through criticism can we discover our errors and learn how to do better in the future. If we are not making mistakes, we are not learning. So we should try to avoid mistakes, but as Popper notes, we should be on the lookout for them including mistakes in our cherished theories. Many obstacles stand in the way of gaining such feedback, including administrators reluctant to examine the effectiveness of services. This reflexivity in which we review our knowledge skills, values, and other characteristics as they may influence client outcomes is one of the vital characteristics of professionals (Schön, 1990). It calls for questioning what we do, what effects we have on others, and what we have to change in order to fulfill our ethical obligation to do more good than harm. Here are some examples that do not reflect a commitment to enhancing self-awareness and continued learning:

Supervisor to student: I really don't care what the research says. I love to do play therapy and use it with all my clients.

Student to instructor: What does evidence have to do with social policy? My agency knows what it is doing.

Student to supervisor: I can instantly tell if someone has post traumatic stress disorder, all I have to do is look at him. I am never wrong.

9. *Empathy both for ourselves and others is vital.* Only if we have empathy for the plights of others, as well as for ourselves, will we turn toward rather than away from avoidable suffering and attempt to understand its causes and what can be done to minimize it (e.g., see Bandura, 1999). Empathy requires caring enough to look, see, feel, and recognize shared human experiences. This takes courage, a key ingredient of social workers (as well as of clients).

10. *The need for courage.* Circumstances requiring courage include: (1) seeing clients' depth of need rather than turning a blind eye, (2) questioning authorities (e.g., raising questions of supervisors, administrators, educators, and researchers), (3) accurately informing clients, (4) candidly reviewing your knowledge and skills and the match between them and your responsibilities and (5) recognizing uncertainty in making decisions (e.g., see Chalmers, 2007; Marris, 1996). I do not recall the word "courage" ever being mentioned in my own professional education. It was mentioned often in my liberal arts education. Great literature is in part about courage in the face of adversity (or its lack) and the varied consequences that may

occur. Why this difference in different educational venues? It certainly is not because courage is not needed in social work. Indeed there are so many circumstances in which it is required that it is astonishing that it is not a key topic in social work education programs. Consider the need to raise questions about practices and policies that others may uncritically embrace. Questions such as "Does it work?" "Has what we have been doing for the last 10 years worked?" are not necessarily met with open arms and responses such as "Thank you for raising this question." Raising such questions requires courage—courage to handle negative reactions including ridicule, abuse, and not being liked—not being one of the in-crowd. You may be labeled a "trouble maker." Those who care enough about clients to raise questions and have the courage to do so may be marginalized. Yet our code of ethics requires such courage—courage to candidly face need in the face of scant resources and the courage to bring this to the attention of others—to make this visible. It requires that we develop this courage and do so in a way that mobilizes us to take action, together with others, to minimize avoidable miseries.

11. *Advocacy efforts are vital. Changes and resources needed to help clients are identified, documented, exposed, and advocated for, especially for disadvantaged clients.* In the section on "Social and Political Action" (p. 27, section 6.04), the NASW Code of Ethics (2008) requires social workers to

engage in social and political action that seeks to ensure that all people have equal access to the resources, employment, services, and opportunities they require to meet their basic human needs and to develop fully;

be aware of the impact of the political arena on practice and advocate for changes in policy and legislation to improve social conditions in order to meet basic human needs and promote social justice;

act to expand choice and opportunity for all people, with special regard of vulnerable, disadvantaged, oppressed, and exploited people and groups;

promote conditions that encourage respect for cultural and social diversity within the United States and globally... and

act to prevent and eliminate domination of, exploitation of, and discrimination against any person, group, or class on the basis of race, ethnicity, national origin, color, sex, sexual orientation, gender identity or expression, age, marital status, political belief, religion, immigration status, or mental or physical disability.

This book highlights common mismatches between resources needed and what is available. A central theme throughout this book is the need to work at multiple levels if we are to honor our code of ethics. To honor these we must offer whatever help we can to our clients in their present circumstances, as well as work on other levels (policy and related legislation), to decrease the likelihood of adverse circumstances occurring in the first place. It is not an either/or choice, it is a "both"—meaning that in addition to developing competence in working with clients, families, and groups, you should develop knowledge and skills needed to pursue changes in organizations, policies, and legislation that affect clients' opportunities to enhance the quality of their lives. This highlights the importance of knowing how to form coalitions to work together to seek changes in practices, programs, and policies that hinder clients' opportunities to seek the good and avoid the bad. Calls to correct avoidable injustices and change dysfunctional agency practices are all too often just that, words with no actions. Advocacy for clients requires attention to agency practices and policies that affect clients' access to resources; there is a requirement not just to complain, but to take steps to change unjust/dysfunctional practices. Increased attention has been devoted to links between practice and policy.

Individual counseling is too often offered when, in addition, advocacy is needed to alter public policies and legislation related to personal problems. Mismatches are influenced by how problems are framed, for example, as mental illnesses of individuals or as due to public policies that limit access to resources such as health care and high-quality education. Agency practices and related funding sources and policies (e.g., managed care) that require use of short-term interventions at the individual level (e.g., use of motivational interviewing to encourage homeless people to stop drinking and/or using drugs) may lure you away from recognizing and working with others to address systemic causes of homelessness, drinking, and drug use such as lack of affordable housing and jobs. (See also discussion of the Professional as Social Reformer in chapter 3.)

12. *Actions correspond to values claimed.* Only if values are acted on are they meaningful (Perlman, 1976). This requires a correspondence between values, words, and actions. If you claim to value informed consent, a review of your interviews with clients should show that you inform clients about the costs and benefits of both recommended methods and alternatives (including doing nothing) and clearly describe the criteria you rely on to recommend plans. (See chapter 4.) If you say you build on clients' strengths, a review of your work should show that you help clients to identify and use personal assets of value. If you claim to advocate for needed services, your actions should reflect this.

Summary

Throughout time, some have needed help and some have offered it. Social workers provide help for a broad range of problems, including child and adult abuse and neglect, material concerns such as lack of food, clothing, or housing, parent–child conflicts, chronic illness and disability, and loneliness and depression. The struggle to establish social work as a profession was hard fought. As with other professions, schools were created,

a national organization formed, a code of ethics developed, and licensing laws passed. Social work gradually changed from using volunteers who worked with the poor to paying staff to provide services to both poor and middle-class persons. Not everyone welcomed professionalization; some viewed it as drawing attention away from a need for social reform and as contributing to the welfare of professionals rather than clients.

Social work is carried out in a political, social, and economic context that shapes the definition of problems and their proposed resolutions. The history of social work reflects the strains in the profession between reform and control and between individual and community. The different functions of social work and social welfare inevitably lead to controversies about what these functions should be and help explain the problems that continue to plague social work, such as relying on ideology instead of evidence to support claims of effectiveness and a social control function mixed with a preference for helping within a voluntary context. The purpose of the social services is to help clients, yet the services offered may contribute to inequalities that perpetuate problems. Social control goals can be seen in distinctions between the deserving and undeserving poor and between "normal" and "abnormal" behavior. Characteristics that protect the rights and welfare of clients include a focus on helping and avoiding harm, attention to individual differences, fully informing clients regarding the evidentiary status of practices and policies, taking responsibility for decisions made, and making well-reasoned decisions.

Reviewing Your Competencies

1. Describe the difference between social welfare and social work.

2. Describe the major functions of social work and social welfare.

3. Give examples of the social control functions of social welfare.

4. Describe controversial issues regarding the different functions of social work and social welfare.

5. Describe controversial issues concerning professionalization.

6. Discuss the value of a philosophy of practice and identify components that contribute to honoring ethical obligations.

Suggested Activity

Review the characteristics of professionals described in this chapter and check those you also value. If you disagree with any, describe why and add others that you consider important, offering reasons for your beliefs.

Appendix: Educational Policy and Accreditation Standards (2008) Council on Social Work Education

Educational Policy 2.1.1—Identify as a professional social worker and conduct oneself accordingly.

Social workers serve as representatives of the profession, its mission, and its core values. They know the profession's history. Social workers commit themselves to the profession's enhancement and to their own professional conduct and growth. Social workers

- advocate for client access to the services of social work;

- practice personal reflection and self-correction to assure continual professional development;

- attend to professional roles and boundaries;

- demonstrate professional demeanor in behavior, appearance, and communication;

- engage in career-long learning; and

- use supervision and consultation.

Educational Policy 2.1.2—Apply social work ethical principles to guide professional practice.

Social workers have an obligation to conduct themselves ethically and to engage in ethical decision-making. Social workers are knowledgeable about the value base of the profession, its ethical standards, and relevant law. Social workers

- recognize and manage personal values in a way that allows professional values to guide practice;

- make ethical decisions by applying standards of the National Association of Social Workers Code of Ethics and, as applicable, of the International Federation of Social Workers/International Association of Schools of Social Work Ethics in Social Work, Statement of Principles;

- tolerate ambiguity in resolving ethical conflicts; and

- apply strategies of ethical reasoning to arrive at principled decisions.

Educational Policy 2.1.3—Apply critical thinking to inform and communicate professional judgments.

Social workers are knowledgeable about the principles of logic, scientific inquiry, and reasoned discernment. They use critical thinking augmented by creativity and curiosity. Critical thinking also requires the synthesis and communication of relevant information. Social workers

- distinguish, appraise, and integrate multiple sources of knowledge, including research-based knowledge, and practice wisdom;

- analyze models of assessment, prevention, intervention, and evaluation; and

- demonstrate effective oral and written communication in working with individuals, families, groups, organizations, communities, and colleagues.

Educational Policy 2.1.4—Engage diversity and difference in practice.

Social workers understand how diversity characterizes and shapes the human experience and is critical to the formation of identity. The dimensions of diversity are understood as the intersectionality of multiple factors including age, class, color, culture, disability, ethnicity, gender, gender identity and expression, immigration status, political ideology, race, religion, sex, and sexual orientation. Social workers appreciate that, as a consequence of difference, a person's life experiences may include oppression, poverty, marginalization, and alienation as well as privilege, power, and acclaim. Social workers

- recognize the extent to which a culture's structures and values may oppress, marginalize, alienate, or create or enhance privilege and power;

- gain sufficient self-awareness to eliminate the influence of personal biases and values in working with diverse groups;

- recognize and communicate their understanding of the importance of difference in shaping life experiences; and

- view themselves as learners and engage those with whom they work as informants.

Educational Policy 2.1.5—Advance human rights and social and economic justice.

Each person, regardless of position in society, has basic human rights, such as freedom, safety, privacy, an adequate standard of living, health care, and education. Social workers recognize the global interconnections of oppression and are knowledgeable about theories of justice and strategies to promote human and civil rights. Social work incorporates social justice practices in organizations, institutions, and society to ensure that these basic human rights are distributed equitably and without prejudice. Social workers

- understand the forms and mechanisms of oppression and discrimination;
- advocate for human rights and social and economic justice; and
- engage in practices that advance social and economic justice.

Educational Policy 2.1.6—Engage in research-informed practice and practice-informed research.

Social workers use practice experience to inform research, employ evidence-based interventions, evaluate their own practice, and use research findings to improve practice, policy, and social service delivery. Social workers comprehend quantitative and qualitative research and understand scientific and ethical approaches to building knowledge. Social workers

- use practice experience to inform scientific inquiry and
- use research evidence to inform practice.

Educational Policy 2.1.7—Apply knowledge of human behavior and the social environment.

Social workers are knowledgeable about human behavior across the life course; the range of social systems in which people live; and the ways social systems promote or deter people in maintaining or achieving health and well-being. Social workers apply theories and knowledge from the liberal arts to understand biological, social, cultural, psychological, and spiritual development. Social workers

- utilize conceptual frameworks to guide the processes of assessment, intervention, and evaluation; and
- critique and apply knowledge to understand the person and environment.

Educational Policy 2.1.8—Engage in policy practice to advance social and economic well-being and to deliver effective social work services.

Social work practitioners understand that policy affects service delivery, and they actively engage in policy practice. Social workers know the history and current structures of social policies and services; the role of policy in service delivery; and the role of practice in policy development. Social workers

- analyze, formulate, and advocate for policies that advance social well-being; and
- collaborate with colleagues and clients for effective policy action.

Educational Policy 2.1.9—Respond to contexts that shape practice.

Social workers are informed, resourceful, and proactive in responding to evolving organizational, community, and societal contexts at all levels of practice. Social workers recognize that the context of practice is dynamic, and use knowledge and skill to respond proactively. Social workers

- continuously discover, appraise, and attend to changing locales, populations, scientific and technological developments, and emerging societal trends to provide relevant services; and
- provide leadership in promoting sustainable changes in service delivery and practice to improve the quality of social services.

Educational Policy 2.1.10(a)–(d)—Engage, assess, intervene, and evaluate with individuals, families, groups, organizations, and communities.

Professional practice involves the dynamic and interactive processes of engagement, assessment, intervention, and evaluation at multiple levels. Social workers have the knowledge and skills to practice with individuals, families, groups, organizations, and communities. Practice knowledge includes identifying, analyzing, and implementing evidence-based interventions designed to achieve client goals; using research and technological advances; evaluating program outcomes and practice effectiveness; developing, analyzing, advocating, and providing leadership for policies and services; and promoting social and economic justice.

Educational Policy 2.1.10(a)—Engagement.

Social workers

- substantively and affectively prepare for action with individuals, families, groups, organizations, and communities;
- use empathy and other interpersonal skills; and
- develop a mutually agreed-on focus of work and desired outcomes.

Educational Policy 2.1.10(b)—Assessment.

Social workers

- collect, organize, and interpret client data;

- assess client strengths and limitations;

- develop mutually agreed-on intervention goals and objectives; and

- select appropriate intervention strategies.

Educational Policy 2.1.10(c)—Intervention.

Social workers

- initiate actions to achieve organizational goals;

- implement prevention interventions that enhance client capacities;

- help clients resolve problems;

- negotiate, mediate, and advocate for clients; and

- facilitate transitions and endings.

Educational Policy 2.1.10(d)—Evaluation.

Social workers critically analyze, monitor, and evaluate interventions.

2

Clients and Services

OVERVIEW   This chapter describes a contextual view of helper–client exchanges. It is informed by research that shows that both parties influence each other and, in turn, are influenced by their environments, including agency practices and related public policies and legislation. In turn, industries such as the media and the biomedical industrial complex influence these policies and legislation. As Mills (1959) noted, the personal is political. That is, client concerns are often directly related to decisions regarding resource distribution reflected in public policies. Earlier experiences in help-seeking influence later ones. Beliefs, goals, and expectations of both clients and helpers are other influences.

YOU WILL LEARN ABOUT

- The route to the agency

- Helping as a social influence process

- Clients' beliefs, expectations, and goals

- Helpers' beliefs, expectations, and goals

- The influence of the profession and related industries

- Clients' cultural diversity

- Overcoming barriers to cross-cultural counseling

The Route to the Agency

Social workers see particular samples of individuals who have certain characteristics or confront certain experiences. For example, only some people with relationship or drinking problems see social workers. Only some people who commit crimes are caught, prosecuted, and found guilty and thus meet a probation or parole officer. Only some individuals who are poor, live in crime-ridden neighborhoods, and who have recently immigrated to the United States seek help from social service agencies. Many people who are eligible for certain benefits such as food stamps do not seek them. Many people with drinking or drug problems do not seek help. They may come to the attention of social workers through their involvement with the criminal justice system. Seeking help from an agency may be preceded by requesting help from friends or relatives (Kung, 2003; see Exhibit 2.1).

On the other hand, people may be reluctant to talk to friends or relatives because of their involvement in problems, fears about how they will react, and concerns about confidentiality, indebtedness, and negative impressions. Some people seek the advice of clergy, elders, indigenous healers, and even hairdressers and bartenders. Strategies these helpers use may be the same as those used by social workers, such as offering support,

---

EXHIBIT 2.1

Examples of Help-Seeking Efforts Before Seeking Help from Professionals

THE GREEN FAMILY

Mrs. Ryan, age 89, had been living for 6 years with her son-in-law (Mr. Green), her daughter, and their two teenage children. This arrangement was made when Mr. Ryan died. Since her daughter and her family had an extra room in their home and since Mrs. Ryan wanted to live with them, they had all agreed that this would be a good plan. Now, 6 years later, Mr. and Mrs. Green were not so sure any longer that this arrangement was a good idea. They felt that Mrs. Ryan was becoming an increasing burden. The help she had provided, such as straightening up after dinner and cleaning, decreased as her health became more fragile owing to a heart condition. And as the children became older and more able to care for themselves, her babysitting services were no longer of benefit to the family. As the children advanced into their teens, value differences between Mrs. Ryan and her grandchildren became accentuated. She was appalled, for example, at the TV shows they watched and was shocked about their open discussion of birth control and the possibility of what might be done if the daughter became pregnant. At first, Mrs. Ryan had expressed her differences of opinion, but since this seemed to result in conflict and hard feelings, she had increasingly withdrawn from discussions and spent more and more time in her room. The Greens were very concerned about this state of affairs. They did not seem able to help Mrs. Ryan and their children achieve a more satisfying means of discussing their differing values, and they were torn between their loyalty to their children and their loyalty to Mrs. Ryan. The increased care that Mrs. Ryan required was an additional burden on the Greens, both of whom worked full time. The Greens also worried about what they would do if Mrs. Ryan had another heart attack, one that left her with substantial disabilities. How would they then care for her? They were worried about the financial burden this might entail, as funds were not overly plentiful in the household. Mrs. Green was a practical nurse, and her husband worked as a truck driver in a nearby lumber company. They were in their early fifties.

The Greens had many discussions between themselves about what to do. Should they bring up the possibility of Mrs. Ryan entering a home for the elderly that was located about 20 miles away? Wouldn't it be better to make arrangements now rather than wait until Mrs. Ryan became more frail and more of a burden to the household? They had also sought the opinion of a couple with whom they were good friends. The couple had advised them to act now rather than later, that is, to place Mrs. Ryan in the home. They talked to the minister of their church, even though they went to church only sporadically. He suggested that they talk with Mrs. Ryan. But they did not take the minister's advice, since they thought she would feel that they did not want her and would insist on moving out. They went to the library and took out a couple of books on living with old people to try to find suggestions.

None of these efforts seemed to help matters. Finally, Mrs. Green decided that she would talk to the social worker at the hospital and ask her advice. The social worker referred the Greens to a local service for the elderly.

MR. RIVERA

Mr. Rivera contacted a community health center because of his health problems. He has been diagnosed as having AIDS and contacted the agency for medical help. He is 48 years old and lives in a small studio apartment in a rundown section of the city. He has no source of income other than disability payments. He describes himself as heterosexual but has frequent sexual relations with men. He is pale and disheveled and clearly seems in distress. He has a number of skin problems and a persistent cough. He had sought help at a local emergency room hospital but after waiting 4 hours he left. He is tired and hungry and discouraged.

THE LAKELAND FAMILY

For the past year, Mr. and Mrs. Lakeland had been having difficulty with their 14-year-old son. In addition to Brian, two other children lived in the home, a girl aged 11 and an older brother aged 18. Brian would not follow his parents' instructions, would often tease his sister and the dog, and would disappear without telling his parents where he was going. The parents also had received many complaints about his behavior from the school authorities—that he got into fights at school and was failing in many subjects.

(continued)

EXHIBIT 2.1 (Continued)

Mrs. Lakeland had spoken with her mother about their problems with Brian, and she suggested that "time would work things out." However, time did not seem to be working things out, and the Lakelands grew increasingly restive about their relationship with Brian and his relationships with others, including his interaction with the family dog, since Brian's teasing was beginning to take a cruel cast: he would twist the dog's tail or kick him. The Lakelands sought the help of their family doctor, who had been seeing Brian since Brian was 4 years old. At this time he had been diagnosed as having epilepsy. Brian was supposed to take medication twice a day, and this seemed to control his seizures if he remembered to take it, which was another problem; Brian often forgot to take his medication. It was because of this diagnosis of epilepsy that the Lakelands had extended extra leeway to Brian in terms of his behavior. They felt that "he couldn't help himself as much as the other children." Dr. Bernard, the physician, suggested that the parents be very firm with Brian and place strict limits on his behavior. They did this; that is, they "laid down the law" to Brian, told him that he was not to tease the dog anymore, was to take his medication every day, was to mind his parents, and so forth—or else. "Or else" was left simply to imply that they would take other steps. This seemed to have an effect for a day or two, and then the situation became even worse. Brian threatened his father with a knife when one evening right after supper Mr. Lakeland had demanded that he stop teasing his sister and the dog.

Mrs. Lakeland decided to contact the Family Service Agency. She knew about this agency, since she passed it on her way to work every day. She thought that maybe they would be able to offer the family some help.

JULIE

Julie had never thought she would get pregnant. She thought that she had timed everything right and that there would be no chance. But here she was, pregnant at age 15. What would she do? She became so upset every time she tried to think about it that it was hard for her to see clearly the possible alternatives and their advantages and disadvantages, let alone decide among them. Should she have the baby or not? If she did, what would she do with it? Would her parents keep it? Should she have the baby and give it up for adoption? What would she do about school? If she had an abortion, where would she go for it? Who would find out? Would she be able to have more children if she had an abortion? Would it hurt a lot? What would her parents say and do? She knew how strict her parents were about their religion and how much against abortion they were. If she talked to a friend, even her best friend, wouldn't she tell others and wouldn't her mother find out? Where could she go for help? She didn't even want to share her predicament with her boyfriend. He would think she was dumb for getting pregnant. After all, she had told him it was safe.

Still she had to do something. Time was passing, and she knew that if she had an abortion, it should be done within the first 3 months.

Maybe the laboratory where she had had the pregnancy test would know about someone to talk to. She remembered that she had seen a notice on the bulletin board when she was there about some service. She decided that she would go back to the laboratory and look up the address.

---

listening, suggesting alternatives, pointing out and supporting strengths, and sharing personal experiences. Clients may find out about social services through relatives or friends, the Internet, the Yellow Pages, a community center, radio, or television. Other professionals may refer clients. Requesting help from a social service agency may be a last resort. It may be viewed as a sign of weakness or immaturity or as a negative reflection on the family.

Clients, Applicants, and Resisters

A *client* is defined as someone who makes an explicit agreement with a social worker about the purpose of their work together. Many people who come to social service agencies are not clients. Some are *applicants* who request something, such as a teacher who seeks help with a "hyperactive" child. Applicants may become clients. Many people social workers see have had their freedom limited against their will, such as parents suspected of child abuse, youths or adults on probation, and residents of mental hospitals. Helen Harris Perlman calls such individuals "resisters." "They come unwillingly, dragging their feet and their spirit, feeling coerced, robbed of their free will by other persons or conditions they oppose. Sometimes they want help but not the kind that is to be had or not the kind under the conditions to be required" (1979, p. 115). They may deny that there is a problem, blame others, and be antagonistic. Resisters may become clients when, for example, a parent whose children have been removed may agree to participate in a plan to regain custody of her children. Social workers often act as though they are working with a client when in fact they are talking to an applicant or a resister, that is, someone with whom they do not have an agreement to work toward a goal. They may not understand why this person does not do what they recommend, failing to realize that he or she never agreed to pursue certain goals. If you have trouble involving your clients (e.g., they don't complete agreed-on tasks), check to see whether you have an agreement to work toward a goal that will offer more benefits than costs for clients. (See chapter 14.) A cost-benefit analysis of pursuit of a goal may show that attaining it would have more costs than benefits—an indication of outcome resistance. The client will lose more by achieving the goal than he will gain.

Previous Contacts with Professionals

People's previous help-seeking experiences influence how they respond when they go to an agency and also what they expect from future meetings. Prior experiences are not always satisfactory. Clients who have encountered rude or insensitive professionals may be hostile or reserved, expecting more of the same. Negative or unhelpful experiences may make them unwilling to seek further help.

All those &%$@**# did was ask dumb questions and take our money. They never gave us any help at all! When they told us that we might as well put him in an institution because he would never be able to count money or even talk, I sort of lost my mind. I was so sad that I was in a fog for about a week. Then I heard a voice inside me telling me that I would have to do the job by myself. (Kozloff, 1979, p. 17)

Helping as a Social Influence Process

Helpers and clients influence each other. Therefore, if we want to understand the helping process, we must explore the transaction (i.e., the interactions) between helpers and clients and the context in which it occurs (e.g., Norcross, 2011). Jerome Frank notes that research has not altered his earlier view of helping as an interpersonal process in which the helper's beliefs, values, and optimism overcome the client's demoralization and offer hope (Frank & Frank, 1991). Studies of helping highlight the social influence process that takes place even in "nondirective" approaches (Duncan, Miller, Wampold, & Hubble, 2010; Truax, 1966; see also chapter 15). Helpers reinforce some behaviors, ignore others, and punish still others. In turn, clients influence the helpers' behavior. The subtlety of these social influence processes (they may not be obvious) does not remove the fact that they occur. Some authors, such as Margolin (1997), argue that this subtlety allows helpers to misuse their power to the detriment of their clients. Cultural differences between clients and helpers may increase the likelihood of miscommunication.

Prior help-seeking experiences, as well as the match between the helpers' and clients' goals, influence what occurs. Client goals include obtaining help with problems, preserving self-respect, limiting invasions of privacy, and perhaps seeking assurance that nothing is wrong. The social worker's goals include demonstrating competence and helping clients.

The possibility of mismatches has led some authors to describe helper–client interactions as *problematic social situations* (Stone, 1979, p. 46). Waitzkin describes exchanges between physicians and patients as "micropolitical situations" in which the control of information reinforces the power relations that parallel those in the broader society, especially those concerning social class, gender, race, and age (1991, p. 54). These power imbalances highlight the importance of ethical components of evidence-based practice such as transparency regarding what is done and involving clients as active, informed participants in decisions (see also Heritage & Clayman, 2011).

Although a transactional model may seem reasonable, some professionals neither subscribe to it nor act on it. Instead, they may blame lack of client participation on their clients, overlooking their responsibility to do what they can to increase participation (see chapter 14). Or, they may assume too much responsibility, neglecting clients' responsibilities and rights to make their own choices (how or if to participate and in what ways with what consequences). With many problems such as homelessness, lack of medical services, unemployment, and lack of day care, client participation is a moot point, since even maximal participation would not succeed in attaining needed resources.

Clients' Beliefs, Expectations, and Goals

Clients' goals and beliefs regarding their lives and possibilities, what services will be offered, and what results are likely influence the helping process. Clients have expectations about what will happen in and result from their meetings with social workers. The extent to which their expectations match those of helpers will affect the outcome (see Exhibit 2.2). Ignoring or misunderstanding client expectations may result in premature dropout. Some clients may be helped in one meeting (Talmon, 1990). Others may drop out because they do not feel helped and believe that further visits would be a waste of time, money, and effort.

Beliefs About Life and Its Joys and Adversities

We each have beliefs about life and the meaning of both joys and adversities and the suffering the latter may create. What is the unique social significance and moral meaning of adversity? (See Wilkinson, 2005.) Clients assume different degrees of responsibility for adversities and solutions. A client may approach the social worker as an outsider who will join him in blaming family members for his problems. A client may feel depressed and hopeless because of an ongoing lack of material resources. Frank (1961) suggested that we seek help when we are demoralized. According to the *moral model,* a person is responsible for both

EXHIBIT 2.2

Clients' Expectations

JULIE

As Julie approaches the agency, she has a last-minute wish to turn around and go home. What will happen? What will she have to tell the social worker? Will the social worker want to know all the details of her sexual relations with her boyfriend? Won't the social worker think Julie is stupid for not taking more precautions? Will she jump on her for thinking about having an abortion? Will she jump on her for wanting to have her child and raising it herself? Here she is at the door. She can always say she feels sick and leave.

Julie arrives at the door of the agency and goes inside. A woman is sitting at a desk, says hello in a pleasant manner, and asks Julie if she can help her. Julie tells her she has an appointment. The woman says "fine" and asks her if she has been there before. Julie says "no" and begins to feel like going home. The woman at the desk says, "Could you please fill in the information on this form? It will just take you a minute." This request bothers Julie. She starts to wonder again if they will tell her mother. She looks at the form and sees that it just calls for some very basic information: her age, year in school, address, and phone number. She completes the form and sits down in the waiting room. She asks herself again for about the thousandth time— what do I want to do? And the same thought comes to her. I want to have an abortion. She cannot imagine herself taking care of a baby right now.

THE LAKELAND FAMILY

The interview with the social worker has been set for 7 p.m. to accommodate the Lakelands, both of whom work. As they think about the upcoming interview, they become uneasy. Maybe this mess is all their fault. Maybe they have not done a good job as parents. Maybe it is because they both work full time. Maybe Brian has epilepsy because he fell when he was 2, and Mr. Lakeland should have caught him before he hit his head. And what is there new to try? They already tried being firm with Brian; they tried putting him on medication. But he won't take it. Maybe the social worker will get him to take it. Maybe she will lay down the law to Brian, and he will begin acting like a human being.

Brian reluctantly agreed to accompany his parents on the visit to the social worker. He dreads this. Every time he sees his counselor at school, all he (the counselor) does is yell at him. "Why can't you be like all the other students? What's the matter with you? Why don't you take your medication?" He does do some nasty things—but they are fun, and they really don't hurt anyone. Why can't anybody else see that? The social worker probably won't see it either. Well, he'll go along, but he's not going to admit that he is the bad guy in all this. If his parents treated him better, none of this would happen. They're always talking about what a goody-goody his older brother is—in college and all of that. Why don't they just leave him alone? He (Brian) gets so mad at his father sometimes.

MR. WONG AND HIS FAMILY

Mr. Wong lives with his woman partner and 6-year-old son. He works as a cook in Chinatown, where he lives. He moved to the United States from Hong Kong 4 years ago. The mother of his child, with whom he has little contact, still lives in Hong Kong. He and his partner share the care of his 6-year-old son. He was contacted by the social worker at his son's school because of complaints by his son's teacher that he (Jason) was not doing his work and would not follow instructions. Mr. Wong's English is fair. He is concerned about these complaints and is eager to see what can be done about them. There are also problems at home; that is, here too his son often does not follow instructions—especially from his companion, Jeanne, with whom he and his son have lived for the past 3 years. He hopes that he can get help to resolve his concerns. He hopes to get some clear advice.

MRS. GRANDER AND HER FAMILY

Mrs. Grander is a 55-year-old African American grandmother who is taking care of her daughter's 2-year-old daughter. The child's mother is addicted to cocaine and the grandmother hopes to apply for guardianship of this child. The grandmother works part time and currently feels quite depressed and is under the care of a psychiatrist who has placed her on medication. She often feels that she cannot manage raising another child at her age and expresses feeling fatigued and "blue." She was referred to an agency that offers support for kin caregivers. She hopes to get some relief from the care of her granddaughter and to find resources to help her to get guardianship of this child.

his or her problems and their solution. This model contrasts with a *medical or disease model,* in which the client is assumed to be responsible for neither the problem nor its solution (Brickman et al., 1982). In the *compensatory model,* the client is viewed as being responsible for the solution but not the problem. In the *enlightenment model,* a person is viewed as responsible for the problem but not its solution. What are clients' views?

Clients' Expectations About Services and Outcomes

Clients may not know what to expect, or they may have preconceived notions about the type of social worker who can help them. A client may believe that only someone who has had similar experiences can be of help; thus an elderly widow may believe that only another elderly widow can appreciate her loss. The less familiar clients are with services offered, the more important it is to describe them carefully. Some clients prefer a direct approach, in which the social worker offers advice and guidance in a collaborative exchange. This advice and guidance may not be provided by professionals, however. Significant others—such as an elder in a Native American group or an older brother in a Chinese family—may be the adviser. The greater the cultural differences between helpers and clients, the greater the need to attend to differences that may affect the helping process.

People on probation or parole may view social workers as disliked and feared authorities who will or can limit their freedom and interfere in their lives. In a classic study of helpers and clients, Mayer and Timms (1970) found that clients expected workers to agree with their view of the solution and to help change the situation. They were puzzled and surprised at the workers' emphasis on talking, their failure to take a stand against an offending significant other, their interest in exploring the clients' past, their focus on feelings, and their interest in them rather than in the people the clients considered responsible for the problems. Social workers attributed their clients' reluctance to engage in expected behaviors to their resistance to acknowledging their role in creating their own problems. The most satisfied clients were those who requested material aid and received it.

Clients' views about services may be related to their beliefs about problems they confront and how (or if) they can be resolved. Clients may expect their problems to be resolved quickly, even when this is unlikely.

I had been so unhappy for so long that when my mother suggested I go to the agency I thought…"Wow! I'll be all fine and cured!"…So…when I first went in there, I went with this kind of illusion that there was this Good Fairy who was going to wave the magic wand and I'd just be so happy and peaceful!…Well, it took me a couple of months to realize that the counselor wasn't a Good Fairy. Oh, she was just a nice lady to talk with.…She gave me time to talk about myself and after a while I began to feel better…but it didn't happen overnight. (Maluccio, 1979, pp. 55–56)

Or clients may not believe that their problems can be solved. Skill in creating positive expectations contributes to success in all forms of helping, psychological as well as medical, perhaps by mobilizing hope (Frank & Frank, 1991) and creating placebo effects (Benedetti, 2009).

Clients' Expectations About How They Will Be Evaluated

A client who complains about a family member may worry that the social worker will blame him for contributing to a difficult situation. He may worry that someone of a different race or ethnicity will not be sympathetic or be able to understand his concerns. The norms for asking for certain types of aid in the community in which a client lives affect expectations. For example, in some communities, seeking help may be viewed as a sign of personal deficiency. Asking for material aid may be hard, even though clients have a legal right to such aid.

Helpers' Beliefs, Expectations, and Goals

Helpers also have beliefs, expectations, and goals. Their evaluation of clients is influenced by the attributions they make about their behavior. Lack of client participation may be attributed to characteristics of clients, overlooking environmental causes including cultural differences, and the fact that change is difficult. Social workers also have beliefs about what behaviors are appropriate, what causes particular behaviors, whether and how behavior can be changed, and how much responsibility clients have. Consider two different social workers who may interview Julie:

Mrs. Kulp works at a family service agency. Most of the clients she sees have problems with their children, but occasionally she interviews unwed pregnant teenagers. She is scheduled to talk to Julie the next day. As the time for the interview approaches, the following thoughts drift through her mind: Another unwed teenager. I just don't understand why they have such loose moral values. Teenagers have to face up to the consequences of their actions. But because the agency's policy is to explore alternatives with young unwed mothers, I guess I'll have to do this. I hope Julie isn't thinking of having an abortion!

Mrs. Landis works at the same agency. As the time for her appointment with Julie approaches, she thinks: Why doesn't this community provide better family-planning services for teenagers? If better services were available, there would not be as many unwanted pregnancies. I wonder what Julie will want to do. Even if she has decided on an alternative, I'll encourage her to at least take a look at other possibilities so that she will be aware of all the available options.

These two workers' different attitudes may influence how they act when they interview Julie, as well as the options they offer to her and how they describe them. Social workers may predict outcomes in advance, and these judgments may influence how they will act. Expectations of failure may result in less effort.

The helpers' reactions are influenced by their views of the ease with which people become involved in a helping relationship, clients' motivation for change, how predictable clients' behavior is, and their estimates of how much a client will benefit from assistance. Helpers' views may be less favorable than laypersons' views. Wills (1978) found that professionals tend to focus on negative traits and this focus increases with increasing experience: "Experience produces an increased emphasis on negative characterological aspects, particularly an increased perception of maladjustment, and a less generous view of clients' motivation for change" (p. 981). Are judgments made by professionals more accurate compared to those of lay persons? It depends on the task and the particular kind of training in relation to the task (e.g., see Garb & Boyle, 2003). The best way to guard against negative expectations is to be aware of and question them and to focus on client strengths such as persistence in the face of adversity and problem-solving skills. It is the unexamined assumption that may cause the most mischief. Recognition of environmental circumstances related to problems clients confront, including unequal educational, housing, health, and recreational opportunities, should discourage negative biases.

The Influence of the Profession and Related Industries

Each profession claims to have special skills in responding to certain kinds of complaints, and each uses a certain ideology to justify its actions and assure the public that it is working in its best interests, such as the ideology of doing good. In his study of the professions, Abbott (1988) described the delicate balance between clarity and obscurity that is needed to maintain professional jurisdiction over certain kinds of problems. If the methods used are clear, people with fewer or no credentials may usurp areas from the domain of professionals. The ideology used to support claims and the technologies used in their service influence the services clients receive. Although there is a great deal of rhetoric in social work urging pursuit of societal level change, in the everyday world of practice, the focus is typically on individuals and families. Leslie Margolin (1997) argues that many professionals mystify not only their clients (as to their real purpose) but also themselves about the covert functions of social work. He views home visits, interviewing, record keeping, and record sharing as technologies used to justify taking actions that affect clients "for their own good."

Social Policy and Agency Influences

Agencies have policies concerning what services they provide, who is eligible to receive them, and what fees (if any) are charged (see Exhibit 2.3). In turn, agency programs and procedures are influenced by public policies and related federal, state, county, and city regulations, funding, and legislation. How services are organized affects clients. Some scholars argue that the investigative/coercive and helping/supportive roles that characterize child welfare services are incompatible (e.g., Lindsey, 1994). Privatization of services has increased in many sectors, including nursing homes, residential treatment, day care, mental health, and substance abuse treatment. Public agencies often contract out services to nonprofit organizations, which may offer poor services (Gainsborough, 2010). Professionals may try to block policies and practices designed to protect clients and actively resist describing what they do to what effect. For example, case records of child welfare staff in the State of New Jersey were opened to review only after a court order (DePanfilis, 2003). Professions are influenced by their environments. Social welfare policies and related legislation are influenced by the biomedical industrial complex, which includes pharmaceutical and biotechnology companies, and the diagnostic and classification industry, including the highly profitable *DSM* industry. The *Diagnostic and Statistical Manual of Mental Disorders* brings in millions of dollars a year to the American Psychiatric Association. The media is controlled by fewer and fewer corporations rendering diverse views less likely in newspapers. Ownership decreased from 50 in the 1980s to 29 today (Bagdikian, 2004).

Even the manner of the agency's receptionist—whether it is curt and cold or welcoming and sensitive to cultural differences—can influence how people respond (e.g., see DuBois, 2010). In a classic study, Hall (1974) found that the receptionist at a social service agency could discourage a client by withdrawing her advocacy activities. Unclear policies and lack of staff training in decision making may interfere with equitable practices (Weiner, LaPorte, Abrams, Moswin, & Warnecke, 2004). The physical characteristics of waiting rooms affect clients. Are accurate, up-to-date educational brochures, as well as access to the Internet, describing the agency's services and alternatives and their costs and benefits available in waiting rooms? Reviews of written material for clients and content on websites show that content may be misleading (e.g., Jørgensen & Gøtzsche, 2004). Are play materials available for children? Preferred practice frameworks influence which services are provided and what outcomes are achieved.

The Technology Used and the Criteria Used to Select It

Agencies use different methods and rely on different criteria to select them, for example, tradition or popularity. Examples include social planning, community organization, research, supervision, consultation, management practice, case management, individual,

EXHIBIT 2.3

Describing Your Agency

1. What are your agency's goals? Are they clear?

2. What services are offered to what clients in what geographical area? What percentage of clients who could benefit from services receive them? Is transportation to the agency readily available? Is the agency accessible to people with physical disabilities?

3. Describe the evidentiary status of services provided by your agency and discuss implications for clients. (What services have been critically tested and found to help clients?)

4. What are the agency's funding sources? How do they influence choice of clients and services provided?

5. How closely does staff match clients in terms of ethnicity, age, sexual orientation, and gender? Discuss the implications of degree of match.

6. Who are the gatekeepers in your agency and how do they affect services?

7. Describe the waiting room in your agency. Could it be made more welcoming and useful to clients (e.g., provision of educational brochures and access to computers describing various services and their track record of success in helping clients achieve certain outcomes)?

8. How does your agency evaluate the quality of services offered and their outcomes? Do these methods provide an accurate picture?

9. Are needed training opportunities provided to staff? What criteria are used to select them? How are their outcomes evaluated?

10. Describe your agency's administrative style and how it may affect services.

11. Describe any specific policies, programs, and practices that detract from the quality of services provided to clients.

12. Identify external groups that influence services offered.

13. Describe your agency's links with other agencies.

14. What changes should be made to enhance quality of services?

15. What public/social policies and related legislation affect services offered (e.g., laws, rules, regulations, funding streams)?

16. Are staff available who speak the language of the clients?

17. Are discriminatory practices identified and plans made and acted on to remove them?

18. Is it clear and easy for clients to establish eligibility for services or benefits?

19. Do staff help clients overcome barriers to access to needed resources?

family, and group work. These may be used with individuals, families, small groups, organizations, communities, regions, or entire countries or groups of countries. These various technologies may be used with the elderly, children, those involved in the criminal justice and/or mental health systems, in public welfare or health care, employment counseling, rehabilitation, and substance misuse. Stephen Fawcett and his colleagues define social technology as "a replicable set of procedures that is designed to produce an effect on socially important behaviors of relevant participants under a variety of real-life conditions" (1984, p. 147).

Some agencies focus on "people-change" technologies; others, on "environmental-change" technologies. Some focus on processing people (giving them labels and referring them elsewhere). Some focus on community development and advocacy to alter policies and related legislation. Exhibit 2.4 provides an opportunity to review the service methods used in your agency. Which services have been critically evaluated and been shown to do more good than harm? Which ones have not been critically tested? That is, they may do more good than harm but no one knows. Are services used that have been shown to do more harm than good? Are services provided attentive to cultural differences? What services have been critically tested and found to help clients such as those seen in your agency but are not offered? If there are such services, why doesn't your agency offer them?

Clients often need a number of services. The term *case management* refers to the arrangement, coordination, and evaluation of services offered to an individual or family. Case managers often are responsible for screening potential clients, assessing their needs, developing service plans, linking clients with needed resources, and monitoring and evaluating services provided. Effective case management often requires a continuum of care levels that match the client's need and help maintain independence, including in-home, community-based, and institutional services. The term *case management* also can have a negative meaning, referring to the speedup of work and the lowering of service quality because of monetary concerns. For example, a key responsibility of discharge planners in a hospital is to get patients out of the hospital as quickly as possible.

Agencies differ in the criteria that staff rely on to choose service methods. The same kind of methods may be offered to all clients, regardless of their suitability. For example, when asked why she was using play therapy for a 6-year-old Chinese American boy referred because he was not following instructions at school or home, the social worker answered, "That's what the agency offers." Tradition may not offer the best guidelines. Leslie Margolin (1997) suggests that in the early part of the century, social workers used the technologies of the telephone, the case record, and the interview to gain and maintain a power position in relation to their clients. He suggests that they used the techniques of friendliness, an expressed interest in doing good, and an apparent absence of self-interest to gain entry into the once private homes of the poor, where they could collect information that was not necessarily related to concerns of clients. They kept case records on clients to which they could refer to justify their

---

EXHIBIT 2.4

Reviewing Agency Services and Criteria Used to Select Them

A. What are the main services your agency offers?

_____ Case management	_____ Skill training	_____ Community development
_____ Support	_____ Brokering	_____ Social action
_____ Outreach	_____ Advocating	_____ Other _____
_____ Cognitive-behavioral	_____ Education	_____
_____ Crisis intervention	_____ Insight development	

B. Check those factors that affect your agency's choice of services.

_____ Funding	_____ Evidentiary status[a]	_____ Personal preferences of staff
_____ Staff knowledge and training	_____ Popularity	
_____ Staff time	_____ Tradition	_____ Administrative decisions
_____ Staff hired	_____ What seems interesting	_____ Other _____

C. Please answer the following using a scale of 1 (not at all), 2 (a little), 3 (a fair amount), 4 (a great deal), 5 (best that could be):

	1	2	3	4	5
1. Practices and policies are evidence-based (they are acceptable to clients and are most likely to help clients achieve desired outcomes as demonstrated via critical tests of related claims, see chapter 11; best that can be, given available knowledge).	1	2	3	4	5
2. Fidelity[b] of practices and policies used is high.	1	2	3	4	5
3. Fidelity of services is routinely reviewed.	1	2	3	4	5
4. Each staff member receives constructive feedback each month on fidelity of methods used.	1	2	3	4	5
5. Technology used is routinely updated, based on related empirical literature.	1	2	3	4	5
6. Staff at all levels welcome questions about the effectiveness of agency practices and policies.	1	2	3	4	5
7. Client feedback regarding the acceptability of methods and their outcomes is regularly collected and reviewed and corrective action taken as needed.	1	2	3	4	5
8. Staff have the knowledge and skills required to provide effective services.	1	2	3	4	5

[a] See 1 under C.
[b] Fidelity refers to the degree to which services match those that maximize likelihood of success.

---

decisions. The biographical entries in these records might have been incomplete and inaccurate. Clients did not have access to them; today many clients still do not. The telephone was used to pass on information in records to other social workers, again without allowing clients to make corrections. Now e-mail is used, with ever greater opportunities for loss of confidentiality as when agencies sell old computers without erasing data from them.

Clients' Cultural Diversity

Social work in the United States is practiced in an increasingly diverse society. Patterns of behavior in different groups may overlap to a large or small degree depending on past and present shared experiences. Everyone has a culture (see Glossary at the end of this chapter). We all grow up in a particular social environment that shapes our behavior (Plomin, 2011). Each individual has a unique identity that is influenced by cultural values and practices, as well as by unique family experiences, geographical setting (e.g., rural/urban/suburban), gender, and generation. Identity may change over time. We may go through different stages in forming our identity, such as accepting the dominant cultural values and then rejecting them and accepting what we view as best from different perspectives. Different cultures create and maintain certain patterns of behavior and values. Culture is passed on in part by language, the arts, and other symbols. Just about every immigrant group has experienced discrimination as it entered the United States. It is easy to forget the hatred toward Italians, the Irish, and in Benjamin Franklin's time, the Germans, for example. Perhaps the harshest oppression was against those who were already here: Native Americans.

Not all people value individualism and competition for status and recognition; rather, the family and community may be at the top of the list. Likewise, the self-exploration valued in Western culture may be considered by others as a cause of problems. Some parents may encourage children who are experiencing problems to think more about their family and less about themselves. For instance, social connectedness and endurance are emphasized in Japanese culture (Turner, 2002). Not all may wish to be fully informed about their health status and to participate actively in decisions about life support.

Cultural adaptation refers to a gradual change in behavior toward prevailing cultural patterns. *Cultural change* may result from the intrusion of outsiders or a gradual change in values and behavior within a group. *Cultural relativism* refers to the belief that a culture should be evaluated in terms of its own standards. *Acculturation* is the integration of one's original values, traditions, and behaviors with those of the prevailing culture (Chun, Organista, & Marin, 2009). A person's rate of acculturation is influenced by the length of residence in the new country, income, educational level, age, and language. People who belong to two cultures may feel marginal in both (i.e., not feel fully a part of either). Diane de Anda (1984, p. 102) suggests that the following factors influence the degree of "bicultural" socialization and nature of exchanges with the dominant group:

- Degree of commonality between the cultures regarding norms, values, beliefs, and perceptions, including conceptual style and problem-solving approach.

- Availability of cultural translators, mediators, and models.

- Amount and type (e.g., positive or negative) of feedback provided by each culture in relation to efforts to encourage normative behaviors.

- Degree of bilingualism.

- Degree of dissimilarity in physical appearance from the majority culture (e.g., skin color, facial features).

Common Classifications

Different cultures use different classification systems. Other than native Americans, the United States is a country of immigrants and different waves of people have sought new lives here over hundreds of years including recent immigrants from Somalia and from Arab countries with continuing wars. In the United States, we live in a culture that emphasizes differences in race, gender, and ethnicity. Class differences are often ignored even though they have a profound effect on people's options (Liu, 2011; Reiman, 2004). Other common classifications are based on sexual orientation, age, and physical ability. The classifications we use frame our thinking. For instance, ethnicity is a common classification (see Glossary at the end of this chapter). The term *Native American* refers to North American native peoples. Values common to many Native Americans include sharing, cooperation, harmony with nature, and noninterference with others. Native Americans often view themselves as an extension of the tribe, in which older people are respected and valued. The importance of the extended family thus should suggest to social workers the value of meeting with Native American clients in their homes so that significant others can participate. Storytelling is often used to encourage change. Direct confrontation is considered rude and inappropriate. Respect is shown by the avoidance of direct eye contact, and firm handshakes are out of place with Native American clients. Poverty, as well as substance abuse, remains high among Native American people. The Indian Child Welfare Act (PL 95–608) of 1978 mandated that when children are removed from their homes, preference for placement must be given to placing the child with relatives, members of the tribe, or to other Native American families.

The term *Asian American* includes both Asians and Pacific Islanders. About 85% fall into six groups: Chinese, Filipino, Japanese, Korean, Asian Indian, and Vietnamese. Other groups include Cambodian, Burmese, Indonesian, Thai, Samoan, Guamanian, Laotian, Khmer, and Hmong. Differences among individuals in these groups are related to different histories, acculturation patterns, different geographical regions, different socioeconomic classes, family experiences, and reasons for immigration. Characteristics shared by many Chinese and Japanese Americans include deference to authority, emotional restraint, clear roles and hierarchical family structure, and an orientation to the family and extended family. Over 100,000 Japanese Americans were confined in concentration camps during the Second World War. Thousands of Chinese immigrated to the United States in the 1800s to work in mining, farming, and railroad industries.

Chinese Americans are the fastest growing group of Asian Americans in the United States. Religious affiliations include Roman Catholicism, Protestantism, and Buddhism. Some of their values have Confucian and Taoist roots. Very generally, Buddhists believe that we can transcend suffering by avoiding desire or attachment to this world. They believe that living a virtuous life will eliminate desire and that this consists of following the Eightfold Path: right views, right intention, right speech, right conduct, right livelihood, right effort, right mindfulness, and right concentration (Lynch & Hanson, 1992, p. 188). Confucian ideals include loyalty, selfless friendship, filial piety, and a duty to country and family. Certain obligations, responsibilities, and privileges are believed to accompany each family role (father, mother, son, daughter). Compared with European Americans, Asian Americans have a more holistic view of health that includes social, physical, psychological, and cultural factors. Inner conflicts are often expressed in the form of physical complaints. A focus on psychological factors may be embarrassing.

Focused, structured, short-term intervention may be preferred over more nondirective counseling. Helpers are expected to be active and to offer solutions. Japanese culture values indirect over direct communication. Here, too, respect for elders is emphasized, and self-disclosure to strangers may seem foreign and inappropriate. Containment, cooperation, and endurance under extreme pressure were in full display during and following the massive Tsunami that hit Japan in 2011.

As with other groups, African Americans and their families vary widely in their histories, values, and socioeconomic status. Most African Americans are descendants of West Africans who were brought to this country as slaves. From that time until the present, the U.S. class structure has been racialized, leading to the overrepresentation of African Americans in the prison population, unemployment rate, and juvenile delinquency rate. Racism and its reflections in disparities in health care, employment, housing, and educational venues such as inner city schools continues (e.g., CDC Health Disparities and Inequalities Report—United States, 2011). Concerns about racism may be reflected in distrust of white social workers and sensitivity to signs of racism and disregard. African Americans raised in the inner city may speak black English, which uses more nonverbal cues, shorter sentences, some different vocabulary, and less elaboration than does white English. Such differences may lead to misinterpretations or negative stereotypes.

The term *Latino* is preferred by many people from Mexico, Puerto Rico, Cuba, and Central and South American countries who live in the United States. The Latino population is the fastest growing minority population in the United States. Here, too, different groups have different norms, values, and communication styles. In general, cooperation is preferred to competition. Traditional Latino families are patriarchal, having the father as the primary authority figure. Different generations confront different problems in language, strain between cultures, and intergenerational conflicts. Arab Americans are another varied group and, as this population has grown in the United States, the Muslim population has increased.

Class differences refer to differences in economic opportunities, resources, and occupations or positions. Styles of interaction among working-class people differ in certain ways compared with styles of interaction among middle-class people. Racial and ethnic disparities in the quality of and access to services and in diagnoses of psychopathology may reflect class differences (e.g., Gray-Little & Kaplan, 2000; Smedley, Stith, & Nelson, 2003). Inequalities and discrimination as a result of poverty are often ignored. For example, in *The Rich Get Richer and the Poor Get Prison*, Reiman (2004) argues that the wealthy are protected by their wealth from having their crimes recognized and, if recognized, prosecuted with the same vigor with which poor people are prosecuted. This has certainly been born out in the financial meltdown of 2008. The wealthy have effective options to protect themselves from being labeled and prosecuted as criminals, for example, access to high-quality lawyers. General Electric Company, which made a profit of over 26 billion dollars in the last 5 years paid not one penny of federal income taxes thanks in part to the 975 employees in its tax department (Kocieniewski, 2011). In 2010, 25 hedge fund managers received a total of 22.07 billion dollars. "At 50,000 a year, it would take the salaries of 441,400 Americans to match that sum" (Creswell, 2011). CEOs of publicly supported hospitals may make millions of dollars a year. Unions are under attack. The role of economic advantage is illustrated in a report on developmental differences among children in three kinds of families: welfare, working-class, and professional (Hart & Risley, 1995). The investigators studied language development in the children in these three groups during their first 3 years in relation to learning experiences provided by their parents. The average "number of words children heard per hour was 2,150 in professional families, 1,250 in working-class families, and 620 in welfare families" (p. 132). Only relative economic advantage related to differences, not race or ethnicity, gender, or birth order.

The term gender refers to the social representation of an individual (e.g., as male or female) as well as their self-presentation that is culturally produced. The term sex refers to biological classification based on reproductive organs and functions; this is also influenced by hormones and chromosomes. Women's and men's socialization experiences differ as a result of cultural practices and beliefs, though not necessarily to the degrees or in the ways frequently assumed. Differences in gender-based experiences can be seen at a very early age, as demonstrated in studies of the different ways that parents respond to boy and girl infants and that elementary school teachers respond to boys and girls (e.g., see Martin, 1998; Raffaelli & Ontai, 2004). Currently there is considerable exploration of different approaches to gender on the part of young people (e.g., "gender bending") (Spade & Valentine, 2011). Barnett and Rivers (2004) argue that similarities between men and woman have been consistently downplayed and the differences exaggerated with a number of negative effects on both men and women. (See also MacGeorge, Graves, Feng, Gillihan, & Burleson, 2004. For other views on gender differences, see Halpern, 2004; Rhoads, 2004. For a discussion of flaws in related research see Jordan-Young, 2010.)

Clients differ in their sexual orientation. Differences in sexual orientation usually are not visible, thereby creating special opportunities and problems (e.g., the ability to "pass" and the tendency to hide one's sexual orientation because of potential negative reactions). Prejudice and societal hatred pose unique risks for gay and lesbian young people as shown by their high suicide rates (Suicide Risk and Prevention for Lesbian, Gay, Bisexual and Transgender Youth, 2009). Violence and attempts to pass laws mandating discrimination against gay/lesbian individuals highlight the strains that confront gay/lesbian people. The "Don't ask, Don't tell" rule in the military was only recently overturned. In clinical encounters, lesbian and gay people may have to defend their sexuality when their goal is to deal with a relationship problem, "come out" on the job or with family and friends, or handle some situation unrelated to their sexuality. Over 200 gay/lesbian/transgender health centers have been established in the United States to offer services to this population in a nondiscriminatory manner. Persons who are gay or lesbian can be just as effective parents and can fulfill other social roles just as well as can heterosexuals (e.g., Patterson & Wainwright, 2011; Stacey & Biblarz, 2001.) (See Mallon, 2009.) Questions such as the following may help heterosexual people understand how discrimination based on sexual orientation feels:

- What do you think caused your heterosexuality?

- When and how did you first decide you were heterosexual?

- Is it possible that your heterosexuality is just a phase you will grow out of?

- Is it possible your heterosexuality stems from a neurotic fear of people of the same sex? Maybe you just need a positive gay experience?

- Heterosexuals have histories of failures in gay relationships. Do you think you may have turned to heterosexuality because of a fear of rejection?

- To whom have you disclosed your heterosexual tendencies? How did they react?

- Why must you heterosexuals be so blatant, making a public spectacle of your heterosexuality? Can't you just be what you are and keep it quiet?

People who live at a certain time (different cohorts) have different experiences that create unique ways of viewing the world. Some older people are discriminated against because of their age, as are recent refugees because of their immigrant status. There also are regional differences; growing up in New York City is quite different from growing up on a farm in Nebraska. People hold different religious beliefs. Physical disabilities may create unique challenges and needs, such as wheelchair access to transportation. Harlan Lane (1992) argues that deaf people have a distinct culture (e.g., sign language). Although some differences are readily observable, others are not. For example, physical illness may or may not be accompanied by observable indicators.

Thinking Critically About Multiculturalism

Thinking critically about beliefs requires raising questions about views, including "politically correct" ones. It calls for distinguishing between what is simply asserted as true and what is suggested as accurate based on a critical evaluation of claims and concepts. Here too, in the area of multiculturalism, we can find helpers imposing their values on clients, relying on pseudoscience, making false claims, and using empty words (e.g., Ortiz de Montellano, 1992). Here, too, we should examine the

soundness of classifications and theories. Common assumptions that require examination include the following:

- Gender, class, race, and ethnicity are reasonable categories (e.g., there is greater variation among people in different categories than within each group).

- Better services are provided by helpers who match clients (e.g., in race, ethnicity, gender, or sexual orientation).

- In order to offer services to different groups, different knowledge is required.

- Emphasizing cultural differences does more good than harm.

- The less frequent use of mental health services by minority clients deprives them of valuable and needed services.

- All clients want to increase their "critical consciousness" of how their personal problems are affected by economic, political, and social factors.

- Training in multicultural counseling enhances the quality of services.

One myth is that cultural clashes are new, but this is not so. Karl Popper (1992) suggests that cultural clashes resulted in the discovery by the Greeks of critical discussion as a way to gain knowledge. Social workers have always confronted cultural clashes. Another myth is that only certain people or groups have a culture. Everyone has a culture.

Overcoming Barriers to Cross-Cultural Counseling

NASW (2001) Standards for Cultural Competence in Social Work Practice include the following:

1. *Ethics and Values*—Social workers shall function in accordance with the values, ethics, and standards of the profession, recognizing how personal and professional values may conflict with or accommodate the needs of diverse clients.

2. *Self-Awareness*—Social workers shall seek to develop an understanding of their own personal, cultural values and beliefs as one way of appreciating the importance of multicultural identities in the lives of people.

3. *Cross-Cultural Knowledge*—Social workers shall have and continue to develop specialized knowledge and understanding about the history, traditions, values, family systems, and artistic expressions of major client groups that they serve.

4. *Cross-Cultural Skills*—Social workers shall use appropriate methodological approaches, skills, and techniques that reflect

the workers' understanding of the role of culture in the helping process.

5. *Service Delivery*—Social workers shall be knowledgeable about and skillful in the use of services available in the community and broader society and be able to make appropriate referrals for their diverse clients.

6. *Empowerment and Advocacy*—Social workers shall be aware of the effect of social policies and programs on diverse client populations, advocating for and with clients whenever appropriate.

7. *Diverse Workforce*—Social workers shall support and advocate for recruitment, admissions and hiring, and retention efforts in social work programs and agencies that ensure diversity within the profession.

8. *Professional Education*—Social workers shall advocate for and participate in educational and training programs that help advance cultural competence within the profession.

9. *Language Diversity*—Social workers shall seek to provide or advocate for the provision of information, referrals, and services in the language appropriate to the client, which may include use of interpreters.

10. *Cross-Cultural Leadership*—Social workers shall be able to communicate information about diverse client groups to other professionals.

Barriers to cross-cultural helping and suggested ways to address them are discussed in more detail in the section that follows (also see Exhibit 2.5).

1. *Become informed about and take actions to reduce discrimination and oppression.* A familiarity with research documenting the prevalence of discrimination will help you appreciate the unequal hands some people are dealt (e.g, Centeno & Newman, 2010; Wacquant, 2009). Without understanding the effects of oppression and discrimination on creating and maintaining social and personal problems, you may make incorrect assumptions about their causes (e.g., Reiman, 2004). Discriminatory policies and procedures (institutional discrimination) are often the most difficult to identify because they are the "taken-for-granted" background in which we carry out our everyday activities. Examples include real estate agents who screen out African American people, police who use racial profiling, and counselors who give nonwhite clients a higher rate of diagnosis of "psychotic" than

---

EXHIBIT 2.5

Barriers and Remedies Related to Cross-Cultural Helping

Barrier	Remedy
1. Discriminatory and oppressive practices, policies, and legislation.	1. Work together with concerned others to identify, document, expose, and alter related practices, policies, and legislation. A contextual assessment should suggest leverage points for change. (See chapter 12.)
2. A focus on punishing prejudicial statements and actions rather than reinforcing positive ones.	2. Reinforce positive alternatives to prejudice; reeducate, win over.
3. Biases, prejudices, and stereotypes.	3. Identify and alter them.
4. Lack of knowledge about a group's history, norms, expectations, and values and individual differences within it.	4. Become informed.
5. Lack of communication skills required to negotiate differences.	5. Acquire needed skills (e.g., active listening, empathy).
6. Lack of facility in client's language.	6. Learn the language; use translators; hire bilingual staff.
7. Fear of differences.	7. Value cultural differences as opportunities to forward understanding, solve problems, and to learn.
8. Uncritical acceptance of common classifications (e.g., Asian, white, black).	8. Critically evaluate common classifications and their consequences.
9. Organizational barriers (e.g., service patterns based on beliefs, values, and norms that conflict with those of clients).	9. Involve other concerned professionals in identifying and changing dysfunctional/unfair procedures and policies.
10. Confusing pursuit of personal and political goals with the pursuit of knowledge.	10. Be honest about personal and political agendas. Evaluate the evidence for claims.
11. Not recognizing our shared humanness (e.g., of problems, potentials). Relying on stereotypes (e.g., race, ethnicity).	11. Recognize our shared humanness and experiences.
12. A belief that empathy is enough to help others.	12. Combine empathy with offering help.

white clients. Work together with concerned others to alter practices, policies, and related legislation that restrict opportunities for certain groups. You may help your clients become more aware of the political, social, and economic factors that contribute to their problems; that is, you may raise their critical consciousness (Freire, 1973). You may help clients to realize that change in individual situations "is often critically dependent on wider structural alterations fought for collectively" (Brookfield, 1995). This will require a familiarity with legislation in your area of interest.

2. *Confront racist and other prejudicial statements and actions and support positive alternatives.* When confronted with discriminatory practices and prejudiced behavior, you have choices about how and whether to respond. Your actions will be influenced by your goals. Possible goals may be to put the offender in his place, let him know that you are not going to put up with _____, reeducate him, or work together with others to reduce prejudice and discrimination. Your goals may differ depending on the situation. You may lose an opportunity to win over and reeducate an offender in your rush to bring prejudiced remarks to his attention. Consider Fineberg's (1949) example of a woman who attended a dinner party at which another woman made a racist remark. On their way home, her partner asked why she did not "call her" on her remark. The woman replied that she did not think that the woman was really prejudiced and that she had bigger plans for her—to reeducate her and to get her actively involved in an antiracist organization—which she was able to do. We may accomplish more by reinforcing alternative positive behaviors than by punishing undesired behaviors.

3. *Identify and neutralize biases, prejudices, and stereotypes.* A bias is an emotional leaning to one side in regard to a person, group, or issue; a prejudice is a negative, preconceived judgment that is not supported by fact and that may result in unequal treatment (see Glossary to this chapter). We often seek data consistent with our biases and prejudices and ignore contradictory evidence. Prejudice does not always result in discrimination. Critically examining assumptions is a characteristic of reflective helpers. Prejudice is more likely when two groups compete with each other, a contact is unpleasant, involuntary, and tense, and a group's prestige or status may decrease as a result of contact. It is more likely when one group's moral or ethical standards are objectionable to another group and the members of a group are of lower status or lower in some other characteristics compared with the majority group.

What are your biases and stereotypes regarding different groups or problems? How do they affect your practice decisions? Prejudices are often based on stereotypes. A *stereotype* refers to responding to a person as if he or she were a member of a group and, in so doing, overlooking differences between the individual and the group. Stereotypes often are caricatures of supposed group traits. For example, if you believe that all Mexican American husbands expect to make all important decisions, you may incorrectly assume this about a Mexican American couple who prefer to make decisions together. We may not even be aware of our biases as shown by comparison of verbal statements and physiological reactions (Greenwald, Poehlman, Uhlman, and Banaji, 2009). Familiarity with a group does not always increase understanding and liking. Beliefs related to racism include the following:

- The belief that there are well-defined and distinctive ethnic groups and races.

- The belief that racial mixing lowers biological quality.

- The belief that some races are superior to others.

- The belief that some groups are naturally prone to criminality, sexual looseness, or dishonest business practices.

- The belief that the "superior" races should rule and dominate the "inferior" races.

- The belief that there are temperamental differences among races.

Gender discrimination is prevalent in all socioeconomic classes. Gay, lesbian, and transgender individuals often confront harassment, discrimination, and physical abuse as illustrated in efforts to legislate discrimination against them. Familiarity with research documenting the prevalence of biases, prejudices, and stereotypes and their effects will help you to appreciate their pervasiveness and the seriousness of their consequences. Biases and stereotypes are not figments of an overly active imagination (as some might have us believe). Racist attitudes and actions are rife. An attitude can be defined as holding certain beliefs about certain individuals and being predisposed to act toward them in certain ways. Attitudes and behaviors may not be closely related. Literature describing efforts to alter attitudes toward certain groups (e.g., people with disabilities, gay/lesbian people, people of certain ethnic groups) suggests that altering attitudes may be slow going, perhaps because programs address only one of multiple interlinked contingency systems that influence attitudes (e.g., the individual level) leaving in place contingencies at other levels (e.g., cultural practices) that maintain certain attitudes.

4. *Learn about and be attentive to cultural differences.* Individually tailoring services to each client's unique circumstances, expectations, values, and customs as needed to help clients and avoid harm may require becoming informed about the disadvantages poor people confront (e.g., Reiman, 2004). It may require learning about the ghettos in which many poor African American youth grow up (Wacquant,

2009) and understanding the meaning of certain nonverbal behaviors in different cultures. Consider, for example, the meaning of the following nonverbal behaviors to people with Filipino roots:

- Beckoning someone with an index finger may be interpreted as a sign of contempt.

- Showing anger or criticizing someone in public is discouraged. People are expected to control their emotions and avoid direct confrontation.

- Some Filipinos smile when upset or embarrassed (Lynch & Hanson, 2011, pp. 350–361).

Information about refugees' experiences when leaving their country of origin and their difficulties in adjusting to a new culture may be vital to obtain. Challenges that refugees and immigrants may confront in their new homeland include an unfamiliar language, new customs and values, a lack of work opportunities, possible discrimination, and scarce low-cost housing.

You might assume that a client who is reluctant to make decisions without consulting family members is excessively dependent, when in fact her wish reflects the norms and values of her culture. Cultures also have different norms regarding expressiveness. Whereas helpers may expect their clients to discuss openly their feelings and problems, clients may be reluctant to share their personal feelings and experiences with strangers. Overlooking cultural differences may result in inaccurately viewing clients as inhibited and/or repressed. Assertion training that emphasizes the open expression of feelings is not appropriate for all clients.

You may win a client's trust by candidly discussing the differences between the two of you. Think of a scale ranging from 0 (no cultural differences) to 10 (great differences) in relation to the degree of match between two people. The higher up the scale one goes, the more important relevant cultural knowledge, open-mindedness, and skill in negotiating differences may be. Seek useful training opportunities, and consult other sources for further detail about multicultural counseling and the history, language, and culture of different groups, such as *Guidelines in Multicultural Education, Training, Research, Practice, and Organizational Change,* 2003; Hays & Erford, 2010; Lum, 2004; Lynch & Hanson, 2011; Ponterotto, Casas, Suzuki, & Alexander, 2010; Sue & Sue, 2008.

5. *Acquire and use skills in negotiating differences.* Knowledge of cultural differences will be of little value if this is not accompanied by skills and values that encourage its use. Use the communication skills described in chapter 15 (e.g., active listening and empathy) to put your knowledge about differences to good use. Recognizing each client's individuality should help you to avoid imposing your values on clients.

As Sue and Sue (1990) note, "qualities such as respect and acceptance of the individual, positive regard, understanding the problem from the individual's perspective, allowing the client to explore his or her own values, and arriving at an individual solution are core qualities that may transcend cultures" (p. 187). Be aware of your own communication styles and how they influence others. Alter those that get in the way.

6. *Acquire or arrange for needed language skills.* If you work with clients who do not speak your language, learn their language, use translators, or encourage your agency to hire bilingual staff members. It is hard enough to communicate when we speak each other's language. Seek clarification when you are unsure what a client means. Misunderstandings may lead to incomplete or incorrect views of client concerns and result in selection of ineffective or harmful services.

7. *Value culture clashes.* We tend to like people who are similar to ourselves and to dislike and fear differences. The greater the differences, the greater our fears may be. Creating such fears is encouraged by the media (Altheide, 2002). Cultural differences are often regarded as negative, as hampering communication and resulting in stress and misunderstanding. However, such differences may be essential to attain shared hoped-for outcomes and to advance knowledge (Popper, 1994).

> Culture is the widening of the mind and of the spirit.
> —Jawaharal Nehru

8. *Critically evaluate common classifications and their effects.* Classifications are based on certain presumed characteristics. For example, we may think of ourselves as black, white, a lesbian, or a senior citizen. Common classifications (e.g., race, ethnicity) require critical appraisal. Are they sound? Do they do more good than harm? What evidence do you have for your views? What is normal? What is abnormal? Who is to say? And on what grounds? (See chapter 6.) Although many people in a group may share a certain history, they may do so in different ways and with different outcomes. It is easy to assume that the categories we use to classify people are inevitable and correct when in fact they may be neither. Perhaps we should classify people in relation to their altruistic contributions, their civility, and their environmental caring (contribution to rather than denigration of the environment). Yheudi Webster (1992), an African American sociologist, argues that categories such as race and gender are social classifications used to limit opportunities for certain kinds of people (those who are poor, dark skinned, and female). He believes that categories such as gender, class, race, and ethnicity perpetuate discrimination and oppression by encouraging classifications that do not accurately define the group's variability and that the very notions of "black" and "white" people as classifications are self-defeating and dangerous political myths

(see also Webster, 1997). He emphasizes *racialization* (rather than race), referring to race as a distinguishing characteristic because of political and social interests (see the discussion of racial, ethnic, and class theories of social problems in chapter 6).

Some writers suggest that a focus on cultural groups allows us to avoid the responsibility and effort required to make our own reasoned moral judgments (Finkielkraut, 1995). That is, we may fall back on a general classification, such as sexual orientation, as a reason for our beliefs or actions, rather than thinking things through for ourselves. We may say, "I'm Chinese. That's what we believe." In this way, we may become "subservient" to a "culture" that may not really exist because it contains so many different subcultures. Use your critical thinking skills to examine the inferences on which common classifications are based and the effects of such classifications. Classifications have consequences. Uncritical acceptance of common ones may result in thinking less of a person because he or she is in a certain category or in setting ourselves apart as better. In either case our shared humanness may be obscured and learning opportunities lost.

9. *Remove organizational barriers.* Western-style mental health and psychotherapy may not be appropriate for some clients. Clients may prefer structured approaches that address economic, educational, vocational, and material needs. Examine both your agency and interagency relationships, and identify changes that could be made to enhance the effectiveness of services, such as hiring bilingual staff. Just as our bodies are embodied theories (Popper, 1994), organizations are embodied repositories of values and related practices and policies. Work with colleagues who share your concerns and select one or two changes to pursue systematically that would increase culturally appropriate services. How do formal and informal communication channels in your agency and among agencies influence services offered? What changes would be helpful and possible? Hyde (2003) suggests that multicultural initiatives in agencies may do more harm than good by wasting resources on ineffective training programs, not investigating the impact of such programs on services clients receive (lack of accountability), and "objectifying" clients by ignoring the environmental context in which a client resides.

10. *Don't confound personal and political agendas and the search for truth.* We all have political and personal agendas—interests we would like to advance. It is easy to confuse them with the pursuit of truth. Community organizers may claim, "We need money for more recreation centers. We know that this will decrease crime," even though they may have no evidence that such centers will decrease crime and it is not obvious that it will do so. (Not every claim requires testing. The consequences of some actions are quite clear such as jumping out of a flying airplane (Smith & Pell, 2003)).

Instead, they should say: "We will test whether they do affect crime." Confounding political agendas and evidentiary issues obscures what has been critically appraised and what has not, making it more difficult to accurately inform clients and other interested parties. Advantages of being honest about which practices and policies have been critically tested and which have not include preventing harming clients in the name of helping them.

11. *Recognize our shared humanness.* Emphasizing differences prevents us from recognizing shared hopes, values, problems, and experiences and may decrease our empathy for others. It may preclude forming the broad-based coalitions needed to make changes valued by many people, regardless of race, class, gender, ethnicity, sexual orientation, age, or physical ability. Yheudi Webster believes that classifications such as race, class, and ethnicity should be abandoned because they perpetuate the consciousness of difference that underlies "dehumanization" (1992, p. 264) and that social problems should be classified as human problems. (See chapter 6.) It is human beings who are discriminated against and oppressed. In this human-centered theory, human beings are viewed as the victims of deficient government and corporate policies. Such an approach reflects a human rights approach as described in chapter 3.

12. *Don't be satisfied with empathy.* In his passionate book *The Night Is Dark and I Am Far from Home* (1990), Jonathan Kozol suggests that we often confuse an empathy for others' plights with doing something to help them. That is, we use caring as an indication that we are doing something to relieve misery and injustice when, in fact, we are doing nothing.

Problems and Their Prospects

Problems differ in their prospects for resolution. Clients' interests in acquiring hoped-for outcomes may not be possible to meet because of gaps in services. They may not be solvable because of need for changes in discriminatory legislation. Only if you attend to the close relationship between the personal and the political are you likely to see "the big picture" and identify needed changes at this level. Without this, you are likely to become accustomed to offering less than clients deserve (e.g., individual counseling).

Summary

Only some people with certain kinds of problems seek aid from, or are referred to, social service agencies. Those who do typically pursue other options first, such as talking to friends and relatives. It may be difficult to find out where to go for different kinds of aid, and it is the agency's responsibility to make its services known and to integrate them with those of other agencies. The expectations and goals of both clients and social workers, eligibility requirements, time limits, preferred practice frameworks, and criteria used to select them influence the quality of services clients receive. Cultural differences influence whose help is sought, what are viewed as problems, what causes are favored to account for them, and what methods and outcomes are preferred. Western-style service approaches are not appropriate for all clients. Many clients are forced to see social workers; they are reluctant participants. Acknowledging coercive aspects of client presence is vital.

Barriers to helping include the service providers' prejudices and stereotypes and a lack of knowledge about cultural differences. An uncritical acceptance of questionable classifications such as race may get in the way of recognizing common human needs and individual differences related to concerns and options for resolution. Lack of communication skills needed to negotiate differences and lack of language facility may present obstacles. Barriers suggest ways to overcome them, for example, to learn about differences that help you work effectively with clients, to become aware of biases and stereotypes and change dysfunctional service delivery systems.

Exploring Your Expectations, Values, and Beliefs

1. Imagine that you need money and are on your way to the local welfare office to ask for aid. Describe your thoughts and feelings. Complete the following items:

   a. People who ask for financial help are _____

   b. Giving financial aid to people is _____

2. Whom do you seek help from when you have a problem? Give an example and explain why you would consult this person.

3. Did you ever seek help for a problem? If not, what are your reasons?

4. Do you have any biases that might affect how you would react to Julie? (See the case example in this chapter.) Complete the following:

   • Abortion is _____

   • People who have abortions are _____

   • If I had an unplanned pregnancy, I would _____

5. Would you have any biases about Mrs. Ryan if the Greens consulted you? (See the case example in this chapter.) Complete the following statements:

   a. People over 75 are usually _____

   b. If an elderly relative wanted to live with me, I would _____

   c. If I were over 75, I would _____

6. Describe one of your "differences" that you are willing to discuss and how it has affected your life.

Reviewing Your Competencies

Reviewing Content Knowledge

1. Describe some reasons why people may not seek help either from service agencies or informal sources.

2. Distinguish among resisters, applicants, and clients.

3. Describe helpers' expectations and goals and explain why they are important to consider.

4. Describe clients' expectations and goals and factors that influence them.

5. Describe the characteristics of Western-style mental health agencies and how they may differ from what some clients may expect or value.

6. Give examples of "blaming the victim" that result from stereotypes and prejudice.

7. Give examples of content knowledge that may help you in working with different kinds of clients.

8. Describe different definitions of culture.

9. Discuss problems with classifying people by race, class, or ethnicity.

Reviewing What You Do

1. A review of your audiotaped or videotaped interviews shows that you are sensitive to differences among clients, applicants, and resisters. You

   a. Discuss the resisters' feelings and possible objections.

   b. Do not respond in kind to hostile or negative comments; you offer disarming responses.

c. Use a range of methods to "engage" people (see chapter 14).

d. Do not act as if you are working with a client when the person is an applicant or resister.

2. You clarify expectations about what will occur.

3. Your language and the helping methods you select reflect sensitivity to individual differences.

4. You avoid judgmental responses.

5. You seek information about your clients' expectations and desired outcomes.

6. Given a case example, you can describe cultural differences that you should consider.

7. You can identify sources of discrimination and oppression that may be related to certain kinds of personal and social problems.

8. Given a case example, you can identify your biases and stereotypes.

Reviewing Results

1. Applicants and resisters become clients.

2. Clients achieve desired outcomes.

Glossary

Acculturation: The integration of values, behaviors, and traditions of a dominant culture with those of another.

Assimilation: The blending of the culture of one group with that of another. By adopting the customs, beliefs, and norms of the dominant culture, a group loses its unique identity.

Bias: Partiality shown in relation to an individual or group.

Bicultural: Being a part of two or more different cultures.

Class: Differences in economic opportunities, resources, and certain occupations or positions. Education, occupation, income, and relationship to the means of production determine social class.

Class theory of social relations: An appeal to economic differences to account for social problems.

Cultural pluralism: The existence of many cultures in a region. Certain groups maintain their own social structure, values, and patterns of behavior. This term is also used to reflect the values of harmonious relationships among groups and a lack of discrimination and dysfunctional competition for resources.

Culture: The values and beliefs and related social contingencies that guide a group's conduct, passed on from one generation to another. A culture includes language, values, religious beliefs and customs, art forms, and patterns of social relationships.

Discrimination: The differential treatment of individuals on the basis of their social category by people or as a result of institutional policies they create and enforce. Discriminatory actions deprive certain persons or groups of valued opportunities; the unfair treatment of one group by another. Those who discriminate against others may or may not be prejudiced against them (Merton, 1949).

Ethnic identity: A person's particular values, traditions, and behaviors that are assumed to be based on cultural differences related to ancestry, national origin, or religion.

Ethnic theory of social relations: Reliance on ethnic differences to account for social relations.

Ethnicity: An identity and sense of belonging assumed to be based on cultural differences in values, attitudes, customs, and rituals related to a common ancestry, national origin, or religion. People who are part of a particular ethnic group often believe that they are different from other groups in important ways. An ethnic group is assumed to "differ from a racial group, which is defined with references to anatomical similarities" (Webster, 1992, p. 14).

Ethnocentrism: Reliance on the cultural practices in one's ethnic group as a central reference point.

Genocide: The systematic killing of members of a particular group with the intention of eliminating the whole group.

Individual Racism: Feelings of superiority to another racial group. Negative views of the cultural differences of different racial groups. Racism may be overt or covert. It may result in calling people names, social exclusion or violence.

Institutional Discrimination: Discriminatory acts against a group in the educational, legal, law enforcement, economic, or political areas. These acts are incorporated in the operating procedures of bureaucracies and lead to unequal outcomes for certain groups of people.

Marginality: Being a part of different groups without fully being part of either. An example is a client with an invisible (not observable) illness.

Minority group: A group of persons with unequal access to power that is considered by the majority group to be in some way unworthy of sharing power equally and that is stigmatized in terms of assumed inferior traits or characteristics (Mindel & Habenstein, 1981, pp. 7–8).

Oppression: The discriminatory treatment of an individual or group based on (for example) gender, age, or sexual orientation.

Prejudice: "A faulty generalization from a group characteristic (stereotype) to an individual member of the group, irrespective of either (1) the accuracy of the group stereotype, or (2) the applicability of the group characterization to the individual in question" (Jones, 1986, p. 288).

Race: Grouping people based on skin color and other anatomical characteristics as a social construction, not a biological construction.

Race relations: Racialized social relations.

Racial theory of social relations: A combination of racial classification (reliance on anatomical criteria to form distinct populations) and racial causation (the imputation of a determining status to racial attributes in the explanation of behavior) (Webster, 1992). The victimization of nonwhites by whites and the uniqueness of each race's immigrant experiences are emphasized.

Segregation: Confinement of a group to particular areas (geographical/institutional).

3

Values, Ethics, and Obligations

OVERVIEW This chapter provides an overview of practice-related ethical concerns. The relationship between values and ethics is discussed, and key social work values and ethical principles are described. Ethical obligations to clients provide a guide for what to do in challenging circumstances such as raising questions about services that may harm clients. Giving clients options to enhance the quality of their lives and involving clients as informed participants in decisions made are emphasized. The close relationship between evidentiary and ethical issues is highlighted. Additional discussion of ethical concerns related to engaging clients, assessment, selection of plans, and evaluation of outcomes is included in chapters dealing with these topics.

YOU WILL LEARN ABOUT

- Values and ethical obligations

- Critical thinking and evidence-informed practice and policy as guides

- Self-determination and empowerment as key values

- Informed consent

- Respect for the dignity and worth of each person

- Confidentiality: Ethical concerns and legal regulations

- Ethical issues related to competence

- Ethical and legal issues related to case records

- Ethical issues related to sexual conduct

- Other ethical concerns

- The importance of knowledge about legal regulations and resources

- Liability (bases for lawsuits and how to avoid them)

- Clients' options when confronted with illegal or unethical behavior on the part of professionals

- Ethics and ideology

- Can the fox guard the chickens?

- Encouraging ethical behavior

Values and Ethical Obligations

Values can be defined as the social principles, goals, or standards held by an individual, group, or society (see Exhibit 3.1). Values state preferences regarding certain goals and how to attain them. They are used in support of decisions at many different levels (e.g., policy, legislation, agency practice, and helper decisions). The preamble to the Code of Ethics of the National Association of Social Workers (NASW) states, "The mission of the social work profession is rooted in a set of core values. These core values, embraced by social workers throughout the profession's history, are the foundation of social work's unique purpose and perspective" (2008). Core values emphasized are (1) service, (2) social justice, (3) dignity and worth of the person, (4) importance of human relationships, (5) integrity, and (6) competence. Ethical issues are moral-value issues suggesting that some ways of acting

---

EXHIBIT 3.1

Ethical Principles of the NASW Code of Ethics

VALUE I: SERVICE

Ethical Principle: *Social workers' primary goal is to help people in need and to address social problems.*
Social workers elevate service to others above self-interest. Social workers draw on their knowledge, values, and skills to help people in need and to address social problems. Social workers are encouraged to volunteer some portion of their professional skills with no expectation of significant financial return (pro bono service).

VALUE II: SOCIAL JUSTICE

Ethical Principle: *Social workers challenge social injustice.*
Social workers pursue social change, particularly with and on behalf of vulnerable and oppressed individuals and groups of people. Social workers' social change efforts are focused primarily on issues of poverty, discrimination, and other forms of social injustice. These activities seek to promote sensitivity to and knowledge about oppression, and cultural and ethnic diversity. Social workers strive to ensure access to needed information, services, and resources; equality of opportunity; and meaningful participation in decision making for all people.

VALUE III: DIGNITY AND WORTH OF THE PERSON

Ethical Principle: *Social workers respect the inherent dignity and worth of the person.*
Social workers treat each person in a caring and respectful fashion, mindful of individual differences and cultural and ethnic diversity. Social workers promote clients' socially responsible self-determination. Social workers seek to enhance clients' capacity and opportunity to change and to address their own needs. Social workers are cognizant of their dual responsibility to clients and to the broader society. They seek to resolve conflicts between clients' interest and the broader society's interests in a socially responsible manner consistent with the values, ethical principles, and ethical standards of the profession.

VALUE IV: IMPORTANCE OF HUMAN RELATIONSHIPS

Ethical Principle: *Social workers recognize the central importance of human relationships.* Social workers understand that relationships between and among people are an important vehicle for change. Social workers engage people as partners in the helping process. Social workers seek to strengthen relationships among people in a purposeful effort to promote, restore, maintain, and enhance the well-being of individuals, families, social groups, organizations, and communities.

VALUE V: INTEGRITY

Ethical Principle: *Social workers behave in a trustworthy manner.*
Social workers are continually aware of the profession's mission, values, ethical principles, and ethical standards, and practice in a manner consistent with them. Social workers act honestly and responsibly and promote ethical practices on the part of the organizations with which they are affiliated.

VALUE VI: COMPETENCE

Ethical Principle: *Social workers practice within their areas of competence and develop and enhance their professional expertise.*
Social workers continually strive to increase their professional knowledge and skills and to apply them in practice. Social workers should aspire to contribute to the knowledge base of the profession.

Source: National Association of Social Workers (2008). *Code of ethics*. Retrieved November 1, 2011, from http://www.socialworkers.org. Reprinted with permission.

are bad, good, wrong, or right. Related differences of opinion are at the heart of different points of view about the "best way to live," the most moral way to behave, and how to structure society (e.g., Sen, 2009). Decisions we make about ethics include:

- What questions we view as a matter of ethics.

- What principles to use as a guide.

- How consistently to act on them: Are they universal?

- What to do if we cannot fulfill them.

- Whether to involve others in confronting ethical challenges.

- How to appraise ethical dilemmas: as burdensome, or as inevitable challenges to be struggled with in an honest, open, professional manner in which we learn how to best handle them in a just way.

Values are reflected in ethical principles and related actions. In consequentialism, acts and intentions are morally evaluated by their consequences. Deontologists argue that some choices are morally forbidden no matter how good their consequences. Duties and rules are emphasized. Virtue ethics emphasize moral character. (See other sources for more detail such as the *Stanford Encyclopedia of Philosophy*.) Some values stress fairness for the least advantaged individuals in society. People differ in their values, even within an agency. For example, some staff may believe corporal punishment of a child is necessary (allowed in Mississippi). Others may not. Clients and social workers may differ in their values. The greater the diversity of cultures, the greater the potential differences. More attention has been paid to the ethics of helping over the past years (e.g., Gambrill, 2009; Reamer, 2006). The field of bioethics has mushroomed so much that there is a counter-reaction to this. Greater attention has been given to a human rights perspective (e.g., Cemlyn, 2008; Hickey & Mitlin, 2009). Such an approach emphasizes the dignity and worth of all human beings and is reflected in a number of national and international statements. The U.K. human rights law has been drawn on to reveal abuses within immigration detention.

Helping (Beneficence) and Avoiding Harm (Non-malfeasance) as Key Principles

Service is the first value listed in the NASW Code of Ethics, which also is included in the philosophy of practice described in chapter 1. Some procedures designed to protect people may have the opposite effect. The juvenile court system stripped juveniles of the basic rights available to adults (*In re Gault*, 387 U.S. 1, 87 S. Ct. 1428 18 L.Ed.2d 527 (1967)). Harm includes removing valuable opportunities, locking people up against their will for victimless crimes, stigmatizing them by means of negative diagnostic labels, and not fully informing clients, with the result that they make decisions they otherwise would not make. Consider

the allegations that a government report made concerning treatments for head injuries:

> Unethical marketing (e.g., lying to the families of people suffering recent brain injuries and pressure tactics to gain access to hospital records of patients with substantial insurance).
>
> Bad care. Patients who said they were promised intensive therapy report finding quadriplegic children unattended, having lain for hours or days in vomit or feces. Others said their children's condition seriously deteriorated from neglect.
>
> Expensive rehabilitation programs that admit and keep patients who cannot benefit from them, simply to garner insurance payments. One researcher found that for an average nine-month stay, patients were charged $106,000 for treatment not justified by the results. Patients released after less than six months did just as well, the researcher found.
>
> Companies instructing medical staff members to file false or misleading reports of patient progress to insurance companies. (Kerr, 1992a, p. A1)

Reports in our daily newspapers describe harming in the name of helping, for example, in residential facilities for juveniles (use of excessive force by staff), in skilled nursing facilities (e.g., overmedication), and residential centers for children and adults with disabilities (e.g., Levy, 2002; Pear, 2004). Staff are often overwhelmed with cases and poorly trained.

Mandated services designed to protect clients may fail to do so as illustrated in a review of 129 randomly selected child welfare case records in the state of New Jersey (DePanfilis, 2003). These records were made available for examination only after a successful lawsuit.

> One of the most dramatic findings from this study relates to the poor quality of decision-making. Based on the facts documented in the files, the decisions were found to be professionally unreasonable 25% of the time. The research team found numerous examples of cases that documented unjustified actions or omissions of the caregiver, which resulted in substantial harm or risk of harm to children, yet the investigation concluded with a finding of "not substantiated." Such case findings are inconsistent with the exercise of reasonable professional judgment, and put children at risk of ongoing harm in out-of-home care settings that are not closed to further placements.
>
> For example, one case was unsubstantiated even though a foster mother admitted striking a child with a belt resulting in a 4 inch linear belt mark on the child's face. This foster mother had two prior substantiated incidents of abuse or neglect. There were equally serious examples of neglect to children that were classified as not substantiated, such as medically documented serious neglect of hygiene and nutrition that resulted in developmental delays, low weight, and pain and irritation to the child's skin.

Specific findings included:

- Only 12% (15 cases) of alleged maltreatment in out-of-home placements were substantiated, although 33% of the cases (40 cases) should have been substantiated if reasonable professional judgment had been exercised.

- Risk of harm to children was noted in 40% of investigations, and removal of victims from unsafe placements was recommended in 29% (35) of the cases, even though only 12% of all cases were substantiated.

- First-hand observations by DYFS workers of serious abuse and neglect in out-of-home placements were repeatedly discounted.

- 58% of the cases that were "unsubstantiated" should have been substantiated.

- 17% of the cases that were "unfounded" should have been substantiated. (p. 7)

State child welfare services have been deemed so poor in many states that judges have ruled they be placed in conservatorship (Eamons & Kopels, 2004; Gainsborough, 2010). (See also the website of Children's Rights <http://www.childrensrights.org>.) Many consumer groups, as well as scholars such as Thomas Szasz (2002), describe coercion in the helping profession and argue that it is unethical. Increasing attention has been given to conflicts of interest of researchers and professionals (e.g., Lo & Field, 2009).

Social Justice

Social justice is another value emphasized in professional codes of ethics. Clearly many people suffer from profound injustices including abuse and lack of basic services such as health care (e.g., see Farmer, 2004; Ptacek 2010). The NASW Code of Ethics emphasizes the social justice mission of social work on behalf of "vulnerable, disadvantaged, oppressed, and exploited people and groups." It advises social workers to "act to prevent and eliminate domination of, exploitation of, and discrimination against any person, group, or class on the basis of race, ethnicity, national origin, color, sex, sexual orientation, gender identity or age, marital status, political belief, religion, immigration status, or mental or physical disability" (6.04). It calls on social workers to "engage in social and political action that seeks to ensure that all people have equal access to the resources, employment, services, and opportunities they require to meet their basic human needs and to develop fully" (6.04). Can social workers achieve these aims? Beneficence as related to an individual client may clash with increasing justice for others (e.g., a more equitable distribution of opportunities). What may be justice for some may be injustice for others.

Hayek (1976) views the belief in social justice as "the gravest threat to most other values of a free civilization" (p. 67) and contends that there is no agreement on standards to evaluate the extent to which there is social justice. Therefore, some people must impose their standards on others. He argues that the belief in social justice "has lured men to abandon many of the values which in the past have inspired the development of civilization" (p. 67), that this goal is unattainable, and that striving for it creates undesirable consequences such as further limiting personal freedom. (See critiques and responses by Lukes, 1997; Johnston, 1997; and Feser, 1998.) Those who advocate "social justice" as a goal should consider concerns raised by Hayek to make sure that in pursuit of justice for some, injustices are not imposed on others. Popper (1994) suggests that we do not know how to make people happy, but we could agree on avoidable miseries. Taking steps to decrease them would move us toward justice. (See discussion of social workers as social reformers in chapter 1.)

A key way forward is to be clear as to what we mean by social justice. Reichert (2007) and others (e.g., Wronka, 2012) suggest moving to a Human Rights Perspective to address oppression (e.g., unjust use of authority and power) and to enhance empowerment (increased access to resources) (e.g., see Ensalaco & Majka, 2005; Hertel & Libal, 2011). Human rights have been defined as "those rights, which are inherent in our nature and without which we cannot live as human beings. Human rights and fundamental freedoms allow us to fully develop and use our human qualities, our intelligence, our talents and our conscience and to satisfy our spiritual and other needs" (Universal Declaration of Human Rights, 1948; United Nations High Commission for Human Rights, 2005). Key ideas in the declaration of human rights include human dignity, nondiscrimination, civil and political rights, economic, social, and cultural rights, and solidarity rights (see Wronka, 2012). Everyone "…has the right to a standard of living adequate for the health and well-being of himself and of his family, including food, clothing, housing and medical care and necessary social services." In addition, "motherhood and childhood are entitled to special care and assistance" and all have a right to a free education at the elementary level (Universal Declaration of Human Rights, 1948, Articles 16–27).

Ethical Dilemmas

In ethical dilemmas, two or more principles or values conflict or it is difficult or impossible to be faithful to an ethical principle. For example, should people who have repeatedly assaulted others and caused serious injury and/or loss of life be paroled, even though there is a high probability that they will continue such actions? Here, self-determination and protecting others from harm are in conflict. Factors to consider include:

1. Client interests.

2. The interests and rights of other involved parties such as family members or victims.

3. Professional code of ethics.

4. Personal values of the social worker.

5. Agency policy.

6. Legal regulations.

7. Related empirical literature.

Reaching decisions agreeable to all interested parties will often be difficult (or impossible). "Practitioners are asked to solve problems every day that philosophers have argued about for the last two thousand years and will probably debate for the next two thousand. Inevitably, arbitrary lines have to be drawn and hard cases decided" (Dingwall, Eekelaar, & Murray, 1983, p. 244). This remains true today. Certain action may be legally mandated. Legal issues concern legislated rights or obligations, which may or may not be possible to act on. For example, parents may have a legal right to educate their children at home but not be able to do so because of insufficient funds. Some rights are both moral and legal, such as the right to free speech. They conform to a standard of behavior and also are legally mandated.

Critical Thinking and Evidence-Informed Practice and Policy as Guides

Ethical choices involve assigning values to different options after reviewing the likely results of each. Critical thinking is integrally related to making ethical decisions (e.g., Baron, 1985). Both critical thinking and evidence-informed practice encourage us to prefer truth to ignorance and prejudice (for example, to draw on practice and policy-related research findings concerning decisions that affect clients' lives), to avoid bias, and to think carefully about our responsibilities and the match between what we say we value and what we do. Decisions often have unintended and unwanted consequences. Critical appraisal of options can help us to catch and avoid some of these. This includes seeking clarity, questioning assumptions, and considering different perspectives. This can help you to identify involved participants and their interests (e.g., clients, significant others, the agency, community) and the possible consequences of different courses of action. Ask yourself the following questions:

- What exactly is the issue? (e.g., what resources are involved? freedom? money?)

- Who is involved and in what ways?

- What are alternative options?

- What are the likely consequences of each option for those who may be affected?

- What may be the unintended consequences of each option?

- What research findings (if any) provide a helpful guide (e.g., about the accuracy of claims and practice frameworks)?

- What grounds would best serve as a guide (e.g., equity in resource distribution, reduction of avoidable misery)?

- What changes could (and should) be made at what levels (individual, family, community, agency, service system, policy, legislation) to honor ethical principles?

Clients are often encouraged to consider both future as well as immediate consequences, for example, of smoking and unprotected sexual intercourse. Reflecting critically on the decisions you make (referred to as as reflexivity by some) will increase the likelihood of making ethical decisions. For example, you will be more likely to question initial assumptions and consider other points of view. You will be more likely to spot questionable appeals and arguments that, if acted on, would harm clients. Exhibit 3.2 provides an opportunity to critically review an ethical concern.

Thinking critically about ethical issues related to practice and policy will help you to discover unrecognized concerns and balance the advantages and disadvantages of acting versus not acting (see Exhibit 3.3). You will see many injustices in your role as a social worker, both within social work and without. Will you do anything? Will you work with others to minimize avoidable injustices, such as hostile staff in immigration centers, rude receptionists, and social workers who offer services that are ineffective and often unwanted (and unneeded in the sense that outcomes addressed are self-chosen and do not harm others)? Thinking critically about decisions you make will help you to distinguish between legitimate and illegitimate uses of authority and power. (See also later discussion of victimless crimes.) The influence of professionals is not always obvious. In fact, the more subtle it is, the more controlling it may be because it is not noticed as with social psychological persuasion strategies (Cialdini, 2001; Pratkanis, 2007).

The Close Connection Between Ethical and Evidentiary Issues

Most books and articles on ethics focus on concerns related to direct work with clients such as confidentiality and maintaining appropriate boundaries with clients. These concerns are important. However, there are many other ethical concerns

EXHIBIT 3.2

Thinking Critically About an Ethical Dilemma

Select an ethical dilemma related to social work practice that you have encountered or know about.

1. Describe the dilemma.
2. Note how the following are involved and may conflict:
   - Client's interests (this may be a community or group).
   - Interests of involved others.
   - Agency policies/interests (e.g., obligation to colleagues).
   - Public and social policies.
   - Legal regulations (as relevant).
   - Professional code of ethics (note values that conflict).
3. Describe possible courses of action (or inaction), including their feasibility, evidentiary status,[a] acceptability to participants, and likely positive and negative side effects.
4. Select the option that seems ethically best.
5. Explain your reasons for selecting this option. Place your argument in diagram form. Is this a well-reasoned argument?
6. How much did you rely on each of the following in the list below in deciding what to do?

	Not At All	A Little	Some-what	A Great Deal
Critical reflection	—	—	—	—
Discussions with other staff	—	—	—	—
Related research findings[a]	—	—	—	—
Discussions with clients	—	—	—	—
Discussions with my supervisor	—	—	—	—
Discussions with an administrator	—	—	—	—
Discussions with agency's legal consultant	—	—	—	—
Professional code of ethics	—	—	—	—
My own moral standard	—	—	—	—
Discussions with friends	—	—	—	—

[a] For example, has a service been critically evaluated and found to be effective?

EXHIBIT 3.3

Failing to Act

Just as we may act when we should not, resulting in doing more harm than good, we also may do more harm than good by failing to act. We often overlook ethical concerns related to *not* acting (omissions) (Baron, 1994). This exercise provides an opportunity for you to consider the consequences of an omission.

Situation: _____

Omission (what was not done): _____

Consequences: _____

Discussion: _____

Suggestions for discussion:

1. Would you act differently in the future? If so, what would you do, and why?
2. What factors influenced your decision (e.g., agency policy, legislation, related research, feared risks)?
3. Can you think of other examples of failing to act when you think you should have acted?
4. What could be done to prevent omissions that limit the quality of services clients receive?

You may even act on them, that is recommend certain services to clients based on inaccurate assumption about related causes. You may assume they are accurate. Your ethical obligations include:

- The obligation to develop self-awareness (reflexivity) regarding your knowledge, skills, and values that affect clients.
- The obligations to understand different kinds of claims that can affect clients' lives (e.g., about what is a problem or risk, alleged causes, potential remedies).
- The obligation to critically evaluate claims that affect clients' lives.
- The obligation not to make bogus claims yourself.
- The obligation to speak up when others make bogus claims that may harm clients (see chapter 16).
- The obligation to avoid oversimplifications that harm clients. This includes attending to vital cultural differences.

that too often receive little attention. These are more challenging, one reason being that they are harder to recognize. These include bogus claims in the professional literature about "what is known" about the causes of client concerns, what is "a problem," and what services may be best. Because such claims appear in the professional literature, you may assume that they are accurate.

The philosophy of evidence-based practice, as described by its originators, emphasizes the importance of honoring ethical obligations to clients such as drawing on practice and policy-related research and involving clients as informed participants. The close relationship between evidentiary and ethical concerns is illustrated in these examples from Leever et al. (2002):

Case Study 3-5. Tami is a new caseworker. One of her first clients is Liz. Liz has been ordered by the court to participate in a drug treatment program. Tami located such a program near Liz's house, gives Liz the address, and tells her that she must attend the program. Has Tami obtained informed consent from Liz? What else could she have done? (p. 40).

Case Study 3-6. The caseworkers at XYZ Agency routinely refer clients to a parent training program that does not conduct individual assessments of clients enrolled in the program. The program offers one training package for all parents. What are the ethical issues that this situation raises? What should the staff at the agency do? (p. 40).

Case Study 3-7. Henry is Beth's coworker. He refers Beth to a substance abuse program, but he does not tell her that the program keeps very poor records about clients' progress. He is concerned that if Beth knows about this, she will lose hope that she can change her drug behavior. What issues does Henry's decision raise? (p. 41).

Case Study 3-10. Mrs. Olsen referred her client to a parent-training program that research suggests will be effective if implemented as designed. She does not know how well the staff implements the program nor does she have any idea about the agency's record of success in helping people similar to her client. Is this client able to give informed consent under these circumstances? (p. 41).

Self-Determination and Empowerment as Key Values

Self-determination refers to a belief that people should be allowed to arrange their lives in accord with their preferences. Stephen Fawcett and his colleagues define empowerment as the process of gaining some control over those events, outcomes, and resources important to an individual or group (1994, p. 472), for example, enhancing neighborhood residents' influence on programs, policies, and practices that affect them. Lorraine Gutierrez defines *empowerment* as "a process of increasing personal, interpersonal, or political power so that individuals can take action to improve their life situations" (1990, p. 149). Self-determination and empowerment involve giving clients real (rather than merely perceived) influence over the quality of their lives and involving clients in making decisions that affect them. They require a candid recognition and discussion of any coercive aspects of contact between social workers and clients. Focusing on outcomes that clients value (whenever they do not compromise the rights of others) respects self-determination.

Ethical practice requires involving clients in selecting outcomes, forming a clear agreement about what specific outcomes will be pursued, considering the interests of all involved parties, and focusing on *functional* objectives (those that improve the quality of clients' lives) (see also discussion of respect and informed consent). Vague statements such as "enhance social functioning" or "empower clients" may obscure different views of what to focus on, as well as outcomes that do the opposite (e.g., decrease empowerment). Only when objectives are clearly described can differences of opinion be discovered. Professionals who have authority over people in a supervisory or monitoring role, as in child welfare departments and institutional settings, should be especially vigilant to make sure they have a legitimate reason for intervening, for example, to protect children from physical abuse.

Clearly describing goals and methods (including their risks and benefits, as well as alternative options) and any coercive aspects of meetings (including negative consequences dependent on participation) provides a degree of self-determination that contrasts with the pursuit of vague goals and use of vaguely described methods (see also discussion of informed consent). Leslie Margolin (1997) suggests that discussions of empowerment in social work in the public social services disguise investigatory and judgmental aims. He argues that social workers say the right thing, but an examination of what they do with what results reveals a different picture. He suggests that the very notion that social workers can empower clients places power firmly in the hands of social workers—they give it to clients.

Avoidance of Coercion

Coercion has always played a role in efforts to deal with troubled, troubling, and dependent behaviors (see chapter 1). This is reflected in the criminal justice, mental health, and child welfare systems. Many behaviors once viewed as sins, then as crimes, are now viewed as mental illnesses warranting coerced treatment including outpatient or inpatient commitment. Both consumer groups such as Mindfreedom (http://www.mindfreedom. org) and watchdog groups such as Alliance for Human Research Protection (http://www.ahrp.org) and Citizens Commission on Human Rights International (http://www.cchr.org) and scholars such as Peter Breggin (1991) and Thomas Szasz (1994) highlight coercion in the "helping" professions. Professionals who have authority over people in a supervisory or monitoring role as in child welfare agencies and institutional settings often engage in unwanted actions such as removing children from the care of their biological parents. Such power requires vigilance to make sure there are legitimate reasons for intervening (e.g., to protect children from physical abuse). Szasz (1987) argues that in victimless crime, there is no ethical or principled basis on which professionals should impose treatment on unwilling clients. Some argue that circumstances may warrant unwanted change attempts. Robinson contends that "individuals presented for treatment...for reasons of having physically harmed others can lay no moral claim on the right not to be changed" (1974, p. 236).

(The right to be different in terms of physically harming others is a separate issue from the question of whether society has a right to force such persons to accept treatment.) Others argue that criminal behavior should be handled by the criminal justice system but that this does not warrant coerced "treatment" (e.g., Szasz, 1994).

Feeling Free and Being Free

Only when we clarify such vague terms as *self-determination* and understand how our behavior is influenced by our environments (some of which we create by our behavior) can we discover how "free" we are and how we can expand our freedom. Only then can we see whether the freedom we feel matches our actual freedom and whether what we believe we have freely chosen is what our culture has socialized us to value (Skinner, 1971). (See also Freire, 1973.) Consider women who have breast augmentations. Is this a free choice? Is it encouraged by a society's standards of beauty? Values and norms regarding ideal weight and breast size, what kinds of cars are status symbols are socially constructed; we are not born with them.

Constraints Imposed by Being a Double Agent

In the public social services, conflicts between individual rights and state's rights (as reflected in legislation and public policies) compromise the self-determination of both social workers and clients. Staff in public agencies work as social agents, not as clients' agents. That is, they are obligated to carry out the policies of the agencies in which they work, and their duties are structured by institutional arrangements. They are not free agents to pursue the broad call to provide service to clients, as in the NASW Code of Ethics. Indeed, they are double agents—of the client and of the agency. They are mediators between clients' needs and constraints imposed by policies and related legislation, for example, regarding the distribution of scarce resources (e.g., see Goldiamond, 1978; Handler, 1973; Hasenfeld, 1987a; Szasz, 1994). Russell Hardin argues that professional ethics in public agencies are "the ethics of the role holders in institutions" (1990, p. 528), not the ethics emphasized in the NASW Code of Ethics, which primarily concern the individual relationship between clients and social workers.

The NASW Code of Ethics states that "social workers may limit clients' right to self-determination when, in the social workers' professional judgement, clients' actions or potential actions pose a serious, foreseeable, and imminent risk to themselves or others." Who is to say what a "threat" is? Overlooking constraints may result in misleading both ourselves and our clients about what we can offer and how effective it is likely to be. For instance, social workers may invade their clients' privacy and interfere in their family life (e.g., remove children from the care of their parents) and confine people against their will (e.g., for psychiatric evaluation). The law views these intrusions as necessary on the grounds that they further interests of social importance (e.g., protect children from neglect or abuse).

Constraints Posed by a Lack of Resources

You cannot empower clients if you yourself are not empowered (i.e., do not have the resources needed). The degree to which you can "empower" clients thus depends partly on the extent to which your knowledge, skills, and other resources match what is needed to help clients attain outcomes they value. Accurately estimating this match (e.g., by becoming informed about the evidentiary status of different options) is one way you take responsibility for your decisions. You may have to refer clients elsewhere if you do not have needed knowledge, skills, or resources and other sources do have these (see discussion of evidence-based purchase of services in chapter 21). Clear description of desired outcomes and related contingencies will help you to accurately estimate what can be accomplished, given constraints and resources. An understanding of interlinked contingencies among different levels (e.g., how a public policy and related legislation affects options) will help you to identify constraints to and opportunities for helping clients (see chapter 7.) Lack of needed resources is common. It may be due to institutional discrimination. Documenting lack of resources needed to help clients is a key ethical obligation of social workers at all levels as emphasized in the philosophy of social work described in chapter 1.

Informed Consent

Integral to informed consent is the competence to offer it, and the extent to which it is offered voluntarily and is informed (see also Foundation for Informed Medical/Decision Making and discussion of self-determination). Being informed requires adequate information. Requirements include the following:

- An absence of coercion and undue social psychological influence.

- A description of anticipated benefits of recommended services.

- A description of possible discomforts and risks (including effects on a client's job, family, independence).

- The capability of clients to provide consent.

- A clear and complete explanation, in the client's language and at his or her level of comprehension, of aims and methods, including their purposes.

- A description of potential benefits and risks of alternative methods (e.g., the extent to which each has been critically tested and found to be effective, ineffective, or harmful).

- An offer to answer any questions.

- Informing clients that they are free to withdraw their consent and discontinue their participation at any time and describing consequences of such a step. (Leever et al., 2002).

Informed consent obligations may be violated by not sharing uncertainties regarding possible harms and benefits associated with use of a given assessment method, such as a measure for depression, or intervention method (e.g., parent training). Not sharing uncertainties may hide the fact that decisions involve a value judgment about how to balance risks and harms. Decisions about trade-offs between harms and benefits related to use of a practice or policy may be a subjective judgment that cannot be answered on evidentiary criteria (e.g., has a recommended service been critically tested and found to be effective). In public agencies such as protective service units for children, clients should be fully informed about the potential consequences of different degrees of participation. There are many opportunities to honor informed consent even in nonautonomous situations (Gambrill, 2008). Evidence-informed patient choice (EIPC) entails three criteria: (1) the decision involves which intervention a person will or will not receive; (2) the person is given research-based information about effectiveness (likely outcomes, risks, and benefits) of at least two alternatives (which may include the option of doing nothing); and (3) the person participates in the decision-making process (Entwistle, Sheldon, Sowden, & Watt, 1998). Evidence-based practice involves sharing responsibility for decision making in a context of recognized uncertainty. The importance of acknowledging uncertainty is highlighted in the Database of Uncertainties about the Effects of Treatment (DUETS) website (http://www.library.nhs.uk/duets).

Informed consent requirements are usually not followed (see Braddock, Edwards, Hasenberg, Laidley, & Levinson, 1999). One in three doctors do not inform patients about services they cannot have (Gottlieb, 2003). Although statutory and regulatory policy require psychiatrists to disclose the risks of neuroleptic medication (e.g., of tardive dyskinesia), a study of 540 psychiatrists from 94 state and county mental hospitals in 35 states found that only 54% of psychiatrists told their patients about the possibility (Kennedy & Sanborn, 1992). (Tardive dyskinesia is an irreversible neurological condition characterized by involuntary muscular movements.) Cohen and Jacobs (1998) describe a model consent form. Your knowledge (e.g., about alternative procedures) limits the extent to which you can provide informed consent. That is, if you are not informed, you cannot inform your clients.

What if clients refuse to give their consent? Should you help parents acquire more effective parenting skills even if their child does not agree? Comparing current and future risks and benefits to all affected parties of different options and involving all participants in making decisions will guard your clients' interests. Be sure to consider the consequences of inaction, as well as action. For example, refusing to help if one party does not agree to participate may allow an intolerable situation to continue

or worsen. (See, for example, the work of Edwin Thomas and his colleagues, 1996 e.g., Thomas & Ager, 1993.) Ethical issues come to the fore when clients cannot give informed consent. Clients labeled *mentally ill* may be (incorrectly and unethically) assumed to be unable to make their own decisions, and so decisions may be made for them. This assumption of "lack of agency" (the inability to make decisions) lies behind intrusive methods used in psychiatry since the beginning of this profession's history (Szasz, 1994). Special safeguards are required to increase the likelihood that objectives pursued and methods used are in the client's interest while also protecting society's interests in preventing harm to others. The approval and ongoing surveillance of all programs by a board composed of a representative of the client, laypeople not associated with the agency, experts in the practices and policies in effect, and a representative of the institution help to provide a safeguard for institutionalized residents. Advance directives such as living wills may protect clients' wishes.

Respect for the Dignity and worth of Each Person

The NASW Code of Ethics calls on social workers to "respect the inherent dignity and worth of the person" to "engage people as partners in the helping process," and to "promote conditions that encourage respect for cultural and social diversity within the United States and globally" (see Exhibit 3.1). Respect requires honesty (fully informing clients), involving clients and significant others in making decisions that affect their lives, giving clients in similar circumstances a similar quality of services, and using service methods that are most likely to result in outcomes clients value with due consideration for possible risks, discomfort, and client preferences. Respect for clients requires acting and speaking in considerate ways, whether or not you are in their presence. It involves identifying and supporting clients' strengths and avoiding unnecessary and/or harmful pathologizing. For instance, professionals sometimes assume that people believed to have Alzheimer's disease or people labeled *schizophrenic* cannot make decisions for themselves, an assumption that is likely to result in coercive interventions that ride roughshod over self-determination (Szasz, 1994). This is especially questionable when there is no evidence that forced intervention is effective.

Selecting assessment, intervention, and evaluation methods based on the following criteria shows respect for clients: (1) there is evidence that the methods will help clients (i.e., they are effective); (2) they are acceptable to clients and significant others; (3) they do not harm clients; (4) they help clients attain outcomes they value; (5) they are the least intrusive; (6) they build on the clients' assets; and (7) helpers are competent to use them effectively. Respect requires attending to individual differences that influence the outcome of service, which may involve considering differences in ethnicity, race, sex, sexual orientation, age, class, and physical and intellectual capabilities. Characteristics central to culturally sensitivity include the following:

- An interest in understanding other cultures.

- Awareness of your values and biases (e.g., stereotypes) and how these may affect clients.

- Recognizing differences between yourself and your clients.

- Identifying situations in which a client should be referred to someone who speaks his or her own language or someone (for example) of his or her own race, culture, sexual preference.

- Being accurately informed concerning cultural differences among different groups.

Concerns for respect call on social workers to "behave in a trustworthy manner." Value 5 in the Code of Ethics is called integrity. Trust and integrity imply predictability, being competent, and a correspondence between words and actions. That is, clients can count on you to do what you say you will do.

Confidentiality: Ethical Concerns and Legal Regulations

Confidentiality refers to professional ethics that regulate against disclosure of information about a client without the client's permission (Galambos, Watt, Anderson, & Danis, 2005). This differs from *privileged communication,* which refers to legal rights that (under certain circumstances) protect clients from having their communications revealed in court without their permission (Dickson, 1998; Glosoff, Herlihy, & Spence, 2000). The Health Insurance Portability and Accountability Act (HIPAA) is designed to increase privacy protection for health information. If information must be shared because of legal requirements (e.g., the duty to report suspected child or elder abuse and neglect), clients should be so informed. The duty to warn includes suspected institutional maltreatment of residents by staff. Some of the concern about the confidentiality of records is due to undocumented negative material in records. Such material should not be there in the first place. Talking about clients to friends, family, and acquaintances is unethical. "Bad-mouthing" clients by name in informal staff get-togethers may create a negative set toward clients by other staff and is equally unacceptable.

Waivers of Privileged Communication

In *Tarasoff v. Regents of the University of California* (17 Cal. 2d 425 [1974]), the parents of a young woman who was murdered sued the regents because a university psychologist did not tell the woman

that his client intended to kill her. The plaintiffs argued that the psychologist had an obligation to warn the woman of his client's intent. They won their case. (See current state civil codes.) The many grounds for waivers of privileged communication, which include the following illustrate the limits of confidentiality.

- The client waives her privilege.

- The client introduces privileged material into the litigation.

- The social worker is called to testify in a criminal case.

- A client sues his counselor.

- A client commits or threatens a criminal act.

- A client threatens suicide.

- A client threatens to harm his therapist.

- A minor is involved in criminal activity.

- Child abuse or neglect is suspected.

- A client is using certain types of drugs.

- A client's condition is alleged to make his employment hazardous to others.

- The court orders a professional examination.

- It is assumed that involuntary hospitalization is needed for the client's protection.

- The client dies.

- A professional needs to collect fees for services rendered.

- Information is learned outside the service relationship.

- Information is shared in the presence of a third person.

- The federal government needs certain information.

- It is assumed that emergency action is needed to save the client's life.

- It is assumed that legal action is needed to protect a minor.

- A presentence investigation report is prepared.

- The professional is employed in an agency or institution.

- A social worker is employed in a military setting.

- Claims are filed for life and accident insurance benefits (e.g., Dickson, 1998; Polowy, Morgan, Khan, & Gorenberg, 2011).

You should be familiar with the legal requirements in your state to report HIV infection to public health authorities. As in many situations, what is ethical may not be a legal issue. Courts have allowed material from confidential psychotherapy sessions to be used as evidence in trials in cases in which the confidentiality of the client–therapist relationship has been ruled as no longer applying because the therapist exercised his or her "duty to warn" a third party of threats made by a client (see In Court: "Duty to Warn" v. Confidentiality, *NASW News,* July 1990, p. 16). For example, in 1982 a former client set fire to his social worker's home, killing her husband and leaving the social worker badly burned. The accused never denied the act and told a court-appointed defense therapist of his intent to kill the social worker's brother, as well as other persons. The potential victims were informed at the therapist's request, and the therapist's testimony was used in evidence during the murder trial.

Ethical Issues Related to Competence

Value VI in the NASW Code of Ethics calls for workers to "practice within their areas of competence and develop and enhance their professional expertise." The Code of Ethics recommends that social workers "provide services and represent themselves as competent only within the boundaries of their education, training, license, certification, consultation received, supervised experience, or other relevant professional experience" (1.04). They "should accept responsibility or employment only on the basis of existing competence or the intention to acquire the necessary competence" (4.01). The Code does not specify the criteria to be used to assess proficiency or competence. (See also NASW Standards for Cultural Competence in Social Work Practice, 2001; Cultural Competence Self-Assessment Instrument, 2002.) The Code of Ethics further advises social workers to "critically examine and keep current with emerging knowledge relevant to social work and fully use evaluation and research evidence in their professional practice" (5.02). "When generally recognized standards do not exist with respect to an emerging area of practice, social workers should exercise careful judgment and take responsible steps (including appropriate education, research, training, consultation, and supervision) to ensure the competence of their work and protect clients from harm" (1.04, c). Further, the Code calls on social workers to "work toward the maintenance and promotion of high standards of practice" (5.01), but it does not mention the criteria to be used to determine whether social workers have reached these practice ideals.

Incompetence may be related to a lack of required skills and knowledge, faulty ethical judgments or standards (either intentional or due to ignorance), or personal impairment (the social worker may have a substance abuse problem or be overworked). High caseloads, insufficient resources, excessive recording requirements, and inadequate training and supervision increase the likelihood of inadequate handling of cases, the results of which are described in daily newspapers (e.g., a child known to child welfare authorities is killed by his biological parents; the infamous baby P case, Batty, 2009). Lack of a systemic focus is a key problem (e.g., see Gambrill & Shlonsky, 2001; Munro, 2010).

Accountability and Competence

To some social workers, accountability means having their clients' best interests at heart, maximizing their self-determination, and respecting them. Such vague language allows great leeway in actions and outcomes, some of which may not be in the clients' best interests. John Kunkel, for example, argues that projects that "are simply designed to do good," without delineating *specific* goals and without regard to learning principles and behavioral procedures, are practically guaranteed to be unsuccessful and to "do evil" (1970, p. 315). In the practice model described here, it is assumed that accountability requires offering services that are most likely to help clients attain outcomes they value (when acceptable to clients), avoiding harm to clients and others, focusing on objectives that enhance the quality of clients' lives, and evaluating progress in an ongoing manner using valid measures and sharing the results with clients. This kind of accountability requires accurate estimates of the degree to which your knowledge and skills match what is needed to help clients, informing them about mismatches, and referring them to other sources as needed.

Involving clients as informed participants in decisions is emphasized in evidence-based practice, and many procedures and tools have been designed to facilitate this, such as interactive decision aids (O'Connor, Bennett, Stacey, Barry, Col, Eden et al., 2009) (see also discussion of informed consent). My students tend to overestimate their competence (knowledge and skills) to provide certain kinds of services (e.g., social skills training, parent training) and to underestimate the domain-specific knowledge and skills available. Indeed, research shows that we are all subject to self-inflated assessments (Dunning, Health, & Suls, 2004). Clients rarely know that their helper is not adequately trained or supervised. If more competent help is not available, you can offer to work with clients, with their full knowledge of the limits of your expertise.

The NASW Code of Ethics calls on social workers to "monitor and evaluate policies, the implementation of programs and practice interventions" (5.02). (It does not call for social workers to share this information with clients.) Ongoing monitoring based on valid progress measures allows timely decisions and keeps clients informed about degree of progress. This kind of accountability is important for both practical and ethical reasons. A concern for accountability highlights the importance of attending to process (what is done), as well as outcome (what is achieved). *Procedural fidelity* refers to the match between how a method should be implemented for maximal effect and how it is implemented.

Ethical Issues Related to Case Records

Clients should be informed about who will have access to their records and under what circumstances access will be granted (see also the section on confidentiality). Access may be legally mandated. Giving clients access to their records would allow them to correct errors. Such access is vital if you accept Margolin's (1997) view that the case record is the main way in which social workers create biographies that are used to justify investigating, classifying, and judging clients. The confidentiality of others mentioned in records should be protected. Clients should have an opportunity to challenge items in their records and either have them removed or insert rebuttals. The clients' permission should be obtained before sharing case-record data with others, unless such sharing is legally required.

The NASW Code of Ethics calls on social workers to "include sufficient and timely documentation in records to facilitate the delivery of services and to ensure continuity of services provided to clients in the future" (3.04). That is, records should facilitate the coordination and evaluation of services. The importance of records was highlighted in *Whitree v. New York State* (290 N.Y.S. 2d. 486 [ct. Claims] [1968]), in which the records' inadequacy was cited as the reason that a client was confined in a mental hospital for 12 years. The court held that the inadequate records hindered the development of treatment plans. Including irrelevant negative material and fudging records to protect service providers are examples of unethical recording practices (see also Luepker, 2012).

Ethical and Legal Issues Related to Sexual Conduct

The NASW Code of Ethics explicitly prohibits sexual activities with current clients, "whether such contact is consensual or forced" (1.09). It also states that social workers should not engage in sexual activities or sexual contact with former clients because of the potential for harm to the client. Questions here are: What is a "former client"? Over what duration of time should this be extended? Consider a community organizer who may work with scores of "clients." According to California law, "any kind of sexual contact, asking for sexual contact, or sexual misconduct by a psychotherapist with a client is illegal as well as unethical" (Business and Professional Sections 726 and 4982k). *Sexual contact* means touching another person's intimate parts (sexual organ, anus, buttocks, groin, or breast). *Touching* means physical contact with another person, either through the person's clothes or directly with the person's skin (Section 728). The code also proscribes offering clinical services "to individuals with whom they have had a prior sexual relationship." A review of ethics cases filed with the National Association of Social Workers from 1986 to 1997 revealed that the most commonly reported violations are sexual activity, dual relationships, and other boundary violations (Strom-Gottfried, 2003). Data collected from 1990 to 2005 show that the most frequent classes of suits brought against individual social workers ranked in order from most to least were incorrect treatment, sexual misconduct,

suicide or attempted suicide, and dual relationship (nonsexual) and reporting of abuse to authorities. Clients may sue when they are disappointed with services, blame a negative outcome on incompetence or neglect, get a bill larger than expected, or believe they have been exploited (dual relationship) (http://www.socialworktoday.com/archive/julyaug2007). For further discussion of boundary issues, see Reamer (2003a).

Other Ethical Concerns

Other ethical issues concern employer/employee relationships, conflicts between loyalties to colleagues and clients, and agency policies and procedures that hinder service. Conflicts may occur between obligations to employers and responsibilities to clients. For example, an agency policy may conflict with providing high-quality services to clients. Services may be compromised by unnecessarily complex forms, long waiting times, shifts from one worker to another, inappropriate referrals, and excessive time spent on paperwork. It is estimated that child welfare workers spend between 50 to 80% of their time on paperwork, leaving little time for client contact (http://www.cwla.org).

The Code of Ethics advises social workers to "avoid unwarranted negative criticism of colleagues with clients or with other professionals. Unwarranted negative criticism may include demeaning comments that refer to colleagues' level of competence or to individuals' attributes, such as race, ethnicity, national origin, color, sex, sexual orientation, age, marital status, political belief, religion, or mental or physical disability" (2.01, b). Given the Code's recommendation to take action when you have good reason to believe that a colleague is engaged in incompetent practice, I assume that this is warranted criticism.

Ethical and Legal Issues Related to Policy and Planning

Policy decisions require deciding what should be, as well as what is. Agency staff and administrators help to create policy by their day-by-day decisions as highlighted in discussion of practice–policy connections. Key ethical dilemmas in public agencies, including health services, involve decisions about allocating (scarce) resources. Moral dilemmas that may arise include: (1) obligations to clients (e.g., compared with the state's obligation), (2) responsibility to different communities, (3) obligations across generations, and (4) collective responsibilities (e.g., of groups). Reamer (1993) views ethical issues related to social planning as one of the three main areas of ethical concerns in social work. Some of the unfortunate events in child welfare, such as children dying at the hands of their foster or biological parents, result from a lack of funds for needed services, including supervisory visits and from purchasing ineffective services from other agencies. Lack of adequate state funds for high-quality community-based group homes may result in institutionalization of residents at an even greater cost to taxpayers and loss of independence for residents. Clients often need a variety of resources that will require coordination among different agencies. This coordination may be lacking.

Burton Gummer (1997) argues that the NASW Code of Ethics is mainly concerned with direct service providers and their interactions with their clients. He argues that the Code is silent on the hard decisions that social workers must make about how to distribute scarce resources. He believes that the Code is remiss in not providing guidelines for problems of concern to managers, such as how to allocate scarce resources. He notes that professional codes of ethics presumes that other attributes of a profession are in place, such as a service ethic, a knowledge base, specialized training, and independent discretionary decisions. He points out that these attributes are missing in the public social services in which helpers are responsible mainly to agency mandates and not to individual clients. (See prior discussion of social workers as "double agents.") Public policies typically allow considerable discretion by administration and line staff. Is this discretion handled in an ethical manner? Can you identify areas of discretion in your current position as a social worker?

Russell Hardin contends that a major role, for example, of doctors today is to mediate conflicts between society and the patient about how to distribute scarce resources (1990, p. 536). He highlights the "costs to new professionals from a code of ethics that so neglects the greatest range of actual cases of difficult moral choices they will face on the job" (p. 540). Gummer (1997) suggests that frameworks for evaluating public officials such as Wilbern's (1984) levels of public morality apply to social work administrators as well, since both bear the responsibility of implementing public policies. The first three (basic honesty and conformity to the law, conflicts of interest, and service orientation and procedural fairness) concern the administrator's moral responsibilities. The other three (the ethics of democratic responsibility, public policy determination, and compromise and social integration) concern the ethics of decisions and actions. He argues that most codes of ethics deal only with personal morality. Critical appraisal of proposed policies, as well as ongoing evaluation of their effects, are necessary to detect unwanted consequences at an early point and take timely corrective action.

Ethical Issues Related to Professional Organizations

The NASW Code of Ethics calls on social workers to "work toward the maintenance and promotion of high standards of practice" (5.01) and "to uphold and advance the values, ethics, knowledge, and mission of the profession," including "responsible criticism of the profession" (though this is not defined). Professionals are ethically bound to work together to achieve the highest quality of services for the greatest number of clients at the least cost. Clearly they do not always do so. An interest in expanding and protecting markets may compete with such aims. There are intense struggles and considerable funds are spent by

professional organizations to maintain and/or expand their turf as illustrated by efforts by psychiatrists to block prescription privileges for psychologists.

In 1989, only after a long struggle by both psychologists and social workers, did Congress pass legislation to include psychologists and social workers in the Medicare programs. Who is to be allowed to provide services in health maintenance organizations (HMOs) is a hard-fought issue. Citing the maintenance of health care standards as a reason to exclude certain professional groups may mask the less altruistic goal of protecting and expanding special interests. Readers of professional newsletters may be "taken in" by criticism of other professional groups and, as a result, may be less willing to try to understand the contributions of other professionals and to work cooperatively with them. Competing for clients is ethically questionable when it results in unnecessarily intrusive care (e.g., hospitalization or prolonged stays in residential centers), lower quality care, higher costs, or the withholding of needed care.

The Importance of Knowledge About Legal Regulations and Resources

You should be familiar with the legal regulations that pertain to your clients and refer them to helpful sources as needed for further information (Batten, 2011; Hudson, 2007; Madden, 2003; Regehr & Kanani, 2006; Slater & Fink, 2012; Stein, 2004). Because they often differ from state to state, you must find out what regulations apply in your state. You can keep up with current information in particular areas by reviewing sources such as *Youth Law News* and related websites. The American Civil Liberties Union publishes handbooks for older persons, crime victims, women, single people, gays and lesbians, prisoners, young people, and students. Legislation concerning clients' rights has increased. Classic decisions include *Wyatt v. Stickney* (344 F. Supp. 387 [M.D. Ala. 1972]), which states that clients have a right to adequate staff and to an individualized intervention program with a timetable for achieving specific objectives, as well as the identification of criteria for the release of clients to less restrictive environments and for their discharge. Juveniles' right to treatment was upheld in *Morales v. Turman* (383 F. Supp. 53 [E.D. Tex. 1974]). The right to treatment in the least restrictive alternative favors community settings. This court, as well as others, called for periodic progress reviews. Children, as well as adults, have a right to refuse treatment.

P.L. 94–142, Individuals with Disabilities Act (IDEA) mandates that all children have a right to education, regardless of their mental or physical disability. This Act calls for an individualized education program (IEP) for each child between the ages of 3 and 21. Basic rights include "1. Free, appropriate public education, 2. Placement in the least restrictive environment, 3. Related services and supplementary aids, and 4. Fair assessment procedures." Other provisions call for participation of parents or guardians in the preparation of educational plans; parental receipt of prior written notice whenever there is a proposed change or referral to initiate a change in the child's educational placement by school authorities; and parental opportunity for an impartial due process hearing when a complaint is received.

You should also be familiar with public laws to which you and your clients could appeal to gain assistance. For example, P.L. 93–112, The Vocational Rehabilitation Act, section 504, guarantees that people with disabilities may not be discriminated against because of their disability. You should also be familiar with mandatory reporting laws regarding non-accidental physical injury, neglect, and/or sexual abuse. Groups of concern include children under the age of 18, the elderly (65 and above), dependent adults with some mental or physical limitation resulting in dependency, and hospital patients transferred from a health or community care facility. Conditions for reporting for children include non-accidental physical injury, sexual abuse including assault and exploitation, any act or omission that comprises willful cruelty or unjustifiable punishment, neglect, and physical dependence on an addictive drug at birth. Conditions for reporting concerning the elderly include physical abuse (assault, battery, unreasonable restraint, sexual abuse), misuse of physical or chemical restraint, neglect, abandonment or isolation, and fiduciary abuse (misappropriation of money or property). Mandatory reporting regarding patients include abuse, neglect, and assaultive injuries. The standard for reporting is to know or reasonably suspect that the condition of concern is present. In California, reporting of domestic violence differs for those professionals who work in a medical setting and those who do not. (For a discussion of dilemmas, see Bergeron & Gray, 2003; see also Madden, 2003.)

Testifying in Court

You may be required to testify in court in regard to civil commitment, child custody, or the termination of parental rights. Court appearances will be less stressful if you prepare for them. The best defense in court is sound practice, including adequate records describing the basis of informed decisions. An *expert witness* is one who is recognized or qualified by the court to offer certain kinds of opinions. The agreement to be an expert witness carries both responsibilities and risks. You should not agree to be an expert witness in areas in which you are not competent. Claims of competence (expertise) may (and should) be tested in court. (See related legal regulations.) Since it is not possible to predict what an individual will do in the future based on data about groups, you should refrain from making predictions about individuals (Ceci & Bruck, 1995; Dawes, 1994a; McCann, Shindler, & Hammond, 2003). Be sure to consider possible conflicts of interest when deciding whether to be a witness. For example, in a custody dispute, a social worker may be asked to offer testimony about a child's feelings about her parents. If one of the parents is a client of the social worker, the social worker's testimony may be biased in the client's favor.

Liability (Bases for Lawsuits and How to Avoid Them)

There are four elements in the definition of malpractice: (1) a helper–client relationship was established; (2) the helper's conduct fell below an acceptable standard; (3) the helper's breach of duty was the proximate cause of an injury; and (4) the client sustained an injury. Injuries may be defined as a worsening of symptoms (the appearance of new problems); a misuse of counseling (e.g., encouraging unnecessary dependency on the social worker); taking on tasks that clients are not ready for resulting in failure or other negative effects such as becoming disillusioned with counseling; and treatment-induced (iatrogenic) loss of a job, divorce, emotional harm, suicide, defamation of character, or abandonment (premature termination) (See Reamer 2003b). Supervisors may not realize that they may be liable for the negligence of those they supervise.

Varieties of Malpractice Claims

Some malpractice claims concern avoidable errors such as the selection of inappropriate or harmful assessment and/or intervention methods that result in harms such as suicide of a client. Claims of incorrect "diagnosis" may allege that medical sources of problems were overlooked. Not seeking expert advice when needed and not referring clients to specialists when problems exceed the limits of your competence may result in a lawsuit. Some lawsuits are based on a violation of clients' civil rights, such as an alleged failure to notify foster parents of the imminent removal of a child from their care and the failure to offer them a hearing or priority in an adoption decision. Alleged breaches of professional behavior, such as not being available when needed and not completing service once it has been started, have also been the basis of lawsuits. (Clients should be able to see another professional when their social worker is not available, and this other individual is required to have the requisite skills.) Alleged sexual contact is a common ground for malpractice claims.

To reduce legal vulnerability you can:

- Become informed about professional liability.
- Follow legal and administrative requirements.
- Draw on practice and policy-related research findings.
- Maintain agency and professional standards of conduct and performance.
- Keep complete records.
- Gain financial protection (e.g., malpractice insurance).
- Involve law enforcement agencies (e.g., in child protection agencies).
- Be sensitive to high-risk situations.
- Advocate for improved services and legal reform. (Besharov, 1985, p. 167)

As Besharov suggests, "Good practice is the best defense" (1985, p. 168; see also Reamer, 2003b).

Agencies may be held responsible for failing to protect workers from assault by clients. Failure to provide adequate care in residential settings continues to receive attention. Consider reports in the *New York Times* regarding residential centers for "mentally ill" clients (e.g., Levy, 2002) and harmful conditions in skilled nursing facilities such as overmedication (Harris, 2011). Suits claiming the neglect of residents (in contrast to active abuse) were won in Mississippi against a nursing home run by the nation's largest nursing home chain, and damages were awarded to the families of residents whose last years of life were diminished by neglect. The dollar amounts included:

> $50,000 for leaving Mrs. Berryhill in her own excrement; $25,000 for verbal abuse of her by the staff, $15,000 for not bathing Mr. Bolian, $15,000 for keeping him in a smelly room, $60,000 for failing to give him the physical therapy he needed....The jury further found that Beverly Enterprises' failure to provide good care was so "willful, wanton, malicious or callous" as to merit another $125,000 in punitive damages to each claimant. (Lewin, 1990, p. A1)

The National Senior Citizens Law Center, a nonprofit advocacy group in Washington, D.C., estimates that such negligence affects residents in 60% of the nation's nursing homes. Inadequate monitoring or intrusive interventions, such as unnecessary confinement may result in lawsuits against social workers and social service agencies.

Clients' Options When Confronted with Unethical or Illegal Behavior on the Part of Professionals

Clients may seek your advice about alleged ethical lapses in professional conduct. What should you suggest? What are your options? What are the clients' options? How can someone know when lack of success or negative effects are a result of professional incompetence? Although this may be easy in some cases, it may not be in others. Our tendency to view professionals as experts contributes to our gullibility in this situation. The Internet provides a source of information for consumers especially if they have the skills needed to locate reliable sources and to critically appraise content found. Such searching is becoming much more common and many professionals welcome this. The first step may be for the client to talk to the social worker, his or her supervisor, or an ombudsperson, if one is available. Every agency should have a clear and readily available complaint process described in brochures available in waiting rooms and on the agency website. A complaint could be lodged with an agency administrator or referring source. The client could request another social worker.

Clients can obtain information and guidance about unethical or illegal professional behavior from state licensing boards, professional associations, or sexual assault/crisis centers. Other resorts include filing a lawsuit in civil court or taking criminal action, for example, filing a complaint with local law enforcement authorities.

Concerns about the emotional drain of conflict and fears about loss of confidentiality or retribution may prevent clients from taking action. Or clients may believe that complaining is useless because "nothing will happen." They may be unwilling to "make a fuss" or to "bother" people. They may not know how to make a complaint and what to do if it is ignored. This highlights the importance of an easily accessible, user-friendly complaint and compliment system in all agencies. Other obstacles include a lack of transportation or required fees and an inability to read or write or to describe complaints clearly. Clients may be reluctant to persevere if initial efforts fail. The potential problems awaiting those who lodge complaints underscores the importance of consumer rights and advocacy groups. Examples include Public Citizen, Alliance for Human Research Protection (http://www.ahrp.org), Coalition Against Institutionalized Child Abuse (http://caica.org; http://healthyskepticism.org), Mindfreedom, American Child Liberties Union, Amnesty International.

Residents of institutional settings should be fully informed of their rights; staff in such settings should consider this one of their responsibilities. Residents' rights councils should be established in all institutional settings to inform staff and residents of resident rights, including access to information, privacy (expecting staff to knock before entering), and participation in decision making. Classic studies show that allowing elderly clients to take part in decision making prolongs life and enhances well-being (Langer & Rodin, 1976; Schultz, 1976).

Does Licensing Protect Consumers?

Do professional licenses protect clients from harm or mediocre practice? Does passing the test required to become a licensed social worker mean that someone is competent? If so, in what areas? What is the correlation between test scores and helping clients achieve outcomes they value? Robyn Dawes (1994a) argues that licensing psychotherapists gives the public a false sense of assurance that they will receive competent services that cannot be provided by lower paid service providers. He notes that a review of psychotherapy research shows that credentialing (e.g., licensing) and experience are not related to success.

Blowing the Whistle

What should you do if you have evidence that a fellow social worker is offering incompetent services? Would you first talk to this person? If this did not help, would you discuss your concerns with your supervisor or with an agency administrator? If these steps failed, would you contact your agency's board of directors or "go public"? The NASW Code of Ethics (2008) states that "social workers who have direct knowledge of a social work colleague's incompetence should consult with that colleague when feasible and assist that colleague in taking remedial action" (2.10). If the colleague "has not taken adequate steps to address the incompetence," he or she "should take action through appropriate channels established by employers' agencies, NASW, licensing and regulatory bodies, and other professional organizations" (see NASW Procedures for Professional Review, 2005). The Code also calls for social workers to "defend and assist colleagues who are unjustly charged with unethical conduct" (2.11).

Agencies and professions may try to block attempts by "whistleblowers" to expose incompetence by claiming that confidential client information was (or would be) revealed. It may be assumed that loyalty to one's profession requires hiding one's "dirty linen." Even in cases in which all agree that the service was inadequate and clients were harmed, exposure of incompetent practice may result in negative sanctions against the whistleblower and persistence is needed (Hartocollis, 2011). There is now legislation to protect whistleblowers in the military from receiving unfair or inappropriate "mental health evaluations" or involuntary commitment for the treatment of "mental health problems." The False Claims Act is often appealed to in whistleblower exposures. In 2010, more money was received under this Act from the pharmaceutical industry than from any other industry (Tanne, 2010) (see also Tanne, 2011).

Ethics and Ideology

Ethical principles often rest on ideologies. *Ideology* has been defined as "a systematic body of ideas which emerge from and justify a state of society or a political program" (Bynum, Browne, & Porter, 1985, p. 199). The term *ideology* can be used in a *descriptive* sense to refer to a system of beliefs or practices or in a *persuasive* sense to refer to efforts to advance a belief system (Thompson, 1987). In the latter sense, it is used to justify and explain a certain way of acting, by providing "vocabularies of motive" (Mills, 1959). Karl Popper (1994) defines ideology as beliefs that are not open to critical discussion. Different ideologies suggest different answers to ethical questions, creating different views about the world and our place in it, as well as about the role of professions and different kinds of "self-knowledge" (what we think we know about ourselves).

Appeal to ideology is used to influence how issues and problems are framed and what actions we take. Politicians, advertisers, and professional organizations spend great amounts of money to encourage views that support their vested interests. Related slogans are often used as a substitute for critical appraisal of claims. Consider the slogan "Knowledge is power" (NASW). Questions here involve power for whom? Are clients' lives really improved? Critically examining ideologies may reveal that although they appear to forward humanitarian aims, they forward actions that harm people. Only by digging beneath the surface can we discover the consequences of ideology.

Uses and Misuses of Ideology

Ideologies can maintain commitment in difficult times. For instance, the professional ideology of "doing good" can provide solace when social workers are hard pressed by excessive caseloads. However, ideologies may compromise services and maintain or increase economic and social inequities by providing false assurances. Awareness of majority ideologies and the ways they may be imposed on minority groups is important in challenging prejudice and related discriminatory patterns of behavior. The ideology of individualism, for example, emphasizes individual rights. However, many people view rights without the resources to act on them as a cruel hoax. Ideological statements may be made to hide reality (e.g., certain consequences of a policy). Statements that appear to support an equality that benefits everyone (e.g., "We believe in individual freedom") may instead forward an economic system that excludes millions from sharing its benefits. Appeals to social justice may refer to efforts to impose unwanted political and economic systems on everyone. Relying on ideology (e.g., appealing to professional values and good intent) in place of critical discussion is ethically questionable if this affects the quality of services clients receive. For example, if we uncritically accept the view that professionals do only good, we will lose opportunities to discover when they do harm or seek aims that do not favor the clients' interests.

Ideology as Propaganda

One way to recognize ideology is by its appeal to authority to support claims, as in "Dr. Z. says that...." If an instructor expects you to believe what he says simply because he said it, he is being ideological. Karl Popper (1994) would say that he is imprisoned by his beliefs rather than using a theory (a guess about what may be true) to pose testable hypotheses. People often claim a certainty that is not possible; knowledge, ignorance, and uncertainty change over time, in accord with new exploration. Other indicators of appeal to ideology to support claims include impatient or defensive reactions when questioned (Nettler, 1970). Ideological statements often have a "slogan" quality, such as "We know social work is effective." The "pronouncement" nature of such claims, unaccompanied by recognizing the need to examine them critically, reveals their ideological nature. Ideological statements are usually general rather than specific. Exactly what actions are called for may be vague, as in the statement "Humanistic practice guards clients' rights." What is humanistic practice? What are the rights referred to? What criteria will be used to determine whether the rights are indeed being guarded?

Ideological statements used as propaganda pitches play on our fears, anger, and self-interest to encourage certain ways of behaving and thinking (e.g., donate money, vote for a certain candidate, seek a certain kind of therapy). Some argue that we live in a culture of fear promoted by the media and the biomedical industrial complex (Furedi, 2006). Ideology and propaganda are closely related. *Propaganda* refers to encouraging beliefs and actions with as little thought as possible (Ellul, 1965). Both ideology and propaganda have an interest in persuading, not through rational discussion, but through emotion. Both play on our emotions and encourage emotional reasoning. We are often unaware of the emotive effects of language and so may act uncritically on statements that sound appealing (such as "We value citizen participation") but may not represent reality (there may be none). Ideological statements also play on our reluctance to raise questions for fear of appearing ignorant, difficult, or disloyal. Scientific theories that become entrenched (not open to critical testing and discussion) become ideologies.

Ideological Clashes

Ethical dilemmas often reflect ideological clashes. Some common ones are highlighted in the sections that follow.

Pessimistic and Optimistic Ideologies

Some beliefs emphasize our passivity and view the environment as inherently hostile and unknowable. Karl Popper (1992) refers to these as *pessimistic ideologies*. In *optimistic ideologies* it is believed that we can discover knowledge about the world, hard as it may be to do so. Karl Popper suggests that "over-optimism about the power of reason…an over-optimistic expectation concerning the outcome of a discussion" (1994, p. 44) may be responsible for a pessimistic ideology. The contextual view described in this book embraces an optimistic perspective that reflects related research findings about the interaction among genes, organisms, and their environments (see chapter 12). We are viewed as active participants in the construction of our environments. This view highlights the interaction between our actions and our environments and opportunities to create new ones, for example, new cultural practices that benefit all.

Service and Professional Ideologies

Service and professional ideologies may clash. The ideology of service emphasizes the importance of serving clients, but the need of a professional organization to reconcile differences among diverse groups in its own membership requires compromises, for example, between calls for using methods that have been critically tested and found to help clients and protecting professional discretion. "The professional association tends more to provide services to their members than to exercise control over their ethical or technical work behavior" (Friedson, 1986, p. 187). Claims made by professional organizations about the unique qualifications of social workers to offer certain services are overstated, reflecting one of the functions of professional ideology to maintain and expand turf. That is, more knowledge and skills and a wider jurisdiction are claimed than are warranted by critical discussion and testing (Friedson, 1973).

A perusal of professional journals reveals a cornucopia of overstated claims about "what is known." Ioannidis (2005) argues that most research findings described in biomedical sources are false. Would this be true also of social work journals? (See, for example, Rubin & Parrish, 2007.) A key function of professional claims of knowledge is to gain public and legislative support for that profession. Reliance on ideology obscures the need to critically test claims that have life-affecting consequences for clients. Indeed, to protect the profession's reputation, its members may try to prevent or discredit whistleblowers who expose ineffective or harmful practices.

Professional, Personal, and Bureaucratic Ideologies

Promoting service and justice is emphasized by the National Association of Social Workers. Most social work practice is carried out in organizations. The bureaucratic ideology and the policies they reflect may conflict with both service (e.g., caseloads may be too high, recording requirements too onerous, and supervision poor) and professionals' interests in maintaining discretion (control over their work). (See earlier discussion of constraints imposed by being an agent of the state.) Bensman suggests that "to a bureaucratic elite, the only acceptable ideologies among their staff are those that support organizational purposes" (1967, p. 197).

The functions of bureaucratic ideology include maintaining a smoothly running agency, implementing agreed-on policies, and staying out of trouble. Management may set requirements that encroach on professional discretion. Line staff typically identify with the clients, whereas administrators focus on "getting the work done." Social workers may have an ideology independent of that of both their profession and the agencies in which they work, which may result in clashes between administrators and employees who set their own goals. Consequently, a welfare worker may learn "how to break the rules, to lie, cheat, to forge or destroy documents in the interest of the client" (Bensman, 1967, p. 161). Administrators may appeal to professional ideology for bureaucratic purposes. Protests by line staff about large case loads and poor supervision may be answered by the administration with "We are committed to serving clients and expect staff to use their professional skills to manage caseloads."

Capitalistic and Socialistic Ideologies

The ideology of a capitalistic market-driven economy assumes that free enterprise (the open market, unrestricted competition) is the most effective economic system and that people have a right to unlimited gain. Recent chaos in the financial system shows that although unregulated financial markets make the richer even richer, it increases poverty and misery for many others. An emphasis on competition and individualism is part and parcel of the ideology of unregulated capitalism. Each person is assumed to be able to control his or her own destiny, fashion his or her own lifestyle, and take responsibility for his or her own problems. Such an ideology stresses individual rights and idealizes the "self-made" man (or woman). Illouz (2008) argues that the methods of clinical psychology (psychotherapy) are used by corporations to create a more productive workforce by training employees in emotion management and interpersonal skills in a way that objectifies emotions and hinders spontaneity. Moncrieff (2008a) suggests that the competition and individualism inherent in consumerism results in feelings of inadequacy that encourage purchase of products (to compete successfully). It thus breeds discontent, assuaged by the latest product, which, in our medicalized culture is often therapy or medication. Timimi (2008) argues that the stress caused by competition in unregulated competitive markets creates feelings of inadequacy that encourage self-examination and a "growth fetish" (p. 171), which benefits the therapy industry and pharmaceutical companies. Like Ellul (1965), he suggests that environmental sources of anxiety and depression (the technological society in which we live) are obscured. Thus, economic systems and the popularity of certain remedies (e.g., psychotherapy and medication compared to advocacy, to create equal educational opportunities and health care for all residents) are intertwined (see also chapter 6). There is a de-politization of personal and social problems in a market-driven economy.

The ideology of socialism regards the economic inequalities in a capitalistic society as unjust. Socialism sees the good of all people as critical and pays particular attention to conflicts of interest among classes. The ideology of individualism and the economic ideology of which it is a part (capitalism) are considered responsible for creating and maintaining economic inequities and encouraging the inappropriate use of psychological approaches with clients who have material and social support needs. Some scholars (e.g., Webster, 1992, 1997) suggest that the recognition of shared interests among economically disadvantaged groups is obscured by ideologies that "balkanize" the working class by setting groups such as poor African Americans and poor whites against each other. They argue that political and economic inequities limiting the extent to which people can be "self-made" are ignored or downplayed, and that the limits of self-determination are obscured by vague statements asserting its ease of accomplishment. Critical, radical, structural, and contextual theories emphasize social, political, and economic influences on personal and social problems. (See, for example, Allan, Pease, and Briskman, 2010; see also chapter 12.)

John Ehrenreich argues that the Progressive Era ideology of the professional middle class that social problems could be viewed as technical problems solvable by "scientific" management offered by middle-class managers, furthered middle-class interests, often at the cost of making working conditions less appealing to those managed (the working class) (1985, p. 134). Demott (1990) argues that even before the turn of the century, prevailing elite ideology described the key division in American society not as that between rich and poor, but as that between industrious and idle, virtuous and vicious, community-minded and selfish. Leslie Margolin suggests that because social work appears to be nonexclusionary and nondivisive, it is able to create and reinforce popular beliefs about who is worthy and who is not (1997).

Social Justice or Psychotherapy

The NASW Code of Ethics emphasizes the social justice mission of social work on "behalf of vulnerable or oppressed individuals and groups of people" (see Exhibit 3.1). (See previous section on Social Justice). People differ as to whether they believe psychotherapy has a legitimate role in social work. Wakefield (1992) argues that it helps people to maximize their potential and that this is a legitimate aim of social work. Others argue that psychotherapy does not have a legitimate role in social work (e.g., Specht & Courtney, 1994). Feminist writers criticize individually based psychotherapy for overlooking social causes of problems (e.g., Kantrowitz & Ballou, 1992; Lerman, 1992). They contend that humanistic ideologies emphasizing authenticity, self-actualization, meaningful human relationships, being in touch with one's inner feelings, expanding one's awareness, and using cognitive-behavioral methods ignore structural factors related to problems, including unequal opportunities for men and women. (See discussion of Capitalistic and Socialistic Ideologies.)

The first clarification needed is a definition of psychotherapy. Unless we describe the helping efforts to which this term refers, we cannot be sure what we are talking about. What are the problems which concern clients? Only when we have answered these questions can we wisely choose the best methods to address them. When confronted with a specific individual, family, group, organization, or community experiencing real-life problems, we can ask, given this situation, what methods are most likely to be effective both now and in the future? (See later section on The Professional as Social Reformer.)

Mental Illness (Biomedical) and Contextual Views

The biomedical industrial complex promotes a medicalized view of personal troubles such as anxiety, depression (mis) use of alcohol and drugs—viewing them as illnesses requiring treatment (e.g., Clarke, Mamo, Fosket, Fishman, & Shim, 2010) including coerced intervention. The state has assumed power over the substances we can place in our bodies (Szasz, 1994; 2001). Some scholars contend that the ideology of mental illness is used to deprive people of their freedom and liberty by labeling them as mentally ill and forcing treatment on them (e.g., Szasz, 1994). Environmental causes of personal problems such as discriminatory policies and practices are often ignored and biological and psychological ones emphasized (Moynihan, Heath, & Henry, 2002; Timimi, 2008). Little attention is given to state and corporate crime compared to crimes of individuals (Chambliss et al., 2010). Client dependency is encouraged by assuming that experts are needed to "treat" an ever-lengthening list of problems-in-living framed as health problems—"mental disorders." Pharmaceutical companies make billions and armies of researchers study the "mentally ill." This is not to say the people do not have problems. It is how these are framed that is at issue here. In contrast, a contextual (ecological) perspective emphasizes the role of environmental factors in creating and maintaining personal troubles and social problems, including class differences in who receives stigmatizing labels (e.g., schizophrenic) and unwanted "treatment" (often the poor and people of color). (See chapter 6.)

Other Ideologies

Religious ideologies emphasize spiritual and moral obligations. Legal ideologies emphasize rights. Cultural ideologies underscore the role of cultural factors in understanding behavior. The ideology of the nuclear family sees this kind of family as providing the optimal setting for raising children. Some scholars argue that the ideology of "doing good" masks the coercive nature of child welfare services (e.g., Margolin, 1997). For example, Sarri and Finn (1992) note the "civilizing mission" that shaped nineteenth- and early twentieth-century federal policy toward Native Americans. "Through the boarding school system, thousands of Native American children were separated from their families, communities and cultures; social control was imposed in the name of education" (p. 224).

Can the Fox Guard the Chickens?

The history of the helping professions shows that there are problems with professions guarding the competency of their members. Consider the troubling history of psychiatry illustrating harming in the name of helping (e.g., Scull, 2005; Valenstein, 1986). Pseudoscience thrives in social work (Pignotti & Thyer, 2009). This is also the case with published research findings (e.g., Ioannidis, 2005). That is, many related knowledge claims are exaggerated. Indeed such problems encouraged the development of evidence-based practice and policy. The reasons are many. They include the tendency of professionals to promote a particular approach to problems, for example, their medicalization (see chapter 6). Professionals often fail to inform clients about the negative effects of recommended services such as neuroleptic medication (e.g., tardive dyskinesia). Most helpers are rarely observed while interacting with their clients. Their behavior is known mainly by indirect means such as reports in staff meetings and case records. The variability of behaviors in relation to particular ethical concerns is unknown. A social worker is held responsible only for meeting the standards of practice in his or her community. These may be poor. The NASW Code of Ethics is vague about what behaviors are involved in what situations. Vague descriptions and lack of transparency of processes and outcomes may conceal avoidable negative outcomes.

The Need for Limits on Professional Discretion

The history of the helping professions highlights the need for limits on professional discretion in choosing (1) objectives (involving clients as informed participants in decisions made),

(2) services offered (least intrusive and restrictive and most effective and efficient), and (3) evaluation methods (keeping track of clear, relevant progress indicators). Judicial and legislative pressures have been necessary to increase professional accountability. It is not unusual for lawsuits to be brought against residential institutions or for state-licensing agencies to warn an agency against further use of policies and practices that harm clients. Lawsuits have been filed against many public child welfare agencies for failing to implement procedural guidelines legislated to protect children (Eamon & Kopels, 2004). The court that reviewed the foster care placement of a disabled child and the services offered held that the agency had not made reasonable efforts to provide either preventive or reunification services to the family because:

1. The family was not referred to parenting classes, identified as a critical service, until nine months after the child was removed from the home.

2. The agency was too slow in providing family and marital counseling and offered no adequate explanation for why it had not offered intensive family counseling from the outset.

3. Efforts to arrange a medical appointment for the mother to determine if she needed medication superseded and interfered with the provision of necessary individual counseling for the mother.

4. The agency failed to provide frequent and appropriate visitation, because it did not attempt unsupervised, extended, overnight, and weekend visits, which the court deemed entirely appropriate.

5. The child's medical exam was not to be considered a reunification service, as it was not given for other than routine purposes. (*Matter of a Child*, no. 88178, 1986; see Shotton, 1990, p. 2)

Avoidable harms occur within the welfare system created to protect children as discussed earlier in this chapter (DePanfilis, 2003). Examination of records in child welfare agencies revealed a variety of avoidable errors (Munro, 1996; Rzepnicki & Johnson, 2005). Systemic factors are often ignored such as lack of high-quality parent-training programs, lack of safe housing, and lack of teamwork across agencies (Broadhurst, Wastell, White, Hall, Peckover, Thompson, et al., 2009). Surrogate indicators of success are often used to evaluate program outcomes such as percentage of children returned home; no information is provided on the quality of these homes.

The potential for professional abuse of power highlights the importance of clear and enforced regulations requiring a clear description of the reasons why clients must have any part of their freedom curtailed and strict limitations of grounds for doing so. The greater the potential influence over clients, the greater the need for constraints on professional behaviors to ensure that clients receive requested services in a manner that does not intrude on their rights including an effective process to review what is done to what effect. Although legislation has been passed to protect clients' rights in many areas, related policies and practices are not necessarily implemented. For example, no longer can children be denied a right to education by being suspended from school because of vague complaints that they are a management problem. The exact nature of the offending behaviors must be described in writing, and the parents and the child have a right to this information. But, in practice, this often does not happen. Guidelines for specific standards of practice already exist in some areas, such as institutional care of developmentally disabled clients, and are described in legislation (see also Exhibit 3.4). Many states have specific written guidelines limiting the use of aversive methods in institutional settings.

However, written guidelines and legislation are not enough to protect clients from harm and to ensure service quality. Contingencies must be arranged that support programs, policies, and practices that guard clients' interests. The call for consumers to help to define the limits of professional discretion is not new (e.g., Lenrow & Cowden, 1980). Including clients as informed participants is emphasized in evidence-based practice (e.g., Cochrane Consumer Network <http://consumers. cochrane.org>; see also Coulter, 2002; Coulter & Collins, 2011). Scores of consumer interest groups have been created to give people information concerning different kinds of problems and methods used to address them. The Public Citizen's Health Research Group publishes material for consumers (e.g., *Health Letter*), as do state boards that regulate professional practice. As with all material, the motto "Buyer Beware" applies. That is,

---

EXHIBIT 3.4

Position Statement on a Clients' Rights to Effective Behavioral Treatment

The Association for Behavior Analysis issues the following position statement on clients' rights to effective behavioral treatment as a set of guiding principles to protect individuals from harm as a result of either the lack or the inappropriate use of behavioral treatment. The Association declares that individuals who receive behavioral treatment have a right to:

1. *A therapeutic physical and social environment*: Characteristics of such an environment include but are not limited to: an acceptable standard of living, opportunities for stimulation and training, therapeutic social interaction, and freedom from undue physical or social restriction.

2. *Services whose overriding goal is personal welfare*: The client participates, either directly or through authorized proxy, in the development and implementation of treatment programs. In cases where withholding or implementing treatment involves potential risk and the client does not have the capacity to provide consent, individual welfare is protected through two mechanisms: Peer Review Committees, imposing professional standards, determine the clinical propriety of treatment programs: Human Rights Committees, imposing community standards, determine the acceptability of treatment programs and the degree to which they may compromise an individual's rights.

3. *Treatment by a competent behavior analyst*: The behavior analyst's training reflects appropriate academic preparation, including knowledge of behavioral principles, methods of assessment and treatment, research methodology, and professional ethics; as well as practical experience. In cases where a problem or treatment is complex or may pose risk, direct involvement by a doctoral-level behavior analyst is necessary.

4. *Programs that teach functional skills*: Improvement in functioning requires the acquisition of adaptive behaviors that will increase independence, as well as the elimination of behaviors that are dangerous or that in some other way serve as barriers to independence.

5. *Behavioral assessment and ongoing evaluation*: Pretreatment assessment, including both interviews and measures of behavior, attempts to identify factors relevant to behavioral maintenance and treatment. The continued use of objective behavioral measurement documents response to treatment.

6. *The most effective treatment procedures available*: An individual is entitled to effective and scientifically validated treatment; in turn, the behavior analyst has an obligation to use only those procedures demonstrated by research to be effective. Decisions on the use of potentially restrictive treatment are based on consideration of its absolute and relative level of restrictiveness, the amount of time required to produce a clinically significant outcome, and the consequences that would result from delayed intervention.

Source: This statement is an abbreviated version of a report by the Association for Behavior Analysis, Task Force on the Right to Effective Behavioral Treatment (see R. Van Houten [chair], S. Axelrod, J. S. Bailey, J. E. Favell, R. M. Foxx, B. A. Iwata, and O. I. Lovas). *Journal of Applied Behavior Analysis, 21* (1988), 381–384. Reprinted with permission.

critically appraise what you read. Who created the website? Who funds it? This may suggest certain biases. Do the creators have a vested interest in overestimating the prevalence of a problem or "condition"? Are specific references related to claims given so you can look these up for yourself? Does it describe negative, as well as positive, effects of methods promoted? A client bill of rights is shown in Exhibit 3.5.

Obstacles to Increasing Ethical Practice

The emphasis on the sanctity of professional opinion and the unquestioned assumption that professionals "do good," are sincere, and engage in ethical behavior are obstacles to identifying policies and practices that harm rather than help clients and to identifying clear standards of practice and arranging monitoring and incentive systems to support them. Agency administrators eager to gain and maintain funding are reluctant to candidly acknowledge what is done to what effect (Altheide & Johnson, 1980). Reasons for the vagueness of ethical codes include their political and economic functions (including asserting good intentions and avoiding the exclusion of constituencies from certain activities). It is in the interest of professionals and administrators to be vague about goals, procedures, and outcomes if clients and other interested parties would raise concerns and possibly remove funding if they knew what was actually done to what effect. The following statement made decades ago is still true today:

> Most institutions protect themselves by assuring a lack of information. In virtually any public institution, the goals are too imprecise to serve as a safeguard against which to judge the workings of the institution. It is impossible to tell by whom important decisions will be made, when they will be made, and what factors will be weighed in the process. Once a decision is made, it is impossible to trace its impact, good or bad. There is not only no feedback within the institution, but also no communication of objective data to the public. (Martin, 1975, pp. 97–98)

Some people argue that vagueness benefits clients, that it allows professionals to define goals and negotiate value conflicts in ways that would not be possible if more specific ethical codes existed. However, the history of the helping professions shows that this flexibility often works against, rather than for, clients. Only when general terms such as respect and empowerment are clearly described regarding what they mean and related actions are taken, do values become meaningful to clients. As Helen Harris Perlman (1976) noted, "a value has small worth except as it is moved, or is movable, from believing into doing, from verbal affirmation into action" (p. 381).

Vague descriptions of goals, procedures, and outcomes provide "a shield for the practitioner," which is not always in the best interests of clients (Rothman, 1980, p. 145). Vague ethical standards offer an illusion of agreement. They provide a false

EXHIBIT 3.5

Patient Bill of Rights

Patients have the right to

- Request and receive information about the therapist's professional capabilities, including licensure, education, training, experience, professional association membership, specialization, and limitations.

- Have written information about fees, payment methods, insurance reimbursement, number of sessions, substitutions (in cases of vacation and emergencies), and cancellation policies before beginning therapy.

- Receive respectful treatment that will be helpful to you.

- A safe environment, free from sexual, physical, and emotional abuse.

- Ask questions about your therapy.

- Refuse to answer any question or disclose any information you choose not to reveal.

- Request and receive information from the therapist about your progress.

- Know the limits of confidentiality and the circumstances in which a therapist is legally required to disclose information to others.

- Know if there are supervisors, consultants, students, or others with whom your therapist will discuss your case.

- Refuse a particular type of treatment, or end treatment without obligation or harassment.

- Refuse electronic recording (but you may request it if you wish).

- Request and (in most cases) receive a summary of your file, including the diagnosis, your progress, and the type of treatment.

- Report unethical and illegal behavior by a therapist.

- Receive a second opinion at any time about your therapy or therapist's methods.

- Have a copy of your file transferred to any therapist or agency you choose.

Source: California Department of Consumer Affairs (2009). *Professional therapy never includes sex* (p. 24). Sacramento, CA. Reprinted with permission.

reassurance that professionals agree on what actions should be taken in given situations and act accordingly. Vague standards obscure areas of disagreement and allow a range of discretion that may not be in the clients' best interests. We need more descriptive studies of ethical dilemmas that arise in everyday practice from the point of view of all involved parties (clients, significant others, social workers, administrators, supervisors) and how they are handled and to what effect. We should develop clear decision-making guidelines related to specific dilemmas. Each should have a level of detail that permits the identification of the potential consequences of different options to those persons involved.

Encouraging Ethical Behavior

If ethical behavior is to occur, it must be supported. Codes of ethics provide the grounds for raising questions about practices and policies that have life-affecting consequences. The steps involved in evidence-based practice and related technological innovations contribute to ethical practice by increasing transparency of what is done to what effect, encouraging informed consent, and taking advantage of practice and policy-related research. Contingency analysis skills will be a value in discovering opportunities to foster ethical practices and policies (see chapters 7 and 12). Evidence-informed standards of practice and effective contingency and audit systems that support them should increase the likelihood that clients receive high-quality services. Highlighting ethical issues, both in work and educational settings, will increase awareness of ethical concerns and dilemmas. Periodic critical reviews by supervisors, administrators, and/or review panels of practices and policies and their outcomes should increase the likelihood that services offered are those most likely to help clients attain outcomes they value. (See Exhibit 3.6 for a model for making ethical decisions.)

EXHIBIT 3.6

Model for Making Ethical Decisions

1. **State the problem.**

2. **Check the facts.** Does the evidence support the alleged facts? Have all needed facts been gathered? What information is irrelevant? Have related research and theory been drawn on?

3. **Develop** a list of alternative courses of action.

4. **Describe what is ethically at stake in relation to each of the alternatives:**

   (a) The relevant ethical principles. Consider the Universal Declaration of Rights and related covenants.

   (b) The likely harms and benefits to the parties involved. Who is the most vulnerable?

   (c) Relevant laws.

   (d) Relevant agency policies and legislation.

   (e) Relevant rights and responsibilities that correspond with those rights.

5. **Evaluate alternatives.** (Consult with others as needed.)

   Ethical standards test: Does one option fit better with ethical principles, agency policies, and laws than other alternatives?

   Outcomes test: Is one option likely to provide more benefit or less harm than others?

6. **Make a decision.** Select the option that is most consistent with important values such as client self-determination and most likely to achieve hoped-for outcomes.

7. **Check the conclusions.**

   Publicity test: Would the decision stand if it were published in a newspaper?

   Goosey-Gander Test: Would the decision stand if the decision maker were adversely affected by it? Is what is good for the goose, good for the gander? (Gambrill & Gibbs, 2002)

   Colleague Test: What would colleagues say about the problem and the selected option?

   Professional Test: What might the profession's governing body or ethics committee say about the option?

   Organization Test: What would the agency's ethics officer or legal counsel say about the selected option?

8. **Plan for prevention of the problem in the future.** Are there steps that could be taken at the professional level to avoid the problem in the future?

Source: Adapted from M. Leever, G. DeCiani, E. Mulaney, & H. Hasslinger (in conjunction with E. Gambrill) (2002). *Ethical child welfare practice* (p. 4). Washington, DC: Child Welfare League of America.

Agencies are obligated to encourage ethical practice by arranging a culture and climate that allows staff to link evidentiary and ethical issues, for example, by providing access to databases needed to discover research related to questions that affect clients' lives. Expected standards of practice should be clearly described and an effective audit system in place to offer staff and clients' feedback regarding the quality and outcome of agency services. Needed training should be offered and incentive systems provided that maximize service quality (e.g., see chapter 27). Such arrangements require transparency regarding what helpers actually do and what they accomplish. Randomly selected interviews can be reviewed by supervisors to identify opportunities for improvement. This review can be used to increase the likelihood that:

- Outcomes of concern to clients are focused on when feasible and ethical.

- Valid assessment, intervention, and evaluation methods are used.

- The least intrusive and restrictive and most acceptable procedures are selected.

- Client assets are supported.

- Clear service agreements exist (see chapter 13).

- Clients and significant others are involved as informed participants in selection of goals and procedures and review of progress.

- Clear, relevant progress indicators are tracked and results are shared with clients on a timely basis.

- Creative, energetic, and informed efforts are made to acquire needed resources and to coordinate them.

- Needed training is provided to staff.

- Advocacy efforts to attain needed funding for effective programs are documented.

Time may have to be put aside for staff to discuss ethical dilemmas that arise and should be if related decisions affect clients' lives.

What Are Your Obligations?

Many social workers tell me that they do not make decisions. Reasons include: "I don't have sufficient resources," "I don't have time," "my supervisor makes the decisions," and "I'm regulated by agency policy." Some of my students tell me that "I just do assessments that I pass on to my supervisor who makes the decisions." Taking responsibility for the decisions you make is a hallmark of being a professional. Accepting responsibility for decisions is a burden. It is also a freedom—a freedom to exercise discretion in the best interests of clients (see Exhibit 3.7). Not taking responsibility leaves you powerless, helpless, unaccountable to clients, and unlikely to recognize social control and

---

EXHIBIT 3.7

Consequences for Assuming or Denying Responsibility for Practice Decisions

Assuming responsibility for your decisions	• People can blame me for poor decisions. • I can blame myself for poor decisions. • I can praise myself for good decisions. • Others can praise me for good decisions. • I am burdened by responsibility for my decisions.
Denying you make decisions	• No one, including clients, can blame me for poor decisions. • No satisfaction in tasks/outcomes achieved. • Feeling helpless/alienated/controlled by fate/others. • I can't blame myself for poor decisions. • I am not burdened by responsibility for making decisions.

---

self-interest masked as "doing good." It takes away what freedom you do have, and some people argue that we have some freedom in making decisions, even in dire circumstances (e.g., Faden, Beauchamp, & King, 1986; Frankl, 1984).

How much responsibility falls on your shoulders for your agency's programs, policies, and practices? Is it ethically acceptable to work in an agency that you know offers ineffective or harmful services? Social workers often do not have the resources needed to help clients. How much responsibility should you take for this state of affairs? What should you do if the resources missing are your knowledge and skills (e.g., you do not have the knowledge and skills needed to help a youth to develop effective social skills)? Who or what is responsible for this (you, your educational program, your agency, or all of these)? What should you do if you work in an agency that transforms clients' goals into other goals that do not benefit clients or may even harm them? What is your responsibility? These are hard questions that you should consider to avoid fooling yourself or your clients about what can be achieved and to avoid overlooking options that do exist (see Exhibit 3.7).

History shows that good intentions do not protect clients from harm. Only by being softhearted (compassionate and caring), as well as hard-headed (clarifying and critically evaluating assumptions) and competent (in possession of knowledge and skills required to address problems), do you have the best chance of helping clients and avoiding harm. Ask yourself, "Would I be satisfied with compassion alone on the part of my physician?"

Does your answer reflect a double standard—art for them and science for me (Gambrill & Gibbs, 2002)?

Handling Discrepancies Between Ideals and Realities

Perhaps in no other profession than in social work is there a greater contrast between the loftiness of service ideals and the stark realities of daily practice in the help that can be offered: "Their jobs [especially in the public social services] force them to see what ignorance, poverty, disease and destitution can do. They are forced to deal with social reality at its worst" (Bensman, 1967, p. 193). Social workers must try daily to resolve problems whose fundamental causes lie outside their field. "In attempting to apply the highest ideals to the most resistant realities, the social welfare worker frequently feels trapped, frustrated, and helpless. How he responds to such situations determines his future and his character as a social welfare worker" (p. 97). Unless you develop skills to cope with mismatches between ideals and realities, you may fall into habits that harm clients, such as pretending that you are competent to offer certain services when you are not, denying that you make any decisions, congratulating yourself for success even when you have had none, offering clients empty promises, or applying rules and regulations in a rigid manner that disregards their needs. You may focus on "interesting" problems, overlooking your client's needs. You may deny rather than examine dilemmas created by conflicting loyalties. You may overlook coercive aspects of practice and make decisions "for your clients' own good" rather than allowing them to make their own choices. Keeping client's interests clearly in view, critically reviewing assumptions (your own as well as those of others), and taking responsibility for your decisions will help you to make ethical decisions.

The Professional as Social Reformer

Social reform has been a key interest in the history of social work. This requires attention to the big picture—to contextual factors that influence the very definition of social and personal problems (see chapter 6). Most social work interventions are at level 1 (the individual) and level 2 (the family). Some occur on the group and community level (3). We need far more attention to higher levels that influence clients' lives, the organizational, policy, and legislative levels. Social workers are in the front lines in terms of daily sight of the results of growing income inequality and its harsh consequences, such as throwing many in the middle class into insecure lives and rendering the lives of the already poor even more difficult. They have daily opportunities to document avoidable miseries caused by political and economic policies that benefit the very rich to the detriment of all others. Financial irregularities include outright fraud on the part of billionaires in the financial industry who are rewarded with bonuses in the millions while poor African American youth in our inner cities are arrested for having small amounts of marijuana. When the

rich break the law, the prosecutors may find themselves on trial; they can afford lawyers. Where is the legal aid for the poor? And how skilled are the lawyers provided for the poor? Do they have a reasonable workload?

Thousands of people sleep in cars, parks, or on the street at night, unable to afford housing. The plights of the poor galvanized social reformers such as Jane Adams. Individual, family, group, and community level intervention goes only so far, often providing a band-aid on a life-threatening wound. It is social workers who can (and should) document the daily miseries of their clients and the need for redress at a systemic level of public policy and related legislation. Policy and practice are intertwined. This is the key thought behind the policy/practice approach to social work. The International Federation of Social Workers statement of purpose calls on social workers to challenge unjust policies and practices. "Social workers have a duty to bring to the attention of their employers, policy politicians and the general public situations where resources are inadequate or where distribution of resources, policies and practices are oppressive, unfair or harmful" (4.1). Other professions also emphasize obligations of professionals to consider the big picture. In their discussion of the philosophy of evidence-based practice, Guyatt and Rennie (2002) call on physicians to be effective advocates for their clients: "physicians concerned about the health of their patients as a group, or about the health of the community, should consider how they might contribute to reducing poverty" (Guyatt & Rennie, 2002, p. 9). Social workers are paying more attention to human rights.

Summary

Ethical practice requires considering the competing interests involved in making decisions: legal regulations, clients' interests, the interests of involved others, professional codes of ethics, agency policy, and personal values. This highlights the prevalence of ethical dilemmas. Ethical and legal issues arise in selecting objectives, service plans, and evaluation methods. Involving clients as informed participants, honoring confidentiality, and working within the limits of one's competence are ethical concerns. Only when ethical concerns are clarified may different interests and levels of influence be revealed. Critical thinking and evidence-informed practice and policy are suggested as guides for making ethical decisions. Both emphasize the close connection between evidentiary and ethical issues. Integral to both are raising vital questions, considering opposing views, and basing decisions on informed judgments in which helpers take advantage of practice and policy-related research findings and consider the interests of all involved parties in a context of transparency regarding what is done to what effect.

Respect for clients requires building on their strengths, offering them the most effective methods, avoiding stereotyping and pathologizing them, and talking to and about clients in a polite manner sensitive to cultural differences. It means offering clients real (rather than merely perceived) influence over the quality of their lives and tailoring methods to each client's unique characteristics as needed, including cultural differences. Self-determination requires involving clients in decisions and ensuring informed consent. Accountability involves focusing on objectives that make a real difference in clients' lives, monitoring progress and sharing the results with clients, and being willing to have one's work evaluated to review the quality of services offered.

Ethical issues and ideologies (beliefs and accepted values of particular groups) are closely related. Ideological clashes—often at the heart of ethical dilemmas in social work—include those between service and professional ideologies and between bureaucratic and service ideologies. Beliefs held dogmatically may obscure sources of influence and hinder change in policies and procedures that harm rather than help clients. Continued vigilance is necessary to protect clients' rights and minimize injustices, both small and large; good intentions and verbal statements of caring are not enough. Your ethical obligations to clients provides a guide for raising vital questions such as "Is this practice working?" They provide a grounding for the courage to raise questions others may prefer to keep hidden.

Reviewing Your Competencies

Reviewing Content Knowledge

1. Describe the key ethical principles in the NASW Code of Ethics.

2. Describe the characteristics of ethical dilemmas and give examples.

3. Identify factors that should be considered when thinking about ethical issues.

4. Describe the relationship between evidentiary and ethical issues.

5. Describe the role of critical thinking in making ethical decisions.

6. Identify the kinds of harms to clients that may result from not recognizing hidden sources of power in social work practice.

7. Discuss the social worker's role as an agent of the state and how this may conflict with being an agent of the client.

8. Explain why professional codes of ethics are vague.

9. Describe the requirements of informed consent.

10. Identify ethical issues related to competence.

11. Describe the components of accountability.

12. Distinguish between privileged communication and confidentiality.

13. Describe common waivers of privileged communication.

14. Identify the ethical and legal concerns related to case records.

15. Describe indicators of respect for clients.

16. Discuss the role (actual and ideal) of professional organizations regarding ethical issues.

17. Identify key regulations related to your area of practice including recent legislation and its possible effects.

18. Discuss the relationship between ethical practice and client empowerment.

19. Describe elements in the definition of malpractice.

20. Give examples of the grounds for malpractice and describe steps you can take to reduce your vulnerability to malpractice lawsuits.

21. Describe clients' options when confronted with unethical or illegal behavior by professionals.

22. Describe the relationship between ethics and ideology.

23. Explain what is meant by the term *ideology*.

24. Identify the functions and indicators of ideology.

25. Identify common ideological clashes in social work.

26. Give examples of ethical issues regarding agency policies and procedures.

27. Give examples of ethical issues related to social and public policies.

28. You can describe the specific steps you can take in your work setting to address specific ethical concerns. You can clearly describe the concerns and identify leverage points for change, as well as constraints and resources (e.g., regarding who will benefit and who will lose from proposed changes).

Reviewing What You Do

1. Given specific examples, you correctly identify ethical issues and legal constraints.

2. You involve clients as informed participants in decisions made.

3. You draw on practice and policy-related research findings to offer your clients effective methods.

4. You participate in joint efforts to alter unethical public and social policies.

5. You provide accurate information to your clients about their legal rights.

6. You demonstrate critical thinking values, knowledge, and skills in discussing ethical issues (see chapter 5).

7. You recognize ideological statements.

8. You explain to your clients the limits of confidentiality.

9. You take appropriate steps to ensure your clients' informed consent.

10. You take appropriate steps to alter unethical agency policies and procedures.

Reviewing Results

1. Legal regulations are honored.

2. Clients receive services that enhance the quality of their lives.

3. The services offered enhance clients' knowledge and skills.

4. Unethical agency policies and practice are changed.

5. Unethical social and public policies are changed.

Part 2

Thinking About Knowledge and How to Get It

4

Different Views of Knowledge

OVERVIEW This chapter introduces you to different views of knowledge and how to get it. Our concern for helping and not harming clients obliges us to critically examine the criteria we use to evaluate claims. Professional codes of ethics require professionals to draw on practice- and policy-related research, to be competent, and to accurately inform clients about the risks and benefits of recommended services and alternatives. The Educational Policy and Accreditation Standards (2008) of CSWE call on social workers to engage in research-informed practice and practice-informed research (2.1.6). This highlights the importance of critically appraising the evidentiary status of claims regarding what is true and what is not. In evidence-informed practice, social workers consider research findings related to life-affecting decisions. But what is evidence? Questionable as well as sound criteria for evaluating claims are described, and you are encouraged to explore your views on this important topic. The close connection between evidentiary and ethical issues is highlighted, including the importance of recognizing uncertainty in making decisions.

YOU WILL LEARN ABOUT

- Different views of knowledge and how (or if) it can be gained

- Evaluating knowledge claims

- Questionable criteria

- Science and scientific criteria

- Relativism

- Quackery

- Propaganda, fraud, and corruption in the helping professions

- Knowledge valued in evidence-informed compared to authority-based practice

- Reviewing your beliefs about learning and your educational environments

- Valuing truth as an ethical obligation

- The importance of a historical perspective

Helping clients, including removing clear injustices, highlights the importance of thinking critically about knowledge and how to get it. It emphasizes the importance of making well-reasoned decisions and valuing truth over prejudice and ignorance. (You can explore your views by completing Exhibit 4.1.) This implies that there is some knowledge to master, that some decisions are better reasoned than others, and that there are differences among truth, prejudice, and ignorance, which have consequences for clients. A concern for helping and not harming implies that certain decisions are better than others. This obligates professionals to be informed about the degree of uncertainty associated with decisions that affect clients' well-being. The closer the match between your knowledge and skills and knowledge available to help clients (or to correctly determine that you cannot), the more likely you are to honor ethical obligations to help clients and avoid harm and the more you can involve clients as informed participants in decisions made.

Mrs. A has to make a decision about how to assess her client's depression. What sources of information should she use and what criteria should she use to evaluate their accuracy? Should she use her intuition? Should she ask her client to complete the Beck Depression Inventory? Should she talk to family members and take a careful history? Ms. Ross has to make a decision about how to help foster parents encourage positive behaviors and enhance the development of a 4-year-old boy who has been removed from his biological parents because of persistent neglect. How can she locate valuable guidelines regarding the most effective methods? What criteria should she use to review the accuracy of a claim such as: "Attention deficit hyperactive disorder (ADHD) is due to a biochemical disorder"? How much evidence is needed to say that a method should be used? What is evidence? These questions highlight the importance of thinking about knowledge and how to get it. Beliefs are based on many different criteria including folklore, practice wisdom, common sense, and research findings. Social work draws on knowledge in many disciplines, each with unique views and perhaps conflicting claims. Mary Richmond (1917) called on social workers to draw on knowledge from the social sciences to help clients.

Professions claim special knowledge and skills to help clients achieve certain outcomes (e.g., decrease child maltreatment or alcohol consumption). Larson (1977) suggests that

> The main instrument of professional advancement, more than the profession of altruism, is the capacity to claim esoteric and identifiable skills—that is, to create and control a cognitive and technical basis. The claim of expertise aims at gaining social recognition and collective prestige which, in turn, are implicitly used by the individual to assert his authority and demand respect in the context of everyday transactions within specific role-sets. (p. 180)

Claimed special knowledge supposedly makes those with certain degrees, training, and/or experience more effective in achieving certain outcomes than those without such "credentials."

That is, the former are supposed to be "experts" in solving certain kinds of problems. The importance of specialized content knowledge and skills is one of the major findings from research in problem solving and decision making, including professional decision making (see chapter 8). *Performance knowledge* refers to knowledge about how and when to use content knowledge in practice and how to automatize procedures so they can be used efficiently. *Inert knowledge* refers to content knowledge unaccompanied by the procedural knowledge required to put it to use in practice (see Exhibit 4.2).

Evidence-based practice arose in part because of flaws in published reports of research findings, for example, inflated claims of effectiveness. But what is a flaw? When is it so significant that we should dismiss a claim? For example are these claims accurate:

- Use of genograms results in better outcomes for clients.

- Multisystemic Family Therapy is more effective than other forms of intervention.

- Brief psychological debriefing is helpful in decreasing post-traumatic stress disorder.

- Brief programs for the depressed elderly are helpful.

- Decreasing plaque decreases mortality.

- Drinking causes domestic violence.

- The DSM is a valid classification system.

Traditional and current criteria include what is "standard or accepted" or what a helper believes to be a client's "best interests." However, as Eddy (1993) notes, "the credibility of clinical judgement, whether exercised individually or collectively, has been severely challenged by observations of wide variations in practices, inappropriate care, and practitioner uncertainty" (p. 521). (See also research comparing clinical and actuarial judgment, Grove & Meehl, 1996; Quinsey, Harris, Rice, & Cormier, 2006.)

Different Views of Knowledge and How (or If) It Can Be Gained

The question "what is knowledge?" has been of concern to philosophers throughout the ages. People differ in their beliefs about knowledge and how it can be gained. Cultural differences influence these beliefs (e.g., Tweed & Lehman, 2002). We are all philosophers in making scores of decisions each day about how to act. Different ways of knowing differ in the extent to which they highlight uncertainty and are designed to weed out biases and distortions. Knowledge serves different functions, only one of which is to encourage the growth of knowledge. Munz (1985) suggests that the function of *false knowledge* (beliefs that

EXHIBIT 4.1

Exploring Your Beliefs About Knowledge

Circle the numbers in the columns that best describe your responses

	SA	A	N	D	SD	
1. Since we cannot know anything for sure, we really do not know anything.	1	2	3	4	5	____
2. Since our beliefs influence what we see, we cannot gather accurate knowledge about our world.	1	2	3	4	5	____
3. It is good not to be too skeptical because anything is possible.	1	2	3	4	5	____
4. Everything is relative; all ways of knowing are equally true.	1	2	3	4	5	____
5. Criticism (critical discussion and testing) provides a valuable route to knowledge.	1	2	3	4	5	____
6. Some things cannot be demonstrated scientifically.	1	2	3	4	5	____
7. Personal experience provides a sound guide, even without corrective feedback.	1	2	3	4	5	____
8. Science is a way of thinking developed by white male Western Europeans that does not apply to other cultures.	1	2	3	4	5	____
9. I rely on the experts to know what is true.	1	2	3	4	5	____
10. It is apparent without elaborate observations that cigarette smoking is associated with cancer.	1	2	3	4	5	____
11. It is important for professionals to have sound reasons for their decisions.	1	2	3	4	5	____
12. The opinions of 10 million qualified and reputable physicians or other professionals are of no value unless they are based on scientific evidence.	1	2	3	4	5	____
13. Just because a famous person makes a claim (e.g., Freud) does not mean it is accurate.	1	2	3	4	5	____
14. It usually is best to go along with what other people accept as true.	1	2	3	4	5	____
15. Tradition provides a sound guide for assessing the accuracy of claims.	1	2	3	4	5	____
16. Newness provides a sound guide for assessing the accuracy of claims.	1	2	3	4	5	____
17. Testimonials and case examples provide a sound guide for assessing the accuracy of claims.	1	2	3	4	5	____
18. Good intentions provide a sound guide for assessing the accuracy of claims.	1	2	3	4	5	____
19. Empirical research has little to offer to social workers.	1	2	3	4	5	____
20. It is obvious that any type of counseling will help people more than none.	1	2	3	4	5	____
21. Experts always know best.	1	2	3	4	5	____
22. Professionals have an obligation to critically evaluate claims of effectiveness no matter who makes them.	1	2	3	4	5	____

Key: SA = strongly agree; A = agree; N = neutral; D = disagree; SD = strongly disagree.

EXHIBIT 4.2

Examples of Different Kinds of Knowledge

Content knowledge

- ethical obligations
- assessment methods
- intervention options
- evaluation methods
- public policies and related legislation that affect clients' options
- developmental norms
- research findings regarding behavior and how it is influenced
- common biases in decision making
- criteria of value in critically appraising different kinds of research
- service systems

Procedural knowledge

- how to use different kinds of assessment methods
- how to use different kinds of intervention methods
- how to critically appraise different kinds of claims and related research reports
- how to search effectively and efficiently for research related to life-affecting decisions
- how to integrate different sources of information in a way that contributes to making sound decisions
- how to accurately evaluate programs
- how to store and retrieve information

Inert knowledge

- content knowledge unaccompanied by procedural knowledge
- failure to use content or procedural knowledge
- censored knowledge

Self-knowledge

- about personal bias
- about gaps between your current knowledge and skills and what is available (e.g., regarding causes, risks, accuracy of assessment methods, effectiveness of intervention methods)
- about your vulnerability to burnout
- about the quality of your learning skills

False knowledge

- beliefs that are not true and are not questioned.

knowledge can only take place in certain circumstances (i.e., cultures)—those in which alternative views are entertained and all views are subject to criticism (see Glossary to this chapter). Only in this way do beliefs confront the environment.

Certain "ways of knowing" compared to others are designed to critically test guesses (e.g., about effectiveness). The purpose of experimental studies is to avoid misleading assumptions about effects. Karl Popper suggests that we do not know more today than we did thousands of years ago because solving some problems creates new ones. Consider, for example, the invention of automobiles. Some people believe that nothing can be known "for sure." This is assumed in science. But does that mean we do not know anything? Can you jump from a high window without harm or walk through walls? Others argue that because we know nothing for sure, we really know nothing. The success of scientific inquiry in hundreds of areas shows that all methods are not equally effective in testing claims. If we know nothing, then what is the rationale for professional education? Exhibit 4.3 suggests responses to the view that we know nothing.

Raymond Nickerson (1986) defines knowledge as information that decreases uncertainty about how to achieve a certain outcome. (I would add—or reveals uncertainty.) We can ask: "What knowledge will help us to solve problems clients confront (e.g., elder abuse, a need for reliable respite care)?" Studies of the development of assumptions about knowledge (e.g., what can be known and what cannot, how we can know, and how certain we can be in knowing) suggest a scale ranging from the belief that we can know reality with certainty by direct observation, to the view that there is never certainty and that we must critically appraise and synthesize information from multiple sources (King & Kitchener, 2002). Karl Popper (1992) defines knowledge as problematic and tentative guesses about what may be true. It results from selective pressures from the real world in which our guesses come into contact with the environment through a process of trial and error (Munz, 1985).

Evaluating Knowledge Claims

The most important decisions you will make in your career concern the criteria you use to evaluate the accuracy of theories and claims of effectiveness. Consider the statements in Exhibit 4.4. Your beliefs about these claims will influence decisions you make. *Theories* are conjectures about what may be true. We always have theories. "There is no pure, disinterested, theory-free observation" (Popper, 1994, p. 8). You will encounter many different theories and claims. How will you choose among them? How will you select those most likely to be of value in helping clients? The criteria you rely on will influence your selection of assessment, intervention, and evaluation methods.

Bogus claims, both in the media and in the professional literature abound. It is vital for professionals to have skill and knowledge in spotting claims, identifying what kind they are and what

are not true and that are not questioned) is to maintain social bonds among people by protecting shared beliefs from criticism (the growth of knowledge). This may be necessary to encourage cooperation in a group. Cultures often thrive because of false knowledge. Such cultures "are doubly effective in promoting social behavior because, not being exposed to rational criticism, they enshrine emotionally comforting and solidarity-producing attitudes" (pp. 283–284). This view suggests that the growth of

EXHIBIT 4.3

Responses to Some Beliefs About Knowledge

Beliefs	Critique
There are things we just cannot know.	It depends on whether a belief can be put into a testable form. Many claims can be investigated through observation and experimentation.
It is not good to be skeptical because anything is possible.	Skepticism is not synonymous with closed-mindedness—quite the opposite. Being skeptical encourages rather than discourages a search for alternative possibilities.
Scientists/researchers do not know everything.	Scientists would agree. However, just because we do not know everything does not mean we do not know anything.
Some things cannot be proved scientifically.	Science deals with questions that are testable. However, many claims that some people believe are untestable can be put into a testable form.
We cannot be certain of anything.	Even if this is the case, some beliefs have survived more rigorous testing than have others.
Human behavior and the mind are mysterious things.	Just because something is mysterious does not mean that it cannot be explored.
Everything is relative.	Is this so? Can you walk through the walls in your home? Are there no moral guidelines for behavior?

Source: Based on W. D. Gray (1991). *Thinking critically about New Age ideas.* Belmont, CA: Wadsworth. Reprinted with permission.

EXHIBIT 4.4

Examples of Practice-Related Claims

A professor tells you: "Some people who have a problem with alcohol can learn to be controlled drinkers; abstinence is not required for all people." Do you believe her simply because she says so? If not, what other information should you seek, and why?

Your supervisor says, "Refer the client to the Altona Family Service Agency. They know how to help these clients." What questions are relevant here?

An advertisement for a residential treatment center for youth claims: "We've been successfully serving young people for more than 50 years." Would this convince you? If not, what kind of evidence would you seek, and why?

An article you read states that "grassroots community organization is not effective in alienated neighborhoods." What questions would you raise?

6. assessment measures (e.g., How valid is _____?);

7. the accuracy of predictions including prognoses;

8. the effectiveness of interventions;

9. prevention (e.g., Can we prevent suicide?)

Avoiding Harming in the Name of Helping

If you rely on false claims or theories, clients may be harmed rather than helped; you may create false hopes and miss opportunities to use effective methods. Consider Emma Eckstein, one of Sigmund Freud's patients (Masson, 1984). He attributed her complaints of stomach ailments and menstrual problems to masturbation. Freud's colleague Fleiss recommended a nose operation, based on his belief that the sexual organs and the nose were connected. Eckstein's subsequent pain and suffering were attributed to her psychological deficiencies. The real cause was a large wad of dressing left in her nose by mistake. Consider the many claims of effectiveness regarding intervention based on anecdotal case reports that were later shown to be false in controlled research. For example, the findings of controlled—in contrast to uncontrolled—studies of the effects of facilitated communication (a method alleged to help nonverbal people talk) "have been consistently negative indicating that FC is neither reliably replicable nor valid when produced" (Jacobson, Mulick, & Schwartz, 1995, p. 754). These controlled studies showed that the communication alleged to be from previously nonverbal people was actually determined by the facilitators. Lilienfeld, Lynn, and Lohr (2003) describe many methods shown to be harmful. (See also Gambrill, 2012a.) Failure to recognize uncertainties about interventions regarding their effectiveness has resulted in considerable harm (Chalmers, 2007).

kind of evidence is needed to explore their accuracy in comparison with what kind is offered (see Exhibit 4.5). These include claims about:

1. problems (Is X a problem? What kind is it claimed to be? Who says so? Who stands to benefit?);

2. risks (e.g., Is X a risk?);

3. prevalence (e.g., Is stranger abduction common? What does "common" mean?);

4. the accuracy of descriptions (e.g., she is depressed);

5. causes (e.g., alcohol use increases domestic abuse);

EXHIBIT 4.5

Different Kinds of Claims and Related Questions

1. About a "problem"
   - Exactly how is it defined? Give specific examples.
   - Who says X is a problem? Do they have any special interests? If so, what are they?
   - What is the base rate?
   - What kind of problem is it?
   - What controversies exist regarding this "problem"?
   - Is there a remedy?
2. About prevalence
   - Exactly what is it?
   - Who or what organization presented this figure? Are special interests involved?
   - How was this figure obtained? Do methods used enable an accurate estimate?
   - Do other sources make different greater estimates?
3. About risk
   - What is the absolute risk reduction? (See chapter 20.)
   - What is the number needed to harm (NNH)?
   - What is the false positive rate?
   - What is the false negative rate?
   - Is risk associated with greater mortality?
4. About assessment and diagnostic measures
   - Is a measure reliable? What kind of reliability was checked? What were the results? Is this the most important kind of reliability to check? (See chapter 17.)
   - Is a measure valid? Does it measure what it is designed to measure? What kind of validity was investigated? What were the results (e.g., correlations of scores with a criterion measure). Is this the most important kind of validity for clients? (See chapter 17.)
5. About effectiveness
   - Were tests of claims carried out? What were the results?
   - How rigorous were the tests?
   - Are reviews of related research of high quality (e.g., rigorous, comprehensive in search and transparent in description of methods and findings)?
   - Was the possibility of harmful effects investigated?
6. About causes
   - Is correlation confused with causation?
   - Could associations found be coincidental?
   - Could a third factor be responsible?
   - Are boundaries or necessary conditions clearly described (circumstances where relationships do not hold)?
   - Are well-argued alternative views accurately presented?
   - How strong are associations?
   - Are interventions based on presumed causes effective?
   - Is the post hoc ergo proc fallacy made?
   - Are vague multifactorial claims made that do not permit critical tests?
7. About predictions
   - Are key valued "end states" accurately predicted (rather than surrogates)?
   - What percentage are accurate?
   - What is the variance in accuracy?

Source: E. Gambrill & L. Gibbs (2009). *Critical thinking for the helping professions: A skills-based workbook* (3rd ed.), pp. 219–220. New York: Oxford University Press.

Questionable Criteria

Propagandists appeal to questionable criteria such as popularity, testimonials, newness, or tradition. These do not provide sound grounds on which to accept claims, often because they consider only part of the picture (e.g., only examples that support a belief). Other examples include manner of presentation and anecdotal experience; see Exhibit 4.6. Before reading the next section, review your answers to the items in Exhibit 4.1 to explore which criteria you use.

Authority

The source of the fallacy of authority is the mistaken assumption that status and opinions are correlated with accuracy. Appeals based on authority can be recognized by the assertion of a claim (e.g., play therapy is the best method to use with acting out children) based solely on someone's status or position, with no reference to related evidence. Let us say that Ms. Sommers, a case manager for the elderly, tells her supervisor that she referred Mr. Rivers to the Montview Nursing Home because Dr. Lancaster told her that this home provides excellent services—even though Dr. Lancaster offered no evidence that it does. It is important to distinguish between cognitive authority (always subject to critical questioning), and institutional or administrative authority (Walton, 1997). Treating an expert opinion that should be open to critical questioning as if it were infallible represents a "shift from one type of 'authority' to another" (Walton, 1997, p. 251; see also Walton, 2008). As Walton highlights, authority based on intellectual or cognitive grounds is always provisional and

EXHIBIT 4.6

Questionable Criteria for Evaluating Knowledge Claims

Criteria	Example
Authority (what do the "experts" say?)	"If Freud said it, it must be true."
Popularity (argument ad populum)	"Eighty percent of social workers use…I'm going to use it, too."
Manner of presentation	"She gave a convincing talk. I'm going to use her methods."
Experience	"I've seen five clients and used facilitated communication successfully with all of them."
Tradition	"That's the way we have always done it. We should continue to use these methods."
What is new	"It's the latest thing. We should try it, too."
Uncritical documentation	Accepting a claim based on vague, undocumented evidence.
Case examples	You present a vivid case example to support a claim. "I used narrative therapy with my client, and she improved dramatically."
Testimonials	"I used it, and it helped."
Characteristics of the person (ad hominem)	"She presents a good argument, but look at the school she graduated from."
Good intentions	In response to a question from a client about an agency's effectiveness, you say: "We really care about our clients."
What makes sense	"I think bioenergetics works. It makes sense."
Intuition	"I just know that support groups will be best."
Entertainment value	"This is a fascinating account of depression. I think it is correct."
Emotional appeals	"I trust my feelings when making decisions."

former sort, is a serious and systematic misuse of argument from authority. It can be a bad error, or perhaps even worse, it can be used as a sophistical tactic to unfairly get the best of a partner in argumentation" (Walton, 1997, p. 252). Appeals to authority are a common persuasion strategy. For example, pharmaceutical companies often use famous people to tout the benefits of their medications (e.g., Moynihan & Cassels, 2005). Appeals to authority are common in the professional literature, such as citing a famous person to support a claim when in fact no evidence is provided. Evidence-based practice arose as an alternative to authority-based practice (Gambrill, 1999; Sackett et al., 1997).

Popularity and Numbers

Popularity and numbers refer to the acceptance of claims simply because many people believe them. For instance, an agency may decide to adopt psychoanalytic methods because other agencies use these methods. Here, too, the question is whether there is any evidence that popular methods are effective.

> How much is spent in the USA every year on magnetic devices to treat pain? $500 million, with a total worldwide market to date above $4 billion.…And what do you think is the evidence for magnets affecting pain? You guessed it. None. There is a trial in a Cochrane review of interventions for plantar heel pain, and that was negative, and poor. A new, well-conducted, randomised trial provides a powerful negative, and a great example of trial design. ("Magnetic insoles for foot pain," 2003 <http://www.medicine.ox.ac.uk/bandolier/>)

A reliance on popularity is similar to a reliance on consensus (what most people think). But what most people think may not be correct.

Tradition

Tradition (what has been done in the past) may be appealed to to support claims. For example, when asked why she was using genograms, a social worker may answer, "That's what our agency has used for the past 5 years." Advertisers often note how long their product has been sold, suggesting that this establishes its effectiveness. Because a method has been used for many years does not mean it is effective. In fact, it may be harmful. Consider Scared Straight programs designed to decrease delinquency. These have been found to increase delinquency (Petrosino, Turpin-Petrosino, & Buehler, 2003).

Newness

Newness (the latest method) is often appealed to, as in "We are using the new co-addiction model with all our clients." Simply because something is new or innovative does not mean it is effective. After all, everything was new at some time.

subject to change, for example, as new evidence appears. "In contrast administrative or institutional authority is often final and enforced coercively so that it is not open to challenge in the same way. Thus treating the authority backing an argument as though it were of the latter sort, when it is really supposed to be of the

Manner of Presentation

We are often persuaded that a claim is correct by the confident manner in which it is presented. This fallacy occurs when (1) a speaker or writer claims that something is true of people or that a method is effective; (2) persuasive interpersonal skills are used (e.g., building the self-esteem of audience members; joking); and (3) data describing the effectiveness of the method is not reviewed (Gibbs, 1991). Being swayed by the style of presentation underlies persuasion by entertainment value. How interesting is a view? Does it sound profound? Does it claim to empower clients? Here, too, the question is whether there is any evidence for the claims made. Testing as well as guessing is needed (systematic exploration) to determine the accuracy of a claim.

Good Intentions

We may accept claims of effectiveness because we believe that those who make them have good intentions; they want to help clients. But, as the history of the "helping professions" shows, good intentions and services that help clients and avoid harm do not necessarily go together. Consider the following:

- People have died as a result of a "rebirthing."

- Scared Straight programs for delinquents increase future delinquency.

- 10,000 babies were blinded as a result of being given oxygen at birth.

- Creating false memories resulted in innocent people being accused of sexual abuse.

Programs that have been critically tested and found to be ineffective or harmful continue to be used. Consider brief (1 hour) psychological debriefing to prevent posttraumatic stress disorder. A systematic review of related research found this to be ineffective, and/or harmful—those experiencing it were more likely (compared to those in a control group) to develop stress (Rose, Bisson, Churchill, & Wessely, 2002).

> Of all tyrannies, a tyranny sincerely exercised for the good of its victims may be the most oppressive. It may be better to live under robber barons than under omnipotent moral busybodies. The robber baron's cruelty may sometimes sleep, his cupidity may at some point be satiated; but those who torment us for our own good will torment us without end, for they do so with the approval of their own conscience. (C. S. Lewis) (See Foner, 1950)

What Makes Sense

You may have read that expressing anger in frustrating situations is helpful in getting rid of your anger. This may make sense to you. But is it true? In fact, the research on anger suggests that it does not have this happy effect (Potegal, Stemmler, & Spielberger, 2010). Explanations always "make sense" to the person who accepts them. "People's thinking is logical if seen on its own premises" (Renstrom, Andersson, & Marton, 1990, p. 556). Whether these premises are accurate is another question. What about common sense? This may refer to cultural maxims and shared beliefs and assumptions about the social and physical world. One problem here is that different maxims often give contradictory advice.

Attacking (or Praising) the Person (Ad Hominem Appeals)

Rather than addressing a person's argument related to a claim (arguing ad rem), the person making the claim may be attacked or praised. For example, you may suggest that an advocacy group should be made up of community residents because they have had experience with advocacy and are eager to work together. A staff member may respond "But how can you say this? You haven't completed your social work degree yet." Rather than addressing your argument, he comments on your education. This example illustrates that ad hominem appeals may function as diversions—an attempt to sidetrack people (a key propaganda ploy).

Entertainment Value

Some claims are accepted simply because they sound interesting, even though interest value does not indicate accuracy. Ellul (1965) suggests that keeping us all entertained distracts us from detecting that we are being manipulated. (See also Huxley, 2005.)

Emotional Appeals

When evaluating claims, we are easily swayed by our emotions, and politicians and advertisers take advantage of this. They may appeal to our self-pity, self-esteem, fears, and self-interest. Vivid testimonials and case examples play on our emotions. For example, a TV commercial for an alcohol treatment center may show an unkempt, depressed man with a drinking problem and describe the downward spiral allegedly caused by drinking, including the loss of job and family. We may then see him in the Detox Treatment Center, which is clean and whose staff seem caring and concerned. Next we see our client shaved, well dressed, employed, and looking happy and healthy. Words, music, and pictures may contribute to the emotive effect. Because of the commercial's emotional appeal, we may overlook the absence of evidence for the effectiveness of the Center.

Case Examples

In the case example fallacy, conclusions about many clients are made based on a few unrepresentative examples (e.g.,

Loftus & Guyer, 2002). The case example fallacy involves faulty generalization. What may be true in a few cases may not be true of many other cases. We tend to overestimate the probability of detailed examples. Gibbs (1991) suggests three reasons why case examples snare the unwary: (1) the detailed descriptions have emotional appeal, especially in comparison to dull data from large samples; (2) social workers become immersed in the details of a particular example and forget that what may be true of this case may be untrue of others; and (3) examples that "prove the point" can always be found. Case examples are easy to remember because they have a storylike quality. Often, extreme examples are selected, making them easy to remember, even though they are unrepresentative of other cases.

Testimonials

Testimonials are reports by people who have used a product or service that the product or service is effective. For example, someone who has attended Alcoholics Anonymous may say, "I tried it and it works." The testimonial is a variant of the case example fallacy and is subject to the limitations of case examples in offering evidence for a claim; neither case examples nor testimonials provide comparative information needed to evaluate whether an assumption is true or false. Testimonials may include detailed vivid descriptions of the method used, the distressing state of affairs prior to its use, and the positive results. Testimonials are widely used in advertising. The problem with testimonials is not that the report about an individual's personal experience with a given method is not accurate, but the further step of making a claim that this experience means that the method works.

Experience

Educational Policy and Accreditation Standards (2008) emphasize the role of practice-informed research. The Society of Clinical Psychology initiated a program to gather practitioners' experiences regarding specific interventions such as cognitive behavior therapy for panic reactions that can inform practice and research (Goldfried, 2011). Professionals often appeal to their anecdotal experience to support claims of effectiveness. A social worker may state, "I know cognitive behavioral methods are most effective with depressed clients because they are effective with my clients." Experience in everyday practice and beliefs based on this are the key source of what is known as practice wisdom and clinical expertise. There has long been an interest in practice-based knowledge in social work and other professions. Both professionals and clients provide vital feedback regarding outcomes of services (see chapter 22). Subjective reports of progress complement objective measures. Other kinds of practice-based knowledge include new ideas for helping clients, sources of harm, and obstacles to helping clients. Whether practice-based knowledge can test a claim depends on

the kind of claim and related data put forward in support. (See chapter 11.)

Anecdotal case reports may be a valuable source of promising hypotheses, for example, regarding adverse events and possible causes, and may provide telling counterexamples to a claim (Aronson, 2003). They may be used to demonstrate diagnostic methods, how to handle challenging clinical situations, or to remind or educate us about important clinical possibilities. And, in some cases relying on experience (as in the recognition heuristic) is best. (See discussion of fast and frugal heuristics in chapter 9.) The key problem with relying on anecdotal experience as a guide to what is accurate is the lack of comparison (Dawes, 1988). An interest in comparison is a hallmark of scientific thinking. Our experience is often not a sound guide because it is restricted and biased (see Exhibit 4.7).

Also, without corrective feedback we cannot learn how to improve our performance in the future. For example, a child welfare worker may assume that few child abusers stop abusing their children because she sees those who do not stop abusing their children more often than those who do stop. Her experience with this biased sample results in incorrect inferences about the recurrence of child abuse (i.e., an overestimate). Relying on a carefully documented track record of success is quite different, as this offers a systematic record. Careful evaluation of practice decisions is emphasized in applied behavior analysis (see chapters 6 and 22).

When relying on experience, we may not recognize that conditions have changed, that what worked in the past may no longer work in the present. For example, Western-style mental

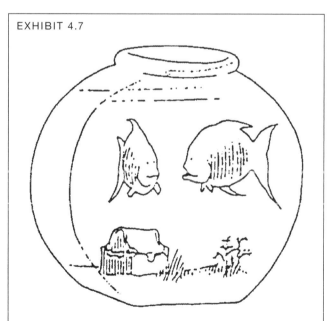

EXHIBIT 4.7

"If I'm right in my guess that this is the Atlantic, then we're the biggest fish in the world."

Source: Used with permission of Richard Guindon.

health services may not be appropriate for many clients. We tend to recall our successes and forget our failures; that is, we tend to selectively focus on our "hits." Unless we have kept track of both our hits and our misses, we may arrive at incorrect conclusions. We tend to be overconfident of our beliefs perhaps because of our interest in predicting what happens in our world. This can encourage an illusion of control in which we overestimate how much control we really have. We do not know what might have happened if another sequence of events had occurred. Overlooking this, we may unfairly praise or blame ourselves (or someone else). A social worker might say, "If only I had focused more on the teenager, Mario and his mother would have returned for a second interview." But maybe if he had concentrated more on the teenager, Mario would have walked out of the first interview. As Dawes (1988) points out, experience lacks comparison. Also, as Dawes (1988) points out, we tend to create our own experience. If we are friendly, others are likely to be friendly in return. If we are hostile, others are likely to be hostile. Dawes (1988) refers to this as "self-imposed bias in our own experience" (p. 106). Another problem with relying on experience concerns the biased nature of our memory of what happened. We may alter views about the past to conform to current moods or views. We tend to remember what is vivid, which may result in biased samples.

Relying on experience opens us to accepting irrelevant causes. We may assume that "mental illness" results in homelessness because many homeless people are diagnosed as "mentally ill." But does it? Does the situation of being homeless, of necessity, create unusual survival behaviors mistakenly labeled as indicators of mental illness? Our tendency to look for causes encourages a premature acceptance of causes that may lead us astray. We tend to see patterns that are not really there. So experience, while honing skills in many ways, may also have negative effects such as a reluctance to consider new ideas and an unwarranted overconfidence in the extent to which we can help clients. Indeed, one advantage of being a novice may be a greater willingness to question beliefs. King (1981) suggests that "For Flexner (1915), as for us today, severely critically handling of experience was an important part of scientific method, applicable to clinical practice as well as to research investigation" (pp. 303–304). With all these concerns about learning from experience, then, what should we do? As Dawes reminds us, we cannot go around conducting controlled experiments. We can, however, be cautious about generalizing from the past and present to the future. "In fact, what we often would do is to learn how to avoid learning from experiences" (1988, p. 120). (See also later section on learning how to learn.) (See also discussion of expertise in chapter 8.)

Intuition

Intuition is another criterion used to evaluate the accuracy of claims. Someone may ask, "How did you know that this method would be effective?" The answer may be: "My intuition." *Webster's*

New World Dictionary (1988) defines *intuition* as "the direct knowing or learning of something without the conscious use of reasoning." Hogarth (2001) suggests that intuitions (inferences) may refer to looking back in time (interpreting experience) or forward in time (predictions). For example, we may predict that a client will act in a certain manner in the future. He also suggests that the content of intuition can represent a "stock of knowledge" (p. 8). The view that intuition involves a responsiveness to information that although not consciously represented, yields productive insights is compatible with the differences that Dreyfus and Dreyfus (1986) found between experts and novices, one of which was that experts rely on "internalized" rules that they no longer may be able to describe. No longer remembering where we learned something encourages attributing solutions to "intuition." When asked what made you think that "Y" service would be effective, your answer may be, "Intuition." When asked to elaborate, you may offer sound reasons reflecting knowledge of content. That is, you used far more than uninformed hunches. Jonathan Baron defines intuition as "an unanalyzed and unjustified belief" (1994, p. 26) and argues that beliefs based on intuition may be either sound or unsound. Therefore, basing beliefs on intuition may have consequences that harm people. Intuition, in contrast to analytic thinking, cannot be defined by a description of steps used in the process (Hammond, 1996, p. 60). This does not mean that intuition is wrong. As Hogarth (2001) suggests, it means "that nonintuitive processes are *deliberative* and can be *specified* after [or before] the fact. Logic and analysis can be made transparent. Intuition cannot" (p. 7).

Although both intuition and experience may be a valuable source of ideas about what may be true, they are not a good guide to their accuracy. Intuition cannot show which method is most effective in helping clients; a different kind of evidence is required for this. Relying on intuition or what "feels right" is ethically questionable when other grounds, including a critical examination of intuitive beliefs, will result in better reasoned decisions. Decisions based on intuition are likely to be inconsistent. But this inconsistency may not be evident because no one keeps track of the decisions made, the grounds for making them, and their outcomes. The greater the number of factors that must be considered in arriving at a well-reasoned decision, and the more that is known about the relevance of considering them, the less likely is intuition to offer the best guide. Attributing judgments to "intuition" decreases the opportunities to teach others; one has "it" but does not know how or why "it" works. If you ask your supervisor, "How did you know to do that at that time?" and she says, "My intuition," this will not help you learn what to do.

Hogarth (2001) suggests that a key step in becoming aware of the limitations of experiential learning is "creating an awareness of the potential deficiencies of experiential (intuitive) learning" (p. 224). He argues that this is a two-step process: (1) people discover that it is to their benefit to "take greater control of their processes" (p. 224) and (2) they must understand why learning from experience has limitations. He suggests that as part of this, it is important to learn about different conditions under which we learn. These range from "kind to wicked." "Whether an environment is kind or wicked depends both on whether feedback is relevant or irrelevant and on whether the task involved is lenient or exacting" (Hogarth, 2001). Child welfare workers who work in intake units usually receive no feedback concerning the outcomes of their decisions—they work in a "wicked" environment. Seek corrective feedback to learn from experience and to test the accuracy of your intuition.

Uncritical Documentation

Simply because something appears in print does not mean that it is true. Consider many of the claims in newspapers such as the *National Enquirer*. Similarly, just because a claim is accompanied by a reference is not a good reason for assuming that it is accurate. Unless the report describes the evidence for this statement, it is uncritical documentation. This statement could be based on someone's uninformed opinion.

Science and Scientific Criteria

A concern for helping and not harming clients obliges us to critically evaluate assumptions about what is true and what is false, as well as their consequences. Relying on scientific criteria offers a way to do so. In 1991 the Council on Social Work Education called for social work curricula to be based on a scientific framework. Propagandists use the discourse of science (e.g., jargon) to promote an illusion of objectivity and scientific rigor. It is important to understand what science is so you can spot look-a-likes that may fool you into embarking on a course of action that does more harm than good and that hides a good option.

Misunderstandings and Misrepresentations

Surveys show that most people do not understand science (National Science Foundation, 2006; also see Exhibit 4.8). Textbooks often omit controversy giving an illusion of a logical progression of uncomplex discovery, when indeed, the process is quite different: chance discoveries, conjecture, and controversies. Journal articles often omit controversy about causes and evidence. Misunderstandings about science may result in ignoring this problem-solving method and the knowledge it has generated to help clients enhance the quality of their lives. For example, a social worker may assume that searching for research findings regarding how to help clients with depression will be of no value when indeed such a search will yield important information. Misunderstandings and misrepresentations

---

EXHIBIT 4.8

Misconceptions About Science

- There is a search for final answers.
- Intuitive thinking has no role.
- It is assumed that science knows, or will soon know, all the answers.
- Objectivity is assumed.
- Chance occurrences are not considered.
- Scientific knowledge is equivalent to scientific thinking.
- The accumulation of facts is the primary goal.
- Linear thinking is required.
- Passion and caring have no role.
- There is one kind of scientific method.
- Unobservable events are not considered.

---

of science are so common that D. C. Phillips entitled one of his books *The Social Scientist's Bestiary: A Guide to Fabled Threats to and Defenses of Naturalistic Social Science* (1992). Even some academics confuse logical positivism (discarded by scientists long ago) and science as we know it today. Logical positivism emphasizes direct observation by the senses. It is assumed that observation can be theory free. It is justification focused, assuming that greater verification yields closer approximations to the truth. This approach to knowledge was discarded decades ago because of the induction problem (see later discussion of justification/falsification), the theory-laden nature of observation, and the utility of unobservable constructs.

Science is often misrepresented as a collection of facts or as referring only to controlled experimental studies. Many people confuse science with pseudoscience and scientism (see the Glossary to this chapter). Some people protest that science is misused. Saying that a method is bad because it has been or may be misused is not a cogent argument. Anything can be misused, including social work services. Some believe that critical reflection is incompatible with passionate caring. Reading the writings of any number of scientists, including Loren Eiseley, Carl Sagan, Karl Popper, and Albert Einstein, should quickly put this false belief to rest. Consider a quote from Karl Popper: "I assert that the scientific way of life involves a burning interest in objective scientific theories—in the theories in themselves, and in the problem of their truth, or their nearness to truth. And this interest is a *critical* interest, an *argumentative* interest" (1994, p. 56).

Far from reinforcing myths about reality, science is likely to question them. (See Kolata, 1998.) All sorts of questions that people may not want raised may be raised, such as: "Does this residential center really help residents? Would another method be more effective? Does what I'm doing really help clients? How accurate is my belief about _____?" Many scientific discoveries, such as Charles Darwin's theory of evolution, clashed with (and still does) some religious views of the world. Consider the Church's reactions to the discovery that the earth was not the center of the universe. Only after 350 years did the Catholic Church agree that Galileo was correct in stating that the earth revolves around the sun. Objections to teaching evolutionary theory remain common (see *Reports* published by the National Center for Science Education). An accurate understanding of science will help you distinguish among helpful, trivializing, and bogus uses. Ignoring available research findings may result in lost opportunities to help clients.

What Is Science?

Science is a way of thinking about and investigating the accuracy of assumptions about the world. It is a process for solving problems in which we learn from our mistakes. Science rejects a reliance on authority (e.g., pronouncements by officials or professors) as a route to knowledge. Authority and science are clashing views of how knowledge can be gained. The history of science and medicine shows that the results of experimental research involving systematic investigation often free us from false beliefs that harm and decrease our susceptibility to fraudulent claims. There are many ways to do science and many philosophies of science. The terms *science* and *scientific* are sometimes used to refer to any systematic effort—including case studies, correlational studies, and naturalistic studies—to acquire information about a subject. All methods are vulnerable to error, which must be considered when evaluating the data they generate.

Nonexperimental approaches to understanding include natural observation, as in ethology (the study of animal behavior in real-life settings), and correlational methods that use statistical analysis to investigate the degree to which events are associated. These methods are of value in suggesting promising experiments, as well as when events of interest cannot be experimentally altered or if doing so would destroy what is under investigation. Frazer (1925) suggested that there is a much closer relationship between magic and science than between science and religion. In both magic and science there is an interest in predicting the environment, for example. Stivers (2001) argues that technology has assumed the status of magic in that simply using a different practice (e.g., management system) is assumed to result in hoped-for changes. That is, the indicator becomes the implementation itself. We are subject to a variety of superstitions (see chapter 7). The occult and mysterious forces have an allure of special powers encouraged by wishful thinking.

Criticism (Self-Correction) Is the Essence of Science

The view of science presented here, critical rationalism, is one in which the theory-laden nature of observation is assumed

(i.e., our assumptions influence what we observe) and rational criticism is viewed as the essence of science (Miller, 1994; Phillips, 1987, 1990; Popper, 1972). Concepts are assumed to have meaning and value even though they are unobservable. Popper's view of science can be summed up in four steps: (1) we select a problem; (2) we try to solve it by proposing a theory as a guess about what may be true; (3) we critically discuss and test our theory, (4) which always reveals new problems ($P_1 \rightarrow$ Th $\rightarrow$ test $\rightarrow$ Error $\rightarrow P_2$). Creative, bold guesses about what may be true are essential to the development of knowledge, especially guesses that can be refuted; that is, we can find out whether they are false. "Religion is a culture of faith; science is a culture of doubt" (See Feynman, 1989, 1997).

This view of science emphasizes the elimination of errors by means of criticism: "Knowledge grows by the elimination of some of our errors, and in this way we learn to understand our problems, and our theories, and the need for new solutions" (Popper, 1994, p. 159). The growth of knowledge is not in accuracy of depiction or certainty but in an increase in universality and abstraction (Munz, 1985). That is, a better theory can account for a wider range of events. By testing our guesses, we eliminate false theories and learn a bit more about our problems. Corrective feedback from the physical world allows us to test our guesses about what is true or false. We learn which of our guesses are false. Evolutionary epistemologists highlight the two different histories of science: the creation of theories (e.g., through random variation) and their selection (by testing) (Munz, 1985).

Scientific Statements Are Refutable/Testable

The scientific tradition is the tradition of criticism (Popper, 1994, p. 42). Karl Popper considers the critical method to be one of the great Greek inventions. Scientific statements are those that can be tested (they can be refuted). Consider the question "How many teeth are in a horse's mouth?" You could speculate about this, or you could open a horse's mouth and look inside. If an agency for the homeless claims that it succeeds in finding homes for applicants within 10 days, you could accept this claim at face value or systematically gather data to see whether this claim is true. Bunge (2003) suggests the possibilities shown in Exhibit 4.9.

The essence of science is creative, bold guessing and rigorous testing in a way that offers accurate information about whether a guess (conjecture or theory) is accurate. Popper argues that "the growth of knowledge, and especially of scientific knowledge, consists of learning from our mistakes" (1994, p. 93). Science is concerned with knowledge that can be pursued through the consideration of alternatives. It is assumed that we can discover approximations to the truth by means of rational argument and critical testing of theories and that the soundness of an assertion is related to the uniqueness and rigor of the relevant critical tests. A theory should describe what cannot occur as well as what can occur. If you can make contradictory predictions based

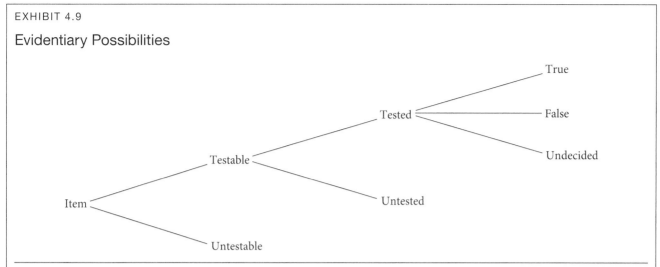

EXHIBIT 4.9

Evidentiary Possibilities

Source: M. Bunge (2003). The pseudoscience concept, dispensable in professional practice, is required to evaluate research projects: A reply to Richard J. McNally. *Scientific Review of Mental Health Practice, 2,* 111–114. Reprinted with permission.

on a theory, it cannot be tested. If you cannot discover a way to test a theory, it is not falsifiable. Theories can be falsified only if specific predictions are made about what can happen and also about what cannot happen.

Many people accept a justification approach to knowledge development, focusing on gathering support for (justifying, confirming) claims and theories. Let's say that you see 3,000 swans, all of which are white. Does this mean that all swans are white? Can we generalize from the particular (seeing 3,000 swans, all of which are white) to the general, that all swans are white? Karl Popper (and others) contend that we cannot discover what is true by means of induction (making generalizations based on particular instances) because we may later discover exceptions (swans that are not white). (In fact, black swans are found in New Zealand.) Popper maintains that falsification (attempts to falsify, to discover the errors in our beliefs) by means of critical discussion and testing is the only sound way to develop knowledge (Popper, 1992, 1994; see Exhibit 4.10). Confirmations of a theory can readily be found if one looks for them. (For critiques of Popper's view of knowledge, see, for example, Kuhn, 1996.)

Popper also uses the criterion of falsifiability to demark what is or could be scientific knowledge from what is not or could not be. For example, there is no way to refute the claim that "there is a God," but there is a way to refute the claim that "assertive community services for the severely and chronically mentally ill reduces substance abuse." We could, for example, randomly distribute clients to a group providing such services and compare those outcomes with those of clients receiving no services or other services. Although we can justify the selection of a theory by its having survived more risky tests concerning a wider variety of hypotheses (not been falsified), compared with other theories that have not been tested or that have been falsified, we can never accurately claim that this theory is "the truth." We can only eliminate false beliefs.

Some Tests Are More Rigorous Than Others

Some tests are more rigorous than others in controlling sources or bias and so offer more information about what may be true or false. Compared with anecdotal reports, experimental tests are more severe tests of claims. (See chapter 11.) Unlike anecdotal reports, they are carefully designed to rule out alternative hypotheses about what may be true and so provide more opportunities to discover that a theory is not correct. Making accurate predictions (e.g., about what service methods will help a client) is more difficult than offering after-the-fact accounts that may sound plausible (even profound) but provide no service guidelines. Theories differ in the extent to which they have been tested and in the rigor of the tests used. Every research method is limited in the kinds of questions it can address successfully. Purpose will suggest the kinds of evidence needed to test different kinds of claims (see chapter 11). Thus, if our purpose is to communicate the emotional complexity of a certain kind of experience (e.g., the death of an infant), then qualitative methods are needed (e.g., detailed case examples, thematic analyses of journal entries, open-ended interviews at different times).

A Search for Patterns and Regularities

It is assumed that the universe has some degree of order and consistency. This does not mean that unexplained phenomena or chance variations do not occur or are not considered. For example, chance variations contribute to evolutionary changes. And uncertainty is assumed. Since a future test may show an assumption to be incorrect, even one that is strongly corroborated (has survived many critical tests), no assertion can ever be proved. This does not mean that all beliefs are equally sound; some have survived more rigorous tests than have others (Asimov, 1989).

EXHIBIT 4.10

Contrasts Between Two Philosophies of Science: Verificationist and Refutationist

Verificationist	Refutationist
Certainty is possible.	Certainty is impossible.
Science is based on proof.	Science is based on disproof.
Observation reveals truth.	Observation involves interpretation.
Recognition of facts precedes formulation of theories.	Theories precede recognition of facts.
A good theory predicts many things.	A good theory forbids many things.
A good theory is probable: it has been repeatedly confirmed.	A good theory is improbable yet it has repeatedly failed to be refuted.
A prediction is more informative the more it conforms to experience.	A prediction is more informative the more it is risky or deviant from expectations.
Induction is the logical foundation of science.	Deduction is the logical foundation of science.
Inductive inference is logical.	Induction is illogical.
A theory can be validated independently, and absolutely.	A theory can be corroborated only relative to other theories.
Among competing theories, the preferable is the one which has been more often verified.	Among competing theories of equal refutability, the preferable is the one which has withstood more diverse tests.
Theories become more scientific the more they have been proven true by objective observations.	Theories become more scientific as they are made more refutable both through reformulations and technological advances in methods.

Source: M. Maclure (1985). Popperian refutation in epidemiology. *American Journal of Epidemiology*, 121(3), 343–350. Reprinted with permission.

Parsimony

An explanation is parsimonious if all or most of its components are necessary to explain most of its related phenomena. Unnecessarily complex explanations may get in the way of detecting relationships between behaviors and related events.

Scientists Strive for Objectivity

Popper (1994) argues that "What we call *scientific objectivity* is nothing else than the fact that no scientific theory is accepted as dogma, and that all theories are tentative and are open all the time to severe criticism—to a rational, critical discussion aiming at the elimination of errors" (p. 160). Basic to objectivity is the critical discussion of theories (eliminating errors through criticism). The theory-laden nature of observation is assumed. Observation is always selective (influenced by our theories, concepts). Scientists are often wrong and find out that they are wrong by testing their predictions. In this way, better theories (those that can account for more findings) replace earlier ones. Science is conservative in its insisting that a new theory account for previous findings. (For critiques of the view that advancing knowledge means abandoning prior knowledge, see Phillips, 1987.) Science is revolutionary in its calling for the overthrow of previous theories shown to be false, but this does not mean that the new theory has been established as true.

Although the purpose of science is to seek true answers to problems (statements that correspond to facts), this does not mean that we can have certain knowledge. Rather, we may say that certain beliefs (theories) have (so far) survived critical tests or have not yet been exposed to them. And some theories have been found to be false. An error "consists essentially of our regarding as true a theory that is not true" (Popper, 1992, p. 4). We can avoid error or discover it by doing all that we can to discover and eliminate falsehoods (p. 4). The study of avoidable errors when making decisions has received greater attention in the past years (e.g., see chapter 9).

A Skeptical Attitude

Scientists are skeptics. They question what others view as fact or "common sense." They ask for arguments and evidence. They do not have sacred cows.

> Science...is a way of thinking...[It] invites us to let the facts in, even when they don't conform to our preconceptions. It counsels us to consider hypotheses in our heads and see which ones best match the facts. It urges on us a fine balance between no-holds-barred openness to new ideas, however heretical, and the most rigorous skeptical scrutiny of everything—new ideas and established wisdom. (Sagan, 1990, p. 265)

Scientists and skeptics seek criticism of their views and change their beliefs when they have good reason to do so. "Science is the belief in the ignorance of experts" (Feynman, 1969).

Other Characteristics

Science deals with specific problems that may be solvable (that may be answered with the available methods of empirical inquiry). For example, is intensive in-home care for parents of abused children more effective than the usual social work services? Is the use of medication to decrease depression in elderly people more (or less) effective than cognitive-behavioral methods? Examples of unsolvable questions are: Should punishment ever be used in raising children? Are people inherently good or evil? Saying that science deals with problems that can be solved does not mean, however, that other kinds of questions are unimportant or that a problem will remain unsolvable. New methods may be developed that yield answers to questions previously unapproachable in a systematic way. Scientific knowledge is publicly reviewed by a community. Science is collective. Scientists communicate with one another, and the results of one study inform the efforts of other scientists.

The Difference Between Science and Pseudoscience

The term *pseudoscience* refers to material that makes science-like claims but provides no evidence for them (Bunge, 1984). Pseudoscience is characterized by a casual approach to evidence (weak evidence is accepted as readily as strong evidence is; see Exhibit 4.11).

Surveys of college students reveal a variety of pseudoscientific beliefs (e.g., see Wilson, 2001). A critical attitude, which Karl Popper (1972) defines as a willingness and commitment to open up favored views to severe scrutiny, is basic to science, distinguishing it from pseudoscience. Indicators of pseudoscience include irrefutable hypotheses, a reluctance to revise beliefs even when confronted with a relevant criticism, and inflated claims of knowledge and ignorance (what is true and what is false). Results of a study may be referred to in many sources until they achieve the status of a law without any additional data being gathered. Richard Gelles calls this the "Woozle Effect" (1982, p. 13). Pseudoscience is a multi-billion-dollar industry. Products include self-help books, "subliminal" tapes, and call-in

advice from "authentic psychics" who have no evidence that they accomplish what they promise. Pseudoscience can be found in all fields, including social work (Thyer & Pignotti, 2010), multiculturalism (e.g., Ortiz de Montellano, 1992), and clinical psychology (Lilienfeld, Lynn, & Lohr, 2003; Sarnoff, 2001). (See <http://www.csicop.org>; <http://www.healthyskepticism.org>.)

The terms *science* and *scientific* are often used to increase the credibility of a view or approach, even though no evidence is provided to support it. The term *science* has been applied to many activities in social work that in reality have nothing to do with science. Examples are "scientific charity" and "scientific philanthropy." They can be seen in bogus uses of the term *evidence-based* (e.g., Gambrill, 2011). The misuse of appeals to science to sell products or encourage certain beliefs is a form of propaganda (encouraging beliefs and actions with the least thought possible, Ellul, 1965). Proselytizers of many sorts cast their advice as based on science. They use the ideology and "trappings" of science to pull the wool over our eyes in suggesting critical tests of claims that do not exist. Classification of clients into psychiatric categories lends an aura of scientific credibility to this practice, whether or not there is any evidence that it is warranted or helpful to clients (Houts, 2002; Kutchins & Kirk, 1997).

Antiscience refers to rejection of scientific methods as valid. For example, some people believe that there is no such thing as privileged knowledge, that is, that some is sounder than others. Typically, such views are not related to real-life problems and to a candid appraisal of the results of different ways of solving a problem. That is, they are not problem focused, allowing a critical appraisal of competing views. Antiscience is common in academic settings (Gross & Levitt, 1994; Patai & Koertege, 2003), as well as in popular culture (e.g., John Burnham, *How Superstition Won and Science Lost,* 1987). Many people confuse science, scientism, and pseudoscience, resulting in an antiscience stance (see Glossary to this chapter).

EXHIBIT 4.11

Hallmarks of Pseudoscience

- Discourages critical examination of claims/arguments.
- The trappings of science are used without the substance.
- Relies on anecdotal evidence.
- Is not self-correcting.
- Is not skeptical.
- Equates an open mind with an uncritical one.
- Falsifying data are ignored or explained away.
- Relies on vague language.
- Is not empirical.
- Produces beliefs and faith but not knowledge.
- Is often not testable.
- Does not require repeatability.

Source: See, for example, M. Bunge (1984). What is pseudoscience? *Skeptical Inquirer, 9*(1), 36–47; W. D. Gray (1991). *Thinking critically about New Age ideas.* Belmont, CA: Wadsworth.

Relativism

Relativists argue that all methods are equally valid in testing claims (e.g., anecdotal reports and experimental studies). It is assumed that knowledge and morality are inherently bounded by or rooted in culture (Gellner, 1992, p. 68). "Knowledge or morality outside of culture is, it claims, a chimera. Meanings are incommensurate, meanings are culturally constructed, and so all cultures are equal" (p. 73). Postmodernism is a current form of relativism. Gellner (1992) argues that in the void created, some voices predominate, throwing us back on authority, not a criterion that will protect clients' rights and allow social workers to be faithful to their code of ethics. If there is no means by which to tell what is accurate and what is not, if all methods are equally effective, the vacuum is filled by an "elite" who are powerful enough to say what is and what is not (Gellner, 1992). Gellner argues that the sole focus on cognitive meaning in postmodernism ignores political and economic influences. He argues that postmodernism "denies or obscures tremendous differences in cognition and technical power" (p. 71). He points out that there are real constraints in society that are obscured within this recent form of relativism (postmodernism) and suggests that such cognitive nihilism constitutes a "travesty of the real role of serious knowledge in our lives" (p. 95). Gellner argues that this view undervalues coercive and economic constraints in society and overvalues conceptual ones. "If we live in a world of meanings, and meanings exhaust the world, where is there any room for coercion through the whip, gun, or hunger?" (p. 63).

Gellner (1992) argues that postmodernism is an affectation: "Those who propound it, or defend it against its critics, continue, whenever facing any serious issue in which their real interests are engaged, to act on the non-relativistic assumption that one particular vision is cognitively much more effective than others" (p. 70). Consider, for example, the different criteria social workers want their physicians to rely on when confronted with a serious medical problem compared to criteria they say they rely on to select a service method offered to clients. They rely on criteria such as intuition, testimonials, and experience with a few cases when making decisions about their clients but want their physicians to rely on the results of controlled experimental studies and demonstrated track record of success based on data collected systematically and regularly when making decisions about a serous medical problem of their own (Gambrill & Gibbs, 2002). Descriptions of what is called "critical postmodernism" include questions that are key to science such as "What constitute acceptable knowledge" (Fawcett, 2011, p. 232).

Quackery

Quackery refers to the promotion and marketing, for a profit, of untested, often worthless and sometimes dangerous health products and procedures, by either professionals or others (Jarvis, 1990; Young, 1992).

> People generally like to feel that they are in control of their life. Quacks take advantage of this fact by giving their clients things to do—such as taking vitamin pills, preparing special foods, meditating, and the like. The activity may provide a temporary psychological lift, but believing in false things can have serious consequences. The loss may be financial, psychological (when disillusionment sets in), physical (when the method is harmful or the person abandons effective care), or social (diversion from more constructive activities). (Barrett, Jarvis, Kroger, & London, 2002, p. 7)

Barrett and his colleagues (2002) suggest that victims of quackery usually have one or more of the following vulnerabilities: (1) lack of suspicion; (2) desperation; (3) alienation (e.g., from the medical profession); (4) belief in magic; or (5) overconfidence in discerning whether a method works. Advertisers, both past and present, use the trappings of science (without the substance) to encourage consumers to buy products (Pepper, 1984). Indicators of quackery include the promise of quick cures, the use of anecdotes and testimonials to support claims, privileged power (only the great Dr. ____ knows how to ____), and secrecy (claims are not open to objective scrutiny). For every claim supported by sound evidence, there are scores of bogus claims in advertisements, newscasts, films, TV, newspapers, and professional sources, making it a considerable challenge to resist their lures. McCoy (2000) describes a cornucopia of questionable medical devices. Reasons suggested by William Jarvis (1990) for why some professionals become quacks include the profit motive (making money) and the prophet motive (enjoying adulation and discipleship resulting from a pretense of superiority). Quacks may award themselves degrees or obtain degrees from bogus institutions. Quacks take advantage of a variety of propaganda methods designed to encourage beliefs and actions with the least thought possible.

Propaganda, Fraud, and Corruption in the Helping Professions

Quackery and pseudoscience make use of propaganda strategies (Best, 2004; Kirsh, 2010; Moncrieff, 2007). Jacques Ellul (1965) suggests that propaganda "is principally interested in shaping action and behavior, and with little thought" (p. 278). A major function of propaganda is to squelch and censor dissenting points of view. The harms of propaganda in the helping professions are varied and may ripple out to clients for decades. Common propaganda methods include oversimplifications, inaccurate generalizations, emotional reasoning, creation of fear, appeal to self-interest, and censorship of alternative views and contradictory evidence (Gambrill, 2012). (See prior discussion of Questionable Criteria.) Internet sources, including those of government agencies such as the National Institute of Health, boldly assert that anxiety in social situations and (mis)behavior in children are "brain diseases," ignoring well-argued alternative views and counter-evidence (e.g., see Moynihan & Cassels, 2005; Timimi & Leo, 2009). Here too, as with fraud, websites and organizations have been developed to counter propaganda (e.g., Alliance for Human Research Protection, National Coalition Against Censorship). The inflation of knowledge claims (puffery) is a key propaganda strategy (Rank, 1984).

Those who market ideas attempt to forward a view, not through a balanced and accurate presentation of related evidence and alternative views, but through reliance on strategies such as distorted presentations of disliked positions, presentation only of data that support a favored position, and question begging (asserting what must be argued). Inflating risk and encouraging fear is a key ploy (Altheide, 2002; Nettleton & Bunton, 1995). Those who have products to sell, including residential centers, pharmaceutical companies, and professional organizations promoting their training programs, take advantage of sophisticated marketing strategies to encourage purchase of their products. Strategies range from the obvious, such as advertisements in professional journals, to the subtle, such as offering workshops or conferences without identifying the funding source of these conferences. Until recently, most continuing education in medicine was funded by the pharmaceutical industry (Brody, 2007). Screening days for anxiety and depression are often funded by this industry. Presenting pitches for a product in an article form ("advertorials") may lull readers into uncritical acceptance of promotional material (Kassirer, 2005; Prounis, 2004). A review of advertising on marketing brochures distributed by drug companies to physicians in Germany revealed that 94% of the content in these had no basis in scientific evidence (reported in Tuffs, 2004). Drug companies promote the creation of new "diseases," such as panic disorder and premenstrual dysphoric disorder, to increase markets for their medications (Conrad, 2007).

Economic interests of pharmaceutical companies in promoting a biomedical view of problems as "mental illnesses" encourage use of propaganda methods, such as simply asserting that depression is a "mental illness" requiring medication (e.g., Antonuccio, Burns, & Danton 2002; Conrad & Potter, 2000; Moncrieff, 2008a; Healy, 2004). Websites sponsored by this industry contain material such as the following:

> If you think you are suffering from depression, panic disorder, obsessive compulsive disorder (OCD), posttraumatic stress disorder (PTSD), or Premenstrual Dysphoric Disorder (PMDD) know that you're not alone. In the United States, millions of people have these disorders. It is important to know these medical conditions are treatable. (December 8, 2003; <http://www.pfizerforwomen.com>)

Psychological and biomedical views ignore contextual factors. This may be the most insidious effect of promoting pharmaceuticals directly to consumers. The message is that problems such as anxiety in social situations, depression, and other alleged "mental disorders" are brain diseases that are biochemically based and that can be treated with medication. This ignores contextual contributors to troubles such as lack of employment, high-cost housing, and poor schools. More attention is being given in professional education programs to helping students understand marketing strategies used, how they may influence professionals, and how to avoid unwanted influences (e.g., Wilkes & Hoffman, 2001). Related research highlights the difficulty of generalizing skills from one situation to another, such as critically appraising assumptions when working with clients and reading a journal that includes advertisements concerning practice.

Fraud and Corruption

Fraud is the intentional misrepresentation of the effect of certain actions, such as taking a prescribed drug to decrease depression, to persuade people to part with something of value (e.g., money) (e.g., see Kerr, 1992b; Levy & Luo, 2005). It does this by means of deception and misrepresentation, drawing on a variety of propaganda ploys, such as the omission of relevant information concerning harmful side effects. Fraudulent claims (often appealing to the trappings of science) may result in overlooking effective methods or being harmed by remedies that are supposed to help. Gould (cited in Jensen, 1989) included fraud (manufacturing evidence, presenting fiction as fact) as one of four pathologies of science (e.g., see Judson, 2004; Tavare, 2012). The three others were propaganda (selective presentations of evidence), prejudice, and finagle. The latter refers to minor hoaxes and intentional errors in data description or recording that result in a misrepresentation of findings. Scientific prejudice involves use of different standards of evidence for preferred and disliked views. That is, less rigorous standards are used for preferred views.

Fraud is so extensive in some areas that special organizations have been formed, newsletters written, and Internet sites created to help consumers evaluate claims (e.g., *Health Letter* published by the Public Citizens Research Group; Federal Trade Commission; National Council Against Health Fraud; Center for Media Education [CME]). Drug makers now top the fraud payout list (Tanne, 2010). For example Allergen paid out $600 million, Novartis was next in line ($422.5 million). (See also False Claims Act (31 USC 3729)). (See also Kondro & Sibbald, 2004.)

Eliot Spitzer, past Attorney General of the State of New York, filed a civil suit accusing the drug giant GlaxoSmithKline of committing fraud by concealing negative information about Paxil, a drug used to treat depression.

> The suit says that the company conducted five clinical trials of Paxil in adolescents and children, yet published only one study whose mixed results it deemed positive. The company sat on two major studies for up to four years, although the results of one were divulged by a whistle-blower at a medical conference in 1999 and all of the studies were submitted to the Food and Drug Administration in 2002 when the company sought approval for new uses of Paxil. At that time it became apparent that Paxil was no more effective than a placebo in treating adolescent depression and might even provoke suicidal thoughts. (*New York Times*, June 6, 2004)

In June 2004 the editors of leading medical journals and the American Medical Association called on drug companies to register all their clinical trials on a website to prevent hiding of negative reports and changing outcomes reported. (See Krimsky, 2003.) Most members of DSM Task Forces have ties to pharmaceutical companies (Cosgrove et al., 2009). Conflicts of interest between academic researchers and pharmaceutical companies have become so common that there has been a backlash

(Angell, 2009). The US Health Department recovered $4 billion through antifraud action in 2010 (Tanne, 2011).

Knowledge Valued in Evidence-Informed Compared to Authority-Based Practice

The phrase *evidence-based practice* (EBP) draws attention to the kind of evidence needed to test different kinds of claims. What is needed depends on the kind of question (e.g., effectiveness, predictive accuracy of a risk assessment measure) as discussed in chapter 11. The philosophy of EBP emphasizes the close relationship between evidentiary and ethical obligations. Knowledge that decreases or reveals the degree of uncertainty about how to attain outcomes that clients value is emphasized. Social workers, as well as other professionals, work under uncertainty. Yet they must act. This uncertainty is often related to our ignorance—what is not understood or known about problems clients confront (e.g., see Proctor & Schiebinger, 2008). EBP is a way to handle uncertainty constructively—to deal "with inadequate information in ways that can help to identify really important uncertainties, uncertainties that are often reflected in dramatic variations in clinical practices and which cry out for coordinated efforts to improve knowledge" (Chalmers, 2004, p. 475). Thus, awareness of the degree of uncertainty associated with decisions is viewed as valuable knowledge.

Failure to recognize uncertainties have caused harm to thousands (Chalmers, 2007). Critically appraising practice and policy claims keeps the uncertainty involved in working with clients in view. We are less likely to promote bogus claims that may harm clients if acted on. Keeping uncertainty in clear view requires knowledge about how to critically test life-affecting practice and policy questions such as "Is this assessment measure valid?" "Does this parent training program enhance positive parenting skills?" Such knowledge can help us to avoid fooling ourselves that we have knowledge when we do not. Mistakes (what kind, when they occur, and what contributes to them) are another kind of valuable knowledge that can help us learn how to do better in the future. Both content and performance knowledge are important. Information concerning application obstacles and how to overcome them, as well as knowledge concerning ethical obligations, is also important. Knowledge of local resources and circumstances is needed (indigenous knowledge).

Other kinds of knowledge valued in EBP include the clients' views about his or her characteristics, circumstances, and values, as well as clinical expertise to identify and integrate information about the unique circumstances and characteristics of a client, including his or her preferences, values, and expectations, and local circumstances in making decisions. Knowledge of common biases that may lead us astray in making decisions is valuable. (See Exhibit 4.2.) The Social Care Institute for Excellence (SCIE) in the United Kingdom uses five kinds of knowledge in preparing research reviews: policy (including related legislation), organizational, practitioner, user, and research knowledge (Coren & Fisher, 2001). Organizational knowledge includes factors at this level that may affect use of research findings regarding the effectiveness of different practices and policies. Practitioner knowledge includes information about obstacles to the use of effective practices, as well as "tacit" knowledge that can give direction to inquiry. User knowledge is vital in planning and reviewing research (Hanley et al., 2001), as well as in evaluating services.

In what Petr (2008) labels "Multidimensional evidence-based practice," knowledge from studies of consumers and practitioners is gathered, as well as knowledge from other research findings, in making decisions about what interventions to use. Input from consumers regarding social validity ("Do they like an intervention?") is important. However, average consumer reactions in such studies may not reflect the unique preferences and values of individual clients. A key characteristic of evidence-based practice as described by its originators is considering the values and preferences of each individual client. Also what clients and professionals believe to be an important contributor to outcome based on experience, may or may not be (it may even be harmful). Only careful investigation could determine this (see chapter 11). (See also prior discussion of Experience and Intuition.)

Criteria used to select knowledge in authority-based practice are quite different: popularity, tradition, status, degrees, or credentials (Gambrill, 2001). Peter Munz (1985) defines *false knowledge* as beliefs that are not true and that are not questioned. This refers to "pieces of knowledge held consciously which have little direct bearing on physical survival" (p. 74). Such beliefs can be held or discarded regardless of the environment in which people who hold them are living. Nevertheless, they frequently serve a useful function. They are used as a social bond so that societies can survive; defined membership makes cooperation and division of labor possible. In this kind of society, membership "depends on being able to give the correct answers to a catechism." Beliefs "are not available for criticism and therefore cannot be examined. They are held dogmatically" (p. 74).

Reviewing Your Beliefs About Learning and Your Educational Environments

Education is conjecture-based rather than belief-based. (See Exhibit 4.12.) It is contextual rather than parochial. It is self-corrective. Education should broaden understanding, encourage well-reasoned beliefs and actions and increase success in helping clients.

Differences between education and schooling/indoctrination highlight the emphasis on students learning to think critically for themselves in the former rather than relying on authority as in the latter (Gambrill, 1997). Education requires presenting

EXHIBIT 4.12

Education Compared With Schooling and Indoctrination

Education	Schooling/Indoctrination
Conjecture based.	Belief based.
Rationally based; guesses are tested; errors are conceded.	Authority based.
Contextual (sensitive to context).	Parochial.
Critical reflection (assumptions are tested).	Uncritical reflection.
Honors standards such as clarity, relevance, breadth, and depth.	Narrow, vague, superficial.
Falsification based (ask: How can I test my assumption? How can I falsify this conjecture?).	Justification based (ask, How can I support my claims?).
Outcome focused (on helping clients achieve hoped-for outcomes).	Focused on what professionals want or find interesting.
Self-corrective.	Not self-corrective.
Problem seeking.	Problem hiding.
Students learn to think for themselves to be "reasonable and exercise good judgment while remaining cautious and open minded" (Lipman, 1991, p. 145).	Conventional; conforming in thought and action.
A high percentage of functional content of value to helping clients.	A high percentage of inert content.
Integrated.	Fragmented (e.g., field and class, different courses).
Data are used to critically test and correct theory.	Guess and guess again.
Concepts and theories are clearly described.	Concepts/theories remain vague.
Discordant views are welcomed.	Discordant views are ridiculed or ignored.
Assume the essence of education is critical inquiry.	Assume the essence of education is a well-stocked and conforming mind.
View knowledge as tentative.	View knowledge as certain.
Students are active, critical inquirers.	Students are passive.

Source: E. Gambrill (1996). Thinking critically about social work education. Address to annual program meeting. Council on Social Work Education, Washington, DC, February 16.

alternative views on subjects discussed, providing arguments for claims, accurately describing well-argued alternative views, questioning accepted views, and offering sound reasons for doing so. Both students and instructors are critically reflective (not just reflective). Understanding is emphasized, rather than memorizing. The interest is in educating minds, not in training memories (Perkins, 1992). Discordant points of view have a quite different fate in education compared to indoctrination. They are welcomed in the former and punished or censored in the latter.

Only a percentage of relevant knowledge that could be presented will be during your education as a social worker. In addition, small or large amounts of inert content (information that is not accompanied by procedural [how to] knowledge) and irrelevant content will be offered. Well-argued alternative views may not be presented. For example, a survey of course outlines on psychopathology given in social work programs revealed that limitations of psychiatric classification system and well-argued alternative views (e.g., Szasz, 1994) were usually not presented to students (Lacasse & Gomory, 2003). The better your learning and critical thinking skills (see chapter 5) are, the more likely you will discover "what's missing" (e.g., alternative well-argued views). You can use Exhibit 4.12 to review your social work program.

> The function of education is to teach one to think intensively and to think critically.
> —Martin Luther King, Jr., *What Manner of Man*, c. 1958

Cultivate Helpful Beliefs About Learning

Effective learners believe that knowing and understanding are products of their own efforts and intellectual processes. As Perkinson (1993) suggests, knowledge does not come to us from without. We are not buckets into which knowledge can be dumped. He argues that learning or growth is up to the student: "It is the student who must modify, or refine his or her existing knowledge when he or she recognizes its inadequacies" (p. 16). (See Exhibit 4.13.)

Teachers are facilitators in this process. Beliefs that promote learning include the following: (1) effort and persistence are required to gain knowledge; (2) we can gain knowledge and solve many problems if we make the effort; (3) knowledge is not certain; (4) we can acquire knowledge by thinking critically for ourselves, not just by relying on authorities (Nickerson, 1988–1989); and (5) "the growth of knowledge depends entirely on the existence of disagreement" (Popper, 1994, p. 34). Beliefs such as "If I don't understand right away, I never will" and "Conflict is bad and should be avoided" are obstacles to learning. Learning requires work, for example, clarifying and understanding other points of view.

Critically Assess Your Values, Knowledge, and Skills

You are more likely to continue to learn over your career if you critically examine your values, skills, and knowledge. Helping

EXHIBIT 4.13

Paradigms of Learning

Old	New
Knowledge-based.	Outcome-based.
Knowing what one should know.	Knowing what one does not know.
Intuition emphasized.	Skill in posing clear questions and searching for, appraising, and acting on evidence to solve it.
Learning as received wisdom.	Question received wisdom.
Learning almost "complete" at end of formal education.	Lifelong learning.
Learning dominated by knowledge from experience.	Learning from experience is complemented by knowledge from research.

Source: J. A. Gray (2001a). *Evidence-based healthcare: How to make health policy and management decisions* (2nd ed.), p. 328. London: Churchill Livingstone. Reprinted with permission.

clients may require gaining new knowledge and skills and winnowing out misleading beliefs and skills. Basic to this process is a willingness to challenge what you believe and do, viewing theories and skills as tools to be judged by their value in helping clients. Your "background knowledge" (current beliefs) will affect how easy it is to understand new concepts. Many beliefs are implicit rather than explicit, making the task difficult. That is why it is helpful to ask yourself: "What do I believe about ____?"

Cultivate Valuable Learning Skills

You will learn more if you use an active learning style, in which you question what you read, summarize points, look for alternative explanations, seek specific examples of general statements, and ask questions, such as "How could this be applied?" Take advantage of opportunities to learn from your experiences with clients by seeking feedback about the accuracy of your decisions. (See prior discussion of intuition.) Question the "obvious" to avoid premature closure and routinized ways of acting (a mindless approach) that may harm rather than help your clients. Effective and creative thinkers are open to new possibilities; they critically evaluate their beliefs. They do not think there is anything wrong with being undecided, changing their minds, or questioning authorities (Sternberg & Lubart, 1995). They seek opposite views to their preferred beliefs (for example, read both pros and cons regarding a question: "Do adults have ADHD?") (See letters, *BMJ*, April 28, 2010.) Differences between deep and superficial learning approaches include the following. The deep approach involves:

- The intention to understand.
- Actively engaging with content.
- Relating concepts to everyday experience.
- Relating new ideas to previous knowledge.
- Relating evidence to conclusions.
- Examining an argument's logic.

The surface approach involves:

- Focusing on completing assignments.
- Memorizing information.
- Failing to distinguish principles from examples.
- Treating a task as an external imposition.
- Focusing on discrete elements without integrating them.
- Not thinking about your purpose or situation. (Entwistle, 1987, p. 16)

Learning requires challenging what you do and think—asking questions, such as "Are there other explanations?" Our tendency to seek material that confirms our views and to ignore contradictory material highlights the importance of active learning. Reviewing how much you understand about what you hear or read and relating new ideas to real-life practice increase learning. Read journals in different fields to discover controversies associated with certain topics.

Take advantage of steps known to be helpful when learning a skill: (1) clear description of skills required to attain valued outcomes, including intermediate steps, that is, designing a learning hierarchy; (2) assessment of pretraining competency levels (baselines); and (3) design of an individually tailored training program using model presentation, rehearsal, and feedback. Learn to be your own best critic (i.e., a constructive one, as all critics should be) and to arrange prompts (cues) and positive feedback for valued behaviors (see chapter 7).

Take Advantage of Useful Material and Educational Opportunities

Effective practice requires updating your knowledge and skills. You will need skills to gain access to helpful material, values that encourage you to do so, and strategies to help you to ferret out biases and misconceptions. You can discover promising assessment, intervention, and evaluation options by consulting practice-related research using the steps in evidence-based practice (see chapter 9). Too many helpers believe too soon that no more information is available or that more does exist but there is no time to find it. Whether you find useful material depends on your skills in posing clear questions related to information needs, knowing where to look and how to evaluate what you find, as well as time and access to tools such as relevant databases. Focus on content that decreases or reveals uncertainty about how to help clients. Seek websites that highlight controversies in a field (e.g., www.procon.org). The Cochrane and Campbell Databases provide many systematic reviews related to goals of value to social work clients (see chapter 10). Effective information retrieval skills are also necessary.

Research on continuing education for professionals indicates that traditional formats are not effective (Forsetlund et al., 2009). Indeed, this was one of the reasons for the development of the process of EBP and the creation of a unique style of problem-based learning in which 5–7 students work in groups with the guidance of a tutor trained in group process and in using the steps of EBP to address real-life problems of clients (e.g., see Straus et al., 2005).

Be Skeptical

Critical appraisal skills will help you to distinguish the wheat from the chaff whether reading, listening, or thinking (see chapter 11). We tend to be impressed with material that is difficult to understand or unintelligible (Naftulin, Ware, & Donnelly, 1973). Armstrong (1980) suggests that we spend more time trying to understand obtuse compared to clear content and rationalize our investment by believing that the material is worthwhile. Questions to keep in mind include the following:

1. Will content help me to answer questions regarding how to attain outcomes of vital concern to my clients?

2. Is relevant literature referred to, including well-argued alternative views?

3. Are concepts clearly defined?

4. Is the derivation of concepts from a theory clear and appropriate?

5. Can the variables be altered in practice situations?

6. Are the data collection methods clearly described?

7. Are measures valid and reliable?

8. Is the study design clearly described?

9. Is the study design sound? (For example, are needed control groups included? Were subjects randomly selected and distributed to groups?)

10. Are data collection methods free of sample bias?

11. Are intervention methods clearly described (who, what, where, when, how long, etc.)?

12. Is there any evidence that services were offered as planned?

13. Is it likely that the intervention caused the changes? Are alternative explanations likely?

14. Were the changes impressive?

15. Is the data analysis appropriate?

16. Were there any negative effects?

17. Are follow-up data available?

18. Can the findings be generalized to other situations?

Be Charitable

"The principle of charity requires that we look for the best, rather than the worst, possible interpretation of the material we are studying" (Scriven, 1976, p. 71). Unless you are charitable, as well as critical, you may overlook valuable material. Make it a habit to look beyond labels (e.g., behavioral, psychoanalytic) to the value of the content.

Getting the Most Out of Supervision

The quality of your supervision will influence what you learn. Field experiences often, if not typically, do not include the detailed guidance and corrective feedback required for learning. Questions to raise are:

1. How informed is your supervisor about the evidentiary status of practices and policies related to clients' concerns?

2. How skilled is your supervisor in gaining access to practice- and policy-related research in a timely fashion and in critically appraising what is found?

3. How skilled is your supervisor in identifying and reinforcing specific positive skills that contribute to helping clients?

4. To what extent does your supervisor use educational formats that contribute to learning such as model presentation, corrective feedback based on viewing or listening to taped exchanges, and, standardized clients?

5. How attentive is your supervisor to ethical concerns such as purchasing services from agencies that offer ineffective programs?

6. How often does your supervisor give you feedback based on direct observation of your work or review of videotapes of your exchanges with clients?

7. Does your supervisor encourage you to ask questions about the evidentiary status of agency services.

You will get more out of supervision if you identify specific competencies you want to acquire, describe intermediate steps between current and desired performance levels, request information, seek clarification, and offer positive feedback for valued supervisory behaviors (for more details, see Drury, 1984; Kadushin & Harkness, 2002). Classic articles by Hawthorne (1975) and Kadushin (1968) describe "games" that supervisors and the supervised play. Well-designed quality assurance programs pay attention to identifying, monitoring, and providing supportive feedback for valued supervisory behaviors. They are characterized by "feedback reciprocity" in which feedback is offered not just down the line (from supervisor to line staff) but also up the line (from line staff to supervisors).

Valuing Truth as an Ethical Obligation

If criticism is the route to knowledge, we must value getting closer to the truth more than winning arguments and maintaining status. We must value "truth, the search for truth, the approximation to truth through the critical elimination of error, and clarity" (Popper, 1994, p. 70), in order to overcome the influence of other values (e.g., trying to appear profound by using obscure words or jargon; see also the discussion of obstacles to critical thinking in chapter 5). Valuing truth calls for making well-reasoned decisions—you can make a sound argument for them. For example, claims have survived risky predictions and are compatible with and informed by empirical data describing relationships between behavior and specific environmental changes. Valuing truth over prejudice and ignorance requires critical testing of claims and conclusions. Only through criticism can we discover our errors and perhaps learn how to do better in the future. A candid recognition of and active search for mistakes keeps the inevitable uncertainty involved in trying to help clients clearly in view. Guesses about the causes of problems should be checked against data gathered in real life. For example, only by collecting detailed observational data in real-life, problem-related settings may informed guesses be made about the causes of client concerns. Collecting systematic data concerning service outcomes provides a guide for decisions and allows us to discover whether we are helping, harming, or having no effect (see chapter 22). It allows clients to find out whether the quality of their lives has improved, remained the same, or diminished.

The Burden of Knowledge

One topic that seems to have been slighted in the literature on the integration of practice and research concerns the burden of knowledge—the consequences of realizing that all is not as it should be regarding services provided to clients, for example, the realization that social workers all too often focus on the alleged dysfunctions of individuals and ignore environmental factors. My students routinely report lapses in agency practices—often

ongoing events in their agency—about which nothing is being done and which are not being discussed. Consider these examples:

- a medical social worker who knows that a client who is dying is not receiving proper pain medication and the medical director will not alter the pain medication schedule,

- a social worker who works in a legal advocates office who knows that a client has been required to attend a drug treatment program even though it is known that the client has no drug problem—a mistake was made by the person who prepared the court report. This parent will not regain custody of her children until she attends a drug treatment program for her alleged drug use,

- a counselor who is getting a kickback from referring clients to a friend's agency,

- a social worker who knows that an agency is using ineffective services (when effective ones are available).

Even among beginning masters students there is a troubling acceptance of practices and policies based on the assumption that nothing can be done. Rarely is the description of the harmful practice, policy, or mistake accompanied by statements such as the following:

- I am going to do something about this.

- I am going to bring this up to my agency team.

- We must work together to change this.

Awareness of avoidable suffering including harming in the name of helping should create concern for the plights of others—even outrage. Forgetting may provide relief. But our ethical obligations to clients require recognition of lapses and action in the face of avoidable suffering. (See chapter 16.)

The Importance of a Historical Perspective

History shows that there is a tendency to travel with the herd in misleading directions encouraged by herd leaders, often members of the establishment, such as academics and professionals (e.g., Bikhchandani, Hirshleifer, & Welch, 1998). False theories about what helped people and what harmed them were believed for centuries such as bleeding, purging and blistering. It also shows that what was proclaimed as impossible (e.g., flying in airplanes) was possible. Major discoveries are often disregarded, such as the discovery that eating citrus fruit can prevent scurvy

(Carpenter, 1986). History shows the prevalence of deception and "disinformation" disseminated in order to make money to our detriment and/or to promote certain political agendas. Consider selective reporting of antidepressant trials (Turner, Matthews, Linardatos, Tell, & Rosenthal, 2008). Political, social, and economic concerns in the helping professions and related venues including pharmaceutical companies, research centers, and governmental organizations often discourage "telling the truth"—pursuit of accurate answers wherever this may lead. Bauer (2004) contends that science is dominated today by research cartels and knowledge monopolies. Recommendations are often accepted uncritically by the media—"passed on as factual and reliable" (p. 650) when they are not.

> What "everyone knows" about the science related to major public issues, then, often fails to reflect the actual state of scientific knowledge. In effect, there exist *knowledge monopolies* composed of international and national bureaucracies. Since those same organizations play a large role in the funding of research as well as in the promulgation of findings, these monopolies are at the same time, *research cartels*. Minority views are not published in widely read periodicals, and unorthodox work is not supported by the main funding organizations. Instead of *disinterested* peer review, mainstream insiders insist on their point of view in order to perpetuate their prestige and privileged positions. (Bauer, 2004, p. 651)

The upshot is that policy makers and the public generally do not realize that there is doubt about, indeed evidence against, some theories almost universally viewed as true, about issues of enormous public import: global warming; healthy diet, heart-disease risk-factors, and appropriate medication;

HIV/AIDS; gene therapy; stem cells; and more. (Bauer, 2004, p. 650)

This does not mean the earth is flat, but that political and economic factors influence what is claimed to be true (or false) in the name of science—the ideology of science rather than the open critical inquiry that is the essence of science.

Summary

Professionals are assumed to have special knowledge that contributes to helping clients. There are many views of knowledge, what it is and how to get it. Some, compared to others, are more likely to result in effective services, avoid harm, and meet ethical obligations to clients. Thus, thinking about knowledge and how to get it is integral to being a responsible professional. If we rely on questionable criteria for evaluating claims, clients may be harmed rather than helped. Some social workers rely on authority as a guide, for example, what high-status people say. Others rely on popularity (how many people use a method) or tradition (what is usually done). These criteria do not provide sound guides.

Avoiding confirmation biases (the tendency to search only for data that confirm your views and to ignore data that do not) will require seeking evidence against favored views and considering well-argued alternative views. Sound criteria for making decisions include well-reasoned arguments and critical tests that suggest that one option is more likely than another to result in valued outcomes. You are more likely to acquire valuable knowledge and skills if you take an active role in critically appraising what you read, hear, and believe.

Reviewing Your Competencies

Reviewing Content Knowledge

1. Describe the relationship between evidentiary concerns and ethical obligations of professionals.

2. Give examples of harm to clients as a result of acting on unfounded claims.

3. Describe a scientific approach.

4. Identify common misconceptions about science.

5. Describe the differences between science and pseudoscience and give examples.

6. Explain why the word *proof* should be avoided (though not as applied to mathematics).

7. Describe the differences between a falsification and a justification approach to knowledge.

8. Give examples of negative effects of a justification approach to knowledge.

9. Describe why parsimonious explanations are of interest.

10. Describe a relativist view of knowledge and the consequences that follow from it.

11. Describe what the term *objectivity* means in science.

12. Identify indicators of quackery.

13. Describe what propaganda is and give examples of related strategies used in the helping professions and related enterprises, such as the pharmaceutical industry.

14. Give examples of appeals to authority.

15. Give examples of the use of case examples and testimonials and describe their limitations in evaluating claims.

16. Give examples of appeals to tradition and popularity.

17. Give examples of ad hominem arguments.

18. Discuss the differences between education and indoctrination/schooling.

19. Discuss the statement "No evidence will sway the true believer."

20. Identify beliefs and strategies that facilitate learning.

21. Describe differences between active and passive learning.

22. Contrast a "bucket" theory of education and a problem-solving one.

23. Accurately describe your knowledge and skill levels in relation to specific hoped-for outcomes.

24. Describe the key provisions of the False Claims Act and its relevance to social work.

25. Describe the relevance of critical thinking knowledge, skills, and values for enhancing clients' opportunities to fulfill their potential and to minimize avoidable suffering.

Reviewing What You Do

1. You ask questions that permit critical appraisal of the accuracy of claims.

2. Your written and spoken communications show that you are a charitable yet critical consumer of the professional literature.

3. Your decisions show that you can distinguish between pseudoscience and science.

4. You rely on sound rather than questionable criteria when making decisions (e.g., see Exercise 1 in Gambrill & Gibbs, 2009.)

5. A review of your written and spoken communications shows that you understand the differences between the accuracy of a belief and the intensity with which it is held.

6. You ask questions that help you to critically appraise what you read in the professional literature.

7. You search for and critically appraise research related to information needs. You pose clear questions, search effectively and efficiently for related research, accurately appraise the evidentiary status of what you find, integrate research findings with other information, and together with clients, decide what to do.

8. You accurately evaluate the extent to which your social work program provides an education rather than indoctrination.

Reviewing Results

1. You are not "taken in" by slick human service advertisements that use testimonials and other weak appeals.

2. Your practice skills increase as determined by a review of the methods you use and goals you achieve.

Glossary

Antiscience: Rejection of scientific methods as valid.

Critical discussion: "Essentially a comparison of the merits and demerits of two or more theories (usually more than two). The merits discussed are, mainly, the *explanatory power* of the theories…the way in which they are able to solve our problems of explaining things, the way in which the theories cohere with certain other highly valued theories, their power to shed new light on old problems and to suggest new problems. The chief demerit is inconsistency, including inconsistency with the results of experiments that a competing theory can explain" (Popper, 1994, pp. 160–161).

Cynicism: A negative view of the world and what can be learned about it.

Eclecticism: The view that we should adopt whatever theories of methodologies are useful in inquiry, no matter what their source and without undue worry about their consistency.

Empiricism: "The position that all knowledge (usually, but not always, excluding that which is logico-mathematical) is in some way 'based on' experience. Adherents of empiricism differ markedly over what the 'based on' amounts to—'starts from' and 'warranted in terms of' are, roughly, at the two ends of the spectrum of opinion" (Phillips, 1987, p. 203).

Evidence: Ground for belief, testimony, or facts regarding a claim or conclusion.

False knowledge: Beliefs that are not true and that are not questioned (Munz, 1985).

Falsification approach to knowledge: The view that we can discover only what is false, not what is true.

Hermeneutics: "The discipline of interpretation of textual or literary material, or of meaningful human action" (Phillips, 1987, p. 203).

Justification approach to knowledge: The view that we can discover the truth by seeking support for our theories.

Knowledge: Problematic and tentative guesses about what may be true (Popper, 1992, 1994); "guess work disciplined by rational criticism" (1992, p. 40). Criticism is "the crucial quality of knowledge" (Munz, 1985, p. 49).

Logical positivism: The main tenet of logical positivism is the verifiability principle of meaning; "something is meaningful only if it is verifiable empirically (i.e., directly, or indirectly, via sense experience), or if it is a truth of logic or mathematics" (Phillips, 1987, p. 204). The reality of theoretical entities is denied. This approach was discarded decades ago. People often confuse logical positivism with postpositivism.

Nonjustificationist epistemology: The view that knowledge is not certain. It is assumed that although some claims of knowledge may be warranted, no warrant is so firm that it is not open to question (see Karl Popper's writings).

Paradigm: A theoretical framework "that determines the problems that are regarded as crucial, the ways these problems are to be conceptualized, the appropriate methods of inquiry, the relevant standards of judgement, etc." (Phillips, 1987, p. 205).

Phenomenology: "The study, in depth, of how things appear in human experience" (Phillips, 1987, p. 205).

Positivism: Many kinds of epistemologies are referred to as positivism (Halfpenny, 1982). Characteristics of positivism include a goal to explain and predict, a reliance on testing, and efforts to be value-neutral. Strong views of positivism (e.g., logical positivism) have long fallen by the wayside. Biases and other limitations are candidly acknowledged in postpositivism.

Postmodernism: Disputes assumptions of science and its products. All grounds for knowledge claims are considered equally questionable (see, for example, Rosenau, 1992; Munz, 1992).

Postpositivism: This is science as we know it today: conjectural, critical, viewing knowledge claims as always open to criticism (see description of science in this chapter). The idea of *incommensurability* of different perspectives (that we cannot understand each other because we have different cultures) is rejected. This approach to science replaced logical positivism decades ago (e.g., Phillips, 1987, 1992; Popper, 1972).

Pseudoscience: Material that makes sciencelike claims but provides no evidence for them.

Quackery: The promotion of products and procedures known to be false or which are untested for a profit (Pepper, 1984).

Rationality: An openness to criticism. "An absolutely limitless invitation to criticism is the essence of rationality" (Munz, 1985, p. 50). Rationality consists in making mistakes and eliminating error by natural selection (p. 16).

Relativism: Relativists "insist that judgments of truth are always relative to a particular framework or point-of-view" (Phillips, 1987, p. 206). This point of view prevents criticism from outside a closed circle of believers.

Science: A process designed to develop knowledge by critically discussing and testing theories.

Scientific objectivity: Scientific objectivity is solely the critical approach (Popper, 1994, p. 93). It is based on mutual rational criticism in which high standards of clarity and rational criticism are valued (Popper, 1994, p. 70). See also **Critical discussion**.

Scientism: A term used "to indicate slavish adherence to the methods of science even in a context where they are inappropriate" and "to indicate a false or mistaken claim to be scientific" (Phillips, 1987, p. 206). Scientism refers to the view that "authority should be conferred upon knowledge and the knower, upon science and the scientists, upon wisdom and the wise man, and upon learning and the learned" (Popper, 1992, p. 33).

Skepticism: A provisional approach to claims; the careful examination of all claims.

Theory: Myths, expectations, guesses, and conjectures about what may be true. A theory always remains hypothetical or conjectural. "It always remains guesswork. And there is no theory that is not beset with problems" (Popper, 1994, p. 157).

Theory ladenness (of perception): "The thesis that the process of perception is theory-laden in that the observer's background knowledge (including theories, factual information, hypotheses, and so forth) acts as a 'lens' helping to 'shape' the nature of what is observed" (Phillips, 1987, p. 206).

Truth: "An assertion is true if it corresponds to or agrees with, the facts" (Popper, 1994, p. 174). We can never be sure that our guesses are true. "Though we can never justify the claim to have reached truth, we can often give some very good reasons, or justification, why one theory should be judged to be nearer to it than another" (Popper, 1994, p. 161).

5

Critical Thinking: Integral to Evidence-Based Practice

OVERVIEW   Clients may be harmed rather than helped if we do not think critically about the decisions we make. Are they well-reasoned? Are they informed by related research? The values, knowledge, and skills described in this chapter are integral to evidence-based practice in which ethical obligations to clients are placed front and center. As Karl Popper points out, "There are always many different opinions and conventions concerning any one problem or subject-matter. This shows that they are not all true. For if they conflict, then at best only one of them can be true" (1994, p. 39). The costs and benefits of critical inquiry are reviewed, barriers to critical thinking are discussed, and remedies suggested. Applying critical thinking to inform and communicate judgments is one of the ten curriculum areas of the Educational Policy and Accreditation Standard (EPAS, 2008, Council on Social Work Education).

YOU WILL LEARN ABOUT

- Hallmarks of critical thinking

- Critical thinking: integral to evidence-based practice

- Related values, skills, and knowledge

- The benefits of critical thinking

- Costs and benefits of critical thinking and obstacles

- Reducing the costs and increasing the benefits of critical thinking

- Review your beliefs about knowledge and how to get it

Hallmarks of Critical Thinking

The term *reflection* is popular. But as Steven Brookfield notes, "Reflection is not by definition critical" (1995, p. 8). Critical thinking is a unique kind of purposeful thinking in which we use standards such as clarity and fairness to evaluate evidence related to claims about what is true and what is not. It involves the careful examination and evaluation of claims and arguments and related actions to arrive at well-reasoned ones (see Exhibit 5.1). Related characteristics are:

- Clear versus unclear

- Accurate versus inaccurate

- Relevant versus irrelevant

- Consistent versus inconsistent

- Logical versus illogical

- Deep versus narrow

- Complete versus incomplete

- Significant versus trivial

- Adequate (for purpose) versus inadequate

- Fair versus biased or one-sided (Paul, 1993, p. 63; see also Paul & Elder, 2012.)

Both critical thinking and evidence-based practice encourage asking questions designed to make the invisible visible including uncertainties related to a decision (e.g., see DUETs <http://www.duets.nhs>). Problems may be created or remain unsolved because we rely on questionable criteria to evaluate claims about what is accurate, such as tradition, popularity, or authority. Consider a claim that recovered memory therapy works. Is this true? Works for what? Propagandists discourage questions that would reveal the evidentiary status of claims such as: "Has anyone been harmed by this method?" This illustrates the difference between propaganda (encouraging beliefs and actions with the least thought possible) and critical thinking (arriving at well-reasoned beliefs and actions). In the former, strategies such as censoring (not mentioning) alternative well-argued views are used to keep the invisible, invisible (see also chapter 4).

Critical thinking involves clearly describing and critically evaluating claims and arguments, no matter how cherished, and considering alternative views. This means paying attention

---

EXHIBIT 5.1

Characteristics of Critical Thinking

1. It is purposeful.
2. It is responsive to and guided by *intellectual standards* (relevance, clarity, depth, and breadth).
3. It supports the development of *traits* of intellectual humility, integrity, perseverance, empathy, and self-discipline.
4. The thinker can identify the *elements of thought* present in thinking about a problem, such that logical connections are made between the elements and the problem. Critical thinkers routinely ask the following questions.

    What is the purpose of my thinking (goal/objective)?

    What precise question (problem) am I trying to answer?

    Within what point of view (perspective) am I thinking?

    What concepts or ideas are central to my thinking?

    What am I taking for granted, what assumptions am I making?

    What information am I using (data, facts, observation)?

    How am I interpreting that information?

    What conclusions am I coming to?

    If I accept the conclusions, what are the implications? What would the consequence be if I put my thoughts into action?

    For each element, the thinker considers standards that shed light on the effectiveness of her thinking.
5. It is *self-assessing* (self-critical) and *self-improving* (self-corrective). The thinker assesses her thinking, using appropriate standards. If you are not assessing your thinking, you are not thinking critically.
6. *There is an integrity to the whole system.* The thinker is able to critically examine her thought as a whole and to take it apart (consider its parts as well). The thinker is committed to be intellectually humble, persevering, courageous, fair, and just. The critical thinker is aware of the variety of ways in which thinking can become distorted, misleading, prejudiced, superficial, unfair, or otherwise defective.
7. It *yields a well-reasoned answer.* If we know how to check our thinking and are committed to doing so, and we get extensive practice, then we can depend on the results of our thinking being productive.
8. It is responsive to the social and moral imperative to argue from opposing points of view and to *seek and identify weakness and limitations in one's own position.* Critical thinkers are aware that there are many legitimate points of view, each of which (when thought through) may yield some level of insight.

Source: R. Paul (1993). *Critical thinking: What every person needs to survive in a rapidly changing world* (Rev. 3rd ed.) (pp. 22–23). Foundation for Critical Thinking, <http://www.criticalthinking.org>. Reprinted with permission.

to reasoning (how we think), not just the product. Consider the statements in chapter 4, Exhibit 4.4. If you carefully examined these using the preceding standards, you thought critically about them. Critical thinking encourages us to examine the context in which problems occur (e.g., to connect private troubles with public issues, Mills, 1959), to view questions from different points of view, to question our assumptions, and to consider the possible consequences of different beliefs or actions. (See Appendix A. Taxonomy of Socratic Questions at the end of this chapter.)

Critical Thinking: Integral to Evidence-Based Practice

Critical thinking knowledge, skills, and values are integral to evidence-based practice as described by its originators (see chapter 9). Critical thinking, evidence-based practice, and scientific reasoning are closely related. All use reasoning for a purpose (i.e., to solve a problem), relying on standards such as clarity, relevance, and accuracy. All regard criticism (self-correction) as essential to forward understanding; all encourage us to challenge our assumptions, consider well-argued opposing views, and check our reasoning for errors. All are antiauthoritarian. Critical appraisal skills are needed to accurately describe the extent to which a given research method can critically test a given practice or policy question. It can protect us from being misled by deceptive descriptions of research (Chalmers, 2003; Rosenthal, 1994; Rubin & Parrish, 2007). Consider the examples below. Each makes a claim.

- Eye movement desensitization is effective in decreasing anxiety.

- Four hours a month can keep a kid off drugs forever. Be a mentor.

- Anatomically detailed dolls can be used to accurately identify children who have been sexually abused.

In each we can ask the following questions:

1. What is the claim?

2. What evidence is provided in support of the claim? What evidence does not support the claim? And, what kinds of evidence are provided? (e.g., testimonials, case examples, expert opinion?)

3. What is the quality of the evidence presented both in support and against the claim?

4. Are there assumptions that affect your weighing of the evidence that should be considered? Are they well-reasoned? An example would be the assumption of

dualism (thinking the mind and body are radically separate things).

5. What are the implications of your conclusion? (Bensley, 1998, p. 55)

Both critical thinking and EBP (as described by its originators) value deep versus superficial analysis and fair-minded versus deceptive practices. Both value transparency (honesty) concerning what is done to what effect, including candid description of lack of knowledge (uncertainty and ignorance). Material referred to as "evidence-based" reflects critical thinking values, knowledge, and skills to different degrees.

Related Values, Skills, and Knowledge

Values, skills, and knowledge related to critical thinking are discussed in the next sections (see other sources for more detail, such as Gambrill, 2012b; Halpern, 2003; Lipman, 2003; Paul & Elder, 2012).

Values, Attitudes, and Styles

Critical thinking is independent thinking—thinking for yourself. Critical thinkers question what others view as self-evident. They ask:

- What is the claim? What kinds of claim is it? (See Exhibit 4.5.)

- Is this claim accurate? Have critical tests been performed? If so, were they relatively free of bias? Have the results been replicated? How representative were the samples used?

- Who presented it as true? How reliable are these sources?

- Are conflicts of interest involved?

- Are the facts presented correct?

- Have any facts been omitted?

- Are there other well-argued points of view?

Critical thinkers are skeptics rather than believers. That is, they are neither gullible (believing anything people say, especially if it agrees with their own views) or cynical (believing nothing and having a negative outlook on life). Cynics look only for faults. They have a contemptuous distrust of all knowledge. Skeptics (critical thinkers) value truth and seek approximations to it through critical discussion and the testing of theories. Criticism is viewed as essential to forward understanding.

Intellectual traits integral to critical thinking suggested by Richard Paul are shown in Exhibit 5.2. Critical thinking requires flexibility and an interest in discovering mistakes in our thinking. Truth (accuracy) is valued over "winning" or social approval. Related values and attitudes include open-mindedness, an interest in the views of others, a desire to be well informed, a tendency to think before acting, and curiosity. Critical thinking involves being fair-minded—accurately describing opposing views and using the same rigorous standards to critique both preferred and disliked views. It discourages arrogance, the assumption that we know better than others or that our beliefs should not be subject to critical evaluation. As Popper emphasized, "In our infinite ignorance we are all equal" (Popper, 1992, p. 50). These attitudes reflect a belief in and respect for the intrinsic worth of all human beings, for valuing learning and truth without self-interest, and a respect for opinions that differ from one's own (Nickerson, 1988–1989). They highlight the role of affective components, such as a tolerance for ambiguity, differences of opinion, and empathy for others. Critical thinkers ask questions, such as: Could I be wrong? Have I considered alternative views? Do I have sound reasons to believe that this plan will help this client?

EXHIBIT 5.2

Examples of Valuable Intellectual Traits

Intellectual autonomy: Analyzing and evaluating beliefs on the basis of reason and evidence.

Intellectual civility: Taking others seriously as thinkers, treating them as intellectual equals, granting respect and full attention to their views, an interest in persuading rather than browbeating. It is distinguished from verbally attacking others, dismissing them, or stereotyping their views.

Intellectual confidence in reason: Confidence that in the long run one's own higher interests and those of humankind will best be served by giving the freest play to reason—by encouraging people to come to their own conclusions through a process of developing their own reasoning skills, forming rational viewpoints, drawing reasonable conclusions, persuading each other by reason, and becoming reasonable people despite the many obstacles to doing so. Confidence in reason is developed through solving problems though reason, using reason to persuade, and being persuaded by reason. It is undermined when we are expected to perform tasks without understanding why, or to accept beliefs on the sole basis of authority or social pressure.

Intellectual courage: Critically assessing viewpoints regardless of negative reactions. To figure things out for ourselves, we must not passively and uncritically "accept" what we have "learned." It takes courage to be true to our own thinking, to tolerate ambiguity, and to face ignorance and prejudice in our own thinking. Examining cherished beliefs is difficult, and the penalties for nonconformity are often severe.

Intellectual curiosity: An interest in deeply understanding, figuring things out, and learning. When we lack passion for figuring things out, we tend to settle for incomplete or incoherent views.

Intellectual discipline: Thinking guided by intellectual standards (e.g., clarity and relevance). Undisciplined thinkers neither know nor care when they come to unwarranted conclusions, confuse distinct ideas, or ignore pertinent evidence. It takes discipline to keep focused on the intellectual task at hand, locate and carefully assess evidence, systematically analyze and address questions and problems, and honor standards of clarity, precision, completeness, and consistency.

Intellectual empathy: Putting ourselves in the place of others to genuinely understand them and recognize our egocentric tendency to identify truth with our views. Indicators include accurately presenting other viewpoints and reasoning from assumptions other than our own.

Intellectual humility: Awareness of the limits of one's knowledge, sensitivity to bias and prejudice, and limitations of one's viewpoint. No one should claim more than he or she actually knows. It does not imply spinelessness or submissiveness. It implies lack of pretentiousness, boastfulness, or conceit, combined with insight into the strengths and weaknesses of the logical foundations of one's views.

Intellectual integrity: Honoring the same standards of evidence to which one holds others, practicing what one advocates, and admitting discrepancies and inconsistencies in one's own thought and action.

Intellectual perseverance: The pursuit of accuracy despite difficulties, obstacles, and frustration; adherence to rational principles despite irrational opposition of others; recognition of the need to struggle with confusion and unsettled questions over time to achieve understanding. This trait is undermined when others provide the answers or do your thinking for you.

Source: R. Paul (1993). Adapted from *Critical thinking: What every person needs to survive in a rapidly changing world* (Rev. 3rd ed.) (pp. 470–472). Foundation for Critical Thinking, <http://www.criticalthinking.org>. Reprinted with permission.

Related Skills and Knowledge

Problem solving, decision making, creative thinking, and critical thinking use similar kinds of knowledge and skills, including identifying claims, accurately weighing the quality of evidence and arguments, identifying assumptions, and recognizing contradictions (see Exhibit 5.3). As discussed in chapter 8, we often

---

EXHIBIT 5.3

Examples of Critical Thinking Skills

Clarify problems.

Identify significant similarities and differences.

Recognize contradictions and inconsistencies.

Refine generalizations and avoid oversimplifications.

Clarify issues, conclusions, or beliefs.

Analyze or evaluate argument, interpretations, beliefs, or theories.

Identify unstated assumptions.

Clarify and analyze the meanings of words or phrases.

Use sound criteria for evaluation.

Clarify values and standards. Detect bias.

Distinguish relevant from irrelevant questions, data, claims, or reasons.

Evaluate the accuracy of different sources of information.

Compare analogous situations; transfer insights to new contexts.

Make well-reasoned inferences and predictions.

Compare and contrast ideals with actual practice.

Discover and accurately evaluate the implications and consequences of a proposed action.

Evaluate one's own reasoning.

Raise and pursue significant questions.

Make interdisciplinary connections.

Analyze or evaluate actions or policies.

Explore thoughts underlying feelings and feelings underlying thoughts.

Compare different views.

Design and carry out critical tests of theories and hypotheses.

Evaluate perspectives, interpretations, or theories.

Source: Based on R. H. Ennis (1987). A taxonomy of critical thinking dispositions and abilities. In J. B. Baron & R. J. Sternberg (Eds.), *Teaching thinking skills: Theory and practice*. New York: Freeman; R. Paul (1993). *Critical thinking: What every person needs to survive in a rapidly changing world*. Santa Rosa, CA: Foundation for Critical Thinking, <http://www.criticalthinking.org>.

---

fail to solve problems not because we are not intelligent but because we fall into intelligence traps, such as jumping to conclusions. This highlights the value of acquiring strategies that avoid these "defaults" in thinking. Critical thinking skills are not a substitute for problem-related knowledge. For example, you may need specialized knowledge to evaluate the plausibility of premises related to an argument. Consider the following example:

- Depression always has a psychological cause.

- Mr. Draper is depressed.

- Therefore, the cause of Mr. Draper's depression is psychological in origin.

Even though the logic of this argument is sound, the conclusion may be false; the cause of Mr. Draper's depression could be physiological. The more information that is available about a subject that can decrease or reveal uncertainty about what decision is best, the more important it is to be familiar with this knowledge. Taking advantage of practice-related research findings is a hallmark of evidence-based practice.

Nickerson (1986) suggests that *self-knowledge* is one of the three forms of knowledge central to critical thinking. Without self-knowledge, content and performance knowledge may remain unused. Self-knowledge includes knowledge of what we take for granted and our points of view. It includes awareness of our personal style of thinking (e.g., the strategies we use) and obstacles such as cultural stereotypes.

The Benefits of Critical Thinking

Honoring ethical obligations to clients is a key benefit, including providing informed consent based on knowledge of research findings. This requires critical thinking skills and related values such as honesty and taking responsibility for drawing on research findings of value in helping clients attain outcomes they value. (See Exhibit 5.4.) Thinking critically about what you hear, read, and think will help you to accurately appraise the accuracy of practice and policy-related claims. You will be less likely to harm clients in the name of helping them by using ineffective or harmful methods.

Consider Context: Avoid Being Bamboozled by the Pied Pipers of the Therapeutic

Critical thinking encourages us to think contextually, to consider the big picture, and to connect personal troubles to social issues. Brookfield argues that reflection becomes critical when it has two purposes: (1) to understand how considerations of power undergird, frame, and distort educational processes and interactions; and (2) to question assumptions and practices that seem to make our lives easier but actually work against our own best

EXHIBIT 5.4

Benefits of Critical Thinking

You Will Be More Likely To

Clearly describe client concerns.

Discover resources and constraints.

See the connection between private troubles and public issues; think contextually.

Focus on outcomes that clients value.

Accurately assess the likelihood of attaining hoped-for outcomes.

Make valuable contributions at case conferences (e.g., identify flawed arguments, suggest alternative views).

Identify the degree of precision required to achieve hoped-for outcomes.

Select practices, programs, and policies that address client concerns with a minimum of harmful side effects.

Make accurate predictions.

Accurately assess the effects of policies, programs, and plans.

Make timely changes in plans based on feedback regarding progress.

Use resources (e.g., time, money) wisely.

Respect and have empathy for others.

Continue to learn and to enhance your skills.

Because You Will

Recognize the vital role of criticism in decision making.

Recognize and avoid influence by propaganda, pseudoscience, quackery, and fraud.

Ask questions with a high payoff value (they decrease uncertainty about how to attain valued outcomes).

Discover contradictions between what you say and what you do.

Recognize mistakes in thinking. Avoid cognitive biases.

Use mistakes and less-than-hoped-for success as learning opportunities.

Communicate effectively.

Identify and minimize personal obstacles to problem solving (e.g., excessive concern with social approval).

Encourage a culture of thoughtfulness (Gambrill & Gibbs, 2009).

Be less likely to "sell out" (act in ways that do not reflect your values).

Be task focused.

long-term interests (1995, p. 8). He highlights the value of critical reflection in the "illumination of power" (p. 9). Only by considering the interlinked contingencies related to a concern may you and your clients understand it and estimate the degree to which it is solvable and, if so, how. Only by seeing the "big picture" may you and your clients and fellow staff identify policies and related legislation that affect clients and that need changing.

Many problems are not solvable by social workers such as lack of well-paying unskilled jobs, poor-quality education, and lack of health care for all residents. Thinking critically will help you to avoid vague descriptions such as "He is aggressive" or "He has a mental disorder" that get in the way of discovering options. It will guide you to be only as precise as you have to be. "One cannot tell truth from falsity, one cannot tell an adequate answer to a problem from an irrelevant one, one cannot tell good ideas from trite ones—unless they are presented with sufficient clarity" (Popper, 1994, p. 71). However as Popper suggests, we should only be as precise as we have to be. "Clarity is an intellectual value in itself; exactness and precision, however, are not" (Popper, 1992, p. 50).

False consciousness and mystification refer to beliefs that obscure or distort, rather than reveal, what is true about the world, such as who benefits from certain practices and policies. Critical thinking is an antidote to being propagandized by others (or propagandizing yourself) in ways that decrease opportunities to help clients (see Exhibit 5.5). Many scholars, although vastly disparate in many or even most of their views, emphasize empowerment through self-education (e.g., Freire, 1973; Popper, 1994; Skinner, 1953). A key part of this self-emancipation through knowledge is the critical appraisal of accepted views. Who benefits from emphasizing "self-esteem" as a cause of problems? Who loses? Don't federal, state, and county governments save millions of dollars by attributing young people's less than hoped for academic and job performance to their low self-esteem rather than providing education, housing, employment, health care, and recreation that provide the successful experiences on which self-esteem is grounded? Although appeals to self-esteem and will power may sound informative and as though they give us control over our fates, do they provide guidelines for achieving hoped-for outcomes? (See critique of self-esteem by Baumeister et al., 2003.)

If we can identify the environmental and personal causes of our problems, we will be in a better position to offer our clients real (rather than merely perceived) influence over the quality of their lives. We are more likely to discover connections between private troubles and social issues. In *Under the Cover of Kindness: The Invention of Social Work* (1997) Leslie Margolin argues that social workers mystify themselves about their motives and actions by emphasizing their essential goodness and services and that this obscures influence over clients and self-interest. He argues that knowledge about clients is used to attain power over their lives and suggests that social work's rejection of political motives encourages an immunity to criticism from clients. Margolin suggests that the great achievement of social workers

---

EXHIBIT 5.5

Hypnotic Effect of One's Own Words

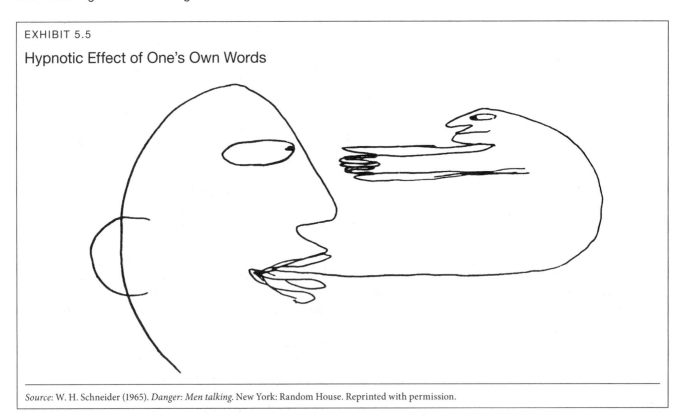

Source: W. H. Schneider (1965). *Danger: Men talking.* New York: Random House. Reprinted with permission.

---

during the twentieth century was gaining access to the privacy of the homes of the poor and that social workers used seductive and manipulative ways to do this including "the hostess technique"—use of a friendly demeanor to hide underlying investigative and judgmental roles. (For a critique of Margolin, see Wakefield, 1998.)

Discourage the Active Promotion of Ignorance

Currently, ignorance is actively promoted in social work in a number of ways. One is through misrepresentation of ideas (e.g., see Gambrill, 2011). A second route is through censorship, for example, not describing well-argued alternatives to popular points of view, such as those questioning the concept of mental illness (Boyle, 2002; Szasz, 1994) and popular diagnostic systems, such as the DSM (e.g., Houts, 2002; Kutchins & Kirk, 1997; Kirk, 2010). Hiding environmental causes of poverty, crime, substance abuse, depression, and anxiety is a key example of promoting ignorance to forward special interests (e.g., sales of medication, increase in the prison industry). The success of disliked policies such as the decriminalization of all drugs as in Portugal in 2001 may be censored by promoters of the "war on drugs" (Hughes & Stevens, 2010). Previous literature may be ignored. Descriptions of strengths-based approaches do not cite the constructional approach described in *Social Casework: A Behavioral Approach* by Schwartz and Goldiamond (1975) and in more recent versions of this (e.g., such as this text). Another

way that ignorance is actively promoted is through social censure (e.g., ridiculing the questioner of popular views) (see also the discussion of ignorance in chapter 4).

Participate in Creating Your Environments

Many writers highlight the emancipating quality of critical thinking and argue that such reasoning is essential to a democracy (e.g., Baron, 1994; Freire, 1973; Paul, 1993). Thinking critically will help you to recognize obstacles to taking any responsibility for the quality of service offered by your agency. These may consist of pressures to conform and to obey authorities and identifying with authorities, so becoming an authoritarian yourself. Brookfield emphasizes that "one fundamental purpose of encouraging adults to become critical thinkers is to help them feel a sense of personal connection to wider happenings" (1987, p. 53). Critical thinking will help you avoid the extremes of helplessness and hopelessness and grandiosity in your professional life. Grandiosity refers to excessive claims of effectiveness (e.g., claiming success, even though no one has cared enough to evaluate it) and impossible expectations, such as ensuring that no child be harmed in foster care. David Stoesz (1997) notes how seldom social workers take collective action to protest the increasingly diminished resources that compromise services. Too seldom do they blow the whistle on scandalous conditions. Consider, for example, ongoing problems in child welfare agencies revealed only by forced public disclosure (e.g., DePanfilis, 2003;

Gainsborough, 2010). Criticism along these lines is increasing as can be seen by related websites and books on critical social work and critical psychiatry (e.g., Cohen & Timimi, 2008; Double, 2006; Rapley, Moncrieff, & Dillon, 2011).

Increase Self-Awareness

Self-awareness and critical inquiry (reflexivity) go hand in hand. Both encourage contextual awareness—exploring how past and present environments and hoped-for futures influence what you do, value, and believe and how, in turn, you influence your environments (see Appendix B). Critical thinking will help you to discover beliefs you have accepted which, on reflection, you find problematic. "Voices" are not necessarily true, nor are they necessarily ours (e.g., accepted after careful review).

> Those who counsel people to accept themselves uncritically lead them into the very trap they claim to be helping them to avoid, the trap of dependence on others.... The only way for people to become individuals is to...carefully examine the self they have taken for granted, identifying the influences society has had on them, evaluating those influences against some reasonably objective standard, and deciding which ones they will strengthen and which ones they will combat. (Ruggiero, 1988, p. 57)

Critical thinking can help us to identify our "logical vulnerabilities," that is, topics or positions to which we have a strong initial reaction in one direction that prevents critical inquiry (Seech, 1993). Thinking carefully about problems and possible ways to solve them can help us to detect contradictions between what we do and what we say we value. It encourages us to become aware of how our emotions influence our beliefs and actions (Gross, 2007). The questionnaire at the end of this chapter, "Are You a Critical Thinker," provides an opportunity for you to explore your experiences and views.

Evaluate Claims and Arguments

Making decisions involves suggesting and evaluating arguments in favor of different options. Consider the following:

- I think Mrs. A's abuse as a child caused her to mistreat her children. We know that a past history of being abused leads to later aggressive behavior. And, this parent denies that she abused her child.

- If Constance developed insight into her past relationships with her father, she would understand how she contributed to the problems in her own marriage and her relationship would improve.

- If we could get money to establish a community service agency, our neighborhood would have less crime.

An argument "is a group of statements, one or more of which (the premises) support or provide evidence for another (the conclusion)" (Damer, 1995, p. 4). Argument is an essential form of inquiry. It provides a way to evaluate the accuracy of different views. For example, if two theories are contradictory, they both cannot be true. Claims asserted with no reasons for them are opinions, not arguments. People use different criteria to evaluate claims and arguments (see chapter 4). We could ask, for example: What evidence is there that money spent on the "war on drugs" has been effective? What evidence is there that genograms contribute to helping clients? (See also Exhibit 5.6.)

What Is a Good Argument? An argument is aimed at suggesting the truth or demonstrating the falsity of a claim. "A good argument...offers reasons and evidence so that other people can make up their minds for themselves" (Weston, 1992, p. xi). As Popper emphasizes:

> Victory in a debate is nothing, while even the slightest clarification of one's problem—even the smallest contribution made towards a clearer understanding of one's own position or that of one's opponent—is a great success. A discussion which you win but which fails to help you to change or to clarify your mind at least a little should be regarded as a sheer loss. (1994, p. 44)

A key part of an argument is the claim, conclusion, or position put forward. A second consists of the reasons or premises offered to support the claim. Indicator terms such as *therefore, because, thus,* and *so* often precede the premises for a claim. Premises can be divided into grounds and warrants. Grounds refer to the data or evidence offered to support the conclusions. Warrants concern the presumed justification for the connection between the grounds and the claim. Grounds and their warrants should be acceptable, relevant, and sufficient. Let's say a teacher consults a school psychologist about a hard-to-manage student. The psychologist diagnoses the student as having ADHD (attention deficit/hyperactivity disorder) and suggests placing him on Ritalin. What is the psychologist's conclusion? What are his premises? To what warrants does the psychologist appeal (e.g., an assumption that hyperactivity has a physical cause)? Are there well-argued alternative accounts and related evidence (rival hypotheses) that suggest a different conclusion (e.g., a poorly designed curriculum that does not match the student's skills and knowledge, so he is bored)? (For practice in identifying rival hypotheses, see Huck & Sandler, 1979.)

Logic, in the narrow sense, is concerned with the form or validity of deductive arguments. "It provides methods and rules for restating information so as to make what is implicit explicit" (Nickerson, 1986, p. 7). Critical inquiry also requires skill in exploring the relevance of data to an argument. It requires raising questions, such as "What is the likelihood that this claim is true given this evidence?" For instance, if a client hears voices,

---

EXHIBIT 5.6

Reviewing Claims and Arguments

1. *Origin.* What is the origin of the material? For example, if an agency claims success in helping clients, can its own evaluation be accepted as the only judge of effectiveness?

- Who is presenting a claim?
- What might be the motives of these involved?
- How accurate are these sources?

2. *Sponsor.* Who pays for promoting a certain policy or point of view?

- Where could I find well-argued alternative views?

3. *Beneficiary.*

- Who stands to benefit? Who stands to lose?

4. *Techniques.* What techniques are used to put across the message?

- How have they tried to persuade me?

5. *Content.* On what "facts" or authorities are the arguments based?

- What do they appeal to? Emotion or reason?
- Is the same point repeated often?
- What facts are selected? What facts are omitted?
- Are the "facts" correct?
- Does the conclusion logically follow from the argument?

6. *Conclusion.* Suggest an interpretation of the overall message based on the above steps (what you think or conclude). In summary consider the:
   - origin
   - sponsor
   - beneficiary
   - techniques
   - content

- What is the overall message?
- What belief or action does the message lead you toward? (Will you be more likely to refer clients to a certain agency or to use of certain assessment tool [e.g., the Family Glee Scale]?)

OVERALL MESSAGE ⟶ Is it accurate? Has the claim been critically tested?

Source: E. MacLean (1981). *Between the lines: How to detect bias and propaganda in the news and everyday life* (p. 63). Montreal, Quebec, Canada: Black Rose Books. Reprinted with permission.

---

is he schizophrenic? (e.g., Layng, 2009). The general rules for constructing arguments are (1) clearly identify the premises and conclusion; (2) present ideas in a natural order; (3) use accurate premises; (4) use specific, concrete language; (5) avoid loaded terms; and (6) stick to one meaning for each term (Weston, 1992, p. v). You could use an outline form:

Premise 1: _____

Premise 2: _____

Conclusion: _____

Be sure to separate inferences and evidence and avoid making inflated claims that may result in harming rather than helping clients. Review your argument for fallacies and search for well-argued alternative accounts. Can you make a strong "rebuttal argument" against your position? Damer (1995) describes a Code of Conduct for effective rational discussion. Components include the fallibility principle (a willingness to admit you could be wrong), the burden of proof principle, and the truth-seeking principle. Others include the clarity principle and the reconsideration principle.

The accuracy of a conclusion does not necessarily indicate that the reasoning used to reach it was sound. For example, errors in the opposite direction may have canceled each other out. Likewise, lack of evidence for a claim does not mean that it is incorrect (nor does it keep people from believing it). (See discussion of "When searches turn up nothing" in chapter 10.) Assigning the proper weight to different kinds of evidence is an important part of analyzing an argument. People often use "consistency" to support their beliefs (e.g., degree of agreement among different sources of data). A helper may say that Mrs. X is depressed because she has a past history of depression. An assertion should be consistent with other beliefs; self-contradictory views should not knowingly be held. However, two or more assertions may be consistent with each other but yield little or no insight into the soundness of an argument. Thus, saying that A (a history of "depression") is consistent with B (alleged current "depression") is saying only that given A, it is possible to believe B. Overconfidence in a belief as a result of gathering redundant data is common.

Recognize Informal Fallacies

Fallacies (such as emotional reasoning—appeal to fear) are often used as ploys to derail critical appraisal of a claim. Walton (2008) defines fallacies in relation to the goal of a discussion. If the goal is to arrive at accurate answers, fallacies are illicit attempts to block critical appraisal of a claim or argument. When seeking accurate answers is the goal of a discussion, questions are never out of order (Walton, 2008). Damer (1995) described a fallacy as a mistake in thinking, "a violation of one of the criteria of a good argument" (Damer, 1995, p. 24). A valid argument is one whose premises, if true, offer good or sufficient grounds for accepting a conclusion. Thus, an argument may be unsound for one of three reasons:

1. There may be something wrong with its logical structure.

   - All mental patients are people.

   - John is a person.

   - Therefore John is a mental patient.

2. It may contain false premises.

   - All social workers are competent.

   - Mrs. Landis is a social worker.

   - Therefore Mrs. Landis is competent.

3. It may be irrelevant or circular.

   - Kicking the dog is a sign of aggression.

   - Brian kicks his dog.

   - Therefore Brian has an aggressive personality.

The last two kinds are *informal* fallacies. They have a correct logical form but are still incorrect. Fallacies result in defective arguments (e.g., the premises may not provide an adequate basis for a conclusion). A premise may be unacceptable or irrelevant or provide insufficient support. Most fallacies are informal (see Damer, 1995; Engel, 1994; Kahane, 1995; Thouless, 1974). They concern the content of arguments rather than their form. These are essentially irrelevant appeals (such as judging the soundness of a position by the confidence with which it is stated), in which the wrong point is supported or premises that are not relevant to an issue are used to support a conclusion. There are many kinds of informal fallacies. Anthony Weston (1992) considers the two greatest fallacies to be drawing conclusions based on too little evidence (e.g., generalizing from incomplete information) and overlooking alternatives.

In the fallacy of *begging the question*, a statement appears to address the facts but does not. Variants of question begging include the use of alleged certainty and circular reasoning. Vacuous guarantees (e.g., "It works") may be offered or an assumption made that because a condition ought to be, it is. Some informal fallacies overlook the facts, as in a *sweeping generalization* in which a rule or assumption that is valid in general is applied to a specific example for which it is not valid. Consider the assertion that parents who were abused as children abuse their own children. In fact, many do not. Other informal fallacies distort facts or positions, as in *straw person arguments* in which a position that is significantly different from the one presented is attacked. Diversions, such as trivial points, irrelevant objections, or *emotional appeals,* may be used to direct attention away from an argument's main point.

Emotional reasoning is a common fallacy. For example, we may be influenced by appeals to pity, fear, or self-interest (such as enhancing self-esteem). Some fallacies work by creating confusion, such as a feigned lack of understanding and excessive wordiness that obscures arguments. *Either-oring* is a common fallacy. That is, we incorrectly assume there are only two options when in fact there are many. This *fallacy of the false dilemma* prevents us from discovering other options. If you are aware of common informal fallacies, you will be better able to detect bogus claims based on faulty arguments.

Some informal fallacies could also be classified as social psychological persuasion strategies. They work through our emotions rather than through the thoughtful consideration of a claim. For example, we like to please people we like and may be reluctant to question claims they make. Influences based on liking (e.g., the "buddy-buddy syndrome") or fear may prevent us from making well-reasoned decisions in case conferences (e.g., Dingwall, Eekelaar, & Murray, 1983; Meehl, 1973). People may try to pressure us into maintaining a position by telling us that we must do so in order to be consistent with our prior beliefs or actions—as if we could not (or should not) change our minds. Or, they may appeal to fears about scarcity (if you do not act now, a valuable opportunity will be lost). Fear mongering is common in our culture (Furedi, 2006; Moynihan, Heath, & Henry, 2002). Learn how to recognize and counter these persuasion strategies (e.g., Cialdini, 2008).

Decrease Influence by Propaganda, Pseudoscience, and Quackery

Thinking critically about claims and arguments will help you detect propaganda, pseudoscience, and quackery and avoid their influence (see chapter 4). It will help you avoid being bamboozled and then misleading your clients. (See Exhibit 5.7.) Censorship of material is a key propaganda strategy (e.g., Ravitch, 2003). We can persuade people (including ourselves) through either well-reasoned arguments or by relying on manner of presentation or appeals to emotions (pity, fear, hate, attraction). The purpose of propaganda is to encourage beliefs and actions with the least thought possible (Ellul, 1965). Its purpose is not to inform but to persuade. Propagandists take advantage of informal fallacies. They encourage mistakes in thinking by trying to persuade us through irrelevant emotional appeals (to pity, anger, or fear) and ad hominem arguments (attacking those who disagree with

---

EXHIBIT 5.7

Mental Illness Model and Rank's Fourfold Classification of Propaganda

1. Overemphasize the positive aspects of preferred model
   - Inflated claims of success in removing complaints (puffery)
   - Inflated claims of success in avoiding problems (puffery)

2. Hide and minimize negative aspects of preferred model
   - Harmful effects of neuroleptic drugs
   - Questionable reliability and validity of psychiatric classifications systems

3. Overemphasize negative aspects of opposing views (e.g., behavior analysis)
   - Associate alternative approaches with negative terms (mechanistic, dehumanizing)
   - Allege that positive effects of alternative approaches are only temporary

4. Hide and minimize positive aspects of opposing views (e.g., behavior analysis)
   - Ignore research showing that nonprofessionals are as effective as professionals with many problems
   - Ignore positive results achieved by alternative approaches

---

them, rather than addressing their arguments). They misrepresent disliked ideas and hide evidence against their preferred views.

Propagandists may misrepresent their position (tell only part of the truth) or rely on slogans and putdowns. Pharmaceutical ads, as well as other human services advertisements, rely on propaganda methods such as vivid case examples (Gambrill & Gibbs, 2009). Critical thinking skills, values, and knowledge will help you spot propaganda (e.g., reliance on testimonials) and avoid its effects, such as recommending ineffective or harmful methods to clients. Rather than addressing cogent criticisms of the diagnosis of ADHD (attention deficit/hyperactivity disorder) and related recommended interventions, the International Consensus Statement on ADHD dismisses all criticisms as dangerous myths (Barkley et al., 2002). (For an example of a critique, see Timimi, 2002.) Indeed, this two-page statement (most pages contain the signatures of 85 people and references) is replete with propaganda strategies such as begging the question and hiding problems with the view presented. Some medical schools now recognize the importance of educating students about strategies used in pharmaceutical promotion (Wilkes & Hoffman, 2001). Examples of such strategies include appeal to anecdotal evidence, exaggerated claims, and hiding adverse effects (see http://www.pharmedout.org).

Communicate Effectively

Effective communication is a vital practice skill. Clear language is important, whether speaking or writing. Indeed, professionals have a responsibility to write and speak clearly. David Perkins (1992) uses the term *language of thoughtfulness* to highlight its role in critical thinking. Clients will not understand obscure jargon or garbled sentences. Critical thinking can be valuable in making presentations at staff meetings and case conferences. This will help you to organize information logically and consider your goals, as well as well-argued alternative views. Clear communication requires use of a language (English, Spanish, French) in accord with agreed-on meanings. The degree to which a "culture of thoughtfulness" exists is reflected in the language used. (See Gambrill & Gibbs, 2009.)

To the gullible, obscurity heightens the appearance of profoundness; indeed, Armstrong (1980) found that clear writing was viewed as less profound than obscure writing. If terms are not clarified, confused discussions may result because of the assumption of "one word, one meaning." Vague terms that may vary in their definitions include *abuse, aggression,* and *addiction.* Technical terms may be carelessly used, resulting in "bafflegarb" or "psychobabble"—words that sound informative but are not. Karl Popper argues that "critical reason is the only alternative to violence so far discovered" and that it is the duty of intellectuals to "write and speak in clear simple language" (which requires hard work) in order to replace violence with critical discussion (Popper, 1994, p. 69). This view conflicts with what Popper calls "the cult of incomprehensibility, of impressive and high-sounding language," and also with the common habit of stating "the utmost trivialities in high-sounding language" (p. 71).

Disagreements often concern how a word is to be used (for example, what is empowerment?). One way to get sidetracked in problem solving is to become caught up in defining words rather than critically testing theories by making risky predictions and testing them. Popper argues that a preoccupation with definition will lead only to an endless regression to other words. What is needed are bold guesses about the nature of a problem (e.g., poverty), combined with critical discussion and a testing of related arguments. Like scientists, professional helpers are concerned with finding real solutions to real problems. "Our aim should not be to analyze meanings, but to seek for interesting and important truths; that is, for true theories" (Popper, 1992, p. 178).

A knowledge of fallacies related to the use of language (see Exhibit 5.8) and care in using words should improve the quality of judgments. We often misuse speculation (assume that what is can be discovered merely by thinking or talking about it). Using a descriptive term as an explanation offers an illusion of understanding. For example, a teacher may state "Ralph is aggressive," and when asked, "How do you know?" she may say, "He hits other children." If then asked why she thinks Ralph does this, she may reply, "Because he is aggressive." This goes around in a circle. It is a pseudoexplanation. Both professionals and intellectuals have a special responsibility to write and speak clearly.

EXHIBIT 5.8

Examples of Misleading Use of Language

Conviction through repetition: We may come to believe something simply because we often hear it reported.

Pseudotechnical jargon/bafflegarb: Vague terms used to conceal ignorance and impress others (e.g., "psychic deficiencies").

Misleading or harmful metaphors: Description of efforts to decrease substance abuse as the "War on Drugs" or labeling a wide range of problems as brain disorders (when there is no evidence for this).

Use of emotional terms and buzz words: They arouse rather than inform.

Uninformative labels: Vague labels that do not inform but do pathologize clients.

Assumption of one word, one meaning: Words differ in their meaning for different individuals and in different contexts.

Use of vague terms: Examples include "uncommunicative," "aggressive."

Reification: Mistakenly assuming that a word corresponds to something real.

Avoid Cognitive Biases

Thinking carefully about claims will help you to avoid the cognitive biases described in chapter 8. Guidelines that you can use to avoid these sources of error are discussed in this chapter, as well as later chapters.

Have Empathy for Others and Ourselves

Critical thinking encourages intellectual empathy and contextual understanding, both of which encourage compassion for ourselves and others. Understanding the context of behavior will encourage empathic rather than judgmental reactions, even when confronted with challenging situations that "push your buttons." Valuing truth means having a sincere interest in understanding other points of view. We know we may be (and often are) wrong. Kuhn (1970) argues that we cannot talk fruitfully (learn from one another) if we have different frameworks. In *The Myth of the Framework* (1994), Karl Popper argues that what is important are theories and problems, not frameworks. He points out that we share many problems, regardless of our particular frameworks.

Costs and Benefits of Critical Thinking and Obstacles

Thinking critically has both costs and benefits that are shared by evidence-informed practice. The costs of critical thinking include

forgoing the comfortable feeling of "certainty" and the time and effort required to clearly describe your views, to understand alternative views, and to seek and critically appraise related research findings. You must abandon intellectual arrogance and instead accept intellectual responsibility. No longer will you be able to say, "Well, that is just what I think should be done" without taking responsibility for providing an argument for your position and a rebuttal to other views. No longer can you rely on unfounded authority, anecdotal experience, or case examples to support your views. Relativists will have to examine contradictions between their views (all knowledge claims are equally valid) and their actions (e.g., driving cars selected for their safety record). (See chapter 4.) Acquiring practice knowledge and skills takes time and effort and often requires abandoning favored beliefs. It may result in loss of a valued "believer group" (Munz, 1985). You may fall into the "sunk costs error" (continuing to invest in a losing option because of previous investments in it). The best option here is to cut your losses by not "throwing good money after bad."

Obstacles to critical thinking include the prevalence of uncritical thinking; a preference for authority-based decision making; differences of opinion about "What is evidence?" and "When do we have enough?"; political and economic interests; and a disdain for intellectual rigor.

The Prevalence of Uncritical Thinking

Thinking critically about claims is not valued by many groups and individuals. To the contrary, they may try to hide the effects of practices and policies by relying on propaganda methods and appealing to pseudoscience. (See chapter 4.) Phillips (1992) argues that raising questions about "truth" has the taboo quality today that talking about sex had in Victorian times. We are surrounded by pseudoscience and propaganda, making it a continuous challenge to resist their allure (e.g., Ellul, 1965; Gambrill, 2012a; Lilienfeld, Lynn, & Lohr, 2003; Thyer & Pignotti, 2010). Burnham (1987) argues that one reason that superstition won and science lost in the United States is the media's role in presenting content in fragmented bits and pieces. The media, pop psychology (such as New Age material), and professional journals often present incomplete accounts of problems. Well-argued alternative views are often not mentioned (e.g., Boyle, 2002). Feelings and thoughts are often more vivid than environmental causes. It is easy to overlook environmental circumstances that contribute to these thoughts and feelings.

Incomplete analyses of client concerns (oversimplifications) contribute to ignoring social, political, and economic factors that affect clients' lives. They obscure context. We may read "Crack-addicted mother kills baby." The focus is on the mother's addiction. Little or nothing may be said about her impoverished life circumstances, both past and present, and related economic and political factors. The media often suppress information and mystify rather than clarify problems as illustrated in the yearly publication *Project Censored, Censored: The News That Didn't Make the News and Why.* (They also take a lead in exposing information hidden by others such as harmful youth homes and corruption and fraud in social services.) Millions watch talk shows and are influenced by claims based on testimonials and manner of presentation (e.g., the confidence with which people speak). For instance, in a show on bullying, an "expert" emphasized that bullies have low self-esteem and that is why they bully others. In fact, research shows that bullies have robust self-esteem (Olweus, 1993). Fewer and fewer organizations control the mass media (Bagdikian, 2004). This decreases exposure to alternative points of view. Fox News is watched by millions

> I lead a life where I hardly have time to think.
> —Nelson Mandela, *Higher Than Hope,* 1991

Work settings differ in the extent to which they support critical inquiry. They may provide no incentives for arriving at well-reasoned beliefs and actions. Locating practice-related research may be difficult because of lack of access to needed databases and busy schedules that allow no time for seeking such material. Staff may be overworked. Supervisors may punish those who raise questions (e.g., ridicule the questioner). Teachers may view students as passive receptacles into which they pour "knowledge." Although clear writing is a responsibility of intellectuals and those who write about practice, we often find obscurantism. Terms may be unclear. Practice methods may not be clearly described or lack of evidence for claims acknowledged.

Differences of Opinion About "Evidence"

The sheer quantity of potentially relevant material is a problem that is aggravated by lack of agreement about criteria to use to select knowledge (see chapter 4). There are many kinds of evidence, including research reports and opinions of clients and practitioners about the effectiveness of services. The question is what types of evidence are needed to answer a particular kind of question (see chapter 11). Do we use different standards in evaluating evidence when making decisions about ourselves than we do for our clients (Gambrill & Gibbs, 2002)? The steps in evidence-informed practice and policy and related tools such as the Cochrane and Campbell databases are designed to decrease costs associated with drawing on related research findings. Client-oriented criteria for selecting material include relevance (how useful it is to achieving clients' goals), evidentiary status (e.g., has a practice or policy been critically tested and found to be effective in achieving these goals?), feasibility (can I use it? do I have needed resources?), and the range of clients/situations to which it can be applied (Rothman & Thomas, 1994).

Social, Political, and Economic Factors

Concerns about protecting vested interests (e.g., economic gain and power) may loom larger than goals of helping people and "telling the truth." The biomedical industrial complex is a multi-billion dollar industry. Social, political, and economic factors such as competition for turf are partly responsible for the fragmentation of knowledge in the helping professions and the ambivalence about what criteria to use to accept "knowledge." Politics thrive on polarization. "So we have behaviorists on the one hand, mentalists on the other, each camp believing the other to be naive, stupid, and occasionally downright evil" (Schnaitter, 1986, p. 265). In *The Mismeasure of Women* (1992), Carol Tavris gives many examples of how stereotypes influence research. The efforts of professional organizations such as the Council on Social Work Education and the National Association of Social Workers (NASW) to protect turf, acquire funds, and enhance the positive image of social workers compete with measured, accurate descriptions of what social work has achieved. Careers are advanced by new "discoveries" (new modes of therapy), encouraging a proliferation of untested therapies, each claiming success (e.g., see Pignotti, & Thyer, 2009). Millions of dollars are spent each year on products that promise cures, relief from distress, or a higher quality sex life despite the absence of evidence that they deliver what they promise. Focusing on individuals as the source of social and personal problems deflects attention from economic and social policies that create unequal opportunities.

Courage Is Required

It takes courage to challenge accepted beliefs, especially when held by "authorities" who do not value a culture of thoughtfulness in which well-argued alternative views are welcomed and arguments critically evaluated. To those who uncritically embrace a "doing good ideology," asking that verbal statements of compassion and caring be accompanied by evidence of helping may seem disloyal or absurd. To the autocratic and powerful, raising questions threatens their power to simply "pronounce" what is and is not without taking responsibility for presenting well-reasoned arguments and involving others in decisions. Even when you ask questions tactfully, people may feel threatened, and their feelings may be hurt. Other people may become defensive, hostile, or angry when you question what they say—even when you do so with courtesy and intellectual empathy and even in a university! Socrates was sentenced to death because he questioned other people's beliefs (see Plato's *Apology*).

Without emotion management skills for handling negative reactions to critical inquiry (your own as well as that of others), you may not challenge fuzzy thinking and bogus claims that may harm clients if acted on. The skills described in chapter 16 will help you to handle challenging situations and to cultivate a "thick skin" where you need it to offer the best to clients. Evolutionary history highlights the powerful role of status (Gilbert, 1989). Thus the student who questions a professor, supervisor, administrator, or physician may be viewed as a threat rather than as a source of knowledge that may help clients attain goals they value. An understanding of social hierarchies and how ranking maintains them will help you view such reactions in their historical and biological context. This evolutionary view will help you not to take things personally. It links our lives to the entire span of animal and human development.

It also takes courage to question our beliefs and candidly examine their accuracy, especially if you do not usually do so. Unless you have grown up in an environment in which critical thinking was valued and modeled, you may feel personally attacked when someone disagrees with or questions what you say. You may have to unlearn part of what you have learned. "Many participants in a rational, that is, a critical, discussion find it particularly difficult that they have to unlearn what their instincts seem to teach them (and what they are taught, incidentally, by every debating society): that is, to win" (Popper, 1994, p. 44).

Personal Characteristics

Not all helpers give first priority to the goals of enhancing the welfare of clients and avoiding harm. Competing goals include maintaining status by appearing more expert than is the case, perhaps even to yourself. The essence of self-deception is not being aware that you deceive yourself (Baron, 2000). A willingness to suspend disbelief and to rush from one task to another, leaving no time to think carefully, is also an obstacle. Vincent Ruggiero (1988) suggests the following obstacles:

1. *Disdain for intellectual rigor.* "Solving problems, making decisions, and evaluating issues is hard work and requires an active approach, perseverance in the face of difficulty and confusion, and refusal to settle for easy answers" (p. 55). As Ruggiero notes, we are accustomed to being passive spectators and to being entertained, whereas learning requires action and may not always be entertaining.

2. *Misconceptions about oneself.* Ruggiero refers to "the romantic notion that the self is effectively insulated from the influences of society" (1988, p. 56). We are encouraged to look within to discover our values as if we have carefully chosen them when we may never have carefully thought about them (see also Rogers & Skinner, 1956). As Ruggiero notes, the influence others have on us in childhood precedes for years our ability to reflect on this. We uncritically absorb much from our parents, peers, and the mass media.

3. *Misconceptions about the truth.* This includes the "view that truth is entirely subjective ... people create their own truth and whatever they accept as true is true for them" (Ruggiero, 1988, p. 58). If one kind of thinking were as good as another, we would not do much of what we do, including designing planes that stay in the air. Ruggiero argues that relativism strips ideas of their interest. All are the same. It undermines curiosity and wonder, robs students of sensitivity to problems, and makes relevant data indistinguishable from irrelevant and promising approaches indistinguishable from unpromising, thereby paralyzing creativity and leaving minds mired in subjectivity. If one idea is as good as another, there is no good reason for students to subject their ideas to critical scrutiny and no purpose in the discussion of issues other than to stroke one's vanity (1988, p. 59).

4. *Confusion about values.* Misconceptions about the truth result in confusion about values. If truth is relative, how can we compare values? Acceptance of moral relativism makes it impossible to judge. If one truth is as good as another, we cannot say which actions are morally correct and which are not. However, as Ruggiero observes, not judging is itself a form of judgment that may permit injustices to continue. "Both relativism and absolutism are extreme positions which should be rejected" (1988, p. 61). (See also Gellner, 1992.)

5. *Basing beliefs on feelings.* We often base our beliefs on what we "feel"—our emotional reactions. This encourages uncritical acceptance of actions and beliefs.

6. These five obstacles lead to intellectual insecurity.

   A disdain for intellectual rigor results in discomfort when problems and issues are not solved quickly and easily. Because students "harbor a misconception about self, they are unprepared to deal with positions that differ from their own and so are ill at ease with dialogue. Because they harbor a misconception about truth, they are not ready to support their views and are nervous and sometimes belligerent when asked to do so. Because they are confused about values, they are defensive when discussions about values arise. Because they are in the habit of basing their belief on feelings, accepted uncritically, they can do little more than assert their views and thus are intimidated by reasoned discourse" (Ruggiero, 1988, p. 64).

Information-Processing Factors

The way we acquire and process information influences our judgments. We are influenced by cognitive biases and tend to fall into certain traps such as not exploring alternative views. We tend to seek data that confirm our views and to overlook those that do not. (See discussion of confirmation biases in chapter 8). This tendency is an obstacle to evidence-informed practice and policy unless you develop skills to counter it. A key contribution of EBP is creating a process and related tools designed to discourage misleading styles, such as "John Wayne reasoning." David Perkins uses this term to describe those who prefer clear-cut black-and-white views to a reflective exploration of pros and cons (1995, p. 129).

Reducing the Costs and Increasing the Benefits of Critical Thinking

Steps you can take to reduce the costs and increase the benefits of critical thinking are described in the next section.

Remember What Is at Stake

Keep in mind that clients benefit or suffer as a result of your beliefs and actions. Concentrating on helping clients attain outcomes they value (when possible) and avoiding harming clients will help you to have the courage and focus needed to use your critical thinking skills to provide evidence-informed practices and policies. The NASW code of ethics lists service first. This focus will help you not to take things personally and to keep your purpose clearly in view: to help clients achieve outcomes they value and to avoid harm. It may help you to have the courage and take the time needed to question assumptions that have life-affecting consequences for clients. Although rapid intuitive thinking may suffice in some situations, at other times analytic thinking is needed as well to make well-reasoned decisions (see chapter 9).

Allocate Resources Wisely

You will not have time to think carefully about all the decisions you make. When working with clients confronting a crisis, you must work fast. You may have a caseload that makes it impossible to carefully plan services. You will have to decide how much time and effort to devote to particular decisions. Like it or not, many social workers have to "triage" problems in terms of what resources to devote to which ones. This problem does not go away by not thinking about it. Rather, by not thinking about it, you may fail to take corrective steps. As your skills increase, you may be able to help clients resolve some problems more swiftly or recognize more quickly that a problem cannot be solved. You can also work together with your colleagues to change policies and practices that limit service options. (See also section on purchasing services in chapter 27.)

View Criticism as Essential to Learning and Problem Solving

The purpose of education is to expand our horizons—to challenge accepted views, to consider new ones, to acquire well-reasoned ways to evaluate beliefs, and to increase understanding. Many scholars suggest that we cannot learn unless there is conflict. Never put your "whole self" on the line when threatened by a question or disagreement (e.g., think you are "stupid," slow, uninformed). It is precisely when you feel attacked (but in reality may be confronted with a good question asked in a respectful manner) that you can use your philosophy of practice as a guide to choose wisely among competing goals (e.g., to discover the most accurate account rather than to "win" an argument).

When a critical discussion of your views reveals flaws, you may feel disappointed, uncertain, anxious, or angry. Perhaps a Buddhist perspective on feelings (acceptance) will help you to view negative feelings as momentary experiences that are a necessary part, even important part, of helping clients and avoiding harm by discovering the evidentiary status of beliefs. Questioning the accuracy of judgments, yours as well as those of others, will help you to pay attention to the uncertainty involved in making decisions and to shift from being a "believer" who does not question beliefs, to a "questioner." (Editors of the *BMJ* (*British Medical Journal*) view recognition of uncertainties as so important, they have added an Uncertainties page.)

Value Mistakes, Errors, and Lack of Success as Learning Opportunities

Feedback is an essential part of learning. If you are not making mistakes, you are probably not learning. The outcomes of your actions provide valuable feedback. Did you achieve what you had hoped? Mistakes are inevitable, and we can learn from them. This is recognized in many areas, including medicine, aviation, and nuclear power where there is an active search for them. Only by recognizing our mistakes can we make better guesses about how to overcome difficulties in solving a problem. Lack of success provides an opportunity to do better in the future. "The growth of knowledge always consists in correcting earlier knowledge.... Settled knowledge does not grow" (Popper, 1994, p. 156). Popper contends that there "is only one way of learning to understand a problem which we do not yet understand—and that is to try and solve it and fail.... Our failure hopefully provides information about where the difficulties lie and we can use this information to make better tests in the future" (pp. 157–158). So by criticizing our efforts, "we learn more and more about our problem: we learn where its difficulties lie" (p. 158).

Pay Attention to What You Do Not Know

If additional information will help your clients attain valued outcomes, it is important to estimate accurately your current (background) knowledge and, if it is lacking, to fill in the gaps. This is a hallmark of EBP and great attention has been devoted to developing tools (such as the systematic review) to help you to do this (see chapter 10). Proctor and Schiebinger (2008) argue that the study of ignorance is just as important as the study of knowledge. Appraisal of claims often reveals that little is known. Informed consent requirements obligate us to share what we find with clients. In a course on medical ignorance at the University of Arizona School of Medicine, Witte, Witte, and Kerwin (1994) stressed the importance of attending to what we do not know. You can use Venn diagrams to estimate knowledge needed, what is available, and how much of this you are aware of. Keep in mind that most guesses (theories) about what is true are wrong, as the history of science, psychiatry, and medicine suggests. As Socrates stated, "I know that I know almost nothing, and hardly this."

Plan Time-outs for Critical Reflection

In the fast moving everyday world of practice, you may not have time for critical reflection; you may have to act and reflect later. Keep track, in a critical thinking log, of exchanges, decisions, or questions you want to review, and consider them later when you have time. For example, you might note decisions you want to think about, such as how to ration scarce resources, arguments in favor of different views on a controversial issue, and useful websites. The points you note could become topics for staff meetings and, if they affect the quality of services, should be discussed. Stay informed by seeking out sources that present well-argued alternatives to popular views. Ask: What is missing? Have there been any critical tests of this claim? Are there other well-argued points of view? Otherwise you may be lulled into accepting dubious claims and faulty arguments.

Review Your Beliefs About Knowledge And how to Get It

As discussed in chapter 4, our beliefs about knowledge and how it can be acquired affect how we think and what we learn. It is thus important to examine them.

Practice

Practice is important to learning all skills, including those that contribute to critical thinking. Practice using critical thinking skills when thinking, reading, writing, listening, or speaking. Scores of opportunities arise each day in work-related contexts and when reading, listening to the radio, watching television, searching the Internet, or talking to your friends. Take advantage of books with useful exercises (e.g., Gambrill & Gibbs, 2009;

Huck & Sandler, 1979), user-friendly checklists (e.g., Greenhalgh, 2010), and reporting guidelines such as CONSORT that can help you to critically evaluate different kinds of research.

Use Helpful Maxims and Questions

Helpful maxims include the following:

- Focus on helping clients and avoiding harming them.
- Check it out.
- Search for well-argued alternative views.
- Get the whole picture; pay attention to context.
- Be suspicious of vivid material.
- Acknowledge uncertainty about decisions you must make.
- Watch out for misleading influences of language.
- Beware of personally relevant data.
- Look for material that is both true and informative.

Helpful questions include the following:

- Is it true?
- Is there evidence against my point of view? (See Exhibit 5.9.)
- Are there alternative well-argued views?

EXHIBIT 5.9

Evaluating Inferences About a Behavior

Select a behavior of interest to you. Describe this and two different inferences about why it occurs, as well as an example of supporting and disconfirming evidence.

Behavior _____

_____

Inference	Supporting evidence	Counterevidence
1. _____ _____ _____	a. _____ b. _____ _____	a. _____ b. _____ _____
2. _____ _____ _____	a. _____ b. _____ _____	a. _____ b. _____ _____

Which inference has survived the most critical tests? _____

_____

- What is missing? What is wrong with this picture?

- What are my assumptions?

- Has this claim been critically tested? If so, what was found?

- How accurate is my background knowledge about this topic?

- What is the relative frequency? (See chapter 20.)

- What about the other three cells? (See chapter 20.)

- How can I test my predictions?

- Is it a question of fact? (Data can be gathered to answer it.)

- What is the sample size in this study?

- Where did the sample come from? How representative is it?

- Are my metaphors misleading?

- Given this evidence, what is the likelihood that this claim is accurate? (See Exhibit 5.9.)

Carroll (2001) includes ignorance questions in his classes to promote critical thinking. (See discussion of ignorance in chapter 4.)

Take Advantage of Visual Representations and Technology

Take advantage of visual tools that can help you and your clients clarify problems and related factors (Tufte, 2006). You can use decision aids and trees, flowcharts, or Venn diagrams (see chapter 10). You can use concept maps to explore assumptions (i.e., to identify associations with a concept). You and your clients can use balance sheets to guide decision making (Eddy, 1990).

Take Advantage of Available Knowledge

Take advantage of information that reveals or decreases uncertainty related to decisions. Evidence-based practice is designed to help us to do this, as well as to recognize our ignorance about many questions. For example, being aware of research showing that some allegations of sexual abuse are false should caution you not to jump to the conclusion that claims of abuse are always true. Being aware that interviewer bias is common should remind you to question other helpers' reports. Being aware that correlational research concerning the relationship between a symptom (e.g., depression) and an outcome (e.g., a suicide attempt) does not permit you to predict what a particular client will do will help you to avoid unwarranted assumptions. Helpful websites can be seen in Exhibit 5.10.

EXHIBIT 5.10

Examples of Useful Websites

Alliance for Human Research Protection
<http://www.ahrp.org>

Austhink (argument mapping)
<http://www.austhink.com>

Bandolier
<http://www.medicine.ox.ac.uk/bandolier/>

Campaign for Commercial-Free Childhood
<http://commercialfreechildhood.org>

Center for Media and Democracy's PR Watch
<http://www.prwatch.org>

Consumer Health Digest
<http://www.consumerhealthdigest.com>

CSI/Skeptical Inquirer
<http://www.csicop.org>

Fallacy Files
<http://www.fallacyfiles.org>

Healthy Skepticism
<http://www.healthyskepticism.org/global/>

International Society for Ethical Psychology and Psychiatry
<http://www.PsychIntegrity.org>

MindFreedom International
<http://www.mindfreedom.org>

National Council Against Health Fraud
<http://www.ncahf.org>

Overcoming Bias
<http:www.overcomingbias.com>

Pros and Cons of Controversial Issues
<http://www.procon.org>

PsychDiagnosis.net
<http:www.psychdiagnosis.net>

The Quack Files
<http://www.quackfiles.com>

Quackwatch
<http://www.quackwatch.com>

Skeptic
<http.www.skeptic.com>

The Skeptic's dictionary
<http://www.skepdic.com>

Take Advantage of Helpful Distinctions

Distinctions that will help you critically evaluate different views of problems, their causes, and possible solutions are described next.

Truth and Credibility

Credible statements are those that are possible to believe. As Dennis Phillips (1992) points out, just about anything may be credible (believable). This does not mean it is true. Thus the distinction between truth and credibility is an important one. History shows that often, what once seemed credible was false (e.g., the belief that tuberculosis was inherited) and what once seemed incredible was true (e.g., people could fly in airplanes). Accounts are often accepted when they "make sense," even though there is no evidence that they are accurate. Only by critically appraising beliefs can we evaluate their soundness.

Reasoning and Truth

Reasoning does not necessarily yield the truth. "An assertion is true if it corresponds to or agrees with the facts" (Popper, 1994, p. 174) (also see the Glossary at the end of chapter 4). People often take and are able to defend opposing views on controversial issues. However, effective reasoners are more likely than are ineffective reasoners to prefer theories that are closer to the truth. Some beliefs are closer to the truth than are others.

Widely Accepted Versus Well Supported

What is widely accepted is not necessarily accurate. For example, many people believe in the influence of astrological signs (i.e., their causal role is widely accepted). However, there is no evidence that they influence behavior.

A Feeling That Something Is True and Whether It Is True

A "feeling" that something is true may not (and often does not) correspond with what is true. Not making this distinction helps to account for the widespread belief in many questionable causes, such as astrological influences. Basing actions and beliefs on feelings discourages an examination of their soundness, and in professional contexts, this may result in decisions that do not benefit clients.

Bias/Propaganda/Point of View

Bias refers to an emotional leaning to one side. Biased people may or may not be aware of their biases. Propaganda refers to encouraging beliefs and actions with the least thought possible (Ellul, 1965). Examples of related strategies include appealing to emotions or status, presenting only one side of an argument, and deflecting criticism by attacking the critics' motives. Propagandists are often aware of their interests and often disguise them. People with a point of view are aware of their interests but describe their sources and do not use propaganda ploys. Their statements and questions encourage rather than discourage critical review; they state their views clearly so that they can be critically examined. People with a point of view are open to clarifying their views when asked to do so.

Beliefs, Facts, Opinions, and Reasoned Judgments

Some beliefs are statements (guesses/inferences/assumptions) that can be shown to be false. If I say, "Play therapy helps children overcome anxiety," I can test this to find out whether it is accurate. There is no way to test other beliefs, such as whether there is a God. Belief may imply a commitment, a reluctance to criticize a view. Facts can be defined as beliefs that have been critically evaluated and/or tested. *Facts* are capable of falsification, whereas beliefs may not be. *Opinions* are statements of preferences and values. It does not make sense to consider opinions as true or false, because people have different preferences, as in the statement: "I prefer cognitive explanations for behavior." This differs from the claim "What people say to themselves influences their behavior," because we can explore through critical testing whether this statement is accurate. Reasoned judgments consist of sound arguments based on good evidence (see discussion of evidence in chapters 4 and 11).

Summary

Critical thinking encourages us to reflect on how we think and why we hold certain beliefs. It requires an acceptance of well-reasoned conclusions even when they are not our preferred ones. Critical thinkers question what others take for granted. They challenge accepted beliefs and ways of acting. They ask questions, such as: Have there been any critical tests of your claim? Could there be another explanation? Critical thinking requires a careful examination of the evidence related to beliefs and a fair-minded consideration of alternative views. Critical thinking and evidence-based practice are closely related. Both encourage values, knowledge, and skills designed to help practitioners and clients make well-reasoned decisions and avoid misleading directions and bogus claims, that if acted on, may harm rather than help clients. Both encourage critical appraisal of the evidentiary status of claims and a search for alternative well-argued views. Both encourage us to be skeptical. Benefits include honoring ethical obligations to clients to make informed (rather than misinformed or uninformed) decisions.

Many of the costs of not thinking carefully about beliefs and actions are hidden, such as being a patsy for propaganda distributed by the pharmaceutical industry resulting in harm to clients. Curiosity may languish when we accept oversimplified accounts that obscure the complexity of issues and give the illusion of understanding but offer no guidelines for helping clients. Hoped-for outcomes may not be attained because causes remain hidden. It is not in the interests of many groups to reveal the lack of evidence for claims made and policies recommended; fuzzy thinking is the oppressor's friend. Focusing on helping clients and avoiding harm provides the ethical grounding for intellectual virtues related to critical thinking and evidence-based practice and policy, such as accurately representing disliked as well as favored points of view and having the courage to ask "hard" questions.

Reviewing Your Competencies

Reviewing Content Knowledge

1. Describe values, skills, and knowledge related to critical thinking.

2. Describe the relationship of critical inquiry to ethical obligations of professionals.

3. Describe the relationship among critical thinking, scientific inquiry, and evidence-based practice and policy.

4. Explain the difference between a cynic and a skeptic (critical thinker).

5. Explain what is meant by the term *propaganda* and give examples.

6. Describe the parts of an argument.

7. Give examples of the influence of language on practice decisions.

8. Identify reasoning errors in the following statements:

   a. That may be true, but the last five clients I saw did not show this behavior.

   b. If this is what nursing homes are like, I do not look forward to getting old.

   c. All I know is that the alcoholics we see here never recover.

   d. I just do not understand it; we know that Mrs. Jones is a schizophrenic, but she does not act like one.

9. Identify your sources of "logical vulnerability" (see the section on increasing self-awareness).

10. Describe the costs and benefits of critical thinking, as well as obstacles.

Reviewing What You Do

1. You seek out and draw on research findings in your work with clients.

2. You seek information that contradicts your views.

3. You review and revise your assumptions as called for when given new information.

4. Observation of your work demonstrates that you value intellectual virtues inherent in critical inquiry.

5. You ask questions that are valuable in assessing the accuracy of claims.

6. You can identify vague terms.

7. You clearly identify assumptions related to your arguments.

8. You can accurately diagram practice-related arguments and identify flaws in them.

9. You seek opportunities to examine the accuracy of your beliefs (e.g., request constructive criticism), as shown in discussions with colleagues and clients.

10. You clearly identify assumptions in arguments.

11. You thank others for pointing out flaws in your arguments.

12. You listen carefully to other people's ideas; you can accurately describe other people's views.

13. You correctly describe both preferred and opposing views on topics discussed.

14. You can give examples of the connection between private troubles and public issues.

15. You can accurately identify fallacies in practice-related material.

16. You identify and overcome personal obstacles to critical thinking.

17. You reinforce behaviors integral to critical thinking.

Reviewing Results

1. Your practices and beliefs are well reasoned.

2. You make ethical decisions.

Appendix A: A Taxonomy of Socratic Questions

Questions of Clarification

- What do you mean by _____?
- What is your main point _____?
- How does _____ relate to _____?
- What do you think is the main issue here?
- Let me see if I understand: do you mean _____ or _____?
- How does this relate to our discussion (problem, issue)?
- Could you give an example?
- Would you say more about that?

Questions That Probe Assumptions

- What are you assuming?
- What could we assume instead?
- You seem to be assuming _____ Do I understand you correctly?
- All of your reasoning depends on the idea that _____ Have you based your, reasoning on _____ rather than _____?
- You seem to be assuming _____ How would you justify taking this for granted?
- Is it always the case? Why do you think the assumption holds here?

Questions That Probe Reasons and Evidence

- What would be an example?
- Are these reasons adequate?
- Why do you think that is true?
- Do you have any evidence for that?
- How does that apply in this case?
- What difference does that make?
- What would change your mind?
- What other information do we need?
- Could you explain your reasons to us?
- Is there good evidence to believe that?

- Is there reason to doubt that evidence?
- Who is in a position to know if that is so?
- How could we find out whether that is true?

Questions About Viewpoints or Perspectives

- You seem to be approaching this issue from _____ perspective. Why have you chosen this one?
- How would other groups/types of people respond? Why?
- How could you answer the objection that _____ would make?
- What would someone who disagrees say?
- What is an alternative?
- How are Ken's and Roxanne's ideas alike? Different?

Questions That Probe Implications and Consequences

- When you say _____ are you implying _____?
- But if that happened, what else would happen as a result? Why?
- Would that necessarily happen or only probably happen?
- What is an alternative?
- If this and this are the case, then what else must also be true?
- If we say that _this_ is unethical, how about _that_?

Questions About the Question

- Is this the same issue as _____?
- What does this question assume?
- Why is this question important?
- How could someone settle this question?
- Can we break this question down at all?
- Is the question clear? Do we understand it?
- Is this question easy or hard to answer? Why?
- Does this question ask us to evaluate something?
- Do we all agree that this is the question?
- To answer this question, what questions would we have to answer first?

Source: Adapted from Paul (1992). _Critical thinking: What every person needs to survive in a rapidly changing world_ (rev. 2nd ed.) (pp. 367–368). Foundation for Critical Thinking, <http://www.criticalthinking.org>.

Appendix B: Are You A Critical Thinker?

	SD	D	N	A	SA
1. I think it is important to examine the accuracy of my beliefs.	1	2	3	4	5
2. I critically evaluate claims of effectiveness.	1	2	3	4	5
3. I dislike ambiguity and search for certainty.	1	2	3	4	5
4. I often discover that something I believe is incorrect.	1	2	3	4	5
5. I am grateful to people who point out flaws in my thinking.	1	2	3	4	5
6. It is important to examine the accuracy of claims that affect clients' lives.	1	2	3	4	5
7. I search for evidence against my assumptions.	1	2	3	4	5
8. It is embarrassing for me to admit that I was wrong or made a mistake.	1	2	3	4	5
9. I like to discuss controversial issues with people who disagree with me.	1	2	3	4	5
10. Changing one's mind is a sign of weakness.	1	2	3	4	5
11. People do not respect me if they ask me to support my claims with evidence.	1	2	3	4	5
12. Professionals should base their decisions on well-reasoned arguments.	1	2	3	4	5
13. Learning something from a discussion is more important to me than winning an argument.	1	2	3	4	5
14. I take responsibility for explaining the reasons for my views.	1	2	3	4	5
15. I can spot questionable claims.	1	2	3	4	5
16. I often say, "I could be wrong."	1	2	3	4	5
17. I take responsibility for evaluating the consequences of actions I propose.	1	2	3	4	5
18. I seek only data that support my point of view.	1	2	3	4	5
19. I take responsibility for clarifying vague statements I make.	1	2	3	4	5
20. I change my mind when I have good reason to do so.	1	2	3	4	5

Source: See, for example, R. Paul (1992). *Critical thinking: What every person needs to survive in a rapidly changing world* (rev. 2nd ed.) (pp. 367–368). Foundation for Critical Thinking, <http://www.criticalthinking.org>.
Key: SD = strongly disagree, D = disagree, N = neutral, A = agree, SA = strongly agree.

Part 3

Thinking About Problems and Causes

Competing Views of Personal and Social Problems and Their Causes

OVERVIEW   This chapter highlights the importance of understanding the context in which social work practice takes place, including competing views of personal and social problems and their causes. The contextual nature of problem framing is discussed, and ongoing controversies are noted. Theories of behavior are described, together with the implications of different views. The importance of distinguishing among facts, concepts, and evaluations is highlighted, and guidelines are suggested for reviewing theories (guesses about what may be accurate). A developmental-contextual model is suggested that attends to multiple levels of influence.

YOU WILL LEARN ABOUT

- Professionals as problem framers
- The politics and economics of problem framing
- Problem definition and prevalence as controversial
- Deviance as a problem
- Ongoing controversies
- Theories of behavior (guesses about what may be true)
- A contextual view
- Thinking critically about theories
- The value of translation and integration skills

Professionals as Problem Framers

The goal to help clients sounds straightforward. However, considering the other functions of social welfare and social work (social control and social reform) suggests that conflicts may occur. As you become immersed in the everyday world of practice, it is easy to forget about the economic, political, and social context in which problems are defined including our increasingly diverse society; increasing economic, health, and educational disparities; and the biomedicalization of problems-in-living such as anxiety and depression (viewing them as health issues in need of medical remedies) encouraged by corporate interest in profit (e.g., see Healy, 2004). You may forget that how problems are framed changes in accord with popular ideas and forget to ask who benefits and who loses from a particular problem framing (e.g., as a human rights issue or a biomedical malady remedied by a professional in a managed care organization). Many scholars argue that professionals are involved not so much in problem-solving as problem-setting (e.g., Schön, 1990). Gusfield (2003) suggests that "the development of professions dedicated to benevolence, the so-called 'helping professions,' depend upon and accentuate the definition of problem populations as 'sick,' as objects of medical and quasimedical attention" (p. 9). (See also Foucault, 1973; Illich et al., 1978.) Social workers are the main providers of mental health services in the United States. This is not to say that people do not have problems and pose them for others, for example, by misuse of alcohol or drugs. It is to say that the meaning of related behaviors is contested.

Social welfare agencies address problems in ways that reflect assumptions about their causes. The assumptions underlying different functions of social work are based on different beliefs about human nature—why people do what they do, how they change, if they can change, and different views of human rights—what is a right? For example, social reform efforts emphasize the influence of political, economic, and social conditions such as the quality of educational opportunities. Problems and the approaches to them are institutionalized in organizational structures and related mission statements. Practice is carried out in the context of social and public policies and related legislation that certain behaviors (e.g., smoking marijuana) are problems and certain remedies (e.g., arrest) are appropriate. To give a name to a problem is to recognize or suggest a structure to deal with it.

Child abuse, juvenile delinquency, mental illness, alcoholics all have developed occupations and facilities that specialize in treatment, prevention, and reform (Gusfield, 2003, p. 8). Once these are developed there is an interest in maintaining related views of problems (e.g., that (mis)use of alcohol or drugs is an addiction, that anxiety in social situations is a mental illness). Who should receive welfare, how much, when, and for how long are vigorously debated. Are poor single parents who neglect their children bad people who should be punished or overburdened people who should be helped? Are they themselves victims of the inequitable distribution of employment, housing, and education opportunities that limit their freedom to enhance their human potentials? Who is hurt by current definitions? Who gains? What are the costs and benefits to different involved parties of certain definitions and proposed remedies? Recognizing the links between problem framing and current policies and practices will help you to identify options for and constraints on helping clients.

The Politics and Economics of Problem Framing

There is a long and rich history of scholarly writings highlighting the construction of social problems. Too seldom are helping professionals informed about this. This prevents awareness of the social construction of categories of social problems based on political, social, and economic grounds. Uninformed students and professionals may assume an "objective" status of "social problems" that does not exist separate from political powers to make it so. (See also discussion of the social control functions of social work in chapter 1.)

> The idea of "social problems" is unique to modern societies…modern societies, including the United States, display a culture of public problems. It is a part of how we think and how we interpret the world around us, that we perceive many conditions as not only deplorable but as capable of being relieved by and as requiring public action, most often by the state. The concept of "social problems" is a category of thought, a way of seeing certain conditions as providing a claim to change through public actions. (Gusfield, 2003, p. 7)

Gusfield (2003) notes that there are many human problems that are not considered to be public problems, such as disappointed friendships and unrequited love.

> Again and again sociologists have pointed out how the conditions said to define the social problem are socially constructed, are only one of several possible "realities." The attempt to pose as the arbiters of standards is less and less taken for granted and more and more seen as an accompaniment to social control, to the quest for hegemony. (p. 15)

Without a contextual understanding of behavior, you may miss the relationship between the personal and the political (Mills, 1959). You may accept views that limit opportunities to help clients. Without a contextual understanding, it is easy to fall into "blaming clients" and focusing on "changing them" or giving them a rationale for their plights rather than working together with others to alter related environmental conditions. Thinking critically about personal and social problems and proposed remedies commits you to the effort and courage required to question popular assumptions and examine underlying points of view. For example, who promotes a certain view? Who stands to benefit? Who loses?

Clarifying and critically examining basic assumptions is a key component of critical thinking. Recognizing underlying goals and points of view is not easy; they are often implicit rather than explicit. They may be part of the basic social fabric and related belief systems in which we live, perhaps unquestioned or even unrecognized. They may be deliberately suppressed. Related facts and figures may be hidden or distorted (see yearly publication of *Project Censored*, http://www.projectcensored.org). Billions of dollars have been and are being spent on "the drug war" in the United States. Fallouts from these drug wars include discriminatory patterns of arrest and incarceration of thousands of African American youth as described in *The New Jim Crow Laws* by Alexander (2010).

The "drug war" has been so unsuccessful in achieving its goals that the Cato Institute, a conservative think tank, recently issued a report calling for the decriminalization of all drugs, as was done in Portugal in 2001 (Greenwald, 2009). "Drug Czars" continue to promote the "drug war" and hide its negative consequences. The hundreds of thousands of drug counselors and substance addiction programs and residential centers all benefit from the criminalization of drugs. Here too we can use Hugh Rank's four-part analysis to identify the kinds of propaganda used, for example, hiding the benefits of medical marijuana and exaggerating the harms of recreational use (alleging that it will transform your brain into a scrambled egg). As Ellul (1965) suggests, propaganda (encouraging beliefs with the least thought possible) is unavoidable in our technological society. Raising questions about accepted views may be met with attempts to discredit (or cajole) the questioner. Multicausal views that assign equal weight to many factors may be used to avoid dissent (Tesh, 1988).

Reframing Political Conflicts Over Values as Personal Troubles/Sickness

Sociologists emphasize the social construction of problems—the framing of political concerns such as equality of rights or freedom from unwanted control into personal ones over which the state has power. What is a political issue is transformed into a "social problem" (see Mills's (1959), as well as related writings by Foucault, Ilich, and Szasz). "If, however, the difficulties are understood to be those of moral diversity, of contested meanings, then the problem is a political issue, and no system of training can provide help" (Gusfield, 2003, p. 9). Consider views of homosexuals. "If the condition is perceived as that of individual illness or deficiency, then there can be a social technology, a form of knowledge and skill that can be effectively learned. That knowledge is the mandate for professions licensed to 'own' their social problem" (p. 9). However, some groups successfully resist an unwanted view.

The gay rights movement is perhaps the most salient example of how the ability to mobilize has enabled a subject group to transform its status. During this century, homosexuals have been thought of as sinful and as sick, objects of condemnation or of medical benevolence. What the gay rights movement did was to resist the public designation of deviance, of abnormality, by attacking the presumed norms and denying that homosexuality constituted a social problem. In the process the phenomena of homosexuality lost its status as a "social problem" and became a matter of political and cultural conflict over the recognition of alternative sexual styles. What had been an uncontested meaning has been transformed into a political contest. (p. 15)

There are great stakes in how problems are framed, and people with vested interests devote considerable time, money, and effort to influence what others believe (Loeske, 1999). Costs and benefits to society and involved individuals may not be apparent until later developmental stages, as illustrated in follow-up studies of antisocial children (e.g., Scott, Knapp, Henderson, & Maughan, 2001). "Problem crusaders" (people with an interest in a certain view of a problem) forward favored definitions and may exaggerate potential risks and prevalence (e.g., MacCoun & Reuter, 2001). Economic interests influence problem definition. For example, the definition of anxiety in social situations and depression as "brain diseases" requiring medication benefits the pharmaceutical industry (which has more lobbyists in Washington than all senators and representatives combined). These lobbyists actively advocate biochemical views of problems in living. They are key players in the biomedical industrial complex. Problem definition is influenced by professionals' interest in maintaining and gaining power, status, and economic resources, as well as by differences of opinion about what makes one explanation better than another. Profit making is the key aim of for-profit, and many (supposedly) nonprofit organizations in the health care industry. Residential psychiatric facilities for youth and nursing homes are multimillion-dollar businesses. The concern for profit rather than service is reflected in the mistreatment (e.g., unneeded hospitalization) of clients in order to make money.

Different Problem Framings Have Different Consequences

Different ways of defining problems have different consequences. Thomas Szasz (1987, 1994) argues that many people who injure others and are labeled mentally ill have committed criminal offenses and should be treated accordingly. Others believe that many criminals are mentally ill and should receive psychiatric care. Throughout history, poverty has been variously viewed as a crime, a personal limitation, or a reflection of discrimination and oppression (social injustice). Views about problems and their causes affect who receives aid and who does not, as well as what is offered and the spirit in which it is offered. Defining behaviors as indicators of mental illness results in quite different consequences than does defining them as criminal. A moralistic definition of problems encourages the belief that people with these problems are bad people who deserve whatever ill fate awaits them, including "justified" punishment or enforced "treatment."

Feminist scholars and advocates have been in the vanguard in emphasizing the relationship between personal problems and social issues ("the personal is political"). Understanding the context in which problems occur provides opportunities to destigmatize clients. Tavris (1992) argues that there has been a turning away from the environmental context of personal problems in the current focus on individual characteristics (e.g., past history of abuse, low self-esteem). This is not to say that individual past histories are not important. It is to say that contextual factors such as gender role expectations comprise a part of individual histories. In a contextual view of behavior, behavior always makes sense, although often at a high cost as discussed in chapter 12. Programs that focus on altering the behavior of battered women so that their partners will stop abusing them encourage the view that women can control the behavior of their abusive partners if they change their own behavior. Focusing on the victim discounts the social roots of domestic violence such as norms that support male dominance over women (see Cavanaugh & Gelles, 2012; Gilbert, 1994). A study of 6,000 sheltered women revealed that access to resources permitting independent living (e.g., transportation, child care, and a source of income after leaving the shelter) was the best predictor of whether a woman would remain away from her abusive partner (Gondolf & Fisher, 1988).

Problem Definition and Prevalence as Controversial

People have different opinions about what a problem is, who and what is responsible for it, and how it can be resolved (see Exhibit 6.1). Some scholars argue that some state of affairs becomes a social problem when an objective state exists. Others believe that social problems are socially constructed. They argue that although certain needs of the sick, poor, elderly, and very young have been recognized throughout the centuries, they have been defined differently at different times and receive more or less attention at different times. One of the ongoing debates concerns the extent to which people are responsible for their problems: whether to locate the source of problems in the people who have them and to focus on changing individuals and/or to examine related environmental causes and pursue environmental changes. If someone drinks too much, is homeless, is unemployed, is this "her fault"? Don't environmental conditions such as high unemployment, poor-quality education, and lack of low-cost housing contribute to these problems? Moral views of problems emphasize individual responsibility.

The freedom to choose is a foundation requirement of moral behavior. Consider pathological gambling. Is it a learned behavior maintained by a complex reinforcement schedule? (See chapter 7.) Is it a "moral failing"? The American Psychiatric Association (2000) views this as a mental disorder. Is this a disease? Is there a (1) known etiology, (2) predictable course, and (3) worsening without treatment? Is anxiety in social situations a "mental illness"? (For critiques, see Cottle, 1999, and McDaniel, 2003; Moynihan & Cassels, 2005.) In his article "The Invention of Post-Traumatic Stress Disorder and the Social Usefulness of a Psychiatric Category," Summerfield (2001) suggests that "a psychiatric diagnosis is not necessarily a disease, distress or suffering is not psychopathology, post-traumatic stress disorder is an entity constructed as much from sociopolitical ideas as from psychiatric ones and that the increase in [this] diagnosis…is linked to changes in the relation between individual 'personhood and modern life' "(p. 95). Thomas Szasz has been emphasizing such

---

> **EXHIBIT 6.1**
>
> ## Proposed Causes for Problems
>
> *Moral:* They are due to moral deficiencies of individuals.
>
> *Psychiatric/medical:* It is assumed that problems result from a disease (mental illness) that has a biochemical and/or constitutional base.
>
> *Psychological:* Problems result from individual characteristics, such as differences in personality traits. These may unfold in stages. Examples include psychodynamic, developmental, and cognitive models.
>
> *Social interactional:* Problems result from the interaction between personal characteristics and social experiences. This includes social learning theory.
>
> *Sociological/cultural/critical school analysis:* Problems are related to social/cultural characteristics (e.g., disorganization, contingency patterns, socioeconomic status, discrimination). Problem categories are created and remedies proposed in accord with values and vested interests.
>
> *Ecological/contextual:* Both personal and environmental factors are considered, including social, political, and economic factors. This includes systems models and radical behavioral theory.
>
> *Philosophical/moral* (humanistic, hermeneutic linguistic, phenomenological/existential, and moral/1egal). An example of a moral/1egal cause is the argument that mental illness is rare and that many behaviors (e.g., assault), labeled as indicators of mental illness, should be criminalized or considered to be one's own business (e.g., suicide, drug use) and decriminalized and demedicalized.

points for decades (e.g., 1961, 1987, 1994). Spirited controversies continue about the prevalence of stranger abduction of children and sexual assault against women.

Deviance as a Problem

From a purely descriptive point of view, deviance refers to the variability of behavior (the range of behaviors that occur, their form, variety, and timing). Variability of behavior is a key factor in evolutionary history and it is essential to creativity. Some variations in behavior are labeled as problems, such as child and elder abuse. A *positivistic view* of deviance dominates many helping efforts. It is assumed that deviance is definable in a straightforward manner as behavior not within permissible conformity to social norms (beliefs about expected behaviors in given situations that are part of a known and shared consensus). This view searches for biological ("It's in the genes"), and/or psychological ("It's in the thoughts") causes. Questions focused on are: "Why do they do it?" and "How can we make them stop?"

In an *interactional view* of deviance, behavior is considered to be socially constructed (not given) relative to actors, context, and historical time (see Exhibit 6.2). Social problems are viewed as "constructed" in accord with cultural, political, and economic influences (e.g., Conrad & Schneider, 1992; Lemert 1967; Loeske, 1999). "A social problem is a putative condition or situation that (at least some) people label a 'problem' in the arenas of policy discourse and action, defining it as harmful and framing its definition in particular ways" (Hilgartner & Bosk, 1988, p. 70). The interactional view assumes the following:

- Deviance is universal, but there are no universal forms of deviance.

- Deviance is a social definition, not a property inherent in any particular behavior.

- Views of deviance are related to beliefs about what is right or wrong.

- Social groups create roles and enforce their definitions through judgments and social sanctions.

- Deviance is contextual; what is labeled as deviant varies in different social situations.

- Defining and sanctioning deviance involves power.

What is considered right (or wrong) is viewed as the product of certain people making claims based on their particular interests, values, and views. Deviance becomes defined as actions or conditions regarded as inappropriate to or in violation of certain powerful groups or conventions. Those who have more power are usually more successful in creating and imposing rules and sanctions on those who are less powerful.

Changing Views

Many behaviors once condemned as sinful were later considered crimes and are now defined as medical or psychological problems. This view of "heretical actions" as sinful is alive, as illustrated by Bishop Michael J. Sheridan of Colorado Springs "who said in a pastoral letter that Catholics who vote for candidates who support gay marriage, euthanasia or abortion rights must confess their sin before receiving communion" (Woodward, 2004, p. A23). The changing ways in which certain behaviors have been viewed supports a contextual view of deviance. For instance, only when women gained more political and economic

---

EXHIBIT 6.2

Some Important Views and Concepts

Deviance as a problem	Variations in behavior that are negatively defined or condemned in a society.
Interactional-contextual view	Deviance is an ascribed status. It involves the classification of behavior, persons, situations, and things into categories of condemnation and negative judgment, which are constructed and applied successfully to some members of a social community by others. The essence of deviance is not the actors' behaviors but is "a quality attributed to such persons and behaviors by others."
Positivistic view	Deviance is inherent in particular kinds of behavior.
Biomedicalization of deviance	The expansion of medicine and related areas (e.g., public health) as an agent of social control.
Politics	"How control and power are gained, shared, abdicated, protected, abused and delegated" (Brookfield, 1987, p. 164). "Process by which decisions are made, wealth is distributed, services are regulated, justice is maintained, and minority interests are protected" (p. 164).
Social control	Means by which society secures adherence to social norms. The greatest power comes from having the authority to define certain behaviors, persons, or things as "deviant." They "define the problem (e.g., as deviance), design what type of problem it is, and indicate what should be done about it" (Conrad & Schneider, 1992, p. 8).
Social problem	A condition/behavior of people or their environment that is viewed as undesirable.
Social policy	Social policy involves the definition of social problems and decisions about how to approach them.

Source: Based on P. Conrad & J. W. Schneider (1992), *Deviance and medicalization: From badness to sickness.* Philadelphia: Temple University Press; and S. D. Brookfield (1987), *Developing critical thinkers: Challenging adults to explore alternative ways of thinking and acting.* San Francisco: Jossey-Bass.

independence was greater attention given to battered women. Advances in knowledge often force changes in how people view a problem. It had been assumed that tuberculosis was inherited because people who lived together tended to "get it." When the bacillus responsible for tuberculosis was isolated, people were no longer blamed for developing it. Changing ideas about what is and what is not mental illness illustrate the consensual nature of psychiatric diagnoses. As mentioned earlier, homosexuality was defined as a mental illness until 1973, when under pressure from gay and lesbian advocacy groups and bitter infighting, the American Association, (by a vote) decided that it was not.

Problems have careers. You could take any pattern of behavior (e.g., drug use, delinquency) and explore the different ways it has been viewed. Consider masturbation. At one time it was thought to be responsible for an enormous range of problems, including mental retardation (see Szasz, 1970). Cultural values, common metaphors, as well as political and economic pressures, influence the decisions we make about problems. In the past, housewives who wanted to work were often regarded as pathological (Oakley, 1976). The metaphors used to describe problems influence how we view them and what solutions we propose. Consider the "war on drugs." This metaphor may encourage use of force against those who sell and use drugs, as well as feelings of "us against them" (see Exhibit 6.3 for a historical note; for critiques of crime and drug policies, see Szasz, 2001; Walker, 2011).

The Biomedicalization of Deviance

The biomedical industrial complex has been very successful in forwarding medical definitions of problems-in-living as illustrated by the ever lengthening list of behaviors, thoughts, and feelings viewed as health problems (mental illnesses) requiring

---

EXHIBIT 6.3

Historical Note

The belief that Satan causes disliked behavior or attributes is an ancient one. Magicians were viewed as active agents of dethroned gods (devils), and many people who practiced magic promoted the belief that they had supernatural powers (White, [1896] 1993). Christianity forbade the practice of magic, and the fourth-century Roman Emperor Constantine decreed that offenders be buried alive. From ancient times, society has distinguished between good and bad magic: Good magic could be used to cure diseases and protect crops, whereas bad magic was used for evil purposes, such as bringing bad luck to others. In the Middle Ages when Christianity was at its height in Europe, "the terror of magic and witchcraft took complete possession of the popular mind" (White, [1896] 1993, p. 383). Women were the principal targets of this persecution. During the Inquisition, not believing in magic was grounds for punishment, as it implied also not believing in Satan and thus God.

---

the help of experts (Conrad, 2007). (See also later discussion in this chapter.) The coffers of helping professionals grow rich from the medicalization of problems. The promotion of the belief that deviant or troubling behaviors are caused by an illness (a brain disease) has spawned scores of industries and thousands of agencies, hundreds of research centers, and thousands of advocacy groups which forward this view. Ivan Illich (1976) emphasized the medicalization of problems in his famous book *Limits to Medicine*. Indeed he used the term "the medicalization of life." The pharmaceutical industry promotes the view of depression and anxiety in social situations as biochemical illnesses requiring medication (e.g., Clarke et al., 2010; Moynihan & Cassels, 2005; Moynihan, Heath, & Henry, 2002; Starcevic, 2002). Professional experts (often in the pay of pharmaceutical companies) set the rules for what is and what is not "normal." The number of listings in the *Diagnostic and Statistical Manual* of the American Psychiatric Association continues to increase (from 185 in 1968 to 365 in 2000).

With the development of the therapeutic service sector of the economy, an increasing proportion of all people come to be perceived as deviating from some desirable norm, and therefore as clients who can now either be submitted to therapy to bring them closer to the established standard of health or concentrated into some special environment built to cater to their deviance. (Illich, 1976, p.123)

[M]edicine is becoming a major institution of social control, nudging aside, if not incorporating, the more traditional institutions of religion and law. It is becoming the new repository of truth, the place where absolute and often final judgments are made by supposedly morally neutral and objective experts. And these judgments are made, not in the name of virtue or legitimacy, but in the name of health. Moreover, this is not occurring through the political power physicians hold or can influence, but is largely an insidious and often undramatic phenomena accomplished by "medicalizing" much of daily living, by making medicine and the labels "healthy" and "ill" *relevant* to an ever increasing part of human existence. (Zola, in Conrad, 2009, p. 470)

Appeal to the trappings of science (pictures of brains) is one of the many strategies used to forward a belief in biomedical causes. Other strategies used include sheer repetition in thousands of journal articles, books, and workshops—and now webinars, direct to consumer advertisements, and in the halls of academia in which professional schools of social work, psychology, and psychiatry are located. Thomas Szasz (1961, 1994) has been the most consistent critic of the assumption that mental illness is a cause of distressed and distressing behavior. Szasz (1994) argues that we now live in a therapeutic state (a pharmacracy) characterized by psychiatric control of (mis)behaviors, primarily via prescribed medication. Psychiatrists have the power to coerce people to participate in interventions "for their own good."

Coercion is now defined as "treatment." Common variations in behavior are transformed into potential risk factors dubbed "unhealthy" and in need of treatment.

The Language of Problem Definition

The words we use influence how we think about problems and behaviors. Certain definitions of problems are forwarded by "claims makers" who try to influence others to accept their views. Consider the widespread use of medical language: healthy/unhealthy, wellness/sickness, health/disease. The word *health* has been applied to an ever wider range of behaviors, feelings, and thoughts. More and more everyday human problems are viewed as mental health problems remediable by experts. This increasing medicalization has resulted in a backlash (e.g., Angell, 2004, 2009; Brody, 2002). Thomas Szasz views the very notion of "mental illness" as a rhetorical device designed to obscure the real differences between physical illness and problems-in-living, such as anxiety and depression in order to exercise control over disliked behaviors. The metaphor of war, as in the "war against drugs," makes it easier to use violent means against "them" (e.g., seizing property) and to hide alternative views and policies such as the successful decriminalization of all drugs in Portugal in 2001.

Societal factors related to use of drugs are obscured. Labels and classifications (e.g., black, white, race, ethnicity) have policy implications and thus warrant careful analysis. Language and the ideology it reflects play a key role in obscuring economic differences. For instance, both working-class and upper-middle-class people may be labeled as middle class, creating the illusion that most people belong to the middle class. Many problems created in part by inequities in housing, job opportunities, education, health care, and the court system are treated as separate from one another, which makes it difficult to detect shared causes. DeMott (1990) suggests that differences in economic circumstances are daily translated into other terms, including moral differences. What is major becomes minor or is ignored as peripheral. Complexities are obscured. If it is "their" fault, what responsibility do we have to do anything about it?

Ongoing Controversies

Controversies include the relative importance attributed to biological, psychological, and environmental factors and how the "environment" is defined. Consider controversies concerning the cause of ADHD (Conrad & Potter, 2000). Some investigators assume that this is based in the brain: "Because ADHD is a behavioral and emotional disorder this is based in the brain" (Barkley et al., 2002). Others view disturbing behavior on the part of children as due to changes in work and family life (less time spent by parents with their children) and dulling school environments (Timimi, 2008). These views have different intervention implications (e.g., medication compared to altering environmental

circumstances) (see also chapter 12). Views that emphasize the interaction among genes, organisms, and their environments differ in how reciprocal these relationships are assumed to be and in the range of environmental events considered.

What System Levels to Focus On

The search for explanations reflects a shifting balance between a focus on individual characteristics (e.g., biological or psychological) and environmental causes (e.g., economic policies). Theories of practice and of behavior differ in what they include in "the environment," ranging from political, social, and economic influences to a narrower focus on the influence of family relationships. One option points to the individual as the source of problems and the key to their resolution (see Exhibit 6.4). Let us call this level 1, the individual focus. For example, in trait approaches, individual or psychological processes are focused on. Biological and/or early experiences, especially in childhood, are regarded as causes of stable personality qualities that are more or less independent of current environment. Modern-day versions of trait views include some genetic theories and psychoanalytic theory, with its emphasis on the enduring influence of early childhood development.

Between 1917 and 1929, a vocal minority of social workers embraced Freudian theory, despite the absence of evidence that this would be useful in helping clients attain outcomes they valued. This view encouraged a focus on individual pathology as the cause of human maladies. It emphasized the role of unconscious, instinctual drives and the influence of early childhood experiences. Inherent in a psychoanalytic framework is the assumption that observable problems are only the outward signs of some underlying process, which must be altered to bring about lasting change. Some social work scholars suggest that social workers turned to individually focused methods because altering environmental conditions was so difficult or impossible. The stress on the power of positive thinking (Peale, 1952) and the "self-made man" (Cawelti, 1965), the idea that people can better themselves through their own efforts (if they want to), focus attention on the individual.

A second option (level 2) includes an interest in families. Considerable attention is given to the family in social work. It is a key interpersonal context in which behavior develops and

---

EXHIBIT 6.4

Different Levels of Focus

Level 1   Individual focus on the person

Level 2   Focus on family

Level 3   Social groups and community

Level 4   Service system

Level 5   Political, economic, and social influences and related policies and legislation

is maintained. In level 3, social groups (e.g., self-help and social advocacy) and community characteristics are also considered, such as quality of housing, transportation, and recreational opportunities. A fourth option (level 4) includes attention to service systems. A fifth level attends as well to political, economic, and social factors and related values including their reflection in policies and legislation. Confining attention to levels 1 and 2 often results in incomplete assessment and selection of ineffective services. The wide variety of services that may be needed to help clients is suggested in the referrals made in a program for runaway and homeless youth (Rothman, 1991):

Counseling and individual treatment (74%)

Health service (55%)

Housing and placements (50%)

Family counseling (44%)

Educational services (31%)

Sex information (26%)

Vocational services (20%)

Legal services (15%)

Substance abuse services (9%)

Perhaps the most common mismatch is using level 1 services for client concerns that require level 3, 4, and 5 solutions. Some scholars suggest that the emphasis on the individual as the cause of problems is responsible for the overrepresentation of the poor and minorities in institutional settings. Policies that focus on changing individuals or families and ignore related political, economic, and social factors, in effect, "blame the victim" (Ryan, 1976). Consider the focus on the "alcoholic" rather than on the economic factors that foster substance abuse, including the multimillion-dollar advertising industry. Goldenberg suggests that an ideology that encourages people to view problems as the result of personal deficiencies is one of four factors that make up and encourage oppression. He defines *oppression* as: "a state of continual marginality and premature obsolescence." Other factors are

- Containment, which restricts and narrows the scope of possibilities (e.g., a reservation)

- Expendability, which assumes that specific groups are expendable and replaceable without loss to society

- Compartmentalization, which prevents people from living an integrated lifestyle (e.g., little relationship between life interests and work) (1978, p. 3).

The Relationship Between Inside and Outside

Different views of problems and related behaviors are based on different assumptions about the interaction among genes, organisms, and their environments. These range from a view in which inside (genes) and outside (the environment) are rigidly separated, as in the incorrect belief that genes cause behavior, to the view that environmental factors are all important. Lewontin (1994) argues that separation between the outside and the inside is not compatible with what we know about the interactions among genes, organisms, and environments (see also Strohman, 2003). This reveals a close relationship among our genes, our environments, our actions, and those around us. There is a co-evolution of organism and environment (Lewontin, 1995). This is not to say that the view that genes cause behavior or the view that environmental variables cause behavior might not be correct under some circumstances, as Lewontin notes. It is to say that under most circumstances, both views will be wrong (Lewontin, 2009). Not only is there a complex interaction (e.g., in relation to the environmental order of events), but in addition, there are unknown sources of variation within an organism. As he notes, this does not mean that we cannot find ruptures or a lack of connections. Nor does it imply that there are no critical points at which small changes may make a big difference. And, our values are influenced by the social circumstances in which we grow up. Malnutrition in childhood affects cognition in old age (Zhang, Gu, & Hayward, 2010). Stress in childhood affects the length of telomeres (Drury et al., 2011).

Construction or Adaptation?

Lewontin (1994) highlights the importance of examining the "metaphors" we use to think about behavior, such as potential, fitness, development, and adaptation. He contends that common metaphors, such as *potential* and *innate capacity*, are wrong. "There are differences among genotypes, with different consequences in different environments, but there is no way in general over environments, to rate these innate or intrinsic properties from 'bad' to 'good,' 'high' to 'low,' 'small' to 'big.' There is complete environmental contingency" (1994, p. 19). Furthermore, we play a great role in creating our environments. Lewontin argues that we must rid ourselves of the metaphor of adaptation, the view that organisms are adapting to a fixed world and either they adapt or they do not (p. 32). He notes that the metaphor of adaptation implies that there is an autonomously determined world to which we change in order to fit. But how do we know what "problems" confront organisms? This is a particularly difficult question in fields such as evolutionary biology. How do we know what particular characteristic of an organism yielded a solution to a problem? He argues that we can only guess at the environment of an organism. Each organism creates and exists in "a set of micro habitats" in which it spends its time, and so we can only guess at what the organism's problems may be. Moreover, an organism has a multitude of problems (pp. 33–34). He views metaphors of stability, harmony, and balance of nature as ideological inventions characteristic of a particularly insecure time in the history of the Western world (p. 47).

Lewontin suggests that based on what little we know about genes, organisms, and environment, a more accurate metaphor is that of construction. "If we want to understand evolution, we must understand it as construction because the actual situation is that organisms make their own environments. They define them. They create them. They change them. They interpret them" (1994, p. 36). He contends that only through careful observation of organisms in their environment can we discover their environments. He gives the example of the use of different parts of his garden by different birds. What is the "environment" to one differs from what it is for others. "There is an external world but there is no single environment out there" (p. 38).

Discrimination and Oppression as Causes

Historical, sociological, and psychological research shows that discrimination and oppression based on skin color, gender, socioeconomic class, sexual orientation, and physical ability are everyday realities. (See, for example, Nelson, 2009; Liptak, 2011a; Pear, 2011). William Goode highlights the roles of stereotyping and discrimination in what he calls "subversion (any special, additional efforts people make in order to get more prestige than their achievements would otherwise elicit, or less disesteem; or to prevent others from getting the respect they would otherwise get or to cause others to receive disesteem they would otherwise not receive)" (1978, p. 262). Increasing concentration of wealth in our consumer-oriented society in which we seek identity through the products we purchase and lack of employment opportunities contribute to (mis)use of alcohol and drugs, anxiety, and depression.

The quality of education provided in many inner-city schools is scandalously poor, and dropout rates are high, especially among poor and minority students. Many students who do graduate are unable to read, which greatly limits their employment options. Some argue that poverty has become increasingly a gender issue. Others believe it always has been so (Abramovitz, 1988). Conditions in inner-city ghettoes such as the lack of "mainstream" employment opportunities for young African American men propels many into the criminal justice system (Wacquant, 2009). Epidemiological data indicate that health problems are related to income inequalities (see Marmot & Wilkinson, 2006).

Mirowsky and Ross (2003) explored the relationship between psychological distress (depression and anxiety) and social factors and concluded that half of all symptoms of depression can be attributed to social factors. The proportion of severe distress attributed to social factors was even more striking: socioeconomically disadvantaged persons experience 83.9% of all severe distress. They argue that there is no evidence that patterns of social distress reflect genetic or biochemical abnormalities. They suggest that skin color affects opportunities which, in turn, affects achievement and a sense of control, which results in depression and anxiety for example.

The patterns of distress reflect the patterns of autonomy, opportunity, and achievement in America. The realities of socio-economic status—amount of education, type of employment or lack of it, family income—have a profound influence on a person's sense of control. Minority status is associated with a reduced sense of control partly because of lower levels of education, income, and employment, and partly because for members of minority groups, any given level of achievement requires greater effort and provides fewer opportunities. (Mirowsky & Ross, 1989, p. 16)

What About Individual Responsibility?

There is no doubt that oppression and discrimination exist, that some people are deprived of options they value because of some ascribed or acquired characteristic. We are dealt uneven hands at birth through no virtue or fault of our own. But are discrimination and oppression the principal causes of social and personal problems? Competing with this is the view that lack of individual initiative and responsibility creates or contributes to problems. Sykes (1993) argues that we have become a nation of victims using past difficult experiences as excuses to continue wallowing in self-sorrow. Existential views emphasize our responsibility for our decisions, no matter what the circumstances. For example, Victor Frankl suggests that each person is responsible for the fulfillment of the specific meaning of his or her own life (1984). He contends that no matter what our circumstances (even if we are in a concentration camp), we cannot escape choosing among possibilities. He views this responsibility as the essence of human existence.

In her book *The Empowerment Tradition in American Social Work* (1994), Barbara Simon suggests that "To ask and keep asking clients for an investment and renewal of their hard work and commitment is to communicate respect and hope" (1994, p. 26). Still, she cautions social workers to avoid the paternalism reflected in working harder than their clients to resolve problems or to enhance the clients' skills. There is no doubt that individual efforts go only so far in many circumstances; for example, if work is integral to mental health and there are no jobs, what then? Income inequality is increased when disability status is considered; that is, a low income may in reality be even more lacking when burdens of disabilities are considered (Sen, 2009). What about individual responsibilities of social workers? Don't they have an obligation to make changes that will decrease injustices in the world, especially when in a position of greater power than others? (See discussion of obligations of power in Sen, 2009.)

Theories of Behavior (Guesses About What May Be True)

Social and personal problems involve behaviors. Some behaviors occur too much, too seldom, at the wrong time, or with the wrong intensity. Elected politicians may refuse to see representatives of community action groups. Recreation centers may not admit certain minority group members. Employers may discriminate against certain kinds of applicants. Theories about behavior differ in a number of ways (see Exhibit 6.5), such as in the degree to which they are molded by the particular time and place in which they developed. For example, scholars argue that Victorian culture influenced psychoanalytic theory. Theories differ in their scope—the range of species, people, and kinds of behavior to which they apply. Views differ in the attention given to the cross-situational consistency of behavior. To what extent are traits such as extraversion, agreeableness, conscientiousness, neuroticism, and openness to experience common in different cultures? (See, e.g., Church et al., 2008.) Evolutionary theory embraces all life-forms, thereby connecting us with the other species of mammals and the rest of nature. Some beliefs are institutionalized in a society and have been referred to as "grand narratives" such as the great religions of the world and major political ideologies (such as capitalism and biomedicine) (Davey & Seale, 2002).

Different practice theories have been influenced by different theories of behavior (Payne, 2009). Psychosocial practice is influenced by psychoanalytic theory. Behavioral practice is based on behavioral theory. A biomedical grand narrative dominates practice in many areas, focusing on the individual as the source of problems. The client is viewed as having an illness (mental) in need of a diagnosis and treatment. A disease model of alcohol and drug (mis)use is widely accepted. (For a contrary view emphasizing choice, see Heyman, 2009). Different beliefs include:

- Genetic determinism: The belief that all behavior is due to genetic differences.

- Cultural determinism: The belief that all behavior is a result of social conditions.

- Radical environmentalism: The belief that behavior is solely influenced by environmental factors.

- Integrative (contextual): The belief that biological, psychological, and environmental variables influence behavior.

Psychological theories focus on the individual. Sociological theories focus more broadly on social structure. Different views of behavior have different consequences in relation to how people are treated. A given view may be used to pursue certain goals even if it is not believed. For example, William Goode notes that "in class relations derogatives can also be a nationally chosen program, a propaganda technique, by which one presents oneself or one's group as honorable and another as worthy of denigration—in order to justify a planned victimization. One can do this without at all believing the accusations made" (1978, p. 367). There is general agreement that behavior varies, that it is influenced by a range of variables, that it can be analyzed at different levels (e.g., physiological, psychological, sociological), and that there is a great deal of individual variation in response to different environmental risks resulting in different degrees of vulnerability and resilience. Examples of variables that may come into play include temperament and other genetic influences, past experiences, the impact of risk experiences at later times, how we view an experience, and protective features that counteract risks (Jensen & Fraser, 2011). Different risks and different forms of resilience may originate from different paths. This should caution us to be wary of simplistic causal analysis in understanding people and their concerns and social problems. Integrative views consider multiple levels of causality.

Genetic Explanations

Currently there is a great interest in searching for genetic markers for certain reactions. Sociobiologists emphasize reproductive success as the main determinant of the development of traits and social strategies and assume that behavior is influenced mainly by genetic differences. Critics of sociobiology claim that ideology is used to legitimize current patterns of inequality as a biological inevitability. They contend that the biological and the social are neither separable, nor antithetical, nor alternatives, but

---

EXHIBIT 6.5

Ways in Which Theories of Behavior Differ

- Degree to which behavior is viewed as knowable.
- Goals pursued (e.g., explanation and interpretation alone, understanding based on prediction and influence, political interests).
- Criteria accepted to evaluate claims (e.g., tradition, consensus, authority, scientific, critical testing).
- Range of problems addressed with success (inclusiveness/scope).
- Causal importance attributed to psychological factors (e.g., feelings/thoughts).
- Causal importance attributed to biological characteristics (e.g., genetic and/or brain differences).
- Attention devoted to evolutionary influences.
- Importance attributed to developmental stages.
- Range of environmental factors considered (e.g., family, community, society).
- Importance attributed to past experiences.
- Degree of optimism about how much change is possible.
- Degree to which critical testing of claims is possible and valued. (Some guesses are not falsifiable; you cannot find out whether they are accurate.)
- Degree of empirical support (evidence for and against a theory).
- Ease with which service guidelines can be developed.
- Degree to which a theory accounts for and is compatible with related knowledge.

complementary (see Lewontin, 1991). Rutter and Taylor (2002) argue that "research over recent decades has made it abundantly clear that genetic factors play an important part in the origins and persistence of all forms of behavior, including all forms of psychopathology" (p. 26). Research findings suggest that the different diagnoses at different ages (ADHD, antisocial personality disorder in adult life) reflect the same underlying genetic liability (Rutter & Taylor, 2010). It is estimated by some that 50% of personality and 80% of intelligence is inherited (Charlton, 2009). Genetic differences influence vulnerabilities to certain risk factors. (For further discussion, see Worthman et al., 2010.)

Some argue that genotype (genetic makeup) can never be separated from phenotype (visible characteristics that result from the interaction between genotype and the environment), because both the environment and random developmental factors affect how genotype is expressed (Lester, Tronick, Nestler, Abel, Kosofsky, Kuzawa, et al., 2011; Lewontin, 1994; Strohman, 2003). They contend that the biological and the social are neither separable, nor antithetical, nor alternatives, but complementary. Meany (2010) reported that the quality of maternal care influences the expression of genes that regulate behavior and neuroendrocrine reactions to stress, as well as hippocampal synaptic development. (See also Cohn, 2011.) This epigenetic view in which environmental influences are recognized as a key contributor to gene expression is now widely accepted but not promoted by those who benefit from a simplistic genetic view.

> Certainly genes are essential for defining any phenotype, but by themselves they remain just inert materials. In order for genetic information to be replicated or "decoded" and used to assemble phenotypes, the DNA must first be manipulated by systems of enzymes and small molecules that constitute the efficient cause for constructing phenotypes. Nearly all biologists now acknowledge this reality...this second informational system: an epigenetic system, [is] so named because of its ability to activate and silence elements of DNA and thereby to produce specific patterns of gene expression and proteins in a context-dependent (time and place) manner. (Strohman, 2003, p. 190)

People with a common genetic history may share a similar environmental history. Even when a genetic influence is found, it may account for only a small portion of the variance in understanding a problem or behavior. Although many people accept the findings of twin studies purporting to show a strong hereditary component to developing schizophrenia, others do not, pointing out methodological flaws (e.g., see Boyle, 2002). Thus, with rare exceptions, attributing behavior to genes is typically a false claim. Questions here include "What percentage of the variance do genes account for?" From a helping point of view, a key question is: "Can influential characteristics be altered to help clients achieve desired outcomes?" (See also earlier discussion of inside and outside.)

Biomedical Explanations

The grand narrative of health rules the day promoted by the biomedical industrial complex including biological psychiatry. Engaging in a growing list of activities too much or too little is now viewed as unhealthy. In his classic article, Zola (1972, reprinted in Conrad, 2009) argues that medical control has increased, not only by finding new diseases, but by creating new ones and claiming jurisdiction over new problems. One out of five people are supposed to have a diagnosable mental disorder. "Experiences of loss, sadness, insomnia and fatigue have become 'depression.' Low self-esteem, excessive sleep, and overeating may be labeled 'dysthymia'" (U'ren, undated, p. 7). Are not problems an escapable part of life? Great literature throughout the ages highlights life's trials and tribulations (e.g., Unamuno, 1972). Do we not, as Thomas Szasz argues, trivialize and stigmatize them by viewing them as pathology? Szasz (1994) suggests that suffering is no longer permitted, we must be happy and healthy. (See also Biehl, Goode, & Kleinman, 2007.)

It is widely believed that mental illness is the cause of troubled, troubling (not working for example) and very dependent behaviors. (Mis)behaviors, troubled or troubling feelings and thoughts, are translated into illness such as bi-polar disorder, schizophrenia, attention deficit hyperactivity disorder, and hundreds of others including gambling, and "female sexual dysfunction" (Moynihan, & Mintzes, 2010). In her chapter on "The Triumph of Suffering," Illouz (2008) points out how more and more people are considered to be victims requiring the help of professionals. Biomedical psychiatry is the main instigator and promoter of this view. This category error, assuming that behavior—what people do—equals illnesses, is widely ignored by players in the mental health industry and their audiences. Indeed, to question it, is often viewed as heretical and deluded. This reaction shows the spectacular success of propaganda equating (mis)behavior and illness.

Psychiatrists and pharmaceutical companies have been very successful in forwarding medical views of problems including transforming everyday behaviors, thoughts, and feelings into illnesses requiring medical solutions (medication), as illustrated by the ever lengthening list of behaviors viewed as signs of mental illness and promotion of medical remedies (prescribed medication). The boundaries around categories of alleged disorders such as "social anxiety" continue to expand. The client is viewed as having an illness (mental) in need of a diagnosis and treatment. Now mental health is considered to be a public health problem warranting screening of the entire population for "mental health" problems (e.g., Lenzer, 2004). Factors focused on include alleged "chemical imbalances," brain damage, and genetic differences. It is assumed, for example, that certain behaviors are related to too much or too little of certain biochemical substances (chemical imbalances). Beliefs that "something in the blood" or "something in the food" is related to mental illness have a long history. This focus on the individual as the cause of problems is compatible with capitalist beliefs regarding the role of individual effort. Zola (1972, reprinted in Conrad, 2009) suggests that this medicalization of society "is as much a result of medicine's potential as it is of society's wish for medicine to use that potential" (p. 477). Here again we see a symbiotic relationship. Moral dilemmas reflected in social and personal problems are transformed into medical concerns. More and more everyday problems are viewed as "health" problems, remediable by experts (Conrad, 2007; Zola, 1972). Although some troubled or troublesome behaviors, thoughts, and feelings may indeed be due to brain dysfunction, if they are so caused, they would become a subject for neurology (not psychiatry) as Szasz suggests.

The finding of biochemical abnormalities related to certain behavior patterns only establishes that abnormalities in biochemistry are present, not that they cause the behavior (see Exhibit 6.6). (See also critiques of neuroimaging methods, Leo & Cohen, 2003; Vul et al., 2009.) Biochemical changes may result from stress caused by limited opportunities due to discrimination. Psychotherapy changes the brain (Karlsson, 2011). In 1999 the U.S. Surgeon General concluded that there was no anatomical, biochemical, or functional sign that reliably distinguishes between the brains of mental patients and those of others. This remains true today. Physical abnormalities in the brain are often assumed to be responsible for certain kinds of mental illness, as well as hyperactivity and explosive temper. Another kind of biophysical explanation assumes that brain damage causes a "disorder." Here, too, even when brain damage

can be detected, it does not necessarily indicate that it causes any particular behavior. Additional problems with these kinds of explanations include limited intervention knowledge and predictive validity.

To say that Rachel can't walk, talk, or feed herself because she is retarded tells us nothing about the conditions under which Rachel might learn to perform these behaviors. For [someone] to explain Ralph's failure to sit down on the basis of hyperactivity caused by brain damage does not provide any useful information about what might help Ralph learn to stay in his seat. Even apparently constitutional differences in temperament are so vulnerable to environmental influences as to provide only limited information about how a child is apt to behave under given conditions. (Alberto & Troutman, 1990, p. 9)

The premature acceptance of biophysical explanations will interfere with discovering alternative explanations that yield intervention knowledge. Alberto and Troutman (1990) argue that biophysical explanations give teachers excuses not to teach. Such explanations are incomplete. For instance, environmental factors may also be important. Locating deficiencies within individuals supports the ideology of capitalism "that success or failure—in work, in emotional life—is largely an individual matter" (U'ren, 1997, p. 6). (For a critique of biological approaches to deviant behavior, see, for example, Boyle, 2002; Gorenstein, 1992.)

EXHIBIT 6.6

Critically Appraising Common Assumptions

Student 1: Look at this advertisement for a new workshop: "Learn about the latest research about brain diseases, alcohol and drug dependence, schizophrenia, and depression."

Student 2: What makes you think that depression is a brain disease?

Student 1: They said they found differences in the brains of people who are depressed and the brains of people who are not depressed. This shows that it is a brain disease.

Student 2: What's the size of these differences? Is there an overlap in differences between nondepressed and depressed people? If so, how do they account for it?

Student 1: You're getting too technical for me. They are the experts. They know how to do and evaluate research.

Student 2: That may be. But we are supposed to learn how to evaluate research too. I don't want to jump to conclusions about the causes of problems of concern to my clients. For example, what about research that shows a relationship between being poor and being depressed. Isn't this appeal to brain disease in depression an example of the medicalization of problems? Now if you are depressed, you have a brain disease. You go to a doctor (maybe soon a psychologist with newly acquired prescription privileges) and she prescribes medication. If it is a brain disease, how come cognitive behavioral methods compare favorably in outcome with medication? I think we have to examine the brain disease assumption more critically. After all, what is a disease?

Student 1: Anyone knows what a disease is. It's something wrong with the brain or physiological functioning. They found differences in the brains of people who are labeled schizophrenic and the brains of people who are not so labeled.

Student 2: Some people argue that the differences found result from taking neuroleptic medication. What about that argument?

Student 1: Gee, I didn't think of that.

Developmental Explanations

The term *development* refers to "the process of continual change during the lifetime of an organism" (Lewontin, 1995, p. 121). There is an "unfolding" metaphor associated with it emphasizing the role of internal characteristics. Lifespan developmental views are popular in social work (e.g., Santrock, 2003). Developmental accounts describe differences and related factors at different ages (e.g., childhood, adolescence, adulthood, and old age) and/or speculate about such differences (e.g., Cicchetti & Cohen, 2006; Rosales-Ruiz & Baer, 1997). Knowledge about developmental norms and transitions that occur at different ages in different cultures may be valuable in discovering risks and opportunities, when planning for smooth transitions (e.g., from adolescent to adulthood) and predicting the likelihood of success. For example, divorce or separation may initiate a sequence of changes, such as loss of social support, that produce other changes, such as increased sadness and irritability, that in turn may compromise parenting skills (Patterson, 2002). How parents respond to their infant influences the infant's reactions including his or her attachment reactions and emotional regulation. (See Exhibit 6.7.) (See also Bergman et al., 2008.) For example, a depressed parent may not respond to her infant's efforts to alter her behavior, and the infant may develop increasingly self-directed regulatory behavior. Lack of appropriate emotional regulation may pose problems when the child enters preschool, as well as at later stages (see discussion in Chamberlain, 2003). Parents differ in the kinds of opportunities they provide children in terms of patterns of attachment.

Although it is generally accepted that development is contingent on environment, there is disagreement about the relative importance of (1) genetically or physically determined processes, (2) environmental conditions, and (3) the actions of the organism and those around it. Development is often described as a series of stages, as in Freud's theory. Core beliefs about the self and others are assumed to be related to early childhood experiences, and people may become fixated at a certain stage, resulting in abnormal development. Developmental theories of moral development have also been described (Gilligan, 1982; Kohlberg & Lickona, 1986) and critiqued (Summers, 1996). In complex developmental views, social learning variables are considered, as well as the effects of earlier stages on later ones (Jensen & Fraser, 2011).

Some argue that what are viewed as developmental changes in fact reflect changing environments. Variables such as age and social class are "marker variables" that correlate with many problems but do not explain them or provide service guidelines (Baer, 1984, 1987). The similarities of circumstances for many people at a given age in a society may lead one to assume (incorrectly) that biological development is responsible, overlooking the role of similar contingencies. In a contextual perspective, it is assumed that people confront different tasks in different environments at different times and may respond to similar situations in different ways. For example, although some women experience the "empty nest syndrome" when their grown children leave home, many do not. Acceptance of a stage theory of development may get in the way of identifying environmental factors that can be prearranged. That is, it may be incorrectly assumed that a person "is stuck" in a given stage and there is nothing to do but wait for time to pass. Some scholars suggest that acceptance of Piagetian stages resulted in withholding valuable learning experiences from children, on the grounds that they were "not ready."

Cognitive Explanations

In cognitive explanations, a causal role is attributed to thoughts. There is an interest in identifying and altering mental events such as expectations, schemas (views of the self and world), and attributions. There is no doubt that people differ in what they say to themselves and that certain kinds of thoughts are correlated with certain kinds of overt behaviors. For example, people who are effective in social situations attend to different social cues and say different things to themselves during social exchanges than do people who are not as effective. Depressed compared to nondepressed college students attribute negative outcomes to personal, unchangeable, global causes and positive outcomes to environmental, changeable, specific causes. Seligman (1975) suggests that people who are depressed have developed a learned helplessness and so make little or no effort to gain valued outcomes (see also Peterson, Maier, & Seligman, 1993). Cognitive accounts differ in their answers to (and interest in) the question, "Where do thoughts come from?" Other questions are: Do thoughts function in a causal role? Are they responsible for behaviors and feelings? Do they serve a mediating role in which they function as parts of "chains of behavior" with thoughts being one kind of behavior? For example, you may think about an upcoming exam, feel anxious, and then study. Do thoughts serve both functions?

Behavioral Explanations

In behavioral views, actions, thoughts, and feelings are considered to be largely a function of our learning history. Varied social histories result in a wide range of behavior. Biochemical and genetic influences are assumed to play a role; however, their interaction with learning variables is emphasized. In addition, different species have their own "biological boundaries" on learning. Behavior that may seem bizarre typically serves adaptive functions (often at high cost), but only when contingencies of reinforcement (relationships between behaviors and their consequences) are clarified may they become apparent. In this way, behavior always "makes sense." (See, for example, behavior analysis of hallucinations in Layng and Andronis, 1984.) An emphasis on the role of learning experiences in developing and maintaining behavior decreases the likelihood of imposing negative labels on clients. Different behavioral views (e.g., cognitive-behavioral/radical behavioral) reflect different assumptions about the causes of behavior and what intervention

EXHIBIT 6.7

Developmental Model of Child Antisocial Behavior

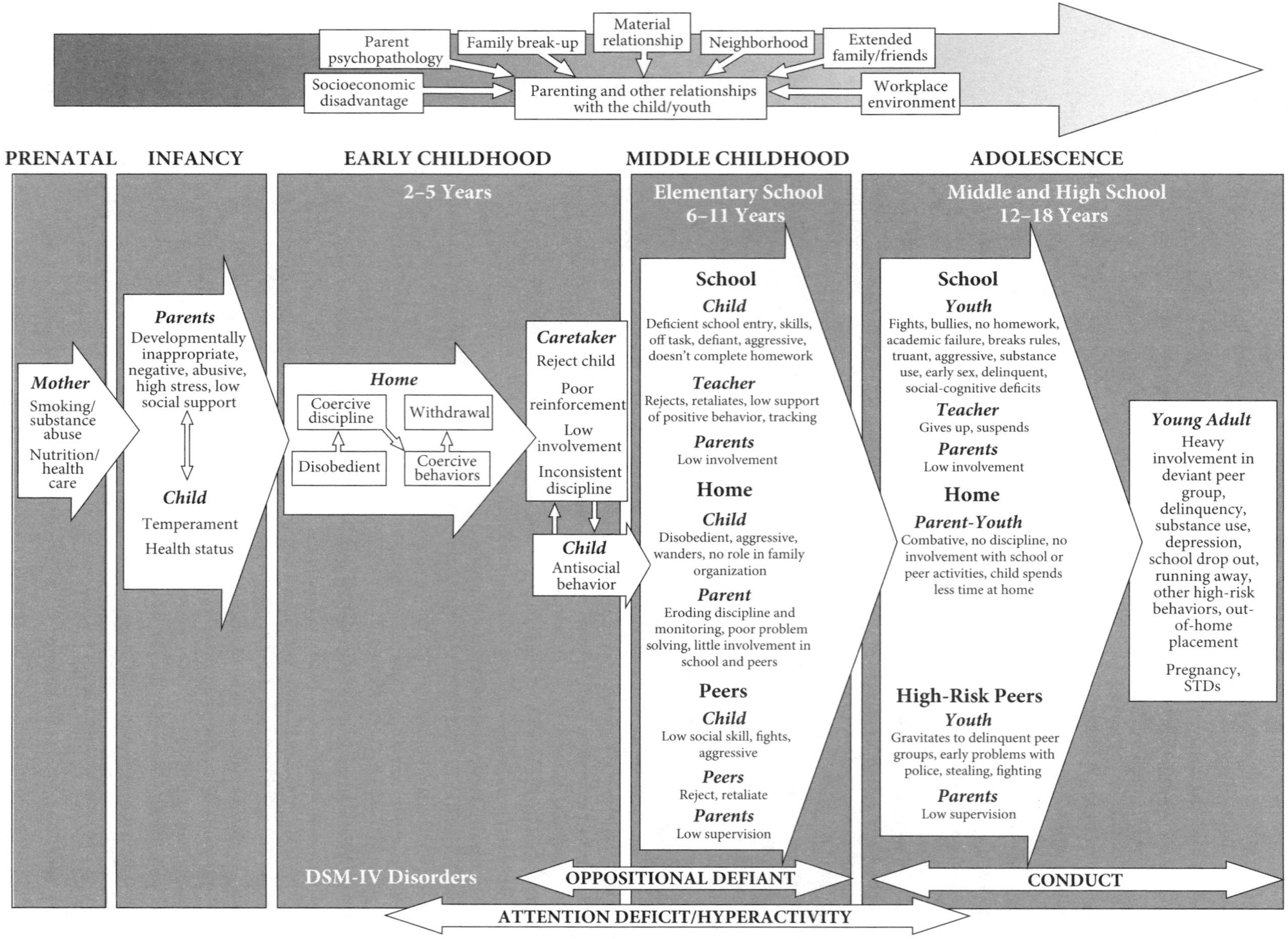

Source: J. B. Reid & J. M. Eddy (1997). The prevention of antisocial behavior: Some considerations in the search for effective interventions. In D. M. Stoff, J. Breiling, & J. D. Maser (Eds.), *Handbook of antisocial behavior* (p. 346). New York: Wiley. Reprinted with permission.

should focus on (e.g., thoughts and/or environmental factors) and also different preferred methodologies (the intensive study of individuals or the study of group differences).

Applied Behavior Analysis

Behavior analysis involves the systematic investigation of variables that influence behavior. Applied behavior analysis involves the application of findings from the experimental analysis of behavior to concerns of social importance (Baer, Wolf, & Risley, 1968, 1987). It is assumed that most behaviors are learned through interaction with the environment, that behavior is selected by its consequences. Research has repeatedly illustrated that it is possible to have reliable influence over behavior by systematically varying associated antecedents and consequences. It is this research that yielded the principles of behavior described in chapter 7. Applied behavior analysts have taken a leading role in developing and evaluating programs of benefit to a wide range of clients, including students at all levels of education, people with developmental disabilities, people with chronic pain, the unemployed, the elderly, parents, and children.

As used here, the term *applied* refers to the extent to which a behavior is socially important. *Behavior* refers to what people do. Behavior—and the translation of problems into behaviors that if changed would resolve them—is of central interest (see Exhibit 6.8). *Analytic* requires "a believable demonstration of the events that can be responsible for the occurrence or non-occurrence of that behavior" (Baer, Wolf, & Risley, 1968, p. 94). "The analytic challenges for anyone who deserves to be called an 'applied behavior analyst' are (1) to restate the complained-of problem in behavioral terms; (2) to change the behaviors indicated by that restatement; and then (3) to see whether changing them has decreased the complaining response" (Baer, 1982, p. 284). The analysis of behavior has been achieved when you can influence it in predicted ways.

The effects of altering a given variable are tracked on an ongoing basis. It is assumed to be just as important to carefully measure behavior in real-life settings such as classrooms, organizations, and groups as it is in laboratory settings. The social validity of outcomes is emphasized; that is, services must improve the behavior focused on in a *socially significant way*. Significant others such as teachers, parents, or residential staff are included in assessing the value of service. Another characteristic of this framework is a concern with generalization. Are positive outcomes maintained? Do they occur in other environments or involve other behaviors? The hallmarks of applied behavior analysis offer important safeguards for clients: goals focused on must be of direct concern to clients, and success must be measured in terms of real-life gains.

Radical Behaviorism

There are different kinds of behaviorism which are often confused. Radical behaviorism is the philosophy related to applied

---

EXHIBIT 6.8

Loneliness in a Retirement Home

Behavioral questioning revealed that one of the indicators of complaints of loneliness was receiving few letters (Goldstein & Baer, 1976). The next question was, "What behaviors of whom were responsible for that low rate?" (Baer, 1982, p. 285). An examination of letters written by residents revealed that residents who complained of receiving few letters were punishing letter writing (e.g., they reproached their correspondents for not writing). The residents were prompted to write nonreproachful letters to relatives or old friends who rarely or never wrote to them. A nonreproachful letter including at least one question requiring an answer was modeled, and the next several letters written by the elderly residents were read and the content commented on before they were mailed. Within a very few tries, residents wrote nonreproachful, nonaccusatory letters. They now wrote about their daily lives, happenings of interest, and memories of past experiences with their correspondents. The residents were coached to include self-addressed, stamped envelopes in their letters, with comments explaining that they wanted to make replying easy. These changes in letter writing were made in a multiple baseline design, across three residents. "In perfect response to the staggered timing of that design, the three complainers began to receive prompt replies to their letters, almost tripling their average rate of receiving letters. Furthermore, they began to receive letters from new correspondents. This led them to begin writing to yet other potential correspondents and to receive prompt answers, accomplishing still higher rates of letters received—and letters to answer. All this activity filled time in otherwise often empty days. That behavior change and its snowballing effects were accompanied by a thorough absence of complaints about loneliness" (Baer, 1982, p. 286).

---

behavior analysis, as well as a theoretical account of behavior. It "is the attempt to account for behavior solely in terms of natural contingencies—either contingencies of survival, contingencies of reinforcement, or contingencies of social evolution" (Day, 1983, p. 101). Culture is viewed "as the contingencies of social reinforcement maintained by a group" (Skinner, 1987, p. 74). Pursuit of a "science of behavior" is a basic goal. It is not claimed that a radical behavioral perspective is the only scientific psychology; it is contended that a scientific approach is most likely to yield knowledge about behavior and how it can be altered in comparison with other approaches. Radical behaviorism is perhaps more misunderstood and misrepresented and attracts more objections than any other perspective in psychology (Thyer, 2005; Todd & Morris, 1983). One objection is that it ignores the meaning of events. In fact, attention is devoted to discovering the unique meanings of events (their functions) through exploration of the relationships between behavior and related cues and consequences. Misunderstandings result in ignoring this framework, which has been applied to help a wide range of clients attain outcomes they value such as participating more effectively on community board meetings, obtaining employment, and maintaining independent living arrangements.

The term *radical behaviorism* is so named because it represents a sharp break with earlier forms such as John Watson's methodological behaviorism. Not only are private events such as thoughts and feelings not dismissed, they are viewed as behaviors that themselves require an explanation (traced to their environmental, evolutionary, and/or physiological origins). Private events (such as thoughts and feelings) are believed to operate as elements in chains that begin with observable environmental events and end with observable responses (Baer, 1982, p. 278). Both thoughts and feelings may play a mediating role in chains of behavior.

Behaviorists argue that environmental contingencies associated with feelings, expectations, moods, or "states of mind" often remain unknown in cognitive accounts of behavior. To understand thoughts and feelings, we would have to explore past and present environmental histories. Feelings can be used as clues to contingencies (relationships between behavior and environmental events). For example, keeping a daily log of what happens before and after feelings of anger may reveal related punishing contingencies (e.g., criticism by a supervisor). Our experiences with others result in different feelings about them. We like people who offer us positive consequences, such as praise and respect, and dislike those who offer us negative consequences, such as insults and ridicule. Family members' emotions and attitudes about one another indicate who is being punished and reinforced and who is doing the punishment and reinforcement. The advantage of viewing thoughts and feelings as behaviors is that they cannot as readily be inaccurately presumed to be the causes of behavior. They themselves are behaviors in need of explanation.

Social Learning Theory (SLT)

Social learning theory underlies cognitive behavioral methods (Bandura, 1986). Thyer and Wodarski (1990) suggest this as a comprehensive conceptual framework for social work education. As in radical behaviorism, a reciprocal interaction is assumed between people and their environments (i.e., we both influence and are influenced by our environment). SLT accepts cognitive explanations in contrast to applied behavior analysis and behavioral approaches emphasizing learning histories as explanatory. It is assumed that we present an important part of our environment through our expectations, goals, and standards. Thoughts are considered to play an important role in the complex processes that affect attention and in the degree to which different kinds of interventions are effective. Observational learning is given a key role. This refers to acquiring new behavior by observing modeled behavior. Bandura argues that cognitive mediation is required for the delayed performance of observed behavior. Group experiments are typical in SLT in contrast to intensive study of single cases. Both applied behavior analysis and cognitive-behavioral approaches emphasize careful evaluation of results, relying on observable outcomes. If this focus were lost, efforts would fall outside what would be considered a behavioral perspective.

Racial, Ethnic, Gender, and Class Theories of Social Problems and Relations

Gender, class, culture, and race influence how certain behaviors and the rights to engage in them are viewed. In the *Mismeasure of Women*, Carol Tavris (1992) suggests that labels such as *dependent personality disorder*, which are most often given to women, punish women for fulfilling expected roles. She contends that we should examine the conditions in society that result in so many women showing these characteristics such as expected gender roles and unequal educational and job opportunities and alter them. Women often accept a psychiatric view of problems and related labels that obscure environmental causes and related options. Indeed, women are the primary consumers of psychotropic medication and are labeled more often than are men (Herzberg, 2009).

In a racial theory, socioeconomic conditions are viewed as racial and as requiring racial explanations. Racial differences are often appealed to as key in understanding social relations in the United States, including inequalities in health care. Discrimination and oppression based on skin color is a past and present reality. White middle- and upper-class people can buy prescribed medications to alter their moods; use of street drugs by poor African American youth results in arrest and imprisonment (Alexander, 2010; Herzberg, 2009). White middle-class people have access to high quality educational opportunities. African Americans living in ghettos may refuse a life of "slave labor" (low paid jobs with no future) and pursue illegal routes to obtain money such as selling drugs (Wacquant, 2009).

Problems are viewed as ethnic, not racial, in an ethnic theory of social relations. It is assumed that solutions must address cultural stereotyping and ethnocentrism. A class analysis of social relations categorizes people according to their economic characteristics. Policies, behavior, and problems are viewed as shaped by economic interests. Both in the past and present, medicine attends more to diseases of the rich than of the poor. A number of physical illnesses, such as heart disease and the incidence of cancer, are higher in low-education and low-income groups (see CDC Health Disparities and Inequalities Report—United States, 2011, and Wilkinson & Pickett, 2010). Economic inequality has increased in the United States; the gap in income between the poor and the rich has vastly increased (see chapter 1). Sen (2009) argues that use of income alone to measure poverty reflects conceptual conservatism because it ignores disabilities and the extra economic burden they place on individuals and families.

Are race, ethnicity, and class sound classifications? Are there greater differences among different races, ethnic groups, and classes than within them? Is there some essence that all members of a group share? There has been a great genetic intermingling among peoples of different ethnicities and races. Attempts to categorize people into different races based on clear differences have repeatedly failed (no clear dividing lines emerged). Gender is a complex classification with many overlaps at different levels of analysis (biological, social, and psychological) (see Spade & Valentine, 2011). Do racial, ethnic, or class theories provide a satisfactory explanation of social relations? Does race or ethnicity imply a certain cultural experience? We speak of black and white cultures as if they existed. But aren't there thousands of different "African American experiences"? What is an ethnic group? Aren't there many different Chinese American groups? Is there an equation of culture and ethnicity (or culture and race)? Don't we overlook individual differences by classifying diverse experiences on the basis of one characteristic? Sociologists and biologists agree that no basis can be found for racial classification: "anatomical criteria such as skin color, facial form and hair type cannot be decisive as means of demarcating racial types, for there are different gradations of each of these characteristics" (Webster, 1992, p. 47; see also Katz, 1995). The populations of India, Pakistan, and Indonesia do not fit the threefold classification of Caucasoid, Mongoloid, and Negroid. The number of races suggested varies from 3 to 113. Races identified are phenotypically distinct within one set of criteria, but not in another. They are often genetically indistinguishable. The DNA of most individuals in the United States reflects a mix of heritage.

Yehudi Webster views racial classification as part of a racial theory of social relations in which persons are racially classified and their biological and moral attributes are viewed as explanations of their behavior and historical developments. He argues that racial and ethnic descriptions focus on selected anatomical and cultural differences for moral-political purposes (1992). By assigning themselves to a race by virtue of their skin color, some humans initiated the racialization of themselves and others. Racial classification was initiated as a justification for certain political and economic decisions and arrangements. He argues that the view that certain physical differences imply a racial identity is propagated by social scientists, governmental institutions, and the media. He contends that social scientists generally justify use of terms such as *race, ethnicity*, and *class* with reference to a reality that is itself a product of the dissemination of racial, ethnic, and class theory. Once persons are racially classified, there is no escaping the implications of racial motives (e.g., racism). Webster views racial classification itself as racism. (He notes that *racism* refers to many things, including "a belief system or ideology, discriminatory policies and behavior, theories of genetic inferiority, and socioeconomic inequality," 1992, p. 241.)

Webster argues that racial and ethnic descriptions of events are "forms of propaganda, an indoctrination into a conviction that U.S. society has different racial and ethnic groups that are locked in a relationship of domination/oppression" (1992, p. 13). He suggests that the continued daily use of racial categories racialize our experiences. Indeed, the government, social scientists, and the media daily saturate us with the alleged validity of

categories based on race, ethnicity, and class, which he considers bogus categories that do more harm than good (i.e., they underplay our shared humanness and, in so doing, make it easier for us to dehumanize others). Some of our most inspiring leaders, such as Martin Luther King, Jr., also emphasized our shared humanness.

A Contextual View

A contextual view highlights the interaction between people and their environments. It directs attention to *both* personal and environmental characteristics and emphasizes the mutual influence of people and their environments. It emphasizes that the environment differs for each person and that people are doing the best they can given their environments and problem-solving skills. The terms *contextual* and *ecological* are used interchangeably here. Ecological models are contextual and historical. Our environments can be viewed as multiple interlinked ecological levels, each of which holds certain risks and provides certain opportunities (see Exhibit 6.9). The competencies and values we develop and the environments we create for ourselves are related to these risks and opportunities, as well as by what we bring to them and how others respond. Different levels (e.g., family, community) have unique characteristics and may influence other levels. Consider youth who are "turned off" to learning because of punishing educational experiences and the potential consequences of this. Warmth of parents affects stress that develops in infants and young children which in turn affects the immune system (Lester et al., 2011). Policies regarding immigration such as access to educational opportunities and health care affect those who travel to new countries.

As emphasized throughout this book the personal and the social are interlinked. Consider child maltreatment (see Exhibit 6.10). Why is it that so many adolescent suicides involve gay or lesbian youth? Could homophobia (irrational hatred or fear of gay and lesbian people) and resulting discrimination be a contributing cause? Societal tolerance of violence, as well as accepted gender roles, contributes to the battering of women. Overlooking these important influences yields an incomplete view of the causes of behaviors. Women often accept society's framing of their problems (e.g., they are depressed; they are anxious) in ways that obscure related social, political, and economic policies including those that create gender disparities in income. For example, a woman may inaccurately view her low-paid job as a result of her deficiencies (e.g., low self-esteem). Natural biological changes such as menopause are viewed as needing the help of experts to negotiate. The influence of culture is often overlooked, such as different reactions to menopause (Lock, 1993, 1998). U'ren (1997) suggests that

> Capitalist society has brought into existence a class of experts trained to deal with the negative consequences of the very

EXHIBIT 6.9

The Ecology of Sociocultural Risk and Opportunity

Ecological Level	Definition	Examples	Factors Affecting Children
Microsystem	Situations in which the child has face-to-face contact with influential others.	Family, school, peer group, church.	Is the child regarded positively? Is the child accepted? Is the child reinforced for competent behavior? Is the child exposed to a diversity in roles and relationships? Is the child given an active role in reciprocal relationships?
Mesosystem	Relationships between microsystems.	Home/school, home/church, school/neighborhood.	Do people in different settings respect each other? Do settings present a consistency in values?
Exosystem	Settings in which the child does not participate but in which significant decisions are made affecting the child or adults who do interact directly with the child.	Parents' place of employment, school board, local government, parents' peer group.	Are decisions made with the interests of the parent and children in mind? How well do supports for families balance stresses for parents?
Macrosystem	"Blueprints" for organizing the institutional life of society.	Ideology, social policy, shared assumptions about human nature, the "social contract."	Are some groups valued at the expenses of others (e.g., sexism, racism)? Balance of individualistic and collectivist orientation? Is violence a norm?

Source: J. Garbarino (1992). Adapted from *Children and families in the social environment* (2nd Ed.) (p. 30). New York: Aldine de Gruyter. Reprinted with permission.

conditions that, historically, capitalism itself has helped bring about: disruption of local community life and emotional bonds, depersonalization of work, the anomie of urban life. Psychiatry and psychotherapy represent modes of treatment that have evolved not only to provide relief of symptoms, but also to bring comfort, encouragement, and personal attention to lonely and demoralized individuals in a society where close personal relationships and community are often absent. Like all goods and services, care is distributed unevenly in a capitalist society depending upon ability to pay. The upper strata, at least until recently, have received therapy that is oriented toward insight and understanding, while those in the lower socio-economic strata get hospitalization, briefer more directive psychotherapy, and tranquillising medications. (Garfield, 1994), retrieved November 24, 2011, from http://www.academyanalyticarts.org)

He argues that "to the extent that psychiatry isolates the individual and leaves untouched real social problems and conflicts,

its role is one of obfuscation" (p. 8). Personal problems become "commodified" and subject to corporate control in for-profit companies such as Aetna, United Health, and Prudential. (See also U'ren, 2011.)

The Advantages of a Contextual Model

A contextual view highlights the influences clients have (and could have) over their environments. It emphasizes the importance of attending to each client's unique characteristics and circumstances including available repertoires that can be used to gain hoped-for outcomes. It emphasizes the multiple identities we each have. A contextual perspective highlights the importance of taking advantage of opportunities for growth such as transitions as well as preventative efforts to avoid or mute risk factors that limit opportunities. For example, building on and enhancing social problem-solving skills may prevent adverse events associated with transitions such as marriage, birth of a child, or retirement. It draws attention to limitations of commonly accepted

EXHIBIT 6.10

Risk, Protective, and Promotive Factors for Juvenile Delinquency

Level	Risk Factors	Protective/Promotion Factors
Individual: Biological and Genetic	Gender (male) Absence of MAOA gene Neuropsychological defects Cognitive defects—low IQ Difficult temperament Hyperactivity/ADHD Perinatal trauma Neurotoxins Maternal AOD* use in pregnancy	Gender (female) High IQ Easy temperament
Individual: Psychological and Behavioral	Aggression Beliefs favorable to deviance Alienation Rebelliousness Impulsiveness Risk taking	Assertiveness Pro-social beliefs Social problem-solving skills Self-efficacy Self-esteem Internal locus of control
Family	Family management problems Family conflict Lack of parental involvement Low level of parental education Child maltreatment Family history of crime Parental antisocial personality Parental psychopathology Parental attitudes favoring deviance Parent-child separation Divorce Large family size	Positive discipline techniques Supportive relationships Monitoring & supervision Parent w/HS education or more Good communication Family advocacy Achievement orientation Strong spiritual values Racial pride Extended family bonds Fewer siblings
Other Adults		Presence of caring adult
Peers	Antisocial peers Delinquent siblings Gang membership	Pro-social peer group
School	Early academic failure Low school commitment Aggressive behavior in school Poor quality schools Truancy Frequent school transitions	Academic success Positive bonding to school High quality schools
Neighborhood	High population density High population mobility Physical deterioration High crime rates Availability of drugs/weapons Lack of social cohesion Low resident attachment	Collective efficacy Nondisadvantaged neighborhood Low neighborhood crime

(continued)

EXHIBIT 6.10 (Continued)

Level	Risk Factors	Protective/Promotion Factors
Social/ Community	Antisocial community norms/laws	Pro-social community norms/ laws
	Expose to violence Racial prejudice and Discrimination	Support
	Few education/employment opportunities	Employment
	Poverty	Many education/employment opportunities
		Boundaries and expectations
		Constructive use of time
		Regular church involvement

Source: J. M. Jenson and M. R. Fraser (2006). *Social policy for children & families: A risk and resilience perspective* (pp. 240–241). Thousand Oaks, CA: Sage. Reprinted with permission.
Note: AOD = alcohol or drug use.

metaphors such as "adaptation" in emphasizing the importance of understanding a person's multiple environments and what options they provide. It reminds us that change on one level can be used to create opportunities on another. For example, gaining and maintaining paid employment for clients with developmental disabilities may require enhancing their social and vocational skills as well as persuading employers to offer them jobs.

If it is not possible to work on one level, it may be possible to work on another. If teachers refuse to participate in programs to help their students, peers may be involved or students "empowered" by enhancing their social influence skills. In his work with runaway youths, Jack Rothman (1991) notes that in 48% of the cases, options other than working with parents must be found. Efforts to attain needed resources from agencies through cooperative means may fail, whereas social action may succeed. Appreciation of the connections between the personal and the political will help you to avoid focusing on psychological or biological characteristics of individuals and overlooking environmental influences. A feminist perspective has been valuable in pointing out macrolevel influences on women's risks and opportunities (see Tavris, 1992). Without a contextual understanding of client concerns, including those created by professionals themselves (e.g., giving clients psychiatric labels that limit rather than broaden their options), you will lose opportunities to help clients. The preamble of the NASW Code of Ethics states, "Fundamental to social work is attention to the environmental forces that create, contribute to, and address problems in living" (2008).

A contextual framework encourages us to keep in mind that what are defined as social problems may disguise social conflicts among values and competing efforts to control resources. For example, what is viewed as a "racial problem" may reflect disagreements about opportunities open to African Americans. Overlooking macrolevel influences may result in overestimating what can be accomplished at the individual and family levels. On the other hand, considering only organizational, community, and societal influences may result in not recognizing the

contribution of individual characteristics to problems, such as a lack of social support and effective problem-solving skills. A contextual approach encourages us to consider the origin of our values and goals—to examine the context in which we develop our values rather than to accept them as given. Only by viewing possible solutions in both a historical and a contextual perspective are we likely to discover variables that influence opportunities for preventing and resolving them. Exhibit 6.11 provides an opportunity to review a client concern that interests you.

A historical view will avoid mistaken beliefs that result from "cohort centrism" (e.g., assuming that people who live at a given time, age in the same way). *Cohort effects* refer to changes in society at a particular historical time that affect people. *Cohort centrism* is responsible for the mistaken assumption that differences found in cross-sectional studies such as physical health show that age was responsible for them (Riley, 1988). In fact, people in a given cohort may change biologically, psychologically, and socially in quite different ways. Different cohorts influence social change in different ways. (See Exhibit 6.12.)

Why Isn't a Contextual View Used More Often?

There are many reasons why a contextual view may not be used. It may not be possible to implement plans based on this view or even to gather the information required to identify, document, expose, and advocate for changes in oppressive conditions due to censorship for example. A contextual view is inherently political. It emphasizes the role of value judgments and conflicting interests in the very definition of personal and social problems. It emphasizes the importance of understanding contingencies and the power relationships they represent. The light shed may be far too bright for those profiting by deceiving others. Consider efforts to block access of photographers to toxic dump sites and factories and farms raising live animals (Silver, 2011). Some approximation may have to be used. Social workers and clients are often disempowered; they do not have the resources needed to attain

EXHIBIT 6.11

Thinking About a Social Problem

Select a problem such as depression, homelessness, elder abuse, or poverty, and answer the following questions:

1. Exactly what is the problem? Clearly describe related behaviors (e.g., their form and frequency) and/or other indicators (e.g., income below a certain level, lack of low-cost housing). Have accepted indicators changed over time?

   What is known about the prevalence of related circumstances and/or behavior?

   What is known about their variability (e.g., do they differ in different groups, times, or settings)?

   Do people agree on whether the selected indicators reflect a problem? If not, what are key differences?

2. What causes were commonly accepted in the past for this problem?

3. What causes are now proposed (e.g., genetic differences, moral lapses, discrimination/oppression) in professional and lay sources (e.g., mass media)? What is known about correlated factors?

4. What are the consequences of each view? Who loses and gains from each account?

5. What guesses about causes have been critically tested? Which one(s), in what way(s), and what are the findings?

6. What point of view do you think is most useful in understanding this problem? On what criteria do you base your choice?

7. Can your preferred view account for related empirical findings?

8. Do vested interests and/or discrimination influence how the problem is defined and proposed remedies? If so, how? Do they influence the definition of related behaviors or circumstances as a problem rather than as an asset or a basic constitutional right? Are political or personal agendas confounded with scientific ones? If so, in what ways? Give examples.

EXHIBIT 6.12

Relating Individual Problems to Social Issues

A. Presenting problem: a family's homelessness
B. Related structural factors
   1. Economic: _____

      _____

      _____

   2. Social/cultural/values/norms: _____

      _____

      _____

   3. Political: _____

      _____

      _____

   4. Cohort effects: _____

      _____

      _____

   5. Service system: _____

      _____

      _____

valued goals. Chronic lack of resources may create a helplessness and hopelessness, a giving up on working together with clients to increase resources at whatever system level is needed. A contextual assessment may reveal a need to work at the community, service system, and policy and legislative levels. Not only may this require greater resources compared to working with individuals and families, it may threaten vested interests and create opposition. Consider the negative reactions of legislators and politicians to presenting data to elected officials concerning a bill on child passenger safety and the provision of subsidized "lifeline" utility rates for low-income families (Fawcett, 1991).

Contextual preventive efforts can be expensive, and so public officials may ignore or suppress information reflecting the role of social, economic, and political factors in creating and maintaining avoidable suffering. It is easier to focus on dysfunctions of individuals than to consider the big picture and corporations can make a tidy profit in the process (e.g., see U'ren, 1997). Conflicting interests may result in foot-dragging, even with successful programs. Neither line nor supervisory staff may have required knowledge, skills, or time to address problems clients have. They may not know how to think and act contextually, that is, to connect the personal and the political. They may prefer working with individuals and families on a psychological or family level. Chronic gaps between needs and resources may result in burn out. Psychological and psychiatric views dominate the media, making contextual models less available. Questioning accepted values and practices takes time

and effort, as well as courage and an interest in thinking things out for yourself. It requires digging beneath the surface of fine-sounding words and asking: What is actually done? Does this practice or policy work? Who benefits from a view? Who loses? Do the rich pay their share of taxes? Do corporations pay their share? (See Exhibit 6.13.) A contextual approach highlights both our opportunities and responsibilities for creating the environments in which we live. Taking responsibility can be a burden. This is suggested by the many ways in which we try to escape from freedom (Fromm, 1963), for example, through being constantly busy. There are many ways to step out (Kozol, 1990). You will have to balance caring with a realistic appraisal of what you can do and create support networks of like-minded social workers and other interested parties.

Thinking Critically About Theories

Theories are guesses about what may be true. You will come across many theories in the course of your career. There are competing views of how to evaluate their accuracy as discussed in chapter 4. Karl Popper, considered by many thoughtful people to be the greatest twentieth-century philosopher, suggests criteria for selecting theories that are especially pertinent to professions dedicated to helping people. One is a theory's *potential refutability*: Can you determine whether it is false? Is it testable?

EXHIBIT 6.13

Senator Bernie Sanders' Guide to Corporate Freeloaders

1. Exxon Mobil's 2009 profits totaled $19 billion yet according to is SEC filings, the company received a $156 million rebate from the IRS. Plus, it did not pay any federal taxes.

2. Bank of America made $4.4 billion in profits last year. This was after it received a $1 trillion bailout from the Federal Reserve and the Treasury Department and a $1.9 billion tax refund from the IRS.

3. General Electric has made $26 billion in profits in the United States over the past five years. It has also received a $4.1 billion tax refund from the IRS. GE has cut a fifth of its American jobs in the past nine years and is boosting jobs overseas—where tax rates are lower. And where it can continue evading U.S. taxes.

4. Chevon's IRS refund last year totaled $19 million, but its 2009 profits came to a whopping $10 billion.

5. Boeing received a $30 billion contract from the Pentagon to build 179 airborne tankers. It also received a $124 million refund from the IRS.

6. Valero Energy made $68 billion in sales and received a $157 million tax refund check form the IRS. Over the past three years, it has received $134 million in tax break thanks to the oil and gas manufacturing tax reduction.

7. Goldman Sachs paid 1.1% of its 2008 income in taxes. Yet it made a profit of $2.3 billion. And guess how much it received from the Federal Reserve and U.S. Treasury Department? $800 billion.

8. Citigroup profits last year totaled more than $4 billion. But it paid zero dollars in federal income tax, and received a $2.5 trillion bailout from the Federal Reserve and U.S. Treasury.

9. ConocoPhillips profits from 2007 through 2009 totaled $16 billion, but it was still awarded $451 million in tax breaks because of the oil and gas manufacturing reduction.

10. Carnival Cruise Lines is apparently getting pretty good business. Its profits over the past 5 years totaled more than $11 billion. Its federal income tax rate however, came to just 1.1%. Reprinted with permission.

Is it falsifiable? Popper argues that we can only eliminate false beliefs in our search for knowledge (see chapter 4). A second criterion is whether a theory has *survived rigorous tests* and the variety of tests it has survived (its *scope*). Theories that are broad in scope yield many testable hypotheses and can be applied successfully to a range of problems. New theories should account for all previous findings and more (Popper, 1994). In this sense, progress is both conservative (a new theory must account for prior findings) and revolutionary (it replaces earlier theories). Although selection of a theory can be justified by having survived more risky tests concerning a wider variety of hypotheses than other theories, it can never accurately be claimed to be "the truth." All knowledge is conjectural. Another theory, broader in scope, may override earlier ones.

Theories should be *logically consistent*. That is, they should not contain contradictory predictions, for if they do, they cannot be tested. *Parsimony* (simplicity) is another valuable characteristic of a theory. The rule of parsimony calls for choosing the simplest explanation, which is useful in avoiding unnecessary concepts that can be misleading. *Applicability* is especially important in professions. From an ethical and practical point of view, the bottom line is whether theories (guesses about what may be true) are useful in helping clients attain valued outcomes. Are they helpful in clarifying problems, identifying related factors, and selecting effective services?

Avoiding the Prisons of Theories

We often think within a belief system or framework, rather than about it. We may assume that a feminist, behavioral, or multicultural framework is best. This is quite different from proposing a theory or hypothesis about what may be true or false and then critically evaluating our guesses (e.g., searching for well-argued alternative views). If we do not critically evaluate our theories (assumptions), they function as prisons that limit our vision rather than as tools to discover what is false (Popper, 1994). Keep in mind that most theories about what is true are wrong (see, for example, any history of science or medicine). As Socrates said, "I know that I know almost nothing, and hardly this." A theory believed too soon stifles further inquiry. Those who are opposed to what Popper calls the myth of the framework "will welcome a discussion with a partner who comes from another world, from another framework for it gives them an opportunity to discover their so far unfelt chains, to break these chains, and thus to transcend themselves" (1994, p. 53).

of translation skills contribute to helping clients. Social workers often work in interdisciplinary teams requiring understanding of different views. This may require translating concepts from one discipline or profession into those of another or combining them in a way that yields a more comprehensive view. A psychologist may approach a problem of homelessness from a different point of view than may an economist, biologist, anthropologist, or sociologist. Each discipline has a domain of knowledge that overlaps with other domains to different degrees. Translation is required even among those who speak the same language. What does a client mean when she says, "My neighbors are driving me crazy"? Does her meaning of "crazy" match yours? Recognizing the need for translation is a vital first step. As Alfred Kadushin noted, the "assumption of ignorance" increases the likelihood that you hear and understand what others say.

Different Levels of Abstraction

We can discuss problems and related behaviors and causes at different levels of abstraction, ranging from the concrete (e.g., "He does not follow his teacher's instructions") to the abstract (e.g., "He is hyperactive"). It is important to distinguish among three kinds of statements in thinking about problems: (1) factual (did a father assault his child?), (2) conceptual (why did he do it?), and (3) evaluative (was it right or wrong?). Questions of fact (what is) and explanation (why it is) differ from those of values (what should be) and definitions (meaning questions) (e.g., see Baker et al., 1993). As we move from facts to theories, we become more removed from concrete data. What is useful depends on our purpose. If we think we know what "the facts are" but do not (because we are being too vague about events of interest), we may make faulty decisions. We may confuse descriptions (what occurs) and inferences (guesses about why it occurs).

If you want to clearly describe what people do, a concrete level is needed. Let us say that you believe that your supervisor does not speak to you in a "respectful manner." What is a "respectful manner"? What does your supervisor do or not do (and when and where) that relates to respect? This example illustrates the key role of classification in thinking about behavior. You must decide what behaviors to include in the category "disrespectful." Considering different levels of abstraction will help you distinguish between theoretical concepts and how they are measured. Consider anxiety. This complex concept is a key one in some theories of behavior. What is anxiety? How should (or can) this be measured? Do measures used accurately represent the theoretical concepts? Are measures used meaningful to clients?

The Value of Translation and Integration Skills

We often associate the word *translation* with translating words and sentences in one language into those of another. Other kinds

Summary

Professionals are integrally involved in problem framing. They, in turn, are influenced by popular problem definitions in society. They may not be aware of how their views of problems are shaped by their culture. The helping professions have been influenced by different views of behavior to different degrees, including medical, sociological, and psychological perspectives. Views differ in their attention to political, economic, and social influences, which create and/or contribute to personal and social problems. Theories differ in their attention to environmental factors such as poor quality educational opportunities. Many focus on interiors (thoughts, feelings) neglecting environmental contributors. The success of a biomedical approach to problems can be seen in the very words we use: therapy, diagnosis, pathology, prognosis, and treatment. Sociological perspectives involve the study of political, economic, and social factors as they influence problem construction and related behaviors; sociologists study behavior in the context of the structures that influence it. Anthropological views explore cultural variations among people and contexts in different settings worldwide.

The context in which problems are defined and services are created influences what problems are addressed and how. Behaviors once viewed as sins were later viewed as crimes and are now viewed as symptoms of mental illness. It is easy to lose sight of the consensual nature of what is defined as a problem. It is easy to take "what is" as the way they should be or inevitably are. Controversies related to problem definition include what is viewed as a problem, what its related causes are, and what remedies are proposed. People have different beliefs about the causes of problems and how they can be resolved and prevented. Biological, psychological, and sociological accounts (or some mix thereof) may be drawn on. Different points of view entail different ways of approaching problems. In professions, perspectives that offer leverage in helping clients are of unique interest. The question, "Will this theory help me help my clients?," is a key one.

Reviewing Your Competencies

Reviewing Content Knowledge

1. Describe the role of professionals in defining problems.

2. Identify controversial issues in problem definition.

3. Discuss deviance as variations in behavior that contribute to evolutionary change and adaptation.

4. Describe an interactional-contextual view of deviance.

5. Describe "the medicalization of deviance" and give examples.

6. Identify different system levels that may be focused on to understand problems and discuss how they may affect one another.

7. Give empirically based examples of the relationship between social conditions and psychological distress.

8. Describe sound criteria for evaluating the usefulness of a theory (a guess about what may be true).

9. Distinguish among facts, concepts, explanations, beliefs, and evaluative statements related to a problem that interests you.

10. Describe and critique racial, ethnic, and class theories of social problems and relations.

Reviewing What You Do

1. You pose questions about problems that forward understanding about them.

2. You can accurately critique different kinds of explanations for behavior.

3. You can accurately describe different views of problems in the professional literature and media, and identify and critique underlying assumptions.

4. You take steps to discourage problem-related language (e.g., negative labels) that obscure uncertainties and value judgments involved in problem definition. For example, rather than saying "She is a schizophrenic" you say "She has been labeled as a schizophrenic."

Reviewing Results

1. You select theories (guesses about what may be true) that are helpful in resolving client complaints.

2. Other staff in your agency raise more questions regarding how problems are defined.

7

Taking Advantage of Research Findings About Behavior and How It Is Influenced by the Environment

OVERVIEW   This chapter introduces you to some of the complex interactions between behavior and its environmental contexts. Understanding these influences will help you (1) identify environmental influences related to outcomes of interest, (2) select appropriate intervention levels (e.g., individual, family, community, organization, state or federal policy and related legislation), (3) recognize incomplete accounts, (4) discover available resources such as positive alternative repertoires for gaining valued consequences, and (5) accurately assess the likelihood that hoped-for valued outcomes can be attained given current circumstances. EPAS (2008) calls on social workers to apply knowledge of human behavior and the social environment (2.1.7).

YOU WILL LEARN ABOUT

- Why a chapter on behavioral principles is included in a book on practice

- Contingencies: their variety and importance

- Reinforcement

- The role of antecedents

- Verbal influences

- Motivation

- Variables that influence operant learning

- Respondent behavior

- Evolutionary influences

Why a Chapter on Behavioral Principles is Included in a Book on Practice

Doesn't a discussion of behavioral principles belong in a book on human behavior and development rather than in a book on social work practice? My answer is that it belongs in both, for four reasons. First is the fundamental attribution error. We tend to overlook environmental causes and attribute behavior to personality characteristics of clients. Environmental influences are often less vivid and thus easy to overlook. This error may result in incomplete accounts that result in incorrectly attributing problems to clients' personal characteristics. Our feelings and thoughts are readily accessible to us and thus easily viewed as causes. It is easy to overlook less vivid but influential environmental circumstances such as oppressive police surveillance of youth. Both individual and cultural differences influence how attention is balanced between environmental and psychological variables (see Nisbett, 2003). Awareness of environmental influences on behavior including public policies and related legislation decrease the likelihood of focusing on "fixing" people and overlooking opportunities to alter oppressive, racist, impoverished contexts. There is a focus on altering dysfunctional environments rather than altering "dysfunctional" clients.

The second reason is that the transfer of knowledge is a key problem (knowledge developed in one situation may not be used in others in which it would be of value). Including this material here may help you to integrate and transfer knowledge about behavior to practice and policy contexts. A third reason is that the principles of behavior described in this chapter are empirically based (i.e., they describe relationships between behavior and environmental events that have been found through systematic exploration). Beliefs about the causes of behavior should be reviewed in light of these findings just as those who construct airplanes must consider empirical findings about gravity. Incorrect beliefs about behavior may result in lost opportunities to help clients because understanding is incomplete or inaccurate. A fourth reason is that this knowledge is usually not covered in courses on human behavior and the social environment.

The subject of applied behavior analysis is behavior in real-life settings and the alteration of behavior in ways valued by clients (Fisher, Piazza, & Roane, 2011; Luyben, 2009; Madden, 2013). (See chapter 6.) It is a contextual approach calling for description of environmental factors that influence behavior at multiple levels. Our behavior is influenced by the environments in which we live, including social institutions that reflect certain values such as child welfare systems, the courts, and schools. A contextual approach (similar to an ecological approach) highlights the reciprocal interactions between our behavior and our environments—it emphasizes opportunities we have to change our environments by changing our behavior. The greater our understanding of client circumstances, the more likely we are to identify what is needed to help them attain valued outcomes and the less likely we are to focus on alleged internal "disorders." We can draw on what has been discovered about the relationships between behavior and the environment to understand options and constraints. This knowledge provides guidelines for gathering information that will help clients attain valued outcomes. It has been successfully applied to help a wide variety of clients, including people with depression, anxiety, and developmental disabilities; the unemployed; community residents who want more influence over their environments; and parents who want to enhance their parenting skills. Without this knowledge, you

and your clients will overlook opportunities to help clients and potentials for change including taking advantage of available repertoires and environmental resources. Without it you may skim the surface missing key environmental influences such as the effects of laws, public policies, and impoverished environments. The International Federation of Social Workers' definition of social work (2000) recognizes the importance of drawing on theories that recognize the role of environmental factors:

> The social work profession promotes social change, problem-solving in human relationships, and the empowerment and liberation of people to enhance well-being. Utilizing theories of human behavior and social systems, social work intervenes at the points where people interact with their environments. Principles of human rights and social justice are fundamental to social work.

Why This Knowledge Is Often Ignored and Misrepresented

Knowledge about contingencies of reinforcement is often ignored and misrepresented, even though it has been used successfully to help clients attain a wide array of valued outcomes (e.g., see Thyer, 2005; Wyatt, 1990). (See also discussion of myths and misconceptions about rearranging contingencies in chapter 25.)

1. The Appeal of the Pathological

Many helping frameworks focus on what is wrong with people such as a biopsychiatric problem framing. This results in a focus on eliminating behaviors rather than constructing repertoires and realizing that clients are doing the best they can, under often adverse circumstances. It results in overlooking valuable client repertoires of use in seeking hoped-for outcomes. A focus on eliminating repertoires (e.g., stopping drug (mis)use, crime, and so) encourages attention to deficiencies of individuals, overlooking environmental factors such as institutional discrimination, classism, and racism creating disparities, for example, in health care and educational opportunities.

2. A Focus on Characteristics of Individuals as Causes of Behavior

The culture of therapy in which we live encourages a focus on interiors, "managing" emotions is of great interest in work environments such as corporations (Illouz, 2008). This culture encourages us to attribute behavior to feelings, as in "He hit her because he was angry." This is an incomplete account. We should go on to ask: "Where do these feelings come from?" If we appeal to personality traits, we should ask: "What are they?" and "What are their origins?" Saying "He hit his wife because he was angry" does not explain why he was angry. Both the behavior (hitting his wife) and the emotion (anger) may be the result of environmental contingencies yet to be described. Perhaps in the past his wife complied with his requests after he hit her; that is, in the past, hitting his wife may have been reinforced. Consider another example. Let us say that a social worker writes in her record, "Mrs. Jones tried to kill herself because she felt lonely and believed that no one cared about her." Why did she feel lonely? What is going on in her life that produced these feelings, thoughts, and the suicide attempt? These accounts stop too soon because they do not identify the contingencies (the relationships between behavior and environmental factors) related to feelings, thoughts, and behavior. Feelings and thoughts are vivid, thus readily available to regard as causes of behavior. Environmental changes are often less vivid, and so are easily overlooked.

3. Those Who Create and Maintain Influential Contingencies Benefit from Obscuring Them

Those who create and maintain contingencies that influence our behavior, such as government policies and the laws to enforce them, often benefit from them. For example, a recent book published by the National Association of Social Workers entitled *Alcohol, Tobacco and Other Drugs: Challenging myths, assessing theories, individualizing, interventions* (Abbott, 2010) does not mention the decriminalization of all drugs including heroin and cocaine in Portugal in 2001. The topic "decriminalization of drug use" appears in the index, but there is no mention on related pages of this successful policy initiated a decade ago. Why? Don't scholars and professional organizations have an obligation to describe alternate policies and practices, especially those that seem successful? Officials may say, "We're doing it for you," when a careful analysis of the contingencies reveals that they are "doing it for themselves" in relation to the main beneficiaries. (See also the discussion of critical thinking as a demystifying process in chapter 5.) Ignorance of political, social, and economic consequences may be bliss for those who create and maintain these consequences but injustice and suffering for those whom they affect.

4. Confusing Feeling Free with Being Free

We often confuse feeling free with being free (Skinner, 1971). Simply because we feel free does not mean that we are not influenced by our environments. Consider a comment from John Kunkel's *Society and Economic Growth*:

> It is evident that the behavioral perspective of development includes political phenomena as important determinants of both the replication and modification of behavior. The explanation of "apathetic peasants," for example, will lead the investigator from the study of the various contingencies that maintain "apathetic" activities through community power structures, officials, and land owners to the operation of regional and national governments. How much more comfortable and inoffensive are the implications of a psychodynamic perspective! Here "apathy" is assumed to be due to some characteristics of the internal state and the investigator is led into the study of personality and child-raising practices.... With the rise of a behavioral perspective, a new series

of often uncomfortable questions arises: "what activities in the population do governmental operations maintain?" "why does the government not shape different behavior patterns?" and "what changes in government operations are required. (1970, p. 277)

Appealing to personality traits of individuals to account for personal and social problems allows the creators of influential contingencies to blame others less powerful (see also chapter 6).

5. Developing a Working Knowledge of Behavioral Principles Takes Time and Effort

Acquiring a working knowledge of the principles of behavior requires careful study. Many social workers choose not to take the time to acquire this knowledge. This can be seen in the many misrepresentations of the behavioral perspective in the professional literature (e.g., see Thyer, 2005). (For accurate descriptions, see Malott, 2007; Martin & Pear, 2010; Michael, 2004; Miltenberger, 2008; Sundel & Sundel, 2005.)

6. Implementing Behavioral Programs Effectively Takes Time and Effort

A behavioral assessment may reveal complex social contingencies that require considerable effort and skill to alter, compared to focusing on altering thoughts and feelings that may take less time but allow limited (if any) change. Consider focusing on altering self-esteem of children in classrooms when change is needed in teachers' curriculum design skills (so children are not under- or overchallenged) and in the teachers' behavior change skills (decreasing attention to undesired behaviors and increasing attention to desired behaviors).

For a review of the literature on self-esteem, see Baumeister, Campbell, Krueger, & Vans (2003).

7. Misunderstandings of Science and Antiscience

Our knowledge of behavioral principles is the result of systematic research over many years. The experimental analysis of behavior reflects a scientific approach to understanding behavior. Guesses about what may be true or false are tested. The prevalence of misunderstandings of science and antiscience is discussed in chapter 4.

8. The Mistaken Belief That Being Guided by Behavioral Principles Allows No Room for Influencing Our Lives

Behavioral principles describe relationships between our behavior and certain environmental circumstances. We can influence our environments by rearranging what happens before and after. Thus, far from decreasing our influence over our environments, a knowledge of behavioral principles offers options for changing them.

9. A Search for Quick Remedies

Problems can seem overwhelming. Consider youth violence, police surveillance that does more harm than good in African American communities and child abuse. It is tempting to search for easy answers rather than do the hard work necessary to understand and alter the multiple interlinked contingencies related to problems.

Contingencies: Their Variety and Importance

Contingencies are relationships between behavior and related cues and consequences. Depending on what happens after our behavior, we are more or less likely to repeat that behavior in similar situations in the future. Depending on what happens after behavior (its consequences), behavior may be established, maintained, decreased, or increased. Decades of research in both applied and laboratory settings show that our behavior is influenced by its consequences (e.g.,Fisher, Piazza, & Roane, 2011). If you reveal an error you have made to your supervisor and she tells you, "You did the right thing to tell me," and works with you to correct it, you may tell her about other errors in the future. On the other hand, if your supervisor severely criticizes you, you may be less likely to reveal errors again. A *contingency* is the complete description of a specific operant. It includes a definition of the range of behaviors that will result in a specific consequence and the situations in which that consequence influences the future probability of the behavior The term *operant* refers to a class of behaviors, all of which have the same effect on the environment (see the Glossary at the end of this chapter). A child may get his mother's attention by yelling, by tugging on her clothes, or by hitting his brother. He may do so only in certain situations—those in which he has been reinforced for such behavior in the past. The concept of the operant highlights the fact that different forms of behavior can have the same function. The components of an operant are influenced by cultural practices.

Contingency analysis can help you discover environmental factors related to oppression and discrimination as well as client concerns. A contingency analysis will often reveal that changes are needed at many different interrelated levels to achieve an outcome. Consider the many parties and influences at many levels involved in successful pressures on the tobacco industry. Anthony Biglan (1995) argues that change efforts were successful (e.g., laws regarding smoking were changed) because the involved parties (1) shared a common verbal analysis about the effects of smoking and its causes, (2) held overlapping memberships in organizations, (3) held joint meetings, and (4) had ample funding. Decreasing discriminatory practices and policies against LGBT individuals (Lesbian, Gay, Transgender and Bisexual) has occurred only by persistent organized efforts at

many levels and discrimination is still rife calling for development of LGTB health centers. Contingencies related to outcomes of concern are often complex and discovered only by systematic observation in real-life settings. Consider children and their families. "Child behavior is functional [affects others] at the micro-social level [the child's unique environment] and theory building [guesses about what may be maintaining problem-related behaviors] at a minimum, needs to focus on understanding processes that are actually formative to the [unique] response styles children display in various settings" (Dishion, Patterson, & Kavanagh, 1992, p. 277). Exhibit 7.1 describes contingencies affecting families, and Exhibit 6.7 illustrates the many influences on families.

A contingency analysis will often reveal *perverse incentives*, incentives that work against positive change and maintain unwanted behaviors. Consider the incentive structure suggested by Caplow (1994) created by the war on drugs. To young people, specially minority males, it offers:

- More sexual opportunities than they can obtain any other way
- More money than they can expect to earn any other way
- More respect from peers and from strangers than they can obtain any other way
- Easy access to drugs, weapons, cars, and other luxury goods
- An exciting and glamorous way of life

To law enforcement agents, it offers:

- Opportunities for personal and collective advancement
- An inexhaustible supply of suspects
- Opportunities for illicit profit
- Easy access to drugs, weapons, cars, and other luxury goods
- An exciting and glamorous way of life

To professional criminals and criminal organizations, it offers:

- Larger profits than are available from any other kind of criminal activity
- Opportunities for organizational development
- Opportunities for manipulating the justice system

To the farmers in exotic lands who grow opium, coca, and marijuana for export to the United States, it offers:

- More profit than they can obtain from any legal crop (1994, pp. 99–100)

EXHIBIT 7.1

Contingencies Affecting Families

For decades, Gerald Patterson and his colleagues have studied interaction patterns in families that produce antisocial children. Their research shows that children and parents actively participate in creating their family environments shaping antisocial children. Parenting behavior has been found to be a key factor in doing so. A child learns his or her interpersonal style in the family.

The coercion process begins with something that is intrinsically normal, a rather high level of child noncompliance and continued employment of aversive behaviors that are maintained because they work (escape conditioning). The parents fail both in teaching the prosocial behaviors that would replace the coercive ones, and they also fail to use effective discipline strategies for the deviant behaviors that do occur. The process moves out of control when the frequencies of these coercive behaviors reach very high levels (Chamberlain & Patterson, 1995, p. 213).

This research shows that parenting practices, including noncontingent reactions and low supervision and involvement are important in creating antisocial children (see also Reid, Patterson, & Snyder, 2002). "Noncontingent means that their reactions are not significantly correlated with what the child is doing. For example, if the child behaves in a prosocial fashion, the mother is no more likely to react in a positive, interested, supportive fashion than if the child is being neutral or deviant" (Chamberlain & Patterson, 1995, p. 212). Coercive behaviors common in families with antisocial children include:

1. *Punishment acceleration,* in which parents' reprimands accelerate aggressive behavior.

2. *Crossover,* in which a family member responds with negative behavior to positive behavior of another.

3. *Counterattacks,* in which negative behavior of one family member is responded to with negative behavior by another family member.

4. *Continuance,* in which family members continue to behave in a negative way, regardless of how others behave.

Families in turn are influenced by their environment, including employment opportunities and the quality of education for children. The media daily depict violent acts. Mothers of aggressive children behave more aggressively toward their children on days when they have unpleasant exchanges with people outside the family (Wahler, 1980).

And, we should add the following:
To helping professionals including social workers it offers:

- Any endless supply of clients/resisters

- Employment opportunities

To researchers it offers:

- Opportunities to gain grants to study the "drug problems"

Consider the consequences suggested by a student concerning a low income pregnant immigrant seeking prenatal care in the first trimester (S − = punishing consequences, S + = positive consequences):

S + = Confirmation of pregnancy (may be S—if the pregnancy is unwanted).

S + = Promise of desired medical care.

S − = Might find a problem with the pregnancy.

S − = Costs (of visit, transportation, wages lost).

S + = Individual attention.

S − = Medical system often depersonalizing, sometimes humiliating.

S − = Taboos in regard to undressing in front of men (many physicians are male).

S − = Language barriers.

S + = Advice about diet and care of self.

S − = This advice might not be culturally appropriate.

S − = Long wait for an appointment in waiting room.

S + = Contact with other pregnant women (in waiting room).

S − = Unfamiliar technological devices and practices.

S − = Difficulty obtaining child care or leaving work.

Some contingencies are remote, that is, they will not occur until some future time. For example, even if you do not exercise, you may not have heart trouble for decades (if ever)—a remote consequence. Other contingencies are immediate; they have an immediate effect on the future probability of our behavior. Some contingencies are natural, such as falling off your bike if you tip too far to one side. Others are *arbitrary*; they are arranged by other people, such as government officials. Still others are *self-arranged,* such as spending an hour on Facebook after reading a chapter in this book. We often must rearrange contingencies at many different system levels to support valued behaviors, because natural related contingencies are remote, aversive, or inconsequential. Consider the interlinked contingencies related to the use of seat belts (see Exhibit 7.2). Contingencies at one level (e.g., individual, family, community, city, nation) influence those at other levels. Consider the influence of social and public policies and related legislation on funding patterns for services that, in turn, influence individuals.

Chains of Behavior

A given behavior is usually part of a sequence, or *chain,* of behaviors. We extract from this sequence one reaction that is called problematic. For example, a client may tell you that he often feels angry. He may feel angry after he has not asked for what he wants in a series of exchanges at work and at home. Clients often describe their exchanges with others as a trichotomy of events that starts with another person's behavior, minimizing their own contribution (Watzlawick, Beavin, & Jackson, 1967). A husband may say in response to his wife's complaint

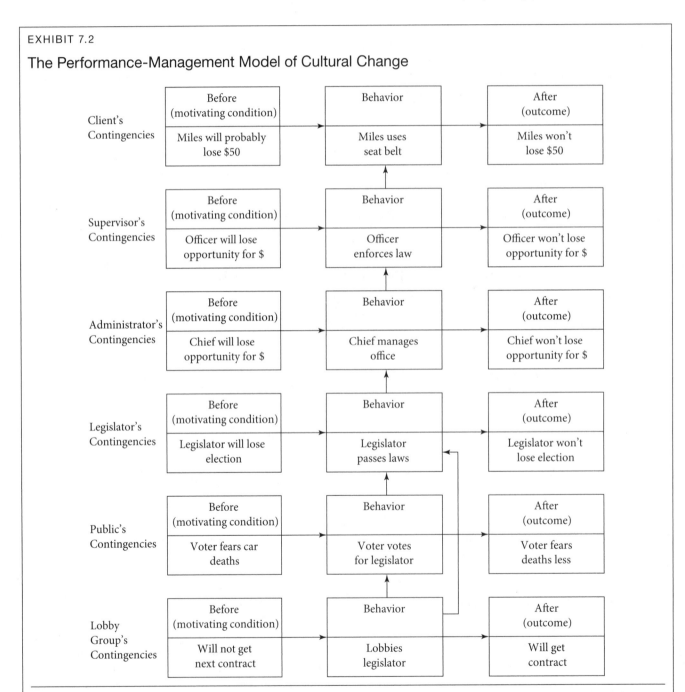

EXHIBIT 7.2

The Performance-Management Model of Cultural Change

	Before (motivating condition)	Behavior	After (outcome)
Client's Contingencies	Miles will probably lose $50	Miles uses seat belt	Miles won't lose $50
Supervisor's Contingencies	Officer will lose opportunity for $	Officer enforces law	Officer won't lose opportunity for $
Administrator's Contingencies	Chief will lose opportunity for $	Chief manages office	Chief won't lose opportunity for $
Legislator's Contingencies	Legislator will lose election	Legislator passes laws	Legislator won't lose election
Public's Contingencies	Voter fears car deaths	Voter votes for legislator	Voter fears deaths less
Lobby Group's Contingencies	Will not get next contract	Lobbies legislator	Will get contract

Source: R. W. Malott (1994). *Rule-governed behavior, self-management, and performance management* (p. 54). Kalamazoo. MI: Department of Psychology, Western Michigan University. Reprinted with permission.

that he is rude, "If you didn't nag me, I wouldn't have to tell you to shut up." He may not mention what he does (or does not do) before his wife starts to "nag" him. Perhaps he ignored his wife's friendly attempts to start a conversation.

Cultures and Contingencies

Differences in cultural norms and values reflect different reinforcement histories. For example, one group may ignore a behavior that to another group may be the occasion for a gang fight. "Behavior is the joint product of (i) the contingencies of survival responsible for the natural selection of the species, (ii) the contingencies of reinforcement responsible for the repertoires acquired by its members including (iii) the special contingencies maintained by an evolved social environment" (Skinner, 1981). Cultural practices (not individual persons) survive over time as a result of natural selection by differential consequences. Such practices involve interlinked contingencies of reinforcement in which the behavior and resultant products of each person function as environmental events that influence other participants (e.g., Glenn, 1991; see also Biglan, 1995; Mattaini & McGuire, 2006). For each cultural practice we can ask: Who is involved? What are related antecedents and consequences? How do different practices at different levels influence one another? Cultural practices affect our behavior, and we in turn affect cultural practices. A cultural practice may survive or disappear depending on its outcome. (What is beneficial for the individual or culture may not benefit the species.) Different cultures create different learning histories as a result of different reinforcement patterns.

Events have different meanings (influences on thoughts, feelings, and behavior) for different people because of unique histories in particular groups. Being born at a particular historical time (e.g., during the Vietnam War) may create unique influences on behavior known as *cohort differences*. A verbal analysis of contingencies at different levels (individual, family, group, organization, legislation, policy), including their interrelationships can help us understand who benefits and who loses from a certain practice and policy program (e.g., see Wacquant, 2009).

Reinforcement

Behavior may be established or maintained by either positive or negative reinforcement. Positive and aversive influences differ in important ways and are accompanied by different emotions. Positive reinforcement is associated with positive feelings, a decreased likelihood of aggression, and an increased likelihood of offering positive consequences to others. Aversive control, which involves both punishment and negative reinforcement, is associated with negative feelings such as anger, an increased likelihood of responding aggressively to others, and a decreased likelihood of offering positive consequences to others. Aversive

events increase aggression, whether or not the aggression is reinforced, as described later in the discussion on punishment.

Positive Reinforcement

The term *positive reinforcement* refers to a procedure in which an event is presented following a behavior and there is an increase in the future likelihood of that behavior (see Exhibit 7.3). The definition of positive reinforcement has two parts: a procedure (a behavior is followed by the presentation of an event) and an effect on behavior (the probability that the behavior will occur in the future on similar occasions is increased). If you do a favor for a friend and she thanks you, you are more likely to do another favor for her in the future. If a teenager steals a car, has a great ride, and receives admiration from his friends for his "feat," he is more likely to steal another car in the future.

The term *positive reinforcement* refers to a procedure, whereas the term *positive reinforcer* refers to an event that, when presented contingent on a behavior, increases the future likelihood of that behavior. Positive reinforcers please people and are accompanied by positive feelings. Reinforcement may be contingent on a low rate of behavior. For example, a teacher may praise a student only if the student talks out of turn less than once a day. Or a high rate of behavior may be reinforced. Some reinforcers are on a limited hold; they are available only until a certain time. Driving to a restaurant will be reinforced only if you arrive before closing time.

Most reinforcers are *conditioned,* or *secondary, reinforcers,* in contrast to *primary reinforcers,* such as food, which function as reinforcers without any prior learning history. Positive *conditioned reinforcers* often are events that consistently precede contact with other positive reinforcers. If a parent's smile is repeatedly associated with food and physical contact, the smile will become a conditioned reinforcer for an infant and may then increase the behavior that it follows. An event may also assume a reinforcing function by being associated with the removal of negative events. Money and approval acquire their function

---

EXHIBIT 7.3

Some Procedures and Their Effects on Behavior

Procedure	Effect on Behavior	
	Behavior Increases	Behavior Decreases
An event is presented following a behavior	Positive reinforcement	Punishment
An event is removed following a behavior	Negative reinforcement	Response cost
What usually happens no longer does	Prior punishment	Operant extinction

as reinforcers by being paired with things that are already reinforcing. Conditioned reinforcers such as money and approval that are paired with a variety of reinforcers become *generalized reinforcers* capable of maintaining a range of behaviors independent of particular states of deprivation. Attention and affection "are conditioned reinforcers which maintain behavior because they are discriminative stimuli for future behavior in other chains of performances leading ultimately to other reinforcers. The approval of one's friends, for example, makes possible their acceptance and issuance of invitations for social occasions...and so forth" (Ferster, Culbertson, & Boren, 1975, p. 381).

Because of different learning histories, an event that functions as a reinforcer for one person may not do so for another. We each have a unique reinforcer profile, those consequences that function as reinforcers. Thus, reinforcers are known not by their physical characteristics but by their functional effects; an event that functions as a reinforcer in one situation may not do so in another. Significant others, such as parents, spouses, or teachers, often assume that what is reinforcing for them is also reinforcing for those with whom they interact (their significant others). This may not be so. Such events could, however, be developed as reinforcers. For example, a teacher's approval could be established as a reinforcer by pairing it with events or items that already function as a reinforcer. On the other hand, because of similar learning histories in a given society, the same reinforcer may have identical functions for many people. Some reinforcers are substitutable; they may satisfy the same or similar needs. Other reinforcers are not.

Negative Reinforcement

Behavior can be established and maintained by preventing, reducing, or removing unpleasant events following its performance. We repeat not only those behaviors that result in pleasurable consequences but also those that remove annoying or painful events (see Exhibit 7.3). If the sun is shining in your eyes and you pull down a shade that removes the glare, your behavior is maintained by negative reinforcement (getting rid of something annoying). Tantrums may be maintained by escaping from or avoiding difficult tasks, especially if socially acceptable forms of escape are not available. The definition of negative reinforcement includes two parts: the description of a procedure (the removal of an event contingent on a behavior) and a behavioral effect (the subsequent increase in the future probability of the behavior). Like positive reinforcers, aversive stimuli create physiological reactions. In both positive and negative reinforcement, actions are followed by a change in the environment. In the former, something is presented and in the latter, something is removed. Both procedures increase the future probability of behavior, and both involve contingencies (relationships between behavior and the environment).

Negative reinforcement is involved in both avoidance and escape behavior. Avoidance behavior is maintained by the removal of anticipated unpleasant events, for example, not starting a conversation with someone because of fear of rejection. Escape behavior is maintained by the removal of a negative event that is already present, for example, ending a conversation with someone who is abusive. Much of our everyday behavior is maintained by negative reinforcement (the removal of aversive or negative events). Aversive events are often used to influence others. For example, people may present unpleasant events to a person, such as critical comments, until that person performs some desired behavior, at which time the events (critical comments) are removed, as illustrated in the example in the following paragraph of the child asking for candy. Our society relies heavily on negative reinforcement. Most of our laws function by means of negative reinforcement. We act in accordance with the law to avoid imprisonment. Consider also religious proscriptions. We avoid an unpleasant afterlife by acting piously in this life. Many advertising campaigns are based on hoped-for negative reinforcement effects, such as using a certain deodorant to avoid social rejection or taking a drug to prevent or decrease anxiety or depression. Negative reinforcement plays a role in maintaining aversive behavior in families (see Exhibit 7.1). Aggression by family members is often negatively reinforced by a decrease in aggressive behaviors by other family members.

As with positive reinforcers, classifying an event as a negative reinforcer depends on its effects on behavior. We cannot tell for sure whether an event will function as a negative reinforcer until we arrange its removal following a behavior and see whether the behavior increases in the future. Aversive events function as reinforcers when they are decreased in intensity or ended. If a child nags his mother to buy a candy bar, repeating over and over, "Buy me a candy bar," the mother may finally buy one, resulting in removal of nagging. Her behavior succeeds in removing an unpleasant event. When the mother and her son are next in a store, her son might again ask her to buy him a candy bar, since he received one in the past. The mother, because he was quiet after she bought him candy in the past, will be more likely to again do so. (Her child will be more likely to whine on similar occasions in the future, since he was reinforced for whining.)

Just as there are many different kinds of events that may function as positive reinforcers, there are many that may function as negative reinforcers, including social ones (disapproval, criticism), undesired tasks (cleaning), and negative self-statements ("I'm really stupid"). Most are conditioned reinforcers; their reinforcing effects are acquired through learning. Just as what functions as a positive reinforcer may vary from person to person depending on his or her unique learning history, what may function as a negative reinforcer may also vary as a function of past history. The same factors that are important with positive reinforcement (immediacy, amount, schedule, and frequency) are important with negative reinforcement.

Natural contingencies involving negative reinforcement (moving out of the sun on a hot day) differ in important ways from socially imposed ones—a parent's request to a child to pick up his toys may carry an implied threat of an unpleasant event for noncompliance. Natural contingencies usually allow a range of behaviors that will remove an unpleasant event. For example, to escape the sun's heat, you could find a shady spot, go inside, or use an umbrella. Socially arranged contingencies are often more controlling in requiring a particular behavior (e.g., apologizing). Behavior that is under the control of natural contingencies benefits the person. The controller is often the beneficiary in socially imposed contingencies.

Superstitious Conditioning

Some behaviors are maintained by the accidental pairing of a behavior and a consequence. This is known as *superstitious conditioning*. For instance, carrying a lucky charm may be followed by an absence of a feared event, thus increasing the tendency to carry this around.

A "Why do you carry that lucky charm?"
B "To keep lions away."
A "That's crazy, there aren't any lions around here."
B "See?"

Superstitious conditioning may be responsible for some ineffective parenting practices. That is, parents may make inaccurate attributions about the causes of a child's behavior because of accidental reinforcement. Such superstitious beliefs may hinder the discovery of real contingencies. Because you think you "know the answer" you may not consider alternative possibilities. Can you think of any behaviors of your own that may be maintained by superstitious conditioning?

Punishment

Consequences may also decrease behavior. If behavior is followed by an aversive event (punishment) or by the removal of a positive reinforcer (response cost), or is no longer followed by reinforcing events (operant extinction), it will decrease in frequency. If a child's request for a cookie results in a slap from his mother (an aversive event) or if the mother consistently ignores his requests (no longer attends to them, that is, operant extinction), he will eventually make fewer requests. Drivers who are caught speeding and receive a fine (response cost) may be less likely to speed in the future. Thus, what happens after a behavior makes it more or less likely in the future. Punishment is a procedure in which an aversive event is presented following a behavior and there is a subsequent decrease in that behavior. The definition includes two factors, the description of a procedure and an effect on behavior. In order to determine whether an event is a punishing one, a contingency must be arranged and the future probability of behavior observed. Aversive events should be distinguished from punishment. There are many types of aversive events, including withholding reinforcement (extinction), removing a positive reinforcer (response cost), and presenting an aversive event contingent on a behavior (punishment). The same variables that influence the effectiveness of reinforcement

also influence the effectiveness of punishment, including the immediacy with which a negative event follows a behavior, the intensity of this event, and the schedule of punishment.

Punishment is an inescapable part of life. We learn through both punishing and positive consequences. For example, if we don't watch where we are going, we will fall when learning to ride a bike. We learn not to lean too far to one side because this is punished by falling, whereas maintaining a straight position is reinforced by avoiding unpleasant falls. This illustrates the close relationship between punishment and negative reinforcement. To arrange for the negative reinforcement of a behavior, a negative event must be presented that can be removed contingent on behavior. This event is presented after some preceding behavior (or its lack) and functions as a punishing event for that behavior.

Punishment is widely used in everyday life to influence the behavior of others. The mother who slaps her child, the supervisor who tells you that your reports are bad, and the teacher who sends a child to the principal's office—all hope to change behavior. They hope for an increase in desired behaviors and/or a decrease in undesired behaviors. The supervisor hopes to increase good report writing and decrease bad report writing. The mother hopes to increase polite verbal behavior and to decrease rude back talk. However, all too often, desirable alternatives are not identified and reinforced. Rather, people often attempt to prod others into acting in expected ways by punishing behavior (or its lack) and removing this contingent on compliance. A mother may stop nagging her daughter to do the dishes when the daughter finally gets up and does them. Power differentials between people (e.g., between police and youth, parents and children, or teachers and students) make it possible for the more powerful to coerce behavior from the less powerful by threatening some aversive event (e.g., jail) or the withdrawal of some privilege for failure to comply. There is usually something readily at hand to remove. The threat is removed contingent on compliance. Use of punishment is encouraged by its immediate (but often temporary) effects, lack of skill in the use of positive methods of influence, and a low tolerance for disliked behaviors.

Disadvantages of Punishment

Behavioral researchers have taken the lead in identifying the negative effects of punishment (e.g., Azrin & Holz, 1966; Fisher et al., 2011). Noncontingent aversive events increase both the probability of aggressive behavior and behavior reinforced by the opportunity to engage in aggressive behavior. Both *elicited* and *operant* aggression may result. The former refers to aggressive reactions that have no influence on the probability of further punishment. For example, if a monkey is shocked in a chamber, he will attack a tennis ball in the chamber, even though this action will in no way influence the probability of future shocks. Consider how this might apply to violence in families. In *operant aggression,* behavior does influence the probability of further punishment. For example, a potential victim may punch a bully, who then retreats. Aversive events are more likely to suppress prosocial and neutral behaviors than aggressive behaviors perhaps because they tend to encourage aggressive behavior (Biglan, Lewin, & Hops, 1990). Abuse was found to predict aggressiveness even after factors such as social class, family disruption, and exposure to spousal violence were controlled.

Modeling aggressive behavior is another disadvantage of punishment. The person delivering the punishment serves as a model for aggressive behaviors such as hitting and yelling. Physically abusing children increases the likelihood that they will develop aggressive behavior, perhaps because effective ways of relating to others are not established. An example of a parent without a clue regarding this is the father who strikes his child saying, "I told you not to hit your brother." Another disadvantage is that the punisher may be avoided. For example, if parents often punish their children, the children may avoid them, and so the parents will have less influence on the children's behavior using positive means.

Neutral cues that are present when punishment is delivered may acquire aversive properties by being paired with punishing events. At a future time, these cues may elicit emotional responses, resulting in avoidance behaviors. If the punishment is intense, the probability of a variety of behaviors, including desirable ones, may be lessened. For example, if parents severely punish sexual exploration in young children, the children may avoid all sexual behavior in the future—appropriate as well as inappropriate. If a negative event serves as a cue for a positive reinforcer to follow, the presentation of negative events may increase the frequency of undesired behaviors. For example, if a mother is affectionate to her child only after she beats him, the behaviors that lead to beatings may increase. The discomfort involved in punishment is unpleasant for the recipient, and permission to use punishment allows one to do so from anger.

Punishment teaches only what not to do and leaves the development of desirable behaviors to chance. It does not eliminate reinforcement for inappropriate behavior. Neither does it undo any damage caused by such behavior. If behavior is punished in a situation that differs from those in which a decrease in response is hoped for, changes may be confined to the original context in which punishment occurred. Creativity and persistence often are required to persuade significant others—such as supervisors, the police, teachers, parents, and staff members—to use positive rather than coercive methods.

Response Cost

Response cost involves the contingent removal of a positive reinforcer following a behavior; access to reinforcers is removed contingent on behavior. Like operant extinction and the use of punishment, response cost, by definition, results in a decrease in behavior. Unlike extinction, this procedure involves a contingency (a relationship between behavior and its consequences). Some reinforcer that is already being sampled (such as watching television), some opportunity or privilege that is normally available (such as use of the car on the weekend), or some reinforcer that has been accumulated (such as money) is removed contingent on a behavior or its absence (e.g., not doing chores).

Removing the opportunity to visit a friend because of stealing or being fined points for not completing a chore are examples of the use of response cost. In everyday life, punishment is often combined with response cost, as when a parent tells a child she must help with the dishes because she teased her sister. If doing the dishes is aversive and also deprives the child of opportunities to engage in pleasurable activities, response cost as well as punishment is involved. Only by using threats of monetary fines or infractions (response cost) and threats of imprisonment (punishment) may companies alter practices that many people believe to be dangerous.

Extinction

If behavior is no longer followed by reinforcing events, it will decrease in frequency. If a mother consistently ignores a child's requests, he will eventually make fewer of them. In operant extinction, there is no longer any contingency between a behavior and the reinforcer that followed it in the past. The schedule on which the behavior was reinforced influences how rapid this decrease will be (see the later discussion of schedules). If a behavior has been reinforced on a continuous schedule, there may be an initial increase in the frequency and intensity of the behavior when reinforcement is withheld. However, this usually is followed by a decrease. For example, if a child's rude requests have typically been granted and then such behavior is consistently ignored, the child may at first shout even louder and more often. The decrease in behavior will be more gradual, and an initial increase in behavior is less likely, if behavior has been maintained on an intermittent schedule of reinforcement. The initial increase in behavior that usually occurs when an extinction procedure is used can be avoided by providing positive reinforcement for alternative behaviors. Note that for an extinction procedure to be in effect, the behavior must occur without being reinforced and there must be a resultant decrease in behavior over the long term. Differential reinforcement consists of positive reinforcement of desired behaviors and use of extinction with undesired behaviors.

Nonreward (e.g., extinction) creates emotional effects similar to those of punishment. Jeffrey Gray (1987) views these as so similar that he defines anxiety in terms of both frustration (nonreward) and punishment. Both increase arousal and attention and behavioral inhibition. This helps explain the intense reactions to social rejection, which may include nonreward as well as punishment of social behaviors. Nonreward may occur when previous behaviors have not been reinforced and also when they have been reinforced, as in extinction.

The Role of Antecedents

Our behavior is influenced by what happens before it, mainly (but not totally) because it is reinforced in particular circumstances (see Exhibit 7.4). A given change in the environment

EXHIBIT 7.4

A Contingency Diagram Analyzing Criminal Activities by Members of Youth Gangs

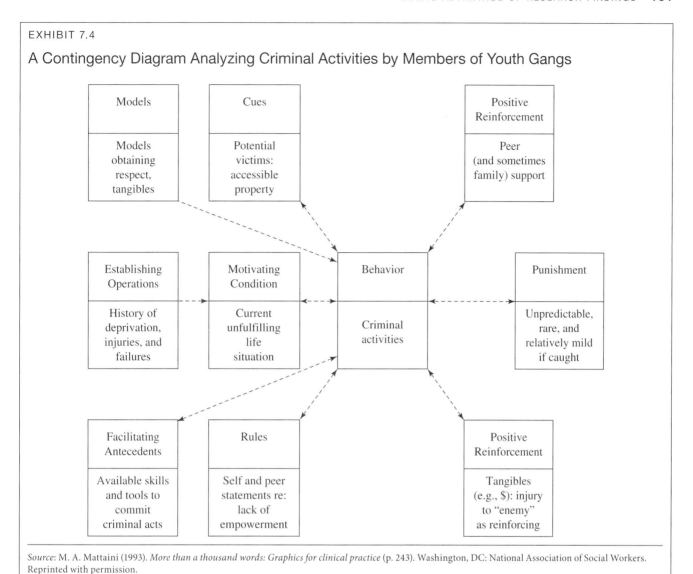

Source: M. A. Mattaini (1993). *More than a thousand words: Graphics for clinical practice* (p. 243). Washington, DC: National Association of Social Workers. Reprinted with permission.

(stimulus) may have a variety of functions (influences on behavior). Consider Mrs. R., who seeks help because of a fear of cars that prevents her from accepting a job in which she has to drive. We can ask: "What functions do cars have at this point?" First, they serve as eliciting stimuli for anxiety. When Mrs. R. thinks of cars or approaches them, she starts to sweat and becomes tense. Second, cars are a cue for avoidance behavior. Mrs. R. avoids riding in cars and avoids being around them as much as possible. Third, cars function as negative reinforcers; that is, they reinforce behavior that removes or avoids them. So cars function as (1) eliciting stimuli for sweating and muscle tension, (2) discriminative cues for avoidance behavior, and (3) negative reinforcers for escape and avoidance behaviors. Successful intervention would reverse these functions (for example, cars would cue approach behavior in relevant situations). Rearranging antecedents (e.g., planning positive activities for children) is a valuable option for increasing positive exchanges and avoiding unpleasant ones between parents and children. Consider the parent who brings toys that a child likes to play with on a long plane trip, compared with the parent who does not prepare in this way.

Occasions for Behavior

Most of our behavior is reinforced only in certain situations and is therefore associated only with certain stimuli. Antecedents acquire influence over our behavior because of their association with behavior and its consequences. For example, we ask certain kinds of questions of others only in certain kinds of situations, such as "How do you feel?" or "How are you?" We are more likely to perform behavior in situations in which it has been reinforced in the past and are less likely to perform behavior in situations in which it has been punished or has not been reinforced. Thus, antecedent events acquire influence over behavior through their association with reinforcing events.

Suppose that Mr. Smith typically adjourns to the living room and reads the paper after dinner and that earlier in the marriage, his wife attempted to initiate a conversation with him at this time and received only a "humm" or a rattle of the paper. She probably no longer tries to initiate conversations with him during this time, since her efforts were not reinforced in this situation. Her husband's reading the paper in the living room after dinner is a cue that attempts to make conversation will not be reinforced. But if Mrs. Smith's attempts are successful when her husband puts the paper down, this may be a cue for initiating a conversation.

Most of our behavior consists of *discriminated operants,* behaviors that occur only in certain situations (those in which they are reinforced). An antecedent event that increases the probability of a behavior is called a *discriminative stimulus* (S^D). (A *stimulus* is defined as any change in the environment that can influence behavior.) Those stimuli signaling that a behavior will probably not be reinforced are called S deltas ($S^{\Delta S}$). A discrimination can be established by reinforcing a behavior in one situation and not reinforcing it in other situations (i.e., differential reinforcement). A discrimination has been established when there is a high rate of a behavior in one situation and a low rate in all other situations. Establishing appropriate discriminations is a key aspect of developing effective repertoires. For example, people who do not do well in social situations, such as meeting people and making friends, may not perceive (notice) signs of friendliness by others and so not initiate conversations. Social skills training may include helping clients learn how to recognize such clues (see chapter 24).

Inappropriate or inadequate discriminations are often involved in presenting problems. Examples include continuing to drink alcohol even when signs of intoxication are evident or a student's incorrect assumption that a teacher's facial expressions indicate disapproval. It is not unusual for children to be well behaved in school but difficult to manage at home or vice versa, reflecting different contingencies of reinforcement in the different settings. Parents may reinforce annoying behaviors at home (and not reinforce desired behaviors), whereas the teacher may reinforce desired behaviors and ignore unwanted behaviors. The teacher thus becomes a cue for desired behaviors because she reinforces them; the parents become a cue for undesired behaviors because they reinforce them and ignore desired behaviors.

Antecedent events that are similar to those present during learning will elicit or occasion similar behaviors. If a person slows down when he sees a police car in back of him, he may also have this reaction when he spots cars that are similar to police cars. This is known as *stimulus generalization* and occurs with both operant and respondent behavior. Situational factors that are not related to whether a behavior is reinforced but that are usually present may affect behavior if these change radically. The term *response generalization* refers to the fact that behaviors that are similar to a behavior that is reinforced will also tend to increase in future probability. If you reinforce a friend for telling particular types of jokes, he may tend to tell you similar jokes. Generalization across time is of major importance in the helping professions (Do valued outcomes persist?) (see chapter 23).

Establishing Operations

If we want to increase the frequency of certain behaviors, we must arrange relevant establishing (motivating) conditions. *Establishing operations* alter the effectiveness of other events as forms of reinforcement (produce a motivational state) and evoke the type of behavior that has been reinforced in the past by those events (Michael, 1993, p. 78). The first effect is described as *reinforcer establishing.* The second is referred to as an *evocative effect.* Examples of establishing operations include deprivation, satiation, and painful stimulation. Food deprivation increases the effects of food reinforcers and increases behaviors that result in access to food. Painful stimulation makes the reduction of pain a powerful reinforcer and also evokes behaviors that previously ended pain. Establishing operations "motivate" behavior (see also the later section on motivation).

Necessary and Facilitating

Necessary and facilitating refer to personal and environmental characteristics that influence how easy it is to carry out a behavior. For example, we are not capable of certain acts (e.g., levitating). Problem-solving styles and nutrition may affect the probability of behavior. The availability of certain items and contexts (weapons, isolated spots, alcohol, drugs) may increase the likelihood of assaults (see Exhibit 7.4). Behavior may also be influenced by events removed in time. These are referred to as "setting" events. For example, a child may have had a very upsetting day with her teacher and be irritable at home later in the day. You may have had a frustrating drive to work and feel irritable when seeing your first client.

Models

The influence of behavior by observing others is known as *observational learning.* By observing others, we may learn new skills. Observing what happens to others may inhibit or disinhibit behavior (Bandura, 1986; Olsson, 2012). Concerns are often raised about the prevalence of models of violent behavior in movies, TV, and newspapers. If a model's behavior is followed by punishing consequences, we are less likely to engage in that behavior. On the other hand, if their behavior is followed by positive consequences, we are more likely to engage in the behavior. If a student sees another classmate get caught cheating, he may be less likely to cheat himself. But if he sees a fellow student get away with cheating, he may be more likely to cheat. Emotional responses can be conditioned or extinguished simply by observing what happens to other people. A child's fear of thunderstorms may be related to his mother's fear reactions on such occasions. Watching someone approach a feared object increases the probability that someone who fears such objects will approach it (Bandura, Blanchard, & Ritter, 1969). Watching others may facilitate behavior (cue behavior not subject to inhibitory processes). For example, if we smoke, we may smoke more when we are around others who smoke.

Verbal Influences

Human beings are unique in the development of complex verbal repertoires that influence behavior in a variety of ways. Verbal behavior includes talking, thinking, imagining, and writing (e.g., see Hayes, Barnes-Holmes, & Roche, 2001). It is our main source of communication and a key source of influence. Verbal behavior is *socially* mediated; that is, it is largely developed and maintained by the behavior of other people. Parents ask children, "Why did you do that?" "Why don't you like it?" and so on. Thus, children's verbal repertoires are created by adults. Verbal behavior may have all the functions other kinds of behavior may have (e.g., cue overt behavior, elicit emotional reactions, and function as reinforcers). For example, our feelings and behavior are influenced by what we say to ourselves (Bandura, 1986). Ideologies function as cues for behavior (e.g., who to vote for). Metaphors such as the "War on Drugs" influence how we view events. Our complex learning history develops unique meanings of words that may appear bizarre to others but "make perfect sense" given a client's unique learning history. Only if we understand these histories may we be able to help a client. Such understanding requires empathy and deep listening, as well as a recognition of the role of our learning histories (e.g., Goldiamond, 1974).

Verbal behavior acquires its influence over our actions because of its association with certain consequences. Instructional control (by either others or ourselves) is created through individual learning histories. Instructions given by others are effective by influencing self-instructions (what we say to ourselves).

> By behaving verbally, people cooperate more successfully in common ventures. By taking advice, heeding warnings, following instructions, and observing rules, they profit from what others have already learned. Ethical practices are strengthened by codifying them in laws, and special techniques of ethical and intellectual self-management are devised and taught. Self-knowledge or awareness emerges when one person asks another such a question as "What are you going to do?" or "Why did you do that?" (Skinner, 1981, p. 502)

Rule-Governed Behavior

Rule-governed behavior is behavior influenced by descriptions of contingencies (e.g., in a book or lecture). A book on bowling may state: "If you hold your arm steady, you will get a strike." "We tend to follow a rule because previous behavior in response to similar verbal stimuli has been reinforced" (Skinner, 1969, p. 148). One reason we follow rules is to escape from or avoid aversive events. For example, studying for final examinations may be maintained by ending self-blame, guilt, or anxiety (negative reinforcement). Rules can be learned quickly, are valuable if contingencies are complex or unclear, and make it easier to profit from similarities between contingencies (Skinner, 1974, p. 125). For example, many contingencies are remote, such as the relationship between smoking cigarettes and developing lung cancer. Competing contingencies often are present (e.g., pleasing others while also pursuing personal goals). "Correspondence training" is used to increase the match between what people say they will do and what they actually do (e.g., Deacon & Konarski, 1987). Describing contingencies that work is just as important as describing those that do not. Rules provide a way to understand how self-talk influences behavior. A rule functions as a discriminative stimulus and, as such, can be effective as part of a set of contingencies. The links between verbal and overt behavior underscore the importance of assessing the role of self-statements in problems (see chapter 24).

Rule-based learning is based on a description of contingencies, and so it differs from contingency-shaped learning, which is based on direct experience (Skinner, 1969). The effects of rule-based contingencies depend on the extent to which they accurately describe what is likely to happen. Reading the descriptions of a contingency in this book (if you do x, y will occur) will generally not be as effective in developing skilled behavior as learning experiences in which direct feedback is used to shape behavior. Rule-governed behavior is more variable. Descriptions of contingencies may or may not be accurate. For example, the likelihood of unpleasant consequences may be greatly exaggerated, as when a client has an excessive fear of social disapproval. Rules often are incomplete. Neither the consequences related to behaviors of interest nor the cues may be described. Rules may reflect impossible goals (Baron, 2000). That is, they may not reflect real-life contingencies and so result in punishing consequences. Consider self-statements such as "Everyone should like me." We may overgeneralize or attend to only part of a situation (focus on negative outcomes and ignore positive ones). Excessive rule following that decreases sensitivity to real-life contingencies is a common side effect of verbal influence.

"Equivalence classes" are classes of events that may differ in form but are linked by a common learning history (see Hayes, Barnes-Holmes, & Roche, 2001). This linking may occur through verbal associations (verbal stimuli associated with events) created by unique learning histories. What on the surface may seem to be unrelated may be related by a common association based on a unique learning history. For example, based on his learning history, a man may equate his wife's expressing an opinion with disrespect to him and may then feel he has a right to hit her. That is, he equates expressing an opinion and disrespect.

Motivation

Motivational variables are related to differences in the reinforcing effects of environmental events. *Motivation* can be viewed as a relationship between a set of operations (e.g., deprivation of a reinforcer, such as social approval) and their effects on behavior (increased persistence in overcoming obstructions and increased resistance to extinction) (Leslie & Millenson, 1996). As discussed earlier in this chapter, establishing operations (e.g., deprivation of water) influence motivational conditions (conditions of our body or environment) that influence our motivational level (sensitivity to reinforcement). Defining motivation in this way provides guidelines for understanding and altering behavior. For example, antecedents related to behaviors can be identified and changed. Identifying problem-related contingencies will help you and your clients understand the motivation for them (their meanings).

Emotions

Emotion can also be viewed as a relationship between certain antecedent conditions (an abrupt stimulus change, such as experiencing an intense pleasant or unpleasant event) and their effects on behavior (Leslie & Millenson, 1996). (See Exhibit 7.5.) Here, too, the reinforcing value of events and general activity level are altered. Characteristics of emotion identified by Paul Ekman (1994) include the following: (1) presence in other primates, (2) distinctive physiology, (3) universal commonalities in antecedent events, (4) quick onset, (5) brief duration, (6) automatic appraisal, and (7) unbidden occurrence. Some emotions have a distinctive universal signal. There is a rich literature on the origins and functions of emotions (Ekman & Davidson, 1994; Lewis, Haviland-Jones, & Barrett, 2011). Large changes in the schedule or amount of reinforcement or punishment are usually accompanied by emotional reactions or a disruption of ongoing behavior. If a teacher severely criticizes a child, the child may have difficulty continuing to work. If a person gets a call while reading a magazine informing him that he has just won a $5,000 trip for his jingle about Crispy Cracky cereals, he is unlikely to continue reading the magazine.

Just as a large change in the amount of a reinforcer or aversive event can alter behavior, so can a large change in the schedule of reinforcement (see later discussion of schedules of reinforcement). This, too, is likely to create emotional effects that disrupt behavior, such as when a companion who supported most of another person's behavior dies. High levels of emotion decrease our skill in making discriminations. High levels of stress may result in emotional effects that decrease parents' skills in identifying specific desired behaviors to reinforce on the part of their children. An evolutionary view highlights the communication and survival functions of emotions. One of the main functions of emotion is mobilizing us to deal quickly with environmental threats (e.g., from predators). We appraise events as harmful or beneficial. An anatomical perspective highlights the role of our "reptilian" brain in our emotions. (See also Reuter-Lorenz, Baynes, Mangun, & Phelps, 2010.) In a review of research related to fear and anxiety, Ohman writes:

Responses of fear and anxiety originate in an alarm system shaped by evolution to protect creatures from impending danger. This system is biased to discover threat, and it results in a sympathetically dominated response as a support of potential flight or fight. This response system can be triggered from three different levels of information processing, the first two of which are inaccessible to introspection. The first level concerns a direct link to an arousal system from elementary feature detectors geared to respond to biologically relevant threats. Thus, the arousal system becomes collaterally and automatically activated with the activation of

further information-processing stages, whose functioning may be influenced by the arousal. The second level concerns a schema-driven nonconscious bias to discover threat in the environment, which delivers information to conscious perception, but has no effect or only a weak effect on physiological arousal. The third level concerns the direct effect of expectancy and physiological arousal on the cognitive-interpretive activity resulting in perceived threat. (1993, pp. 529–530) (see also Antony & Stein, 2009)

The emotions and accompanying behaviors common to a culture depend on the basic forms of social organization that are favored (e.g., see Stets & Turner, 2006). In competitive, power-based groups, fear and appeasement are common. In cooperative, reassurance-based groups, playfulness, problem solving, and sharing are common (Gilbert, 1989; see also the later discussion of respondent behaviors). Emotions offer vital clues to contingencies. We can use them as an occasion to explore our behavior and its consequences (e.g., when we drink alcohol and when we do not and what happens).

Variables That Influence Operant Learning

A knowledge of variables that influence operant learning will help you and your clients to design effective plans. These variables include timing, magnitude, frequency, and schedule of reinforcement. *Timing* refers to the period of time between a behavior and the presentation of a reinforcer. For maximum effect, a reinforcer should immediately follow the behavior. Excessive delays are one of the principal errors made in using reinforcement. *Frequency* refers to how often a behavior is reinforced; *magnitude* refers to how much of a reinforcer is offered; and *quality* refers to the reinforcing potential of one event relative to others. Although awareness of the relationship between behavior and its consequences facilitates learning, it is not essential. Many contingencies influence our behavior that we either cannot identify or misidentify (e.g., see discussion of cognitive biases in chapter 8). We may learn about contingencies through direct experience (contingency-shaped behavior) or what we hear or read (rule-governed behavior). Beliefs about rule governed contingencies are less likely (compared with contingency-shaped behavior) to accurately reflect contingencies (relationships between our behavior and environmental changes). Beliefs about a contingency may override the effects of real-life contingencies. *Consistency* refers to the use of an established schedule. If schedules vary a great deal, developing new behaviors may be more difficult.

Schedule of Reinforcement

The *schedule of reinforcement* refers to the particular pattern that describes the relationship between a behavior and its consequences. Different schedules produce different patterns of behavior.

Why It Is Important to Know About Scheduling Effects

Understanding schedules of reinforcement is important because they influence the rate of behavior, its maintenance, and its resistance to extinction (how difficult it is to decrease a behavior). Consider the "addictive" effects of variable ratio schedules of reinforcement in gambling. Scheduling effects are often overlooked, resulting in serious assessment errors. Sudden changes in response requirements may disrupt behavior. Children have different histories in terms of how much output has been required before reinforcement in a given situation. If a teacher requires the same output for all children, those who are not accustomed to this requirement will not meet her expectations. The teacher may label such children as lazy or unmotivated (she may "blame the victim"), when in fact, environmental factors are responsible (a change in the schedule of reinforcement). This teacher may refer these children to a social worker because of "lack of motivation," not realizing that she must arrange the motivating conditions for the children's behavior by offering schedules of reinforcement that match each child's unique reinforcement history. She could then provide new histories by gradually changing the requirements. Transitions, such as retirement, usually involve changes in reinforcement schedules, which may account for some of the changes in behavior and emotions at such times. Behaviors that are maintained on "thin schedules" of reinforcement are especially likely to be disrupted by punishment that would otherwise have little effect.

Schedule changes may result in attack (e.g., when a schedule is thinned and reinforcement is given less often) or changes in the frequency of other behaviors, such as water drinking (Epling & Pierce, 1988). Such behaviors are called *adjunctive behaviors.* Examples are time-filling behaviors such as idle conversation, habits such as nail biting, smoking, hand washing, self-stimulating rituals, manic episodes, and rage outbursts (Foster, 1978; Kanter, Cantilli, Busch, & Baruch, 2005). A further influence of schedules is shown by the effects of preceding schedules on later ones.

Different Kinds of Schedules and Their Effects on Behavior

Some behavior is followed by a reinforcer on every occasion (a *continuous schedule* of reinforcement). If your favorite coffee shop always opens at 9 a.m. on Tuesdays, walking to this shop to get some coffee at that time will always be reinforced. Most behavior is maintained on an *intermittent schedule* (a consequence does not follow every instance of a behavior). For example, only on some occasions do you hit the jackpot when you pull a slot machine handle. The advantages of intermittent reinforcement include its value in maintaining behavior and resistance to

extinction (a behavior persists longer when reinforcement is no longer provided).

There are two main types of intermittent schedules. In *ratio schedules,* either a fixed or variable number of behaviors are required before a consequence occurs. Such schedules usually produce high performance rates. An example of a fixed ratio schedule is piecework production in a factory. In a *fixed-ratio schedule,* a pause in responding typically occurs after reinforcement, followed by a fairly steady rate of behavior until the next reinforcer occurs. Difficulty in starting a new project (e.g., a new term paper) may reflect the pause in responding that occurs in fixed-ratio schedules. Emotional reactions, such as anxiety, are more likely to disrupt behavior maintained on fixed-ratio schedules in which there are long pauses after reinforcement, than with behaviors on variable ratio schedules in which small response requirements are occasionally reinforced. Pushing a button on a slot machine is an example of a *variable-ratio schedule.* This schedule generates behaviors that have a high stable rate and are difficult to decrease. In fixed-ratio schedules, the higher the ratio, the higher the rate of behavior (one reinforcement for every 10 behaviors is a higher ratio than one reinforcer for every five). In a variable-ratio schedule, the higher the average ratio (the average number of behaviors required before a reinforcer follows), the higher the rate of behavior will be. Parents who reinforce undesirable behaviors on high-ratio schedules ensure a high rate of this behavior.

In *interval schedules,* behavior is reinforced only after a fixed or variable amount of time has passed. The first behavior that occurs after a certain time interval is reinforced. Behaviors that occur before this are not reinforced. Waiting for a bus that arrives only on the hour is an example of a fixed-interval schedule. Interval schedules differentially reinforce low rates of behavior, whereas ratio schedules differentially reinforce high rates of behavior. An example of a behavior on a variable-interval schedule is a child's request for an ice cream cone when the mother buys one only when she thinks enough time (which is variable) has passed since the child last had one. Variable-interval schedules create behaviors that occur at a low rate and are difficult to decelerate. A low rate results because the reinforcement is not dependent on response output. Many factors influence the rate of behavior on interval schedules. For example, if the behavior is very strong, such as waiting for an ambulance, there may be a fairly steady output of behavior, such as looking in the direction in which the ambulance is to approach, even though it is not due to arrive for a set period of time. When a variable schedule is used, it is more difficult to decease behavior. Parents who try to decrease behavior by no longer reinforcing it often do this for only a certain period of time. That is, they provide periodic reinforcement that will create behavior that is difficult to decrease. Occasional reinforcement may maintain behavior.

Complex Schedules. In everyday life, reinforcement is often available for more than one response from more than one source. Many behaviors, each of which is on a certain schedule of reinforcement, may compete with one another. For example, an elementary school student may receive reinforcement from his peers for making funny faces and concurrently receive criticism from his teacher for getting the incorrect answer on a problem. In *concurrent schedules,* two or more schedules are in effect independently and at the same time for two or more different behaviors. The *matching law* refers to the finding that we tend to match our behaviors in choice situations to the rate of reinforcement for each choice. This provides valuable guidelines for altering behavior. We can increase valued behaviors by enriching their schedules of reinforcement while decreasing or holding constant reinforcement for other behaviors. Some schedules combine both a response and an interval requirement. For example, a teacher may require a certain number of problems to be completed and evaluate the students' progress after a certain amount of time has passed. She is using a *conjunctive schedule.* Different schedules of reinforcement may be in effect for the same behavior in different situations. For example, saying "How are you?" to some people you know may always be reinforced by a friendly response, but this may not be true for other people.

Respondent Behavior

Respondent behaviors include those that involve the autonomic nervous system, such as heart rate and blood pressure, whereas operants (behavior that "operates" on or influences the environment) involve the skeletal muscles (walking, running). We usually associate respondent behaviors with involuntary reactions and operants with voluntary behaviors. Examples of respondent reactions are an increased heart rate before going on stage to give a speech, sweaty palms before a test, and goose pimples on a chilly day. Respondent behavior plays a key role in many problems, including depression, anxiety, chronic pain, aggression, and child abuse. Some events (unconditioned stimuli) elicit behavior without any previous learning.

> The ability to respond automatically to certain stimuli is part of the genetic endowment of each organism. Such behaviors function as protection against certain harmful stimuli (e.g., pupil contraction in bright light) and help regulate the internal economy of the organism (e.g., changes in heart rate and respiration in response to temperature and activity levels); these responses evolved through natural selection because of their survival value to the species. (Cooper, Heron, & Heward, 1987, p. 19)

Respondent learning involves pairing neutral events with cues that already elicit a given reaction (see Lavond & Steinmetz, 2003). Ivan Pavlov (1927), a famous physiologist who won a Nobel Prize for his studies of digestion in dogs, spent the major part of his career investigating conditioned reflexes. Stimuli that affect behavior only after being paired with events that already elicit a response are known as *conditioned stimuli.* For example, only after an experience of painful drilling at a dentist's office may approaching the

office cause discomfort. In higher order respondent conditioning, neutral events become conditioned stimuli by being paired with conditioned stimuli. Knowledge of respondent learning can help you understand the complex interactions between respondent and operant behavior (e.g., between anxiety and avoidance reactions). The placebo effect can be viewed as a conditioned response (e.g., see Stewart-Williams & Podd, 2004). The placebo effect is a positive response to the act of treatment rather than the treatment itself; cues associated with receiving a certain treatment may result in effects associated with that treatment.

Variables That Influence Respondent Learning

Classical conditioning is complex in the associations that may be formed. The characteristics of conditioned and unconditioned stimuli as well as physical relationships among them influence whether a conditioned response is acquired. Prior learning history influences later experiences through preexisting associations. Recent discussions of Pavlovian (respondent) conditioning emphasize the overlap between cognitive and conditioning influences. The associations formed are influenced by the "net" of associations related to a particular stimulus, including inhibitory and excitatory associations (Lavond & Steinmetz, 2003; Rescorla, 1988). Thus classical conditioning entails much more than the establishment of single associations between specific cues. Consider the "blocking" effect that one stimulus may have on another. That is, conditioning to a particular stimulus may be prevented by previous conditioning to another event. There are biological boundaries and specific differences in the particular responses that can be associated with particular stimuli. We are biologically prepared to experience certain kinds of reactions in certain kinds of situations. (See also Domjan, 1983.) Our evolutionary history influences emotional reactions such as anger, panic attacks, social anxiety, and shyness (Gilbert, 1989; Trower, Gilbert, & Sherling, 1990). Neutral events that are paired with aversive stimuli become conditioned aversive stimuli. The avoidance of such events is reinforcing.

The intensity of the unconditioned stimulus (US) relative to other background events and the number of pairings (up to a point) between it and a neutral stimulus influence the effects of pairing a neutral event with a conditioned or unconditioned stimulus. A single pairing may result in a conditioned response as in long-lasting taste aversions to particular kinds of food. Conditioned taste aversions are a concern when patients undergo treatments that induce nausea, such as chemotherapy for cancer. A third variable is the time between the presentation of the neutral and conditioned stimulus. With humans, close contiguity between two events is not necessarily required because of the influential role of thoughts (e.g., reminders about contingencies). Contiguity between events may not produce an association, and failure to arrange contiguity does not preclude associative learning. Even *backward conditioning* (presentation of the unconditioned event before the neutral one) may be effective with humans, whereas it usually is not with animals.

The intensity of the eliciting stimulus affects the magnitude and latency of respondent reactions. In general, the greater the intensity of the eliciting stimulus and the shorter the time period between its presentation and the occurrence of a response (the shorter the latency), the greater the magnitude of the response. Intensity is influenced by preexisting associations. With conditioned responses, the likelihood of a reaction, its magnitude, and its latency are related to the degree of similarity of an event (or complex of events) to the one (or those) present during conditioning. Thus, in the example of the dentist's office, the probability and magnitude of conditioned reactions on future occasions will be influenced by the similarity of the events presented on the next visit to those originally present. Is the dentist wearing the same white coat? Is the client again there to have a cavity filled? Thoughts about feared events will influence reactions. What is similar depends on the events associated with a stimulus (see the discussion of stimulus equivalence).

Respondent extinction involves repeated presentation of an event without pairing this with events with which it has typically been associated in the past. For example, a child may be gradually exposed to speaking in front of adults, thus avoiding intense anxiety reactions usually experienced when his mother tried to force him to speak. As extinction progresses, the magnitude of the reaction decreases, and the latency between the presentation of the conditioned stimulus and the conditioned response increases. Empirical research on anxiety suggests that exposure to feared events is the principal factor in the success of anxiety reduction methods (e.g., see Barlow, 2002; Richard & Lauterbach, 2007). *Counter conditioning* involves pairing an event with a response that is incompatible with the reaction typically elicited. For example, in systematic desensitization based on relaxation, feared events are presented in a context of relaxation.

The Interaction Between Respondent and Operant Behaviors

In the past, a wide separation was made between respondent and operant behavior in terms of their controlling variables; respondent behavior was thought to be influenced mainly by antecedents (what happens before the behavior), and operant behavior, mainly by its consequences (what happens after behavior). We now know that the difference between these two types of reactions—whether they can be influenced by their consequences—has been exaggerated. Heart rate, blood pressure, and a range of other responses can be brought under operant control. That is, they can be influenced by what happens after they occur (e.g., see literature on behavioral medicine). Both respondents and operants are involved in most reactions and chains of behavior. Seeing a lover after a long absence, for instance, may elicit warm feelings and cue greeting behaviors. Thus, the same event may elicit respondent reactions and occasion operant behaviors. Each person may have a different pattern of responses in a situation.

Different response systems may or may not be related, depending on the unique learning history of each person: (1) overt behavior (e.g., avoidance of crowds and verbal reports, such as descriptions of anxiety), (2) cognitions (thoughts about crowds), and (3) physiological reactions (increased heart rate).

Physiological reactions, such as a rapid heart beat, may or may not accompany verbal reports of fear or avoidance of related situations. Thoughts may or may not trigger anxiety reactions, depending on the person's learning history. Failure of a reaction to follow the principles of respondent behavior should be a signal that other factors are involved, such as reinforcement from significant others or that eliciting events (those that result in the response) have not been identified. A respondent reaction should be observed every time the *eliciting* stimulus is presented, given that other factors are held constant. In contrast, we speak of operant behavior as being *emitted*—the antecedents (S^{Ds} as establishing operations) set the occasion on which a behavior is likely to be reinforced. Exhibits 7.5 to 7.7 offer examples of the application of behavioral principles.

Limitations of this kind of analysis include: (1) lack of knowledge about important relationships between behaviors and their context in real-life settings, (2) lack of influence over important contingencies (see chapter 19), and (3) high cost in time and effort involved in some (not all) programs.

Evolutionary Influences

We have a history both as individuals and as a species. Both histories influence what environments we create and their risks and opportunities. It is easy to lose sight of the fact that we carry anatomical, physiological, and psychological characteristics related to our evolutionary history. This history influences biological selection (some living beings are more likely to survive), behavioral selection (we act on the environment and are affected by the consequences), environmental selection (through our behaviors we create our own unique environments), and cultural selection (patterns of behavior in a network of individuals). Variability of behavior is a key building block of evolutionary theory. Variations followed by positive consequences or the removal of negative consequences are likely to recur in the future. Those that are followed by the removal of positive consequences or the presentation of negative ones are less likely to recur.

There is a complex interaction among biological, behavioral, and cultural selection. Behavior changes over time for an individual, family, and culture in accord with changes in contingencies. This happens not only over someone's life-time but also over the evolutionary history of a species. Goals and related social strategies may change, such as care eliciting (recruiting help and life-sustaining resources), caregiving, competition (power seeking), and cooperation (sharing). We learn about our world through our interactions in it with other people, other species, and our physical environment. That is, we evolve in certain ways depending on our experiences. In this sense, we are "embodied theories" about what works and has worked in the past (what has solved problems we confront) (Munz, 1985). Karl Popper views evolution as the history of problem solving for a species.

Evolutionary psychology is the attempt to understand behavior in relation to the process of evolution (Buss, 2011).

EXHIBIT 7.5

Behavioral Analysis of Problems and Interventions for Response Functions

Functional Problem	Description	Example	Possible Interventions
Deficient or ineffective behavioral repertoire	Behaviors do not lead to reinforcement	Poor social skills, parental skills, deficits, social isolation, and assertion deficits	FAP (functional analytic therapy); parent effectiveness training
Aversive behavioral repertoire	Exhibits behavioral excesses or controlling behaviors that others find aversive	Aggressive or coercive behavior	Self-control training
Inappropriate conditioned emotional response	Has classically conditioned responses	Phobia and excessive fear	Exposure; modeling
Excessive self-monitoring of behavior	Is overly concerned with form of behavior rather than function	Perfectionism that impairs efficiency; obsessive-compulsive behavior	Thought stopping; response prevention
Behavioral excess	Exhibits excess behavior that interferes with access to reinforcers	Panic/anxiety; obsessive-compulsive behavior	Systematic desensitization flooding; panic control therapy

Source: W. C. Follette & S. C. Hayes (2000). Contemporary behavior therapy. In C. R. Snyder & R. E. Ingram (Eds.), *Handbook of psychological change: Psychotherapy processes and practices for the 21st century* (p. 394). New York: John Wiley & Sons, Inc. Reprinted with permission.

Contingencies consist of relationships between behavior and their consequences and antecedents. Contingencies critical to our survival in early times may now hamper rather than help us. For instance, we seem to have difficulty decreasing our use of punishment, with all the negative consequences of relying on coercion (Sidman, 1989). Paleopsychology emphasizes the importance of archaic biological roots on complex human behavior. An evolutionary perspective adds a historical dimension to understanding aggression and caregiving in society, as well as what Paul Gilbert (1989) refers to as "defeat states," such as depression and the experiences that may be responsible. Threats to survival and ecological imbalances are just as important today as they were millions of years ago, and phylogenetic carryovers influence our behavior, especially our emotions in certain situations (e.g., when we are threatened). Threats occur both from outside organized groups (e.g., predators, strangers) and within them (from dominant individuals) (Gilbert, 1993). Both social and nonsocial defense systems evolved over time. "The defense system is essentially concerned with the avoidance of all forms of threat, injury and attack. It is a self-protective system with attentional, evaluative, affective and behavioral components designed to protect the animal" (Gilbert, 1989, pp. 42–43). The nonsocial defense system evolved to defend against predators. This includes (1) hypersensitivity to sensory data; (2) rapid increases in arousal-startle, alertness; and (3) rapid, unpredictable movements, as in rapid flight, freezing, and automatic aggression. Once initiated, it tends to be controlled internally. You can see the potential relevance of such reactions to human behavior (e.g., panic attacks and aggression; see also Gilbert, 1993).

Paul Gilbert (1989) argues that social defense systems evolved in order to facilitate interaction within species (e.g., to regulate control over territory, allow breeding) and to protect against predators (e.g., parents act to reduce physical dangers to their offspring). There also are social and nonsocial safety systems. Gilbert suggests that social signals (such as smiling) evolved to facilitate cooperative behavior. Cooperative behavior can be viewed as an evolutionary adaptation designed to permit caregiving to infants who cannot defend themselves. Defense and safety systems interact. For example, anxiety may result because of an increase in fear or a loss of safety. "Defeat states" are assumed to be involved in depression, whereas submissive behavior reflects anxiety. Consider battered women who are habitually forced into a submissive role (Gilbert, 1994).

Reassurance or Threat: Different Modes of Group Interaction

Group organization requires close proximity and thus special processes to regulate behavior. Gilbert highlights the role of ranking in regulating social interaction. For example, "in order for a lower ranking animal not to be chased away, injured or even killed, the lower rank must be able to send signals of submission which inhibit the attack of the more dominant animal" (Gilbert, 1989, p. 46). In what he calls the hedonic mode, behavior is regulated by the exchange of reassuring signals.

The social structure is one of *mutual dependence* rather than (as in the agonic mode) *mutual defensiveness*. Whereas

EXHIBIT 7.6

Behavioral Analysis of Problems and Interventions for Reinforcing Stimulus Functions

Functional Problem	Description	Specific Problem Example	Possible Interventions
Behavior ineffectively controlled	Commonly controlled social/legal contingencies do not sufficiently reinforce or restrict behavior	Antisocial behavior	Establishment of conditioned reinforcers; environmental restriction
Inappropriate contingent control	Reinforcers socially unacceptable or lead to unacceptable outcomes for client or others	Pedophilia; substance abuse	Self-control training; social skills training; environmental restriction
Insufficient environmental reinforcement	Reinforcement of appropriate behaviors lacking	Living in social situation where some prosocial behavior is not adequately supported	Pleasant activities planning and social skills training; environmental restructuring
Restricted range of reinforcement	Has limited set of reinforcing stimuli	Excessively dependent relationships; vulnerability to depression	Reinforcer sampling
Noncontingent reinforcement	Receives significant reinforcement for inadequate performance	Spoiled; school or work difficulties	Parent training; business management training
Overly punitive environment	Behavior is under aversive control rather than positive control	Mistrust; over caution; misses opportunity for expanding behavioral repertoire	Social skills training; relationship-oriented approach
Excessively stringent self-reinforcement strategies	Standards set too high	Perfectionism; frequently disappointed in self or others	Self-instructional training; discrimination training
Excessive schedule dependence	Behavior is too dependent on high rates of reinforcement	Insecurity; easily frustrated and gives up too easily; does not attempt complex new skills	Self-control procedures; reinforcement schedule management

Source: W. C. Follette & S. C. Hayes (2000). Contemporary behavior therapy. In C. R. Snyder & R. E. Ingram (Eds.), *Handbook of psychological change: Psychotherapy processes and practices for the 21st century* (p. 395). New York: John Wiley & Sons, Inc. Reprinted with permission.

in the agonic mode arousal tends to be high (e.g., with braced readiness) and priming of self-protective behaviors, the hedonic mode maintains arousal at lower levels. It facilitates increased proximity to others and deactivates defensive behaviors which would otherwise be aroused by close proximity. This allows for a safer exploration of the social environment without a major preoccupation with potential threat from within the social domain. (Gilbert, 1989, p. 52)

Rather than submissive appeasement, reassurance signals are offered (e.g., hugging, sharing). Exploration, problem solving, and cooperative behavior are characteristics of the hedonic mode. The absence of threat signals reduces defensive reactions and increases trust. The response to predator threat is a group one rather than an individual one. In the hedonic mode, prestige depends on the ability to control positive (rather than defensive) attention of others. Prestige may be measured by the amount of positive attention that others direct toward an individual.

EXHIBIT 7.7

Behavioral Analysis of Problems and Interventions for Discriminative Stimulus Functions

Functional Problem	Description	Specific Problem Example	Possible Interventions
Defective stimulus control	Response emitted under wrong conditions	Client gives too much interpersonal information for a given occasion	Social skills training
Discrimination deficits of private events	Person does not accurately tact (label) feelings	Client mislabels lust as love	Training in self-labeling
Inappropriate self-generated stimulus control; poor self-labeling	Self-generated cues for behavior lead to poor outcomes	Person inappropriately limits or emits behavior by under or overestimating ability	Behavioral rehearsal
Overly rigid rule governance	Client is not under contingent control of environment or sensitive to environmental changes	Client does not see actual relationship between behavior and consequences	ACT (acceptance and commitment therapy)
Ineffective arrangements of contingencies	Immediate environment not arranged to usefully influence behavior	Inefficient dietary management; problems with schoolwork	Stimulus control and problem-solving training

Source: W. C. Follette & S. C. Hayes (2000). Contemporary behavior therapy. In C. R. Snyder & R. E. Ingram (Eds.), *Handbook of psychological change: Psychotherapy processes & practices for the 21st century* (p. 393). New York: John Wiley & Sons, Inc. Reprinted with permission.

An evolutionary perspective helps us to explore the question "What is human nature?" Understanding evolutionary influences on human behavior may help us understand how to shift further toward a society regulated by caring and cooperation. An appreciation of the evolutionary roots of human behavior allows us to realistically view the potential for change. For example, the evolutionary functions of status hierarchies (ranking) suggest how difficult it will be to alter the reinforcing value of status and dominance. Karen Pryor (1999) suggests that some people use punishment to control others in order to assert their dominance (their rank). Here, too, it is important to examine the soundness of commonly accepted but incorrect metaphors, such as the view of evolution as a ladder or cone leading to human beings as the pinnacle of success. Stephen Jay Gould (1995) notes that these misleading images of evolution continue to constrain our vision.

Summary

The unique relationships between behavior and its consequences result in unique reinforcement histories, which vary from person to person and culture to culture. Human behavior is complex, and each person's repertoire is different. Patterns of social interaction and the accompanying emotional reactions that evolved over millions of years continue to influence our behavior, although to be sure, these are modified by higher order cognitive processes. Natural selection through differential biological, behavioral, and cultural consequences influences our behavior and the cultural practices we create and maintain. Both immediate and remote contingencies affect behavior, and they often are difficult to identify. Some contingencies, such as punishment and response cost, decrease behavior, whereas others, such as positive and negative reinforcement, increase behavior. The cues associated with reinforcement (or its absence) acquire influence over behavior through this association, Thus, both antecedents and consequences affect our behavior. Verbal behavior (talking, thinking, imagining, writing) has a variety of influences on behavior as a result of past and current contingencies of reinforcement. The principles related to respondent conditioning offer valuable information about emotional reactions. Knowledge about the complex interactions between behavior and environmental changes provides a valuable tool for clarifying the context in which problems occur and for discovering options for helping clients enhance the quality of their lives.

Reviewing Your Competencies

Reviewing Content Knowledge

1. Describe different kinds of behavior.

2. Define the term *contingency* and give examples.

3. Distinguish between respondent and operant behavior and give examples.

4. Define the term *operant*.

5. Define *operant conditioning* and give examples.

6. Discuss the role of the variability of behavior in the "selection of behavior."

7. Distinguish between the form and the function of behavior and give examples.

8. Define *positive reinforcement* and give an example.

9. Define *negative reinforcement* and give an example.

10. Describe the difference between positive and negative reinforcement.

11. Describe how positive and negative reinforcement are similar.

12. Explain what is meant by the statement "reinforcers are relative" and give examples.

13. Discuss the role of negative reinforcement in families.

14. Define two types of punishment and give an example of each.

15. Describe the disadvantages of using punishment.

16. Define and give examples of operant extinction.

17. Describe the difference between punishment and operant extinction.

18. Distinguish between punishment and response cost.

19. Discuss the differences between positive and aversive control in relation to their effects.

20. Describe variables that influence operant learning.

21. Explain why schedules of reinforcement are important.

22. Describe how a discrimination is established and the criteria used to determine if one has been established.

23. Describe different kinds of changes that may be achieved through model presentation.

24. Explain what is meant by "establishing operations" and give examples.

25. Distinguish between rule-governed and contingency-shaped behavior and explain why this is an important distinction.

26. Identify the variables that influence respondent learning.

27. Give some examples of the influence of antecedents on behavior.

28. Describe some of the effects of our evolutionary history on our behavior.

29. Define the term *behavior chain* and give examples. Explain why chains of behavior are important to consider during assessment and intervention.

30. Describe three functions a stimulus may have and give an example of each.

31. Mr. L. reports that he has a severe fear of cars. He goes out of his way to avoid the sight and sound of cars. Cars have acquired three functions as stimuli. What are they?

32. Define the term *stimulus generalization* and gives examples.

33. Define the term *response generalization* and give examples.

34. Describe different causes of a low frequency of a behavior in a given situation.

35. Describe the components of "differential reinforcement."

Reviewing What You Do

1. You identify consequences that function as reinforcers.

2. You teach someone the meaning of "contingency management."

3. You can correctly apply behavioral principles to problems of concern to clients at many different levels (communities, organizations, groups, families, and individuals).

Reviewing Results

1. Given specific examples you can describe and implement effective, well-designed plans to alter behavior.

Glossary

Avoidance behavior: Behavior maintained by delaying, preventing, or minimizing aversive events.

Behavior: What people do, acting on or having commerce with the outside world. In radical behaviorism, thoughts and feelings are viewed as behaviors.

Behavior chain: A sequence of responses, each associated with a particular cue and reinforcer.

Behavior cusp: A behavior change that brings our behaviors into contact with other contingencies that have important consequences.

Concurrent contingencies: Multiple, perhaps competing consequences in a given context.

Contingency: An association between a behavior and its related cues and consequences.

Contingency management: Rearranging contingencies between a behavior and related cues and consequences that results in a change in behavior and the conditions that influence behavior.

Cultural practice: Interlinked contingencies of reinforcement in which the behavior of each person and its results influence the behavior of other participants.

Culture: Practices characteristic of a group and their associated interrelated contingencies.

Culture clash: Differences in norms, values, beliefs, and related contingency systems.

Culture shock: Feeling of confusion and anxiety as a result of being in a new environment (e.g., accustomed behaviors may no longer be reinforced).

Discrimination: A high rate of a particular behavior in one situation and a low rate in all others.

Discriminative stimulus: A cue that signals the availability of reinforcement if a behavior occurs.

Ecological niche: A particular environment that creates particular behaviors and in turn is affected (altered) by them.

Ecology: The study of the interrelationships between organisms and their environments.

Eliciting stimulus: A cue that elicits a respondent behavior.

Equivalence class: Types of events that differ in form but which occasion a similar response because of our learning history (e.g., see Sidman, 1994).

Escape behavior: Behavior maintained by removing aversive events.

Establishing operation: An event, such as deprivation or pain, that alters the reinforcer effectiveness of some events and evokes the type of behavior reinforced by those events in the past.

Extinction: A procedure in which the usual reinforcement for a behavior is withheld, resulting in a decrease in the probability of that behavior in the future.

Generalization: The occurrence of a behavior in situations in which it was not learned.

Imitation: The duplication of a behavior that is modeled.

Interlinked: Contingencies that influence one another at different contingency system levels (individual, group, family, organization, community, society).

Learning: Any relatively enduring change in behavior as a result of experience.

Matching law: When two behaviors are available (they are current), the relative rate of each and the time spent in each are a function of the relative rate of reinforcement for the two behaviors (McDowell, 1988).

Metacontingency: Dependence between a cultural practice and its outcome for a group (Glenn, 1991).

Model presentation: Displaying an example of behavior.

Negative reinforcement: A procedure in which an event is removed following a behavior and there is a future increase in the probability of that behavior in similar circumstances.

Negative reinforcer: A stimulus that increases behavior that removes it and decreases behavior that results in its presentation.

Noncontingent reinforcement: Delivery of reinforcers independent of responses.

Operant: A class of behaviors, all of which have a similar effect on the environment.

Operant behavior: Behavior maintained by its consequences.

Operant learning: The selection of behavior by its consequences.

Positive reinforcement: A procedure in which an event is presented following a behavior and there is an increase in the future probability of the behavior in similar circumstances.

Positive reinforcer: A stimulus that increases behavior that it follows and decreases behavior when it is removed contingent on that behavior.

Premack Principle: Using a high probability behavior to reinforce a low probability behavior.

Punishment: A procedure in which an event is presented following a behavior and there is a decrease in the future probability of the behavior.

Respondent behavior: Behavior elicited by antecedent stimuli.

Respondent extinction: The conditioned or unconditioned stimulus is no longer paired with stimulus, resulting in the CS gradually ceasing to elicit a CR.

Respondent learning (also known as classical conditioning): The process by which neutral stimuli acquire the ability to elicit responses through their association with stimuli that elicit a response.

Response cost: A procedure in which an event is removed following a behavior and there is a decrease in the future probability of the behavior.

Rule-governed behavior: Behavior influenced by verbal descriptions of contingencies.

Satiation: When a reinforcer loses its effectiveness through overuse.

Schedule of reinforcement: The pattern of reinforcement related to a behavior.

Self-efficacy: Performance efficacy refers to the belief that we can perform a task and outcome efficacy refers to the belief that we will be successful if we perform it (e.g., fulfill role expectations).

Shaping: The reinforcement of successive approximations to a desired behavior.

Social control: Contingencies that regulate behavior by means of norms, laws, rules, and regulations.

Social exchange theory: A theory of behavior emphasizing the costs and benefits of interacting with another person or group.

Socialization: The social influence process by which behavior and values are shaped and maintained.

Stimulus: Any aspect of the environment that can be distinguished; any condition, event, or change in the physical world (inside or outside the body). Examples include people, places, things, light, sound, and odors.

Part 4

A Decision-Focused Practice Model

8

Problem Solving and Decision Making: Integral to Helping Clients

OVERVIEW   Helping clients, like life itself, involves solving problems and making decisions. Problems differ in their prospects for resolution. Obstacles to making sound decisions, such as propaganda in the helping professions and in the media, as well as cognitive biases and agency cultures that discourage well-reasoned decisions are discussed. Being forewarned is being prepared. If you are aware of obstacles and know how to avoid them, your clients are more likely to attain outcomes they value. We can draw on literature concerning problem solving, judgment, and decision making to make sound decisions.

YOU WILL LEARN ABOUT

- Advantages of a practice model emphasizing problem solving and related decisions

- The relationship between problem solving and decision making

- Taking advantage of related research

- Approaches focusing on bias

- Fast and frugal heuristics

- Errors we tend to make

- Barriers to problem solving

- We can become better problem solvers

Advantages of a Practice Model Emphasizing Problem Solving and Related Decisions

Clients, whether individuals, families, groups, organizations, or communities, have real-life problems. They may need concrete services, such as housing, food, or health care. Family caregivers of elderly relatives may need respite care and information about different kinds of resources. Residents of an inner-city neighborhood may need guidance in how to influence the agenda of local board meetings. A person with a developmental disability may need help locating a job. Social policy analysis involves trying to understand and solve social problems such as unemployment, lack of health care, and domestic violence. A problem-solving model has long been of interest in social work (Perlman, 1957). We are all engaged in problem solving on an everyday basis. Karl Popper views problem solving as our primal activity, one needed for our very survival. He views evolution as the history of problem solving. Based on trial solutions we eliminate certain errors (if we are lucky) and are confronted with new problems. Asking "What problems are clients trying to solve?" grounds activities on outcomes of concern to clients (see Exhibit 8.1). Such a focus in no way implies that clients' strengths are overlooked. This approach and its undesirable effects (e.g., blaming clients for their problems and overlooking environmental causes) are critiqued throughout this book. It would be a poor problem solver indeed who did not take advantage of available resources including clients' strengths.

A problem-solving model emphasizes the importance of critically reviewing assumptions and drawing on practice- and policy-related research findings to inform decisions including

---

EXHIBIT 8.1

Advantages of Focusing on Problem Solving and Related Decisions

1. Grounds activities on problems and related outcomes of concern to clients.

2. Evaluates effectiveness by the degree to which outcomes that clients value are achieved and outcomes that harm clients are minimized.

3. Emphasizes the importance of an active search for resources including client assets of value in solving problems.

4. Encourages use of research related to problem solving, judgment, and decision making.

5. Highlights the value of mistakes in learning how to do better in the future.

6. Emphasizes the value of critical appraisal of claims (e.g., in avoiding common biases).

7. Emphasizes the value of functional knowledge (that which decreases or reveals uncertainly about how to attain valued outcomes).

8. Emphasizes the importance of self-reflection (e.g., appraising the gap between your knowledge and what is available).

9. Minimizes irrelevant activities/discussion.

10. Encourages contextual understanding of the relationship between the personal and the political.

---

material concerning problem solving, critical thinking, and decision making. This literature describes errors we tend to make and steps we can take to avoid them. It describes differences in how experts and novices approach and solve problems. It highlights the importance of considering the context in which problems occur, including resource constraints. A problem-solving model highlights key decisions across service levels and common questions, actions, needed resources, and errors in different problem-solving phases. It serves as a guide to how precise we have to be. Karl Popper (1994) suggests that we should never be more precise than we have to be when trying to solve problems. Guidelines Sternberg (1986) recommends include the following:

1. *Recognize that a problem exists.* What kind is it? How is it reflected at different system levels (individual, family, community, society)? At what levels (if any) can it be resolved and how? Do you question the obvious? Do you use multiple representations of the problem (including visual ones)?

2. *Identify and order steps needed to achieve hoped-for outcomes.* Review data, sift out relevant from irrelevant data; simplify or redefine goals as needed.

3. *Resource allocation (planning how to spend time).* Is high-level planning required? Can you use prior knowledge in planning and allocating resources? Are you flexible and willing to change plans and resource allocation? Are you on the lookout for new resources?

4. *Monitor adequacy of solution.* Seek feedback: beware of "justification of effort" effects. Seek external feedback.

The Relationship Between Problem Solving and Decision Making

Problems involve gaps between some current and desired state of affairs. Problems differ in the possibilities of solving them. (See Exhibit 8.2.) Solving problems requires making decisions about the reasons related to gaps between current and desired situations and what plans are most promising to close them. This is true whether you are considering a social policy, helping a community gain better services, helping family members resolve disagreements, or working with a depressed single parent. A major purpose of this book is to increase your awareness of the decisions you make and the basis on which you make them, and the kinds of errors that may be made at different decision points and how to minimize them. Encouraging this "reflexivity" has long been a concern (e.g., Schön, 1990). You and your clients decide how to frame problems (e.g., is lack of a job due to lack of job skills and/or limited employment opportunities?), who to involve, what data to collect and how to gather it, how to evaluate the accuracy of data gathered, and how to integrate it. You

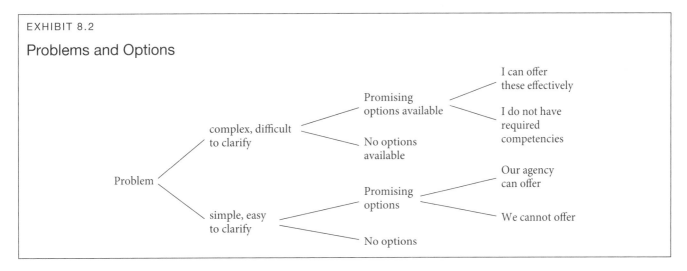

EXHIBIT 8.2

Problems and Options

make decisions about what causes to focus on, what outcomes to select, what plans are most promising, and how to evaluate progress. Decisions include moment-to-moment ones about what to say next. Decisions made in work with parents alleged to have abused or neglected their children include: (1) substantiating maltreatment, (2) assessing risk, (3) determining child safety, and (4) determining emergency needs (DePanfilis & Salus, 2003). Different problems clients confront involve different levels and kinds of uncertainty and conflicts of interest and may require different kinds of information. Reviews of decisions made by professionals reveals a variety of avoidable errors, often caused by miscommunication between different service providers. We may be over- or underconfident in the accuracy of our views. We may be unaware of or reluctant to admit uncertainty. We may refuse to make a decision or cause a delay in making a decision, which may harm clients.

Decisions and Options (Menus)

Decision making requires choosing among different (often competing) goals and related courses of action. One of the purposes of decision making is to reveal possibilities (Baron, 2000). You may have to decide whether lack of needed concrete resources is related to lack of information, poor marketing of services, policies restricting access to resources, lack of skills needed to attain resources, or beliefs that interfere with accepting help. How we frame a problem (e.g., in terms of potential gains or losses) influences our decisions (Hastie & Dawes, 2001). Our decisions tend to be more extreme when posed in terms of possible losses rather than gains. We tend to be "risk adverse" (see Paling, 2006). The list of options (the "menu") related to a decision differ in number, variety, and whether they include feasible options. Exhibit 8.3 illustrates decisions you will make and options you may consider. Cultural differences may influence the acceptability of options.

Lists of options (menus) differ in their "noise level" (number and vividness of irrelevant and misleading options). Misleading items may be included (those that will take you and your clients in unhelpful directions) such as results of an invalid measure.

You may, incorrectly attribute the cause of problems to psychological characteristics of the client and overlook environmental causes. Valuable options may be missing. When I ask students what sources of data they draw on, they often list client self-report, reports from significant others, other professionals' opinions, the results of standardized paper-and-pencil tests (another form of self-report), and case records in which data from one or more of these sources are described. Observation in role-play or real-life settings and self-monitoring (clients or significant others collect data in real-life settings) are rarely mentioned. If these methods would be of value in selecting effective plans, then this list of options is incomplete.

Valuable options may be included but not be possible to pursue, perhaps because of limited resources. You and your clients may be forced to rely on some approximation. For example, rather than helping community members to organize to improve the quality of their neighborhood, you may have to settle for the more modest goal of helping residents to make their homes more secure from crime. Application problems may prohibit use of valuable practice methods. The accuracy and completeness of your background knowledge will influence success.

What Is a Good Decision?

As Jonathan Baron (1994) points out, the whole point of good thinking is to increase the probability of good outcomes. A good outcome is one that decision makers value; it results in valued goals (Baron, 2000). Good decision makers "do the best they can with what is knowable." Clearly this is not always done (Tetlock, 2005). Herek, Janis, and Huth (1989) examined the thinking of U.S. presidents (and their advisers) in making decisions related to international crises. They noted the following indicators of defective decision making based on a review of historical records:

1. Gross omissions in surveying alternatives (inadequate search for possibilities).

2. Gross omissions in surveying objectives (inadequate search for goals).

EXHIBIT 8.3

Examples of Decisions and Options

What kind of problem it is
- Lack of concrete resources
- Lack of information
- Lack of skills
- Emotional/affective
- Lack of social support
- Interpersonal (between people)
- Lack of insight
- Decision problem
- Discrimination/oppression
- Group process
- Legal
- Community problem
- Transition problem
- Cultural conflict
- Service system problem
- Public and social policy problem
- Organizational problem
- Legislation problem

What theory to draw on
- Psychoanalytic
- Cognitive
- Family systems
- Social learning
- Radical behavioral
- Life span developmental
- Contextual (ecological)
- Interpersonal

What to explore to find out what kind of problem it is
- Psychological characteristics
- Biological factors
- Family environment
- Community influences
- Cultural differences
- Legal complications
- Material circumstances
- Recent events
- Service systems
- Public and social policies
- Political, social, and economic influences

How to explore (i.e., what kinds of assessment data to rely on)
- Self-report in interview
- Standardized tests
- Self-monitoring
- Observation in role plays
- Observation in real life
- Physiological measures
- Case records

How to evaluate claims
- Rely on common sense
- Authority

- Intuition
- Tradition
- Consensus (what most people believe)
- Testimonials/case examples
- Anecdotal experience
- Systematically collected data
- Scientific criteria (e.g., critical tests of claims)

How to integrate data
- Sequentially review data
- Try to examine all data at once
- Rely on intuition
- Use an "expert" computer-based program
- Consult the professional literature

What to do if you do not have resources to help clients attain outcomes they value
- Offer support
- Refer elsewhere
- Help clients form self-help advocacy groups
- "Problem shift" (focus on another area)
- Pretend you do and forge ahead
- Pursue changes in policy and legislation

What intervention level(s) to focus on
- Individual
- Family
- Group
- Community
- Service system
- Public and social policy and related legislation

How to evaluate progress
- Your opinion
- Self-report of clients
- Self-report by significant others
- Standardized questionnaires
- Observation of behavior in role play
- Observation of behavior in problem-related real-life settings
- Archival records
- Pre-post data
- Single case designs (see chapter 22)

How to encourage generalization and maintenance of positive outcomes
- Train and hope
- Involve significant others
- Focus on behaviors of value to clients in real life
- Focus on behaviors that will continue to be reinforced in real-life settings
- Shift to naturally occurring schedules of reinforcement
- Provide relapse training

3. Failure to examine major costs and risks of the preferred choice (inadequate search for evidence).

4. Selective bias in processing information (biased interpretation).

Taking Advantage of Related Research

There is a rich literature on problem solving and decision making in many different fields. (See Gambrill 2012b; Schraagen et al., 2008.) This indicates that:

- Problem definition is a critical phase.

- Uncertainty abounds.

- Creative, as well as critical thinking is required.

- Situation awareness is important (attending to what is going on in related environments).

- Some ways of structuring problems are more productive than others.

- Degree of expertise in an area varies greatly.

- Domain-specific knowledge may be vital.

- We often satisfice rather than optimize.

- Our goals direct our actions.

- We fall into a number of "intelligence traps" such as jumping to conclusions (deciding on one option too soon) and overlooking promising alternatives.

- Experts compared to novices organize knowledge in a different way (e.g., pattern recognition), approach problems on a more abstract level, and can more readily identify what additional information would be helpful.

- Learning from experience via corrective feedback is vital (not experience per se).

- The strategies we use influence our success.

- Monitoring our progress is important (e.g., to catch false directions).

- Errors of both omission and commission occur.

- How we allocate our resources influences our success (e.g., time spent in planning).

- Both problem-related knowledge and self-knowledge influence success.

- We can learn to become better problem solvers.

Successful compared to unsuccessful problem solvers think more about their thinking. They critically review their assumptions and reasoning. They are their own best critics. They ask questions about the accuracy of data. They ask: What evidence supports this claim? What evidence contradicts this claim? Has it been critically tested? With what results? Are there well-argued alternative views?

Problem Solving Is Uncertain

Making decisions in the helping professions is an uncertain activity. However, professionals, including social workers are typically uninformed about uncertainty and how to handle it ethically and effectively. Professionals, as well as clients, vastly overestimate the predictive accuracy of tests (Gaissmaier & Gigerenzer, 2011; Wegwarth & Gigerenzer, 2011). Many authors describe our "innumeracy," referring to difficulties in reasoning correctly about uncertainty. Uncertainty may concern: (1) the nature of the problem; (2) the outcomes desired; (3) what is needed to attain valued outcomes; (4) likelihood of attaining outcomes; and (5) measures that will best reflect degree of success. Information about options may be missing, and accurate estimates of the probability that different alternatives will result in desired outcomes may be unknown. Preferences may change in the very process of being asked about them. Failure to recognize uncertainties has resulted (and does result) in considerable harm to clients. They are so important to recognize that an Uncertainties Page has been initiated in the *British Medical Journal* to bring these to the attention of physicians (see also Database of Uncertainties about the Effects of Treatments (DUETS). Shouldn't we have a similar page in *Social Work?*

Problems that confront clients (e.g., lack of housing or day care) are often difficult ones that challenge the most skilled of helpers. They are often unstructured. Rarely is all relevant information available, and it is difficult to integrate different kinds of data. We work under constraints such as time pressures. Knowledge may be available but not used. Even when a great deal is known, this knowledge is usually in the form of general principles that do not allow specific predictions about individuals (Dawes, 1994a). For example, many convicted rapists rape again when released from prison; this does not allow you to accurately predict whether a particular person will rape again if released. You can only appeal to the general information (see also critiques of expert testimony). Problems may have a variety of causes and potential solutions.

The Role of Creativity and Intuition

Successful problem solvers draw on their creative talents to discover options.

The scientist and the artist, far from being engaged in opposed or incompatible activities, are both trying to extend our understanding of experience by the use of creative imagination subjected to critical control, and so both are using irrational as well as rational faculties. Both are exploring the unknown and trying to articulate the search and its findings. Both are seekers after truth who make indispensable use of intuition. (Magee, 1985, pp. 68–69)

Styles, attitudes, and strategies associated with creativity include:

- Readiness to explore and to change.

- Attention to problem finding, as well as problem solving.

- Immersion in a task.

- Restructuring of understanding.

- A belief that knowing and understanding are products of one's intellectual efforts.

- Withholding of judgment.

- An emphasis on understanding.

- Thinking in terms of opposites.

- Valuing complexity, ambiguity, and uncertainty combined with an interest in finding order.

- Valuing feedback but not deferring to convention and social pressure.

- Recognizing multiple perspectives on a topic. See for example Kaufman & Sternberg, 2010.

The Importance of Domain-Specific Knowledge and Skills

Nickerson (1988–89) points out, "To think effectively in any domain one must know something about the domain and, in general, the more one knows the better" (p. 13). *Content knowledge* includes facts, concepts, principles, and strategies that contribute to problem solving. *Procedural knowledge* includes the skills required to implement content knowledge. Let us say that you have been asked to help homeless people form self-help groups. What information may be important to know? What theories and concepts will be helpful? What skills do you need to use this knowledge effectively? Knowledge that could be helpful may remain unused (inert). Perhaps you never understood a concept in the first place. Content knowledge without performance skills to put this into use remains unused. This is known as the *"parroting problem"*; we can describe what should be done but cannot put this knowledge to use.

Experts compared to novices in an area possess domain-specific knowledge and can move rapidly to identify what information is needed to solve a problem. Indeed, they seem to use a different reasoning process compared to novices based on many experiences providing corrective feedback (e.g., Salas & Klein, 2001; Schraagen et al., 2008). Expert decision makers quickly size up a situation based on recognition of important cues. Klein calls his model "recognition primed decision-making" (RPD). Related research highlights the importance of situation awareness, that

is, having an accurate understanding of what is occurring in a situation from moment to moment as circumstances change (see also Nutt & Wilson, 2010; Phillips, Klein, & Sieck, 2005).

Different Problem-Solving Phases

Questions, actions, resources needed, and common errors in different phases can be seen in Exhibit 8.4. Initial steps influence later ones unless you use strategies to avoid this effect. Many of the errors shown reflect a confirmatory bias (seeking only data that support favored views). Imagine that you are a community organizer in a low-income neighborhood and believe that new immigrants moving into the neighborhood are the least likely to become active in community advocacy efforts. Because of this belief you may concentrate your attention on long-term residents. As a result, new resident immigrants are ignored with the consequences that they are unlikely to become involved. This will strengthen your original belief.

Problem Framing as a Critical Phase

Clarifying and deciding how to structure a problem is a critical step in problem solving. Vague descriptions get in the way of identifying related behaviors and the circumstances in which they occur. Different theories involve different problem spaces (i.e., how a problem is represented). (See chapter 6.) Consider homelessness. This could be viewed as: (1) the client's own fault (he is lazy); (2) a family problem (relatives are unwilling to help); (3) lack of low-cost housing; (4) a problem with service integration; (5) due to a "mental disorder"; (6) a result of our basic economic structure (e.g., unskilled jobs have decreased); (7) discrimination based on racial prejudice; and (8) some mix of these possibilities.

Experts structure problems at a deeper (more abstract) level compared to novices, who tend to accept problems as given. For example, experts in applied behavior analysis use their knowledge of principles of behavior to identify contingencies related to behaviors of concern (associations between behaviors and what happens right before and after; see chapter 7). Only by clarifying and restructuring a problem may it be solved or may you discover that there is no solution (see Exhibit 8.5). Creative (bold guesses) and contextual thinking will often be needed to describe the "problem space" in a way that yields a solution. Only in this way may you discover interrelationship among different levels of influence (e.g., individual, family, community, service system, policy).

> A problem well stated is a problem half solved.
> —Charles F. Kettering

There Are Different Decision-Making Styles

Dual process theories of decision making suggest that we use both a rapid intuitive style, as well as a more deliberative analytic style as needed, depending on the situation (Kahneman, 2011).

EXHIBIT 8.4

Problem-Solving Phases and Related Questions, Actions, Resources, and Common Errors

Steps	Questions	Actions	Resources Needed	Common Errors
1. Clarify the problem	• What kind of problem is it? • Who is involved? • How does it affect clients and significant others? • What would happen if nothing were done? • What are influential contingencies? • What is the base rate? • What solutions have been attempted to what effect? • Do attempted solutions make problems worse? • What are clients' and significant others' views of concerns and how they can be solved?	• Gather and evaluate the accuracy of data. • Accurately identify knowledge gaps between personal and available problem-related knowledge. • Fill in the gaps as needed and as possible. • Pose well-structured questions related to information needs (e.g., description, risk, and assessment questions). • Search effectively and efficiently for related research. • Critically appraise what you find.	• Problem-related domain-specific knowledge. • Knowledge, skills, and tools (e.g. access to needed databases) to gain access to related research findings in a timely manner. • Time and materials needed for assessment. • Access to relevant environments (e.g., homes, classrooms). • Knowledge about assessment methods and skills in using them. • A willingness to recognize uncertainties.	• Jump to conclusions (overlook alternative views). • Seek to justify views rather than critically evaluate them. • Ignore environmental causes. • Gather irrelevant data. • Ignore available related research. • Rely on invalid data (e.g., small biased samples). • Disregard conflicting evidence. • Stereotyping.
2. Search for solutions	• What are options? • How feasible is each? • How likely is it that each will result in desired outcomes? • What resources are needed to address concerns at different levels? • What resources are available at different levels? • What resources could be created? • What constraints must be considered? • What have clients tried?	• Critically review alternatives. • Estimate the likely success of each. • Review and seek needed resources. • Identify constraints. • Pose clear relevant questions regarding information needs • Search for and critically appraise what you find. • Assess the relevance of research findings to your client.	• Domain-specific knowledge (e.g., about problem-related factors). • Access to information about resources. • See also items listed under 1 above and under questions to the left.	• Overlook options (e.g., to rearrange environmental cues and consequences). • Look only for data that confirm your assumptions. • Overlook constraints. • Overlook resources. • Not revising views based on new information. • See other errors under step 1.
3. Decide on a plan	• Can you provide help needed? • What plan is least costly, most likely to be successful, and most acceptable to clients? • How likely is it to be successful? • Should you refer clients elsewhere?	• Integrate data collected, drawing on your clinical expertise, as well as client values and preferences. • Review soundness of arguments for different plans. • Review feasibility of plans.	• Knowledge, resources, and skills required to implement plans with the fidelity needed for success.	• Overlook promising options. • Overlook constraints. • Do not fully inform clients about options and their advantages and disadvantages.

(continued)

EXHIBIT 8.4 (Continued)

Steps	Questions	Actions	Resources Needed	Common Errors
4. Implement plans	• Can the plan be implemented? With what fidelity can you implement it?	• Arrange requisites needed. Fill in gaps in content and procedural knowledge and skills.	• Knowledge, resources, and skills required to implement plans with fidelity.	• The "dilution" effect (i.e., offer ineffective version of plans).
5. Evaluate results	• How can progress be accurately assessed with the least cost? • Was the plan implemented with fidelity? • Have we succeeded? • If so, how can gains be maintained? • If not, what should we do next?	• Select relevant, sensitive, feasible outcome measures. • Design a feasible, acceptable monitoring procedure. • Collect data regarding outcome. • Alter plans as necessary in accord with degree of progress.	• Knowledge and skills related to evaluation and troubleshooting. • Someone (e.g. the client) who agrees to gather needed information.	• Use vague outcome measures. • Use inaccurate measures. • Do not gather both subjective and objective measures. • Post-hoc fallacy (assume that because there was a change, your services were responsible). • Overlook harmful effects. • Not revising plans as needed based on outcome data.
6. Try again?	• Can the plan be implemented more effectively? • Should we circle back to assessment? • Is another plan likely to be successful? • Can constraints be addressed?	• Circle back to assessment—check problem structuring. • Search again for related research. • Proceed through other phases.	• Time. • Troubleshooting skills.	• Give up too soon. • Fail to critically examine favored views. • Believing you can help everyone.

EXHIBIT 8.5

Problem-Solving Flow Chart

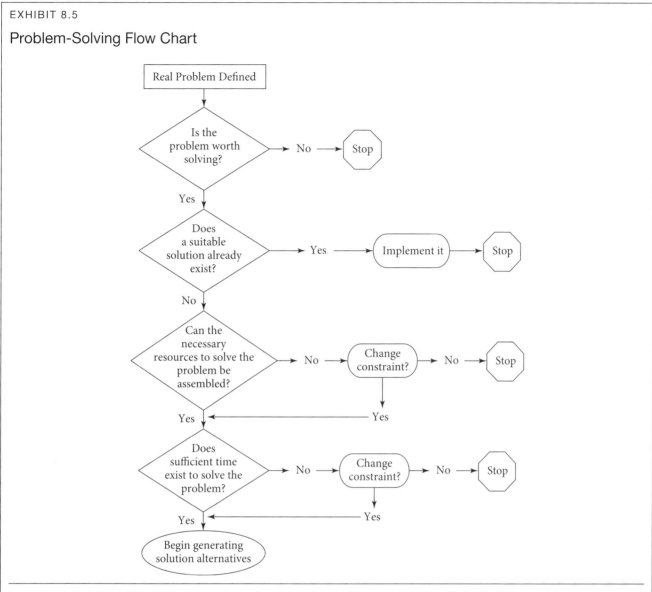

Source: H. S. Fogler & S. E. LeBlanc (2008). *Strategies for creative problem solving* (p. 75). Upper Saddle River, N.J.: Prentice Hall. Reprinted with permission of Pearson Education Inc.

(See also Glockner & Witteman, 2010; Kruglanski & Gigerenzer, 2011). Steps presumed to be of value in a rational model of decision making in which we identify alternatives, estimate the probability that each will yield hoped-for outcomes, assign values to different options, and select the alternative with the greatest value are often impossible to satisfy, and may be less effective than intuitive styles. Expert decision makers develop "situation awareness" based on corrective feedback from past experiences and act swiftly based on this, as they often must (e.g., fire fighters). They satisfice rather than optimize.

We Use Simplifying Strategies (Heuristics)

The term "heuristic" refers to a "rule of thumb" (strategy). Our information is typically incomplete. We can consider only so

much information at one time. The consequences of this may include: (1) selective perception (we do not necessarily see what is there); (2) sequential (rather than contextual) processing of information; (3) reliance on heuristics (rules-of-thumb) to reduce effort (e.g., frequently occurring cues); and (4) faulty memory. In his discussion of bounded rationality Simon (1982) suggested that we use heuristics (simplifying strategies) to solve problems.

Approaches Focusing on Bias

Nisbett and Ross (1980) and others, such as Tversky and Kahneman (1973), emphasized errors that result from use of simplifying heuristics. They suggested availability and representativeness (similarity) as reasons related to a variety of errors.

Availability

We often rely on what is available, for example, a preferred practice theory or a vivid testimonial. We tend to seek information that is consistent with our preconceived notions; we tend to disregard conflicting evidence. Let us say that one of your clients has a substance-abuse problem and that you recently went to a workshop on self-esteem. This concept (self-esteem) is readily available in your thoughts. You may associate self-esteem with your client's problems and believe that low self-esteem is mainly responsible for this person's substance abuse. Behaviors such as hitting and yelling are more vivid compared to polite requests and following instructions. Resources available may guide choices rather than those that may not be obvious but be of greater value.

Observers tend to attribute the cause of other people's behavior to characteristics of the person rather than to situational factors (Pronin, Puccio, & Ross, 2002) (the fundamental attribution error). The "actor's" behavior is more noticeable compared to more static situational events. The client in the interview is more vivid than his or her home and neighborhood, which you may not see. Many factors that are not correlated with the frequency of an event influence how important it seems, such as how visible it is, how vivid it is, and how easily it can be imagined (that is, how available it is). We tend to overestimate the prevalence of illnesses that receive a great deal of media attention and underestimate the prevalence of illnesses that receive little media attention (Slovic, Fischhoff, & Lichtenstein, 1982).

The Influence of Preconceptions and Preferred Theories "The impact of preconceptions is one of the better demonstrated findings of twentieth-century psychology" (Nisbett & Ross, 1980, p. 67). Consider the classic study in which teachers were told that certain children in their classroom did very well on a nonverbal intelligence test that predicts intellectual blooming (Rosenthal & Jacobson, 1992). These children showed superior gains over the next 8 months. Actually, they were randomly selected. Differences in expectations create different interactions. For example, teachers pay greater attention to students for whom they have high expectations (see Rosenthal & Jacobson, 1992). Our expectations alter what we do and do not attend to as suggested in Exhibit 8.6. If we are not aware that we have a preconception that people 85 years old are "over the hill," we may focus on an elderly client's deficiencies and overlook her assets. We may overlook environmental factors related to her concerns, such as reactions of significant others. These may be less vivid. Our preconceptions and theories affect which concepts and beliefs are available. They influence what events we notice or inquire about. Beliefs about the causes associated with a problem may result in selective inquiry during assessment.

Preconceptions can lead to incorrect inferences when a theory (1) is held on poor grounds (there is not adequate reason to believe it is relevant); (2) is used unconsciously; or (3) it preempts examination of the data (Nisbett & Ross, 1980, p. 71). We may hold theories that have not been critically tested as dearly as theories that have been critically tested and found to help clients attain outcomes they value. Unwarranted confidence in a theory increases chances of incorrect views of concerns. Stereotypes are a kind of preconception. They influence what we do and what we believe (e.g., Nelson, 2009). Stereotypes can be created remarkably quickly. For example, children told that a visitor to their school was clumsy resulted in many of the children holding him responsible for knocking over a cake (when in fact he had not) (Leichtman & Ceci, 1995). Stereotyping is an incorrect assessment of variability, "a set of people who are labeled as belonging to a given group is presumed to be more homogeneous than is in fact the case" (Holland, Holyoak, Nisbett, & Thagard, 1986, p. 245). It is a false estimate of the complexity of a group.

The fallacy of stereotyping (Scriven, 1976, p. 208) consists of treating a description as if it represents all the individuals in a group of which it may (or may not) be a fairly typical sample. We tend to overestimate the variability of in-groups (groups of which we are a member) and underestimate the degree of variability in out-groups (groups of which we are not a member). For

---

EXHIBIT 8.6

The Preconceived Notion

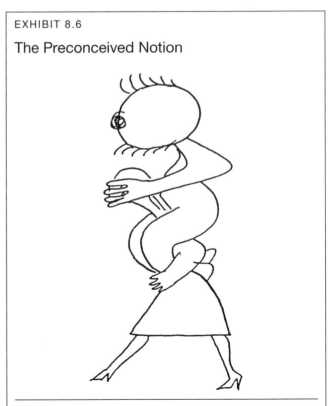

Source: W. H. Schneider (1965). *Danger: Men talking.* New York: Random House. Reprinted with permission.

example, people who are not gay or lesbian may underestimate the degree of variability among people who are gay or lesbian. On the other hand, gay men and lesbians may overestimate the degree of variability of gay or lesbian people. Underestimating the variability of groups with which we are not familiar results in believing that we learn more (than we in fact do) from experience with one member of that group. If you have never before met a Native American, you may be inclined to make greater generalizations about what all Native Americans are like than if you have met many. Ceci and Bruck (1995) note that "Failure to test an alternative to a pet hunch can lead interviewers to ignore inconsistent evidence and to shape the contents of the interview to be consistent with their own beliefs" (p. 80).

Vividness The vividness or concreteness of material influences how available it is. Vivid case examples are easy to recall and crowd out data that, although less vivid, may be more informative. Vivid material is more likely to be remembered and is thus more likely to influence the collection, organization, and interpretation of data. Advertisements take full advantage of this to encourage us to buy their products such as medications, for example, vivid testimonials and before and after pictures. Events that do not take place are not as vivid. This type of information tends to be overlooked when it can be crucial. Sherlock Holmes solved a case based on the fact that a dog did not bark at an intruder.

> Vision is the art of seeing things invisible.
> —Jonathan Swift

Vivid information can be misleading, especially when duller but more informative material is not considered. Helpers often discount statistical information by citing a single case that supposedly contradicts this information. Testimonials and case examples are vivid as is personal experience: "I have seen this in my own practice" (see Exhibit 4.5). The greater vividness of case examples compared to statistical data may explain why research reports are often of little interest to helpers. A vivid case example, unless it is known to be typical, ought to be given little weight in making decisions. It rarely warrants the inferential weight assigned to it. You should certainly give less weight to a single example than to relevant statistical data. If vividness reflects valuable clues, then relying on this should facilitate speedy, accurate decisions.

Anchoring and Insufficient Adjustment We often form impressions quickly. Nisbett and Ross (1980) attribute primacy effects to our tendency to generate theories that bias the interpretation of data. These effects are encouraged by premature commitment to one assumption and insufficient revision of beliefs, as well as the tendency to believe (often falsely) in the consistency of behavior across different situations. One way to avoid anchoring effects is to consider an alternative estimate at

another extreme. We are influenced by recency—what we last see or hear. You may attend a workshop on child abuse and as a result suspect child abuse more readily in families.

Influence by Resemblance

We often make judgments based on the degree to which a characteristic seems to resemble or be similar to another characteristic or theory (Tversky & Kahneman, 1974). We may assume that causes resemble their effects when this may not be so. Representative thinking is mainly an associative process in which the associations we have with a certain characteristic (such as the label "mental patient") influence our judgments. The problem is, similarity is not influenced by factors we should consider: (1) whether a person/object belongs in a certain group; (2) the probability that an outcome was a result of a particular cause; and (3) the probability that a process will result in a certain outcome. Reliance on representative thinking may yield incorrect beliefs about the degree to which: (1) outcomes reflect origins; (2) instances are representative of their categories; and (3) antecedents are representative of consequences. Overestimating the relationship between abuse as a child and abuse of one's own children reflects reliance on resemblance criteria. Consider some other examples:

- Foxes have remarkable lungs. Therefore, the lungs of a fox will remedy asthma.

- Turmeric (which is yellow) will cure jaundice.

- Unwillingness to discuss "homosexual feelings" reflects excessive interest in them. (Here and in the next two examples we see the assumption of opposites.)

- A generous action reflects underlying stinginess.

- Permissiveness when raising children leads to radicalism as adults.

Associative thinking may occur unnoticed (automatically, mindlessly) unless we question our assumptions, search for alternative possibilities, and review the evidentiary status of claims. Reliance on representativeness results in errors when we use clues that do not accurately predict an outcome. For example, we may incorrectly assume that because a homeless child is similar to another client we just saw, similar causes are involved. Often, as in recognition primed decision making, our associations reflect accurate information about frequencies that help us to make sound decisions (Gigerenzer, Hertwig, & Pachur, 2011). But they may not. (For readers who want to pursue this further, see Appendix A.) How likely is it that a sample (e.g., of behaviors, thoughts, or feelings) accurately represents the population from which it is drawn? How likely is it that what you see during 1 hour in a residential center accurately reflects the usual pattern of interaction between staff and residents?

Fast and Frugal Heuristics

There has been a shift to highlighting the adaptive nature of our decision making as it fits certain environments—a realization that heuristics often work well and save time and effort. Gigerenzer (2005) argues that many events that have been viewed as cognitive illusions are reasonable judgments given the environmental structure. Their use has been referred to as the "fast and frugal" approach to decision making (Gigerenzer, Hertwig, & Pachur, 2011). Such strategies often (but not always) suffice, and when "ecologically relevant," may surpass more deliberative approaches. Advocates of the "fast and frugal" approach argue that rather than our limited information-processing capabilities being a handicap, they are an advantage, because they facilitate rapid decisions based on recognition of relevant environmental cues. They encourage attention to cues that are most relevant (situation awareness), so avoiding errors introduced by too much information, including misleading and irrelevant data. Consider the recognition heuristic: "If one of two objects is recognized and the other is not, then infer that the recognized object has the higher value with respect to the criterion." Such a strategy is fast because it can solve problems quickly and frugal because it requires little information and effort; but it works only when recognition validity is greater than .5.

Gigerenzer and his colleagues (2011) argue that availability and representativeness are labels for a wide variety of events such as ease of recall. They argue that these are not theories but labels, surrogates for theories. He and his colleagues focus on the selection of heuristics in specific contexts—how do we select one in a given situation and how effective is it? He and his colleagues argue that problems posed in laboratory experiments do not reflect real-life situations, for example, information search is ignored. They highlight the important distinction between cue validity (what is in the mind) and ecological validity (what is in the environment).

Gigerenzer suggests that there are two kinds of search: an optimizing and a heuristic search. In the former there is a kind of sequential analysis. In the second, we do not try to optimize; we exploit characteristics of particular environments to make sound decisions. This view is a continuation of Simon's (1982) bounded rationality—that satisficing is sufficient in many situations—that the time and effort required to identify many alternatives and evaluate their soundness is not only unnecessary in many situations to arrive at a sound decision, it may result in more errors, perhaps because too much information is considered; cues that are most valuable are lost in a sea of data. Research regarding the development of expertise shows that primed decision making based on repeated past experiences providing corrective feedback enables speedy pattern recognition (Klein, 1998). Gigerenzer and his colleagues argue that the "heuristics and biases approach" (e.g., Nisbett & Ross, 1980) views rationality as logical instead of *ecological*. Typically, as they point out, optimization is not possible, let alone necessary; we rarely know all the factors influencing a behavior/event.

Thus, we have the "less is more" effect, in which accuracy "is always relative to the structure of the environment" (p. 9); error is confined to acceptable limits, for example, in making a prediction. The key question is: "Are the decisions that result those most likely to help clients attain outcomes they value?"

Too much information may decrease our effectiveness by creating distracting "noise" that results in overlooking central clues that enable speedy action (e.g., Zsambok & Klein, 1997). Gigerenzer (2005) suggests that a rule functions as a heuristic (rule-of-thumb) when it exploits our evolved capacities, as well as structures of environments. All heuristics are domain-specific to some degree, designed to solve certain kinds of problems. Heuristics differ from optimization, in which we try to attain the optimal solution to a problem. Thus, as he and his colleagues (2011) note, "Heuristics are not good or bad, rational or irrational, per se, but only relative to an environment.... The same holds for optimization methods" (p. xix). Gigerenzer and his colleagues have pursued a research agenda to identify components of what they call "The adaptive toolbox." This includes search rules, stopping rules, and decision rules. Since these heuristics ignore information and enable fast decisions they are called "fast and frugal." There is a trade off between accuracy ("good enough") and effort and time. A "take the best" approach consists of three building blocks.

1. *Search rule*: Search through cues in order of their validity.

2. *Stopping rule*: Stop on finding the first cue that discriminates between the objects.

3. *Decision rule*: Infer that the object with the positive cue value 1 has the higher criterion value. (Gigerenzer & Brighton, 2011, p. 7)

Errors We Tend to Make

Studies of decision making in professional contexts reveal a variety of avoidable errors (e.g., Munro, 1996; Rzepnicki, Johnson, Kane, Moncher, Coconato, & Shulman, 2012) Studies in child welfare show the effects of *ratcheting* (persisting with a point of view in spite of evidence that it is wrong) and *templating* (inappropriately applying correlational data to individual clients) (Howitt, 1992). We may fail to recognize important cues or focus on irrelevant content/events. Many errors occur because of confirmation biases (searching only for data in support of a preferred view) and reliance on questionable criteria, such as popularity for evaluating the accuracy of claims. Errors are usually due to systemic factors, including poor training (e.g., Reason, 2001). There may be a "cascade effect" in which one error, if not caught and countered, leads to another in a chain that results in harmful consequences. This highlights the value of identifying errors at an early point. As Woods and Cook (1999) note, "Because there are a set of contributors, multiple opportunities arise to redirect the trajectory away from disaster" (p. 144) (see also Boal & Meckler, 2010). In some instances, making rapid decisions with little reflection may work fine. However, in other instances both analytical and intuitive thinking may be needed to make sound decisions and solve problems.

Many errors occur because of reliance on questionable criteria, such as anecdotal experience, to evaluate the accuracy of claims as discussed in chapter 4. In errors of commission we do something that decreases the likelihood of discovering valuable options. We may:

- Look only for data that confirm our beliefs.

- Jump to conclusions.

- Stereotype people or theories.

- Misinterpret cues.

- Assume that correlation reflects causation.

- Prematurely discard a valuable opinion.

In errors of omission we fail to do something. We may:

- Not question initial assumptions.

- Fail to seek out and critically appraise research related to practices and policies.

- Ignore environmental causes.

- Overlook cultural differences.

- Overlook client assets.

These two kinds of errors are interrelated. For example, jumping to conclusions (an error of commission) can occur only if you do not question initial assumptions (an error of omission). These errors may result in:

- Inaccurate descriptions (e.g., assuming a client is being abused when she is not). This involves misclassification.

- Incorrect estimates of covariations (e.g., assuming all people who were abused as children abuse their own children).

- Inaccurate description of causal relationships (e.g., assuming that abuse as a child is responsible for abuse of one's own children later).

- Inaccurate predictions (e.g., incorrectly predicting that participation in parenting classes will prevent a parent from abusing her children in the future).

Common defaults in thinking emphasized by David Perkins (1995) include:

- *Hasty thinking*: Impulsive and mindless; we do not reflect on what we think or do.

- *Narrow thinking*: Tendency to think in a narrow context; we overlook the "big picture" (e.g., my side bias).

- *Fuzzy thinking*: Imprecise, unclear; we overlook key differences; we do not question vague terms (e.g., "support," "ego strength").

- *Sprawling thinking*: Wandering aimlessly in a disorganized manner without integrating data from diverse sources; we bounce from one view to another without ever deciding on an overview (p. 153).

They occur because of a lack of critical questioning. Consider the Barnum effect. This refers to accepting vague personality descriptions about ourselves that could be true of just about anybody.

We Learn Through Our Mistakes

One of your greatest challenges in becoming a successful problem solver is reappraising the value of mistakes. We are often taught to hide rather than reveal them. Hiding them makes it less likely that they will be corrected in the future. Mistakes are inevitable and provide valuable learning opportunities. Reason (2001) distinguishes among violations, lapses, and slips that may occur during planning, recalling intentions, carrying out a task, or monitoring. A violation entails knowingly omitting an important step. A lapse involves not recalling an intention to carry out an important item at the needed time. A slip entails unwittingly omitting an important task in a sequence and/or not detecting it. Failures and mistakes offer information that may yield better guesses next time around. Principles that Popper (1998) suggests for recognizing and learning from our mistakes include the following:

1. To recognize that mistakes will be made; "it is impossible to avoid all mistakes" (p. 63).

2. To recognize that it is our duty to minimize avoidable mistakes.

3. To learn how to do better from recognizing our mistakes.

4. To be "on the lookout for mistakes" (p. 64).

5. To embrace a self-critical attitude.

6. To welcome others pointing out our mistakes; criticism by others is a necessity.

7. "Rational (or objective) criticism must always be specific: it must give specific reasons why specific statements, specific hypotheses appear to be false, or specific arguments invalid. It must be guided by the idea of getting nearer to objective truth. In this sense it must be impersonal, but also sympathetic" (pp. 64–65).

Unavoidable mistakes are those that could not have been anticipated. They occur despite taking advantage of available knowledge and critical thinking skills—in spite of making and acting on well-informed judgments. You may have worked with caregivers of an elderly relative to identify activities the relative enjoys but find that they do not function as reinforcers. Even though you and your clients do your best to identify reinforcers, you cannot know whether particular events will function as reinforcers until you try them out (see chapter 19). Avoidable mistakes are mistakes that could have been avoided, for example, by being better informed regarding practice-related research findings and by thinking more critically about assumptions and their possible consequences or by arranging reminders to help you to remember an important task. They may occur because of faulty decision-making styles, such as jumping to conclusions, and/or agency policies and procedures that interfere with sound decision making, such as an autocratic administrative style. We may forget to carry out an important step in a practice method. We may not monitor progress so that we can detect need for change in a program.

Perkinson (1993) notes that many teachers including Socrates emphasized that "all education is self-education; the student educates himself or herself. The teacher's task is simply to facilitate this self-education" (p. 20). But improvement or growth is up to the student. The student is the one who modifies his or her present knowledge. The teacher facilitates growth of knowledge by creating an environment that allows the student to engage in those trial-and-error activities through which growth takes place. (See also Freire, 1973; 1996.) Perkinson (1993) argues that "students must become critical of their own performances and their own understandings—while remaining confident in their ability to 'do better' if they are to continue growing" (pp. 40–41). This philosophy of education is reflected in evidence-based practice and problem-based learning and their goal to develop lifelong learners. It is also compatible with research findings regarding knowledge and how we acquire it. Only by seeking and acting on feedback about the outcomes of our decisions and critically evaluating our ideas may we enhance our success on future occasions; "we can do better only by finding out what can be improved and then improving it…critical comments from others, far from being resented, are an invaluable aid to be insisted on and welcomed" (Magee, 1985, p. 37).

Failures Are Inevitable

Even in the best of circumstances, given the uncertainty surrounding problems and missing options for altering circumstances, failure to help clients will occur. Some failures are avoidable, as suggested by the research by DePanfilis (2003) based on reviews of case records of children in care. Others are not. Calling for a perfection that is not possible can be demoralizing and can impede looking closely at outcomes (since we know we are unlikely to find such perfection). And bad outcomes do not necessarily reflect poor decisions. Illusions that we can always succeed are likely to result in feelings of regret that hinder rather than facilitate better decisions in the future.

Barriers to Problem Solving

Identifying and decreasing barriers to effective services is a priority of evidence-informed practice; for example, providing access to databases describing practice and policy-related research (see also Exhibit 8.7).

Confirmation Biases

We tend to seek and overweigh evidence that supports our beliefs and to ignore and underweigh contrary evidence (Nickerson, 1998). That is, we try to justify (confirm) our assumptions rather than to falsify them (seek counterexamples and test them as rigorously as possible). Consider the classic study by Snyder and Swann (1978) in which students were asked to test the hypothesis that a person was either an extrovert or an introvert. Those who believed he was an extrovert asked questions that prompted data in support of their view. Students who believed he was an introvert selected questions that prompted answers supporting this view. Both created a *self-fulfilling prophecy*. Studies of medical reasoning show that *overinterpretation* is a common error. This refers to assigning new information to favored hypotheses rather than exploring alternative accounts that more effectively explain data or remembering this information separately (Elstein et al., 1978). Data that provide some support for and against views increase confidence for holders of both views (Lord, Ross, & Lepper, 1979). (See also Berner & Graber, 2008.)

These confirmation biases are also illustrated in research on interviewer biases. As a result of considering only one hypothesis (e.g., that a child's behavior is a result of sexual abuse) and ignoring an alternative hypothesis (e.g., that he has not been so abused), false allegations of sexual abuse have occurred (Ceci & Bruck, 1995). Social workers often assign psychiatric labels to clients based on the *Diagnostic and Statistical Manual of Mental Disorders* (American Psychiatric Association, 2000). Such labels may result in a selective search for data that confirm the label; contradictory data may be ignored. We use different standards to criticize opposing evidence than to evaluate supporting evidence. Confirmation biases influence judgment in all phases of work with clients: defining problems, deciding on causes, and selecting service plans.

Knowledge Is Limited

Our ignorance is vast. Overlooking ignorance and uncertainty encourages attitudes (e.g., overconfidence) and problem-solving styles (e.g., jumping to conclusions) that may get in the way of helping clients or delude clients that help is at hand when it is not. This also will result in misinforming clients. Ignoring uncertainties has resulted in harm to thousands. The true prevalence of a behavior or its natural history may not be known. The probabilities of different outcomes given certain interventions may be unknown. Every source of information has a margin of error that may be small or large. We often do not know how great the range of error is or if it is random or biased. Theories (guesses about what is true) differ in the extent to which they have survived

EXHIBIT 8.7

Barriers to Problem Solving

1. **Limited Knowledge Is Available**
   - Little is known about the prevalence of a problem or course without intervention.
   - Little is known about the causes of a problem.
   - Little is known about what methods will be most effective in solving a problem.
2. **Ignorance Is Deliberately Created**
   - Censorship is common in all venues including the helping professions (e.g., negative findings regarding claims are hidden).
   - Distortion of disliked views is common.
3. **Information Processing Barriers**
   - We can only consider so many different kinds of data at one time.
   - Our memory is often inaccurate.
   - We process information sequentially rather than contextually.
   - We rely on misleading "rules" to simplify tasks (see discussion on biases).
4. **Task Environment**
   - Reliance on questionable criteria to evaluate claims.
   - Lack of resources (e.g., time, services, money).
   - Lack of service coordination and team cooperation.
   - Autocratic bosses (value only their own ideas).
   - Overvalue of tradition (as preferable to change).
   - Taboo topics (e.g., questioning claims of effectiveness).
   - Distractions (constant interruptions) and time pressures.
   - Reluctance to examine the results of policies, programs, and practices.
5. **Motivational Blocks**
   - Value winning over learning.
   - Vested interest in an outcome.
   - Interest in predicting our environment.
   - Cynicism.
6. **Emotional Blocks**
   - Fatigue.
   - Anger.
   - Anxiety.
   - Low tolerance for ambiguity/uncertainty.
   - Lack of zeal.
   - Appeal of vivid material.
7. **Perceptual Blocks**
   - Defining concerns too narrowly (e.g., overlooking environmental causes).
   - Overlooking alternative views.
   - Stereotyping.
   - Judging rather than generating ideas.
   - We see what we expect to see.
8. **Intellectual Blocks**
   - Reliance on questionable criteria to evaluate claims (e.g., popularity).
   - Failure to critically appraise claims.
   - Inflexible use of problem-solving strategies.
   - Lack of accurate information.
   - Limited use of decision tools (e.g., flow charts, decision aids, illustrations).
   - Arrogance.
9. **Cultural Blocks**
   - Disdain for intellectual rigor.
   - Valuing John Wayne thinking (strong pro/con positions with little reflection).
   - Fear that the competition of ideas would harm the social bonding functions of false beliefs (see chapter 4).
   - Ignorance of important cultural differences (e.g., of communication styles).
10. **Expressive Blocks**
    - Lack of skill in writing and speaking clearly.
    - Social anxiety.

Source: Adapted from J. L. Adams (1986). *Conceptual blockbusting: A guide to better ideas* (3rd ed.). Reading, MA: Addison-Wesley.

---

critical tests and in the range of situations to which they can be applied with success. The process of evidence-informed practice is designed to reveal not only knowledge related to decisions, but also ignorance and uncertainty.

Ignorance Is Deliberately Created: The Role of Propaganda

We are surrounded by propaganda (material that encourages beliefs and actions with the least thought possible) (Ellul, 1965). Distortions and misrepresentations of the origins and philosophy of evidence-informed practice is a key example. (See chapter 9.) Other examples include framing common problems-in-living such as anxiety in social situations as mental illnesses in need of biomedical interventions (Moynihan & Cassels, 2005). Lack of awareness regarding the role of the media and the biomedical industrial complex in promoting misleading claims is a key barrier to helping clients arrive at informed decisions. It is a key barrier to recognizing social, political, and economic causes of personal and social problems (such as poor health, homelessness, and poverty) (see Gambrill, 2012a).

Information Processing Factors

We tend to disregard data that do not support preferred beliefs and assign exaggerated importance to data that do support our beliefs. We can consider only so much information at one time. The consequences of this may include: (1) selective perception (we do not necessarily see what is there); (2) sequential (rather than contextual) processing of information; (3) reliance on "heuristics" (strategies) to reduce effort (e.g., frequently occurring cues, vivid case examples); and (4) faulty memory (our memory is inaccurate). Although shortcuts may often work for us, they may also result in errors. The primed decision-making approach emphasizes the value of fast and frugal strategies, indeed arguing that limited information-processing ability may be an asset rather than a liability by decreasing the misleading influences of excessive data. Questions may remain unanswered because you move too fast. For example, a social worker may say that a client is reluctant to participate in setting up a plan. She may ignore coercive aspects of the clients' presence or ambivalence due to ignoring of cultural differences in problem-solving styles. She may not have a client (someone with whom there is a clear agreement to work toward certain outcomes), but a resister (someone present against his or her will). Helping clients requires laying a sound foundation including offering hope, giving support, clearly describing hoped-for outcomes and a thorough search for client strengths and environmental resources.

Memory Is Reconstructive

We rely on our memory when processing and organizing data. Memory is a "reconstructive process." With the passage of time, proper motivation, certain questions, or the introduction of interfering facts, memory may change (Ceci & Bruck, 1995; Loftus, 2004). We tend to recall our successes and overlook our failures. This is one reason "intuition" may lead us astray. False memories can be created through biased interviewing methods (Ceci & Bruck, 1995; Ofshe & Watters, 1994). Simply being asked a question repeatedly can result in memories of events that did not happen (Ceci & Bruck, 1993, 1995). Our memories change in accord with our stereotypes. Consider a study in which subjects were read a description of some events in a woman's life (Gahagan, 1984, p. 93). Some subjects were told that the woman had met a lesbian and had started a homosexual relationship with her. Other subjects were told that she met a man and initiated a relationship with him. A third group received no information about sexual relationships. A week later, all participants were asked to recall details of the woman's earlier life. Subjects who were told that she had initiated a homosexual relationship showed strong distortion effects in their recall in accord with stereotypes about "typical characteristics of lesbians" (p. 93).

Memory may be imperfect because events were not accurately noted in the first place. Even if we observe a sequence of events, our memory of these events may not remain accurate. Although some details may be correctly recalled, we may make up events to fill in gaps in our memory, to create what seem to be "logical sequences" of actions. We then imagine that we really saw these events. We thus may have false memories (e.g., see Roediger & Bergman, 1998). The illusion of having a memory of an event can be created by including inaccurate descriptive data in a question. For example, subjects who watched a car accident and who later received new information about the accident changed their description (Loftus, 1979). High anxiety decreases attention to detail so events may not be noticed. Drugs and alcohol also affect memory. Methods explored to "jog memory" include multiple probes, use of different question forms, hypnosis, and monetary incentives (Loftus & Ketcham, 1994) (see also Tulving & Craik, 2000).

The Task Environment

Decisions are influenced by the environment in which they are made, including the approach to framing problems in your agency and preferred criteria for evaluating the accuracy of claims about causes and remedies (see chapter 6). Funding patterns influence services available. Pressure to conform may result in poor decisions. In "Why I Do Not Attend Case Conferences," Meehl (1973) describes a tendency to reward anything anybody says, "gold and garbage alike." Time pressures and distractions may encourage a mindless approach in which we make decisions with little thought. Supervisors may have little or no time to carry out their educational role in helping supervisees enhance their skills. Agencies differ in the extent to which they encourage a culture of thoughtfulness in which critical inquiry is valued and mistakes are viewed as learning opportunities. (See Culture of Thoughtfulness Scale in Gambrill & Gibbs, 2009.) Authoritarian administrators may squelch critical discussion of claims made about services (e.g., do they do more good than harm?). Agencies differ in provision of tools that facilitate informed decisions, such as access to up-to-date databases that can be searched to seek answers needed to make sound decisions.

Personal Blocks

Some barriers to problem solving are self-imposed, such as failure to revise our views when needed (see Exhibit 8.8). The accuracy of our beliefs about clients' concerns affects our success in helping clients as do our beliefs about ourselves (e.g., whether we think we can make a difference). Our background knowledge (assumptions that we bring to a question) may help us to solve problems and make sound decisions, or they may have the opposite effect, hinder solving problems and learning. You may believe (falsely) that all people who were abused as children abuse their own children. As a result, you assume (incorrectly) that a client who was abused as a child is now abusing her children and remove her children. Only if you are aware of your assumptions can you critically examine them. Motivational barriers include lack of interest in helping clients. You may believe that good intentions are enough to protect clients from harmful or ineffective services when history shows they are not. Professionals, as well as clients, are vulnerable to propaganda such as false claims about the effects of practices and policies. They are easy prey for marketing pitches including

Why Intelligent People Fail

1. Lack of motivation

2. Lack of impulse control

3. Lack of perseverance

4. Inability to translate thought into action

5. Lack of goal orientation

6. Task completion problems/lack of follow-through

7. Failure to initiate

8. Fear of failure

9. Procrastination

10. Misattribution of blame

11. Excessive self-pity

12. Excessive dependency

13. Distractibility/lack of concentration

14. Spreading oneself too thick or too thin

15. Inability to delay gratification

16. Failure to see the forest from the trees

17. Poor balance between critical, analytical thinking, and creative thinking

18. Too little or too much self-confidence

19. Have not learned how to detect and avoid influence of propaganda.

Source: Based on R. J. Sternberg (1987). Teaching intelligence: The application of cognitive psychology to the improvement of intellectual skills. In J. D. Baron & R. J. Sternberg (Eds.) (1993), *Teaching thinking skills: Theory and practice* (pp. 212–213). New York: W. H. Freeman.

smooth talkers who hype untested methods that may be ineffective or even harmful. Academics presenting at conferences may be receiving money from sources with special interest such as pharmaceutical companies (Brody, 2007). Emotional barriers include fear of making mistakes and a low tolerance for uncertainty. We may fear taking risks or feel helpless in the face of great need.

> Many people fear nothing more than to take a position which stands out sharply and clearly from the prevailing opinion. The tendency of most is to adopt a view that is so ambiguous that it will include everything and so popular that it will include everybody.
>
> —Rev. Martin Luther King Jr.

Lack of knowledge about practice-related research may get in the way of offering clients valuable options. Statistical innumeracy is strikingly high both among professionals and clients, often resulting in faulty assumptions that harm clients (e.g., Gaissmaier & Gigerenzer, 2011). Alarmingly, professionals who make gross errors are often highly confident in their false estimations. Our beliefs about behavior may have little overlap with knowledge about behavior based on systematic investigation. Let us say you are working with a child labeled "autistic" and know little about autism. Your domain-specific knowledge will differ considerably compared to a well-informed professional who specializes in this area. Perceptual blocks, such as stereotyping, may hinder accurate understanding of clients and their concerns.

Intellectual barriers include inflexible use of problem-solving strategies that result in getting caught in "loops." Focusing on justifying our beliefs rather than on critiquing them is a major obstacle. This encourages confirmation biases in which we seek only data that support our assumptions. Self-criticism is essential to problem solving. Only if we critically evaluate beliefs and actions, including our most cherished views, can we discover flaws in our thinking and prejudices that may get in the way of helping clients. A preoccupation with finding the cause of a problem can be a barrier rather than asking how behaviors or events can be altered to attain desired outcomes (Feinstein, 1967). Exhibit 8.9 offers an opportunity to explore your problem-solving style.

Relying on Questionable Criteria to Evaluate Claims

Problems may remain unsolved because we rely on questionable criteria to evaluate claims. We may rely on tradition, popularity, or authority (see chapter 4). Review Exhibit 4.6 in chapter 4 and become familiar with misleading criteria for evaluating the accuracy of claims (see also Appendix B. A Catalog of Faulty Inferences at the end of this chapter). Focusing on service goals will help you to choose wisely among different criteria.

We Can Become Better Problem Solvers

The good news is that we can learn to become better problem solvers (see Appendices A and B). We can overcome statistical innumeracies that may harm clients (see Gigerenzer, 2007). We can learn how to allocate our resources such as planning time wisely. We can become familiar with barriers to helping clients and develop skills for minimizing them. We can acquire critical thinking values, knowledge, and skills that contribute to decision making. We can make it a rule to "consider the opposite" (Larrick, 2005; Lilienfeld, Ammirati, & Landfield, 2009)). The term *metacognitive* refers to awareness of and influence on our reasoning processes (e.g., monitoring our thinking by asking questions, such as "Is this correct?" "How do I know this is true?" "What

EXHIBIT 8.9

Exploring Your Decision-Making Style

Please circle the numbers in the columns that best indicate your degree of agreement with each statement

	SD	D	N	A	SA
1. I go to the original sources for information.	1	2	3	4	5
2. When my first efforts fail, I try again.	1	2	3	4	5
3. I seek out points of view that differ from my own.	1	2	3	4	5
4. I arrange a way to see if I have resolved problems I tackle.	1	2	3	4	5
5. I welcome criticism of my views.	1	2	3	4	5
6. I break up complex problems into subproblems.	1	2	3	4	5
7. I consider constraints that affect the potential to solve problems.	1	2	3	4	5
8. I get frustrated when I cannot solve problems rapidly.	1	2	3	4	5
9. I usually accept the first option I can think of.	1	2	3	4	5
10. I consider the consequences of each alternative.	1	2	3	4	5
11. I review arguments against, as well as for different options.	1	2	3	4	5
12. I enjoy working on difficult problems.	1	2	3	4	5
13. I take time to clearly describe and understand problems before seeking solutions.	1	2	3	4	5
14. I consider the "big picture" when thinking about problems and options.	1	2	3	4	5
15. I critically assess the accuracy and completeness of my background knowledge and skills.[a]	1	2	3	4	5
16. It is easy for me to say "I don't know."	1	2	3	4	5
17. I change my mind when I have good reason to do so.	1	2	3	4	5
18. I like to probe deeply into issues.	1	2	3	4	5
19. I tend to go along with what others think and want.	1	2	3	4	5
20. I seek out other people's ideas.	1	2	3	4	5
21. I usually rely on intuition to speculate about what may happen.	1	2	3	4	5
22. I welcome critical feedback from others.	1	2	3	4	5

Key: SD = strongly disagree; D = disagree; N = neutral; A = agree; SA = strongly agree.
[a] Background knowledge refers to your current beliefs about a topic; these may or may not correspond to empirical findings regarding the topic.

are my biases?" "Is there another way to approach this problem?" "Do I understand this point?"). These questions highlight the importance of *self-correction* in helping clients. Related behaviors are strategies used to guide our thinking. They can help us to avoid common intelligence traps that hinder problem-solving. Increasingly metacognitive levels of thought include: (1) *Tacit*: Thinking without thinking about it; (2) *Aware*: Thinking and being aware that you are thinking: (3) *Strategic*: Organizing our thinking by using strategies that enhance its efficacy; and (4) *Reflective*: Reflecting on our thinking (pondering how to proceed and how to improve) (Swartz & Perkins, 1990, p. 52).

Summary

Helping clients involves making decisions. The personal and social problems your clients confront will usually be unstructured ones in which there are differences of opinion about how success should be evaluated and in which alternatives may be unknown or not possible. No matter what our intelligence, we are likely to fall into common intelligence traps unless we develop values, knowledge, and skills that help us avoid them. Personal blocks to sound decision making include emotional barriers, such as fear of criticism if dubious views are questioned and motivational barriers, such as lack of interest in helping clients. Environmental blocks include noisy offices, time pressures, and authoritarian cultures in which those who question bogus claims of effectiveness are punished. We are subject to a variety of cognitive biases, such as looking only for data that support our beliefs (confirmation biases) and being influenced by vivid case examples. The good news is that we can become more effective decision makers by taking advantage of debiasing strategies including the process of evidence-informed practice. We can learn how to minimize and learn from errors and lack of success, for example, by drawing on practice- and policy-related research findings regarding clients' hoped-for outcomes. We can become informed about important cultural differences that influence success in helping clients.

Reviewing Your Competencies

Reviewing Content Knowledge

1. Describe the advantages of a critically reflective decision-focused practice model.

2. Discuss the relationship between problem solving and decision making.

3. Describe some of the major research findings regarding decision making and problem solving.

4. Describe the role of creativity in problem solving.

5. Give examples of incorrect problem structuring.

6. Discuss the role of resources in decision making and problem solving.

7. Describe common errors in making decisions and judgments.

8. Discuss the influence of heuristics in decision making and give examples.

9. Describe how vivid data may lead us astray.

10. Give an example of the misleading influence of resemblance.

11. Give examples illustrating the negative effects of stereotyping.

12. Describe personal barriers to decision making and why they pose a barrier.

13. Describe environmental barriers to problem solving and decision making.

14. Discuss the role of mistakes and lack of success in learning.

15. Describe common errors of omission in decision making.

16. Compare the criteria you use to make decisions concerning clients with those you use to make decisions about your own health. (See Exercise 1 in Gambrill & Gibbs, 2009.)

Reviewing What You Do

1. You accurately identify fallacies in case examples and describe why they are of concern.

2. You recognize cognitive biases in practice examples.

3. A review of your case records shows that you avoid common errors in decision making.

4. You accurately recognize when nothing can be done to achieve hoped-for outcomes.

Reviewing Results

1. Clients attain outcomes they value.

2. You make effective, efficient use of available practice- and policy-related research findings.

Appendix A

Avoiding Errors Caused by Relying on Similarity

Representative thinking is an association process in which some characteristic "triggers" an associated theory, belief, or schema. An example given by Howitt (1992) is assuming that a man abused his stepson because there is a correlation between being a stepfather and abuse of children. You can draw on rules of probability theory to avoid errors caused by representative thinking. Consider the example of a college admissions committee reviewing applicants given by Dawes (1988). One applicant was outstanding in all areas; however, she misspelled a word on her application. One committee member believed that this indicated that she was dyslexic and her application was denied. Let's call misspelling a word c and the associated schema (dyslexia) the symbol S. We can then ask about *conditional* probabilities: What is the probability of c given S or S given c? The probability that members of S have characteristic c $p(c|S)$ is likely. People with dyslexia often do misspell words. However, the probability that the characteristic c implies membership in S (dyslexia) is given by the conditional probability $p(S|c)$ (the probability that people with characteristic c are members of S), which is the inverse of $p(c|S)$. Misspelling is a characteristic of dyslexia, however, many more students cannot spell certain words who are not dyslexic than who are dyslexic.

EXHIBIT 8.10

Hypothesized Venn Diagram of Pot Smokers and Hard Drug Users

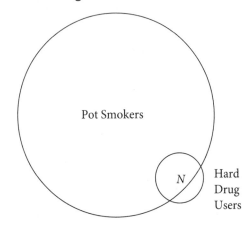

Pot Smokers

N   Hard Drug Users

N represents people who both smoke pot and use hard drugs

Source: R. Hastie & R. Dawes (2001). *Rational choice in an uncertain world: The psychology of judgement and decision making.* Thousand Oaks, CA: Sage. Reprinted with permission of Sage Publications.

Thus, "the basic problem with making probability judgments on the basis of representative characteristics is that the schema accessed [dyslexia] may in fact be *less* probable, given the characteristic, than one not accessed when the schema not accessed has a much greater *extent* in the world than the accessed one" (p. 70). The number of people who are not dyslexic is much larger than the number of people who are dyslexic. The problem is that when a schema (i.e., dyslexia) is accessed (considered), the actual extent of the class is usually not, resulting in faulty decisions. As Dawes points out, representative thinking does not distinguish between the probability of *c* given *S* and the probability of *S* given *c*. Most associations are not symmetric.

Consider another example. It is often said that smoking marijuana leads to heroin use. Let us call smoking marijuana *c* and heroin use *S*. Thus, this assumption can be written $p(c|S)$. What should be considered is $p(S|c)$. Venn diagrams can be used to represent conditional probabilities (the ratio of the area in the overlap to the area in the large circle) (see Exhibit 8.10). This illustrates the nonsymmetrical nature of conditional probabilities. You cannot simply reverse them. The probability that marijuana smokers also use heroin is much smaller than the probability that heroin users smoke marijuana. Can you apply this analysis to the stepparent "template" mentioned in the first paragraph?

Appendix B

A Catalog of Faulty Inferences

1. *Relying on similarity.* Assuming that two or more things or events are related simply because they resemble each other.

   Foxes have remarkable lungs. Therefore the lungs of a fox will remedy asthma.

2. *Irrelevant conclusion.* A conclusion is irrelevant to the reasoning that led to it.

   I do not think Mr. Jones abused his child. He acts like a normal father; he even spends time on the weekend repairing his car.

3. *Fallacy of division.* Assuming that what is true of the whole is necessarily true of each individual part of the whole.

   Staff at the Mixer Community Mental Health Center are psychoanalytically oriented. Mary M., who works there, is psychoanalytically oriented.

4. *Fallacy of labeling.* Labeling yourself or others when the label is unjustified by the circumstances, or when the label is inappropriately used as a reason for behavior or lack of behavior (Sternberg, 1986, p. 96).

   You have worked hard to help a client to little avail. You say to yourself, "I'm a failure."

5. *Hasty generalization.* Incorrect assumptions about the informative value of a single (or few) instance.

   Bill and a friend were discussing the director of their agency. Bill said, "He is a total failure because he has not increased funding for our agency."

6. *Overlooking the role of chance.* Assuming that an outcome due to chance is related to past occurrences.

   My next baby must be a boy. We've had five girls.

7. *Fallacy of composition.* Assuming that what is true of parts of a whole is true of the whole.

   Jane is behaviorally oriented. Therefore staff at her agency are behaviorally oriented.

8. *False cause.* Relying on the mere fact of coincidence of temporal succession to identify a cause.

   You walked under a ladder and a few second latter were hit by a car and believe that walking under the ladder caused the accident.

9. *Invalid disjunction* (either/oring). Considering only two options when more than two should be considered.

   We must either hospitalize him or leave him to wander the streets.

10. *Relying on recency.* Accepting the first explanations that occurs to you without considering other possibilities.

    I can see he is an angry man by how he acts in the office. I think he is guilty of abusing his wife.

11. *Argument from ignorance.* Assuming that something is true simply because it has not been shown to be false, or that it is false simply because it has not been shown to be true.

    You don't have any proof that your method works. Therefore I don't think it does.

12. *Appeal to authority.* Arguing that a claim is true based purely on an authority's status with no reference to evidence.

    Dr. Monston said…

13. *Argumentation ad populum.* Assuming that "if everyone else thinks this way, it must be right." Appeal to popularity.

    Everyone is using this new method. I think we should use it too.

14. *Argumentum ad hominem.* Attacking or praising some aspects of a person's character, lifestyle, race, religion, sex, and so on, as evidence for (or against) a conclusion, even when these circumstances are irrelevant to the situation being examined.

    He has a point. But look at how he is dressed.

15. *Inference by manner of presentation* (how believable is this person?).

    She gave a convincing talk. I'm going to use her methods.

16. *Appeal to anecdotal experience.*

    I've seen three clients and used *x* successfully with all of them. It works!

17. *Appeal to tradition.*

    That's the way we have always done it. We should continue to use these methods.

18. *Influence by testimonials.*

    I believe it works because Mrs. Rivera said she tried it and it helped.

19. *Appeal to newness.*

    It's the latest thing. We should try it too.

20. *Assume hard headed therefore hard hearted.*

    She can't really care about her clients if she spends that much time questioning our agency's methods.

21. *Assume that good intentions result in good services* (e.g., protect clients from harm).

    In response to a question from a client about an agency's effectiveness, you say: "We really care about our clients."

22. *Weak documentation.*

    Accepting a claim based on vague, undocumented evidence.

23. *Personalization.* Assuming you are the cause of some event for which you were not primarily responsible or taking personally a statement that is not directed toward you.

    A client failed to keep an agreement that you believe he could have kept. You say to yourself, "It's my fault."

24. *Magnification/minimization.* Magnifying our negative characteristics or mistakes or minimizing positive characteristics or accomplishments.

    Mrs. Silvers (a supervisor) congratulated Max on his success with his client. He said, "Oh, it's really not a big thing."

25. *"Should" statements* (e.g., "I must do this," "I should feel that," "They should do this") are fallacies when they are used as the sole reason for behavior.

    A supervisor tells her staff: "You should evaluate your practice."

26. *Mental filter.* Picking out some small aspect of a situation (often a negative one) and focusing on that one small aspect so that the "bigger picture" is ignored. All events are viewed through the filter of one aspect of the situation.

    I just don't like the way my director dresses.

27. *Emotional reasoning.* Using our emotions or feelings as evidence of a truth.

    This is true because I feel it is true.

Evidence-Based Practice: A Decision-Making Process and Philosophy

OVERVIEW   The origins and hallmarks of evidence-based practice (EBP) are described in this chapter, as well as common misrepresentations and implementation challenges. Professional codes of ethics, as well as EPAS (2008), call for key characteristics of EBP, such as drawing on practice- and policy-related research and involving clients as informed participants. There are many alternatives to evidence-informed decision making, for example, basing decisions on criteria such as popularity or what is new. Given that evidence-informed practice as described in this chapter is not the norm today, it is clear that alternative methods are popular and pose an obstacle to integrating evidentiary, ethical, and application concerns.

YOU WILL LEARN ABOUT

- Evidence-based practice: What it is and what it is not

- Origins of evidence-based practice

- Hallmarks and implications of the philosophy of evidence-based practice

- Misrepresentations and objections to evidence-based practice

- Controversies regarding evidence

Evidence-Based Practice: What It Is and What It Is Not

Descriptions of evidence-based practice and policy differ greatly in their breadth and attention to ethical issues ranging from the broad, systemic philosophy and related evolving technology envisioned by its originators to narrow, fragmented views and total distortions. The most popular is the EBPs approach in which academics, researchers, and administrators decide what is effective and mandate or recommend use of these methods. This approach is quite different from the process and philosophy of EBP described in original sources (e.g., Sackett, Richardson, Rosenberg, & Haynes, 1997; Straus, Richardson, Glasziou, &

Haynes, 2005). Given the different views of EBP, it is important to review the vision of EBP as described by its creators. Otherwise, potential benefits to clients and professionals may be lost. Evidence-based practice (EBP) is a decision-making approach to practice and policy designed to handle uncertainties in an informed, honest manner within the context of a supportive helping relationship drawing on practice theory. EBP describes a process and a professional education format—problem-based learning in which students work in small groups of five or six guided by a tutor trained in both group process and the process of EBP—designed to help practitioners to link evidentiary, ethical, and application issues. The idea of integrating practice and research in professional contexts is not new, nor is attention to ethical issues as they relate to evidentiary ones. What is new about EBP is a unique process and attention to evidentiary, ethical, and application concerns in all professional venues (practice and policy, research, and professional education) taking advantage of the Internet.

EBP arose in part because of troubling gaps between available knowledge and what is used by professionals. Evidence-based practice and policy reflect a particular philosophy of knowledge, ethics, and technology. EBP involves the "conscientious, explicit and judicious use of current best evidence in making decisions about the care of individual [clients]" (Sackett, Richardson, Rosenberg, & Haynes, 1997, p. 2). It calls for "the integration of the best research evidence with our clinical expertise and our [client's] unique values and circumstances" (Straus et al., 2005, p. 1). (see Exhibit 9.1). It is assumed that professionals often need information to make important decisions, for example, concerning risk assessment or what services are most likely to help clients attain outcomes they value. When evidence is not used important failures in decision making occur:

- ineffective interventions are introduced;

- interventions that do more harm than good are introduced;

- interventions that do more good than harm are not introduced;

- interventions that are ineffective or do more harm than good are not discontinued. (Gray, 2001a, p. 354)

Client values refer to "the unique preferences, concerns and expectations each [client] brings to an…encounter and which must be integrated into…decisions if they are to serve the [client]" (Straus et al., 2005, p. 1).

Clinical expertise is used to integrate information about a client's unique characteristics and circumstances, with external research findings, client expectations and values, and their preferences and actions (Sackett et al., 1997; Haynes, Devereaux, & Guyatt, 2002). Such expertise includes use of effective relationship skills and the experience of individual helpers to rapidly identify each client's unique circumstances and characteristics, and "their individual risks and benefits of potential interventions, and their

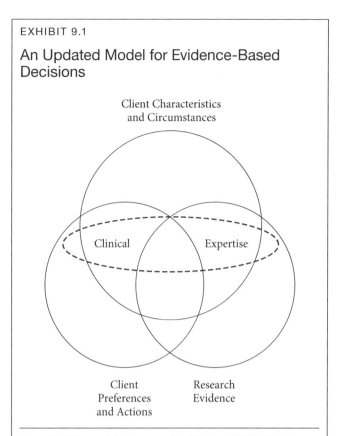

EXHIBIT 9.1

An Updated Model for Evidence-Based Decisions

Client Characteristics and Circumstances

Clinical   Expertise

Client Preferences and Actions   Research Evidence

Source: R. B. Haynes, P. J. Devereaux, & G. H. Guyatt (2002). Clinical expertise in the era of evidence-based medicine and patience choice. *Evidence-Based Medicine, 7*, 36–38. Reprinted with permission.

personal circumstances and expectations" (Straus et al., 2005, p. 1). It is reflected in many ways including "the more thoughtful identification and compassionate use of individual [clients'] predicaments, rights and preferences in making clinical decisions about their care" (Sackett et al., 1997, p. 2). "External clinical evidence can inform, but never replace, individual clinical expertise and it is this expertise that decides whether the external evidence applies to the individual [client] at all and, if so, how it should be integrated into a clinical decision. Similarly, any external guideline must be integrated with individual clinical expertise in deciding whether and how it matches" the client's characteristics and circumstances including their preferences and thus whether it should be applied (Sackett et al., 1997, p. 4).

An ongoing concern is how to use clinical expertise to integrate external research findings, information about client characteristics and circumstances, and client preferences and actions in order to maximize the likelihood of attaining hoped-for outcomes (Haynes, Devereaux, & Guyatt, 2002; see chapter 10). Research shows that helping clients is both an art and a science. Certain aspects of the "art" have been identified such as empathy and other communication skills (see chapter 15). Aspects of the science have also been identified including rapid identification of assessment patterns based on experience providing corrective feedback (see chapter 9). More attention has been given to the gap between client actions and their stated preferences because what clients do (e.g., carry out agreed-on tasks or not), so often differs from their stated preferences, and helper estimates of participation are as likely to be inaccurate as accurate (Haynes, Devereaux, & Guyatt, 2002). (See Exhibit 9.1.) Evidence-Based Health Care (EBHC) is informed not only by the best available evidence that is up-to-date, valid, and relevant but also by the values of those receiving care, and the experience of those providing it in the context of available resources (Sicily Statement on Evidence-based Healthcare, 2004).

An Alternative to Authority-Based Practice

Evidence-based decision making arose as an alternative to authority-based decision making in which decisions are based on criteria, such as consensus, anecdotal experience, or tradition. It is an evolving process. It describes a philosophy and process designed to forward effective use of professional judgment in integrating information regarding each client's unique characteristics, circumstances, preferences, and actions, and external research findings (see Exhibit 9.2). "It is a guide for thinking about how decisions should be made" (Haynes, Devereaux, & Guyatt, 2002).

Although its philosophical roots are old, the blooming of EBP as a process attending to evidentiary, ethical, and application issues in all professional venues (education, practice and policy, and research) is fairly recent, facilitated by the Internet revolution. It is designed to break down the division between research, practice, and policy—highlighting the importance of honoring ethical obligations. Although misleading in the incorrect assumption that EBP means that decisions are based only on evidence of the effectiveness of different services, use of the term does call attention to the fact that available evidence may not be

used or the current state of ignorance shared with clients. It is hoped that professionals who consider related research findings regarding life-affecting decisions and inform clients about them, will provide more effective and ethical care than those relying on criteria such as anecdotal experience, available resources, or popularity. The following examples illustrate reliance on authority-based criteria for selection of service methods:

Ms. Riverton has just been to a workshop on eye movement desensitization therapy. The workshop leader told the participants that this method "works and can be used for a broad range of problems." Ms. Riverton suggests to her supervisor at the mental health clinic where she works that agency staff should use this method. When asked why, she said because the workshop leader is a respected authority in the field.

Mr. Davis read an editorial that describes the DARE programs as very effective in decreasing drug use. No related empirical literature was referred to. He suggested to his agency that they use this effective method.

In the first example, the authority of a workshop leader is appealed to. In the second, the authority of an author of an editorial is appealed to. Evidence-based decision making involves use of quite different criteria; a key one is information about the accuracy of practice- and policy-related claims. Is eye movement desensitization effective for certain kinds of problems? Are DARE programs effective? EBP draws on the results of systematic, rigorous, critical appraisals of research related to different kinds of practice questions, such as "Is this assessment measure valid?" "Does this intervention do more good than harm?" For example, review groups in the Cochrane and Campbell

---

EXHIBIT 9.2

Differences Between Authority-Based and Evidence-Informed Practitioners

Authority-Based Practice	Evidence-Informed Practice
• Clients are not informed or are misinformed.	• Clients are involved as informed participants.
• Ignores client preferences ("We know best").	• Seeks and considers client values and preferences.
• Does not pose specific questions about decisions and does not search for and critically appraise what is found and share results with clients.	• Poses clear questions related to information needs, seeks related research findings, critically appraises them, and shares what is found with clients and others.
• Motivated to appear well informed, to preserve status and reputation.	• Motivated to help clients and be an honest and competent broker of knowledge and ignorance.
• Ignores errors and mistakes.	• Seeks out errors and mistakes; values criticism as vital for learning.
• Accepts practice- and policy-related claims based on misleading criteria, such as tradition, expert consensus.	• Relies on rigorous criteria to appraise practice claims and select practices and policies (e.g., those that control for biases).
• Relies on self-report of clients and anecdotal observations.	• Seeks both subjective and objective information.

Collaborations prepare comprehensive, rigorous reviews of all research related to a question.

Three Philosophies of Evidence-Based Practice

Evidence-based practice and policy involve a philosophy of ethics of professional practice and related enterprises, such as research and scholarly writing, a philosophy of science (epistemology—views about what knowledge is and how it can be gained), and a philosophy of technology. Ethics involves decisions regarding how and when to act; it involves standards of conduct. Epistemology involves views about knowledge and how to get it or if we can. The philosophy of technology concerns questions such as: Should we develop technology? What values should we draw on to decide what to develop? Should we examine the consequences of a given technology? Evidence-based practice emphasizes the importance of critically appraising research and developing a technology to help clinicians to do so; proponents of EBM "emphasized that clinicians had to use their scientific training and their judgment to interpret [guidelines] and individualize care accordingly" (Gray, 2001b, p. 26).

EBP offers practitioners and administrators a philosophy that is compatible with obligations described in professional codes of ethics and accreditation policies and standards (e.g., for informed consent and to draw on practice- and policy-related research findings), as well as an evolving technology for integrating evidentiary, ethical, and practical issues. Related literature highlights the interconnections among these three concerns and suggests specific steps (a technology) to decrease gaps among them in all professional venues, including practice and policy (e.g., drawing on related research), research (e.g., preparing systematic reviews and clearly describing limitations of studies), and professional education (e.g., exploring the value of problem-based learning in developing lifelong learners). The uncertainty associated with decisions is acknowledged, not hidden. EBP requires considering research findings related to important practice/policy decisions and sharing what is found (including nothing) with clients. Transparency and honesty regarding the evidentiary status of services is a hallmark of this philosophy.

The Process: Steps in Evidence-Based Practice

Steps in evidence-based practice include the following:

1. converting information needs related to practice decisions into clear questions;

2. tracking down, with maximum efficiency, the best evidence with which to answer them;

3. critically appraising that evidence for its validity (closeness to the truth), impact (size of effect), and applicability (usefulness in practice);

4. using clinical expertise to integrate information regarding the client's unique characteristics and circumstances and research findings. This involves deciding whether evidence found (if any) applies to the decision at hand (e.g., is a client similar to those studied, is there access to services described) and considering client values and preferences in making decisions, as well as other applicability concerns such as resources available;

5. evaluating our effectiveness and efficiency in carrying out steps 1–4 and seeking ways to improve them in the future (Straus et al., 2005, pp. 3–4).

Evidence-based practitioners conduct electronic searches to locate the current best evidence regarding a specific question. (See chapter 10.) Thus, EPB emphasizes information literacy and retrievability (Gray, 2001a). Information literacy includes recognizing when information is needed, knowing how to get and evaluate it, and developing and using lifelong learning skills.

Different Kinds of Questions

Kinds of questions include the following:

- *Effectiveness*: Do job training programs help clients get and maintain jobs?

- *Prevention*: Do Head Start programs prevent school dropout?

- *Screening (risk/prognosis)*: Does this measure accurately predict suicide attempts?

- *Description/Assessment*: Do self-report data provide accurate descriptions of parenting practices?

- *Harm*: Does (or will) this intervention harm clients?

- *Cost*: How much does this program cost compared to others?

- *Practice guidelines*: Are these practice guidelines valid and are they applicable to my client/agency/community?

- *Self-development*: Am I keeping up-to-date? How can I keep up-to-date?

Different questions require different kinds of research methods to critically appraise proposed assumptions (e.g., Greenhalgh, 2010; Guyatt et al., 2008). These differences are reflected in the use of different "quality filters" to search for research findings (see chapter 10). Thus, it is not true, as some have claimed, that only randomized controlled trials are considered of value.

Different Styles of Evidence-Based Practice

Sackett and his colleagues (2000) distinguish between three different styles of EBP, all of which require integrating research findings regarding life-affecting decisions with the unique characteristics of a client and their circumstances. All require step 4 (see prior list of steps in EBP), but they vary in how other steps are carried out. They suggest that for problems encountered on an everyday basis, you should invest the time and energy necessary to carry out both searching and critical appraisal of research reports found. For level 2 (problems encountered less often), they suggest that you seek out critical appraisals already prepared by others who describe and use explicit criteria for deciding what research they select and how they decide whether it is valid. Here, step 3 can be omitted and step 2 restricted to sources that have already undergone critical appraisal. A third style applies to problems encountered very infrequently in which we "'blindly' seek, accept, and apply the recommendations we receive from authorities" (p. 5). As they note, the trouble with this mode is that it is "blind" to whether the advice received from the experts "is authoritative (evidence-based, resulting from their operating in the 'appraising' mode) or merely authoritarian (opinion-based, resulting from pride and prejudice)" (p. 5). Lack of time may result in using style 2 with most problems. Literature in social work suggests that social workers do not draw on practice-related research findings to inform practice decisions (e.g., Rosen, 1994; Rosen, Proctor, Morrow-Howell, & Staudt, 1995). Not keeping up with new research findings related to important decisions renders knowledge increasingly out-of-date. As a result, decisions may harm rather than help clients (e.g., Jacobson, Foxx, & Mulick, 2005; Jacobson, Mulick, & Schwartz, 1995; Thyer & Pignotti, 2010). Many helpers do not honor informed consent obligations (e.g., Braddock, Edwards, Hasenberg, Laidley, & Levinson, 1999). Views of EBP are promoted that ignore its ethical hallmarks, such as involving clients as informed participants.

Examples of EBP

Richard works in a child protection agency that uses a consensus-based risk assessment to estimate the likely recurrence of child abuse among parents alleged to have abused their children. This is based on the opinions of a group of experts on what they consider risk factors. His question was: Among parents alleged to have abused their children, are actuarial compared to consensus-based measures most accurate in predicting the likelihood of future abuse? This is a question about risk. Actuarial measures are based on empirical relationships between certain factors and the likelihood of an outcome, such as abuse. (See chapter 15 for further discussion.) He looked at www.childwelfare.com, as well as the Internet, and discovered a report by Barber and his colleagues (2008) that concluded that an actuarial method was most accurate. He discovered an article by Johnson (2011), which reported similar results.

Dr. Price works in a mental health crisis center. The administrator of this agency sent a memo to staff that he had heard that brief psychological debriefing was effective in decreasing Post Traumatic Stress Disorder following a crisis, and he suggested that his staff use this method. His question was: In clients experiencing a potentially traumatic event, is brief, one-hour psychological debriefing, compared to no service, more effected in preventing Post Traumatic Stress Disorder? This is an effectiveness question. He found a systematic review prepared by Rose, Bisson, Churchill, and Wessely (2002). (See also Bisson, 2003.) To his surprise, this review concluded that not only was this method not effective, there was some indication that it had harmful effects; one study reported that those receiving such counseling were more likely to experience stressful reactions a year later. Based on this review, he sent an e-mail to his colleagues questioning the use of this method for clients.

Origins of Evidence-Based Practice

Sackett and his colleagues (2000) suggest four realizations made possible by five recent developments for the rapid spread of EPB. Realizations include: (1) practitioner need for valid information about decisions they make; (2) the inadequacy of traditional sources for acquiring this information (e.g., because they are out-of-date, frequently wrong, overwhelming in their volume, variable in their validity); (3) the gap between assessment skills and clinical judgment "which increase with experience and our up-to-date knowledge and clinical performance which decline" (p. 2); and (4) lack of time to locate, appraise, and integrate this evidence (p. 2). There were increasing gaps between information available on the Internet that could be of value to clients and clinicians in making decisions and what was drawn on. Developments that Sackett and his co-authors (2000) suggest that have allowed improvement in this state of affairs included: (1) the creation of strategies for efficiently tracking down and appraising evidence (for its validity and relevance); (2) the invention of the systematic review and concise summaries of the effects of health care (epitomized by the Cochrane Collaboration); (3) the creation of evidence-based journals of secondary publication; (4) the creation of information systems for bringing the foregoing to us in seconds; and (5) the creation and use of effective strategies for lifelong learning and for improving the soundness of decisions made (p. 3). Reasons Gray (2001b) suggests for the development of EBP include those discussed next.

Variations in Services Offered

EBP and health care originated in medicine in part because of variations in services offered and their outcomes (Wennberg, 2002). As Gray (2001b) notes, variations occurred between countries, between services in a country, between services in an area, and between staff in an agency. Variations in services naturally raise questions, such as "Are they of equal effectiveness?" "Do some harm?"

Gaps Among Ethical, Evidentiary, and Application Concerns

Although interlinked in professional codes of ethics and accreditation standards, ethical and evidentiary issues are often far apart in practice. Consider gaps between obligations described in the Code of Ethics of the National Association of Social Workers (2008) and everyday practice regarding informed consent, self-determination, empowerment, and drawing on practice- and policy-related research. Ineffective and harmful services continue to be used and effective services are often not used. Gray (2001a) suggests that current service patterns have the following characteristics:

- overenthusiastic adoption of interventions of unproven efficacy or even proven ineffectiveness;

- failure to adopt interventions that do more good than harm at a reasonable cost;

- continuing to offer interventions demonstrated to be ineffective;

- adoption of interventions without adequate preparation (such that the benefits demonstrated in a research setting cannot be reproduced in the ordinary service setting); wide variations in the rates at which interventions are adopted or discarded. (p. 366)

The following quotes from the NASW Code of Ethics highlight obligations:

> Social workers should provide services to clients only in the context of a professional relationship based, when appropriate, on valid informed consent. Social workers should use clear and understandable language to inform clients of the purpose of the services, risks related to the services, limits to services because of the requirements of a third-party payer, relevant costs, reasonable alternatives, clients' right to refuse or withdraw consent, and the time frame covered by the consent. Social workers should provide clients with an opportunity to ask questions. (1.03a)

> Social workers should critically examine and keep current with emerging knowledge relevant to social work. (4.01)

Sheldon and Chilvers (2000) found that 18% of social workers surveyed had read nothing related to practice within the last 6 months (total n = 2,285). If professionals are not familiar with the evidentiary status of practices and policies, they cannot pass this information on to their clients; they cannot honor informed consent obligations. Clients may be deprived of opportunities to achieve hoped-for outcomes. Currently there are large gaps between what research suggests is effective and what services are provided. For example, rarely do we compare services offered by an agency, such as parent training programs, and what research suggests is effective and disseminate this information to all involved parties. Clients are typically not informed that recommended services are of unknown effectiveness or have been found to be ineffective or harmful.

Economic Considerations

No matter what system of care exists, resources are limited with subsequent pressures to use them justly and wisely. Wasting money on harmful or ineffective services leaves less for effective services. The concern in EBP to consider both individuals and populations (do all residents with a particular need have access to similar quality care?) encourages evidence-informed decision making.

Increased Attention to Harming in the Name of Helping

The history of the helping professions shows that common practices thought to help people were found to harm them (e.g., see Sharpe & Faden, 1998; Valenstein, 1986). Consider the blinding of children by routine use of oxygen at birth (Silverman, 1980). Such reports increased awareness that services designed to help clients, including assessment measures, may result in negative effects.

Limitations of Traditional Methods of Knowledge Dissemination

There are also troubling gaps between obligations of researchers to report limitations of research, prepare systematic reviews, and accurately describe well-argued alternative views and what we find in published literature (see Exhibit 9.3). Examples of flaws and fallacies in the medical literature include Significance Turkey (Lauds significant results even if they are not clinically significant. Even if a finding is statistically significant, is it large enough to make any real difference to clients?) Another is Diagnostic Zealot (Overzealous peddler of the latest diagnostic test. He has fooled himself (and may fool you too) into untested belief in the benefits of a diagnostic test) (Michael, Boyce, & Wilcox, 1984). Poor quality research continues to appear in professional journals (Altman, 2002). Ioannidis (2005) argues that most published research findings are false. Lack of transparency regarding limitations of research remains common as does the publication of incomplete, unrigorous reviews of research. There are many reasons for this including the special interests of those who fund research such as pharmaceutical companies that censor negative findings (e.g., Angell, 2004) and conflicts of interest between academics/researchers and Big Pharma (Lo & Field, 2009). Related concerns were key in the development of EBP and health care (Gray, 2001a and 2001b). In discussing the origins of EBP, Gray (2001a) notes the increasing lack of confidence in data of potential use to clinicians: peer review, which he subtitles feet of clay, flaws in books, editorials, and journal

EXHIBIT 9.3

Gaps Between Ethical Obligations of Scholars and Researchers and What We Find

- Inflated claims.

- Biased estimates of the prevalence of a concern, propagandistic advocacy in place of careful weighting of evidence.

- Hiding limitations of research.

- Preparing haphazard reviews.

- Ignoring counterevidence to preferred views.

- Ignoring or distorting well-argued alternative perspectives and related evidence.

- Pseudo inquiry; little match between questions addressed and methods used to address them.

- Ad hominem rather than ad rem arguments.

- Ignoring unique knowledge of clients and service providers in making decisions about the appropriateness of a practice guideline.

articles. Conclusions drawn based on haphazard reviews are often misleading (Littell, 2008). As Rosenthal (1994) suggests in his description of hyperclaiming (telling others that proposed research is likely to achieve goals that it will not) and causism (implying a causal relationship when none has been established), "Bad science makes for bad ethics" (p. 128). Chalmers (1990) argues that failure to accurately describe research methods used is a form of scientific misconduct.

Invention of the Systematic Review

Recognition of limitations in traditional research reviews encouraged the development of the systematic review for synthesizing research findings. (See Exhibit 9.4.) The Cochrane Collaboration was created in 1992 to prepare, maintain, and disseminate high-quality research reviews related to a specific practice/policy question. Such reviews "state their objectives, ascertain as much of the available evidence as possible, use explicit quality criteria for inclusion or exclusion of studies found, use explicitly stated methods for combining data, produce reports which describe the processes of ascertainment, inclusion and exclusion, and combining data" (Gray, 2001b, p. 24). (See also description of the Campbell Collaboration in chapter 10, as well as Littell, Corcoran, & Pillai, 2008.)

The Internet Revolution

As Gray (2001b) notes, "The Internet stimulated the development of a number of software tools which allowed international organizations such as the Cochrane Collaboration to function efficiently" (p. 25). The Internet provides rapid access to databases that facilitate speedy searches. The limitations of traditional forms of knowledge diffusion was a key reason for the decision to make the Cochrane database of systematic reviews electronic, with routine updating by review groups.

The Appeal of EBP to Professionals and Clients

Gray (2001b) highlights the rapid spread of EBP and attributes this in part to its appeal to clinicians and to clients. He notes that clients initially experience surprise to the concept of EBP because they thought doctors were basing their decisions on best current evidence.

> It also came as a shock that even the knowledge, where it was available, was often deficient (or commonly not even utilized by doctors who had been left behind the knowledge frontier). They therefore welcomed EBM enthusiastically and it is remarkable how quickly that access to information has turned the table on professional expertise and power. It is no longer feasible to feign knowledge: patients are just as likely to have searched for the evidence before they consult a clinician. (p. 27)

Other Views of EBP

The most popular view is the EBPs approach. For example, Rosen and Proctor (2003) state that "we use evidence-based practice here primarily to denote that practitioners will select interventions on the basis of their empirically demonstrated links to the desired outcomes" (p. 743). Making decisions about individual clients is much more complex. There are many other considerations such as the need to consider the unique circumstances and characteristics of each client as suggested by the critiques of practice guidelines and manualized treatments (e.g., Norcross, Beutler, & Levant, 2006). Practice guidelines are but one component of EBP, as can be seen by a review of topics in Sackett et al. (2000). The view that EBP consists of requiring practitioners to use empirically based treatments also omits attention to client values and their individual circumstances and resource constraints. The broad view of EBP involves searching for research related to important decisions and sharing what is found, including nothing, with clients. It involves a search not only for knowledge but also for ignorance. Such a search is required to involve clients as informed participants.

Many descriptions of EBP in the social work literature could be termed business as usual, for example, publication of unrigorous research reviews regarding practice claims, inflated claims of effectiveness, lack of attention to ethical concerns such as involving clients as informed participants, and neglect of application barriers. In addition to those who seek to forward EBP as envisioned by its originators in an atmosphere of open, rigorous critical inquiry (transparency and accountability), there

EXHIBIT 9.4

Examples of Differences Between Systematic and Haphazard Reviews

Haphazard Reviews	Systematic Reviews
1. The search process is not described.	1. The search process is clearly described.
2. The review omits many related studies.	2. All currently available research related to a question, both published and unpublished in all languages, is sought.
3. Criteria used to review research are not described.	3. Criteria used to appraise research are clearly described.
4. Criteria used to appraise the quality of studies are not rigorous.	4. Criteria used to appraise research are rigorous (e.g., were evaluators of outcome blind to group assignment?).
5. Readers were not provided with sufficient information about each study to judge its quality for themselves.	5. Readers are provided with enough information about each study to judge its quality for themselves.
6. Inflated claims of effectiveness and validity.	6. Claims match descriptions of related evidence.

are those who adopt the external features of EBP (e.g., its language) and forgo the substance as the latest guise for authoritarian practice. Indications that EBP will be used as a new cloak for authority-based practice include material labeled as evidence-based that is not. The same product is offered in a different wrapper. A common reaction is simply relabeling the old as the new (as EBP), using the term *evidence-based* without the substance, for example, including uncritical reviews in sources labeled evidence-based. In many sources, we find no description of the unique process of EBP. Indeed many authors have used their discretion to misinform rather than inform readers about the origins and characteristics of EBP (Gambrill, 2011).

Hallmarks and Implications of the Philosophy of Evidence-Based Practice

The philosophy and related technology of EBP has implications for all individuals and institutions involved with helping clients, including educators, researchers, practitioners/policy makers, and those who provide funding (Gambrill, 2006) (see Exhibit 9.5). Interrelated implications include focusing on client concerns and hoped-for outcomes; increased transparency and attention to ethical obligations; consideration of populations, as well as individuals in the distribution of scarce resources; a systemic focus attending to multiple factors that influence decisions, including quality of professional education; maximizing the flow of knowledge and minimizing the flow of ignorance and propaganda; exploring the effectiveness of new professional education formats in preparing helpers who are lifelong learners; rigorous testing of claims; and systematic research reviews in place of haphazard ones. Hallmarks of EBP, such as considering the values and expectations of clients, involving clients as

informed participants in decisions that affect their lives, and making what professionals do to what effect transparent, should help to counter influences that contribute to ignoring outcomes of interest to clients and using ineffective or harmful services.

Research, practice, and educational issues are closely intertwined. For example, poor-quality reviews of research may result in misleading "practice guidelines," which result in poor-quality services for clients. Social workers may be misinformed about the evidentiary status of practice and policy claims and so harm rather than help clients or forgo opportunities to achieve hoped-for outcomes. Hallmarks and implications are interrelated. For example, promotion of transparency contributes to both knowledge flow and honoring ethical obligations (see Exhibit 9.5).

Move Away From Authority-Based Practices and Policies

The key contribution of EBP is encouraging social work to move from an authority-based profession to one in which ethical obligations to clients and students (for example, to draw on related research findings) are honored and critical appraisal and honest brokering of knowledge and ignorance thrives (Gambrill, 1999; see also Exhibit 9.2). Indicators of the authority-based nature of social work include basing decisions on criteria such as consensus and tradition. Propaganda (encouraging beliefs and actions with the least thought possible, Ellul, 1965) thrives as can be seen by censorship of certain kinds of knowledge such as variations in services and their outcomes. Other examples include misrepresenting disliked views, hiding limitations of research studies, and ignoring counterevidence to preferred views.

Honor Ethical Obligations

Evidence-based practice has ethical implications for practitioners and policy makers, as well as for researchers and educators (see Exhibit 9.6). Hallmarks of EBP include focusing on client

EXHIBIT 9.5

Interrelated Hallmarks and Contributions of EBP

1. **Move away from authority-based practices and policies.**
   - Clearly describe gaps among evidentiary, ethical, and practical concerns.
   - Be honest brokers of knowledge and ignorance; clearly describe limitations of research; accurately describe well-argued alternative views and evidence against favored views.
   - Avoid pseudo-inquiry (research that cannot critically test questions raised).
   - Avoid influence by and promotion of human service propaganda.
   - Do not rely on questionable criteria for making decisions (e.g., popularity, what is new).

2. **Honor ethical obligations.**
   - Focus on client concerns and hoped-for outcomes.
   - Attend to individual and cultural differences in client circumstances and characteristics including client values and preferences.
   - Involve clients as informed participants.
   - Clearly describe evidentiary status of recommended services.
   - Describe and take proactive steps to minimize errors.
   - Minimize harming in the name of helping.
   - Consider populations, as well as individuals, in the distribution of scarce resources.
   - Provide clear descriptions of services used and to what effect; be accountable.

3. **Promote transparency and accountability regarding what is done to what effect.**
   - Describe variations in services and their outcomes.
   - Acknowledge ignorance and uncertainty associated with decisions.

   - Encourage rigorous testing and appraisal of knowledge claims.
   - Avoid inflated claims.
   - Describe gaps between research findings regarding the causes of problems and services provided.
   - Blow the whistle on pseudoscience, propaganda, quackery, and fraud.

4. **Encourage a systemic approach for integrating ethical, evidentiary, and application issues.**
   - Highlight application challenges and explore how to decrease them.
   - Attend to management practices and policies that influence services.
   - Consider the implications of scarce resources; consider populations, as well as individuals.
   - Educate professionals who are lifelong learners.
   - Educate professionals who can spot and avoid the influence of human service propaganda.
   - Promote accurate reporting of research findings.

5. **Maximize knowledge flow (see also number 3).**
   - Increase use of available knowledge.
   - Welcome criticism.
   - Prepare, maintain, and disseminate systematic reviews (e.g., see Cochrane and Campbell databases of reviews).
   - Teach helpers and clients how to rapidly locate and critically appraise relevant research and provide resources needed.
   - Use professional education programs that develop lifelong learners.
   - Create accountable agency complaint systems.
   - Create effective programs for identifying errors and their causes and use this information to minimize avoidable errors.

Source: Based on E. Gambrill, Evidence-based practice: Implications for knowledge development and use in social work. Paper presented at Conference on Developing Practice Guidelines for Social Work Interventions. George Warren Brown School of Social Work. Washington University, May, 2000. Shortened version in A. Rosen & E. K. Proctor (Eds.). *Developing practice guidelines for social work intervention: Issues, methods and research agenda* (pp. 37–58). New York: Columbia University Press, 2003.

concerns and hoped-for outcomes, attending to individual differences in client characteristics and circumstances, considering client values and expectations, and involving clients as informed participants in decision making. Ignoring practice- and policy-related research findings and forwarding bogus claims of effectiveness violates our obligation to provide informed consent and may result in wasting money on ineffective services, harming clients in the name of helping them, and forgoing opportunities to attain hoped-for outcomes.

A striking characteristic of EBP and related developments is the extent to which clients are involved in many different ways.

One is reflected in the attention given to individual differences in client characteristics and circumstances in making decisions (e.g., see earlier description of EBP). A second is helping clients to develop critical appraisal skills. A third is encouraging client involvement in the design and critique of practice- and policy-related research (e.g., Hanley et al., 2001). A fourth is attending to outcomes that clients value, and a fifth is involving clients as informed (rather than as uninformed or misinformed) participants. A sixth is recognizing their unique knowledge in relation to application concerns. The client-focused nature of evidence-based decision making requires helpers to attend to

EXHIBIT 9.6

Contributions of Evidence-Based Practice and Policy to Honoring Ethical Obligations

Ethical Obligation	Contribution
A. Professional Helpers	
1. Help clients and avoid harm.	1. Draw on practice- and policy-related research to maximize success and minimize harm.
2. Maximize autonomy/self-determination.	2. Minimize coercion and involve clients as informed participants. Accurately describe the evidentiary status of recommended methods and alternatives.
3. Respect and integrity.	3. See 2.
4. Competence.	4. Have the knowledge and skills required to provide services that maximize success.
5. Accountability.	5. Arrange ongoing feedback about progress.
6. Promote social justice.	6. Advocate for changes in social conditions that contribute to problems.
7. Lifelong learning.	7. Develop tools to help practitioners become lifelong learners.
B. Researchers	
1. Accurately describe research methods used and make accurate conclusions.	1. Encourage accurate reporting of research limitations and measured (rather than inflated) claims.
2. Use research methods that can critically test questions posed.	2. Encourage match between research methods used and questions pursued.
3. Focus on outcomes of value to clients.	3. Involve clients in design and/or interpretation and critique of research.
C. Educators	
1. Help students to become lifelong learners.	1. Use educational programs that create lifelong learners.
2. Be honest up-to-date brokers of knowledge and ignorance.	2. Accurately describe both preferred and disliked views and related research findings.
3. Involve students as informed participants.	3. Accurately describe biases, conflicts of interest, and scope of knowledge.
4. Treat students equitably.	4. Do not show favoritism.
5. Competence.	5. Possess knowledge claimed.

client interests: what are *their* desired outcomes, what information would *they* like, what are *their* preferences regarding practices and policies. Sharpe and Faden (1998) describe the struggle in medicine, a continuing one, to focus on client outcome and highlight how recent this focus is and what a contentious issue it has been and continues to be. A concern for involving clients in making decisions that affect their lives highlights the importance of informed consent (e.g., Edwards, Elwyn, & Mulley, 2002). EBP involves sharing responsibility for decision making in a context of recognized uncertainty. Although professional codes of ethics call on practitioners to inform clients regarding risks and benefits of recommended services and alternatives, this is typically not done. Decisions concerning the distribution of scarce resources are a key ethical concern in the helping professions. This requires consideration of populations, as well as individuals.

Reduce Harm by Learning From Our Errors

EBP encourages programmatic research regarding error, both avoidable and unavoidable, its causes and consequences for clients and other involved parties, and exploration of methods designed to minimize avoidable errors, including agency-wide risk management programs (e.g., Reason, 1997, 2001; Munro, 2010). A careful review of the circumstances related to errors offers information about how to minimize avoidable ones. Research regarding errors points to systemic causes including quality of staff training and agency.

Make Practices, Policies, and Their Outcomes Transparent

Enhancing the visibility of what is done to what effect is a key contribution of EBP. Consider the study of variations in service patterns. If a variety of services is used to pursue a certain outcome (e.g., enhance positive parenting skills), questions arise, such as "Are they of equal cost and effectiveness?" EBP calls for candid descriptions of limitations of research studies and use of research methods that critically test questions addressed. A key contribution of EBP is discouraging inflated claims of knowledge that mislead involved parties and hinder the development of knowledge. Consider terms such as *well established* and *validated* that convey a certainty that is not possible (see chapter 4). Ignorance and uncertainty are recognized rather than hidden. EBP is a democratic endeavor in which transparency is highlighted and clients are involved as informed participants. There is candidness and clarity in place of secrecy and obscurity and paternalism. These characteristics are at odds with authority-based practice (e.g., Chalmers, 1983; Gambrill, 2001). EBP emphasizes the importance of accurately describing the evidentiary status of claims about assessment, intervention, and evaluation methods and avoiding propaganda ploys, such as hiding counterevidence to views promoted, hiding well-argued alternative accounts, and misrepresenting EBP and then attacking the distorted view. For example, is there evidence for the following claims:

- Scared Straight programs decrease delinquency.

- Brief psychological debriefing programs prevent posttraumatic stress disorder.

- Eyewitness testimony can be trusted.

- Genograms have been shown to be valuable in achieving client goals.

- Screening for depression on the part of general practitioners contributes to identification of clients in need of services.

- Anger management programs for adolescents are effective.

Indeed, research shows that some of these claims are false.

Evidence-based practice encourages transparency of what is done to what effect in all venues of interest, including practice and policy, research, and professional education. It has implications for the conduct, reporting, and dissemination of research findings. We will find that some programs do more good than harm, some more harm than good, and that many have not been critically tested. Involvement of clients as informed participants increases transparency of what is done to what effect. Transparency encourages clear descriptions of variations in services and their outcomes. It calls for critical appraisal of the evidentiary status of services and for blowing the whistle on pseudoscience, fraud, quackery, and propaganda (see chapter 4).

Increased transparency will highlight gaps between resources needed to attain certain outcomes and what is used. It will reveal gaps between causes of client problems and interventions used and promoted as of value. It will help us to identify ineffective and harmful services, as well as practices, programs, and policies that help clients. Transparency will also reveal the extent to which ethical obligations are met, such as involving clients as informed participants in making decisions in which uncertainty is acknowledged. It will draw attention to opportunity costs. That is, whenever we decide to provide service, there is less money for other services. It will reveal services that are ineffective, allowing a more judicious distribution of scarce resources (see Eddy, 1994a, 1994b). And it will suggest impossible tasks. Consider the requirement to "ensure" that children in protective care will not be harmed. This cannot be done. Pretending that it is possible is demoralizing to staff. Increased transparency requires clear language. This will discourage ploys that hide what is done to what effect and confuse pseudo-inquiry (efforts that cannot test claims addressed) with critical appraisal of claims.

Encourage a Systemic Approach for Integrating Practical, Ethical, and Evidentiary Issues

Evidence-based practice involves a systemic approach to improving quality of services: (1) educating professionals who are lifelong learners, (2) involving clients as informed participants, (3) attending to administrative practices and policies that influence practices (i.e., purchase of services), (4) considering the implications of scarce resources, and (5) attending to application challenges such as the development of strategies for efficiently tracking down and appraising evidence (for its validity and relevance) and the identification and application of effective strategies for lifelong learning and for improving clinical performance (e.g., see Gray, 2001a).

Quality of services is unlikely to improve in a fragmented approach, that is, without attending to all links in the system of service provision. EBP encourages the creation of tools and training programs designed to develop and encourage use of critical appraisal skills (see chapter 10). The evidence-based literature describes a wide variety of efforts to address application concerns (see chapter 10), some of which may be so severe that Sackett and his colleagues (2000) refer to them as "Killer Bs" (for example, organizational barriers and reliance on tradition or authority when making decisions) (p. 181).

Maximize Knowledge Flow

EBP is designed to maximize knowledge flow (see earlier discussion of reasons for developing EBP). In a culture in which knowledge flow is free, puffery (inflated claims of knowledge) is challenged and such challenges are welcomed. Evidence-based decision making emphasizes the importance of breaking down divisions between research and practice, and its advocates have actively pursued the development of a technology and political base to encourage this, for example, involving clients in the design and interpretation of research. Gray (2001a) suggests that evidence-based organizations should include systems that are capable of providing evidence and promoting the use of evidence, including both explicit (created by researchers) and tacit (created by clinicians, clients, and managers).

Clinicians and clients are involved as informed participants—there is no privileged knowledge in the sense of not sharing information about the evidentiary status of recommended methods. Such sharing poses a threat to those who prefer authority-based decision making, who forward bogus claims, and carry out pseudo-inquiry perhaps to maintain and gain funding and maintain status. Benefits of a democratic knowledge market include:

1. Critical appraisal of knowledge claims.

2. Increased staff morale because decisions will be more informed (e.g., regarding important uncertainties) and staff are rewarded for sharing knowledge and are free to discuss questions and learn from their colleagues and others throughout the world.

3. Increase in the ratio of informed to uninformed or misinformed decisions.

4. Candid recognition of uncertainty and ignorance. This is often swept under the rug, and staff may be blamed for not acting with knowledge that in fact does not (or did not) exist.

Exploration of ways to disseminate knowledge is key to maximizing knowledge flow, and literature on EPB is rich in the variety of efforts described. Rigorous appraisal of practice- and policy-related claims maximizes knowledge flow by reducing bogus assertions about what is true and what is not that may result in harm to clients. Accountable complaint systems are another way to increase knowledge flow. Evidence-based agencies encourage knowledge flow by using services found to maximize the likelihood of attaining hoped-for outcomes and not using ineffective services or services found to do more harm than good. Minimizing censorship of well-argued alternative views and counterevidence regarding popular views are additional ways to increase knowledge flow.

Misrepresentations and Objections to Evidence-Based Practice

Straus and McAlister (2000) suggest that some limitations of EBP are universal in helping efforts, such as lack of scientific evidence related to decisions and challenges in applying evidence to individuals. Barriers include the need to develop new skills and limited resources including access to needed databases. Many objections result from misunderstandings and misrepresentations of EBP including the following:

- Evidence-based practice denigrates clinical expertise.

- It ignores client's values and preferences.

- It promotes a cookbook approach to medicine (e.g., ignores clients' unique circumstances and characteristics).

- It is simply a cost-cutting tool.

- It is limited to clinical research.

- It is an ivory-tower concept (it cannot be done).

- Only randomized controlled trials are considered.

- It leads to therapeutic nihilism in the absence of evidence.

- We are already doing it; there is nothing new.

Reading original sources shows the incorrectness of the above. (Replies to objections based on distortions of EBP can be seen in Gibbs and Gambrill, 2002.) Unique characteristics and circumstances of clients including cultural differences prohibit a "cook book" approach and review of research related to a question may show that effective programs will cost more, not less. Many (most?) practitioners do not search for external research findings related to important practice decisions. Many (most) do not inform clients about the criteria they use to select service methods or describe the risks and benefits of recommended services and alternatives.

Professional codes of ethics require characteristics of EBP including informed consent and drawing on practice-related literature. EBP calls on professionals to search for practice-related research findings and share what is found (including nothing) with clients and to involve clients in decisions made as informed participants. If no research findings are located, clients are so informed and well-argued practice theories are drawn on. EBP describes a philosophy and unique process for integrating research and practice facilitated through innovations such as the Internet. Such advances have been applied to practice primarily during the past two decades. They are new. So too is the ease of accessibility to checklists guiding critical appraisal of different kinds of research studies and programs designed to help both professionals and clients critically review research. It is true that there is a preference for certain methodologies; EBP favors methods that critically appraise claims so that we do not misinform ourselves and our clients. Randomized controlled trials are important in evaluating many kinds of questions such as those that concern effectiveness and prevention. Other research methods are required to critically appraise other kinds of questions such as description questions.

Some claim that if you look diligently enough, you can always find a study that will support your conclusion and you can always find fault with a study that does not support favored views. Ethical reviewers seek all published and unpublished research that meets standards for inclusion in a review, regardless of whether that research supports or refutes their assumptions. Efforts are made to minimize the play of biases in critical appraisal of practice-related research literature by clear description of search procedures used and use of rigorous criteria to evaluate studies located. Historically, those in professions such as social work have turned to medicine as a guide to practice (e.g., Richmond, 1917). There have been spirited critiques of such an approach. Medicine, like other professions, requires complex decisions in uncertain environments. It is true that there are *signs*, as well as *symptoms* in medicine. That is, if we feel warm (a symptom) we can take our temperature (a sign) to check on this. However, similarities outweigh the differences, including a reluctance to face uncertainty, the vital role of communication skills, the play of political and economic influences, and ethical obligations. Medical experts note that the typical physician works in an atmosphere of uncertainty. Physicians too must struggle with deciding how (or if) research findings apply to a particular client. Here too self-reports may be unreliable and misleading, and there may be missing information. Informed consent obligations apply to all helping professions.

Obstacles

There are many obstacles to using the process of evidence-informed practice. Encouraging practitioners to try to integrate evidentiary, ethical, and application issues may clash with current practices in agencies; in authority-based agencies, staff may be punished for asking questions about the effectiveness of agency services. Resources required for EBP may be lacking. However, professional codes of ethics require us to make informed decisions, thus, we are obligated to advocate for needed tools. Both professionals and clients may lack health and statistical literacy. The Institute of Medicine (IOM) defines health literacy as "the degree to which individuals can obtain, process, and understand basic health information and services they need to make appropriate health decisions." Statistical literacy refers to the ability to understand numbers, proportions, and probabilities. Both professionals and clients typically lack both kinds of literacy, which is a major obstacle and a major focus of attention in literature concerning EBP. (See also discussion of application challenges in chapter 10.)

Controversies Regarding Evidence

Both the origins of EBP and objections to it reflect different views of "evidence." When do we have enough to recommend a practice or policy? Differences of opinion regarding evidence can be seen in the professional literature, as well as in the media. Concerns about inflated claims of knowledge and ignorance was a key reason for the origin of EBP. There are many kinds of evidence (see Exhibit 9.7). Different opinions about how much "we know" (or "don't know") reflect use of different criteria. How should these differences be handled? Given the history of the helping professions (e.g., bogus claims of effectiveness and

---

EXHIBIT 9.7

Different Kinds of "Evidence"

- legal regulations
- ethical issues
- folklore
- common sense
- practice wisdom; received wisdom (experiences, beliefs, and skills of professionals)
- cultural differences
- superstition
- values
- social care system, rules, resources, and finances
- descriptive/analytical data (e.g., prevalence and incidence of a problem)
- description of a client's circumstances or career of a problem
- experience of clients, practitioners, or researchers
- resources available
- people's attitudes
- statistical information
- economic data
- implementation
- habits/tradition

---

harming in the name of helping), is not the ethical road to make measured rather than inflated claims so that we are not misled and in turn, mislead clients?

A key way in which views of EBP differ is in the degree of rigor in evaluating knowledge claims. Such differences are illustrated by the different conclusions concerning the comparative effectiveness of Multi-systemic Therapy (MST). This program is typically described as an effective, evidence-based treatment model. Littell, Popa, and Forsythe (2005) conducted a systematic review of related RCTs and concluded that MST is no more effective than alternative treatments. Concerns identified in related studies included: (1) inconsistent reports on the number of cases randomly assigned; (2) unyoked designs; (3) unstandardized observation periods within studies; (4) unclear randomization procedures; (5) subjective definitions of treatment completion, and (6) no intention to treat analysis. Do uncritical reviews contribute to helping clients and involving clients as informed participants?

If there are no randomized controlled trials regarding an effectiveness question, we may have to rely on findings from a pre-post test. As this example illustrates, the term "best evidence" may refer to different kinds of tests that differ in their ability to critically test claims. The Task Force on Psychological Intervention Guidelines of the American Psychological Association (1995) used the criterion of two well-designed randomized controlled trials showing a positive outcome, as representing a "well-established claim." Within a more skeptical approach to knowledge (see chapter 4), we would say that a claim has been critically tested in two well-controlled randomized controlled trials and has passed both tests. This keeps uncertainty in view.

Davies (2004) suggests that a broad view of evidence is needed to review policies including (1) experience and expertise, (2) judgment, (3) resources, (4) values, (5) habits and traditions, (6) lobbyists and pressure groups, and (7) pragmatics and contingencies. He suggests that we should consider all of these factors in making decisions about whether or not to implement a policy. He describes six kinds of research related to policy impact: (1) implementation evidence, (2) descriptive analytical evidence, (3) attitudinal evidence, (4) statistical modeling, (5) economic/econometric evidence, and (6) ethical evidence. Hierarchies of evidence with systematic reviews at the top that are used to select interventions for individuals may not be appropriate for selection of policies because of all the different kinds of relevant evidence.

Summary

The helping professions are characterized by troubling gaps between obligations described in professional codes of ethics and accreditation standards and everyday practices and policies, and between responsibilities of researchers and scholars to be honest brokers of knowledge and ignorance and what we find in professional venues such as published literature—inflated claims, hiding limitations of research methods, and misrepresentation of new developments. The study of variations in practices and policies reveals that clients may be harmed rather than helped because of neglect of related research findings and that clients are typically not involved in decisions as informed participants. Evidence-based practice describes a decision-making process designed to integrate ethical, evidentiary, and application concerns. It is assumed that we and our clients often need information to make important decisions, for example, about how to decrease risk of child abuse or what method is most likely to help a client attain a job. It is a process in which the uncertainty in making decision is highlighted, efforts to decrease it are made, and clients are involved as informed participants. It is as much about the ethics of and pressure on academics and researchers as it is about the ethics of and pressures on practitioners and agency administrators.

Evidence-based practice and policy call for honest brokering of knowledge and ignorance, for example, clear descriptions of criteria used to make decisions. They are an alternative to authority-based practice. They encourage us to attend to ethical obligations (e.g., to draw on practice and policy research, to involve clients as informed participants), to be systemic (e.g., to decrease the division between research and practice by creating evidence-based agency cultures and creating lifelong learners), and to be realistic (e.g., identify and minimize application problems). There are many challenges and obstacles. It is important to distinguish between objections based on misrepresentations of EBP and those based on an accurate understanding. Otherwise, we may prematurely discard this approach that is so compatible with ethical obligations of social workers and lose opportunities to help clients. An EBPs approach in which some authority designates what is effective and should be used is quite different from the process and philosophy of EBP as described by its originators.

Reviewing Your Competencies

Reviewing Content Knowledge

1. Describe the philosophy of evidence-based practice as developed by its originators.

2. Describe how the EBPs approach differs from the process and philosophy of EBP.

3. Distinguish between authority-based and evidence-based practice.

4. Describe key reasons for the development of EBP.

5. Give examples of different kinds of questions that arise in everyday practice.

6. Describe different styles of EBP and their advantages and disadvantages.

7. Describe hallmarks of EBP.

8. Discuss the relationship between EBP and ethical obligations.

9. Describe the relationship between knowledge flow and EBP.

10. Describe what the term *transparency* means and its relationship EBP.

11. Identify common misrepresentations of EBP.

12. Describe application challenges in using EBP.

Reviewing What You Do

1. You can accurately describe EBP to others.

2. You accurately describe the difference between an EBPs approach and the process of EBP to others.

3. You do well on a test of competence in EBP (e.g., Ramos, Schafer, & Tracz, 2003).

4. You check what people mean when they use the term EBP to avoid confused, unproductive conversations.

5. Given objections to EBP, you can accurately identify which ones are based on misunderstandings or distortions of EBP.

Reviewing Results

1. You can teach someone else the process of EBP.

2. You take effective steps to address application challenges.

3. See self-evaluation questions at the end of chapter 10.

10

Posing Questions and Searching for Answers

OVERVIEW This chapter describes the steps involved in the process of evidence-informed practice, as well as related challenges and evolving remedies. Evidence-based practice (EBP) is a decision-making process designed to help you to integrate evidentiary, ethical, and application concerns. It is designed to reveal or decrease the uncertainty surrounding decisions that affect your clients and to involve clients as informed (rather than uninformed or misinformed) participants and so honor ethical obligations to clients. Access to related tools, such as relevant databases, is vital. Ongoing challenges include integrating diverse sources of information in a context of uncertainty, scarce resources, and bureaucratic obstacles such as a preference for authoritarian decision-making styles.

What You Will Learn About

- The first step: A willingness to say "I don't know"

- Posing well-formed questions

- Searching effectively for research findings related to information needs

- Critically appraising research located

- Integrating research findings with other information and applying the findings

- Evaluating and learning from what happens

- Evaluating your skills in evidence-based practice

- The question of motivation

The First Step: A Willingness To Say "I Don't Know"

Evidence-based practice requires a willingness to say "I don't know"—to acknowledge that there may be a gap between your current knowledge and skills and what is needed to help clients and to avoid harm. It is a process for handling the uncertainty surrounding decisions. It requires a willingness to recognize this uncertainty. Sources of uncertainty include limitations in knowledge, lack of familiarity with knowledge that is available, difficulties in distinguishing between personal ignorance and lack of competence, and actual limitations of knowledge (Fox & Swazy, 1974). That is, what is the gap between your knowledge and skills and what is available that could be used to help clients? Uncertainties may be related to lack of information about clients' circumstances, ambivalence about pursuing certain goals, and availability of resources. A willingness to say "I don't know," combined with taking steps to see if needed information is available, increases the likelihood that you will accurately identify important uncertainties (Chalmers, 2007). This helps you to honor ethical obligations to involve clients as informed participants.

Application Challenges

The steps in EBP may sound as if they are easy to carry out but that is often not the case. You need skills in critical thinking and the courage to use them—to ask questions others may find disturbing such as "Does a service used by your agency really help clients?" You need skills in searching, appraising, and storing information and the motivation to use them. And, competence does not guarantee good performance; the distinction between performance and competence is an old and continuing concern. Gray (2001a) suggests that performance (*P*) is directly related to our motivation (*M*) and competence (*C*) and inversely related to the barriers (*B*) we confront (p. 13):

$$P = \frac{M \times C}{B}$$

Special training, guided practice, and related tools and resources are needed to carry out the steps of EBP on the job, in real time. Challenges include gaining timely access to research findings and critically appraising this knowledge. Creating technologies to address application problems has been a key contribution of evidence-informed practice. This is an ongoing challenge (Greenhalgh et al., 2004; Lavis, Oxman, Moynihan, & Paulsen, 2008.)

Posing Well-Formed Questions

A key step in EBP is translating information needs, for example, about causes related to a problem, into questions that facilitate a search for related research (Sackett et al., 2000). Reasons include the following (Gambrill & Gibbs, 2009):

- Vague questions lead to vague answers; specific questions are needed to gain specific answers to guide decisions.

- If we do not pose clear questions, we are less likely to discover helpful research findings and change what we do; we may harm clients or offer clients ineffective methods.

- It is a countermeasure to arrogance that interferes with learning and the integration of practice and research; if we seek answers, we will discover important uncertainties (Chalmers, 2004).

- It can save time during a search. The better formed the question, the more quickly may related literature (or the lack of it) be revealed.

- It is necessary for self-directed, lifelong learning.

Translating information needs concerning important decisions into well-formed questions can be difficult. There is a tendency to underestimate the difficulty of this step. Posing well-formed questions that allow rapid access to related research findings requires training and practice. The better formed the question, the greater the efficiency of searching should be. A well-formed question should meet the following criteria:

- It concerns problems of concern to clients.

- It affects a large number of clients.

- It is probably answerable by searching for related research findings.

- It is clearly posed to facilitate an efficient, effective electronic search.

The originators of EBP (Sackett et al., 1997, 2000) suggest posing four-part questions that describe the population of clients, the intervention you are interested in, what it may be compared to (including doing nothing), and hoped-for outcomes (PICO questions). Gibbs (2003) refers to these as COPES questions (see Exhibit 10.1). They are *Client Oriented*. They are questions posed by practitioners in their daily practice that affect clients' welfare (the word *client* may refer to an individual, group, or community.) Second, they have *Practical* importance. They concern problems that arise frequently in everyday practice and that are of concern to an agency. For example, child protective service workers must assess risk. Asking the question about what types of clients present the greatest immediate risk for child abuse is a critical one. Third, COPES questions guide an *Evidence Search* for related research findings. The process of forming a specific question often begins with a vague general question and then proceeds to a well-built one. Fourth, hoped-for outcomes are identified. Synonyms can be used to facilitate a search (e.g., Gibbs, 2003; Glasziou, Del Mar, & Salisbury, 2003). For example, if abused children are of concern, other terms for this may be *maltreated children, neglected children, mistreated children*. Background reading may help you to focus your question. You may rapidly find relevant research by searching in Google.

Different Kinds of Questions

Different kinds of questions (about effectiveness, prevention, risk, assessment, or description) require different research

EXHIBIT 10.1

Kinds of Questions and Corresponding Components of a Well-Structured Question

Question Types	Client Type and Problem	What You Might Do	Alternate Course of Action	Hoped-for Outcome
	Describe a group of similar clients. (Be specific.)	Use an intervention to prevent a problem; assess a problem; screen clients to assess risk.	Describe an alternative.	Valid measure? Accurate risk estimation? Accurate description of need?
Effectiveness	If disoriented elderly persons residing in a nursing home	who receive reality orientation therapy	compared to validation therapy	which results in better orientation to time, pace, and person?
Prevention	In sexually active high school students at high risk for pregnancy.	who are exposed to baby—think it over	compared to didactic material on the use of birth control methods	which group has fewer pregnancies during an academic year and more knowledge of birth control methods?
Assessment	In elderly nursing home residents who may be depressed or have Alzheimer's disease or dementia	who complete a depression screening test	compared to a short mental examination test	which measure most efficiently and reliably discriminates between depression and dementia?
Description	In children	raised with depressed mothers	compared to mothers who are not depressed	which group has the greatest prevalence of developmental delays?
Prediction	In preschool children	with antisocial behavior	compared to children who do not display such behavior	what percentage will display antisocial behavior in adolescence?
Risk	In mothers alleged to maltreat their children.	who complete an actuarial risk-assessment measure	compared to a consensus-based measure	which measure best predicts future abuse?
Harm	In adults	who participate in a depression screening program	compared with those who do not	which results in the least harm?
Cost-benefit	In offering parenting classes to mothers whose children have been removed from their care	will purchasing services from another agency	compared to offering such training in-house	be more cost effective and effective?

Source: The first three questions are from L. E. Gibbs (2003). *Evidence-based practice for the helping professions* (p. 59). Pacific Grove, CA: Thomson/Brooks-Cole. The format of all questions is based on D. L. Sackett, W. S. Richardson, W. Rosenberg, & R. B. Haynes (1997). *Evidence-based medicine: How to practice and teach EBM* (p. 29). New York: Churchill Livingstone.

methods to critically test them (see chapter 11). A variety of questions may arise with one client or family. Let us say you work in a hospice and counsel grieving parents who have lost a child. *Descriptive* questions include "What are the experiences of parents who lose a young child?" "How long do these last?" "Do they change over time and if so, how?" Both survey data and qualitative research, such as focus groups, in-depth interviews, and participant observation, can be used to explore such

questions. Research may be available that describes experiences of grieving parents based on a large randomly drawn sample of such parents. A research report may describe the experiences of clients who seek bereavement counseling using in-depth interviews. Questions concerning *risk* may arise (such as "In parents who have lost a young child, what is the risk of depression?"), as well as questions about *effectiveness*: "For parents who have lost a young child, is a support group compared to no service more effective in decreasing depression?" *Prevention* questions may arise. "For parents who have lost a young child, is brief counseling compared to a support group more effective in preventing depression from interfering with care of other children?"

Effectiveness Questions

Many questions concern the effectiveness of services. A question may be: "In people recently exposed to a catastrophic event, would brief psychological debriefing or nothing avoid or minimize the likelihood of posttraumatic stress disorder?" Ideally we would discover a related systematic review or meta-analyses of randomized controlled trials such as Rose, Bisson, Churchill, and Wessely (2002).

Prevention Questions

Prevention questions direct attention to the future. These include questions about the effectiveness of early childhood visitation programs in preventing delinquency at later developmental stages. Examples are: "In young children, do early home visitation programs, compared with no service, influence the frequency of delinquency as adolescents?" "For parents who have lost a young child, is bereavement counseling or a support group most valuable in decreasing prolonged dysfunctional grieving?" Here, too, well-designed randomized controlled trials control for more biases than do other kinds of studies.

Prediction (Risk/Prognosis) Questions

Social workers often have to estimate risk, for example, of future child maltreatment. A key question here is: "Is the risk assessment measure valid?" What is the rate of false positives (clients incorrectly said to have some characteristics such as be suicidal) and false negatives (clients inaccurately said not to have this characteristic, not be suicidal). You can use a four-cell contingency table to review the accuracy of measures (see chapter 20). A well-built risk question is: "In abused children in foster care, will an actuarial risk assessment measure, compared to a consensus-based measure, provide the most accurate predictions regarding re-abuse of children returned to their biological parents?" (e.g., Barber Shlonsky, Black, Goodman, & Trocmé, 2008; Johnson, 2011).

Assessment Questions

Professionals use a variety of assessment measures. These measures differ in their reliability (for example, consistency of responses in absence of change) and validity (do they measure what they purport to measure?) (See chapter 17 for further discussion of reliability and validity.) Inflated claims regarding the accuracy of assessment measures are common. The sample used to gather data and provide "norms" on a measure (scores of a certain group of individuals) may be quite different than clients with whom you work, and so these norms may not apply. Key concepts in reviewing assessment tools are also reviewed in chapters 11 and 17. A well-built assessment question is: "In detecting frail elderly people who are depressed, is the Beck Depression Inventory or the Pleasant Events Schedule more accurate?"

Description Questions

You may also need descriptive information, such as the experiences of caregivers of frail elderly relatives. A question here is: "In those who care for dying relatives, what challenges arise and how are they handled?" Some description questions call for qualitative research. For example, questions concerning experiences related to events such as loss of an infant or living in a nursing home call for research methods that can provide such accounts (e.g., in-depth interviews and focus groups). Other kinds of description questions require survey data, involving large samples. Survey data may provide information about the percentage of grieving parents who continue to grieve in certain ways with certain consequences over the years. It may provide information about the percentage of divorces and other consequences and describe how parents cope with them. Here, too, we should consider the quality of related research (see chapter 11).

Questions About Harm

How many people have to receive some assessment measure or service for one to be harmed? This is known as number needed to harm (NNH). Related questions are: "How many people would we have to screen to identify one person who could benefit from help?" and "How many of these would be harmed by simply taking the test who are not at risk?" As Gray (2001a) suggests, any intervention including assessment methods may harm as well as help.

Questions About Cost-Benefit

Limited resources highlight the importance of cost-benefit analyses. "What is the cost of offering one service compared to another and how many people benefit from each service?" Criteria for reviewing cost-benefit studies can be found in Gray (2001a) and Guyatt, et al. (2008).

Questions About How to Encourage Lifelong Learning

Integrating practice and research requires lifelong learning. An example of a question here is: "In newly graduated social workers, will a journal club, compared to a 'buddy system,' be most effective in maintaining evidence-based practice skills?"

Common Errors in Posting Questions

Errors that may occur when posing questions include having more than one question in a question, trying to answer the question before stating it clearly (posing vague questions). Gibbs (2003) notes that students often do not distinguish between a practice or policy question useful to guide a search, and a research question requiring collection of data using an appropriate research method. Novices may pose different questions compared to experts in an area who are familiar with research, for example, regarding prevalence of a concern (such as depression) and the complexity of related factors, such as lack of social support, negative thoughts, recent losses, poor nutrition, and so on. A lack of knowledge may contribute to posing misleading questions that overlook important individual differences in a client's circumstances or characteristics. For example, posing an effectiveness question before discovering factors that contribute to depression (such as "In adults who are depressed, is cognitive-behavioral therapy, compared to medication, most effective in decreasing depression?") may overlook the fact that, for this client, recent losses in social support are uppermost, which suggests a different question, such as "In adults who are depressed because of a recent loss in social support, is a support group or individual counseling most effective in decreasing depression?"

Obstacles to Posing Well-Structured Questions

Posing well-formed questions can be difficult. One obstacle is thinking it is easy and giving up when difficulty occurs. Ely and his co-authors (2002) conducted a qualitative study investigating obstacles to answering physicians' questions about patient care with evidence. Participants included 9 academic generalist doctors, 14 family doctors, and 2 medical librarians. They identified 59 obstacles. Obstacles related to formulating questions included the following:

- Missing client data requiring unnecessarily broad search. Questions that include demographic or clinical information and information about client preferences may help to focus the search. The kind of information of value will vary depending on the question and may not be clear until the search is under way.

- Inability to answer specific questions with general resources. Questions such as "What is this rash?" and vague cries for help "I don't know what to do with this client" cannot be answered by a general resource.

- Uncertainty about the scope of the question and unspoken ancillary questions. For example, the original question may have to be expanded to include ancillary questions.

EXHIBIT 10.2

Obstacles to Posing Well-Formed Questions

1. Lack of training (e.g., confusing research questions and practice questions, trying to answer a question before clearly posing it, including more than one question in a question).

2. Lack of information about client characteristics.

3. Lack of training on the part of agency supervisors.

4. Lack of related tools, such as access to computerized databases.

5. Lack of motivation to honor ethical obligations to draw on practice- and policy-related research.

6. Lack of support in agency, e.g., threatening nature of clear questions to those who favor use of authority-based criteria to select services (such as tradition, popularity).

7. Lack of patience in crafting a well-structured question.

- Obstacles related to modifying the question include unhelpful changes, perhaps due to misunderstandings between helpers and clients, trying to answer too many questions at once, and trying to answer the question while posing it (see Exhibit 10.2).

Posing clear questions may be viewed a threat. Questions are not benign as illustrated by the fate of Socrates. Staff who pose questions in their agency may create discomfort among other staff, perhaps because they are doing something unfamiliar or perhaps because others view such staff as impertinent or disloyal to the agency or profession. Supervisors may not have experience in posing clear questions and wonder why it is of value; learning to pose well-formed questions has probably not been a part of their education. Other obstacles include lack of training in how to pose well-structured questions, lack of needed tools to follow through on searches, lack of motivation to consider criteria on which decisions are made, and fears that there are more questions than answers.

Options for Decreasing Challenges

Options for addressing challenges include gaining guided experience in posing both clinical and research questions. The more we practice a skill, the more facility we gain with it, if we also gain corrective feedback. Unless we try to perform a skill, we cannot discover our baseline competency level. Posing questions sounds easy, but can be difficult. Practice posing a well-structured question by completing the Form for Posing Questions at the end of this chapter. (See also Gambrill & Gibbs, 2009.)

Searching for Research Findings Related to Information Needs

Searching effectively and efficiently for research related to important decisions is a key competency. It is perhaps at this step that the most revolutionary changes have occurred to help searchers, including invention of the systematic review and creation of Internet databases, such as the Cochrane and Campbell Collaboration Libraries. The Internet has revolutionized the search for information, making it speedier and more effective. Google searches can be swift and productive. Sources differ in the degree of "quality control" regarding accuracy of reporting of the evidentiary status of claims. Keep in mind that flaws in published research (inflated claims, incomplete searches, for example, omitting studies with negative or harmful effects, and out-of-date material) was a key reason for the development of the process and philosophy of EBP (Gray, 2001a, b). You will not have time to seek and appraise research findings related to all decisions. Sackett et al. (2000) suggest that research should always be sought and critically appraised with questions that arise often. The better formed the question, the more likely it is that the terms used will yield relevant information. Steps in searching include the following:

- Form a well-structured question (see Exhibit 10.1).

- Select the appropriate quality filters related to question type.

- Plan a search strategy (e.g., select the most appropriate databases).

- Conduct your search.

- Evaluate the results and revise the strategy as needed.

Use of Quality Filters

Different kinds of questions require different kinds of research to critically appraise them, and related terms are of value in a search. Such terms are referred to as *quality filters*. Gibbs (2003) refers to these as MOLES (methodologically oriented locators for an evidence search). (Criteria suggested to critically appraise different kinds of research are discussed in chapter 11.) The use of quality filters relevant to the type of question posed will facilitate a search. Examples are shown in Exhibit 10.3. If a question concerns effectiveness, quality filters include terms, such as random or controlled trials, meta-analysis, or systematic review. Systematic reviews and meta-analyses include a search for and critical appraisal of related studies. Cochrane and Campbell reviews are based on a search for all high quality research, published and unpublished, in all languages, concerning a question and critical appraisal of what is found. Campbell Reviews include those related to education, child welfare, and the criminal justice system.

EXHIBIT 10.3

Examples of Quality Filters Regarding Different Kinds of Questions

Effectiveness and Preventive	Risk/Prognosis	Assessment	Description
random OR controlled Trial OR meta-anal OR systematic review	risk assessment OR predictive validity OR receiver operat OR sensitivity OR specificity OR false positive OR prognos AND predict	inter-rater OR sensitivity OR specificity OR false positive	Survey OR Representative Sample *qual studies*: Qualitative analys OR content analys OR in-depth Interview OR Focus group

Source: See, for example, L. E. Gibbs (2003). *Evidence-based practice for the helping professions* (p. 100). Pacific Grove, CA: Thomson/Brooks-Cole; and A. McKibbon, A. Eady, & S. Marks (1999). *PDQ evidence-based principles and practice*. Hamilton, U.K.: B. C. Decker.

A search strategy consists of identifying important search terms. (See Exhibit 10.4.) Let us say you are interested in locating research concerning brief psychological debriefing to prevent posttraumatic stress. Terms selected might be *stress, psychological debriefing,* and *systematic review*. A careful search requires seeking information that challenges (disconfirms) your initial assumptions, as well as for information that supports them. You can keep track of how many "hits" you obtain using a certain search strategy in a search log (Gibbs, 2003). A finding that an intervention harms clients or that there is no guiding research also provides important information that permits accurate appraisal of the uncertainty surrounding a decision.

Ease of searching depends on access to relevant databases. Some sites are available only by subscription, but a library near you may have a subscription. Use of Boolean search terms is helpful (see Exhibit 10.5). Examples include "and," which retrieves only articles with *both* words (child abuse and single parents), and "or," which locates all articles with either word (alcohol abuse or cocaine abuse). The term NOT excludes material containing certain words. Synonyms and key words can be combined by placing parentheses around OR statements such as (parent training OR parent education). You can limit searches in a variety of ways, for example, by date. Parentheses can be used to group words such as (*frail* and *elderly*). Different databases have different rules about how search terms should

EXHIBIT 10.4

Search Planning Worksheet

Question: In families experiencing youth–parent conflict, is conflict resolution training, compared to behavioral training, more effective in decreasing conflict?

	Client Type and Characteristics	Course of Action	Alternate Course of Action	Intended Result	Relevant Quality Filters
Row 1 Terms from your Question	Family with youth–parent conflict	Conflict resolution training	Behavioral training	Decrease family conflict	Random, controlled trial, meta-analysis, systematic review
Row 2 Possible Synonyms	Adolescent, at risk child/youth	Problem solving	Contingency management	Improved relations, increased communication	Effectiveness, best practice, program evaluation
Row 3 Terms Chosen and Combined	(Troubled family OR parent-child conflict)	(Conflict resolution OR problem solving)	(Behavioral training OR contingency management	(Decrease OR reduce conflict)	(Effectiveness OR systematic review)

Source: Amanda Reiman, UCB.

be entered for maximum effect, and you should seek specific information about how to use these effectively from other sources. Experience in using relevant databases is an important skill. An informatist may be available to help you search in relevant databases. Searches can be facilitated by careful selection of words including a relevant quality filter such as "systematic review." If you get too many "hits," narrow the search by using more specific terms and more selective quality filters. If you get too few, widen the search by using more general terms.

Relevant Sources

Searches will be more productive by focusing on sources that contain high quality reviews. Different databases may have different rules about how search terms should be entered for maximum effect. Experience in using relevant databases is an important skill.

The Cochrane and Campbell Databases of Systematic Reviews

The Cochrane Collaboration prepares, maintains, and disseminates high quality reviews of research related to particular questions in the area of health. The Cochrane Library is an electronic publication designed to supply high quality reviews to those providing and receiving care and those responsible for research, teaching, funding, and administration at all levels. It is published on the Internet and is distributed on a subscription basis. Abstracts are available without charge and can be searched. Reviews are based on hand-searches of relevant journals, as well as a search for and critical appraisal of relevant unpublished material. They are prepared by a review group, which is also responsible for periodically updating the review. Entries include completed reviews available in full text, protocols that are expressions of intent, and a brief outline of the topic and a submission deadline. Reviews are prepared and maintained, based on standards in The Reviewers' Handbook, which describes the process of creating Cochrane systematic

EXHIBIT 10.5

Boolean Searching

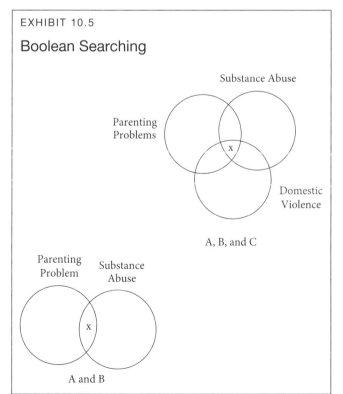

reviews. It is revised often to ensure that it remains up-to-date (Higgins & Greene, 2008).

The Campbell collaboration, patterned after the Cochrane Collaboration, prepares reviews related to education, social intervention, and criminal justice. Coordinating groups include communication and dissemination, crime and justice, education, social welfare, and a methods group. Like the Cochrane Collaboration, detailed instructions are followed for preparing reviews, and reviews are routinely updated. Like the Cochrane Collaboration, there is an annual conference, and both are attended by methodologists, as well as those interested in particular problem areas (http://www.campbellcollaboration.com). Thousands of systematic reviews have been completed. Here are some examples:

- Amphetamines for Attention Deficit Hyperactivity Disorder (ADHD) in adults.

- Day care centers for severe mental illness.

- Dietary advice for reducing cardiovascular risk.

- Discharge planning from hospital to home.

- Parent training support for intellectually disabled parents.

- Peer support telephone calls for improving health.

The Internet

Search engines such as Google provide a key source for locating practice- and policy-related research findings. For example, a search on Google using the question "What is the prevalence of bedwetting among 5-year-olds?" produced an answer of 16% in 5 seconds (http://www.emedicinehealth.com). Sources include web sites concerned with a unique topic such as anxiety, sites prepared by businesses, those concerned with fraud and quackery, consumer protection sites, , web sites concerned with harm (http://www.cchr.org; http://www.healthyskepticism. org), and those of various advocacy groups (e.g., Commercial Free Childhood, http://www.commercialfreechildhood.org). Material differs greatly in accuracy of content (e.g., Kunst, Groot, Latthe, Latthe, & Khan, 2002). As always, "buyer beware" applies. Consider Anxiety Disorders Association of America. You will find a biomedical framing of anxiety. Is this the most accurate framing (e.g., see Lane, 2007; Moynihan & Cassels, 2005; Gambrill & Reiman, 2011). And, just because a source has a reputation for providing accurate appraisals, this does not guarantee that all material will be accurate. Criteria that can be used to appraise the accuracy of material include the source which funds it (does it have a reputation for critical appraisal and accurate presentation of well-argued alternative views), clarity of writing, completeness of description of studies (e.g., sample size, measures used), and citation of references so you can review original sources for yourself.

Examples of databases, together with their subject coverage and focus, are given in Appendix A. Some sites are available only by subscription. Databases relevant to the interpersonal helping professions include: PsychInfo, Social Science Citation Index, Social Work Abstracts, Sociological Abstracts, ERIC, Evidence-based mental health, MEDLINE, EMBASE, CINAHL (nursing and allied health professionals), Health Technology Assessment Program, Effective Health Care Bulletin, and Clinical Evidence. SIGLE (System for Information on Grey Literature in Europe) can be used to locate hard to find and nonconventional literature. Libraries are a key resource. Newspapers are another source. Governmental agencies provide free statistical information of potential value. (See examples of U.S. federal agencies and departments in Appendix B.)

Centers and Organizations

Many centers and organizations promote an evidence-informed approach and provide related support and resources. The National Health Service (NHS) Research and Development Centre for Evidence-Based Medicine at the John Radcliffe Hospital in Oxford was the first of several similar centers in the United Kingdom. (See http://www.cebm.net.) The Centre for Evidence-Based Child Health is located at the Institute of Child Health, London. Short courses, workshops, and training opportunities are offered by many centers. The Centre for Evidence-Based Mental Health contains resources designed to promote and support the teaching and practice of evidence-based mental health care, including a list of links to evidence-based mental health web sites; a toolkit of teaching resources, including examples of scenarios used in teaching EBP in mental health. (See http://www.cebmh. com.) The Centre for Evidence-Based Nursing is designed to help nurses, researchers, nurse educators, and managers to identify evidence-based practices and to encourage use of evidence.

Common Errors in Searching

Errors at this stage are related to the clarity of questions posed; they may be too narrow or too broad, resulting in too few or too many reports. Giving up too soon is a common error; it takes persistence to reframe search strategies more effectively. Lack of information about valuable sites may result in overlooking helpful sources.

Obstacles and Evolving Remedies

You may not be aware of important databases or have access to skilled librarians. There may be no rigorous research related to a question. Gray refers to this as the *relevance gap* (Gray, 2001a). Another is failure to publish research results—the *publication gap*. A third difficulty is finding published research—the *hunting gap*. Yet another is the need for critical appraisal—the *quality gap* (p. 107). Of the 59 obstacles to EBP identified by Ely and his colleagues (2002), five they considered most important involved search problems:

- Excessive time required to locate information.

- Difficulty selecting an optimal search strategy.

- Failure of a seemingly relevant resource to cover the topic.

- Uncertainty about how to know when all relevant evidence has been found.

- Inadequate synthesis of multiple sources of evidence into a conclusion that is clinically relevant.

The resources that enable an efficient search illustrate challenges that lie in the path of the professional or client who would like to make evidence-informed decisions. There may be no library in an agency, let alone a librarian. There may be no access to relevant databases. The importance of immediate access to needed databases is illustrated by the failure to use agency-based libraries even though they are conveniently located. There may be no access to a reference management system. Only via providing access to a knowledge manager as suggested by Gray (1998) may speedy access to needed information be possible. This person's role is to locate and critically appraise practice- and policy-related research findings in a timely manner. Searching widely is one way to protect yourself from influence by bogus presentations from a single source. For example, material on the web site of the American Psychiatric Association may be compared with the material on the web site of The International Society for Ethical Psychology and Psychiatry (www.PsychIntegrity.org) or the web site of the Citizen's Commission on Human Rights International (www.cchr.org).

Critically Appraising Research Located

Critically appraising the quality of different kinds of research is a key competency in EBP (see chapter 11). Developing and using critical appraisal skills will help you to avoid being bamboozled by inflated claims about causes, risks, and remedies. It will allow you to be an informed user of the professional literature rather than being misled by bogus claims. Guyatt and Rennie (2002) suggest that such skills allow professionals to be effective leaders in introducing the process of EBP into their agencies. As emphasized earlier, the kind of research that may provide answers to important questions that affect client well-being differs depending on the question. Some questions call for qualitative research methods, such as in-depth interviews. Questions pertaining to intervention, prevention, accuracy of diagnostic method, or harm may most rigorously be explored using randomized controlled trials. Often, a mix of both qualitative and quantitative research is best.

Skill in critically appraising research related to different kinds of questions should be acquired during your professional education. Valuable resources for gaining this information include books such as Guyatt et al. (2008), Greenhalgh (2010), and Straus et al. (2005). Checklists for reviewing different

kinds of reports differ in degree of detail. (See chapter 11.) The Critical Appraisal Skills Program (CASP) was initiated in 1993 to help decision makers and those who seek to influence them to acquire skills in locating, critically appraising, and changing practices and policies based on research findings. The EBM toolkit is a Canadian-based collection of resources to support EPB. It includes appraisal checklists and methodological filters (http://www.ebm.med.ualberta.ca/). The Cochrane Consumer Network offers a variety of resources for consumers (see http://www.consumers.cochrane.org).

There is no perfect study. All research has flaws that may compromise its value in exploring a question. Biases that may limit the value of findings are always of concern. Questions to ask of all research reports include the following (see chapter 11 for more detail).

- Is there a clear research question?

- Is the study design appropriate? Does it match the question?

- What is the sample size and source? Is the sample representative of the population of interest?

- Are measures used valid and reliable?

- Are claims made accurate?

- Is the data analysis appropriate?

- Does the study offer information that can guide decisions?

The research methods used may be appropriate for the question, and rigorous, but the findings may not apply to your clients or community because of the sample or setting involved or the measures used. Important cultural differences may be of concern (e.g., see Lynch & Hanson, 2011).

Common Errors

Common errors include: (1) not critically appraising what you find, (2) becoming disheartened when you find little, and (3) misinterpreting a lack of evidence that a method is effective as evidence that it is not effective. (See also discussion of misinterpretation of statistical testing in chapter 11.) A method that is untested may be effective. Or, may be harmful. Gray (1997) recommends placing untested methods that are used in a research program designed to test their effectiveness. Ethical obligations to help clients and avoid harm obligates social workers to seek research findings related to decisions that affect clients' lives. It obligates them to accurately describe to clients the state of knowledge, ignorance, and uncertainty about life-affecting decisions. When little or no research is available regarding important questions, you must draw on practice theory, as well as your client's ideas and preferences in a supportive exchange of shared uncertainties. (See also later discussion about how to handle this possibility.)

Obstacles and Evolving Remedies

You can save time by drawing on high quality critical appraisals of research related to a question when these are available such as systematic reviews in the Cochrane and Campbell Databases. Palm pilots are available for evaluating tests, as well as for other goals (e.g., Clinical Decision Making Calculators). Take advantage of user-friendly checklists that will help you to critically appraise different kinds of research (e.g., see Greenhalgh, 2010), as well as reporting guidelines such as CONSORT (http://www. consort-statement.org), PRISMA (Liberati et al., 2009), and STARD (Bossuyt et al., 2003). Statistical literacy is a common obstacle among professionals and clients alike. (See Gaissmaier & Gigerenzer, 2011.)

Integrating Research Findings With Other Information and Applying the Findings

You must decide whether external research located apply to a client and consider his or her preferences and whether you have access to needed resources. Starting where the client is has long been emphasized in social work. Unless we understand each client's unique characteristics and circumstances, including their strengths, we cannot make decisions that are tailored as necessary for each client. Thus, this step requires integration of different kinds of information. It requires drawing on your clinical expertise to integrate information concerning research findings with characteristics of the client and his or her circumstances, including their values and expectations, and a consideration of application problems, such as available resources and deciding what to do together with the client. "Without clinical expertise, practice risks becoming tyrannized by external evidence, for even excellent external evidence may be inapplicable to or inappropriate for an individual patient. Without current best external evidence, practice risks becoming rapidly out of date, to the detriment of patients" (Sackett et al., 1997, p. 2). Many application barriers may enter at this stage. Examples of obstacles reported by my students include:

1. Lack of needed resources (e.g., programs that offer the best likelihood of helping clients achieve a certain outcome are not available).

2. Chaotic working space—shared phone, desk, and computer and no private space for confidential conversations.

3. Disparity between evidentiary standards advocated in school and those used in agencies (e.g., relying on popularity or entertainment value to select service in agencies).

4. Staff work mainly in a crisis mode, which results in lack of time to make informed decisions.

5. Providers feel overwhelmed by the problems and issues clients bring. This may be due to large caseloads and lack of resources.

6. Unsupportive administrative practices such as failure to reinforce staff for raising questions about the effectiveness of services and dysfunctional micro-management.

7. Unclear mission of organization or agency (confusion about what services we are supposed to provide).

8. Poor inter-agency communication and collaboration.

Acceptability of plans to clients must be considered. A search for research related to a life-affecting question may reveal that little or nothing is known. Information may be available about certain kinds of clients, but these clients may differ from your client and so findings may not apply. Here, too, our ethical obligations to inform clients and to consider their preferences provide a guide (e.g., to clearly describe limitations of research findings). Questions include: Do research findings apply to my client? Is a client similar to clients included in related research findings? Can I use this method in my setting (e.g., are needed resources available)? If not, is there access to some other program found to be effective. Will the benefits of service outweigh the harms for this client? Is this method acceptable to my client? What if I do not find anything? Lack of resources is a common problem. Here, ethical obligations include blowing the whistle—involving others in keeping track of needed resources such as effective parent-training programs, collating and sharing this information with others, and advocating for creation of these services.

Do Research Findings Apply to My Client?

A great deal of research consists of correlational research (e.g., describing the relationship between characteristics of parents and child abuse) and experimental research describing differences among groups (e.g., experimental and control). In neither case may the findings apply to a particular client. Samples used in research studies may differ from a client. Will these differences influence the potential costs and benefits to a particular client of an intervention? The unique characteristics and circumstances of a client may suggest that a method should not be used because negative effects are likely or because such characteristics would render an intervention ineffective. Your knowledge of behavior and how it is influenced and what principles of behavior have been found to apply to all persons provide helpful guidelines (see chapter 7). Social or cultural factors may affect the suitability or acceptability of a method. Is a practice guideline applicable to a particular client, family, or community? Questions here are:

1. Is the relative benefit of the intervention likely to be different because of a client's characteristics?

2. Are there social or cultural factors that might affect the suitability of a practice or policy or its acceptability?

3. What do the client and the client's family want? (Sheldon, Guyatt, & Haines, 1998)

Norms on assessment measures may be available but not for people like your client. Note, however, that norms should not necessarily be used as guidelines for selecting outcomes for individual clients because outcomes they seek may differ from normative criteria and norms may not be optimal (e.g., low rates of positive feedback from teachers to students in classrooms).

How Definitive Are the Research Findings?

Reviews found may be high quality systematic reviews or haphazard narrative ones (Littell, Corcoran, & Pillai, 2008). In the former, there may be strong evidence not to use a method or strong evidence to use a method. Usually, there will be uncertainty about the evidentiary status of a method (e.g., is it effective?). Research regarding causes may not allow ruling out rival explanations including placebo effects, the cyclic nature of a concern such as depression, or the influence of other remedies being used.

Can I Use This Method in My Agency?

Can a plan be carried out in a way that maximizes success? Are needed resources available? Do participants have the skills required to carry out plans? Can needed resources be created? Are those responsible for offering service competent to do so? How do you know? Competence in applying a method does not necessarily reflect competence to teach others, such as parents (McGimsey, Greene, & Lutzker, 1995). Consultation skills are required to teach others successfully, such as providing a rationale for methods used, demonstrating steps while describing them, arranging role plays for each step, and providing corrective feedback. Current service patterns may limit options (see discussion of purchase of services in chapter 27). Problems may have to be redefined from helping clients attain needed resources to helping them to bear up under the strain of not having them or involving clients with similar concerns in advocacy efforts to acquire better services.

Are Alternative Options Available?

Are other options available, perhaps another agency to which a client could be referred? Perhaps self-help programs are available. Here, too, familiarity with practice and policy-related research can facilitate decisions.

Will Benefits Outweigh Harms?

Every intervention, including assessment measures, has potential risks, as well as benefits. Diagnostic tests may result in false positives or false negatives. Will the benefits of an intervention outweigh potential risks and costs (e.g., see Woloshin, Schwartz, & Welch, 2008). Do you and your clients know what the benefits and risks are? This will require statistical literacy (e.g., see Gigerenzer & Gray, 2011) Calculating number needed to treat (NNT) may yield valuable guidelines about options. How many clients have to receive a harm reduction program to help one person? Is there any information about NNH (the number of individuals who would have to receive a service to harm one person)? (See also later section on helping clients make decisions.)

What If the Experts Disagree?

We often appeal to the authority of experts. How can we make wise decisions regarding the accuracy and candidness with which an expert describes controversies and uncertainties? Recommendations of clinical experts often do not match what is suggested based on results of carefully controlled research (Antman, Lau, Kupelnick, Mostellar, & Chalmers, 1992). In some situations we could seek and review the evidence for ourselves. Checking the evidentiary status of claims by an expert may be fairly easy. Suppose a lecturer claims that psychiatric classifications are valid categories. Critiques of this classification system are readily available (e.g., Frances, 2010; Houts, 2002; Kutchins & Kirk, 1997). At other times checking the accuracy of claims may require greater effort. Perhaps a Cochrane or Campbell review is available. How can you check the ethics (honesty regarding controversies and uncertainties) of an expert? Indicators of honesty include: (1) accurate description of controversies in an area including methodological and conceptual problems; (2) accurate description of well-argued alternative views; (3) critical appraisal of both preferred and well-argued alternative views; (4) nondefensiveness when confronted with probing questions; (5) inclusion of references to sources cited so others can look these up; and (6) candid description of any conflicts of interests (e.g., owning stock in a pharmaceutical company or being a highly paid consultant).

How Can I Help My Clients to Make Decisions?

Research concerning preferences show that we often do not know what we want and that our preferences change in accord with a variety of factors, including the visibility of related consequences. Although many people say they want to achieve a certain goal, such as to stop drinking, exercise more, meet more people, be less depressed, eat a healthier diet, their actions do not reflect their preferences. Both process resistance and outcome resistance may be an issue. (See chapter 14.) Shared decision making between clients and professionals is increasingly emphasized. Many decision aids are available for people confronted with making a decision about what to do, for example, take a screening test or a prescribed medication. Decision aids may be self- or practitioner-administered in one-to-one or in group sessions. Formats include interactive videos, audio-guided workbooks, and pamphlets (O'Connor Bennett, Stacey,

Barry, Col, Eden, et al., 2009). Such aids increase client's involvement and are more likely to lead to informed value-based decisions (O'Connor, et al., 2009). They prevent overuse of options that informed patients do not value (O'Connor, Wennberg, Legare, Llewellyn-Thomas, Mouton, Sepucha, et al., 2007). Use of decision aids improves accuracy of risk perception but they do not necessarily improve general or specific health outcomes. (See Shaffer and Hulsey, 2009, for a discussion of why this may be so.)

Decisions often involve trade-offs between risks and benefits, both short and long term. A decision aid can help an individual to weigh factors according to his or her unique values while being accurately informed about possible consequences of different options, including the uncertainty associated with each one. Information is provided on available options and related outcomes, including how they may affect the client and the probabilities associated with such outcomes. Exercises are used to carefully consider the personal importance of each benefit or harm using strategies such as cost-benefit balance sheets. Woltman and her colleagues (2011) developed an electronic decision support system to enhance shared decision making between community mental health clients and their case managers. Occasions when discovering client preferences is especially important include those in which:

- Options have major differences in outcomes or complications.

- Decisions require making trade-offs between short-term and long-term outcomes.

- One choice can result in a small chance of a grave outcome.

- There are marginal differences in outcomes between options. (Kassirer, 1994)

Clients differ in how "risk adverse" they are and in the importance of particular outcomes. Benefits of decision aids noted by O'Connor (2001) include the following:

- Reducing the proportion of clients who are uncertain about what to choose.

- Increasing clients' knowledge of problems, options, and outcomes.

- Creating realistic expectations of outcomes.

- Improving the agreement between choices and a client's values.

- Reducing decision conflict (feeling uncertain, uninformed, unclear about values, and unsupported in decision making).

- Increasing participation in decision making without adversely affecting anxiety. (p. 101) (See also O'Connor et al., 2009.)

Client satisfaction with use of decision aids is more uncertain. Scales have been developed to measure client involvement (e.g., Elwyn, Edwards, Wensing, Hood, Atwell, & Grol, 2003).

What If Clients Prefer an Untested Method?

What if the client prefers a method that has not been critically appraised regarding its effectiveness or one that has been tested and been found to be ineffective or harmful? Most interventions used by social workers have not been tested; we do not know if they are effective, not effective, or are harmful. Certainly you should not use a method shown to be harmful. What about untested methods? If there is an effective method you could describe the costs and benefits of using this compared to an untested method. Untested methods are routinely offered in both health and social care. Whether you should offer them depends on many factors including acceptability to clients and scarcity of resources. (See Domenighetti, Grilli, & Liberati, 1998.)

What If I Do Not Find Any Relevant Research?

What if a search reveals that there is no research that can guide decisions? Let us assume that your search has been sound and that no one else could find anything either. This is an important finding. Ethical obligations to clients require sharing what you find (including nothing) and drawing on practice theory to guide your work (e.g., see chapters 6 and 12). Providing empathy and support is also called for here. EBP involves sharing ignorance and uncertainty, as well as knowledge in a context of ongoing support.

What If There Is Relevant Research but It Is of Poor Quality?

This will be a common finding. Your search will often reveal uncertainty about the effectiveness of a practice or policy. Share what you find with your clients. You and your clients will typically have to make decisions in the context of uncertainty. The term *best practice* is used to describe a hierarchy of evidence (see chapter 11). Available resources may be low on this hierarchy in relation to critical tests of a method (tests that control for biases that may result in misleading conclusions). However, this may be all that is available. If there are no randomized controlled trials regarding an effectiveness question, then we move down the list. Instead of well-designed randomized controlled trials you may discover pre-post tests (see chapter 11). This term *best evidence* could refer to tests that differ greatly in whether they critically test claims. The position of the American Psychological Association is that if two well-designed randomized controlled trials (RCTs) shows a positive outcome, this is a "well-established" method. This conveys an unwarranted certainty. Within a Popperian approach to knowledge (see chapter 4), we would say that a claim has been critically tested in two well-controlled RCTs and has passed both tests. This keeps uncertainty in view. The next two RCTs may not yield positive findings. The first two RCTs may be revealed to be flawed (e.g., Ioannidis, 2005).

What If Research Is Available but It Has Not Been Critically Appraised?

One course of action is to critically appraise the literature for yourself. In the everyday world, you may not have time to do this. If this concerns a problem that occurs often, involve interested others in critically appraising related research.

Balancing Individual and Population Perspectives

One challenging aspect of the process of EBP is considering both individuals and populations. Decisions made about populations limit options of individuals. Ethical issues regarding the distribution of scarce resources are often overlooked. But we overlook these only at the peril of making unjust decisions. There is only so much money and time.

Common Errors in Integrating Information

Cognitive biases, such as overconfidence, influence by redundant information, and confirmation biases contribute to errors in integrating information (see chapter 8). Eagerness to help clients may encourage unfounded confidence in methods suggested and premature advice and assurances. Lack of validity of measures may be overlooked resulting in faulty inferences. Jumping to conclusions may result in misleading oversimplifications about the causes of client concerns. Or the opposite may occur—posing overly complex accounts, none of which provide practice or policy guidelines. Lack of evidence may be shared with clients in an unempathetic, nonsupportive manner. King (1981) suggests that use of the term *critical* implies alternative choices and a means of discrimination and evaluation of these choices relative to a standard (p. 304). He suggests that the physician who is not critical corresponds to the empiric. The empiric "does not consider alternatives, does not discriminate among their features and does not attend to any detailed congruence with a pattern. He acts reflexively instead of reflectively" (p. 304). King argues that characteristics such as observation and reflection, consideration of alternatives, discrimination, and deliberate choice have "characterized the good physician throughout medical history and comprise a constant methodology of good medicine" (pp. 300–310). Isn't this true of social workers also? (p. 301). By *empirically,* he refers to lacking any method to tell the difference between apparently similar phenomena, and ignorance of causes. Ignoring the possibility of making mistakes is related to jumping to conclusions. What do you think?

1. Do social workers make incorrect judgments at times?

2. May the consequences of such judgments harm clients?

3. Does professional education decrease the likelihood of making avoidable mistakes?

4. Can reading practice- and policy-related research help you to avoid making mistakes?

5. What do you do to avoid mistakes?

6. Do you view mistakes as learning opportunities?

7. Do you keep track of mistakes you make in your practice?

8. Give an example of a mistake that you made with clients and describe possible consequences, as well as how you could avoid it in the future.

Obstacles and Evolving Remedies

Helping professionals to learn from their experience in ways that improve the accuracy of future decisions is a key priority. EBP highlights the play of bias and the uncertainty involved in helping clients and attempts to give helpers and clients the knowledge and skills to handle this honestly and constructively. Consider the attention given to training both clients and helpers in critical appraisal skills and use of "quality filters" in reviewing research findings related to decisions. Biases intrude both on the part of researchers when planning and conducting research and preparing reviews, and at the practitioner level when making decisions as described in chapters 8 and 11. Biases related to a preferred practice theory and stereotypes may interfere with sound integration of research findings and client characteristics and circumstances. Many components of EBP are designed to minimize biases, such as "jumping to conclusions," for example, by using "quality filters" when reviewing research related to a question.

We can draw on literature investigating expertise and take advantage of guidelines described in the literature on critical thinking to minimize biases (see chapter 5). Use of clinical pathways and palm pilots with built-in decision aids, such as flow charts, can be helpful, and many are already in use in the health area. Use of hand-held computers to guide decisions may be of value in decreasing errors and biases, for example, by providing reminders to check certain things. Computer-based decision aids may be used to prompt valuable behaviors, to critique a decision (for example, purchasing services from other agencies), to match a client's unique circumstances and characteristics with a service program, to suggest options, and to interpret different assessment pictures (see Guyatt & Rennie, 2008). And, just as the narratives of clients may help us to understand how we can improve services, so the narratives of practitioners may help us to identify challenges and opportunities for providing quality services (e.g., Greenhalgh & Hurwitz, 1998).

Evaluating and Learning From What Happens

Arranging for evaluation of outcome allows you and your clients to assess degree of success. Depending on what is found, services may be altered or continued, and you can learn from this how to do better in the future. Selection of valid, feasible progress measures will facilitate accurate appraisal of degree of progress (see chapter 22). The cruder the measure in scoring options (e.g., yes/no compared to a continuum of ratings), the less sensitive the measure may be. Utility is also important. Is a measure easy to interpret? Is it feasible? Will it tell you and your clients what you want to know? For example, some measures may be satisfactory for assessing pre-post change, but not for detecting day-to-day changes in outcomes of interest. There is a rich literature suggesting valid, feasible ways to evaluate outcomes including complex ones such as quality of life (see chapter 22). Keep track of the questions you ask, important research findings and client progress to learn how to improve future decisions. Gray (2001a) emphasizes the importance of information storage and retrieval skills; if you cannot find information when you need it, it is not of value to clients.

Common Errors

A variety of biases may contribute to incorrect views of progress, including wishful thinking. Selection of vague outcomes will make it impossible to carefully evaluate any progress (see chapter 22 for further discussion). You may incorrectly assume that negative outcomes are due to poor decisions.

Obstacles and Evolving Remedies

Lack of time and training in selecting relevant, feasible progress indicators interferes with evaluation that can guide decision making. Fears about revealing lack of progress or harmful effects may discourage careful evaluation. Calls for accountability and the transparency of results that this requires, as well as selection of user-friendly, valid tools for assessing progress, will facilitate evaluation.

Evaluating Your Skills in Evidence-Based Practice

Self-evaluation is the fifth step in EBP. How can you evaluate your current skills and progress in order to become a lifelong learner? The Self-Evaluation Questions in Appendix 10C at the end of this chapter can serve as a guide. You may want to make a plan regarding:

- How many hours each week do I want to spend searching for research findings relevant to my clients?

- What sources do I want to scan regularly?

- How can I increase the likelihood of not missing important new knowledge?

- What self-management skills can I use to increase my success? (See chapter 19.)

Tests have been developed to evaluate evidence-based practice skills (Ramos et al., 2003). Try out your skills by completing the form in Appendix 10D.

The Question of Motivation

Gibbs (2003) lists getting motivated to use EBP as the first step. Some helpers are motivated already. How do we get motivated? Does awareness of harming in the name of helping help us to get motivated? Not necessarily. Many professionals are aware of harming in the name of helping but do not think this possibility applies to their practices and policies. Our motivation is related to our values and our skills in "getting motivated." We must believe that it is important to prevent harming in the name of helping and to provide services most likely to help clients (given that they are acceptable to clients). Agency incentive systems such as encouraging use of effective practices must support this commitment.

It is important to recognize gaps in your personal knowledge and what is available—to recognize your ignorance. We must be willing to acknowledge uncertainty—to say "I don't know." And, we must have the "courage to fail" (Fox & Swazey, 1974)—the courage to recognize that we will make mistakes and a commitment to learn from them. If we work in environments in which supervisors and administrators have little interest in discovering whether clients are helped or harmed (indeed, they may block such efforts), it may be difficult to maintain values and behaviors related to evidence-informed practice. We may get "worn down" as our efforts are not reinforced or are punished. We may even forget the value of asking hard questions (e.g., Does play therapy help children?); we may come to view such questions as irrelevant or disrespectful. Questions that can help us to remain faithful to our ethical obligations to help clients and avoid harming them include:

- Will it help clients if I use assessment measures of dubious validity?

- Will it help clients if I hide the evidentiary status of service programs?

- Will it help clients if I use outcome measures that are not valid?

- Will it help clients if I attribute (mis)behaviors to alleged pathology of clients ("mental disorders") and ignore environmental factors shown to influence related behaviors?

We can draw on theory and research regarding motivation to suggest answers to the "motivation problem." Theories differ in how much influence is attributed to internal compared to external influences. Related research suggests that we cannot simply wave a magic wand to "become motivated." That is, we cannot simply want to act a certain way and then do so regardless of our skills in altering our behavior and regardless of environmental influences. Getting and staying motivated is closely linked to a commitment to honoring ethical obligations to clients and to becoming a lifelong learner. Chapter 28 suggests strategies you can use to get and stay motivated.

Summary

Key steps in EBP include posing well-formed questions that highlight information needs related to important decisions, seeking efficiently and effectively electronically for related research, critically appraising what is found (or drawing on high quality systematic reviews prepared by others), using practice expertise to integrate diverse sources of information (including knowledge about the clients' values, expectations, and preferences and available resources), making a decision together with clients about what to do, trying it out, evaluating what happens, and learning from this experience how to do better next time. These steps increase the likelihood that you and your clients will be informed about the kinds and levels of uncertainties associated with decisions and will make well-reasoned decisions. Although the steps involved in EBP may sound simple and straightforward, they are often difficult and sometimes impossible to carry out in the real world. There are many challenges including learning new skills and acquiring access to needed resources, such as high quality training programs and needed databases and arranging for ongoing feedback to keep skills well honed. Perhaps the greatest challenge is a willingness to recognize gaps in current knowledge regarding decisions and what is "out there"—a willingness to say "I don't know"—and a commitment to clients to see what is out there.

Reviewing Your Competencies

Reviewing Content Knowledge

1. You can accurately describe the steps in EBP.

2. You can identify databases relevant to decisions.

3. You are familiar with different kinds of reference tools and major reference sources and can download the end products of a search into a reference management software system.

Reviewing What You Do

1. You pose well-structured questions related to decisions.

2. You carry out effective, efficient searches for research findings related to questions that affect clients' lives using Boolean operators (*and* or *or*).

    You efficiently locate a systematic review related to a question.

    You distinguish between primary and secondary sources.

    You are familiar with relevant Internet resources.

3. You critically appraise articles concerning services, tests, screening programs, and social policies in relation to: (a) effectiveness, (b) safety, (c) acceptability, (d) cost effectiveness, (e) quality, and (f) appropriateness.

4. You accurately appraise the quality of systematic reviews, RCTs, case-control studies, cohort studies, surveys, decision analysis, and qualitative research. (See also chapter 11.)

5. You accurately assess the individual and population outcomes of an intervention using the following criteria: (a) acceptability, (b) equity, (c) effectiveness, (d) safety, (e) client satisfaction and experience of care, (f) cost-effectiveness, and (g) quality.

6. You consider client preferences and experiences when making decisions, as well as their unique circumstances and characteristics including cultural differences.

7. You accurately describe the evidentiary status of recommended methods to your clients to involve them as informed participants.

Reviewing Results

1. Clients are involved as informed participants.

2. Cultural differences are considered as they influence relevance of research findings.

3. Clients are offered "best practices" (those most likely to help them achieve hoped-for outcomes).

Appendix 10A   Examples of Web Sites

- *Bandolier.* <http://www.medicine.ox.ac.uk/bandolier/>. A web site about evidence-based healthcare.

- *BestBETS.* <http://www.bestbets.org/>. Best Evidence topics provide answers to clinical questions, using a systematic approach to reviewing the literature.

- *California Evidence-Based Clearinghouse for Child Welfare (CEBC).* <http://www.cebc4cw.org/>.

- *Campbell Collaboration.* http://www.campbellcollaboration.org/

- *Center for Evidence-Based Mental Health.* <http://www.cebmh.com/>. This site provides materials to help develop skills in practicing EBMH. Also provided are links to other resources including the full text online journal *Evidence-Based Mental Health.*

- Center for the Study and Prevention of Violence. <http://www.colorado.edu/cspv/blueprints>.

- *Centre for Evidence-Based Medicine.* <http://www.cebm.net/>. This site includes a toolbox for practicing and teaching EBM, the CATMaker (a software program for creating 1-page summaries of evidence), a calendar of EBM events, and links to other EBM sites.

- *Centre for Health Evidence.* <http://www.cche.net/>. This site includes the User's Guides to the Medical Literature produced by *JAMA.*

- *Child Trends.* <http://www.childtrends.org>.

- Child Welfare Information Gateway. <http://www.childwelfare.gov/>.

- CINAHL is a nursing and allied health database, including health education, occupational therapy, emergency services, and social services in health care (United States). <http://www.cinahl.com>.

- *Clinical Evidence.* <http://clinicalevidence.bmj.com/>. This site provides a concise account of the current state of knowledge, ignorance, and uncertainty about the prevention and treatment of a wide range of clinical conditions based on careful searches of the literature.

- *ClinicalTrials.gov.* <http://clinicaltrials.gov>.

- *Cochrane Collaboration.* <http://www.cochrane.org/>.

- *Coalition for Evidence-Based Policy.* <http://www.coalition4evidence.org/>.

- *DUETS.* Database of uncertainties about the effectiveness of interventions. <http://www.library.nhs.uk/duets>.

- *EBP Substance Abuse Database.* <http://lib.adai.washington.edu/ebpsearch.htm>.

- *EPPI-Center.* <http://www.eppi.ioe.ac.uk>. Provides an evidence library; provides training and workshops.

- *EQUATOR.* This is an international initiative designed to increase the value of medial research by promoting transparency and accurate reporting of studies. <http://www.equator-network.org/>.

- *ERIC.* This is a database of educational literature, sponsored by the U.S. Department of Education. It contains Resources in Education (RIE), Current Index to Journals in Education (CIJE) and ERIC Digest for overviews of educational topics. <http://www.eric.ed.gov/>.

- *The Evaluation Center's EBP Metabase.* <http://www.tecathsri.org/ebp>.

- Evidence-Based Behavioral Practice (EBBP). <http://www.ebbp.org>.

- *Evidence-Based Group Work.* <http://www.evidencebasedgroupwork.com/>.

- *Evidence-Based Medicine.* <http://ebm.bmj.com/>. *Evidence-Based Medicine* is a bimonthly journal, which alerts clinicians of important advances in general and family practice, internal medicine, surgery, psychiatry, pediatrics, and obstetrics and gynecology.

- *Evidence-Based Mental Health.* <http://ebmh.bmj.com/>. *Evidence-Based Mental Health* is a journal that appears four times a year. It describes clinically relevant advances in treatment, diagnosis, aetiology, prognosis/outcome research, quality improvement, continuing education, economic evaluation, and qualitative research.

- *Institute of Research and Innovation in Social Services (IRISS). <http://www.iriss.org.uk/>www.iriss.org.uk*

- *James Lind Library.* <http://www.jameslindlibrary.org/>.

- *MedlinePlus.* <http://medlineplus.gov/>.

- MINCAVA electronic clearinghouse: Minnesota Center Against Violence and Abuse. Provides information and resources on violence and abuse. www.mincava.umn.edu

- National Working Group on Evidence-Based Health Care. <http://www.evidencebasedhealthcare.org>.

- *NHS Centre for Reviews and Dissemination (CRD).* <http://www.york.ac.uk/inst/crd/>. It produced reviews of the effectiveness and cost-effectiveness of healthcare interventions and provides access to several databases including a database of structured abstracts of good quality systematic reviews (DARE). It also provides the Effective Health Care Bulletin that examines the effectiveness of a variety of health care interventions.

- *Netting the Evidence.* <http://www.shef.ac.uk/scharr/netting>. Provides a variety of related resources.

- *Ovid.* <http://www.ovid.com>. Provides access to a variety of related resources including access to 300 full text journals.

- *Patient Decision Aids.* <http://www.decisionaid.ohri.ca>.

- *PubMed: Medline.* <http://www.nlm.nih.gov/pubs/factsheets/pubmed.html>.

- *Social Care Institute for Excellence (SCIE).* <http://www.scie.org.uk>. Established in the United Kingdom

in 2001 to provide reports regarding best practices in social care emphasizing value of services to consumers. They produce "knowledge reviews" combining research knowledge with knowledge from practitioners and consumers.

- *Social Programs That Work.* <http://www.evidencebasedprograms.org/>.

- Suicide Prevention Research Center: Best Practice Registry. <http://www.sprc.org/featured_resources/bpr/index.asp>.

- *Trip Database.* <http://www.tripdatabase.com/>. The TRIP Database searches over 75 sites of high quality medical information. It provides direct, hyperlinked access to the largest collection of "evidence-based" material on the web, as well as articles from journals such as the *BMJ, JAMA, NEJM* etc.

Appendix 10B   Examples of U.S. Federal Agencies and Departments

Administration for Children and Families (ACF): <http://www.acf.hhs.gov/>

Administration on Aging: (AoA): <http://www.aoa.gov/>

Agency for Healthcare Research and Quality (AHRQ): <http://www.ahrq.gov/>

Bureau of the Census: <http://www.census.gov/>

Centers for Disease Control and Prevention (CDC): <http://www.cdc.gov/>

Centers for Medicare & Medicaid Services (formerly the Health Care Financing Administration): <http://www.cms.hhs.gov/>

Civil Rights Division, Department of Justice: <http://www.justice.gov/crt/>

Department of Health and Human Services (HHS): <http://www.hhs.gov/>

Drug Enforcement Administration (DEA): <http://www.dea.gov>

Fair Housing and Equal Opportunity: <http://www.hud.gov/offices/fheo/index.cfm>

Food and Drug Administration (FDA): <http://www.fda.gov/>

General Accounting Office (GAO): <http://www.gao.gov/>

healthIT.gov

Health Resources and Services Administration: <http://www.hrsa.gov/>

HLWIKI.Canada

House of Representatives: <http://www.house.gov/>

Indian Health Service: <http://www.ihs.gov/>

Justice Programs Office (Juvenile Justice, Victims of Crime, Violence Against Women, Family Violence, and more): <http://www.ojp.usdoj.gov/>

Legal Services Corporation: <http://www.lsc.gov/>

National AIDS Policy Office: <http://www.whitehouse.gov/onap/aids.html>

National Center for Complementary and Alternative Medicine (NCCAM): <http://nccam.nih.gov/>

National Center for Telehealth & Technology: <t2health.org>

National Center for Research Resources (NCRR): <http://www.ncrr.nih.gov/>

National Council on Disability: <http://www.ncd.gov/>

National Council on Disability: <http://www.ncd.gov/>www.ncd.gov

National Health Information Center: <http://www.health.gov/NHIC/>

National Institute of Child Health and Human Development (NICHD): <http://www.nichd.nih.gov/>

National Institute of Justice: <http://www.nij.gov/>

National Institute of Mental Health (NIMH): <http://www.nimh.nih.gov/>

National Institute on Aging (NIA): <http://www.nia.nih.gov/>

National Institute on Deafness and Other Communication Disorders (NIDCD): <http://www.nidcd.nih.gov/>

National Institute on Minority Health and Health Disparities (NIMHD): <http://www.nimhd.nih.gov>

National Institute on substance use and Addiction Disorders

National Institutes of Health (NIH): <http://www.nih.gov/>

National Library of Medicine (NLM): <http://www.nlm.nih.gov/>

Office of Justice Programs: <http://www.ojp.usdoj.gov>

Office of Scientific and Technical Information: <http://www.osti.gov/>

Office of Special Education and Rehabilitative Services: <http://www.ed.gov.osers>

Rural Development: <http://www.rurdev.usda.gov/>

Substance Abuse and Mental Health Services Administration: <http://www.samhsa.gov/index.aspx>

U.S. Citizenship and Immigration Services: <http://uscis.gov/graphics/index.htm> U.S. Department of Veterans Affairs <www.va.gov>

Appendix 10C Self-Evaluation Questions

Asking Answerable Questions

1. Am I asking any practice or policy questions at all?

2. Am I asking well-formed (three- or four-part) questions?

3. Am I using a "map" to locate my knowledge gaps and pose questions?

4. Can I get myself "unstuck" when asking questions?

5. Do I have a way to save my questions for later answering?

6. Is my success rate of asking clear questions rising?

7. Am I modeling the asking of clear questions for others?

Finding the Best External Evidence

1. Am I searching at all?

2. Do I know the best sources of current evidence for decisions I make?

3. Do I have immediate access to searching hardware, software, and the best evidence for questions that arise?

4. Am I finding useful external evidence from a widening array of sources?

5. Am I becoming more efficient in my searching?

6. How do my searches compare with those of research librarians or other respective colleagues who have a passion for providing best current care?

Critically Appraising the Evidence for Its Validity and Usefulness

1. Am I critically appraising external evidence at all?

2. Are critical appraisal guides becoming easier for me to apply?

3. Am I becoming more accurate and efficient in applying critical appraisal measures such as pretest probabilities and NNTs?

Integrating the Critical Appraisal with Clinical Expertise and Applying the Results

1. Am I integrating my critical appraisals in my practice at all?

2. Am I becoming more accurate and efficient in adjusting some of the critical appraisal measures to fit my clients?

3. Can I explain (and resolve) disagreements about decisions in terms of this integration?

4. Have I conducted any clinical decision analyses?

5. Have I carried out any audits of my EBP performance?

Helping Others Learn EBP

1. Am I helping others learn how to ask clear questions?

2. Am I teaching and modeling searching skills?

3. Am I teaching and modeling critical appraisal skills?

4. Am I teaching and modeling the integration of best evidence with my clinical expertise and my clients' preferences?

Continuing Professional Development

1. Am I a member of an EBP-style journal club?

2. Have I participated in or tutored at a workshop on how to practice EBP?

3. Have I joined an evidence-based e-mail discussion group?

4. Have I established links with other practitioners of EBP?

Source: Adapted from D. L. Sackett, S. E. Straus, W. S. Richardson, W. Rosenberg, & R. B. Haynes (2000). *Evidence-based medicine: How to practice and teach EBM* (2nd ed.) (pp. 220–228). New York: Churchill Livingstone. Reprinted with permission.

Appendix 10D   Posing Questions and Searching for Answers

Important decision you must make:

_____

_____

_____

_____

_____

Well-structured question related to this decision:

_____

_____

_____

_____

_____

_____

_____

Question type: _____ Effectiveness _____ Risk/Prognosis _____ Description _____ Assessment _____
Prevention _____ Other (please describe): _____

_____

_____

_____

_____

_____

Your best answer before searching for external evidence:

_____

_____

_____

_____

_____

Resources used:

_____

_____

_____

_____

_____

Your best answer based on a review of external research:

_____

_____

_____

_____

_____

Source: See E. Gambrill & L. Gibbs (2009). _Critical thinking for helping professionals: Exercises for the helping professions_ (3rd ed.) (p. 242). New York: Oxford University Press. Based on format described in Sackett et al. (1997).

11

Critically Appraising Research: Thinking for Yourself

OVERVIEW   This chapter offers a bare-bones guide for critically appraising practice-related research related to different kinds of questions that arise in everyday practice. You are urged to consult other sources for additional details. Many excellent sources are described in this chapter. Indeed a key contribution of evidence-based practice is developing user-friendly tools for critically appraising different kinds of research. Here, an overview is offered, and common biases are described.

WHAT YOU WILL LEARN ABOUT

- The need for skepticism

- Common myths that hinder critical appraisal

- The question of bias

- Questions to ask about all research

- Levels of evidence

- Questions about effectiveness and prevention

- Systematic reviews and meta-analyses

- Questions about causes

- Questions about prevalence and incidence (frequency and rate)

- Questions regarding experiences

- Questions about diagnosis and screening

- Questions concerning prognosis, risk, and protective factors (prediction)

- Questions about practice guidelines

- Controversial issues

- The relationship between research methods used and views of knowledge

- Obstacles

The Need for Skepticism

Simply because something appears in print does not mean that it is accurate. Indeed flaws in published research were key to the development of evidence-based practice and policy (see chapter 9). Thornley and Adams (1998) reviewed data in 2,000 trials on the Cochrane Schizophrenia Group's register and found consistently poor quality of reporting, which they suggest "is likely to have resulted in an overly optimistic estimation of the effects of treatment" (p. 1181). And, as Rosenbaum (2002) suggests, we should also be skeptical of the skeptics. Just because someone says a study is flawed does not mean that it is. Learning to critically appraise different kinds of research studies for yourself frees you from misleading influences by others, including researchers, academics, and journalists, allowing you to accurately inform your clients about the potential of given options for attaining outcomes they value. As Chalmers (2003) notes, "Because professionals sometimes do more harm than good when they intervene in the lives of other people, their policies and practices should be informed by rigorous, transparent, up-to-date evaluations. Surveys often reveal wide variations in the type and frequency of practice and policy interventions, and this evidence of collective uncertainty should prompt the humility that is a precondition for rigorous evaluation" (p. 22).

Being informed about different kinds of research and their advantages and disadvantages, including biases that result in misleading results, will help you to draw on practice- and policy-related research in an informed manner. This kind of research savvy is closely related to meeting your ethical obligations to clients (see chapter 3). Without this, you may recommend ineffective or harmful methods and overlook effective programs. And you will be a pushover for those who try to persuade you to use certain methods that may not be in the best interests of clients (see discussion of human service propaganda in chapter 4). For example, phrases such as "has not been established" may really mean that a medication has been tested with equivocal results. Drawing on rigorous appraisals of research related to practice and policy decisions and creating tools and training programs designed to facilitate this are hallmarks of EBP. Gaining access to practice-related research will help you and your clients to make more informed decisions, some of which will increase the likelihood that clients attain outcomes that they value and avoid services that result in harm. Professional codes of ethics obligate us to draw on practice-related research and to involve clients as informed participants.

> The censorship of uncertainty is the enemy of evidence-based care
>
> —Alderson & Roberts, 2000

There are many kinds of research reports (see Exhibit 11.1). They differ in their purpose (the questions raised) and the likelihood that the method used can provide accurate information about the question (see Exhibit 11.2). Examples include:

Analytic: Designed to make causal inferences about relationships, for example, between certain risk factors (such as poverty) and an outcome (such as child abuse). Two or more groups are compared.

Descriptive: Designed to provide information about the prevalence or incidence of a concern (for example, "mental disorder") or about the distribution of certain characteristics in a group.

Prospective: Subjects are selected and followed up.

Retrospective: Events of interest have already occurred (for example, children have been abused) and data is collected from case records or recall as in case-control studies.

Contemporary Comparison: Groups that experience a risk factor at the same time are compared.

A key question is what works, for what client, in what circumstances, to what effect. Unique characteristics of clients and their contexts may potentiate or hinder achievement of positive outcomes. Different kinds of research design control for different kinds of biases that may result in misleading conclusions, for example, about causal relationships to different degrees. Sackett (1979) identified thirty-five different kinds of biases in case-control studies. Many excellent sources provide more detail, including the user-friendly book *How to Read a Paper* (Greenhalgh, 2010).

Common Myths That Hinder Critical Appraisal

A variety of myths hinder critical appraisal of the quality of research.

It Is Too Difficult for Me to Learn

The ease of identifying key characteristics of rigorous studies regarding certain kinds of questions is suggested by the fact that six different samples of social workers wanted their physicians to rely on the results of randomized controlled trials when making recommendations about interventions (Gambrill & Gibbs, 2002). However, respondents relied on weak criteria (such as intuition) when making decisions about their clients. Guidelines have been developed to report and/or review different kinds of research, including guidelines for reviewing RCTs (Schulz, Altman, & Moher for the CONSORT Group, 2010) and PRISMA for reviewing research reviews (http://www.prisma-statement.org). Items regarding methodology are listed, such as allocation concealment, blinding, and follow-up, that may bias estimation of effects in

EXHIBIT 11.1

The Major Types of Studies Found in the Literature

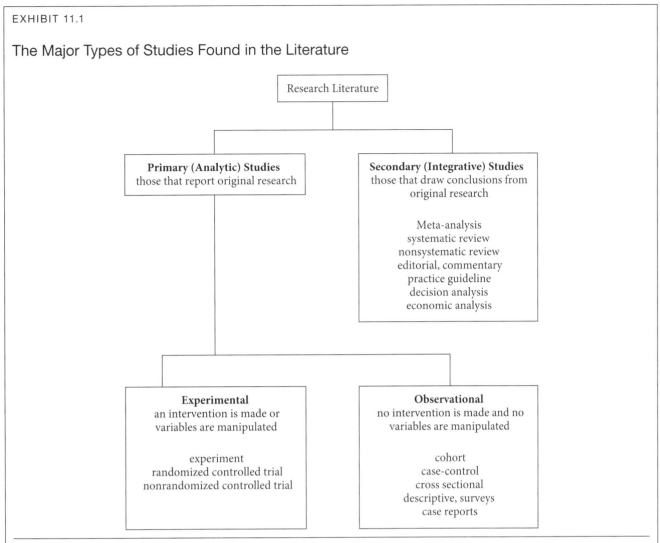

Source: W. F. Miser (2000). Critical appraisal of the literature: How to assess an article and still enjoy life. In J. P. Geyman, R. A. Deyo, & S. D. Ramsey (Eds.) (2000), *Evidence-based clinical practice: Concepts and approaches* (p. 42). Boston: Butterworth Heinemann. Originally published W. F. Miser (1999). Critical appraisal of the literature. *Journal of the American Board of Family Practice, 12*, 315–333. Reprinted with permission of the American Board of Family Medicine.

an experimental study. The Critical Appraisal Skills Program (CASP) in Oxford has been offering workshops on critical appraisal to professionals for years.

All Research Is Equally Sound

You may be a relativist—at least regarding clients. Different views of knowledge and how or if it can be gained are discussed in chapter 4. All research is not equally informative. Research designs differ in the questions that can be carefully explored; they differ in the extent to which biases are controlled for that may contribute to incorrect conclusions that may harm clients if acted on. A variety of errors can be and are made in designing and interpreting research. Because of this, you may conclude that a method was effective when it was not; it may even be harmful. You may conclude that a method was not effective when it is effective. A research design may be used that cannot critically

test the question raised. Chalmers (2003) defines reliable studies as "those in which the effects of policies and practices are unlikely to be confused with the effects of biases or chance" (p. 28). Less rigorous studies report more positive results than do more rigorous studies.

I Should Trust the Experts

You will often have to depend on the experts. Depending on expertise is risky because experts may all be biased in a certain direction. That is, they may share a bias toward a commonly favored view of a certain problem and how to minimize it. In fact, experts in an area prepare more biased reviews than do individuals who are well trained in methodological issues but who do not work in that area (Oxman & Guyatt, 1993). But you can learn about criteria of value in discovering whether a person is an honest expert. Do they, for example, use clear language that

EXHIBIT 11.2

Types of Studies

The types of studies that give the best evidence are different for different types of questions. In every case, however, the best evidence comes from studies where the methods used maximize the chance of eliminating bias. The study designs that best suit different question types are as follows:

Question	Best Study Designs	Description
INTERVENTION	Randomized controlled trial	Subjects are randomly allocated to treatment or control groups and outcomes assessed.
ETIOLOGY AND RISK FACTORS	Randomized controlled trial	As etiology questions are similar to intervention questions, the ideal study type is an RCT. However, it is usually not ethical or practical to conduct such a trial to assess harmful outcomes.
	Cohort study	Outcomes are compared for matched groups with and without exposure or risk factor (prospective study).
	Case-control study	Subjects with and without outcome of interest are compared for previous exposure or risk factor (retrospective study).
FREQUENCY AND RATE	Cohort study	As above.
	Cross-sectional study	Measurement of condition in a representative (preferably random) sample of people.
DIAGNOSIS	Cross-sectional study with random or consecutive sample	Preferably an independent, blind, comparison with "gold standard" test.
PROGNOSIS AND PREDICTION	Cohort/survival study	Long-term follow-up of a representative cohort.
PHENOMENA	Qualitative	Narrative analysis or focus group; designed to assess the range of issues (rather than their quantification).

Source: P. Glasziou, C. Del Mar, & J. Salisbury (2003). *Evidence-based medicine workbook*. London: BMJ. Reprinted with permission.

you can understand? Do they describe well-argued alternatives and contradictory evidence to preferred views?

Intuition Is a Better Guide

Myths that hinder critical appraisal include the belief that intuitive beliefs about what may help people do not result in harmful consequences. But harm occurs because of reliance on such criteria. Chalmers (2003) points out that "as Donald Campbell (1969) noted many years ago, selectively designating some interventions as 'experiments'—a term loaded with negative associations—ignores the reality that policy makers and practitioners are experimenting on other people most of the time. The problem is that their experiments are usually poorly controlled. Dr. Spock's ill-founded advice [to parents to let babies sleep on their stomachs] would probably not be conceptualized by many people as a poorly controlled experiment, yet that is just what it was" (p. 30). As a result, many babies died. "The clinician who is convinced that a certain treatment works will almost never find an ethicist in his path, whereas his colleague who wonders and doubts and wants to learn will stumble over piles of

them" (Medical Ethics, 1990, p. 846, quoted in Chalmers, 2003, p. 30).

Only Certain Kinds of Research Must Be Rigorous

Another myth is that only certain kinds of research must be rigorous to avoid biased results. A concern to avoid biases that may result in misleading conclusions is relevant to all research, including qualitative research. Misleading conclusions may result from not checking assumptions by, for example, using different kinds of qualitative research (see later discussion of qualitative research).

One or Two Studies Can Yield Conclusive Findings

Yet another myth is that one or two well-controlled studies yield the "truth." Such an assumption reflects a justification approach to knowledge in which we assume that certainty is possible (see chapter 4).

A Study Must Be Perfect to Be Useful

Yet another myth is that a study must be perfect to yield valuable findings. All studies are flawed. The question is, are the flaws so great that they preclude any sound conclusions?

Quantitative Research Is Best/Qualitative Research Is Best

Another myth is that quantitative research is better than qualitative research, or vice versa. It depends on the question. And pursuit of many questions is informed by both kinds of research. Consider, for example, *Labeling the Mentally Retarded* (1973) by Jane Mercer, in which community surveys, official records, and unstructured interviews were all used.

The Question of Bias

The notion of bias is central to critically appraising the quality of practice- and policy-related research. Bias is a systematic "leaning to one side" that distorts the accuracy of results. Bias can be of two types: (1) systematic, in which errors are made in a certain direction; or (2) random fluctuations. It has long been of interest. Consider Francis Bacon's ([1620] 1985) four idols of the mind:

The Idols of the Tribe have their foundation in human nature itself, and in the tribe or race of men. For it is a false assertion that the sense of man is the measure of things...and the human understanding is like a false mirror, which receiving rays irregularly, distorts and discolors the nature of things by mingling its own nature with it.

The Idols of the Cave are the idols of the individual man. For everyone (besides the errors common to human nature in general) has a cave or den of his own, which refracts and discolors the light of nature; owing either to his own proper and peculiar nature; or to its education and conversation with others; or to the reading of books, and the authority of those whom he esteems and admires; or to the differences of impressions, accordingly as they take place in a mind preoccupied and predisposed or in a mind indifferent and settled;...

There are also Idols formed by the intercourse and association of men with each other, which I call Idols of the Market-place, on account of the commerce and consort of men there....And therefore the ill and unfit choice of words wonderfully obstructs the understanding....But words plainly force and overrule the understanding, and throw all into confusion, and lead men away into numberless empty controversies and idle fancies.

Lastly, there are Idols, which have immigrated into men's minds from the various dogmas of philosophies and also from wrong laws of demonstration. These I call Idols of the Theater, because in my judgment all the received systems are but so many stage-plays, representing worlds of their own creation after an unreal and scenic fashion...

Biases occur in the design of research, in how it is interpreted and in how it is used (MacCoun, 1998). There are publication biases. For example, studies reporting negative results are less likely to be published than studies reporting positive results. "Studies that show a statistically significant effect of treatment are more likely to be published, more likely to be published in English, more likely to be cited by other authors, and more likely to produce multiple publications than other studies" (Sterne, Egger, & Smith, 2001, p. 189). Examples of biases in published research include the following: "submission bias (research workers are more strongly motivated to complete, and submit for publication, positive results), publication bias (editors are more likely to publish positive studies), methodological bias (methodological errors such as flawed randomization produce positive biases), abstracting bias (abstracts emphasize positive results), framing bias (relative risk data produce a positive bias)" (Gray, 2001b, p. 24). Allegiance effects (preferences for a certain kind of therapy) contribute to differences in outcome (Luborsky & Barrett, 2006). Campbell (1996) suggests, "Our culture (and our test-constructing psychologists) tends to create problem disabilities on every dimension flattering to elites and relevant for our competitive status-seeking. In the name of a higher objectivity (and an emancipatory social science) we should not take these culturally imposed category systems for granted, but seek a methodology that can avoid reifying them as part of nature" (p. 162). The steps involved in evidence-based practice are designed to decrease confirmation biases, such as looking only for data that support a preferred theory.

Bias and Validity

Biases may influence both internal and external validity. *Internal validity* refers to the extent to which a design allows you to critically test and come up with an accurate answer concerning the causal relationships between some intervention and an outcome. Threats to internal validity have been masterfully described by Campbell and Stanley (1963) (see Exhibit 11.3). These threats are rival hypotheses to the assumption that a service method was effective, for example. Biases include *selection bias* (e.g., biased allocation to experimental and control groups), *performance bias* (unequal provision of care apart from the methods under evaluation), *detection bias* (biased assessment of outcome), and *attrition bias* (biased loss of participants to follow-up). Such sources of bias are rival hypotheses to claims, for example, that a particular service method resulted in observed outcomes. *Confounders* may occur—variables that are related to a causal factor of interest and some outcome(s) that are not represented equally in two different groups. "Zero time bias" may occur in which people in a prospective study are enrolled in a way resulting in systematic differences between groups (as in prospective cohort studies). Well-designed randomized controlled trials contain more

EXHIBIT 11.3

Possible Confounding Causes (Rival Explanations) for Change

1. *History.* Events that occur between the first and second measurement, in addition to the experimental variables, may account for changes (e.g., clients may get help elsewhere).

2. *Maturation.* Simply growing older or living longer may be responsible, especially when long periods of time are involved.

3. *Instrumentation.* The way that something is measured changes (e.g., observers may change how they record).

4. *Testing effects.* Assessment may result in change.

5. *Mortality.* There may be a differential loss of people from different groups.

6. *Regression.* Extreme scores tend to return to the mean.

7. *Self-selection bias.* Clients are often "self-directed" rather than randomly selected. They may differ in critical ways from the population they are assumed to represent and differ from clients in a comparison group.

8. *Helper selection bias.* Social workers may select certain kinds of clients to receive certain methods.

9. *Interaction effects.* Only certain clients may benefit from certain services, and others may even be harmed.

Source: Based on D. T. Campbell & J. C. Stanley (1963). *Experimental and quasi-experimental designs for research.* Chicago: Rand McNally.

control for different kinds of biases compared to weaker studies, such as quasi-experimental studies. Unless a study is replicated we are not sure whether there were problems (flaws) that resulted in misleading findings. History illustrates that many results based on a single study could not be replicated and were found to be false.

External validity refers to the extent to which you can generalize the findings in a study to other circumstances. These other circumstances may include other kinds of clients (e.g., age, risk factors, severity of problem), settings, services offered (e.g., timing, number of sessions (dosage), other concurrent services) or kinds of outcomes reviewed, and length of follow-up. To what extent can you generalize the causal relationship found in a study to different times, places, and people, and different operational definitions of interventions and outcomes? Farrington (2003) uses the term *descriptive validity* to refer to "the adequacy of the presentation of key features of an evaluation in a research report." Unblinded rating of outcome can result in misleading conclusions of effectiveness.

The literature on experimenter and subject biases highlights the importance of research that controls for these (e.g., Rosenthal, 1994). For example, we tend to give socially desirable responses—to present ourselves in a good light. Knowing a hypothesis creates a tendency to encourage the very responses that we are investigating. Experimenter effects are not necessarily intentional; even when we do not intend to skew results in a certain way, this may occur. Experimenter biases influence results in a number of ways. If the experimenters know the group a subject is in, they may change their behavior, for example, subtly lead the person in a certain direction. This is why it is vital in randomized controlled trials for raters of outcome to be blind—unaware of the group to which a person is assigned.

Questions to Ask About All Research

Certain questions are important to raise across research methods because of the potential for flaws that may result in misleading conclusions. These include concerns about the size and source of samples used, whether there is a comparison group, the accuracy and validity of measures used, and the appropriateness of data analysis. Answers to these characteristics will shed light both on the internal and external validity of a study. Methodological quality criteria suggested by Cook and Campbell (1979), as well as Shadish, Cook, and Campbell (2002) include four criteria: statistical conclusion validity, internal validity, construct validity, and external validity. The term *validity* refers to the accuracy of assumptions in relation to causes and effects. Classic criteria for assuming a causal relationship include: (1) the cause precedes the effect, (2) the cause is related to the effect, and (3) other plausible alternatives of the effect can be excluded (John Stewart Mill, 1911). As Farrington (2003) notes, "If threats to valid causal inference cannot be ruled out in the design, they should at least be measured and their importance estimated" (pp. 51–52). Too often the limitations of studies are not mentioned, are glossed over, or are minimized. Keep in mind that flaws in traditional methods of dissemination (journals and peer review journals) were one of the reasons for the origins of evidence-based practice (see chapter 9). Poor reporting of a randomized control trial does not necessarily mean that a trial was poorly constructed; it may be only poorly reported (e.g., see Soares, Daniels, Kumar, Clarke, Scott, Swann, & Djulbegovic, 2004).

Is the Research Question Clear?

Do the authors clearly describe their research question or is this vague or confusing? Examples of clear research questions are: "What factors contribute to the reabuse of children returned to their biological parents?" or "Do substance abuse programs to which parents are referred help them to decrease alcohol consumption compared to no intervention?" Unclear questions do not allow for clear tests at the point of data analysis—set in advance so all are clear on key concerns.

What Kind of Question Is It?

Does the article address the effectiveness of a practice method? Is it an assessment question? Does it describe a new risk assessment measure for depression in the elderly? What kind of question does it concern?

Is It Relevant to My Clients?

Does the question apply to your clients? If you knew the answer, could you and your clients make more informed decisions? Does it concern outcomes of interest to your clients? Have key ones been omitted? Is the setting similar to your practice setting? Are the clients similar?

Who Sponsored the Study?

Sponsorship of a study may suggest possible biases (see also discussion of propaganda in chapter 4). Sponsorship of research by a company with vested interest in a product, such as a pharmaceutical company or child welfare training program offered to all staff in a state, may encourage biased material.

Does the Research Method Used Match the Question Raised?

Can the research method used address the question? Different questions require different research methods. That is why discussing whether qualitative or quantitative research is best is unproductive—it depends on the question. Oxman and Guyatt (1993) suggest a scale ranging from 1 (not at all) to 6 (ideal) in relation to the potential that a research method can critically test a question.

Is There a Comparison Group?

Critically testing certain kinds of questions requires a comparison. A hallmark of randomized controlled trials is distributing clients to two or more different conditions. An intervention group (cognitive behavioral therapy for depression) may be compared to a no-treatment group or to a comparison group (interpersonal therapy). Only if we have a comparison can we identify which might be better than the other. If all we have is a pre-post test describing how depressed people are before and after some intervention, there is no comparison with a group receiving no service or a different service. Thus, there could be a variety of other reasons for any changes seen (see Exhibit 11.3).

Is the Study Design Rigorous?

The general research method may be appropriate but be carried out in a sloppy, unrigorous manner that allows the play of many biases. (See other questions in this section.)

What Is the Sample Size and Source?

Most research involves a sample that is assumed to be characteristic of the population from which it is drawn. Selection biases are one kind of bias related to how subjects were selected. Does the sample on which a study was based offer an opportunity to answer questions raised? (Some research deals with an entire population such as all graduates of the University of California at Berkeley's social work master's degree program in the year 2004.) A key question is "Can we accurately generalize from a sample to the population from which it is drawn or from one population to another (other year)?" Does the sample represent the population to which generalizations will be made? Questions that arise include the following:

- Is the sample selection process clearly described?
- How was the sample selected?
- From what population was it selected?
- Is it representative of the population?
- Were subjects lost for follow-up?

The answers to these questions provide clues about biases that may limit the value of a study to answer questions. For example, small samples drawn by convenience, rather than by random selection in which each individual has an equal chance of selection, may not provide information that reflects characteristics of the population of interest. Often, researchers do not clearly describe the source of their sample. A number of "filtering" decisions may be made to obtain a final sample. Consider the complexity of the source of samples of child welfare clients in some studies. CONSORT guidelines include a flowchart to describe samples used in randomized controlled trials (Schulz, Altman, & Moher for the CONSORT Group, 2010). Readers can determine how many people were excluded at different points and for what reasons. Readers can see for themselves possible sources of bias in the final sample on which conclusions are based.

Sample size and the critical testing of hypotheses are closely related. That is, some studies do not find effects not because there are no effects to be found, but because the sample size does not have the power to critically test whether there is an association or not. As Farrington (2003) notes, "A statistically significant result could indicate a large effect in a small sample or a small effect in a large sample" (p. 52). Researchers should base selection of their sample size on a statistical power analysis. Use of a very large sample may yield many significant differences that may not be illuminating. Clear description of the source of samples used is important in qualitative, as well as quantitative research.

Are Measures Used Reliable and Valid?

Particular measures of certain concepts, such as self-esteem and substance abuse, are used in research. Do they measure what they purport to measure? Are measures used relevant to your clients? To what extent are measures used in a study accurate? The validity and accuracy of measures are key concerns in all research. Reliability refers to the correlation of ratings, for example, between different administrations of an assessment measure for an individual at different times (stability) or between two observers of an interaction at the same time (interrater reliability). Validity refers to the extent to which a measure reflects what it is designed to measure. There are many different kinds, as discussed in chapter 17. Reliability places an upward boundary on validity. That is, a measure cannot be valid if it is not reliable (cannot be consistently assessed). And a measure may be reliable but invalid perhaps because of shared biases among raters—including peer reviewers of manuscripts. Research using one kind of data (self-report) may present an inaccurate picture. Observation of children's behavior on the playground to identify instances of bullying may not match a student's self-report.

Did Authors Report Attrition (Drop-Out Rates)?

In many studies, some subjects drop out over the course of the study. This number should be reported and is reflected in "intention-to-treat" analysis. This is "an analysis of a study where participants are analysed according to the group to which they were initially allocated. This is regardless of whether or not they dropped out, fully complied with the treatment, or crossed over and received the other treatment. It protects against attrition bias" (Center for Research and Dissemination, University of York, April 4, 2004).

Was There Any Follow-Up—If So, How Long?

An intervention may be effective in the short term but not in the long term. How long were subjects followed up? The effects of many programs are short term.

Are Procedures Clearly Described?

Are practice methods used clearly described? If not, it will not be possible to replicate them. For example, in effectiveness studies, only if methods are clearly described can readers understand exactly what interventions were used and determine if methods used were offered in an optimal manner.

Are the Data Analyses Sound?

Statistics are tools used to explore whether there is a relationship between two or more variables. We ask what is the probability of finding an association by chance in samples of different sizes. We do this by estimating the probability of getting a result in a sample of a certain size. The null hypothesis (the assumption that there is no difference between two variables we think are associated or two groups that we think will differ) is tested. We could make two kinds of errors. We may assume that there is a relationship when there is not (Type I Error) or assume there is no relationship when

there is (Type II Error). The term *statistical significance* refers to whether a test falls below a 5% probability. Practitioners and administrators should have a rudimentary knowledge of statistics so that they can ask cogent questions in terms of the adequacy of statistical analyses (see Penston, 2010). Researchers, as well as practitioners, make mistakes in how they word findings. For example, rather than stating that there was "no statistically significant difference," they may say there was "no difference/change" (Weisburd, Lum, & Yang, 2003). Statistical testing is not without controversy; for example, there are arguments against statistical testing (e.g., see Oakes, 1986). Complex statistical methods will not correct major flaws in the design or conduct of a study. This is why care in planning studies is so important.

In addition to insufficient sample size to critically test the relationship between two or more variables, another problem is the use of inappropriate methods of statistical analysis. Incorrect statistical methods may be used, leading to bogus claims. Different statistical tests make different assumptions about variables in relation to their underlying distributions. A statistical method may be used that requires interval data (reflecting continuous data in which points are separated by equal intervals) for ordinal data in which you can rank order differences but in fact do not have any idea about how much difference there is between points. It is like using a rubber ruler. Many constructs are continuous. Consider drinking. One could have no drinks, one drink, or many drinks per day. However, often this is treated as a binary variable (categorically defined); either one is or is not an alcoholic; a continuous variable is transformed into a binary one. Data are lost in changing a continuous variable to a dichotomous one—individual variations are omitted. Research texts describe a number of problems in relation to inappropriate use of statistical tests, such as fishing (running scores of statistical tests to see if any would be significant). You may read an article that uses many different variables with a large sample in which authors claim that 15 significant differences were found. The question is: How many correlations were run? A certain percentage would be significant by chance.

Are Claims Made Accurate?

Problems in any of the characteristics described above, such as samples and measures used, may not allow clear conclusions. Inflated claims are common. That is why is it important to learn how to critically appraise research findings for yourself. Do claims made match the kind of design used? For example, many authors use pre-post tests. Such a design cannot tell us whether the intervention was responsible for the results because there is no comparison group. Yet the author may say, "Our results show that X was effective." This is a bogus claim.

Are Findings Clinically Important?

Will research findings from a study help you to help your clients? How many clients would have to receive a service for one to be helped? (See discussion of Number Needed to Treat in chapter 21.) Here too, people differ in their views about when there is "enough evidence" to recommend use of service or to recommend that a program not be used because it is harmful. For example, the 10% reduction in prevention of delinquency reflected in controlled studies may be considered an important reduction (e.g., Weisburd, Lum, & Yang, 2003). Many other kinds of "evidence" will come into play (see Exhibit 9.7).

Did the Authors Describe Any Special Interests and Their Biases?

Special interests may bias results (see chapter 4). We should be informed about any conflicts of interest authors have that may bias conclusions (e.g., see Cosgrove, Bursztajn, Krimsky, Anaya, & Walker, 2009). For example, did a drug company fund a study?

Levels of Evidence

The concept of levels of evidence draws attention to the fact that different kinds of research related to a certain kind of question offers different degrees of control regarding potential biases that may limit conclusions that can be drawn. A hierarchy regarding levels of evidence for studies of effectiveness is shown below:

1. Systematic review (SR) of RCTs

2. Experimental studies (e.g., RCT with concealed allocation)

3. Quasi-experimental studies (e.g., experimental study without randomization)

4. Controlled observational studies

   a. Cohort studies

   b. Case control studies

5. Observational studies without control groups

6. Expert opinion, for example, based on consensus.

Hierarchies should not be rigidly used. And, many questions are informed by more than one kind of research (see Davies, 2004). Glasziou, Vandenbroucke, and Chalmers (2004) note that "criteria designed to guide inferences about the main effects of treatment have been uncritically applied to questions about etiology, diagnosis, prognosis, or adverse effects" (p. 39). A key point they make is that whatever the kind of report, including case studies, it is important to do a systematic review. Balanced assessments should draw on a variety of types of research and different questions require different types of evidence.

Questions About Effectiveness and Prevention

We often seek information about the effects of different practices and policies. How can we discover if a practice or policy does more good than harm? We could ask our colleagues what they think. But on what do they base their views? Examples of effectiveness questions are:

- In youth with antisocial behavior, is group cognitive behavioral training or individual counseling more effective in decreasing such behaviors and increasing positive behaviors?

- In young adults diagnosed with AIDS, are education and group support compared to individual counseling more effective in increasing safe-sex behaviors?

A key concern with testing effectiveness questions is: Is there a comparison group that allows us to determine whether different results would be attained with different groups? For example, has a medication for depression been compared with a placebo?

Randomized Controlled Trials

In experimental designs, such as randomized controlled clinical trials, there is a comparison between different groups, which may be an experimental group that receives a special treatment (the independent variable) and a control group in which there is no special treatment (see Exhibit 11.4). Or, a comparison group receiving a different service may be used; two different services may be compared. Factorial experimental designs explore the effects of more than one independent variable. Interaction effects are often of interest here, for example, between personality, peer rejection of youth, and school environment. Random distribution of subjects to different groups using an effective randomization procedure is a key feature of rigorous experimental designs.

Randomisation in clinical trials is the use of a chance procedure, such as coin tossing or computer-generated random numbers, to generate an allocation sequence. It ensures that participants have a prespecified (very often an equal) chance of being assigned to the experimental or control group. This means that the groups are likely to be balanced for known as well as unknown and unmeasured confounding variables. To protect against selection bias, concealment of the randomly-generated allocation sequence is essential. This is because foreknowledge of group assignments leaves the allocation sequence subject to possible manipulation by researchers and participants. Randomisation without allocation concealment does not guarantee protection against selection bias. (Center for Research and Dissemination, University of York, April 4, 2004)

EXHIBIT 11.4

Validity Screen of an Article About Therapy

1. Is the study a randomized controlled trial? How were patients selected for the trial? Were they properly randomized into groups using concealed assignment?	Yes (go on)	No (stop)*
2. Are the subjects in the study similar to mine?	Yes (go on)	No (stop)
3. Are all participants who entered the trial properly accounted for at its conclusion? Was follow-up complete and were few lost to follow-up compared with the number of bad outcomes? Were patients analyzed in the groups to which they were initially randomized (intention-to-treat analysis)?	Yes (go on)	No (stop)
4. Was everyone involved in the study (subjects and investigators) "blind" to treatment?	Yes	No
5. Were the intervention and control groups similar at the start of the trial?	Yes	No
6. Were the groups treated equally (aside from the experimental intervention)?	Yes	No
7. Are the results clinically as well as statistically significant? Were the outcomes measured clinically important?	Yes	No
8. If a negative trial, was a power analysis done?	Yes	No
9. Were other factors present that might have affected the outcome?	Yes	No
10. Are the treatment benefits worth the potential harms and costs?	Yes	No

*A "stop" answer to any of the questions should prompt you to seriously question whether the results of the study are valid and whether you should use this intervention.
Source: W. F. Miser (2000). Critical appraisal of the literature: How to assess an article and still enjoy life. In J. P. Geyman, R. A. Deyo, & S. D. Ramsey (2000), *Evidence-based clinical practice: Concepts and approaches* (p. 46). Boston: Butterworth Heinemann. Original source: W. F. Miser (1999). Critical appraisal of the literature. *Journal of the American Board of Family Practice, 12*, 315–333. Reprinted with permission of the American Board of Family Medicine.

Without a comparison group (for example, a group that did not receive a service), we do not know what would have happened in the absence of a service (see Exhibit 11.4). This is a key problem in pre-post studies. Failure to check the effects of an intervention has been responsible for much harm, include blinding 10,000 babies by giving them oxygen at birth (Silverman, 1980). Random distribution of subjects to groups is designed to minimize selection bias—differences in outcomes due to differences in subjects in different groups (see CONSORT guidelines). You should always ask how subjects were randomly distributed to groups because some methods of random distribution do not guard against selection biases that may skew the results. Blinding is another method designed to decrease bias.

Blinding is used to keep the participants, investigators and outcome assessors ignorant about which interventions participants are receiving during a study. In single blind studies only the participants are blind to their group allocations, while in double-blind studies both the participants and investigators are blind. Blinding of outcome assessment can often be done even when blinding of participants and caregivers cannot. Blinding is used to protect against performance and detection bias. It may also contribute to adequate

allocation concealment. However, the success of blinding procedures is infrequently checked and it may be overestimated. (Center for Research and Dissemination, University of York, April 4, 2004)

Farrington (2003) suggests that the SMS is the most influential methodological quality scale in criminology. This scale was used to rate prevention programs using ten criteria on a scale from 0 to 5: (1) adequacy of sampling, (2) adequacy of sample size, (3) pretreatment measures of outcome, (4) adequacy of comparison groups, (5) controls for prior group differences, (6) adequacy of measurement of variables, (7) attrition, (8) post-intervention measurement, (9) adequacy of statistical analyses, (10) testing of alternative explanations. Brounstein and his colleagues (1997) used this scale to review 440 evaluations. Only 30% received a score of 3 to 5 on a scale ranging from 0 (no confidence in results) to 5 (high confidence in results) (p. 57).

It is difficult to carry out experiments in applied settings. However, we should not overlook the fact that many investigators do manage to carry out controlled studies that provide rigorous tests of claims in real-life settings. There are hundreds of RCTs in the area of prevention of delinquency. Joan McCord (1978) investigated the effectiveness of special services to youth designed to prevent delinquency. Youth were randomly distributed to the usual services or to a special group receiving a variety of services. The independent variable is the service program. The dependent variable is the outcome of interest. These two groups were tracked over 30 years. This study thus represents a longitudinal experimental study. Among the 253 matched pairs assessed for follow-up, 125 of the treatment boys had been sent to summer camp, and 128 were not. None of the treatment approaches showed measurable benefits, and some, repeated placement in summer camps, resulted in harm. McCord (2003) summarizes the study as follows:

1. The Cambridge-Somerville Youth Study was carefully planned.

2. It was based on knowledge that poor families in disorganized neighborhoods were at high risk for crime.

3. Counselors had been trained to carry out their roles, and weekly conferences ensured that they were doing so.

4. Counselors integrated services provided by other available agencies with their own.

5. The program included youth with good as well as bad prognoses so that participation was not stigmatizing.

6. The youth study aimed to change many features of the environment, providing the boys with prosocial guidance, social skills, and healthful activities.

7. The program gave medical assistance and tutoring as well as guidance to both parents and youth.

8. Clients, for the most part, were satisfied with the program.

9. The program lasted five and one-half years, covering the period when the boys were between the ages of 10.5 and 16.

10. The program could be scientifically evaluated because its founder insisted that evaluation was central to the advance of social intervention practices. (pp. 22–23)

Had there been no control group, evaluators might have concluded that the program was beneficial because so many of the treatment boys were better adjusted than anticipated. Or because two-thirds reported beneficial effects for themselves, evaluators might have judged that the program was effective. But these judgments would have been contrary to objective evidence that the program resulted in adverse outcomes for many of the participants.

Let me emphasize again the fact that the Cambridge-Somerville Youth Study was effective. The intervention had lasting effects. These effects were not beneficial. The important legacy of the program, however, is its contribution to the science of prevention. Because the design supports scientifically credible conclusions, it showed that social interventions can have long-term [negative] effects. (McCord, 2003, pp. 22–23)

Effect size is one statistic used to describe the effects of an intervention in an experimental study. This indicates the strength of a relationship between, or among, two or more variables. Effect sizes range from 0 to 1. Larger effect sizes indicate stronger relationships. Cohen (1977) suggests that small effect sizes are about 0.2, medium ones about 0.5, and larger effect sizes about 0.8 or greater. Effect sizes should be reported. These can be calculated in different ways, all of which are designed to describe the relationship between the effect found in the intervention group and the effect found in a comparison group. One is to divide the mean difference between the experimental and control groups by the standard deviation of the control or alternative treatment group. The narrower the confidence interval, the stronger the effect size (see later discussion).

Randomized N of 1 controlled trials involving the detailed description of an individual over a period of time provide useful information about effectiveness (see chapter 22). What may be true of a group may not be true of an individual. Thus, aggregate studies must be interpreted with caution in relation to generalizing to an individual. Otherwise you may make the "ecological fallacy"—assume that what is true of a group is true of an individual. Questions Guyatt and Rennie (2002) suggest for deciding on the feasibility of such a study include: "1) Is the client eager to collaborate? 2) Does the program have a rapid onset and offset? 3) Is an optimal duration of service feasible? 4) What important targets of service should be measured? And 5) What dictates the end?" (p. 278).

In quasi-experimental studies, allocation of participants to different groups is arranged by the researcher but there is no genuine randomization and allocation concealment, thus selection biases are of concern, as well as a number of other biases, depending on the design (see Exhibit 11.3). Pre-post studies are one variety; they do not include a comparison group so we cannot determine causation. Time series designs are another kind of quasi-experimental study (see Campbell & Stanley, 1963; Cook & Campbell, 1979; Shadish, Cook, & Campbell, 2002).

Observational Studies

In observational studies, unlike RCTs, assignment of subjects to different groups is not under the control of the investigator. Different groups are self-selected or are "natural experiments" (Campbell, 1969). Subjects are not randomly assigned to different services or exposed to different kinds of risks. Such exposure or service occurs by choice or circumstance. Examples include exposure to lead in houses and to family violence. Those who are exposed and those who are not exposed may differ in important ways, thus introducing selection biases.

An observational study concerns treatments, interventions, or policies and the effects they cause and in this respect it resembles an experiment. A study without a treatment is neither an experiment nor an observational study. Most public opinion polls, most forecasting efforts, most studies of fairness and discrimination, and many other important empirical studies are neither experiments nor observational studies. (Rosenbaum, 2002, pp. 1–2)

Experimental studies may be impossible to conduct because of ethical or logistic reasons. They may not be necessary. They may be inappropriate or inadequate. Important roles for observational methods suggested by Black (1994) include the following:

1. Some interventions have such a large impact that observational data are sufficient to show it.

2. Infrequent adverse outcomes would be detected only by randomized controlled trials so large that they are rarely conducted. Observational methods may be the only alternative.

3. Observational data provide a means of assessing the long-term outcome of interventions beyond the timescale of many trials.

4. Many clinicians will not share their concerns and will be opposed to a randomized controlled trial; observational approaches can then be used to demonstrate clinical uncertainty and encourage a trial.

5. Some important aspects of care cannot be investigated in a randomized trial for practical and ethical reasons. (Adapted from Black, 1994)

Observational studies include: (1) cohort studies, (2) case control studies, (3) pre-post studies, and (4) case series. This order reflects the level of evidence provided regarding effectiveness questions, although there are exceptions (see discussion, for example, of case control studies). Observational studies may be descriptive or analytical. Analytical include cohort and case control studies.

Observational studies differ in their *ecological validity*, that is, the extent to which the study is carried out in contexts that are similar or identical to the everyday life experiences of those involved. A variety of strategies are used to detect hidden biases in observational studies, such as inclusion of a number of control groups to try to identify hidden covariates (characteristics that influence the results other than the one focused on). And, as Rosenbaum (2002) suggests, "even when it is not possible to remove bias through adjustment or detect bias through careful design, it is nonetheless possible to give quantitative expression to the magnitude of uncertainties about bias, a technique called *sensitivity analysis*" (p. 11).

Cohort Studies

In cohort studies, a group of individuals that has experienced a certain situation (for example, witnessed domestic violence) is compared with another group that has not been so exposed. Both groups are followed up at a later time in order to determine the association between exposure and an outcome of interest (such as subsequent abuse of one's own children). Cohort studies are prospective and analytical. Because of lack of random assignment, they are prone to a number of biases, such as lack of control over risk assignment and uneven loss to follow-up. Cohort studies are often used to describe different kinds of risk. Questions to ask about cohort studies include the following (see Gray, 2001a):

- Is there sufficient description of the groups (how they were recruited) and the distribution of prognostic factors?

- Are the groups assembled at a similar point in relation to (for example) their disorder progression? (Were decisions made that could have included or excluded more severe cases?)

- Is the intervention/treatment reliably ascertained?

- Were the groups comparable on all important confounding factors?

- Was there adequate adjustment for the effects of these confounding variables?

- Were measures used valid?

- Was a dose-response relationship between intervention and outcome demonstrated?

- Was outcome assessment blind to exposure status?

- Was the presence of co-occurring disorders considered?

- Was follow-up long enough for the outcomes to occur?

- What proportion of the cohort was followed-up?

- Were drop-out rates and reasons for drop-out similar across intervention and unexposed groups? (CRD, University of York, Phase 5, 2001, p. 11)

Gray (2001a) notes that "the main abuse of a cohort study is to assess the effectiveness of a particular intervention when a more appropriate method would be an RCT" (p. 150).

Case Control (Case-Referent) Studies

In a retrospective case control study, we start with people who have a particular characteristic (a certain illness) and look back in time in relation to certain outcomes. Samples may be small in such studies yet suggest strong relationships. Consider the case-referent study reporting a relationship between the drug diethylstilbestrol (DES), given to pregnant women, and vaginal cancer. Herbst, Ulfelder, and Poskanzer (1971) included 8 women who had vaginal cancer and 32 who did not in relation to use of DES during pregnancies. Seven had taken DES in the group with vaginal cancer and none had taken it in the referent group. This study illustrates the value of case-referent studies regarding rare conditions or for risk factors that have long development phases. Criteria for reviewing case control studies are suggested below:

- Is the case definition explicit?

- Has the illness state of clients been reliably assessed and validated?

- Were the controls randomly selected from the source of population of the cases?

- How comparable are the cases and controls with respect to potential confounding factors?

- Were interventions and other exposures assessed in the same way for cases and controls?

- How was the response rate defined?

- Were the non-response rates and reasons for non-response the same in both groups?

- Is it possible that over-matching has occurred in that cases and controls were matched on factors related to exposure?

- Was an appropriate statistical analysis used (matched or unmatched)? (CRD, University of York, Phase 5, 2001, p. 11)

Cross-Sectional Study

In a cross-sectional study, a snapshot is taken of people at a particular time. Such studies may be used to describe the frequency or rate of a behavior or to try to identify the relationship between one or more factors and a problem, such as child abuse. Unfortunately, such research does not show which came first.

Pre-Post Study (Before and After)

Responses are compared before and after some intervention. Such designs do not provide information about the causal relationship between an intervention and an outcome unless perhaps the change is very large and is replicated. They do provide information about change.

Case Series Study

Another kind of clinical study consists of describing characteristics of a series of case examples. Because of the lack of comparison we cannot make assumptions about causes. Questions for reviewing case series studies include the following:

- Is the study based on a representative sample selected from a relevant population?

- Are the criteria for inclusion explicit?

- Did all individuals enter the study at a similar point in the progression of the problem?

- Was follow-up long enough for important events to occur?

- Were outcomes assessed using objective criteria or was blinding used?

- If comparisons of sub-series are being made, was there sufficient description of the series and the distribution of prognostic factors? (CRD, University of York, Phase 5, 2001, p. 11)

A case report is essentially an anecdotal report—a description of a single case. Such reports differ greatly in their rigor.

Questions About Harm

Just as we can ask about number needed to treat (NNT), we can ask about number needed to harm (NNH). That is, how many people would have to receive a service for one to be harmed? Many studies do not offer any information about possible harms of interventions, including assessment and diagnostic measures. Petrosino, Turpin-Petrosino, and Buehler (2003) presented a meta-analysis of seven randomized experiments regarding recidivism data concerning scared-straight programs. All seven indicated that this program was harmful; that is, the experimental group had higher recidivism rates. More recent reviews including more studies have arrived at the same conclusions.

Systematic Reviews and Meta-Analyses

In systematic reviews there is a search for all evidence related to a question. For example, Cochrane review groups search for published and unpublished research reports related to a specific question. The search process is clearly described so readers are apprised of how this was conducted. Authors describe how they searched, where they searched, and what criteria they used to appraise the quality of studies. Systematic reviews involve the following basic components:

1. State the objectives of the research.

2. Describe eligibility criteria for studies to be included.

3. Identify (all) potentially eligible studies.

4. Apply eligibility criteria.

5. Assemble the most complete data set feasible.

6. Analyze this data set, using statistical synthesis and sensitivity analysis, if appropriate and possible; and prepare a structured report of the research. (Chalmers, 2003, p. 25)

Rigorous reviews "are designed to minimize the likelihood that the effects of interventions will be confused with the effects of biases and chance" (Chalmers, 2003, p. 22). Systematic reviews are of value in relation to all questions. There are vast differences between haphazard (incomplete, uncritical) and rigorous, exhaustive reviews—garbage in, garbage out. (See Exhibit 11.6)

Differences in the rigor of research reviews are illustrated by reviews of multisystemic therapy. Most sources describe this as an effective treatment. A systematic review shows this to be no more effective than other interventions (Littell, Popa, & Forsythe, 2005). Overlooking important methodological concerns encourages inflated claims of effectiveness that provide misleading conclusions. A key contribution of systematic reviews is an exhaustive search for research findings related to important practice and policy questions, a clear description of the search process used to locate studies, rigorous review of each study located, and a clear description of the criteria used to appraise research reports. Not wasting data is one aim of thorough reviews; that is, there is a search for all well-designed related research studies, including unpublished studies. Reviewers may have access (or gain it) to raw data and reanalyze the data. Criteria for assessing the methodological rigor of reviews include the following (see, for example, Oxman, Cook, & Guyatt, 1994, p. 128):

1. Did the overview address a focused practice-related question?

2. Were the search methods reported?

3. Was the search comprehensive?

4. Were the inclusion criteria reported?

5. Were criteria for inclusion appropriate?

6. Was selection bias avoided?

7. Were the validity criteria reported?

8. Was validity assessed appropriately?

9. Were the methods used to combine studies reported?

10. Were the findings combined appropriately?

11. Does it list, in tabular form, indices of effect size?

12. Do the conclusions match the data reported?

13. What was the overall scientific quality of the review?

14. Can the results be applied to my clients?

15. Were all important outcomes considered?

16. Are the benefits worth the harms and costs? (See also Exhibit 11.5.)

Little if any of this information is given in incomplete reviews. Without this, readers are not provided with the information needed to make up their own minds about the evidentiary status of claims. Farrington (2003) suggests five methodological criteria: (1) *internal validity*—demonstrating that the intervention caused an effect on the outcome: (2) *descriptive validity*—without information about key features of research it is hard to include the results in a systematic review; (3) *statistical conclusion validity*; (4) *construct validity*; and (5) *external validity*. He suggests that these occur in order of importance, at least concerning systematic reviews of impact evaluations. He views information about the external validity of a single research project as "the least important to a systematic reviewer since the main aims of a systematic review and meta-analyses include establishing the external validity or generalizability of results over different conditions and investigating factors that explain heterogeneity in effect size among different evaluation studies" (p. 61).

There is no way to get around the time it takes to carefully appraise each research report reviewed. Critical appraisal of a study takes a great deal of time. That is probably why it is often not done. The abstract and discussion sections of reports become the least important and the method and results sections of key concern. Remarkably, some authors of alleged research reviews actually say that they did not have time to carefully review each study included but blithely go on to make conclusions about effectiveness (Mueser, Bond, Drake, & Resnick, 1998). Randomization procedures in RCTs are carefully reviewed. Measures used are critically appraised regarding their reliability and validity. Results are carefully reviewed, including the validity of outcome measures and the extent to which descriptions in the text match data presented in tables and figures. Statistical methods used are carefully reviewed for their appropriateness. And conclusions are carefully appraised. Are they warranted? For example, an outcome measure of fewer hospital days may be a result of an administrative decision not to hospitalize clients in one group (Gomory, 1999). Conceptual critiques are also needed. For example, the influence of moderating variables may have been glossed over, personal problems may be assumed to have a biomedical cause when little or no evidence exists for such an assumption. Counterevidence to assumptions may be available but not be mentioned. Reviews that claim to be systematic may not be rigorous in their methods of review.

The logo of the Cochrane Collaboration illustrates a program that is effective (see Cochrane web site). The solid line running down the center indicates the point where there is no difference between treatment and control groups. Each horizontal line represents one trial and the length of each line shows the confidence interval (CI). The smaller this is, the less the variability in results in a study. The larger it is, the greater the variability in a study. If a confidence interval crosses the vertical line, the range of estimated effects of the treatment includes the possibility both of getting better and of getting worse. Generally, if the whole CI is on the left of the line, the treatment improves the situation, and if it is on the right of the line, it makes the situation worse. The CI shows the precision of the estimate. The power of a study to detect a real difference is reflected in the narrowness of the range: the shorter the length of the CI, the more precise the estimate is. The odds ratios and 95% confidence intervals for effect of home visiting on child injury (Roberts, Kramer, & Suissa,

EXHIBIT 11.5

Steps in Determining the Validity of a Meta-Analysis

1. Was the literature search done well?		
a. Was it comprehensive?	yes	no
b. Were the search methods systematic and clearly described?	yes	no
c. Were the key words used in the search described?	yes	no
d. Was the issue of publication bias addressed?	yes	no
2. Was the method for selecting articles clear, systematic, and appropriate?		
a. Were there clear, preestablished inclusion and exclusion criteria for evaluation?	yes	no
b. Was selection systematic?	yes	no
Was the population defined?	yes	no
Was the exposure/intervention clearly described?	yes	no
Were all outcomes described and were they compatible?	yes	no
c. Was selection done blindly and in random order?	yes	no
d. Was the selection process reliable?		
Were at least two independent selectors used?	yes	no
Was the extent of selection disagreement evaluated?	yes	no
3. Was the quality of the primary studies evaluated?		
a. Did all studies, published or not, have the same standard applied?	yes	no
b. Were at least two independent evaluators used and was the interrater agreement assessed and adequate?	yes	no
c. Were the evaluators blinded to the authors, institutions, and results of the primary studies?	yes	no
4. Were results from the studies combined appropriately?		
a. Were the studies similar enough to combine results?	yes	no
Were the study designs, populations, exposures, outcomes, and direction of effect similar in the combined studies?	yes	no
b. Was a test for heterogeneity done and was its P value nonsignificant?	yes	no
5. Was a statistical combination (meta-analysis) done properly?		
a. Were the methods of the studies similar?	yes	no
b. Was the possibility of chance differences statistically addressed?	yes	no
Was a test for homogeneity done?	yes	no
c. Were appropriate statistical analyses performed?	yes	no
d. Were sensitivity analyses used?	yes	no
6. Are the results important?		
a. Was the effect strong?	yes	no
Was the odds ratio large?	yes	no
Were the results reported in a clinically meaningful manner, such as the absolute difference or the number needed to treat?	yes	no
b. Are the results likely to be reproducible and generalizable?	yes	no
c. Were all clinically important consequences considered?	yes	no
d. Are the benefits worth the harm and costs?	yes	no

Source: W. F. Miser (2000). Applying a meta-analysis to daily clinical practice. In J. P. Geyman, R. A. Deyo, & S. D. Ramsey (Eds.), *Evidence-based clinical practice: Concepts and approaches* (p. 60). Boston: Butterworth Heinemann. Reprinted with permission.

1996) is illustrated in Exhibit 11.6. This visual description allows you to quickly see how many studies fall to the left or to the right of the midline.

Criticisms of meta-analyses suggested by Rosenthal (2001) include the following:

1. Retrievability bias.

2. Overemphasis on a single value rather than a description of central tendency and variability in findings.

3. Glossing over important details.

EXHIBIT 11.6

Odds Ratios and 95% Confidence Intervals for Effect of Home Visiting on Child Injury

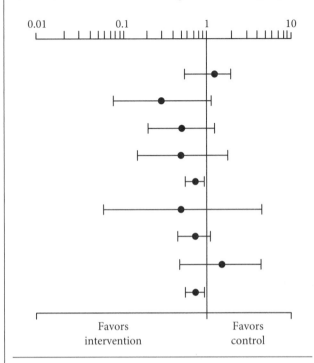

Source: I. Roberts, M. S. Kramer, & S. Suissa (1996). Does home visiting prevent childhood injury? A systematic review of randomized controlled trials. *BM J, 312,* 29–33. Reprinted with permission.

4. Overlooking heterogeneity of studies.

5. Overlooking heterogeneity of outcomes and the potential contributions of moderating variables (such as psychotherapy).

6. Inclusion of poorly designed studies that contain many sources of bias.

7. Inclusion of multiple dependent variables (outcomes) with different effect sizes, perhaps due to variables, such as different laboratories. (Workshop on meta-analysis, March 2000, UC Berkeley)

Questions about Causes

Consider Mindy, a school social worker who was asked by a teacher to help her with a second-grade student whom she described as out of control; he shouts out in class and tears up his work. A well-formed question might be: "In elementary school children who are a classroom management problem, what are common causes?" We could use a variety of methods to try to identify related factors. We could create a survey and ask teachers what they think. We could compare this with results of a descriptive and functional analysis of classroom contingencies (see chapters 7 and 25). The latter form of investigation suggests that being under or over challenged may contribute to disruptive behavior in a classroom (problems in curriculum design) and/or classroom contingencies may maintain such behavior (being reinforced for inappropriate behavior and ignoring desired behaviors). Would a survey reveal the same thing? See Exhibit 11.7 for questions to raise concerning articles about causation.

Surveys

Surveys are used for many purposes including describing the prevalence of certain conditions (such as depression), to gather people's views about quality of care and services, and to try to identify causes using complex statistical tools, such as regression analysis. The purpose of correlational research is to investigate the relationship among two or more variables using statistical analysis. Pearson product moment correlation coefficients are typically used as the statistic to represent the degree of association. This ranges from −1 to +1, both indicating a perfect correlation. For example, we may ask, "What is the relationship between college grade-point average (GPA), scores on the Graduate Record Examination (GRE), and performance in graduate school?" Do GPA and GRE predict performance in graduate school? Correlational designs differ in their ecological validity (the extent to which findings can be generalized to other groups). We cannot draw causal assumptions based upon correlational data; associations do not necessarily reflect causal relationships. There may be some other variable that is responsible for the association. It could even be that there is reverse association. Gray (2001a) suggests the following questions in critically appraising a survey:

- How was the population to be surveyed chosen? Was it the whole population or a sample?

- If a sample, how was the sample chosen? Was it a random sample or was it stratified to ensure that all sectors of the population were represented?

- Was a valid questionnaire used? Did the authors of the survey mention the possibility of different results being obtained by different interviewers, if interviewers were used?

- What procedures were used to verify the data?

- Were the conclusions drawn from the survey all based on the data or did those carrying out the survey infer conclusions? Inference is acceptable, but it must be clearly distinguished from results derived solely from the data. (Gray, 2001a, p. 153)

EXHIBIT 11.7

Validity Screen for an Article About Causation

1. Was a clearly defined comparison group of those at risk for having the outcome of interest included?	Yes (go on)	No (stop)*
2. Were the outcomes and exposures measured in the same way in the groups being compared?	Yes (go on)	No (stop)
3. Were the observers blinded to the exposure of outcome and to the outcome?	Yes (go on)	No (stop)
4. Was follow-up sufficiently long and complete?	Yes (go on)	No (stop)
5. Is the temporal relationship correct? (Does the exposure to the agent precede the outcome?)	Yes (go on)	No (stop)
6. Is there a dose-response gradient? (As the quantity or the duration of exposure to the agent increases, does the risk of outcome likewise increase?)	Yes (go on)	No (stop)
7. How strong is the association between exposure and outcome? (Is the relative risk or odds ratio large?)	Yes (go on)	No (stop)

*A "stop" answer to any of the questions should prompt you to seriously question whether the results of the study are valid and whether the item in question is really a causative factor.
Source: W. F. Miser (1999). Critical appraisal of the literature. *Journal of the American Board of Family Practice, 12*, 315–337. Reprinted with permission. of the American Board of Family Medicine.

Questions about Prevalence and Incidence (Frequency and Rate)

In the course of your education and professional career, you will come across estimates of the prevalence of certain problems. Making informed decisions may require accurate information regarding the incidence and prevalence of a concern. Prevalence refers to the number of instances of an illness or other characteristic in a population at a given time. Incidence refers to the number of new events in a given population in a given time. Epidemiology is the study of the distribution and determinants of health-related states or events in specific populations, and the application of this study to the control of health problems (Last, 2001).

Let us say that a parent seeks help because she is worried about her child being abducted by a stranger. She has read a report in the newspaper saying that stranger abduction is common and parents should be careful. Because of this she rarely allows her children to go out unaccompanied. She and her husband disagree about this—he believes that his wife is overconcerned and because of this, depriving her child of freedom and opportunities to learn and grow. As with other decisions, we can translate information needs into well-formed questions that allow us to search for related literature. The following questions may guide a search:

- In suburban neighborhoods, what is the incidence and prevalence of stranger abduction of young children?

- Does the media exaggerate the prevalence of stranger abduction?

Other kinds of questions that are relevant here include: "For young children, are there effective preventative steps that can be taken to decrease stranger abduction?" "Under what circumstances does stranger abduction occur?" Quality filters for description questions can be seen in chapter 10, Exhibit 10.3. A search of the literature revealed that the prevalence of stranger abduction is often exaggerated by the media. Ecological studies are descriptive in nature and use data collected for a variety of purposes, including administrative needs. An example is comparison of the different rates of child abuse in different communities that have different levels of social support. Both cohort studies and cross-sectional studies may be used to gather information about frequency or rate.

Questions Regarding Experiences

Examples of questions that arise here include:

- In social workers in child welfare agencies, what are current sources of strain and perceived causes?

- In elderly clients entering a nursing home, what are feelings and thoughts?

Different Kinds of Qualitative Research

Qualitative research may be of many different kinds, including case studies, narrative analyses, focus groups, and participant observation. The concern in ethnographic research is to describe people's experiences as they see them. Social workers must understand events from a client's point of view in order to plan, together with the client, what might be helpful. If they do not understand this, if they misattribute motives and values to clients, hoped-for outcomes and related factors may not be accurately identified. This illustrates the closeness between good ethnographic research and a sound contextual assessment—a social worker's attempts to describe factors that influence problems of concern to clients. Case studies consist of detailed descriptions of individuals, groups, organizations, or neighborhoods. There are a wide variety of case studies ranging from detailed accounts of one particular individual, family, group, community, or organization to collection of information about a variety of individuals, groups, or organizations with less detail. Case studies differ in the method used to select the sample and thus how representative it may be to the larger population.

As Becker (1996) suggests, "we *always* describe how they [other people], interpret the events they participate in, so the only question is not whether we should, but how accurately we do it." He suggests that "it is inevitably epistemologically dangerous to guess at what could be observed directly. The danger is that we will guess wrong, that what looks reasonable to us will not be what looked reasonable to them. This happens all the time, largely because we are not those people and do not live in their circumstances" (p. 58). Observational data differ in its rigor, ranging from careful systematic observation including reliability checks reflecting degree of agreement between raters to unsystematic, anecdotal observation. Anecdotal research may be of value, for example, in suggesting more rigorous research (Aronson, 2003). As Becker (1996) notes, "The variety of things called ethnographic aren't all alike, and in fact may be at odds with each other over epistemological details" (p. 57). He suggests that attribution errors are common in many fields. "Misinterpretations of people's experience and meanings are commonplace in studies of delinquency and crime, of sexual behavior, and in general studies of behaviors foreign to the experience and lifestyle of conventional academic researchers" (p. 59).

Ethnographic Research Compared to Surveys

Data gathered via participant observation may be more valid than information collecting on self-report surveys people are paid to complete. Consider the question "What kinds of risks (if any) do street addicts take?" In their article describing HIV risk among homeless heroin addicts in San Francisco, Bourgois, Lettiere, and Quesada (2003) argue that ethnographic methods in which people spend time on the street, with addicts, provide more accurate information than does information gathered through a survey. "Virtually all our network members have told us that they distort their risky behavior on questionnaires" (p. 270). They argue that ethnographic research in which one spends time with those studied provides a fuller understanding of what actually occurs and the possible reasons for this.

Qualitative research may have intervention implications. "The challenge is not merely to access, document and explain

the dynamics of every day suffering; but also to translate it into meaningful interventions that do not unconsciously reproduce structures of inequality and discourses of subordination" (Bourgois, Lettiere, & Quesada, 2003, p. 272). This example illustrates different methodologies used to gather descriptive data. The question is: What kind of qualitative research will provide the most accurate answer to questions of interest? Campbell (1996) agrees with Becker about over-stretching quantitative research.

He stresses that those whose scientific evidence is mean differences and correlations on quantified questionnaire items go on to interpret them in terms of the meanings and actions of respondents. Not only are these interpretations very often wrong, they could have been made right by participant observation. Quantitative data often represents low-cost, mass-produced research and is often wrong. The others' meanings as inferred from questionnaire averages are overly determined by the ethnocentric subjectivity of the researcher. (p. 161)

Campbell (1996) notes that "questionnaires, fixed interviews, and experimental designs limit the dimensions of inquiry in advance. Often this precludes learning information that would have discredited the validity of the quantitative results and the hypotheses that guided the research" (p. 162). Becker suggests that the very methods of the field workers, if conducted properly, are designed to ferret out biases and expectations of the field workers themselves through constantly checking assumptions and by using varied methodologies, for example, interviews and observation. Field workers are coached to always be ready and take advantage of the unexpected. Campbell considers the "most ubiquitous source of error in efforts to know the other" to be "to interpret as a cultural difference what is in reality a failure of communication....I personally am convinced that many of the cultural differences reported by psychologists and others using questionnaires or tests come from failures of communication misreported as differences" (p. 165). One of the most insightful discussions of the differences and commonalities in epistemology and methods between qualitative and quantitative research can be found in *Ethnography and Human Development*, edited by Jessor, Colby, and Shweder (1996). A checklist for critically appraising a qualitative research report is shown below (see other sources for additional descriptions of qualitative research methods):

1. Did the article describe an important clinical problem examined via a clear question?

2. Was the qualitative approach appropriate?

3. How were the setting and the subjects selected?

4. What was the researcher's perspective and has this been taken into account?

5. What methods did the researcher use for collecting data; are these described in enough detail?

6. What methods did the researcher use to analyze the data—and what quality control measures were used?

7. Are the results credible, and, if so, are they clinically important?

8. What conclusions were drawn, and are they justified by the results?

9. Are the findings of the study transferable to other clinical settings? (Greenhalgh, 2010, p. 227)

Questions About Diagnosis and Screening

Social workers provide most of the mental health services in the United States today. They are required to use psychiatric classifications in their work using the DSM. If they work in health care, they may have to understand a variety of medical diagnoses that apply to their clients in order to understand related prognoses. Tests are used for many purposes, such as to make a diagnosis. It is important to learn how to critically appraise related research. Otherwise you may impose bogus labels on your clients, scare people about irrelevant risks, and overlook important risks or protective factors. You may make avoidable faulty predictions based on avoidable misestimates of protective and risk factors. The professional literature describes scores of tests. The key question here is: Can a test accurately detect a certain condition or characteristic, such as depression, in an elderly client?

Diagnostic tests are used on symptomatic clients, screening tests are used on asymptomatic clients. Tests may be used to predict future behavior. They should be used to revise subjective estimates that is, to change a decision. Clinicians tend to overestimate the predictive accuracy of test results. One cause of this error is ignoring base-rate data (see chapter 20). The predictive accuracy of a test depends on the initial risk of a condition in the person receiving the test. The probability that a client with a positive (or negative) test result for dementia actually has dementia depends on the prevalence of dementia in the population from which the client was selected—that is, on the pretest probability that a client has dementia. Because there is little appreciation of this point, predictive accuracy often is overestimated.

Tests may provide helpful guidelines or be misleading—appear to inform but do the opposite, perhaps harm rather than help clients. Consider the reflex dilation test. In Britain, Hobbs and Wynne (1989) (two pediatricians) suggested that a simple medical test could be used to demonstrate that buggery or other forms of anal penetration had occurred. Because of this test many children were removed from their homes on the grounds that they were being sexually abused. Questions that should have been asked to critically appraise this test are noted next.

Critically Appraising Reports of Diagnostic Accuracy

Like investigations of the effectiveness of an intervention, a variety of biases, as well as incomplete reporting of how a test was developed and tested, can lead to problems in interpreting accuracy. And there always are challenges. For example, classification is involved in testing—placing people into categories. Surprisingly few reference standards are clear for making unequivocal classifications. The best type of evidence in relation to how test results relate to benefits of intervention is a randomized controlled trial. If these are not available, cohort studies may provide information. Bossuyt, Reitsma, Bruns, Gatsonis, Glasziou, Irwig, et al. (2003) includes a checklist and flow chart that can be used to estimate bias in a diagnostic study and to judge the usefulness of findings. Greenhalgh (2010) suggests the following points for critically appraising related articles:

1. The test is potentially relevant to my practice.

2. The test has been compared with a true gold standard.

3. The validation study included an appropriate spectrum of clients.

4. Work up bias was avoided.

5. Observer bias has been avoided.

6. The test has been shown to be reproducible both within and between observers.

7. The features of the test as derived from this validation study are described.

8. Confidence intervals are given for sensitivity, specificity, and other features of the test.

9. A sensible "normal range" has been derived from those results.

10. The test has been placed in the context of other potential tests in the assessment sequence for the problem. (p. 225)

These points were not considered in reviewing the accuracy of the reflex dilation test. As a result, many people were harmed. The false positive rate was not reported (the percentage of persons inaccurately identified as having a characteristic). Nor was the false negative rate reported (the percentage of persons inaccurately identified as not having a characteristic). Nor was sensitivity and specificity reported. Key concepts in reviewing the validity of tests include the following: These concepts can be illustrated by a four-cell contingency table (see Exhibit 11.8).

- *Sensitivity*: among those known to have a problem, the proportion whom a test or measure indicates as having the problem.

EXHIBIT 11.8

Definitions and Calculation for a Perfect ("Gold Standard") Diagnostic Test. Definitions of Sensitivity, Specificity, Predictive Values, and Posttest Disorder Probability

Test	Disorder Present	Disorder Absent	Total
Test Positive	A	B	A + B
Test Negative	C	D	C + D
Total	A + C	B + D	N = (A + B + C + D)

Definitions
Sensitivity: A/(A + C)
Specificity: D/(D + B)
False-negative rate: C/(C + A)
False-positive rate: B/(B + D)
Positive predictive value: A/(A + B)
Negative predictive value: D/(C + D)
Pretest disease probability: (A + C)/(A + B + C + D)
Posttest disease probability, positive results: A/A + C)
Posttest disease probability, negative result: (C/C + D)

	Disorder Present	Disorder Absent	Total
Test Positive	100	0	100
Test Negative	0	100	100
Total	100	100	200

Calculations
Sensitivity: 100/(100 + 0) = 100%
Specificity: 100/(100 + 0) = 100%
Positive predictive value: 100%
Posttest disease probability negative test: 0%

Source: J. G. Elmore & E. J. Boyko (2000). Assessing the accuracy of diagnostic and screening tests. In J. P. Geyman, R. A. Deyo, & S. D. Ramsey (Eds.), *Evidence-based clinical practice: Concepts and approaches* (p. 85). Boston: Butterworth Heinemann. Reprinted with permission.

- *Specificity*: among those known not to have a problem, the proportion whom the test or measure indicates as not having the problem.

- *Pretest probability (prevalence)*: The probability that an individual has the disorder before the test is carried out.

- *Post-test probability*: The probability that an individual with a specific test result has the target condition (posttest odds/[1 + posttest odds).

- *Pretest odds*: The odds that an individual has the disorder before the test is carried out (pretest probability/[1—pretest probability]).

- *Posttest odds*: The odds that a client has the disorder after being tested (pretest odds × LR).

- *Positive predictive value (PPV)*: The proportion of individuals with positive test results who have the target condition.

- *Negative predictive value (NPV)*: The proportion of individuals with negative test results who do not have the target condition.

- *Likelihood ratio*: Measure of a test result's ability to modify pretest probabilities. Likelihood ratios indicate how many times more likely a test result is in a client with a disorder compared with a person free of the disorder. A likelihood ratio of 1 indicates that a test is totally uninformative.

- *Likelihood ratio of a positive test result (LR +)*: The ratio of the true positive rate to the false positive rate: sensitivity/(1—specificity).

- *Likelihood ratio of a negative test result (LR –)*: The ratio of the false negative to the true negative rate: (1—sensitivity)/specificity. (Adapted from Pewsner et al., 2004)

Only if a test increases accuracy of understanding should it be used. Often in social work, psychology, and psychiatry, there is no gold standard against which to compare a test (see related discussion in chapter 12). An example of a "gold standard" is reviewing an X-ray to detect pneumonia when someone has a bad cough.

Screening

Screening is a key public health strategy that has been broadened to concerns such as depression and anxiety. The New Freedom in Mental Health Commission (2004) recommends universal screening for mental health. The benefits of screening should outweigh any harms. Requirements for a screening program include the following:

- The benefit of testing outweighs the harm.

- The problem is serious with a high burden of suffering.

- The natural history of the problem is understood.

- The problem occurs frequently.

- Effective treatment exists, and early treatment is more effective than late treatment.

- The test is easy to administer.

- The test is inexpensive.

- The test is safe.

- The test is acceptable to participants.

- The sensitivity, specificity, and other operating characteristics of the test are acceptable. (e.g., see Gray, 2001a)

Questions Concerning Prognosis, Risk, and Protective Factors (Prediction)

Both prognosis and risk project into the future; related tests attempt to predict events in the future. Depending on a diagnosis (for example, of depression) one has a certain prognosis, which in turn is related to certain protective and risk factors. Risk assessment is of interest in a number of areas including suicide and violent acts, such as domestic and child abuse. Thousands of children are on "at risk" registers on the assumption that they are at continuing risk of abuse. Child welfare workers make predictions about future risk of abuse. Thus, both prognosis and prediction look into the future, and as with all such looks, there will be errors. Errors in earlier stages (e.g., assessment) may result in errors at later stages (selection of service plans). Examples of questions here are:

- In elderly, frail clients living alone, what is the risk of hip fracture?

- In young children abused by their parents, what is the risk of future abuse?

- In young adults who have unprotected sexual intercourse with multiple partners, what is the risk of developing AIDS?

Prognostic studies include clinical studies of variables that predict future events, as well as epidemiological studies of risk factors. This information may provide a guide for choice of services. In ecological (aggregate) studies, secondary data are often used to identify associations in a population between risk factors and outcomes, such as a certain illness. Generalization from aggregate data to individuals is problematic because of the ecological fallacy (assuming what is true for a group is true for an individual). Considerable attention has been devoted to trying to identify risks and protective factors related to antisocial behavior of children and health concerns (e.g., Jensen & Fraser, 2011). Actuarial methods using the results of empirical investigations of the relationships between certain characteristics and an outcome have been found to be superior to intuitive methods for making accurate predictions in a number of areas (e.g., see Hilton, Harris, & Rice, 2006). Both cohort and case control studies have been used to try to identify and quantify risk factors. Problems in trying to describe risk include naturally occurring fluctuation of risks. Protective as well as risk factors are of importance in prevention.

Critically Appraising Related Research

Guyatt and Rennie (2002) suggest the following questions:

- *Are the results valid?*

- Was the sample of clients representative?

- Were the clients sufficiently homogeneous with respect to prognostic risk?

- Was follow-up sufficiently complete?

- Were objective and unbiased outcome criteria used?

- *What are the results?*

- How likely are the outcomes over time?

- How precise are the estimates of likelihood?

- *How can I apply the results to client care?*

- Were the study clients and their management similar to those in my work?

- Was the follow-up sufficiently long?

- Can I use the results in my setting?

Both absolute and relative risks should be given. The latter sound impressive in relation to risk reduction compared to absolute risk reduction and are misleading.

Questions about Practice Guidelines

Many sources purport to describe practice guidelines. Indeed, this term has become a buzzword, together with terms such as "best practice," "empirically validated methods," and "evidence-based practice." Criteria used to decide whether a guideline should be used differ. The American Psychological Association Task Force on Psychological Intervention Guidelines (1995) recommends that if two randomized controlled trials show the effectiveness of an intervention, then this method has been established as valid. Notice the justificatory nature of such a claim (certainty is suggested by the term "established") when two randomized controlled trials, even though well designed, cannot certainty make (see chapter 4). The next two trials may show different results. Some interpret EBP to consist of using practice guidelines.

Questions to Ask When Reviewing Practice Guidelines

Inflated claims are common regarding the effectiveness of practice guidelines (Grilli et al., 2000). Thus, it is important to learn how to evaluate their quality. A key question is "Is the guideline valid?" "Has it been rigorously tested regarding effects?" "Has its *effectiveness* been tested, not just its *efficacy*—that is, has it been tested in real-world circumstances (e.g., clinics) in addition to research-based hospitals?" Questions that arise here include the following:

1. Were all important decisions, options, and outcomes clearly described? For example, has a well-tested alternative, such as the use of contingency management, been ignored for altering behavior of children labeled ADHD?

2. Is there a rigorous effort to identify and locate all related research? Were studies located and appraised using rigorous criteria?

3. Are the benefits and risks clearly described, as well as costs for each outcome of interest, including the views of different stake holders? (Lawrie, McIntosh, & Rao, 2000).

4. Does the guideline apply to your clients?

Greenhalgh (2010) suggests also inquiring whether the preparation and publication of the guidelines involved a significant conflict of interest.

Lawrie, McIntosh, and Rao (2000) suggest the following questions in reviewing the potential usefulness of a clinical guideline: (1) Is the guideline valid? (2) Is it important? and (3) Can I use it in helping my clients? Questions suggested under number (2) include: (1) Is there currently a large variation in clinical practice? (2) Does the guideline contain new evidence or old research findings that are not acted on (p. 168)? and (3) Would use of a guideline have major effects on outcomes? Questions that arise regarding whether a guideline can be used with a particular client include: (1) Are there barriers to implementation? Can I enlist the cooperation of colleagues? and (2) Can I meet the "educational, administrative, and economic conditions necessary for implementation of the guidelines?" (p. 170). As Gray (2001a) emphasizes, the experts regarding application barriers are staff and clients. They are in a position to identify, and indeed reflect in their behaviors, application barriers, such as beliefs about what methods are effective. Although the *efficacy* of a method may be tested under ideal conditions, this same program may not achieve the same results when used in real-life settings (when its *effectiveness* is tested).

Controversial Issues

It is generally agreed that there is no certainty in science. It is also generally agreed that some tests are more rigorous than others. In the presence of such agreement, people still differ in the certainty with which they make claims, based on given kinds of research. There are differences of opinion about how critical appraisal of different questions should proceed even within a particular research tradition (e.g., Becker, 1996). Baer (1982) argues that marker variable research (e.g., correlational research) is often continued when it is time to conduct more rigorous experimental tests, such as RCTs, where possible and relevant. Ethical and application issues will suggest criteria of importance.

The Relationship Between Research Methods Used and Views of Knowledge

The research design used to explore a question reflects the researchers' views about knowledge and how it can be gained and/or their ethical views about being honest brokers of knowledge and ignorance. If they make inflated claims, this suggests one of a variety of possibilities: (1) they are uninformed about the limitations of the research design in critically testing a question; (2) they are aware of this, but do not care; or (3) they care but need a publication. Ioannidis (2005) argues that most published research findings are false. Claims may be inflated in a number of ways—claims of effectiveness or claims of no effectiveness. And, just because a program has been found to be effective or ineffective in critical tests does not warrant claims of certainty. Also, other criteria come into play in addition to evidentiary status, such as importance of outcomes attained to clients and transferability of research findings.

Obstacles

Obstacles to acquiring skills in critically appraising research and using these to enhance the quality of services occur in all professional venues including educational programs, published literature, and agencies. They include both personal and environmental obstacles. Research courses are given separately from practice courses in most professional education programs. This discourages integration of practice and research skills. This is not the case with problem-based learning now used in many medical schools (e.g., Straus et al., 2005). Agencies may discourage evidence-based services and purchasing and not provide needed training and tools, such as relevant educational programs and access to needed databases. Exploration of how to address application problems is an active area of research with many exciting developments, such as involving clients as informed participants in making decisions (see Coulter, 2002, 2006; Coulter & Collins, 2011).

Summary

Different kinds of practice and policy questions require different kinds of research methods to critically test them. Different kinds of research have different goals. Some questions are exploratory and descriptive. Their intent is to describe the relationships among different variables. A question may be: "What is the relationship between certain characteristics of a helper (e.g., warmth) and outcome?" Another question may be: "What are characteristics of single parents on welfare who succeed in getting a job and getting off welfare, compared to people who do not?" Some kinds of research involve testing a hypothesis. Their aim is to identify causal relationships among variables in a rigorous manner. Research methods differ in the degree to which they control for bias. A key concern is the match between a question and the likelihood that the method used to test it can do

so. Currently, literature in the helping professions abounds with poor matches.

Evidence-informed practice encourages attention to the limitations of research designs. Keep in mind that one of the key reasons for the origin of EBP was a concern about flaws in published research, such as inflated claims of knowledge (see chapter 9). Bogus claims are problematic in a profession in which clients are affected by beliefs in such claims that may result in use of ineffective or harmful methods. A variety of tools and enterprises, such as the Cochrane and Campbell collaborations, have been developed to replace bogus claims with measured ones. These include user-friendly checklists for critically appraising the quality of different kinds of research.

Reviewing your Competencies

Reviewing Content Knowledge

1. You can accurately describe what kind of research design matches different kinds of questions.

2. You can explain concepts such as intention to treat analysis, sensitivity, and specificity.

Reviewing What You Do

1. You accurately appraise different kinds of research reports.

2. You effectively use statistical tools, such as the number needed to treat and likelihood ratio.

Reviewing Results

1. You accurately describe the evidentiary status of recommended services and alternatives to your clients.

2. You offer or refer clients to services most likely to help them to achieve outcomes they value.

Part 5

Getting Started

12

A Contextual Assessment Framework

OVERVIEW The chapter describes guidelines for clarifying client concerns and hoped-for outcomes and identifying related factors. A detailed guide is described in chapter 13, and additional guidelines for assessing families, group, organizations, and communities can be found in chapters 26 and 27. Assessment knowledge and skills should contribute to provision of valuable services and, if you are a case manager and coordinate services provided by others, help you to select those most likely to help your clients. A multilevel contingency analysis informed by related research findings may be needed to understand client concerns. Such an analysis is typically not carried out. An example would be simply prescribing Ritalin to a difficult to manage child rather than exploring related environmental circumstances and altering them when indicated. Reasons include lack of time in a resource-scarce climate, as well as lack of required knowledge and skills, for example, in discovering competing alternative repertoires. Such obstacles have ethical implications that require exposure.

YOU WILL LEARN ABOUT

- What is involved

- Kinds of questions

- What is at stake

- The difference between diagnosis and assessment

- Thinking critically about labels

- Making assessment of value to clients

- Characteristics of a contextual assessment framework

- Important distinctions

- Sources of influence that should be reviewed

- Ethical issues

What Is Involved

Assessment lays the groundwork for selecting plans. It should indicate how likely it is that hoped-for outcomes can be attained.

The likelihood may be slim when needed resources are not available or when related circumstances cannot be arranged. This phase is an ongoing process in which assumptions are altered as needed in response to new information, such as degree of progress. Assessment should suggest "leverage points" for pursuing valued outcomes. It should suggest: (1) objectives that if attained would resolve problems, (2) how they can be pursued most effectively, and (3) the probability of attaining them, given current resources and options. Interrelated goals (sometimes referred to as "case formulation") include: (1) identifying hoped-for outcomes, (2) detecting related characteristics of clients and their environments, and (3) interpreting and integrating the data collected. This lays the groundwork for selecting intervention plans.

A key part of assessment is making the invisible visible. Consider a child who has temper tantrums. Related behaviors, such as screaming, throwing objects, and hitting, are visible. What is not visible is the environmental history in which such behaviors developed. Reactions of teachers and parents who reinforce hitting, screaming, and throwing objects and fail to provide positive feedback for desired behaviors are not as vivid. Consider also the following examples:

- Mrs. Rivera, a client of the Sumner Mental Health Clinic, is depressed. How can I discover what factors may be related to this?

- Ralph, a 17-year-old foster child, will soon be emancipated from care and needs to find a job. How can I determine the adequacy of his job-seeking skills?

- The Riverdale Community Center has acquired money to improve the quality of their neighborhoods. How can residents determine how to use this money most effectively?

Critically Appraising Assessment Frameworks and Methods

Assessment frameworks differ in what is focused on and in the degree to which they can be and have been critically tested. They differ in how compatible they are with empirical data regarding how behavior develops, changes, and is maintained, and how successful they have been in attaining hoped-for outcomes. History suggests that some approaches are more successful than others. For example, trying to assess people by examining the bumps on their head was not very fruitful; however, for decades many people believed it was useful (Gamwell & Tomes, 1995; McCoy, 2000). Assessment frameworks differ in their vulnerability to certain kinds of errors. Some focus on describing what is wrong with people (e.g., giving clients psychiatric diagnoses). Approaches that focus on alleged pathologies of clients (eliminative approaches) may result in overlooking valuable resources including client assets. Such approaches can be contrasted with a contextual-constructional approach that includes attention to

client characteristics and circumstances including alternative behaviors that compete successfully with undesired ones, environmental resources such as sources of social support, and policies and related legislation that influence resources available such as health care and financial aid. The contextual model described in this chapter is a constructional one. Rather than focusing on deficiencies, there is an interest in identifying valued repertoires that clients can use to attain hoped-for outcomes. Such an assessment encourages a contextual understanding of concerns and potential for resolution. There is an interest in the use of and construction of repertoires that enhance the quality of clients' lives rather than in eliminating behavior (Layng, 2009). This kind of analysis is often ignored in practice. (See Exhibit 12.1).

EXHIBIT 12.1

Contextual Assessment: Honored in Words and Ignored in Practice

Concerns found by Alessi almost a quarter of a century ago are in even greater evidence today as biopsychiatric framing and disease mongering (see chapter 6) has become ever more popular propelled by pharmaceutical companies and biopsychiatry. Alessi (1988) noted that behavior and learning problems in school may be associated with one or more of five broad areas: (1) the child may be misplaced in the curriculum or the curriculum may contain faulty teaching routines; (2) the teacher may not be using effective teaching and/or behavior management practices; (3) the principal and other school administrators may not be using effective school management practices; (4) the parents may not be providing the home-based support necessary for effective learning; and (5) the child may have physical and/or psychological problems that may be contributing to the learning problems (see Alessi, 1988, for supporting references).

To find out whether school psychologists consider these multiple influences, Alessi asked several groups of school psychologists (about 50 in each), in different areas of the country, whether they agreed that each of these five factors played a primary role in a given school learning or behavior problem. They almost always agreed. He then asked for the number of cases each psychologist had examined in the past year to determine the source of learning problems. The answer was about 120. Rounding this to 100 and multiplying by 50 yielded about 5,000 cases studied by the group in the past year. Next, Alessi asked how many of their psychological reports concluded that the referred problem was due primarily to one of these factors. For curriculum factors, inappropriate teaching practices, and school administrative factors, the answer was none. For the parent and home factors, the answer ranged from 500 to 1,000 (10 to 20%). When he asked how many of their reports concluded that child factors were primarily responsible for the referred problem, the answer was 100%.

Assessment frameworks are more likely to be useful if they take advantage of knowledge about factors related to behaviors of concern and related circumstances and the accuracy of different kinds of data. (See Exhibit 12.2.) They should be instrumental, that is, help clients achieve hoped-for outcomes. It is not very useful to carry out an assessment that offers few, if any, guidelines for discovering options for helping clients. If factors related to concerns are not identified, plans may be misdirected and clients harmed rather than helped, for example, referred unnecessarily to a psychiatrist who medicates a client. Focusing solely on personal characteristics may result in psychologizing rather than helping clients. Focusing solely on environmental characteristics may result in overlooking relevant individual characteristics.

Key implications of evidence-based practice for assessment include: (1) drawing on relevant research, for example, about related factors; (2) selecting assessment frameworks that reflect research findings regarding outcomes of interest; (3) using reliable, valid assessment measures including those designed to assess risk; (4) avoiding common errors in collecting and integrating data; and (5) involving clients as informed participants and considering their values and preferences. Evidence-informed assessment calls for asking questions such as:

- What assumptions am I making? Can I provide a sound argument for them, for example, demonstrate compatibility with research findings regarding behaviors of concern?

- Are there well-argued alternative views?

- Have I relied on accurate sources of information? Are assessment measures valid? Do they measure what they purport to measure? Do they apply to my client?

- Are measures used reliable? Do they provide consistent data by the same person at different times and over different practitioners?

- Are norms available for assessment measures that involve people like my clients?

- Does my assessment provide clear guidelines for selecting service plans? Is it helpful in estimating the probability of attaining hoped-for outcomes?

- Have I avoided common errors such as searching only for data that confirm my preferred views

- Have I considered my clients' values and preferences, as well as those of their significant others (those who interact with and influence clients)?

- Is there evidence that assessment methods do more good than harm?

Concerns about the evidentiary status of assessment frameworks and tools are illustrated by the following examples:

- Genograms are commonly used and claimed to be of value in assessment in spite of a lack of rigorous appraisal of claims.

- The Rorschach Ink Blot Test is used in spite of a lack of evidence for its validity (Hunsley, Lee, & Wood, 2003).

- Clients receive psychiatric labels based on the DSM-IV-R in spite of problematic reliability and validity of this classification system (see later discussion).

EXHIBIT 12.2

Content Knowledge of Potential Value in Assessment

Type of Information	Potential Value
1. Prevalence of a problem	1. Share this information with clients, normalize concerns, estimate the likelihood that a client has a concern, estimate benefits and harms of screening
2. Factors related to a complaint such as depression.	2. Provide guidelines for assessment and intervention
3. Reliability and validity of assessment measures including measures of risk	3. Make evidence-informed selection of measures
4. Beliefs of clients regarding problems and possible solutions	4. Allows determination of match between your views and the clients; permits support of promising views
5. Acceptability of different frameworks and methods to clients	5. Match views offered to client preferences
6. Evidentiary status of assessment frameworks	6. Allow informed selection of frameworks
7. Validity and reliability of diagnosis	7. Allow critical appraisal of diagnostic classification systems
8. Facilitating relationship factors	8. Maximize sharing and client engagement

- Counselors may create false memories (e.g., Ofshe & Watters, 1994).

- Practitioners often rely on self-report of clients and ignore other valuable sources of information such as observation in real-life contexts such as classrooms to check the accuracy of such reports (Budd, et al., 2001).

- Most practitioners do not know how to carry out a descriptive and functional analysis of behaviors of concern and related competing behaviors.

Critical appraisal of different assessment frameworks can help you to discover which views have been found to enhance the likelihood of helping clients, including decreasing avoidable social injustices such as not providing needed resources to a family caring for a relative with a disability. This example illustrates that assessment is not only a practical matter, it is also an ethical and political activity as Charles Cowger (1994) noted. Thinking critically about your beliefs about behavior and how (or if) it can be changed can help you to identify related assumptions, their possible consequences, and their evidentiary status (e.g., are they true?). It can help you to spot inflated claims disguised as scientific guidelines. (See discussion of propaganda in the helping professions in chapter 4.)

Assessment should indicate how likely it is that hoped-for outcomes can be attained. The possibility may be slim when needed resources are not available or when the environment cannot be rearranged. Initial assessment will point to areas requiring more detailed review. Assessment should indicate what factors influence options, make demands on clients, or create discomfort (see Exhibit 12.3). Consider a client who is said to neglect her child because of her heroin addiction. A contextual analysis requires information about the pattern of heroin use (assuming that the parent does use heroin and that this does interfere with her parenting), including high-risk situations (those in which she is likely to use heroin) and low-risk situations (those in which she is unlikely to use heroin). It also requires a clear description of "neglect" and related factors. Detailed information is needed about the mother's parenting skills and the personal and environmental factors that affect them (e.g., a belief in the value of severe physical punishment, an abusive partner, lack of money for needed medical services, and her alleged heroin use). What parenting skills does the mother possess? Which ones are absent? What factors interfere with the use of positive parenting skills? What cultural factors play a role? What environmental factors and policies are related to heroin use and the quality of parenting, such as legislation regarding fathers' obligations for contributing financially to the care of their children?

Helpers differ in their skill in avoiding misleading accounts. They differ in the quality of their interpersonal skills for placing clients at ease and involving them in the helping process. (See chapter 15.) Knowledge about the accuracy of assessment frameworks and measures can help you to select referral sources most likely to help clients and to evaluate data gathered by others. Evidence-informed selection of assessment methods maximizes opportunities for accurate understanding including discovery of alternative behaviors that can successfully compete with disturbing behaviors. This encourages you to build on client strengths and is one of the many positive features of a constructional approach to understanding and changing behavior. Observation in real-life settings may be required to clarify client concerns and to discover valuable client repertoires. This may reveal discrepancies between self-report data and what is observed. Here, as well as in other helping phases, specialized knowledge and critical thinking skills may be needed to appraise the accuracy of claims and to integrate diverse sources of information including findings from practice- and policy-related research and the unique circumstances and characteristics of a client, including cultural differences, for example, in problem-solving styles. Let us say a parent tells you that she knows how to use positive methods to discipline her child. How can you find out if this is accurate? Or, let us say that your supervisor asks you to use the Beck Depression Inventory to assess a client's complaint of depression. What information do you need to judge for yourself whether this measure is a good choice—Is it reliable and does it provide an accurate account of depression for this client?

Decisions

Decisions must be made about what data to collect as well as how to gather and organize it (see chapter 17). These decisions will be influenced by preferred practice theories, for example, cognitive-behavioral, family systems, interpersonal, radical behavioral, or psychoanalytic (e.g., see Payne, 2009).You will have to decide:

- What data will be most helpful in describing and understanding concerns?

- Where and how can I obtain the data?

- How will I decide when I have enough information?

- What should I do if I obtain contradictory data?

- What criteria should I use to check the accuracy of data?

- How can I avoid inaccurate and incomplete accounts?

- How can I communicate most effectively with clients to obtain needed information?

Let us say that you work in a college student counseling center and a 19-year-old young woman is referred to you because she is having trouble studying and is receiving failing grades. What information will be useful in helping her? Will you focus on her study habits? What are her grades? Have they changed recently? Did she want to attend college? Will you explore her "self-esteem"? Will you explore her current life circumstances, including financial resources, family responsibilities, and significant others? Will you consider cultural differences that may be related to her concerns? How will you identify strengths that can be supported and used to forward success, such as a desire to obtain a good education? How will you translate "trouble

EXHIBIT 12.3

Characteristics That May Be Related to a Problem at Different System Levels

Level 1: Individual

_____ Health
_____ Developmental Level
_____ Temperament
_____ Intelligence
_____ Problem-solving skills
_____ Social skills available
_____ Recreational skills
_____ Economic resources

_____ Vocational skills
_____ Self-management skills
_____ Reinforcer profile
_____ Acculturation level
_____ Cultural background
_____ Emotion management skills

Level 2: Family

_____ Problem-solving skills
_____ Family composition
_____ Income
_____ Cultural norms
_____ Interaction patterns

_____ Extended family network
_____ Living space
_____ Goals and values
_____ Cultural conflicts

Level 3: Neighborhood and Community

_____ Recreational opportunities
_____ Crime rate
_____ Educational resources
_____ Physical environment
_____ Kinds of stores
_____ Cultural norms

_____ Accessibility of services (e.g., medical, legal)
_____ Cultural diversity
_____ Social support available
_____ Transportation available
_____ Police presence

Level 4: Service System

_____ Kind of problem framing favored (see chapter 6).
_____ Interrelationships among agencies

_____ Eligibility requirements
_____ Favored intervention methods

Level 5: Political, Economic, and Social Influences and Related Policies and Legislation

_____ Cultural diversity
_____ Tolerance for violence
_____ Immigration policies
_____ Services funded
_____ For profit agencies
_____ Health disparities
_____ Options for influencing policy
_____ Public policies and related legislation.
_____ Global influences (e.g., wars, famines, international industries)

_____ Emphasis on consumerism
_____ Patterns of discrimination and oppression
_____ Expected gender roles
_____ Educational opportunities
_____ Media (e.g., diversity of points of view available)
_____ Surveillance patterns
_____ Level of corruption (e.g., parasitic enterprises which feed on productive businesses, Meblum, Moene, & Torvik, 2006).

studying" and "receiving failing grades" into specific outcomes that, if attained, will resolve her concerns?

What questions can you pose to locate valuable research? Where and how will you look for related research findings? How will you evaluate the quality of research you find? Perhaps the student has high anxiety in test situations. She may have poor time management skills or have little interest in the classes she is taking. She may try to study in distracting situations and so get little accomplished. You may find that the student is very motivated but has poor study skills. Here, you will have to identify specific study skills needed,

including time management skills, and then select relevant intervention methods. Search terms may include: "Students with poor study skills and failing grades and effectiveness and systematic review." If you find that the student has good study skills but is not motivated, this calls for further inquiry regarding possible reasons for lack of motivation such as a disinterest in particular subjects, a punishing teacher, and/or competing repertoires such as watching television or spending time on Facebook.

What knowledge and skills will you use to avoid misleading accounts? Your knowledge about behavior and how it is maintained and can be changed will influence what information you gather. A "gated" approach includes an initial screening using a valid indicator of the need for further assessment. Related screening tools are designed to identify the most severe level of a problem. For example, intake workers in child welfare agencies use risk assessment measures to identify high-risk children. Such a measure may divide children into low, medium, and high risk categories (e.g., see Johnson, 2011). Depending on the classification, further assessment is carried out and service provided as needed.

Kinds of Questions

Questions that arise in this phase concern description, assessment, and risk (see Exhibit 12.4). All three may arise with one client. Each can be translated into a well-formed question that facilitates a search for external research findings. Assessment is more likely to be useful if we take advantage of research related to information we need—for example, information about factors related to client concerns and the accuracy of different kinds of data. Many areas of research are of potential value in assessment as reflected in the kinds of questions that arise in this phase of helping. Consider a young single mother who is depressed. Information needed may include description (for depressed single adults living in poor neighborhoods, what factors have been

found to be related to depression?), assessment (for such adults, what is the most accurate measure of depression?), and risk (for someone like this client, what is the risk of a suicide attempt over the next 6 months?). Different questions call for a different kind of research to pursue answers as described in chapter 11. User friendly sources for additional detail include Greenhalgh (2010).

Description Questions

Social workers often seek descriptive information, such as challenges faced by youth transitioning out of foster care or by caregivers of frail elderly relatives. A question may be: Among caregivers of frail elderly relatives, what problems arise in offering care? Results of survey data, as well as qualitative research, may be of value. The need for critical analysis to understand complex phenomenon, such as the relationships between work and family life is illustrated by Hochschild's research (e.g., 2003). She argues that survey data describing attitudes toward work and family life do not "question the construction of the social worlds that shape how people feel about their families" (p. 202). She suggests that some researchers omit mention of what she views as "the symbiotic—even parasitic—relationship between work and family" (p. 202). She suggests that much of the literature describing the relation of work to family "is based on the unquestioned assumptions about what families and workplaces feel like and mean" (p. 202) and that we can only understand the work–family balance by considering the larger context. (See also Gilbert's (2008) critique of policies urging women to enter the workforce.)

Questions About Assessment Measures

Social workers use a variety of assessment measures (e.g., Corcoran & Fischer, 2009; Jordan & Franklin, 2010). Examples of an assessment question are: "In couples who have communication problems, what is the most accurate measure of related concerns?" "For youth transitioning out of foster care who need employment, what is the most accurate way to determine their employment skills?"

Questions About Risk/Prognosis

Over the past years, there has been great interest (many argue excessive) in identifying "alleged" risk factors for certain problems and conditions viewed as unhealthy or troubling. Indeed "at risk" categories are proposed for inclusion in DSM V, which some argue will result in many false positives—(people identified as having a risk who do not) (Frances, 2006, 2010). A large portion of public health endeavors is occupied with identifying risks of certain diseases and promoting strategies to minimize them such as screening programs. Professionals often attempt to estimate risk, for example, of future child maltreatment or of suicide. An example of a risk question is: "For children who have been physically abused by their parents, which risk assessment measure best predicts the likelihood of further abuse?" Another example is: "In elderly clients diagnosed with depression, what

---

EXHIBIT 12.4

Examples of Assessment Questions

Description
- In adolescents with anger management problems, what social skills do they often lack?
- In frail elderly adults, what are common needs?
- In 5-year-olds boys, what is the prevalence of enuresis?

Assessment
- In students with behavior management problems in the classroom, is classroom observation compared to teacher self-report more accurate?
- In foster care youth transitioning out of care, is a social skill self-report inventory or observation in role plays more accurate in identifying needed skills?

Risk
- In children who are prescribed antidepressants, what is the risk of a suicide attempt?
- In frail elderly people, what is the risk of falls in those who have incorrect vision corrections compared to those whose vision correction is correct?
- In children who have been physically abused by their parents, what is the risk of further abuse?

is the risk that they will make a suicide attempt in the next 6 months?"

What Is at Stake

Although decisions typically must be made on the basis of incomplete data, without a sound assessment, interviews may drift, opportunities to gather useful data may be lost, and assessment may be incomplete, resulting in selection of ineffective or harmful plans (see Exhibit 12.5). Clients may be referred to agencies that offer ineffective or harmful services. Here, as well as in other phases of helping clients, knowledge may be available regarding client concerns and related factors that will contribute to making sound decisions. Balancing benefits and harms related to a practice or policy will often require a subjective judgment based on a different kinds of evidence (see Exhibit 9.7). Not sharing uncertainties may hide the fact that decisions involve a value judgment about how to balance risks and harms. Many measures used by professionals are pseudoscientific; there is no evidence that they are accurate and do more good than harm; there is no evidence that they contribute to accurate assessment (see Thyer & Pignotti, 2010, in press, as well as chapter 17). If this is true, they waste money and time and may suggest misleading directions. Thus, it is important to critically appraise them.

- Does a risk assessment instrument accurately predict further likelihood of child abuse?

- Does an anxiety measure accurately identify clients with high levels of anxiety??

- Does a measure designed to assess the effects of traumatic life experiences accurately identify those who benefit from counseling?

Here too, as when making decisions regarding selection of service plans (see chapter 21), you should inquire about the evidentiary status of the method being considered in comparison with alternatives. Standardization in how a measure is administered and interpreted is important not just for scientific purposes but also to ensure the accuracy of a test. If we read a claim that a measure is reliable and valid, is this true and what kind of reliability and validity were assessed? (See chapter 17 for discussion of reliability and validity.) Are claims made about usefulness sound? We must be careful because limitations are often not candidly acknowledged. The assessment industry is huge with millions of dollars at stake (Gambrill, 2012a). Rarely will you find a statement such as the following: "We only examined interitem reliability (correlation among items). We do not know if the measure is stable over time. That is, we do not know whether a person who takes the inventory today, will get a different score 4 weeks from now in the absence of intervention." Unstable measures cannot accurately reflect change that may result from provision of services. Thus, if a measure is unstable, feedback from the test may be misleading. For example, it may be assumed that positive changes have occurred when there has been no change. Have the validity and reliability of a test been independently investigated or have only the creators of a test investigated its

---

EXHIBIT 12.5

An Example of Incomplete Assessment

John, a social work student, works in a crisis center. One of the clients to whom he provides ongoing services is a 46-year-old African American woman, Mrs. K., who lives in a "satellite" home for psychiatric patients. Her 12-year-old daughter lives with her in the home. Mrs. K. had what was called an "acute psychotic episode," which led to a short hospitalization and her current residence in the community care home. John decided to focus on decreasing Mrs. K's "sense of shame." No information was provided about what was happening in her life at the time of the "acute psychotic break" or what had been happening over the past 10 years; the whereabouts of her relatives (including her three other children); her assets, work, medical, and educational history; or a description of changes she wanted in her life. The student had never visited the home where she lived (and was not sure his supervisor would approve of such a visit), had never seen Mrs. K. and her daughter together, and had no contact with Mrs. K.'s other children.

Obtaining additional information revealed a fuller picture of this woman and her situation that called into question the focus on shame. Mrs. K., who was originally presented as a debilitated, problem-ridden psychiatric patient with few assets, was discovered to be a woman who had held a responsible job for 15 years. She was in good health, had many interpersonal skills, and enjoyed being around people. She loved her children and was concerned about creating a good environment for her youngest child, who lived with her. Her concerns were: improving her relationship with her youngest daughter, getting along better with the people in the community home, and decreasing negative thoughts about herself. Mrs. K. had many assets, including relatives with whom she could gain social support.

This example of incomplete assessment is not unusual; it is common even among second-year master's degree students with whom I have worked. Often, as in this case, premature closure results in selection of a negative outcome (decreasing shame) rather than a positive one (e.g., increasing enjoyable exchanges with others and locating suitable housing in the community).

reliability and validity? To what extent does a measure provide accurate information about clients in real-life situations? Responsibility for gathering such evidence falls not to those who raise questions regarding the accuracy of a measure, but to those who claim it is accurate.

Problems and Their Prospects

Problems differ in their prospects for resolution. These prospects are influenced by the accuracy of assessment. That is, client concerns may be framed in a way that facilitates or hinders discovery of options. A biopsychiatric approach focuses on identifying "disorders" of clients—what is "wrong with them." A constructional approach focuses on identifying client strengths and other resources useful in pursuit of hoped-for outcomes (Schwartz & Goldiamond, 1974, 1975; Layng, 2009). Prospects for resolution are influenced by resources available and obstacles including both personal and environmental. Identification of resources and obstacles is a key assessment task. Problems clients confront often arrive unwanted on their doorsteps such as removal of children by child protective workers.

Personal and social problems may have many causes that vary in complexity and are interlinked; unemployment is related to job openings. The social problems focused on in a society and their framing affect the kinds and prevalence of personal problems. Consider drug policies in the United States. The "war on drugs," which criminalizes sales and use of nonprescribed drugs, creates a billion-dollar addiction and criminal justice industry to address (mis)use of drugs and contributes to the multi-billion dollar pharmaceutical industry, which in turn creates problems of (mis)use of prescribed medications. The "war on drugs" has filled our jails with African American youth raised in neighborhoods with few mainstream opportunities resulting in arrest for selling and/or using drugs) (Wacquant, 2009). Portugal decriminalized all drugs in 2001 with a subsequent decrease in use and related negative events (Hughes & Stevens, 2010). Questions to ask include the following:

- How do current policies and related legislation affect options (e.g., eligibility requirements, discriminatory practices)?

- Are needed resources available such as staff who speak the client's language?

- Are contexts available that will facilitate change?

- What strengths do significant others and clients bring such as alternate positive behaviors?

- Are multiple concerns interlinked?

Characteristics of the client (for example, motivation to change, willingness to carry out agreed-on tasks), as well as characteristics of their environment (social support available), are related to outcome (Norcross, 2011). Significant others may have interfering beliefs or be threatened by proposed changes. A problem may be linked to other areas that must be addressed, such as a lack of vocational skills. A grandparent may visit a family and reinforce a child's annoying behavior. Staff may complain about the "dependency" of residents, not realizing that they themselves encourage and maintain dependent behaviors. They may oppose a plan in which independent behaviors will be reinforced, viewing this as bribery. Attempts to resolve concerns may create more problems. Distinguishing between problems and efforts to resolve them will help you and your clients to avoid confusing the results of attempted solutions and the effects of the original concern (Watzlawick, Weakland, & Fisch, 1974).

Limited resources (such as day care, legal and health care, job training programs, housing, recreational centers, high quality educational programs, parent training programs) and limited influence over environmental circumstances often pose an obstacle. For example, you may have little influence over teachers who do not know how to plan effective curricula or encourage valued behaviors using positive methods. Discriminatory police practices in ghettoes pose an ever-present danger to African American young men (Alexander, 2010; Wacquant, 2009). Expected role behaviors may limit change. For example, a father may view child-rearing as his wife's responsibility. You may have little influence over inadequate housing or access to crack cocaine that contributes to a parent's neglect of a child. Agency policies and practices and the physical characteristics of the environment affect client options. Lack of coordination of services may limit access to needed resources. Clients may receive fragmentary, overlapping, or incompatible services. Policies and related legislation and its implementation (or lack thereof) influence options (e.g., services provided to immigrants).

Problem Solving or Strength Enhancing: A Dysfunctional Either/oring

Either/oring (considering only two options) is a common informal fallacy in which we often get caught. An example is: "Should I send this child to a group home or to residential care?"—when there are other possibilities. "Problem-based" or "strength-based" is another dysfunctional example. Everyone has problems (some sought, some not) and everyone should take advantage of personal and environmental resources to address them. Indeed, we seek and create problems and risks on an everyday basis, for example, in our search for entertainment such as sky driving and car racing. Artists and researchers thrive on solving problems. Solving problems involves seeking solutions. What social worker would be so callous as to ignore problems clients confront such as institutional racism, gender discrimination, lack of access to needed health care, lack of housing, or maltreatment of children or elders. Consider the 4-year-old who weighed 18 pounds at her death in March of 2011 (Kleinfield & Secret, 2011). She was bound to her bed everyday as witnessed by her grandmother. Her child welfare worker forged records to attempt to show that he had visited more often than he had. This sad situation illustrates problems at multiple levels requiring solutions. Social workers confront problems every day (e.g., "What should I do about lack of effective parent-training programs in our area?"). There is a rich literature in every field devoted to helping people solve problems. We can draw on this to help clients. We use resources, both personal and environmental, to pursue hoped-for outcomes.

Common Errors

An accurate assessment avoids incomplete causal accounts that may result in focusing on irrelevant outcomes or choosing ineffective or harm-inducing (iatrogenic) plans. Collecting irrelevant data wastes time and money and increases the likelihood that you and your clients will be misled by such material. Assessment frameworks differ in their vulnerability to certain kinds of errors. Approaches that focus on alleged pathologies of clients may result in overlooking valuable client strengths, such as caregiving skills. Such approaches can be contrasted with a constructional approach (Schwartz & Goldiamond, 1975). Unexplained speculation may result in incomplete views of client concerns. Examples of incomplete assessment include the following:

- Hoped-for outcomes are not identified.

- Behaviors of concern are not clearly described including positive alternatives to undesired behaviors.

- There is a focus on pathology rather than a search for and support of client strengths.

- Cultural factors are overlooked.

- The functions of behaviors of interest are unknown (e.g., related environmental consequences, such as reactions by significant others are not identified).

- Related setting events and antecedents are not identified.

- Baseline data are not available (e.g., description of the frequency rate of behaviors, thoughts, or feelings prior to intervention).

- Related physical characteristics of the environment are overlooked.

- Higher-level contingencies are overlooked, such as loss of financial aid.

Inaccurate or incomplete accounts may occur because attention is too narrowly focused on one source (e.g., thoughts). Important environmental contingencies may be overlooked. Objectives may be selected prematurely. Sources of error that result in inaccurate or incomplete views include:

- Vague descriptions of hoped-for outcomes

- Focusing on pathology and overlooking client positive alternative repertoires (assets)

- Confusing the form and function of behavior

- Hasty assumptions about causes

- Failure to search for alternative accounts

- Ignoring practice-related research findings

- Speculating when data collection is called for (e.g., observation in real-life settings)

- Using uninformative labels

- Confusing motivational and behavior deficits

- Collecting irrelevant material

- Relying on inaccurate sources of data

- Being misled by first impressions

- Being misled by the client's superficial resemblance to another client

- Overlooking important cultural differences

Focus on collecting information that decreases uncertainty about how to attain outcomes clients value (or if they can be attained). Hasty, incomplete assessment may result in selecting outcomes that are not of concern to clients or do not address circumstances that must be altered to attain desired outcomes. You may accept an incomplete account because you attribute behaviors of concern to other behaviors. A teacher may attribute poor academic performance to low self-esteem because a student often "puts herself down" (has a high frequency of negative self-statements). This assessment is incomplete. Factors related to both self-esteem and negative thoughts (such as past history of punishment in schools and current punishing consequences provided by teachers) have not been identified. (For a critique of self-esteem as a causal account, see Baumeister et al., 2003). The fundamental attribution error is made when behavior is attributed to characteristics of the individual, overlooking environmental causes.

Assessment may reveal that change efforts should focus on significant others who maintain undesired behaviors by reinforcing them and by failing to reinforce valued behaviors. Understanding their role may call for a restructuring of how a concern is defined. Rather than depression and drinking, resulting in marital discord, the association may be the reverse. That is, marital discord may result in depression and drinking.

What About Person-Environment Fit?

The concept of person-environment fit has been suggested as a key one in social work. Problems are viewed as mismatches between environmental and personal characteristics. Examples include lack of a ramp allowing persons in wheelchairs to enter buildings and lack of information needed by clients to obtain food stamps. Indeed the environment, rather than the client, may require change. Thus, although there may appear to be a "fit," pursuit of changes may benefit clients. Consider an elderly person living alone who tells a social worker that she is satisfied with the few social contacts she has. This person may have adapted to (learned to be happy with) few social contacts but would be happier if she had more. Our ability to do well in many different environments is suggested by the fact that income level is not necessarily correlated with happiness (Diener & Seligman, 2004). Rachlin (1980) suggests that we feel happiness and sadness when we move from one level of reinforcement to another and, that when we "get used to" a new level, we may be as happy as we were with a richer one.

The Difference Between Diagnosis and Assessment

The term *diagnosis* was borrowed from medicine, in which a physician makes a diagnosis and then recommends a treatment based on this diagnosis. A staff member in a mental hospital may say that "Mr. Smith tries to hit staff and spits on them." When asked for an explanation, he may say, "Mr. Smith is psychotic." Observed behavior is used as a sign of more important underlying processes, typically of a pathological nature. Assessment differs from diagnosis in a number of ways. An evidence-informed contextual assessment includes a clear description of behaviors of concern and related factors and a description of what a person can do and cannot do, what he or she can learn to do, and what is expected of him or her, as well as environmental factors that influence behaviors. (See Exhibit 12.6.) Research regarding problems and possible causes and ways to discover them are drawn on. This kind of assessment often reveals that environmental factors contribute to problems (e.g., a lack of recreational opportunities, an abusive partner, lack of day care, low wages). Assessment encourages the description of processes rather than the study of conditions. For example, rather than describing a client as anxious, assessment requires the description of the contexts in which the anxiety occurs and the patterns of related behaviors, thoughts, and feelings. "A fitting metaphor is the motion picture rather than the still photograph" (Peterson, 1987, p. 30). Behaviors including thoughts are not used as signs of something more significant but as important in their own right.

Assessment requires a clear description of relevant behaviors and their consequences including positive alternative behaviors. These alternative positive repertoires can be used to attain valued consequences such as attention. Focusing on the adaptive value of behavior in specific circumstances encourages understanding the meaning of seemingly unusual, even bizarre reactions including hallucinations (e.g., Goldiamond, 1974; Layng & Andronis, 1984). (See later description of a contextual assessment.) Trait labels such as aggressive personality do not offer information about what people do in specific situations, what

occasions cue their behavior, and what reinforces it. Attributing the cause of behaviors of concern to character traits ("She's just lazy") or to thoughts or feelings increases the likelihood of "pseudoexplanations" (circular explanations that are not helpful). For example, a parent may describe a child as "lazy" referring to the fact that she does not complete her homework. When asked, "Why doesn't she complete her homework?" the parents may say, "She is lazy." Nothing new is added. Clients are often assigned a diagnosis as a requirement for third-party reimbursement. Providing a diagnosis does not and should not preclude a contextual assessment. One danger is believing there is no need for an assessment because a label has been given.

Thinking Critically About Labels

Labels are classifications and thus can suffer from all the ways in which classifications are wrong such as over or under inclusion. Clients may be given an incorrect label (it does not really describe them), or a label that does accurately describe them may not be used and valuable services may be withheld. (See discussion of false positives and false negatives in chapter 20.) Social workers use labels in two main ways. One is as a shorthand term to refer to a cluster of specific behaviors. The term *unmanageable* may refer to the fact that a student often gets out of his seat and talks out of turn in class. Labels are also used as diagnostic categories assumed to indicate the cause of problems and to suggest remedies. Here, labels are used to refer to (mis)behaviors, thoughts, and/or feelings thought to reflect an underlying disorder ("mental illness") such as "social anxiety disorder." Such terms are useful only if they do more good than harm, for example suggest causes and point to promising intervention options (or their lack). A teacher may conclude that a child has ADHD (attention-deficit/hyperactivity disorder) because he has difficulty concentrating on tasks and sitting in his seat. She may further assume that he should be medicated (e.g., take Ritalin). Notice the circularity here:

Observed Behavior	Inference	Reasons for Inference
Does not work on assigned tasks	Hyperactive	Does not work on assigned tasks
Often gets out of his seat	Hyperactive	Often gets out of his seat

This label is based on the two observed behaviors, and no such underlying condition may exist. If this is the case, a descriptive term is used as a *pseudoexplanatory* term. The use of labels in this manner can be frustrating, since although it may seem that more is known, no additional information is available. Indeed, misleading directions may be offered. We should think critically about labels and ask: When are they helpful? When are they irrelevant? When are they misleading or harmful? Do they offer guidelines about how to help clients? What are underlying

EXHIBIT 12.6

Is This Report Evidence-Based?

Guevara and Stein (2001) published an article titled "Evidence based management of attention deficit hyper-activity disorder." This article generated many letters, as well as a review and integration of their content by Greenhalgh and Smyth (2002). One indication that this is not an evidence-informed report is lack of critique of the diagnostic category of attention-deficit/hyper-activity disorder (ADHD). There is no mention of the controversy surrounding this label. Guevara and Stein (2001) state that: "You confirm the diagnosis of attention-deficit/hyperactivity disorder by using the DSM-IV diagnostic criteria and the Conners parent and teachers rating scales. You inform the parents of the potential risk of additional psychiatric disorders and persistence of symptoms into adolescence. You prescribe a stimulant drug and arrange review" (p. 1235). Letters written in response to this article note the reliance on the DSM checklist of symptoms and parent and teacher behavior checklists in lieu of conducting an individualized assessment. In one letter entitled "A naive use of evidence," Coghill (2001) wrote, "They justify this approach by quoting the impressive effect sizes, sensitivity and specificity of the Conners rating scales." Coghill notes that this is problematic because the studies were "conducted under ideal conditions; actual performance on the scales in a physicians' offices would be expected to be poorer." He also notes that the authors simply informed the parents of the risk that their child suffered from a comorbid disorder when they should have described any other concerns. In integrating reactions regarding this report, Greenhalgh and Smyth (2002) described the following limitations: the case description is extremely brief; we do not have the details that would allow us to carry out an individualized assessment. She also noted the problem of the great variation in the prevalence of ADHD over different studies ranging from 4.2% to 26%.

Some argue that ADHD refers to (mis)behaviors normal children engage in. William Carey (2003), in testimony to a panel on prescribing Ritalin, noted that only a small percentage of children would meet the criterion of ADHD (June 19, 2001). "Abundant evidence supports the conclusion that one–two percent of children are so pervasively over-active or inattentive that those qualities by themselves severely impair chances for normal living and make these children very hard for any caregivers to manage" (p. 2). Carey (2003) argues that this raises concern not for this 1% to 2% (that he argues are accurately diagnosed), "but for the rest of the 3 to 5 or up to 10 to 15% of American children who today are being diagnosed with ADHD and usually being treated with stimulants inappropriately." He suggests (as do others) that the ADHD diagnosis is seriously flawed. (See also Timimi, 2008.)

Critics of this diagnosis argue that ADHD diagnostic criteria ignore the role of environmental causes, that diagnostic criteria and questionnaires used for assessment are subjective and impressionistic, and that other problems with the current ADHD diagnosis include: overlooking learning problems, overcrowded classrooms, and lack of cultural and historical perspectives (e.g., see Diller, 2006; Timimi & Leo, 2009; Timimi & Taylor, 2004). One of the letters in response to the Guevara and Stein (2001) article entitled "Real or Imagined" (Lake) said as follows, "As a society we now seek not to tolerate deviations from the normal in young children because of breakdown of both nuclear and extended family support and mothers away at work." For a view of ADHD as a "brain disease," see Barkley et al. (2002). Thus, there is a controversy about the use of this label, so much so that bills have been passed in some states limiting the pressure schools can exert on parents to medicate their children. Thus, one way to recognize material that is not evidence-informed (even though it is so labeled) is not mentioning controversial issues regarding problem framing.

assumptions? Are they well argued? For example, what is a "disorder"? Many people believe that there is convincing evidence that a disorder called schizophrenia exists and has a biological cause. Others present cogent arguments against these beliefs (Boyle, 2002). Some scholars argue that the concept of mental disorder is culturally relative. Others argue that it is not.

A classification system may be faulty in not distinguishing among different "syndromes;" that is, there may be "boundary" problems (overlap between two or more categories). This is a problem with the DSM (2000) classification system. Does a given diagnostic category represent a "syndrome" (a cluster of symptoms) that can be distinguished from others? Does a label differ from others concerning basic features external to the behaviors that define a hypothesized diagnostic construct? Correlates might include genetic influences, course and response to specific

treatments. How many different classifications can one person fall in? Is there any hierarchical order to these—that is, are some more primary than others? We may think our work is over when we give a person a diagnostic label rather than realizing it is just beginning in relation to the need for a contextual evidence-informed assessment.

Labels can obscure important cultural and individual variations among people; it encourages the "patient uniformity myth." Use of labels also contributes to the "psychopathologist's fallacy"—the belief that because a child has been brought in as a patient there must be something wrong with him or her (Taylor & Rutter, 2002, p. 4). We may start to think of a person as the label he or she is given. Indeed the DSM (2000) warns readers against this possibility. Saleebey (2001) suggested a "diagnostic strengths manual" as an alternative to a system focused on pathology.

Being labeled may result in attention only to characteristics that complement the label. (See discussion of confirmation biases in chapter 8.) Use of a psychiatric label such as "social anxiety disorder" may obscure the relationship between different concerns such as anxiety and depression, which are often co-occurring.

> Few options for change are generated by an assessment that regards Mary to be an "inadequate personality."…[T]his kind of diagnosis doesn't indicate what needs to be changed. The vagueness of the label can prevent us from knowing when that label is no longer deserved or appropriate. It will be difficult for Mary to prove her labelers wrong. If we deal with the specifics of the children being clean, going to the doctor if they have earaches, and receiving proper nutrition, the directions for change become clear. It will also be clear to everyone when the problems are resolved. (Kinney, Haapala, & Booth, 1991, p. 86)

Labels often do not reflect changes that take place. That is, even though changes may be made, the same label (e.g., "developmentally disabled") may be applied to a client. Labels often provide an illusion of understanding. You may think you know more about how to help a client (or discover that you cannot), but in fact know nothing more about the client's concerns, the factors related to them, and how to attain desired outcomes (see earlier discussion of circular accounts). Accepting a label may prematurely close off consideration of promising options. Labels that limit exploration do not have to be fancy ones like *hyperactive* or *paranoid*; they can be everyday ones like *old lady*. The tendency to use an either/or classification system (people either have or do not have something, e.g., being an alcoholic or not) obscures varied individual patterns that may be referred to by a term. Within labeling theory, the label itself is considered to be partially responsible for deviant acts (Scheff, 1984). For example, applying labels such as *delinquent* or *shy* may encourage behaviors that match this label and hinder change. A client who has trouble making friends may think of himself as shy and may use this label as an excuse not to initiate conversations. An adolescent labeled *delinquent* may begin to think of himself as a "delinquent" and so engage in other acts compatible with this label. Labeling is viewed as a behavior that varies from culture to culture, from person to person, and from time to time. This point of view is very different from a psychiatric one in which there is a search for a correct diagnostic label for a client.

Controversies Regarding Psychiatric Labels

Psychiatric labels have been applied to an ever-increasing variety of behaviors viewed as mental disorders (see also the discussion of the biomedicalization of deviance in chapter 6). The hundreds of alleged "mental disorders" in the DSM are based on consensus—a vote by alleged experts, many of whom have conflicts of interests, for example, receive money from pharmaceutical companies (Cosgrove et al., 2009). Indeed most members

of some task forces concerned with the DSM have financial ties to Big Pharma (Cosgrove, 2010). DSM diagnoses are required for access to care. The latest edition of the *Diagnostic and Statistical Manual of Mental Disorders (DSM-IV-R)* (2000) of the American Psychiatric Association contains hundreds of diagnostic categories, DSM-V will include even more. Axes include the following:

Axis I	Clinical disorders.
Axis II	Personality disorders. Mental retardation.
Axis III	General medical conditions.
Axis IV	Psychosocial and environmental problems.
Axis V	Global Assessment of Functioning, or "GAF scores." A score of (1–100) is assigned regarding psychological, social, and occupational functioning. Zero indicates insufficient information to assign a score.

For each "disorder" the following is described: diagnostic features, subtypes/specifiers, recording procedures, associated features and disorders, specific culture, age, and gender features, prevalence, course, family pattern, and differential diagnosis. People differ in their beliefs about the usefulness of psychiatric labels. The controversies concerning the empirical status of psychiatric diagnoses and resultant consequences are so sharp, that if you are interested in pursuing this further, you should read related material for yourself. Some argue that psychiatric labels are valuable in communicating among different professionals. This would only be true if such labels were valuable in helping clients.

Pharmaceutical companies describe the DSM as their most helpful marketing aid; a diagnosis is required for prescribing medications so the more diagnoses, the more pills can be sold. Moynihan and Cassels (2005) document the creation of "social anxiety disorder" by a public relations firm hired by a pharmaceutical company. (See also Lane, 2007.) Conflicts of interests between academic researchers (especially psychiatrists) and Big Pharma are rife, including fraud and corruption (e.g., failing to report income from pharmaceutical companies to universities where researchers are employed (e.g., Lo & Field, 2009; Gambrill, 2012a). In *Follies and Fallacies in Medicine* (1998), Skrabanek and McCormick suggest that "because there is no need to confirm diagnosis by strict, objective criteria, psychiatry is at a particular risk of creating diseases" (p. 79). They suggest that the use of "Latin and Greek helps to reify dubious entities" (p. 79) and that a knowledge of Greek "is particularly useful in describing new diseases: silurophobia, fear of cats; kynophobia, common in postmen, fear of dogs; iatrophobia, fear of fear" (p. 84). Skrabanek and McCormick argue that new terms for diseases may serve as a camouflage for a lack of understanding. "By pronouncing Greek or Latin, the doctor pretends to be in charge of the daemon of disease" (p. 85). "As doctors [social workers too?] are generally uncomfortable about exposing their ignorance, there is a temptation to 'diagnose,' to label inappropriately, to create non-diseases. Training in use of the DSM increases the diagnosis of "mental disorders" (Pottick, Wakefield, Kirk, & Tian, 2003).

Although the American Psychiatric Association claims that its classification system is based on scientific evidence, critics question this claim (e.g., Houts, 2002; Kirk, & Kutchins, 1992b Kutchins & Kirk, 1997). In *The Selling of DSM* (1992a), Kirk and Kutchins (1992a) document reliability and validity problems with this system, still a problem (Kirk, 2010). These include the consensual nature of what is included (agreement among individuals is relied on rather than empirical criteria), lack of agreement about what label to assign clients (poor reliability), and lack of association between a diagnosis and indications of what plans will be effective (see Exhibit 12.7). Given the questionable reliability and validity of psychiatric diagnoses, the enormous success of the DSM is remarkable. Client ethnicity and race, as well as other client characteristics such as obesity, influence helpers' views (e.g., Garb, 1997). Some writers argue that psychiatric classification systems trivialize problems in living and encourage blaming victims for their plights rather than examining the social circumstances that are often responsible. In *The Mismeasure of Woman* (1992), Tavris contends that labels newly included in the DSM-IV (1994) continue to misdirect attention away from political, social, and economic conditions related to expected gender roles and toward supposed individual deficiencies.

Thomas Szasz (1961, 1987) has been the most persistent and penetrating critic of the very concept of "mental illness," arguing that this is a rhetorical device (a metaphor) obscuring the difference between real diseases (e.g., syphilis) and (mis)behaviors. He argues that its true role is to allow the "therapeutic state" and its thousands of social workers, psychiatrists, and psychologists to control troubled, troubling, and very dependent behaviors. Kirk and Kutchins (both social workers) highlight the role of political and economic considerations in the creation and "selling" of the DSM. Moncrieff (2008a) suggests that a psychiatric framing of problems complements conservative political views by framing discontents such as depression and anxiety as caused by individual deficiencies, overlooking related political and economic factors such as lack of jobs. Indeed suicide rates are affected by economic factors (Carey, 2011b; Luo et al., 2011). Many scholars argue that labels, such as "mental illness," are used for social control purposes and often result in harming rather than helping people (see books on critical psychology and critical psychiatry and related web sites). Consider labels such as *drapetomania* (an irresistible propensity to run away). This "disease" was allegedly common among slaves in the southern United States in the past. Hobbs (1975) suggests that: "Categories and labels are powerful instruments for social regulation and control, and they are often employed for obscure, covert, or hurtful purposes: to degrade people, to deny them access to opportunity, to exclude 'undesirables' whose presence in some way offends, disturbs familiar custom, or demands extraordinary effort" (p. 11).

Status offenders have been labeled as mentally ill and confined, without due process, to inpatient psychiatric and chemical dependency units of private hospitals (Schwartz, 1989). (The term *status offender* refers to youths who fall under juvenile court jurisdiction because of conduct prohibited only because of their juvenile status, e.g., disobedience, curfew violations, running away, and truancy.) Schwartz (1989) argues that reasons include insurance policies favoring inpatient care, widespread advertising describing residential treatment centers, lack of community-based services for status offenders who cannot be confined in juvenile correctional institutions and too many hospital beds. He refers to this relabeling of typical teenage behavior as "mental illness" as "the medicalization of defiance." Increasing concern has been raised regarding the relentless medicalization of problems as discussed in chapter 6.

Howitt (1992) contends that labels given to clients often obscure lapses in agency services that create problems (e.g., via false assumptions due to uncritical thinking). Many social workers believe there are serious misuses of the DSM, including assigning an inappropriate diagnosis simply for reimbursement reasons (Kirk & Kutchins, 1988). Diagnostic labeling implies the need for specialists to help people with their problems. As more and more behaviors are assigned a label, the mental health industry can grow ever greater (Moynihan, Heath, & Henry, 2002). Key conceptual questions (such as "What is mental illness?" "What is a disease?" "What is a disorder?") are often glossed over. Psychiatric labels are stigmatizing. They say too little about positive attributes, potential for change, and change that does occur and too much about presumed negative characteristics and limits to change. People labeled are often regarded as if they possess only the characteristics of a category (e.g., "schizophrenic").

Although they may sound sophisticated, too often labels offer few if any guidelines about what to do to resolve problems. The introduction to the DSM emphasizes that giving a psychiatric label to a client provides no implications of etiology or selection of intervention (American Psychiatric Association (2000)). However, hundreds of (mis)behaviors included therein, are

---

EXHIBIT 12.7

Problems with Psychiatric Labels

Are typically vague, resulting in low reliability.

Lack validity.

Do not offer information about how to resolve problem.

Are often used for reasons that benefit professionals rather than clients (reimbursement, creation of an aura of expertise).

Pathologize clients.

Are based on shifting consensual grounds.

Discourage search for environmental causes.

Are used for social control purposes.

May encourage behavior in accord with the label (argued by labeling theorists).

Create an illusion of understanding.

assumed to be "mental disorders." Psychiatric labels are not explanatory. Just how descriptive they are in terms of clarity is another question. From a behavioral point of view, most are quite fuzzy. Consider these two examples of diagnostic criteria for ADHD (Attention-Deficit/ Hyperactivity Disorder): "Often fails to give close attention to details or makes careless mistakes in school work, work, or other activities;" "Is often forgetful in daily activities." What is "often"? What is a "careless mistake"? Neither trait nor diagnostic labels offer enough detail about what people do in specific situations and what personal and environmental events influence their behavior to be of value in clarifying concerns and related factors. The individual variability of behavior is overlooked, resulting in lost opportunities to discover unique relationships between a client's behavior and his or her environments. Dispositional attributions shift attention away from observing what people do in specific situations to speculating about what they have done. General predictions about a person based on tiny samples of behavior in one context are not likely to be accurate, especially when behaviors of interest occur in quite different situations.

Evidence-Based Diagnosis?

The term *diagnosis* refers to accurately identifying the cause(s) of symptoms. Evidence-based diagnosis can be defined as the use of certain symptoms and signs (feeling hot and having a fever as determined by a thermometer) to identify an underlying condition (a bacterial infection). Such a diagnosis is evidence-informed in two senses: (1) signs and symptoms accurately indicate the underlying condition, and (2) accurate identification of these conditions points to an effective remedy (e.g., antibiotics). (See also discussion of appraising research regarding diagnostic measures in chapter 11.) Let us say you have a persistent cough. A guess on the part of your physician that you have pneumonia can be checked by obtaining an X-ray. This example illustrates that in medicine, we often have both signs (an X-ray) and symptoms (complaints of a cough). Is this true of concerns such as depression and anxiety? The answer from psychiatry is yes. It is assumed that symptoms (for example, anxiety in social situations) reflect an underlying disorder (or dysfunction). But what signs do they use? A "sign" is defined as "an objective manifestation of a pathological condition. Signs are observed by the examiner rather than reported by the affected individual" (American Psychiatric Association (2000)). Observed behaviors are used as signs. A social worker observes that a person appears nervous—they sweat, they tremble.

Consider Judy, who was referred to a counselor because of anxiety. She reported being nervous around people and having difficulty approaching them and that this got in the way of making friends. A psychiatric narrative here would argue that Judy has a "mental illness" ("social anxiety disorder"). This "diagnosis" would be based on her symptoms (self-reported complaints), the clinician's observation that she appeared nervous in social situations, and perhaps responses on a self-report measure. Now how does this situation differ from seeing a doctor because of

a persistent cough? There are things that are called signs such as scores on an anxiety inventory, but there are no signs of biochemical or anatomical dysfunction. The term *disease* is used as a metaphor here. This is why Thomas Szasz refers to such uses as rhetorical—a concept (diseaselike) is reified into an alleged reality. There has been an intense interest in identifying possible brain differences in people showing a certain pattern of behavior, for example, by using brain imaging. Some claim that genetic and biochemical differences have been found. Critics argue that correlations do not causations make, that correlations found explain only a small portion of variance, and that studies are flawed methodologically (e.g., Vul et al., 2009). (See discussion of biomedical factors in chapter 6.)

Now where does this leave us regarding our question "Are there evidence-based diagnoses in the interpersonal helping professions?" How does this question apply, for example, to depression and anxiety? Here we have symptoms without signs—that is, there is no independent objective indicators of the alleged underlying pathology. It is here that differences arise between a contextual assessment and a psychiatric diagnosis. These are competing grand narratives. (See chapter 6.) The answer depends on whether you accept helper-observed signs as indicators of biochemical dysfunctions.

Diagnosis and Assessment: Not an Either/Or Matter

From an evidence-informed point of view, diagnosis and assessment are not either/or endeavors. Providing a diagnosis for clients is a requirement for third-party payment. This does not mean that you cannot or should not carry out a contextual assessment describing, for example, personal and environmental factors that create risks and contribute to resilience (e.g., Jensen & Fraser, 2011). Thus, you can satisfy the requirements of your agency to diagnose clients (for third-party reimbursement) and still honor your responsibility to complete an assessment, drawing on relevant research findings. See also discussion of transdiagnostic assessment and intervention (e.g. Johnston, Titov, Andrews, Spence & Dear, 2011; Nolen-Hoeksema & Watkins, 2011).

Risk, Protective Factors, Diagnosis, and Prognosis

A client may be diagnosed with depression and then, based on a contextual assessment, receive a certain prognosis. For example, based on related research findings, you may predict that a client will have recurrent bouts of depression—that is, you may make a prognosis. Both protective and risk factors enter at many points (Biglan, Flay, Embry, & Sandler, 2012; Yoshikawa, Aber, & Beardslee, 2012). They enter prior to a diagnosis; for example, certain people are prone to depression. They enter following diagnosis; certain environmental factors such as social support may yield positive prognosis. This is a recursive process. The relationship among these factors is illustrated in Exhibit 12.8. This highlights the

EXHIBIT 12.8

The Relationship Between Risk, Protective Factors, Diagnosis, and Prognosis

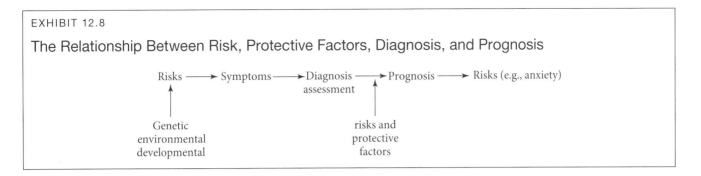

importance of being informed about research findings regarding risk and protective factors (e.g., resilience) and skill in critically appraising related research and understanding the relationship among these factors.

What About P-I-E?

The National Association of Social Workers helped fund the development of Person-In-Environment (PIE) (Karls, & Wandrei. 1994). Although its creators argue that it is useful, others believe that the same concerns that apply to the DSM apply as well to P-I-E, such as a lack of validity (e.g., Kutchins & Kirk, 1997).

Making Assessment of Value to Clients

Assessment should help clients achieve valued outcomes. You can make assessment of value by helping people to clearly describe hoped-for outcomes and related factors. If concerns remain vague (a teacher does not clearly describe what she means by a student's "aggressiveness" or a supervisor does not identify what she means by staff's poor recording skills), it will be difficult or impossible to identify specific behaviors of concern and associated causes. If maintaining conditions are not identified, opportunities to help clients may be lost. Focus on collecting data that decreases uncertainty about how to attain outcomes that clients value. Assessment should offer clients more helpful views of their concerns and a more helpful vocabulary for describing them that points to how to achieve hoped-for outcomes.

Relationship skills such as empathy, warmth, and genuineness contribute to positive expectations and encourage hope, a vital aspect of helping (see chapter 15). A key way to make assessment of value to clients is to attend to their assets: to help clients identify their strengths, their support systems, what is going well in their lives, and what they can contribute. Assessment should be strength-based. It should empower clients by building on their assets. Explore client views, acknowledge and validate their frustration and anger regarding difficult situations, and help them to focus on successes in influencing behaviors of concern.

Labels that are instrumental (i.e., they point to effective plans or indicate accurately that there are no effective options)

are helpful. Recognizing signs of pathology is important if this increases understanding of what can be accomplished and how. Some elderly clients do have dementia. Labels can normalize clients' concerns. Parents who have been struggling to understand why their child is developmentally slow may view themselves as failures. Recognizing that their child has a specific kind of developmental disability that accounts for this can be a relief. Failing to use labels may prevent clients from receiving appropriate help. Consider the Japanese custom of labeling clients as *neurasthemic* to protect them and their relatives from the social stigma associated with "mental illness." Munakata (1989) suggests that the use of such a "disguised diagnosis" given to the pilot was responsible for the 1982 crash of an airliner in Tokyo. The pilot, who had hallucinations and delusions at the time of the crash, had a history of psychiatric problems.

Social Workers as Consultants Involved in a Collaborative Process

Social workers often help mediators (e.g., parents, teachers, residential or agency staff) acquire knowledge and skills to address problems with their significant others (e.g., children, students, residents, or other staff). Potential sources of support for mediators include the person with the presenting problem, others they see, and the consultant (you). The term *consultation* highlights the collaborative nature of helping relationships, including the joint decision-making process that is ideally involved in practice. Clients and significant others make decisions about whether to share or collect data, whether to carry out assignments, what plans are suitable, and whether they are satisfied with outcomes of service. You should do your best to encourage helpful actions, but clients and significant others play a key role in what results.

Characteristics of A Contextual Assessment Framework

The characteristics of a contextual-constructional assessment framework are described in the next section. This framework decreases the likelihood of errors, such as emphasizing people's deficiencies rather than their strengths, neglecting environmental causes and resources, and focusing on outcomes that will not resolve problems. It encourages a broad review that may reveal leverage points otherwise overlooked.

Individually Tailored

Individualized assessment does not mean you focus on individuals as the locus of problems. It means that whether individuals, families, groups, organizations, communities, policies, or global events such as famine and genocide are involved, a careful assessment may be required, including an understanding of historical events and unique subjectivities and related environmental circumstances. This term subjectivities refers to each person's unique experiences of local and global events. We each differ, for example, in the extent to which we have been influenced by the increased biomedicalization of behavior. These larger changes shape our individual identities to different degrees in different ways (e.g., Biehl, Good, & Kleinman, 2007). Although we talk about the importance of "starting where the client is" and respecting individual differences including cultural and environmental differences, we may not do so. For example, information about behaviors of concern and related circumstances based on observation in real-life settings may not be collected even when this is needed to understand concerns and related circumstances and it is feasible and ethical to do so. Why should clients and/or significant others (e.g., politicians) participate?

What objections might clients have? (See chapter 14.) If the costs of changing a behavior outweigh the benefits, it is unlikely that clients will engage in pursuit of changes. Individualized assessment avoids the patient uniformity myth in which individuals, families, groups, organizations, or communities are mistakenly assumed to be identical (Wolpe, 1986). Indicators of this myth are:

- Speculating about causes without checking beliefs against data gathered in real-life settings.

- Using vague labels and description of problems.

- Stereotyping (talking about clients as if they were the same as all other members of a group).

An individualized assessment decreases the likelihood of errors, such as focusing on people's deficiencies and ignoring their strengths, ignoring important cultural differences, and neglecting environmental causes and resources. Attending to each client's unique circumstances and characteristics, including their values and preferences, is a hallmark of evidence-based practice (Straus et al., 2005).

Clear Description of Client Concerns and Hoped-For-Outcomes

Identifying clients' hoped-for outcomes is a first concern. How will things be different if problems are resolved? How would we know if outcomes were achieved? A focus on vague concerns may prevent the discovery of related factors. If hoped-for outcomes are not clearly described, it will be difficult to determine the actual frequency of behaviors of interest or to assess progress.

The specific referents to which clients refer when using vague terms such as *uncooperative, immature,* or *aggressive* may differ. One person may define aggressive behavior as hitting, shoving, or slapping. Another person may include verbal responses such as yelling, shouting, and name-calling. Adults who are thought by many people to have been abused as children (e.g., they were beaten with straps and locked in closets for long periods) may not define this as abuse. They may say, "I was bad" or "I deserved it." Exhibit 12.9 gives examples of clearly described outcomes, and Exhibit 12.10 illustrates presenting problems, their referents, and related outcomes.

Focus on outcomes that succeed in removing complaints. Some can be identified early on, such as need for a different kind of housing, creation of a neighborhood mediation center, and arrangement for day care for children.

Evidence-Informed

Assessment is more likely to help you and your clients to make informed decisions if you use methods that provide accurate information and a practice framework informed by empirical information about behavior and how it is influenced (e.g., take advantage of the science of behavior) (See chapter 7.) Some practice frameworks have been well tested regarding their value in helping clients. Others have not. This does not mean that they are not helpful; it means that their evidentiary status is unknown. Constructional assessment rests on a rich laboratory and clinical literature describing behavior and how it is influenced. You may find a particular model interesting, even though, compared to others, it has not been found to help clients. A focus on helping clients requires asking, "What framework has been found to be most effective in helping clients achieve hoped-for outcomes?" Sources of information differ in their accuracy. Self-report may not reflect what occurs in real life. Observers may be biased.

A Preference for Testing Inferences. Unexamined speculation may result in incomplete or incorrect accounts of client concerns and related circumstances. Consider a social worker who saw a family because the mother was concerned about her 10-year-old child's behavior at school. The social worker believed that the child's "misbehavior" in class occurred because the mother's boyfriend had left her and the child was upset about it. The social worker did not observe the child in the classroom or obtain any information about her academic progress. I asked the social worker when the boyfriend had left the mother, and she said he left 8 months before the problems at school started. According to the mother, these problems started in the last month. The social worker reported that because the child was no longer worried about the boyfriend's leaving (this change was not explained) and because classroom behavior was no longer a problem (no evidence was provided for this claim), she decided not to address the mother's original concern but to offer her supportive counseling for herself. What are some of the inferences here? One is that the child was indeed misbehaving in class. This inference should have been tested for its accuracy, for example, by observing the child in her classroom. Since the social worker never

EXHIBIT 12.9

Examples of Outcomes at Different Levels of Intervention

Level	Examples
Individual	Increase parenting skills (e.g., giving clear instructions and offering positive feedback for accomplishments). Increase daily number of planned activities from zero to five.
Family	Increase weekly time spent in shared activities from 0 to 2 hours a week. Hold a 1-hour problem-solving session each week.
Group	Increase number of positive comments exchanged among group members from zero to two for each group member. Increase percentage of group members who complete assignments. Increase leadership skills (e.g., suggest agenda items, refocus discussion on topics of interest).
Organization	Increase weekly positive comments given by supervisors to staff for valued behaviors from zero to two. Increase number of people who offer valuable suggestions at case conferences.
Community	Increase the percentage of residents involved in local planning from 5 to 20. Establish a neighborhood mediation board by December 30. Increase percentage of parents who attend parent–teacher meetings at school. Increase percentage of youth who help elderly residents with chores.
Service system	Increase percentage of agreed-on reports received on time. Increase positive feedback to staff for specific behaviors that contribute to service delivery. Increase percentage of successful referrals (those that result in receipt of requested service).

observed the child in the classroom, we do not know whether or not this was true (or if this child misbehaved any more or less often than did other children in the class). Speculation was relied on when observation was called for. Untested speculation can get in the way of identifying outcomes that, if achieved, would resolve problems. For example, if you limit your source

of information to a teacher's report about an "unmanageable child," you may assume that (1) the child's behavior is unmanageable; (2) it is worse than that of the other children in the classroom; and (3) the causes of behavior can be discovered by relying on reports of significant others (e.g., teachers). This is a classic example of "working in the dark." Another inference is that the child misbehaved in the classroom because the mother's boyfriend had left. There is little evidence on which to base this and some counterevidence as well (the time lapse between the boyfriend's leaving and the start of the alleged misbehavior).

Parsimonious accounts that involve limited inferences (they are closely tied to data) are easier to test than those that include many, perhaps conflicting, theories. A key advantage of evidence-informed practice is encouraging you to question assumptions by consulting related research (see Exhibit 12.11). Questions may pertain to the accuracy of measures or of practice frameworks. Validity is a concern in any kind of assessment; however, the nature of the concern differs in sign and sample approaches. In a *sign approach* to assessment, behavior is used as a sign of some entity (such as personality trait) at a different level. The concern is with *vertical validity*. Is the sign an accurate indicator of the underlying trait? In a *sample approach* such as the model described here, different levels (such as behavior and personality dispositions) are not involved. Questions here are: (1) Does self-report provide an accurate account of behavior and related circumstances? (2) Does behavior in role play reflect behavior in real life? (3) Do changes achieved remove complaints? (Different kinds of reliability and validity are discussed in chapter 17.)

A Preference for Observation. An interest in discovering important contingencies related to hoped-for outcomes highlights the value of observing behavior in real-life settings when feasible or by means of client-gathered information. (See chapter 17.) This may be needed to discover the functions of behaviors of interest. Self-report in the office may offer incomplete or inaccurate account of behaviors of concern and related circumstances.

Constructional Rather than Eliminative: Building on Client Assets

Many practice models, including a biopsychiatric one, are eliminative; they focus on what is wrong with people. A constructional approach focuses on client assets—discovering and creating repertoires that can be used to attain hoped-for outcomes. There is an emphasis on the use of available repertoires and their construction rather than on eliminating repertoires (e.g., Layng, 2009; Schwartz & Goldiamond, 1975). This kind of nonlinear analysis is needed to reveal positive ways to achieve valued outcomes. (See Exhibit 12.12.) As Goldiamond (1974) suggests, attaining valued outcomes "requires the *establishment* of repertoires, an eliminative approach gets in the way" (p. 124). Complaints (e.g., depression, anxiety) are viewed as important guides for discovering reinforcers that can be used to increase alternative positive behaviors for example (gaining attention from a neglectful husband via appropriate assertive behaviors rather than by a fear of roaches or recurrent stomach pains) (e.g.,

---

EXHIBIT 12.10

Examples of Presenting Problems, Specific Referents, and Desired Outcomes

Presenting Problem	Specific Referents	Desired Outcomes
My 14-year-old daughter is uncontrollable.	She stays out beyond curfew time. She calls me names.	Return home by agreed on time. Discuss issues without name-calling.
Loneliness (80-year-old male).	No one ever visits me at home. I never speak to anyone on the phone. I never go to the senior center.	Have one person visit each week. Have three telephone conversations per week. Visit the senior center for 1 hour once a week.
Lack of participation at community-board meetings.	I do not say anything.	Offer three elaborated opinion statements at each board meeting.
Children have no proper care.	Children are left by themselves for 3 hours when they return from school.	Arrange care for children between return from school and the time parent finishes work.

Goldiamond, 1974). As Goldiamond (1974) noted, "Clients are treasure chests of repertoires." Emphasizing the *construction of repertoires* has many advantages.

Both applied and laboratory research demonstrate the value of increasing alternative positive behaviors to achieve hoped-for outcomes. First, you are less likely to pathologize people. Second, it encourages a search for client assets—available positive alternative behaviors that can be used to obtain valued reinforcers currently maintaining unwanted behaviors. Increasing alternative positive behaviors is often the most effective way to decrease unwanted behavior. This enables access to valued consequences via less costly behaviors. Third, attending to clients' assets helps them focus on their strengths and to use these to pursue valued outcomes. Behaviors of interest may be related to fulfilling roles (parent, husband, wife, daughter, or employee). Consider adult children caring for an elderly relative in their home. Valued behaviors included reinforcing independent behaviors on the part of the elderly relative, providing opportunities for recreation and social contacts, arranging time-outs from caregiving responsibilities, planning shared positive events among family members, and constructive problem solving to address concerns that arise. This constructional nature of behavioral practice is typically ignored in discussion of "strength-based social work."

Focus Is on the Present

There is a focus on present concerns and related factors. The biopsychosocial approach favored in social work emphasizes current concerns and circumstances. This is also true of ego psychological and behavioral approaches. The circumstances in which a reaction originally developed, such as a fear of crowds, may be different from those that currently maintain this fear. Perhaps the fear is now maintained by attention from significant others and by the avoidance of disliked tasks, such as working. Understanding clients often requires an overview of their current lives, including relationships with significant others, employment, physical health, recreational activities, and community and material resources, such as housing and income. What is a client's typical day like? Does a client like her work? Does she have any friends? How is her physical health? Whom does she live with? Does she have enough money to feed her children? Is her housing situation stable? Are circumstances in any of these areas related to presenting concerns?

What About Past History?

Although all practice perspectives recognize the role of past history in influencing thoughts, feelings, and behavior, they differ in how much attention is given to the past and what is focused on (e.g., feelings, thoughts, or experiences). More traditional psychoanalytic practice emphasizes helping people understand

---

EXHIBIT 12.11

Testing Assumptions: Is It True?

- Joan, a school social worker, was taught by her supervisor that observing in the classroom was a waste of time because it was impossible to gather accurate information because of the students' focus on the observer.

- Ralph preferred to use a n-grams to understand the personality of his clients.

- Pat relies on genograms to help her to understand families.

- Robert relies on transactional analysis to understand his clients.

EXHIBIT 12.12

Behavior Always Makes Sense: Cost-Benefit Analyses

Different kinds of behavior analyses include *topical*, *nonlinear*, and *systemic* (e.g., see Goldiamond, 1984). Only the latter attends to the total context related to behaviors of interest, and thus only this kind of analysis may provide effective guidelines for intervention. Behaviors that appear irrational could have been shaped by environmental contingencies and be maintained by current reinforcers. No matter how bizarre or dysfunctional a disturbing behavior may seem (the DB), when the context is explored including available alternative behaviors (AABs), and the costs and benefits related to these different behaviors are compared, we can see that DBs have been selected by the social environment. For example, only by acting "crazy" may a person gain access to resources provided only to those who act "crazy."

In a topical analysis there is a direct focus on a disturbing behavior (DB), for example, hallucinations or talking out of turn in class. Topical analyses may be linear or nonlinear. The effects on the DB of consequences attached to AABs are ignored in a linear analysis (Goldiamond, 1984, p. 535). In linear analyses ("eliminative" or "pathological" approaches), there is a direct focus on the DB and eliminative methods are used such as extinction, punishment, and/or response cost to decrease the DB. Let's say the DB is yelling in class and the teacher makes the student stay 10 minutes after class each time he yells out. She is using an eliminative method focused on the DB. *Topical nonlinear analyses* also focus on the DB such as yelling out in class, but a desired alternative such as raising his hand and waiting to be called on is identified and reinforced. The focus is still on the DB but a constructional approach is used.

A *systemic behavior analysis* broadens assessment to include identification of current relevant alternative repertoires that can be used to alter the frequency of DBs. Current available repertoires (behaviors the client already has, such as social skills) are transferred to new situations. (See cost/benefit matrix.) Emotions and thoughts can be used to identify related contingencies. Both this kind of analysis and a nonlinear topical analysis are constructional approaches that require consideration of what is *not* occurring such as for example positive social contacts. Both offer guidelines for decreasing the DB by improving the cost-benefit ratio of AABs. Target behaviors (those focused on to change) are selected based on a review of the costs and benefits associated with DBs and AABs. Target behaviors should "depotentiate" (decrease the likelihood of) costly DBs; they should be less costly than the DB and provide more benefits to both the client and significant others. A target behavior could be on-task behavior encouraged by providing instructional tasks that engage the student's attention. Notice that in plans based on a systemic analysis,f the conditions that "potentiate" a reinforcer, such as escape from boring or overchallenging material, are removed; there is no need to escape because the instructional material now engages the students. A constructional analysis requires information about available alternative repertoires. (See chapters 12 and 25, as well as Goldiamond, 1974, 1984.) It may require observation in real-life settings (see chapter 18).

Cost-Benefit Matrix

	Costs	Benefits
Disturbing Behaviors		
Available Alternative Behaviors		
Target Behaviors		

Source: Based on material distributed at a workshop on systemic, nonlinear, and constructional approaches to behavior change given by P. T. Andronis, T. V. J. Layng, & K. Johnson, International Conference on Applied Behavior Analysis, Chicago, IL, May 1997. Reprinted with permission.

(gain insight into) their past experiences and the relationship of these experiences to the present. In a behavioral perspective, past history is assumed to be reflected in current behavior, feelings, and thoughts. The influence of the past is suggested by research in many areas including attachment (e.g., see Cassidy & Shaver, 2008). This does not mean that later change is not possible. Information about the past allows you and your clients to view current events in a more comprehensive context (Wolpe, 1990). Major areas include immigration history, medical history, educational and work history, significant relationships, family history, and developmental history.

Valuable coping skills may be identified by inquiring about what clients have done in the past to achieve hoped-for outcomes. You may discover family ties that have languished. Knowledge about past contingencies may be of value when it is difficult to identify current maintaining factors and may be helpful in predicting future problems (keeping in mind that current maintaining conditions may differ from those present when a behavior was established). Although effective intervention does not require discovering historical causes, understanding initiating circumstances can help clients "make sense" of current reactions. New ways of viewing past events may be helpful. Demographic indicators reflecting past behavior and social competence, such as work history and marital status, are better predictors of future behavior than are personality tests or clinical judgments (Dawes, 1994a). The more that past situations resemble current ones, the more informative data about the past may be in predicting future behavior.

Information about the past may increase understanding of current reactions. A client may understand how past discrimination based on gender or race resulted in limited opportunities. Helping clients to understand the effects of the political on the personal is key in feminist counseling. As Mills (1959) long ago noted, "The personal is political." A client may be willing to learn and use positive communication skills if she sees how negative behaviors resulted in the loss of valued consequences in the past. Disadvantages of excessive focus on the past include offering clients an excuse for not addressing current concerns and slowing down progress in understanding current circumstances. Excessive attention to past troubles may create pessimism about the future and encourage rationalizations and excuses that get in the way of helping clients. And, descriptions of past events may not be accurate.

Contingencies Are of Interest

A contingency analysis involves describing the context in which problems occur (i.e., the relationships between behavior in real-life settings and what happens right before and after), including alternative behaviors that, if increased, would compete successfully with undesired behaviors. The International Federation of Social Workers' definition of Social Work (2000) "recognizes the complexity of interactions between human beings and their environment, and the capacity of people both to be affected by and to alter the multiple influences upon them, including biopsychological factors." Considerable advances have been made

in some areas in identifying important contingencies. For example, assessment protocols have been developed to identify the cues and consequences related to severe self-injurious behavior of children. This is truly "starting where the client is." Discovering options for attaining valued outcomes may require a multilevel analysis including agency policy and related social policies and legislation. This will often reveal contingencies that may interfere with attaining valued goals. Some of the myths and misconceptions about contingency analysis are as follows:

- It is easy.

- I can do it sitting in my office.

- Thoughts and feelings are not considered.

- It dehumanizes people.

- The helper–client relationship is not important.

The interest in behavior and related circumstances calls for the translation of concerns into observable behaviors of involved parties and the discovery of options for rearranging them.

A *descriptive analysis* involves identification of problem-related behaviors and associated setting events, antecedents, and consequences. Helpful questions here are: What does this behavior communicate? What is its "meaning"? Behaviors have a communication function. They communicate a desire for or a dislike of something. Accurate description of contingencies will help you to discover options for change. For example, methods required to decrease self-injurious behavior will differ depending on whether this behavior is maintained by positive reinforcement such as attention from adults or negative reinforcement such as escape from difficult tasks. An accurate description will help you avoid victim blaming (attributing the cause of problems to clients when the causes lie in their environments). Accounts that do not include a description of related environmental contingencies are incomplete ones that may interfere with the discovery of options. A *functional analysis* requires demonstration that certain antecedents and/or consequences influence behaviors of interest. This involves the systematic variation of selected variables (e.g., certain consequences), noting changes that occur.

A focus on contingencies has a number of implications for assessment. One is observing people in real-life contexts when it is feasible, ethical, and necessary to do so to clarify concerns and related factors. A second is an emphasis on collecting information about individuals and their interactions with others. The very term "social work" emphasizes social interaction. Data describing group differences does not offer information about what an individual does in specific situations and what cues and consequences influence his or her behavior, although it may offer clues about how an individual may react. Clients are encouraged to recognize and alter the role they play in maintaining disliked circumstances. For example, teachers and parents often reinforce behaviors they complain about. If you play a role in creating and maintaining behaviors, you can play a role in altering them. This is not to say that clients can change social, political, and economic factors related to personal troubles. Clearly the homeless have few resources to change conditions such as shortages of affordable housing. But you can seek to give clients as much influence as possible over the quality of their lives. And, together with others, you can pursue changes in policies and practices that create avoidable miseries, for example, via community organizing, coalition building, and seeking changes in legislation.

The Importance of Consequences

The consequences that follow behavior affect its future probability. (See chapter 7.) A contingency analysis often reveals that desired behaviors are ignored and undesired ones are reinforced. Studies of residential centers show that contingencies often are counterhabilitative rather than habilitative; they discourage independence and client engagement (Meinhold & Mulick, 1990). Policies and procedures may contribute to the neglect and abuse of residents (Favell & McGimsey, 1993; Schemo, 2007), consider inappropriate medication of elderly residents (Levinson, 2011). Significant others may not realize that they maintain the very behaviors they complain about through the consequences they offer (e.g., attention); what they believe are positive reinforcers may have the opposite effect (punish behavior).

Different Kinds of Consequences

Behavior is affected by many kinds of consequences, including reactions from significant others, changes in the physical environment, and physiological changes. Consider test anxiety. The term *anxiety* may refer to physiological changes (increased heart rate), to related thoughts (worries about failure), and/or to behaviors (avoidance of test situations). Taking a test may be followed by negative self-statements (thoughts), increased muscle tension (physical changes), and social consequences (parents calling and saying, "I hope you did as well as your brother"). An alternative set of consequences might be positive self-statements for a job well done or anticipation of a high grade; a friend suggesting, "Let's go out and celebrate;" and a pleasant tiredness from a job well done.

The sum total of consequences that follow a behavior has been called the *reinforcing event* (Tharp & Wetzel, 1969). This may be mostly positive, mostly negative, or balanced (e.g., see Daniels, 2000). Behaviors are often followed by more than one change in the environment. For example, drinking alcohol may be followed by increased physical relaxation (a positive consequence) and a decrease in anxiety-provoking thoughts (the removal of a negative event). A contingency analysis will often reveal that undesired behaviors are reinforced positively, immediately, and with certainty and desired behaviors are not positively reinforced or reinforcement is uncertain and delayed. Discovering the function of a behavior (its effects on the environment) may be difficult when it is followed by both punishing and reinforcing consequences. In these instances, strong behavior may be observed only indirectly because it is displayed in only indirect forms. You may, for example, want to talk to someone you are attracted to but approach the person indirectly because of a fear

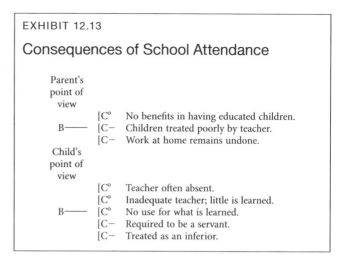

EXHIBIT 12.13

Consequences of School Attendance

Parent's
point of
view

           [C°   No benefits in having educated children.
B—— [C− Children treated poorly by teacher.
           [C− Work at home remains undone.

Child's
point of
view

           [C°   Teacher often absent.
           [C°   Inadequate teacher; little is learned.
B—— [C°   No use for what is learned.
           [C− Required to be a servant.
           [C− Treated as an inferior.

of rejection. Consequences for school attendance may be negative including punishment for being late and not completing assignments. (See Exhibit 12.13.)

The Importance of Antecedents

Behaviors tend to occur in situations in which they have been reinforced. Cues associated with reinforcement increase the probability of behaviors reinforced in their presence, whereas cues associated with punishing consequences (i.e., behavior is punished in their presence) decrease the probability of behaviors. Brian found that when the dog began to snarl, he might get bitten (see chapter 7). When this happened, he stopped teasing the dog. Snarling was a cue that continued teasing may result in a nasty bite. We usually say hello only when there is someone present. Their presence is the antecedent for saying hello. An elderly resident of a retirement home may snap at the staff when she is asked to carry out a task that is too difficult for her. In these instances, altering antecedents (sometimes other people's behavior) is a valuable approach (see e.g., Luiselli, 2008). One goal of assessment is to identify antecedents that influence behaviors of interest.

Like consequences, antecedents have a variety of sources. If you are relaxed during written examinations, you may think about past successes, share reassurances with a friend, and feel rested after a good night's sleep. If you are anxious, you may anticipate failing (cognitive cue), have had a telephone call from your parents reminding you how important it is to pass the exam (social cue), and be tired from staying up all night (physiological cues) (see Exhibit 12.14). We may make past or future events current by thinking about them, and they in turn, influence what we do, feel, and think. The sum total of antecedents related to a behavior can be termed the *antecedent event*. This may increase or decrease the probability of the behavior in the future. Assessment includes identification of both high-risk and low-risk situations for undesired behaviors. Examples of common antecedents for disruptive behavior of developmentally disabled children and youth can be seen in Exhibit 12.15. Notice that some are demand-based (disruptive behavior occurs when an instruction or demand is given and succeeds in getting rid of

EXHIBIT 12.14

Reviewing Antecedents

One hour before examination.	A^-	
Thoughts of failure.	A^-	
A nervous roommate who also has exams.	A^-	Anxiety
Reassurance by a friend.	A^+	
Supervisor seems in a good mood.	A^+	
All important work has been completed.	A^+	
It is near the end of the day.	A^+	Asking supervisor for the rest oft he afternoon off.
Worry that you will be considered undependable.	A^-	

unwanted tasks). What are low-risk situations (those in which problematic behavior rarely occurs)?

Rearranging antecedents (stimulus control) is one way to change behavior (see chapter 7). A *setting event* is a kind of antecedent that is closely associated with a behavior but is not in the immediate situation in which behaviors of interest occur. For example, because of an unpleasant exchange with a teacher, a child may respond angrily to a request by his parents when he comes home. The setting event alters the likelihood of certain reactions in later situations.

Behavior Always Makes Sense

An individual contextual analysis will yield detailed information about a client's characteristics and circumstances. It will typically reveal that behaviors, even those that appear bizarre and irrational "make sense." That is, there is a payoff for the client but at a high cost. For example, rather than focusing directly on undesired behavior (e.g., eating and binging), Israel Goldiamond (1984) helped a client take advantage of naturally competing

EXHIBIT 12.15

Examples of Antecedents of Disruptive Behavior

People	Places	Social Interactions
Specific staff	Novel places	Refusal of a request
New staff	On the bus	Given an instruction (e.g.,
Parent(s)	At work	to transition)
Doctors	Bathrooms	Provocation by peers
Peers		Difficulty communicating
Medical	Self-Created	Ecology/Atmosphere
During illness	Moodiness	Crowds/Noise
Drug side effects	Withdrawal	Absence of schedule
Prior to menses	Agitated	Personal space violation

Source: Adapted from C. Schrader & M. Levine (1994). *PTR: Prevent, teach and reinforce* (ch. 2, p. 3). San Rafael, CA: Behavioral Counseling and Research Center.

activities, such as enriching her social life. (See Exhibit 12.16.) Layng and Andronis (1984) describe how behaviors such as hallucinations often make sense, but only when we understand a client's history and current circumstances. This constructional view of behavior encourages identifying and building on client assets including alternative repertoires. (See also Exhibit 12.12.)

Clear Description of Assessment Methods

Clear description of assessment methods fulfills one of the conditions for informed consent. If you clearly describe your methods, your colleagues will be able to duplicate those that are successful and your supervisors will be able to offer you more specific feedback. Clear description makes it possible to gather information about useful methods.

A Close Relationship Between Assessment and Intervention

Assessment should offer guidelines for selecting plans. It should help you and your clients discover "leverage points" for attaining valued outcomes. It should indicate (1) objectives that must be reached to achieve hoped-for outcomes, (2) what must be done to achieve them, (3) how objectives can be pursued most effectively, and (4) the probability of attaining them given current resources and options.

Important Distinctions

Three important distinctions are discussed in this section: (1) form and function, (2) motivational and behavior deficits, and (3) response inhibition and behavior deficits. Overlooking these may result in selection of ineffective plans.

Form and Function

The form of a behavior (its topography) does not indicate its function (why the behavior occurs). Identical forms of behavior may be maintained by different contingencies. Someone might run down the street because he is being chased by someone (whom you cannot see because he has not yet rounded the corner),

EXHIBIT 12.16

A Case of Bulimia: Intervention Rationale

Occasion	Alternative Behaviors	Costs	Benefits
Client alone with child at home, in kitchen while husband at work; housework done; 2:00, 3:00 P.M., 6:00 P.M.	Disturbing behavior (DB) 1. Eating excessively, vomiting.	Medical and psychological risks, worry over interpretation; food and money wasted.	Whiles away her time; occupies her while watching child and after housework is done.
	2. Same pattern.	Same costs	Child having slept, bathed, and now playing, foregoing benefits are potent; leaves her time to prepare supper thereafter.
Sunday, client at her parents' house in afternoon.	3. Eating mother's cakes, ice cream, and cookies to excess.	Same costs, plus risk of discovery of pattern.	Mother expresses delight that her daughter enjoys her cooking; whiles away boring afternoon.
Afternoons	Target behavior (TB)		
	1. Find other young mothers with similar problems; new circle of friends.	Usual risks attached to forming friends; arrange for friends and husbands to meet husband; keep him informed; thank him for release of time.	Enjoyable time occupies her while child is cared for; housework done (other mothers have same problem)
Evenings	2a. Arrange with new friends to go shopping for meals, in early evening; start other activities	Same, plus scheduling problems and breakdowns	Child is cared for, client does things with friends; leaves her time to prepare supper.
	2b. Go out with own circle of friends twice a week.	See above.	Friendships, social circle.
Sundays	3. Arrive Sunday morning, go to Mass with parents; leave after luncheon snack.	Stress and indicate importance of marriage; stress and plan afternoon.	Mother and father express joy over lost daughter found; avoids boring afternoon; afternoon with husband and son.

Note. Bulimic nonlinear intervention: Daily event logs kept by client, turned in weekly, food eating and vomiting to be recorded. RE: Targets—
1. Discuss and check on social resources for groups of young mothers: neighborhood churches—no resources, community colleges—no groups, women's groups—none in neighborhood, local Y—regular classes for mothers during afternoons, swimming periods, with supervised children "dribs" (shallow pools) in some room as pool. Register in courses there.
2. Find friends from Resource 1, make arrangements for shopping, swapping child care. Discuss ways to have husband take over child care two evenings a week, while group goes out.
3. Discuss with husband change in Sunday pattern.

Intervention with spouse:
1. Program and rationale discussed; consent obtained.
2. Come home early two afternoons a week. (Spouse's initial reaction: "Good, then we'll go out together." Therapist's answer: "You go out with the boys, don't you? Let her go out with the girls.")
3. Spouse to get up early to allow his wife to attend Mass. (Had no objections to wife's religion, feared possible use by parents to get her back completely. Agreed that they would not try to break up their marriage, which could be strengthened by having Sunday afternoons to themselves.) To read paper at her parents' house while waiting; babysit.
4. To move to better house as job prospers.

Source: I. Goldiamond (1984). Training parent trainers and ethicists in nonlinear analysis of behavior. In R. F. Dangel & R. A. Polster (Eds.), *Parent training: Foundations of research and practice* (pp. 504–546). New York: Guilford. Reprinted with permission.

because he enjoys running, or because he is hungry and lunch is waiting for him at home. Thus, running may be maintained by either positive or negative reinforcement or both. A client may drink alcohol to avoid worrying about unpaid bills, because he enjoys the resulting relaxed feeling, because it upsets his mother and he enjoys her discomfort, or for all these reasons. A child saying the word *toast* might be reading a word, or she may be hungry and this prompts her to say *toast* because this produced food on previous occasions. Or she might be telling her parents that there is no toast as described in the classic book by Ferster,

Culbertson, and Boren (1975). Just as the same behavior may have different functions, different behaviors may have identical functions. Saying the word *toast,* banging on the table, or throwing cereal all may be maintained by attention from parents; that is, all three behaviors may belong to the same response class, or operant. A behavioral analysis includes a description of behaviors of concern, as well as evidence that specific antecedents and consequences affect them; thus it requires both a functional and a descriptive analysis.

Motivational Versus Behavioral Deficits

When someone does not know how to carry out a given behavior, there is a *behavior deficit*—a lack of needed behavioral skills. When someone knows how to perform a behavior but is not reinforced on an effective schedule or is punished, there is a *motivational problem.* If a desired behavior does not occur, its absence may point to either a behavioral or a motivational problem. Motivation and behavior deficits can be distinguished by arranging the conditions for the performance of behavior. A client could be asked to role-play behaviors of interest and also asked whether she uses similar behaviors in other situations. If she does engage in desired behaviors in other situations, then there is a motivational concern. If a client can perform a behavior if he is paid $500 to do so, motivation is the problem. The distinction between motivational and behavioral concerns is important because different intervention methods are usually called for. Altering motivation requires rearranging contingencies, but there is no need to establish a behavior, although prompts such as verbal instructions may be needed. If a client lacks a certain repertoire, then new behaviors must be established, perhaps by model presentation or shaping as described in chapter 24.

Motivational concerns are often mistaken for behavioral ones. A teacher may say that a student does not know how to do addition problems, or a husband may say that his wife does not know how to talk to him about his work. The student and the wife may indeed have these skills in their repertoire but not use them because they are not reinforced.

Interfering Emotions Versus Lack of Skills

Emotional reactions may interfere with desired behavior. For example, a client may not initiate conversations, not because he does not know how to, but because of social anxiety. Role playing can be used to find out whether required skills are available (see chapter 17). If they are, then interfering factors can be sought (e.g., anxiety, lack of knowledge about when to use skills, lack of reinforcement, and/or punishment). A disruption of behavior may suggest that the behaviors were easily disruptable to begin with. Anxiety, for example, "is not so much a thing of itself as it is a general condition of a larger repertoire" (Ferster, 1972, p. 6). If the behaviors were better maintained through positive consequences, a punishing consequence could not disrupt them so easily.

Sources of Influence That Should Be Reviewed

A contextual assessment requires a review of both personal and environmental factors that may influence options. Possible influences include global effects on local contexts, social policies and related legislation, other people, the physical environment, physiological changes, thoughts, genetic differences, and developmental factors. Material and community resources and related policies and legislation affect options. (See Exhibit 12.17.)

Global Influences on Local Circumstances and Subjectivities

Long ago Jane Jacobs highlighted the importance of local communities being appraised of developments at the state and federal levels as they may influence local neighborhoods. Today we live in an ever more globalized world in which developments in distant areas may affect local communities. Examples include the outsourcing of jobs to other countries, transnational corporations, wars, famine, and genocide. These global factors affect not only local resources, but our very subjectivities—how we each experience these changes. The personal and the social are inextricably mixed. This interaction shows the harm of a simplistic use of practice theory in trying to understand individuals. "Experience, then, has as much to do with collective realities as it does with individual translations and transformations of those realities. It is always simultaneously social and subjective, collective and individual" (Kleinman & Fitz-Henry, 2007, p. 53). Only by understanding the unique circumstances of women living in impoverished neighborhoods in Brazil can we understand why they did not grieve for their young children who died (Scheper-Hughes, 1992).

Big Pharma is a global multi-billion dollar industry that influences us on a daily basis, for example, promoting problems-in-living as mental illnesses. The biomedical industrial complex has every incentive to minimize contextual causes of personal troubles such as lack of affordable housing and discriminatory hiring practices and maximize promotion of individual deficiencies as causal. Moncrieff (2008a) suggests that the chemical imbalance model of human illness "is a perfect companion to the ideology of consumerism and helps the neoliberal project in various ways" (p. 247). It creates a dissatisfaction (lack of an ideal chemical balance) that is vital to the purchase of products (e.g., prescribed medications).

Social Policies and Related Legislation and the Values They Reflect

A contextual assessment calls for attention to the relationship between personal problems and public issues (between the personal and the political as reflected in service systems)

EXHIBIT 12.17

Domains Selected to Reflect Quality of Life in New Zealand Cities

1. **People**—Information about the people in New Zealand's largest cities helps build an understanding of the nature of urban communities and how they are changing. This information provides a context for the rest of the indicators report. The indicators in this domain highlight key demographics about New Zealand's city dwellers.

2. **Knowledge and skills**—Knowledge and skill attainment are essential for effective participation in society and hence, quality of life. The indicators in this domain provide an overview of the state of educational participation and achievement in New Zealand's largest cities.

3. **Economic standard of living**—Levels of income and socio-economic position determine ability to purchase goods and services and ability to obtain adequate food and housing. They also influence people's ability to participate in the wider community. The indicators in this domain look at aspects of the economy that impact at the personal and household level.

4. **Economic development**—Economic growth and development help underpin quality of life and enhance prosperity in cities. The indicators in this domain explore aspects of the broader economy and its impacts on New Zealand cities.

5. **Housing**—Housing is the base from which people interact with and participate in their wider communities. It has one of the biggest impacts on people's well being. The indicators in this domain identify issues related to general housing trends and crises in New Zealand cities and how these issues have flow-on effects for communities in areas such as health, education, and community cohesion.

6. **Health**—The overall physical and mental health of city population impacts significantly on quality of life and is closely related to many other areas such as socio-economic status and employment. The indicators in this domain focus on a holistic view of health and address aspects of physical and mental well being.

7. **Safety**—Feeling and being safe and secure in homes, communities, and cities are basic human rights. As cities grow, a key challenge is the provision of safe social and physical environments where people are able to participate fully in their communities. Indicators in this domain present an overview of perceptions of safety, aspects of physical safety for key population groups and general law and order issues.

8. **Built environment**—The built environment is an important contributor to the way people feel about their city. It also has a huge impact on the sustainability of the natural environment. Indicators in this domain look at aspects of the developed environment that make up cityscapes.

9. **Natural environment**—The quality of the natural environment impacts directly on people's quality of life. Increases in a city's population can place increasing pressure on the sustainability of the physical environment. The indicators in this domain look at aspects of the natural environment that are significant to city living.

10. **Social connectedness**—Connecting with other people and networks are important in the development and maintenance of strong communities. The rapid pace of change and diversity in cities has an impact on the way people connect with one another. The indicators in this domain highlight how people develop and maintain social connectedness.

11. **Civil and political rights**—Effective civil and political systems allows communities to be governed in a manner that promotes justice and fairness and thus a better quality of life. Participation of residents in representative governance and decision making processes at local and national levels is central to the concept of democracy. Indicators in this domain look at the effectiveness of civil and political systems that are important to decision making in cities.

Source: K. Jamieson (2004). A collaborative approach to developing and using quality of life indicators in New Zealand's largest cities. In M. J. Sirgy, D. Rahtz, & Tong-jin, Yi (Eds.), *Community quality of life indicators: Best cases* (pp. 78–79). Boston: Kluwer Academic. Reprinted with permission.

(e.g., Mills, 1959). The values and norms in a society and conflicts about them are reflected in public policies and related legislation and social institutions that influence availability of resources. Those who have power use this to frame problems in a certain manner (e.g., as individual deficiencies). Those who have influence over socialization institutions such as schools and the media promote certain views, which may become internalized; we ourselves come to believe them; we become our own oppressors. "Eventually, people come to regulate themselves through the internalization of cultural prescriptions. Hence, what may seem on the surface as freedom may be questioned as a form of acquiescence whereby citizens restrict their life choices to coincide with a narrow range of socially approved options" (Prilleltensky, Prilleltensky, & Voorhees, 2008).

Disciplinary techniques and moralizing injunctions as to health, hygiene and civility are no longer required; the project of responsible citizenship has been fused with individuals' projects for themselves. What began as a social norm here ends as a personal desire. Individuals act upon themselves and their families in terms of the languages, values and techniques made available to them by professions, disseminated through the apparatuses of the mass media or sought out by the troubled through the market. (Rose, 1999, p. 88)

Thus, as Skinner (1956) long ago noted in a debate with Carl Rogers, we have to ask why we want a certain item. Prilleltensky and his colleagues (2008) distinguish between political and psychological oppression. This contextual view requires attention to macro, meso, and micro influences on oppression, liberation, and well-being. (See Exhibit 12.18.)

Policies and related legislation affect both for-profit and not-for-profit organizations and their interrelationships. Problems clients confront may require societal-level change because related contingencies are influenced by people at many different system levels. (Consider Exhibit 7.2.) Policies regarding housing influence availability of low-cost rentals. You may be able to influence only some levels. Understanding the big picture may avoid inaccurate estimates of what can be accomplished. Hasenfeld (2000) argues that human service organizations are integrally involved in making judgments about moral worth. Many scholars have lamented the residual nature of child welfare (Pelton, 1989). Depending on policies and related funding, agencies may or may not have the resources needed to help clients. Consider lack of availability of evidence-informed parent-training programs resulting in parents being referred to programs that are not likely to help them (e.g., Barth, Landsverk, Chamberlain, Reid, Rolls, Hurlburt, et al., 2005). Financial considerations may create competition among agencies that harms clients.

Changes in funding encouraged by managed care policies and related practices constrain what can be offered, for example, number of sessions and follow-up of clients. The growth of managed care has been accompanied by a rise in bureaucracy and "managerialism"—the influence of administrators on the discretion and tasks of front-line staff including ever-increasing paperwork. This has been particularly marked in countries such as the United Kingdom where required documentation has decreased time available for direct work with clients in public agencies. This has become so intrusive that there has been a backlash including the creation of a special review panel (e.g., Munro, 2011). Rogowski (2010) attributes these trends to the intrusion of neoliberal ideology into the welfare sector. The latter refers to the ideology that the market is superior to the state in that public services should be managed in ways common in the private sector, thus the ever-increasing role of managers. He suggests that this rise of managerialism is closely related to "marketization," which refers to the sponsored development of competition in the provision of welfare services together with the development of internal markets within public agencies in order to imitate market relationships. The idea was to get out of the care business including returning care to the community. The message was, people have to help themselves and if they did not, they may be fined as were parents whose children did not attend school. Key to managerialism is increased regulation of professionals via centralized financial control and creation of performance targets and measures of success in achieving them. This highlights yet again the close connection between what you can offer to clients and ideologies about welfare—who should provide what to whom and under what circumstances. We live in an era of retrenchment—moving away from helping those who confront adversity or create it for others. Keeping these higher-level contingencies in mind will help you to avoid incorrect accounts of problems that limit clients' options or promote false promises of change.

Other People Including Social Support Systems

What social supports do clients have? What kind can be created? Are there extended kinship networks that can be involved? Can neighbors or local groups be involved? What is the role of peers? (Dodge, Dishion, & Lansford, 2008)

What public places provide opportunities to make friends and gain support? Social support plays a critical role in our lives at all ages. How do significant others such as family members view a problem, and what will they gain or lose if particular outcomes are achieved? Supportive relationships are a key factor in both developing and maintaining resilience (coping well with stress and adversity). Social support provides many potential benefits including enjoyable social contacts, material aid, and guidance in times of need, support of values, predictability of social contacts, and being a valued part of different groups. Lack of or decrease in social support is a key vulnerability factor for many personal and social problems. Uncertainty created by a lagging economy may result in moving away from sources of social support to seek employment. Migration and immigration also profoundly affect social support available.

Attention from others may become an important maintaining factor for behavior, even though it was not involved in encouraging an initial reaction. For example, a woman may become anxious when she is away from home. Her family members may respond with sympathy and support, which may increase her reports of fear, especially if she receives little attention at other times. Family members may not recognize their role in maintaining behaviors they dislike. Brian's parents were unaware of how their reactions helped maintain Brian's behaviors that they found annoying. That is, they attended to (reinforced) him when he teased the dog and ignored him when he played nicely with the dog. Brian, in turn, influenced his parents' behavior. Staff in residential settings are often unaware that they reinforce behaviors they complain about. (See Dodge, Dishion & Lansford, 2008.) They may ignore desired behaviors and reinforce (mis)behaviors with attention. Supervisors who complain about line staff behavior may not realize that they ignore desired behaviors. Current life circumstances influence whether significant others participate effectively. Mrs. Lakeland's full-time job, coupled with running a household in which the children shouldered few chores, left her tired and, in her words, "more likely to fly off the handle." Her husband worked full-time on one job and three nights a week on another to help his older son pay for college.

The Community and Physical Environment

The influence of the physical environment is often overlooked. Consider the impact of environment pollutants (Pellow &

EXHIBIT 12.18

Attention to power in Understanding Clients and Their Circumstances

Stages of wellness/ Empowerment ▸ Level of analysis/ Intervention ▾	Oppression (state)	Liberation (process)	Well-being (outcome)
Macro/collective/ structural/community	Context minimization error: failing to assess for and highlight the role of macro-level systemic factors (i.e., poverty, neighborhood violence), as well as social policies and cultural norms (i.e., xenophobia; blame the victim mentality) that increase problematic functioning and decrease well-being. In a similar vein, failing to assess macro-level factors (i.e., greater gender equality) that enhance well-being.	Highlighting macro-level constraints and their correlation with problematic functioning at the personal, interpersonal, and familial level.	Highlighting the interdependence between personal, organizational, and collective well-being. Acknowledging that micro-level interventions are necessary but insufficient and must be supplemented with meso- and macro-level interventions. Must realize that personal well-being cannot be attained in the absence of organizational and collective well-being.
Meso/organizational/ group/relational	Failing to assess for, or giving insufficient weight to, contextual factors and organizational structures (i.e., school climate, work environment) that increase problematic functioning and decrease well-being. Failing to assess for contextual factors and organizational structures that reduce problems and enhance well-being, as well as factors and structures that have the potential for doing so.	Identifying meso-level constraints that increase dysfunction and reduce well-being (i.e., bullying at school; an unhealthy work environment) Identifying and amplifying meso-level factors that currently serve as protective factors (i.e., positive school climate, collaborative work environment). Assessing ways of building on healthy structures and affecting those that impede well-being.	Clear guidelines for meso-level interventions designed to alleviate distress, dysfunction, and/or mental illness. Clear guidelines for meso-level interventions designed to enhance well-being, flourishing, and mental health. Clear guidelines for strengthening and building on positive structures.
Micro/individual/ Personal/ Psychological (emotional, cognitive, behavioral, spiritual)	Amplifying deficits and dysfunction. Ignoring strengths and resilience. Focusing exclusively on alleviating illness and distress. Overlooking potential for flourishing and well-being.	Supplementing problem assessment with situations when said problem was resisted or overcome. Assessing for internalized oppression. Inquiring about health-enhancing relationships and problem-free spheres in the client's life. Assessing for personal strengths, assets, and examples of thriving and well-being.	A balanced assessment process that builds on personal strengths, assets, and resources (i.e., good social skills; perseverance). Clear guidelines for individually based interventions designed to alleviate distress, dysfunction, and/or mental illness. Clear guidelines for individually based interventions designed to enhance well-being, flourishing, and mental health.

Source: I. Prillelkensky, O. Prillelkensky, & C. Voorhees (2008). Psychopolitical validity in the helping professions: Applications to research, interventions, case conceptualization and therapy. In C. I. Cohen & S. Timimi (Eds.), *Liberatory psychiatry: Philosophy, politics and mental health* (pp. 118–119). New York: Cambridge University Press. Reprinted with permission.

Brulle, 2007). Housing policy affects residents (Schwartz, 2010). Rates of schizophrenia are two times higher among people in cities (see Silversides, 2004). Temperature changes, crowding, and noise level affect behavior. Violent acts may be discouraged by decreasing physical spaces that are not open to scrutiny by others (e.g., see Astor, Meyer, & Pitner, 1999). The characteristics of the neighborhoods and communities in which clients live influence their options as described by Wacquant (2009) in *Punishing the Poor*. (See also Kling, Liebman, & Katz, 2001; Mohnen, Groenewegen, Volker, & Flap, 2011) Neighborhood variables include level and kind of police surveillance, recreational opportunities, poverty, immigrant concentration, stability, networks/exchanges, transportation availability, and collective efficacy (Burton, Kemp, Leung, Matthews, & Takeuchi, 2011; Sutton & Kemp, 2011). Lists of potential indicators of quality of life include arts and culture (e.g., venues for art events), economy and economic vitality (e.g., poverty level), education and life long learning (e.g., libraries available), environment (e.g., air quality, open space, parks, litter), government (e.g., hours people spend volunteering), health and welfare (e.g., infant mortality, prenatal care, substance abuse), human services (e.g., child abuse, senior housing), land use, housing and transportation (e.g., public transit hours, average rent), and public safety (e.g., hate crimes, police response time).

Over 30 years ago, Homel and Burns (1989) found that children who live in poor-quality environments (e.g., little play space, industrial neighborhoods, littered streets) were less satisfied with their lives, experienced more negative emotions, and had more restricted and less positive friendships compared with children who lived in higher quality settings. Hazards in the rundown housing in which many poor families live include lead poisoning and unprotected windows. Poor people have fewer options in dealing with potential hazards. They may not be able to afford baby sitters or bars on windows. They may fear that, if they complain about dangerous conditions, they will be evicted. They may not be able to make changes in their home that would allow an elderly relative to safely navigate the house.

Air pollution has been linked to poorer student health and academic performance (Erickson, 2011). Physical arrangements in residential and day care settings influence behavior. Unwanted behaviors may be encouraged by available materials. For example, toys may distract children from educational tasks. Brian did not have a room of his own and had no place where he could work on his hobbies without being interrupted. Board-and-care operators may crowd residents into small rooms, provide few if any social opportunities, and fail to make needed repairs. Shelters for the homeless may be more dangerous than the streets for those they claim to help. Community characteristics contribute to resilience of residents, including children, via availability of diverse social organizations, consistency of guidance regarding behavior, and opportunities to take part in varied social groups.

Available Repertoires and Reinforcers

We can use a client's unique available repertoires and reinforcer profile to help them to attain valued outcomes. Examples of repertoires include self-management skills (e.g., getting up, dressing and arriving at work on time, refusing drinks, studying an hour a day), social skills (e.g., making friends, maintaining intimate relationships, supporting family members, dealing with difficult supervisors), work skills (e.g., locating employment), problem-solving and emotion management skills, and recreational skills. Identifying available repertoires is an integral aspect of a constructional approach. Reinforcers include valuing social contacts, helping others, and solving problems.

The Match Between the Tasks We Confront and Our Resources

The kinds of tasks we confront influence our behavior. In such cases, focus may be on altering the task environment. Behaviors of concern may occur because of boredom or excessive demands. For example, there is a relationship between tasks children confront and injurious behavior (Luiselli, Russo, Christian, & Wilczynski, 2008). The quality of the curriculum in classrooms influences children's behaviors. Low income may be compounded by need to care for a disabled family member.

Biomedical Factors

Overlooking physical causes may result in incorrect inferences about the causes of problems. For instance, certain illnesses are associated with psychological changes. Examples are hyperthyroidism in a young refugee woman referred by an internist because of anxiety; an orange-sized (and curable) meningioma in a middle-aged refugee woman referred by a family physician with a diagnosis of depression; and pellagra in a refugee teacher who suddenly became socially withdrawn, confused, and silly (Westermeyer, 1987). One of my students had her field placement in a school. An 8-year-old girl was referred to her for behavior problems both at home and at school. There were certain indications that some medical cause may be responsible (she felt dizzy at times) and she was referred to a physician for a checkup. He said that she was fine. The student noticed that the little girl appeared to falter sometimes when walking and pressed for a referral to a specialist. This referral was made and an MRI revealed a brain tumor, which was thought to be responsible for the problem behaviors. The sources of information drawn on here included signs (results of an MRI), as well as symptoms.

Environmental pollutants, nutritional deficiencies, and food allergens may affect health and behavior (e.g., see Gatrell & Elliot, 2009). Lack of sleep may lower our ability to solve problems. Hormonal changes associated with menopause may result in mood changes that may be mistakenly attributed to psychological causes. On the other hand, psychological changes may be mistakenly attributed to hormonal changes. For example, a coworker may incorrectly attribute disliked behavior to pre-menstrual tension. Great attention has been given over the past years to trying to identify biochemical correlates of behaviors labeled as mental disorders, some argue with little success (for critiques of some popular methods, see Vul et al., 2009; for critiques of biomedical narratives, see, for example, Clarke et al., 2010.)

Clients may not have access to health care or be reluctant to seek it because of fears such as disclosure of undocumented status. (See literature describing health disparities.) Chronic health problems increase with age. Health problems are a major concern for clients with AIDS. A physical examination should be required whenever physiological factors may be related to a problem (e.g., seizures, depression, fatigue, or headaches). Be sure to explore the adequacy of nutrition and coffee, alcohol, or drug intake. Drugs, prescribed or not, may influence how clients appear and behave. Fetal alcohol syndrome and drug-affected infants have received increasing attention. If you work with clients who are taking prescription drugs you should become familiar with their effects. (See http://www.criticalthinkrx.org.) Experiences affect biomedical factors (e.g., see Shonkoff & Garner, 2012). The more time Romanian children spent in an orphanage before age 5 the shorter were their telomeres (Tyrka, Price, Kao, Porton, Marsella, & Carpenter, 2010).

Cognitive and Perceptual Characteristics

Clients differ in their intellectual functioning and problem-solving skills, for example, their flexibility in approaching concerns (Jacobson, Mulick, & Rojahn, 2007). (See chapter 19 for more detail.) (Mis)use of substances may compromise decision-making skills. Clients differ in how they view their potentials (their self-efficacy/self-concept). This may be over or underestimated. People differ in their views of the world. Some view this as hostile and threatening. Others view it as full of opportunities. Some view their world as controlled by others; others believe they have considerable influence over their lives. Clients differ in how accurately they view their environments and themselves and in their moral values, for example, obligations to help others. Misconceptions (e.g., that everyone will like them) may be an obstacle. Thoughts may function as cues in chains of behavior and may contribute to anxiety, anger, and depression (for more detail, see chapter 7). A depressed client may have a high frequency of negative self-statements and a low frequency of positive self-statements. The thoughts and feelings we have in a situation are related to past and current experiences in that situation and those that are similar or associated in some way.

A causal role may be mistakenly attributed to thoughts because the learning histories related to their development, as well as current related contingencies are unknown or ignored. It is not that an explanation that attributes the cause of problems to thoughts is wrong; it is that such accounts are incomplete. A change in thoughts and feelings often occurs as a result of behavior changes. We can examine the role of thoughts by varying certain ones and determining the effects on behaviors. The heuristics approach suggests that the particular "toolbox of heuristics" we have is more descriptive of human nature than are "traits, attitudes, preferences or similar internal explanations" (Gigerenzer, Hertwig, & Pachur, 2011, p. 25). Rather than looking inside, such heuristics consider ecological rationality; does a heuristic work in real life? (For further discussion, see chapter 8.)

Emotions and Feelings

Clients differ in the range of emotions they experience, the situations in which they occur, and in their skills in influencing their feelings including coping with stress (e.g., see literature on emotional intelligence). They may be subject to wide mood swings. They may (mis)use drugs or alcohol to regulate their moods. A past history of trauma may result in a blunting of emotions or a heightened vigilance for adverse events. Feelings and mood states such as depression, anxiety, and anger may be presented as a problem or be related to other problems. (See discussion of affective disorders in the DSM.) For example, a parent's depression may encourage neglect of her child. The absence of certain feelings may be of concern such as not having empathy for harm to others. Feelings, thoughts, and behavior are interrelated. Feelings and thoughts may influence our behavior and, in turn, our behavior may influence our thoughts and feelings. Theories of behavior differ in whether causal status is given to feelings and in the variables believed to account for them such as early childhood experiences and current contingencies. Emotions are important cues to contingencies—who is reinforcing or punishing what behaviors? Indeed in a constructional approach to helping clients, clients learn how to use their emotions to identify important contingencies.

We can draw on literature concerning emotions to understand how they develop and change. Paul Ekman's (1992) research suggests that each emotion has unique behavioral display patterns, motivational value, and physiological arousal patterns. Cultural norms influence what is viewed as appropriate in specific circumstances. Different people express their feelings in different ways. Just because someone does not cry when a relative dies does not mean she does not care. Mesquita (2001) notes that "The research generally supports the hypothesis that equivalent emotions in different cultures are characterized by similar appraisal patterns" (p. 229). For example, "Across culture, the situations that produce fear were conceived of as unpleasant, obstructing goals and hard to cope with. Anger was provoked in situations that were seen as unexpected, unpleasant, obstructing goals, unfair, and caused by other people" (p. 229). Changing feelings will not make up for a lack of skills required to attain a valued outcome or rearrange related environmental contingencies. Here, too, as with thoughts, it is not that attributing the cause of problems to feelings is wrong, it is that the account is incomplete. The relative importance of behaviors, thoughts, affect, and physiological responses for a given client has implications for selecting plans. For example, if social anxiety is mainly related to muscle tension, relaxation training may be called for. If it is mainly cued by negative self-statements such as "I bet I'll be a flop again," cognitive restructuring combined with exposure to feared situations may be best. If it is related to a lack of effective social skills, social skills training may be required (see chapter 24).

Motivational Differences

Motivation is (and has been) of great interest in psychology. Motivation can be defined as a relationship between behavior and various operations such as deprivation that influences behavior (e.g., Leslie & Millenson, 1996). We each have a unique reinforcer profile (consequences we like or dislike) shaped by our past history. For example, a client may have sought relief from economic adversity by drinking alcohol, resulting in further adversity. Drinking alcohol is used to remove unpleasant events in his life. Lack of motivation may be related to beliefs about problems and potential solutions. A client may believe that a label given to him by a psychiatrist (bi-polar) means that he can never change. He may believe that his life is unchangeable because he resembles his father who spent his life in prison. Our values influence what we find reinforcing or punishing. For example, valuing removal of avoidable injustices may provide the courage (the motivation) to identify, document, expose, and advocate for removal of avoidable miseries.

Religion and Spirituality

Greater attention has been given to client's spirituality and religion over the past years and how they may influence concerns and options. Religion refers to formal institutional structures (e.g., Is a client Catholic or Muslim?) Spirituality refers to experiences of transcendence and search for personal meanings (e.g., Hill, Pargament, Hood, McCullough, Swyers, Larson, et al. 2000). Some authors recommend that an understanding of a client's religious values and spiritual experiences and meanings and goals should be a part of assessment (e.g., Richards & Bergin, 1997). You should be sensitive to the role that religion and different kinds of spirituality play in the life of a client, especially as this relates to outcomes a client hopes to achieve. Here too, a variety of measures are available.

Cultural Differences

Cultural differences in values and norms may influence the problems clients confront, preferred communication styles, and service options (Pederson, Lonner, Draguns, & Trimble, 2007; Sue & Sue, 2002). Geertz suggests that "culture is best seen not as complexes of concrete behavior patterns…but as a set of control mechanisms-plans, recipes, rules, instructions…for the governing of behavior" (quoted in Becker, 1996). Norms for behavior differ in different groups. These differences involve far

more than race and ethnicity. They include differences related to gender, physical abilities, sexual orientation, geographical region, religion, and age. Identity politics encourages us to think of ourselves as but one of our many identities to the exclusion of others; we each have many identities, affiliations, and associations. "Proposals to see a person merely as a member of one social group tend to be based on an inadequate understanding of the breadth and complexity in any society in the world" (Sen, 2009, p. 247).

Cultural differences may be reflected in preferred coping styles and beliefs about the causes of problems. Lack of knowledge about cultural differences may result in incorrect assumptions about clients and their circumstances. Degree of acculturation may be important to assess (Roysircar-Sodowsky & Maestas, 2000). Differences in acculturation among family members may create strains in families. De Anda (1984) suggests that the interaction of ethnic minority clients with mainstream culture is influenced by the following:

- Degree of overlap between cultures regarding norms, values, beliefs, perceptions, and related contingencies.

- Availability of "cultural translators, mediators, and models."

- Nature of contingencies.

- Overlap between the conceptual style and problem-solving approach of the minority individual and the prevalent styles of the majority culture.

- Degree of bilingualism.

- Similarity in physical appearance to that of the majority culture (e.g., skin color, facial features).

Level of acculturation may influence stress, experiences, attitude toward helpers, and the process and goals that are appropriate (Kohatsu, Conception, & Perez, 2010; Sue & Sue, 2008). The stresses of migration and immigration may linger for years (e.g., see Furman & Negi, 2010). More people now go back and forth between two or more countries. Thus, the increasing interest in social work with transnational clients (Negi & Furman, 2010). Standardized assessment instruments have been developed to assess acculturation. Knowledge of problems faced and preferred communication styles of different generations within different cultures will be valuable. We are influenced by popular culture including the culture of therapy to different degrees (e.g., Illouz, 2008).

Developmental Considerations Including Transitions

Knowledge about required tasks and related behaviors at different ages and life transitions can be helpful in making decisions.

Information concerning typical behaviors at different times (developmental norms) offers information about the prevalence of a behavior. This knowledge can be used to "normalize" behavior (help clients realize that reactions they believed to be unusual or abnormal are typical). For example, a parent may believe that his child is doomed to a career of crime because he was caught stealing. The parent may not know that most children steal some object at some time. This is not to say that nothing should be done to discourage stealing. Information about common changes in different life-cycle phases (e.g., parenthood, retirement) can help in preventive planning, for example, offering support groups for people nearing retirement, or for couples about to have their first child. Being misinformed about the nature of some developmental tasks (for example, assuming incorrectly that certain behaviors have to be learned before others) may hinder effective case planning because of the mistaken belief that a client is not yet "ready."

Considerable attention has been devoted to identifying risk and protective factors, for example, for child abuse and neglect (e.g., see Jensen & Fraser, 2011). This public health approach is reflected in life stage development models. The risk factors that initiate a problem may differ from those that maintain or exacerbate a concern. Some risks contribute to the development of problems; others to their maintenance. Thus, there are proximal and distal risk factors. Experiences during childhood such as degree and kind of parental nurturing influence behavior at later ages. Parents offer different kinds of attachment opportunities to their children, for example, secure or insecure (see Cassidy, & Shaver, 2008). Such experiences may influence skills in tolerating unpleasant emotional reactions. Knowledge concerning genetic and developmental influences is of value in understanding different patterns of behavior at different ages (e.g., Cicchitti & Cohen, 2006). Examples of recommendations suggested by Holmbeck, Greenley, and Franks (2003) for considering developmental principles in clinical and research work include the following:

- Stay current with developmental literature.

- Consider developmental tasks and milestones.

- Think about the total context.

- Help parents and other relevant adults such as teachers, become developmentally sensitive; familiarity with norms will help people to understand transitional changes that might occur, for example, in adolescents.

- Anticipate future developmental tasks and milestones and plan for them, for example, arrange a divorce support group for children whose parents are getting divorced.

- Consider the concept of equifinality; different developmental pathways may lead to the same outcomes. This is a major reason people object to being guided simply by diagnostic category.

Ethical Issues

Assessment frameworks and methods can be harmful, as well as helpful. For example, they may provide misleading estimates of problem severity and misleading directions. They can shrink or expand opportunities to help clients. Informed consent obligations may be violated by not sharing uncertainties regarding possible harms and benefits associated with use of a given framework and method (e.g., a screening test for depression). Discovering whether hoped-for outcomes can be achieved may be possible only via a sound assessment. Professionals have an obligation to consider how problem framing may influence the prospects of achieving hoped-for outcomes without adverse effects such as irreversible tardive dyskensia as a result of neuroleptic medication. Human experience is complex, affected not only by biological factors but by unique environmental circumstances as shown even in infant and twin studies (e.g., see also Plomin, 2011). Kleinman and Fitz-Henry (2007) argue that biological reductionism fails "to account for the enormous complexity of human social experience—war, genocide, structural violence, poverty and displacement—and the highly nuanced subjective states that those experiences engender…or even the more 'routine' violences of social neglect and institutionalized racism" (p. 53). Anthropologists highlight the interplay of individuals and their unique circumstances. Experience "has as much to do with collective realities [e.g., dependence on medication] as it does with individual translations and transformations of those realities. It is always simultaneously social and subjective, collective and individual" (Kleinman & Fitz-Henry, 2007, p. 53).

Although decisions must typically be made on the basis of incomplete data, without a sound assessment framework, opportunities to gather useful data may be lost, and assessment may be incomplete, resulting in selection of ineffective or harmful plans. This highlights the importance of thinking critically about assessment frameworks and measures: for example, are they compatible with empirical information about behaviors, thoughts, and feelings?

Summary

Assessment frameworks differ in the extent to which they have been critically appraised regarding their accuracy and usefulness in providing guidelines about how to attain valued outcomes or if they can be attained. The perspective preferred affects choice of data to collect and how to collect it. Honoring ethical obligations to clients requires selection of frameworks that are compatible with empirical data regarding behavior and use of measures that provide accurate information that contributes to making well-reasoned decisions. Assessment should indicate the likelihood of attaining valued outcomes. This may be slim because needed resources are not available or because related environmental or personal characteristics cannot be altered. Taking advantage of the steps involved in evidence-based practice, for example, consulting practice-related research regarding life-affecting decisions will contribute to making well-informed decisions.

Assessment should be of value to clients and significant others by offering some immediate benefits, such as hope and concrete help. It is an ongoing process in which decisions are altered as necessary in response to new information. A contextual analysis should indicate the levels of intervention required to attain hoped-for outcomes whether at the individual, family, group, community, agency, service system, and policy and/or legislative level. Characteristics of a contextual assessment include use of frameworks and methods that are most likely to offer accurate data, including observation of relevant interactions when needed and clear descriptions of hoped-for outcomes. There is an interest in constructing repertoires. Presenting concerns are translated into outcomes that, if attained, will remove or minimize them. This may require changes in the behaviors of service providers as well as those of clients and significant others. There is an interest in understanding the function (meaning) of behaviors of concern; what do they communicate? Assessment should be individually tailored as needed for each client and include a search for both personal and environmental resources. Cultural differences should be considered as they relate to possible resolutions. A contextual assessment avoids blaming clients for their problems, relying on oversimplified stigmatizing labels, and offering incomplete accounts. A procedural guide for carrying out an assessment is described in the next chapter.

Reviewing Your Competencies

Reviewing Content Knowledge

1. Describe the basic characteristics of a contextual assessment framework.

2. Describe the differences between sign (diagnostic) and sample (assessment) approaches.

3. Describe the kinds of questions that arise during assessment related to information needed to make decisions.

4. Describe criteria of value in reviewing different practice frameworks.

5. Describe assessment errors that result in incomplete or incorrect problem analyses.

6. Describe the difference between a descriptive and a functional analysis.

7. Give an example of a pseudoexplanation.

8. Describe four ways assessment can be of value to clients.

9. Explain why significant others are important to include in assessment and give examples.

10. Give examples of the difference between motivation and behavior deficits.

11. Give examples of the difference between topographic and functional descriptions of behavior.

12. Describe what is meant by "the client uniformity myth."

13. Describe the differences between a constructional and a deficiency approach to helping.

14. Discuss the role of past history in a contextual assessment.

15. Describe the disadvantages of focusing on the past.

16. Describe the limitations of psychiatric labels and give examples.

17. Describe the difference between setting events and antecedents.

18. Accurately describe different kinds of contingencies and their effects on behavior.

19. Give examples of the influence of the physical environment on behavior.

20. Discuss the roles of thoughts and feelings in different practice perspectives.

21. Discuss the relationship between behavior deficits and behavior surfeits (behaviors that occur too often).

22. Give examples of inadequate and inappropriate stimulus control.

23. Give examples of inadequate or inappropriate reinforcing functions.

24. You can review a case example and accurately critique it from an evidence-informed, contextual, strengths-oriented assessment perspective.

25. You can review a case example and accurately describe the kinds of information you would need.

Reviewing What You Do

1. You pose well-structured questions regarding assessment needs that allow an efficient, effective search for related research findings.

2. You clearly describe client concerns and related hoped-for outcomes.

3. You identify environmental factors related to client concerns including setting events, antecedents, and consequences, as well as structural factors such as policies and related legislation.

4. You involve significant others in assessment.

5. You identify personal assets and environmental resources.

6. Your inferences about the causes of problems are informed by related research findings.

7. You avoid noninstrumental labels.

8. You focus on appropriate systems levels (e.g., individual, family, group, agency, community, policy, and legislative).

Reviewing Results

1. Clients form more helpful views of their problems.

2. Clients report that assessment was helpful.

3. Clients increase their problem-solving skills.

4. Plans selected help clients to attain outcomes they value.

13

Beginning: A Practice Guide

OVERVIEW Social work practice has beginnings, middles, and endings. This chapter describes decisions, tasks, and accompanying skills involved in the beginning phase. Goals in initial interviews include offering introductory information, identifying hoped-for outcomes, initiating a collaborative working relationship, and encouraging positive expectations. The value of gathering an overview of problems/desired outcomes and setting priorities are described, as are the advantages of clear agreements and access to resources, such as relevant databases that permit effective, efficient searches for practice- and policy-related research findings. Guidelines are offered for clarifying client concerns and related factors and selecting objectives. A careful assessment will help you tailor your decisions to the unique characteristics and circumstances of each client (individual, family, group, organization, or community) as needed to help clients attain outcomes they value. It will allow you to build on client assets including alternative available repertoires. Your success will be related to the "goodness of fit" between client circumstances and characteristics and what is offered. Common errors include trying to work on too many concerns at once, seeking vague outcomes (not clarifying hoped-for outcomes), choosing process goals that do not identify hoped-for outcomes (e.g., attend counseling for addiction) and confusing clients with resisters.

YOU WILL LEARN ABOUT

- A problem-solving guide

- Initial interviews/exchanges

- Gathering an overview of concerns and related desired outcomes

- Deciding whether services can be provided

- Deciding on priorities

- Encouraging a collaborative working relationship

- Clearly describing problems and their context

- Offering support

- Encouraging helpful views of problems and their causes

- Identifying specific outcomes to focus on

- Forming a service agreement
- Selecting progress indicators
- Culturally sensitive practice
- Reporting maltreatment
- Assessing the risk of self-harm, suicide, and abuse
- When there is a crisis

A Problem-Solving Guide

Responsibilities of social workers differ greatly ranging from providing no direct services (as in a case management role in which you coordinate services provided by others) to provision of direct services yourself. The latter may range from working intensively with clients, families, groups, or communities over many weeks or months to a more sporadic and limited role, as in some outreach services for homeless youth or some protective services for the elderly. (See, for example, the descriptions of social workers given in chapter 1.) Follow-up is usually limited—unfortunately, since this provides opportunities to catch and reverse downward trends in positive outcomes. (See chapter 22.) The detailed examples given in this chapter illustrate provision of direct services to individuals and families. Understanding requisites for providing direct services is important if you function as a case manager of services provided by others. (chapters 26 and 27 describe work with groups and communities.) Questions of concern and a related constructional questionnaire are shown in Exhibits 13.1 and 13.2. Initial meetings set the stage for later ones and influence whether or not there will be later meetings.

Many decisions, tasks, and accompanying skills in the beginning stages are common to all levels of service with a wide variety of problems and clients. Examples are: (1) identifying hoped-for outcomes and related factors, (2) offering support and empathy, (3) describing services, (4) clarifying what will be expected of clients and what clients can expect from you, (5) offering timely concrete help, (6) involving significant others (those who interact with and influence clients), (7) identifying resources and obstacles, and (8) forming collaborative working relationships. You and your clients will have to decide whether you can offer any help; what outcomes to pursue; what behaviors, thoughts, feelings, or environmental factors are related to these outcomes; whom to involve in assessment; what settings to explore; and what referrals to make (if any). Knowledge about human behavior and development will be valuable in making these decisions, as well as skill in posing questions that guide a search for relevant research findings. Knowledge about factors related to particular concerns and about cultural differences and developmental norms will be useful. Differences in acculturation between generations in a family may be related to problems. Depending on your background knowledge, you may have to consult practice-related literature to obtain information regarding client

EXHIBIT 13.1

Assessment: Questions and Reasons for Asking Them

Question	Rationale
What is the problem?	Clear description increases the likelihood of selecting relevant outcomes, identifying related factors, and accurately estimating the likelihood of attaining hoped-for outcomes.
What does it communicate?	Provides information about the functions that behaviors of concern may serve (e.g., prevention of worse problems, obtaining certain reinforcers).
Who is affected and how?	Provides information about who to involve and who may help or hinder change efforts.
Why now?	Offers clues about related factors, possible obstacles, and sources of help.
What would happen if nothing were done?	Helpful in understanding how problems influence clients' lives.
How will I know if related hoped-for outcomes are achieved? What would be different?	Identifies specific outcomes of concern and clear criteria to assess progress.
Who and/or what influences concerns? What makes them worse? What makes them better?	Provides information about related contingencies.
What efforts have been made to resolve the problem? What happened?	Offers information about options and the effects of attempted solutions; provides opportunities to support helpful options.
What obstacles must be overcome?	Assess feasibility of attaining outcomes and helpful in planning services.
What resources are needed and what resources are available including client assets?	Assess likelihood of achieving hoped-for outcomes; helpful in planning what to do.
What could be done to prevent the problem from recurring?	Provides information about how to prevent problems in the future.

Source: E. Gambrill (2012). Social work practice: A critical thinker's guide (3rd Ed.). New York: Oxford.

EXHIBIT 13.2

Constructional Questionnaire

The purpose of these questions is to obtain information; hence, their wording should be tailored to the occasion.

(QUESTION 1: OUTCOMES)

a. Presented outcome: Assuming we were successful, what would the outcome be for you?

b. Observable outcome: What would others observe when the successful outcome was obtained?

c. Present state: How does this differ from the present state of affairs?

d. Examples: Can you give me an example?

(QUESTION 2: AREAS CHANGED, UNCHANGED)

a. Areas unchanged: What is going well for you now; what areas of your life would not be affected by our work together?

b. By-products: What areas other than those we would directly work on would change?

(QUESTION 3: CHANGE HISTORY)

a. Present attempt: Why now?

b. First attempt: When did it first occur to you to try to change? What was going on? What did you do? How did it come out?

c. Intervening attempts: What did you do then? What was going on? How did it come out? (Series continues until present.)

(QUESTION 4: ASSETS)

a. Related skills: What skills or strengths do you have which we can use to attain these outcomes?

b. Other skills: What other skills do you have?

c. Stimulus control: Are there conditions when the present problem is not a problem?

d. Relevant problem-solving repertoire: In the past, what related problems did you tackle successfully? How?

e. Other problems solved: What other problems did you tackle successfully? How?

f. Past influence: Did you once have mastery of the present problem? If so, when, and under what circumstances? Any idea of how?

(QUESTION 5: CONSEQUENCES)

a. Symptom reinforcer-positive: Has your problem ever produced any special advantages for you? (Examples: in school, job, at home). Please give specific examples.

b. Symptom reinforcer-negative: As a result of your problem, have you been excused for things—or from things—that you might not be otherwise?

c. Symptom cost: How is your present problem a drag, or how does it jeopardize you? (Note: Omit if answered in 3a. Why start now?)

d. Possible reinforcers: What do you really like to do, or would like to do?

e. High probability behaviors: What do you find yourself doing instead? (or getting instead?)

f. Social reinforcers: Who else is interested in the changes you are after?

g. Past social reinforcers: What people have been helpful in the past? How did they go about it? How did you obtain this from them?

(QUESTION 6: COMPLETION)

Is there anything we left out or did not get enough information about? Was there something we overlooked—or made too much or? Are there any impressions you would like to correct?

(QUESTION 7: TURNABOUT)

We have asked a lot of questions. Are there questions you would like to ask? Anything you would like to know about our goals or approach?

Source: A. Schwartz & I. Goldiamond (1975). *Social casework: A behavioral approach* (pp. 79–81). New York: Columbia University Press. Reprinted with permission.

concerns and related circumstances (see chapter 10). Examples of questions that may arise include:

- In family members caring for elderly relatives, what problems are common and what are related factors?

- In adolescents with unwanted pregnancies, is there a risk of depression?

Complaints should be translated into objectives that if achieved would solve the problem (Baer, 1982). What are client's hoped-for outcomes? How would you and your clients know you have been successful? Valued outcomes may involve the behavior of service providers, as well as significant others and clients. If you are a successful broker and advocate for your clients, you influence the "gate-keepers" of resources needed by your clients. Find out why complaints are made at this time and what would happen if nothing were done (unless this is obvious). What has been tried, to what effect? How do the potential benefits of change compare with possible losses? Do potential losses outweigh the benefits? If so, it will be difficult or impossible to involve the client in a change effort. Burns (1999) asks his client to list benefits and costs of achieving an outcome such as to stop drinking. (See also Janis & Mann, 1977). This list may reveal that there are more costs of stopping than continuing drinking. Is there any overarching contingency that will make it difficult to attain outcomes that clients value? For example, a client who wants to keep her Supplementary Security Income benefits (SSI) may also want to overcome her depression, but if she did, she would lose this source of income. Clients must be *involved*—encouraged to discuss personally relevant topics and to move from the general to the specific. (See chapter 14.) Both voluntary and involuntary clients are more likely to participate in helpful ways if you focus on outcomes that they value. Your tasks include providing support and reassurance, maintaining focus, and helping clients and significant others to clearly describe valued outcomes and associated factors. You could review your practice skills using the checklist at the end of this chapter.

A contextual assessment framework suggests the steps described in Exhibit 13.3 (Gambrill, Thomas, & Carter, 1971). This guide can be used to answer the questions in Exhibits 13.1 and 13.2. In practice, steps often overlap and do not necessarily occur in the order shown. In some settings, such as outreach services for the homeless and psychiatric emergency centers, contacts with clients may be sporadic, with little opportunity to

---

EXHIBIT 13.3

Phases and Tasks: A Problem-Solving Guide

Preparation
1. Prepare (see chapter 14).

Engagement and Exploration
2. Offer crisis services as needed.
3. Identify client's hoped-for outcomes and related problems.
4. Initiate a collaborative working relationship.
5. Identify and support client strengths.
6. Decide on priorities together with the client; describe outcomes of greatest concern, as well as related behaviors, antecedents, and consequences. Gather baseline data, if possible.

Syntheses
7. Organize and interpret data.
8. Review resources and obstacles and decide whether you can provide effective services drawing on practice-related research findings (see chapter 10). If you cannot, refer clients elsewhere to gain access to effective services.
9. Form a clear service agreement.

Intervention
10. Select plans that are feasible and acceptable to clients and likely to result in hoped-for outcomes.

Implementation
11. Implement plans, paying attention to needed intermediate steps and the fidelity of plans to maximize the likelihood of success.

Evaluation
12. Evaluate progress using valid, acceptable measures.
13. Alter plans as needed.
14. Arrange maintenance plans as needed (see chapter 23).
15. Plan endings (see chapter 23).

Follow-up
16. Follow up with clients and provide additional services as needed.

work systematically. You will have to vary your actions in accord with each unique situation and what the client wants and what you can provide. Assessment should precede selection of plans unless a crisis is at hand. If there is a crisis (a situation requiring immediate attention), exploring why it occurred so that future crises can be avoided may have to take second place.

The construction of social problems is emphasized in chapter 6. That is, different societies at different times decide that certain circumstances, such as poverty, lack of health care for residents, or crime constitute a problem requiring attention. This attention molds the problem as a certain kind, for example, as a consequence of individual characteristics such as "mental illness" and/or social, political, and economic factors, and draws on this framing to suggest and enact related practices, programs, and policies. So too do clients and social workers in their exchanges mold problems in certain ways. The client may have a firm belief in the causes of problems that he or she confronts, such as family disputes. The social worker's beliefs are also influential; she may believe that family problems are systemic in nature, that they arise from and are located in the interactions between family members rather than in the characteristics and actions of individual family members.

Different views are shared including arguments for them in the exchanges between social workers and their clients. These views are shaped by those who have the power to control major sources of socialization such as school curriculums, as well as by the media as discussed in chapter 6. Our understanding of such exchanges has been advanced by their detailed review. In *Talk of the Clinic: Explorations in the Analysis of Medical and Therapeutic Discourse,* Morris and Chenail (1995) describe the complexity of the discourse related to a discussion of problems—how problems are constructed and how they are responded to. There is a negotiation regarding views of concern—whether there is a problem, if so, what kind it is, and what should be done about it (see also Heritage & Clayman, 2010).

Clients may think they have a problem when indeed what they refer to is normative. Or, they may deny they have a problem because they think they have a right to act in a certain way even though others complain, for example, a husband who batters his wife. The only problem he may have is that his wife complains about being hit and the police bother him. Thus, problem framing at the personal level, like problem framing at the societal level, is often complex. Although many problems are not complex in their need to be addressed, such as lack of access to needed health care or housing, addressing such needs at higher levels may be very complex indeed, requiring advocacy for legislation requiring the building of more low-cost housing. This may involve a process requiring years of effort by many different groups and individuals.

Initial Interviews/Exchanges

Although initial exchanges with clients may be in the form of a scheduled interview, in many other settings it may not.

For example, in outreach services to the homeless, encounters may be unplanned. There are different kinds of interviews, including assessment interviews (e.g., determining people's eligibility for certain services). Objectives of initial interviews are to:

- Identify hoped-for outcomes and get an overview of concerns.

- Offer support and encouragement; identify what is going well.

- Describe the agency's services.

- Offer concrete, material help.

- Establish rapport and increase client comfort.

- Engage clients.

- Determine if (and how) you can help clients.

- If you can be of help, reach an agreement about outcomes to pursue.

- Help clients to clearly describe concerns and discover related factors and explore how they may be resolved.

- Arrange conditions for continuance or discontinuance.

In some agencies, intake workers refer clients to staff, who provide ongoing services. If this is the case, clients should be informed about this so that they will be prepared to meet someone new on their next visit. Interviews should be goal directed. Multiple purposes may be served by any one exchange, such as providing concrete help and information, making a decision (e.g., whether an applicant meets eligibility requirements), and offering support. With resisters, as in the child welfare and criminal justice systems, the purpose of the interview might be to explore how you could help them, as well as meet goals imposed by other sources, such as the court (for example, to gain an earlier release from detention).

Your tasks include arranging a distraction-free environment, guiding the focus of interviews, avoiding interviewer biases, and making the exchange as comfortable as possible. Interviewer biases include the following (Ceci & Bruck, 1995):

- Repeating a question *within* an interview, which may encourage clients to report events that did not occur.

- Stereotype induction: transmitting a negative view of a person or event to a client (e.g., telling a child that a suspect "does bad things").

- Searching only for confirmatory evidence for assumptions.

Draw on your interviewing skills to encourage clients to share needed material, explore concerns, and identify personalized goals (steps clients can take to achieve hoped-for outcomes). Encourage solution talk rather than problem talk. Relationship skills of value in helping clients move from sharing, exploring, and understanding to acting are described in chapter 15. The greater burden for being courteous and considerate and effectively handling cultural differences falls on you. This will require not taking negative or rude behavior "personally" (it gets under your skin and/or you react in kind). (See chapter 16.) Stay focused on service goals. Decide on mutually understood, feasible, and acceptable goal(s) for each interview. Use language that is clear and intelligible to clients, and personalize your comments and questions (e.g., use examples from their lives). (See Exhibit 13.4.)

Whenever possible, end interviews on an up-beat. For example, reaffirm your agreement to work together to achieve agreed-on outcomes, encourage positive expectations, review what has been accomplished, and support clients' assets. People's lives are made up of more than their problems.

Offer Introductory Information and Help Clients to Feel Comfortable

If clients are not familiar with services available, one of your tasks will be to describe them. You can allay concerns about what to expect by informing clients about services available, fees (if any), time limits, mutual responsibilities, and the approach that will be used. This will help to demystify what may occur and take the client "off the hook" in being expected to talk right away. Clients are more likely to participate in helpful ways if they understand the rationale for and activities involved in assessment. You can ease the transition into the interview by small talk (a brief discussion of a neutral topic), unless this is inappropriate because of the urgency of a problem or client anxiety or anger. You could note that initial discomfort is common. You could gather some basic descriptive information to put the client at ease, even though this is already available. Sometimes, novice interviewers are so nervous themselves that they forget basic amenities, such as helping clients feel physically comfortable, for example, by suggesting that they take off their coat (see "Initial Interview Checklist" at the end of this chapter).

An introductory statement offers an opportunity to establish your role in guiding the helping process and to clarify expectations (see Exhibit 13.5). Ambiguous statements of purpose may increase client anxiety about what will happen especially with nonvoluntary clients. Checking client expectations provides an opportunity to correct misunderstandings. Correcting misconceptions and encouraging helpful views is often a gradual process. Be honest about your agenda and describe the limits on confidentiality. You may postpone introductory information if clients are eager to talk. Or you may suggest that it will be helpful to first describe what you can offer, especially if clients seem to misunderstand this. Introductory statements may not be necessary if clients are familiar with the agency's services. Other information you are ethically obligated to share with clients include your competence to address clients' concerns. What are your areas of expertise? Will you be supervised? How will you evaluate progress? What criteria do you use to select services including assessment frameworks and measures? Such information is typically not provided to clients as Pignotti and Thyer (2009) note. However clients have a right to this information. (See discussion of Informed Consent in chapter 3.) Here is one of many opportunities you will have in your career to enhance attention to ethical requirements of social work.

Gather an Overview of Concerns and Related Desired Outcomes

Clients often have many concerns. One helpful way of proceeding is to first get an overview of client concerns and related desired outcomes (assuming that one concern does not take precedence) (unless a crisis is at hand, see later discussion). This will help you and your client discover interrelationships among valued outcomes and to set priorities. Kinds of problems include (1) individual mood problems such as anxiety or depression, (2) relationship problems such as anger or conflicts with family members, friends, or colleagues, (3) habits or addictions such as procrastination, drug or alcohol abuse, eating disorders, or (4) a non-problem (e.g., sadness or grief when no therapeutic methods other than empathic listening is needed). Some clients have problems in all of the first three areas, as well as lack of health care, money, and/or suitable housing. If additional concerns emerge later, they can be added and priorities changed as needed. If several family members are present, ask each one to identify desired outcomes and to indicate their importance. Use your knowledge of cultural norms to decide whom to ask first. For example, if the father is viewed as the authority in a family, he may be insulted if you speak first to his wife or children.

Encourage clients and significant others to talk to one another (if this is culturally appropriate). You may have to prompt clients to do this: "Maria, could you tell John what changes you would like?" Then if Maria starts to talk to you, prompt her to speak to John. Exhibit 13.6 describes concerns of Brian and his parents, and Exhibit 13.7 illustrates a profile for a homeless client, which was prepared by Joe Neifert, one of my students. His client, a 28-year-old African American woman, reported being homeless since the age of 20 and had no identified family or relatives. She had never been employed. Note that room is included on the profile to indicate who labels a given area as a problem and who has the problem. This offers valuable information about degree of agreement about concerns and related hoped-for outcomes. Teachers, social workers, the school nurse, and parents all may note problems with a youth, none of which he considers a problem. Problem solving in organizations and communities will involve a wider variety of interested parties compared to working with individuals and families. Here, too, identifying concerns of all involved parties, understanding different points of view about why they occur and how they can be solved, and

EXHIBIT 13.4

Example of a Beginning Interview

Mr. and Mrs. Lakeland consulted a social worker, Mr. Colvine, about problems with their son Brian, aged 14. This exhibit continues the description of the Lakeland family presented in chapter 2. Most of the reflective and paraphrasing statements have been omitted to save space. One of Mr. Colvine's goals was to help his clients to feel at ease. Other goals were to find out what changes family members wanted and to gather information about how these could be achieved. Notice the focus on the present and the interest in clearly describing concerns and hoped-for outcomes and related setting events, antecedents, and consequences. Brian and his parents were on time for their first interview with Mr. Colvine. Brian looked sullen, and his parents seemed anxious.

MR. COLVINE: (To all three clients.) Could you tell me about your family? Who lives at home, for example?

MR. LAKELAND: Well, my wife and I, our oldest son Bob, Brian, and his little sister Joan. Joan's only 11, and Bob is 18. Oh, yes, we also have a dog. (He glares at Brian, who continues to look down at the floor.)

MR. COLVINE: Is there anything else you would like to tell me about your family?

MR. LAKELAND: We both (looks at his wife) work hard. My wife works full-time and I have a part-time job three nights a week. We need the extra money for Bob, since he just started community college.

MR. COLVINE: Is this the first time you have sought help with the family problems?

MRS. LAKELAND: No, we saw a social worker at another agency 2 years ago about Brian. We were having trouble with him then. She was nice to talk to, and we kept on going, since we didn't want to show disrespect. But she didn't help us much.

MR. COLVINE: What did the social worker suggest?

MRS. LAKELAND: She said we should learn to talk to each other and listen to each other and wanted to see the whole family together. We did talk, but it didn't seem to change anything at home.

MR. COLVINE: Was there any other time you sought help?

MR. LAKELAND: Yes, we also went to see our doctor, and he said that we should be real strict with Brian and get him to take his medication. We were strict for a while, but then things just returned to their usual miserable state.

MR. COLVINE: I would like to find out what changes you would like to see in your family. This will help me know how I can be of help to you. Brian, let's start with you. What changes would you like to see in your family?

BRIAN: Gee, I don't know. Why don't you ask them? (He points to his parents.)

MR. COLVINE: I'll also be asking your father and mother what changes they would like to see, but I want to know what changes you would like, too. Could you give me one example?

BRIAN: Well, you could get them off my back.

MR. COLVINE: Could you give me an example of what happens when they "are on your back"?

BRIAN: Sure, they nag me all the time; don't do this, do that. It's really a pain.

MR. COLVINE: Could you tell me what was happening the last time they asked you to do something?

BRIAN: Yeah, just today. I was playing with the dog, and they said to cut it out. I wasn't hurting anyone.

MR. COLVINE: Can you tell me what you were doing?

BRIAN: I was picking him up by his tail. He really likes this. (Brian smirks, and his parents look at him in disgust, and with an air of helplessness, they sigh.)

MR. COLVINE: Can you think of another example of when your parents are "on your back"?

BRIAN: They're on my back all the time—take my medication, have good table manners, don't tease my sister, get better grades. They're always threatening me, too—we'll send you away.

MR. COLVINE: OK. That's helpful. Now I'd like you to describe something that your parents do that you like. Think back over the past week.

BRIAN: (Looks at his parents.) Well… (pause) they try their best. (Silence.)

MR. COLVINE: Think back over the past week, Brian. Give me an example of something either your Dad or Mom did that you liked.

BRIAN: Well, Dad took me around to collect the money for my papers.

MR. COLVINE: How about your Mom?

BRIAN: (Looks at his mother.) Gee, that's hard (he grins). (His mother rolls her eyes upward.) Well, she told me she liked my new haircut yesterday.

(continued)

EXHIBIT 13.4 (Continued)

MR. COLVINE: OK, Brian. We'll come back to you in a minute. Mr. Lakeland, could you tell me what changes you would like to see in the family.

MR. LAKELAND: (Pause.) Well, things seem to be getting out of hand lately with Brian. We've always had trouble with him. You know he is epileptic and has to take medication. He often forgets to take this. He never did too well in school, but lately his grades have been getting really bad. But I guess what really concerns us most is that he is getting more violent. He threatened to hit his mother the other day and threatened to throw a knife at me last week. Things are getting out of hand. I don't know how much longer we can go on like this.

MR. COLVINE: I can see that you are concerned about what is happening in your family, and I hope that we can work together and see that some changes can be made. It sounds like changes you would like are for Brian to take his medication regularly, for him not to physically threaten you or your wife, and for him to get better grades in school.

BRIAN: I was just kidding.

MRS. LAKELAND: No, you were not.

MR. LAKELAND: Yes, and mainly to mind us, do what we say.

MR. COLVINE: Now, Mr. Lakeland, give me an example of something you like about Brian. What are some of the things he does that you like?

MR. LAKELAND: He helps me in the yard. He is pretty good, too, about delivering the papers on his route. Sometimes I have to keep reminding him to get up. But after he is up, he usually gets right out there. He doesn't always remember to collect the money though, and that's a problem.

MR. COLVINE: Let's keep focused on the positives right now. It seems that there are a number of things that Brian does that you like. And how about you, Mrs. Lakeland? What changes would you like to see in the family?

MRS. LAKELAND: My husband has picked out the big ones. It really bothers me when he talks nasty to me.

MR. COLVINE: Could you give me an example?

MRS. LAKELAND: Well, yesterday when I asked Brian to take out the garbage, he said, "Do it yourself, bitch." (Mrs. L. looks like she is going to cry, and Brian looks very sheepish.)

MR. COLVINE: Does he talk to you that way very often, Mrs. Lakeland?

MRS. LAKELAND: No, but it really hurts me and makes me mad when he does.

MR. COLVINE: I can see that it is upsetting to you. (Pause.) Can you think of anything else?

MRS. LAKELAND: Not really.

MR. COLVINE: Mrs. Lakeland, what are some things that Brian does that you like?

MRS. LAKELAND: Well, I really don't feel that he means to be so bad. I think he just gets beside himself. He can be nice at times.

MR. COLVINE: Could you give me an example?

MRS. LAKELAND: Well, he brought me some flowers for my birthday last week. He helps his father with the yard work, sometimes.

MR. COLVINE: What else does he do that you like?

MRS. LAKELAND: Sometimes he makes a special dessert for the family, one that is also his favorite. (She smiles for the first time.) He lets Bob help him with his homework sometimes.

MR. COLVINE: Brian, you said that you would like your parents to "get off your back." Are there any other changes you would like to see in your family?

BRIAN: Well, yeah, I'd like to have my own work space. I have no place to work on my models. My stuff always gets pushed out of the way.

MR. COLVINE: OK. let's note that down too. (He writes this change under the column "Changes Brian would like.") Is there anything else?

BRIAN: (Pause.) No, nothing I can think of.

MR. COLVINE: (To the parents.) What have you done to try to change Brian's behavior?

MR. LAKELAND: We've tried everything. We tried to talk to him, and that didn't work. We tried to punish him by removing privileges, and that didn't work. He just seemed to get madder. We talked to our doctor, and he said to be firm with Brian. That worked for about a day. Nothing seems to work, and things seem to be getting worse.

(continued)

EXHIBIT 13.4 (Continued)

MRS. LAKELAND: Nothing we have tried has had any effect.

MR. COLVINE: Well, we will try to find some ways that will be helpful. I can see that you are discouraged about how things are now. It is frustrating to try to make things better and not be as successful as you would like. (The Lakelands nod in agreement.)

MR. COLVINE: Brian, what have you tried to change your parents' behavior?

BRIAN: Are you kidding? You can't change them. They're old stick-in-the-muds.

MR. COLVINE: But what have you tried?

BRIAN: I tried to tell them I just forget. But they don't believe me.

MR. COLVINE: Have you tried anything else?

BRIAN: No, what's the use?

MR. COLVINE: (Pause.) I'd like to find out a bit more about what happens when things get really bad at home. Can you tell me about a recent incident?

MRS. LAKELAND: How about when he threatened to hit me. He said, "I'm going to punch you" and raised his fist to me.

MR. COLVINE: Were you present too, Mr. Lakeland?

MR. LAKELAND: Yes, and Brian's older brother and his sister were there, too.

MR. COLVINE: OK. What was going on before he threatened you?

MRS. LAKELAND: We were having dinner, and Brian was teasing his little sister. He was calling her "Cutesy," which she hates, and making fun of her new haircut. She started to cry, she was so upset. I twice asked Brian to stop this, and he just kept on. Then I finally shouted at him that if he didn't stop, he was to leave the table. That's when he threatened me.

MR. COLVINE: Then what did you do?

MR. LAKELAND: I told him that he better not threaten his mother, and I told him to leave the table and go up to his room. Instead, he went out of the house and slammed the door.

MR. COLVINE: Brian, is this how you would describe what happened?

BRIAN: They just kept nagging me. I was just having some fun. (Mr. Colvine obtains specific descriptions of three other incidents that occurred at home, including what happened right before and right after each one.)

MR. COLVINE: Brian, what other things do your parents do that you like?

BRIAN: Well, Dad takes me fishing once in a great while, but not very often. Mom makes my favorite dishes sometime. But they sure do nag me.

MR. COLVINE: Is there anything else you can think of, Brian?

BRIAN: They used to stick up for me when I got into trouble at school, but now they just think I'm always in the wrong.

MR. COLVINE: Could you give me an example?

BRIAN: Sure, last week I got kicked out of my math class for no reason and sent to the principal's office. They called my Mom at work the next day to complain about me. They (points to his parents) didn't even stick up for me.

MR. COLVINE: What do you mean, Brian?

BRIAN: They didn't even let me give my side of the story.

MR. COLVINE: (To the parents.) Is this how you see the situation?

MRS. LAKELAND: I guess I did get upset. I hate to be bothered at work and just tried to get off the phone. When I saw Brian later, I did hop on him.

MR. COLVINE: We'll get back to this topic later, too. Let me get a better idea of what your family is like. When was the last time you did something as a family, all of you did something together?

MRS. LAKELAND: (Looks at her husband.) I can't remember. Can you, Bill?

describing attempted solutions and their effects, provide valuable information.

Encourage clients to focus on *present* concerns/desired outcomes. Obtain specific examples of each, including a description of related situation(s), who has the concern, and who would like to see changes. You may discover desired outcomes by asking questions like "How would you like your life to be different?" "How would we know if we were successful?" (see Exhibit 13.2). Use prompts as needed, such as "Is there anything else that concerns you right now?" You and your clients can then review the

EXHIBIT 13.5

Examples of Introductory Statements

This example is what Mr. Covine said to the Lakeland family

1. Let me tell you about our agency and some of the things that will happen in our work together. We'll make a tentative agreement today about how many times we will see each other. I know that it's difficult for you to come to the agency, and we could have some of our meetings in your home if this would be convenient for you. I'd like to meet your other children so I can get a picture of your whole family. Today we'll identify changes that each of you here today would like to make in your family and then we'll have a better idea of what other information we'll need to see how these can be accomplished. I'd like you to focus on present concerns—changes that you would like to see right now. I'll be asking you to do some homework between sessions. These tasks won't take up much of your time, and they will be very valuable in our work together. This will allow us to make use of time between our meetings.

If anything comes up and you cannot make a meeting, please give me 24 hours' notice. If I have to rearrange a meeting, I'll give you at least 24 hours' notice. We'll have periodic telephone contact with each other between sessions. I'll be helping you this morning to identify changes each of you would like in your family.

2. *An example of an introductory statement about a parent-training program follows. Responsibilities of the parents are highlighted, skills they will learn are noted, as well as the need to alter old beliefs and habits, and benefits of the program are described. Note the positive spirit of this statement and the attention to the parents' feelings:*

Basically, we are here so that together we can help you to take charge of your children's future. We will help you to learn and to use important skills for planning, running, and keeping track of a home-education program that may change your children in a big way. Make no mistake about it, though. This means learning new skills on your part. It may even mean changing some basic ideas of yours and some habitual ways in which you deal with your children, yourselves, and with other people

. . . . Your kids do a lot of things that are driving you up the wall and that do, or will, get your children into trouble and keep them from enjoying many of the good things in life. We can teach you how to reduce and replace those problem behaviors with behaviors that are helpful for your children to learn and do, which are considered appropriate, normal, some of which may even be expected or demanded if your child is to have a place in this society.

The second reason you should be involved in this program has to do with the relationship between home and school. Even if your children are in a terrific program and are learning all kinds of things, that does not mean that they are going to do any of them, or do them well, in the home. You have to learn some of the skills your kids' teachers have, if it is a good program, or else a lot of the progress they are making in school may have no effect on your child at home. On the other hand, if you are not satisfied with your children's school program, this program teaches you not only how to provide your children with a partial substitute, but how to evaluate your children's school program and to make important comments on how it can be improved. In fact, imagine what a group of motivated and skillful parents could do to help change the school programs their children are in!

And if your children are not even in a program anywhere, you certainly need to learn how to teach your children in the home.

Third, many of you have said that you've had a rough time getting help over the years. And you may be pretty bitter as a result of your experiences. Well, we can't make excuses for others, but the truth is that many people and many facilities have just not been geared to meet your needs and the needs of your children. Some, as you know, have not seemed to be interested in the particular problems of your kids.

But things have been changing and can be changed even more. One benefit of this program, then, is that it can help to prepare your children for evaluations because, as you know, if your children are screaming their heads off or do not pay attention, it is hard to pinpoint their strengths and weaknesses. In addition, we can help you to use available services such as physicians or speech therapists, and to seek outside help when it is needed.

Finally, the program will help you to establish networks between families, so that you all can maintain your efforts and home programs, and can help others to do what you will have learned.

Source: M. A. Kozloff (1979). *A program for families of children with learning and behavior problems* (pp. 152–153). New York: Wiley. Reprinted with permission.

problem/outcome profile to decide which areas to focus on first. Areas listed may be interrelated. Coach clients to think in terms of outcomes related to their concerns (see Exhibit 13.8).

You may need more information to identify specific outcomes (see chapters 17 and 18). Helping clients to clearly describe hoped-for outcomes and related factors is a key practice skill. Clients may describe problems in vague terms like "Everything is

a mess," "He is impossible," "We can't talk," or "He is always that way." They may use general metaphors, such as "He is smothering me." Help them identify specific behaviors to which these terms refer, as well as the context in which they occur (what happens right before and after them). You might ask: "What would you do differently if you were not depressed?" The reply might be: "I would go out more, not sit around the house."

EXHIBIT 13.6

Problem/Outcome Profile

Case: Lakeland
Worker(s): Colvine

Number	Problem/Label	Who Labels	Who Has Problem	Date Noted	Examples	Situational Context	Desired Outcome
1.	Call mother names	Mrs. L.	Brian	10/13	Calls Mrs. L. a grouch.	In evening.	Refers to Mrs. L. as "Mother."
		Both parents	Brian	10/13	Refers to Ms. L. as "she" rather than as "Mother."	No particular context other than Mrs. L.'s presence.	Decrease negative labels for Mrs. L.
2.	Mean to dog.	Both parents	Brian	10/13	Holds radio in dog's ear; plays too roughly; holds dog's head between knees.	Mainly in the evening.	Pet dog gently. Do not hold dog "against his will" (criterion—struggling to get away).
3.	"Not appreciative" re: sister.	Mrs. L.	Brian	10/13	Does not say "thank you" when Joan does something for him.	At home.	Thank his sister when she does something for him.
4.	Teases Joan.	Both parents	Brian	10/13	Plugs transistor into her ear when she does not want it; punches her.	When she is around.	Decrease hitting; do not force her to do things.
5.	Not home on time after school.	Both parents	Brian	10/13	Comes in later than 3:30 on days when could be home by 3:30.	Weekdays.	Come straight home from school, arriving home at 3:30.
6.	Not enough time spent with Joan.	Mrs. L.	Brian	10/13	Rarely plays games with her.	When Joan is home.	Spend more time with Joan.
7.	Does not follow instructions; argumentative.	Both parents	Brian	10/13	Does not make bed; turn radio down; go to bed; come to dinner table; stop playing roughly with Charlie.	At home.	Follow instructions; complete agreed-on chores.
8.	Does not sit at dinner table.	Mrs. L.	Brian	10/13		Fridays or late school days are excluded.	Sit at dinner table with rest of family except Friday and late school days.
9.	Parents don't do what they say they will.	Brian	Both parents	10/13	Mr. L. does not take trips as promises; Mrs. L. doesn't give what she promises, didn't start bank account when promised.	Something else comes up, or fatigue prevents follow-through.	Parents keep their promises.
10.	Nagging.	Brian	Parents	10/13	Parents ask him to do something many times.	At home.	Ask him to do something only once.

No.	Problem			Date	Current behavior	Setting	Objective
11.	Brian leaves house without telling parents where he is going.	Parents	Brian	10/13		After school.	Leave note or inform someone when leaving house; indicate when will be back.
12.	Brian does not straighten room daily.	Parents	Brian	10/13	Bed not made, clothes thrown on floor.	At home.	Make bed, hang clothes up, put dirty clothes in hamper each morning.
13.	Brian does not clean room on weekend.	Parents	Brian	10/13	Does not vacuum, dust, change bed.	At home.	Brian will vacuum and dust his room each Saturday and change sheets on bed.
14.	Not allowed in store by himself.	Brian		10/13	Caught but not prosecuted for shoplifting.		Be allowed to go to store by himself.
15.	Does not always take medication (for control of epilepsy).	Parents	Brian	10/13	Did not take medication and had seizures.	Taking pills at school makes him late for class.	Take medication three times a day (morning, afternoon, and evening).
16.	Won't take tranquilizers.	Parents	Brian	10/13	Refuses to take tranquilizers.	Brian says tranquilizers make him sleepy.	Take tranquilizers as recommended by doctor (note—check whether needed).
17.	Physical threats on family member.	Parents	Brian	10/13	During argument with parents threatened to throw a knife at Mr. L.	At home after dinner.	Do not physically assault or threaten family members.
18.	Rough physical interaction with a family member.	Parents	Brian	10/13	Pushes sisters or parents when talking to them.	At home when disagreement occurs or when "playing."	Do not push or shove any family member, even "in play."
19.	Brian does not come home when told in evening.	Parents	Brian	10/13	Returns home an hour or two later than agreed.	Evenings.	Return home at agreed-on time.
20.	Mrs. L. is a grouch.	Brian	Mrs. L.	10/13	Doesn't do any work when comes home; always asking children to do things for her.	When Mrs. L. comes home.	Mrs. L. will smile more when she comes home from work; do chores and not ask children to do things she can do herself.
21.	Poor grades.	Parents, Brian		10/13	Gets C's, D's, and F's.	School	Get more B's and C's.

EXHIBIT 13.7

Problem Profile of a 28-Year-Old Homeless Woman

Number	Problem/Label	Who Labels	Who Has Problem	Date Noted	Examples	Situational Context	Desired Outcome
1.	Chronic drug use (cocaine).	Society, staff at services, client	Client	11/95	Smokes crack cocaine daily.	Smokes crack in the North area of Berkeley.	To enter recovery and stop using drugs/cocaine.
2.	Prostitution.	Police, society, client	Client	11/95	Client prostitutes herself for money and crack cocaine.	Client regularly is assaulted and abused. Client does not inform her clients that she is HIV positive.	Practice safe sex. Stop being a prostitute to prevent future abuse.
3.	Does not treat her HIV.	Staff	Client	11/95	When client gets ill, she rarely takes her antibiotics and other meds. Decompensates to the point that she ends up in the county hospital.	Client feels she will die from AIDS, so she does not treat it. Continually ill.	Get client to follow a medical and health plan.
4.	Unprotected & uninformed sex.	Staff, client	Client, society	11/95	Public health concern when client has sex with drug users to get money and/or drugs. Client does this at least 4 to 5 times a week.	Client normally has unprotected sex. She does not inform her partners that she is HIV positive.	Practice safe sex. Inform partners she engages in sexual activities.
5.	Living outdoors.	Staff, society	Client	11/95	Being homeless for 8 years, has negatively affected the client's health.	Homeless people in Berkeley are exposed to easy access to drugs and being physically abused. She does not want to live indoors.	Get client to be housed on a consistent basis.
6.	People do not like me.	Client	Client	11/95	Her prostitution clients abuse her. People on the street take her drugs and money.	Prostitution sets up the client to be a victim.	Discontinue drug use, prostitution, and seek healthy environment. People should be nice to me.
7.	Don't have enough money.	Client	Client	11/95	Don't have enough money to buy food and drugs that I want.	I spend my general relief in a week. No money left for the rest of the month.	County should give me more money.

Source: J. Neifert (1995). Field work report. Unpublished paper, School of Social Welfare, University of California at Berkeley.

EXHIBIT 13.8

Differences Between Presenting Problems and Desired Outcomes

Presenting Problems	Desired Outcomes
Vague	Specific
Stated in negative terms	Stated in positive terms
Viewed in noninstrumental ways*	Instrumental
Seem impossible to alter	Personalized (indicate how client may change situation)
Not measurable	Measurable
Not observable	Observable
Do not point to an agenda	Suggest an agenda (initial and intermediate steps)

*No information is offered about how to achieve valued outcomes.

Obtain an Overview of Current Life Circumstances and Past History

Find out what the client's life is like in major areas (e.g., work, family, friends, money available, and recreational interests). What is a typical day like? What is a typical week like? What are living conditions like? Without an overview of a client's current real-life circumstances, you may overlook important factors. Information about a person's thoughts will indicate the contribution of dysfunctional beliefs and expectations. Past history is pertinent to review when exploring the present leaves questions unanswered or when a review of the past suggests patterns that are helpful to point out. For example, dysfunctional communication patterns in an agency may be related to a particular history. Organizations, like people, have histories. A parent's low self-esteem may be related to a past history of "put-downs" throughout childhood and adolescence. Work history is important to review when employment is a concern. Structured interview schedules have been developed to obtain a "psychosocial history" and to gather information about specific concerns (see chapter 17). Examples of content reviewed in such schedules include demographic data, current living arrangements, educational history, relationship history, work history, financial circumstances, and physical illnesses and current physical symptoms.

Decide Whether Services Can Be Provided

An overview of concerns and desired outcomes, together with information you gain from the related research literature, will indicate whether the services you can offer match those needed

to help clients attain goals they value. This decision should be informed by research regarding the effectiveness of services your agency offers in relation to hoped-for outcomes, as well as your expertise (see discussion of posing questions and critically appraising what you find in chapter 10). If there is a match, then the conditions for continuing can be discussed, including the client's willingness to participate in the process most likely to result in valued outcomes. For example, there is a high correlation between willingness to carry out homework assignments and overcoming depression (Burns, 2004). Is the client willing to do so? If not, is it reasonable (or ethical) to proceed? If you do not have the knowledge or skills required to offer help, do not have the authority or resources to do so, or have biases that might get in the way, you may have to refer the client elsewhere. You will have to assess your knowledge and skills in relation to services needed. Only when you clarify client concerns and related contingencies may it be obvious that little leverage is possible in attaining outcomes that clients value. Gaps between what clients need and what can be offered are common. Here are some examples:

- You are a social worker working in an inner-city school in which bullying is a recurring problem. Research suggests that a school-community wide program is most effective in decreasing bullying, but there is no such integrative program.

- You work with inner-city youth to enhance educational and recreational opportunities. The neighborhoods in which they live are high crime areas in which police have an antagonistic surveillance role with these young people. Past efforts to change this relationship have failed.

- You work in a child protection agency and have no access to parent training programs found to be effective in enhancing positive parenting skills and must refer clients to programs unlikely to help them.

Make Referrals as Needed

Brokering (linking clients to needed resources) is a key helping role. Making effective referrals requires matching the client's goals and characteristics to resources that provide services likely to achieve these goals. This will require knowledge about the relative effectiveness of different methods in achieving them. Effective referrals involve gaining an agency's agreement to see a person, encouraging clients to keep appointments, and provision of benefits to the client through service received. The following steps will be helpful.

1. Clearly describe desired outcomes.

2. Identify resources that provide effective services related to outcomes of interest (those critically tested and found to be of value in attaining hoped-for outcomes).

3. Describe relevant resources to the client and how they may help.

4. Find out if the client is interested in using the resource.

5. If so, assess the client's motivation and capacity to contact the resource.

6. Offer help as needed based on item 5 (e.g., you may telephone the referral source and set up a specific time with a specific person for the client).

7. Follow up to find out whether the client did seek services recommended and what happened. (See Gray, 2001a.)

Clients are more likely to keep an appointment at another agency if it is arranged beforehand. Clear description of desired outcomes will make it easier to pose well-structured questions that allow you to search for related research findings regarding options and their evidentiary status. The services offered in an agency can be divided into the following categories:

- Interventions that have been critically tested and found to be effective.

- Interventions of unknown effectiveness.

- Interventions that have been critically tested and found to harm clients.

- Interventions that have not been critically tested but that are in a high-quality trial to test their effectiveness (Gray, 2001a).

Knowledge of the evidentiary status of different methods in relation to what different agencies offer will allow you to make informed referrals, for example, to avoid those that offer ineffective or harmful services. If your agency does not maintain an up-to-date list of resources, develop your own. Include information about services that each agency offers, as well as data about their track record in helping clients with particular problems. Agencies differ in criteria used to select methods, attention to evaluation, and obstacles that clients confront when seeking services, such as long waiting lists and complex forms. Use your knowledge about obstacles to prepare clients for them or use other agencies.

You may have to accompany a client to an agency and advocate in his or her behalf (try to convince staff that the client is eligible for service). Follow up on referrals to see how successful these have been. This provides information about the need for different linkages with, within, or among agencies. (See discussion of advocacy in chapter 27.) For further discussion of purchase of services from other agencies, see chapter 27. What if no agencies in your area offer intervention methods found to be effective in helping a client achieve certain outcomes (such as more positive parenting skills)? Should you just refer clients to such agencies any way? What are the ethical implications here?

One option is to work together with other staff to provide such services.

Decide on Priorities

If you will continue to work with clients, reach a clear mutual agreement about the focus of contact as soon as possible. Otherwise, interviews may drift, and opportunities to help clients may be lost. Agreeing on priorities involves reviewing the problem profile, finding out the client's priorities, and identifying areas that are interlinked (e.g., a client with a drinking problem who also wants to find a job may first have to stop drinking). Criteria to consider include the following:

1. Preferences of clients (e.g., annoyance level to significant others and/or clients).

2. Urgency or danger.

3. Interference in the client's life.

4. Ease in attaining desired outcomes; consult practice-related research findings as necessary.

5. Likelihood of early progress.

6. Centrality of the concern in a complex of problems.

7. Cost of services (e.g., time, money, energy).

8. Ethical acceptability.

9. Likelihood that gains will be maintained.

10. Possible consequences if hoped-for outcomes are attained; do potential benefits outweigh potential losses? (List both costs and benefits.)

With some clients, a high-priority outcome, such as the need for housing, is clear right away, and you and your client can concentrate on that. Often, there is an overarching agreed-on goal such as getting out of a detention facility or reunifying children who have been removed by the court with their biological parents. This over-arching goal provides the focus of your work. Objectives required to achieve it must be identified. For example, objectives that must be met to return a child in foster care to her biological parents may include increasing positive parenting skills and arranging supervisory care of children. The distinction between goals and objectives is useful in reminding you and your clients that many objectives may have to be attained to reach a goal.

If there are many different problems (or many objectives related to a goal), focus on those of greatest concern. Baseline data describing the current frequency or rate of behaviors, thoughts, or feelings of interest may reveal that a behavior is less (or more) frequent than a client thought (see later discussion of baseline data). Considering the importance of a problem in relation to the client's overall life will suggest priorities. For example, unless a client stops drinking, he may lose his job. Some behaviors pose a serious threat to clients or significant others. Problems are often interrelated. For example, Brian's concern about his parents' "nagging" was related to his behaviors that annoyed his parents. If there is more than one client, find out about each person's preferences. The following questions will be helpful in understanding the effects of behaviors of concern:

- What do they communicate?

- What would happen if nothing were done?

- Do their benefits outweigh their costs?

Selecting outcomes that are easy to attain has been suggested as a criterion because this will provide early success. Skills learned in handling easier problems may be of value with more difficult ones. This criterion must be balanced against annoyance value. Both criteria can be considered by selecting concerns with the highest annoyance value and pursuing them in small steps, each of which has a high probability of being achieved. Outcomes that are not likely to be achieved should usually not be chosen. However, at times such outcomes may have to be pursued because of court involvement or the client's wishes. For example, a child may have been removed from his parents' custody on grounds of neglect and one condition of his return may be his parents' not using drugs. If the parents want their child back and if more drug-free days is a court requirement, this objective may have to be pursued, even though there may be little hope of success.

Some outcomes are likely to occur in the natural course of events and so may not warrant intervention. A parent may complain that her 4-year-old son wets his bed at night. Many 4-year-old boys wet their bed at night, and most stop without any special intervention. This does not mean, however, that steps should not be taken to decrease bed wetting, especially if the parents respond adversely to the child because of it. You may reframe problems as reactions that are typical in certain situations. A client who has recently lost a spouse may believe that she is abnormal because she cries often: She may not be aware that crying is typical in the grieving process. Research regarding developmental norms and common reactions in given situations will help you to discover whether certain feelings, thoughts, and behaviors are typical in certain circumstances and their "developmental trajectory," for example, whether they are "time limited."

Encourage a Collaborative Working Relationship

A collaborative framework involves *working with* clients, as well as clients working with significant others, to achieve outcomes of mutual interest (significant others are people who influence the clients' behavior). In a collaborative relationship, both parties have responsibilities. You and your clients *work together* to achieve desired outcomes. You can encourage this by:

- Focusing on goals and objectives valued by clients and significant others.

- Seeking feedback from clients about suggested procedures.

- Considering cultural differences.

- Seeking client commitment to participate.

- Supporting clients' assets.

- Helping clients to identify what is going well.

- Responding to clients' suggestions and feedback.

- Agreeing on assignments that will be carried out between meetings both for clients and social workers.

When significant others are involved, encourage the view that they, as well as clients, will work together to achieve agreed-on outcomes—if this is culturally appropriate. You can do this by seeing clients and significant others together and suggesting assignments that highlight how they influence each other's behavior. If significant others refuse to participate, you may have to work with the client alone (e.g., Thomas & Ager, 1993). Seeing clients and significant others together offers opportunities to observe how they interact. An excessive focus on forming a collaborative relationship is not appropriate if clients have quite different expectations about what will occur. Identify hesitations, unrealistic expectations, and fears clients have so that you can address them at an early point (see chapter 14). Ignoring such reactions may result in lost opportunities to overcome obstacles and waste time setting up agreements that are not really agreements, or clients may "drop out."

Encourage Trust and Rapport

Establishing a collaborative working relationship requires trust and mutual respect. Showing concern for a person's troubles will encourage rapport and trust. Be sure to listen attentively to what is said (see chapter 15). You do not have to agree with people to understand their perspective. Clients may be hostile, rude, aggressive, or sullen. Children and adolescents in trouble may be aggressive and hostile because of past traumatic experiences and related fears (e.g., see Chamberlain, 2003). The more vulnerable clients feel, the more negative they may be. Responding to a client as a fellow human-being lays the basis for offering high-quality empathic responses, such as disarming (finding the truth in critical and angry reactions). (See chapter 15.) A contextual analysis of a client's life circumstances will help you understand the unique situations that confront each client. There are always two (or more) sides to a story. Each involved person may have their own narrative. Only by gathering all narratives may you understand client circumstances. As Leroy Pelton (1989) notes, parents who abuse their children are often victims themselves—victims of impoverished childhoods, second-class educations, poor health care, chaotic living conditions due to lack of resources, dangerous housing (poor wiring, broken toilets and furnaces), and no cushion of money or social support in times of need. Another way to encourage liking is to keep in mind that family members usually do care about one another. Their motivation and intentions are usually positive. A classic study of more than 800 instances of child abuse indicated that 87% were in the context of parents trying to discipline their children (Kadushin & Martin, 1981). The parents' intent was not to abuse their children. Husbands who batter their wives often believe that their actions will improve their relationship.

People who seek or are referred for help may be ambivalent about the time and effort that may be involved. They may worry about whether they will be helped or can trust a stranger, how they will be evaluated, and what they will have to reveal. Involuntary clients, such as parents alleged to have abused their children or elderly clients in need of protective care, may be angry about unwanted intrusions into their privacy that they view as unnecessary. Identifying and focusing on goals that clients value will encourage participation. For example, clients may want to prevent their children from being taken away from them or to have children who have been removed to be returned. This does not mean that they will take part in agreed-on ways. This remains to be seen. However, you can increase the likelihood that clients will participate by selecting an agreed-on goal, and being trustworthy, friendly, competent, clear, and empathic. (See Exhibit 13.9.)

Be Honest

It is important to be honest with clients, for both practical and ethical reasons. For instance, withholding bad news may create more worry. If a medical social worker withholds information, the client may reach even more alarming conclusions about what is wrong. Social workers in public agencies sometimes have hidden agendas—goals that are not shared with clients. A child welfare worker may secretly hope that a parent who has neglected her child will not show up for visits so that a petition for abandonment can be filed. Potential consequences of participation or its lack should be candidly discussed in a supportive manner (see also later section on service agreements). Any involuntary pressures on clients and their feelings about this should be recognized and ways in which meetings might benefit clients explored. Examples of what you could say are:

- "I know you didn't come here of your own free will and that you may be angry about being here."

- "You probably don't feel like seeing me…"

- "I think there are some ways I can be of help."

If feelings are brought out into the open, you can explore what might be accomplished within the present constraints. You may have to discuss certain topics even if it is uncomfortable for clients.

What if no agency, including yours, offers services likely to help clients? What do you do in this common circumstance? What if you know you are uninformed about research related to a client's concerns? Or what if there are effective programs but you do not offer them, nor are they available in your community? Should you share this information with clients? And if you do,

---

EXHIBIT 13.9

Helping Clients Feel at Ease

CONSULTANT: I'm glad to see you, Mr. and Mrs. Blake. (Parents are offered and take seats at a comfortable distance from consultant. If parents seem tense or shy, the consultant encourages a little ice-breaking small talk about the weather, or some encouraging developments in the child's education, and possibly offers clients coffee or a soft drink.)

PARENTS: (Return greeting and participate in small talk.)

CONSULTANT: (Makes sure to smile at parents as they indicate that they are more at ease.) This is our first meeting. And it may be the first of some valuable meetings to come. I think we can get a lot done together.

CONSULTANT: (Smiles and speaks softly.) It's natural to feel a bit uneasy. I sometimes get butterflies too, when I first meet parents. I don't know how they feel about things. And, you know, some parents have gotten so little help, that they may not have much trust in new people who offer them help. And I don't blame them at all. If I were you, I wouldn't trust me, at least not yet! (Anticipates possible distrust or hostility of parents toward professionals. Remains alert for any movements indicating parents' agreement, such as a smile, nod of the head, or a settling into a more comfortable position, and reinforces such movements by smiling.)

Source: M. A. Kozloff (1979). *A program for families of children with learning and behavior problems* (pp. 61–62). New York: Wiley. Reprinted by permission.

EXHIBIT 13.10

Possible Gaps Between Needs and Resources Available

Situation	Suggested Ethical Action
1. You are not informed about research regarding problems clients confront including the evidentiary status of different assessment or intervention options.	1. Become informed and share what you find with clients (see chapter 10).
2. Your agency does not offer services found to be effective in achieving desired outcomes but another one does.	2. Share this information with clients and arrange a referral.
3. Neither your agency nor any other local agency offers services found to be of value in addressing concern to clients.	3. Share this information with clients and draw on practice theory to guide selection of services. Offer support and work with other staff and interested parties to provide effective services in your community.
4. A review of related research shows that no services have been found to be effective in achieving hoped-for outcomes.	4. Share this with clients, draw on practice-related theory to make suggestions and offer support.

are you left with nothing to offer? What are ethical issues here? Options are suggested in Exhibit 13.10. (See also chapter 10.)

Clearly Describe Problems and Their Context

Clarifying client concerns and their context is a key assessment task. Without this, the specific changes needed to attain valued outcomes will remain a mystery. Explain this to clients so they understand your interest in clarity regarding outcomes and related factors. You may have to observe behavior in real-life settings to discover behaviors of concern, desired alternatives, and related antecedents and consequences (see chapter 18). Only if the *function(s)* of behaviors (their meanings) are understood, can plans be soundly based. Basing plans on a behavioral analysis is now mandated by law for special education students in California (Positive Behavioral Intervention Regulations, California Department of Education, 1993).

Find out what clients refer to when they use vague terms, such as *lack of communication, vandalism,* and *assault.* People often have different meanings for the same words. What specific behaviors, thoughts, or feelings occur too often, too seldom, at the wrong time, or in the wrong place? Ask questions that focus on behavior and related events, such as:

- Can you give me an example?

- What was going on when this occurred?

- Could you describe the most recent time this happened?

- Are there things he does not do that are related to _____?

When you have one example, seek others until you have identified the referents to which a general term refers. If you assume that you and the client share the same referents for vague terms, you will not ask such questions and may be biased by cultural stereotypes that get in the way of clarifying problems. Use *what, who, when,* and *where* questions rather than *why* questions (see Exhibit 13.11). For example, if your client says he is an alcoholic, find out the referents for this term so that you can understand what he means. What specific behaviors (or their absence) are referred to? Helpful questions are: What do you drink? How much do you drink? How often do you drink? Where do you drink? Where do you not drink? The client may not be able to clearly describe behaviors of concern and related circumstances. If feasible and relevant, you may observe clients in real-life settings to identify relevant behaviors and associated cues and consequences or clients may collect information. (See chapter 18.) Terms that refer to emotions, such as *anxiety* and *anger,* must be clarified; each person may refer to somewhat different reactions when using such words. Useful questions include: How do you know when you are anxious? What do you do when you are anxious? What situations increases anxiety? Which ones decrease it?

Asking people why something occurs presumes that they know the answer. This can be frustrating to clients, since they probably do not know, but since the question was asked, it seems that they should know the answer. Instead, ask "What happens when..." or "What makes you think...?" *Why* questions encourage motivational accounts. A student may say, "I'm just lazy," or "I'm just shy." Such statements are often offered as explanations for problems. They may be used as excuses not to change. *Why* questions *are* useful in discovering a client's point of view about the causes of a problem and how they can be resolved. For example, a teacher may believe that a student's "out-of-control" behavior is due to a poor home environment. She may not realize that

EXHIBIT 13.11

Case Example of a Beginning Interview with a Teacher

CONSULTANT: (1) Jody, what are your general concerns regarding Candy's behavior? (2) In very general terms, tell me about her behavior.

CONSULTEE: She is a very complicated child. She has had quite a difficult background. Mainly, I guess it's her adjustment to her new home, her adjustment to the new class situation, and being able to get along with her peer group.

CONSULTANT: (3) OK.

CONSULTEE: All of these things are based on what has been happening to her in the past.

CONSULTANT: (4) As far as adjustment to her classroom situation is concerned, what are some of the things you are talking about?

CONSULTEE: Her behavior is inappropriate in that she has a hard time staying in her seat. She has a hard time knowing when to speak out and when not to. She does a lot of blurting out of things when she shouldn't. She has been taking things from other children but wants very much to be their friend and to be my friend.

CONSULTANT: (5) The general area then appears to be social, getting along with other children.

CONSULTEE: Right. Rather than academics.

CONSULTANT: (6) Academic behavior is not uppermost in your mind?

CONSULTEE: She does quite well.

CONSULTANT: (7) In the area of social concerns, it would be adjustment to the classroom situation, staying in the seat, speaking at appropriate times, and taking things from others that are the concerns you have about her social behavior.

CONSULTEE: She just doesn't know how to go about getting along with other people, There are a lot of little things that happen that cause her not to be liked by the other children, Yet, they are trying, in part, to overlook things. She doesn't seem to be willing to try to work things out by herself, nor does she seem to understand what is necessary, She just seems to go down her own little path.

CONSULTANT: (8) So that the major goals that you have, or the direction that you would like to move in, is for her to be able to get along better with others and to adjust to the classroom situation better. (9) You see those as two separate areas: adjusting to the classroom and getting along better with others?

CONSULTEE: Separate, yes. But it is important to work on them together.

CONSULTANT: (10) As far as getting along better with others is concerned, what are some of the things you would like her to do?

CONSULTEE: I would like her to learn to understand others. What are some of the necessary social skills she needs to have? She needs to know when children want to be her friend. She often puts the children in a position where she demands this friendship. When she doesn't get it, she turns kind of vengeful instead of trying to figure out what she is going to do in order to get them to be her friend.

CONSULTANT: (11) All right, she demands friendship, and (12) what exactly does she do in these kinds of situations?

CONSULTEE: When she is wanting to have friends?

CONSULTANT: (13) Yes.

CONSULTEE: She will pull at them physically, handle them in trying to get them away from other children. She often tries to give things to the children and then expects them to turn around and be her friend because she has given something to them. She tries to get up and be by a particular person at a time when she shouldn't be out of her seat. The other child knows that what is going on is wrong and tries to ignore it or tells her to sit down or something. She still stays right there.

CONSULTANT: (14) Then, in getting along with peers, it is to know when she is with friends not to demand their friendship or to get them away from other children or to try to bribe them into being her friend, but to understand the ways in which she can get other children to like her. (15) Is that right?

CONSULTEE: Yes.

CONSULTANT: (16) In the area of adjustment to the classroom, what are some of the skills that you would like her to have?

(continued)

EXHIBIT 13.11 (Continued)

CONSULTEE: I would like her to stay in her seat when it is the appropriate time to be in her seat. I would like her to listen when I say, "Please go sit down," rather than have to get to the point that I am having to get mad at her. I don't like to get to that point. She won't listen at first. She won't listen a second time and so on. I would like her to raise her hand instead of just blurting out in class. These are the main things she needs to work on, I think.

CONSULTANT: (17) Our two major areas of concern are getting along with other children and adjusting to the classroom situation. (18) Which of these areas would you want to concentrate on?

CONSULTEE: I think working on the classroom behavior. I think that if that can begin to come around, the children would in turn understand and like her better.

CONSULTANT: (19) Under classroom behavior, what do you want to work on first? (20) You mentioned staying in her seat, listening when spoken to, and raising her hand to be called on. (21) Which of those would you like to work on first?

CONSULTEE: I would like to work on the one that I think we could remedy the fastest and easiest so that the other things could come around. So I would say following directions.

CONSULTANT: (22) The situation we would like her to follow directions in is in the classroom. (23) Is there any particular time?

CONSULTEE: During direct teaching time. During the time that they do independent work. I think it would be mostly when it is teacher-directed.

CONSULTANT: (24) So, whenever you are doing direct teaching to the group, you would like her to follow whatever directions you give to the group?

CONSULTEE: No. Wait a minute. I think I want to change that. I would say, actually, that we have the most trouble in between subjects, while we are changing over, when we are changing the activity or something. That is when she has the hardest time.

CONSULTANT: (25) So, whenever you are changing from one activity to another and you give a direction to the class, you would like her to follow the direction immediately. (1) Would you be able in the next few days, until I get back here on Tuesday, to keep track of how many times you give a direction and it is not followed by her? (2) It could simply be just keeping a running tally during these times.

CONSULTEE: Shall I keep track of what the specific direction is?

CONSULTANT: (3) If you can, because there may be one type of direction that she is not following rather than another. (4) The type of direction and whether she follows it would be a simple thing. (5) Record every time you give a direction and whether she follows it so we have a percentage.

CONSULTEE: OK. Sure.

CONSULTANT: (6) Then, our goal is to get her to adjust to the classroom, (7) and our first step is to get her to follow directions. (8) Once we have helped that, we can concentrate on staying in her seat and that sort of thing.

CONSULTEE: I think that is good.

CONSULTANT: (9) Can we get together, then, next Tuesday, look at the data, and go from there?

CONSULTEE: Yes. This same time?

CONSULTANT: (10) Fine. (11) Thanks.

Source: J. R. Bergan & T. R. Kratochwill (1990). *Behavioral consultation and therapy* (pp. 307–310). New York: Plenum. Reprinted with permission.

she reinforces the very behaviors she complains about. You may help her to understand the role she plays via your questions.

Descriptions should refer to observable characteristics of behavior or the environment. Boundary conditions should be clear so that behaviors to be included and excluded can be readily distinguished. Examples of clearly defined behaviors are snacking (eating between meals) and initiating a conversation (a verbal exchange lasting at least 3 minutes), introducing agenda items at a local citizen board meeting, and thanking others for their contributions to team meetings. Examples of vague terms are *aggressive, unmanageable, sad, insecure, anxious, depressed,* and *overly dependent*. Ask: Would people agree on its occurrence based on this description? If the answer is no, further clarification is necessary. Try to select behaviors that have a definite beginning and end, such as offering opinions at citizen board meetings, following instructions, requesting help when needed, and initiating conversations. Discourage use of vague negative labels, such as shy or aggressive. General labels get in the way of discovering relevant behaviors and related causes. When possible, and ethical, obtain a sample of the behaviors of concern and the context in which they occur by observing relevant behaviors in role plays or real life.

Identify Client Strengths Including Positive Alternative Behaviors and Related Contingencies

Be sure to identify and support client strengths such as valuable coping skills, as well as other valuable resources such as local community groups. Clients may have access to vital resources such as caring relatives. As many have said, clients are more than their problems. Many clients have shown impressive creativity and resilience in dealing with the effects of racism, oppression, and their sequela such as poor quality schools for their children, lack of health care, and few (if any) opportunities for employment. Practice/policy highlights the close connection between client concerns and related political and economic factors such as stingy, punitive financial aid policies (Trattner, 1999).

Clients often present desired changes in negative terms, such as "being less miserable" or "feeling less nervous." Find out what they would *do* if they were less miserable or less nervous. Possible questions are: How would you know if you were less miserable? What would you do differently? What would you do more often? What would you do less often? Focus on increasing positive alternatives to undesired behaviors. Relying first on positive intervention programs is now mandated for special education students in the State of California (Positive Behavioral Intervention Regulations, 1993).

Understanding the *communicative functions* of behaviors of concern will help you to identify positive alternatives. For example, children's noncompliance and "out-of-control" behavior in class may be maintained by getting rid of unwanted demands (e.g., tasks that are too difficult). Identifying positive alternatives may require observation in real-life settings. Clients often have difficulty describing behaviors they want to see more of, because they focus on behaviors they dislike. So many unpleasant exchanges may have taken place between family members that they become negative scanners of each other's behavior, attending only to disliked reactions. Helpful questions are: What does he do that you like? What would you like him to do? The answer to the first question sometimes is, "Nothing." Most clients need help in identifying specific behaviors to be increased, as well as approximations to them. You could ask clients what an ideal friendship or child would be like (when relevant) and then identify specific behaviors related to general terms. You may discover important objectives by asking a client what he would do if he behaved in a way opposite to that complained about. You could ask a child, "What would your teacher do if he liked you?" Be careful not to impose your assumptions on clients.

Some positive alternatives become obvious once disliked behaviors have been noted. Two behaviors may be physically incompatible in that they cannot be performed at the same time: a child cannot sit in his seat and run around the room at the same time. In other instances, competing behaviors may be more difficult to identify. This requires searching for behaviors and circumstances that are not correlated with problematic behavior. A child may not cry while playing with other children. If so, play could be increased to decrease crying. A woman may not feel depressed when talking to friends. These behaviors could be encouraged to decrease depression. When desired behaviors are identified, you and your clients can explore how contingencies could be altered to increase them. Examples of positive alternatives to undesired behavior are:

- Praising staff (criticizing them).

- Following instructions (not following instructions).

- Talking with roommate for 5 minutes when entering the house after work (not communicating).

- Sharing toys (keeping toys to self).

- Initiating conversations (avoiding people).

When low-frequency behaviors (such as occasional school vandalism or fire setting) are of concern, identify and reinforce behaviors that are functionally incompatible with them and occur often. For example, Patterson and Reid guessed that a youth's occasional fire setting was related to low rates of positive reinforcement for desired behaviors at school, at home, and on the playground. Their intervention centered on increasing reinforcement of such behaviors in these contexts (Patterson & Reid, 1970). This is an example of a *nonlinear approach* often required to address concerns (see Exhibit 12.12).

Describe the Context in Which Problems Occur

Clients often overgeneralize. They may not realize that behaviors of concern usually occur only in certain situations. For example, a parent may say that her daughter is *always* out of control or that she feels angry *all* the time. Behavior usually varies in accordance with the presence or absence of certain events. A child may wet the bed only at home and never when visiting friends or relatives. No one is always shy or always aggressive. You can review data collected, highlighting situational variations. Helpful questions in identifying antecedents and consequences are:

- When does this usually occur?

- What is going on when this happens?

- Are there any times when this does not occur?

- Does this happen at certain times of the day more than others?

- What happens right afterward?

- What happens right before?

- Are there some things that make it worse (or better)?

For example, Brian's leaving the house without telling his parents where he was going was usually preceded by what he described as "their nagging." Leaving the house resulted in getting rid of the "nagging" and so was negatively reinforced. Brian's parents positively reinforced many behaviors that they complained of and failed to attend to desired behaviors, such as playing ball with the dog, helping his sister with her homework, and offering to help around the house. They did not intend to reinforce behaviors they disliked; however, the effects of our behavior often do not match our intentions.

Focus on behavior and surrounding environmental cues and consequences—what occurs in what situations and how others respond before and after behaviors of concern. Find out what happens in real life. What situations increase the likelihood of behaviors of concern? What situations make them less likely? Questions such as "When did this start?" may offer clues about environmental changes related to problems. What we do and think influence what we feel, and so it is helpful to identify actions and thoughts along with environmental factors that influence feelings. *We can use feelings as clues* about who has (or is believed to have) influence over important consequences. Use information gained to complete a contingency analysis form (see Exhibit 7.4). You can review this in relation to resources at hand (see chapter 19) to evaluate your options.

Collect Baseline Data When Possible

A *baseline* is a measure of how often a behavior occurs before intervention. This allows comparison of the frequency (or duration, intensity, or latency) of a behavior (or thought, or feeling) before intervention with the frequency after intervention. Information about antecedents and consequences related to behaviors of concern and desired alternatives is often collected at the same time. Baseline data provide valuable information about the severity of problems and their context and a comparative point for you and your clients to track degree of progress. For instance, a second-grade teacher may complain that a student's misbehavior is worse than that of other students in her class. Observation may indicate that this student's rate of annoying behaviors (talking out of turn, getting out of his seat) is no higher than that of other students.

Baseline data may be collected by clients, or they may already be available (e.g., frequency of arrests). The data gathered by Brian and his parents revealed a high frequency of noncompliance by Brian right before and during dinner when the entire family was present. His noncompliance was much lower when only Brian and his parents were at home. For a week, Julie kept track of the times she was free from worrisome thoughts about her decision. Mrs. Landis gave her an index card divided into 1-hour periods for each day. Julie put a check mark in each 1-hour period during which she did not worry. She also wrote down in a small diary what she worried about. Julie's record indicated that she was better able to deal with intrusive thoughts at school than when she was at home with her parents or on weekends. Because

behavior often differs in different situations, you should gather baseline data in all relevant situations if possible, if this is needed to understand concerns and/or determine baseline levels so that progress can be reviewed.

The skills required for gathering and using baseline data include (1) identifying specific behaviors, thoughts, or feelings; (2) selecting feasible methods to monitor them; and (3) summarizing data. If a behavior occurs only in certain contexts (such as the classroom), collect it only there. With low-frequency behaviors or when it is necessary to intervene immediately, you may rely on a *prebaseline* (an estimate of the current frequency of a behavior). When low-frequency behaviors are of concern such as setting fires, identify related behaviors that occur frequently. For example, stealing a car may only happen once every six weeks, but criticism from parents and teachers may occur every day, as well as a lack of praise for desired behavior. Praise for desired behaviors can be offered often each day. Explosive anger on the part of an administrator may occur only once a month, but situations in which she does not say what she wants may occur several times each workday.

Offer Support

Offering support is an important aspect of all phases of work with clients. Support is the context in which other kinds of help are offered. Functions of support include reducing stress, restoring hope, and enhancing recognition of resources, both personal and environmental. Normalization of concerns is one aspect of support; clients learn that their feelings, behaviors, or thoughts or the situations they experience are not odd or pathological but common for many people. Related helper skills include attentive listening, structuring, presenting a helpful model, being concrete and respectful, identifying and reinforcing valuable repertoires, and being nonjudgmental, empathetic, warm, and genuine (see chapter 15). Helping clients to understand environmental factors related to problems should decrease tendencies to blame themselves for outcomes over which they have little control. Support will not be enough when clients need material resources such as money, housing, food, clothing, jobs, or health services or do not have the knowledge and required skills to attain valued outcomes.

Encourage Helpful Views of Problems and Their Causes

Find out how clients view concerns and possible solutions. Placing yourself in other people's "shoes" will help you understand their viewpoints. What have clients and significant others tried to resolve problems? Beliefs about problems and their causes are reflected in attempted solutions. Attempted solutions may create more problems and be an obstacle to change (Watzlawick, Weakland, & Fisch, 1974). If you understand your client's point of view, you will be in a better position to suggest solutions compatible with this or to discuss advantages of other views. The match between helpers' and clients' views is related to outcome. People who insist that you do not understand their perspective—when you do—may mistakenly equate understanding and agreement. Understanding a viewpoint does not mean that you agree with it—or that it is accurate. Help clients view concerns in *instrumental* ways that suggest what can be done to solve them. If a client says: "If only my Uncle George had not drunk himself to death, I wouldn't be miserable today," point out that since there is no way time can be turned back and Uncle George cured of his drinking, this offers no clues about how to attain hoped-for outcomes.

Coach clients to think in terms of desired outcomes related to problems. Help them discover steps *they* can take to resolve concerns. To identify these, clients may have to understand their own role in relation to a problem. For example, a caregiver of an elderly homebound relative who complains about her "endless talking" may not realize that she supports this behavior by attentively listening to her. This problem can be reframed from the caregiver's view that the elderly woman is to blame, to a view that people influence one another and thus the caregiver can do something to change disliked behaviors (e.g., reinforce desired alternatives). This new view increases her influence over her environment. Avoid negative labels.

Some concerns may be "normative"—experienced by most people in a given situation. If so, point out their common occurrence. This will help reduce any sense of stigma clients may feel. This highlights the value of being informed about the prevalence of certain reactions and their developmental characteristics (for example, at what life stage they occur). This does not mean concerns should be minimized or ignored. It does mean questioning clients' views of themselves as sick or pathological for having problems. Clients may accept society's definition of problems as being one's own fault. They may have little or no awareness of the relationship between the personal and the political (Mills, 1959)—that their troubles are related to political, social, and economic ideologies and policies that influence the quality of their neighborhoods and schools and their access to health care and employment. (See chapter 27.)

Clients may agree to participate after they understand how current patterns of behavior work against them. Many people get caught up in the "reinforcement trap." That is, they give in to (reinforce) annoying behavior, gaining temporary respite at the cost of increasing the probability of annoying behavior in the future. Overgeneralizations such as "it will never change" or "he's always that way" can be challenged by collecting data showing they are inaccurate. For example, a parent may learn from data she collects that the child she describes as never following instructions does follow some instructions.

Decrease Blame and Negative Labels

Clients may blame themselves or others for their troubles. Blame encourages defensiveness and fear and gets in the way of identifying *personalized goals,* steps that the complainer can take to make positive changes. There are a number of ways to nudge clients toward less negative views of themselves or significant others, including suggesting other views (see chapter 15). When appropriate, "normalizing" concerns helps clients realize that their complaints are not unusual. You could point out that 5,000 other people have also lost their jobs because of recent business closures in a community, that complaints about lack of communication between adolescents and their parents are common, and that fears about having cancer when one has certain symptoms are not unusual.

Identify Specific Outcomes to Focus on

After you and your clients have decided on priorities (what to focus on first), identify specific related objectives that describe:

- What behaviors are to occur.
- With what frequency, duration, or intensity.
- In what situations.
- When they are to occur.
- Who is to offer them.
- Intermediate steps.

Examples of clear objectives are as follows:

- Set up a community-police review group within six months designed to increase positive and decrease negative exchanges between police and community residents (e.g., "stop and frisk" incidents of youth decrease).
- Form a citizens review board in three months.
- Increase the percentage of eligible clients who receive food stamps.
- Identify clear, criterion-referenced performance standards for staff within six months.
- Each weekday after school, spend one-half hour talking about your child's work.
- Return greetings (say hi or hello, look at the person, smile).
- Attend school 4 days a week.

- Within 1 week, sign up for food stamp program.

- Wear an orthodontic device during all waking hours.

Objectives should be achievable, relevant (related to concerns focused on), and measurable. Relevance can be determined by asking: Will meeting these objectives solve this problem? Moving from vague complaints to clear, relevant objectives usually requires gathering data from a variety of sources (see chapter 17).

Clearly describing concerns and related factors will help clients move from vague goals that do not offer information about how to attain them, to *specific, relevant* objectives (see Exhibit 13.12). A clear description of agreed-on objectives ensures that you and your clients understand the purpose of your contacts, guides selection of plans by helping you to pose and pursue answers to information needs by consulting related research, and allows you to judge whether needed resources are available. Examples of such questions are:

- For community members who want to improve the quality of their neighborhood schools, what strategies are most effective in gaining the attention of local politicians?

- For parents and adolescents who often argue, is conflict resolution training or insight counseling more effective in decreasing conflicts and increasing positive resolutions?

- For families caring for elderly relatives, is behavioral family therapy or negotiation training more effective in decreasing negative interactions and increasing positive interactions?

Objectives will often involve changes in the environment, such as altering how significant others respond, gaining needed resources, and creating significant others. Explain the purposes of identifying specific objectives. These include making sure they are relevant to concerns focused on, selecting effective plans, evaluating progress, avoiding sidetracks, and identifying intermediate steps.

Plan an Agenda

An agenda includes description of baseline levels, intermediate steps, and desired outcomes. Examples of baseline levels and desired outcomes are given in Exhibit 13.13. The first two examples involve behaviors to be increased. Examples 3 and 4 involve behaviors to be decreased. The goal may be to stabilize a variable behavior or to vary a stable behavior. For instance, a woman may seldom visit places where she can start conversations so the goal may be to visit such places more regularly. Or she may always use the same remark to initiate conversations so the goal may be to vary what she says. Another goal may be to

maintain a behavior at its current level, such as help an elderly client maintain her current frequency of daily social contacts or help an administrator maintain her current level of positive feedback (verbal praise, letters of appreciation) for valued staff behaviors.

You may also have to identify *intermediate behaviors* (behaviors that lie between what the client is now doing (baseline levels) and desired outcomes. Intermediate steps may involve gradually increasing or decreasing the frequency of the same behavior or introducing different behaviors. A *task analysis* may be required to discover related behaviors (see chapter 18). The description of initial, intermediate, and desired objectives provides a step-by-step agenda. Each step should be clearly described (require a minimum of interpretation), including specific criteria that will be used to assess performance. For example, if *neatness* is used to assess homework of a child, clearly define what this means. To what does "neat" refer?

Attaining desired outcomes often involves pursuit of many objectives. Let us say a teacher complains that a 6-year-old is unmanageable. This vague term may refer to behavior surfeits, such as shouting in class or hitting other students, as well as a lack of desired behaviors, such as not completing assignments, not following instructions, and not playing cooperatively with peers. The objectives might be to increase assignments completed on time from zero to all assigned, increase instructions followed from 25% to 80%, and increase time spent in cooperative play with peers during free time from 10% to 60%. A series of intermediate steps may have to be pursued to achieve each objective. It may be necessary to identify levels of correctness and neatness, and to clearly describe desired social behaviors. Even when the objective is to increase a behavior that already exists, this may have to be done gradually. If the aim is to increase homework assignments completed from 1 per week to 10 per week, intermediate steps might be 2 assignments, 4, 6, and so on. Clear description of approximations to desired outcomes will make it easy to identify and to reinforce these.

Guidelines for Selecting Goals and Related Objectives

Focus on outcomes that are important to clients and significant others. People will not be interested in pursuing outcomes that do not interest them. Select objectives that involve changing the circumstances related to concerns. This will require distinguishing between *indirect* and *direct* methods. (See Exhibit 13.14.) For example, a direct approach to altering eating patterns would be to focus on eating. An indirect approach would focus on the conditions related to problematic eating patterns, such as boredom. Indirect approaches are generally more effective than direct approaches. Consider Jenny, a college student who wanted to lose weight. She had moved to San Francisco four months ago, had no friends there, and could not find a job. She

EXHIBIT 13.12

Examples of Objectives

The Lakeland Family

Changes Mr. and Mrs. Lakeland wanted:
1. Brian would treat the family dog respectfully: pet the dog gently if he touches him, not pick him up by the tail, not kick the dog.
2. Brian would take his medication (three times each day—morning, afternoon, and evening).
3. Tell his parents (or leave a note) where he was going when he left the house and planned to be away for more than 1 hour.
4. Address his mother politely (not call his mother negative names, such as "old bag").
5. Not physically threaten his parents.
6. Get better grades in school (a C average) and complete homework assignments on time.
7. Reach agreements with Brian in a positive way. (Each person would have a chance to state his or her wishes, and all would be responsible for suggesting possible solutions, identifying their advantages and disadvantages, and reaching compromises.)
8. Brian would take out the garbage each evening within 1 hour after dinner and cut the grass once a week in the spring, summer, and fall (or shovel snow in winter).

Changes Brian desired:
1. His father would help him collect the money for his paper route once a month.
2. His father would take him fishing once a month.
3. His parents would not "nag" him (they would ask him to do something only once).
4. His brother Bob would help him with his homework twice a week.
5. To solve conflicts with his parents in a positive way (see number 7 above).
6. A "special dinner" (something he chose) cooked by his mother once a week.
7. His parents to be "nicer to him" (to say more positive things to him).
8. He would get along better at school (his teachers would not yell at him as much).
9. He would have a place to do his homework.

Mrs. Ryan and the Greens

Outcomes Mrs. Ryan wanted:
1. Have more contact with other people (about 2 hours a week).
2. Take a 30-minute walk every day.
3. Write four letters a week.
4. Have more family conversations (at least once or twice a week for an hour or more).
5. Do more chores around the house (dust every third day, clean the kitchen counters each day, and vacuum once a week).

Outcomes the Greens wanted:
1. Gain information about the aging process.
2. Have some time to themselves (about 2 half-hour talks a week).
3. Gain information about Medicare.

Joint outcomes:
1. Decide where Mrs. Ryan will live.
2. Share their feelings constructively.

Julie

Desired outcomes:
1. Decide whether to have an abortion or to have her baby.
2. Decide whether to involve her parents in this decision.
3. Learn how to avoid future pregnancies.
4. Decide how to handle the situation with her boyfriend.
5. Not worry about this decision all the time.

ate when she was home alone. Rather than focusing directly on eating, boredom, lack of friends, lack of a job, and negative self-statements were addressed. Since the most effective way to decrease undesired reactions is to increase desired alternatives, pick objectives that involve increasing desired behaviors, thoughts, or feelings. Focus on the *construction* of repertoires rather than their elimination. A client may learn to replace worrisome thoughts with task-focused self-statements. Caregivers can be encouraged to focus on and reinforce behaviors they want to see more often.

EXHIBIT 13.13

Examples of Baselines and Related Objectives

Baseline Levels	Objectives
1. Zero assignments completed per week.	1. All assignments completed each week.
2. Zero initiations of conversations. (A conversation is more than a greeting and at least 1 minute in length.)	2. Four conversations initiated per week.
3. Five temper tantrums per day.	3. Zero tantrums per day.
4. Five criticisms of staff a day.	4. Zero criticism of staff; praise staff three times a day.

The *relevance-of-behavior rule* emphasizes selecting behaviors that will continue to be reinforced after contacts with clients end. Objectives should involve behaviors and situations that "make a difference" in the client's life. Selecting objectives that result in benefits for clients and significant others in real-life settings requires a clear description of the contexts in which new behaviors will take place and anticipation of possible consequences of new ways of acting. The call for functional significance is legally mandated for some populations. Consider these regulations mandating that educational services be appropriate for students with disabilities: "Behavioral interventions" are designed to give people greater access to a variety of community settings, social contacts, and public events and to ensure individuals their right to placement in the least restrictive educational environment as outlined in that person's IEP (individual education plan) (Positive Behavioral Intervention Regulations, 1993, p. 2).

Being functional (behaviors are relevant) is a key characteristic all objectives should share. This rule is often violated. For example, staff in residential settings may focus on behaviors that benefit them rather than the residents. Staff may offer unneeded help that erodes independent self-care behaviors because it is easier for them (i.e., residents would take longer to complete tasks themselves).

A Five-Step Approach

Mager (1972) has identified five steps in the process of goal analysis. *Step 1* entails writing down the goal, using whatever words seem reasonable, no matter how vague. *Step 2* involves writing down what someone would say or do if they attained the goal. Questions here are: What will I accept as evidence that the goal has been achieved? How would someone know if he saw

a person who had achieved the goal? People who represent the goal (e.g., good parents) could be identified and relevant behaviors noted. Be sure to include positives (what a person would do or say), as well as omissions (what she would not do or say). For example, perhaps a good parent would:

Positives	*Negatives*
Take children for required medical checkups.	Do not hit children.
Feed children a balanced diet.	Do not leave children unsupervised.
Dress children properly.	Do not allow husband to abuse children.
Keep children clean.	Do not call children names like "stupid."
Provide appropriate play opportunities	
Use instructions effectively.	

Step 3 involves going back over the list and tidying up. As Mager suggests, there are bound to be "a number of fuzzies" (1972, p. 53). There may also be redundancies and items that describe procedures rather than outcomes. Remove items that describe *procedures* (e.g., attend parenting class). The task at this point is to identify *outcomes,* not to describe how to attain these. Other examples of process goals are joining Alcoholic Anonymous, attending a drug treatment program, and seeing a psychotherapist for six months. None of these describes desired outcomes, ways in which a person should be different, after the program. Describe the specific outcomes hoped for as a result of suggested procedures. Cross out duplications and place terms that are still vague on separate pages for further analysis.

Step 4 involves further clarification. For example, *effectively* must be clearly defined in the statement "uses instructions effectively." *Step 5* consists of scanning objectives to make sure they are clear and relevant. Are all relevant behaviors identified? Could the clients act in ways that would match your description but would not be helpful in attaining desired outcomes? For example, a goal of "attend school more often" could be met by going to school 3 days a week rather than 1. What may be desired is for a student to go to school 5 days a week. If fuzzies are found, performance criteria are not yet complete. Have you clearly described the situations in which behaviors are expected? Have you set a frequency or duration criterion? Will achieving objectives benefit both the client and significant others? Will there be any negative effects if outcomes are attained?

The first steps encouraged should be the closest approximations to desired outcomes that are comfortable and achievable. If a "lonely" client wants to meet more people, a first step may be to locate promising places to meet people (i.e., to gain information). The next may be to visit one or two places a week and start one conversation while there. Others might be arranging future meetings and introducing more personal topics (Gambrill &

EXHIBIT 13.14

A Planning Guide

1. Sensible behavior. Present a coherent picture of a person functioning highly competently, given the circumstances and implicit or explicit goals and available alternatives. Infer how the present pattern may have been shaped, and why the patterns are now "costly" enough to seek professional help. Infer what consequences are currently maintaining the "symptomatic pattern." Use a cost/benefit matrix to make sense of these patterns and their available alternatives. Show how the person's reason giving, stated thoughts, and reported emotions are sensible outcomes of the contingencies described by your matrix. Describe any systemic relations, i.e., indicate if contingencies other than those presented may be potentiating the costly contingencies, thereby occasioning the presenting complaints.

2. **Outcomes**. State the outcomes that seem reasonable as targets. Support each of your targets with evidence from the interview. Describe the relation between the targets and the consequences maintaining the symptomatic pattern. Describe any additional benefits (reinforcers) that might occur as a result of reaching the targets. Enter these targets into your cost benefit matrix. Using your cost/benefit matrix describe how the target patterns will provide greater or similar benefits at reduced cost. Describe the terminal analytic repertoire that may be established along with the other defined outcomes (self-control). Describe the emotions, thoughts, and self-descriptions that should occur as by-products of reaching program goals.

3. **The program**. Describe the topical, nonlinear topical, or systematic components of your intervention. (See Exhibit 12.12.) Describe the program sequence. Describe how components of past repertoires may be transferred to new situations or used as part of new composite repertoires. Describe how you will use the client's emotions and thoughts as "contingency descriptors" so as to help the client discriminate the relevant consequential contingencies governing his or her behavior. Specify any shaping, modeling, transfer, or instructional procedures that may be required.

4. **Current repertoire as starting point**. Describe the current relevant repertoires you can draw on. What assets, social, educational, environmental, or professional might be helpful? State if you think the client will be able to keep records, and if the client will be able to quickly use them as analytical tools. Where should the program begin? State an entry repertoire for each of the targets. Provide evidence from the interview for your inferences.

5. **Obstacles**. Speculate on what the developmental costs might be for establishing the target patterns.

6. **Maintaining consequences**. Describe the consequences that will maintain the client's behavior through the program. Indicate whether progress toward stated outcomes (both behaviors and consequences) will serve as program-intrinsic reinforcers. Describe how quickly following the program sequence greater benefits, less cost, or both can be expected. If contrived (social or tangible) program-extrinsic consequences are to be used, describe them, and describe how they will be potentiated. Indicate when they will be faded from the program. Describe any "behavior trapping" procedures.

Source: Andronis, Layng, & Johnson (1997). Adapted from Goldiamond (1974). Toward a constructional approach to social problems: Ethical and constitutional issues raised by applied behavior analysis. *Behaviorism*, *2*, 1–84.

Richey, 1988). Describe each step in specific terms that require a minimum of interpretation. Progress with initial steps provides guidelines for moving on to more advanced ones.

Selecting Objectives as a Negotiation Process

Deciding on goals and objectives involves a process of negotiation between you and your clients. It is better to select too few than too many outcomes to pursue, so that those of most concern are addressed. Agreement may not be possible because of ethical objections you may have. You may be reluctant to pursue a goal that concerns someone else without that person's involvement. If significant others refuse to participate, you will have to decide whether it is practical and ethical to proceed without their involvement. Let us say a teacher refers a 7-year-old to you because of his "out-of-control behavior" in class. The teacher may expect you to remove this child from class and to work with him individually. Observation in the class-room may reveal that the teacher provokes out-of-control behaviors and does not reinforce desired behaviors. If you cannot involve this teacher, you will have to decide whether outcomes can be attained without his participation. Perhaps you could persuade the child's parents to offer reinforcement at home for behaviors at school. Or you could help the student learn how to prompt more positive feedback for desired classroom behaviors (see the classic study by Graubard, Rosenberg, & Miller, 1971).

If family members or others differ in what they want or clients cannot decide what they want, the agreed-on goal could be to help them reach a decision (Stein, Gambrill, & Wiltse, 1978; Stuart, 1980). This goal could be pursued when parents and children cannot decide whether they want to live together again or when an elderly client is trying to decide whether to move from her apartment to a sheltered living condition. You might work with community residents to help them to decide on priorities. (See chapter 27.) Exhibit 13.15 provides a checklist for reviewing objectives.

Working with Mandated Clients

Many clients that social workers encounter are mandated to see them, for example, in child protection and criminal justice agencies. Questions of value with voluntary clients apply to these clients: What outcomes are important? (such as getting one's children back or getting out of jail). What has to occur to achieve valued outcomes? Can this be arranged? Use of effective practice skills can change a resister into a client. For example, parents may be required to attend parenting classes or men may be required to attend a program for men who batter their wives. You may know that a program is not effective but neither you nor the client may have any control over the requirement to participate in the program and alternative programs may not be available. You can empathize with the client and provide support. It is especially important to empathize with the client's frustration and anger at having to participate in programs unlikely to help them. (See also discussion of use of authority in chapter 14.)

Form A Service Agreement

Service agreements describe the goals and conditions of service. Written agreements encourage helpers and clients to be specific about goals, related objectives, and mutual responsibilities and help prevent hidden agendas objectives that are not shared. The term *agreement* is preferable to *contract* because the latter implies a legal status that service agreements do not possess. Service agreements contain the following information:

- Overall goal (if relevant).
- Objectives that must be achieved to attain this goal.
- Consequences if objectives are or are not met.
- Responsibilities of participants.
- Time limits.
- Signatures of participants.

Written agreements are especially important when working with involuntary clients in clarifying expectations and responsibilities and making transparent any coercive aspects of exchanges (for example, noting possible consequences if objectives are not fulfilled).

EXHIBIT 13.15

Checklist for Reviewing Objectives

_____	1. They are specific (i.e., clearly described).	0	1	2	3
_____	2. They address clients' concerns (if achieved, they will resolve problems).	0	1	2	3
_____	3. An agreement has been made to pursue them.	0	1	2	3
_____	4. They build on client assets.	0	1	2	3
_____	5. They are personalized (they offer clients and significant others influence in achieving desired outcomes).	0	1	2	3
_____	6. They are attainable as illustrated by related research.	0	1	2	3
_____	7. They focus on behaviors that will continue to be reinforced after service ends.	0	1	2	3
_____	8. They focus on increasing positive alternatives to unwanted behaviors.	0	1	2	3
_____	9. They offer both immediate and long-term benefits to clients and significant others.	0	1	2	3
_____	10. Intermediate steps are identified.	0	1	2	3
_____	11. Progress will be easy to assess.	0	1	2	3
_____	12. They provide the most effective way to resolve concerns.	0	1	2	3
_____	13. Achieving objectives will not result in negative consequences for clients, significant others, or society.	0	1	2	3
_____	14. If achieved, they will prevent future problems.	0	1	2	3

Key: 0 = not at all, 1 = somewhat, 2 = mostly, 3 = completely. Scores may range from 0 to 42.

Forming a service agreement involves a negotiation process between you and your clients in which objectives and mutual responsibilities are clarified. Your responsibilities include providing competent services, involving clients and significant others as informed participants (describing fees if any, risks and benefits of recommended practices and alternative options, and protection for clients regarding confidentiality). The clients' responsibilities include sharing needed information, carrying out agreed-on assignments, and keeping appointments except when emergencies arise. Specific times to evaluate progress should be described in the agreement, as well as the criteria that will be used to measure success. Exhibit 13.16 shows a service agreement drawn up by a social worker and parents who wanted their child returned to their care. A goal is identified, as well as objectives and the consequences if these are not attained.

Agreements should focus on goals selected by clients. Clients will have little interest in working toward aims they do not want and value. (You cannot agree to pursue goals you believe are unethical, such as helping a person become a better shoplifter, or are unattainable, such as securing the release of a prisoner in a week.) Some social workers object to allowing clients to select the overall goal, on the grounds that if the goal were attained, it would be a "bad outcome." Or they may ask, "How do you know the goal can be achieved?" Agreeing on a goal is only a first step. The specific objectives required to meet the goal must be identified and met. Both you and your clients (and perhaps the court) participate in selecting objectives so that a "bad outcome"

should not result if they are met. Identifying a goal gives direction to your work together, but it does not guarantee that it will be reached.

Agreements may be formed at different points during assessment. Agreements written during the early stages of assessment describe expectations relevant to work with all clients and describe the conditions required to gather needed data about others (e.g., home visits). The results of assessment, such as specific objectives to focus on, can be included in agreements written after assessment has been completed. Agreements can be amended as needed as additional information is gathered. Specific plans related to each objective should be described in writing in attachments. Mutual signing of the agreement highlights that both parties have responsibilities, that these should be clear, and that progress will be reviewed at agreed-on times. Signing the agreement may increase the clients' commitment to participate. If clients are reluctant to do so, explore the reasons for their refusal. If this reflects a reluctance to sign anything, work can proceed as usual. If it stems from a lack of commitment to pursue agreed-on goals, additional discussion is needed about the basis for your work together.

Be Clear

Vague agreements are unfair to both clients and social workers. Statements such as "use reasonable discipline" or "work cooperatively with parents" are vague. Process objectives such as "participate in counseling" should be accompanied by a clear

---

EXHIBIT 13.16

Service Agreement with W. Family

This agreement is between _____, child welfare worker for _____ County, and Louise and Stewart W., parents of Steven W., who is a dependent of the _____ County Juvenile Court.

Both parents want Steven returned home on a trial basis, and Steven agrees with this goal. _____ agrees to recommend a trial visit if parents achieve the following objectives:

1. Increase the frequency with which the children complete household chores (see attached).
2. Decrease Mr. W.'s alcohol consumption to two or fewer drinks per day (see attached).
3. Increase Mrs. W.'s free time from 0 to 2 hours per week.
4. Visit Steven in accord with the attached schedule.

Failure to do so will result in a statement to the court that in the opinion of the worker, trial visit is not feasible at the present time.

The agreement is in effect for ninety (90) days beginning _____ and ending _____.

_____
Stewart W. (father)

_____   _____
Louise W. (mother)   Child Welfare Worker

Source: Adapted from T. J. Stein, E. D. Gambrill, & K. T. Wiltse (1978). *Children in foster homes: Achieving continuity of care* (p. 231). New York: Praeger.

description of the specific objectives hoped for as a result of participation. What would a client do differently at the end of the class compared with the start? Participation in a program does not necessarily mean that anything has been achieved. Although initial agreements may contain vague descriptions of objectives related to an overall goal (such as deciding where someone will live), as assessment progresses, specific related objectives and plans to achieve them should be clearly described.

Decide on Time Limits

Time limits may be suggested by legislation, agency policy, clients, the court, or practice-related literature. Time limits are a key part of managed health care. Separate time limits may be selected for an overall goal (e.g., returning a child from foster care to his biological parents) and for attaining objectives necessary to reach this goal (e.g., locating a two-bedroom apartment in three months). A client may be willing to pursue a time-limited goal but not a long-range one. Overextending the length of service may have negative effects by suggesting that problems are greater than people thought. A study of clients seen at Kaiser Permanente clinics found that short-term treatment was more effective than long-term treatment for 85% of the clients and that long-term treatment produced negative effects for 5% to 6% of clients (Cummings, 1977). (See also Lambert & Ogles, 2004.)

The Pros and Cons of Written Service Agreements

Some writers argue that agreements should be used only between equal partners, which does not apply to social workers and clients, especially involuntary clients. Others (including me) believe that service agreements help protect and inform clients by encouraging clarity of objectives and consequences depending on whether these are met. This view highlights the importance of clearly describing goals and objectives, as well as mutual responsibilities and consequences. Service agreements help identify legitimate areas of exploration and those that are out of bounds. As with any other practice tool, they will not always be appropriate. Using vague service agreements in a routinized, mechanical fashion is a waste of time and provides only an illusion of agreement about focus and methods.

Select Progress Indicators

Help clients identify relevant, clear progress indicators that accurately reflect outcomes. If objectives are clear, it will be easier to identify specific, relevant indicators of success. Questions such as "How would you know if we were successful?" are helpful here. Be sure to select measures that are meaningful to clients. This will require involving them in decisions made. Self-report may not be a sound guide. Different people (e.g., children, peers, parents, teachers) perceive change differently and may report

change even when there is none. They may be influenced by a variety of biases such as self-interest. Supplement self-reports with observation when needed and feasible. Guidelines for evaluation are discussed in chapter 22.

Culturally Sensitive Practice

Differences in race, age, gender, class, ability, ethnicity, or sexual orientation between you and your clients may require specialized knowledge and skills to ensure that lack of knowledge, biases, and stereotypes on your part do not get in the way. In Thailand—a Buddhist nation that encourages children's inhibition, peacefulness, politeness, and deference and discourages aggression—children and adolescents are referred for clinic treatment more often for "overcontrolled syndrome" (fearfulness, sleep problems, and somaticizing) (Weisz, Suwanlert, Chaiyasit, & Walter, 1987). In the United States, where independence, competitiveness, and differentiation from the family are emphasized, children and adolescents are referred more often for "undercontrolled syndrome" (disobedience, fighting, and arguing). An American social worker might inappropriately pathologize a Thai child referred for "overcontrolled behavior." Class differences are often overlooked in the United States. Liu (2011) describes a social class and classism-conscious model ranging from the status of unaware to equilibration. Prejudice and discrimination may go upward (against those viewed as in a higher social class) or downward (against people or groups viewed as below the viewer). "Lateral classism" is viewed as "keeping up with the Jones" because one "is constantly reminded of personal deficiencies" unrelated to being a member of a certain social class (p. 200).

Efforts to reassure clients that you can be of help, even though you are of a different race, culture, age, class, ethnicity, or sexual orientation, may not always work out well. Time may be needed to establish trust and to encourage clients to discuss personal matters with a stranger. Taking time to get acquainted is especially important when a rapid task focus would be viewed as unpleasant and abrupt, for example, as with many Native Americans. There are hundreds of tribes with different values, language, cultural norms, and preferred communication styles. Viewing each client as an individual will make you less likely to stereotype others. If you cannot overcome interfering reactions, refer clients elsewhere if possible. If this is not possible, then it is your responsibility to overcome your personal biases and stereotypes.

Most guidelines recommended for working with different groups are important for all clients. Consider the suggestions by Sue and Sue for working with African American clients. Only the first two pertain to clients of a different ethnicity or race:

- Find out how the client feels about working with someone from a different ethnic group.

- If appropriate, discuss issues related to racial identity and associated personal conflicts.

- Identify client expectations.

- Describe what will occur and find out whether clients believe this process will be useful.

- Describe the limits of confidentiality.

- Explore the history of the problem, the client's views of causes, and outcomes valued.

- Gather information about the family.

- Identify strengths of clients and significant others. What resources are available? What problems have been successfully handled?

- Identify factors related to problems.

- Establish mutually agreed-on goals.

- Discuss how goals will be pursued.

- Discuss the number of sessions required to achieve outcomes and the responsibilities of the helper and client.

- Find out whether the client thinks you can work together. If not, explore other options. (1990, p. 225)

Most guidelines suggested for working with Asian immigrants and refugees also are appropriate for all clients.

- Use restraint when gathering information.

- Prepare clients by engaging in role preparation.

- Focus on problems of concern to clients and help clients decide on their goals.

- Identify material needs (e.g., food, money, and shelter).

- Provide information on services and help in filling out forms and dealing with agencies.

- Consider intergenerational conflicts. (See Sue & Sue, 1990, pp. 199–200.)

For further detail, see, for example, Ponterotto, Casas, Suzuki, and Alexander (2010) and Thyer, Wodarski, Myers, and Harrison (2010).

Common Errors

One common error is focusing on outcomes that are the consequences of behavior change rather than on the changes required to achieve these results. For example, improving family life will be a result of changes in the behaviors of family members. Objectives should refer to these behaviors (thoughts or feelings), not to their indirect consequences (e.g., improvement in family life). "Being happier" will be a result of changes in related behaviors which must be identified. Objectives related to a goal of returning a child to her family must be clearly described. Vagueness is a common error (pursuing outcomes such as increasing communication, enhancing caregiving, decreasing abuse, providing support). Stating objectives negatively (in terms of not doing something) is another error

(e.g., not being rude, not getting upset). It does not indicate exactly what should occur. Whenever possible, describe objectives in positive terms. Identify what could be done more often to achieve desired outcomes (e.g., increase polite requests, remain calm). This allows you and your clients to rely on positive methods to achieve valued outcomes (e.g., positive reinforcement). Focusing on personal characteristics and overlooking environmental factors related to desired outcomes is a common error. Focusing on too many outcomes at one time is common. Ask clients: What is most important to work on right now?

Disregarding the relevance-of-behavior rule is another error (focusing on objectives that do not really make a difference to clients in real life). Defining the problem to be time spent in an activity rather than identifying specific behaviors or outcomes also is common. Spending more time at a task does not necessarily result in a greater amount of a desired product. If "increasing study time" is accepted as a goal, the client may spend more time "studying" (perhaps sitting with a book in hand), but there may be no improvement in comprehension. Help clients select outcomes that refer to specific behaviors or their products. Selecting process goals is a common error. Avoid process goals (e.g., complete a parenting course) and focus on outcome goals (e.g., increase praise for desired behaviors). "Enrolling a parent in a parenting class" describes how the goal is to be reached, not what is to be achieved. Try to avoid this confusion of means and ends.

Perhaps the most common error my students make is acting as if they have a client (someone with whom they have a clear agreement to work to achieve certain outcomes) with a resistor who is forced to see you or with someone who does not want to change. They may just like to talk to you. Whether the latter is a concern to you (and your agency) depends on your agency's objectives and policies and whether there is a waiting list of individuals needing/wanting service. Certainly you should try to "engage" such clients. Indeed motivational interviewing, which incorporates techniques from many areas including the behavioral area, is often used. (See chapter 14.) However, I often find that students continue on for weeks or months with a client who has no interest in working toward specific changes. Ethical concerns such as other clients in need must be considered. You have to know when to "move on." If continuing supportive counseling is called for and your agency permits this, that is a different story. Lastly, is the failure to select assessment frameworks and measures based on their evidentiary status—have they been critically tested and found to be of value in understanding client concerns and selecting effective services? Currently social work abounds with use of untested and bogus assessment frameworks and measures.

Reporting Maltreatment

Maltreatment includes neglect (e.g., inadequate supervision), physical abuse, sexual abuse, and emotional or verbal abuse (e.g., see Myers, 2011). Domestic violence has received increasing attention (e.g., see Cavanaugh and Gelles, 2012). You should be familiar with mandatory reporting laws regarding non-accidental physical injury, neglect and/or sexual abuse. Groups of concern include children under the age of 18, the elderly (65 and older), dependent adults with some mental or physical limitation resulting in dependency, and hospital patients transferred from a health or community care facility. Conditions for reporting for children include non-accidental physical injury, sexual abuse including assault and exploitation, any act of omission that comprises willful cruelty or unjustifiable punishment, neglect, and physical dependence on an addictive drug at birth. Conditions for reporting concerning the elderly include physical abuse (assault, battery, unreasonable restraint, sexual abuse, misuse of physical or chemical restraint), neglect, abandonment or isolation, and fiduciary abuse (misappropriation of money or property). The standard for reporting is to know or reasonably suspect that the condition of concern is present. Financial abuse of the elderly is increasingly common. (See Bonnie & Wallace, 2003.) Social workers are legally required to report suspected elder and child abuse and inattention to physical needs. Suspected abuse or neglect may be encountered in many kinds of social work in addition to protective services for the elderly and for children. Signs of maltreatment include the following:

- Physical injuries: Burns, bruises, cuts, or broken bones for which there is no satisfactory explanation; injuries to the head and face.

- Negligent physical care: Malnourishment, poor hygiene, unmet medical or dental needs.

- Unusual behaviors: Abrupt changes in behavior, withdrawal, aggression, sexualized behavior, self-harm, fearful behavior in the presence of a caregiver or when mentioning him or her.

- Financial irregularities: These include missing money or valuables, unpaid bills, and coerced spending for the elderly.

Assessing the Risk of Self-Harm, Suicide, and Abuse

Youth and/or adults may have a history of self-harm and may be at risk for future self-harm (e.g., see Nock, 2009). Indications of further self-harm on the part of children and young adults include a clear statement of further intent to harm, depression, continuing family problems, hopelessness, a clear plan, and previous attempts.

You should be familiar with the risk factors related to suicide. These include:

- Feelings of despair and hopelessness; feelings of worthlessness.

- Previous suicidal attempts.

- Concrete, available, and lethal plans to commit suicide (when, where, and how).

- A family history of suicide.

- Perseveration about suicide.

- Lack of support systems; isolation.

- Belief that others would be better off if he or she were dead.

- Elderly (especially for white males).

- Substance abuse.

This is not to say that you can prevent suicide. The identification of risk factors is based on correlational research that does not allow you to predict what a particular person will do (Dawes, 1994a). You can, however, take steps to decrease risk, for example, offer support, discuss concerns, and offer hope. Scholars disagree about hospitalizing "suicidal" people against their will to prevent suicide. Some argue that not only is this unethical—it cannot be done (i.e., be used to prevent suicide) (e.g., Szasz, 1994). Others argue that suicidal individuals may, because of temporary distorted view of their future, not themselves have the autonomy necessary to make an informed decision (Halpern, 2001).

Child welfare workers estimate risk of further abuse. Risk assessment involves use of predictors of risk. Methods of assessment may include structured interviews, observation in related environments, psychometric testing, risk assessment protocols, perhaps even physiological assessment in relation to patterns of arousal. Actuarial methods based on empirical relationships between prediction and outcome are often used to make such estimates (e.g., see Barber et al., 2008; Johnson, 2011). Such methods are also used in predicting future criminal behavior (Quinsey et al., 2006). As important as it is to detect abuse when it is present, it also is important not to falsely accuse people of abuse. False allegations create havoc in families. Consider results of false charges of sexual and ritual abuse (Ofshe & Watters, 1994).

A critical question in risk assessment is: What is the reliability and validity of the data (measures) relied on in arriving at an overall assessment of risk? For example, safety and risk inventories regarding children require child welfare staff to indicate whether a number of items, such as history of abuse, apply to a case. Is there a history of alcohol abuse? But what does "a history of alcohol abuse" mean? Does it mean that alcohol abuse was noted in a record somewhere at some time? What severity of alcohol abuse should be noted? Over how long of a period? Social workers often depend on secondary sources of information and should have the knowledge and skills needed to evaluate the accuracy of data in such sources such as court reports (see chapter 17).

Many biases may interfere with accurate assessment of risk at any stage of risk assessment: (1) initial estimate of risk using a screening measure or system, (2) subsequent assessment, (3) selection of services, and (4) evaluation of outcome. (For a detailed discussion of reliability and validity, see chapter 17.) The complexity of estimating risk is highlighted by the recommendation by Azar, Lauretti, and Loding (1998) that we should exercise "extreme caution in conducting such evaluations due to limitations of our current technology and the potential for biases to enter reports" (p. 78). For example, they note that "what exactly is minimally adequate parenting is unknown; tests and measures to assess questions relevant to issues of parenting abilities in child maltreatment are limited" (p. 132). (For an effort to identify minimal parenting competencies, see Budd, 2005.) Forensic risk evaluations involve some kind of legal question. For example, estimates of risk could result in removal of children on legal grounds from the care of their parents.

When There Is a Crisis

Social workers often provide help in crisis situations (concerns that require immediate attention). Perhaps a family has been evicted and must find housing immediately. A crisis can be defined as a situation that temporarily overwhelms a person's coping skills. Situational crises include natural disasters, assaults, loss of a job, or the sudden death of a relative. Maturational crises include life changes, such as the birth of a child, divorce, or retirement. A crisis may be accompanied by an openness to change. This possibility underscores the importance of providing timely services. Relieving distress and helping clients recapture previous levels of functioning may require a more directive approach than usual (such as recommending some immediate action). Finding out why the crisis occurred (if it is not obvious) and planning how to prevent future ones (if possible) may temporarily take a back seat to pursuing more immediate goals.

Providing support and encouraging positive expectations are important tasks. Child welfare workers have been criticized for having a crisis mentality—going from crisis to crisis rather than carrying out systematic case planning. To the extent to which problems are inaccurately labeled as a crisis and prevent systematic planning, such a work style is dysfunctional both to clients and to social workers: to clients in that problems may not be resolved; to social workers in that they feel buffeted about by circumstances beyond their control. If something is presented as a crisis, ask, "Is it something that precludes systematic attention to concerns?" (For a more detailed discussion of working with clients confronting a crisis, see James, 2008; Roberts, 2005; Roberts & Yeager 2009; Thompson, 2011).

Summary

Common tasks in beginning work with individuals, families, groups, organizations, and communities include identifying and clarifying problems, related factors, and desired outcomes; supporting client assets; offering support; and deciding whether help can be provided by drawing on practice-related research. The interview is a typical setting for initial meetings. If ongoing services are to be offered, or arranged and monitored, other tasks include reaching a mutual agreement on the focus of contact, gathering information about individual characteristics and environmental circumstances related to desired outcomes, consulting related research as needed guided by clear questions related to information needs, forming helpful views of concerns, selecting outcomes to focus on, and encouraging positive expectations.

Special attention should be given to identifying and supporting clients' strengths. Moving from vague to clear descriptions of outcomes and related factors and from dysfunctional to instrumental views of concerns is usually a gradual process. A written service agreement can be helpful in clarifying expectations and responsibilities. Indicators of success are that clients attain outcomes they value and/or seek and obtain needed help from referral sources. Any coercive aspect of contact should be candidly acknowledged. This is also true of gaps between needs and available resources.

Reviewing Your Competencies

Reviewing Content Knowledge

1. Describe specific steps you can take to increase the client's comfort during interviews.

2. Explain what is meant by role induction and its purpose.

3. Describe information that should be offered to clients in introductory statements.

4. Explain what is meant by a collaborative working relationship and how it can be encouraged.

5. Describe the advantages of getting an overview of problems/desired outcomes.

6. Give examples of questions you can ask during interviews that are helpful in clarifying concerns and hoped-for outcomes.

7. Describe criteria for establishing priorities.

8. Distinguish between goals and objectives, and give examples of each.

9. Describe the characteristics of clear objectives and give examples.

10. Identify common errors in identifying objectives.

11. Identify the "fuzzies" in the following list and items that refer to a process outcome:
    a. Attend parent training program.
    b. Improve housing and financial status.
    c. Develop nurturing skills.
    d. Improve child behavior.

12. Describe important characteristics of written service agreements and their rationale.

13. Explain the purposes of gathering baseline data and give an example of a baseline.

14. Describe the differences between direct and indirect problem-solving approaches and give examples.

15. Describe cultural differences that should be considered in the beginning stages of work with clients.

16. Describe common errors in beginning interviews.

17. Describe well-structured questions related to information needs (see chapter 10).

18. Identity databases useful in answering these questions (see chapter 10).

19. Accurately appraise the quality of related research (see chapter 11).

Reviewing What You Do

1. You normalize client concerns as appropriate.

2. You offer effective introductory statements (see Initial Interview Checklist at the end of the chapter).

3. You involve resisters in useful exchanges.

4. You identify intermediate steps related to valued outcomes.

5. You and your clients select objectives that meet the criteria in Exhibit 13.15.

6. You form collaborative working relationships with your clients.

7. You attend to cultural differences when deciding how and when to involve significant others.

8. You gather helpful information.

9. You include problem/outcome profiles in your case records and review these with your clients when deciding on concerns to focus on first.

10. You form written service agreements, when appropriate, that clearly describe objectives and mutual expectations.

11. You can accurately critique written service agreements.

12. You rely on communication styles that are compatible with those of your clients.

13. You encourage instrumental views of problems.

14. You identify relevant, feasible progress indicators.

15. You gather relevant background information and descriptive data about the client's current life circumstances.

16. You identify specific desired outcomes that clients want to pursue.

17. You identify both environmental and personal problem-related factors.

18. Your interviews reflect a clear, agreed-on focus.

19. You encourage clients to identify what is going well in their lives.

20. You note and support clients' assets.

21. You collect baseline data when possible.

22. You encourage positive expectations.

23. You can distinguish between vague and clear objectives.

24. You can accurately critique a beginning interview.

25. You involve clients as informed participants (e.g., share relevant research findings regarding important decisions and describe any coercive aspects of your contact).

26. You pose well-structured questions related to information needs.

27. Your decisions are informed by research findings as needed to make sound decisions.

Reviewing Results

1. Clients attain hoped-for outcomes.

2. Clients keep subsequent appointments.

3. Clients report that meetings were helpful.

4. Useful information is shared.

5. Specific assignments are agreed on.

6. Assignments are completed.

7. Clients seek out and benefit from referral sources.

8. Clients feel more hopeful.

9. A high percentage of your comments and questions yield valuable information.

Initial Interview Checklist

1. Initial Behaviors

    _____ Greet the person.

    _____ See that clients are as comfortable as possible.

    _____ Recognize any difficulties clients may have had in attending the interview.

    _____ Speak clearly a friendly and respectful manner; do not be hostile, sarcastic, or condescending.

    _____ Recognize any coercion concerning clients' presence.

2. Offer Introductory Information About Agency Services

    _____ Purpose of initial meeting.

    _____ Overview of services and framework used (e.g., focus on current concerns, involvement of significant others, number, frequency, and length of interviews, home visits).

    _____ Description of other types of contacts that may be involved.

    _____ Fees (if any).

    _____ Information about confidentiality.

    Responsibilities of Clients

    _____ Carry out agreed-on tasks (e.g., keep logs of value in assessment; collect data concerning progress).

    _____ Share difficulties that occur.

    _____ Participate in decisions made.

    _____ Share relevant information.

    _____ Keep scheduled appointments.

    _____ Provide requested notice when an appointment must be canceled.

    _____ Pay agreed-on fees (if any).

    Your Responsibilities

    _____ Keep scheduled appointments.

    _____ Help client identify clear hoped-for outcomes.

    _____ Clearly describe recommended interventions, reasons for suggesting them, as well as alternatives and their costs and benefits.

    _____ Plan and stick to an agenda focused on outcomes of most concern to clients.

    _____ Build on client strengths (e.g., identify valuable alternative repertoires).

    _____ Recognize and address motivational obstacles (e.g., see also 3, 4, and 6).

    _____ Maintain confidentiality.

    _____ Offer effective services.

    _____ Involve clients as informed participants.

    _____ Arrange for feedback concerning progress.

3. Encourage a Collaborative Working Relationship

    _____ Include significant others as relevant.

    _____ Seek client's commitment to participate.

_____ Offer empathy.

_____ Seek feedback and suggestions from clients.

_____ Check clients' understanding as needed.

_____ Support valuable suggestions by clients and validate their feedback.

_____ Anticipate hesitations (e.g., motivational obstacles) and discuss them with clients.

4. Obtain Relevant Information (additional interviews will be required to complete some items)

_____ Create a profile of hoped-for outcomes and related concerns for each person.

_____ Identify costs and benefits of attaining hoped-for outcomes.

_____ Find out why people sought help at this time.

_____ Find out what would happen if concerns were ignored.

_____ Get an overview of clients' current life circumstances and obtain relevant historical information.

_____ Determine clients' and significant others' views of concerns and solutions, as well as their expectations.

_____ Find out what efforts have been made to attain desired outcomes and what resulted.

_____ Establish priorities. (Review problems/outcome profile with client.)

_____ Identify antecedents, consequences, and setting events that influence behaviors of concern, including desired alternatives to disliked behaviors.

_____ Seek related research findings guided by well-formed questions as needed, critically appraise what you find and share results with clients. (See chapter 10.)

_____ Find out what efforts have been made to attain desired outcomes and what resulted.

_____ Identify personal and environmental resources.

_____ Identify personal and environmental obstacles.

_____ Collect prebaseline information.

_____ Identify relevant, feasible, and accurate progress indicators.

5. Arrive at Joint Decisions

_____ Agree on focus of contact—hoped-for-outcomes. Review problem/outcome profile.

_____ Make an explicit verbal or written service agreement.

_____ Select helpful assignments.

_____ Arrange next meeting.

_____ Make appropriate referrals as necessary (those that offer services likely to be effective).

6. Be of Help

_____ Provide support.

_____ Help clients identify what is going well in their lives.

_____ Identify personalized, achievable, desired outcomes.

_____ Encourage positive expectations.

_____ Draw on related research to guide decisions.

_____ Offer more helpful views of concerns.

_____ Build on client's assets.

Appendix 13A
Reviewing Your Practice Skills

Your Name: _____   Date: _____   Instructor: _____

	Would Like to Work on	Fairly Competent	Very Competent
1. Preparing for interviews	_____	_____	_____
2. Offering welcoming behaviors	_____	_____	_____
3. Providing introductory information	_____	_____	_____
4. Clearly describing client's hoped-for outcomes	_____	_____	_____
5. Obtaining a problem/outcome profile	_____	_____	_____
6. Deciding on priorities	_____	_____	_____
7. Identifying client strengths, including alternative positive repertoires	_____	_____	_____
8. Completing a descriptive analysis of relevant contingencies	_____	_____	_____
9. Identifying progress indicators	_____	_____	_____
10. Forming clear service agreements	_____	_____	_____
11. Establishing collaborative working relationships	_____	_____	_____
12. Offering high-quality empathic responses	_____	_____	_____
13. Encouraging positive expectations	_____	_____	_____
14. Helping clients identify their strengths	_____	_____	_____
15. Posing well-formed questions regarding information needed (see chapter 10)	_____	_____	_____
16. Searching efficiently and effectively for research findings related to information needs (see chapter 10)	_____	_____	_____
17. Critically appraising research discovered (see chapter 11)	_____	_____	_____
18. Anticipating obstacles including client hesitations	_____	_____	_____
19. Selecting helpful assignments	_____	_____	_____
20. Responding effectively to cultural differences	_____	_____	_____
21. Offering concrete help at an early point	_____	_____	_____
22. Identifying resources	_____	_____	_____
23. Organizing and interpreting information	_____	_____	_____
24. Selecting effective intervention plans	_____	_____	_____
25. Involving clients and significant others in carrying out plans	_____	_____	_____
26. Implementing plans	_____	_____	_____
27. Monitoring progress	_____	_____	_____
28. Following through with commitments	_____	_____	_____
29. Making effective referrals	_____	_____	_____
30. Monitoring progress	_____	_____	_____
31. Designing plans to maintain changes	_____	_____	_____
32. Implementing maintenance plans	_____	_____	_____
33. Ending skills	_____	_____	_____
34. Follow-up	_____	_____	_____

Source: E. Gambrill (2012). *Social work practice: A critical thinker's guide* (3rd Ed.). New York: Oxford.

14

Engaging Clients

OVERVIEW   This chapter describes steps you can take to engage clients in collaborative working relationships. Client participation can be viewed as a set of behaviors, such as sharing information and completing agreed-on tasks, which like any other behaviors, are influenced by the circumstances in which they occur including the skills of social workers. A contextual approach requires attending to both personal and environmental factors that influence participation, including the transaction between helpers and clients, the helper's knowledge and skills, and the agency context.

YOU WILL LEARN ABOUT

- Thinking critically about client participation

- Factors that influence participation

- Steps you can take to encourage participation

- Focusing on concerns that are important to clients

- Being helpful

- Anticipating hesitations

- Understanding and respecting differences (tailoring)

- Focusing on strengths

- Being honest about coercive aspects of the situation (use of authority)

- Using effective relationship skills

- Encouraging positive expectations

- Enhancing credibility

- Encouraging helpful views

- Discouraing negative labels and minimizing blame

- Using formal client feedback

- Arranging helpful organizational policies and procedures

- Other steps

- Preparing for interviews as a way to enhance participation

- Ethical issues

Thinking Critically About Client Participation

The term *client participation* refers to engaging in a collaborative working relationship such as sharing information and completing agreed-on tasks. Lack of participation is not a mystery and is not something that should be blamed on clients. Rather, it is an occasion to examine what can be done to increase it (e.g., Lister & Gardner, 2006). Attending to clients' concerns such as preserving privacy will help you to respond effectively. Lack of participation is often blamed on clients. Terms such as *compliance* and *resistance* focus attention on the client, omitting contextual influences and rights of clients. In a contextual view of client participation, we must consider the agency setting, the influence of the helper, the match between helpers and clients, and the clients. A focus on the transaction between you and your clients highlights the ebb and flow of exchanges; there will be ups and downs, ruptures and repairs in your alliances with clients (Safran, Muran, & Eubanks-Carter, 2011). External stressors, views of problems and related hoped-for outcomes, and remedies suggested influence participation. This contextual view offers many options for increasing participation that respect and involve clients as informed participants. It highlights the importance of recognizing the boundaries between your responsibilities (to do the best that is possible under the circumstances) and the clients' responsibilities (to work toward agreed-on outcomes).

Some clients are not in your presence by choice. They have been forced to see you and are subject to unwanted restrictions you may impose such as removal of children from their care. Staff may hospitalize a client they view as suicidal against the person's wishes. In such cases there is actual or potential coercion that may affect client participation. Clients may participate only because they are goaded into it by avoiding even more disliked or feared potential consequences. Informed consent and respect for clients calls for candid recognition of any coercive aspects in exchanges. (See chapter 3, as well as later discussion in this chapter of the use of authority.) Clients may seek contact only because significant others, such as family members, are at the end of their rope in dealing with behaviors such as drinking or gambling.

You may jump to the conclusion that nothing can be done because the client is "nonvoluntary" or that you can help a client attain a desired outcome when you can offer only support. Faulty assumptions that get in the way of encouraging participation of ambivalent and nonvoluntary clients include beliefs that (1) they will not participate, (2) involving them requires pursuit of impractical or unethical goals, or (3) methods used to engage voluntary clients are not useful. You may mistakenly assume that goals nonvoluntary clients value cannot be found. You indeed may have to reframe problems to discover shared goals. Let us say that a youth is brought, by his parents and against his will, to a community mental health center. You could suggest helping

him to reduce his parents' complaints about his behavior. The objectives involved in "getting social workers off his case" may be the same as those required to attain goals you and/or significant others value (e.g., Stein, Gambrill, & Wiltse, 1978).

You often have to be creative to discover promising options. This, combined with avoidance of dead ends such as jumping to the conclusion that nothing can be done because a client is nonvoluntary, will increase your chances of involving clients. Consider Mr. Ashly, who complains that because his clients are involuntary, they will not participate (see Exhibit 14.1). Is Mr. Ashly focusing on goals that are important to his client? Mr. Ashly may say (thinking that his supervisor just "isn't with it") that this is the very point, that his clients are nonvoluntary and so agreed-on goals cannot be found. Can you illustrate his faulty assumption using a Venn diagram? (See Exhibit 10.5.) How about Ms. Wan, who complains that her clients will not follow through on seeking needed resources? Here too, there are many possibilities to consider before concluding that nothing can be done: (1) Does the client value the resources? (2) Does she need help in getting to interviews? (3) Does she believe that this particular resource will be helpful? The more challenging the problem, the more creative you may have to be to discover options.

Factors That Influence Participation

Client participation is a complex topic because it involves many different behaviors and related factors including characteristics of the client, agency setting (e.g., coercive or not), your relationship with the client, the nature of client concerns, and environmental factors such as resources available and reactions of significant others) (Kissane, 2003; Littell, Alexander, & Reynolds, 2001). You may assume that because a client says they want to achieve a certain outcome, it can be attained, when, in fact, he or she is not willing to participate in the process required to do so (process resistance). A resistance analysis related to both process and outcome will help you to anticipate hesitations and obstacles (Burns, 2004). *Process resistance* refers to an unwillingness to engage in the work that is necessary to attain hoped-for outcomes such as confronting feared situations. *Outcome resistance* refers to benefits of current patterns of behavior, such as drinking or using drugs, that outweigh the costs of these behaviors. The latter may be revealed by preparing a table listing both costs and benefits of current patterns of behavior (Burns, 2004). A cost-benefit analysis related to an outcome may reveal that there will be more costs than benefits if the client achieves this outcome (e.g., stops drinking to excess). This kind of analysis, at an early point in contact with a client, is of value in anticipating outcome resistance.

Change is often difficult. Clients often have to act in new ways in old situations or enter unfamiliar ones. Acting in new ways usually requires effort. Typical experiences, even if painful, are at

---

EXHIBIT 14.1

What Do You Think?

Mr. Ashly works in a child protection unit. All his clients are involuntary. The main reason they consent to see him is that if they do not, their children will be taken away. He complains to his supervisor that because his clients are involuntary, there is little that he can do to involve them in a helping relationship. What do you think? How would you respond if you were Mr. Ashly's supervisor?

Ms. Wan is a social worker attached to a homeless shelter, many of whose residents are alleged to be "mentally ill." She works as a case manager for some of the residents. Her job is to try to ensure that their basic needs are met and to provide other resources as available, such as substance abuse treatment programs. At the monthly staff conference, she tells the rest of the staff that there is little she can do for many of the residents, especially those who are "mentally ill" and do not keep the agreements she makes with them. She gives an example of making an appointment for one of the residents to visit an apartment-finding program. He did not keep it. Furthermore, this was the third appointment that he had not kept. She said that she can do little with such clients. She also reports that residents with drug abuse problems do not keep their appointments with drug treatment programs. How would you handle these complaints?

Mrs. Rodriguez, an elementary school teacher who has sought your help about a difficult-to-manage child, did not gather the data that she had agreed to collect over the past week. She tells you that she forgot. What would you do?

Mrs. Kandice is a an elderly resident living in a single room in an inner-city hotel. Recently she has become more frail. She has difficulty getting up and down the stairs to her third-floor room and the hotel manager reported that she seems forgetful and appears unkempt. He is worried about her and called the local protective services worker for the elderly. Mr. Jenkins, a social worker at the agency, visits Mrs. Kandice. She denies any need for help. What can be done to encourage her participation?

Ralph works at a day care center for emotionally disturbed adolescents. The staff are having increasing difficulty with a 14-year-old resident. He refuses to follow instructions, swears at the staff, and occasionally becomes violent (hits other residents). He tells Ralph to "get lost" when Ralph approaches him to discuss his behavior. What can Ralph do to encourage his participation?

---

least familiar and often predictable. The new and unknown may not be. Nonvoluntary clients may be angry and suspicious—with good reason. Many medical patients do not follow the treatments prescribed for them, even when instructions are clear. Many clients forget information provided or do not read materials given to them. Clients are often ambivalent about giving up behaviors that create problems for themselves, as well as for significant others, such as heavy drinking.

> To know one's feelings is to know that they are often many-sided and mixed and that they may pull in two directions at once. Everyone has experienced this duality of wanting something strongly yet drawing back from it, making up one's mind but somehow not carrying out the planned action. This is part of what is meant by ambivalence. A person may be subject to two opposing forces within himself at the same moment—one that says, "Yes, I will," and the other that says, "No, I won't"; one that says, "I want," and the other, "Not really"; one affirming and the other negating. (Perlman, 1957, p. 121)

Clients labeled as having a "personality disorder" are (almost by definition) difficult to engage in a collaborative working relationship. A lack of relationship skills on the part of clients (or helpers) and dysfunctional attachment experiences may make engagement more difficult. (See Levy, Ellison, Scott, & Bernecker, 2011.)

The particular match between a client and helper may aggravate or lessen resistance as may blunders on your part, such as not providing reactions such as empathy that convey respect, compassion, and understanding of clients' feelings (e.g., see Upmark, Hagberg, & Alexanderson, 2009). Sensitivity on your part to the degree of directiveness different clients prefer will help you to respond appropriately. Burns (2004) advises us not to try to persuade, analyze, help, or use logic when a client resists but to empathize with the client—there are always reasons for resistance. (See also descriptions of motivational interviewing e.g., Arkowitz, et al., 2008.) High-quality empathic skills are vital here (see chapter 15). These include disarming methods in which you find truth in what the client says, including harsh criticisms of you or your agency ("Aren't you only a student?"). A reply may be: "Yes, I am a student and I can see how this may be a concern to you. However, I am supervised by a credentialed social worker who routinely reviews my work. I hope that this is reassuring to you." Defensive reactions are not helpful.

Other factors are related to environmental variables such as anticipated loss of support from significant others (see Exhibit 14.2). Ambivalence about change may be due to anticipated negative reactions from relatives. Personal and social factors are especially influential in the initial stages of helping, whereas efforts to intervene (teach or confront) play an increasingly important role during the middle and later stages of intervention in influencing participation (Patterson & Forgatch, 1985). Signs of resistance include interrupting and not tracking. Some signs of resistance are easy to spot, such as anger directed at you or expressions of dissatisfaction with seeing you. Others are subtler. In either case, there are a number of steps you can take to try to decrease such reactions such as showing empathy

EXHIBIT 14.2

Factors That Discourage Client Participation

Agency Variables

Inefficiency, unfriendly personnel.

Long waiting time.

Lack of resources (money for transportation).

Long time between referral and appointment.

Ineffective management practices (e.g., related to staff training and supervision).

Lack of individual appointment times.

Poor reputation of agency.

Inconvenience (e.g., location of clinic, limited transportation).

Helper Characteristics (examples)

Lack of problem-solving skills and knowledge (e.g., regarding contingencies) (see chapter 7).

A focus on outcomes that clients do not value.

Lack of skill in identifying obstacles to completing agreed-on tasks.

Failure to consider clients' views of concerns and causes.

Lack of knowledge about cultural differences.

Relationship Variables

Negative transference or countertransference effects.

Other errors in relating to clients (e.g., pacing, negative comments, few empathic statements).

Problem-Related Variables

Competing, conflicting, or other pressing demands (poverty, unemployment).

Negative expectations and attitudes of significant others.

Intervention Variables

Overly complex recommendations.

Long duration of intervention.

Intrusiveness (e.g., interferes with other goals).

Expense.

Selection of plans that conflict with the client's beliefs about the cause of problems.

Lack of continuity of care and/or lack of integration of services.

Client Characteristics

Certain diagnoses (e.g., "personality disorder").

Sensory deficits.

Lack of understanding.

Conflicting beliefs about problems and resolutions; sense of fatalism.

Negative past experiences with other helpers.

Belief that the effort, expense, and side effects outweigh potential benefits.

Embarrassment about seeing a professional.

Pessimism or skepticism about the value or recommended methods.

Desire to maintain control over one's life.

Impatience with degree of progress or the helping process.

View participation as interfering with values, beliefs, future plans, family relationship patterns, social roles, self-concept, emotional equilibrium, or daily life patterns.

History of lack of participation.

Lack of confidence.

Source: Adapted from D. Meichenbaum & D. C. Turk (1987). *Facilitating treatment adherence* (pp. 43–44, 51). New York: Plenum. See also Longtin, Sax, Leape, Sheridan, Donaldson, & Pittet (2010).

and clearly explaining procedures and the reasons for them, including any legal constraints that influence what is happening to the client.

Clients may say that suggested plans are irrelevant or impossible. They may have negative emotional responses to a program (e.g., see Korfmacher, Green, Staerkel, Peterson, Cook, Roggman, et al. , 2008). The client's life circumstances must be considered (see Exhibit 14.3). These include economic and cultural factors, attitudes and behavior of family members, and the physical environment. The nature of concerns and suggested services influence participation. Following recommended actions is greatest with acute, serious illness and least with chronic conditions. It rapidly decreases as the complexity of intervention increases. Participation increases with age, education, and socioeconomic status (SES), and is higher in white populations. However, these demographic characteristics are often confounded with other factors, such as different patterns of service use among different groups.

Steps You Can Take To Encourage Participation

Participation may be enhanced by (1) educational means (offering information and instructions), (2) behavioral strategies (such as self-monitoring, reminders, reinforcement), and (3) organizational changes (such as flexibility in place and timing of contacts). (See for example Mitchell, 2009; Shuman & Shapiro, 2002.) Encouraging participation requires planning and consistent attention (see Exhibit 14.4).

EXHIBIT 14.3

One Drug-Using Mother's Story

Michelle (not her real name) was an AFDC recipient with a 7-year-old child when she found out she was pregnant. She was also a heroin addict. Determined to minimize the harm to her fetus, she contacted every agency she could think of that might be able to help her obtain drug treatment, including health and mental health clinics and the county child welfare agency. She even contacted local media, in the hope that a journalist would have information about drug treatment programs.

In Butte County, California, where Michelle lived, there was not a single treatment program available to her. She did learn, however, that methadone maintenance was the preferred treatment for pregnant heroin addicts. On the street, she heard about a methadone maintenance clinic in Sacramento, the state capital, 65 to 70 miles away. Methadone maintenance requires daily treatments.

The Sacramento clinic had a 2-year waiting list, but because Michelle was pregnant and especially because she was very persistent, she was admitted to the program. She paid the $200 monthly fee from her AFDC grant and drove everyday to Sacramento, a 140-mile round trip.

After months of commuting daily, Michelle's car broke down. Still she managed to get to Sacramento nearly every day, begging family and friends to give her rides, paying people to give her rides, and on occasion even hitchhiking. These added costs out of her meager income, however, caused her to fall behind in her payments to the clinic.

Eight and one-half months pregnant, with no dependable way to get to the clinic and no way to pay its fee, Michelle gave up on the Sacramento program. Again she tried to find help closer to home. As part of the methadone treatment she had been getting regular prenatal care and was being seen at home by a student intern public health nurse, who also searched for some form of treatment for Michelle. They both came up empty-handed.

Finally, unable to get any help, Michelle did the responsible thing: she went back to using illegal drugs. This choice was in her baby's best interest, since sudden withdrawal from opiates can be deadly to a fetus.

When her baby was delivered, Michelle immediately told the doctor and other medical personnel about her drug use, so they would be able to provide appropriate treatment to the baby. The following day, Michelle was visited in the hospital by representatives of the district attorney's office and the child welfare agency. Again, she recounted her drug use, her attempts to get treatment, her inability to continue with the methadone program in Sacramento, and her return to drug use. Child Protective Services took the baby away from her.

Shortly before Michelle gave birth, the Butte County District Attorney had announced a new policy of criminally prosecuting any woman who gave birth to a baby who tested positive for drugs. According to the policy as stated by the DA, such women would not be prosecuted, however, if they went into a treatment program. Nevertheless, despite having complete information about Michelle's unsuccessful attempts to obtain treatment locally and her daily trips to Sacramento, the district attorney announced plans to prosecute her for use of a controlled substance. Following a great deal of publicity about the case, he did not pursue the charges.

Source: M. Henry (1990). One drug-using mother's story. *Youth Law News* 11, 19. Reprinted with permission.

EXHIBIT 14.4

Checklist for Enhancing Participation

_____ 1. Focus on outcomes that are important to clients.

_____ 2. Encourage positive expectations.

_____ 3. Clarify expectations, including time limits, and clearly describe what will be expected of clients and services offered.

_____ 4. Avoid labeling and blaming.

_____ 5. Focus on strengths and build on clients' assets.

_____ 6. Offer empathic responses; validate client concerns and feelings.

_____ 7. Tailor your style as needed to individual and situational differences including cultural differences.

_____ 8. Develop instrumental views of concern (they offer guidelines for achieving desired outcomes); reframe concerns in helpful ways.

_____ 9. Anticipate hesitations, including those related to cultural differences between you and your clients.

_____ 10. Avoid negative comments.

_____ 11. Use high-quality attentive listening skills.

_____ 12. Involve significant others.

_____ 13. Acknowledge any coercive constraints on meetings.

_____ 14. Encourage open discussion of feelings.

_____ 15. Neutralize conflicting advice.

_____ 16. Be courteous.

_____ 17. Offer choices, identify possibilities.

_____ 18. Emphasize the importance of participation.

_____ 19. Clearly describe suggested steps and the rationale for them in a framework that makes sense and is acceptable to clients.

_____ 20. Select feasible tasks.

_____ 21. Prepare clients for setbacks.

_____ 22. Use a step-by-step approach that offers opportunities for "small wins."

_____ 23. Select tasks that result in valued outcomes.

_____ 24. Seek commitment.

_____ 25. Arrange helpful organizational policies and procedures.

_____ 26. Empathize with reasons for reluctance to participate.

_____ 27. Form an agreement clearly describing outcomes that will be pursued and mutual responsibilities.

_____ 28. Review results of assignments.

_____ 29. Arrange reminders as needed.

_____ 30. Arrange positive consequences for participation and remove or minimize negative consequences.

_____ 31. Don't rush people.

_____ 32. Don't reinforce pessimistic statements.

_____ 33. See also Checklist for Assignments in chapter 21.

Special arrangements must often be made (e.g., Haynes et al., 2008). What works best depends in part on the helping stage (e.g., before you meet clients, during interviews, between sessions). For example, clarifying expected roles in initial interviews may encourage participation. Being familiar with factors related to lack of participation and skill in minimizing these should increase your success in involving clients. Exhortation (asking a person to behave in a certain manner or telling him why he should or ought to do so) is notoriously ineffective. Effective persuaders emphasize the benefits of change and prompt and support desired behaviors. They do not assume that people should or will change. Clients are more likely to participate in helpful ways if they value the goals focused on, and if services offered are compatible with their view of problems and possible solutions. Participation is related to how successful you are in encouraging clients to believe that methods will be effective. Obstacles to participation should be removed and aids offered that enhance participation. You may identify obstacles to change by asking clients how they could stop themselves from making progress or what would be the best way to bring on a relapse.

Low participation may be related to anxiety, low motivation, lack of information, and misinformation. Clients may have interfering beliefs and attitudes, be distracted, or lack support from significant others. Life circumstances, such as poverty or social isolation, may be an obstacle. High levels of stress or depression may interfere with observation and the judgments based on this that are needed to respond in new ways. Process mistakes such as not involving clients in selecting goals and procedures, not respecting clients, and ignoring cultural differences in values, communication styles, and norms will compromise participation. Steps you can take to encourage participation are discussed in the sections that follow.

Focusing on Outcomes That Are Important To Clients

Focus on outcomes that are of concern to clients whenever feasible, ethical, and legal. Outcomes of concern to clients are often not addressed without good reason. Good reasons are that they cannot be addressed given current resources or pursuing them would be illegal or unethical or would hurt clients or significant others. Poor reasons include agency policies that get in the way, social workers' personal preferences for working on certain kinds of problems, and lack of knowledge about effective service methods. Why should clients participate in plans when the outcomes focused on are of little or no interest to them? Too often, helpers assume that they have the right to say what is and is not important for clients.

Being Helpful

A guiding question should be: How can this meeting have some immediate benefit for this client? What concrete services can I provide? What steps can I take to reduce distress? How can I restore client morale (Frank, 1976)? Help clients to identify specific outcomes they would like to attain and a step-by-step agenda for pursuing them, as well as valuable assets they can draw on such as a desire to be a good parent. Perhaps clients have not achieved hoped-for outcomes on their own because they do not know how to design a step-by-step agenda. Point out and illustrate the relationship of intermediate steps (subgoals) to desired outcomes so that clients see their value. For example, initiating conversations and arranging brief contacts with new acquaintances are intermediate steps to making friends. Select plans that are efficient and effective, as well as acceptable to clients. This will require knowledge about the evidentiary status of different assessment and intervention methods (see chapter 11). Be sure to consider cultural and developmental issues that may influence success.

Anticipating Hesitations

Many clients have hesitations and concerns about working with social workers or other helping professionals in terms of what is expected of them, involvement of family members, and so on. Indicators include attacks directed toward you, silence,

intellectualizing, flooding you with details, repeated rejections of your suggestions, and yes-buts. Involuntary clients may be actively resistant. Offering information may decrease concerns and help clients to become engaged. Anticipating hesitations may increase participation by (1) increasing trust and credibility, since you show that you recognize client concerns, (2) encouraging liking because it shows that you care about the client's concerns, (3) addressing objections before they are raised, and (4) increasing options by removing obstacles to valuable alternatives. Being prepared for different kinds of objections will help you respond effectively.

Hesitations About the Likelihood and Course of Change and Who Will Control This

Clients may have doubts about whether change is possible, perhaps because of lack of success with other "helpers." Describe why you think you can be of help and explain how methods you suggest differ from previous ones (see also section on encouraging positive expectations). Let clients know when they can expect to see positive changes if plans are implemented. Practice-related research may provide information about this. Establishing a collaborative working relationship and involving clients in decisions is vital here. Change rarely occurs in a smooth fashion. Prepare clients for plateaus and temporary downward trends. This will increase the likelihood that clients will tell you about them when they occur. They become expected hardships rather than unexpected disappointments. Be sure to collect and review data about degree of progress to see if the overall trend is in a positive direction.

Hesitations About Confidentiality and Required Time, Effort, and Costs

Clients have concerns about how much time and effort will be involved, what they will be expected to disclose, what they may have to give up, and who will have access to material shared. Anticipate these concerns in introductory statements. Describe the number and length of meetings, mutual responsibilities, limits on confidentiality, and costs involved (if any). Just because clients do not ask about an issue does not mean that it is not a concern. You may entice a reluctant client to participate by suggesting a time-limited (e.g., 1 week) commitment.

Hesitations Related to Beliefs About Behavior and Its Causes

Clients may have hesitations about your approach. Clients have beliefs about behavior (e.g., how and if it can be changed). They may object to positive incentives as bribery or believe that people should not be reinforced for doing "what they should do." They may believe that bad behaviors should be punished, that all people should be treated alike, or that methods you suggest are simpleminded or mechanical. Listen carefully to and empathize with their points of view so that you can respond effectively. This does not mean that you agree with them. Nor does it mean that you should challenge them. Challenging objections is likely to increase resistance. (See prior discussion of disarming.) There are more effective ways to encourage consideration of new views and approaches. Some hesitations may have been created by the very professionals from whom no help was received or harm done. You can also anticipate objections by informing clients that certain views do not represent a correct picture of your approach.

Clients may blame significant others for their problems and believe that they themselves have no part in maintaining unpleasant exchanges (e.g. see Yeh & Weisz, 2001). In this case, you may have to help clients and significant others understand how they influence each other (how their behaviors are interrelated), perhaps through data clients collect. (See chapter 17.) You can do this by seeing clients and significant others together and suggesting assignments that demonstrate mutual influences. Helping clients to understand that significant others usually have good intentions is valuable. New ways of acting will often feel unnatural, and clients may complain about this. Anticipate this objection by pointing out that acting differently *will not* feel natural at first. Emphasize that it is what happens in the long run that counts.

Hesitations About How They Will Be Judged

Clients may have fears about what you will think of them if they disclose their thoughts and experiences. They may think you will blame, ridicule, dismiss, or pathologize them. They may believe that their concerns are not worth mentioning. Your support here is vital. Shulman (2006) notes the importance of supporting clients in "taboo" areas. Clients may worry that their status as an illegal immigrant may be reported.

Hesitations About Helper–Client Differences

It may be useful to ask how a client feels about differences from you in regard to ethnicity, sexual orientation, race, age, or gender. Anticipating concerns lets clients off the hook for bringing them up and will show that you are sensitive to these differences. These hesitations highlight the role of establishing and maintaining a collaborative working relationship with clients. (See also chapter 15.)

Mrs. Ryan and the Greens

Mrs. Slater is a 28-year-old social worker. How will her client Mrs. Ryan (aged 87) react to her? How will Mr. and Mrs. Green, Mrs. Ryan's daughter and son-in-law (in their fifties), react? Won't they expect to meet an older person who is closer to their age? If they have concerns about this, will they express them, and how can Mrs. Slater reassure them? Mrs. Slater decided to address these questions directly by saying, "I wonder if you are concerned about whether I'll be able to understand your situation, since I am younger." They all said yes. Mrs. Slater explained why she felt that she could be of help but

also said that she would be happy to refer them to an older worker if they would prefer. The Greens said no, they would like to talk to her. Mrs. Slater's anticipatory empathy helped her to respond effectively to her clients' concerns.

Understanding and Respecting Differences (Tailoring)

Lack of participation may be related to your lack of knowledge about client values, norms, and preferred communication styles. One of the themes of this book is the importance of avoiding the "client uniformity myth" (the false belief that all clients and their environments are the same). You can do this by focusing on outcomes that clients value, matching procedures to individual circumstances and characteristics including client preferences, and suggesting methods that are compatible with the client's point of view and unique life circumstances, including cultural differences. Avoid stigmatizing labels (see chapter 12). An awareness of class differences and animosities will help you understand negative reactions by poor and working-class clients. Ehrenreich notes: "For working-class people, relations with the middle class are usually a one way dialogue. From above come commands, diagnoses, instructions, judgments, definitions—even, through the media, suggestions as to how to think, feel, spend money, and relax" (1990, p. 139). As a 56-year-old mother of three diagnosed as suffering from a character disorder said of her social worker: "God I hate that woman. She makes me feel so stupid. Seems like everything that I do is wrong—the way I am with my kids, with my husband, even my sex life. She knows it all. Personally, I think her ideas are a little screwed up, but I can't tell her that" (Ehrenreich, 1990, pp. 139–140).

Recent research suggests the importance of assessing a client's stage of change (Norcross, Krebs, & Prochaska, 2011). (See Littell & Girvin, 2002, for a critique of the underlying theory.) The assumption of stages of change is key in motivational interviewing that is designed to engage clients in working toward certain outcomes. Stages suggested include *precontemplation* in which the client has no interest in altering his or her behavior. (See Exhibit 14.5.) Clients that social workers see are often pressured to seek help by others. They may be unaware that behaviors such as drinking alcohol is a problem for others even though family members have complained about this. Counselor skills here include being empathic and encouraging "change talk." In the next stage, *contemplation*, clients are aware that there is a problem and are thinking about taking some action. They may have a balanced cost-benefit analysis of behaviors of interest; that is, the list is evenly balanced between costs and benefits of achieving related outcomes. Interventions here include providing information about the change process, acknowledging ambivalence about change and suggesting benefits of change. You can encourage clients to identify changes they have made in the past. The third stage is *preparation*. Here clients intend to

EXHIBIT 14.5

Stages of Change and Related Intervention

Stage	Description	Helper Role/Intervention
Precontemplation	Sees no need to change or is unwilling to change. Denial, minimization, blaming, and resistance are common. Clients may be discouraged.	Provide information and increase awareness of negative effects of current behavior pattern. Encourage positive views of the possibility of change. (Avoid prescriptive advice.)
Contemplation	The idea of change is considered but there is ambivalence. Client may seek information and consider the losses and benefits of change, but no action is taken.	Help the client to see the benefits of changing and the consequences of not changing.
Preparation	Decided to do something about the problem but needs help. Identify lessons from past attempts to change.	Help the client to find acceptable and effective change strategies; suggest alternatives; encourage "experiments" with change and evaluate outcome.
Action	Steps taken to change started. Client acquires behavior change skills such as stimulus control and contingency management. (See Exhibit 14.6.)	Support and advocate for the client. Help the client to accomplish change and identify situations that may encourage relapse.
Maintenance	Reaches goals; the challenge here is to sustain changes. This will often require developing skills to prevent backsliding.	Encourage strategies to prevent relapse; offer support.

Source: See J. C. Norcross, P. M. Krebs, & J. O. Prochaska (2011). Stages of change. In J. C. Norcross (ed.), *Psychotherapy relationships that work: Evidence-based responsiveness* (2nd ed.) (pp. 279–300). New York: Oxford.

make a change. They are prepared to take action and may have taken a small step and intend to take more. Here, you may suggest alternatives including "experiments with change." In the *action* stage clients actually alter their behavior or environment to achieve a change. Finally in the *maintenance* stage, steps are taken to prevent relapse and maintain gains. Offering support is important in all stages. Process of change, both overt and covert, can be seen in Exhibit 14.6. "Each process is a broad category encompassing multiple techniques, methods, and relationship stances traditionally associated with disparate theoretical orientations" (p. 281). Common mismatches between stages and process used include pressing contemplators to engage an action and lingering too long in the contemplation stage.

Focusing on Clients' Strengths

A focus on clients' strengths has many advantages:

1. Increasing positive behaviors is often the best way to decrease disliked ones. (See Chapters 7, 12, and 25.)

2. Clients can put their skills to good use; they can generalize them to new situations.

3. Clients can take credit for success; their self-efficiency will increase.

4. Clients may be more willing to carry out agreed-on tasks, since they will be more hopeful about achieving valued outcomes.

5. Clients develop more positive views of significant others, as well as of themselves.

Focusing on clients' deficiencies is not helpful. Knowing what to do less of does not necessarily provide information about what to do more of or how to go about doing it. A focus on deficiencies may encourage a client's tendency to attend to negative aspects of himself, his environment, or significant others. Avoid thinking about clients in negative terms (e.g., "he's hostile," "she's unmotivated," "she's borderline"). Focus on clients' strengths.

Being Honest About Coercive Aspects of the Situation: Handling Authority

As discussed at the beginning of this chapter, contacts between social workers and clients may have a coercive aspect. Many social work services are provided in public agencies in which the staff's principal obligation is to carry out state and federal policies (Gummer, 1997). Candid recognition of any coercive aspects of contact is important for both ethical and practical reasons. Pretending that coercive contingencies do not exist, that clients

---

EXHIBIT 14.6

Process of Change and Related Examples of Intervention

Process	Interventions
Consciousness raising	Increasing information about self and problem: observations, confrontations, interpretations, awareness exercises, bibliography.
Self-reevaluation	Assessing how one feels and thinks about oneself with respect to a problem: value clarification, imagery, corrective emotional experience.
Dramatic relief (emotional arousal)	Experiencing and expressing feelings about one's problems and solutions: psychodrama, cathartic work, grieving losses, role-playing.
Self-liberation	Choosing and commitment to act or believe in ability to change: decision-making methods, motivational interviewing, commitment-enhancing techniques.
Counterconditioning	Substituting alternative or incompatible behaviors for problem: relaxation, desensitization, assertion, cognitive restructuring, behavioral activation.
Stimulus control	Avoiding or controlling stimuli that elicit problem behaviors: restructuring one's environment, avoiding high-risk cues, fading techniques, altering relationships.
Reinforcement	Rewarding one's self or being rewarded by others for making changes: contingency contracts, overt and covert reinforcement, self-reward.

Source: J. C. Norcross, P. M. Krebs, & J. O. Prochaska (2011). Stages of change. In J. C. Norcross (ed.), *Psychotherapy relationships that work: Evidence-based responsiveness* (2nd ed.) (p. 281). New York: Oxford. Reprinted with permission.

---

participate out of their "own free will," creates dangers for clients, such as not being fully informed and being subject to decisions made for "their own good," that in fact, deny people their civil and human rights (e.g., labeling a client schizophrenic and locking him up in a mental hospital rather than giving him a right to stand trial before a jury of his or her peers). Also, reasons for lack of participation may be missed. Honest recognition of coercive contingencies will help you and your clients to discuss options with a clear picture of actual and potential consequences given certain courses of action. Whether coercive or not, you should offer support, empathy, and help.

Using Effective Relationship Skills

Your self-presentation is more than a personal matter; it influences how much help you can offer to your clients. Communicating caring, concern, friendliness, warmth, and respect will facilitate participation. (See Exhibit 14.7.) Empathy is vital for encouraging clients to feel supported and to understand their feelings. Relationship behaviors and styles that may limit success are as follows:

- Distracting mannerisms or facial expressions.

- Poor attending skills.

- Difficulty following and focusing on the client's statements.

- The use of closed-end questions and an interrogative style.

- Frequent interruptions.

- Noting the surface messages of what clients say rather than their deeper-level messages.

- Relying exclusively on what is said, rather than affect or process.

- Excessive self-disclosure. (See Haley, 1969.)

- Excessive passivity.

- Difficulty in tolerating silence.

- Appearing cool and aloof.

- Being overly friendly, seductive, or informal.

- Being aggressive or punitive. (See Kottler & Blau, 1989, pp. 80–81.)

If clients trust and like you, they are more likely to participate in effective ways. Active listening, recognition of cultural differences, and validation of concerns encourage trust and liking. If staff at other agencies like you, they will be more willing to provide needed resources.

Considerable attention is given to *transference effects* in psychoanalytic practice. These refer to feelings, attitudes, or behaviors the client has toward the helper because of his or her resemblance to someone in the past. It is not surprising that clients may react to similarities between helpers and others in their past and that these reactions may influence their participation.

EXHIBIT 14.7

The Value of Just Listening

My second assignment after joining Homebuilders was a particularly difficult one for me. The presenting problems centered around 5-year-old Jason, whose mother complained that he was almost impossible to control—setting fires, destroying property, running through the neighborhood in the middle of the night, pillaging the refrigerator, etc. Jason seemed incapable of sitting still or of following a single request his mother would make of him.

But all this was not what made this family a difficult one. To all appearances Jason had been, from the beginning of his life, a neglected and abused child. As an infant, on three different occasions he had been hospitalized as a failure-to-thrive child. There had been at least eight prior CPS referrals that had faulted the parents as neglectful. Jason had been dismissed from a day-care treatment program on the grounds of noncooperation on the part of his mother.

It was difficult for me in this particular case not to cast blame on Jason's parents for these problems. I got little or no response from his mother, who seemed only to complain of Jason's behaviors, but who did not seem willing to try the suggestions I made. (Jason's dad was not living at home and was for the most part only an occasional and equally passive participant in the sessions.) To top things off, during the first week of our intervention, Jason's maternal grandmother entered the hospital for a serious operation, making it even more difficult for the mother to stay focused.

I remember so clearly the day that things shifted. I was feeling more and more frustrated and was going to confront Jason's mother on what I felt to be her lack of cooperation. What I somehow ended up doing instead was just listening to her as she told me something about her own life as a child in her family, how she had been the one in the family who was always called upon to support her mother and sisters when they had problems. As I listened, I felt touched with compassion and realized how superficial my judgments had been. All of us are just doing the very best we can.

Things changed after that—not all at once and not dramatically. I talked more with Jason's mother about her own life goals and took her one day to the local community college where she was interested in studying—of all things—early childhood education. Jason ended up in excellent day-care and school programs. His behaviors began to fall more into the normal range. A number of months later I visited Jason's school to see another client and met Jason's teacher. She told me that he was not only doing well, but was showing signs of real leadership in the class. I also learned that Jason's parents were close to getting back together. As Jason's mother wrote in the evaluation: "Jim was very supportive. He brought us back together so that we're very close."

The lesson for me is that we really cannot judge anyone, no matter how bad the evidence looks (Jim Poggi).

Source: J. Kinney, D. Haapala, & C. Booth (1991). *Keeping families together: The Homebuilders model* (pp. 85–86). New York: Aldine de Gruyter. Reprinted with permission.

Similarly, helpers may react to clients in certain ways based on their resemblances to people in their past. These are known as *countertransference effects* (see Hayes, Gelso, & Hummel, 2011). They may affect participation by altering the helper's behaviors in positive or negative ways. Not recognizing these influences may result in errors such as mistakenly attributing a lack of progress to environmental obstacles rather than to relationship factors. Kottler and Blau (1989) discuss a number of errors that may result from lack of awareness of countertransference effects, such as prematurely ending helping efforts because of an unrecognized dislike of the client. Thus, either underinvestment or overinvestment in clients may result in less than optimal decisions. Examples of errors described by Herbert Strean in one of his cases that he attributed to his negative attitude toward a client are as follows:

- He lost his objectivity and let himself be pulled into the client's manipulative ploys.

- Because of feelings of threat, jealousy, and competition, he perpetuated a continual power struggle.

- He often made the "correct" interpretation or said the "right" words, but in a tone of voice that was more hostile than empathic.

- He spent much of the time trying to prove to the client that he knew what he was doing.

- Although he was aware his countertransference feelings were getting in the way, he could not monitor or confront them sufficiently, nor did he seek supervision or therapy to resolve them.

- He retreated behind the mask of cold, objective analyst. (Cited in Kottler & Blau, 1989, p. 132.)

Attentive listening and empathizing with the client's perspective and the difficult situations he or she faces contribute to collaborative working relationships. There are many ways to encourage liking even when clients have hard-to-like characteristics. One is to keep in mind that clients are doing the best they can and that there are always two or more sides to every story.

Responding to Silence

A client's silence may reflect underlying feelings of anger, anxiety, confusion, or time to think. Use silence as a cue to try to discover concerns clients may have. Shulman (1991) reports that "reaching inside of silences" was one of four skills used to help clients manage their feelings. Related reactions convey a sense that helpers care. His research showed that this skill is underused. He concluded that helpers are often reluctant to explore silences and suggested that silence often means the helper is doing something right (rather than something wrong). Helpers who are willing to "reach into a silence" to discover negative client reactions have an opportunity to bring them out into the open for discussion.

Encouraging Quiet Clients to Talk

Steps you can take to encourage quiet clients to talk include the following:

- Offer active listening (e.g., reflections, paraphrases).

- Seek out concerns clients may have.

- Avoid making critical comments.

- Consider cultural differences.

- Ask clients for suggestions.

- Reinforce clients for participating.

- Do not rush clients; match their pace as appropriate.

- Pick settings for meetings that encourage clients' involvement.

- Watch for small signals that clients want to say something and invite their comments.

- Encourage clients to share their reservations.

What is useful in encouraging clients to talk depends on why they are silent. They may say little because they do not want to see you, are not interested in goals you focus on, or do not believe that change is possible. Cultural differences should also be considered. Anticipating reluctance to share certain information and giving clients a choice about when to share this may be useful. You may say, "You might be hesitant to tell me certain details about yourself. If I were in your shoes, I might feel the same way. Don't tell me anything until you're ready." This changes the issue from whether a client will do something (share information) to when she may do so. Offering a choice between alternatives is similar. A staff member at a residential center could ask a child which shower, bathroom, or color of towel he would like, rather than asking him whether he is ready to take a bath or shower. Be alert for clues that clients would like to say something and invite them to contribute. Encourage clients to express their reservations. If you do not know what they are, you will not be able to "fine-tune" your answers.

Calming Clients

You can use active listening skills to calm clients. Homebuilders has a rule: when in doubt, listen (Kinney, Haapala, & Booth, 1991, p. 68). Following this rule will help you avoid trying to "fix things" and take control. Just listening helps clients feel understood and respected. Active listening skills may decrease threats clients may feel and contribute to a positive working relationship.

Holding the Clients' Attention

Clients' attention may drift if they cannot follow or are not interested in what you are saying or if you talk too long. Clients may lose interest because of a monotone manner of speaking or "tune out" because of excessive affect on your part that alarms or offends them. When their attention flags, ask yourself the following:

- Is my language and speaking style compatible with my clients? Can they understand what I am saying? Have I avoided "turn-offs" (e.g., excessive jargon or patronizing comments)? Is my pace too fast or too slow?

- Do we have a clear agreement on hoped-for outcomes the client values?

- Have I avoided critical comments?

- Do I offer a credible image (do clients believe I can help them)?

- Have I encouraged positive expectations?

- Have I encouraged a collaborative working relationship in which we share responsibility?

- Do I seek clients' feedback (invite them to respond to what I say)?

Using the Telephone

You may spend some time on the telephone (calling clients, making referrals, and returning calls). You can make this less of a burden and increase the likelihood of attaining your goals by scheduling time for these calls and preparing for them. Before you telephone, identify your goals and plan how to pursue them.

- What do I want? What is my goal?

- How can I increase the likelihood of achieving it?

- What objections or obstacles might arise? What can I do to prevent or handle them?

- What can I do to make the call pleasant for myself and the other person?

- What reminders would be helpful?

Reminders might include:

- Introduce myself.

- Describe what I want.

- Do not talk too fast.

- Wait for an answer to questions.

- Do not talk too long.

- Be positive.

- Be polite.

- Ignore hostile, curt, negative responses.

- Keep focused on my goal.

- Use active listening skills to calm people and to help others feel understood and validated.

Requesting Work From the Client

Many clients in social work settings are reluctant participants, or they want to change but do not want to do the work necessary for change (process resistance). Here you will have to clearly describe the need to work to attain hoped-for outcomes, for example, carry out tasks associated with success. This is usually an ongoing requirement in working with clients. Various ways to do this include being clear about hoped-for outcomes, clearly describing the client's responsibilities, and forming a service agreement. (See Chapter 13.) Requesting participation of clients is preceded by discussion of the client's situation and feelings, pros and cons of change, obstacles, discussion of difficult topics, acknowledging client ambivalence, and describing a change agenda (e.g., identifying intermediate steps). (See chapter 13.) Shulman (2006) highlights the importance of "challenging the illusion of work"—for example, talking about peripheral concerns (pp. 153–154). Ethical concerns here include a just distribution of available time and money (providing services to clients on a waiting list).

Encouraging Positive Expectations

Positive expectations contribute to positive outcomes. This is the main element in the placebo effect (a favorable effect as a result of the act of intervention rather than the intervention itself) (Benedetti, 2009). Encourage positive expectations by providing estimates of success based on research findings. Be honest about uncertainties. You cannot guarantee success, but based on research findings you can indicate how likely certain

changes are. (See, for example, discussion of number needed to treat in chapter 10). Fulfilling the requirements for informed consent requires sharing related research findings with clients. Competence in sharing such information with clients in understandable language is an important practice skill. Beginning helpers are sometimes diffident and timid when they should be firm and confident. If you offer suggestions hesitantly, your clients may not be interested in trying them. However, as with all general guidelines, there are exceptions. Tentative descriptions may be more effective when clients are sensitive to the appearance of "being told what to do" and when your goal is to have clients make suggestions by prompts such as "Could it be that . . . ?" "Do you think that . . . might work?"

Highlight methods associated with success. For example, when describing a parenting program, prospective clients were told that successful parents required their children to earn rewards (no freebies), were satisfied with small changes leading to big ones, cooperated and worked together as a team, took scheduled breaks, and reinforced themselves as progress was made (among other things) (Kozloff, 1979, p. 159). Encourage questions and comments about what you have shared, and support optimistic statements, as well as efforts to generalize new information. In offering guidelines to helpers who use parent training programs, Kozloff cautions:

> Do not reinforce pessimistic statements! Get parents thinking and talking in a positive, prescriptive way. For instance, if parents indicate that they do not think that they have the skill, again stress that they are probably no different from other parents, either in their abilities or in their feelings: that other parents soon found out just how competent they could become.
>
> If parents assert that their child is somehow different from the children seen on the tapes or films (implying that the methods might not work with their children), ask them to be specific. Then, explain that no two children are alike! It is not that one type of child can learn whereas another "type" cannot, because the principles of learning and of good teaching are the same. Rather, the details of the teaching programs might be different for each child. In sum, using the videotapes, films, or descriptions, do your best to help the parents believe that they may well do the same thing with their children that the other parents have done (again, cautious optimism). (1979, p. 159)

Discourage negative talk about suggested methods by supporting positive expectations and enhancing your credibility. This does not mean that you should not use your active listening skills to understand and validate your clients' concerns. Rather, if you have done your best to accomplish such ends and negative talk persists, try other options. Emphasize the differences between what has been done in the past and your approach. To do this, you will need information about what clients have tried and what resulted (see Exhibit 14.8).

EXHIBIT 14.8

Setting the Stage for a New Way of Approaching a Problem

PARENT: Jane used to scratch her hands a lot.

CONSULTANT: Umm hmm. What did you do about it?

PARENT: Well, we were taking her to see Dr. Blither. He told us just to ignore it, that Jane was scratching her hands to get attention. And we did, for weeks!! But she kept it up—no more, no less than before. (Parent looks disgusted.)

CONSULTANT: Did Dr. Blither ever see Jane at home? (Consultant subtly indicates that she may question Dr. Blither's advice, because Blither was not around to conduct a behavioral analysis.)

PARENT: No.

CONSULTANT: Well, you see, attention is only one reason why Jane might have been scratching her hands. (Indicates an alternative to Blither's analysis and advice.)

PARENT: Oh?

CONSULTANT: Well, she might have scratched her hands because she had an allergy. Or she might have been turned on or reinforced by the feelings in her hands when she scratched them. You see, before you decide what to do to handle a problem, you have to analyze the behavior and the situation—and that means that you have to examine the child, sometimes medically, and observe the child's behavior before you can really tell why the child seems to be doing the behavior. (Consultant points out that she might have offered different advice.)

PARENT: I see. And besides, she scratched her hands even when she was by herself. We never really did think that she did it just for attention.

CONSULTANT: That's a good observation! (Reinforces parents.) And what about her scratching now?

PARENT: She still does it. (Gives consultant a chance to offer her own suggestion.)

CONSULTANT: See, there are several reasons why she might be scratching her hands. Allergy, attention, self-stimulation. In fact, they all may be true at the same time. So, we have to check out the possibilities and try to eliminate the ones that do not apply. It might be a good idea to have an allergist see her. If she does not have an allergy, then we can observe Jane's behavior more carefully to see what else might be causing her scratching. And, you know, even if attention has something to do with her scratching, ignoring it does not teach her other, proper ways to get attention. In addition to not rewarding or reinforcing her scratching with attention, we have to teach her alternative ways to get attention. (Presents main features of a problem-solving strategy and points out importance of teaching alternative behaviors.)

Source: M. A. Kozloff (1979). *A program for families of children with learning and behavior problems* (pp. 68–69). New York: Wiley. Reprinted with permission.

Clients may believe that change is unlikely because they have failed in the past. They may feel hopeless and helpless. They may be in a "defeat state" from repeatedly submitting to others, for example, battered women (Gilbert, 1989). Only gradually, by "small wins" may hope increase. Successful assignments will encourage the belief that change is possible. Clients may overlook modest gains that show that they can have some influence over their lives. Help clients to identify positive changes that have occurred (see chapter 22). When working with clients in crisis, you may have to take major responsibility at first for identifying goals and pursuing them.

Enhancing Credibility

The more credible you appear, the more likely it is that clients will listen to what you say and participate in helpful ways. Credibility is influenced by (1) degree of expertness as indicated, for example, by professional credentials and type of agency; (2) reliability as an information source (e.g., dependability, predictability, and consistency); (3) motives and intentions—the clearer it is to clients that it is their interests toward which you are working, the greater your credibility; and (4) your dynamism—apparent confidence, forcefulness, and activity level. (For a review of therapist variables as they relate to outcome, see Norcross, 2011.) Your credibility will be influenced by the success of your suggestions. If they decrease client distress, your credibility will improve. If they do not, it may diminish. Your suggestions are more likely to be accepted by clients if they are compatible with your client's point of view. Similarity to clients in age, gender, ethnicity, or some other key characteristic may increase credibility. Clients who differ in ethnicity, race, gender, age, physical abilities, or sexual orientation may have doubts about whether you can understand them and be of help. You can anticipate questions by bringing them up yourself. Helpful rules for handling challenges include:

- Do not be defensive.
- Acknowledge and anticipate clients' concerns.
- Do not downplay differences.
- Describe how you can be of help despite such differences.
- Relax and listen; try to understand the client's point of view (see also chapter 15).

Encouraging Helpful Views

Help clients frame problems in a way that gives them influence over their lives and a feeling of hope. The goal is to arrive at a view that points to steps clients can take to enhance the quality of their lives. They may not know how to break a problem down into a number of specific steps. Shulman (2006) refers to this as partializing. Clients may not accurately estimate how much influence they can have over what happens to them. They may be "stuck" in attempted solutions that maintain or worsen rather than lessen problems. They may blame significant others for problems. They may blame society. Clients may believe that they should be in complete control of what happens to them and feel guilty because they are not. Their usual attributional style (e.g., blaming others) and problem-solving approach may conflict with a view that highlights their options and responsibilities for influencing their environments. The question is: Does a particular view offer guidelines for attaining desired outcomes? That is, is it instrumental?

Clients with an internal locus of control (they believe that what happens to them is largely a result of their own actions) are more likely to participate than are clients who have an external locus of control (they believe that they have little or no control over what happens to them). The view that we have little or no control over what happens to us decreases our efforts to change disliked conditions. Involving clients in making decisions promotes a sense of choice and freedom and increases the likelihood of collaborative efforts. You can foster shared views by the questions you ask, interpretations you give, assessment methods you use (e.g., gathering data describing the patterns of interaction between clients and significant others), rationales you offer, and homework assignments you suggest.

When you discuss data clients collect, use questions and interpretations that encourage more helpful views and highlight relationships between behaviors of concern and their consequences. Be sure to personalize discussions by using examples from the client's own life. If you find yourself saying "most people ..." or "They say that ..." you are probably not making points uniquely relevant to your clients. Emphasize positive motivations. For example, you could point out to an "overprotective mother" that it is natural for her to be concerned about her children. You can suggest plans that allow this mother to continue to see herself in the role of a "good parent." Family members usually care about one another. Their behavior is usually well intended even if their actions have negative effects on significant others. (See discussion of Behavior Always Makes Sense in chapter 12.)

Discouraging Negative Labels and Minimizing Blame

Encouraging helpful views will often require minimizing blame and discouraging negative labels, such as *drunkard*, *hostile*, and *unmotivated*. Negative labels that have no intervention guidelines and that encourage negative expectations get in the way of seeing the potential for change. They may increase hopelessness on the part of both clients and social workers, whether directed by social workers toward clients or by clients toward themselves or significant others. Negative labels do not have to be terms from the DSM-R-IV (2000), such as *bipolar*. They can be labels, such as *unmotivated* or *hostile*, that you apply to clients. Professional education programs for social workers emphasize reliance on diagnostic categories (Lacasse & Gomory, 2003). Labels are commonly used in everyday life (e.g., "He's stupid," "I'm lazy"). Labels have an either/or quality that interferes with discovering unique patterns of behavior and related circumstances and initial steps that can be taken to attain desired outcomes. The disadvantages of labeling are described in Exhibit 14.9 (see also the discussion of labeling in chapter 12).

Using Formal Client Feedback

Gaining formal, real-time feedback from clients about the process used and outcomes attained in your meetings contributes to retention and outcome (Miller, Duncan, Brown, Sorrell, & Chalk, 2006). Ongoing monitoring of the quality of your alliance with your clients will help you maintain a positive alliance. Certainly this will not be feasible in some situations but in many others it will. You can gain this important feedback by asking clients to complete a brief rating scale following each meeting (Owen & Imel, 2010). This provides vital information about the alliance, which is so key to outcome. (See chapter 15 for further discussion.) Gathering this kind of feedback from clients enhances outcome, one reason being that you can discuss client concerns at an early point. (See, for example, the four-item Session Rating Scale (Duncan, Miller, Sparks, Claud, Reynolds, Brown, & Johnson, 2003.) The four items on the scale concern the relationship, goals and topics, approach and method, and

---

EXHIBIT 14.9

Disadvantages of Negative Labels

Labels such as "unmotivated" or "resistant" define clients as adversaries with bad intentions and little common sense or desire to overcome their problems. Labels can position us to demean clients, disagree with them, and pressure them to do things "for their own good" rather than because the courses of action we recommend make sense to them. Labeling makes it harder for us to be warm and supportive, if we're thinking about coping with the negative traits we've assigned to our clients. Instead of calling clients "resistant" or "unmotivated," it's more helpful to describe them as worried about failing again, feeling hopeless, feeling helpless, lacking the skills necessary to begin thinking about the problems, or unable, at the moment, to formulate goals that seem worthwhile and obtainable. . . .

Once we begin to think of a client as "antagonistic" or "vindictive," we are likely to believe it, and to feel some pressure to justify our initial impressions, hindering us from being open to the whole picture and to more positive interpretations. It will be more helpful to redefine "vindictive" as "focusing on past hurts," and "antagonistic" as "afraid of being disappointed again."

Other labels, such as "sociopathic" or "psychotic," can also have a tremendous impact on the client–counselor relationship. Not only do clients not like having these labels, the labels also scare us and make us think the situation is hopeless—much more hopeless than if we stuck to the specifics such as "Jerry took his grandmother's medicine and flushed it down the toilet," or "Sometimes when Susie talks, her sentences don't make sense," or "Theron some-times hits Judy when they fight." When clients are labeled by referring workers, it is particularly easy for us to look at the referral sheet and say, "Oh, no, a chronic psychopath, nobody can work with those!" rather than remembering that the label resulted from some specific things the client did that are not half as scary as the label might imply.

Labels can also harm our goal of helping clients feel hopeful because they imply an all or nothingness about problems. If someone is something, like pathological, or if they *have* something, like low ego strength, the implication is that that is the way they are, and that is the way they always will be. They have a condition. We think it's more helpful to define problems in terms of things that people do or do not do . . . It is possible to set small goals of changing only one or a few behaviors at a time. The goals begin to seem possible. There is hope.

Source: J. Kinney, D. Haapala, & C. Booth (1991). *Keeping families together: The Homebuilders Model* (pp. 84–85). New York: Aldine de Gruyter. Reprinted with permission.

---

overall view. (See <http://www.talkingcure.com>.) David Burns has also developed a brief form that clients complete after each session. Possible scores range from 1 to 21. He suggests you are in trouble if your score is under 19. Correlations between client ratings and counselor ratings of sessions were found to be low (Burns, 2004).

Arranging Helpful Organizational Policies and Procedures

Attitudes toward clients are shown not only by how helpers act during interviews but also by characteristics of the agency in which services are offered (see Exhibit 14.2). Organizational barriers may prevent clients from seeking services and compromise participation of those who do. Long waiting times and delayed appointment times may discourage clients. Agency policy regarding appointment reminders affects participation. Attractiveness of decor, degree of privacy for interviews, safety of waiting rooms, and flexibility in scheduling times and places to meet reflect how the agency views clients. The typical helping relationship may not be appropriate for some clients and/or desired outcomes and a different format may

have to be arranged. Examples are peer tutoring (parents may be trained to help other parents) and self-help groups. Participatory community-based programs may be the best choice rather than one-on-one counseling or family-focused change (see chapter 27). Inadequate links among or within services, such as vague referrals with no follow-up, may discourage participation. Seek changes in agency policies and procedures that discourage participation (see Exhibit 14.10). Use your obligation to help clients to identify and alter dysfunctional policies and practices that hinder correction of avoidable injustices.

Other Steps

Arrange reminders and incentives that increase participation. Without special prompts and incentives, clients may forget to carry out agreed-on tasks. You may have to reframe concerns and proposed solutions to engage clients (e.g., encourage perspectives that are consistent with effective methods). (See, for example, the classic book by Watzlawick, Weakland, & Fisch, 1974.) Enlist the support of significant others. If they understand the rationale for programs and the steps required for success and

---

EXHIBIT 14.10

EXHIBIT 14.10

Practice Example Practice Example

Describe one way in which your agency's policies or procedures could be changed to encourage client participation. Clearly describe this and suggest specific changes based on a contextual assessment.

1. What is the current practice or policy?

_____

_____

_____

2. How does it affect client participation?

_____

_____

_____

3. How should it be altered?

_____

_____

_____

---

if the outcomes also will benefit them, they are more likely to work with rather than against clients.

Agreed-on tasks are more likely to be carried out if clients give their verbal and/or written commitment to do so. You should seek such a commitment. Forming a written service agreement and clarifying expectations may enhance participation. Be sure to review the outcomes of assignments; this will increase the likelihood that future ones will be completed. You may have to repeat important content and should check understanding. Lack of participation may result from rushing clients, from not respecting their pace. You may have to cycle back to initial steps.

Preparing for Interviews as a Way to Enhance Participation

Client participation can be enhanced by preparing for interviews. Being informed about outcomes of concern to clients and their life circumstances and history shows them that you care enough to be prepared. Even though you have not seen a client before and have no information about this person's concerns and circumstances, there are ways you can prepare (see Exhibit 14.11). You can arrange a place to meet that is convenient for the client and that will facilitate your exchange, empathize with the client no matter what the problem (to get his or her side of the story), and be familiar with research findings regarding problems clients frequently bring to your agency, as well as resources that may be of value. Preparing for meetings is a sign of respect for clients. Excessive time pressures may make it impossible to be prepared. However, it is important not to lose sight of what is best.

Review Helpful Information

If you do have information about a client, review it before your meetings so you can be prepared with resources and anticipate obstacles. Records may contain information about the client's age, family composition, employment history, and prior experiences with other agencies. Reviewing available information will help you to anticipate clients' concerns, offer clues about how to tailor your language to match your clients', and suggest cultural and value differences and the effect they may have. Be careful not to pick up negative views of clients. Records often focus on what is wrong with clients, with little content on client assets. If you have prior knowledge of what concerns may be shared, you can collect information about helpful resources and decide what information to get in the interview. Be prepared by being up-to-date about available services, including information about potential obstacles. Familiarity with the neighborhoods and communities in which clients live often offers valuable information about related circumstances such as poorly maintained housing.

If you have advance information about a client's concerns and have little or no related knowledge in these areas, consult relevant literature before the interview. This may suggest helpful assessment methods and intervention options and their likely success (see Exhibit 14.12). Reviewing related literature will help you to spot and counter biases and challenge inaccurate assumptions about problems and how (or if) they can be resolved. Professionals have an ethical obligation to be knowledgeable about the outcomes they pursue—about what is known and what is not (ignorance and uncertainty)—as well as about biases that may get in the way of helping clients. The

---

EXHIBIT 14.11

Checklist for Preparing for Meetings

_____ Prepare a tentative agenda.
_____ Review relevant information (if available).
_____ Arrange a facilitating context.
_____ If you have information about the nature of a client's concerns, consult related research as needed regarding valuable assessment, intervention, and evaluation options.

_____ Have useful forms available.
_____ If you have knowledge beforehand about what may be needed, gather information about resources including possible referrals.
_____ Engage in anticipatory empathy.

---

greater the gap between your personal knowledge and related research findings that can be of benefit to clients, the more ethically questionable it is to work with them in the absence of this information.

Anticipatory Empathy

Anticipatory empathy refers to trying to understand another person's point of view and experiences (placing yourself in another's shoes) (Kadushin & Kadushin, 1997) (see Exhibit 14.13). This will help to correct stereotypes and biases that get in the way of understanding and helping people. It is also important to be aware of _your_ feelings. It may be useful to recall what you thought and felt in situations similar to those of your client. However, be careful not to assume that your experiences mirror those of others. They may be quite different. Let clients tell their own story, to relate their experience as they see it. Anticipatory empathy is especially important with clients who may have committed acts such as child abuse. Be honest with yourself about your own feelings so they do not get in the way of helping clients. Recognizing

---

EXHIBIT 14.12

Case Examples of Reviewing and Updating Background Knowledge

THE LAKELANDS

Mr. Colvine had never worked with youth with epilepsy, nor did he know anything about it. So when he learned over the phone that Brian had epilepsy, he decided to become informed before seeing the Lakelands. He was interested in learning about the physical and psychological effects of epilepsy (as far as they are known) and the possible side effects of the various drugs used to control epilepsy. He posed the following questions to guide his search: "In youth with epilepsy, what are common physical and psychological effects?" "In youth with epilepsy who are taking certain kinds of medication, what are common side effects of the medication?" This would be important to know, since Brian complained about the effects of the prescribed dosage. He also posed a general question related to family conflict: "In families having conflict, what are effective interventions?"

MRS. RYAN AND THE GREENS

Mrs. Slater had little experience in working with what she called "old people" and did not know anyone over the age of 70. Her parents died when they were young, and she had never known her grandparents. She felt an immediate sympathy for the problems the Greens said they were having with Mrs. Ryan, their elderly relative. Her first reaction was to help the Greens locate another living arrangement for Mrs. Ryan. Clearly, she had a bias against "old people." However, she also had a rule to question her beliefs. What was known about people over 80 who lived with family members? Mrs. Slater posed the following question and used this to guide her search for related research findings: "In multigenerational families, what are common sources of satisfaction and strain?" Her search revealed a wide variation in experiences. Many older people live with family members and get along well, although this is not to say there are no problems. Caring for an elderly relative can be a strain, as well as a source of satisfaction. Mrs. Slater found that significant others often had inaccurate beliefs about their aging relatives and often acted in accord with those beliefs. For example, the differences of opinion expressed by older relatives that were considered as signs of lively interest 20 years earlier may now be viewed as stubbornness and combativeness—even senility. Mrs. Slater found that as people get older, they often have negative feelings about still being alive (since many of their friends have died) and feel guilty about being a burden to their families. Consulting the professional literature before her first interview thus helped Mrs. Slater to correct her biases and appreciate environmental influences. She would have to consider the entire family situation. She could not focus solely on Mrs. Ryan in order to understand concerns and options.

EXHIBIT 14.13

Examples of Anticipatory Empathy

Julie's social worker once thought that she was pregnant at a time when she did not wish to be. She remembered the panic she felt, the feeling that things were out of control, the uncertainty about where to turn for help, the feeling that there was no good solution. Recalling her own past helped her understand Julie's concerns.

Ms. Landis knew that she tended to use big words that clients might not understand. So she reminded herself before her interview to use words that would be familiar to Julie and that would help Julie understand her. She knew that clients may not ask what a word meant even when they did not understand her. She recognized that most pregnant unmarried teenagers worried about reactions of their parents and that the extent of their involvement must be discussed. (Laws about whether parental consent must be obtained before a minor may have an abortion vary from state to state. It was not a requirement in the state where Julie lived.) Ms. Landis reminded herself to describe agency rules about confidentiality, that nothing would be said to her parents without her permission, and that she would not be pressured to tell her parents.

---

that each person has his or her own view of a situation and realizing the importance of understanding that view may help you avoid messages of disapproval (Perlman, 1979).

Anticipatory empathy may help you to notice subtle clues to concerns clients may have and understand reactions that may appear puzzling. For example, Julie worried that she would be asked about her sexual behavior. She decided that if Mrs. Landis brought up this topic, she would say, "I think I'll work this out on my own." Hostile statements may mask feelings of vulnerability, embarrassment, or fear. Concerns and expectations clients may have are discussed in chapter 2. Keep this in mind when preparing to meet people. Questions that encourage anticipatory empathy are:

1. What might it be like to be in this person's situation?

2. Do I have any stereotypes about this person or his or her circumstances? Am I viewing him or her as a "type" rather than as a unique human being? You can test this by completing sentences illustrated in chapter 2.

3. Have I had a similar experience? What did I feel and think? Have I known anyone else who has? What did she think and feel?

4. How might my experience differ from her experience?

5. How should I modify my language?

6. What concerns might this person have about me?

7. What concerns might he have about coming to this agency?

8. What cultural, ethnic, racial, age, sexual orientation, religious, or class differences are important here?

Arrange a Facilitating Context

Exchanges are influenced by the context in which they occur. Perhaps you work in a large public agency in which there is little privacy, high noise levels, and frequent interruptions. Try to minimize the interruptions. Involve other interested colleagues

in changing dysfunctional policies, procedures, or physical arrangements. The agency is not necessarily the best place for meetings. The client's home, a playground, or a school may be a better setting. If clients are distracted by competing activities (a teacher may be trying to maintain control of her class), they may not get involved in a discussion. Taking a walk or meeting in a public place such as a fast-food restaurant may provide a better atmosphere for a talk than an office does. Try to allow sufficient time for each interview so that you and your clients do not feel rushed. If possible, allow some time between interviews to reflect on your exchange, to make required or helpful notes, and to prepare for the next interview.

Decide on a Tentative Agenda

Planning what you can accomplish during an interview will help you to focus on important points and avoid drift. Agendas will differ depending on the helping phase. Some tasks, such as describing the reasons for your suggestions, are common to all meetings. Others are unique to particular phases or kinds of interviews. Agendas should be tentative and open to change as necessary. For individuals or families with many problems, crises that require attention may arise daily or weekly (see also the discussion of structuring in chapter 15). If pressed for time, scale down your agenda. Have helpful forms readily available.

Arrange Helpful Prompts

If you tend to forget important items, prepare a prompt list as a reminder. You could note points you want to discuss or helping behaviors you tend to forget. For instance, you may forget to "empathize" with resisters or to seek input from everyone when interviewing a family. You could jot down a word or phrase to remind yourself to do so. You could include reminders of how to handle difficult situations. For example, you may become exasperated with "Yes, but ..." responses. A prompt will remind you to use this reaction as a cue to try to understand the function (meaning) of the "Yes, buts ..." Perhaps these reflect that you have lost your way—that there is a failure of agenda setting—identifying and focusing on outcomes clients hope to attain. Fade out prompts when you no longer need them.

Use your emotions as cues to contingencies (see chapter 7)—as clues to identifying actions (or inactions) of others for example that trigger these emotions. You could review the Initial Interview Checklist in chapter 13 prior to interviews.

Should You Use Social Psychological Persuasion Strategies?

Knowledge about social psychological persuasion strategies is useful in both resisting unwanted influences and persuading others to participate in desired ways (see Cialdini, 2008; Pratkanis, 2007). These strategies work through emotional associations and appeals rather than through a thoughtful consideration of arguments for and against a position. Persuasion by affect comes into play when we are influenced by how attractive a person is or how confidently they present their views.

Is it ethical to use social psychological persuasion strategies with either clients or other professionals who serve as gatekeepers to needed services? Consider the *scarcity principle*. This rests on the fact that opportunities seem more valuable when they are limited. A client may be more eager to participate in a program that is available for only a limited time. Scarcity may be a reality. If so, there is no ethical problem with noting it. However, as with other persuasion strategies, it can be used dishonestly. For example, a nursing home intake worker may tell a caller, "If you don't decide now, space may not be available" (when this is not true). We are also influenced by the *contrast effect*, which also may be a reality. Immediately providing concrete help to a client who has not received help elsewhere may be a contrast to past experiences and so encourage participation. Helpers also are influenced by contrast effects. After an interview with a "challenging" person, you may regard a client as very cooperative who is actually only fairly cooperative.

The *reciprocity rule* lies behind the success of the "rejection-then-retreat technique," in which a small request follows a large one. The small request is viewed as a "concession" and may be reciprocated by a concession from the other person. For example, when college students were asked to chaperone a group of juvenile delinquents on a day trip to the zoo, 83% refused. When this was first preceded by a bigger request (to spend 2 hours a week for 2 years as a counselor to a delinquent), three times as many students agreed (Cialdini, 1984, pp. 50–51). (The contrast effect is also at work here.) Obtaining an initial concession or offering a favor may encourage participation through the reciprocity rule because we feel obligated to return favors.

The *principle of liking* is a frequently used persuasion strategy. We like to please people we know and like (i.e., to comply with their requests). Physical attractiveness, similarity, compliments, familiarity, and cooperation encourage liking. The good guy/bad guy routine takes advantage of the liking rule. We like

the good guy (in contrast to the bad guy), so comply with what he wants. Persuasion strategies based on liking and authority are effective partly because of affective associations. Another persuasion strategy is based on the *desire to be (and appear) consistent* with what we have already done. Obtaining a commitment puts the consistency rule into effect. "Commitment strategies are … intended to get us to take some action or make some statement that will trap us into later compliance through consistency pressures" (Cialdini, 1984, p. 75), Someone may say "You already agreed to give me _____. How about _____?" (which is similar). Or you may ask a person to come for "just one interview," hoping that if he does, he will attend other meetings.

The *principle of social proof* involves being influenced by what other people think is correct (consensus). Describing other clients who have overcome problems may create hope and a willingness to try suggested methods. Relying on testimonials and case examples to encourage clients to use suggested services is ethically questionable if it increases the likelihood that clients will rely on such grounds when making other life-affecting decisions (see chapter 4). Both uncertainty and similarity heighten persuasion effects. We are more likely to go along with what other people do in ambiguous situations and when we observe others who are similar to ourselves.

The principles on which social psychological persuasion strategies are based provide convenient shortcuts that often work for us. But if we accept them "automatically" they can work against our best interests and the best interests of clients, and other people can exploit them for their own purposes.

Ethical Issues

Many of the practice skills described in this chapter are an integral part of ethical practice, such as fully informing clients of any coercive aspects to contacts with your agency, supporting client strengths, involving clients in selecting outcomes and plans, and considering cultural differences. You are less likely to blame clients (or yourself) unfairly for a lack of participation if you understand related reasons such as environmental obstacles. A key ethical issue concerning preparing is accurately estimating the gap between your knowledge and skills and what is needed to help clients (e.g., the gap between personal and available knowledge). Informed consent requires accurately describing the evidentiary status of recommended methods and alternatives in clear language that clients can understand. Have the methods you recommended or use been found to help clients? (See also chapter 3.)

Summary

A contextual view requires attention to both personal and environmental factors that influence participation. Many clients are nonvoluntary and have concerns about what will be involved and what consequences will result. There is an asymmetry of power that requires special vigilance on your part to use this power for the benefit of clients and significant others. Clients' lack of participation may be related to agency characteristics, such an inhospitable waiting room and long waiting times. Vague instructions and mismatches between client skills and expectations may be responsible. Encouraging participation requires effective use of practice knowledge and skills, including knowledge of cultural differences, offering concrete help, building on clients' assets, and encouraging positive expectations. Enhancing your credibility and involving clients in making decisions increases the likelihood that clients will participate. You can encourage participation by agreeing on a clear agenda (outcomes clients hope to achieve), helping clients replace interfering beliefs and attitudes with instrumental ones, seeking commitment, and clarifying expectations. Arrange agency policies and procedures that maximize participation. Other steps include anticipating hesitations, individually tailoring methods to cultural differences, and preparing for meetings. You can show that you care about clients by being informed about research findings concerning outcomes they hope to attain.

Reviewing Your Competencies

Reviewing Content Knowledge

1. Describe methods you can use to increase client participation.

2. Describe how you can increase your credibility.

3. Discuss different kinds of attributions and their relationship to participation.

4. Describe how you can encourage helpful views of problems.

5. Describe methods you can use to encourage positive expectations.

6. Discuss hesitations clients may have about participating and how they can be addressed including cultural differences.

7. Describe what you can do to prepare for interviews.

8. Identify agency policies or practices that influence participation.

9. Describe relationship factors that influence participation.

10. Define the placebo effect and give examples.

11. Discuss ethical questions about relying on testimonials and case examples to encourage participation.

12. Accurately describe social-psychological persuasion strategies.

Reviewing What You Do

1. Your questions and statements in interviews demonstrate advance preparation.

2. You anticipate client hesitations.

3. You clearly describe client expectations.

4. You focus on client concerns and hoped-for outcomes.

5. You identify and support client strengths.

6. You take effective steps to enhance participation as demonstrated in interviews and role plays.

7. You consider client preferences in arranging meeting times and places.

8. You can carry out a contingency analysis of an agency policy or procedure that interferes with client participation and make specific recommendations for change based on this.

9. You avoid premature advice and promises of help.

10. You meet resistance with empathy.

11. You gain written client feedback after each session and use this to enhance your working alliance with your clients.

Reviewing Results

1. Clients share relevant information.

2. Positive expectations are encouraged.

3. Clients accept more helpful views of problems and possible solutions.

4. Clients express hope that desired outcomes can be attained.

5. Clients give you high ratings of warmth, empathy, and helpfulness on after-session questionnaires (see http://www.talkingcure.com; and Burns, 2004).

6. Clients complete agreed-on assignments.

7. Clients' knowledge and skills increase.

8. There are no physical assaults on social workers.

9. Blaming statements and negative labels become less frequent.

10. Hoped-for outcomes are attained.

Part 6

Relationship
Skills

15

Interpersonal Helping Skills

OVERVIEW   This chapter describes relationship skills of value in helping clients, including empathy, structuring, attentive listening, and confronting clients. These skills contribute to engaging and supporting clients, as well as understanding their concerns and related factors. They contribute to the formation of a positive alliance with both clients and significant others, which is related to positive outcomes. Many skills useful in everyday life are also of value with clients, such as attentive listening and offering positive feedback. The term *exchange* or *meeting* is used to highlight the variety of encounters involved in social work (e.g., with clients, significant others, and colleagues). One way to use this chapter is to select one or two skills to work on through guided practice opportunities arranged by your instructors. When reviewing the checklists in this chapter, keep in mind that you may have to change some items, depending on your goals and cultural differences in communication styles.

YOU WILL LEARN ABOUT

- Helping as a social influence process

- Empathy

- Warmth and genuineness (congruence)

- Attentive listening

- Respect/positive regard

- Asking helpful questions

- Structuring exchanges

- Encouraging helpful views and behaviors

- Self-disclosure

- Clarity/Concreteness

- Other important relationship skills

- Challenges

- Improving your skills

- Components of effective social behavior

- Verbal behavior (what is said)

- Nonverbal behavior

Helping as a Social Influence Process

Whether we intend to or not, our actions influence how others perceive and react toward us. As the saying goes: "You cannot not communicate." Studies of helping highlight the social influence process that takes place, even in "nondirective" approaches (Truax, 1966). Statements that match the therapist's views are reinforced; this may increase the congruence between therapist and client views. Helpers reinforce some behaviors, ignore others, and punish still others. In turn, clients influence the helpers' behavior. The quality of your communication skills influences client options. For example, you may obtain needed resources from another agency because you have been empathic,

persuasive, and polite when talking to their staff. Exhibit 15.1 gives examples of useful relationship skills. We differ in whom we feel most comfortable interviewing. We differ in the feelings we have in certain situations. Being a professional requires responding to feelings in a manner that contributes to helping clients attain outcomes they value. Being aware of your feelings, such as anger or anxiety, will help you to identify emotional triggers and respond appropriately. Similarly, being aware of the social signals you send can help you to alter these in directions that contribute to forming collaborative helping relationships with clients and others.

The helping relationship has been a topic of interest for decades. Consider the classic work of Carl Rogers (1957), who suggested congruence (genuineness), positive regard (non-possessive warmth), and empathy as the necessary and sufficient

---

EXHIBIT 15.1

Reviewing Your Relationship Skills (See also Chapter 16)

	Would Like to Work On	Fairly Competent	Very Competent
_____ 1. Observing and accurately translating social signals; recognizing attitudes and feelings.	_____	_____	_____
_____ 2. Avoiding judgmental reactions.	_____	_____	_____
_____ 3. Speaking clearly and at an effective pace.	_____	_____	_____
_____ 4. Prompting, modeling, and reinforcing helpful behaviors.	_____	_____	_____
_____ 5. Offering empathic responses.	_____	_____	_____
_____ 6. Offering an effective self-presentation.	_____	_____	_____
_____ 7. Using nonverbal signals consistent with your intent.	_____	_____	_____
_____ 8. Conveying a friendly attitude.	_____	_____	_____
_____ 9. Asking helpful questions.	_____	_____	_____
_____ 10. Active listening.	_____	_____	_____
_____ 11. Structuring exchanges.	_____	_____	_____
_____ 12. Being clear (e.g., explaining the purpose of meetings).	_____	_____	_____
_____ 13. Offering effective greetings.	_____	_____	_____
_____ 14. Providing constructive feedback.	_____	_____	_____
_____ 15. Normalizing concerns.	_____	_____	_____
_____ 16. Planning how to achieve social goals.	_____	_____	_____
_____ 17. Discouraging unhelpful behavior.	_____	_____	_____
_____ 18. Confronting clients when necessary.	_____	_____	_____
_____ 19. Requesting behavior changes.	_____	_____	_____
_____ 20. Offering encouragement.	_____	_____	_____
_____ 21. Avoiding distracting mannerisms	_____	_____	_____
_____ 22. Sharing personal information when appropriate.	_____	_____	_____
_____ 23. Ending exchanges in a timely and polite way.	_____	_____	_____
_____ 24. Offering compliments/expressing appreciation.	_____	_____	_____
_____ 25. Expressing liking and affection.	_____	_____	_____
_____ 26. Conveying respect.	_____	_____	_____
_____ 27. Making amends (e.g., apologizing).	_____	_____	_____
_____ 28. Selecting appropriate social goals.	_____	_____	_____

conditions for therapeutic change. In his classic book *Persuasion and Healing* (1961), Jerome Frank emphasized the helping skills involved in moving clients from a demoralized position to one where they felt hopeful about the future. The quality of communication between clients and helpers is important in all helping professions including medicine (Katz, 2002). Questions and related controversies suggested by Norcross (2002) include: (1) Do particular characteristics of a helping relationship contribute to positive outcomes and, if so, what are they? (2) What percentage of the variance of outcomes attained is related to relationship variables, the person of the helper, or the particular intervention used? and (3) Can important relationship variables be enhanced through training? Skills identified as contributing to relationship building and helpfulness include the following (e.g., see Duncan, Miller, Wampold, & Hubble, 2010; Norcross, 2011; Shulman, 1977, 2006):

- Sharing personal thoughts and feelings.
- Understanding clients' feelings.
- Supporting clients in taboo areas.
- Encouraging feedback concerning purpose.
- Putting clients' feelings into words.
- Partializing concerns.
- Providing information.
- Clarifying roles.
- Displaying feelings openly.
- Supporting strengths.
- Dealing with authority.
- Assessing people accurately (attending to and accurately interpreting social signals).
- Using effective communication skills.
- Discovering how to satisfy shared interests.
- Adjusting your behavior to that of others.
- Making appropriate demands.

Effective relationship skills, such as high-level empathic reactions including disarming reactions that communicate respect and understanding even in the face of criticism and anger, will add to your effectiveness with clients, as well as your own comfort. Such reactions acknowledge the truth in a criticism. For example, a youth may say "How can an old person like you help me?" You might say, "It's true. I really know nothing about your life. But I hope you can help me to understand it." The importance of relationship factors is suggested by research showing that nonprofessionals are as effective as are those with professional degrees, training, and experience in helping clients

achieve a range of outcomes (Dawes, 1994a; Christensen & Jacobson, 1994). Personal barriers to communication include a lack of respect for others and a lack of relationship skills and knowledge of when to use them. Some helpers are "hyper." Others are depressed or self-centered. Countertransference effects may result in being underprotective of clients or assuming too much responsibility for their lives. Environmental barriers include being overworked, high noise levels, and frequent interruptions.

Effective relationship skills increase the likelihood of establishing rapport with clients, gaining their participation, and avoiding drop out. Empathy, warmth, and credibility increase liking, respect, and trust, which in turn increase openness and communication and strengthen the helping alliance. It is estimated that about two-thirds of the observed small differences between psychotherapies in relation to outcome can be attributed to investigator allegiance (preferences of helpers for a particular method) (e.g., Luborsky & Barrett, 2006; Luborsky, Diguer, Seligman, Rosenthal, Krause, Johnson, et al., 1999; Lambert & Barley, 2002). Strupp suggests that all forms of helping involve a relationship "characterized by respect, interest, understanding, tact, maturity…a firm belief in [one's] ability to help" and influence through suggestions, encouragement of open communication, self-scrutiny, honesty, interpretations of material that people are not aware of (such as self-defeating strategies in interpersonal relations), offering examples of "maturity" and "capacity and willingness to profit from the experience" (1976, p. 97). Lambert and Barley (2002, p. 27) suggest that "in addition to providing the facilitative conditions in a positive alliance, therapists must avoid the negative communication patterns that detract from outcome, especially in working with difficult clients. These include comments or behaviors that are critical, attacking, rejecting, blaming, or neglectful" (see also Najavits & Strupp, 1994).

Therapist variables that have a positive impact on outcome include credibility, empathic understanding and affirmation of the client, skill in engaging the client, a focus on client's concerns, and skill in directing the client's attention to his or her affective experiences (Lambert, 2004; Norcross, 2011). Therapists differ in the extent to which they can form a positive working alliance with clients, which in turn, is related to positive outcome (Duncan, Miller, Wampold, & Hubble, 2010; Horvath, Del Re, Flückiger, & Symonds, 2011). They differ in their skill in repairing alliance ruptures (Safran, Muran, & Eubanks-Carter, 2011). Some therapists are more understanding and accepting, empathic, warm, and supportive than are others. They have lower rates of negative behaviors such as blaming, ignoring, and rejecting. Positive alliances encourage sharing of information needed to arrive at well-reasoned decisions and working to achieve hoped-for outcomes. Relationship skills are a critical ingredient of evidence-informed practice; they are a vital part of clinical expertise. Helpers who are cold, closed down, and judgmental are not as likely to involve clients in collaborative working relationships as are those who are warm, supportive, and empathic.

The Nonspecific Factors Versus Specific Intervention Debate

There is a spirited debate regarding the relative contribution of nonspecific factors including the alliance (the helper–client connection), helping skills used, and the person of the helper compared to the specific interventions used. Common factors refer to "variables found in most therapies regardless of the therapist's theoretical orientation such as empathy, warmth, acceptance, encouragement of risk taking, client and therapist characteristics, confidentiality of the client–therapist relationship, the therapeutic alliance or process factors" (Lambert & Barley, 2002, pp. 17–18). Wampold (2001) suggests that the specific intervention account for only 1% of outcomes attained, whereas relationship skills account for 5% and the person of the therapist accounts for 8%. Others disagree (e.g., Shadish, Navarro, Matt, & Phillips, 2000; Weisz, Jensen-Doss, & Hawley, 2006). (See also Wampold, 2006.)

Based on his review of the literature, Wampold (2006) sums up his views as follows: "In clinical trials, the variability of outcomes due to therapists (8%–9%) is larger than the variability among treatments (0%–1%), the alliance (5%), and the superiority of an EST [empirically established treatment] to a placebo treatment (0%–4%), making it the most robust predictor of outcomes of any factor studied, with the exception of the initial level of severity" (p. 204). Wampold (2001) concluded that "a preponderance of evidence indicates that there are large therapist effects...and that the effects greatly exceed treatment efforts" (p. 200). (See also Imel, Wampold, Miller, & Fleming, 2008; Wampold, 2010; more recent inquiry supports this statement.) Thus, as Norcross (2011) suggests, the person of the helper is intertwined with outcome. So too are the preferences of clients (e.g., see Swift & Callahan, 2009, 2010).

Lambert and Barley (2002) describe percent improvement as a function of different therapeutic factors: expectancy 15%, common factors 30%, techniques 15%, and extra therapeutic change 40%. (However, unexplained variance accounts for 40% of total outcome). Extra therapeutic factors include spontaneous remission, fortuitous events, and social support. They include factors outside of counseling that contribute to improvement. Improvement (or its lack) is also related to client characteristics, such as motivation to change and environmental circumstances. Clients differ in access to social support including friends, family members, and self-help groups. Clients viewed as "untreated" receive psychological interventions from their natural environment or through self-study or participation in various kinds of self-help or other groups led by people with some training (e.g., Finch, Lambert, & Brown, 2000). Lambert and Barley (2002) conclude that "Measures of therapeutic relationship variables consistently correlate more highly with client outcome than specialized therapy techniques. Associations between the therapeutic relationship and client outcome are strongest when measured by client ratings of both constructs" (p. 20). Knowledge of receiving help or the client's belief in the methods used and the rationale

for them (separate from specific effects) may result in positive effects. A placebo is an intervention that is objectively without any specific effect on a problem of concern but which induces an effect. It is a part of all interventions (e.g., see Benedetti, 2009).

Empathy

Empathic responses communicate that you understand what others say or experience. Carl Rogers defines *empathy* as "the therapist's sensitive ability and willingness to understand the client's thoughts, feelings, and struggles from the client's point of view." In *primary-level accurate empathy,* you try to let clients know that you understand what they explicitly expressed. In *advanced accurate empathy,* you comment on what clients have implied and left unstated, as well as what they have expressed openly. Both *reflections of feelings* ("You feel like everyone is against you") and *paraphrases of content* (e.g., "You're not sure what to say to him") may be used to communicate understanding. Reflections can be used for other purposes as well, including encouraging clients to talk more about their feelings, to increase awareness of feelings, and to check your understanding. Paraphrasing can also be used for other purposes, including guiding clients to focus on certain content and checking understanding. Empathy requires an assumption of ignorance (about the other); an assumption of a learner rather than expert role.

Empathy, warmth, positive regard, and genuineness create a context in which other important elements of helping are offered, such as inspiring hope, supporting client assets, clarifying goals, and planning services. Empathy is positively associated with outcome (Elliott, Bohart, Watson, & Greenberg, 2011). It may contribute to successful outcomes by increasing client satisfaction, so increasing participation including disclosure. Other benefits include decreasing isolation, feeling respected and encouraging productive exploration, all of which may contribute to valuable self-change efforts. Empathy facilitates selection of interventions that are compatible with the client's frame of reference. It requires individualizing responses for particular clients. Some clients may find expressions of empathy intrusive or foreign. Other clients may view these as efforts to control them. Sensitivity to a client's reasons will cue you as to when (and when not) to respond empathically. Research that shows that nonprofessionals are as effective as professionals in helping clients highlights the importance of empathy and other "nonspecific" relationship factors (Dawes, 1994a).

The goals of empathy include helping clients (1) to identify their feelings associated with their experiences, (2) to share relevant material, and (3) to feel accepted and understood (Shulman, 2006). Empathic responses let clients know that you are listening and understand what they have said. Because you go beyond what has been explicitly stated in advanced accurate empathy, be sure to make statements tentatively. What may be viewed as empathic and caring by one client may be viewed as insensitive and intrusive by other clients. Statements intended to be empathic that confuse, frighten, or anger clients are not successful. If you put yourself "in the other person's shoes"—you are more likely to accurately observe and translate social signals (such as smiles or frowns). Empathy training has been suggested as a way to decrease errors due to biases and stereotypes (e.g., see Arnoult & Anderson, 1988).

Related Behaviors

Many behaviors involved in offering accurate empathy are discussed later in this chapter. These include nonverbal behaviors such as posture, how we say things (for example, voice quality), and the words we use. In a classic study, Haase and Tepper (1972) found that nonverbal behaviors such as eye contact, trunk lean (forward or backward), body orientation (toward or away from a person), and distance from a person accounted for more than twice as many judgments of empathy as did verbal behaviors. If we are not good listeners, we cannot offer empathic statements. Low-quality listening will give clients the impression that you are not interested in or cannot help them. If you interrupt clients often and give excessive advice, they will not view you as empathic. Types of empathic responses include: (1) communicating understanding; (2) affirmations—validating client's experiences; (3) evocations which try to bring a client's experience alive, such as suggesting an appropriate metaphor, and (4) explorations that attempt to encourage clients to discover important information.

Common Errors

You may say nothing when you should offer an empathic comment (e.g., see Haley, 1969). You may offer advice when you should empathize with the client. You may respond to content rather than to feelings and content. Reflections, paraphrases, or interpretations may distort rather than correspond to a client's feelings, beliefs, or experiences. Stereotypes may interfere with offering empathic responses. You may offer solutions prematurely. Avoid statements like "I know what you are feeling," since you may be wrong and clients will think that you do not know what you are talking about or view you as patronizing. Examples of how to show that you appreciate someone else's experience are: "I think I'd feel the same way in your situation"; "This must be very difficult." Other errors include labeling and diagnosing (e.g., you have a dependent personality) and judging and evaluating (you were really aggressive). Avoid moralizing and preaching, as in "You should respect your parents," and patronizing reactions like "You'll get over it."

Other errors are (1) telling people what they should feel (e.g., "That's not the way to feel when you see her"), (2) an interrogative interview style, (3) overinterpretation, (4) self-disclosure that distracts attention from service goals, and (5) encouragement of dependence by offering excessive help. Examples of physicians' poor attempts at empathy when they must deliver bad news to patients are as follows:

> One 72-year-old woman with breast cancer confided to her consultant surgeon that she did not want to lose her breast, only to be told: "At your age, what do you need a breast for?" A woman of 40 with the same disease asked a different hospital consultant if there was any way she could avoid a mastectomy. He said: "There is not much there worth keeping, is there?"
>
> An elderly man with terminal lung cancer was asked by a junior hospital doctor why he was crying, and [he] explained that he did not want to die. The house officer's unsympathetic response was: "Well, we all have to die some time." (Collins, 1988, p. A7)

Being excessively self-preoccupied will limit empathy for others. Another way to fail to be empathic is by not giving clients the same choices you yourself would like to have (e.g., be informed about the likely effectiveness of different intervention methods).

Warmth and Genuineness (Congruence)

Warmth refers to the extent to which you communicate nonevaluative caring and positive regard for clients. Many behaviors discussed in this chapter, such as attentive listening, positive feedback, and respect, contribute to warmth. *Genuineness* can be defined as the extent to which helpers are not defensive, real, and not phony in their exchanges. They are themselves. They are "present." They are mindful. Congruence also refers to the capacity to communicate your experience with the client to the client (Kolden, Klein, Wang, & Austin, 2011). As with other skills, their use may have to be individually tailored for different clients. Questionnaire items tapping congruence include "I feel that he is real and genuine with me" and "He is openly himself in our relationship" (p. 193). Genuineness may entail sharing life experiences such as "I feel _____ when _____." *Phoniness* refers to saying one thing and doing another. Like other attributes, being genuine involves offering some actions and avoiding others such as intellectualizing and distancing responses. Not hiding behind a professional role to protect yourself or to substitute for helping clients is one aspect of genuineness discussed by Egan (1994). An example of hiding behind a professional role is saying, "I'll decide whether or not we are making progress at the proper time" in response to a question about progress. *Spontaneity* involves weighing what is said only as necessary and otherwise drawing on skills in a flexible way.

Nondefensiveness refers to responding in a nonhostile, non-aggressive exploring fashion when confronted with disagreement or negative information about yourself and an openness to listening to criticism in which negative comments are viewed as an opportunity to explore what you can learn and/or how a goal can be achieved (see chapter 16 for guidelines on responding to criticism). *Consistency* means matching words, feelings, and actions.

Other aspects of genuineness include *self-disclosure, confrontation,* and *immediacy.* The purpose of immediacy is to help clients understand themselves better by discussing some aspect of the immediate exchange. For example, perhaps a client often interrupts you. You could point this out, discuss the effects of such behavior, and suggest alternatives. As with any other skill, effective use is demonstrated both by engaging in it when it would be helpful and by not engaging in it when it would not.

Attentive Listening

Good listeners are oriented to other people rather than to themselves. They are good observers of other people. They accurately note what others say and how they say it, as well as nonverbal cues. "Good listeners are committed to listening, are physically and mentally ready to listen, wait for others to complete their statements before speaking, and use their analytic skills to supplement rather than to replace listening" (Stuart, 1980, p. 224). They listen rather than judge. These features increase the likelihood of understanding clients' experiences and feelings and communicating this to clients. A commitment to listening means believing that what other people say is important, suspending your assumptions and judgments about people, not asking for additional information until people complete their statements, and making comments and questions that follow from other people's statements. Careful listening is aided by the assumption of ignorance (Kadushin & Kadushin, 1997). Thinking that we know something may prevent hearing what is said. We tend to see what we expect to see and readily infer trait like qualities about others and overlook situational influences (see chapter 8).

Accurate paraphrases and reflections are part of attentive listening. They communicate that you are interested in understanding what is said and offer an opportunity to check your understanding. In addition, they help clients clarify their thoughts, focus attention on particular topics and encourage further exploration, and convey concern for what clients view as important. Meanings that are only hinted at may have to be checked out, being sensitive to clients' comfort. Nonverbal behavior is important in showing that you are listening (see Exhibit 15.2). Avoid reactions that suggest disapproval (e.g., rolling your eyes, frowning).

Attentive listening increases the likelihood that clients share useful information and participate in agreed-on plans.

EXHIBIT 15.2

Checklist for Reviewing Listening Skills

_____ 1. Arrange a distraction-free environment.

_____ 2. Avoid interruptions and talking for clients (e.g., finishing their sentences).

_____ 3. Avoid distracting mannerisms.

_____ 4. Use facial expressions that reflect interest and concern.

_____ 5. Use postures that reflect interest and concern (relaxed but attentive, oriented toward others).

_____ 6. Use appropriate eye contact.

_____ 7. Match verbal and nonverbal behaviors.

_____ 8. Ask questions that reflect attention and concern.

_____ 9. Use facilitating seating arrangements.

_____ 10. Take appropriate steps to avoid or remove obstacles to communication.

_____ 11. Time paraphrases and reflections well and use empathic skills to communicate understanding of what clients say.

_____ 12. Use an effective variety of responses.

_____ 13. Use minimal encourages effectively.

_____ 14. Indicators of success:

  • Clients share relevant material.

  • Clients explore new views of concerns.

  • Clients complete agreed-on assignments.

  • Clients feel supported and more hopeful.

  • Clients keep agreed-on appointments.

Common Errors

Advice giving is a common error. People often want to be heard, to be understood without being given advice, suggestions, or interpretations, and they want recognition that they have been heard. Think about your own experiences. Sometimes you may just want to share your feelings about some event without being given suggestions about what you can or should do. Poor substitutes for listening include *responding with a cliché,* such as "That's the way the ball bounces," or *parroting* (repeating exactly) what was said (Egan, 1994). Minimal responses (e.g., "hmm") may not be enough to communicate understanding. Egan refers to these as *inadequate responses;* others may feel that they did not say anything worth responding to. *Ignoring what has been said* is another form of inadequate response.

Your statements may reflect inaccurate understanding, which is why you should offer paraphrases and reflections tentatively. *Tentativeness* indicates that you are aware that you may misrepresent what has been said and are open to being corrected. You might say, "You sound like you're angry with me, but I might be wrong." Do not *pretend understanding.* If you cannot follow what has been said, ask for clarification. You might say, "I'm not sure

I follow you. Could you go over that again?" Being long-winded may convey that you are more interested in talking about yourself than in understanding your clients. *Interpretations* of why a person feels a certain way is another poor substitute for listening. *Patronizing* comments like "You'll get over it" will offend people. Matching a person's tone and manner of speaking ("mirroring") can convey an understanding of his or her feelings. If someone is very sad, a happy tone will not demonstrate understanding. Avoid distracting mannerisms such as saying OK after each of your client's statements, rapidly nodding your head, or frequently gesturing with your hands. Some people jump in too quickly after others have finished speaking, thereby cutting off others who want to speak. Pausing a few seconds after someone stops speaking will give you time to decide what to say next and will avoid interrupting others.

Reflective and paraphrasing statements should be frequent enough to demonstrate understanding but not so often that they function as interruptions. A mix of paraphrasing content and reflecting feelings may be most effective. If a client stops speaking abruptly when you start to speak, it may indicate that you interrupted her. If you do not offer any feedback that you understand what has been said, clients may stop speaking because they assume that you are not interested in what they say. The percentage of time you spend listening rather than speaking will vary, depending on your goals. Criteria that you can use to judge the quality of your listening skills are that (1) clients share relevant material and participate in exploring factors related to complaints; (2) clients seem comfortable; and (3) you, your peers, or your supervisor can check many of the items on Exhibit 15.1. You could identify your biases about clients that may get in the way of effective listening by noting what you think a person will say at specific points.

Respect/Positive Regard

Respect includes involving clients as informed participants in decisions made, considering cultural differences, and not imposing values on clients. Considering client preferences and values is a hallmark of evidence-informed practice (see chapter 9). Other indicators that reflect the close relationship between evidentiary and ethical issues include use of effective intervention methods and monitoring progress so clients can see whether their time, effort, and perhaps money have been well spent. Avoid responding mechanically (conveying a lack of interest or regard), displaying a passivity that communicates a lack of regard, and imposing values on clients. If you show respect for clients, they are more likely to discuss difficult topics, explore how they may contribute to concerns, carry out agreed-on plans, feel better about themselves, and be more hopeful (see Exhibit 15.3). Conveying liking and respect for clients is related to positive outcome. Carl Rogers (1957) emphasized the importance of positive regard, genuineness, and empathy. Such regard may be especially important

---

EXHIBIT 15.3

Checklist Regarding Respect

_____ 1. Take the time to be informed about research findings that could benefit clients.

_____ 2. Accurately describe the evidentiary status of recommended methods and alternatives.

_____ 3. Offer clients effective methods.

_____ 4. Suspend judgment about people's actions until hearing their side of the story.

_____ 5. Focus on hoped-for outcomes of concern to clients.

_____ 6. Avoid offering premature advice.

_____ 7. Do not impose stereotypes or unhelpful negative labels on clients.

_____ 8. Actions reflect sensitivity to cultural differences in values, norms, and preferred communication styles.

_____ 9. Be aware of and alter personal biases that interfere with service.

_____ 10. Explain the rationale for recommended methods in language clients can understand.

_____ 11. Fully inform clients about the limits of available services (see number 2).

_____ 12. Identify and support clients' strengths and environmental resources; encourage helpful behaviors and beliefs.

_____ 13. Avoid imposing beliefs or outcomes on clients.

_____ 14. Offer attentive listening (see Exhibit 15.2).

_____ 15. Point out negative consequences of behavior when doing so is in the client's best interest.

_____ 16. Do not support dependent behaviors.

_____ 17. Follow through on promised actions.

_____ 18. Avoid criticizing or lecturing clients.

_____ 19. Indicators of success:
  • Clients discuss difficult topics.
  • Clients carry out agreed-on tasks.
  • Clients report that meetings were helpful.
  • Clients feel more hopeful.
  • Clients attain valued outcomes.

---

when there are differences between clients and helpers and/or coercive circumstances such as involvement of the criminal justice system. Conveying positive regard will help to support clients and their beliefs in themselves and encourage engagement (e.g., see Farber & Doolin, 2011).

Being Nonjudgmental

There is no more important task than being nonjudgmental. This does not imply that you should not identify and respond differently to helpful behaviors that should be supported and dysfunctional ones that should not. Indicators of judgmentalness include blaming or criticizing clients, imposing personal values about what outcomes are good or bad, and ignoring cultural differences in values, norms, or preferred styles of communication. Some helpers believe (incorrectly) that because they are trying to be neutral, they are not communicating their values to clients. In fact, helpers usually do communicate their attitudes and feelings to clients, either wittingly or unwittingly. Being nonjudgmental is difficult, since we are often unaware of our biases and how we communicate them. (See descriptions of the Implicit Association Test.) Biases may be difficult to identify because they are inherent in how problems are defined in a particular society, profession, or practice framework (see chapter 6). Judgments about what is best may be imposed on clients in the guise of "expertise" or "science" (see chapter 4). Exploring your own reactions to specific individuals, problems, or groups will help you identify biases that may affect your work.

Asking Helpful Questions

The questions you ask, the information you offer, and the behaviors you reinforce influence the focus of interviews. The importance of questions is emphasized at many points in this book (see, for example, chapters 10 and 15). Your questions direct attention to areas that you think are important. In this sense, they indicate what you think is relevant. Questions typically progress from the general, to the specific, to feelings. Functions of questions include expressing interest, encouraging participation, arousing interest, obtaining information (e.g., clarifying hoped-for outcomes and related circumstances), holding the client's attention, and encouraging new perspectives (e.g., see Cormier, Nurius & Osborn, 2009). Questions vary on a number of dimensions, including focus and allowed freedom of response. They may be open invitations (e.g., "What brings you here today?") or more direct (e.g., "Are you employed?"). They may ask for clarification ("Can you give me an example?") or encourage new ways to view concerns (e.g., "Could it be that…?"). They may direct attention to the past or present, feelings or actions, the self or others. Some questions encourage clients to offer more specific information (e.g., to move from vague to specific descriptions of concerns and related situations, such as "What did he do?" "What happened then?" "What did you want to happen?"). Whether you get a useful response is the key indicator of a successful question.

Ask *instrumental questions,* questions that contribute to helping clients. For example, ask yourself, "If I had this information, would it help resolve the problem?" A question may not be instrumental, for three reasons: (1) the hoped-for outcome is appropriate, but the question is asked in a way that is unlikely to achieve it (e.g., it is leading or garbled); (2) the outcome sought will not be helpful, no matter how the question is phrased; (3) the outcome sought is appropriate, but the person cannot provide it. Common errors include:

- Asking leading questions.
- Asking questions at the wrong time (they serve as distractions or interruptions).
- Asking closed-end questions calling for a yes or no answer when more information is desired.
- Asking irrelevant questions (knowing the answer will not be helpful).
- Asking more than one question at a time.
- Asking complicated questions.
- Asking a person why something occurs with the assumption that she knows the answer. (See also discussion of interviewer biases in chapter 17.)

The order in which questions are asked and whether they are framed in terms of possible gains or losses influences how people will respond. Unless you want to encourage a specific reply, your questions should not suggest answers. Some clients may feel uncomfortable and confused by an open invitation to talk. More focused questions may be required. Culturally preferred styles of communication will influence what is appropriate. Explaining the rationale for asking certain questions will help clients understand why you want this information.

Use *probes* (follow-up questions) to clarify ambiguities and seek additional details (e.g., "Could you tell me more about that?" "What do you mean by…?"). Sensitive topics are usually best approached in a gradual fashion in which less threatening questions are first posed (e.g., asking a client how she feels about someone else engaging in a certain act). More personal questions can then be asked (asking how she feels about doing this). You can introduce questions later if they make clients uncomfortable or if they do not respond. Hypothetical questions may be of value when clients are reluctant to share their views. You could ask a client who has difficulties with her partner what she thinks an ideal relationship would be like. Ask for clarification when a statement is unclear. You can check out your understanding by rephrasing the client's statements. The skills modeled in seeking clarification can be of value to clients.

Ask questions in a way that encourages clients to consider new, more helpful ways of viewing concerns and solutions. You could phrase them in a "Columbo" style: "Could it be that…?" Don't worry about asking questions in a standardized way. Let's say that you need examples of what a client refers to when she says that her son is "out-of-control." You might ask:

- Could you give me an example?
- Could you tell me about the last time this happened?
- What does he do when he is out of control?

EXHIBIT 15.4

Checklist for Reviewing Questions

_____ 1. Do not suggest answers (unless this is your aim).

_____ 2. Ask one question at a time.

_____ 3. Use probes to clarify content and direct exchanges.

_____ 4. Reflect understanding and consideration of clients' feelings and points of view.

_____ 5. Be brief and to the point.

_____ 6. Be well timed.

_____ 7. Relate to current concerns and related factors.

_____ 8. Ask what, when, where, who, and how often questions.

_____ 9. Avoid inappropriate "why" questions.

_____ 10 Reflect sensitivity to environmental causes of problems.

_____ 11. Reflect sensitivity to individual differences (e.g., in ethnicity, class, gender, sexual orientation).

_____ 12. Describe the rationale for asking questions as necessary.

_____ 13. Use intelligible and acceptable language.

_____ 14. Avoid intrusive questions (e.g., they interrupt clients).

_____ 15. Indicators of success:
  • Clients accept more helpful views.
  • Clients use constructive problem-solving language.
  • Valued outcomes and related factors are clarified.

You can use questions to regulate participation. People who hog the conversation do not ask many questions, do not bother to wait for answers to their questions, do not seem interested in what others say, and violate the question-listen-question rule, in which the conversation is turned back to the speaker. Use the following criteria to judge the effectiveness of your questions: (1) useful outcomes result, (2) questions make sense to clients, and (3) you (or your coworkers or supervisor) can check off most of the items on the checklist in Exhibit 15.4 when reviewing an interview.

Structuring Exchanges

Structured, time-limited approaches that are goal directed (that is a clear agreed-on agenda), clarify the roles of participants, and build on available assets in a step-by-step manner are more effective than less predictable approaches and have fewer negative effects (e.g., see Lambert & Ogles, 2004). Many

minority-group clients prefer these characteristics. Structured frameworks avoid Haley's (1969) prescriptions for failure: be passive, inactive, silent, and beware. Structuring interviews requires effective pacing and timing, maintaining focus, beginning and ending interviews effectively, and making smooth transitions (see Exhibit 15.5). The functions of structuring include:

• Creating a readiness appropriate to a task.

• Relieving anxiety due to uncertainty about what will happen.

• Gaining attention.

• Determining expectations and knowledge of a topic.

• Increasing motivation.

• Focusing on important tasks.

• Identifying ambivalence.

• Describing expectations and responsibilities.

• Offering information about tasks.

• Creating links with previous meetings.

Structuring should be carried out in a polite and informative manner. Role induction interviews, in which you review expected behaviors and the format you will follow, may encourage behaviors that "move things along." Written manuals or audio and videotape presentations may be used to inform clients about what will occur (e.g., Barlow & Craske, 2000).

Maintaining Focus

One of your tasks is to help people discuss concerns in a useful goal-directed fashion. It is your responsibility to maintain focus and to do so in an efficient yet comfortable way. Lack of focus results in drift. Reasons for a lack of focus include unclear goals, not identifying intermediate steps, stress (too much work), ineffective social influence skills, lack of assessment knowledge and skills, and a lack of preparation for interviews. A client's lack of focus may be related to fear of change, stress, fatigue, or avoidance of touchy topics. You can encourage focus by:

• Planning an agenda.

• Checking to see whether the agenda will contribute to helping your client.

• Identifying and focusing on outcomes that clients value.

• Enhancing your assessment knowledge and skills.

• Using effective social influence skills.

• Summarizing at the end of the interview what was achieved and the next steps to be taken.

EXHIBIT 15.5

Checklist for Structuring Interviews

_____ 1. Arrange a nondistracting environment.

_____ 2. Offer appropriate greetings.

_____ 3. Make a tentative agenda.

_____ 4. Review the results of assignments at the beginning of the interview.

_____ 5. Emphasize the purpose of the interview and seek the client's agreement.

_____ 6. Avoid irrelevant digressions.

_____ 7. Offer opportunities to clients to introduce material.

_____ 8. Make effective transitions.

_____ 9. Consider cultural differences.

_____ 10. Introduce difficult topics at appropriate times.

_____ 11. Maintain a comfortable pace (e.g., regarding sensitivity of content).

_____ 12. Use an effective speed of talking (not too slow or too fast).

_____ 13. Focus on client concerns.

_____ 14. Agree on helpful assignments.

_____ 15. Allow time for a comfortable ending.

_____ 16. Provide useful summaries.

_____ 17. Clarify the time and purpose of the next meeting.

_____ 19. Indicators of success:

- Useful outcomes result (e.g., helpful tasks are agreed on, useful data are gathered).
- Clients are as comfortable as possible.
- Clients report that the interview was useful.
- Clients feel more hopeful.

Focusing requires holding the clients' attention, encouraging them to participate, and redirecting the discussion when necessary in a respectful manner. Your options will depend partly on whether you are talking to clients, coworkers, or supervisors.

Clients may prefer to talk about topics that do not forward progress. Discomfort when discussing a topic or emergencies may require a temporary diversion from the main focus. Otherwise, center on key goals as efficiently and effectively as possible without unduly rushing clients, with due respect for cultural differences and attention to maintaining a collaborative working relationship. You may have to lead clients back to a question or reaffirm the purpose of the interview or remind clients of time limits. The focus of an interview may change based on new information. However, if problems shift often, possible reasons should be explored. Perhaps you have not identified areas of greatest interest to clients. Clients may be reluctant to assume any responsibility for achieving hoped for outcomes. They may anticipate negative consequences if outcomes are achieved. Perhaps you have not sought their commitment to pursue certain goals;

you do not have a client (see chapters 2 and 14). Clients may hope for instant change (a "magic bullet") and be disappointed and ready to move on to another area that may be addressed more quickly. Additional reassurance and encouragement may be required when clients are anxious or depressed. Encouragement and support may be needed to draw out quiet clients. You may have to restate questions in different ways, review the reasons for your questions, and offer reassurance about the likelihood of positive outcomes.

Punctuating Exchanges

Interviews have beginnings, middles, and endings and transitions within them. Greetings and partings are social "routines" that require certain reactions from participants. The word _routine_ highlights the importance of certain behaviors. Errors in greeting behaviors include mumbling (people cannot hear what you say) and asking a question but not waiting for an answer.

Transitions occur within interviews such as a change from clients describing concerns in a relatively uninterrupted fashion at the beginning of an initial interview to responding to questions designed to obtain specific information. Prepare clients for transitions by explaining why you are guiding the discussion in a certain direction, for example, toward specific examples of hoped-for outcomes.

Summaries provide an opportunity to check your understanding of what clients say and can serve as a transition to a new topic. You might say, "Mr. Rivera, let me see if I understand what you have said. You...Is this correct?" Be sure to wait for an answer. Breaking silences too quickly is a common error of beginning interviewers; clients may need time to think about your question and their answer.

Endings provide an opportunity to summarize accomplishments, offer encouragement and support, agree on and practice tasks to be carried out between meetings, reaffirm the importance of carrying out agreed-on tasks, and arrange the next meeting or review steps to be taken in contacting other sources. Summaries are selective. They emphasize important points and describe what remains to be done. Plan for endings in the beginning and middle phases of your interviews (consider how much time is available, what can be accomplished in this time, and next steps needed). People may feel rejected if you end conversations abruptly. Partings, like greetings, involve a social routine, a series of moves and options that offer opportunities for ending or extending conversations.

Clients may be reluctant to end a meeting because important topics have not been discussed. They may enjoy the conversation or still have unanswered questions. How you handle their reluctance to end an interview will depend on your goals. You might say, "Let's discuss this on _____ when we meet." Or you could extend the interview if it is possible and is warranted by what has been disclosed. If you do not want to continue the exchange, remain politely firm without being harsh or rude. Do not allow yourself to be pressured into continuing conversations that you want to end. (See chapter 16.) An example of a closing summary statement follows:

> Let's review what we accomplished. We've identified some changes you would like in your family and decided on a plan to get more information. Do you have any questions? (Pause for an answer. The client indicates that he has no questions.) If you have any questions when you get home, call me at the number I gave you or e-mail me and we'll see whether we can take care of them. We'll meet again on _____ of next week. I look forward to working with you, and I think we can make your family life a more pleasant one.

Meshing Skills and Pacing

Meshing skills ensure the continuity of content, timing, and turn taking (Trower, Bryant, & Argyle, 1978). Timing refers to the smooth sequencing of speaking turns and the avoidance of interruptions and speech delays. It also refers to the point in a conversation when a certain reaction occurs. Skill in turn taking will avoid interruptions and help you take up and hand over conversations. Interviews differ in their pace (duration of pauses between questions, speed of topic transitions, pattern of sharing feelings and discussing difficult topics, and rapidness of speaking). It may take time to remember what happened at a certain time. Describing difficult exchanges may take time and rekindle emotions. It may take time to tell the story related to concerns and hoped-for outcomes or difficult life events, such as the death of a partner. Given sufficient time, this sharing itself may have beneficial effects—but not if it is rushed (see also next section on silences). Clients may feel rushed and not understand what you say if you speak quickly and allow few pauses. Quick topic transitions may be confusing or anxiety provoking. Be sure to allow pauses after clients stop talking so that you do not cut them off prematurely. On the other hand, try not to waste time by allowing long pauses and speaking very slowly. It usually is best to introduce difficult topics gradually.

Avoid ending meetings with discussions of unsettling topics. Allow time at the end to shift to neutral content (if appropriate) and to reaffirm agreed-on tasks and the next meeting time. Research on psychotherapy emphasizes the importance of compatible matches between clients and helpers in style and communication in maximizing the likelihood of positive outcomes. An effective helper can be defined as someone who offers strong supportive relationships, and who individually tailors both discreet methods and relationship skills to the individual client and circumstances (see Norcross, 2011).

Silences

Silences serve many functions. They provide transitions to new topics and allow time for clients to recall important events, think about what has been said, and decide what they will say. Many silences are natural pauses in speech. Others are attempts to gain control of the interview or to avoid talking about unpleasant subjects. They may reflect uncertainty about what to say or an interest in letting others speak. Understanding the reasons for silences and responding correctly to them was found to be one of the three most important skills differentiating a positive skill group of social workers from a negative skill group (Shulman, 1977). When confronted with a long silence by a client, you could offer a minimal comment ("I see"), repeat or emphasize the client's last few words, or rephrase his or her last thoughts.

Encouraging Helpful Views and Behaviors

Encouraging helpful behaviors and discouraging dysfunctional ones is a key influence process during interviews (see Exhibit 15.6). Your questions and feedback focus clients on particular aspects of their environment, behavior, or feelings rather than others. Support desired behaviors by reinforcing them and modeling helpful reactions. You could, for example, model constructive reactions to mistakes by pointing out that everyone makes mistakes, describing one of your own, and reframing mistakes as learning opportunities. Your influence as a model will be greater if your clients view you as competent and as similar enough to them that you can understand them. Model presentation can be used to show clients how to carry out agreed-on assignments and to develop new skills. Helping clients become more aware of what they do and why they do it is a feature of all

---

EXHIBIT 15.6

Checklist for Encouraging Helpful Behaviors

_____ 1. Model helpful behaviors.

_____ 2. Prompt and reinforce helpful behaviors.

_____ 3. Do not reinforce unhelpful behaviors.

_____ 4. Avoid criticism and negative comments.

_____ 5. Use personalized examples.

_____ 6. Encourage process language.

_____ 7. Avoid unnecessary confrontations.

_____ 8. Avoid premature interpretations and advice.

_____ 9. Avoid unsupported (or wild) speculations.

_____ 10. Seek clients' reactions to views suggested.

_____ 11. Use language that is intelligible to participants.

_____ 12. Note disadvantages of behaviors that lead to unwanted consequences.

_____ 13. Indicators of success:
- an increase in helpful behaviors
- a decrease in unhelpful ones

helping approaches. Characteristics of helpful feedback include the following:

- It is descriptive rather than evaluative.

- It refers to specific behaviors.

- It focuses on positives.

- It uses process rather than terminal language (i.e., it concerns things that can be changed).

- It is offered when people are most open to receiving it.

- It is offered in an appropriate manner so that clients will be most likely to receive it.

- Statements should begin with "I."

- It is based on data that support it.

Be sure to reinforce clients for clearly describing concerns, desired outcomes, and related factors including statements recognizing the role they play in maintaining problems. This can be done by prompts (e.g., questions) and feedback (head nods and minimal encouragements such as "Go on, please"), interpretations, and reflections. You can play an active role in laying the groundwork for helpful statements by the questions you ask. A teacher may say, "I wonder if I am encouraging this annoying behavior by attending to it every time it occurs." You might say, "That's a good point, and it is a possibility." In this statement you support the teacher's efforts to be helpful and encourage her to consider the role she may play in maintaining behaviors of concern. Reactions that are not helpful can be discouraged by ignoring them (if appropriate) and by prompting and reinforcing desired alternatives. Clients often accept causal assumptions or make statements of blame that do not offer any clues to how things can be improved (e.g., "I was born this way," "You're just like your mother," "It's in my genes"). This kind of terminal language (no guidelines for removing complaints are offered) prevents the discovery of useful options and encourages negative expectations. More helpful alternative views can be suggested.

Confrontation

Gerald Egan defines confrontation as "a responsible unmasking of the discrepancies, distortions, games, and smoke screens the client uses to hide both from self-understanding and from constructive behavior change" (1975, p. 158). It is "an invitation to examine some form of behavior that seems to be self-defeating or harmful to others and to change the behavior if it is found to be so" (Egan, 1982, p. 186). One purpose of confrontation is to help clients increase their awareness of discrepancies in what they do, think, or feel. For example, a client may say his problems really do not matter but show by his demeanor and past actions that they do. A client may say she is comfortable but reveal by her nonverbal behavior (fidgeting and trembling) that

she is not. Not following through on agreements is common. For example, a client may agree to carry out a task, but not do so. Possible reasons should be discussed. You might say, "Let's make sure that we both understood and agree on what was to be done and why." You can be firm and supportive at the same time. You could remind clients that they will have to shoulder some of the responsibility for achieving desired outcomes, empathize with the effort that will be involved, and reaffirm your support. Per-haps you should reassess your overall service agreement. Discussing discrepancies may encourage more helpful views of events and new ways of acting.

The term *confrontation* implies conflict and negative impact. Negative (compared with positive) feedback decreases risk-taking and performance. Thus, be cautious in using it. Avoid criticism and lecturing. Such behavior may result in "alliance ruptures—a breakdown in a collaborative working relationship" (see Safran, Muran, & Eubanks-Carter, 2011). Confronting and teaching increase client resistance (Patterson & Forgatch, 1985). These behaviors are less likely to have this effect if used together with supportive or joining responses, as well as reframing of concerns and goals in a way that complements clients' views (Chamberlain & Baldwin, 1988). The purpose of confrontation is to help clients, and so it should be done in a manner that minimizes the likelihood of defensive reactions. It should not be accusatory but, rather, constructive. Use specific examples. Timing is important. That is, consider the client's readiness to handle the confrontation.

Examining your motives will increase the likelihood that confrontations are for the benefit of clients rather than for your benefit (to defend yourself, for example). Clients may be pessimistic about the prospect of change or whether a procedure will be effective. Directly confronting negativism ("I won't" or "I can't") is *not* likely to be helpful. Clients often have good reason to think that assurances of success are empty, especially if they have a history of failing to resolve a problem. You may learn valuable information by exploring the reasons for negative reactions. You may decide to focus on the positive aspects of your clients' statements and to ignore the negative comments. Or you could relabel or reframe negative views in a positive way. For example, the loss of a job may be viewed as an opportunity to find more rewarding employment. Clients may react to confrontation by questioning your credibility, trying to convince you that your views are wrong, minimizing the importance of what you say, seeking support elsewhere, or agreeing with your views but saying "I can't." Take advantage of disarming comments—recognize the truth in critical comments to convey empathy for clients (Burns, 2004).

Practice in some contexts such as child protection and criminal justice often requires confrontation. A reluctance to do to when needed may result in inappropriate reactions such as being placating or evasive to avoid negative reactions. Some examples are noted below:

1. Not asking difficult questions or challenging inconsistencies and evasion.

2. Giving unrealistic assurances. (For example, saying, "This will not result in your child being taken into care" when that is a possibility.)

3. Crossing professional boundaries in a desire to establish your credentials or concern, for example, by discussing your personal problems.

4. Avoiding meeting hostile family members, so missing out on part of the picture.

5. Denying what you have observed, for example, giving an account of a case to a supervisor in which you do not give the full story, or put a favorable gloss on it.

6. Avoiding the child who is the subject of concern and forming an alliance with the parents (Beckett, 2003, p. 48).

Beckett suggests that resorting to punitive practices is another dysfunctional way of handling confrontational situations. Examples include: (1) adopting a cold official manner; (2) making threats; (3) hiding behind the system. Statements that reflect this approach are:

- "Of course, if it were up to me, I wouldn't make you go through this.

- I don't want to call a child-protection conference, but my boss says I've got to.

- I know there are a lot of stupid questions, but I'm afraid we've got to fill in this form for the file." (p. 49)

Interpretations

Interpretations often refer to material expressed only implicitly. In this way, they differ from listening responses. This view of interpretation is similar to Egan's advanced accurate empathy (see the earlier discussion). Interpretations may help clients to understand relationships between events, consider troubling feelings and behaviors from a different perspective, and act more effectively in real life. The emphasis of many practice approaches, including the one described here, is on current behaviors, thoughts, or feelings and related factors, not on past hidden meanings. Avoid premature interpretations and suggestions (those that result in negative reactions rather than enhanced understanding). Premature interpretations decrease the likelihood of client engagement. Overuse of interpretations may reflect a belief that you have "an inside track" on "the real meanings" or an unwarranted belief in a client's potential to alter behavior, thoughts, or feelings based on interpretations.

Focus on service goals to guide your actions. More helpful views may emerge only after behavior changes. Do not offer advice or suggestions unless you have a sound basis for doing so, for example, as a result of consulting related research findings. This may offer the information necessary to identify promising options. (However, you may have to take immediate action if there is a crisis.) Clients may react to inquiries or statements not intended as suggestions as advice. To avoid this, you could preface your comments or questions with "I am not suggesting this, but…" Be sure to consider cultural and educational differences when planning what to say and how to say it.

If you follow these guidelines, you will be less likely to be met with negative reactions, such as clients' saying "It's not so," "It won't work," "I won't do it," "I can't do it," or "This is a waste of time." You can judge your success in part by the absence of these responses. Keep in mind that interpretations will not change behavior if needed resources, skills, or incentives are absent. In order to achieve most hoped-for outcomes, clients (or other persons) must act differently in real-life settings, and additional methods usually are required to bring this about.

Self-Disclosure

Sharing information about yourself can serve a number of purposes. You can use self-disclosure to encourage clients to share information or to appear less aloof and more similar to your clients. Answering personal questions can normalize concerns. Consider a developmentally disabled adolescent who asked his male social worker, "Do you masturbate?" This client had been referred because he was caught masturbating in a public men's room. The social worker's direct "yes" conveys the message that masturbation is not something to be ashamed of. The social worker helped this client distinguish between situations in which masturbation is acceptable and those in which it is not. Clients may ask personal questions because of concerns they have or because of a desire to become closer to you. Avoid brusque refusals to answer questions, throwing questions back in a condescending manner ("I wonder why you find it necessary to ask that?"), and giving overly long or involved answers that deflect attention from service goals.

Sharing personal experiences can encourage a positive relationship by conveying understanding of others' experiences. You can use self-disclosure to describe new ways of viewing a situation and possible options. You may share your reactions to a client to indicate how others may respond to him in situations of concern. Let's say that you are helping a shy client increase her social contacts and you notice that she rarely looks or smiles at you. You may point out that if you met her in a social situation and she acted this way, you would think she was not interested in meeting people or was depressed.

Too little disclosure maintains distance between people. Too much may create embarrassment and reluctant reciprocation of disclosures (Hill & Knox, 2002). Self-disclosure is dysfunctional if it takes up valuable time in non-goal-directed ways or if it is done in a "can you top this" fashion ("You think you have a problem? Let me tell you about mine"). Avoid self-disclosures that diminish your credibility. Self-disclosures that are not related to service goals are inappropriate, such as disclosures made because of a need for approval or to encourage a sexual interest. Cultural differences influence what, when, and how information is best shared.

Clarity/Concreteness

One of your tasks is to help clients clarify concerns and related factors in order to reveal options. The term *concreteness* refers to the clarity of questions, statements, and information. Clarity is necessary in regard to feelings, thoughts, behavior, and related factors, as well as personal, family, and community resources. Because it is so important, it is singled out here for a separate discussion in addition to related content in chapters 12 and 13. Encourage clients to move from vague to specific descriptions. If problems and related factors remain vague, identifying hoped-for outcomes and choosing effective plans to achieve them will be difficult. Speaking in generalities will be helpful only if you wish to avoid clear identification of an issue or concern. And clients may wish to do so. Use the following criteria to explore whether questions, statements, and information are clear:

- Specific examples of concerns and desired outcomes are obtained.

- Cues and consequences related to behaviors of concern are clearly described.

- Plans for achieving desired outcomes are clearly described.

- Clear relevant progress indicators are identified.

Other Important Relationship Skills

Helpers differ in the warmth and friendliness they show to clients. Helpers who had higher scores on the Helpers Alliance Scale showed greater warmth, friendliness, and more affirmation and understanding compared to counselors with scores that were lower (Najavits & Strupp, 1994). If you are friendly (smile, offer attentive listening), other people are more likely to be friendly in return. These reactions contribute to empathy, which is related to outcome. On the other hand, if you act superior to others, contradict them, and "put people down," they are likely to offer you negative reactions and to dislike you. Friendly people offer attention, share information about themselves, and are supportive rather than rejecting. You can enhance your rewardingness by pointing out similarities between yourself and others, offering praise, indicating a willingness to help out of genuine concern for others, and conveying that others are worthwhile despite their shortcomings. People viewed as friendly keep criticism to a minimum and offer positive feedback. They use praise, encouragement, compliments, and sympathy. People viewed as unfriendly or anxious are not as supportive. They often turn

or look away when others speak or may "look through" people. They may assume a defensive, closed posture. They might recoil or flinch when touched or approached; they frown and may be preoccupied with self-grooming and offer only brief glances.

Helping clients may require negotiating, mediating, and bargaining skills, as well as skills in chairing meetings and participating in case conferences. You often will have to be persistent and should use language that is compatible with the values and language of others. You will have to learn how to handle difficult people and turn potentially negative encounters into positive ones (see chapter 16).

Offering support and providing reassurance are key helping skills. This involves relationship skills such as attentive listening, being nonjudgmental, and showing respect, empathy, and warmth. You may validate clients' concerns and highlight client strengths (e.g., particular coping skills). Offering support and reassurance encourages clients' involvement and helps create an atmosphere of warmth and understanding. Effective helpers encourage clients to feel more hopeful and to give themselves positive feedback for useful skills and viewpoints. Flexibility in creating and maintaining a relationship that matches the needs and characteristics of each client contributes to positive outcomes (see Norcross, 2011). Successfully presenting yourself to clients as competent—as someone who has the knowledge and skills needed to be of help and the motivation to use this knowledge in the client's best interests—contributes to positive exchanges.

Humor may lighten a difficult conversation or put matters in a more realistic, hopeful perspective. Some helpers take themselves too seriously. They may appear depressed but may not be aware of this. Humor can transform a potentially divisive exchange into a positive one. What is funny varies from person to person. Timing is important, as well as similarity of values and attitudes (for more detail, see Strean, 1994).

Challenges

Challenges include gaining access to effective training programs and ongoing feedback that will help you to enhance your relationship skills. Factors that Lambert and Barley (2002) believe compromise helpers' skill in relating in an empathic and genuine manner include: the increasing influence of managed care, insistence on cost-effective symptom reduction, ascendancy of manual-based therapy, increasing caseloads, and an increase in paperwork (p. 27). These concerns highlight the relationship between work stress and relating sensitively and flexibly to each client (maximizing components of the helping relationship that contribute to positive outcomes). Monitoring the helping alliance is important. Client change occurs sooner rather than later over meetings, and it is thus important to gain feedback. Gaining such feedback enhances retention and outcome (Miller et al., 2006). Many helpers do not detect deteriorating client–helper relationships. This is why regular feedback is so important via a user-friendly checklists completed by clients after every session. David Burns (2004) has collected hundreds of these which show a low correlation between client and helper views. That is, helpers who think the session was great are usually wrong and vice versa. Owen and Imel (2010) describe a number of easy-to-use client feedback forms. (See also http://www.talkingcure.com; and Miller, Duncan, Brown, Sorrell, & Chalk, 2003.) Regular checks on the alliance allows discussion of client concerns at an early point. This serves a preventative function. It also provides vital feedback that can help you to enhance your skills. Electronic forms of feedback could be used. (See Lambert & Shimokawa, 2011 for further detail.)

Improving Your Skills

One of the advantages of being a professional is that you can continue to learn during your career. For any situation there is a range of options (the operant class) that may be used to attain a given outcome (see chapter 7). This is partly what accounts for "style." You can increase your success by becoming familiar with what impressions you make on others and by acting in ways that complement your goals. There is a relationship among self-concept (what we believe about ourselves), social identity (how others regard us), and impression management (signals we offer to others to influence our social identity) (Schlenker, 2003). Our self-presentation may be faulty in a variety of ways. We may offer too little, too much, too dull, or misleading information. The social signals we offer influence other people. For example, if a client tries to define a situation as one in which sexual advances are permitted, you can discourage this view by offering incompatible images (e.g., being task focused).

Components of Effective Social Behavior

Your behavior is effective if you influence the behavior and feelings of others in ways that you intend and that benefit clients. Exhibit 15.7 shows possible goals. Effective behavior avoids problematic situations and/or alters them so they are no longer worrisome and offers a maximum of positive consequences and a minimum of negative ones to you and others. Understanding the components of effective social behavior will help you plan how to improve your relationship skills and to help clients to enhance their skills.

Knowledge of Situational Requirements and Options

As with all skills, their effective use requires identification of when they will be of value. Effective social behavior is situationally specific. The particular behaviors required for success

---

EXHIBIT 15.7

Examples of Goals in Helping Clients

1. Provide support. Provide a warm, empathic environment, increase trust and rapport, and establish a positive relationship; help clients feel accepted, understood, comfortable, and reassured; give clients a chance to talk about their feelings and concerns.

2. Set limits. Establish goals, objectives, rules, or parameters (e.g., time, agreed-on tasks).

3. Obtain information. Clarify concerns and related factors; identify resources.

4. Give information. Share relevant research findings, correct misperceptions or misinformation, and explain reasons for recommended procedures. (See chapter 24.)

5. Maintain focus; structure the discussion.

6. Increase hope; increase expectations that positive outcomes are possible and that you can help clients.

7. Relieve distress.

8. Identify helpful and unhelpful thoughts or attitudes (e.g., "I must be perfect").

9. Identify and give feedback about behaviors of concern and/or their consequences.

10. Increase self-management skills of value in attaining hoped-for outcomes.

11. Help clients identify, alter, and/or accept their feelings as appropriate.

12. Increase clients' understanding of factors related to complaints.

13. Enable change; enhance clients' skills; create more helpful views.

14. Support new ways of acting.

15. Overcome obstacles to valued outcomes.

16. Prevent or repair problems in the helping relationship.

17. Meet your needs; protect yourself.

Source: Based on C. E. Hill & K. E. O'Grady (1985). List of therapist intentions illustrated in a case study and with therapists of varying theoretical orientations. *Journal of Counseling Psychology, 32,* 8.

---

depend on the situation. Each situation can be considered in terms of:

- *Goals* that are attainable.

- *Rules* about what may or may not be done in the situation.

- *Special skills* that are required.
- *Roles* that are required or acceptable.

Rules are shared beliefs about what reactions are permitted, not permitted, or required in certain situations. Knowledge about required or expected roles in specific situations and about typical behaviors in them will help you to accurately interpret reactions and respond effectively. Cultural differences must be considered (e.g., Ponterotto et al., 2010). Roles are positions occupied by people in a situation and are associated with certain expected behaviors. Examples include parent, client, and counselor. Lack of knowledge about expected behaviors in given roles may result in inappropriate behavior and negative consequences. For example, putting your feet up on your desk when interviewing a client is not likely to create rapport and communicate respect. Power relationships between people influence options. French and Raven's (1959) classic description of different sources remains a useful one:

- Reward power (the ability to reward others).
- Coercive power (the ability to punish others).
- Expert power (others believe that you possess knowledge and/or skills that are useful to them).
- Referent power (influence based on liking).
- Legitimate power (others comply because they believe they should; for example, a security guard asks people to leave the premises).

Goals, Plans, and Feedback

Whether you achieve your goals depends in part on whether your goals complement those of others. You are more likely to be successful if you identify your goals, plan how to achieve them, and pursue realistic ones. You can increase your effectiveness by paying attention to how others respond and modifying your behavior accordingly. People who are not effective often fail to pay attention to the impressions they create, misinterpret reactions, or do not change their behavior to enhance their success. Some helpers fall into *social traps* (actions that result in immediate positive effects but have long-term negative consequences). For example, a clever put-down may give you some immediate pleasure but may create negative feelings that decrease the likelihood of influencing others in the future, such as the gatekeepers of services that clients need. People differ in how much attention they pay to themselves in social situations. Low or high degrees of self-monitoring interfere with the effective use of feedback from others. Setting goals in a "must" or "should" form ("I must get this teacher to cooperate") may interfere with accurate perception and interpretation of social signals, as well as with skilled reactions on your part. For example, your urgency may dampen your sense of humor. Feelings of entitlement tend to generate dysfunctional emotions such as anger.

Perception and Translation of Social Cues

You will be more effective if you accurately perceive and translate (interpret) social cues. Not only is it important to perceive that a person is smiling, it also is important to translate the meaning of this smile accurately. Is it a sign of friendliness or a sign of hostility? Skill in one area (interpreting facial expressions) does not necessarily mean that other skills are present (communicating emotions accurately). Accurate perception and translation of social cues depends in part on your knowledge of the preferred communication styles of others. Communication patterns are influenced by our past experiences. African Americans' history of slavery encouraged use of indirect expressions of hostility, aggression, and fear. This history increased sensitivity to nonverbal cues and encouraged use of subordinating behaviors to avoid negative consequences. Compared with whites, African Americans place greater emphasis on nonverbal behaviors and believe that they are more accurate indicators than verbal behaviors are of how people feel and what they believe. In the Chinese culture, eyes are used as key cues to identify and interpret the facial expressions and social intention of others (Mai, Ge, Tao, Tang, Liu, & Luo, 2011). Past experiences with oppression and discrimination may make it difficult for African American clients to respond to a white social worker as an individual person rather than as a symbol of the establishment. Mistrust and guarded reactions are understandable. No matter how good your cross-cultural helping knowledge and skills may be, they may not alter reactions based on past experiences. Understanding the origin of reactions that make helping difficult (e.g., "testing," anger, mistrust, and/or accusations of racism) increases the likelihood of effective responses.

Verbal Behavior (What Is Said)

The verbal behaviors discussed in this chapter include clarity, self-disclosure, and questions. Length of speaking also is important: you may speak too little or too much in interviews. What is "too much" or "too little" depends on your goals, as well as client preferences perhaps influenced by cultural differences. Try to balance talking and listening in a way that maximizes the likelihood of helping clients. Guidelines for increasing or decreasing participation are described in chapter 16. Norms concerning directness vary from culture to culture (e.g., regarding how to refuse requests). Differences in communication styles may result in misunderstandings if overlooked. English people tend to be direct and frank, even blunt in public discussion. Anglo-Americans are less so and Asian Americans tend to be less direct than Anglo-Americans. Chinese Americans and Japanese Americans may view bluntness as rude, even when frank discussion is needed to make decisions (Nisbett, 2003).

Voice Qualities

Our attitudes are communicated more by how we speak than by the words we use. The word *paralanguage* refers to qualities such as voice loudness, silence, hesitations, speed of talking, and inflections.

Loudness

If you speak too softly, you might irritate others or be ignored. A soft voice volume can indicate submissiveness or sadness, whereas a louder volume can indicate confidence and dominance. Talking too loudly may offend people. Changes in voice volume can be used in conversation to emphasize points. Asians, Latinos, and Native Americans tend to speak more softly compared to Anglo-Americans.

Tone

Some people have nasal, thin voices, and others have full, resonant voices. Different tones convey different emotions. For instance, a flat, monotonous tone may give the impression of depression.

Pitch

Different combinations of pitch and loudness communicate different attitudes and emotions. People may be perceived as more dynamic if they often change the pitch of their voices during a conversation. You can increase or decrease the pitch of your voice to indicate that you would like someone else to speak.

Clarity

Some people slur their words, and others speak with a heavy drawl or accent or in a clipped or choppy manner. These speech patterns can be difficult to follow. A very clipped manner of speaking might suggest anger or impatience, whereas a drawl might suggest boredom or sadness and be difficult to understand.

Pace

If you speak very slowly, listeners may become impatient and bored. On the other hand, people may have difficulty understanding you if you speak rapidly. Slow speech can indicate sadness, affection, or boredom. Rapid speech can indicate happiness or surprise.

Speech Disturbances

Hesitations, false starts, and repetitions are common in everyday conversations. However, if they are excessive, they may detract from your effectiveness. Speech disturbances include many unfilled silences and excessive use of "filler words" during pauses (e.g., "you know" or sounds such as "ah"). A third type of disturbance includes repetitions, stammers, mispronunciations, and stuttering.

Silences

Silences have different meanings in different ethnic groups. In some Asian cultures, silence is a sign of respect for elders. Rather than a signal for someone else to take up the conversation, it may indicate an interest in continuing to speak. Effective interviewing requires a skillful use of silences (not jumping in too soon and interrupting others, not allowing long silences that make people uncomfortable).

Nonverbal Behavior

Nonverbal signals are more important than verbal behaviors in expressing attitudes such as friendliness. We can use nonverbal behaviors to indicate how we would like a message to be viewed (as serious or funny) and to mask negative reactions. Nonverbal and verbal behaviors may be used to detect deception (Vrij, Granhag, & Porter, 2010). Make sure your nonverbal and verbal behavior match (e.g., smiling when you praise someone). If you do not, people may think you are insincere. Gestures and facial expressions can make conversations more interesting, illustrate or give emphasis to what is said, and indicate topic transitions. We use nonverbal behaviors to "frame" statements (e.g., to indicate whether we want a statement to be viewed as funny or serious) and to regulate turn taking (to indicate that we are finished speaking or would like to speak). (See Knapp and Hall, 2010; Matsumoto, 2010; Richmond, McCroskey, & Hickson, 2008, for further details about nonverbal behavior.)

Nonverbal behavior reflects status differences. For example, women tend to smile more than men do and, in general, are more polite and accommodating. Be sure to consider gender, race, class, and ethnic differences when interpreting nonverbal behavior. Overlooking such differences may result in incorrect assumptions that clients are "out of touch" with their feelings. For example, the timing and duration of shaking hands differs in different cultures. Oppression, racism, and discrimination encourage sensitivity to nonverbal cues as a protection against negative consequences. One way to dismiss biased attitudes or patronizing reactions is to claim that the person is being overly sensitive.

Facial Expression

Facial expressions are indicators of emotions and attitudes, as well as "stress markers." For example, to change a statement into a question, you might raise your eyebrows as you raise the pitch of your voice at the end of a sentence. Facial expression and voice tone are the most important channels for indicating emotions and attitudes (Ekman & Davidson, 1994). Your facial expression should be compatible with your intentions. If you look angry while trying to convey a friendly attitude, you are not likely to be successful. Norms describe standards regarding what can and should be expressed and where. Norms related to the expression of emotions (masking and neutralizing what is felt, as well as regulating the intensity of emotions) vary among cultures. Smiling and laughter by Japanese clients may convey embarrassment, discomfort, or shyness rather than liking and positive affect. Skill in controlling emotions is valued in traditional Latino and American cultures. Lack of knowledge about cultural differences may result in incorrectly describing clients as inhibited or repressed or agitated and excitable.

Gaze

The term *gaze* refers to a person's "looking" behavior. Gaze has an important information-gathering function. Although gaze avoidance (not looking at others) deprives us of valuable information about how others respond, this may be the norm in some cultures in some situations. Gaze avoidance may occur because of deference to the speaker, fear of revealing feelings, or fear of negative feedback. We use gaze to express feelings, intentions (e.g., a readiness to communicate), and attitudes. Gaze also helps us regulate turn taking. There are strong norms regarding gaze, as shown by the discomfort we feel when someone stares at us. Norms regarding gaze vary in different groups. Looking at others when they are speaking is likely to increase the amount of time they speak, although in some groups, norms may dictate that the listener not look at the speaker, especially if the listener is in a subordinate position. Looking at others while speaking may add emphasis to what is said. African American people make more eye contact when speaking than when listening. Asians and Native Americans, compared with whites, have less eye contact. Head nodding and minimal responses such as "uh-hum" when listening are not as common among African American people. Not recognizing such differences can result in inappropriate reactions, as shown in the following example:

> For instance, one Black female student was sent to the office by her gymnasium teacher because the student was said to display insolent behavior. When the student was asked to give her version of the incident, she replied, "Mrs. X asked all of us to come over to the side of the pool so that she could show us how to do the backstroke. I went over with the rest of the girls. Then Mrs. X started yelling at me and said I wasn't paying attention to her because I wasn't looking directly at her. I told her I was paying attention to her (throughout the conversation, the student kept her head down. avoiding the principal's eyes), and then she said that she wanted me to face her and look her square in the face like the rest of the girls [all of whom were white]. So I did. The next thing I knew she was telling me to get out of the pool, that she didn't like the way I was looking at her. So that's why I'm here." (Smith, 1981, p. 155)

Posture and Position

We indicate our attitudes and emotions not only by our gaze and facial expressions but also by our posture and body position. The object is to convey a relaxed and confident posture while maintaining a socially appropriate posture and position. Tightly crossing your arms over your chest may give the impression of anger or tension. A forward lean (leaning toward rather than away from others) and arms and legs relaxed communicate warmth and friendliness. Indifference may be communicated by shoulder shrugs, raised arms, and outstretched hands. Anger is conveyed by clenched fists and forward lean. Slouched shoulders may convey a lack of confidence. In contrast, good posture—with the shoulders back in a relaxed position (not "at attention")—makes it more likely that others will view you as self-confident. How we position or orient our bodies (e.g., whether we face toward or away from others) communicates different degrees of intimacy or formality. The meaning of and reactions to different body orientations depend on a number of factors, including ethnic, status, and gender differences.

Proximity

Rules for proximity vary in different countries and ethnic groups. Knowledge about preferred distances will help you to respond appropriately. Preference for spacing will influence where people sit or stand. If you remain distant from others when you speak to them, you may unintentionally communicate unfriendliness or disinterest. If you approach people too closely, they may feel uncomfortable. People who like each other tend to stand closer together than people who do not like each other.

Gestures

We use gestures such as head and hand movements to reveal or conceal feelings. We can use them to add emphasis, to illustrate points, and to manage turn taking. You can encourage others to continue talking by nodding periodically. Some gestures, such as scratching yourself, covering your eyes, picking at your clothing, tapping your feet, or wringing your hands, can, if excessive, communicate discomfort or some other negative emotion. Both regional and ethnic differences may influence the kind of gestures and the situations in which they are used.

Touch

Touch communicates and influences emotion, status, and attitudes. It takes on different meanings depending on the situation. What kind of touch is appropriate depends on the situation and the relationship between the people involved. Norms for touching vary from culture to culture. Touching plays a role in communicating status or dominance. High-status people engage in more touching of lower-status persons. Norms for touching between men and women reflect status differences;

men touch women more than women touch men. People are more likely to touch each other when they are:

- Giving information or advice (rather than receiving it).

- Giving an order (rather than responding to one).

- Requesting a favor (rather than reacting to it).

- Attempting to persuade someone (rather than being persuaded).

- Engaging in deep rather than casual conversation.

- Attending social events such as parties (rather than being at work).

- Receiving reactions of worry (rather than communicating them).

You can avoid misinterpretations by complementing touches with other cues that match your intentions. For example, to get someone's attention, you could touch him on the arm while saying "Excuse me." You could avoid the mistaken perception of a touch as aggressive by accompanying it with a smile and appropriate comments. Here, too, cultural differences influence what will be effective.

Physical Appearance

You can influence how others respond by offering a physical appearance that complements your goals. Components of physical appearance include hair style, accessories such as jewelry, cosmetics (makeup, perfume), posture, neatness, cleanliness, and style of clothing. These characteristics convey impressions to others about our attractiveness, status, degree of conformity, intelligence, personality, social class, style and taste, sexuality, and age. Your skills, the extent to which people view you as similar or compatible to themselves, and their confidence in your ability to get things done affect how credible and attractive you appear to others.

Paying Attention to Cultural Differences

In our increasingly diverse society, attention to cultural differences is an ever greater concern. They range from language differences to subtleties in the meaning of specific nonverbal reactions (e.g., looking or not, expression in the eyes, smiling or not in certain situations) (e.g., see Cornish, Schreier, Nadkarni, Metzger, & Rodolfa, 2010). Familiarity with cultural metaphors and specific modes of expression will encourage engagement. Interviewing styles may have to be modified to consider cultural differences including differences in acculturation among different individuals (e.g., see Kohatsu, Concepcion, & Perez, 2010). As with all clients, attention to client values, hopes, and expectations is vital.

EXHIBIT 15.8

Troubleshooting Checklist

_____ 1. Were my goals clear?

_____ 2. Were they achievable?

_____ 3. Did I focus on common goals?

_____ 4. Did I focus on positive goals?

_____ 5. Did I have a plan? Was it likely to be effective?

_____ 6. What cues did I attend to? Were they relevant or irrelevant? Distracting or helpful?

_____ 7. Did I offer others a rewarding experience?

_____ 8. What did I do or think that was helpful?

_____ 9. What did I do or think that was *not* helpful (e.g., behaviors that occurred too often, too seldom, at the wrong time, or in the wrong form)?

_____ 10. Did I consider the perspective of others?

_____ 11. Were there special skills that I needed but don't have?

_____ 12. Was my self-presentation effective? Could it be improved?

_____ 13. Did I overlook cultural differences?

Enhancing Your Skills

There is a rich literature you can draw on to enhance your understanding of social behavior and to hone your relationship skills (see the references in this chapter, as well as Hargie, 2006; Cormier, Nurius, & Osborn, 2009; Duncan, Miller, Wampold, Hubble, 2010). Knowledge about cultural differences in interaction styles may be needed to respond effectively. First, identify the skills you would like to enhance. Find out if there is information available about what behaviors contribute to or detract from achieving a certain goal. You could use role playing to explore your current skill levels in relation to outcomes of interest. The more clearly you describe your goals and related skills, the easier it will be to determine your current skill levels, plan a learning agenda, and monitor your progress. You could videotape some of your interviews (with the clients' permission) and review them to discover skills that you would like to improve. You could keep a diary of situations you find difficult, noting the situation, your goal, and suggestions for increasing success. You could arrange "prompts" to remind yourself to use new skills (e.g., placing some object on your desk as a reminder). Exhibit 15.8 is a troubleshooting checklist.

Summary

Effective helpers have effective relationship skills, such as structuring meetings, attentively listening, offering constructive feedback, and being clear, respectful, empathetic, warm, and nonjudgmental. These skills are important to use with coworkers, supervisors, and other professionals, as well as with clients and significant others. Understanding the components of effective social behavior, such as selecting appropriate goals, knowing the rules concerning what may and may not be done in specific situations, and accurately perceiving and translating social signals will help you to discover what has "gone wrong" in problematic social situations. Knowing what not to do is as important as knowing what to do. Whether you achieve your goals will depend not only on your skills but also on the skills of involved others and the degree to which styles and goals are shared or compatible. Skill in avoiding or removing barriers to communication and sensitivity to cultural differences in preferred styles of communication also are important.

Reviewing Your Competencies

Reviewing Your Knowledge

1. Describe criteria for judging the effectiveness of questions.

2. Give examples of clear statements and questions.

3. Describe five ways to structure exchanges.

4. Describe behaviors that you should model during interviews.

5. Describe components of attentive listening, as well as common errors.

6. Distinguish between advanced and primary accurate empathy.

7. Identify poor substitutes for empathic responses.

8. Identify behaviors that should be avoided in order to be nonjudgmental.

9. Describe the functions of self-disclosure and give examples of situations in which this would be helpful.

10. Describe voice qualities and nonverbal behaviors that influence how others respond.

11. Identify components of a "friendly attitude."

12. Describe common errors in offering feedback.

13. Describe preferred styles of communication of different cultural groups.

14. Describe behaviors that communicate respect.

15. Clearly define your goals in specific social situations, and identify verbal and nonverbal behaviors that will help you attain them. Include behaviors you should avoid, as well as those you should offer.

16. Describe changes you could make in your self-presentation that would enhance your effectiveness in specific social situations.

17. Identify social skills you would like to improve, as well as the situations in which these would be of value. Design a program to increase your skill based on a description of specific verbal and nonverbal skills that influence success.

18. You can distinguish between attentive and nonattentive listening and identify related behaviors based on observation of videotaped exchanges.

Reviewing What You Do

1. You offer attentive listening (you can check many items in Exhibit 15.2).

2. You maintain a comfortable and effective pace during interviews, in both rapidness of talking and sensitivity of content discussed.

3. Your ratio of instrumental to noninstrumental questions is high (see Exhibit 15.4).

4. Your questions and comments encourage clear descriptions. (Rate each question and statement during an interview on a scale from 1 (not at all clear) to 5 (very clear).

5. You use personalized examples to support your explanations.

6. Your physical presentation increases the likelihood of attaining valued goals.

7. You provide helpful feedback.

8. You structure interviews effectively (see Exhibit 15.5).

9. You start and end interviews smoothly.

10. A review of your interviews shows that you are nonjudgmental.

11. You adjust your style of communication to match the styles of your clients.

12. You offer high levels of empathy and respect (see Exhibit 15.3).

13. You accurately identify the impressions you convey to others and their consequences.

14. You can describe what you would do differently to create more effective impressions in specific situations.

15. You use self-disclosure effectively.

16. Your nonverbal behavior matches your verbal behavior.

17. You take advantage of opportunities to prompt and support positive behaviors.

18. You ignore irrelevant and inappropriate behaviors.

19. You give criticism in a nonthreatening, constructive manner.

20. Your paraphrases and reflective comments are accurate.

21. You appropriately confront clients.

Reviewing Results

1. You attain a high percentage of your goals during social exchanges.

2. Other people succeed in attaining goals that are important to them in a high percentage of their exchanges with you.

3. Clients feel better about themselves.

4. Clients describe their exchanges with you as useful.

5. Clients carry out agreed-on tasks.

6. Clients achieve outcomes they value.

7. Clients give you high ratings of empathy, helpfulness, and warmth after each session.

16

Handling Challenging
Social Situations

OVERVIEW This chapter could be the most important chapter you read in this book to clients! It offers guidelines for creating and handling challenging social situations in your everyday work. These include introducing unpopular points of view, responding to criticism, and making and refusing requests. Advocating for clients requires speaking up rather than remaining silent in the face of discrimination and oppression. It requires taking action in the face of unfair agency practices that harm rather than help clients. Thinking critically about life-affecting decisions will involve asking colleagues to clarify points that they may view as self-evident when they are not. Helping clients requires critical appraisal of views, your own as well as those of others, including "experts." Making decisions that contribute to client well-being will require questioning claims made by your supervisor, your professor, and by authors of articles in professional journals and books. Raising questions that affect clients' lives is vital to a learning organization that values client safety and maximizes quality of services. Options for avoiding and handling emotional abuse, sexual harassment, and discrimination at work are also discussed in this chapter. Clients should not be patronized, abused, or treated unfairly, nor should you. The guidelines offered may have to be modified to consider different cultural norms for social behavior. For example, although not losing face is important in all cultures, the particular situations that result in "loss of face" may differ.

YOU WILL LEARN ABOUT

- Creating, as well as responding to, difficult social situations

- Assertive, passive, and aggressive behavior

- Interpersonal problem solving

- Raising questions and disagreeing

- Responding to criticism (feedback)

- Refusing requests

- Requesting behavior changes

- Responding to put-downs

- Handling emotional abuse, sexual harassment, and discrimination on the job

- Speaking more

- Listening more

- Obstacles to handling difficult social situations effectively

- Safety

Creating, as Well as Responding to, Difficult Social Situations

Client-centered social work practice requires creating, as well as responding to, difficult social situations, such as requesting changes in harmful agency policies . These situations may arise with colleagues, politicians, legislators, community members, administrators, and professionals in other agencies, as well as with clients (e.g., see Kowalski, 2002). Placing clients front and center requires thinking critically about decisions that affect their well-being. It requires raising questions that others may

prefer to remain unasked. Examples of useful skills are shown in Exhibit 16.1. Knowledge about cultural differences will help you to respond effectively.

Nonverbal behaviors such as eye contact or smiling may have different meanings in different cultures. Laughter may reflect embarrassment. Lack of eye contact may reflect deference (not disinterest). Misunderstandings due to cultural differences may result in lost opportunities to understand clients and their circumstances. Your past experiences will influence whether you view a situation as irrelevant, positive, or stressful (one in which there is some actual or potential harm or challenge). You could (1) seek information, (2) take direct action (change the environment and/or your own behavior), (3) do nothing, (4) complain, or (5) use a cognitive coping strategy. The last option involves altering what you attend to or how you view events. Examples include denial, avoidance, and detachment. You could, for example, reassess an imagined slight as irrelevant. Denial is often used in everyday life (Taylor & Brown, 1988). You may have grown up in a culture in which questioning authorities (e.g., your supervisor) was not allowed. Raising questions vital to client's well-being may feel unnatural and perhaps wrong. But helping clients, especially in these times of shrinking resources and continuing

---

EXHIBIT 16.1

Examples of Useful Social Skills

	Would Like to Work On	Fairly Competent	Very Competent
1. Raise questions about claims/points of view in a tactful manner.	_____	_____	_____
2. Request clarification (e.g., of vague concepts).	_____	_____	_____
3. Listen attentively (see chapter 15).	_____	_____	_____
4. Communicate understanding of other views.	_____	_____	_____
5. Prompt and reinforce desired behaviors.	_____	_____	_____
6. Remove cues for and ignore undesired behaviors.	_____	_____	_____
7. Recognize and accurately interpret social signals.	_____	_____	_____
8. Recognize and use feelings as clues to contingencies (see chapter 7).	_____	_____	_____
9. Balance talking and listening.	_____	_____	_____
10. Manage anger and anxiety.	_____	_____	_____
11. Refuse requests.	_____	_____	_____
12. Request behavior changes.	_____	_____	_____
13. Request favors.	_____	_____	_____
14. Respond constructively to criticism.	_____	_____	_____
15. Apologize when appropriate.	_____	_____	_____
16. Respond effectively to put-downs and discriminatory comments.	_____	_____	_____
17. Clearly describe expectations.	_____	_____	_____
18. Respond effectively to unwanted sexual advances.	_____	_____	_____
19. Neutralize and/or avoid hostile and violent reactions.	_____	_____	_____

bogus claims about what is true and what is not, obligates you to raise questions about practices, programs, and policies.

You can often avoid unpleasant social situations by planning ahead. For example, you may avoid social predicaments by reinforcing valued behaviors. Disliked behaviors often occur because positive alternatives are not reinforced (including approximations to them). So when you complain about someone, ask yourself: Am I reinforcing behaviors I want to increase or maintain? Am I reinforcing behaviors I dislike? Supervisors who complain about staff may not offer positive feedback for behaviors they value. Beliefs such as "She gets paid for this" or "She should know this" may interfere with supporting such behaviors. Developing effective skills for interacting with supervisors and agency administrators will help you avoid predicaments and acquire needed training. Drury recommends: "Don't undermine their authority; build a strong case for change (the more specific the better) and recognize norms and power dynamics in organizations" (1984, p. 255).

Assertive, Passive, and Aggressive Behavior

Some people are passive (e.g., say nothing) when they must speak up in order to attain valued outcomes such as decreasing discriminatory practices. Others are aggressive, they put people down and harshly criticize them. Assertive behavior involves expressing preferences without undue anxiety in a way that encourages others to take them into account and does not infringe on their rights, for example, to disagree with you (Alberti & Emmons, 2008). There is a focus on the situation or behavior rather than the person. Alternatives to aggressive reactions include clear requests and emphasizing common interests, for example, to help clients. Behaviors and outcomes associated with passive, aggressive, and assertive reactions are illustrated in Exhibit 16.2. Respect for your rights, as well as those of others, is integral to the philosophy underlying assertiveness. It is not a "do your own thing" approach in which you express your wishes, regardless of their effects on others, nor does it guarantee that you will achieve your goals. As with any new behavior, learning to be more assertive may feel awkward and unnatural at first. And, what will be effective in one social situation may not be effective in another.

Interpersonal Problem Solving

Your skills will be more than adequate in many situations, and you will not have to think much about what to do. In others, you may have to "problem solve" to decide what to do. Examples include:

- Staff who do not return your calls.
- Clients who talk too much.
- Clients who repeatedly interrupt you.

- Supervisors who harshly criticize you.
- Clients who physically threaten you.
- Supervisors who make sexual advances.
- Coworkers who put you down (e.g., make demeaning remarks).
- Coworkers who bad-mouth clients.
- Coworkers who arrive late for meetings.
- Situations that create anxiety or anger.

The problem-solving steps described in chapter 8 also are helpful in interpersonal problem solving (e.g., Beyth-Marom, Fischhoff, & Quadrel, 1991).

- Stop, calm down, and think.
- Describe the problem and how you feel.
- Select a positive goal.
- Identify options and consider the consequences.
- Try the best plan.
- Evaluate the results.

Stop, Calm Down, and Think

Stopping, calming down, and thinking will help you avoid escalating negative emotions that may result in selection of ineffective options. You could have a rule to count to 10. In most situations, it is good advice. However, there are situations in which this advice is not wise, those in which quick action is called for to prevent harm and violence. Use your relaxation skills to stay calm or to calm down. Helpful rules for keeping interfering emotional reactions in check are:

- Consider other people's perspectives (cultivate empathic understanding).
- Focus on service goals (shared interests).
- When in doubt, think the best (give people the benefit of the doubt).
- Ignore minor annoyances.
- Be sensitive to cultural differences in values, norms, and preferred communication styles.
- Catch and counter emotional "triggers" (e.g., "He is a _____," "I can't stand this").
- Reinforce behaviors you want to encourage.
- Do not reinforce behavior you dislike.
- Take a deep breath; count to ten.

EXHIBIT 16.2

Comparison of Passive, Assertive, and Aggressive Styles and Their Effects

	Passive	Aggressive	Assertive
Behavior Patterns	No expression of expectations and feelings.	Critical expression of expectations and feelings.	Clear, direct descriptions of unapologetic expectations and feelings.
	Views stated indirectly or apologetically.	Blaming and judgmental negative intentions attributed to others.	Descriptive instead of judgmental criticisms.
	Complaints are made to the wrong person.	Problems acted on too quickly.	Persistence.
	Problems not confronted soon enough. No persistence. Unclear negotiation and compromise.	Unwillingness to listen. Refusal to negotiate and compromise.	Willingness to listen. Negotiation and compromise.
Word Choices	Minimizing words. Apologetic statements. Statements made about people in general instead of to a specific person. General instead of specific behavioral descriptions. Statements disguised as questions.	Loaded words. "You" statements. "Always" or "never" statements. Demands instead of requests. Judgments disguised as questions.	Neutral language. Concise statements. Personalized statements of concern. Specific behavioral descriptions. Cooperative words. Requests instead of demands. No statements disguised as questions.
Voice Characteristics and Body Language.	Pleading or questioning voice tone. Hesitation. Lack of eye contact. Slumping downtrodden posture. Words and nonverbal behavior do not match.	Sarcastic; judgmental, overbearing voice tone. Interruptions. "Looking-through-you" eye contact. Tense, impatient posture.	Even, powerful voice tone. Eye contact. Erect, relaxed. Words and nonverbal messages that match.
Results	Rights are violated; taken advantage of. Not likely to achieve goals. Feels frustrated, hurt, or anxious. Allows others to choose for him or her.	Violates other people's rights; takes advantages of others. Achieves goals at other people's expense. Defensive, belligerent; humiliates and depreciates others. Chooses for others.	Respects own rights, as well as those of others. Achieves desired goals without hurting others. Feels good about self; is confident. Chooses for self.

Source: (First three sections only). S. S. Drury (1984). *Assertive supervision: Building involved treatment* (pp. 294–295). Champaign, IL: Research Press. Reprinted with permission.

Describe the Problem and How You Feel (to Yourself)

What exactly is the problem? Who is doing what (or not) to or for whom? Clearly describe the five W's: context (who, where, when), behavior (what), and effect (why). Use feelings of wanting to blame and punish others as clues to identify what you want and how you can achieve it. Awareness of how you feel in certain situations can help you understand and empathize with how others feel. Expand your vocabulary of words that describe different kinds and intensities of feelings. Larson (1993) underscores the importance of identifying your "emotional allergies" (incidents that "get under your skin" and interfere with task performance). If you know what these are and decide they get in your way, you will be ready to ignore them when they occur and to focus on helping clients.

Select a Positive Goal

What do you want? What would have to be different for the problem to be solved? The more clearly you describe what you want, the more information you can offer to others. Focus on positive goals. Rather than telling your supervisor, "I was dissatisfied with our last meeting," say, "I'd like more specific feedback from you about how I'm evaluating progress with Mrs. L."

Identify Options and Related Consequences

How can you achieve your goal? What are different options and the likely consequences of each? What obstacles might get in the way of promising options? What cultural differences should be considered? Ethnic and cultural factors influence what emotions people feel and how they express them. Unless you consider cultural differences, you may offend, frighten, or anger others. Indirectness is highly valued in some cultures. For example, people of Japanese origin consider it a sign of maturity and power. In his article "Sixteen Ways to Avoid Saying 'No' in Japan," Keiko Ueda (1974) includes the options of silence, ambiguity, and expressions of apology. Skill in carrying out on-the-spot cost-benefit analyses in which you review potential short- and long-term consequences of an action will help you make decisions (see Exhibit 16.3). Be sure to consider both personal outcomes (effects on yourself) and social ones (effects on others). Consider what you may lose by not doing anything. For example, if you do not ask your supervisor for more specific feedback, you may lose learning opportunities.

Try the Best Plan and Evaluate the Results

Try out the alternative that seems most promising for reaching your goals with a maximum of positive and a minimum of negative consequences to others, as well as yourself. If it is successful, use it on future occasions. If not, circle back to earlier steps. Have you overlooked cultural or ethnic differences?

The Importance of Flexibility and Persistence

Creating positive working relationships requires flexibility in adjusting your behavior to the behavior and interests of others. Such adjustments may involve pacing, content to focus on, degree of directiveness, and kinds and timing of encouragement to offer. In some situations, direct action (requesting or negotiating changes) may be most effective. In others, indirect methods may be best such as calming self-talk or delaying a reaction. What will be effective in one situation may not be in another. Your skills, the skills of others, the match between styles, the degree to which goals and values are shared, and the kinds of power people rely on (for example, punishment or reward) will influence options. You may decrease your success by relying on the wrong power base. For example, perhaps you have been trying to encourage an administrator to like you when demonstrating your competence would be more successful. Or you may be relying on criticism rather than praise. Keep in mind that agreements based on affection and understanding are more likely to be carried out in the absence of external control.

You will often have to be persistent to help your clients. Your first attempt to question a generally accepted point of view in a case conference may be ignored (see Exhibit 16.4). You may have to introduce your point more than once and should do so if this would be of value in helping clients and avoiding harm. For example, staff at a case conference may recommend that a youth be sent to a residential facility they saw advertised in

---

EXHIBIT 16.3

Cost-Benefit Analysis: Expressing Anger

Advantages	Disadvantages
1. I will enjoy telling him off.	1. Telling him off will make it more difficult to work together.
2. I have a right to tell him off.	2. He will avoid and not trust me.
3. I'll feel better letting him know how I feel.	3. Clients may suffer because we cannot work together well.
4. Other people will not give me grief.	4. I will be a poor model for others.
5. He won't bother me any more.	5. Telling him off will not solve the problem.
6. Others will see that I can take care of myself	6. He may make plans to get back at me.

Source: Adapted from D. D. Burns (1990). *Feeling good: The new mood therapy* (p. 151). New York: Morrow. Reprinted with permission.

EXHIBIT 16.4

Being Persistent in a Discussion

Situation:	Case conference
Supervisor:	Blandy Residential Center was advertised in *Social Work*. I think this setting would be a good one for Jim.
Social Worker 1:	Yes, I've heard about the center. Other agencies also refer to Blandy.
Social Worker 2:	I've visited the center and the staff seem very dedicated.
Social Worker 3 *(you)*:	Do you know anything about their success in helping adolescents like Jim?
Supervisor:	Well, they've been around for 50 years. They must be doing something right.
Social Worker 3 *(you)*:	Fifty years is a long time. I wonder if they've collected any data about how effective they have been.
Social Worker 1:	Well, let's see. Here's their brochure. It says they offer high-quality services and are sensitive to young people's needs. Sounds good to me.
Social Worker 3 *(you)*:	Sending Jim to Blandy means removing him from his home and neighborhood. I wonder if we could think of other alternatives.
Social Worker 2:	You're new here and don't know the limitations of our resources. I think we should refer him to Blandy.
Social Worker 3 *(you)*:	Yes, I am new to this agency, but I do think we are approaching this is in either/or terms—either leave him home or send him to Blandy. I think we need information about this center's success rate.

Social Work, which includes only testimonials in support of claims of effectiveness, and there are less intrusive options such as working with the youth in the community, which have been critically appraised and found to be effective. You may have to be persistent to obtain services for a client.

> As a youth [Pablo] sustained a traumatic amputation of his left leg below the knee. He lived alone and worked long hours as a cook....He kept himself isolated with few friends and no family....He worked for cash, had little savings and, of course, no health insurance. When his prosthesis broke, he could no longer stand without crutches. He lost his job and wound up in a shelter....We treated his stump, and referred him to the hospital-based clinic for a new prosthesis but learned that the "healthcare" to which shelter residents were entitled did not include prostheses. The shelter case worker deemed him ineligible for Medicaid. But an experienced social worker, new to our team, was sure that despite his alien status he was entitled to emergency coverage. She set out relentlessly to obtain it. After six months of filing applications and placing telephone calls on his behalf, the social worker obtained approval. (Savarese & Weber, 1993, p. 4)

You may have to keep trying to contact staff at another agency. You may have to e-mail a social worker to obtain housing for a client many times, as well as call her. Be sure not to criticize staff for not returning your calls when you do contact them. You might say "Hello, my name is _____ I am...I would like to talk to you about _____." Focusing on service goals will help you to handle difficult situations constructively.

Raising Questions and Disagreeing

Making well-informed decisions requires critical appraisal of claims about what is true and what is false. Thinking carefully about decisions requires raising questions such as: Do we know if this service really helps clients? Have there been any critical tests of the effectiveness of this service? Are there any data suggesting that this method may harm rather than help clients? Questions are needed to understand clients and to discover options. Disagreements are opportunities to forward understanding of clients and to discover options. One of the key ways you can contribute to offering clients services that do more good than harm is by learning how to raise questions in a way that encourages attention rather than dismissal or punishment. Also, being open to question yourself is vital. Your own views of asking questions may get in the way:

- Don't ask! It may have been discussed before.

- Don't ask. It may slow down the discussion or group.

- Don't ask. You may be the only one who does not know.

- Don't ask. If it is important, someone else will ask it.

- Don't ask. The other person (or group) may not want to deal with it now.

- Don't ask. Your question may be difficult to describe correctly.

- Don't ask! It may be too big an issue to discuss! (Matthies, 1996)

Raising questions requires courage. Focusing on helping clients will encourage speaking up (see Exhibit 16.5). Questions are welcomed in a learning organization in which freedom to raise concerns is recognized as vital to protecting clients from avoidable harms. Your work and learning environments may not reflect a culture of thoughtfulness in which alternative views are sought and welcomed (Gambrill & Gibbs, 2009). Raising questions may be viewed as signs of disloyalty, impertinence, or rudeness. Supervisors or teachers may respond negatively to questions and differences of opinion. They may confuse biased people with those who are expressing a point of view (and who are open to changing their minds). They may respond to questions as unwelcome challenges to their authority rather than as efforts to understand different points of view and to make sound decisions My students tell me that they are often punished for asking questions about what their professors say or field supervisors promote. This will not help clients.

Effective Disagreement

The answer to the question "What is effective disagreement?" depends on your goals, which could include the following:

- To discover options.
- To recognize shared concerns.
- To make sound decisions.
- To show how smart you are.
- To show people how stupid they are.

Pursuing the first three goals is more likely to foster constructive exchanges in which well-informed decisions are made. Be sure you understand a position before you criticize it. Check our your understanding of other views by paraphrasing what others say (see chapter 15). People are more likely to consider what you say if they are not offended by your style of expression. Recognizing points of agreement decreases the likelihood of defensive reactions and improves the chances of discovering shared concerns and goals. You are more likely to "be heard" if you raise questions tactfully at an appropriate time and acknowledge other views. You might say:

- "That's an interesting view. I like the way you.... Another approach might be..."

EXHIBIT 16.5

To Speak or Not To Speak

You will have many opportunities to protect clients from harm and ineffective service by questioning decisions and claims. Raising questions about ideas or claims other people take for granted requires courage, especially in environments in which disagreements are not viewed as opportunities to make sound decisions. You may overestimate the risk of negative consequences such as being "put-down" or being labeled a troublemaker. Think of a practice related situation in which questions should be raised about claims but are not. Clearly describe the situation, the claim made, questions you think should be raised, and why. Last, describe any obstacles and possible remedies.

Situation (what was said, where, when, by whom):

_____

_____

_____

What I wanted (or would want) to say:

_____

_____

_____

Describe possible positive and negative consequences of speaking up for clients, colleagues, the agency, the profession, and for you. Also, describe possible negative consequences for these groups.

_____

_____

_____

- "It sounds as if we both agree that this program would be helpful, but we seem to differ in how to pursue it…"
  "I think…because…"

Cultural differences influence who can question or disagree with whom, about what, when, and what style is most effective. Preferred styles range from indirect to blunt. In some cultures it is important to avoid conflict. Hierarchical relationships in some families and cultures require respect for certain speaking patterns (e.g., who speaks first).

Take responsibility for points you make by using a personal pronoun such as "I" or "my" and explain the reasons for your views. You might say, "That's an interesting point; however, I think…because…" Questions or disagreements that do not include elaborations may appear abrupt and do not explain the reasons for your position. Practice raising questions tactfully and responding constructively to reactions that do not foster a critical appraisal of claims that affect client well-being (e.g., put-downs and question begging). A constructive response results in minimal negative reactions and maximal positive reactions, including forwarding service goals. If you start to get upset, focus on service goals and do not take things personally.

Be sure to reinforce tolerant and open-minded reactions by attending to and commenting on them. You might say, "It's great to talk to someone willing to consider other views." If you change your point of view after a discussion, tell the other person. You might say: "I did not think of that. Yes, they offered only testimonials to support their claim that their residential program is 'effective.'" Do not let people neutralize you; if you do, clients may lose (see Exhibit 16.6). Whether used intentionally or not, they may derail critical appraisal of claims about what may help or harm a client.

Timing

Wait until other people finish talking before starting to speak, unless you are not receiving your share of talk time. If you interrupt other people, they might react negatively to the interruption and not consider your ideas. Raising questions and disagreeing with someone in front of others may be inappropriate in some cultures. This may result in a "loss of face" for the other person. Try not to violate the "pleasantness norm" during initial encounters by introducing a topic or opinion that will lead to conflict. Overlook minor differences.

What to Avoid

Avoid comments that put others down or embarrass them. Examples are: "You don't know what you're talking about" and "That's a stupid idea." Such comments are likely to result in counter aggression or avoidance. Excessive negative emotion will encourage defensive reactions and increase the likelihood of unproductive conflict. Your nonverbal behavior might communicate anger or annoyance as you express an otherwise effective message. Avoid the buildup of anger by learning to identify the beginning signs of irritation such as increased body tension and negative thoughts and using constructive self-statements (e.g., "Take it easy," "What's my goal?"). Unrelenting disagreeing or questioning with the goal of changing someone's mind can be unpleasant and is not likely to be effective. Furthermore, if you disagree with many small points, your disagreement with the big points may not be taken seriously. Some people show disagreement by withdrawing their attention (for example, looking away), leaving the conversation, or avoiding future contact. Silence is not a good option if you can achieve your goals only by expressing your views.

EXHIBIT 16.6

Responding to Neutralizing Attempts

Criterion	Reply
You're always questioning others.	I question myself, too. I think we have to raise questions about our decisions. They affect clients' lives. For example,…
You're not working as a team member.	I thought our purpose was to help clients and I think my questions forward this aim. For example,…
You're always bringing up minor points.	I think this point is important. For example, if…
We don't have time for these questions.	My questions concern the quality of services we offer clients. For example,…
I don't think you should be so critical of your colleagues.	My points are directed toward ideas, not people. Only if we are open to criticism can we learn from one another.
You're being hardheaded; it's caring that counts.	If we care about our clients, we will ask searching questions about whether our services help or harm them.

Handling Conflict

If a discussion seems to be escalating into a conflict, you could comment on this and suggest that you move on to another topic or remind participants about service goals. You might say, "We seem to have strong feelings about this issue," "Let's keep our clients' needs in view," or "Let's table this discussion for now and talk about…" (pause). You may have to bring in a mediator to move a discussion in a positive direction. Exhibit 16.7 is a checklist for disagreeing.

Responding to Criticism (Feedback)

Responding effectively to criticism, whether from yourself or others, is essential to learning and to maintaining constructive working relationships. Empathic reactions may help you to understand emotions and thoughts underlying criticism and to avoid defensive responses. People may criticize claims you make, the soundness of your reasoning, or your behavior.

EXHIBIT 16.7

Checklist for Raising Questions and Disagreeing

_____ Ignore minor differences.

_____ Focus on common goals (helping clients).

_____ Acknowledge other points of view.

_____ View disagreements and raising questions as learning opportunities.

_____ Make sure you understand other views. Acknowledge other people's cogent points, points of agreement, and mutual concerns.

_____ Avoid derogatory critical comments and negative nonverbal reactions (e.g., scowling).

_____ Don't interrupt people.

_____ Explain why you disagree or question views/claims (use elaborated opinion statements).

_____ Express differences as they arise when appropriate; don't allow frustration to build up or time for effective action may pass you by.

_____ Reinforce others for listening.

_____ End or avoid unconstructive exchanges if possible (you could suggest another time for discussion or involve another person).

_____ Consider cultural differences in norms, values, and preferred styles of communication.

Differences provide opportunities to make sound decisions and to strengthen working relationships. Different kinds of criticism include teasing, blowing off steam, and attempts at problem solving. Teasing may or may not reflect a real concern that should be addressed. Techniques Drury (1984) recommends for responding to teasing include using humor, ignoring, fogging (e.g., agreeing with some aspect of the implied criticism without agreeing with the implied judgment ("that may be"), asking the person to stop teasing, and commenting on the process (making an observation such as "I notice that…" and asking a question like "Is there a problem we should discuss?"). If teasing reflects an underlying concern, bring this into the open and discuss it. Blowing off steam is another kind of criticism in which someone may simply want to express frustration or anger. Attempts to solve a problem comprise a third form of criticism.

Common reactions to criticism (whether of a belief or a behavior) are (1) withdrawal (avoiding the person, escaping from the situation), (2) attack (name-calling, threats), and (3) defensiveness (counteraccusations, excuses, nonverbal indicators). Signs of defensiveness and closed-mindedness include an unwillingness to listen, raised voices, ridicule/mockery/disgust, crossed arms, shaking the head, rolling the eyes (e.g., Seech, 1993). Criticism may reflect a desire to maintain status or unrealistic expectations rather than the quality of your reasoning or the appropriateness of your behavior. Misunderstanding work roles may also be the cause. Consider the example Drury (1984) gives of the employee who accused a supervisor of being uncaring because the supervisor asked the employee to finish her work. That is, she saw the supervisor as uncaring because the supervisor was doing her job.

Responding constructively to criticism can prevent unfair blame. Intense reactions to criticism (prolonged sadness, anger, or hostility) may reflect unrealistic expectations about yourself (e.g., "I must never make mistakes") or others (e.g., "They have no right to question my behavior"). The guidelines discussed next mainly concern criticisms that are problem solving attempts. What you should do depends partly on the kind of criticism, how it is given, and your relationship with other participants.

View Feedback as a Learning Opportunity

The reactions of others offer clues about what they want and think. A supervisor who appears angry may not have shared all her concerns. Recognition of these "anger cues" can prompt a response such as "Is there anything else I should know?" Your critic may help you to discover flaws in your thinking or show you how to use a practice skill. They may locate a vital systematic review related to a decision you and your clients must make. Focus first on understanding your critic's point of view (e.g., what she wants, feels, or thinks) rather than defending yourself, making suggestions, or giving advice. Clients may "test" you by critical comments to see whether you are biased or uninformed about their culture. Being prepared for such tests will help you respond effectively.

Relax and Listen (as Appropriate)

Relax and listen (unless someone continues to verbally abuse you or there is a danger of violence). Attend to what is expressed both verbally and nonverbally. If the person is very upset (e.g., speaking loudly and fast), let him "run down" before you respond, unless he is offensive or potentially dangerous. When you do respond, avoid attacks and negative labels so you do not contribute to the emotionality of the exchange. Taking time to understand the criticism will help you learn, remain calm, and respond effectively. Other people will feel listened to. Steps that Drury (1984) recommends when criticism represents blowing off steam are (1) correcting misperceptions, (2) listening and asking for details to allow others to calm down, (3) identifying problems that should be discussed, (4) acknowledging the other person's feelings and perspectives, and (5) setting limits when people are violent or abusive, or when the time or place is inappropriate.

Check Your Understanding and Ask for Clarification When Needed

Check your understanding of what has been said by paraphrasing it and reflecting the feelings expressed (see chapter 15). This will indicate that you take the other person's concerns seriously and will allow him to correct any misunderstandings. People may tell you what they do not want but not what they do want. You might say "It sounds as if you want me to.... Is this right?" If the criticism is vague, ask for clarification. If a client accuses you of being rude, ask for specific examples of what you said or did (or did not say or do) so that you can clearly understand their complaint. Only if you understand what people want, can you decide whether their requests or objections are reasonable and/ or possible to fulfill. Your critics have a responsibility to clearly describe their criticisms and the reasons for them.

Offer Empathic Reactions

Empathic responses can diffuse negative emotions and create a more congenial problem-solving atmosphere. Examples are "I can see how this would be difficult" or "I think I'd feel the same way if I thought that." You do not have to agree with criticisms to offer empathic statements. Avoid comments such as "I know how you feel," which may appear patronizing. Recognize points of agreement. Some people confuse a lack of understanding with a lack of agreement. You may understand what a person wants but not agree that it is a problem. In any case, you can demonstrate your understanding by accurately describing his or her position.

Accept Responsibility for What You Say and Do

If the criticism is sound, acknowledge it. You might say, "Yes, you're right, I did interrupt you several times." If appropriate, consider apologizing when you agree with the feedback, but do not be overly self-critical or apologetic. You could ignore unfair or abusive comments and respond only to the sound criticism. If someone says, "You interrupted me several times, and each time your remark was pointless," you could acknowledge that you did interrupt and then reintroduce your point if you still think it is a worthwhile one. If someone says, "That was a silly thing to ask," your reply might be, "There are times when I could be more on my toes, but I do think my question is a good one that still has not been answered. My question is…"

Don't Let People Continue to Abuse or Neutralize You

Don't listen to or tolerate abuse. If you do, you will probably receive more. You could say (interrupting the person), "I can't allow you to talk to me that way." As a last resort, you could walk away (see the later section on safety). In reply to unfair criticism or to valid criticism delivered in an offensive way or at an inappropriate time, you might say, "I appreciate your suggestion, but I was embarrassed that you brought up the topic when other staff members were around. I'd prefer you to…" Saying "It's difficult for me to accept criticism about this" communicates vulnerability that might encourage others to soften their approach.

Seek and Offer Solutions

The best way to react to valid criticisms is to offer desired outcomes. This will satisfy your critics more than verbal assurances or excuses will. If the criticism is valid, ask for or offer suggestions to encourage people to become involved in a solution. You might say, "I do tend to interrupt you. How about giving me a signal when I do, so I can learn to stop myself?" If you say, "Since you're the one who's upset about this, you find a solution," others will feel that you do not care about or cannot respond to their concerns.

Take Time to Think If You Need It

If you feel unable to consider negative feedback or to sort out your reactions to it, arrange to discuss the criticism at another time. You might say, "I'd like to think about what you've said. How about discussing this on Friday?" Scheduling a future time to discuss concerns is important if someone introduces an issue when you have little time or privacy to discuss it. If the conversation begins to escalate into an argument or if you begin to feel confused or angry, suggest a time-out. You might say, "I think I understand and accept part of your criticism, and I've offered some solutions. However, you're repeating your original complaint and are now bringing up new ones. I'm feeling overwhelmed and would like a break."

Arrive at a Clear Agreement and get Back on Track

If appropriate, reach a clear agreement on what will be done. Compromise and negotiation may be required to reach a mutually

---

EXHIBIT 16.8

Checklist for Handling Criticism

_____ View feedback as a learning opportunity.

_____ Don't take it personally.

_____ Relax and listen (unless the feedback is abusive).

_____ Check your understanding and ask for clarification as needed.

_____ Offer empathic responses (consider the other person's perspective).

_____ Avoid defensive, aggressive, and overly apologetic replies.

_____ Accept responsibility for what you say and do.

_____ Don't let people abuse or neutralize you.

_____ Seek and offer solutions.

_____ Take time to think if you need it.

_____ Arrive at a clear agreement about what will be done and get back on track.

---

acceptable agreement. Focus on common goals (those shared by you and the other person), such as offering effective services (Fisher & Ury, 1991). You may have to use the "broken record" technique (repeat a statement such as "Let's get back to…") (see Exhibit 16.8).

Refusing Requests

You may have to refuse requests from clients, coworkers, supervisors, or other professionals; it is best to do so in a way that maximizes positive feelings and minimizes negative ones. Be sure to consider preferred styles of communication when deciding whether to refuse a request and how to do so. Indirect ways are more acceptable in some groups (e.g., expressing regret, not using the word *no*). People who are uncomfortable with being direct even when this is appropriate often never use word the word *no*. They might say, "Well, I just don't know…" or "I'm sorry. I don't think so…" If direct styles of refusal are appropriate, face the person, use the word *no* (as a signal that you have made up your mind and have no intention of changing it), look at the person, speak loudly enough to be heard and slowly enough to be understood, and try not to stammer and hesitate. You may have to repeat your refusal. If you offer a reason for your refusal and the person rejects it, do not offer new reasons; just repeat the one you gave. The more excuses you give, the more opportunities others have to counter them. Shorter refusal statements may be more effective than long ones.

Refusing unreasonable demands from supervisors is important. In these times of shrinking resources, staff are often pushed to work longer and harder. Patronizing slogans are sometimes used, such as "work smarter not harder" (as if you were not already working hard and smart). Know your rights and stick to your guns; do not be "guilt tripped." For example, a common ploy in response to your refusal may be to say, "But this work must be done" or "Your clients need your help." You could answer, "That's a good point, but I can't do it. Perhaps you should hire some temporary help." In their book *You Don't Have to Take It!* Ginny Nicarthy and her colleagues (1993) provide several examples of how to refuse unreasonable work requests. You as well as your clients can be exploited. Those in helping professions such as social work can perhaps be more easily guilt tripped into exploitive working conditions because of calls to elevate service to others above self-interest. Limited resources do not mean that your work climate should be punitive (e.g., complaints are punished and staff are excessively burdened).

Requesting Behavior Changes

Sometimes you will have to ask people to change their behavior. You may ask a supervisor for more detailed feedback, request a coworker to stop bad-mouthing clients, or a client to stop interrupting you, or request friends or coworkers to return borrowed items (Kowalski, 2001). Requesting behavior changes is often regarded as criticism. However, problems provide an opportunity to strengthen a relationship and should be approached from this viewpoint. Success in resolving concerns will increase your confidence that you can establish and maintain good relationships. Be sure to consider your goals. Goals such as making people feel guilty or making them pay for bad behavior carry the cost of people disliking you, and, you probably will not achieve them anyway. A reluctance to request behavior changes may be related to inaccurate or dysfunctional beliefs about social relationships (e.g., "I have no right to ask others to change") or fear of disapproval. Supervisors' rights include saying directly what they want or expect (e.g., be on time for work), asking employees to do the job they were hired to do, saying "no" when it is in the agency's best interest, confronting failure to perform, and asking employees to stop behaviors that prevent others from doing their work.

We often (incorrectly) assume that other people know when their action or inactions bother us. Or we may assume that we are helpless when we are not. The most positive and effective way to change offending behaviors is to reinforce positive alternatives. Suppose you dislike coworkers' dropping by your desk to chat. If they check with you before they come over, tell them you appreciate this. If indirect efforts fail (ignoring unwanted behaviors, prompting and reinforcing positive alternatives), discussing your concerns may be the next step. If you ignore your discomfort, hoping that it will go away or will magically change, you may start to dislike the person, become angry or hopeless about the situation, and may start to avoid the "culprit."

Ask: Does It Really Matter?

Is this a minor matter that should be ignored? If so, why mention it? Is it likely to happen again? If not, forget it. Is it a picky concern? If so, do not worry about it. Perhaps you are oversensitive to disapproval. You may have unrealistic beliefs (e.g., being asked a question by your supervisor shows disrespect or means that you are a bad person). You may confuse a problem you have with a problem you blame on someone else. On the other hand, something may matter a great deal (e.g., emotional abuse) and call for a clear request to stop (see the later section on handling emotional abuse).

Consider the Other Person's Perspective

Considering a situation from the other person's point of view will help you to focus on common interests and shift from "winning" to reaching a mutually acceptable resolution. Empathy lessens anger and anxiety and encourages you to consider whether the other person can change. Two kinds of handicaps may compromise job performance: (1) personal concerns (e.g., poor training or problems at home) or (2) conditions such as large caseloads, poor supervision, and unrealistic administrative expectations. Rather than arguing about such handicaps, acknowledge them (e.g., that case loads are large), work together with others to change them if this is possible, and seek options for doing the best that can be done given the handicap and options for removing it.

Plan and Practice What to Say

Plan how to ask for changes in a positive way. You could prepare a script of what you will say and practice it. If defensive or hostile reactions are likely despite a positive approach, rehearse constructive responses to them.

Choose the Right Time and Place

If there is time and privacy to share concerns and it is appropriate to do so, express them as they arise rather than allowing them to build up. If you want to discuss an issue that occurred earlier, arrange a time to talk it over. You might say, "I'd like to talk with you about something that's been on my mind. Do you have time now?" Try not to surprise others with such requests when they might not be willing or have time to discuss them. Avoid criticizing people in front of others and talking about people behind their backs.

Start with Positive Feedback

Before you share a concern, comment on something the person does that you like or on a positive quality of your relationship.

Reassure the person that you like him or her and want to maintain a positive working relationship (if this is true). An example is, "Lee, I think we work together well but I would like to discuss…" Combining a request for a change of behavior with a recognition of appreciated behaviors will help to maintain these behaviors and increase the likelihood that your requests will be considered. This approach might be viewed as manipulative if you offer positive feedback only when you give negative feedback as well.

Be Specific About What You Want and Why

Effective feedback is objective rather than judgmental. It focuses on behaviors of concern (see Exhibit 16.9). By being specific, you

---

EXHIBIT 16.9

Checklist for Requesting Behavior Changes

_____ Ignore minor annoyances.

_____ Consider the other person's perspective. Find out if there are any handicapping conditions that get in the way and use the "given that" method.

_____ Plan and practice beforehand.

_____ Select an appropriate time and place.

_____ Give positive recognition first, as appropriate.

_____ Focus on common interests.

_____ Be specific. Describe what you want and why; give examples.

_____ Focus on the situation (the behaviors desired), not on the person. Be brief and to the point; don't overload others with criticisms.

_____ Check out the other person's understanding of what you have said and clarify as needed.

_____ Avoid accusatory "you" statements and name-calling.

_____ Share concerns as they arise—if they are really important.

_____ Use nonverbal behaviors that communicate your seriousness.

_____ Offer specific suggestions or solutions.

_____ Remain firm when challenged (unless it is a lost cause).

_____ Use concerns as opportunities to strengthen relationships.

_____ Persist when necessary.

_____ Seek the person's commitment to follow through.

_____ Reinforce desired alternatives.

avoid "characterological blame" (attacks on the whole person) (Janoff-Bulman, 1979). Clearly describe what you want and why. Give specific examples and describe particular situations. When requests for change are specific, other people are more likely to respond to them as information rather than attacks. Vague complaints are likely to result in defensiveness and counter blame and do not inform people about what you want.

Be brief and to the point. Lengthy criticism can be difficult to understand and accept; people will not know what issues are most important to you and might feel overwhelmed with complaints. Limit your feedback to one or two specific concerns. Recognize and focus on common interests. Examples of common goals are providing high-quality service and maintaining enjoyable and productive working relationships. Describe the positive consequences of changing and the negative ones of not doing so. This may increase motivation to alter behavior and is especially important in work situations in which the consequences may include loss of a job or negative comments in personnel records. Supervisors who have difficulty requesting behavior changes may threaten a staff person, without prior warning, with losing his or her job. This is not fair and, in fact, may be grounds for a successful grievance or lawsuit.

Personalize and Own Feedback

Use personal pronouns (I, me) rather than the accusatory "you," which connotes blame. You could say, "I feel uncomfortable when you criticize me in front of other students" rather than "You make me angry when you…" It is better to say, "It gives the agency a bad image when you talk so negatively about the agency in front of other people" than "You're giving the agency a bad name." Begin your comments with a personal pronoun to indicate that you take responsibility for your feelings and reactions. Including the following five components is helpful:

- **I feel** (describe your feelings, using words that refer to feelings)
- **when** (describe the behavior of concern)
- **because** (describe how the behavior affects you).
- **I would prefer** (describe what you want)
- **because** (describe how you would feel).

The first step reminds you to use "I" statements and to express what you feel (sad, mad, happy, angry). The error you are most likely to make here is to refer to complaints or beliefs rather than feelings, as in the following: "I feel you should give me more feedback" or "I don't think you like me." Neither statement refers to a specific feeling. If you do not want to start off with "I feel…" start with a clear description of the requested behavior change and the reasons for your request. One disadvantage of starting with a "feeling statement" is that it opens you up to attacks on your feelings (e.g., "You women are so sensitive"). If this happens,

focus on what you want—do not get sidetracked. The second step calls for a clear description of your concern. The third reminds you to describe why it is a concern. The fourth involves taking responsibility for clearly describing what you want, and the last one brings you back to sharing your feelings about the desired change. Some examples are as follows:

- **I feel** frustrated
- **when** you ask me to do extra work late in the afternoon
- **because** I have made plans for the evening and cannot stay late
- **I would rather** you give me new work earlier in the day
- **because** that would help me plan my day.

People are more likely to consider your requests if you use words that communicate mild emotions (e.g., "I feel annoyed" rather than "I feel furious"). Use your feelings as clues as to what you want. Avoid words such as *should, ought, have to,* and *must* that may promote guilt, anger, and defensive statements. Share any discomfort you feel by saying, "This is difficult for me, but I do want to talk about…" Knowing that you are honestly struggling with being direct might put others at ease. Self-disclosure of this kind communicates that you are vulnerable, too, and do not see yourself in a superior position. There is no need to apologize or say you are sorry. You have a right to make requests as long as you do not do so in an objectionable manner.

Avoid Negative Comments

Avoid loaded words—judgmental comments and put-downs such as "You're inconsiderate (cold, uptight, unfair)." Moralizing and excessive questioning (e.g., "Why did you…"), giving orders, and "diagnosing" the other person ("You're doing this because you have a…") will decrease your effectiveness.

Match Your Style of Presentation to Your Message

Make your request in a manner that matches your message. When asking for a change in an annoying behavior, be serious and thoughtful; do not giggle, smile, or laugh. You do not have to act out your feelings to communicate them.

Offer Specific Suggestions for Change

Before you bring up a concern, identify what changes you would like. How would you like things to be different? By offering specific suggestions for change, you share responsibility for improving the situation. Rather than saying, "You're really thoughtless" when you mean that someone interrupts you, you could say, "I'd like you to let me finish speaking before you start to speak."

Be Willing to Compromise

Demonstrating a willingness to compromise will help keep discussions on a positive note. Perhaps you had some role in an annoying event. For example, if you were kept waiting, perhaps you did not set a definite time. A willingness to share responsibility shows that you are flexible.

Offer Positive Feedback

You might say, "I'm glad we talked. I feel relieved and think we'll be able to work together better in the future. I appreciate your willingness to talk about this." You could also point out how good it is that the two of you can discuss your differences.

Avoid Sidetracks

People might try to sidetrack you by changing the subject or bringing up the past. Many informal fallacies, such as ad hominem attacks (e.g., personal criticisms), serve as distractions from addressing the real issue (such as the weakness of an argument). You can either ignore the sidetrack and repeat or elaborate your request or statement or comment on the distraction. You might say, "My point is…" Do not react in kind and do not back down when confronted with hostile or defensive reactions unless the other person is becoming very upset or threatening. Here the best option may be to postpone the discussion. You might say, "This does not seem like a good time to talk about this. Let's discuss it later." Try to stay calm. In some cases, you may have to take special precautions (see later discussion of safety in this chapter).

Persist

Discussing your concerns will accomplish little unless you arrive at a clear agreement that a change will be made and describe exactly what it will be. You might say, "I'd feel better if we reached a clear agreement about how to handle this." But you cannot force people to change. If you are getting "hot under the collar" or ready to "go over the top" you probably have an expectation that this person "must," "ought to," or "should" change. Focusing on common interests rather than on winning increases the likelihood of an agreement.

When to Keep Silent

When thinking about asking people to change their behavior, consider the following:

- Does it really matter?
- Is this a matter of cultural differences that should be respected, not altered?
- Can this person change?

- Will a request encourage physical aggression?
- Will making the request have short- and long-term positive or negative consequences?
- Are legal or ethical issues involved?

Responding To Put-Downs

Put-downs are often based on stereotypes related to gender, religion, race, ethnicity, physical abilities, age, or sexual orientation. Put-downs ("zaps" as Patterson calls them) are in the eye of the beholder. They are defined by their function, not their form (i.e., they result in negative reactions on the part of the target). Regardless of the intent of the person making the remark (the person might not have intended to belittle or demean you), its effect is an important criterion for deciding whether it is a put-down. Name-calling may be used in ad hominem arguments (attacks on the person) to deflect attention from a weak argument. Whether a comment is directed toward you as a person, toward a general group, or toward someone else, you must decide whether to ignore or address it. What is most appropriate will depend in part on the source of the criticism. Consider your goals and the chances of achieving them. Focusing on put-downs may get in the way of pursuing service goals. If so, ignore them and attend to service tasks. Or you could offer a disarming reaction—acknowledge the truth in the put-down (see Burns, 1999). If they are recurrent in a continuing relationship, you may decide to try to change this behavior.

Verbal put-downs based on race, gender, sexual orientation, age, or ethnicity are a kind of verbal harassment and could be reported to appropriate authorities (see the next section). (See conversational terrorism, http://www.vandruff.com/art_converse.html.) Guidelines proposed many years ago by Naomi Gottlieb (1978) still hold true today (see also Nicarthy, Gottlieb, & Coffman, 1993):

- *Take time to respond in your own way.* Do not feel pressured to react immediately.
- *Avoid responding in kind* and using aggressive reactions. Use "I" statements to express your feelings and opinions.
- *Make it clear that you do not accept stereotypes* (e.g., "Women are emotional"). Show by your manner of speaking, as well as by what you say, that you do not accept this sexist stereotype.
- *Complement what you say with appropriate nonverbal behaviors.* Do not laugh or smile at offensive comments. You could say, "I don't think that was funny." If the reply to this is "What's the matter, no sense of humor?" you could repeat your initial comment without getting into a prolonged discussion or defense of your reaction. Look at the person; do not smile; maintain a relaxed and

confident body position; do not speak in a high-pitched or whiny voice; empathize as appropriate with the feelings underlying the put-down.

- *Offer and reinforce desired alternatives.* At work, in response to being called "honey" or some other inappropriate term, you might say, "I would prefer to be called Mary."

- *Ignore the comment or put-down and focus on your goals.*

- *Know when to stop.* If there is little change in unwanted behavior, introduce another topic or end the conversation.

- *Be prepared with effective reactions.* Have a few stock replies on hand, such as "that sounds like a put-down to me."

Handling Emotional Abuse, Sexual Harassment, and Discrimination on The Job

Bullying has received considerable attention over the past years, including related behaviors in work settings (Einsaren, 2010). Sexual harassment is a form of sex discrimination. The legal definition of sexual harassment is "*unwelcome* verbal, visual, or physical *conduct of a sexual nature* that is *severe or pervasive* and *affects working conditions or creates a hostile work environment*" (http://www.equalrights.org/). Ginny Nicarthy and her colleagues define emotional abuse at work as "a pattern of intimidation, harassment, emotional manipulation, or excessive or illegitimate control of a worker" (1993, p. 5). They identified eight kinds based on interviews and focus groups with women (see Exhibit 16.10). This book is a valuable source for becoming informed about work-related emotional abuse, as well as options for dealing with it.

Sexual harassment or discrimination on grounds of gender, race, age, sexual orientation, pregnancy, or disability are not legal and should not be tolerated. In 1986 the U.S. Supreme Court unanimously recognized that sexual harassment is a form of sexual discrimination and that hostile environments and sex-for-jobs harassment violate the Civil Rights Act (*Meritor Sav. Bank v. Vinson*, 477 U.S. 57 (1986)). The NASW Code of Ethics states that "social workers should not sexually harass supervisees, students, trainees, or colleagues" (2.08). A sexual harassment policy may ban:

- Verbal harassment, including making sexual comments about a person's body, telling sexual jokes or stories, spreading rumors about a coworker's sex life, asking or telling about sexual fantasies, preferences, or history.

EXHIBIT 16.10

Examples of Emotional Abuse on the Job and Related Reactions

1. Isolation
   - Ignore or cancel your request for meetings or feedback?
   - Isolate you from others who are also angry about the abuse?

2. Threats
   - Imply that you will be sorry if you don't do exactly what she or he wants down to the finest detail?
   - Shout, pound the desk, raise a fist, or slam doors?

3. Degradation and humiliation
   - Call you names like stupid or crazy?
   - Ignore your ideas and accept them from a male coworker or someone else who has more status or power than you?
   - Criticize or ridicule you in front of others?
   - Check and recheck all your work?

4. Enforcing unreasonable demands
   - Set unnecessary, arbitrary deadlines?
   - Insist you do work that is someone else's responsibility?
   - Assign tasks he knows you haven't learned to do and refuse to provide instruction?

5. Occasional indulgences
   - Treat your rights to break times, vacations, and so forth as if they were personal favors?

6. Demonstrating power
   - Take credit for your production, work, or ideas?
   - Arbitrarily change agreements without consulting you?

7. Monopolizing your attention
   - Worry about whether the boss or coworker will approve of unimportant things such as the state of your desk?
   - Worry that she will yell at you or act in an angry, punishing, or critical manner?

8. Exhaustion and lowered competency
   - Work so hard to please that you feel exhausted?
   - Feel less competent to perform tasks than you used to?

Source: Adapted from Ginny Nicarthy, Naomi Gottlieb, and Sandra Coffman (1993). *You don't have to take it! A woman's guide to confronting emotional abuse at work*. Seattle, WA: Seal Press.

- Nonverbal harassment, such as giving unwanted personal gifts, following a person, staring at a person's body, displaying sexually suggestive material such as pornographic photos.

- Physical harassment, including touching yourself in a sexual manner in front of another person, brushing up against another person suggestively. (Petrocelli & Repa, 1992, p. 4/9)

You can recover damages if you have lost a promotion or your job because you refused sexual demands if you can prove that:

- You were validly working when the harassment took place.

- The person who harassed you knew of the employment relationship.

- Your harasser intentionally and improperly interfered with your employment relationship.

- You suffered damages such as loss of your job, a demotion or a failure to get a promotion because of the interference. (Petrocelli & Repa, 1992, p. 8/16)

Concentrating on the task and not offering "mixed messages" make unwanted sexual advances less likely. Be sure your nonverbal behavior reflects the message you want to get across. Effective refusals of sexual overtures communicate a clear "no" without being abusive. Guidelines for refusing unwanted requests, discussed earlier, include not smiling or flirting, including the word *no* in your statement, and sticking with your explanation for refusing (if you gave one) rather than making up additional reasons or excuses. Make it clear that you choose to say no. Say "I don't want to" rather than "I can't," "I'm not supposed to," or "I'm sorry." Conveying that you have made the decision will make it clear that you are not a victim of constraints imposed against your will. You may have to persist in your refusal and directly discuss the offensive behavior, noting why it is inappropriate and undesired. If the offensive behavior persists, you could file a formal complaint through the appropriate channels, at either the state or federal level. Petrocelli and Repa also give a checklist for evaluating your case (8/13). Seek support from others who share your concerns.

Speaking More

Perhaps you rarely express your opinions or offer ideas at meetings. If so, practice speaking more often. Skill in resisting interruption and breaking into conversations is helpful. Elaborated opinion statements are useful for increasing participation (see the discussion of disagreeing). How can you tell if you talk too much or too little? The key question is "Do you meet your goals?" In addition, you could ask other people what they think.

Breaking into an Ongoing Conversation

In a fast-moving conversation, you will have to speak up during brief pauses. If you wait for a long pause, the topic might change before you get a chance to share your ideas. This does not mean that you should interrupt people while they are talking but, rather, that you should speak after they finish talking. Practice coming into conversations quickly by using short sentences at first. You might say, "Yes, I think that's true." The sooner you come in, the more likely you will be viewed as an active participant. Questions, opinions, and the use of people's names are different ways to enter a conversation. You can use hand gestures or a light touch on the arm or shoulder to let people know you want to speak. Sitting forward in your chair or standing closer might capture attention. People are more likely to offer you an opportunity to talk if you sit in a visible location.

Resisting Interruptions

One way to resist interruptions is to raise your voice slightly when someone tries to break in. If you are with several people, direct your communication toward the receptive ones. Another technique is to pause briefly when someone tries to interrupt and then repeat what you just said. Or, you could ignore the interruption and continue talking. You could comment on the interruption by asking the person to wait. A hand signal or touch indicating "stop" or "hold it" could be added to a verbal request such as "just a minute." Interrupters may not be aware of their behavior or know how to change it. You could suggest a cue, such as raising your hand slightly, to alert them whenever they interrupt you. Commenting on interruptions at the time they occur may not be appropriate. You could raise the issue later.

Handling Monopolizers

What is best when faced with a monopolizer depends on your goals and the context. One strategy is to start speaking during a pause between the person's sentences. You could try this when waiting for a natural pause has not been successful. You could let the person know you want to speak by saying, "I'd like to respond to your first point." You could stop reinforcing their talking (e.g., not look or smile at the person) or discuss your concern with him (see discussion of requesting behavior changes) (see Exhibit 16.11). A key function of group facilitators (paid or unpaid) is to help a group balance talking and listening of each member.

Listening More

Perhaps you talk too much in some situations. Pay attention to other people's nonverbal signals. Do they look bored or like they are "spacing out" when you talk? Do they fidget and tap

---

EXHIBIT 16.11

Increasing Your Participation

_____ Do you hesitate too long before trying to enter a conversation?

_____ Can people hear you?

_____ Can people understand you; do you speak clearly?

_____ Do you use overly subtle signals to indicate that you would like to speak?

_____ Do you prepare what you want to say?

_____ Do you believe you have valuable contributions to make?

_____ Do you wait until you are angry before speaking up?

_____ Do you directly express your desire to talk after more subtle approaches fail?

---

their feet? You could use shorter, simpler sentences and limit your examples. You might mistakenly interpret a brief pause between statements as an end to a person's speech when it is a transition from one sentence to the next. To prevent this, wait a few seconds after others stop speaking before you talk. Follow the "ask-listen-ask rule" (handing back the conversation after listening to responses to a question) (Stuart, 1980). You could say, "Well, what do you think?" Be sure to offer positive feedback for other people's contributions (e.g., head nods) (see chapter 15 for a discussion of active listening). Perhaps other people are not as talkative as you would like because you show little interest in understanding their point of view (e.g., ask no questions, offer little eye contact) or have been overly critical of their remarks. You may disagree too often or point out faults in what has been said in ways that offend others (see guidelines for disagreeing). You may forget to point out areas of agreement (see Exhibit 16.12).

EXHIBIT 16.12

Encouraging Others to Talk

_____ Do you follow the "ask-listen-ask" rule?

_____ Do you offer high quality listening?

_____ Are you interested in what other people say?

_____ Do you focus too much on yourself and not enough on what other people do, feel, and think?

_____ Do you miss or misinterpret social signals that other people want to speak?

_____ Do you forget to wait a few seconds after people finish talking before speaking?

Obstacles to Handling Difficult Social Situations Effectively

Both environmental and personal obstacles may interfere with effective social behavior (see Exhibit 16.13). Environmental factors include lack of opportunities for positive informal exchanges such as a staff lounge and an agreed-on time and place for staff to discuss issues such as a support group or journal club. You may work in an agency that does not value a culture of thoughtfulness in which differences of opinion are viewed as learning opportunities. If so, work together with colleagues who share your interests to change your work climate and culture. Guidelines that contribute to making well-informed decisions in groups are shown in Exhibit 16.14.

Not being familiar with the norms, values, and preferred styles of communication in different groups may get in the way. Needed skills may be absent, such as empathic reactions including disarming responses, in which you see the truth in a critic's remarks (see chapter 15). You may have needed skills but not use them because they are not reinforced and/or are punished. For example, your requests for more specific supervisory feedback may have been ignored or punished. As a result, you may no longer ask, and even thinking about doing so may create anxiety. You can lessen anxiety by imagining the "worst-case scenario" and realizing that even this would not be a catastrophe. Your beliefs about how people should act may be an obstacle. They may not reflect real-life contingencies. You may feel "entitled" to being treated in a certain way with no responsibility for taking positive action to change a disliked situation. Here are some examples of unrealistic expectations:

- Everyone must like and approve of me at all times.

- I must be perfect, totally competent, and productive in order to consider myself worthwhile.

- It is a catastrophe when things are not the way I want them to be.

- Past events control my present behavior.

- Other people should act as I want, and I can and should control the behavior of those around me.

- There is always a correct and perfect solution to a problem, and it is a catastrophe if I do not find it.

- When people do something bad, they should be blamed and punished.

- My happiness is externally caused and controlled. (See, e.g., Ellis, 1996.)

A belief that everyone must like you or that you must never make mistakes will get in the way of raising questions. Neither belief is likely to be confirmed and thus may result in anger if you sense disapproval or anxiety as a result of nonreward and

---

EXHIBIT 16.13

Factors Related to Ineffective Social Behavior

Problem	Remedy
1. Lack of knowledge about social rules/norms.	1. Acquire knowledge.
2. Lack of needed skills.	2. Acquire skills.
3. Interfering behavior (aggressive reactions).	3. Replace with effective reactions.
4. Inappropriate or inadequate stimulus control (e.g., skills are available but not used).	4. Develop effective stimulus control.
5. Interfering emotional reactions (anxiety, anger).	5. Identify related factors (e.g., lack of skills or knowledge, taking things personally, fear of negative evaluation, unrealistic expectations), and make needed changes.
6. Fear of negative evaluation.	6. Decrease sensitivity to social disapproval.
7. Unrealistic performance standards.	7. Moderate standards, identify unrealistic expectations (e.g., "I must please everyone"), and replace with realistic ones (e.g., "I can't please everyone").
8. Lack of respect for others.	8. Increase empathic understanding.
9. A focus on winning.	9. Focus on shared goals (e.g., to help clients).
10. Few settings that encourage positive exchanges.	10. Increase access to such settings.
11. Agency culture (e.g., contingency systems, see chapter 27).	11. Rearrange contingencies, involve coworkers.

---

punishment. Use your feelings as clues to identify your emotional "triggers" (such as unrealistic expectations) and replace them with helpful self-statements (see Exhibit 16.15). Unrealistic expectations include the belief that you must be successful with all your clients and be respected and loved by all your colleagues

and clients (Ellis & Yeager, 1989). Inaccurate beliefs about conflict may also get in the way (e.g., it should be avoided at all cost, there is something wrong if you have conflicts, and there must be winners and losers).

EXHIBIT 16.14

Case Conference Guidelines That Contribute to Ethical Decisions

1. It is "safe" to disagree.
2. It is safe to reveal ignorance and error (participants recognize that knowledge develops through error and correction through criticism).
3. Uncertainty in making decisions is recognized.
4. Participants avoid propaganda methods such as ad hominem arguments and glittering generalizations (e.g., inflated claims of effectiveness of a method).
5. Alternate views are sought.
6. Critical appraisal of all views is the norm.
7. Blameless: seek information about how to minimize avoidable errors.
8. Recognize conflicts between educational needs and clients' rights.
9. Focus on maximizing quality of care provided to clients (how best to address client concerns).

Safety

Safety is an issue in some social work positions. Take special precautions with clients who have a history of violence, such as having direct access to an exit, leaving your office door open, having access to an alarm that is in working order, and being trained to recognize and respond effectively to the initial stages of aggressive chains of behavior (e.g., limit testing, agitation, irritability). Insisting that a client confront negative information or refusing to meet her request may only make her more aggressive. Try meeting in a neutral place such as a restaurant or community center. You could visit together with another worker. You can ask referring professionals about a client's potential for violence and past violence. Addressing outcomes of interest to clients, showing respect, and avoiding unnecessary provocations decrease the likelihood of violent behavior.

Discuss the situation with your supervisor if you are concerned about danger. Make arrangements to send help if you do not call your agency at an agreed-on time. Carry a cell phone and call in after each visit. Have a colleague call you after you arrive to check if all is ok. You could agree on a code word for needing help. If driving, park close to the client's home and be alert when entering the home. If the family has a telephone, call beforehand to set up

EXHIBIT 16.15

How to Overcome Difficulties in Being Assertive

Difficulty	How to Overcome It
Guilt	1. Become aware of guilt feelings and guilt triggers. 2. Uncover irrational beliefs, cognitive distortions, and parent messages and decide if the guilt is appropriate. 3. Develop an antidote statement.
Fear of consequences	1. Uncover your catastrophic fantasy and exaggerate it. 2. Ask yourself, "What's really likely to happen?" and be alert for irrational beliefs and cognitive distortions. 3. Weigh the risks of being assertive and the costs of not being assertive. 4. Assess what you need to do to protect yourself from negative consequences.
Fear of being taken advantage of	1. Recognize your fear and the assumptions behind it. 2. Dispute your assumptions.
Anxiety	1. Realize you can still act rationally when you're anxious. 2. Practice relaxation techniques. 3. Use deep breathing or a short meditation before confrontations.
Doubt	1. Do your homework—know what you want to accomplish and the facts of the situation. 2. Substitute positive pep talks for negative pep talks. 3. Focus on supervisory rights and responsibilities.
Anger	1. Examine negative assumptions and look for more benign alternatives. 2. Look for and dispute irrational beliefs and cognitive distortions. 3. Watch for anger triggers, especially red-flag people. 4. Empathize—put yourself in the other person's shoes.
Inflexible self-image	1. Realize that one or a few interactions will not make or break your image. 2. Remind yourself that you can act in opposing ways and still maintain your image.
Negative self image	1. Identify and dispute ways that you undermine yourself. 2. Give yourself credit for your strengths. 3. Forgive yourself for your flaws.
Sexual and racial blocks to assertiveness	1. Dispute internal programming that keeps you from being assertive. 2. Define negative reactions as inevitable responses to changes in the traditional distribution of power. 3. Build a power base to support your assertiveness.

Source: S. S. Drury (1984). *Assertive supervision: Building involved teamwork* (pp. 304–305). Champaign, IL: Research Press. Reprinted with permission.

an appointment. Use active listening skills to calm angry clients and respect the clients' personal space. If you know that a situation may be dangerous, ask about it (e.g., "Are there guns in the house?"). Family members themselves may be worried and suggest a plan. Techniques for deescalating anger include the following:

- Remain calm; try not to show fear or anxiety.

- Be firm without raising one's voice.

- Make statements simple and direct.

- Recognize and address feelings and do not take hostile statements personally.

- Offer the person a choice between positive alternatives.

- Be alert for the possibility of aggression.

- Attempt to have the person sit down and distract him or her from the source of anger.

- Give the person lots of space; do not touch them.

- If the person attacks, use only enough force to protect yourself or restrain him or her.

- Remember it takes a person 30–40 minutes to calm down physiologically.

- After the visit, do not sit in front of the house to write notes.

- Carry a cell phone, whistle, or personal alarm and use it, if appropriate.

- Pay attention to your intuition or "gut instinct" and leave if warranted. (DePanfilis & Salus, 2003, p. 22, based on Griffin, Montsinger, & Carter, 1995)

If talking to an entire family is chaotic or tensions escalate, you could suggest talking to each person separately. You could talk to the most difficult person first. If everyone tries to talk at once, point out that it is difficult for you to hear anyone and ask that just one person speak at a time. Inform family members of the consequences if a situation seems to be getting out of hand, as in the following example:

The family consisted of 15-year-old Mary and her 36-year-old mother, Rita. Mary had been on the run at referral and presenting problems were truancy, alcohol abuse and sexual involvement. She and her mother had had many conflicts over these issues and sometimes became physical with one another.

During one session Rita and Mary became angry with one another. Their anger quickly escalated to the point of yelling. During this initial stage I fell back on a rule of thumb I had learned in my training ("when in doubt: listen") and made several listening responses. However, Rita and Mary continued to scream at one another. Mary ran upstairs with Rita in close pursuit. I followed them. When they reached the top of the stairs, they began slapping one another, pulling each other's hair, and wrestling. I began expressing my concern and fear that one or both of them would be hurt. I made several statements such as "I'm afraid someone is going to get hurt," "I don't want anyone to get hurt," "I'm worried that you will hurt each other," but they continued screaming and fighting.

Next, they headed back downstairs with me close behind expressing my concern. In the living room, Mary knocked everything including the telephone off a table and yelled "I'm going to call the police" to which Rita yelled back "I'm going to call the police." In as calm a voice as I could muster at that point, I said "If you don't stop, I will call the police." They stopped wrestling, hitting and pulling hair but continued yelling. I resumed listening to their feelings and as they began to deescalate, I was able to convince Mary to go out on the front porch. Afterward I spent time with each of them individually and Mary said "It was weird to hear you say you would call the police." Until then, I did not know what had made the difference. (Jack Chambers). (Kinney, Haapala, & Booth, 1991, p. 51)

You could suggest a time out to get a glass of water. Other steps are calling your supervisor or the police or simply leaving.

Summary

Both you and your clients will confront a variety of challenging social situations. Options for handling them such as being criticized, requesting behavior changes, and refusing unwanted requests include seeking information, taking direct action, doing nothing, and changing how a situation is viewed. Your problem-solving skills will help you plan what to do. Steps include calming down, describing the problem and what you want, identifying your options and considering the consequences, trying the best plan, and evaluating the results. You can often head off unpleasant situations by planning ahead and supporting desired behaviors. You can enhance your success by attending to cultural differences in preferred communication styles.

Reviewing Your Competencies

Reviewing Content Knowledge

1. Identify situations which call for speaking up rather than remaining silent to protect clients from harm and to maximize service quality.

2. Identify specific social situations that are difficult for you. Select two examples and describe how you handle them and how you can increase your effectiveness.

3. Describe behaviors and beliefs associated with passive, assertive, and aggressive behavior.

4. Describe "emotional allergies" that get in your way of raising vital questions and responding effectively to difficult social situations.

5. Describe effective ways of handling specific problematic social situations.

6. Describe helpful social problem-solving steps.

7. Give examples of the statement "Feelings are clues to contingencies" Describe why this is important to understand.

8. Identify positive alternatives to dysfunctional social goals in specific situations.

9. Suggest promising options for attaining goals in given social situations.

10. Describe factors related to ineffective social behavior.

11. Describe helpful ways to overcome specific communication barriers.

12. Describe components of effective disagreement.

13. Describe helpful steps in asking others to change their behavior.

14. Describe constructive reactions to criticism that promote client welfare.

15. Give specific examples of cultural differences in responding effectively to challenging social situations.

16. Give examples of work-related obstacles to valuable social behaviors.

17. Describe steps you can take to encourage others to talk.

18. Describe alternatives to aggressive reactions in specific situations.

19. Describe useful coping skills for regulating emotions.

20. Describe nonverbal cues you can use to recognize different feelings and attitudes.

21. Identify indicators of emotional abuse at work.

22. Identify power differences at work and their relationship to dysfunctional social behaviors.

Reviewing What You Do

1. A review of your work related exchanges shows that you raise vital questions that affect clients' lives, request behavior changes, respond to criticisms, and balance talking and listening in a way that increases the likelihood of making sound decisions and helping clients.

2. In role plays, you demonstrate constructive feedback and effective refusal of requests.

3. A review of your interactions with others, including exchanges during staff conferences, shows that you:

   - Acknowledge and seek to understand other points of view.
   - Offer opinions effectively.
   - Avoid put-downs.
   - Raise questions about claims that affect clients' lives (e.g., about what is effective).
   - Request clarification/information/feedback as needed.
   - Recognize the need for evidence to accompany claims of what is true (or false).

   - Support suggestions with evidence or acknowledge its lack.
   - Clearly describe behaviors/situations of concern.
   - Compromise when appropriate.
   - Provide and request constructive feedback.
   - Change your opinions when you have good reason to do so.
   - Accurately identify other people's emotions and attitudes.
   - Convey attitudes and emotions you intend to offer.

4. You can teach someone one of the skills described in this chapter. Criteria for success: Valued goals are attained in real-life situations.

5. You do well on "Exercise 7. Reasoning and Practice Game B: Group and Interpersonal Dynamics" in Gambrill and Gibbs (2009).

Reviewing Results

1. Unfair or ineffective discriminatory agency practices decrease.

2. Clients attain hoped-for outcome.

3. Well-informed decisions are made.

4. Other people like and/or respect you.

5. There are few social predicaments.

6. Stress levels in exchanges are low.

7. You develop and maintain constructive working relationships.

8. You like and respect others.

9. Clients and coworkers compliment you on your knowledge of cultural difference in preferred communication styles.

10. Evaluation of specific skills you wish to improve (e.g., speaking up rather than remaining silent, avoiding influence by ad hominem comments in case conferences) shows that you take advantage of an increasing number of opportunities to do so.

Part 7

Gathering and Organizing Information

17

Where to Look: Deciding How to Gather Needed Information

OVERVIEW   The assessment framework described in chapters 12 and 13 offers a guide as to *what* data to collect. The next two chapters provide guidelines for gathering data. Sources include self-report, standardized questionnaires, self-anchored scales, self-monitoring, observation in role plays or in real-life contexts such as the classroom, physiological measures, and case records. Measures may be used to describe, screen, assess, monitor, or predict future behavior. The potential inaccuracy of any one source calls for use of multiple sources when possible. Criteria to consider when making choices such as reliability and validity of measures are reviewed, and advantages and disadvantages of different methods discussed.

YOU WILL LEARN ABOUT

- Decisions and options
- Critically appraising data
- Self-report
- Standardized measures
- Asking clients to collect data—self-monitoring
- Observing in the natural environment: seeing for yourself
- Physiological measures
- When to insist on a physical examination
- Case records
- Data provided by other professionals
- What to do about discrepancies
- Keeping track of material
- Ethical issues

Decisions and Options

If you provide direct services to clients, then knowledge of and skill in using feasible, informative assessment methods are essential (see Exhibit 17.1). Kinds of questions that arise include description, assessment, and risk/prognosis. You could talk to clients, observe them in real-life settings (if feasible and relevant), or ask them to role play behavior in situations of concern. Knowledge about the potential risks and benefits of different assessment frameworks and measures will help you to select referral sources that use evidence-informed practices and evaluate data gathered by others (e.g., see Hunsley & Mash, 2008).

Measures reflect an underlining theory regarding causes (e.g., see Matson, Andrasik, & Matson, 2009). There are many competing grand narratives regarding alleged causes of behaviors, feelings, and environmental circumstances. If contradictory, they cannot all be accurate. The view favored influences the creation and use of diagnostic and assessment measures. Thus, a key question is, what is the theory related to a recommended measure? Has it been tested? If so, with what results? A colorful array of theories have been suggested over the centuries including the four humors, still appealed to in some alternative healing methods: earth, fire, water and air. Some methods such as phrenology were enormously popular for years and many famous people including Walt Whitman sought the services of a phrenologist. Required decisions include the following:

- What data will be most helpful in making sound decisions, for example, about factors related to hoped-for outcomes, how to achieve them, and whether they can be achieved?

- How can I obtain such data?

- How will I decide when I have enough information?

- What should I do if I obtain contradictory data?

- What criteria should I use to check the accuracy of data?

- How can I avoid inaccurate and incomplete accounts?

EXHIBIT 17.1

What Do You Think?

Imagine that your job includes helping community residents to enhance the quality of their neighborhood. What information will you gather and why? What question will you pose? A descriptive question may be: In inner city, poor neighborhoods what characteristics hinder and facilitate opportunities for employment?

Mr. Young, an elderly man living with his family, was referred because family members are concerned about his "increasing social isolation." How will you clarify this concern? How will you identify environmental factors that influence related feelings, thoughts, and behaviors such as opportunities for enjoyable social contacts. Describe a well-formed question concerning your information needs (see chapter 10).

Sarah works in a community mental health center. She has just interviewed Mrs. Rivera, who described herself as "always depressed." Mrs. Rivera lives with her two small children, ages 2 and 5. She is a divorced parent with a part-time job. Her mother helps out with the children. Sarah suspects that Mrs. Rivera is not *always* depressed—that this varies depending on certain circumstances. How can she test out this assumption? Sarah's supervisor suggests that she use the Beck Depression Inventory to find out Mrs. Rivera's degree of depression, as well as suicidal potential. What questions should Sarah ask about this inventory before using it with her client? What other source of information might be of value? Describe a well-formed question regarding this example, as well as databases you may use to search for related research. Questions may be:

- For inner city, depressed women, what factors are associated with depression?
- For depressed women, what assessment measure will be most accurate in assessing level of depression?

Brian and his family have been having trouble for months. Brian complains that his parents nag him. His parents complain that Brian is out of control (mistreats the dog, speaks in a nasty way to his parents, will not follow instructions, is doing poorly at school, and has threatened his father with violence). How can you clarify these concerns and discover related circumstances? A contextual assessment would lead you to guess that family members influence each other. How can you test this guess? What questions would you pose? Examples are:

- In families experiencing adolescent–parent conflict, what are common sources of conflict?
- What percentage of families experience parent–adolescent conflict?

Imagine that you work in a neighborhood mediation center and a resident complaints about his neighbor's "intrusions on his privacy" (playing loud music, throwing trash on his property, swearing at him, and so on). Are these reports accurate? How will you find out? Questions may be:

- In neighbors experiencing conflict with each other, what are common resources?
- What percentage escalate into violence?

Options

No matter what our preferred practice framework, we have a limited number of sources of information: (a) various forms of self-report (e.g., what clients or others say, written measures), (b) self-monitoring (clients or significant others keep track of some behaviors, thoughts or feelings, or events in real life), (c) observation in role plays or real life, and (d) physiological measures. Case records and administrative data contain information based on one or more of these sources. Your decisions will be influenced by your knowledge about various methods, client preferences, your practice framework, and feasibility (whether it is possible to use a method). Each method has advantages and disadvantages and certain requisites. Judging whether a particular method provides reliable and valid data requires skill in locating related research, as well as knowledge and skills in critically appraising what is found. Clients may not be willing to use certain methods. You may not have the skills required to administer and interpret a measure. Some sources such as self-report are easy to use and are flexible in the range of content provided; however, accuracy varies considerably.

In addition to deciding on *sources* of data (e.g., self-report, observation), you and your clients will decide on a *type* of measure. What is best will depend on the particular outcome focused on. Options include the following:

- *Frequency:* How often a behavior, thought, or feeling occurs in a fixed period. This may be expressed as rate (number of behaviors divided by a time measure such as number of hours) or percentage (proportion of occurrences in total opportunities; e.g., percentages of conversations initiated over ten opportunities).

- *Latency:* Time interval between presentation of a cue and a behavior (e.g., time elapsing between a question and an answer); time elapsing between writing to a city official and receiving an answer.

- *Duration:* Length of time over which a behavior occurs (e.g., time spent studying; time spent arguing by family members).

- *Amount:* This involves a "how much" dimension and includes amplitude and intensity, such as intensity of anxiety or anger.

- *Form*: Exactly what is the behavior? What criteria will be used to identify the behavior?

- *Competence*: The effectiveness of a behavior in resulting in a given outcome.

- *Variety*: Different forms of behavior resulting in a given outcome (operant class).

Professionals tend to base decisions on a small amount of data even though they collect a great deal. One problem with

---

EXHIBIT 17.2

Guidelines for Collecting Data

- Focus on gathering information that decreases or reveals uncertainty about how to attain desired outcomes.

- Watch out for vivid data that may be misleading or uninformative; attend to what is *not* there, as well as what is.

- Beware of confirmation biases (collecting only data that support initial assumptions).

- Use multiple sources.

- Use valid methods (those that measure what they purport to measure).

- Critically evaluate the accuracy of data collected.

- Search for data that allow you to explore alternative views of concerns and related hoped-for outcomes.

- Consider cultural differences.

- Use observation in real-life settings when needed.

- Describe behavior in its context (clearly describe behaviors of concern, as well as their antecedents and consequences).

- Identify positive alternatives to undesired behaviors.

- Critically evaluate your beliefs about presumed cause(s). Could they be wrong? Can you offer a well-reasoned argument for them? Are alternative views likely? If so, what are they?

---

collecting lots of data is that decisions may be influenced by irrelevant data. Incorrect beliefs about the causes of client concerns may be strengthened by gathering redundant data (data that do *not* provide any additional information). You can improve accuracy by using multiple methods, relying on those most likely to offer accurate, relevant data. You can save time and effort by focusing on information that provides the best guidelines for making informed decisions—they help you and your clients to select successful plans (see Exhibit 17.2).

Critically Appraising Data

Because you and your clients make life-affecting decisions based on information collected, it is important to critically evaluate it (complete Exhibit 17.3). Have you relied on self-reports? Do these provide a sound basis for decisions? Should you check the accuracy of self-report by observing behaviors of interest in real life? Will this provide a sounder basis for decisions? Let us say a parent tells you that she knows how to use positive methods with her child. How can you find out if this is accurate? Or let

EXHIBIT 17.3

Reviewing Data Relied On

Select a client with whom you have recently worked (or are seeing). First, circle each number on the far left that describes a source you used. For each source circled, complete the three scales shown. If your values are low, discuss possible reasons for this. *Suggestions for discussion:* How do your ratings of relevance compare with those of accuracy and completeness? Data could be accurate but not relevant.

	Accuracy[a]				Completeness[a]				Relevance[a]			
1. Client self-report.	0	1	2	3	0	1	2	3	0	1	2	3
2. Significant others' self-report.	0	1	2	3	0	1	2	3	0	1	2	3
3. Observation of clients during interview.	0	1	2	3	0	1	2	3	0	1	2	3
4. Standardized measures.	0	1	2	3	0	1	2	3	0	1	2	3
5. Projective tests.	0	1	2	3	0	1	2	3	0	1	2	3
6. Self-monitoring by clients.	0	1	2	3	0	1	2	3	0	1	2	3
7. Anecdotal observation in role plays.	0	1	2	3	0	1	2	3	0	1	2	3
8. Systematic observation in role plays.	0	1	2	3	0	1	2	3	0	1	2	3
9. Anecdotal observation in problem-related real-life contexts.	0	1	2	3	0	1	2	3	0	1	2	3
10. Systematic observation in real-life problem-related contexts.	0	1	2	3	0	1	2	3	0	1	2	3
11. Physiological measures.	0	1	2	3	0	1	2	3	0	1	2	3
12. Case records.	0	1	2	3	0	1	2	3	0	1	2	3
13. Other (please describe).[b]	0	1	2	3	0	1	2	3	0	1	2	3

Key: 0 = (not at all); 1 = (somewhat); 2 = (fairly); 3 = (very).
[a] Overall ratings may range from 0 to 39 on each scale if no other sources are noted.
[b] Are these examples of one of the items already listed? If so, do not include here.

us say that your supervisor asks you to use the Zung Depression Inventory to assess a client's depression. What information do you need to judge for yourself whether this measure is a good choice (i.e., is it reliable; does it provide an accurate account of depression for this client)? Observation in real-life settings may be required to clarify problems and identify related circumstances. This may reveal discrepancies between self-report data and what is observed. Here, as well as in other helping phases, specialized knowledge may be required, as well as critical thinking skills, to weigh the accuracy of claims and soundness of different views and to integrate different kinds of information, such as research findings and the unique circumstances and characteristics of a client. Knowledge about the accuracy of different assessment frameworks and measures can help you to select referral sources that offer sound methods and evaluate data gathered by others. Judicious selection of assessment methods maximizes opportunities for understanding clients and their circumstances, including discovery of alternative behaviors that will compete with undesired behaviors. This allows you and your client to use positive methods to achieve hoped-for outcomes.

Assessment methods can be harmful, as well as helpful. Limitations of and related potential adverse consequences of assessment/diagnostic methods such as anxiety, worry, and unnecessary interventions because of a high rate of false positives, are often *not* candidly acknowledged. Even when the decision to use a test is well-argued, there may be risks that should be clearly described to patients. Hiding potential harm and inaccuracy of assessment methods is a common form of propaganda in the helping professions. Each source of information is subject to error. This may be random (unsystematic, varying) or systematic (biased in one direction).

Sources of random error include measurement changes (observers may fluctuate in their ratings) and changes in client characteristics (for example, in mood). Sources of systematic error include *demand characteristics* (characteristics of a situation that encourage responses in one direction). For example, we tend to present ourselves in a good light. This is known as *the social desirability effect*. Both random and systematic error may interfere with discovering a client's "true score" on a measure. Common errors when gathering data can be seen

EXHIBIT 17.4

Common Errors in Gathering Assessment Data

- Gathering irrelevant data (e.g., redundant data).

- Gathering only data that support preconceived views (confirmation bias).

- Using invalid, standardized measures (they do not measure what they are supposed to measure).

- Overlooking the role of environmental factors.

- Overlooking cultural differences that influence the validity and acceptability of given sources of data.

- Forgoing opportunities to observe behavior in real life or role plays when needed to clarify client concerns and options.

- Not involving significant others in collecting data.

- Vagueness (data do not clarify problems).

- Not describing setting events, antecedents, and consequences related to behavior of interest.

- Relying on unsupported opinions of other professionals.

- Relying on unsupported data in case records.

- Not performing function tests in which antecedents or consequences are altered to determine their effects on behaviors of interest.

- Disregarding an otherwise valuable measure because of a minor flaw.

- Relying on biased, unrepresentative samples (sampling too narrowly, for example, observing behavior on only one occasion that may not provide information about what usually occurs).

in Exhibit 17.4. Many errors involve or result in inappropriate speculation (assuming what is can be discovered simply by thinking about it). The question is: What method will offer information that will help you to help your clients? Criteria to consider in judging the value of data include: (1) reliability, (2) validity, (3) sensitivity, (4) utility, (5) feasibility, and (6) relevance. Karen Budd and her colleagues (2001) reviewed the content and legal relevance of clinical evaluations of parents conducted in child abuse and neglect (n = 190) mental health evaluation reports.

Evaluations of parents typically were completed in a single session, rarely included a home visit, used few if any sources of information other than the parent, often cited no previous written reports, rarely used behavioral methods, stated purposes in general rather than specific terms, emphasized weaknesses over strengths in reporting results, and often neglected to describe the parent's caregiving qualities or the child's relationship with the parent. (p. 93)

Assessment methods can be harmful, as well as helpful. For example, they may provide misleading directions for understanding of client concerns. Informed consent obligations may be violated by not sharing uncertainties regarding possible harms and benefits associated with use of a given method (e.g., a screening test for depression). Not sharing uncertainties may hide the fact that decisions involve a value judgment about how to balance risks and harms.

- Does a risk assessment measure accurately predict further likelihood of child abuse?

- Does a measure designed to assess the effects of traumatic life experiences accurately identify those who could benefit from counseling?

Many tests used by professionals are pseudoscientific; that is, there is no evidence that they are accurate and do more good than harm; there is no evidence that they contribute to accurate assessment. If this is true, they waste money and time. Focus on material that helps you and your clients to make informed decisions. Careless use of assessment measures and frameworks may result in oversimplification of client's characteristics and circumstances. Many tests focus on negative characteristics and may result in ignoring client assets. Standardized tests can give an illusion of rigor because of related scoring protocols and published material. They may be based on a faulty theory.

Here too, as when making decisions regarding selection of intervention plans, seek information about the evidentiary status of the method being considered in comparison with alternatives. If we read a claim that a measure is reliable and valid, is this true and what kind of reliability and validity were assessed? Are claims made about its usefulness accurate? Is there a better measure? We must be skeptical because limitations of practices and policies are often *not* candidly acknowledged. Professionals should be well informed regarding reliability and validity concerns of both assessment and evaluation methods so they are not mislead by bogus claims of accuracy. For example, standardization in how a measure is administered and interpreted is important to increase the accuracy with which a test is used. Rarely will you find a statement such as the following: "We only examined inter-item reliability (correlation among items). We do not know if the measure is stable. That is, we do not know whether a person who takes the inventory today, will get a different score four weeks from now in the absence of intervention." Unstable measures cannot accurately reflect change that may result from services provided. Thus, if a measure is unstable, feedback from the test may be misleading.

It may be assumed that changes have occurred when there has been no change. Has the validity and reliability of a test been independently investigated? Have only the creators of a test investigated its reliability and validity? (See later discussion.) And to what extent does a measure provide accurate information about clients in real-life situations? Responsibility for gathering such evidence falls, not to those who raise questions regarding the accuracy and reliability of a measure, but to those who forward claims about it.

Examples of Questionable Assessment Methods

Hunsley, Lee, and Wood (2003) describe a number of assessment techniques they regard as questionable based on a review of related empirical literature. These tests included the Rorschach inkblot test, the Thematic Apperception test, projective drawings, anatomically correct dolls, and the Myers-Briggs type indicator. (See also Lilienfeld, Wood, & Garb, 2000; Thyer & Pignotti, in press.)

Rorschach Inkblot Test

Surveys of psychologists suggest that many use this test in their everyday practice. Respondents are requested to describe what they see in 10 cards depicting a variety of inkblots that are purposely ambiguous. *Projective tests* such as the Thematic Apperception test, incomplete sentences test, and the Rorschach inkblot test are purposefully vague and ambiguous. It is assumed that each person will impose on this unstructured stimulus unique meanings that reflect his or her perceptions of the world and responses to it. Proponents argue that clinicians can gain insight into unconscious processes related to problems by what clients report seeing on the cards. Although different raters can attain high reliability with this test, there is no evidence for the validity of this test. Questions have been raised about the extent to which the use of the Rorschach is standardized; that is, do people use it in the same way, and are norms for different groups available? Investigations of test/retest reliability are difficult because people may remember what they said on the first test. Hunsley, Lee, and Wood (2003) conclude that "Despite decades of research, there has been no convincing accumulation of data supporting the use of the Rorschach in routine clinical practice" (p. 50).

Projective Drawings

Here too, there is a problem with use of different methods of administration and scoring making it difficult to explore reliability and validity. Here too, many clinicians continue to use projective drawings in spite of a lack of evidentiary status of their usefulness.

Anatomically Correct Dolls

The terms "anatomically correct" or "anatomically detailed" refer to the fact that such dolls have penises and orifices and breasts as appropriate. Such body parts are often exaggeratedly large. A wide variety of uses for such dolls is suggested, including comforting the child, forming an icebreaker, demonstrating certain things, as a memory stimulus, and as a diagnostic test to determine if a child has been sexually abuse or not (e.g., Everson & Boat, 1994). Advertisements for anatomically correct dolls (ACDs) (such as teach-a-bodies) routinely appeared in the National Association of Social Workers (NASW) monthly newsletter with no accompanying statement alerting readers to the questionable evidentiary status of this method for assessment. Potential consequence of errors (false positives and false negatives) are great. For example, a parent could be falsely accused of sexual abuse of a child.

A task force organized by the American Psychological Association (Koocher et al., 1995) concluded that ACDs did not meet any of the criteria for a valid psychological test or projective technique. However, this task force still suggested their use. Hunsley, Lee, and Wood (2003) suggest that this reflects "the tensions in psychological practice, and the lip service paid to science by some psychologists who are willing to examine research literature, but equally willing to dismiss it if it does not correspond to views founded on their clinical experience" (p. 60). These authors also note the importance of incremental validity: "that the use of any particular method including [ADDs] must be shown to consistently add to our ability to determine whether a child has been abused above and beyond all readily available information, such as interviews, observations, and rating scales" (p. 60). They suggest that the argument that ACDs are no worse than other assessment strategies is a discouraging position to take. Lack of standardization in the use of such dolls poses a problem for investigation of reliability and validity; if the way a test is used varies from time to time, there is no way it can be valid. Hunsley, Lee, and Wood (2003) conclude that there is no support for the use of anatomically detailed dolls as a screening instrument for evidence of sexual abuse. Given the implications of false positives and false negatives, as a result of reliance on ACDs, Cronch, Viljoen, & Hansen (2006) discourage their use.

> Overall, research in this area indicates that anatomically detailed dolls should be avoided with preschool children due to the suggestibility and lack of self-representational skills found in this age group. They may be useful tools with school age children, but should be used with caution and only when necessary to facilitate communication (p. 201).... Anatomically detailed dolls should be used cautiously, should be avoided with very young children, and should be introduced to obtain further details only after the child has already disclosed. (p. 205)

Such dolls were used by a social worker in the infamous McMartin Preschool trial in 1980, in which staff were accused of sexually abusing children in their care. All claims of abuse were unsubstantiated.

One could conclude from this discussion that considering the evidentiary status and practical utility of assessment measures is a hopeless matter. Reasons for optimism include strides that have been made for greater honesty, transparency, and client and practitioner involvement in critically appraising claims to avoid using measures that are not valid. The concerns raised here apply not only to claims that appear in professional newsletters but also to material in peer-reviewed professional and academic journals. Keep in mind that one of the key reasons for the development of EBP was the poor quality of peer review. Gray (2001b) described it as having feet of clay and noted the variety of biases that contribute to false information in journals.

Expert Testimony and Eyewitness Accounts

Professionals are often called on to testify as experts in hearings concerning child custody and allegations of sexual abuse. Weighty consequences rest on the accuracy of such testimony. Experts testify regarding the characteristics of a person. For example, did he have road rage? Does he have a personality disorder? A key question is whether such experts have the knowledge needed to make accurate assertions (see critique of expert testimony by Gigerenzer, 2002a; McCann, Shindler, & Hammond, 2003 for example). Consider the overturning of murder convictions because of flawed expert testimony (Sally Clark, 2003). We can protect ourselves from being misled by alleged "expert testimony" by being informed about factors that influence the accuracy and reliability of such reports (e.g., see Cutler, 2009). This also applies to eyewitness accounts. Research regarding the questionable reliability of eyewitness testimony should increase skepticism among all involved parties about the accuracy of such reports. (See also Goode & Schwartz, 2011; Weiser, 2011.)

Not for Researchers Alone: Concerns About Reliability and Validity

Concerns about validity and factors that influence this (e.g., reliability) are not confined to researchers. They are also relevant to everyday practice. If you rely on irrelevant or inaccurate measures, you may select ineffective or harmful plans because of faulty assumptions. If you rely on an inaccurate measure of social skill, you may assume incorrectly that a client has the skills required to succeed in certain situations when he does not, resulting in punishing consequences such as rejection.

Validity concerns the question: Does the measure reflect the characteristic it is supposed to measure? For example, does behavior in a role play correspond to what a client does in similar real-life situations? *Direct* (e.g., observing teacher–student interaction) in contrast to *indirect* measures (e.g., asking a student to complete a questionnaire assumed to offer information about classroom behavior) are typically more valid. Different kinds of responses (overt behavior, thoughts) may or may not be related to certain events. Clients may report being anxious but show no physiological signs of anxiety. This does not mean that their reports are inaccurate. For these individuals, the experience of anxiety may be mainly cognitive rather than physical. Types of *validity and reliability* include the following:

- *Predictive validity:* This refers to the extent to which a measure accurately predicts behavior at a later time. For example, how accurately does a measure of suicidal potential predict suicide attempts?

- *Concurrent validity:* This refers to the extent to which a measure correlates with a validated measure gathered at the same time; for example, do responses on a questionnaire concerning social behavior correlate with behavior in real-life contexts? Concurrent and predictive validity are sometimes referred to as *criterion validity*. In both, scores on a measure are compared to a criterion that is assumed to be accurate. For example, scores on a self-report measure of social skill could be compared with behavior in a role-play simulation.

- *Content validity:* This reflects the degree to which a measure adequately samples the domain being assessed. For example, does an inventory used to assess parenting skills include an adequate sample of such skills?

- *Construct validity:* This term refers to the degree to which a measure successfully measures a theoretical construct— the degree to which results of a measure correspond with assumptions about the measure. The finding that depressed people report more negative thoughts on the Automatic Thoughts Questionnaire (Hollon & Kendall, 1980) compared to nondepressed people adds an increment of construct validity to this measure. Evidence should be available showing that different methods of assessing a construct (e.g., direct observation and self-report) yield similar results (convergent validity) and that similar methods of measuring *different* constructs (e.g., aggression and altruism) yield different results (discriminant validity). That is, evidence should be available that a construct can be distinguished from other different ones.

- *Face validity:* This term refers to the extent to which items included on a measure make sense "on the face of it." Would you expect the items to be there given the intent of the measure?

- *Reliability:* This term refers to the consistency of results (in the absence of real change) provided by the same person at different times (time-based reliability), by two different raters of the same events (individual-based reliability as in interrater reliability), or by parallel forms or split-halves of a measure (item-bound reliability). Homogeneity is a kind of item-bound reliability assessing the degree to which all the items on a test measure the same characteristics. Homogeneity of a test is important if all items are supposed to measure the same characteristics. If a scale is *multidimensional* (many dimensions are assumed to be involved in a construct such as "loneliness" or "social support"), then homogeneity would *not* be expected.

Reliability places an upward boundary on validity. For example, if responses on a questionnaire vary from time to time (in the absence of real change), it will not be possible to use results of a measure to predict what a person will do in the future. Reliability can be assessed in a number of ways, all of which yield some measure of consistency. In test-retest reliability, the scores of the same individuals at different times are correlated with each other. Correlations may range from +1 to –1. The size of the correlation coefficient indicates the degree of association. A zero correlation indicates a complete absence of consistency. Correlations of +1 or –1 indicate perfect positive or negative correlations. The stability (reliability of a measure at different times) of some measures is high. That is, you can ask a client to complete a questionnaire this week and five weeks from now and obtain similar results (in the absence of real change). Other measures have low stability. Coefficients of reliability are usually sufficient if they are 80 or better. However, the higher the better (interrater reliability is discussed in the next chapter).

Other Important Considerations

The *sensitivity* of measures is important to consider; that is, will a measure reflect changes that occur? Insensitive measures will not offer information about progress or factors related to presenting problems.

The *utility* of a measure is determined by its cost (time, effort, expense) balanced against information provided.

Feasibility is related to utility. Some measures will not be feasible to gather. For example, clients who cannot read will not be able to complete written questionnaires. Utility may be compromised by the absence of empirically derived norms for a measure.

Relevance should also be considered. Is a measure relevant to desired outcomes? Do clients and significant others consider it relevant?

Norms offer information about the typical (or average) performance of a group of individuals. You can compare your clients' results with those of similar clients. Cut points in the distribution of scores are used to decide whether a client is in the "normal" range on a given characteristic and to make predictions about future behavior. Their placement will affect the rate of false positives and false negatives. Placing people into categories based on cut-points in a continuous distribution encourages pathologizing clients because what is in reality a continuous dimension (e.g., number of alcoholic drinks a day) is treated as categorical (e.g., normal or not). Be sure to consider the representativeness of norms in relation to your client. How similar is the client to the people whose norms were obtained? Are there cultural differences? The more representative the sample is to your client, the greater the utility of the measures in relation to a client.

Relying on the criteria discussed above will help you to select accurate, relevant measures. Resist the temptation to choose measures that are available and easy to use but are irrelevant or misleading. Compromises will often be necessary between feasibility and accuracy. The most valid measure may not be possible to use. You will often have to settle for measures that, although imprecise, provide helpful guidelines. You can improve accuracy by using multiple methods, relying especially on those most likely to offer accurate, relevant data. Take advantage of new technologies such as aps on iphones that help clients gather data.

Self-Report

Self-report is the most widely used source of information. There are many different types of self-report including verbal reports in interviews and answers on written inventories. Advantages of self-report include ease of collecting material and flexibility in the range of information that may be gathered. Some information can be gathered only through self-reports, such as beliefs about the cause of problems, plans for the future, and many past events. Only via self-report including narratives shared by clients may we understand their unique experiences—their unique subjectivities. "Always social, subjectivity encompasses all the identifications that can be formed by, discovered in, or attributed to the person" (Biehl, Good, & Kleinman, 2007, p. 348). Methods such as observation may not be feasible.

Structured interviews have been developed for both children and adults in a number of areas (Segal & Hersen, 2010). Some structured interviews provide a "psychosocial history" (description of the client's concerns and relevant current and past circumstances). Others are designed for a more specific purpose. For example, topics included in structured interviews regarding drinking problems may concern development of the problem, present drinking pattern and pattern history, alcohol-related problems, drinking settings and associated behaviors, beverage preferences, relevant medical history, reasons for drinking, effects of drinking, other life problems, and motivation for treatment. Even if you do not use these interview schedules as designed, they may be helpful to review to identify areas to explore. Many structured interviews are costly and time-consuming to administer. Like unstructured ones, they also are subject to error.

Critically Appraising Self-Report Data

When assessing the accuracy of self-reports, consider the following questions:

- Does the situation encourage an honest answer?

- Does the client have access to the information?

- Can the client comprehend the question?

- Does the client have the verbal skills required to answer questions?

- Is the interviewer familiar with and skilled in avoiding interviewer biases such as leading questions?

Familiarity with sources of interviewer bias may help you to avoid them (see Exhibit 17.5). The accuracy of self-reports is influenced by questions asked and characteristics of the interviewer (Stone, Turkkan, Bachrach, Jobe, Kurtzman, & Cain, 2000). (See also chapters 13 and 15.)

- Questions or terms may be vague or ambiguous.

- A particular sequence of questions may suggest certain answers.

- Too many questions may be asked (the inquisitor).

- Assumptions may be implicit in questions asked, as in leading questions.

- More than one question may be embedded in a single question.

- Interviewer preferences, emotional reactions, and biases may influence what is noted.

- Answers may be misunderstood.

- Recording errors may be made.

Client characteristics also influence self-reports.

- Desire to give socially desirable answers.

- Lack of understanding of questions.

- Faulty memory.

- Anxiety.

- No true opinions/preferences.

- Distracted because of poor timing of interview.

- Misunderstandings about the purpose of the interview.

The questions you ask reflect your beliefs about what is and is not important. They may obscure or clarify problems. Clients' answers may reflect popular beliefs proposed in pop psychology sources. For example, parents may inaccurately report that their child's problems started at a time suggested by certain popular psychological theories. We tend to ask questions that confirm our beliefs. This *confirmatory bias* may result in overlooking contradictory data and alternative (more accurate) views.

The response format used influences what is reported. Clients may give different reports if you ask closed-end questions calling for a "yes–no" answer than if you ask open-ended questions. Some people may have an *acquiescent response set* (a tendency to say "yes"). Use of inexact adjectives such as *often* or *seldom* can

---

EXHIBIT 17.5

Empirical Findings Regarding Children's Suggestibility

1. There are reliable age differences in children's suggestibility, with preschoolers being more vulnerable than older children to a variety of factors that contribute to unreliable reports.
2. Although young children are often accurate reporters, some do make mistakes—particularly when they undergo suggestive interviews; and these errors are not limited to peripheral details, but may include salient events that involve children's own bodies.
3. Measures can be taken to lessen the risk of suggestibility effects. To date, the factors that we know most about concern the nature of the interview itself: its frequency, degree of suggestiveness, and demand characteristics.

   - A child's report is less likely to be distorted, for example, after one interview than after several interviews. (The term *interviews* includes any conversations between adults and children about the target event.)
   - Interviewers who ask nonleading questions, who do not have a confirmatory bias (i.e., an attachment to a single hypothesis), who do not inculcate a negative stereotype about the defendant, and who do not repeat close-ended, yes/no questions within or across interviews are more likely to obtain accurate reports from young children.
   - Interviewers who are patient and nonjudgmental, and who do not attempt to create demand characteristics (e.g., by providing subtle rewards for certain responses) are likely to elicit the most accurate reports from young children.
   - Thus, at one extreme we can have more confidence in a child's spontaneous statements made prior to any attempt by an adult to elicit what they suspect may be the truth. At the other extreme, we are more likely to be concerned when a child has made a statement only after prolonged, repeated, and suggestive interviews.

4. Finally…as in most areas of social science, effects are rarely as straightforward as one might wish. For example, even though suggestibility effects may be robust, they are not inevitable, nor are they ineluctably large in magnitude.

Source: S. J. Ceci & M. Bruck (1995). *Jeopardy in the courtroom: A scientific analysis of children's testimony* (pp. 271–272). Washington, DC: American Psychological Association. Reprinted with permission.

give an illusion of precision and agreement that does not exist. We differ in our interpretation of vague terms such as *frequent* or *seldom* (Pepper, 1981). Repeated suggestions that a certain event occurred (when it did not) may result in inaccurate reports. For example, 58% of preschool children produced false stories to at least one fictitious event after 10 weeks of thinking about both real and fictitious events (Ceci, Crotteau-Huffman, Smith, & Loftus, 1994). Consider the report from Bill, a 4-year-old.

> My brother Colin was trying to get Blowtorch (an action figurine) from me, and I wouldn't let him take it from me, so he pushed me into the wood pile where the mousetrap was. And then my finger got caught in it. And then we went to the hospital. And my mommy, daddy, and Colin drove me there, to the hospital in our van, because it was far away. And the doctor put a bandage on this finger (indicating). (Ceci & Bruck, 1995, p. 219)

As this example suggests, the very process of thinking about a question may alter our memories (see also Loftus & Ketcham, 1994). Consider critiques of recovered memory therapy. Scholars such as Richard Ofshe present a compelling argument that not only may these alleged memories be false, they create havoc in people's lives, as well as in the lives of those they accuse (see Ofshe & Watters, 1994). This is not to say that all memories of past abuse are false. It is to say that some are, especially those that violate what we know about how memory works. Also, we must examine all four possible relationships between whether someone who reports being abused as a child remembers abuse, and whether it really occurred (Dawes, 1994b). This is usually *not* done, resulting in false estimates.

Often, we do not know what influences our behavior and so will not be able to identify relevant events. Our memories change over time (e.g., Loftus, 2004). We often overlook environmental causes. The more specific the question as to what a person would do in a specific context, the more likely self-report is to accurately reflect real-life behavior, given that motivational factors also favor an honest reply. A client may not understand a question and so offer incorrect material. Subtle differences in how questions are asked may yield different expressions of preferences. Thus, when inquiring about values and preferences, it is best to ask about these in different ways. Otherwise, the very process of asking about preferences may shape the responses given.

Clients may offer inaccurate reports because they are embarrassed over a lack of information, fear the consequences of offering correct accounts, or do not understand a question. If it is not in the clients' interests to share material, they are less likely to do so (e.g., see Ackerman, 2010; Rogers, 2008). Incorrect accounts may be given even though you do your best to put clients at ease. Descriptions offered may be related more to clients' beliefs about how they are expected to act than to what they really do. They may give incorrect descriptions about significant others because they dislike them or want to avoid responsibility for remedying troubling situations. *Social desirability* influences reports (we

tend to present ourselves in a positive light). Our views about a person's current personality influence recall of past events. Your confidence in the accuracy of a report may be increased by identical independent accounts. However, all observers involved may have been influenced by biasing factors. Examples of guidelines suggested by the National Center on Child Abuse and Neglect for interviewing parents in cases of suspected maltreatment include the following:

- Tell the parents that the child's physical condition or behavior is a matter of concern.

- Focus initially on the child's condition and its possible causes.

- Use open-ended questions (e.g., ask the parents if they know what happened).

- Do not try to prove abuse or neglect through accusations or demands.

- Do not display anger, repugnance, or shock.

- If appropriate, tell the parents that a report of suspected child maltreatment will be made and offer your continued support and assistance during the investigation.

Interviewing Children

As suggested earlier, special knowledge and skills may be required when interviewing children (e.g., Ceci, Gilstrap, & Fitneva, 2002). The importance of avoiding leading questions is demonstrated by the disregard for interview data collected in cases of alleged sexual abuse because of such questions. Guidelines for interviewing children recommended by the National Center on Child Abuse and Neglect include the following:

Do
- Make sure the interviewer is someone the child trusts.

- Conduct the interview in private.

- Sit next to the child, not across a table or desk.

- Ask the child to indicate words or terms that are not understood.

- Tell the child if any future action will be required.

Don't
- Allow the child to feel "in trouble" or "at fault."

- Disparage or criticize the child's choice of words or language.

- Suggest answers to the child.

- Display shock or disapproval of the parents, the child, or the situation.

- Force the child to remove clothing.

- Conduct the interview with a group of interviewers.

- Leave the child alone with a stranger (for example, a CPS worker).

DePanfilis & Salus (2003) suggest that the ideal interview setting is a comfortable room where stress is minimized for the child.

- A neutral setting where the child does not feel pressured or intimidated. The alleged maltreating person should not be in the vicinity.

- A room with a one-way mirror. This enables one person to be with the child while other professionals who need information can observe.

- A small table and chairs or pillows or rugs for sitting on the floor.

- Availability of anatomical dolls, felt-tipped markers or crayons and paper, toy telephones, doll house with dolls, Play-dough, puppets, etc. (p. 62)

A variety of methods including play materials, anatomical dolls, "guided imagery," or "memory work" storytelling may be used to gather data about children's feelings and experiences. As with any source of data, the validity and reliability of such methods should be explored. (See earlier critique of using anatomically correct dolls.) Both practical and ethical reasons encourage caution in using conjoint parent–child interviews to evaluate child allegations of sexual abuse by the parent. Faller, Froming, and Lipovsky (1991) suggest that such interviews are potentially traumatic for children and can be misleading. The child's developmental level should also be considered. (See also Faller, 2007.) DePanfilis & Salus (2003) note that:

- Preschool children's thinking is very concrete, and their ability to think abstractly is still developing. Since irony, metaphor, and analogy are beyond their grasp, it is very important not to assume that children understand concepts.

- Preschool children's…narratives tend to be disjointed and rambling, resulting in the need for the interviewer to sort out relevant from irrelevant data; it is beyond the children's cognitive capacities to do this alone. It is important not to ask them leading questions, however.

- Preschool children's understanding of space, distance, and time is not logical or linear, generally…

- Issues of truth versus lying are particularly complex in preschool years. Children in this age group may tell lies under two circumstances: to avoid a problem or punishment, or to impress adults or get attention.

- Preschool children generally…do not usually think of what effect their actions will have on others….As a result, interviewers of young children must be aware that

children may be emotionally spontaneous in ways that are occasionally disconcerting to adults.

- The attention span of preschool children is limited. Long interviews are not possible…

- Many 2- and 3-year-olds are afraid to talk with an unfamiliar person without a parent present. The interviewer should work slowly to help children separate from the parent, when possible. If this process is difficult, the interview may need to begin with a parent present working toward separate interviews at a later time, once the child feels more comfortable. (pp. 61–62)

This overview should caution you against uncritical acceptance of self-reports.

Standardized Measures

Standardized measures have uniform procedures for administration and scoring and are accompanied by certain kinds of information, including data concerning reliability, validity, and norms (average scores of certain groups). Standardized measures are used to: (1) describe populations or clients; (2) screen clients (e.g., make a decision about the need for further assessment or find out if a client is eligible for or likely to require a service); (3) assess clients (a more detailed review); (4) evaluate progress; and (5) make predictions about the likely futures of clients.

Varieties of Standardized Measures

Thousands of standardized questionnaires have been developed related to hundreds of different purposes (see, for example, Corcoran & Fischer, 2009; Jordan & Franklin, 2010; Lopez & Snyder, 2003). They include personality inventories, ratings scales, checklists, and surveys (see Exhibit 17.6). Some require only yes or no answers, others call for longer responses as in paper-and-pencil analogs in which clients note what they would do or say in specific situations. Many require little time and expense and are useful when methods such as observation are not possible. Others such as structured interview schedules may require considerable time (e.g., see Segal & Hersen, 2010). Some provide an overview of many areas. Others focus on one kind of situation.

Questionnaires can be used to gather demographic information (e.g., family composition, income, work history, and age), to explore attitudes, or to assess knowledge (e.g., of effective behavior in specific situations). You can compare the responses of your client to normative data (responses of others who complete the same measure). Be sure to explain the purpose of a measure before asking clients to complete it, and encourage them to be as accurate and honest as possible. Consider reading levels required, as well as cultural differences that influence

---

EXHIBIT 17.6

Examples of Standardized Measures

Measure	Purpose
Brief Anger Measure (Novaco, Swanson, Gonzales, Gahm, & Reger, 2012).	Determine degree of anger aroused by different situations with U.S. soldiers.
Automatic Thoughts Questionnaires (Hollon & Kendall, 1980).	Identify negative thoughts associated with depression (37 items).
Multidimensional Acculturative Stress Inventory (Rodriguez, Myers, Mira, Flores, & Garcia-Hernandez, 2002).	A 36-item measure designed to assess acculturation stress among persons of Mexican origin living in the United States.
Pleasant Events Schedule (MacPhillamy & Lewinsohn, 1982).	Identify pleasant activities engaged in over the past month and degree of enjoyment for each (320 items). Used to identify activities that may function as reinforcers for depressed clients.
Social Support Inventory (Barrera, Sandler, & Ramsey, 1981).	Assess perceived social support.
Abusive Behavior Inventory (Shepard & Campbell, 1992).	Assess domestic violence (30 items).
Attributional style questionnaire (Peterson et al. 1982).	Assess attributions.

---

the appropriateness of items. If a client cannot read, you could present items out loud. And, you should inform clients of any potential disadvantages of completing a measure such as false positives or false negatives (see chapter 11).

Objective tests include specific questions, statements, or concepts, and respondents are asked to reply with direct answers, choices, or ratings. Some focus on one area. Others review many dimensions. Julian Rotter's (1966) locus of control scale is an example of the former, and the MMPI is an example of the latter. Personality tests such as the MMPI (Minnesota Multiphasic Personality Inventory) offer data that are used as signs. Inferences are made about underlying dynamics, traits, or future behavior that may be determined by those traits. Other measures seek information about specific behaviors in specific situations. In the latter approach, it is assumed that the more specific the items, the more helpful the answers. The distinction between these approaches is known as the *sign* versus *sample* approach to assessment. A sample approach is preferred in contextual practice, because this offers more specific data about behaviors and related cues and consequences compared to sign approaches.

Projective tests (such as the Rorschach inkblot test) focus on assessing general personality characteristics and uncovering unconscious processes. Psychoanalytic concepts underlie use of most projective tests. Projective tests have little predictive validity and provide little guidance about what methods will be most helpful in resolving complaints. Little or no information is provided about environmental factors that may influence problems. (See prior discussion in this chapter.)

Checklists and rating scales consist of a series of items, for example, a list of behaviors. Respondents indicate which ones are descriptive of themselves or of significant others. Responses may call for a simple yes or no, or a scale may be used. For example, the Assertion Inventory (Gambrill & Richey, 1975) lists 40 behaviors, such as "resisting pressure to drink," and the

respondent is asked to indicate degree of discomfort on a scale ranging from 1 (none) to 5 (a great deal) and the likelihood of engaging in the behavior if the situation arose on a scale from 1 (always do it) to 5 (never do it). Scores on given item clusters can be used to discover areas of concern. More specific information about these areas can then be gathered. Rating scales are easy to score and take little time to complete. Responses on checklists are subject to the same type of demand characteristics as other types of self-report data. Items included are often vague (for instance, "impertinence"). Another disadvantage is the tendency to use overall scores to describe a person, which may obscure the situational variability in behavior. Many checklists emphasize problems rather than assets (e.g., Eyberg Child Behavior Checklist).

Paper-and-pencil analogs are designed to offer a sample of behavior that is assumed to reflect what a person would do in real life. They may be presented in a written form (paper-and-pencil analogs) in which specific situations are described and the client indicates what he would do in each one. Notice that this is a form of self-report and so subject to sources of inaccuracy in self-report data. Clients may write down what they would do in each situation or select an option from a list of alternatives. Paper-and-pencil analogs tap "content" knowledge. Content knowledge (knowing what) may not reflect performance skills (knowing how). Such measures may underestimate or overestimate what clients can do.

Critically Appraising Standardized Measures

As always, a key question is: " Is the measure valid?" Does it measure what it claims to measure (see Exhibit 17.7)? Is a person who has a high score on the Beck Depression Inventory really depressed? Do items included represent the domain of interest? Is there any evidence that scores on a measure will allow you to predict future behavior? What about concurrent validity? Do

Checklist for Reviewing Standardized Measures

_____ 1. Data are available showing that the measure is valid (measures what it is supposed to measure).

_____ 2. Data are useful in understanding client concerns.

_____ 3. Test-retest reliability is high (in the absence of real change).

_____ 4. Easy to complete and does not take much time.

_____ 5. Acceptable to clients.

_____ 6. Required reading levels match client skills.

_____ 7. Sensitive (small changes can be detected).

_____ 8. The user has the knowledge required to make effective use of the measure.

_____ 9. Norms are available for populations of concern.

_____ 10. Data concerning reactive effects are available.

_____ 11. Responses are quantifiable.

_____ 12. The false positive rate is low.

_____ 13. The false negative rate is low.

_____ 14. Biases are minimal (e.g., social desirability, response set)

_____ 15. Instructions for administration, scoring, and interpretation are clear.

_____ 16. Cultural differences are considered in relation to content.

scores correlate in expected ways with other measures that are accepted as a criterion? For example, do scores on a social skills inventory correlate with behavior during role plays? How high is the correlation? Can a measure be used to discriminate between people who have a certain characteristic and those who do not? For example, do scores on the Beck Depression Inventory help you to predict who will attempt suicide in the next 6 months and who will not? What about construct validity? Does a scale designed to assess altruism positively correlate with measures used to assess similar characteristics and negatively correlate with measures used to assess quite different characteristics (e.g., stinginess)? Direct measures (observing people in real-life situations) are often more valid than indirect ones (asking people what they do). Reliability should also be considered (e.g., see Urbina, 2004). How stable are responses on a measure given a lack of real change? Reliability should be 80 or better. Unstable measures are not likely to be valid. With unidimensional scales (those that include only one dimension in assessing a concept), find out about homogeneity (correlation between items). A measure may

not be valid because only one dimension of a multidimensional concept is included on a scale. For example, loneliness may be related to a number of different factors. Reliance on a scale that taps only one dimension may not offer an accurate view.

Will a measure detect change that occurs in events of concern? The cruder the measure in scoring options (e.g., yes/no compared to a continuum of ratings), the less sensitive the measure may be. Utility is also important. Can the measure be used? Is it feasible? Is it easy to administer? Is it easy to score and interpret? Will it offer you and your clients helpful information? For example, some measures may be satisfactory for assessing pre-post change but not detect day-to-day changes in behaviors of interest. Are norms available describing the scores of similar individuals? If there were no norms for the Beck Depression Inventory, you could not determine whether a client's score indicates an unusual level of depression. Norms may be available but not for people like your client. For example, your clients may be Latino, and available norms may be for Chinese Americans. These norms may not represent responses of Latinos. Norms should not necessarily be used as a guideline for selecting outcomes for individual clients because outcomes they seek may differ from normative criteria.

Limitations of Standardized Measures

As with verbal reports, responses on standardized measures may not offer an accurate picture. One disadvantage of standardized measures is overconfidence in the accuracy of a measure because of the appearance of rigor. Sources of error and bias that influence verbal reports also influence written measures. Factors that influence accuracy include response biases on the part of respondents (e.g., the tendency to answer in socially desirable ways); reactivity (completing the measures creates changes); and clarity of items (the more vague the questions, the more likely clients will interpret them in different ways). Questionnaires should be designed to avoid a yes/no response set by varying how items are worded (some in a positive direction and some in a negative one). Questions may be leading (suggest answers). Responses will be influenced by demand characteristics (pressures in a situation to offer a certain type of report). For example, clients may exaggerate problems when seeking help and exaggerate positive change following intervention—the hello-goodbye effect (Hathaway, 1948).

The language used may be biased. Words may be incomprehensible to respondents or have a different meaning than the one intended. The behavior of the test administrator, as well as the context in which a measure or test is completed, may bias results. Measures may not be accurately coded. Normative data may not be available allowing comparison of client responses with other similar individuals. Measures differ in the percentage of _false positives_ (respondents incorrectly assumed to have a certain characteristic) and _false negatives_ (respondents incorrectly assumed not to have a certain characteristic) (see chapter 20 on evaluating test accuracy).

Measures may have to be altered to increase their relevance for different cultural groups. Do not discard an otherwise valuable measure because of the inappropriateness of one or two items.

Change the wording or omit the items. Keep in mind, however, that if you alter a measure, available data about reliability, validity, and norms may no longer apply. Standardized personality inventories lack the detail necessary to plan for behavior change. Answers usually do not offer information about specific behaviors and related events. The use of such inventories may be helpful in selecting plans if there is evidence of correlations between certain traits and service outcomes. The criteria suggested 30 years ago for reviewing assessment measures for elderly clients shown in Exhibit 17.8 remain valuable today.

Interpreting Tests

Professionals tend to make certain kinds of errors in interpreting test results. For example, Steurer and his colleagues (2002) found that most in a sample of Swiss general practitioners (n = 263) "were unable to interpret correctly numerical information on the diagnostic accuracy of a screening test" (p. 826); only

22% selected the correct answer for the posttest probability of a positive screening test when given only the test result. Might the same apply to social workers informing clients about the results of tests for HIV? (See Gigerenzer, 2002.)

Professionals estimate the likelihood that a person has a certain problem such as depression. This is known as the initial *base rate probability*. They then may consider whether asking a client to take a test will be of value. The question here is: "To what extent is taking a certain test likely to decrease uncertainty about a particular assessment or diagnostic picture?" It serves little purpose to ask a client to take a test that will not change the base rate probability of the person *prior* to taking the test, or, if there is no change in what would be done, depending on what the test reveals, perhaps because there is no effective intervention. Thus, as many authors note, taking a test is only useful if it moves a client across an "*action threshold*." This refers to the point at which a different action will be taken depending on what is revealed in assessment.

EXHIBIT 17.8

Criteria for Reviewing Assessment Measures Used with Elderly Clients in Need of Care

- It offers comprehensive information about the client and the client's situation, providing the basis for an individualized understanding of concerns and selection of a service plan.

- It helps providers to make decisions with and on behalf of a client by providing information about functional abilities and suggesting the cause of observed problems and how they might be remedied. Information about potential to attain valued outcomes is offered.

- It is sensitive to changes in functional status over time.

- It is keyed to thresholds with practical significance for the client's well-being or independence.

- It provides an equitable way of making decisions about eligibility for services.

- It distinguishes small changes allowing distinctions among different levels of functioning at the lower end of the continuum where slight improvement or worsening might be significant.

- It provides information about both performance and opportunity. Performance is influenced by motivation and opportunity. For example, in some nursing homes residents are not allowed to bathe themselves. Case managers and caregivers need to determine capabilities apart from environmental constraints to select plans that maximize functional potential.

- It is acceptable to clients.

- It is acceptable to providers. The purposes of the questions are clear, the instrument is streamlined, and raters are capable of making accurate judgments.

- Costly or bulky equipment is not needed.

- A branching procedure is used so that it is suitable for clients whose functional status varies widely without requiring respondents to answer questions that are too difficult, too simple, or irrelevant.

- A branching format is used that allows exploration of areas of particular concern for individual clients.

- It produces categories of need that satisfy equity requirements in beginning and ending services across clients.

- It is supplemented with a brief screening procedure to determine the need for full-scale assessment. The initial intake assessment can be streamlined, with branching for reassessments and monitoring that emphasize collection of specific data at specific intervals, depending on the nature of desired outcomes.

- Decision rules are described to decide when the client is an appropriate informant and when reliable information should be sought elsewhere.

Source: Adapted with permission from R. A. Kane & R. L. Kane (1981). *Assessing the elderly: A practical guide to measurement* (pp. 248–249). Lexington, MA: Lexington Books.

In making this decision, it is important to consider where a test has been normed. Has it been tested for validity on clients with a known condition? For example, has a test of depression been normed using a sample of people known to be depressed by criterion indicators? The test will have different accuracy readings in a population in which there is a much smaller percentage of individuals with known depression. If used in such a population there will be a high *false positive rate*. That is, there will be a high rate of individuals labeled with the condition (depression) who do not have it. This has been found in many tests in the medical area, including mammograms used to diagnose breast cancer. This also applies to measures used to assess risk of further child abuse (Munro, 2004) (see chapter 20). Let us say a social worker works in an agency where staff see a high frequency of children who have been sexually abused. If such a test is used in an agency that sees a wide variety of children with a much lower base rate of sexual abuse, there will be a high rate of false positives. Thus, you should ask: "How will this test perform with my clients?" Does the pretest probability for my clients differ from the pretest probability of clients who were subjects in the study for which the test was developed?

We can estimate the test performance by using likelihood ratios. (See chapter 11.) A likelihood ratio nomogram can be used to visually depict the relationship between pretest and posttest probability in relation to likelihood ratios. Gilbert and Logan (2000, p. 26) note, "When faced with a [client], all you know is the test result—you do not know whether the test result is correct." The consequence of a positive or negative test will differ depending on the pretest probability. Evaluations that we may think are quite accurate, when carefully examined, often reveal considerable variability even in areas in which we assume that there is a high agreement such as judgments concerning cell pathology. There will typically be an overlap in test scores between what is considered normal and abnormal. Cut-off points are selected to try to optimally balance the kinds of errors that occur. The higher the cut point, the more you will make mistakes of false negatives. The lower the cut point, the more you will make mistakes of false positives.

Thus, in using a test to try to increase assessment accuracy, describe the client's probability of having a certain condition (e.g., being clinically depressed) prior to giving them a test. You could then search the literature to identify the best available study or systematic review that indicates whether a test will improve accuracy over pretest probability. Review research found using appropriate quality filters (e.g., sensitivity, specificity). Did the study include an independent blind comparison with an adequate reference standard and an appropriate variety of clients with whom the test would be used in everyday practice? Other questions include the following: (1) What is the likelihood ratio? (2) How precise is it? (3) Will the test help you and your clients to make sound decisions? (4) What is the posttest probability of the condition and does it cross your action threshold? (5) Were the methods for performing the test described in sufficient detail to be reproducible in your work? 6) Is the test feasible, and affordable, accurate, and precise in your setting? (Gilbert & Logan, 2000, pp. 32–33). You should also consider the extent to which test results will affect decisions you make in relation to initial severity and potential benefits of intervention and the extent to which it outweighs potential harms.

Special Precautions When Using Screening Measures

Standardized measures can be used to screen clients (e.g., to decide which clients are most at risk of abuse or most likely to benefit from a service). Unless you would do something different as a result of screening and unless an effective intervention is available (i.e., some decision rests on screening), it should not be done. Important characteristics of screening tools include brevity, lack of expense, and ease of use by people with little or no training. Accuracy in identifying those who do and those who do not have a certain characteristic or problem is a key concern. For example, what are the false positive and false negative rates? (See discussion of using tests to make decisions in chapter 20.)

Two purposes of screening can be easily confused: (1) case finding and (2) describing a population. These two purposes require different methods for selecting samples and tests and interpreting results. With case finding, the measure should be keyed to appropriate thresholds (e.g., cut points on measured scores) for identifying cases, and the sampling should focus on specific populations at risk. Using data derived from screening to estimate the prevalence of a concern in a population will result in overestimates of the prevalence (base rate). The higher the prevalence of some characteristic in a population (the higher the *base rate*), the higher the sensitivity threshold should be set; otherwise, most of the population would be screened in. A representative sample is needed to describe a population, as well as a measure that offers relevant data about areas of concern.

Screening Can Harm, as Well as Help

People often assume that screening cannot harm, but it can. As Gray (2001a) suggests, "Screening programs, like any other intervention, have a potential to do both good and harm," and "The balance between good and harm will change with the frequency of testing and the quality of the program" (p. 87). Eddy (1990) notes that the likelihood of a false positive in a high-risk person screened from ages 50 to 75 for colorectal cancer is about 40%. He argues that this information should be shared with clients before they are tested and, that without such information, clients are not accurately informed about the balance of good and harm from taking a test. Studies both in the health area and in psychology show that involving people in screening programs can increase anxiety and fear that one may have a disease or alleged psychological disorder. Thus, screening decisions should be made carefully. The following concepts are of value when searching for relevant research regarding tests: sensitivity, specificity, predictive value, false-negative rate, false-positive rate, diagnosis, differential diagnostic test, diagnostic service, routine diagnostic test, and diagnosis (see also chapter 20). The best method for appraising a test is a large well-designed RCT including outcomes such as survival or quality of life. Such studies are rare. Studies usually report better test performance (rather than quality of life and survival as endpoints), which may not be related to long-term survival or quality of life.

Asking Clients to Collect Data—Self-Monitoring

Clients often gather valuable information (see Exhibit 17.9). New technology such as smart phones allows user-friendly self-monitoring of relevant indicators such as emotional experiences (e.g., see http://www.usmedicine.com/psychiatry/new-smart-phone-application-designed-to-help-users-monitor-emotional-health.html). (See also http://quantifiedself.com/guide.) As with any other source, not all clients will be able or willing to participate. Benjamin Franklin kept track of his daily successes and failures in relation to virtues such as temperance (eat not to dullness, drink not to elevation), silence (avoid trifling conversation), order (keep things in order), resolution (meet goals set), frugality (avoid waste), industry (lose no time), tranquility (be not disturbed by trifles), and chastity (rarely use venery but for health or offspring; never to dullness, weakness, or the injury of your own or another's peace or reputation) (Silverman, 1986, pp. 91–92).

I determined to give a Week's strict Attention to each of the Virtues successively. Thus in the first Week my great Guard was to avoid even the least Offense against Temperance, leaving the other Virtues to their ordinary Chance, only marking every Evening the Faults of the Day. Thus if in the first Week I could keep my first Line marked T clear of Spots, I suppos'd the Habit of that Virtue so much strengthen'd and its opposite weaken'd, that I might venture extending my Attention to include the next, and for the following Week Keep both Lines clear of Spots. (Silverman, 1986, pp. 91–94)

Extensive education, training, and time are not required to gather data in real-life settings. Consider work with single mothers following divorce (Patterson & Forgatch, 1990). Fifty-five percent of these mothers received public assistance. The mothers kept track of daily pleasant and unpleasant events in structured diaries. Data were summarized over 6 days to determine the mean proportion of negative to total events. An irritability measure was also gathered. The mothers rated their mood twice a day on a 7-point scale ranging from irritable to calm. The mean of 12 scores over 6 days was used as an overall measure. The mothers also rated their anger each day on a 5-point scale. In addition, the sum of five items that made the mother angry that day was obtained. Social isolation was assessed based on three items: feeling lonely, without anyone to talk to, and without anyone to share experiences with. Percent of positive contacts was also obtained. The data provided valuable planning guides, as well as a basis for evaluating progress.

Advantages of self-monitoring include lack of intrusion by outside observers and an educational function in helping clients

---

EXHIBIT 17.9

Monitoring the Behavior of Others: Examples

Brian kept track of the number of times his parents praised and criticized him and noted what happened right before and afterward on an ABC form. His parents also kept track for one week of how often they praised and criticized Brian and what happened right before and afterward on a similar form. Mr. Colville (the social worker) showed Brian and his parents how to use the form and offered practice opportunities in recording before they left the office. Mr. Colvine thought that what was noted in the before columns would help the clients to identify relationships between their own behavior and that of other family members. He was familiar with the research showing that desired behaviors are often ignored and annoying ones reinforced in families experiencing problems. Mr. Colville calculated the mean rate for praise and criticism and reviewed what happened right before and after to identify related factors. Data were converted to rates since behavior was observed for different time periods. His summary was as follows:

Mrs. Lakeland's hourly rate of praise was .23 compared with an average rate of criticism of 1.5. Mr. Lakeland's average rate of praise was .24 and his average rate of criticism was .62. Mrs. Lakeland offered six times more criticism than praise and her husband offered over two times as much criticism compared to praise. The data indicated a low rate of interaction between Brian and his parents with Mr. Lakeland having an especially low rate. This low level was also reflected in statements Brian made during the interview and in observation of the family during interviews.

A review of antecedents suggested that Mr. Lakeland intervened when he thought that "things were getting out of hand" (he waited until high-level aversive behavior occurred before taking some action, usually a punitive one). Criticism rarely resulted in positive changes. Brian's response to praise was usually silence. Praise offered tended to be vague and mixed with criticism. Many reactions recorded as praise probably did not serve this function. This was supported by Brian's data recorded the same week. He noted only one incident of praise from his father and one from his mother and reported more criticism.

learn a useful skill; clients gain practice in clarifying concerns and identifying related factors. Client-recorded logs may reveal food allergies related to developmental delays in children. Attending carefully to the details of client concerns increases the likelihood that related circumstances will be discovered. The frequency of some events, such as thoughts and urges, can only be determined by self-monitoring. A mother could monitor her urges to hit her child; self-monitoring may be a first step in helping her to recognize and control such feelings. Identification of urges and engaging in alternative behaviors at this early point may help her to change her usual ways of acting. A daily record of dysfunctional thoughts and constructive responses may be kept.

Decisions

You and your clients will have to decide the following:

- What to observe and record.
- Who is to do it.
- When and where it is to be done.
- How it is to be done.
- Who has access to data collected.
- What prompts to arrange.
- What incentives to arrange.
- Over how many days information is to be gathered.
- What to do if difficulties arise.
- How to summarize data collected.

In choosing who is to observe and record, keep two criteria in mind. (1) Can the person provide reasonably accurate information? (2) How easy will it be to do so? Clients may collect useful information about exchanges with significant others. Whether they will collect data and how accurate they will be depend in part on whether you help them to create a recording method that is easy to use and provides valuable information. You will have to decide *how* events of interest (e.g., behaviors) are to be recorded. Decisions will depend on information needed, how frequently related events occur, and practical considerations such as time available. If a behavior occurs frequently, you could select one representative period to explore contingencies. If behaviors of interest vary in different situations, you may have to collect data in each one. You will have to decide on the daily length of the sampling period. Select recording assignments that are easy to complete and that provide valuable planning information.

Increasing the Likelihood That Clients Will Gather Useful Data

Designing successful self-monitoring tasks is a skill that develops with practice. You may discover valuable, easy-to-use

---

EXHIBIT 17.10

Checklist for Reviewing Self-Monitoring Tasks

1. The client knows what, when, where, and how to record.
2. Clients understand the purpose of self-monitoring.
3. Data gathered will be of value in case planning.
4. An easy-to-use recording method is used.
5. Positive behaviors are emphasized.
6. Practice opportunities have been given.
7. Prompts and incentives are arranged as necessary.
8. Clients are coached to continue acting as they normally would.
9. Recording will not interfere with daily activities.
10. An agreed-on date when data are to be shared is set.
11. Decisions have been made about who is to have access to records.

---

recording forms by consulting practice-related literature (e.g., Bloom, Fischer, & Orme, 2009). Be sure to select methods that do not intrude unduly on daily activities. Review points noted in Exhibit 17.10 before clients start to gather data. What is often blamed on clients or on limitations of self-monitoring as a source of information is often due to lack of skill on the part of helpers in selecting relevant, feasible procedures. Methods selected should match each client's unique skills and interests. Design or have on hand recording forms that permit easy, accurate collection of data. Codes may be used to make recording easier (e.g., S = social situation; W = work).

Be sure that forms are easy to fill out and readily accessible. Self-monitoring assignments are more likely to be carried out if obstacles are identified and arrangements made to overcome them. A recording method may be too cumbersome or times selected to observe too intrusive. If so, design an easier method and select more convenient times. Show clients how to record and provide practice opportunities before they try to collect data in real-life settings. Vague instructions or failure to check that clients know how to collect data will decrease the likelihood that useful information will be collected. Encourage clients to record observations as soon as possible after behaviors of interest occur as memory is fallible. Clients could videotape relevant exchanges on their cell phones for later review. You may have to arrange cues to remind clients to observe and record relevant information. They could use a kitchen timer, watch, or reminder via phone cues. And, you may have to arrange special incentives to encourage data collection. You can make recording easier for children by using drawings such as faces indicating different moods or degrees of pain or stick figures indicating different actions. They can circle the face that represents their mood or place a check next to the appropriate stick figure to indicate their responses. Clients may ask you to accept their recollections in lieu of recorded data. Such recollections may be inaccurate and are often vague. You could make access to further help contingent on receiving needed data. If data is really necessary to plan wisely, this makes good sense.

Telephone calls and e-mail provide an opportunity to collect data, to support clients for their efforts, and to troubleshoot (catch and correct problems at an early point). (See chapter 21 for additional guidelines concerning assignments.) If clients have difficulty, you may have to arrange additional practice and provide more detailed instructions. Further contact could be made contingent on receiving needed data. Support clients for initial efforts, no matter how far removed from the ideal. If they bring in *any* data at all, praise them for this and review how this is of value. If it is not feasible for clients to gather data, or if this is tried and is unsuccessful, other methods will have to be used.

Exploring Contingencies: Narrative Recording

This form of recording describes behavior and related events (what happens before and after specific behaviors of interest) (see Exhibit 17.11). It is used to identify events that cue and maintain behaviors of concern. Information about the frequency or rate of behavior is often provided at the same time. Smart phones allow videotaping and audio-recording of key interactions for later review. Teenagers who have problems managing aggressive responses could keep track of provoking antecedents, consequences, and self-ratings of anger. Feelings and thoughts, as well as behavior, could be monitored. An ABC recording form can be used in which three columns are listed: (1) what happened right before; (2) the behavior thought or feeling; and (3) what happened right afterward. Common errors in using narrative recording include the following:

- Not noting events that happen *immediately* before and after behaviors, thoughts, or feelings of concern.

- Concentrating on feelings and thoughts rather than behaviors.

- Recording too little data about specific behaviors of concern.

- Not being clear about what to record.

You could use code categories for frequently related situations to make recording easier. The recorder enters the relevant code to indicate what he was doing when a behavior occurred. For example, the categories (R) reading, (E) eating, and (W) working are some that have been used when keeping track of smoking. A chart can be made with days along the top and times along the sides (e.g., 7–8 A.M., 8–9 A.M.). The appropriate code can be noted when the behavior occurs. This information will indicate times and situations when a behavior is most and least likely. Be sure to clearly define what is to be recorded. An anxious client could record the date, time, and anxiety level on a scale ranging from 1 (very low) to 100 (very high), as well as what happened at that time. Data can be categorized in terms of intensity of anxiety (0–25, 26–50, 51–75, and 76–100) and records examined to identify events related to different levels. Information about factors related to social situations of concern could be collected by using a form with the following categories: date, time, situation, who was present, what I wanted, what I did, and what happened. Thoughts could also be noted to identify unhelpful and helpful self-statements. You could ask clients to write down what they *could* have done, said, or thought to assess their knowledge of effective reactions. Clients may prefer to record data in a diary.

Exploring How Often Problem-Related Behaviors Occur

Data describing the frequency or magnitude of relevant behaviors, thoughts, or feelings collected prior to intervention offer information about behaviors of concern and provide a baseline comparison point for evaluating progress. Behavior can be monitored in many different ways, including frequency recording (sometimes called event recording), in which the number of times a behavior occurs is counted; time samples, interval recording, and duration measures that are based on units of

---

EXHIBIT 17.11

Example of Narrative Recording

Date	Time	What Happened Right Before	Behavior	What Happened Right Afterward
10/15	4 P.M.	Brian lying on couch.	I said, "Get up and do something useful."	Brian said, "Ah, shut up—you do something useful."
10/15	5 P.M.	Brian refused to come to dinner.	I said, "You give me such aggravation—this is the last time I'm calling you."	Brian said, "Who cares?"
10/15	5:15 P.M.	Brian teasing his sister.	I said, "Stop. You are impossible."	Brian said, "Don't be an old nag."

time rather than on discrete behaviors; and measures of behavior products, magnitude, and distance. Data may be collected by clients or by significant others, depending on interest, time, and skills. A variety of aids are available for making recording easy and even fun. These include wrist counters, timers, biofeedback devices, and smart phones. Many items are inexpensive and can be loaned to clients. Audiotape recorders are useful for recording exchanges. Videotape recording may offer a valuable adjunct.

Ease of collecting data and the likelihood that relevant, representative information will result are key criteria to consider in making decisions. These criteria should be considered when deciding what to record, in what situations, how long observation periods will be, and who will collect data. Well-designed forms and readily available aids such as wrist counters increase the ease and accuracy of recording. If a client feels anxious only in certain kinds of social situations, data can be gathered only in these situations. If a mother has trouble at bedtime with her child, she can collect data only at this time. Clients could collect data about what happens before and after behaviors of interest at the same time they record data concerning frequency (see prior discussion of narrative recording). For example, a father who had physically abused his child while drinking kept track of what he drank, the situation, how much he drank, and the time, as well as his thoughts and feelings before and afterward (Stein, Gambrill, & Wiltse, 1978). This provided baseline data related to drinking, as well as information about related cues and consequences.

Frequency (Event) Recording

This refers to a count of the number of times a behavior, thought, or feeling occurs during a period of time (for example, hour, day, or week). This method is valuable when behaviors or events of interest have clear beginnings and endings. The rate must be low enough to count and individual instances relatively similar in duration. Thoughts or feelings may be recorded. For example, a client may be asked to note when she has an urge to eat. Behaviors can be listed along the top of a page and days down the left and a check made in the appropriate square each time a behavior occurs. This form is sometimes called a behavior checklist. It could be small in size (e.g., to place in a pocket) or large (if it is to be posted so that clients can easily see it). Recording forms or devices should be readily accessible and behaviors to be noted clearly described. If only one behavior is counted, a wrist counter can be used.

Total frequency counts are often too troublesome to obtain. An alternative is to record how often a behavior occurs during some time period, focusing on periods in which behavior is of particular concern. Recording responsibilities could be divided among significant others (e.g., staff and residents, family members). A disadvantage of recording only during selected periods is that the frequency of a behavior may vary in different situations. So recording only in one may not offer accurate accounts of the frequency in other situations. If behaviors

of interest occur often and regularly, sampling periods can be short while still providing a reasonable estimate of frequency. Time periods must be selected carefully if a behavior occurs only under certain situations or varies in different contexts.

Rate of Behavior

If observation periods differ from day to day, then you will have to use the rate of behavior as a measure. Divide the number of hours or minutes of observation into the number of behaviors that occurred. Let us say that a mother keeps track of how often she praises her son. On Saturday, she was home for 7 hours, and praised her son three times and on Thursday she was home for 3 hours and praised her son once. Her hourly rate of praise was 43 on Saturday and 33 on Thursday. If saying pleasant things was monitored over a 7-hour day, and the frequency was 5, the rate per hour would be 5 divided by 7, or about 0.7 per hour. Finding the rate of behavior in terms of some common index, such as number per day or hour, allows comparison of different behaviors. A convenient recording form includes room for the date, time (start and stop), total time, number of behaviors, and daily rate. Daily rate can be graphed for review.

One-Shot Recording

Some behaviors can occur only once in a given period. The behavior either does or does not occur during this time, which can be a month, week, day, or hour. Examples include making breakfast for children before they go to school and being on time for work. The behavior check sheet or a recording form allowing room to note the date and whether the behavior occurred can be used. The percentage of days on which the behavior occurred can be found by dividing the total number of days into the number of days in which it occurred.

Time Samples

Clients may not have time to record the frequency of a behavior even during a selected period. Or this may be difficult because what is of interest may not have a definite beginning and ending or may last for varying times (e.g., wearing an orthodontic device). Time sampling, in which behavior is sampled at fixed or random times, provides an alternative. Select times that offer representative information about behavior and related events. Preselected times can be written down on a form and a yes or no recorded for each, depending on whether the behavior occurred or not. Ideally, random times should be selected so that clients will not be able to predict when behavior will be checked. A cue may be needed to remind clients to check on behavior. Random times can be pre-selected and a timer set for each. Time samples may be gathered without selecting particular times. The observer simply records behavior when she happens to remember to do so or does so an agreed-on number of times during the day. Julie used time sampling to note whether she was worrying about her decision or not, the time she noted this information, and what she was thinking. You can find the daily percentage of times in which the behavior occurred by dividing the number of times the behavior was checked into the number of times it was observed. If a parent checked on her son's behavior five times and recorded only one instance, the daily percentage for that day would be 20.

Gathering information on an hourly basis may be helpful in discovering factors related to complaints. Schwartz and Goldiamond (1975) asked a client to record the following every hour during the day: what he was doing (work); the setting (sitting at desk); who was there (self); what he wanted (to get work done); what happened (little accomplished); and comments (sat and daydreamed). These records revealed events related to difficulty in completing work, such as going to other people's offices rather than having clients come to him.

Duration

Measures of duration are useful when behaviors are continuous rather than discrete and when the objective is to alter the length of time a behavior occurs. The total length of time a behavior occupies either for a single occurrence (duration of a temper tantrum) or over a certain time period such as a day (for instance, daily time spent doing chores) could be measured. Make sure that the onset and ending of a behavior are easy to determine. Use of duration allows you to set approximations to a desired outcome rather than using an either/or criterion as in the one-shot method. Duration is not necessarily the method of choice for behaviors that vary in length of time, such as tantrums, because recording this may be too time-consuming. A time sample could be used instead. A client could check whether the behavior is occurring at random times and find out the percentage of instances in which it did occur, or a required time lapse could be imposed between behaviors before recording another instance. If observation periods differ in length, the proportion of time in which the behavior occurred can be determined.

Magnitude/Intensity

Magnitude (e.g., intensity of pain or anxiety) may be the most relevant measure. Noise level could be recorded by using a decibel counter. Depression could be rated on a scale ranging from 1 (none) to 10 (very high). Self-anchored scales are often used to rate magnitude of emotional reactions.

Self-Anchored Scales

Self-anchored scales are often used to measure thoughts, feelings, and behaviors. These are individually tailored for each client. Clients select anchors at each end of a dimension such as 1 (no energy) to 5 (full of energy). Advantages include flexibility in designing a scale that matches the unique circumstances of each client. Self-anchored scales can be used to assess events (such as

urges and negative thoughts) that cannot be determined by other means. (See Bloom et al., 2009, for more detail.) Disadvantages include lack of norms. Because these are individually constructed, no norms are available allowing comparison of the client's responses with those of others. In addition, no information may be available about reliability and validity. Steps Bloom et al. recommend when creating self-anchored scales include the following:

1. Help clients define problems and desired outcomes using their own words.

2. Decide on the number of scale points. Clients could rate their depression on a scale that includes 1 (none), 2 (a little), 3 (moderate), 4 (intense).

3. Encourage clients to view scale values as equally distant from each other. A thermometer analogy is sometimes used.

4. Use scales with one dimension.

5. Give clear examples of scale values. Examples of values used to rate anxiety in social situations may be as follows:

   25: Mild anxiety that does not interfere with behavior.

   50: Uncomfortable anxiety that affects concentration but does not disrupt behavior.

   75: Uncomfortable preoccupying anxiety (it is hard to concentrate and the client has thoughts of leaving the situation).

   100: The highest anxiety ever experienced or that the client can imagine feeling.

6. Decide how often the client will complete the scale and where.

Other Measures

Keeping track of behavior products may be useful when other forms of observation may affect the frequency of a behavior or when it is too time-consuming to observe behavior directly. Examples include empty beer cans, problems completed, meals prepared, and weight. *Latency* may be the most appropriate measure. Examples include time elapsing between a parent's request and a child's compliance and time between lying down and falling asleep. Use of latency as a measure requires clear description of a cue (e.g., a request) and when a behavior starts and stops. *Distance* will be the choice for some valued outcomes (e.g., when a client wants to travel farther from home without fear).

Reactive Effects of Self-Monitoring

Self-monitoring draws attention to particular behaviors and so may influence their form or frequency. Such changes are called *reactive effects*. They may be negative or positive. Positive effects include an increase in desirable behaviors or decrease in undesired behaviors. Students who monitored their study time had significantly higher grades than those who did not (Johnson & White, 1971). Negative reactive effects include an increase in undesired behavior or a decrease in desired behavior. The effects of self-monitoring usually fade over time (but not always) (Maletzky, 1974).

Factors That Influence Reactivity

Factors that influence the "reactivity" of self-recording (whether self-recording results in a change in the frequency of behaviors, thoughts, or feelings) are described below (for more detail see Korotitsch & Nelson-Gray, 1999).

1. *Motivation.* Self-monitoring may result in greater reactivity if clients are motivated to change their behavior. For example, Lipinski et al. (1975) found that self-monitoring decreased smoking only for people who were motivated to stop smoking. Monitoring resisted urges to smoke decreased smoking, whereas recording number of cigarettes smoked increased it (McFall, 1970). Clients tend to underestimate their undesirable behaviors and overestimate desirable ones.

2. *Setting goals and offering feedback.* Reactivity is greater if specific goals are set and incentives are offered for attaining them; feedback concerning performance increases reactivity. (See, for example, Locke and Latham, 2002.)

3. *Timing.* Recording a behavior before it occurs interrupts the usual chain of behavior and provides an alternative to an undesired reaction such as hitting or yelling.

4. *The recording method.* Intrusive methods are more reactive. A wrist counter may function as a cue that influences behavior.

5. *Schedule of self-monitoring.* Recording behavior at the end of the day or periodically during the day seems to be less reactive than continuous recording. Clients who monitored their mood and recorded their activities hourly reported an increase in pleasant activities and a decrease in depressed mood (Harmon, Nelson, & Hayes, 1980). Self-monitoring was cued by a timer set on a variable-interval (1-hour) schedule. Such effects have not been found for clients who recorded their mood or activities once a day.

6. *Other factors.* Instructions may influence reactivity. If you suggest that a client's worrisome thoughts will decrease, they may. The more behaviors that are monitored, the less the reactivity (and the less likely that the client will monitor them). Reactivity seems to be greater for nonverbal than for verbal behaviors. (For detailed discussion of homework assignments, see Tompkins, 2004.)

Accuracy of Self-Monitoring

Variables that enhance reactivity will decrease accuracy. There are many ways you can increase accuracy. If clients object to recording "negative" behaviors (e.g., yelling at children), ask them to track positive alternatives. Clearly describe behaviors so clients can easily identify them. Use recording methods that are not intrusive and encourage clients to record data right after relevant behaviors occur. Clients will not gather data if recording interferes with their daily life activities. Training and practice increase accuracy. Be sure to consider the potential negative effects of monitoring. For example, monitoring inaccurate solutions on a mathematics task resulted in decreased self-reward and accuracy, and lowered self-evaluations (Kirschenbaum & Karoly, 1977). Asking a depressed client to write down negative thoughts may increase these, and clients should be prepared for this. Individually tailor recording tasks for each client. A particular method may be easy for some clients and difficult for others.

The observer's behavior may change as a result of watching someone else. For example, parents may decrease their use of criticism as a result of using narrative recording in which they note the frequency of their child's annoying behaviors, as well as what they do before and after. Check on the representativeness of data by asking clients and significant others whether exchanges noted are typical of what usually occurs. You will have to decide whether to tell significant others they are being observed. Not telling them may have ethical problems. Telling them may result in changes in their behavior. A child who bullies other children on a playground may not do so when he knows he is being watched by a teacher. The effects of observation typically decrease over time as the usual real-life contingencies take precedence. The main concern is to obtain a reasonably accurate account of behaviors and related events.

Observing in the Natural Environment: Seeing for Yourself

Observing clients and significant others in real-life settings may be needed to identify behaviors of concern and related antecedents and consequences with your client's permission (see chapter 18). Overlooking the value of observation contributes to the *fundamental attribution error* in which problems are incorrectly attributed to clients' personal characteristics and related environmental circumstances are overlooked. No matter how good our reasoning skills are, if we base our decisions on inaccurate data, we will be less likely to help clients. The money and time saved by not observing behaviors of concern in real-life settings when necessary for accurate assessment may be wasted many times over in lost opportunities to help clients because of incorrect views of their concerns. Observing behavior during interviews may offer clues about how other people respond to clients and how clients feel about topics discussed. (See chapter 18 for discussion of use of role plays for assessment.)

Physiological Measures

Measures include heart rate, respiration rate, skin conductance, muscle tension, and urine analysis. Although some measures require expensive equipment, others do not, such as pulse and respiration rate (e.g., see Turk & Melzack 2011). Physiological measures are useful when verbal reports may be inaccurate. Other examples include measuring blood pressure of clients with hypertension, breathing function of asthmatics, and breathalyzer tests to determine blood alcohol levels. Many such measures are used in behavioral medicine. HIV tests are often given. (For a critical view of the latter, see Bauer, 2007; Gigerenzer, 2002.) Here too, technological innovations permit real time data collection. Swyer Syndrome is a rare condition in which an individual female has the male x-y chromosome pattern. DSD (disorder of sexual differentiation) is the medical term for hermaphrodite. Failure to detect this may result in avoidable distress (e.g., Allday, 2011).

When to Insist on a Physical Examination

Anxiety, aggression, depression, headaches, and sexual problems may be related to physical causes. In such instances, a physical examination may be vital. Without this, physical causes may be overlooked. Consider the inaccurate diagnosis of people who have Wilson's disease. Symptoms of this illness include various psychological changes, as well as trembling. Wilson's disease is a result of failure to absorb copper, and it can be diagnosed by a blood test as well as by certain indications in the eye. Nutritional deficiencies may result in psychological changes, as may prescribed medication.

Case Records

Advantages of reliance on archival and case records include savings in time and cost, unobtrusiveness, and availability. Examples of archival records include school grades, police reports, and hospital records. Disadvantages include missing data (see Exhibit 17.12). Records may not contain clear descriptions of problems, desired outcomes, or related contingencies. Vague, obscure language may confuse and mislead rather than enlighten. Assessment methods and services offered may be vaguely described, as may claims about progress. Information about current life circumstances may be missing. It is sometimes even hard to discover what the presenting concerns were. And, often there is a focus on pathology rather than on assets.

EXHIBIT 17.12

Common Problems with Case Records

- Presenting problems are not described.
- Assumed pathology of clients and significant others is focused on; assets are ignored.
- Descriptions of problems, desired outcomes, and related
- circumstances are vague; they do not provide case planning guidelines.
- Environmental causes are overlooked.
- Important demographic information is missing (e.g., age, household members).
- Irrelevant content is included.
- Unsupported speculations are offered (conclusion based on insufficient data); theory is presented as fact.
- Jargon (psychobabble) is used.
- Conclusions are drawn based on small biased sample.
- Descriptions and inferences are confused; descriptive terms are used as explanatory terms (see chapter 12).
- Assessment procedures are not clearly described.
- Service goals are vague.
- Up-to-date information is missing.

The accuracy of archival data such as school or police records is influenced by the biases of those who record data and by policy changes about what, when, and how to record. Material may be hard to find because it is scattered through a lengthy record. Conclusions are often based on vague grounds, and alternative accounts are rarely suggested. Often no information is given about the basis for inferences or how they may be helpful in achieving hoped-for outcomes. We may read "This client is paranoid" with no details presented as to why this conclusion was reached or of what help it will be. Inferences made may be based on one of the questionable criteria described in chapter 4. The sources on which claims are based should be critically examined no matter who prepares a report. Questions include: Are claims well reasoned? What evidence is presented for inferences? Are alternative possibilities noted? Do suggested causes provide clear guidelines about what to do? (See Tallent, 1993.)

Data Provided by Other Professionals

Clients may be referred to other professionals. Whether data provided are helpful (or misleading) will depend on the match between the questions asked and the knowledge and skills of the involved professional, as well as available information regarding questions. Critically review data they provide using the same questions you would use to review material from any source: How valid are tests used? Are inferences well reasoned? Do not be intimidated by credentials and degrees. If you are working with people who are indeed professionals, they will welcome questions about their assumptions and will take the initiative in telling you about any limitations of tests used and assumptions made.

What to Do About Discrepancies

What if reports from different sources provide contradictory data? Certain kinds of discrepancies are common and may provide useful assessment data. They may suggest underlying physical causes (e.g., Rutter & Yule, 2002). Verbal reports of anxiety often lag behind performance measures. For example, clients may report more fear than they show in real-life situations. Lack of agreement may occur because clients differ in their reaction patterns. Some clients have marked physiological changes in anxiety-provoking situations. Other clients may experience anxiety mainly cognitively (have anxious thoughts). Discrepancies between reports of different people are more the rule than not in some areas such as reports from children, teachers, and parents (Angold, 2002). Different parties may attend to different behaviors.

Differences between verbal self-reports and responses on written measures may be a result of different wording or response formats. Overall scores on a measure that reviews behavior in a variety of situations may not reflect reactions in particular situations. Consider the Assertion Inventory, which measures anxiety in a wide variety of social situations (Gambrill & Richey, 1975). Discrepancies between verbal reports of anxiety and overall scores may occur because a client experiences anxiety only in some of the situations described on the inventory. Only one subscale (cluster of items) on an inventory may be correlated with behavior in certain situations, not the overall score. A client may be anxious when initiating conversations and arranging future meetings but not when refusing unwanted requests and responding to criticism.

Keeping Track of Material

There are many ways to keep recording minimally time-consuming and maximally useful, including taking advantage of user-friendly computerized systems. Well-designed forms will make it easy to record and organize data. You may have to take notes during interviews to keep track of material. Note taking does not have to interfere with attentive listening. Be sure to

explain what you are noting and who will have access to your notes. If possible, schedule time between interviews to keep up with recording. You could audiotape interviews for later review with the client's permission. If you do, explain your purpose for taping interviews and inform the client about who will have access to taped material (e.g., your supervisor) and when tapes will be erased. Typing notes directly into a computer saves time. Staff in many agencies routinely do so. Errors may be decreased by use of easily accessible smart phones. Information storage and retrieval skills regarding practice-related research findings and assessment tools is also important (Gray, 2001a). Information that will help you to help your clients is of little use if you cannot quickly find it when you need it.

Ethical Issues

Select measures that are valid and relevant (they provide information that will help you and your clients to make well-reasoned decisions about what to do next). This may require consideration of cultural differences (e.g., Sue & Sue, 2008). Avoid unnecessary tests that waste the client's time and tests and questions that pathologize or stigmatize clients. Be sure to inform clients about any known potential negative effects of a test such as overdiagnosis and overtreatment because of high rates of false positives (see chapter 20). Consider possible negative effects of contacting collateral sources. Contacting a supervisor at work with whom a client is having trouble is not a good idea if it would make things worse for the client. You should use only methods you are competent to use, for example, know how to interpret data collected. Resist temptations to use methods that are easy to use and at hand, but offer few or no guidelines about how to help clients.

Summary

You and your clients will have to decide what data to collect to explore how (or if) hoped-for outcomes can be achieved. You should only be as precise as you have to be to clarify problems and options. Sources of data to choose among include self-reports in the interview, written measures, self-monitoring, role play, observation in real-life settings, case records, and physiological measures. Each source is subject to error. Focus on gathering useful data—data that decrease uncertainty about how to help clients and to determine if you can. Some sources will not be feasible. For example, some clients will not be able to provide needed information in the interview. Some clients will refuse to gather data at home. What is often blamed on clients (they will not or cannot collect data) is often due to lack of care, creativity, and flexibility on the part of helpers in selecting feasible, relevant data collection methods. What is needed is a representative picture, not a totally accurate account—data that will guide next steps (e.g., be of value in selecting plans). If needed, combine self-report data with data collected in the natural environment. The function test (altering circumstances to determine their influence on behavior) is the final arbiter of whether data gathered and assumptions made are accurate. Social workers tend to rely too much on verbal reports, neglecting self-monitoring, role play, and observation in real-life. Being informed about the advantages and disadvantages of different sources of data will help you and your clients to make informed decisions, whether you offer direct services or refer clients elsewhere.

Reviewing Your Competencies

Reviewing Content Knowledge

1. Identify key questions that arise regarding assessment.

2. Describe sources of assessment information and the advantages and disadvantages of each.

3. Identify databases of value regarding information needs concerning assessment methods.

4. Describe conditions under which verbal reports are likely to be accurate.

5. Identify helpful criteria for assessing measures.

6. Define the term *reactivity* and give an example.

7. Describe the difference between a frequency count and a time sample and give an example of each.

8. Given examples of specific client concerns, describe feasible means that clients or significant others could use to collect valuable data.

9. Accurately appraise research reports regarding assessment methods.

10. Identify circumstances in which an assessment measure may not be relevant.

11. Define the terms *reliability* and *validity* and give examples of different kinds of reliability and validity. Describe why each is important.

12. Describe steps you can take to increase the accuracy of self-monitoring.

13. Identify characteristics of helpful self-monitoring assignments.

14. Describe steps you can take to increase the likelihood that clients will gather useful data.

15. Describe how rate of behavior is determined.

16. Identify questions that should be asked about standardized measures.

17. Given specific examples, describe why a data collection method was not successful.

18. Give examples of the value of norms.

Reviewing What You Do

1. You pose well-formed questions regarding assessment needs that permit efficient, effective searches for related research findings.

2. You can accurately identify well-structured questions.

3. You accurately appraise the evidentiary status of an assessment measure based on critical appraisal of related research.

4. You design feasible, relevant self-monitoring assignments.

5. You complement indirect sources (e.g., self-report) with direct ones (e.g., observation) when possible and important.

6. You accurately evaluate the quality of evidence in case records.

7. You make effective use of written questionnaires.

8. You gather valuable case planning information in role plays (see chapter 18).

9. You include graphed baseline data relevant to desired outcomes in clients' case records.

10. You use an effective information retrieval system that allows you to quickly locate needed assessment measures and forms.

11. You use valid assessment methods with your clients.

12. You take advantage of user-friendly technology to gather data.

Reviewing Results

1. You discover practice-related research findings that contribute to selection of valid assessment measures.

2. Clients collect useful data.

3. Clients report that collecting data was helpful.

4. Data collected result in selection of successful plans.

5. Clients acquire useful problem-solving skills, for example, clearly describing desired outcomes and related factors.

18

Observation: Learning to See

OVERVIEW   This chapter offers guidelines for observing behavior in real-life settings and for evaluating data gathered by others. Evaluating observational reports and gathering accurate data based on observation are valuable practice skills. Common sources of error are described, as well as suggestions for avoiding them.

YOU WILL LEARN ABOUT

- The value of seeing for yourself

- Role play (analog situations)

- Observation in the natural environment: seeing for yourself

- Critically appraising observational data

- Observing the physical environment

- The value of observation in task analyses

- Obstacles

- Keeping track of data

The Value of Seeing for Yourself

Observation in real-life settings may be required to understand client circumstances and identify behaviors of concern (see Exhibit 18.1). Without a fine-grained (detailed) description of behaviors and contingencies related to hoped-for outcomes based on careful observation, you may miss opportunities to help clients. (See Exhibit 18.2). You may overlook alternate available repertoires that can be used to attain hoped-for outcomes. Systematic observation of student/teacher behavior is an important skill for school social workers (see Watson & Steege, 2003). It is used to screen children, to identify those in need of further evaluation for assessment of behavior and emotional problems, to describe the ecology of the classroom, to select academic interventions, and to track results of different kinds of interventions (Downer, Booren, Lima, Luckner, & Pianta, 2010; Volpe, DiPerna, Hintze, & Shapiro, 2005). Interactions between peers

---

EXHIBIT 18.1

The Value of Observation

At age 11, Sam Brown burned down his neighbor's garage and was sent to a residential youth facility. Two years later he returned home. The adjustment wasn't easy. Sam fought with his two younger brothers, and their mother (Anne) had difficulty handling them. Sam's father worked at night and was reluctant to discipline the children, fearing he would lose his temper. With all three boys home during summer vacation, tensions mounted. One afternoon, while playing outside, Sam and his 9-year-old brother, Frank, got into a violent fight. A neighbor called the police when Sam began choking Frank. The police took Sam, accompanied by his mother, to a psychiatric emergency room. The hospital called in a social worker from the Home-Based Crisis Intervention Program, who drove Sam and his mother home. The next morning the social worker returned to talk to them.

Over the next 6 weeks, the worker spent almost every other day with the family and was able to observe their daily routines at first hand. He discovered that Sam was not always the instigator of fights with his brothers. In fact, his brother Frank often started a brawl and then blamed it on Sam. (Frank had assumed the role of "number one son" while Sam was away and was upset about giving it up.) The worker brought this to their mother's attention and encouraged her to discipline all three boys and not just Sam. "Anne had good parenting skills," the worker recalls. "What she needed was a lot of reassurance that she could handle them." They worked on building her confidence in her parenting skills and her ability to take charge when a fight broke out.

Source: Adapted from S. Leavitt & B. McGowan (1991). Transferring the principles of intensive family preservation services to different fields of practice. In E. M. Tracy, J. Kinney, & P. Pecora (Eds.), *Intensive family preservation services: An instructional sourcebook* (pp. 61–62). Cleveland: Case Western Reserve University, Mandel School of Applied Social Sciences.

---

may be recorded, as well as interaction between teachers and students using smartphone apps. A wide range of observation systems are available including those for observing and recording collective action (Schweingruber & McPhail, 1999). Each individual and each environment is unique. Only through careful observation may interaction patterns between clients and significant others be understood (e.g., Bakeman & Gottman, 2010; Kerig & Baucom, 2004; Kerig & Lindahl, 2004). As the designers of one observational form note, "It is more respectful of a person's dignity and autonomy to assume that functional reasons exist for challenging behavior rather than to think that it occurs because of some major 'trait or [personality] characteristics'" (O'Neill, Horner, Albin, Storey, & Sprague, 1990, p. 28) (see also Crone, 2003; Repp & Horner, 1999). Sherlock Holmes emphasized the importance of "observing" what others merely "see" (Truzzi, 1976, p. 60). Observation of community and neighborhood characteristics may be vital to understand client circumstances (See chapter 27.).

Overlooking the value of observation contributes to the *fundamental attribution error* in which problems are incorrectly attributed to clients' personal characteristics and related environmental circumstances are overlooked. No matter how good your reasoning skills are, if you base your decisions on inaccurate data, you will be less likely to help your clients. The money and time saved by not observing behaviors in real-life settings when necessary for accurate assessment may be wasted many times over in lost opportunities to help clients because of incorrect views of concerns. Observing behavior during interviews may offer clues about how other people respond to clients and how clients feel about topics discussed. You may note that family members interrupt one another and offer few positive comments. Keep in mind, however, that behavior during interviews may not correspond to what occurs in real life (e.g., at home).

Given the possible lack of agreement between self-report and observational data, gather both when needed and possible (see Exhibit 18.3). If observation in real life is not possible, observation during role plays may be a good alternative. The question is which method offers accurate information about behaviors of concern and related circumstances. The *function test* (altering specific antecedents or consequences to determine their

---

EXHIBIT 18.2

Common Errors Related to Observation in Real-Life Settings

- Not believing it is important when feasible and relevant.
- Using vague descriptions, poorly defined behavior categories.
- Overlooking biases that interfere with accurate observation (e.g., stereotypes).
- Not describing behaviors in their context (setting events, antecedents, and consequences related to behaviors of concern are not described).
- Using invalid coding systems; e.g., behaviors of concern are not included.
- Assuming that what is observed in one setting reflects what occurs in others.
- Confusing inferences and descriptions.
- Assuming that agreement between observers indicates accuracy.
- Not checking reliability (interrater agreement)
- Overlooking reaction effects on individuals observed.

EXHIBIT 18.3

Using Multiple Sources of Information

Elsie Pinkston and her colleagues used observation of problem-related exchanges, as well as other sources of information such as self-monitoring and self-report, in their work with elderly clients and their caregivers. "Very often an observation session follows the initial interview. During this session the practitioner spends an hour or more at the client's home, observing interactions and activities. When possible, another observer besides the practitioner participates....*Anecdotal observations* are usually recorded in three columns: antecedent events, client behaviors, and consequent events, with all client behaviors being recorded in the center column. The arrangement provides the groundwork for a preliminary functional analysis of the client's interaction with the environment and a more accurate guess at appropriate and inappropriate behaviors to be measured. Thus, behaviors of others in the client's environment, as well as the client's behaviors, are included.

Mr. Young was referred to a home health care social worker because the family and the home care nurse were concerned about his low activity level, his refusal to converse or socialize, and his general depression. His severe cardiac condition placed some limitations on active behaviors. During a preliminary anecdotal observation, the practitioner found that Mr. Young was not responsive to efforts by family members to converse with him (he mumbled or answered in very brief sentences). The practitioner also observed that family members had the required prompting and praising abilities to [encourage] behaviors and that Mr. Young's activities were indeed very low level and nonsocial in form. The assessment helped the practitioner and the family select some target behaviors for further assessment and intervention: positive statements by Mr. Young, responses of more than three words, praise by family members, and increasing out-of-home activities."

Source: E. Pinkston & N. L. Linsk (1984). *Care of the elderly: A family approach* (p. 24). New York: Pergamon.

---

influence on behavior) can help you and your clients test your guesses about the functions of behaviors of interest. Only by rearranging the environment in certain ways and observing the effects of these changes may you and your clients detect influential contingencies.

When Observation Is Needed But Is Not Possible

Observation, although needed to clarify client concerns and discover options, may not be possible, perhaps because your agency does not allow time for it or provide the requisite training. You may have to "shoot from the hip" (make inferences) without the minimally needed information to do so (let alone optimal). Deciding on plans without a careful assessment may result in ineffective or unnecessarily intrusive interventions. Consider the following example that one of my students noted in her critical thinking log:

Situation: Case conference at a day care center for clients alleged to have Alzheimer's disease. The staff wanted to ask Mrs. L. to leave because she yells loudly, "because of her dementia."

What you did: I raised the possibility that yelling may not be a result of her dementia but might be maintained by positive consequences such as attention from volunteers and escaping unwanted situations. I noted that as a result of yelling, Mrs. L. had been assigned a one-to-one volunteer and did not have to participate in a group that she did not like. I suggested that we examine the contingencies related to yelling by observing what happens before and after yelling.

What happened: The other staff said, "Look, we know that Mrs. L. is demented. That's why she yells. She does not know what she is doing." I persisted. I pointed out that if Mrs. L. left the day care center, she would be sent to a nursing home, which was an intrusive plan, since she now lived at home. I reintroduced the idea of gathering systematic data that we could then examine.

What should you do in such a situation? First, remember what you are trying to accomplish; otherwise you may forget about or abandon sound assessment guidelines and simply label clients (e.g., as "demented") rather than help them maintain or enhance the quality of their lives. Second, involve interested colleagues in altering agency policies and practices that prevent collection of needed data. Third, you could request clients to record relevant interactions on smart phones.

Role Play (Analog Situations)

Analog situations are designed to simulate real-life conditions. You can use role plays to find out whether clients have needed skills and to identify changes in behavior needed to attain outcomes that clients value, as well as related cues and consequences (see Exhibit 18.4). It is hoped that clients' reactions during role play reflect what clients and/or significant others do (or could do) in real life. Let us say that a father and son argue about who is to do household chores. Audiotaping or videotaping exchanges (with the clients' permission) permits a detailed review. Role plays used to review the communication skills of parents and children or of couples last about 10 minutes. Situations may be presented

EXHIBIT 18.4

An Example of Using Role Playing to Assess Communication Styles

Expressing negative feelings was one situation of concern to Mrs. Ryan and the Greens. Mrs. Ryan, aged 89, lived with her daughter and son-in-law (Mr. and Mrs. Green) and their children. They all were asked to enact how they usually spoke to one another when they tried to share their feelings. Mrs. Ryan chose "feeling left out" at the dinner table. The social worker asked her clients to pretend they were at home talking about this. The following exchange took place:

MRS. RYAN: I never seem to get a chance to talk during supper. All the attention goes to the children.

MR. AND MRS. GREEN (together): Well, the children…(Mr. Green stopped and Mrs. Green continued) Well, we don't get a chance to talk to the children except at dinner.

MRS. RYAN: I don't feel that anyone cares about what I have to say.

MR. GREEN: The kids aren't interested in that old stuff—they get tired of that.

MRS. RYAN (at the words old stuff noticeably flinches): Yes, "old stuff"; I guess I am just old stuff, to be stuffed away in a corner.

MR. GREEN: Don't be ridiculous. You know we care about you.

MRS. RYAN: If you cared about me, you'd listen to me more. But you don't care, either, about "old stuff."

MRS. GREEN: It just seems that you are never interested in what we are doing or in what the children are doing, that you are interested only in your past times, your old friends, people we don't even know.

The conversation continued along these lines with accusations and counteraccusations and a noticeable lack of eye contact, empathic statements, paraphrases of the other person's point of view, or proposed solutions. The social worker praised the clients for taking part in the role play, reaffirming that the criterion for success was acting as they usually did at home. This role play suggested objectives to focus on to enhance positive communication among family members.

by film, audiotape, or videotape on an smartphone (Heyman & Slep, 2004). An example of a situation of concern to "delinquent" adolescents together with possible reactions is as follows.

It is 1:30 at night, and you're walking along a street near your home. You're on your way home from your friend's home, and you know it is after curfew in your town. You weren't doing anything wrong. You just lost track of time. You see a patrol car cruising along the street and you feel scared, because you know you can get into trouble for breaking curfew. Sure enough the car stops next to you, the policeman gets out, and he says, "You there, put your hands on the car. Stand with your feet apart." What do you say or do now? Score:

8   Either the youth does it without saying anything OR he asks a brief general question respectfully. Example: "What's wrong, officer? " "Is something the matter?" OR he explains honestly and convincingly where he was.

6   The youth explains where he was, etc., but in a less assertive or less convincing manner. Examples: "I just got out of Pete Jones's house. You can call him if you want to."

4   No specific criteria…midway between responses scores 6 and 2.

2   The youth is antagonistic or flippant or insolent.

0   Either the youth hits the policeman OR he runs away. (Freedman, Donahoe, Rosenthal, Schlundt, & McFall, 1978, p. 1452)

Compared with paper-and-pencil analogs (see chapter 17), behavioral role plays offer more accurate and more detailed

information about behaviors of interest including skills that are not used to advantage. Exhibit 18.5 gives examples of using role plays for assessment. Role plays have been used to evaluate the quality of care that respite providers give to people with disabilities (Neef, Parrish, Egel, & Sloan, 1986) and the telephone conversational skills of socially isolated, impaired nursing-home residents (Praderas & MacDonald, 1986). They are used in many forms of social skills training. The LIFE coding system is used to describe both depressive and aggressive behaviors (Hops, Davis, & Longoria, 1995). Couple observational coding systems are described in Kerig and Baucom (2004). Some coding systems for assessing interaction patterns may not be feasible because of the time required to learn how to use them reliably and to gather and summarize the data.

You could ask clients to act out exchanges with significant others or with another person and audiotape or videotape these exchanges for review. Exhibit 18.6 shows some common communication problems of couples identified during role-played discussions. Examples include not acknowledging other points of view, vague descriptions, and overgeneralizing. You could ask clients to imagine situations of concern and to act out how they would respond in each; be sure to allow them time to clearly imagine the scene. People differ in their skills in clearly imagining situations.

Advantages and Disadvantages of Role Playing

The advantages of role playing are convenience and efficiency. Exchanges can be videotaped for later review to identify relevant

EXHIBIT 18.5

Examples of Using Role Play for Assessment

Purpose	Task	Possible Measurement
1. Assess couple's communication skills.	Discuss situations they disagree about. Record interactions.	Identify rate of specific behaviors (e.g., questions asked).
2. Assess conflict resolution skills of parents and children.	Discuss conflicts.	Record frequency of behaviors such as proposed solutions.
3. Assess parenting skills.	Request parent and child to interact in a free-play situation in which parent sets rules (parent's game) and then shift and have child set the rules (child's game).	Determine rate of positive feedback or sequential child-parent behavior (e.g., following instruction).
4. Assess social skills of psychiatric patients.	Respond to tape-recorded situations.	Review behavior in terms of previously identified, explicit criteria.

behaviors, cues, and consequences. Gains of efficiency must be balanced against concerns about validity. Does the behavior represent what occurs in real life? Clients may be more (or less) anxious during role plays than they would be in similar real-life situations. Role plays may reveal that a client does have the skills needed to achieve valued outcomes. However, these skills may not be used in real life. Current environments may provide neither opportunities nor incentives.

Making the Most of Role Playing

To make the most of role playing, focus on situations that are directly related to desired outcomes. You may have to sample behavior in a variety of contexts to discover situations in which changes would be desirable. If a client has trouble making friends, social situations of concern include initiating conversations, introducing topics of conversation, sharing personal information, asking questions, and arranging future meetings (Gambrill & Richey, 1988). Take advantage of what is known about the situations of concern to different groups. Clearly explaining the purpose of role playing and criteria for success will help put clients at ease. Reassure them that most people feel awkward and uncomfortable at first. You could ease clients into role playing by asking them to play a role that is comfortable and that will not reflect negatively upon them. They could play themselves with the criterion for success being how well they do so. Another way to relax clients is to use yourself as a model. Support client participation with generous use of praise.

The more similar that role plays are to real-life circumstances, the more likely it is that behaviors observed will represent what usually takes place. It therefore is important to clearly describe specific situations related to valued outcomes. You may have to assume the role of a significant other yourself if only the client is present. If so, find out first how this person usually responds in the situation. Use props to make the scene more realistic. Start the role play based on what occurs in real life. For example, if

you are role playing a job interview, begin by having the client enter the room so that you can see her posture, eye contact, facial expression, and gait.

Clearly describe behaviors related to desired outcomes. Descriptions like "communicates well" are too vague to be helpful. The specific behaviors referred to by these terms, as well as the specific situations in which they can be used with success, must be identified. Attend to nonverbal, as well as verbal behaviors. Nonverbal behaviors such as eye contact, posture, and facial expression influence how we affect others. Check to see whether the client's nonverbal behavior matches his or her verbal behavior. For example, smiling while telling someone bad news is usually not appropriate. How something is said (e.g., tone, loudness, fluency) is as important as what is said. Are statements made loudly enough to be heard? Are facial expressions appropriate? What cultural differences should be considered? You can use checklists or rating scales to assess behavior.

One reason for using role plays during assessment is to identify valuable skills that clients and significant others could use to attain hoped-for outcomes. This highlights the importance of discovering what clients could do, as well as what they usually do, in situations of concern. After role playing a typical exchange, Mrs. Ryan and the Greens were asked to replay the same situation, doing the "best they could." This time they made some empathic statements and paraphrased other points of view. But they did not offer any ideas for resolving their concerns, nor were any requested. Discovering clients' assets is a key assessment goal. If skills are available, they will not have to be developed, although cues and incentives may have to be arranged to encourage their use. Ask clients what they are thinking at certain times during role plays to identify both helpful and unhelpful self-statements. An example of the former is "Good for me for trying." Examples of self-handicapping thoughts are negative labels ("that was stupid") and negative expectations ("I'll fail again").

EXHIBIT 18.6

Examples of Communication Problems

Overtalk. Speaking much more than others.

Rapid latency. Speaking very quickly after the speech of another.

Affective flatness. Speaking without the vocal characteristics usually associated with the content of what is being said.

Obtrusions. Making frequent utterances while others are speaking. Such intrusions become interruptions if they result in an immediate and premature end of the speech by the other.

Quibbling. Efforts to explicate, clarify, or dispute minor, tangential, and irrelevant details.

Underresponsiveness. Saying too little in answer to a question or comment.

Dogmatic statements. Making a statement in a categorical, unqualified, all or none, "black or white" manner.

Overgeneralization. Misrepresenting the frequency or pervasiveness of behaviors or other events (e.g., claiming a behavior "always" occurs in a situation when it occurs only sometimes).

Presumptive attribution. Misrepresenting the motivations, feelings, and thoughts of others (mind-reading).

Topic avoidance. Avoiding opportunities to talk about a topic.

Vague descriptions. Being general and abstract.

Temporal remoteness. Dwelling excessively on the past or hypothetical future.

Positive talk deficit. Failing to compliment or say nice things about the other as a person or about what the other says or does.

Acknowledgment deficit. Failing to admit or give credit when the other person is correct or failing to recognize other points of view.

Opinion deficit. Failing to express a preference or an opinion when the discussion calls for one.

Excessive disagreement. Disagreeing excessively with others.

Negative talk surfeit. Frequent or lengthy negative comments about others, events, or one's surroundings.

Source: Adapted from E. J. Thomas, C. L. Walter, & K. O'Flaherty (1974). A verbal problem checklist for use in assessing family verbal behavior. *Behavior Therapy, 35*, 238–239.

You can use structured role plays to assess interaction patterns. Forehand and McMahon (1981) designed a parents' game and a child's game to explore parenting behavior under different conditions. Parents could be asked to make their child look as good as possible to observe their child-management skills. Some parents who have problems with their children do have effective parenting skills, as shown by studies that found no differences between mothers of problem children and mothers of nonproblem children in altering their child's compliance or in the behaviors they used to obtain compliance and noncompliance (Green, Forehand, & McMahon, 1979). Other studies have found that parents who have difficulty with their children can make them look worse but not better. Use the checklist in Exhibit 18.7 to remind yourself of important points to consider when using role playing for assessment. Common errors are:

- Not using role plays when they would offer valuable information.

- Vaguely describing situations of concern and related behaviors.

- Not recording exchanges (as appropriate and feasible) for detailed review.

- Allowing role plays to last too long.

- Giving punishing rather than positive feedback.

Observing in the Natural Environment: Seeing for Yourself

You may have to observe clients and significant others in real-life settings to identify relevant behaviors and related antecedents and consequences, with your client's permission. You and your clients will have to decide: (1) who will observe, (2) what to observe, (3) when to observe, (4) how long to observe, (5) how to minimize intrusiveness, and (6) how to keep track of data you collect. Observation in real life is a valuable complement to interview data. (Dishion & Granic, 2004; Hartmann, Barrios, & Wood, 2004; Lofland & Lofland, 2003). This may indicate that

EXHIBIT 18.7

Checklist for Using Role Playing for Assessment

_____ 1. Situations are related to client concerns.

_____ 2. The purpose of using role play is clearly described to clients.

_____ 3. Role plays are structured to tap available skills, as well as typical reactions in situations of concern.

_____ 4. The role the client is to assume is clearly described.

_____ 5. Criteria for success are clear and clients can meet them (e.g., act as you typically do in the situation).

_____ 6. Props are used to increase realism.

_____ 7. Situations selected closely resemble those in real life.

_____ 8. Clients will be fairly comfortable during role plays.

_____ 9. Exchanges are recorded for later review.

_____ 10. Praise is offered following each role play.

_____ 11. Specific changes that would be helpful are identified.

a client's views about the causes of problems are incomplete or inaccurate (for detailed examples, see Carr et al., 1994). Observation often reveals that appropriate behaviors are ignored and undesired ones are reinforced. For instance, the staff in a residential center may complain about the residents' behavior. Observation may show that staff ignore desired behaviors (e.g., polite requests and greetings) and reinforce (with attention) disliked behaviors (e.g., shouting). In addition to discovering influential consequences related to behaviors of concern, it also is important to identify related setting events and antecedents. Only when the staff have ignored several requests by the residents may they resort to behaviors such as shouting. Only when a child has had a fight with his parents at home may he hit other children at school. Scatterplots can be used to discover patterns of behavior (see http://www.specialconnections.ku.edu).

You may use initial observation periods to identify relevant behaviors and related events. Since behavior often differs in different situations, you may have to collect data in more than one setting. For example, a child may act quite differently on the playground and in a classroom. You may have to collect data over a few days to allow time for people to become accustomed to being observed and for their behavior to return to its usual pattern. Observation periods often last about 30 minutes. How much

time you will need depends on whether the contingencies of interest are clear. O'Neill and colleagues (1990) recommend that data be gathered for 2 to 5 days or until a minimum of 10 to 15 occurrences of the behavior have been observed. If no consistent patterns emerge, specific antecedents and consequences can be altered and the effects noted. You can use prompts to encourage certain actions. The disadvantages of observation include cost and inconvenience, restriction to overt behavior, intrusiveness, and reactive effects (i.e., your presence may alter behavior). The guidelines discussed next suggest how to minimize these disadvantages.

Guidelines for Observation

The guidelines for making recording easy for clients apply to you as well. Count behaviors only after they have been clearly defined and can be reliably coded. It is frustrating to try to count behaviors when you are not ready to do so. If you are not prepared, this will become obvious when exchanges occur faster than you can record them. Take advantage of computerized handheld observational systems. These provide immediate feedback about interaction patterns between clients (e.g., students) and significant others (teachers). Well-designed systems and thorough training increase the likelihood of gathering accurate data (see Tyron, 1996; Volpe et al., 2005). Success in collecting relevant, accurate data will depend on:

- The observer's skill in identifying specific problem-related behaviors (including positive alternatives to disliked behaviors) and related setting events, antecedents, and consequences (e.g., misapplied and unapplied contingencies).

- The availability of helpful tools such as recording forms/counters/computers.

- Ease of access to relevant contexts.

- Preparation of clients to facilitate the observation of relevant contingencies.

Be sure to describe clearly the purpose of observation to clients and significant others. If you are observing in agencies, hospitals, or residential centers, review the procedures with staff members as ethically and practically necessary before collecting data, and follow the agency's rules and policies. Helpful rules during home observation of family interaction are not speaking to the observer, not permitting TV or phone calls, requesting clients to remain in the room, removing items that might be distracting to small children (such as handbags), and sitting or standing in an unobtrusive place. Observation takes time and effort. Prepare carefully so that you can make good use of these opportunities (see Exhibit 18.8).

The distinction between _description_ and _inference_ is important. Let us say you observe a mother and her son and

Checklist for Observing Interaction in Real-Life Settings

_____ 1. The purpose of observation is explained to participants.

_____ 2. A time and place is selected that will allow observation of relevant behaviors and related events.

_____ 3. Rules are agreed on that increase access to relevant behaviors and related antecedents and consequences (e.g., no interaction with observers).

_____ 4. Easy-to-use unobtrusive and valid recording methods are used.

_____ 5. Behaviors are clearly described.

_____ 6. Antecedents and consequences related to behaviors of interest are noted.

_____ 7. A time to discuss data collected with involved participants is arranged.

write in your case record, "She is hostile." This is an inference based on what you observed rather than a description of what you saw. Be sure to include descriptive accounts relevant to your inferences. Clear descriptions allow others who review your records to understand what you mean by certain terms (see Exhibit 18.9). Mary Richmond (1917) noted that "The gathering of facts is made difficult by faulty observation, faulty recollection, and by a confusion between the facts themselves and the inferences drawn from them" (Richmond, 1917, p. 63).

Distinguishing Inferences from Descriptions

Check those items that you believe are inferences.

1. She is a good parent.

2. She hit her child when he called her "old nag."

3. He is an alcoholic.

4. My supervisor likes me.

5. He fell and hit his head.

6. Mrs. Rivera is a battered spouse.

7. She says that her neighbor hates her.

8. He told her to get lost.

9. Her son is out of control.

10. Mr. Monk is mentally ill.

Sequential Recording

Making sound practice decisions may require detailed information about contingencies related to hoped-for outcomes, including interactions between clients and significant others to determine who reinforces whom, when, and for what. Sequential recording systems have been developed to observe interactions in a variety of settings, including group homes, geriatric nursing facilities, institutional settings, classrooms, nursery schools, and community settings. Systems differ in the number and type of code categories included and in the training required. The Patterson Coding System for observing family interaction (Reid, 1978) contains 29 categories. Examples include hit, talk, command, request, and cry. Interactions are coded sequentially by concentrating on one family member for 5-minute periods and noting his or her behavior, as well as the reactions of other family members to it. For other family observation systems, see Kerig and Lindahl (2004), as well as web sites such as the University of Washington Parenting Clinic (http://www.son.washington.edu/centers/parenting-clinic).

One way to gather sequential data is to describe each interaction (including the context, the behavior, and the consequences) on a separate index card (see Exhibit 18.10). You can also write down your guesses about the function (meaning) of behaviors noted. (Behaviors of interest may have more than one function.) After you record a number of critical incidents, you can review the data collected to explore possible functions (e.g., escape from unwanted attention or tasks, attention from peers or teachers, gaining a valued item). Consider Michael, whose behaviors of concern were slapping and pinching. The initial data suggested that these behaviors were maintained by escape from less familiar, more difficult tasks. His teachers decided to explore this by varying the difficulty of teaching tasks over sessions. Michael's aggressive behavior was consistently higher in conditions requiring difficult tasks. Try the practice exercise in Exhibit 18.11.

Interval Recording

Interval samples are a form of time sampling in which a period is broken into smaller units of time, such as 15-second intervals. Then, for each interval, the observer notes with a check mark whether the behavior occurred. Not every instance of the behavior is recorded—only whether it occurred during the selected time period. Thus, interval recording provides an estimate of the true frequency or duration of behaviors. The maximum frequency of a behavior is determined by the size of the time unit selected, which should be related to the frequency with which the behavior occurs. If a 10-second interval is used, the maximum rate of behavior will be 6 per minute. With a frequent behavior, the unit should be smaller in order to reflect its rate more accurately. Using intervals that are too long underestimates a behavior's frequency. Whenever small time intervals are involved, arrange cues so you will know when to record. (You could use your smart phone for this.)

EXHIBIT 18.10

Three Cards For Gary

Three cards for Gary grouped according to the common theme of response to a request to perform a nonpreferred task within the category of escape-motivated behavior

Name: Gary General Context: Gathering work materials	Observer: Rob	Date: 3/10/87 Time: 9:30 A.M.

Interpersonal Context: Cal asked Gary to bring over a wheelbarrow full of potting soil to the workbench.
Behavior Problem: Gary punched Cal in the chest and tried to punch him a second time in the face but Cal ducked.
Social Reaction: Cal told Gary to "keep cool" and moved away from him. After a few minutes, Cal got the wheelbarrow himself.

Name: Gary General Context: Lunch	Observer: Bob	Date: 6/25/88 Time: 12:30 P.M.

Interpersonal Context. Gary had just finished eating his lunch. Mrs. Ibsen was very busy trying to get a number of things done so that she and Gary could keep a doctor's appointment. Because she was so busy, she asked Gary to clean the table and put away the dishes. She had to make several requests to get Gary moving.
Behavior Problem: Gary responded by biting his hand, spitting, and trying to slap his mother.
Social Reaction: Mrs. Ibsen backed away. When Gary had calmed down, she quickly cleaned up the table and put the dishes in the sink.

Name: Gary General Context: Shaving	Observer: Bob	Date: 4/11/87 Time: 7:30 P.M.

Interpersonal Context: Gary's father asked him to go into the bathroom and shave.
Behavior Problem: Gary shouted, "Go away!" and bit himself.
Social Reaction: Gary's father walked away and Gary did not shave.

Source: E. G. Carr, L. Levin, G. McConnachie, J. I. Carlson, D. C. Kemp, C. E. Smith (1994). *Communication-based intervention for problem behavior: A user's guide for producing positive change* (p. 85). Baltimore: Paul H. Brookes. Reprinted with permission.

You also may record behaviors at the interval rather than within an interval. For example, Goodwin and Coates (1976) developed a procedure for simultaneously recording both behavior and its consequences. Their codes for students included on-task behavior, scanning, social contact, and disruptive behavior. Teacher consequences included instructing, rewarding, neutral behavior, and disapproval. The observer notes at each 5-second interval what the student is doing and the teacher's response and checks the appropriate space. To evaluate progress, the percentage of intervals in which a behavior occurred during baseline can be compared with the percentage after intervention.

Time Sampling

Both time sampling and interval recording depend on units of time rather than discrete behaviors. Both estimate the frequency of a behavior. *Time sampling* refers to recording procedures with a much longer span of time between intervals compared with those of interval recording. Time sampling is useful when a behavior may occur over a long time span and when it does not have a definite beginning or end. For example, ward staff could monitor residents' social exchanges by making 20 observations of each resident every day. *Prompting* is often used when behaviors of interest are under strict stimulus control, such as responding to someone initiating a conversation (e.g., walking up to a person and saying hello). In such cases, it would be a waste of time to wait around until the behavior occurred.

You can use time sampling to discover the range of behaviors that occur in a particular situation. Data can be summarized by counting the total number of times a person was observed and the total number in which each behavior occurred, and dividing the former into the total for each behavior. If behavior were observed at 17 intervals during one shift in a residential setting and a resident were found to be sleeping during 10 and talking during 2, you could determine what percentage of 17 that each of these behaviors occupies. Time sampling can be helpful in discovering antecedents related to behaviors of concern. The observer notes whether or not the behavior occurred in each time block and may also note whether it occurred frequently. The resulting scatterplot indicates the times when there is a high frequency of the behavior and a low frequency of the behavior.

EXHIBIT 18.11

Practice in Observation

Make 5 copies of this form. Choose a behavior you are interested in, and describe 5 related interactions based on your observation. Review this information, and suggest possible function(s) of the behavior.

Name of person(s) observed: _____   Observer: _____   Date: _____

Context: _____   Time: _____

Antecedents (who was present, what happened right before): _____

_____

_____

Behavior (what the person did): _____

_____

_____

Social Consequences (how others responded): _____

_____

_____

Hypothesis (the behavior's probable function): _____

_____

_____

Other Measures

Total frequency counts may be feasible to gather (e.g., number of cigarettes smoked, number of bottles of beer consumed). You can also note related cues and consequences. You may use rate or percentage (see chapter 17). Sometimes a *duration measure* will be most appropriate (e.g., length of conversation, duration of pain). Latency has been used to measure the time between when an instruction is given and when it is followed. Behavior products may be noted, such as amount of litter, energy used, or empty beer cans.

Data Describing a Group

At times a group measure may be best. If you know the rate of positive and negative exchanges between clients during group meetings, you can compare different groups or a behavior of one group over many sessions (see Mattaini, 1993, for examples of visualizing group interaction). If the size of the group differs on different occasions, divide the number of behaviors by the number of people, and then divide this figure by a time measure to obtain the rate of behavior (see Rose, 1989, for other examples). You can use a time sample with fixed or random intervals to observe residents' behavior. A form for the observer to note location, position, whether the person was awake or asleep, facial expression, social orientation, and activities was reliably used by mentally retarded residents of a state school and hospital

(Craighead, Mercatoris, & Bellack, 1974). You can summarize the data by counting the number of residents engaged in each behavior over all intervals. Let us say that you observed 10 residents for 17 intervals and that a total of 35 were watching television. The number of intervals multiplied by the number of residents yields the total number of opportunities for any one behavior over all intervals. To find the percentage contribution of any one behavior, divide the number of people engaging in this behavior by the total number possible. This example illustrates how you can gather observational data that may be valuable in enhancing the residents' quality of life.

Critically Appraising Observational Data

Like other sources of data, observation is subject to error (see Exhibit 18.12). Observation is theory laden. We see what we expect to see and may miss what we do not expect to see (see also discussion in chapter 11). Unless you take special precautions, you may miss what is there to be seen and see things that are not there. Knowledge of sources of bias and error, as well as skill in avoiding them, will help you to make effective use of observation. Be sure to consider reliability and validity when reviewing data (see chapter 17). Basing decisions on small, biased samples may result in poor decisions. Social workers often address "highly

EXHIBIT 18.12

Sources of Error in Observational Data

Type of Error	Description
1. Central tendency error.	Observers tend to select subjective midpoints on rating scales when judging a series of events.
2. Tendency to be generous or lenient.	Observers tend to be lenient or generous when using scales requiring "yes," "sometimes," "rarely," or "no."
3. Primacy or recency effects.	Initial impressions distort later judgments.
4. Logical errors (informal or formal).	Judgment errors due to assumptions (e.g., that because a teacher is warm, she or he is also instructionally effective).
5. Overlooking vested interests and values of observer.	Judgments are influenced by personal biases or expectations.
6. Classification of observations.	Fine distinctions are lost when general categories are used.
7. Faulty generalizations about behavior.	Judgments are based on data from an unrepresentative sample, resulting in false conclusions or incorrect classifications of people or events.
8. Failure to consider the perspective of those observed.	Overlooking participants' perspectives may result in inaccurate accounts.
9. Poorly designed observation methods.	Recording forms may be cumbersome, resulting in low reliability and validity. Recording methods may be vaguely described.
10. Failure to consider the rate of exchanges.	Observers can't keep up with what's happening, resulting in missing data.
11. Reactions of those observed.	Teachers may behave differently when being observed than they otherwise would.
12. Failure to consider the situation or context.	Contextual differences that influence behavior are overlooked. Incorrect assumptions of functional equivalence (e.g., assuming that reading time 1 = reading time 2 may result in overlooking the effects of changes in activities or variations in obligations in different situations).
13. Overlooking the function of behavior.	Incorrect conclusion that a behavior lacks stability because differences in contingencies that influence behavior are overlooked.
14. Overlooking the simultaneity of behaviors of interest.	Errors due to failure to account for multiple activities occurring at one time. For example, more than one message may be sent at a time through different channels (verbal and nonverbal). A message may have more than one function at a time.
15. Assuming that a behavior has only one function.	A behavior may serve many functions (e.g., escape from unwanted tasks, attention). Focusing on one alone will decrease success.
16. Inattention to observer drift.	Errors caused by changes in uses of a coding system over time, resulting in descriptions that do not match the original categories or that vary from one another.

Source: Adapted from C. M. Evertson & J. L. Green (1986). Observation as inquiry and method. In M. C. Wittrock (Ed.) American Educational Research Association (Corporate Author), *Handbook of research on teaching* (3rd Ed.) (p. 183). Gale, a part of Cengage Learning, Inc. Reprinted with permission.

charged" problems. Consider possible differences of opinion among neighborhood residents about what problems should be given greater priority and what should be done to resolve them, or the different views of staff and youth about the cause of fights in a residential setting. The staff may blame the residents, and the residents may blame the staff. Preconceptions about how people will behave based on stereotypes may influence what is seen and reported. Observers of an event may have quite different views about what occurred (see, for example, Brainerd & Reyna, 2005; Liptak, 2011b). Observers may be inconsistent in their use of behavior definitions. Recording methods may be cumbersome. Observers are more accurate when they think that their results will be checked. Vague definitions of behavior are a common cause of error.

Reactive Effects

Behavior may change because it is being observed. Like self-monitoring, observation may also have reactive effects. For example, when parents knew they were being observed, they played more, offered more positive verbal reactions, and structured their children's activities more than when they were not aware of being observed (Zegiob, Arnold, & Forehand, 1975). Reactive effects may be temporary. That is, over time, clients may become accustomed to the observer's presence, and their behavior may return to its natural patterns and rates. The purpose of observation is to obtain a representative picture of behavior and related events. Only if reactive effects are so severe that what is seen is quite unrepresentative of what usually occurs should there be concern.

Reviewing Reliability and Accuracy

How reliable are observations? Do observers agree with one another? You can explore reliability by finding out how closely two or more observers independently agree on what they observe. You can calculate interobserver agreement in a number of ways. One is to divide the number of agreements by the number of agreements plus disagreements and multiply this by 100. Or you could determine the correlations between two raters. Percentage agreement, however, can be misleading because some agreement will occur purely by chance and agreement percentage scores do not correct for this. Point-by-point agreement, in which an agreement is counted only when both observers identify the same behaviors at the same time, provides more accurate estimates than do procedures that do not require point-by-point agreement.

When using interval recording, you should not count those intervals in which neither observer recorded a code, since including them artificially inflates the index of reliability. Reliability can be increased through training. Records can be compared right after observation, disagreements discussed, and rules developed to resolve them. Observers should be familiar with behavioral definitions used, the data sheet, and any timing devices. If an independent assessment of reliability is not possible (i.e., using two observers), the accuracy of response definitions can be checked by periodically gathering examples of relevant behaviors and seeing whether they match agreed-on definitions.

Observer accuracy refers to the extent to which the observer's ratings match the coding of a criterion. Observer reliability may be high but observer accuracy may be low. Even if observers agree on how to describe a behavior, their ratings may not reflect the "meaning" (function) of behavior for those observed. For example, an observer may score the interruptions of one person

as having a negative consequence when in reality it does not. What is a positive or negative consequence for one person may not be to others. Accuracy can be determined by having observers periodically code a criterion tape (an audiotape or videotape of situations of concern) to find out whether coding matches agreed-on definitions. You can detect *observer drift* (changes in recording over time) by comparing data collected with data based on a criterion observer. Exhibit 18.13 suggests questions to ask when reviewing observational data.

Observing the Physical Environment

Valuable options can be discovered by carefully observing the physical environments in which clients live, work, and play. (See Kelly et al., 2002.) Considerable attention has been devoted to describing social environments in order to maximize safety and minimize violence (e.g., Vernberg & Biggs, 2010). Advantages of altering the physical environment may include low cost in terms of training, time, money, and interference with routines and policies. Once in place certain kinds of physical alterations tend to remain. Questions to ask include the following:

- In what ways do physical arrangements encourage valued behaviors?
- In what ways do they discourage valued behaviors?
- In what ways do they encourage undesired reactions?
- How could the physical setting be altered to enhance desired outcomes? (See, e.g., Gawande, 2010.)
- Who would benefit from changes made?
- Who would experience negative consequences?
- Are there hazards in the home that should be removed (e.g., faulty electrical wiring, unprotected windows that could be a danger)?
- Are there pollution hazards nearby such as toxic waste dumps?

EXHIBIT 18.13

Reviewing the Quality of Observational Data

- Are reliability data presented? Are they adequate?
- Are validity data presented? Are they adequate?
- How was the sample of observed interactions selected? Are there biases of concern?
- Does the sample of observed exchanges comprise a representative sample?
- Do data collected help you and your clients make sound decisions?

Bullying and assault can be minimized by making sure all contexts (e.g., in school or in a YMCA) are potentially visible to others.

Examining Residential Environments

Thousands of people spend years of their lives in residential settings including millions of elderly clients. Our prisons are overflowing. We know that life in such settings is often grim. Observation provides a way to discover opportunities to create more humane contexts. For example, Prain and her colleagues (2010) observed behavior and interactions of adults with congenital deafblindness residing in community residences. Codes used to describe behavior of staff included assistance, praise, restraint, conversation, and processing (e.g., holding a resident by the hand while walking). Cohen-Mansfield and colleagues (2006) examined interactions during dressing of cognitively impaired nursing home residents, including types of communication (e.g., announcing a task, giving information, providing choices, affirmation, chatting and positive feedback).

Percent of opportunities to acknowledge client participation and to give appropriate feedback were described. Related data provide guidance for enhancing quality of life for residents.

The Staff-Resident Interaction Chronograph (Paul, Licht, Mariotta, Power, & Engel, 1987a) and the Time-Sample Behavioral Checklist (Paul et al., 1987b) are designed for use in residential settings. (See also Hutchinson et al., 2010.) Rudolph Moos and Sonne Lemke (1994) designed a series of scales to describe residential settings. Areas included in the description of physical features can be seen in Exhibit 18.14. Assessment of the social climate includes scales for cohesion, conflict, independence, self-disclosure, resident influence, and physical comfort. Assessment of policies and services includes scales for expectations of functioning, acceptance of problem behavior, resident control, policy clarity, provision for privacy, health services, daily living assistance, and social-recreational activities. Environmental characteristics that should be assessed in residential settings for elderly persons include structural barriers to wheelchairs and walkers, distance barriers, prompts and cues indicating where and when activities are to take place,

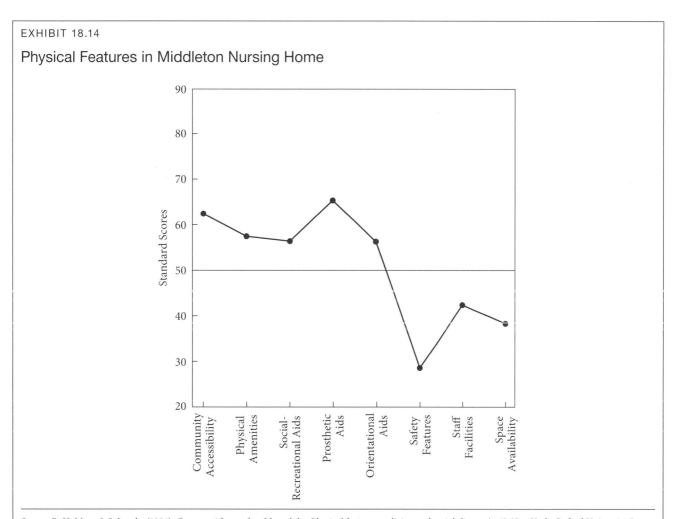

EXHIBIT 18.14

Physical Features in Middleton Nursing Home

Source: R. H. Moos & S. Lemke (1994). *Group residences for older adults: Physical features, policies, and social climate* (p. 5). New York: Oxford University Press. Reprinted with permission.

type of furniture and arrangement, lighting, content of activities and materials used, and scheduling conflicts. Do residents have sufficient privacy? If not, how can it be increased? Are the residents allowed to personalize their rooms? Is the setting free of hazards (are railings in place on all stairs)? Are the beds comfortable? Are the toilet facilities clean and accessible? Are recreational areas available? Are these sufficient? Are residents engaged with their environments or do they sit and lay passively most of the time? A classic study shows that allowing elderly residents to take care of a plant decreased mortality (Rodin, & Langer, 1977). Chairs can be repositioned to increase social exchanges (Peterson, Knapp, Rosen, & Pither, 1977). Food can be served family style rather than institutional style to encourage social exchanges (VanBiervliet, Spangler, & Marshall, 1981). Stores can be placed in the lobby of a nursing home to increase social and leisure time participation (McClannahan & Risley, 1973). Participation of residents in recreational activities can be enhanced by making materials readily available and prompting their use (McClannahan & Risley, 1975). Exploration of variations in the physical design of preschool settings has a long history (Risley & Twardosz, 1976).

Examining the Physical Characteristics of Social Service Agencies

Physical arrangements in an agency influence work climate and effectiveness. Noise pollution, poor lighting, lack of privacy, and few phones may adversely influence the staff's behavior, which in turn compromises the services that clients receive. The agency's physical characteristics may reflect the staff's attitudes toward their work and/or citizens' attitudes toward the particular client group (see Dubois, 2010). For example, a center serving homeless people and families may be in need of paint and have few decorative amenities. Use your observational skills to identify low-cost improvements that could be made and involve interested colleagues in getting them done. Are educational brochures available in waiting rooms, as well as access to computers containing information about agency services, including their track record of success in helping clients attain certain outcomes?

Observing Neighborhoods and Communities

Information about different aspects of neighborhoods and communities (e.g., physical such as transportation and recreational facilities/spaces, political characteristics such as who holds office, and social features such as who talks to whom, where, when, and about what) may be needed to discover options to resolve concerns (see also chapter 27). A visit to a client's neighborhood and community may provide valuable information. Computer programs allowing notation of the geographical location of given types of services can aid in rapidly finding accessible services for a client. In her classic book *The Death and Life of Great American Cities* (1961), Jane Jacobs describes the importance of knowledge about neighborhoods, links of residents with people with influence in their districts, and links of these individuals to people in citywide or even state and federal power positions. The fields of environmental and community psychology suggest valuable ways of describing neighborhoods and communities (e.g., Bechtel & Churchman, 2002).

Sutton and Kemp (2011) describe case studies illustrating inequality and transformation in marginalized communities. As they note, place matters for the quality of our human existence; it influences our social contacts, expresses values, and contributes to our sense of self. Arendt (1958) emphasizes the need for public places where people can engage in conversations about political issues. There are all too few. In *The Paradox of Urban Space* Sutton and Kemp (2011) describe place-based inequalities, as well as their change. They argue that "place matters for low-income communities of color because it is simultaneously a source of inequality and oppression *and* a context for transformation and possibility" (p. 4). (See also Kling, Liebman, & Katz, 2001.)

The Value of Observation in task Analyses

The purpose of a task analysis is to identify the behaviors required to attain a valued outcome. Examples of behaviors involved in putting on a pull-over shirt are:

1. Pick up a shirt/holding at bottom.

2. Open shirt/holding at sides.

3. Place over head.

4. Pull shirt until head emerges.

5. Put right arm in right sleeve.

6. Right arm emerges completely.

7. Put left arm in left sleeve.

8. Left arm emerges completely.

9. Pull shirt down to waist. (Young, West, Howard, & Whitney, 1986)

This information serves as a training guide to develop needed skills. Many helpers ignore the need for a task analysis and in its place use questionable substitutes such as armchair speculation—perhaps abetted or hindered by personal experience. Central to task analysis is observing behaviors in the contexts in which they occur. If behavior by the residential staff is of interest, then their behaviors and the effects on the residents' behavior would be observed. If ordering food in a fast-food restaurant is of concern, then that is the place to observe behavior (see van den Pol, Iwata, Ivancic, Page, Neef, & Whitley, 1981).

Videotapes of behaviors of interest in real-life situations may be useful for discovering effective behaviors, as well as problematic points and options for handling them.

All the questions and concerns that arise with observation of behavior in real-life settings come into play here. Are there reactive effects? That is, does behavior change as a result of being observed? How many different people should be observed to obtain a representative account? Redundancy is one criteria that could be used (i.e., observation ceases when no additional information is provided). Sometimes it will be obvious that certain behaviors must occur to attain a given outcome. For example, you have to remove the toothpaste cap before you can squeeze out the toothpaste. At other times, the required behaviors are not obvious. For example, without careful observation, the relationship between a social behavior and its effects on the environment may not be clear. Or the future effects of certain social behaviors may not be known. A person who talks a great deal at a senior center may get the attention of others at the time but be avoided on future occasions. There may be a variety of ways in which a desired outcome can be achieved. The more accustomed we are to one way of acting in a situation, the harder it may be to think of alternatives. You or your clients could collect data in real-life settings to discover options. Most task analyses provide information about what most people do in a specific situation. Thus, a task analysis may not offer information about creative variations that may result in similar (or valued) outcomes.

The task is broken down into teachable components describing what the learner is expected to do. Each step should be numbered and clearly described. Responsibility for the learner acquiring the task is placed on the trainer. You (the trainer) must decide on the size of the components into which a sequence of behavior is divided and the alternatives that are acceptable at each point. In training to a criterion, you should accept (and encourage) all behaviors in an operant. (The term *operant* refers to a class of behaviors all of which have a similar effect on the environment.) For example, if you do not hold out your hand with the palm turned up when getting change in a fast food restaurant, the chain of behavior required to order food successfully may be disrupted at this point. However, you could hold out your left rather than your right hand or ask the person to put the change on your tray.

Obstacles

Obstacles to observation include overconfidence that you can discover needed information just by "thinking about it" (i.e., speculation). You may overlook sources of bias that enter the picture when just "thinking about it," such as stereotypes and unrepresentative personal experiences. Another obstacle is accepting other people's reports without questioning them. Instead, you should ask: What evidence is there that behaviors said to be important are required to achieve desired outcomes in real life?

Five psychologists may rate a behavior effective in a role play, but does their rating correlate with the behavior's effectiveness in real life? Underestimating the training required to become an expert "task analyzer" is an obstacle. Cost in time, money, and effort is an issue. Observation in real life is time-consuming. However, this must be balanced against the cost of less than hoped-for success if plans are not based on a task analysis.

Keeping Track of Data

Be sure to record clearly and concisely what you observe. You can use special recording forms. Clearly describe behaviors of interest and related setting events, antecedents, and consequences. Base your hunches about causes on descriptive data when suggesting next steps. Next steps depend on your responsibilities and what related research findings suggest is important. Whoever is responsible for providing services can check the accuracy of your written descriptive analyses by carrying out a functional analysis (rearranging setting events, antecedents, or consequences presumed to influence behaviors of interest and determining the effects).

Summary

Observation is a valuable skill at all levels of practice. An accurate assessment may require systematic observation in real-life settings and/or role plays to identify specific behaviors of concern, associated setting events, antecedents and consequences, and resources that can be used. You may discover changes in the physical environment that can contribute to positive outcomes. The time taken to "see for yourself" is usually more than compensated by the value of the data obtained. Sound training in observational methods, as well as knowledge about sources of bias and how you can minimize them, will help you to take advantage of this valuable source of information.

Reviewing Your Competencies

Reviewing Content Knowledge

1. Describe how you can make role plays realistic.

2. Describe steps you can take to increase the likelihood of gathering accurate data by observing behavior in real-life settings.

3. Give examples of the following data collected while observing in real-life settings: sequential, frequency, duration, rate, time samples, interval recording.

4. For various practice examples, describe observational data that would be valuable to collect and design easy-to-use recording methods that would yield helpful data.

5. Describe the difference between a descriptive and a functional analysis.

6. Describe the purposes of a task analysis and its components and give an example.

7. Describe common errors in observation and how to avoid them.

Reviewing What You Do

1. You collect valuable assessment data from role plays.

2. You supplement self-report data with observational data when relevant and feasible.

3. You correctly identify inferences on a list that contains both descriptions and inferences.

4. The data you collect facilitate selection of effective services.

5. Your inferences are based on accurate descriptive data.

6. Given a filmed or videotaped presentation of a behavior to be decreased, you can clearly define the behavior, identify alternative behaviors to increase, and describe a useful recording procedure.

7. You identify valuable ways in which a client's physical environments could be rearranged.

8. You make well-reasoned guesses about the functions of problem-related behaviors based on observation.

9. You accurately identify reliability and validity problems in samples of observational data collected.

10. Your case records contain accurate, clear, concise summaries of data.

11. Inferences in case records are based on relevant descriptive data.

12. You carry out task analyses that are effective in helping clients to acquire valued skills.

13. You use geographic mapping systems to discover the accessibility of services for your clients as needed.

14. You use valid neighborhood observation systems to discover obstacles and options.

Reviewing Results

1. Plans result in valued outcomes.

2. Data collected result in well-reasoned decisions not to intervene (e.g., data show that there is no way to influence relevant contingencies).

19

Reviewing Resources and Obstacles

OVERVIEW   This chapter provides guidelines for reviewing resources and obstacles. Personal resources include valuable coping skills, motivation to resolve problems, and supportive significant others. Family resources include mutual caring. Agency resources include a culture of thoughtfulness and policies that facilitate the use of evidence-informed practices and policies. Neighborhood and community resources include convenient, affordable public transportation, affordable housing, and recreational opportunities. Societal resources include economic, educational, and health policies that help residents enhance the quality of their lives. Options to help clients will often be limited by a lack of resources.

YOU WILL LEARN ABOUT

- Thinking contextually about resources and obstacles

- Resources and obstacles related to service and surveillance systems and related policies and legislation

- Neighborhood and community resources and obstacles

- Social networks and social support systems

- Significant others as resources and obstacles

- Personal resources and obstacles

- When needed resources are scarce or not available

- The need for advocacy

Thinking Contextually About Resources and Obstacles

Problems involve a gap between a current and a desired situation. Only by reviewing resources and obstacles can the potential for closing the gap be estimated. The nature of the problem influences the particular resources and obstacles focused on. Perhaps only a distant approximation to closing the gap is possible. Let's say a client has a history of violence and has been diagnosed with severe and chronic mental illness. Where will the client be located? Cutbacks in funding for psychiatric hospitals may result in placing clients with a known violent history in an inappropriate setting such as a group home. Placement of such a client resulted in a young attendant's brutal murder. She had a BSW in social work (Sontag, 2011a). Staff in this group home received one week of training. Services offered often have a residual nature, waiting until very troubling behavior occurs before help is offered and even then, the help offered may be scant. Policies and laws regarding undocumented residents may hamper provision of and seeking of needed services because of fear of arrest and deportation. Gay/lesbian and transgender people may be wary of seeking help from health providers because of fear of discrimination (for review of social work practice with lesbians, see Hunter, 2012). Staff may not speak the language of clients rendering accurate communication impossible. This is why identifying, documenting, exposing and advocating for enhanced services is so important as described in chapter 1. Your only alternative may be to offer support to help clients tolerate difficult situations and take steps together with others at other levels (e.g., advocacy and community organization) to increase future resources.

The neighborhoods and communities in which families reside influence stress levels which, in turn, may influence health and family interaction. Communities are influenced by historical and current institutional arrangements. Bowles et al. (2006) use the term "institutional poverty traps" to refer to institutions that create and maintain widespread poverty. Consider, for example, unequal educational opportunities. Environmental hazards, such as air pollution, are greater in poor neighborhoods (Pellow & Brulle, 2007). Resources and obstacles are often in the eye of the beholder: that is, what at first may seem to be an obstacle may, when creatively viewed, turn out to be a resource. The very starkness of many clients' needs calls for a creative and energetic search for resources. You may have to create new resources. What you do will depend on whether you are a case manager and so arrange, coordinate, and evaluate services provided by other agencies or whether you offer services yourself. Guidelines for reviewing resources and obstacles are suggested in Exhibit 19.1. Relevant questions are:

- What resources are needed?

- What resources are available?

- Which resources are most likely to be of value?

- What efforts have been made to obtain them to what effect?

- What factors facilitate or hinder access to and use of resources, such as eligibility requirements, high-crime neighborhoods, lack of transportation?

- What can be done to overcome obstacles?

- What resources could be created?

Here, as in other phases of helping, focusing only on the individual or family may get in the way of discovering options.

EXHIBIT 19.1

Guidelines for Reviewing Resources and Obstacles

- Use a contextual approach (a wide-angle lens).

- Identify and build on clients' strengths.

- Involve significant others.

- Take advantage of options for rearranging the physical environment.

- Keep informed about community resources and unmet needs.

- Help clients to take advantage of self-help and support groups.

- Consider cultural differences that affect resources and obstacles.

- Involve other professionals and community residents in improving coordination among services and in creating services.

- Alter agency procedures and policies that interfere with helping clients.

- Alter service system interrelationships that interfere with service.

We live in a society that emphasizes psychological causes of problems. Those who use a "deficiency model" rivet on people's defects, their disabilities, and what they cannot do—as if people are made up of only their problems (Sarason & Lorentz, 1979, p. 128). This deficiency model is promoted by the biomedical industrial complex as described in chapter 6. A contextual view directs attention to both environmental and personal characteristics. Attaining needed resources may require influencing legislation and helping community members with a common interest organize to pursue valued goals.

A variety of steps may be needed to help a client locate and use a resource. For instance, a single parent who wants to enroll in a job-training program may need day care services for her 5-year-old child. First, find out whether the client has tried to find day care and why she was not successful. Help her locate and review the possibilities and decide which one is best for her in regard to hours, cost, location, and quality of care. You may find one that meets her needs but then discover that her child must be toilet trained in order to be eligible. You may have to update your knowledge regarding the evidentiary status of different toilet training programs. A question here might be: "In young children who are not toilet trained, what method is most effective in increasing appropriate toileting behavior?" The next question is: "Are you or staff in other agencies trained to provide such a program? If not, can you acquire the needed skills?"

Obstacles include: (1) lack of resources, (2) a lack of knowledge about resources, (3) organizational and service system barriers, (4) poor management of resources, and (5) an unwillingness to use resources. Clients may not know about valuable resources or have located a resource but encountered barriers. People in need of medical care may not realize that they are eligible for Medicare. One of your tasks is to inform clients about helpful resources. Clients may not be willing to use benefits to which they are entitled. Cultural values and norms influence the kind of help that is acceptable. Understanding the reasons for objections will help you respond effectively.

Resources and Obstacles Related to Service and Surveillance Systems and Related Policies and Legislation

Funding patterns influence access to services. States differ in how actively they pursue implementation of legal regulations, such as pursuit of fathers for financial contributions to their children's care. Cities and states differ in their surveillance patterns—who is watched and in turn, arrested. The war on drugs and related policies mandating arrest for victimless crimes fall especially heavily on African-American youth (Wacquant, 2009). Dwyer (2011) reports that more people are arrested in New York City and accused of possessing marijuana than any other crime and that nearly all are black or Latino males under the age of 25, most with no previous convictions. Fifty thousand people in New York City were arrested in 2010 on marijuana charges. Most are poor with little access to legal advice or help. Many are tricked into displaying small amounts of marijuana and as soon as this is visible, they are arrested for a misdemeanor. These arrests have consequences for those arrested including loss of hard to get jobs (Dwyer, 2011). Even though ineffective, the war on drugs continues to be promoted by the Federal government (Blow, 2011b; Hughes & Stevens, 2010). Most criminal defendants are indigent and unable to hire a lawyer. Public defenders are overloaded (Alexander, 2010). Here yet again the poor are at a disadvantage compared to those with money (e.g., to hire lawyers).

Once arrested, one's chances of ever being truly free of the system of control are slim, often to the vanishing point. Defendants are typically denied meaningful legal representation, pressured by the threat of a lengthy sentence into a plea bargain, and then placed under formal control—in prison or jail, on probation or parole. Most Americans probably have no idea how common it is for people to be convicted without ever having the benefit of legal representation, or how many people plead guilty to crimes they did not commit because of fear of mandatory sentences. (Alexander, 2010, p. 83)

Migrant workers may be harassed rather than helped. Almost a third of Americans have been arrested for a crime by age 23 (Goode, 2011). Resources given to certain groups may be co-opted for others. Consider the 387-acre Pacific Coast home for wounded veterans donated to the federal government over 100 years ago in Brentwood, California. Los Angeles has the largest number of homeless veterans in the United States. Out of an estimated 49,000 homeless people, 8,200 are estimated to be homeless veterans (Nagourney, 2011). Advocates for the homeless are suing The Department of Veterans Affairs "seeking to compel federal officials to use the campus to care for and house the mentally ill veterans" (p. 15). Right now some of this land is leased to car rental agencies, a laundry, a golf course and a baseball stadium for the University of California, Los Angeles. Ineffective marketing of service availability, long and confusing application forms, language difficulties, and poor links among services hinder service use (e.g., Kissane, 2003).

Documentation and audit requirements occupy up to 60% of child welfare workers' time, leaving too little time for face-to-face contact with families and children (Munro, 2011). Agencies differ in their policies regarding exposure of avoidable suffering and advocating for its decrease. Social workers who daily see need for services, as well as need for changes in discriminatory policies or practices, may not be encouraged to work together with agency administrators and clients to advocate for legislation that would address unmet needs. Review of care in many settings including hospitals, nursing homes, and residential care centers for the developmentally disabled continue to show avoidable lapses in standards (e.g., Levinson, 2011). The situation is so bad in hospitals that doctors are now prescribing water for elderly patients to avoid neglect by nurses and subsequent death by dehydration (e.g., see Mooney, 2011). Social workers who work in health care settings have an obligation to work together with others to correct such neglectful practices. Only through exposure of harms may corrective action be taken. Consider steps taken to increase reports of allegations of physical abuse of the developmentally disabled in group homes and institutions in New York (Hakim, 2011).

The results of ineffective supervisors and failure to carry out responsibilities are reported in our daily newspapers such as avoidable death of children known to child welfare agencies. Certainly some, if not many, such deaths are unavoidable. However others are avoidable as shown by cases in which child welfare staff did not make required visits to families. In a recent case both a social worker and his supervisor have been charged with manslaughter in addition to involved family members (Kleinfield & Secret, 2011). Such cases are not new. Consider also 8-year-old Yaakov. His mother "twisted his leg so viciously that she heard his thigh bone crack. The retarded boy, 8-years-old, 3-feet-8 and 48 pounds, was taken to the hospital in a coma and never woke up....At one point a city worker was ending the supervision of [the mother] because she supposedly had learned to be a nonviolent parent—on the same day that another worker was investigating a new report that Yaakov was being abused. And confidentiality laws also played a part, preventing [the mother's] probation officer from finding out about new reports of abuse in her home" (Dugger, 1992, p. A1/16). A pediatrician knew of [the mother's] abusive history and treated Yaakov's wounds several times, but said he did recognize a battered child.

Social workers confront a wide array of situations, even within one area of social work such as child welfare or work with the elderly. No one person can have all the specialized knowledge and experience to skillfully handle this array. Consider a child welfare worker. On the same day, she may have to interview a 3-year-old child and a stressed out aggressive teenager. She may encounter a parent who is being battered by her partner and who is caring for an elderly relative in the same home as a young child. This example illustrates the need for a service system in which individual workers have access to others who have specialized skills. For example, someone who is skilled in interviewing young children can ask another worker skilled in interviewing teenagers to talk to the teenager. This kind of arrangement requires a team approach in which staff know about and can call on others with special skills. A team approach is important in coordinating work among different agencies that have contact with an individual or family, each of which may have an incomplete piece of the narrative of an individual or family. The Munro (2011) report on child protection in the United Kingdom highlights such a need for multi-agency coordination.

Staff may not use evidence-informed practices and policies that maximize the likelihood of attaining valued outcomes. They may not regularly review outcomes, practices, and policies based on ongoing tracking of relevant, valid indicators (see chapter 22). Social service agencies can suffer from all the problems possible in any organization:

- Vague goals.

- Lack of an agreement on goals.

- Pursuit of goals that do not benefit and/or harm clients.

- Ineffective technology; selection of ineffective or harmful services or neglect of those shown to help clients.

- Onerous eligibility requirements.

- Insufficient resources (e.g., money/staff/clerical help).

- Lack of support for valuable practice behaviors.

- Unwelcoming gatekeepers (e.g., receptionists).

- Lack of effective supervision.

- Lack of staff training to develop practice skills and knowledge.

- Within agency communication structure that hinders provision of high-quality service.

- Lack of effective multi-agency coordination of services to individuals and family.

- Too little or too much individual discretion in making decisions.

Howitt (1992) argues that many studies of child sexual abuse so confound client and system abuse that it is impossible to tell whether negative consequences are a result of the alleged perpetrators (e.g., a parent) or the intrusion of social service personnel into the family's lives. Clients may be given incorrect information (e.g., be told they are not eligible for services when they are). They may be expected to conform to a service delivery pattern that is difficult for them (e.g., be required to come to the agency even when transportation is difficult). Agencies may compete with one another for clients resulting in fragmented services, withholding of information about resources, or complicating access to resources. These problems require changes in the service delivery system, such as improving links with, within, and among agencies (Pincus & Minahan, 1973). For further discussion of overcoming organizational obstacles, see chapter 27.

Social workers often refer clients to residential centers and/or work in them. These settings differ in the extent to which they offer and achieve what they claim. They differ in how much control residents have over decisions that affect them (see Exhibit 19.2) and in their physical characteristics. Contingencies may erode rather than enhance and maintain competencies needed in real life. Consider nursing homes. Independent behavior is often discouraged and dependency reinforced (Baltes, 1988). Clients are often overmedicated so they will be less bother to staff (Levinson, 2011). On the other hand, clients may be undermedicated (e.g., for pain), either by error or refusal to take medication and as a result harm themselves and others (e.g., see earlier example of client placed in group home). (For information on medications, see <http://www.criticalthinkrx.org>, <http://www.pharmedout.org>.)

Some scholars suggest using clients' engagement as an indicator of the quality of life in a setting. This refers to their participation in activities in their living environment. "High levels of engagement denote high levels of reinforcement" (Favell & McGimsey, 1993, p. 27). "People have a right to live in an environment that is interesting and appropriate for them.…One of the clearest and most basic indicators of an impoverished unresponsive environment is the lack of activity of its inhabitants" (p. 28). Beneficial effects of engagement include a decrease in unwanted behavior because there is abundant reinforcement of desired behaviors and natural teaching, practice, and play opportunities.

If a client is to be moved from one place to another (e.g., from a mental hospital to a halfway house), explore the extent to which this new environment will support valued behaviors. What behaviors will be reinforced? What behaviors will be punished? Will the behaviors encouraged in day care and residential settings increase clients' opportunities for reinforcement in real-life environments? You should be familiar with the contingencies in settings of interest (e.g., what behaviors are reinforced, punished, or ignored and when, where, and by whom) and with clients' current repertoires to maximize the match between behaviors that will be supported and valued outcomes. (See chapter 18.) Agencies that serve similar clients may be poorly coordinated. Barriers to successful coordination may include

EXHIBIT 19.2

Policies and Services in Middleton Nursing Home

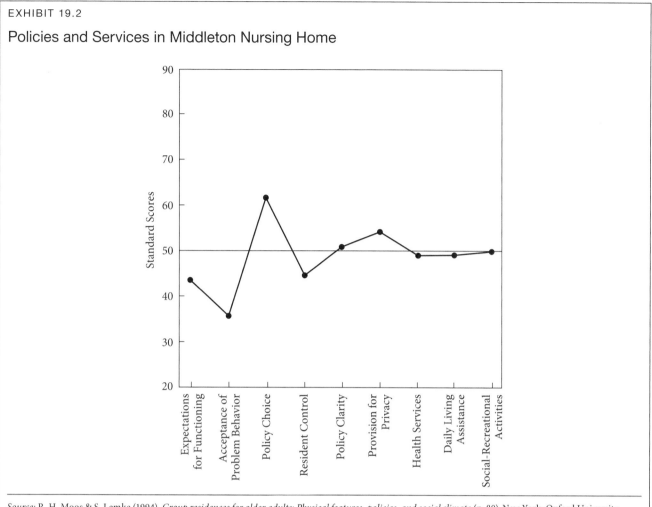

Source: R. H. Moos & S. Lemke (1994), *Group residences for older adults: Physical features, policies, and social climate* (p. 80). New York: Oxford University Press. Reprinted with permission.

personal ones, such as a value on competition, different views of how to frame problems, systemic barriers including limited time and poor communication, and environmental barriers such as political rivalries (e.g., see Anderson, McIntyre, Rotto, & Robertson, 2002).

Neighborhood and Community Resources and Obstacles

Neighborhoods and communities differ in the risks they pose and the opportunities they offer to residents. Characteristics that influence residents include:

- Informal support systems.

- Contexts for positive social exchanges.

- Freedom from crime.

- Opportunities for privacy.

- Quality of educational opportunities.

- Quality of housing.

- Access to health care.

- Access to public transportation.

- Recreational opportunities.

- Income level

- Employment opportunities.

Neighborhood and community characteristics influence the prevalence of substance abuse, delinquency, and child abuse and neglect, as well as health indicators. Guidelines for assessing neighborhoods and communities are suggested in chapter 27. (See also Exhibit 12.17.) Geographic mapping systems have been developed to assess the distribution of services in a community, for example, day care for children, transportation, supermarkets, or recreational settings. Communities and neighborhoods differ in their capacity for change. For example, high crime rates, lack of social connections among residents, poverty, and poor health may interfere with potential for taking action to create change. The concept of social capital has received attention stimulated by Putnam's book *Bowling Alone* (2000). Definitions of social capital differ in their breadth ranging from broad definitions that refer to the social and political environment that influences social structure and norms including the law, court system, and civil liberties, to narrow definitions focusing on people's social networks and associated norms that influence well-being and community resources. Measures used include voting trends, membership in civic organizations, hours spent in volunteer work, and trust in various institutions and individuals.

Neighborhoods and communities differ in their range of contexts, in the overlap among them in terms of participation and in the risks and opportunities provided in each. They differ in the interrelationships among social, cultural, and economic capital. For example, a client may have little economic capital but be rich in cultural and social capital (e.g., Portes, 1998). She may live in a poor section of a large city but have access to libraries, museums, local art shows, and poetry readings at the YMCA. Providing access to social and cultural capital may prevent social exclusion. Enhancing social capital may increase economic capital via local community development (see chapter 27).

Using the least intrusive methods calls for working with clients in their natural environments whenever needed and possible. Take advantage of natural reinforcing communities (real-life settings) that support valued behaviors. What settings encourage valued behaviors? What settings discourage them? Supported employment has replaced sheltered workshops for persons with severe disabilities. This consists of paid employment in an integrated work setting (i.e., persons without disabilities also are employed). An employment specialist helps the employees perform expected tasks and provides follow-up services. Data gathered from job analyses and each client's social and vocational skills are considered when arranging placements and training programs. Placing a person in a group of people with adaptive behaviors provides opportunities for constructive modeling and reinforcement of valued behaviors. Group homes may be a good option. Here, too, find out whether the contingencies and programs provided are likely to enhance or erode the quality of life for residents.

Social Networks and Social Support Systems

Assessing social support systems and social networks is often an important part of assessment. The term *social network* refers to people with whom an individual interacts. Social networks differ in structure, function, and perceived value. "Social support system" refers to social exchanges that offer some resource, such as emotional support or material aid. Rook (1990) distinguishes between the exchange of problem-focused aid and companionship (shared leisure and other activities undertaken mainly for enjoyment) and argues that the latter plays an important (and often unrecognized) role in sustaining emotional well-being.

Networks differ in the number of people in different domains (e.g., work, family, neighbors). They also differ in perceived availability of different kinds of support (e.g., mutual help, information, emotional, problem-solving) and in their stability (how long people have known each other) and frequency of contact (e.g., see Cohen, Gordon, & Gottlieb, 2000). They differ in reciprocity (extent to which help goes both ways), in the size of kinship networks, and interrelationships among different sources (e.g., church and family). Differences have been found between Caribbean Blacks and African Americans in the effects of emotional support on the impact of negative interaction on depression (Lincoln & Chae, 2011).

The distinction between social network and social support highlights the fact that social exchanges (interactions among people in a network) may not be supportive; they can be a source of stress, as well as joy and support. It is not the quantity but the quality of interaction that influences satisfaction (Sarason, Sarason, & Pierce, 1990). Negative (compared with positive) interactions may weigh especially heavily in influencing personal relationships (Rook, 1984a). Inadequate, stress-producing, and/or unwanted deviance-supporting social exchanges are related to many problems. Depression, for instance, may be related to a lack of significant others. An elderly widower may be socially isolated and lack skills in forming friendships and so may start to drink alcohol because this lessens his loneliness.

Sources of Social Support

Sources of social support range from casual associations to intimate, confiding relationships with friends. Social experiences in one area may influence those in others. Consider the classic study illustrating the association between a parent's social exchanges outside the home and how they respond to their children; on high friendship days for the parent, they were less negative toward their children, and their children showed improved behavior (Wahler, 1980). Friends, relatives, neighbors, acquaintances, or "community caretakers" (such as bartenders, hairdressers, and waitresses) may provide support. Neighborhoods differ in the number and variety of settings in which informal meetings are possible. One goal of the Community Networks Strategies (Horner, Meyer, & Fredericks, 1986) was to enhance the social support of severely disabled persons by increasing their access to others and the amount of contact (by decreasing barriers such as inflexible amounts of time allotted to certain social activities) and maximizing the disabled person's contributions to the social network, acknowledging birthdays, and feeding pets. Inventories and/or social network diagrams may be used to identify supportive persons and activities (e.g., Tracy & Whittaker, 1993); and to assess caregiver burden (Braun, Scholz, Hornung, & Martin, 2010).

You may help a client distribute support among providers of care to an elderly relative so that no one person is overburdened. Careful planning for transitions increases the likelihood of success (e.g., see McDonnell & Hardman, 2010). Social agencies may provide mediators, such as Big Brothers and Big Sisters. Settings such as senior centers offer opportunities for supportive social contacts. The level of intervention (e.g., individual, family, or community) required to increase social support depends on each person's skills and circumstances, including the characteristics of the community in which she or he lives. Possible options are:

- Increasing the social skills of clients and/or significant others.
- Creating self-help groups.
- Establishing neighborhood exchanges/block organizations.
- Rearranging the physical environment in order to increase opportunities for positive social exchanges (e.g., increasing recreational space, establishing a community center).

The Functions of Social Support

Social support affects both psychological and physical well-being (e.g., see Martin, Rogers, & Cook, 2004). Positive effects of social support include:

- Reducing the stress of relocating from one place to another.
- Encouraging adherence to health care regimens.
- Encouraging persistence in coping with problems.
- Decreasing vulnerability to physical illness.
- Maintaining positive family relationships.
- Decreasing stress.
- Encouraging constructive problem solving.
- Encouraging a positive outlook.

Informal social support may provide both tangible (e.g., money) and intangible goods (e.g., emotional support). Valued outcomes include financial or physical resources, information, guidelines for fulfilling roles (e.g., as a parent), and opportunities for nurturance and reassurance of one's worth. Additional functions are social integration (feeling part of a valued group) and attachment to others. A study of the kinds of informal help that single mothers exchanged with one another revealed 26 separate behaviors (Gottlieb, 1978), including emotionally sustaining behaviors (listening, encouragement, reassurance, and companionship) and problem-solving behaviors (offering information or a new perspective, providing suggestions, material aid, or direct service). The kind of resource needed will help determine the provider. Some resources can be provided by many different people, whereas others have fewer potential providers.

Obstacles

Personal obstacles to gaining social reinforcers include a lack of required skills (e.g., initiating conversations), as well as interfering behaviors (e.g., aggressive reactions, physiological reactions such as anxiety, and/or negative self-statements such as no one will like me). Little time may be available to make friends. Caregivers may be overburdened. Neighborhoods differ in the variety and number of settings that offer opportunities for positive social exchanges and help in times of need. The residents of poor communities may have few if any extra resources to offer to others in need. They may have little social and economic capital (see previous discussion). A long-term resident of a mental hospital or prison may no longer have any contacts in the community. This situation led Fairweather and his colleagues to establish a network of social contacts among people in the hospital and to move an entire group into a community home (Fairweather, Sanders, Cressler, & Maynard, 1969). Their program remains a classic and underused model, given its success in keeping people in the community (see also Fairweather & Fergus, 1993). (See also Mosher, 2004; Calton, Ferriter, Huband, & Spandler, 2008.) A needs assessment is useful in identifying the kinds of support valued and needed, as well as the stressors (anticipated or actual) that may accompany transitions, such as returning from residential care to the community.

Significant Others as Resources and Obstacles

Significant others (mediators) are people (e.g., teachers, peers, parents, partners) who have an ongoing relationship with the client. They may be the main cause of the client's problems, as when an elderly person is abused or robbed by her own grown children or a woman is battered by her partner. The value of working with significant others lies in their continuing interaction with clients, as part of their real-life circumstances. If a client's complaints are related to how significant others respond, these significant others should be involved when useful and possible. They become the mediators of change by enhancing their knowledge and skills in interacting with their significant others (e.g., children, students, residents). To be effective, mediators must have access to reinforcers of value to clients, as well as the motivation, knowledge, skills, and opportunities to offer them contingently and consistently. Problems such as substance abuse may interfere with the contributions they could otherwise make. In deciding which significant others to involve, assess each one's capabilities to support valued behaviors.

Finding and Creating Significant Others

Teachers, parents, and residential staff often consult social workers about problems with children, youths, or adults. These individuals are significant others for those they are troubled by. Peers provide an important source of reinforcement in many contexts, including classrooms, and have been involved in many programs designed to alter behavior (e.g., Broussard & Northup, 1997; DuPaul, Ervin, Hook, & McGoey, 1998). Preschool children have been enlisted to help parents educate children with disabilities (Cash & Evans, 1975). If significant others are not cooperative or available, you may locate others who can support valued behaviors. For example, foster grandparents may help train children with severe disabilities (Fabry & Reid, 1978). There is a rich literature describing the creation of significant others. Consider, for example, the Fostser Grandparent Program, which links volunteers with youth who need support. Peers provide many sources of reinforcement (Kupersmidt & Dodge, 2004; Rubin, Bukowski, & Laursen, 2009). Knowledge of cultural differences will help you identify significant others (see Exhibit 19.3). (See also Chang-Muy & Congress, 2009; Pederson, Lonner, Draguns, & Trimble, 2007.)

Overcoming Obstacles to the Participation of Significant Others

Obtaining the cooperation of significant others may not be easy. Significant others may not possess effective reinforcers or be willing or able to offer them contingent on desired behavior (see, for example, Greer, 2007). Problems that may occur and suggestions for resolving them are discussed in the next section.

Significant Others May Not Possess Reinforcers

Significant others cannot be used as mediators unless they have access to effective reinforcers. One goal of intervention might be to increase the reinforcing potential of mediators by pairing attention with consequences that already function as reinforcers. For example, parents' attention could be strengthened as a reinforcer by pairing it with access to desired activities (see chapter 25).

Lack of Skill and Knowledge

Many intervention programs involve helping significant others such as teachers acquire the contingency management skills needed to attain valued outcomes (see chapter 25). If reinforcers are not offered following desired behaviors and withheld following undesired ones in a consistent fashion, it is unlikely that change will occur. Significant others may not understand (or may deny) that they influence behaviors they complain about. Family members often do not realize how they influence one another. That is, they may not believe they are "significant." They may protest, "It's her fault," or "If only he wouldn't…" Parents and teachers may believe that a child's disruptive behaviors stem from his "psychological problems" and expect you to correct them by seeing him alone (for example, in play therapy). Or they may attribute them to ADHD and recommend that he be placed on medication. A teacher may be surprised to hear that you would like to observe her exchanges with students in her classroom (see chapter 18). Self-monitoring methods of value in helping people discover how they support disliked behaviors are described in chapter 17.

Clients may lack skills in reinforcing desired behaviors and withholding reinforcement following undesired behaviors. Parents may be unable to contain their angry outbursts when a child engages in annoying behaviors and so may reinforce such behavior. Special procedures such as desensitization may be needed to help mediators tolerate annoying behaviors so that they can refrain from reinforcing disliked reactions while reinforcing desired behaviors. Prompts delivered by mobile phones may be valuable in encouraging desired behaviors (e.g., Aguilera, 2012; L'Abate & Kaiser, 2011) (see also National Center for Telehealth & Technology. http://t2health.org). Significant others may be either underinvolved (offer little aid or support to clients) or overinvolved (e.g., reinforce dependent behaviors). Expressed emotion (EE) refers to criticism and emotional overinvolvement on the part of family members, for example, comments of dislike, resentment, and annoyance and comments indicating overconcern, self-sacrifice, and over-involvement. The level of family and environmental stress is a risk factor for relapse

---

EXHIBIT 19.3

Attending to Cultural Differences: The Hmong

To the Hmong, the family encompasses all relatives who belong to an extended family known as the *clan*. The clan serves as the locus for resolving problems and making decisions and also provides a sense of belonging. There are 18 Hmong clans, and the leader of each clan is the head of all the families belonging to that clan. Clan leaders serve as liaisons between Hmong communities and outsiders.

Working with Hmong children in the school, social service, or health care system may involve decision making by clan leaders, as well as parents and professionals. For example, if a child is referred by a teacher to a school social worker for behavior problems, the social worker may find the Hmong family uncooperative in developing a plan. The family may prefer to seek a clan leader's advice. Hmong families may rely on their own system of foster care. For example, a child may be sent to live with a relative on the clan leader's suggestion. Trying to circumvent clan involvement may result in alienation and withdrawal of a family from any contact with social service personnel.

Source: Adapted from K. McInnis (1991). Ethnic-sensitive work with Hmong refugee children. *Child Welfare, 70*, 571–580.

on the part of a family member with a psychiatric diagnosis (e.g., see Butzlaff & Hooley, 1998). Culturally sensitive programs designed to help family members alter how they express their emotion may be needed.

Fear of Failure

Significant others may be wary of trying anything else because previous efforts were not successful. Arranging some immediate payoff will encourage hope that different methods can be successful.

Being Overburdened Themselves

Personal problems such as marital discord, poor health, substance abuse, or depression interfere with client participation including consistent use of new contingencies. Significant others may lack money or access to health care. Perhaps caregivers of an elderly relative are overburdened. If so, you will have to find a way to remove obstacles (e.g. by providing respite care).

Reluctance to Offer Positive Reinforcers

If significant others are reluctant to offer positive incentives, find out why. Further discussion may be needed to convince them that encouraging valued behaviors by offering positive consequences contingently is a caring act. You may have to explain the difference between bribery and the use of positive reinforcement, pointing out the advantages of positive incentives and the benefits of new ways of acting to mediators. Bribery refers to giving someone something to induce him to do something illegal or wrong (*Webster's New World Dictionary*, 1988). Thus, the use of positive incentives to increase behaviors valued by mediators could not accurately be called bribery. A staff member may object to offering rewards for tasks that "clients should do anyway." Point out that acting in new ways requires finding out that new behaviors have a payoff. You could point out that "unless we reinforce our children with praise while they are struggling with the hard task of learning to read, they may not stick to it long enough to find out that it is enjoyable and beneficial" (Kozloff, 1979, p. 75).

Significant others may worry that clients will become dependent on positive reinforcers and so demand them in the future. Point out that artificial reinforcers (e.g., points or tokens) are only a temporary measure and that as behavior stabilizes, they will be faded out and natural consequences, such as praise, approval, and self-reinforcement, relied on to maintain behavior. Significant others may feel that it is unfair to offer special incentives to only one person. This view assumes that all persons are identical and they are not. "To deny them those [special] environmental conditions in the name of equality may mean that they are denied the very conditions that could help them to be more equal in terms of their behaviors and, hence, in their control of their own future" (Kozloff, 1979, p. 78).

A relationship may have become so negative that it is unpleasant for family members to offer one another positive feedback. Rather, they may get pleasure from hurting one another. In such instances, identify an acceptable approximation such as removing attention contingent on undesired reactions. For example, a husband who is unwilling to reinforce his wife for behaviors he likes may be willing to leave the room when she acts in disliked ways. We must start "where the client is." Backup reinforcers can be offered at home if a teacher is not willing (or able) to offer them at school.

Fear of Loss of Valued Outcomes

Anticipated negative consequences of participation may pose a barrier.

> Our staff strongly urged a widowed mother to call the juvenile authorities when next her daughter, Annie, sneaked out of the house at night. The mother was unable to do so, because this might have resulted in the daughter's being adjudicated delinquent. If the daughter were confined to detention or a correction home, the mother would have lost the pension that she administered for the daughter, and that was the family's major support. It was economically unfeasible for the mother to behave in her daughter's best interest. (Tharp & Wetzel, 1969, pp. 130–131)

A student may worry that his peers will hassle him if his grades improve. Worries about negative consequences should be discussed and steps taken to prevent them or to prepare clients for handling them. A cost-benefit analysis of seeking changes (or not) is useful. The advantages and disadvantages are written down and reviewed.

A Preference for Aversive Control

Significant others may continue to use punishment, even though it is ineffective in the long run and even though you have pointed out its limitations. In this case, you may have to offer incentives to mediators to use positive consequences. Seeing the benefits of positive contingencies may overcome a preference for aversive control.

Overlooking Cultural Differences

A woman's desire to become more assertive with her husband may not be compatible with her culture's norms, and she may be criticized by her husband, children, friends, and other family members for doing so. Consult clients and significant others, and also the literature describing cultural differences, for information about differences that may influence mediating potential (see for example Suzuki et al., 2008).

Other Problems

Mediators may have trouble identifying desired changes. Helping clients clearly describe how they would like their lives to be different is a key assessment task. A reluctance to try new methods may be overcome by making minimal demands.

Personal Resources and Obstacles

You may discover resources by finding out what is going well and what concerns have been resolved successfully. (See Constructional Questionnaire in Exhibit 13.2.) Helpful attitudes, knowledge, and skills may be available but not used in problem-related situations. For example, a client may use effective anger-management skills at work but not at home. Interfering thoughts, behaviors, or emotional reactions may contribute to problems. Clients may not be motivated to address problems. Guidelines for encouraging participation are discussed in chapter 14.

Problem-Solving Styles and Skills

People have different problem-solving styles and skills. A review of past problem-solving efforts may reveal useful skills. Examples are:

- Using confrontive coping (remaining in a situation and pursuing goals, such as requesting behavior changes).

- Regulating emotions (becoming aware of increased tension, using relaxation skills).

- Seeking social support, for example, talking to someone.

- Escaping (leaving the situation) or avoiding it.

- Planful problem solving (reviewing resources and planning how to use them in anticipation of demands; gathering information; planning how to avoid or reduce stressors, for example, clearly describing hoped-for outcomes, identifying options for attaining them and the likely consequences of each, trying out the best option, and evaluating the results).

- Using positive reappraisal (reframing situations such as viewing a social slight as irrelevant in the long term).

Attempted solutions may create more problems. For example, clients may avoid feared situations, forgoing opportunities to decrease anxiety through exposure. Stressful environments may encourage drinking patterns and drug abuse that create further problems. (See discussion of high-cost behavior in chapter 12.) Substance abuse is common, for example, in parents who abuse or neglect their children. Clients may try to solve problems when they are tired, angry, or anxious. They may skip important problem-solving steps (e.g., not clarify goals) or not consider alternatives and their consequences. Examples of "self-handicapping" strategies include a lack of persistence and a low tolerance of failure. Clients may have a pessimistic outlook and feel helpless; they may believe that their problems cannot be solved so there

is a no use trying; they may be demoralized. Self-handicapping behaviors can be self-serving (e.g., protect us from failure). If we do not try, we cannot fail.

Attributions/Beliefs

The term *attribution* refers to beliefs about the cause(s) of behavior and outcomes. Understanding clients' attributions for problems provides a guide for redirecting them in a constructive direction. For example, aggressive and nonaggressive boys differ in their attributions, as well as in their processing of social cues, social problem solving, affect labeling, outcome expectations, and perceived competence (Lochman & Dodge, 1994). MacBrayer, Milich, and Hundley (2003) describe attributional biases of aggressive children and their mothers. Examples of attributional biases are shown in Exhibit 19.4. Debiasing methods include searching for less obvious possible causes.

Attributions influence whom we hold responsible for given behaviors or outcomes, how much control we think we (or others) have over outcomes, and how we view our own or others' intentions. Some people believe that the world is basically a "just place," that events and the relationships among them are predictable and can be discovered. Lerner (1980) suggests that this view encourages the belief that there are right and wrong ways to act, so it makes sense to act responsibly. Some value the obligation of power: if one has more power than another (e.g., parent vs. child, human vs. animal), there is an obligation to use this power to help the less powerful (Sen, 2009). Others believe that the world is basically an unjust place and that events occur randomly and cannot be predicted or understood. An implication of this view is that there are no right and wrong ways to act, so there is little point in trying to understand the world or what is wrong or right. An "unjust" world view may result in apathy and failure to acknowledge responsibility for one's actions, since it makes little sense to try anything. There is a rich literature describing biases (errors and distortions) in viewing interpersonal exchanges, including how we maintain positive views of ourselves (e.g., Pronin, Puccio, & Ross, 2002; Taylor & Brown, 1988).

Attributions may be global or specific, stable or unstable, personal or external (Abramson, Seligman, & Teasdale, 1978). A supervisor may attribute a student's quiet demeanor to a passive-aggressive personality, a stable internal trait over which the student has little control. This is quite different from attributing such behavior to the effects of a new situation (a new field internship) (an external, changeable, specific attribution). Men who are violent toward their partners are more likely, compared to nonviolent men, to attribute negative intentions to their wives (Holtzworth-Munroe & Hutchinson, 1993). How much control we think we have influences whether we will try to attain valued goals and how long we will persist. We are more likely to persist in trying to achieve our goals if we assume responsibility for our behavior, have been successful in the past, and attribute our successes to our efforts rather than to luck. Our self-efficacy

EXHIBIT 19.4

Examples of Attributional Biases

Ignore Consensus Information

We tend to ignore information about what most people do in a situation (we ignore base rates).

Attend to Available Data (Salience)

We are influenced by vivid data.

Fundamental Attribution Error

We tend to overlook environmental causes and focus on dispositional characteristics (e.g., alleged personality characteristics).

Actor's (Versus Observer's) Bias

We explain our own behavior as related to situational factors more often than we do in relation to other people's behavior. Scott Plous sums this up in the phrase "My situation is your disposition" (1993, p. 181).

More Likely to Accept Responsibility for Success Than Failure

We have a self-serving bias in our attributions, due partly to motivational factors (we want to look good).

Positive Effect

We tend to attribute positive behaviors to dispositional factors and negative ones to situational factors.

We Tend to Ascribe Less Variability to Others Than to Ourselves

We view our own behavior as more variable over situations than our friends' behavior.

We see ourselves as more complex and less predictable than others. As a result, stereotypes flourish.

Source: Based on S. Plous (1993). *The psychology of judgment and decision making.* New York: McGraw-Hill.

is related to past successes we have in achieving our goals (e.g., Baumeister, Campbell, Krueger, & Vohs, 2003). Cultural differences in reasoning about social exchanges should be considered. For example, those who live in a culture emphasizing interdependence (Chinese) tend to use contextual explanations compared to people who live in cultures emphasizing independence (Anglo-Americans) who favor dispositional explanations (Nisbett, 2003).

Clients may blame themselves for events that cannot be controlled or assume no responsibility for events over which they do have influence. They may continue to believe something, despite contradictory evidence, or have negative self-fulfilling prophecies. They may use defenses such as projection (e.g., attributing unacceptable thoughts and behaviors to others) or denial (Freud, 1967; Opotow & Weiss, 2000). Over the past years, greater

attention has been given to the positive effects of denial (Lazarus, 1982; Taylor & Brown, 1988; Vos, Putter, van Houwelingen, & de Haes, 2011). That is, sometimes it is best to overlook risks or potential for failure. Attributing disliked reactions to dispositional traits ("he's moody") and overlooking environmental circumstances (being asked to work late) may create ill feelings between partners. People diagnosed as "paranoid" may falsely believe that people want to harm them. Clients' spiritual beliefs may contribute to finding solutions to concerns and bearing up under difficult circumstances. Greater attention has been given to clients' spirituality and religion over the past years. Religion is related to affiliation (for example, is a client a Catholic or a Muslim?) whereas spirituality refers to transcendent and experiential processes of personal meanings (e.g., see Canda & Furman, 2010; Hodge, 2001; Pargament, Koenig, & Perez, 2000).

Self-Statements

Our beliefs and attributions are reflected in what we say to ourselves about ourselves. This in turn influences what we feel and do. Negative self-statements and self-labels may interfere with attaining hoped-for outcomes. Mrs. Ryan thought of herself as "an old lady," "no longer useful" (see case example in chapter 13), and wondered why she was still alive when so many of her friends had already died. She believed she was in the way, useless. These thoughts interfered with improving the quality of her life. Both Mr. and Mrs. Lakeland thought of themselves as "bad parents" and Brian thought that something was "wrong" with him, since he got into so much trouble. Popular—compared with aggressive or withdrawn—children make more facilitating than inhibiting self-statements (Stefanek, Ollendick, Baldock, Francis, & Yaeger, 1987). (See also Cook & Cook, 2009.) A variety of intervention programs are available to help children think more effectively about making friends (e.g., http://www.socialthinking.com).

Self-efficacy (our beliefs about what we can do and what outcomes will result) is reflected in what we say about ourselves. People with a negative self-concept and low self-efficacy say more negative things about themselves and their potential than do people who have a positive self-concept and high self-efficacy. Our self-concept and self-efficacy are influenced by our experiences (past and current environmental contingencies). Consider a client I saw for depression and suicidal attempts who had a "very low self-image." A review of her past revealed many years of being told by her parents that she was limited intellectually and would never amount to much. Pessimistic thoughts may reflect a lack of success in achieving valued outcomes and may discourage efforts to change a troubling situation. Written questionnaires, such as the Automatic Thoughts Questionnaire and the Dysfunctional Attitudes Scale, can be used to explore clients' self-statements and attitudes.

Clients' problems may be related to unrealistic beliefs and related goals such as "Everyone must like me," "I should never make mistakes," "I should never feel frustrated or anxious," or "People should be the way I expect them to be." They may

EXHIBIT 19.5

Examples of Cognitive Distortions

Overgeneralizing.	Generalizing from single examples (e.g., about your overall competence).
Negative scanning.	Attending only to negative events/circumstances.
Assuming excessive responsibility.	Assuming you are responsible for all negative events.
Catastrophizing.	Thinking the worst.
Dichotomous thinking.	Thinking in terms of extremes (e.g., "this will be either _____ or _____").
Emotional reasoning.	Assuming your feelings reflect reality.
Magnifying.	Overestimating the significance of an event.
Minimizing.	Underestimating the significance of an event.
Personalizing.	Assuming events are related to you when they are not.
Selective abstraction.	Attending to only part of the picture and drawing conclusions based on this (e.g., discounting positive events or attributes).

think in terms of "musts" and "shoulds" rather than "wants" and "desires." Albert Ellis (1996) has long suggested that people's irrational beliefs stem from their core philosophies related to life's adversities. Aaron Beck and his colleagues suggest that unrealistic expectations and inaccurate attributions contribute to anxiety and depression (e.g., Beck, 1995). A focus on altering such thoughts is a key part of cognitive-behavioral therapy. Clients may jump to conclusions, overgeneralize, or think in either/or terms (see Exhibit 19.5). Such tendencies may be related to attributional biases shown in Exhibit 19.4. For example, Dudley and Over (2003) suggested that people with delusions jump to conclusions. A history of punishment in a situation may result in a vigilance for negative outcomes and a neglect of positive ones (see literature on post-traumatic stress disorder including critiques, Summerfield, 2001). Positive alternatives to dysfunctional thoughts can be discovered by asking clients to note them in a daily log.

Problem-Related Information

Parents may not be informed about children's typical behavior at different ages. Adolescents may not know about effective birth-control methods. Clients may have incorrect beliefs about problem-related behaviors. On the other hand, client knowledge

about behaviors related to hoped-for outcomes may be valuable in selecting successful plans (see chapter 21).

Intellectual Functioning

The term *intelligence* refers to performing certain tasks at certain levels of competence. Intelligence is a "hypothetical construct" (i.e., it is assessed indirectly by certain measures presumed to reflect intelligence) (see Nisbett, Aronson, Blair, Dickens, Flynn, Halpern, & Turkheimer, 2012). Scholars such as Perkins (1995) criticize traditional ways of measuring intelligence as being too narrow and suggest that there are many kinds of intelligence, including artistic and social. Individual differences in different kinds of intelligence including "emotional intelligence" may influence what outcomes can be attained. It is important to recognize that different people may be able to achieve different outcomes—otherwise inappropriate expectations may be imposed—and, at the same time, not to underestimate what a given person can achieve. A contextual assessment, with its emphasis on exploring interrelationships between environmental and personal factors and in constructing repertoires, is less likely to err in either direction. Perhaps this is why a behavioral approach has been so useful in devising helpful programs for children and adults with developmental disabilities (see Cambridge Center for Behavioral Studies, http://www.behavior.org).

Self-Management Skills

Self-management refers to altering our behavior and/or environment to increase the likelihood of attaining goals we value. For example, you may turn off your cell phone to avoid being distracted while studying. Related skills include:

1. Setting specific goals (clarifying the question "What do I want?").

2. Gathering information about how to attain your goals.

3. Forming a plan.

4. Arranging prompts and incentives.

5. Monitoring progress.

6. Altering plans as necessary. (Watson & Tharp, 2007).

Clients may have some self-management skills such as arranging reminders, identifying specific goals, and collecting useful information but lack others (e.g., rewarding progress). Skills are required to break large tasks into a series of small achievable steps, arrange access to needed tools (such as a computer), and provide reminders and incentives. Meichenbaum and Goodman (1971) found that hyperactive, impulsive children did not use self-instructions that help to maintain their attention, such as setting response standards, noting when their attention is drifting, producing motor reactions (such as shaking their head) to increase vigilance, and playing cognitive games to make the task more interesting. You may help clients respond to problems by first clearly describing them. For example, a client may believe she is not receiving promotions as rapidly as other workers who are "more assertive." What does she mean by "more assertive"? What do these other women do (and not do) that makes them "more assertive"? Only if the behavioral referents for this term are identified can clients discover if they have related skills and, if they do not, whether they want to acquire them.

People have different patterns of self-reinforcement. Depressed compared to nondepressed people offer fewer positive self-statements or reinforcers for accomplishments. They have a high frequency of self-critical statements like "How could I do such a stupid thing?" They have an attentional bias toward negative interpersonal events. You should make separate assessments of positive and negative self-statements because they have been found to be independent. (For further discussion, see, for example, Baumeister & Vohs, 2004).

Stress-Management Skills

Problems may be related to a lack of stress-management skills. Physical complaints such as headaches or high blood pressure may be related to stress. Anxiety or anger may prevent a client from learning and using helpful skills. The skills that will be of value in decreasing stress depend in part on its source. Stress may result from unresolved problems or the absence of hoped-for positive consequences. Clients often struggle with environmental stressors, such as poor housing or a lack of money. Clients may benefit from learning how to replace stress-inducing thoughts with task-focused ones. They may be more successful in job interviews when they learn how to manage their reactions to rejections and slights.

Additional social skills may be needed to avoid conflicts and to obtain emotional support and needed material resources. You may discover helpful skills by asking clients how they usually handle stress. Folkman and Lazarus (1980) investigated the ways people coped with daily life challenges. Both problem- and emotion-focused coping were used in 98% of episodes. Emotion-focused coping skills included trying to forget an unpleasant experience, joking about it, concentrating on something good that could result, and talking to someone about your feelings. Problem-focused coping skills included concentrating on the next step, making and following a plan of action, drawing on past experiences, and coming up with some different solutions (see also the section on problem-solving skills). Clients differ in their skills in forming intimate relationships that may buffer the effects of stress. (See also later discussion of use of written schedules.)

Beliefs About the Helping Process

Beliefs about the helping process (for example, who will have to change and how) may be an obstacle. Clients may have strong beliefs about the causes of problems that do not match perspectives of the professionals they see. They may believe that you will do all the work, that you will make decisions for them. They may be searching for an "instant" cure or believe that change will come about with little or no effort on their part. They may feel hopeless that nothing can be done. They may be in an early stage of considering change. (See Exhibit 14.5.) Clearly describing mutual responsibilities will encourage accurate beliefs about the helping process. David Burns (2004) asks his clients to complete a self-help questionnaire describing what is expected (e.g., complete weekly homework assignments). You can set the stage for viewing concerns in a contextual perspective by seeing clients and significant others together (e.g., parents and children) and providing valuable introductory information.

Relationship Skills

Client concerns often involve social behaviors. For example, not having an intimate relationship is a precursor to depression (Brown & Harris, 1978). Social skills are required for getting along with coworkers, making and keeping friends, relating to family members, and acquiring resources such as support and validation. Interpersonal skills are needed to interact effectively with service providers. Behavior deficits, such as a lack of cooperative and friendship skills, may be related to behavior surfeits such as aggressive behavior. (See Steele, Elkin, & Roberts, 2008.) Explosive anger reactions may result when behavior changes are not requested and feelings are not expressed in appropriate ways. People may lose or not get a job because of disliked social behaviors (e.g., sarcasm). (See discussion of assertive, passive, and aggressive behavior in chapter 16.) Beliefs about rights are related to aggressive behavior. For example, an abusive husband may believe that he has a right (he is entitled) to hit his wife. Anger may be fueled by reliving imagined slights. A lack of social skills may result in loneliness, which in turn contributes to depression or substance abuse. For recently separated or divorced mothers, a lack of relationship competence is a high-risk factor for entering a spiral of negative interactions (Patterson & Forgatch, 1990, 2005).

Clients may lack skills in planning enjoyable activities and encouraging others to talk about interesting topics. They may approach people who do not share any of their interests and rely on punishment to influence others. They may not know how to use the Internet and local newspapers to locate contexts in which to meet people with similar interests. Negative self-statements ("I'm really stupid"), unrealistic expectations ("I have to please everyone"), and excessive concern about negative evaluations may contribute to ineffective social behavior. Role plays are valuable in assessing social behaviors (see chapter 18). You may include situations that are important to address, even though the client did not think of them. For example, psychiatric patients may not realize the value of stigma-reduction skills.

Physical Assets and Obstacles

Skill in certain sports, a high energy level, and good health may contribute to achieving hoped-for outcomes. On the other hand, medical problems and/or limitations in physical functioning may present obstacles. Physical problems may or may not be changeable. Even with an unchangeable situation, such as confinement to a wheelchair, resources may be located that maximize opportunities for reinforcement and minimize negative consequences. Examples are a motorized wheelchair that allows greater freedom and independence or a specially designed computer terminal that offers easy access to friends. In his classic article "Geriatric Behavioral Prosthetics" (1964), Ogden Lindsley highlights the importance of arranging "prosthetics" that allow elderly people to maintain access to valued reinforcers (e.g., railings in bathrooms, response amplifiers in case of physical weakness or sensory deficits, and prompting devices to remind a person to take required medication).

Reinforcer Profile

A reinforcer profile lists events that function as reinforcers for an individual. Helping clients often requires rearranging contingencies (the relationships between behaviors and their consequences). An interest in increasing client skills and using positive change methods highlights the importance of identifying feasible reinforcers. Reinforcers are relative; that is, what functions as a reinforcer for one person may not for another, and what functions as a reinforcer for a person in one situation may not in others. Deprivation level, competing contingencies, and past history influence whether an event will serve as a reinforcer. Thus, each person's reinforcer profile is somewhat different.

The range and kinds of events that function as reinforcers may present an obstacle. A study of car theft from the offender's perspective showed that the main reasons for initial involvement were friends' influence (31%), boredom (18%), excitement (18%), a laugh (10%), and money (10%). The main reasons for persisting were money (42%), a buzz (24%), nothing else to do (10%), somewhere to go (5%), a desire to drive (5%), and a laugh (2%) (Nee, 1993). A client's feelings about significant others may be either an asset or an obstacle. For instance, residential staff who have trouble with residents they like may be more willing to reinforce valued behaviors than may staff who dislike the residents. If children like to help others, such opportunities can be used as a reinforcer.

Types of Reinforcers

There are many different types of reinforcers, including social (approval), activity-oriented (bike riding), edible (cake, ice cream), tangible (marbles), informative feedback (grades), and self-reinforcers (positive self-statements). Clients who complain about other people's behavior often rely on punishment to change it, by criticizing them or withdrawing privileges. Social reinforcers include physical contact (hugs, kisses), proximity (sitting or standing near someone), verbal statements (approving comments), nonverbal expressions of approval (looking, smiling, laughing), and shared activities (talking or playing a game together). Parents and teachers use social approval to establish and maintain a range of behaviors. Social reinforcers have many advantages: they do not take much time to offer and are part of the natural environment. No prior preparation is required, as may be needed to arrange access to an activity, and satiation is not as much of a problem as it is with reinforcers such as food. Social reinforcers typically do not distract recipients from desired behaviors, as does consuming a sweet.

Examples of activity-oriented reinforcers are going to the movies, having lunch with friends, and playing a game. Behaviors that have a high probability can be used to reinforce behaviors that have a low probability (Premack, 1965). If behavior A (drinking a cup of coffee) is more probable than behavior B (completing case reports) in a situation, you can increase the rate of B by making A contingent on B, so that in order to drink a cup of coffee, you must first complete a portion of the report. High-probability behaviors share many of the advantages of social reinforcers. They are readily available and can be used both to maintain and to establish behaviors. They are more distracting than social reinforcers in that engaging in an activity often precludes other behaviors and some activities require preparation. Many high-probability behaviors involve social exchanges:

Behaviors Involving Social Interaction	
Walking with someone.	Introducing people who like each other.
Talking about old times.	
Texting.	Visiting relatives.
Visiting friends.	Meeting someone new.
Playing basketball.	Going to the movies with someone.
Helping someone.	
Playing cards.	Singing in a choir.
Attending a club meeting.	Doing something nice for someone.

Other Behaviors	
Listening to music.	Cooking.
Playing with a cat.	Taking a trip.
Watching television.	Going to the library.
Looking at beautiful scenery.	Swimming.
Playing computer games.	Visiting a museum.
Playing the guitar.	Running.
Shopping.	Visiting garage sales.
Gardening.	Reading a book.
Working on a cross-word puzzle.	Writing letters.
	Watching people.

Preferences	Freedom From Tasks
For vacation days.	Child care.
Choice of dinner.	Sleeping late.
Choice of clothing to wear.	Somebody doing the dishes.
For a night's entertainment.	Longer lunch hour.
Staying out later.	
Staying up later.	

Consumables (e.g., food) can be used as reinforcers. Consequences such as food are valuable when social approval does not function as a reinforcer. Possible disadvantages are satiation and the possibility that consuming food or beverages may distract people from engaging in desired behaviors. Some of these problems can be avoided by using small amounts, which are easy to carry around and do not take long to consume, and by offering them for only a limited time.

Using material items such as books and magazines, tools, CDs, and toys as reinforcers usually involves engaging in an activity. If clothes are reinforcers, related activities may be looking at clothes, wearing them, or showing them to others. The behaviors associated with a given item may not be immediately apparent, however, so it may be helpful to look for the items first and then to think of related activities. The advantages and disadvantages of material items as reinforcers are similar to those for high-probability behaviors. Some reinforcers function as generalized reinforcers. They allow access to a wide range of reinforcers. Examples are money, approval, and tokens. Money can be used to purchase many items or to gain access to a variety of activities, and tokens or points can be traded for a range of items on a reinforcer menu. If we have someone's approval, many different positive consequences may be available from that person.

Feedback may function as a reinforcer. It has two components: evaluative or approval and informative (about progress). Informative feedback can be used when performance criteria are clear, such as when staff are expected to carry out specific tasks in a residential center. Feedback may not enhance performance. For example, some studies have found that offering feedback to staff regarding clients' outcomes does not have any effect on staff behavior (Pommer & Streedbeck, 1974). On the other hand, feedback has been successfully used to encourage behaviors such as approaching a feared object (Leitenberg, Agras, Thompson, & Wright, 1968). Other examples of informative feedback are time spent in an activity (e.g., on Facebook), problems completed correctly, number of cigarettes smoked, tasks completed, calories consumed, or pounds lost. Some writers believe that feedback always entails an evaluative (good/bad) judgment component (Kanfer, 1970).

Self-reinforcers are consequences that are self-presented contingent on certain achievements. They include self-statements (e.g., "It worked—I did it," "Good for me"), as well as social, material, or activity reinforcers that are contingent on carrying out a task. For example, you may make an agreement with yourself that after you read 10 pages of this book, you e-mail a friend.

How to Locate Reinforcers

You can discover reinforcers by using verbal or written reports or observation or by trying out different consequences in real life (e.g., see http://www.interventioncentral.org/behavior). Opinions of others, such as staff, may not accurately represent preferences of clients (Green, Reid, White, Halford, Brittain, & Gardner, 1988). Verbal reports may not be as accurate as information gained from observation. That is, although clients may say that they do not want anything, observation may reveal reinforcing events. And what we say we want may not be accompanied by related actions; that is, our stated preferences may not match our actions. Self-reports point to possible reinforcers. Not until items or opportunities are made contingent on behavior and a future increase in behavior is found can we be sure that a reinforcer has been identified and is being used effectively. The next section describes methods you can use to identify reinforcers. (See also later discussion of the Pleasant Events Schedule.)

Observe Behavior

You can observe behavior in real life to identify behaviors exchanged among significant others and also other sources of reinforcement (see chapter 18). Pace and his colleagues (1985) developed a method for assessing reinforcer preferences among clients with profound retardation by measuring approaches, avoidance, smiling, vocalizations, and compliance with instructions. Only by observing clients at a variety of times and in a number of contexts may reinforcers be discovered.

Ask Clients

Ask clients what they do and with whom they spend their time. What would they like to do more or less often? What did they do in the past that they no longer do? If general terms are used, such as have fun, the referents for these terms, as well as mediators of these events can be identified by asking questions such as "Can you give me an example?" and "Whom do you have fun with?" Items can be ranked in terms of desirability. Pictorial displays have been developed for children. They can look through these and point to valued activities.

Ask Significant Others

You can ask parents what their children like to do, with whom they spend time, and what they do at different times of the day. Significant others may be surprisingly uninformed about what events please family members. They may rely on aversive control. Check out the value of suggested reinforcers by asking the person involved and/or by making the reinforcers contingent on behavior and seeing whether behavior changes.

Reinforcer Sampling

You can use reinforcer sampling to identify or prime (increase) the use of reinforcers. This involves offering a reinforcer noncontingently and allowing people to sample it. Their behavior will reveal whether the item is of interest. For example, when I asked my sister during her illness whether she would like to hear some music, she said no. When I asked her if she would mind if I played some, she said "Not at all." Her next response was "That sounds wonderful. Let's hear some more."

Vary Reinforcers

You can offer variations of a reinforcer and note selections. For example, different magazines or games could be made available to residents of an old age home. Different kinds of groups could be offered or different individuals could approach a resident to start a conversation.

Use Written Schedules

The Pleasant Events Schedule (MacPhillamy & Lewinsohn, 1982) can be used to identify events that may function as a reinforcer (e.g., see Logsdon & Teri, 1997). This schedule lists events that may function as reinforcers, such as taking a walk, reading a book, or talking to a friend. One version lists 160 items. Respondents rate how pleasurable each item is on a 3-point scale, as well as how often each event occurred in the past month. A list can be made of enjoyable items, ranked in terms of importance. Self-report measures include leisure questionnaires (e.g., see Drummond, Parker, Gladman, & Logan, 2001), and the Hassles and Uplifts Scale (Kanner, Coyne, Schaefer, & Lazarus, 1981). (See also Maybery, Jones-Ellis, Neale, & Arentz, 2006; Maybery, Neale, Arentz, & Jones-Ellis, 2007.)

Identify States of Deprivation

Current states of deprivation influence whether a consequence will function as a reinforcer. For instance, if a client lives alone and has little contact with others, social contacts may be a powerful reinforcer.

When Resources Are Scarce Or Not Available

Lack of needed resources is a frequent complaint by social workers. For example, although poor single parents (overwhelmingly women) are encouraged to work, jobs may be scarce, and day care services may be in short supply and costly. Parents are often unable to afford them. Problems such as depression may be related to stressful, impoverished environments in which clients have little control over daily events. They may have little social, economic, or cultural capital they can draw on. Families with a child who has severe emotional disturbances may not have access to needed services. Common components of wraparound programs include vocational services (e.g., job finding), health services (including acute or ongoing care), recreational services (e.g., summer camps for children), mental health services (including emergency and prevention services), social services (financial aid, in home help, respite care, protective services for children and/or elderly clients), substance abuse services (including prevention and inpatient services), and facilitation of self-help (e.g., creating a self-support group, providing transportation or legal services). You may have to fill in resource gaps by creating (often with the aid of other interested people) new services or improving existing services, for example, enhancing accessibility of services, and their integration. Newly arrived refugees may welcome contacts with others from their country; related groups may or may not be available to decrease social isolation and offer mutual help. You may help them to form a group.

The Need for Advocacy

Clients often encounter uncaring, inadequate services that get in the way of resolving problems and achieving related hoped-for outcomes. In *Improving Healthcare Through Advocacy* (2011), Jannson describes seven problems often encountered by clients: (1) lack of money, (2) low standards of care, (3) violations of ethical obligations, such as lack of informed consent, (4) care not culturally competent, (5) insufficient preventative care, (6) unaddressed problems such as anxiety, and (7) failure to link clients to other health care providers. Lack of resources is often a direct result of public policies and related legislation regarding how resources are distributed, which in turn reflect dominant cultural values and economic interests. (See earlier discussion in this chapter.) The Patient Protection and Affordable Care Act of 2010 is designed to address such concerns but, in this day of cutbacks in money for services that provide a safety net, it remains to be seen whether client circumstances will improve. Unemployment is related to decisions made by businesses to relocate. Clients with various kinds of physical disabilities (e.g., hearing, vision, physical) may need ongoing supportive services. Elderly clients with cognitive declines may require in-home help. Is such help available? Lack of funds may make it impossible to move out of high crime areas with few opportunities for social support.

Understanding the "big picture" will help you to identify factors related to resource distribution and discover options for increasing opportunities. This may require action on many different levels—organizational, community, policy, and legislative. It may require identifying, documenting, exposing, and advocating for practices and policies that decrease avoidable injustices. Case advocacy includes components of wraparound programs such as procuring legal aid for individuals and/or families, planning how to increase needed resources, assessing success, and involving concerned others (e.g., in agencies providing services) in pressing for needed resources. Cause advocacy includes proposing and advocating for new legislation, supporting bills already passed by calling for increased implementation, forming coalitions and other groups to press for certain policies and legislation, and organizing protests calling attention to avoidable injustices. Many skills are required including networking, using cogent arguments, managing conflict, focusing on shared interests, using effective assertive skills (see chapter 16), and peer pressure.

Summary

Helping clients requires reviewing resources and obstacles. A lack of resources, such as job-training programs, housing, and health care, is often an obstacle. Agency policies and procedures may interfere with helping clients. Viewing clients and significant others in terms of their strengths rather than their deficiencies will increase your chance of discovering resources. Clients differ in their patterns of coping and reinforcer profiles (what they like and dislike). These differences will influence options. Client attributions for concerns (beliefs about causes) and beliefs about how they can be resolved may help or hinder planning. An emphasis on supporting positive alternatives to problematic behaviors requires a search for reinforcers that will maintain these behaviors. Attention to context emphasizes the value of involving significant others such as family members as mediators when possible. Considering their values, worries, knowledge, and skills will increase the likelihood that they will participate in helpful ways. You may have to advocate to create new resources.

Reviewing Your Competencies

Reviewing Content Knowledge

1. Identify agency procedures and policies that contribute to effective services.

2. Identify agency procedures and policies that interfere with provision of effective services.

3. Identify agencies in your community, the problems they address, and describe their track record of success.

4. Describe relationships among different agencies in your community and how these could be improved to enhance services.

5. Describe gaps between what research suggests is best in achieving outcomes valued by clients and what is offered by your agency and by agencies from which services are purchased.

6. Identify county, state, and federal programs relevant to clients' concerns and describe how they affect clients' options.

7. Given specific examples, describe how a setting's physical characteristics may influence behavior.

8. Explain what is meant by the term *significant other* (mediator) and give examples.

9. Identify valid measures for describing neighborhood and community resources that may affect clients' options.

10. Describe valuable characteristics of mediators.

11. Describe obstacles to involving significant others and options for preventing or overcoming them.

12. Discuss the role of significant others in case examples given in class.

13. Describe the difference between social networks and social support systems.

14. Describe common deficiencies in social networks.

15. Give examples of cognitive coping skills.

16. Give examples of specific social skills and settings in which they could be useful.

17. Explain what is meant by the term *reinforcer profile*.

18. Describe how to find out if a given consequence will function as a positive reinforcer.

19. Explain what is meant by the "relativity of reinforcers."

20. Identify four methods of locating reinforcers.

21. Give examples of using high-probability behaviors as reinforcers.

22. Explain what is meant by the term *attribution*, and give examples of common attributional biases.

Reviewing What You Do

1. You accurately describe client's social network and the "social provisions" (resources) received.

2. You identify feasible reinforcers and significant others who offer these contingent on valued behaviors.

3. You design effective ways to overcome obstacles to involving mediators.

4. You identify personal assets of clients and significant others.

5. You arrange valuable changes of physical environments.

6. You create valuable resources when necessary.

7. You overcome agency obstacles to using resources.

8. You identify neighborhood and community resources related to hoped-for outcomes.

9. You help clients take advantage of social support groups.

Reviewing Results

1. Desired outcomes are achieved.

2. Significant others participate in agreed-on plans.

3. New resources are created that benefit clients.

4. Interagency coordination of services is improved.

20

Putting It All Together

OVERVIEW This chapter offers guidelines for organizing and interpreting data and selecting outcomes. Errors that may occur and guidelines for avoiding them are described. A key question is: Does assessment provide guidelines for helping clients to achieve outcomes they value? Success in earlier phases sets the stage for success in later ones. Disappointing results in later stages may require circling back to earlier phases.

YOU WILL LEARN ABOUT

- Organizing and interpreting data
- If you get stuck
- Choosing among different problem framings
- Thinking about causes
- Guidelines for discovering causes
- Using tests to make decisions
- Reviewing your inferences
- Ideals and actualities
- Ethical issues in the selection of outcomes
- The value of records

Organizing and Interpreting Data

Helping clients requires making decisions about how to organize and interpret data. What does it add up to? Is there a problem? What kind of a problem is it? Who is concerned about it? Do you have a client (see prior distinctions among clients and resisters)? Is there an agreed-on agenda with your client? You will think about different options as you work with clients (see Exhibit 20.1). Your beliefs about behavior and its causes will influence what data you collect and how you organize it. This in turn influences selection of objectives (outcomes to pursue), change agents (whom to involve), and settings (where to intervene). The criteria you use to evaluate claims and

Thinking About Problems: Mrs. Ryan and the Greens

I think this family could learn to live together and have a more enjoyable family life. I think it's premature to place Mrs. Ryan in a retirement home, and from what I can see, the Greens are not ready for this, nor is Mrs. Ryan. I think we should work on the problems they've mentioned and see if this improves the situation. But what if I'm wrong? Maybe the family will break down if Mrs. Ryan is not moved. The marriage could become strained. The children could start to act out. But I don't think that will happen. The Greens seem to love each other and to love Mrs. Ryan. The children's concerns seem typical for their age. If problems start, we can catch them at an early point.

arguments will influence what data you search for and when you stop searching. Your task environment (e.g., time pressures) also will affect the search. Many different kinds of "evidence" may be considered (see chapter 9). Client preferences will influence decisions (see also section on integrating data in chapter 10).

The data collected should indicate the probable difficulty of achieving outcomes and the feasibility and likely effectiveness of different approaches. Discovering all influential factors is not necessary and usually impossible. What you need is information that decreases uncertainty about how to help clients or to determine that little or no help is possible. Information about resources will indicate whether obstacles can be overcome and, if so, how and to what degree. Reviewing resources and obstacles will offer information about:

- Who should and can be involved (including other service providers)

- Who has access to behaviors of concern and is willing and able to support desired behaviors (e.g., teachers, parents)

- Whether clients will participate in helpful ways

- Whether obstacles can be overcome

- What alternative available repertoires of clients can be of value

- Which cultural factors should be considered

- What advocacy efforts are needed (e.g., to increase access to services)

Computerized decision support systems are now common in health care. Karsh and his colleagues (2010) argue that to date, these have been oversold.

If You Get Stuck

If you have difficulty clarifying concerns and discovering related factors, you may have to gather additional data, unless a crisis is at hand and you have to act quickly despite having little information. You could seek consultation from your supervisor. Despite your best efforts to engage clients in participating they may not do so. (See chapter 14.) Assessment will often be incomplete because of inevitable uncertainties and lack of time because of high caseloads and onerous documentation requirements (see Exhibit 20.2). You may have to observe clients in real-life contexts to understand their circumstances (e.g., discover related contingencies). Helpful questions include the following:

- Have I listened carefully to clients about what they value and want?

- Have I identified and discussed clients' concerns about the helping process?

- Have I ignored important contingencies?

- Have I posed well-structured questions concerning decisions and searched for related research findings?

- Have I overlooked benefits clients gain from current problems?

- Are my feelings about clients and/or significant others getting in the way? (Am I over- or underinvolved?)

- Have I made a process error (e.g., tried to move too fast)?

Examples of Incomplete Assessment

- Behaviors of concern are not clearly described.

- The functions (meaning) of behaviors of concern are unknown.

- Cultural factors are overlooked.

- Clients' assets (strengths) are overlooked.

- Positive alternative behaviors to undesired behaviors are not identified.

- Baseline data are not available (i.e., description of the frequency/duration of behaviors, thoughts, or feelings before intervention).

- The cause of behavior (e.g., aggression) is assumed to be another behavior (e.g., low self-esteem).

- Higher level contingencies are overlooked (e.g., loss of welfare payments, poverty, etc.).

- Have I considered cultural differences in values, norms, and preferred communication styles?

- Am I doing the best that can be done under the circumstances?

Choosing Among Different Problem Framings

Problem solving requires making inferences about causes. Just as the expert detective searches for clues, you and your clients also do so. Questions include:

- What are possible causes (e.g., social, psychological, political, sociological, biological); have I paid attention to context?

- What do I think is the most likely account?

- Have I taken advantage of related research findings?

- Is my view compatible with empirical findings?

- Have I left out anything important? Is important information missing?

- Does my assessment provide guidelines for selecting plans that are likely to be effective?

- Have I helped my clients to identify their assets?

- Does my view account for all the information at hand?

- Can I make a stronger argument for an alternative view?

- Do my views match my clients' views?

- Have I considered important cultural differences?

The particular causes focused on depend partly on how advanced knowledge is in an area. Choosing among different views involves reviewing data collected and considering alternative accounts in the light of these data. Both a microscopic and wide-angle lens will be useful. Two questions should be asked about any view: (1) does it offer leverage in achieving hoped-for outcomes? and (2) would an alternative account offer more? Consider the Lakeland family. Are problems related to Brian's characteristics, his parents' reactions or characteristics, experiences in other settings (e.g., school), interactions between Brian and his parents, economic stresses on the family, or all of these possibilities (see Exhibit 20.3)?

Reviewing assessment data with clients provides an opportunity to involve them in making decisions about outcomes and how to pursue them. Be selective to highlight key points and use language that is intelligible to clients. Illustrate your points using examples related to their lives. Encourage positive expectations as appropriate and build on clients' assets and environmental

EXHIBIT 20.3

Reviewing Alternative Accounts: The Lakeland Family

Brian's parents believed that his behavior resulted from epilepsy and that if the epilepsy could be controlled, the problem behaviors would disappear. What evidence do they have for this conclusion? How complete is this view? Are alternative accounts more likely? Perhaps Brian has problems at school that have caused his problems at home. Negative interactions with teachers and other students can serve as "setting events" that increase the likelihood of aggressive behaviors at home. Data suggesting that Brian's parents reinforce behaviors they do not like and ignore behaviors they do like suggest that Brian's epilepsy is not the sole cause.

Perhaps the Lakelands' problems with Brian are due to marital problems that Mr. and Mrs. Lakeland have hidden from the social worker. Some family systems theories assume that if there is a problem in one subsystem (between parents and child), there must be problems in others as well. No such assumption is made in other family system approaches, such as behavioral perspectives. It is assumed that only through assessment can you discover who is involved and in what way. There were no indications that there were problems in the marriage. Mr. and Mrs. Lakeland seemed to work well together to raise their family on a modest income.

resources that can be put to good use. Exhibit 20.4 gives examples of "putting it all together." A search for practice-related literature may reveal helpful information. Possible questions concerning the clients described in Exhibits 20.3 and 20.4 include the following:

- In families caring for an elderly relative, what are common sources of strain?

- In pregnant teenagers, what is the likelihood of depression following abortion compared to having and keeping the child to raise?

- In families having parent–adolescent conflict, is conflict resolution training or insight counseling most effective in increasing positive exchanges and decreasing negative ones.

- In what percentage of families having adolescent–parent conflict is there also marital conflict?

Thinking About Causes

Identifying the causes of behavior is difficult because (1) they may be unknown, (2) they occur at different interrelated levels

EXHIBIT 20.4

Case Examples

MRS. RYAN AND THE GREENS

Developmental Considerations

The Greens' initial interest was to discuss the possibility of finding other living accommodations for Mrs. Ryan. There was a span of 74 years between Mrs. Ryan and the Greens' youngest daughter, who was 15. As Mrs. Ryan grew older, the relationship between her and her daughter and son-in-law changed. They assumed the role of provider. This required adjustments for all of them. The children, too, were experiencing many changes in their lives. Jean, the daughter, was having difficulty freeing herself from her mother's control in order to be able to go out with boys. After the family's move to the suburbs in search of more affordable housing, no transportation was available except by car. Jean spent most of her time watching television, gaining a great deal of weight in the process. She and Mrs. Ryan had many clashes. Mrs. Ryan could not become accustomed to what she considered vast differences in how children were raised today compared with how she was raised almost 80 years ago. Mrs. Ryan also was confronted by her own increasing age and feelings of helplessness and uselessness.

A Review of Assessment Data

Based on the information she collected in interviews, in structured role plays in the office, and by observing the family at home, Mrs. Slater, the social worker, arrived at the following views. In the past, her daughter and son-in-law considered Mrs. Ryan to be an independent, self-sufficient woman and a pleasant companion. Indeed, it was they who insisted that she live with them after Mrs. Ryan's husband died, and they bought a house that was large enough for Mrs. Ryan to have her own bedroom. But this move made a drastic change in her life: Mrs. Ryan never replaced the valuable social contacts in her life when she moved in with the Greens, and she now found herself stranded in the suburbs and dependent on others for transportation. This was quite different from her previous home, which was just half a block away from the main street of a small town filled with friends. Thus Mrs. Ryan lost many of her reinforcers. She also developed a serious heart condition a year after she moved in with the Greens and was told that she must severely limit her activities, in order to decrease the likelihood of another heart attack. Many friends with whom she had corresponded had died. These losses resulted in a depression of varying intensity that was influenced by how much attention she received from her daughter, son-in-law, and their children. In turn, Mrs. Ryan's behavior influenced how her relatives responded to her.

As Mrs. Ryan offered fewer positive events to the Greens, they offered fewer to her. As the children grew older, the differences in their way of life from Mrs. Ryan's caused further conflict. She began to spend more and more time alone in her room and developed the habit of sleeping most of the day and staying up at night doing chores such as the dishes, which kept the family awake. Neither the Greens nor Mrs. Ryan had effective communication skills for discussing and resolving their differences. Mrs. Green was a negative thinker: "Nothing can be done"; "Things won't change, but if they do, it will be for the worse"; "What can we do? This is a terrible situation"; and so on. Mrs. Ryan was overly sensitive to criticism, interpreting requests for behavior changes as slaps in the face, no matter how carefully they were worded. Family members offered too lean of a schedule of positive reinforcement to one another and too many aversive events.

A review of desired outcomes indicated that many were interrelated: the Greens' wish to have more time alone was related to Mrs. Ryan's interest in being more active outside the house. Deciding where Mrs. Ryan would live involved many steps, including sharing feelings and getting information about Medicare and aging.

In Summary

The Greens considered having Mrs. Ryan move because of a decrease in shared positive events and increase in unpleasant exchanges. This change was related to the family members' lack of communication skills and Mrs. Ryan's failing to replace lost sources of enjoyment with new ones. Mrs. Slater reframed the presenting concern from making a decision about where Mrs. Ryan would live to gathering information to make this decision. The question now was: "Could positive events be increased?" A review of the resources available to Mrs. Ryan and the Greens revealed many, perhaps the most important being that Mrs. Ryan, the Greens, and their teenaged children liked one another. This increased their willingness to participate in case plans. Community resources such as a local senior center were available. Although the Greens and Mrs. Ryan had to budget their money carefully, they did have enough to get along on, especially if they took advantage of Medicare.

(continued)

EXHIBIT 20.4 (Continued)

Intermediate Steps

Almost all outcomes of interest to these clients were intermediate steps to deciding where Mrs. Ryan would live. Mrs. Slater discussed the relationship of these steps to this decision and suggested that discussion of that decision be temporarily put aside until the desired changes were pursued over a 2-month period. They identified outcomes related to each area. Baseline data made it possible to select appropriate intermediate steps. One of Mrs. Ryan's goals was to increase her contacts with other people. Other than going to a lunch meeting of retired civil servants twice a year, she saw only her relatives. Assessment information indicated that she did have skills for meeting and talking to other people; she had had many friends in the community where she had lived. Mrs. Slater joined Mrs. Ryan on a brief walk one day and had an enjoyable conversation with her. She was interested in current events and liked talking about a variety of topics.

Mrs. Ryan's reluctance to participate in the activities at the local senior center was partly due to her reluctance to trouble anyone to drive her there. She refused to allow this, even when she learned that the center had a van and would pick up people at their homes. (It was too far for her to walk there.) As a first step, Mrs. Slater suggested that they visit the center together and get a monthly bulletin describing its activities. After some hesitation, Mrs. Ryan agreed. Other intermediate steps included the following:

- Review the monthly bulletin and select two activities each month that you might enjoy.
- Read the description of the transportation service and arrange for the van to pick you up to attend these two events.
- Initiate one conversation at each meeting.
- Obtain the telephone numbers of people you want to contact.
- Telephone one person each week.
- Attend three activities each month at the center.
- Telephone two people each week
- Invite one person over every other week for tea, or arrange a brief outing such as a shopping trip or lunch.

Intermediate objectives were set for other outcomes as well.

BRIAN AND THE LAKELANDS

Developmental Considerations

The Lakelands were a family shifting from raising small children to learning how to handle adolescents. Some of their current difficulties were related to Brian's desire for greater independence. Even though he was 14 and their daughter Joan was only 11, the Lakelands were looking forward to an easing of child-rearing responsibilities.

A Review of Contingencies and Related Effects

This family was typical of many families experiencing parent–child problems: undesired behaviors were reinforced and desired behaviors were ignored. The Lakelands' lack of positive parenting skills resulted in an escalation of aversive exchanges. Brian and his parents had fallen into the habit of looking for disliked behaviors rather than reinforcing one another for valued behaviors. Mr. and Mrs. Lakeland used threats that they did not enforce and that were either too severe and/or threatened positive activities, such as Brian's paper route. They nagged Brian to try to get him to comply with their requests, repeating their requests over and over, but often they just gave in to his wishes. They offered reinforcers noncontingently rather than contingent on desired behaviors. For example, Brian's allowance was not contingent on any specific behaviors. Contributing factors included both parents' heavy work schedules, so they were tired and had less emotional resilience to handle stress. Family members did not have negotiation skills to resolve conflicts. Mr. Colvine, their social worker, had looked into the possible relationship between epilepsy and the behaviors Brian displayed and found that there was no evidence that they resulted from the epilepsy, per se. The family doctor agreed with this conclusion.

In Summary

Brian's inappropriate behavior was maintained by attention from parents and siblings. Desired behaviors were not reinforced. Family members exchanged few positive events, such as outings together, and did not possess effective problem-solving skills. Brian had no study schedule, so his homework often remained undone, which contributed to his poor grades. It also seemed that he could use tutorial help in mathematics and a more suitable place to study. Contingencies would have to be rearranged and constructive problem-solving skills increased.

(continued)

EXHIBIT 20.4 (Continued)

JULIE

Developmental Considerations

Julie was in a stage of rebellion against her parents, who were very strict. She felt overwhelmed by the pressures that seemed suddenly to descend on her, such as deciding what to do about sex, how far she should push her parents, and what she wanted to do with her life.

Review of Assessment Data

Julie's decision was easy for her to put off, since the ultimate aversive consequences were distant. These would have to be made more current through identification of alternatives and the advantages and disadvantages of each. Her stress interfered with careful considerations of different options. This would have to be decreased. This stress also interfered with Julie's enjoyment of her everyday life. Assessment indicated that Julie had inferiority feelings about her looks, was easily pressured into sexual intercourse even though she did not want it, had little information about birth control, and had ambivalent feelings about having sex.

(e.g., physiological, psychological, sociological), (3) they often interact in complex ways, (4) they change over time, and (5) they are influenced by chance occurrences (Haynes, 1992). A given cause may affect behavior differently at different times and places. The organization of knowledge by discipline and profession encourages a fragmented view. The glossary in Exhibit 20.5 suggests the complexity of causes.

EXHIBIT 20.5

Glossary Related to Concepts of Causality

Causal model: Assumptions about the cause(s) of behavior.

Critical periods: The effects of a variable depend on age or developmental stage.

Equilibrium time: Time required for the effects of a causal variable to stabilize.

Latency of causal effects: How long it takes for a cause to affect behavior.

Mediating variable: A variable that can strengthen or weaken the relationship between two other variables.

Necessary cause: Y never occurs without X.

Necessary and sufficient cause: Y occurs whenever X occurs, and Y never occurs without X.

Parameter: Dimensions of a variable (e.g., depression) that can be measured (e.g., magnitude or duration). This term also is used to describe the characteristics of a population, in contrast to the characteristics of a sample.

Probabilistic nature of prediction: Predictions are always imperfect; some are more probable than others.

Sufficient cause: Y occurs whenever X occurs.

Temporal precedence: X must precede Y if X is a cause of Y.

Vulnerability: The probability that a causal variable will result in a certain outcome; the magnitude of the variable that is necessary to do so.

Source: Based on S. N. Haynes (1992). Models of causality in psychopathology: Toward dynamic, synthetic and nonlinear models of behavior disorders (p. 123). New York: Macmillan.

Clues to Causality

Clues to causality include the following:

- Contiguity (events occur close together)
- Temporal order (the presumed cause occurs before the presumed effect)
- Covariation (as one changes, the other changes)
- Alternative explanations can be ruled out
- There is a logical connection between the variables; a sound argument can be made for the link

Attention to only one of the conditions may result in the incorrect belief that because an event follows another, it is caused by it. Haynes (1992) argues that *constant conjunction* (two events always occurring together) is not applicable to the social sciences because of the complexity of causes related to behavior.

Necessary and Sufficient Causes

Variables related to problems may be *necessary* (a condition that must be present if the effect occurs), *sufficient* (a condition that by itself will bring about change), or *necessary* and *sufficient* (a condition that must be present for an effect to occur and one that by itself will bring about an effect). Rarely can we point to necessary and sufficient conditions related to problems.

Interrelated Causes

Explanations differ in the system level(s) to which they appeal (e.g., biological, psychological, sociological) and how integrative they are (the extent to which relationships among different causes are recognized). Contributory causes often come into play that help to create the total set of conditions necessary and sufficient for an effect. Social problems are usually related to factors at many interconnected system levels. For example, poor funding of schools, combined with low income of parents, influences students' opportunities to do well academically. These opportunities, in turn, affect other outcomes such as employability. Consider Brian and his parents. If more money were available for special-education programs and related assessment services and better preparation of teachers, Brian's grades might be better. Differences in temperament may increase the likelihood of certain behaviors, which in turn influence how others respond. A contextual framework will help you to avoid incomplete accounts that focus on only one cause of a problem.

Individual Differences in the Strength of Causal Variables

The strength of causal variables differs among individuals with the same behaviors. People differ on:

- The number of variables that influence a behavior

- Which variables influence onset, magnitude, and duration

- The relative strength of causal variables

- The role of mediating variables

- Predispositions and vulnerability to particular events

- The setting generality of causal relationships

- The paths through which causal effects occur (Haynes, 1992, p. 108)

The variation in causal relationships highlights the importance of a contextual, multifocused assessment. Ideally, intervention should focus on the key causal variables. This requires estimating the weights of different variables.

Causes and Explanations

Causes differ in their explanatory completeness. Identification of causes is not necessarily explanatory. For example, the symptoms of an illness and associated pathology may be known, but the etiology may not be understood. People use different criteria to decide when an explanation is at hand (e.g., it allows accurate prediction, it "makes sense"). (See chapter 4). What is best depends on your purpose. The goal of helping clients highlights the value of explanations that help you to select plans that result in hoped-for outcomes.

Compatibility with Empirical Findings Regarding Behavior

Beliefs about causes differ in the extent to which they are compatible with empirical findings; for instance, claims of "levitation" (the ability to float in the air) are not compatible with the laws of gravity. Lack of generalization of positive outcomes over settings and time is a major problem. Thus, a plan that does not take this into account is not compatible with empirical data about behavior.

The Fallacy of False Cause

In the *fallacy of false cause,* we inaccurately assume that one or more events cause another. Consider Clever Hans, the wonder horse. Clever Hans supposedly could solve mathematical problems. When presented with a problem by his trainer, he would tap out the answers with his hoof. Many testimonials were offered in support of his amazing ability. But then a psychologist, Oskar Pfungst, decided to study the horse's ability. He systematically altered conditions to search for alternative explanations. This exploration revealed that Clever Hans was an astute observer of human behavior. He watched the head of his trainer as he tapped out his answer: His trainer would tilt his head slightly as Hans approached the correct number, and Clever Hans would then stop (reported in Stanovich, 1992). *Confounding factors* (variables that are related to both some characteristic and an outcome) are one reason for the spurious appearances of causation.

Underestimating Coincidences and the Play of Chance

We tend to underestimate the frequency of chance events. What do you think the odds are that in a class of 23 people, two will have their birthday on the same day? The odds are over 50–50. One reason behavior is so difficult to predict is that chance (accidental events) plays a role in our lives. That is, the occurrence of important events may not be predictable because such events are not under our control. Consider fires, earthquakes, and many illnesses. One of the subjects of great literature is the ways in which individual lives are affected by historical events (wars, famines). Unexpected deaths or meetings may change our lives dramatically. Underestimating uncertainty may result in faulty decisions.

Confusing Causes and Their Effects

Is depression a cause of marital conflict, or is marital conflict a cause of depression? Is cognitive disorientation a result of being homeless, or does being homeless contribute to disorientation? Depression may result from limited employment opportunities because of discrimination. The fundamental attribution error may result in mistaking effects for causes. Consider, for example, Jimmy, a 12-year-old African American student, who was referred because of apathy, indifference, and inattentiveness to classroom activities (Sue & Sue, 1990, p. 44). The counselor believed that Jimmy harbored repressed rage that needed to be ventilated and dealt with. He believed that Jimmy's inability to express his anger led him to adopt a passive-aggressive means of expressing hostility (i.e., inattentiveness, daydreaming, falling asleep) and recommended that Jimmy be seen for intensive counseling to discover the basis of his anger. After six months of meetings, the counselor realized the basis of Jimmy's problems. He came from a home of extreme poverty, where hunger, lack of sleep, and overcrowding sapped his energy and motivation. That is, his fatigue, passivity, and fatalism were more a result of poverty than some psychological characteristic. Clearly this counselor had not been educated to employ a contextual assessment (or was and did not use this broad framework).

Mistaking Correlations and Causation

We may assume that because two variables (brain and foot size) covary, one causes the other. Although we may scoff at the idea that brain size causes foot size, other mistaken assumptions based on confusions between correlations and causation may not be so obvious. The history of the professions provides many illustrations of the confusion between correlation and causation. For example, people used to think that tuberculosis was inherited because people who lived together often got it. Consider also the common assumption that low self-esteem causes problems such as depression. In fact, both low self-esteem and depression may be related to other variables (e.g., a high frequency of punishing experiences and a low frequency of positive feedback in the past and the present). Our tendency to overestimate correlations heightens our susceptibility to this error.

Dead-End and Incomplete Accounts

Dead-end accounts are those that do not provide guidelines for achieving valued outcomes. They get in the way of discovering options. "After-the-fact" accounts describing what people did (and why) may sound profound but do not provide "before-the-fact" information that helps you and your clients select effective plans. Dead-end accounts may be incomplete (omit crucial causes). *Incomplete accounts* include only some pieces of a puzzle. They may focus on thoughts without relating them to what people do in specific situations. Another kind of incomplete account is assuming that behavior causes another behavior without asking about the causes of both. For example, self-esteem is often accepted as a cause of behavior. But where does self-esteem come from? You may assume that your success in a job interview is due to high self-efficacy (an expectation that you will succeed). A more complete account would include information about your history in related situations. Rather than self-efficacy (or self-esteem) being the cause of doing well, it may be a product of past successful experiences. We feel confident in situations in which we do well (see Baumeister et al., 2003).

Confusing Form and Function

Focusing on the form of behavior (hitting) and overlooking its function (removing demands) may result in incomplete accounts.

(See chapter 7.) This error is less likely in practice theories that emphasize the distinction between form (the typology of behavior) and function (what maintains the behavior; why it occurs). Simply describing behavior does not provide information about its function (why it occurs). The context in which behavior occurs must also be explored. If you know the circumstances in which a client is likely to engage in certain behaviors, you have information about how you might alter the environment to influence these behaviors. Ignoring context encourages excessive focus on psychological causes. For example, individual counseling may be recommended for an adolescent having problems at school that are related to the reactions of her peers and teachers, as well as to the economic stress experienced by her single parent. A problem-oriented curriculum design (e.g., aging, health, family) may encourage the confusion of form and function. It may discourage recognition of similar contingencies of reinforcement that apply to different problems.

Guidelines for Discovering Causes

The following guidelines should help you to avoid common errors in thinking about causes such as confirmation biases resulting in oversimplifications. Many errors involve partiality in the use of evidence (looking at only part of the picture) (see Exhibit 20.6). The theory we use may lead us astray. Once we have accepted a view, it may bias our subsequent search (what we look for and discover). Overlooking the inaccuracy of data may result in poor decisions.

Clearly Describe Problems, Related Factors, and Hoped-for Outcomes

Vague descriptions make it difficult (or impossible) to discover helpful plans. Another way to get bogged down is to focus on problems rather than related factors. Rather than focusing on elder or child abuse per se, identify factors related to the abuse and address them.

Watch Out for the Fundamental Attribution Error

We tend to focus on attributes of the person and to overlook environmental variables (i.e., fall into the fundamental attribution error). This, combined with the greater vividness of negative behaviors, often results in pathologizing clients. To avoid doing this, be sure to consider the context in which behaviors or events of concern occur. The more clearly you describe this, the more information you will have about client concerns and related factors. You may overlook environmental influences because you focus on psychological characteristics and rely solely on self-report data that may not reflect what is happening. Our thoughts and feelings in situations of concern are often more vivid than associated environmental contingencies, and so it is easy to focus on them as causes and to overlook environmental influences.

EXHIBIT 20.6

Sources of Error That May Result in Inaccurate or Incomplete Views of Client Concerns

Source	Description
1. Partiality in the use of evidence.	Overlooking, distorting, or discounting contradictory evidence. Giving favored treatment to favored beliefs (see, for example, items 2 to 7).
2. Rationalizing rather than reasoning (justifying rather than critiquing).	Focusing on building a case for a position rather than gathering information impartially. This is an example of item 1.
3. Focusing on irrelevant or incorrect reasons (fallacy of false cause).	Selecting irrelevant or marginally relevant reasons or "evidence" to support beliefs or actions. The conclusion may have nothing to do with the reasons provided.
4. Jumping to conclusions.	Failing to treat a belief or conclusion as a hypothesis requiring testing.
5. Unwarranted persistence.	Not changing your mind when there is compelling evidence to do so.
6. Categorical rather than probabilistic reasoning.	Reducing options to two possibilities (either A or B).
7. Confusing naming with explaining (e.g., "diagnosing" rather than assessing).	Assuming that giving something a name (e.g., bipolar disorder) explains it and offers intervention leverage.
8. Confusing correlation with causation.	Assuming that an association between two or more events indicates causation.
9. Confusing shared with distinguishing characteristics.	Focusing on characteristics that may not distinguish among different groups/causes.
10. Faulty generalization.	Relying on small or biased samples; assuming that what is true of the whole is true of the parts, or vice versa.
11. Stereotyping.	Incorrectly estimating the degree of variability in a group.
12. Influence by consistent data.	Being influenced by data that do not offer any new information but are merely consistent with data already available.
13. Lack of domain-specific knowledge.	Not having information needed to understand client concerns (e.g., facts, concepts, theories). This source of error is related to many others in this list.
14. Confusing form and function.	Mistakenly assuming that similar forms of behavior have similar functions and different forms of behavior reflect different functions.
15. Simplistic accounts.	Relying on accounts that ignore important causes and/or overlook uncertainties.
16. Vagueness.	Vaguely describing problems, causes, and hoped-for outcomes.
17. Uncritical acceptance of explanations.	Accepting explanations without evaluating them and comparing them with well-argued alternative accounts; not checking whether a belief is consistent with known facts; selecting untestable beliefs.
18. Assuming that a weak argument is not true.	Assuming that because you cannot offer a convincing argument, a claim is false.
19. Reliance on ad hoc explanations.	Making up explanations as you go along, even though they may contradict one another or be circular (explain nothing).
20. Incorrect weighing of different contributors.	Not weighing contributing factors in relation to their importance.
21. Misuse of speculation.	Believing that you can find out what is going on just by thinking about it.
22. Overcomplex accounts.	Relying on needlessly complicated accounts that obscure causes.
23. Ecological fallacy.	Assuming that an association between two variables on a group level is also true on an individual level.
24. Confusing correlations and base rates.	Incorrectly assuming that a correlation reflects the base rate.
25. Relying on questionable criteria for evaluating the accuracy of claims.	Examples include consensus, anecdotal experience, and tradition (see Exhibit 4.5).
26. Using a general rule that is not applicable to a particular situation.	Assuming that because agency administrators are usually fair that a particular administrator was fair on a certain occasion.

Note: The sources of error described may be (and usually are) not related to intentions; caring about people is not enough to avoid errors.

Pay Attention to Data

Speculative thinking may be relied on "to solve problems which can only be solved by the observation and interpretation of facts." "The belief that one can find out something about real things by speculation alone is one of the most long-lived delusions in human thought" (Thouless, 1974, p. 78). We often are guilty of the contrary-to-fact hypothesis in which we state "with an unreasonable degree of certainty the results of events that might have occurred that did not" (Seech, 1993, p. 131). An example is: "She felt sad because of her neighbor's family problems. If only she hadn't gotten married at such an early age, she would be a happier woman today" (p. 131). Speculation is valuable in discovering new possibilities, but it does not offer information about whether these insights are correct. What is cannot be deduced from what ought to be. Speculation is not without its effects, since our beliefs influence what we look for. In their classic study, Chapman and Chapman (1969) found that clinicians were more likely than naive observers to report illusory correlations. Such studies illustrate that expectations based on theories and semantic associations may overwhelm the influence of data that do not match these expectations or even refute them. This tendency is encouraged by *confirmation biases* (seeking data that confirm our beliefs and overlooking data that do not). For example, we often attend to only the positive-positive cell of a four-cell contingency table (see later discussion in this chapter).

There is nothing odd or negative about weighing data in relation to available theories. The problem arises when we ignore data that allows us to test our guesses about what is accurate. Paying attention to data will help you to avoid premature and excessive reliance on dubious accounts. The more tenuous a theory is, the less you should rely on it when reviewing data, and the more attention you should pay to the data. What exactly is the problem? Exactly how is it manifested? What factors have been found to be associated with it in research reports? (See, for example, Newton, Horner, Algozzine, Todd & Algozzine, 2009.)

Focus on Informative Data

The data you gather could be (1) relevant (help you and your clients select effective service plans), (2) irrelevant, or (3) misleading. Focus on relevant data. Irrelevant data may lead you astray. A few worthless items can dilute the effect of one helpful item. Consider the classic study in which social work graduate students were asked to estimate the likelihood that some people were child abusers. Being told that the person "fixes cars in his spare time" and "once ran away from home as a boy" decreased the effects of the description of this man as having "sadomasochistic sexual fantasies" (see Nisbett & Ross, 1980, p. 155). There is no research showing that people who fix cars in their spare time and once ran away from home as a boy are more (or less) likely to abuse their children. Irrelevant material about this person tended to make him less "similar" to someone who might abuse his child. When irrelevant data are given about a case, we often rely on this and ignore data describing what is "normative" (typical behavior) in a situation. That is, in thinking about what a person might do in a situation, we tend to disregard data that describe how people usually act (i.e., base rate data) even though this may help us predict what an individual would do. Ask: Is this data relevant here? How so?

We tend to focus on vivid events and to overlook those that are important but not vivid. We tend to recall vivid examples that may mislead us about factors related to a problem. In trying to explain why negative exchanges weigh so heavily in basically positive relationships (they may ruin a friendship), Rook (1984a) suggested that positive behaviors became the expected background and so are less vivid than the rare negative events.

Assess Rather Than Diagnose; Explain Rather Than Name

Problem solving can be likened to walking along an unknown path with many dead ends. One kind of dead end is simply naming (e.g., labeling) something (a problem or behavior of interest). Suppose that you see a homeless person on the street gesturing oddly and talking to himself. You may think, "He is mentally ill." Is this label helpful? Does it decrease uncertainty about how you might be able to be of help?

> Intervention programs cannot be based solely on a diagnostic or classification category such as "depression" or "attention-deficit disorder" because such topographically based [description of form] diagnoses do not identify which of many possible determinants are operational for a particular client. Diagnoses typically provide only an array of possible causal factors. The generalizability of the suggested variables and weights to a particular client cannot be presumed.
>
> Diagnosis can facilitate the design of intervention programs only if any of three conditions are met: (1) specific causal paths are invariably associated with specific diagnostic categories, (2) a hierarchy of the most probable paths or their weights is associated with specific diagnostic categories, and/or (3) effective interventions are available for specific diagnostic categories regardless of within-category variance in causality. These conditions are seldom met. (Haynes, 1992, p. 109)

Assessing rather than diagnosing will help you avoid explanatory fictions (terms that seem to offer information but do not). Pseudoexplanations (circular accounts) are prime examples. In a circular account, we use a behavior to infer an explanation and appeal to the same behavior to support our explanation (no additional information is provided). For example, a teacher may "explain" a student's hitting other children by stating that he is aggressive and, when asked how she knows, may say, "Because he hits other children." A lack of situational awareness—failing to elaborate the "problem space" (to pursue a contextual analysis) is a principal cause of ineffective problem solving (Salas & Klein, 2001).

Avoid the Single-Cause Fallacy (Oversimplifications): Ask "What Is Missing?"

Just as an explanation may be overly complex and obscure options, it also may be incomplete (overlook causes) and obscure options. Rarely is behavior related to one cause. Simplistic accounts in which complex problems such as family violence is attributed to one factor (e.g., past history of violence) can be misleading. Thinking in either/or terms and ignoring important uncertainties encourage simplistic accounts. Ask yourself: Have I left out important influences?

Avoid Unnecessarily Complex Accounts

Just as an account may be overly simple (overlook causes related to a problem), it may be overly complex (unnecessary concepts may be used that get in the way of discovering causes). This is why parsimony is emphasized in science (see chapter 4). Although general "sensitizing concepts" can be helpful in the exploratory stage of assessment, they must be clarified to obtain a fuller understanding of concerns and options for resolving them. We tend to believe that vague, jargon-filled accounts are more profound than clearly stated ones (Armstrong, 1980).

Watch Out for Illusory Correlations

Mistaken assumptions about causes may be due to incorrect estimates of the degree to which two or more events covary. Covariations (and thus causal relationships) are often assumed between certain characteristics (e.g., personality traits or recent life changes) and problems or between certain symptoms and diagnostic categories (e.g., vigilance for danger and generalized anxiety disorder). "Everyone possesses what might be called 'data' on the degree of covariation between various socially relevant dimensions and behavior dimensions, but the data are usually skimpy, hit-or-miss, vague, and subject to bias and distortion in both encoding and recall" (Nisbett & Ross, 1980, p. 98). Covariations may be assumed on the basis of a belief that causes are similar to their effects (the representativeness heuristic). We tend to overestimate the size of correlations between factors that we believe "go together" and to underestimate the degree of covariation when we do not have any particular preconceptions about the relationship between two or more factors (Jennings, Amabile, & Ross, 1982). Incorrect estimates often persist despite disconfirming information. For example, a clinician may insist that a woman is schizophrenic because she was once labeled a schizophrenic, even though there is no current evidence to support this diagnosis.

Expectations of consistency encourage illusory correlations. We tend to assume that people behave in trait-consistent ways when, in fact, correlations between personality traits and behavior are often low. One reason for this is that "we tend to see most people in a limited number of roles and situations and thus are exposed to a more consistent sample of behavior than we would obtain from a truly random sample of the person's behavioral repertoire" (Nisbett & Ross, 1980, p. 107). Apparent discrepancies are readily explained away. Subjective feelings of control are enhanced by the belief that other people are consistent in their traits and thus are predictable. (See also Pronin, Puccio, & Ross, 2002.) If our preconceptions are rigid and the feedback is vague or irrelevant, experience will do little to alter incorrect beliefs. Different situations present different kinds of feedback. Consider the consequences of turning the steering wheel when driving a car: each movement has an immediate effect; there is immediate feedback. Such feedback offers an opportunity to correct misleading beliefs about what "ought" to go together. (See also discussion of fast and frugal heuristics.)

Examine All Four Cells

We tend to focus on our "hits" when estimating covariation. This encourages false estimates that may result in incorrect beliefs about causes. For example, parents often worry that their teenaged children will have a car accident. Let's say that a mother worries, and her son then is in an accident. The parent may attribute this to "clairvoyance" or some other mystical power. Only the "hits" (worry followed by accident) receive attention; false alarms, misses, and correct rejections are ignored (see Exhibit 20.7). The tendency to ignore negative instances encourages beliefs in suspect causes such as psychic powers. People who say that their prayers are answered usually do not consider the times they prayed and their prayers were not answered. That is, they do not keep track of all the times they prayed, noting the outcome for each. "Answered prayers" are more vivid. The confirmatory bias (our tendency to search selectively for evidence that supports our preconceptions) encourages a focus on hits. We must examine all four cells on a 2 × 2 contingency table.

Sometimes people make inferences based on only one row in a 2 × 2 table. Consider reports of being abused as a child and whether or not an individual was in fact abused. We must examine all four cells in a 2 × 2 table (Dawes, 1994b). We must consider those who have and have not reported abuse and those who have actually been and those who have not been abused. In everyday practice, only one row of a four-cell contingency

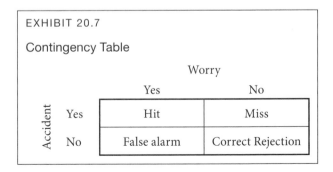

EXHIBIT 20.7

Contingency Table

		Worry	
		Yes	No
Accident	Yes	Hit	Miss
	No	False alarm	Correct Rejection

table is available. Consider people who have or have not been caught for abuse and whether they are or are not abusers. We do not know who would be represented in the not caught row. As Dawes points out, we do not think in comparative terms. "We match (often from memory) rather than compare" (p. 4). Statements that sound convincing may be quite inaccurate. The only way to avoid these errors, as Dawes notes, is to describe joint probabilities, that is, create a 2 × 2 contingency table. (See also Hastie & Dawes, 2001; and the discussion of sensitivity and specificity later in this chapter.)

Pay Attention to Base Rates

Base rates indicate the prevalence of a behavior or event in a population. Only some parents who were abused as children abuse their own children (estimates range from 40% to 60%). We tend to rely on data about a particular case and to ignore base rate probabilities. Imagine that you have just left a staff position in a shelter for battered women where 90% of clients seeking services had been abused. You are now working in a community mental health center in which the base rate of battered women is much lower, say 10%. Ignoring difference in base rates may result in incorrect assumptions that clients have been battered when they have not been. Base rate data are not as vivid as characteristics of the client whom you see during interviews. It thus is easy to overlook this information, even though it is important to consider when making decisions. If we rely on resemblance criteria (similarity) to evaluate probability, we may overlook prior probability (base rate data).

Watch Out for Sample Bias

Decisions are based on samples of behavior or conditions. We make generalizations about what clients do in real-life contexts based on how they act during interviews. Inaccurate assumptions may result from *overgeneralizations* based on small, biased samples. We often overlook *selection bias*. Consider the assumption that since students' achievement in private compared with public schools is superior, private schools are better. What do you think?

Search for Alternative Accounts

We tend to seek data that confirm our views and not to look for evidence against them. This is known as the *confirmatory bias* or *self-fulfilling prophecy*. This style of search often results in faulty judgments (Nickerson, 1998). Studies of medical decisions show that overinterpretation is a key source of error (contradictory evidence is ignored or is incorrectly assumed to support preferred views) (Elstein et al., 1978). We use different standards to criticize evidence against our views than we use to evaluate evidence that supports them. Evidence that is mixed (it provides some support for and some against favored views) increases the confidence of believers of both views (Lord, Ross, & Lepper, 1979). We

readily think up causes. We have an investment in understanding and predicting what happens around us. A premature focus on one possibility will get in the way of considering alternative views. Unless your assumptions about causes provide guidelines for removing complaints or unless you must act quickly ("shoot from the hip"), consider alternative possibilities.

Enhance Your Understanding of Probabilities: Decrease Your Innumeracy

Misunderstanding of probabilities may result in avoidable errors. Different kinds of probabilities include: (1) *compound* (probability of X *and* Y), (2) *conditional* (probability of X *given* Y), and (3) *simple* (X). In the conjunction fallacy, we overlook the fact that the probabilities of A and B *both* occurring must be less than the simple probability of A or the simple probability of B. We often ignore base rates of the characteristic in question. Dawes (1988) gives the example of assuming that low self-esteem (c) results in problems (P) because people who consult counselors regarding problems have low self-esteem. This confuses p (c |S)—the probability of low self-esteem given problems and (p S|c) the probability of problems given low self-esteem. As Dawes notes, we do not know (p S|c) is high "because clients come to [counselors] because they have problems" (p. 76). The counselors' experience is conditional on S. Also, self-esteem may be poor *because* people have problems. (See also Appendix A in chapter 8 illustrating that conditional probabilities are not symmetric.) Readers of books on sexual abuse are often asked to review a list of symptoms to check for indicators of sexual abuse. One problem here is assuming that the probability of a symptom (e.g., suicidal thoughts) is the same as the probability of an underlying problem or experience (e.g., sexual abuse as a child) (Ofshe & Watters, 1994). Symptoms such as depression are much more common than any one underlying cause. When we do not consider this, we are subject to illusory correlations, for example, between symptoms and presumed causes. Another problem is that certain symptoms may not be independent but are assumed to be so when making an overall estimate.

Watch Your Language

The role of language is discussed at many points in this book. Language influences how successful we are in communicating with ourselves, as well as with clients and colleagues. Some uses of language have an almost magical quality, as when we label a behavior and think that we have explained it when we have not (see the earlier discussion of naming compared with explaining). It is easy to slip from describing someone (she complains about being lonely) to a causal inference that provides little or no intervention leverage (she has a dependent personality). We tend to convert trait names (e.g., aggressive) into presumed causes (e.g., aggressive personality) that get in the way of searching for problem-related factors. *Psychobabble* (vague, excessively abstract concepts) obscures rather than clarifies as do weasel words and phrases (vague, uninformative terms).

Be Aware of What You Do Not Know (Ignorance as a Kind of Knowledge)

Be honest about gaps in your knowledge related to decisions you and your clients must make. Available knowledge about how to help clients attain certain outcomes is usually incomplete. Sources of uncertainty include potential effectiveness of different methods, the accuracy of assessment and evaluation measures, and the future course of certain behavior patterns. Recognizing our ignorance and the uncertainties involved in problem solving can help us to avoid misleading influences of overconfidence. Avoidable mistakes may result from lack of knowledge. Witte, Witte, and Kerwin (1994) offered a course on medical ignorance at the University of Arizona School of Medicine to highlight the importance of knowing what is not known as well as what is. Carroll (2001) has his students ask "ignorance" questions based on their reading of texts. (See also discussion of ignorance as a kind of knowledge in chapter 4.)

Acquire Domain-Specific Knowledge and Skills

Specialized content knowledge and skills may be necessary to accurately assess concerns and related circumstances and options in order to help a client achieve hoped-for outcomes. You may have to search for and critically appraise related research findings to discover promising options (see chapter 11). If you are unaware of the influence of schedules of reinforcement on behavior, you may mistakenly attribute the cause of problems to personal characteristics (low self-esteem), overlooking the role of scheduling effects (see chapter 7). Lack of knowledge about the psychological effects of certain physical illnesses, dehydration, or drugs may result in incorrect assumptions about the cause of an elderly client's confusion or "depression."

Watch Out for Redundant Data

Our tendency to collect redundant information encourages a false sense of overconfidence. You may, for example, ask a client who complains of depression about her past history of depression. In selectively scanning for depression, you may overlook periods of happiness and related factors.

Be Flexible

One definition of rationality is changing your mind when the data indicate that you should. Our tendency to be overconfident of our judgments and to look for data that confirm our views (confirmatory biases), contributes to unwarranted persistence. Change your mind when you have good reason to do so. We tend to be influenced by what we first see or think of. This may provide a fast and frugal way to make accurate decisions. (See discussion

in chapter 8.) But it may not. We may have to question initial impressions.

Avoid False Dilemmas

We often think in either/or terms when searching for causes and selecting service plans. We may think it must be either A or B when in fact there may be a number of possibilities. Thinking in either/or terms may result in overlooking promising options.

Take Advantage of Helpful Tools

Making decisions often requires combining different kinds of data (e.g., self-report and observational data). Let us say you have to decide whether to remove a child from his home. You will estimate the probability of further abuse, steps that can be taken to avoid it, and the safety that could be provided in other settings such as foster homes. Integrating different kinds of data is difficult. Actuarial methods have been found to be superior to clinical judgment in making decisions in a variety of areas, including the diagnosis of medical and psychiatric disorders, the prediction of service outcome, the risk of further child abuse, and the length of hospitalization (e.g., Barber et al., 2008; Grove & Meehl, 1996; Johnson, 2011). Statistical or actuarial methods draw on empirical data describing the relationships between certain outcomes (e.g., child abuse), and "predictors" (e.g., a past history of abuse). Computer programs have been designed as decision-making tools to allocate services (e.g., see Hirdes et al., 2008). Use of such programs may enhance both the accuracy and equity of decisions; clients with similar needs receive similar services. A variety of applications on smart phones are used in health care (e.g., Black, Car, Pagliari, Anandan, Cresswell, Bokun, et al., 2011). Visual models such as flowcharts and decision trees may be useful (see Exhibit 20.8). We can use natural frequencies to determine risks (Gigerenzer, 2002). (See also later discussion.)

Using Tests to Make Decisions

Professionals often use tests to understand clients or problems or to predict how people are likely to respond in the future. Social workers often assess risks, for example, of elder or child abuse. Thousands of children are on "at risk" registers on the assumption that they are at a continuing risk of abuse. Tests should be used to revise subjective estimates, to change a decision about what should be done. Otherwise, why bother? You should consider both new information and information you already have. Two kinds of odds are important: (1) prior odds (odds before additional material is available) and (2) posterior odds (odds after considering additional data). The addition of more information should change prior odds. Let us say you suspect (based on an interview) that an elderly client has Alzheimer's disease and you obtain psychological test results as well. You should then use the

EXHIBIT 20.8

Example of a Tree Diagram

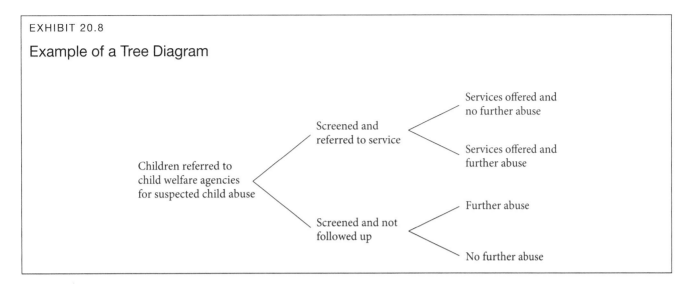

test results to choose among different options in light of your new estimate based on the results. That is, you may revise your estimate of the probability that the client has Alzheimer's disease (see Exhibit 20.9).

Clients should not be asked to take tests simply to satisfy the curiosity of professionals or because the tests are available. This wastes time and provides an illusion of "work being done." Ethical obligations require you to inform clients about the costs and benefits of any recommended test. A balance sheet describing benefits and risks, together with their likelihood (if known) and the subjective value for each, can help clients make decisions (Eddy, 1990). This sheet should include information about the

EXHIBIT 20.9

Should a Test Be Used?

Suppose that the psychologist believes that Mrs. Ryan has "loose associations" and that these are an indicator of dementia. Exactly what are "loose associations"? That is, what is the base rate? What percent of people like Mrs. Ryan have "loose associations"? Keep in mind that symptoms (loose associations) are usually much more frequent than an underlying illness. What is the correlation between "loose associations" and dementia? What is the probability that "loose associations" are predictive of dementia? And if they are, would this change what you would do now or in the future? What is the cost of a test of loose associations to the clients in money, possible anxiety, and stigma? Would family members start to pathologize Mrs. Ryan if additional assessments were recommended? Would positive results on additional "tests" give family members an excuse to "get rid" of Mrs. Ryan, even though they offer no additional information about whether her current complaints could be resolved and, if so, how? On the other hand, could opportunities be lost for preventive intervention?

accuracy of the test (e.g., false positive and false negative rates). Someone may request a test even though it is not very accurate and is costly in money, time, discomfort, likelihood of misclassification (a false positive or a false negative), or harm from the test itself. We differ in the risks we are willing (or eager) to take.

The predictive accuracy of test results is often overestimated. Incorrect estimates of a test's predictive accuracy may result from confusing two different conditional probabilities. We tend to confuse *retrospective accuracy* (the probability of a positive test given that the person has a condition) and *predictive accuracy* (the probability of a condition given a positive test result). Retrospective accuracy is determined by reviewing test results after the true condition is known. For example, an autopsy may show that a woman who had a positive mammogram indeed did have breast cancer. Predictive accuracy refers to the probability of having a condition given a positive test result and the probability of not having a condition given a negative result. A physician may ask a patient to have a mammogram and, if it is positive, may infer that she has breast cancer and recommend a biopsy. It is predictive accuracy that is important when considering a test result for an individual. (See Gøtzsche & Jørgensen, 2011; Welch, Schwartz & Woloshin, 2011; Woloshin, Schwartz, & Welch, 2008.)

Inaccurate estimates based on invalid tests may harm clients. Both test sensitivity and test specificity should be considered, as well as prevalence (base rate) for the problem of concern. *Test sensitivity* refers to a test's accuracy in correctly identifying the proportion of people who have a problem or will engage in a certain behavior (see the glossary in Exhibit 20.10). *Test specificity* refers to the accuracy of a test in correctly identifying the proportion of people who do not have a disorder (or will not engage in a behavior). Both are calculated by examining the columns in a 2 × 2 table as shown in Exhibit 20.11. Neither permits predictions about individuals.

Test sensitivity is often incorrectly equated with the predictive value of a positive test result, and test specificity is often incorrectly equated with the predictive value of a negative test result

EXHIBIT 20.10

Glossary

False negative rate: Percentage of persons incorrectly identified as not having a characteristic.

False positive rate: Percentage of persons inaccurately identified as having a characteristic.

Predictive accuracy: The probability of a condition given a positive test result.

Predictive value of a negative test: The proportion of those with a negative test result who do not have a problem.

Predictive value of a positive test: Proportion of those with a positive test result who actually have a problem.

Prevalence rate (base rate, prior probability): The frequency of a problem among a group of people. The best estimate of the probability of a problem before carrying out a test.

Retrospective accuracy: The probability of a positive test, given that a person has a condition.

Test sensitivity: The proportion among those known to have a problem who test positive.

Test specificity: The proportion among those known to not have the problem who test negative.

True negative rate: Percentage of persons accurately identified as not having a characteristic.

True positive rate: Percentage of persons accurately identified as having a characteristic.

resulting in gross overestimates of predictive value (Dawes, 1988). The positive predictive value of a test depends on the prevalence rate, specificity, and sensitivity. The probability that a client with a positive (or negative) test result for dementia really has dementia depends on the prevalence (base rate) of dementia in the population from which the person was selected (on the pretest probability that the person has dementia). Because there is little appreciation of this point, predictive accuracy is often overestimated. Thus, test accuracy varies depending on whether a test is used as a screening device in which there are large numbers of people who do not have some condition of interest (e.g., depression) or whether it is used for clients with known signs or symptoms. In the latter case, the true positive and true negative rates are much higher, and so there will be fewer false positives and false negatives. Overlooking this difference results in overestimates of test accuracy in screening situations, resulting in a high percentage of false positives.

Communicating Information About Risks and Benefits

Clients cannot be involved as informed participants unless you have the skills needed to communicate information in an understandable way regarding the risks and benefits of recommended practices and alternatives. This includes risks and benefits of screening for depression or anxiety during screening days (often sponsored by pharmaceutical companies). The difficulty of communicating risk is shown by the very different meanings of terms such as "likely" and "rare." A review of material concerning risks and benefits of mammograms on websites provided by pharmaceutical companies, consumer groups, and health agencies revealed biased presentations—for example, inclusion of only relative risks (Jørgensen & Gøtzsche, 2004; Gøtzsche & Jørgensen, 2011). As Edwards, Elwyn, and Mulley (2002) note, "Without the whole truth presenting information in such a way is not consistent with truly informed decision-making" (p. 828). Let us say you are a social worker in a hospital and your client has been encouraged by her oncologist to take chemotherapy and she has been told that there is a 50% benefit. This sounds good doesn't it? But what does this mean? What is the absolute risk? This is what your client should know. Absolute risk is always in relation to a certain number of individuals (e.g., 100, 1,000, 10,000). The absolute risk in this situation is that, instead of six women out of 100 getting a recurrence of cancer in ten years, three do with taking chemotherapy. Would *you* want this information? Providing only information about relative risk in isolation of base rates is very misleading and is considered unethical.

Edwards, Elwyn, and Mulley (2002) highlight the effects of framing and other manipulations in making decisions.

1. Information on relative risk is more persuasive than absolute risk data.

2. "Loss" framing (for example, the potential losses from not having a mammogram) influences screening uptake more than "gain" framing.

3. Positive framing (for example, chance of survival) is more effective than negative framing (chance of death) in persuading people to take risky options, such as treatments.

4. More information, and information that is more understandable to the [client], is associated with a greater wariness to take treatments or tests. (p. 828)

These authors conclude as follows:

- Graphical displays of information increase the effectiveness of risk communication.

- Simple bar charts may be preferred over "representations" (faces, stick figures, etc.).

- Absolute risks (with appropriate scales) should be given greater prominence than relative risks—in both information for [clients] and journals for professionals.

EXHIBIT 20.11

Elements for Judging a Prediction Instrument's Value

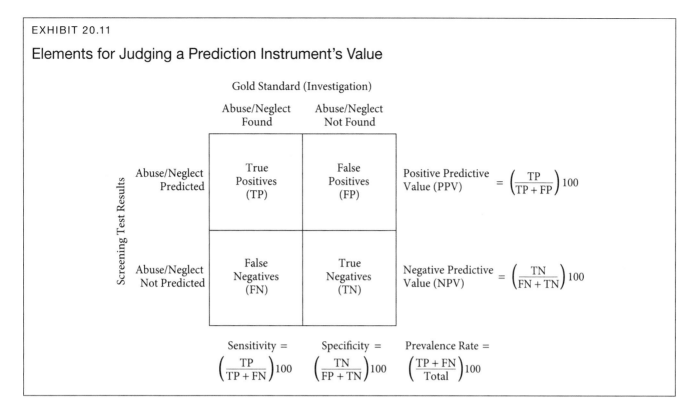

- Lifetime risks should be given, with relevant information about risks in relevant time spans as additional information.

- The influence of framing should be countered by using dual representations (loss and gain, mortality and survival data).

- Comparison with everyday risks is valuable; what is the risk compared with other well-known risks. (p. 830)

Surrogate measures (reducing plaque) should be distinguished from key outcomes (mortality). Decision aids are valuable including visual descriptions of risk and relating information to familiar risks. Paling (2006) suggests use of a scale with standardized terms for specific frequencies. You could inform clients about number needed to treat (NNT) or number needed to harm (NNH) (see chapter 21). We could also share the number needed to screen or the number needed to test.

Using Natural Frequencies to Estimate Risk

Risk assessment is of interest in a number of areas including suicide, domestic violence, and child abuse. Information that would allow you to determine the accuracy of such measures may be missing in research reports. We should be informed about both the sensitivity and specificity of a measure, as well as base rate data (the prevalence of the condition of concern such as physical abuse of children) in the population. Depending on the base rates, the accuracy may be quite different for a measure

of a given specificity and sensitivity. Consider an example Munro (2004) offers of using a risk assessment measure for screening initial referrals to child welfare agencies to determine if the referrals call for investigation. She selects a base rate of 40% with a sensitivity of 69% and a specificity of 74% and calculates the probability that a positive test result would be a true positive using natural frequencies rather than standard probabilities.

In a group of 1000 families, we would expect that 400 would be abusive. Of these 400 families, 276 will get a positive result on using the instrument (sensitivity 69%). Of the other 600 families, 156 will also get positive results (specificity 74%). Therefore, there will be a total of 432 positive results, of which 276 will be true positives. (Munro, 2004, p. 878)

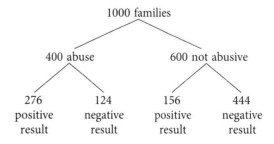

The probability of a positive result being a true positive is equal to:

$$\frac{276}{276 + 156} = 0.64$$

She has calculated the result with a base rate of 4% (four per thousand).

If we take a group of 1000 families, we expect that four will be abusive. Of these four families, three approximately will get a positive result on using the instrument (sensitivity 69%). Of the other 996 families, 259 will also get a positive result (specificity 74%). Therefore, there will be a total of 262 positive results, of which three will be true positives (Munro, 2004, p. 879).

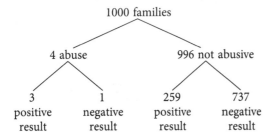

The probability of a positive result being a true positive is equal to

$$\frac{3}{3 + 259} = 0.12$$

As Munro notes:

In both cases, the accuracy is far lower than most people expect intuitively from being told just the sensitivity and specificity and it has serious practice implications. If we are screening the general population, an instrument with this degree of reliability would identify a very large group of families as potentially abusive, but only a tiny percentage would be true positives.... At the same time, it would have to recognize that about a quarter of dangerous families were being overlooked. (p. 879)

Natural frequencies are much easier to use than Bayes Theorem.

Reviewing Your Inferences

Can you make a well-reasoned argument for your assumptions? Guidelines for presenting arguments are as follows:

- Clearly identify your conclusion and premises.
- Separate evidence and inferences.
- Use accurate premises drawing on practice-related research findings.
- Avoid overstating inferences.
- Review your argument for fallacies.
- Search for well-argued alternative accounts.

Can you make a well-reasoned argument that the objectives you and your clients have decided to pursue will result in hoped-for outcomes? Is there a clear relationship between your assumptions about causes and selection of outcomes? Is your account compatible with related research? Can a stronger argument be made for some other account? Focus on criticisms that are relevant to the main thrust of an argument (strong criticisms) rather than nitpick (use weak criticisms). Are there hidden assumptions? What are they? Consider both the factual soundness of an argument and its logical soundness. An argument can be logically sound but lead to false conclusions because of one or more false premises. Examples of inaccurate premises are: "All parents who have been abused as a child abuse their own children"; "Once a problem drinker, always a problem drinker." Inaccuracies may be easier to spot if you translate an argument into visual or diagrammatic form. Consider the argument that smoking marijuana implies a high probability of using heroin (see chapter 8, Appendix A). This argument is an example of the confusion of the inverse (the confusion between the probability of using heroin if you smoke marijuana and the probability of smoking marijuana if you use hard drugs). The two probabilities are quite different.

On the Use and Misuse of Intuition

Although intuition is an invaluable source of ideas about what may be true or false, it is not a sound guide for testing those beliefs, as discussed in chapter 4. There are over 135 studies showing that actuarial methods are superior to intuition in making decisions in a variety of fields (Grove & Meehl, 1996). For a discussion of arguments against actuarial risk appraisal and responses, see Quinsey, Harris, Rice, and Cormier (2006). Jonathan Baron defines intuition as "an unanalyzed and unjustified belief" (1994, p. 26) and argues that because beliefs based on intuition may be either sound or unsound, basing beliefs on intuition may result in consequences that harm people. Arriving at accurate decisions often requires checking of initial assumptions. (See discussion of dual process view of decision making in chapter 8,) Attributing sound judgments to "intuition" decreases opportunities to teach helping skills (one has "it" but does not know how or why "it" works). Relying on intuition, or what "feels right," is not wise if it results in ignoring information about problems, causes, and remedies, including possible consequences of given courses of action and degree of uncertainty associated with them. Knowledge is fragmentary, forcing you to rely on criteria such as intuition to fill in the gaps. What is ethically questionable is relying on intuition when other grounds—including a critical examination of intuitively held beliefs—will result in sounder decisions.

Ideals and Actualities

The purpose of assessment is to find out what is needed and what can be offered. Think of a balance scale. The balance will often reveal many problems and few resources. An "impossible job" is one in which you do not have the resources (e.g., time) to solve the problems you confront or can only minimally address them. Case management, for example, will not substantially change structural and fiscal problems that limit outcomes that can be achieved (Austin, 1992).

When a Contextual Framework Is Not Preferred

Adequate assessment may not be possible because your supervisor or agency relies on practice frameworks that yield incomplete accounts of problems and related circumstances. Some of my students want to use effective methods but cannot do so. They may not be permitted (or may not have the time) to gather observational data needed to clarify problems, outcomes, and related factors. Their options for speaking up and changing inadequate and/or harmful practices and policies may be limited. Practice may be contextual in name only. Staff may say they use a contextual approach but reveal by their actions that they do not. Multiple services may be offered with little integration to avoid duplication and working at cross-purposes.

When a Contextual Assessment Is Not Possible

A contextual assessment may not be possible. Obstacles include heavy caseloads and recording requirements, lack of resources, and time pressures. As resources shrink, "speed-ups" (having to cover more cases in the same amount of time) have become common. You may have neither time nor opportunity to clarify concerns and discover related factors. You may have to make recommendations hastily, with little time for critical reflection. Or, required assessment skills may be missing.

What Can You Do in Such Circumstances?

You can do whatever you can to address your clients' needs and explore what can be done to create additional resources. (See discussion of case and cause advocacy in chapters 19 and 27.) Dysfunctional responses to imbalances between ideals and actualities include focusing on areas of little interest to clients and becoming a "natterer" (merely complaining). You can be aware of the limitations of your assessment (uncertainties)—you can be your own constructive critic. This will help you to accurately appraise the data on which you base assumptions. If you acknowledge the limitations of your assessment, you are more likely to avoid overconfidence (unwarranted belief in assumptions) and to continue to enhance your assessment skills. Avoiding overconfidence does not mean that you do not act in spite of uncertainty; as Thouless (1974) points out, this would be the height of "crooked thinking." It means that you take what actions you must, bearing in mind associated uncertainty and take future steps to enhance your skills and advocate for conditions that would permit sound assessment.

Do What You Can

The concept of "successive approximations" is valuable not only in helping clients, but in helping you to focus on what can be done even in dismal circumstances. Perhaps you can complete some of the steps in a sound assessment. Do what you can. Complete the closest approximation to an informed assessment.

Keep Your Eye on the Gold Standard

The gold standard is that we have sufficient data to make sound decisions. It is not that assessment data be complete. This is usually impossible (and often unnecessary). Plans must typically be made based on incomplete data. However, there are degrees of incompleteness, ranging from totally inadequate (for example, no clear description of problems, hoped-for outcomes, and related factors) to excellent (clear description of all the latter). When we cannot do what we think we should do, we may change our minds about what is "best." Suppose you work in an agency in which you have to make hasty decisions. You may gradually change your beliefs about what is needed. You could form a support group of colleagues with similar values to prevent drift from standards you value. Without this, you may confuse ideals, possibilities, and actualities. You could start a journal club (Deenadayalan, Grimmer-Somers, Prior, & Kumar, 2008).

Be an Advocate: Change Ineffective and Harmful Policies and Procedures

Talk to others who share your concerns and work together to seek changes. Teach clients how to be empowered consumers of services (e.g., see Jannson, 2011). Do not assume that dysfunctional policies and procedures cannot be changed. (See also chapter 27.)

Ethical Issues in the Selection of Outcomes

Ethical practice requires involving clients in selecting outcomes, forming a clear agreement about what outcomes will be pursued, considering the interests of all involved parties, and focusing on functional objectives (those that are of value to clients in real-life environments). A clear service agreement highlights your responsibility to work toward agreed-on objectives and decreases the likelihood of hidden agendas (goals you pursue but do not share with clients). The influence of professionals is often hidden by the vagueness of objectives pursued. The fuzzier the goal, the greater the chance that an outcome will be pursued that is not of interest to clients. Labeling may be used to obscure questionable decisions. For example, labeling a client mentally ill may legitimize the use of intrusive methods that would otherwise be considered unethical, such as outpatient commitment. Informed consent requires describing benefits and costs of recommended plans as well as the benefits and costs of alternatives, including doing nothing (see chapter 3).

You may help clients to recognize the influence of social norms and values on their selection of outcomes. For example, consumerism is a hallmark of American culture, but buying unnecessary items may result in strained family relationships because of financial worries. Stereotypes and a lack of knowledge may result in incorrect assumptions that a problem is related to race, gender, sexual orientation, or age. Differences of opinion about objectives may concern who the target of change is to be, in addition to what is to be altered. Until fairly recently, seeking to change a homosexual orientation to a heterosexual one was accepted as an outcome by many professionals (and still is by some). Many now argue against this on the grounds that it reflects and supports societal biases and the resulting oppression of and discrimination against gay and lesbian people. (See also research illustrating discrimination against transgender clients.)

Empowering Clients

Expanding freedom is a key criterion in selecting objectives. This includes freedom from restrictions that result from a lack of skills, freedom to gain outcomes that do not harm others, and freedom to avoid unfairly imposed or unnecessary negative consequences. You can expand clients' freedom by focusing on *functional objectives*: those that enhance positive outcomes in real-life settings. A focus on objectives that are valuable only in artificial contexts such as a day treatment center violates legal regulations intended to ensure effective services to persons with developmental disabilities (e.g., see *Positive Behavioral Intervention Regulations*, 1993). Both the interests of clients, as well as those of involved others, must be considered to arrive at ethical decisions. When interests conflict, help parties to identify options and the advantages and disadvantages of each. Focusing on shared interests will help clients to identify mutually acceptable outcomes (e.g., see Fisher & Ury, 1991).

Questions to ask if you have authority over people in a supervisory or monitoring role (as in child welfare or correctional settings) include (1) Is there a legitimate reason for intervening? Will the outcomes sought benefit both clients and significant others? Does the behavior occur often enough to justify intervening? (2) Are my judgments free of bias, for example, in relation to gender, sexual orientation, ethnicity, age, or race?

The Importance of Compassion

Your support and caring are especially vital when there are no options for helping clients attain outcomes they value as suggested by the moving example Archie Cochrane gives in *Effectiveness & Efficiency* (1999). As a prisoner of war in World War II he took care of other prisoners of war. He was with a

dying soldier who was in great pain. Neither spoke a word of the other's language. He had no pain medication. He took the man in his arms and held him until he died. "In despair, and purely instinctively, I sat on his bed and took him in my arms. The effect was almost magical; he quieted at once and died peacefully a few hours later. I was still with him, half asleep and very stiff. I believe that by personal intervention I improved the quality of care dramatically in this case, and I know it was based on instinct and not on reason" (pp. 94–95).

The Value of Records

Records can help you decide on plans and review clients' progress (e.g., see Kagle, 2008). If accurate and complete, records protect clients from repetitive questions and may help you to avoid mistakes based on faulty assumptions and recollections. If accurate and complete, they serve as a guide for others who take over a case and allow supervisors and administrators to review the quality of services provided (see also discussion of legal regulations related to records in chapter 3). Are objectives clearly described? Do they address outcomes of concern to clients? Are service methods clearly described? Are records up-to-date? Asking "Is this material useful in planning what to do?" can help you decide what to record. You can save time by eliminating redundant forms and using standardized forms that allow easy recording and review. Common deficiencies of case records and psychological reports include missing data, overly general or unsupported speculations, and vague or overly technical language (Tallent, 1993). Writing tips include the following:

- Be precise; give clear examples (e.g., of terms such as "aggressive").
- Get rid of unnecessary words.
- Never use a long word when a short one will do (see Orwell, 1958).
- Use active verbs.
- Clearly define key terms.
- Focus on main points.
- Clearly identify your conclusions and the premises on which you base them.
- Support your inferences with descriptive data.

Computerized case records are increasingly required. Social workers and allied professionals may input information in the field on handheld computers. These may also provide decision-support systems. Computerized records are not without their hazards (see Hoffman & Podgurski, 2009). Recording requirements may interfere with time with clients (Munro, 2011). Case records may build narratives that harm rather than help clients (Tice, 1998).

Record client's presenting concerns and hoped-for outcomes in the client's (or referral source's) own words. Failure to do this is a key lapse often found in records. This may be due to a "tick-box" format, which does not permit accurate accounts of clients or their circumstances. A log of contacts noting the date, people present, purpose, and type of contact can save time when preparing court reports. Describe sources of data relied on (see Exhibit 20.12). Describing both current and desired levels of behaviors and/or environmental conditions and intermediate steps provides an "agenda" for change individually tailored for each client. Clearly describe plans, including the settings that will be used, who will be involved, what they will do, and the reasons for selections made. Also describe progress indicators and plans for maintaining gains. Ethical issues regarding records include protecting clients' rights to confidentiality (e.g., not sharing records with other people unless you must because of legal regulations or you have the client's permission), avoiding irrelevant negative material, and using records as a tool in planning and evaluating services. For more discussion of case records, see Kagle (2008). Failure to keep records has been the

---

EXHIBIT 20.12

Checklist for Reviewing Case Records

	Not at all	A little	Fair Amount	Ideal
1. Route to agency is clearly noted.	0	1	2	3
2. Presenting problems are described.	0	1	2	3
3. A problem (outcome) profile is included.	0	1	2	3
4. Demographic data are complete.	0	1	2	3
5. Relevant historical data (e.g., work history) are included.	0	1	2	3
6. Current life circumstances are clearly described.	0	1	2	3
7. Problem-related behaviors are clearly described.	0	1	2	3
8. Sources of data relied on are noted.	0	1	2	3
9. Valid assessment sources are used.	0	1	2	3
10. Self-report data are supplemented by observational data.	0	1	2	3
11. Baseline data are available.	0	1	2	3
12. Contingencies related to behaviors of concern are clearly described.	0	1	2	3
13. Client assets are noted.	0	1	2	3
14. Relevant assets of significant others are noted.	0	1	2	3
15. Environmental resources are described.	0	1	2	3
16. Uninformative labels are avoided.	0	1	2	3
17. Objectives, including intermediate steps, are clearly described.	0	1	2	3
18. Inferences about the causes of problems are supported by evidence and are compatible with what is known about behavior.	0	1	2	3
19. Meeting objectives will remove complaints.	0	1	2	3
20. Intervention methods are clearly described.	0	1	2	3
21. Plans selected have an empirically tested track record of success.	0	1	2	3
22. Clear relevant progress indicators are noted.	0	1	2	3
23. Graphs showing degree of progress are included and are up-to-date.	0	1	2	3
24. There is little irrelevant material.	0	1	2	3
25. A log of contacts is included.	0	1	2	3

Key: 0 = not at all, 1 = a little, 2 = a fair amount, 3 = ideal. Total scores may range from 0 to 75.

basis of successful lawsuits (e.g., *Whitree v. New York State* (1968) 290 N.Y.S. 2d 486 (ct. claims)).

Summary

Helping clients requires integrating different kinds of information. You have to make guesses about how to help clients attain valued outcomes. These guesses may be well informed (by drawing on related research) or off-the-cuff. Ideally, objectives are selected that involve a change in problem-related circumstances and build on client assets and environmental resources. Common errors in this phase include acting on hasty assumptions, selecting vague objectives, overlooking client's strengths, and offering incomplete accounts (ignoring environmental causes such as lack of jobs in a community). We tend to be overconfident of our beliefs, to focus on data that support them, and to ignore data that do not. Helpful rules of thumb for avoiding errors include searching for well-argued alternative accounts, drawing on related research, questioning initial assumptions, taking advantage of helpful tools such as actuarial methods, and asking what is missing. Flowcharts and decision trees may be useful in organizing information and seeing what is missing. Limited options call for your support and compassion.

Reviewing Your Competencies

Reviewing Content Knowledge

1. Recognize and give examples of incomplete assessment, including neglect of important cultural differences.
2. Give examples of common errors in organizing and interpreting data.
3. Give examples of naming rather than explaining.
4. Describe helpful rules for avoiding errors in organizing and integrating data.
5. Describe important questions to ask when deciding whether to use a test to make predictions.
6. Explain why it is important to consider base rate data when interpreting test results and give an example.
7. Describe the advantages of actuarial risk assessment tools compared to reliance on intuition.
8. You can use frequencies to determine risks of false positives and false negatives.

Reviewing What You Do

1. The inferences you make are compatible with research findings concerning behaviors of interest.
2. Descriptions, causal analyses, and predictions draw on related research and suggest feasible plans.
3. The objectives you select are relevant to outcomes of most concern to your clients.
4. You advocate for needed resources.
5. Given case examples, you can spot faulty arguments and accurately describe why they are faulty.
6. You take advantage of available decision aids to help clients make informed decisions.
7. You build on client assets.

Reviewing Results

1. Plans selected are effective.
2. Situations in which there are no effective options are accurately identified and support is offered.
3. Clients acquire more influence over the quality of their lives.

Part 8

Selecting Plans and Assessing Progress

21

Selecting and Implementing Plans

OVERVIEW   This chapter describes decisions involved in selecting plans, options you may consider, and guidelines for selecting among them. (See chapter 27 for discussion of purchasing services from other agencies.) Practices, programs, and policies differ in their track record of success and the resources needed to implement them successfully. Identification of common elements in evidence-based practices, as well as common factors that contribute to successful outcomes facilitates decision making. Information collected during assessment should help you and your clients decide whether and how to pursue valued outcomes. Changes may be vital at the policy level including legislation. Problems that may arise when trying to implement plans are reviewed and suggestions for handling them offered. Chapters 26 and 27 provide additional discussion about working with families, groups, organizations, and communities.

YOU WILL LEARN ABOUT

- The relationship between assessment and intervention

- Factors that influence success

- Decisions involved in selecting plans

- Offering support

- Thinking critically about plans

- Implementing plans and programs and trying again

- Ethical issues in selecting plans

- Prevention

The Relationship Between Assessment and Intervention

The distinction between assessment and intervention is somewhat arbitrary, in that assessment may produce change (e.g., clients may become more or less hopeful, politicians may concede that low-cost housing is scarce and advocate for more low-cost dwellings), and additional assessment data may emerge during intervention. The distinction is not arbitrary in that assessment should inform selection of plans. (See Exhibit 21.1.) Assessment should suggest valued outcomes, how to attain them, and the likelihood of success given available resources. If initial plans fail, clients may be less willing to "try again" and feel more hopeless. Community residents may decide that their efforts are useless. Tailoring plans for each client (whether an individual, family, group, community, or organization) and their unique circumstances is a hallmark of a contextual, evidence-informed approach. Conditions must be arranged so that people act, think, or feel differently in relevant situations.

Different views of concerns have different service implications (see Exhibit 21.2). Planning requires determining the degree of match between available resources and what is needed to attaining hoped-for outcomes. What will you and your clients do? Possibilities will be shaped by all that has gone before including the imperfect picture you and your clients have of their options in this uncertain world. There will be a temptation to dismiss these uncertainties, perhaps not even to see them in the first place, but, they are there, seen or not. Options will often be less than hoped for. Our service system is fragmented. Many pieces are missing and your clients will often confront these missing pieces. There may be no low-cost health care for needed care. Temporary cash provided by a program may be at an end. Your job is to try your best to offer what is needed and to provide support in all circumstances and, as emphasized throughout this book, to identify, document, expose, and advocate for filling in of the missing pieces. Work together with others to make the world a more just habitat for all. (See chapter 3.)

The goal is to discover leverage points at different system levels. (See Exhibit 7.2.) Altering behavior and/or circumstances at one level (e.g., helping community residents to participate effectively in community board meetings) will often be needed to achieve valued outcomes at other levels (e.g., change a policy).

EXHIBIT 21.1

Presumed Causes, Service Focus, and Role

Service Focus	Presumed Causes				
	Individual	Family	Neighborhood, Group, Community	Agency	Service System
Individual					
Family					
Group					
Neighborhood/ Community					
Agency					
Service/System					

Focus of Intervention	Possible Intervention Role
1. Provide concrete services.	1. Broker, advocate.
2. Offer support.	2. Enabler.
3. Rearrange contingencies.	3. Enabler, teacher.
4. Provide information or advice.	4. Enabler, teacher.
5. Increase understanding.	5. Teacher, enabler.
6. Enhance skills.	6. Mediator, teacher, enabler.
7. Improve social support systems.	7. Teacher, enabler, mediator, planner.
8. Improve communication.	8. Teacher, broker.
9. Alter physical environment.	9. Teacher, advocate, mediator.
10. Alter agency policies and procedures.	10. Advocate, broker, planner.
11. Alter interactions among agencies.	11. Advocate, mediator, planner.
12. Alter policies affecting resource distribution.	12. Advocate, mediator, planner.
13. Influence legislation.	13. Advocate, mediator, planner.
14. Create new services/programs.	14. Advocate, planner.

EXHIBIT 21.2

Different Accounts Have Different Intervention Implications: The Lakeland Family

Account	Intervention Implications
1. Brian's troubling behaviors are due to his epilepsy. (B)[a]	1. Control epilepsy. Contact family doctor to adjust prescription.
2. The medication Brian takes is responsible. (B)	2. Change medication. Contact family's physician.
3. Developmental changes are responsible. (D)	3. Educate family members about developmental changes; help them acquire skills for handling changes.
4. Brian's behavior is maintained by reinforcement from his parents. (E/F)	4. Alter patterns of reinforcement; teach family members to reinforce desired behaviors and to ignore undesired ones.
5. Problems at home are due to stress at school. (E)	5. Refer to school social worker to address problems at school.
6. Mother's personality disorder is responsible for family's problems. (P)	6. Refer to community mental health center for individually focused counseling.
7. Worry about money and fatigue, coupled with the lack of effective conflict resolution skills, increased stress, which decreases the use of effective parenting skills. (E/P)	7. Relieve fatigue and economic worries (if possible), alter patterns of reinforcement among family members, and enhance conflict resolution skills.
8. Actions by siblings prompt and reinforce Brian's problem behavior. (E/F)	8. Alter siblings' behavior.
9. Family's life developmental stage is the cause of problems. (F/D)	9. Help family members understand the influence of family's life cycle on current experiences.
10. An "enmeshed subsystem" between Brian and his mother is responsible. (F)	10. Help family members, especially Brian and his mother, establish appropriate boundaries.
11. Increased cost of living forces both parents to work full-time, creating strains due to stress and worry. (E)	11. Create changes in the tax system that redistribute income downward to economically struggling families.

[a] The letter following each account reflects the kind of account: B = biological, D = developmental, E = environmental, E/F = family environment, F = family, P = psychological.

Your options will be limited by the influence you and your clients have or can bring to bear on different players in varied systems. They will be influenced by the number and complexity of desired outcomes, the strength of contingencies that compete with those you and your clients try to introduce or maintain, and resources available, including access to effective services. Attaining valued outcomes may be possible only via efforts over years to alter policies that limit client opportunities. Your knowledge of research findings related to important decisions will help you and your clients to identify promising options and to avoid those that are ineffective or harmful.

Factors That Influence Success

Variables associated with success that are common to many helping methods include: (1) support (e.g., relief of isolation, positive helping relationship, trust), (2) learning (e.g., advice, exploring new frameworks, feedback, insight, corrective emotional experiences, changed expectations for personal effectiveness, assimilation of troubling experiences), and (3) action (e.g., changing behavior, facing fears, having successful experiences, reality testing) (Duncan, Miller, Wampold, & Hubble, 2010; Norcross, 2011). The degree of match between your view and the client's view of concerns is critical. Other important influences include positive expectations, helper empathy, timing of service, and support offered in real life. Based on his review of the literature Wampold (2001) argues that specific interventions add little to outcome. Controversies regarding the role of "nonspecific" factors such as empathy and support compared to the role of specific interventions in relation to outcomes are sharp and continuing. Wampold (2006) argues that there is "not a scintilla of evidence to support empirically supported treatments as more effective than other treatments." He suggests that being understood and affirmed in a safe environment promotes positive outcomes. (See also Wampold, 2010). Others argue that research shows that some methods are more effective than a placebo or no treatment (e.g., Ollendick & King, 2006). (See also discussion of nonspecific factors in chapter 15 and later discussion of practice guidelines in this chapter.) Although the equivalence hypothesis (the belief that all methods are equally effective) may be true for some (even many) problems, it is not true for all. Consider, for example, the relationship between exposure and outcome regarding anxiety (e.g., see Richard & Lauterbach, 2007).

Dawes (1994a) argues that there is little relationship between outcome and years of experience or professional degrees and licenses. Indeed, empathic paraprofessionals can be as effective as professionally trained helpers with a range of complaints. Consider the classic study by Strupp and Hadley (1979), in which clients were randomly assigned either to professors with no background in psychology or to professional helpers. The professors achieved the same results as did the professionally trained helpers. Does this mean that training and experience make no difference? Yes and no. Training would make little difference if positive effects could be achieved without it. On the other hand, if specific knowledge and skills are needed to help clients, and training is required to attain them, then programs that provide such knowledge and skills have something to offer. The value of

experience in increasing skills and knowledge depends on the nature of feedback provided (see chapter 4). Thus we should ask: (1) Are special competencies needed to help clients attain certain outcomes? (2) What are they? (3) Are they learned in a program? (4) Are knowledge and skills used on the job? And, if so, with what consequences? (5) If not, why not? It is not hours spent in educational programs that are critical but the demonstrated relationship between the knowledge and skills acquired and success in helping clients achieve outcomes they and significant others value.

Offering clients effective methods requires knowledge of such methods and skill in maximizing their effectiveness. Practice guidelines and "treatment manuals" have been developed for a number of desired outcomes. Chorpita and his colleagues (2007) have examined such manuals and extracted common elements most correlated with positive outcomes (e.g., see Exhibit 21.3). This facilitates your task in selection of evidence-informed methods. (See Barth, Lee, Lindsey, Collins, Strieder, Chorpita, Becker, & Sparks, 2011.) One person cannot be an expert in all interventions. That is why team approaches are often vital. Understanding how behavior is influenced by

EXHIBIT 21.3

Relative Frequency of Practice Elements from Coded Evidence-Based Protocols for Childhood Depression

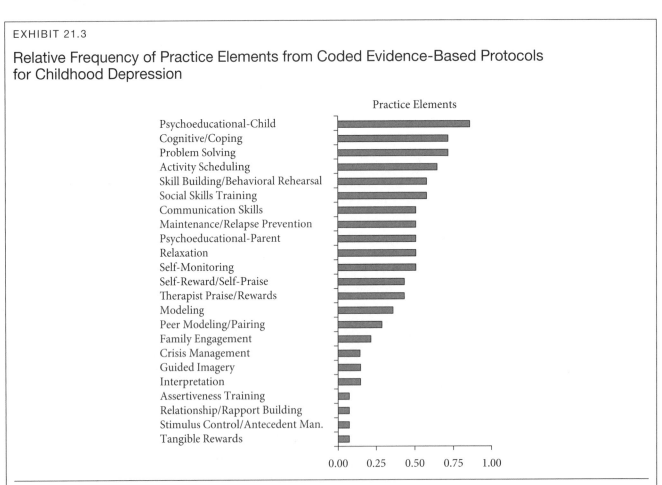

Note: man. = management

Source: B. R. Chorpita, K. D. Becker, & E. L. Daleiden (2007). Understanding the common elements of evidence-based practice: Misconceptions and clinical examples. *American Academy of Child and Adolescent Psychiatry, 46,* 647. Reprinted with permission.

the environment, developmental influences, and changes, and the relationship between personal troubles and social issues will help you to identify options. Intervention fidelity influences success. This refers to the extent to which what is offered matches what has been found to influence success. Shared decision making involves clients as co-participants. Such involvement is a key concern in evidence-based practice. Participatory decision making enhances positive outcomes (e.g. Swift & Callahan, 2009).

Decisions Involved in Selecting Plans

Decisions must be made about whether to (1) change thoughts or feelings, (2) change how people act, (3) alter the environment in which they live, (4) use several approaches, or (5) do nothing (e.g., watchful waiting). Decisions must be made about level(s) of intervention (individual, family, group, organization, neighborhood, community, service system, policy, legislation), location within level (e.g., school, neighborhood center, or agency), what to focus on within levels, intensity of services (e.g., day treatment, residential, time-limited therapy), whom to involve, what particular methods to use, and how to encourage generalization and maintenance. (See Exhibit 21.4.) Will services be preventative and if so, for all people or only certain individuals "at risk"? Familiarity with possible options provides a "menu" from which to choose; you will be less likely to overlook valuable options. Altering the environment may involve changing the behavior of significant others and making linkages with other service providers. Depression may be related to negative self-statements, and a procedure designed to alter what clients say to themselves (their cognitive ecology) may be helpful. Or depression may be related to an unhappy marriage and lack of a job. This suggests a different approach. Depression may be related to stressful circumstances such as raising the 2-year-old grandchild of a drug-addicted daughter in a crime-ridden neighborhood. This suggests yet another approach. (See also Exhibit 12.1.)

Flowcharts describing the implications of assessment for selection of plans may guide decision making by highlighting decision points, options, and criteria for reviewing them. These have been suggested for many years (e.g., see Exhibit 21.5). Decision trees or balance sheets may help you and your clients to weigh the likelihood of different outcomes and balance the risks and benefits. People differ in the risks they are willing to take, and a balance sheet allows inclusion of these preferences (Eddy, 1990). Plans usually involve a number of steps. It may be critical to success to clearly describe and order them. (See discussion of identifying intermediate steps in chapter 20.) Your preferred practice theory will influence how problems are framed and what plans are selected. The decisions made will influence the likelihood of success.

What System Level(s) to Focus On

System levels include: individual, family, neighborhood, community, organization, service system, and public policies and related legislation. Success may require work at several levels with many different people, including significant others and other professionals. Helping clients with problems such as a lack of paid employment may require planned changes at the community, city, state, country, or international level. Attention to both social and economic development is integral to social development perspectives (see chapter 27). A key question is: Are levels focused on likely to result in successful outcomes? Keeping track of discrepancies between what is needed and what can be done will provide a record that you can use to advocate for needed changes in service patterns and policies.

Intervention Roles: How Will You Intervene?

Helping clients often involves one or more of the following helper roles:

- *Broker*: Link clients with needed services. Example: Refer a client to a senior center.

- *Mediator*: Resolve disputes/conflicts. Example: Help community members resolve a conflict.

- *Enabler*: Help clients identify and make effective use of their knowledge and skills (offer support).

- *Teacher*: Provide information and teach new skills. Example: Help a youth acquire skills for making and keeping friends.

- *Advocate*: Argue, mediate, negotiate, alter contingencies on behalf of clients. Example: Accompany a client to a social service agency to help her obtain benefits. Help clients to learn how to advocate on their own behalf (see chapters 19 and 27).

- *Planner*: Create new resources, improve, or create new service programs, evaluate programs.

Carrying out one role may involve other roles. For example, helping clients find and use resources (a broker role) may require accompanying clients to an agency and speaking up in their behalf (advocacy), helping clients acquire skills in requesting services (teaching), and identifying and supporting the skills that clients already possess (enabling). Skill in discovering problem-related contingencies is valuable in all these roles (see chapters 7 and 12).

Broker and Mediator

Offering help may require improving links with, within, or among agencies; coordinating services; creating better outreach

EXHIBIT 21.4

Decisions and Options

What intervention level(s) to focus on
- Individual
- Family
- Group
- Agency
- Neighborhood
- Community
- Service system (e.g., policy legislation)

What to focus on
- Offer support
- Clarify problems and their causes
- Rearrange contingencies
- Provide concrete services
- Provide information
- Enhance skills
- Enhance support system
- Increase cooperation among different service providers
- Enhance support and communication channels
- Alter physical environment
- Redistribute resources via changes in policy and legislation

What helping role(s) to use
- Broker
- Mediator
- Advocate
- Enabler
- Teacher
- Planner

What to focus on at the individual level
- Advocacy skills
- Enhance skills in gaining access to needed material resources
- Attributions (e.g., views about self and/or others)
- Vocational skills
- Relationship skills
- Philosophical/existential dilemmas
- Recreational skills
- Self-management skills
- Emotional/affective patterns

What kind of skills are needed
- Vocational
- Resources acquisition
- Relationship
- Recreational
- Problem solving/critical thinking
- Self-management
- Emotional management

What relationship skills are needed
- Friendship
- Parenting
- Negotiation

- Assertive/advocacy
- Partnership
- Caregiving
- Self (relationship with)

What to focus on at the family level
- Communication styles
- Intergenerational conflicts
- Decision-making styles
- External resources
- Rules
- Shared activities
- Acculturation differences

What to focus on at the group level
- Communication skills
- Information advocacy skills
- Transparency of practices
- Social support
- Group process

What to focus on at the agency level
- Clarify goals
- Leadership style
- Culture/work climate
- Decision-making style norms
- Formal communication systems
- Informal communication system
- Program planning/development
- Obstacles to services (e.g., lack of bilingual staff)
- Links among service providers
- Transparency of practices and outcomes
- Physical environment

What to focus on at the neighborhood and community levels
- Help residents identify needs
- Help residents establish links with people in political power
- Establish neighborhood watch groups or block organizations
- Form political action groups
- Plan effective demonstrations
- Provide information about problems and their causes

What to focus on at the service system level
- Decrease overlap in services
- Increase resources
- Introduce new programs/policies
- Evaluate program effectiveness
- Assess needs
- Compare effects of different programs/policies
- Increase involvement of clients in policy decisions
- Enhance access to services, case advocacy
- Enhance smooth transitions among different services
- Press for change in policies and related legislation

EXHIBIT 21.5

Flowchart for Analyzing Performance Problems

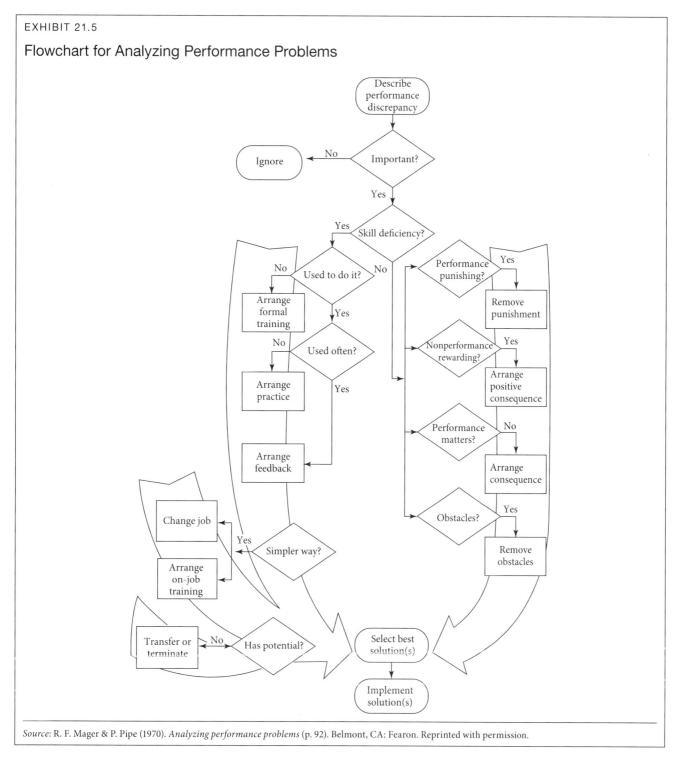

Source: R. F. Mager & P. Pipe (1970). *Analyzing performance problems* (p. 92). Belmont, CA: Fearon. Reprinted with permission.

programs; and designing new services. Often, many different services are needed to help a client (see Exhibit 21.6). You may have to refer clients to other sources for money, clothes, housing, or medical or legal services. A knowledge of practice and policy-related research findings and familiarity with available services will help you to accurately describe the match between what services are needed to attain hoped-for outcomes and what services are available. This will help you to make successful referrals. (See also discussion of purchasing services in chapter 27.) Gaining

needed help requires familiarity with both formal and informal resources and involving "indigenous helpers" such as significant others and neighbors. Valuable information includes familiarity with agency policies and operating procedures and information about barriers to service use. Follow up to make sure effective links have been made. Effective skills in bargaining and negotiating, making requests, and compromising when necessary will increase your success in obtaining resources for clients (see chapter 16).

EXHIBIT 21.6

Involvement of Multiple Service Agencies in Helping Clients

A custodian of a neighborhood tenement reported that one of the tenants spent nearly all her days crying, locked in her apartment. Upon investigation it was realized that...a Vietnam refugee with four children, aged 6 to 14, was the person reported about. This woman had lost her husband and youngest son in Vietnam. She had no relative or friend in this country and did not speak English. Her small apartment was completely bare except for two beds. The allotment she received from public assistance was not sufficient to buy furniture or clothing and no special allowance had been provided for these purposes. The situation was potentially dangerous—all the family possessed was warm weather clothing and winter was approaching.

The children, because of their home situation and inability to communicate, had problems in school. The fact that the family had been affluent in Vietnam compounded the difficulties that they were experiencing. The mother felt that she might be on the verge of a breakdown. Five major problem areas were isolated:

1. Financial—more money required for family's basic needs
2. Socialization—human contact needed particularly by the mother
3. Language—need by all family members to learn English
4. Health—children's teeth particularly in need of work
5. Housing –need for a larger apartment.

A staff worker monitored the provision of services and participation of the client. The following services have been provided to the family as of this date:

1. International Rescue Committee supplied $600 for furniture, $275 for winter clothing, and $80 for a sewing machine.
2. A neighbor agreed to help the mother shop and along with the worker provided some of the human contact that was needed.
3. The mother and children were enrolled in special English classes provided by the Board of Education and Immigration services.
4. Governeur Hospital gave all members of the family physical checkups and provided the dental work required by the children.
5. A local agency contracted to work with the family in finding more appropriate housing.

It is obvious that this woman could not be helped by merely providing emotional insight. Five or six organizations, besides the focal agency that took on her case, had to provide services. Some person had to see to it that all the needed services were arranged for, that they were actually provided, and that they were sufficient to help this woman provide for herself and her family. The role this type of worker plays is the case manager role.

Source: H. Weissman, I. Epstein, & A. Savage (1983). *Agency-based social work: Neglected aspects of clinical practice* (pp. 74–75). Philadelphia: Temple University Press. Reprinted with permission.

Advocate

Advocacy can be defined as "1. the act of directly representing or defending others. 2. in social work, championing the rights of individuals or communities through direct intervention or through *empowerment*...it is a basic obligation of the profession and its members" (Barker, 2003, p. 11). The Internet provides a way to mobilize advocacy efforts (e.g., Hick & McNutt, 2002). (See also related websites and Dartnell, 2006.) In case advocacy, you act on behalf of individuals. In cause advocacy, you help a group or community achieve a valued goal such as receiving more timely services from an agency or gaining access to mandated services. Social workers should always be case advocates. For example, you may accompany a client to an agency, telephone a worker who has denied a request, or contact an administrator. Advocacy may be needed when clients are refused benefits to which they are entitled or when services are provided in a

dehumanizing manner. Denial of civil or legal rights (e.g., discrimination based on ethnicity, race, age, or sexual orientation or gender) may require advocacy. Agency policies and procedures that impede the delivery of services may have to be changed.

Effective advocacy requires knowledge of clients' legal and civil rights, appeal processes, resources, and methods that may be used to attain valued outcomes. Knowledge and skills described in earlier chapters such as clearly describing outcomes will be needed. Contingency analysis skills will help you to identify resources and obstacles, including vested interests of involved others (see chapter 12). Confrontation may be necessary to advocate for clients. You may have to "blow the whistle" to make headway or lobby legislators. Advocating for clients often involves asking people to do something they would not do voluntarily and questioning the decisions and power of others. Be prepared for negative reactions. Emphasizing common goals, thinking the best about others, and empathizing with other points of view (intellectual empathy) will increase your success. Stay focused on your goal—to help clients. This will help you manage your emotions.

Brokering, advocating, and mediating require a familiarity with agency policies, regulations, and administrative structures and how different service systems are connected. Not understanding other approaches and being biased against them may hamper effective coordination of services; there may be little agreement about how to pursue goals because different criteria are used to select knowledge.

Enabler and Teacher

You may help clients make effective use of their own resources and help them to acquire valuable information and skills (see chapters 24 and 25).

Planner

Planning (e.g., deciding what to do, reviewing and creating options) is often a part of other helping roles and may be the key service focus, such as when you help agencies or community residents identify needs, set priorities, review current service programs, and plan new ones. Depending on your job responsibilities, you may be heavily or only slightly involved in program planning (e.g., offering suggestions about needed programs to agency administrators).

Another Way to Think About Service Roles

Being a broker, advocate, enabler, teacher, mediator, or planner may involve (1) talking to clients and significant others, (2) planning and carrying out tasks in real life, (3) practicing relevant behaviors, or (4) directly influencing behavior in real-life settings such as the home or school or state legislature (Kanfer & Phillips, 1969). Specific methods are selected within these roles such as writing letters to state legislators advocating for needed services. Each role has certain requirements for successful use, as well as advantages and disadvantages. Hundreds of different kinds of intervention methods are available that may use one or more of the roles described.

In *enactive* methods, clients carry out behaviors in real-life contexts (or those similar to them). In *symbolic* methods, clients imagine situations or talk about them (Bandura, 1986). Cognitive behavioral interventions make use of both enactive and symbolic methods. Enactive—compared to symbolic—methods provide realistic feedback about what can be accomplished and may encourage greater change in self-efficacy, which influences what we attempt and how long we persist in our efforts. (*Self-efficacy* refers to beliefs about whether we can carry out certain behaviors and their likely success in gaining valued outcomes.) If it is not possible to use enactive methods at first (perhaps because of anxiety), you could start with symbolic procedures in which events and reactions are imagined and then move on to enactive

methods. (Successful performance does not automatically result in increased confidence. Attributing success to external factors such as luck, rather than to personal competency, may discourage this.)

Talking to Clients

Helpers and clients talk to each other. Requirements include verbal facility and the use of "insights" and support gained in interviews to alter behavior, thoughts, or feelings in real-life contexts. Clients may form more helpful views of their problems, discover valuable strengths, and identify new options. Support alone may be of vital concern in stressful times. Expectancy effects and common factors such as empathy and warmth contribute to positive outcomes (see chapter 15). Thus, "talk" is a highly active process.

Using Assignments

Here clients carry out agreed-on tasks in real-life settings such as the home, school, or community. A range of behaviors can be addressed with agreed-on tasks, including those that are private (e.g., thoughts) and behaviors that occur in contexts unavailable to social workers. This role also depends on verbal exchanges, and thus relationship skills are also important here (see chapters 15 and 16). Clients have to remember to carry out tasks and be willing to do them and to share the results. Your support and positive outcomes that result from completing assignments will encourage continued participation. Select assignments that address clients' concerns and match their skill and comfort levels. Characteristics of assignments that contribute to success are illustrated in Exhibit 21.7. Initial tasks often involve collecting assessment data. Selecting feasible, relevant homework assignments is a skill that develops with practice. You may have to arrange cues to remind clients to act in new ways and provide incentives to support related behaviors. (See Tompkins, 2004.) Generalization and maintenance are not as problematic as in a verbal role, since agreed-on tasks are carried out in real life (see chapter 23). The likelihood of task completion may be increased by contact with clients between meetings to "troubleshoot" and collect data, for example, via e-mail. Assignments clients carry out are vital to success of some programs such as behavioral activation to decrease depression.

Practicing

In this role, behaviors of interest (such as offering positive feedback) are practiced in simulated environments. Efforts are made to "replicate" real-life conditions. A parent may practice new ways of praising her child during your meetings. Community members may practice effective ways of introducing issues on community boards. Exposure to feared situations is the key contributor to success in cognitive-behavioral programs designed

EXHIBIT 21.7

Checklist for Reviewing an Assignment

	Not at all	A little	Satisfactory	Ideal
1. It addresses outcome(s) of concern to clients.	0	1	2	3
2. It is clearly described.	0	1	2	3
3. Research shows that if completed, it will contribute to hoped-for outcome(s).	0	1	2	3
4. Clients understand the purpose.	0	1	2	3
5. Participants can accurately describe what is to be done, by whom, where, and when.	0	1	2	3
6. Clients have the skills needed to carry it out.	0	1	2	3
7. It focuses on positive behaviors.	0	1	2	3
8. Clients practice tasks before trying them out in real life.	0	1	2	3
9. Real-life opportunities are available to carry it out.	0	1	2	3
10. Needed cues are arranged.	0	1	2	3
11. Needed incentives are arranged.	0	1	2	3
12. Needed tools are provided.	0	1	2	3
13. Possible obstacles are identified and plans made to overcome them.	0	1	2	3
14. Intrusiveness is low.	0	1	2	3
15. It has a high probability of being correctly completed.	0	1	2	3

Note: This scale can be used in a variety of ways. You could determine the overall score for an assignment. Possible values range from 0 to 45. You could note the percentage of criteria satisfied. You could find the average score for a number of assignments.

to decrease anxiety and anger (Barlow, 2002). Practice is a step closer to real life than simply talking about events. Skills and comfort levels can be assessed more accurately than by simply talking and constructive feedback can be offered. New ways of acting can be practiced in a safe environment. Disadvantages include the possibility that behaviors may not represent what happens in real life. Because behaviors are practiced in an artificial setting (the office), arrangements must be made to encourage their use in real life such as homework assignments. (See prior sections.)

Influencing Behavior in Real-Life Contexts

In this role, you enter the natural environment and directly influence behavior. If a parent is not able to follow instructions to act in new ways with her children, you could cue the mother when she is home with her children to use different consequences, such as praise (e.g., see the classic study by Hawkins, Peterson, Schweid, & Bijou, 1966). You could accompany a client who has difficulty obtaining food stamps to the office and "prompt" effective responses. This role is useful when it is difficult for clients to change their behavior without on-the-spot guidance. Clients can see the effects of new ways of acting, and procedural errors are less likely because an expert trainer is present. The trainer's help should be faded out as clients acquire skills. (See literature on increasing skills and work opportunities of clients with developmental disabilities.) Disadvantages of this role include cost in time (visiting real-life settings), intrusiveness of the trainer, and need to fade out help to maintain gains under natural conditions.

Offering Support

As emphasized in chapter 13, offering support is an important aspect of all phases of work with clients. It provides the context in which other kinds of help are offered. Your support can reduce stress, maintain hope, and encourage clients to carry out helpful assignments. Lack of resources may leave you with little but support to offer. If clients value this, then your time is well spent. However, keep your eyes open for opportunities to change policies, procedures, and programs that leave you with so little to offer. Pursuing vague objectives may result in neglect

---

EXHIBIT 21.8

Support as a Poor Substitute for Needed Services

Joyce works in a community center offering services to poor families. She has been asked to work with a group of parents to help them with any problems they may have. I asked her what she was working on. Let's take a look at the discussion:

EG: How many times does the group meet?

ST: The group meets for 10 sessions.

EG: What are the group's goals?

ST: To get support. To get help for their concerns.

EG: What are you working on now?

ST: Really nothing specific. My goal is to support and help these parents increase their self-esteem. We let the mothers talk about whatever they want to talk about.

EG: Have they mentioned any problems that concern them?

ST: Yes, they want better relations with the school.

EG: What would be different if they had better relations with the school?

ST: I don't know.

EG: Did they give you any clues?

ST: They want to be treated with respect.

EG: What would be different if they were treated with respect?

ST: They would feel better about themselves and the school.

EG: What changes would help them feel better?

ST: The teachers would involve them in the decisions made about their children. They would ask for their opinions at meetings.

EG: Are they invited now?

ST: No.

EG: Do the teachers ever ask the parents for their opinions? Note: The interview progressed in this way with two additional specific changes identified by the parents that would help them "feel respected."

EG: Well, it seems that you do have some specific information about what these parents would like. Do they want to work toward these changes?

ST: I don't know. The group changes from week to week in who comes. I don't really know what they want to work on.

EG: Have they mentioned any other areas?

ST: No, they keep mentioning the school situation.

EG: Note: Is this method of working the best that can be done here? Are attentive listening and empathy enough? What do you think?

---

of effective intervention methods and consequent excessive reliance on support. Ask: "What are my client's goals?" Posing related well-formed questions and searching for related research findings may reveal that more than support is needed to help clients (see Exhibit 21.8).

Thinking Critically About Plans

Sources of error when deciding on plans that may result in choosing ineffective or harmful ones are shown in Exhibit 21.9. Many errors reflect a lack of critical thinking (see chapter 5). Perhaps you have not involved clients in selecting outcomes to focus on and so are trying to pursue outcomes of little or no interest to

them. Pursuing vague objectives is an obstacle because you and your clients are not sure about what you are trying to accomplish and thus have only vague guidelines to follow to discover what might be helpful by taking advantage of the steps in evidence-based practice. You are on a voyage with no clear destination. Overlooking client assets may result in selecting unnecessarily intrusive methods and wasting time. Incomplete assessment is a cause of many errors, for example, overlooking important environmental contingencies (see chapter 12). Lack of resources and time pressures may limit options. You may want to use evidence-informed methods but not be able to because of agency policy and procedures (see chapter 27). The *client uniformity myth*, the belief that plans can be used without regard for situational and individual differences, can be avoided by matching client and environmental characteristics and plans. Plans differ in the

EXHIBIT 21.9

Sources of Error in Deciding on a Plan

- Faulty problem framing (the problem is not understood).

- Incorrect estimates of plan's potential effectiveness due to reliance on weak criteria such as popularity or tradition.

- Overlooking cultural differences that influence preferences and success.

- Time pressures that require "shooting from the hip."

- Social pressures, for example, to conform to choices of other staff.

- Low tolerance for uncertainty/ambiguity.

- Overlooking clients' assets and sources of social support.

- Overlooking opportunities to rearrange the physical environment.

- A "one-size-fits-all" approach—offering the same plan to all clients, ignoring important individual characteristics and circumstances.

- Overlooking lack of needed resources.

- Underestimating the knowledge, time, and skill required to implement a plan successfully.

- Trying to achieve too many outcomes at one time.

- Not involving clients and significant others in selecting plans; ignoring client preferences.

extent to which they increase skills that are valuable in a range of settings and prevent future problems. They differ in the likelihood of immediate results, their complexity, and the amount of training required for competent use. You can use the checklist in Exhibit 21.10 to review your plans.

Clearly Describe Plans and the Reasons for Them

Review assessment data and suggested plans with clients including your rationale for suggesting them and discuss the relationship between what was discovered and plans proposed. Be sure to use clear language that clients understand. Clearly describe plans including intermediate steps. Otherwise, it will be difficult (if not impossible) to estimate their feasibility and the possibility of side effects or to implement them in a planned way. This kind of description is needed for informed consent (see chapter 3). The plan should include a clear description of:

- Hoped-for outcomes, intermediate steps, and a projected timetable for attaining them.

- Who will be involved and how (responsibility of each participant).

- What situations, prompts, and reinforcers will be used.

- What progress indicators will be used.

- Changes to be made depending on degree of progress and criteria used to introduce them.

Many plans require a series of steps. For example, changes in what people think may lay the groundwork for changing what they do. Helping clients to relabel problems as challenges and to accept more realistic expectations provides a framework for acting differently and for viewing these changes positively. A timetable for attaining subgoals provides timely feedback so that you and your clients can change approaches that are not working. Describe the relationship between each component of the plan and each goal so you can make sure you have a plan to meet each objective and protect clients against unrealistic expectations. Identify people responsible for carrying out each part of the plan and make sure they have the knowledge and skills needed and are motivated to use them. You may have to engage clients in learning new skills via practice in the office setting. (See discussion of social skills training in chapter 24.)

Review agreements about records to be kept and how progress will be evaluated to make sure expectations are clear. Ask your clients if they have any questions about the plans and reasons for them. Give them copies of agreed-on tasks so they can refer to them at home as needed. You can highlight important points as reminders. Exhibit 21.11 illustrates a program worksheet used in helping a client. The client wanted to learn to drive a car and then buy one (see item one). The second item concerned career choice. The third concerned both independence and weekend depression resulting from lack of pleasant events on weekends. The fourth addressed loneliness and shyness with women. Review and update plans as needed in accord with degree of progress. This is another way you can be accountable to clients.

Select Plans That Are Acceptable to Participants

A plan may not be feasible because clients and/or significant others do not like it. Agency staff may not like your recommendations for changes in programs. An adolescent who wants to meet more people may not want to join a group designed to achieve this outcome. If so, explore their reasons and, based on what you discover, seek other options. Children, their parents, as well as staff in a psychiatric ward, considered reinforcement of incompatible behavior more acceptable, appropriate, fair, and reasonable in handling child behavior problems, compared to time out or drug therapy (Kazdin, French, & Sherick, 1981). Procedures differ in how much discomfort they entail. What is comfortable varies from person to person. Describe plans in a way that compliments the beliefs and values of clients and significant

EXHIBIT 21.10

Checklist for Reviewing Plans

	Not at all	A Little	Satisfactory	Ideal
1. Assessment data support selection.	0	1	2	3
2. Objective pursued addresses problem-related circumstances.	0	1	2	3
3. Related research findings suggest that plans offer the greatest likelihood of success.[a]	0	1	2	3
4. Requisites can be provided.	0	1	2	3
5. Plans and the rationale for them are acceptable to participants.	0	1	2	3
6. Plans are clearly described, including intermediate steps.	0	1	2	3
7. Positive methods are used.	0	1	2	3
8. Plans allow for the incremental acquisition of skills as needed in accord with baseline levels.	0	1	2	3
9. Plans focus on the construction of repertoires.	0	1	2	3
10. Plans are efficient in cost, time, and effort and are not too intrusive.	0	1	2	3
11. Positive side effects are likely.	0	1	2	3
12. Negative side effects are unlikely.	0	1	2	3
13. Significant others are involved.	0	1	2	3
14. Cues and reinforcers for desired behaviors are arranged.	0	1	2	3
15. Cues and reinforcers for undesired behaviors are removed.	0	1	2	3
16. Plans encourage generalization and maintenance of valued behaviors.	0	1	2	3
17. Settings used maximize the likelihood of success.	0	1	2	3
18. Cultural differences are considered as needed.	0	1	2	3
19. Multiple services are well integrated.	0	1	2	3
20. Clear descriptions of plans are given to participants.	0	1	2	3
21. Plans meet legal regulations and ethical standards.	0	1	2	3
22. Clear, relevant progress indicators are agreed on.	0	1	2	3
23. The probability of success is high.				

Reviewing Plans That You Do Not Think Will Be Effective

Total score can range from 0 to 69. If this is low, or you rate the probability of success low (item 23), review the following questions:

Is there anything more you could do? _____Yes _____No

If no, is this because:

_____ I don't know how to offer effective methods.

_____ I know how but don't have the time.

_____ Needed resources are unavailable.

_____ Agency policies pose an obstacle.

_____ Client is unwilling.

_____ There is no research that provides guidelines about what to do.

_____ Other.

If yes, what could you do? (Describe):

_____

_____

_____

_____

[a] Questions to review when answering item 3:
• There is evidence that your plan will achieve outcomes focused on.
• There are empirically based principles that suggest that the plan will be effective with this client.
• There is evidence that this plan is likely to be more effective than other plans.

EXHIBIT 21.11

Program Worksheet: Robert Jones, June 28

Available Assets	Intermediate Steps
1. Passes written test for drivers license.	1. Pay tuition at auto school. Take at least one lesson.
2. Received catalogues from a school.	2. Discuss with instructors X and Y about next steps.
3. Spent last Sunday in Loop.	3. Plan and carry out activity for Saturday and Sunday in downtown Chicago (or Hyde Park).
4. Had coffee with Jean two times.	4. Ask Jean to lunch.

Program Notes

1. A great step forward toward eventual "independence."
2. Career choice.
3. Break the weekend "depression" also tied to "independence." '

Source: A. Schwartz & I. Goldiamond (1975). *Social casework: A behavioral approach* (p. 120). New York: Columbia University Press. Reprinted with permission.

others including cultural differences. For example, Mrs. Slater presented the suggestion to include Mrs. Ryan in meetings in a framework her clients valued; they were a family and families work together to resolve concerns. There is a rich literature you can draw on for ideas about how to involve clients as informed participants and to consider their values and preferences (e.g., Coulter & Collins, 2011; Edwards & Elwyn, 2001).

Select Plans That Are Effective, Efficient, and Well-Integrated

People use different criteria to decide when a practice or policy is effective, and a variety of hierarchies and levels of evidence have been suggested (see chapter 11). Differences of opinion about what a "good" study is may reflect different levels of education about what research methods are most likely to control for sources of bias that may result in misleading conclusions. When (if ever) is something "well-established"? What kind of research study should be considered good enough to make a definitive claim about the effectiveness of a practice or policy? We should consider many dimensions of "evidence," for example, transportability. Transportability refers to how easily research findings or other forms of evidence can be carried over into another situation. Whether related research findings apply to your client or setting must be carefully considered (see chapter 10). A program found to be effective in a research setting may not

be effective when used in real-life practice environments. Thus, it is important to distinguish between effectiveness and efficacy. Little may be known about the efficiency of certain methods in relation to cost and time. However, data are available in some areas regarding comparative costs and benefits.

A particular approach may not be helpful because of a low acceptance rate, high dropout rate, or expensive training required to offer the service at a high level of fidelity. Generalization may be compromised by a number of factors, including characteristics of the helper such as their training, the degree of supervision required, and contact variables such as how often service must occur. Research by O'Donohue, Fisher, and Plaud (1989) suggest that clients want their helpers to select methods based on past successful personal experience and research. As they note, personal experience is important "because even therapies that are in principle effective can become ineffective when incompetently delivered" (p. 406). Basing decisions solely on experience may result in incorrect estimates of effectiveness (see chapter 4). Although research about the effectiveness of certain methods in achieving certain outcomes is often unavailable, research is available in many areas indicating the greater success (or harm) of some methods compared to others.

A client or family may need a variety of services that require careful planning together with other service providers. Arranging and coordinating multiple services and overcoming barriers to use of services are integral to case management, as well as wraparound services for children and families using a team approach to service coordination (e.g., see Burns & Hoagwood, 2002; Pullman, Kerbs, Koroloff, Veach-White, Gaylor, & Sieler, 2006). Common ingredients include emotional and material support, provision of information, linking clients with needed services, advocacy for clients in gaining access to resources, encouraging positive support systems, and providing parenting support and instruction. Team approaches require skills in advocacy, negotiation, collaboration, networking, and resource development. Guiding principles in arranging systems of care suggested by Stroul and Freidman (1986) include the following:

1. Access to an array of needed services.

2. Individualized services.

3. Offering the least restrictive normative environment possible.

4. Families participate as equal decision-making partners.

5. Services are linked and integrated across agencies.

6. Case management ensures coordination of services.

7. Early identification and intervention is promoted.

8. Transition services to adulthood are available.

9. The rights of children with special needs is protected through advocacy.

10. Services are provided in a culturally responsive manner without discrimination based on race, religion, national origin, sex, or any other characteristic. (See also Friedman & Drews, 2005.)

Build on Client Strengths

Identifying client strengths you can build on, as well as other resources such as neighborhood and community resources, is a key part of assessment. The plans you and your clients develop should build on these assets. You may involve clients with the same interests in advocacy efforts designed to acquire more resources, taking advantage of their motivation, coping and problem-solving skills to help others and to alter discriminatory practices, programs, and policies. Only if parents work together as a group may changes in desired school practices take place such as creating an anti-bullying program or creating an after school day care program. (See chapter 27.)

Select Feasible Plans

How feasible are proposed plans? Can they be carried out in ways that maximize success, or is only a diluted version possible? Review personal and environmental resources and constraints to evaluate feasibility.

- Are needed material resources available?

- If relevant, can eligibility requirements be met?

- Are important contexts and services within them available (e.g., daycare)?

- Can significant others (e.g., parents, teachers) be consistent mediators?

- Do participants have the skills required to carry out the plans?

- Do significant others have access to effective reinforcers?

- Can significant others be created?

- Can needed resources be created?

- Do you have needed knowledge and skills?

Are those who will be responsible for offering services competent to do so? How do you know? Competence in applying a method does not necessarily reflect competence to teach others, for example, parents (McGimsey, Greene, & Lutzker, 1995). Consultation skills are required to teach others successfully such as providing a rationale for methods used, demonstrating the steps while describing them, arranging role plays of each step, providing verbal praise for efforts, accurately describing errors

and desired behaviors, and repeating the process of describing, modeling, and role playing as needed (see chapter 24). Can clients be their own managers of change? Which of their skills can be used to advantage? Do they have any physical conditions that limit the use of certain plans? You can use role playing to find out whether clients have needed skills. If skills are not available, you will have to help clients acquire them or choose other plans. What can be used as reinforcers? (See chapter 19.) Review possible intervention settings (e.g., home, school, work). Perhaps a group would be best.

The list of possible plans will usually be shortened when you and your clients consider the evidentiary status of different options, application problems such as lack of available resources, and client preferences including cultural differences (see also chapter 20). Current service patterns orchestrated by managed care policies may limit options. You may have to move from helping clients attain needed resources to helping them to bear up under the strain of not having them or involve clients with similar concerns in advocacy efforts to alter policies (see chapter 27). You may have to work together with other interested parties to create needed resources, perhaps using methods such as microlending and microinsurance. (See chapter 27.)

Consider Cultural Differences

Our unique culture influences our views about problems, outcomes, and how they can best be attained (Thyer, Wodarski, Meyer, & Harrison, 2010). These are important to consider in all helping phases. Characteristics of culturally sensitive services in health care for Puerto Rican families suggested by Schensul (1993) include the following:

1. A culturally and linguistically accurate assessment of the family and social context of the client focused on the identification of a family caregiver who will act as an advocate, and on the strengths and limitations of the family/household situation in oversight of care and home management.

2. Thorough and rapid diagnosis by experienced physicians or other diagnosticians who speak Spanish or have available professional translators.

3. Accurate, clearly presented, and understood information in the appropriate language about the condition, its cause, treatment, probable outcome, and effects on the family. This information should…be built on the cultural frame of reference of the family with regard to the health concerns and embedded in the context of family life.

4. Accurate information about how to obtain adequate specialized and follow-up care from health professionals familiar with the Puerto Rican experience in the United States and assistance in obtaining this care.

5. Comprehensive clinic, institutional, and social service care and follow-up.

6. Appropriate community-based and institutionalized long-term care and coordinated release to the community to families with the resources and information to manage the situation.

7. Clear and collaborative involvement of the family advocates in all aspects of service delivery including home management of the health problem. (Schensul, 1993, p. 24) (see also Lynch & Hansen, 2011).

Note that most of these are relevant to *all* clients. (See also NASW, 2001.)

Select the Least Restrictive Plan

Restrictiveness is a legal, ethical, and practical concern. It is a practical concern because the more that circumstances during intervention differ from those in real life, the more effort will be required to generalize and maintain gains in the natural environment (see chapter 23). Restrictiveness is an ethical and legal concern because the more intrusive a procedure is, the more it affects people's lives. Some state laws require demonstration that positive procedures were tried and failed before aversive methods such as punishment can be used. Procedures involving punishment are more intrusive than those that rely on positive reinforcement. They create negative emotional reactions and, unless combined with other procedures, do not encourage alternative desired reactions (see chapter 25).

Restraint, including the use of chemical restraint via medication, is intrusive, and there should be good reason for using this (e.g., see Agens, 2010). A report by the Inspector General's Office (Levinson, 2011) found that nearly 1.4 million of Medicare claims for atypical antipsychotic drugs such as Abilify, Seroquel, and Risperdal were for elderly nursing home residents diagnosed with off-label conditions and/or dementia. Such drugs were approved by the FDA for treatment of schizophrenia and bipolar disorder. They are not approved for treatment of agitation and other symptoms of dementia/Alzheimer's. Indeed, the FDA warned against such use—even issuing a public health advisory that risk of death increases between 1.6 and 1.7 times for elderly patients prescribed antipsychotic drugs to treat agitation and other symptoms of dementia. Excessive intrusiveness includes use of the wrong drug, excessive dosage, excessive chronicity of drug use, and use with no clear benefit.

Intrusiveness may involve irreversibility of effects, the extent to which program effects can be voluntarily resisted, or duration of change efforts. Plans that remove people from real-life environments (institutionalizing them or placing them in foster care) are more intrusive than those that do not. It is less intrusive to work with a child and his parents in the home than to move him to a group home and the latter is less intrusive than

placing him in an institution. Avoid offering incentives that undermine natural reinforcing systems that maintain valuable repertoires. Encourage clients and significant others to consider the long-term consequences of not using an intrusive method in the short term; for example, not doing so may result in outcomes that require the ongoing institutionalization of an individual. Axelrod and his colleagues (1993) suggest the following when considering a plan's restrictiveness:

- The urgency with which the behavior must be changed.

- The speed with which a plan works.

- The likely side effects of the method estimated based on a person's past history and the history of the procedure with other people.

- The amount of embarrassment, deprivation, or discomfort the procedure causes.

- The likelihood that the procedure can be applied correctly in normalized environments.

- The social acceptability of the procedure.

- The potential for harm to the individual and program implementers when applying the procedure.

- The degree to which the method reduces educational social, and vocational opportunities (opportunity costs).

Axelrod and his colleagues argue that

in the case of dangerous behaviors, people are entitled to the least restrictive effective treatment from the outset. People should not be exposed to a hierarchy of treatments that are likely to be ineffective when there are treatments available that are likely to be effective. A hierarchical decision-making model stating that a number of "nonrestrictive" procedures be used first fails to hit the target, because it implies that there is nothing wrong with several failures before an effective procedure is identified. This does not make sense in cases of serious self-abuse and aggression. There is an urgency to eliminating some problems, therefore, finding effective procedure from the outset is crucial. (1993, pp. 189–190)

Select Plans Likely to Have Positive Side Effects and Avoid Negative Side Effects

What positive side effects are likely? Are negative side effects likely? A positive change in some behaviors may lead to both positive and negative changes in other behaviors. These are referred to as collateral effects. Encouraging assertive behavior of staff may result in punishing consequences at work from supervisors and administrators. (See chapter 16.) Consider both short- and long-term potential side effects. A decrease in an annoying behavior (such as bedwetting) usually increases positive reactions on the part of significant others such as parents. Helping parents to acquire more positive parenting skills for one child may generalize to other children.

Rely on Positive Methods

Use positive methods (e.g., positive reinforcement and prompting) when possible (see chapter 22). Usually, the most effective way to decrease undesirable behaviors is to increase desired alternatives. Punishing behavior does not necessarily increase any other particular behavior. Other disadvantages include modeling aggressive behavior, creating anger and anxiety, and avoiding the "punisher," for example, socializing agents such as teachers or parents (see also chapter 25).

Avoid Harmful Plans, Programs, and Policies

Professionals often assume that they must do something. Other reasons professionals may use ineffective or harmful methods include: (1) relying on anecdotal experience, (2) overreliance on surrogate outcomes (e.g., Gøtzsche, Liberati, Torri, & Rossetti, 1996), (3) ritual and mystique, (4) no one raises questions, (5) client's expectations, and (6) enchantment with a pathological model that is incorrect (Doust & Del Mar, 2004). The ethical obligation to do no harm requires balancing the risks and

benefits of doing something against the risks and benefits of doing nothing or watchful waiting (active monitoring) (e.g., see Harris, 2004; Cecile & Born, 2009). Offering ineffective methods may increase client demoralization or raise false hopes that change will be easy. Improving students' school performance, for example, may require restructuring the entire school system, with heavy involvement from parents and other local residents (e.g., Sailor, Dunlap, Sugai, & Horner 2009). What is the number needed to harm (NNH)? That is, how many people would have to receive a service for one to be harmed? Just as we can estimate the number of individuals who would have to receive an intervention for one to be helped (number needed to treat), we can estimate the number of individuals who would have to receive an intervention for one to be harmed. (See instructions for calculation on Bandolier website.)

Making a Final Decision

As Gray (2001a) suggests, "There is usually a dilemma associated with every clinical decision" (p. 365). Candidly confronting this fact emphasizes the complexity of making decisions. On what system level(s) will you work? (See Exhibit 21.12.) Consider the balance between potential benefits and harm in relation to costs. (Such analysis also should be carried out by administrators when purchasing services, as discussed in chapter 27.) Be sure to consider what Woods and Cook (1999) refer to as "local rationality"—all those factors that affect decisions in a particular

---

EXHIBIT 21.12

Comparative Model of Schoolwide Versus Family Systems Application of Positive Behavior Support in a Sample Family Support Agency

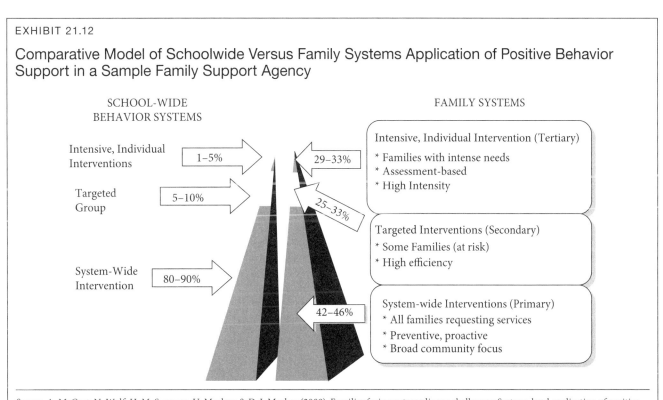

Source: A. McCart, N. Wolf, H. M. Sweeney, U. Markey, & D. J. Markey (2009). Families facing extraordinary challenges: Systems-level application of positive behavior support. In W. Sailor, G. Dunlap, G. Sugai, & R. Horner (Eds.), *Handbook of Positive Behavior Support* (p. 267). New York: Springer. Reprinted with permission.

context. They suggest that competing goals in this context may include:

- Resolving conflicts

- Anticipating hazards

- Accommodating variations and change

- Coping with suspicion

- Working around obstacles

- Closing gaps between plans and real situations

- Detecting and recovering from miscommunications and misassessments (p. 148)

When possible, offer clients the choice of efficient programs that have a track record of success (see later discussion of ethical concerns). Arrange environments that enhance functional skills related to hoped-for outcomes—skills of value to clients in real-life settings (Favell & McGimsey, 1993). Avoid complex methods when simpler, less costly ones (in time, effort, or money) will be effective. Offering permission may be all that is required. For example, a client's reluctance to accept needed financial assistance may be overcome by pointing out that this is a right, not a handout. Worries about being "abnormal" because of some behavior, thought, or feeling can be dampened by normalizing behaviors, drawing on related research concerning prevalence rates of certain behaviors, thoughts, feelings, or circumstances. A socially anxious client may not realize that most people are shy in some situations and that most people sometimes worry about being rejected. On the other hand, a label that accurately reflects the cause of complaints can be reassuring and may point to remedy.

Estimate the likely success of recommended plans in helping clients to attain outcomes they value (10%, 90%) based on related research (see Exhibit 21.13). What is the number needed to treat (NNT); how many people would have to receive a service for one to be helped? If this is low, is another plan more likely to succeed? Be sure to be attentive to how choices are framed in reviewing risks and benefits (see related discussion in chapter 20). Clients may choose to ignore uncertainties. They may view options in either/or terms. Take advantage of decision aids to help clients to make informed choices (e.g., O'Connor, Wennberg, Legare, Llewellyn-Thomas, Moulton, Sepucha, et al., 2007; http://decisionaid.ohri.ca).

Implementing Plans and Programs and Trying Again

The best-laid plans may go awry, and you may have to try again. Obstacles may continue to get in the way, or new ones may arise. Significant others or clients may not complete agreed-on tasks; agencies may not offer services; emergencies may occur.

EXHIBIT 21.13

Estimated Impact of Plans

+3	Maximal:	Clients receive services at levels that maximize the likelihood of success with minimal or no negative side effects.
+2	Moderate:	Partially addresses concerns.
+1	Minimal:	Band-Aid services offered on a crisis basis only. More intensive or varied services are needed to help clients attain outcomes they value.
0	No Effect:	No change.
−1	Slight Harm:	Minimal negative effects.
−2	Moderate Harm:	Moderate harmful effects.
−3	Significant Harm:	For example, problems become worse because clients are referred to an agency that uses ineffective methods.

Initial plans are a best guess as to what will work. Often they will have to be altered. Success in earlier stages influences success in later ones. The more carefully you consider procedural requirements, clients' preferences (including cultural differences) and resources, and obstacles, the more likely it is that plans will succeed and policies will achieve what advocates hoped-for. Clients will not carry out agreements that they do not want to complete, do not know how to complete, or cannot complete because they are too intrusive.

You may have to arrange more prompts and incentives for desired behaviors, remove competing contingencies, and provide additional opportunities to use valued skills or simplify procedures. You may have to involve other change agents or settings. Perhaps you have not involved all significant others (e.g., supervisors, staff on all shifts who work with residents) or arranged regular reviews of programs. If a teacher refuses to participate, parents could offer backup reinforcers at home. Perhaps you are not focusing on outcomes of most concern to clients or have overlooked costs of change. (See chapter 14.) Ongoing evaluation of progress will help you and your clients to make "timely" decisions. If plans succeed, they can be continued or next steps implemented. If progress is nil or limited or negative effects are found, explore related reasons (see chapter 22). Take advantage of technological advances such a mobile phones to encourage helpful changes (L'Abate & Kaiser, 2011).

Mutual Responsibilities

The responsibilities of clients and significant others include participating in agreed-on plans and reporting any difficulties. If possible, clients should also collect information about progress.

Each client's responsibilities should be tailored to his or her unique characteristics and circumstances as needed, including cultural differences and available resources. Your responsibilities are to:

- Select plans that are likely to help clients attain outcomes they value.

- Ensure that clients have the knowledge and skills required to carry out plans.

- Arrange needed prompts and incentives.

- Arrange opportunities for desired behaviors to occur.

- Offer service methods in a way that maximizes the likelihood of success.

- Identify and remove obstacles when possible.

- Arrange ongoing feedback about progress.

- Arrange for the generalization and maintenance of gains.

- Modify plans as necessary (try again).

If you are a case manager and other professionals are providing services, they will be responsible for these tasks. However, as a case manager, you should review methods used and progress made (see discussion of purchasing services in chapter 27). Services offered by different sources may not be well integrated . There may be vital gaps.

Increasing the Likelihood of Success

Clients are more likely to participate in constructive ways if they have been involved in decision making, plans are acceptable to them, plans focus on outcomes they value, and if they understand and agree with the rationale for plans. (Guidelines for encouraging participation are given in chapter 14.) Progress may be hampered by a lack of match in problem-solving approaches, by choosing tasks that are too difficult, by not describing the relevance of tasks to achieving valued outcomes, and/or by process factors such as clashing interaction styles or excessive negativity on your part (see chapter 15). David Burns asks clients to complete a questionnaire in which clients indicate whether they are willing to complete homework assignments, as well as brief weekly questionnaires regarding process variables (e.g., helper empathy and warmth). This provides valuable feedback you can use to review how you can be more helpful and sensitive to client concerns. (See also Duncan et al., 2003; Owen & Imel, 2010.)

Arrange Prompts and Opportunities to Use Valued Skills

Prompts (reminders) may be needed to encourage new behaviors. For instance, Ms. Landis suggested that Julie wear a special bracelet or ring to remind her to redirect her attention from worrisome thoughts to constructive tasks or thoughts. Timing devices, smartphones, and recording forms can be used as prompts. Email prompts may be used. Clearly describing tasks increases the likelihood of successful completion. Collecting information by phone or e-mail may remind clients to complete helpful assignments. Such contacts also provide an opportunity to support clients for their efforts and to catch problems at an early point. Be sure to arrange access to situations in which valued skills can be put to good use. For example, you may help a client who wishes to make more friends to select promising situations in which to initiate conversations. Desired behaviors will not occur if there are no opportunities to use them.

Arrange Supporting Contingencies

Special contingencies may be required to involve clients. (See Exhibit 7.4.) Reinforcers should be individually selected in accord with incentives that are meaningful to each participant. Reinforcers are relative: what is reinforcing to some people is not to others. A promise to work on a problem of concern in another setting, such as school, may be made contingent on progress in altering behavior at home. Try to minimize negative consequences associated with participation. You may have to enhance clients' anxiety-management skills or select assignments that are less stress provoking. Lack of participation may be related to negative reactions from significant others. Consider the effects of plans on significant others, as well as clients. If both clients and significant others value goals pursued, believe that agreed-on plans will work, have the skills and comfort level required to complete tasks, have access to opportunities to use skills, as well as prompts and incentives to do so, agreed-on tasks are more likely to be completed. They are more likely to be completed if environmental stressors are minimized (e.g., worries about money, child care, medical care). If clients do not participate, explore possible reasons why (see chapter 11).

Pay Attention to the Integrity of Plans

Research may offer guidelines for maximizing the likelihood of positive outcomes. See, for example, the modular approach developed by Bruce Chorpita and his colleagues. Use of self-help manuals may increase success. If a plan is not implemented correctly, it is not surprising if little or no progress occurs. If clients keep records, review them to see what they did and what resulted. Ineffective implementation is a major cause of failure. Case records may offer information about the fidelity of methods used and progress made. Reviewing what was done when there is little or no progress may reveal what went wrong.

Track Progress

Tracking progress allows you and yosur clients to make timely changes and also provides motivating feedback. Clients are more likely to collect information about progress if they understand its value; have the required knowledge, skills, and tools to do so; and use unintrusive methods. Be sure to (1) explain the purpose of evaluating progress, (2) select progress indicators that are meaningful to clients, (3) provide needed skills and tools, (4) encourage clients to report any difficulties, and 5) review data collected regularly. If clients do not keep agreed-on records, it may be because you did not explain their purpose, did not choose an easy recording method, and/or do not review records kept.

What About Practice Guidelines and Treatment Manuals?

Practice guidelines and manuals are designed to provide empirically based standardized methods to help practitioners to use particular programs with high fidelity. Such guidelines are available for a wide range of concerns. Use of such manuals does improve the consistency with which a method is offered. Should you use them? One factor to consider is how closely they match your client's characteristics and circumstances. (See Step 4 in the process of EBP in chapter 10.) To what degree can a guideline or manual be applied with no modification called for by a client's unique circumstances and characteristics including cultural differences? Many concerns have been raised regarding "empirically supported" (or "validated") treatments (e.g., Strupp & Anderson, 1997). Controversy surrounding the use of manuals is suggested by a survey of psychotherapists by Addis and Krasnow (2000). Norcross (2002) argues that "lists of empirically supported treatments and practice guidelines give short shrift—some would say lip service—to the person of the therapist, the individual [client's] characteristics, and their emergent relationship. Current attempts are thus seriously incomplete and potentially misleading, both on clinical and empirical grounds" (p. 6).

Lambert and Barley (2002) suggest that manuals and "empirically supported interventions may overemphasize technical procedures and adherence to specific treatment guidelines and deemphasize the necessity to develop and sustain an effective therapeutic relationship" (p. 26). Wampold (2001, p. 200) argues that "a preponderance of evidence indicates that there are large therapist effects...and that the effects greatly exceed treatment effects." Even in carefully designed efforts to completely control what was presented to clients through manualized presentations, there was a therapist impact on outcome. Most manuals are organized around a DSM diagnosis. Many clients have a number of different kinds of concerns. Individual differences are ignored by viewing people through the lens of a label, overlooking unique important variations among those labeled. (See discussion of psychiatric labels in chapter 12.) Another concern is the criteria used to claim an intervention as "well-established." The taskforce of the American Psychological Association on psychological interventions (1995) suggests that if two well-designed randomized controlled trials show that a particular method is effective, it is "well-established." This is one example of many inflated claims in the professional literature (see also Gorman, 1998; Gorman & Huber, 2009). The common elements approach suggested by Chorpita and his colleagues (2007) is an alternative to use of manuals (see Exhibit 21.3).

Ethical Issues in Selecting Plans

Ethical concerns when selecting practices, programs, and policies include the following:

1. Clients are fully informed about the risks and benefits of recommended methods, as well as the risks and benefits of alternatives, include doing nothing (e.g., watchful waiting).

2. Research suggests that agreed-on plans will result in valued outcomes.

3. Plans selected are acceptable to clients.

4. Plans do not harm clients or significant others.

5. Plans increase knowledge and skills that will help clients enhance the current and future quality of their lives.

6. Plans are the least restrictive possible; for example, they occur in real-life contexts.

7. You and your clients can implement plans in a way that maximizes the likelihood of success.

Empowering interventions include action-oriented, community-based programs in which people learn how to help themselves, for example, to form coalitions and self-help groups to pursue program, policy, and legislative changes (Minkler & Wallerstein, 2008).

Allocating Scarce Resources

You may not have the resources needed to help your clients. They may be (and typically are) scarce. How will you allocate scarce resources, including your time, skills, and knowledge? What criteria will you use? Burt Gummer (1997) and Russell Hardin (1990), suggest that the allocation of scarce resources is a major ethical problem, about which the NASW Code of Ethics has had little to say. Do staff in your agency discuss this challenging problem? If so, have they arrived at criteria for distributing resources or, is this left to chance and the discretion of each staff member? If so, is this the best way to operate? (See discussion of purchasing services in chapter 27). If you constructed a pie chart of all services used by staff in your agency, including services contracted out to other agencies, what percentage would fall into the following categories?

1. Services found through critical tests to do more good than harm.

2. Services that have not been tested.

3. Services that have been critically tested and found to do more harm than good.

4. Services of unknown effectiveness but which are being tested in a rigorous design (Gray, 2001a).

What if no agencies in your area offer methods found to be effective in helping a client achieve certain outcomes such as more positive parenting skills? Should you just refer clients to such agencies anyway? What are ethical implications here? One option is to work together with other staff to advocate for effective services.

Involving Clients as Informed Participants

Informed consent is an ethical requirement of professional practice. Honoring this entails informing clients about the track record of success of different methods in achieving outcomes clients value and any associated harms and considering clients' preferences. Procedures recommended, as well as alternative options, should be clearly described to clients and significant others, including their risks and benefits, and decisions about continuing or ending programs should be based on clear outcome criteria. For example, are clients informed about the possibility of memory loss as a result of electroconvulsive therapy for depression (Rose, Fleischman, Wykes, Leese & Bindman, 2003). Refer clients to valuable web sites related to hoped-for-outcomes.

Clients are sometimes said to be "free to participate or not" when in fact if they do not, they may suffer negative consequences such as removal of their children by child protection staff. Fully informing clients requires a candid discussion of any coercive contingencies. Your clients may be on prescribed medications of various kinds. Neuroleptic medication is often prescribed for people labeled as mentally ill. Clients should be informed about the potential negative side effects of medications, such as irreversible neurological damage (see http://www.criticalthinkrx. org; http://www.PharmedOut.org).

Questionable Criteria for Selecting Plans

Examples of questionable criteria for selecting plans include personal preferences (unsupported by empirical research) and what is available. (See chapter 4 for further discussion.) Consider a social worker using narrative therapy with a 7-year-old boy diagnosed as having ADHD (attention deficit hyperactivity disorder) because of misbehaviors at school. She said she chose this because she believes it is helpful. She had not observed this child in his classroom to discover related environmental circumstances such as failure by the teacher to appropriately sequence curriculum content and to reinforce desired behaviors. She had not informed his parents about other options and their track record of success. How, then, could they give informed consent?

What should you do if you cannot offer methods that are most effective and that clients would select if given a choice? Is this a sound and ethical reason to withhold information from them? Not according to your code of ethics. If you were making an important medical decision, wouldn't you like to know about the track record of different methods even when, or perhaps especially when, your physician offers only an option that is unlikely to be effective and that may harm you in the process? Shouldn't we inform clients as we ourselves would like to be informed? Criteria on which social workers base decisions about their clients differ from those they would like their physicians to rely on when making recommendations or from the criteria they ideally would like to use (Gambrill & Gibbs, 2002). They rely on questionable criteria such as intuition and their experience with a few cases in making decisions about clients. In making decisions about their own health, they wanted physicians they consulted to rely on the results of randomized controlled trials and demonstrated track record of success.

Selection of methods may be based on what is available (what resources an agency has to offer) rather than what is needed to help clients achieve hoped-for outcomes. Reasons include economic (the agency will lose money if clients are referred elsewhere) and lack of knowledge about effective methods and who offers them. Resources influence rates of hospitalization and institutionalization. For example, Schwartz (1989) found that the juvenile confinement rate was related to the number of beds available. Basing decisions on such criteria is ethically questionable when relying on other criteria would offer clients a better chance of attaining outcomes they value and avoiding or minimizing negative ones. Because helpers and clients may use different criteria to select plans, O'Donahue and his colleagues (1989) recommend that helpers tell clients what criteria they are using (e.g., personal preference, testimonials, results of experimental studies).

Prevention

There has been increased focus on prevention (e.g., see Lipka & Siegel, 2010; Lösel & Beelmann, 2003; Stagner & Lansing, 2009). *Primary prevention* refers to preventing problems from arising in the first place. For example, all children are required to get a polio vaccination. There is an extensive literature on home-based programs (see http://www.childwelfare.gov). Approaches to preventing child maltreatment suggested by Stagner and Lansing

(2009) include education (distributing educational materials to families), support groups that provide peer support facilitated by trained professionals, visitation programs, and broad public policies that address risk factors such as inequality in income and provide access to services and financial support, individual and family therapy. Programs designed to decrease entry of youth into the criminal justice system have shown success (see The Future of Children, http://www.princeton.edu/futureofchildren; Coalition for Evidence-based Policy). One focus is on helping youth to acquire valuable skills. School-based programs have shown success (e.g., Wilson & Lipsey, 2005). "School violence programs were generally effective at reducing the more common types of aggressive behavior seen in schools, including fighting, name-calling, intimidation, and other negative interpersonal behaviors, especially among higher risk students." The authors suggest that it is unknown whether the types of programs they reviewed (or any others) "would be effective in preventing the rare but serious incidents of school violence perpetrated by very disturbed youth" (p. 2).

Prevention programs, if successful, may have a cascade effect in terms of fostering additional positive consequences and avoiding negative ones such as entry into the criminal justice system. (For further description of early childhood family and community intervention, for example, see Sailor et al., 2009. See also http://preventionaction.org; http://www.colorado.edu/cspv/blueprints.) Cost-benefit analyses of programs supporting families with newborns and toddlers show that money is saved in the long run, in other governmental health care and social costs.

Secondary prevention efforts focus on identifying those at risk of a problem (e.g., child abuse, AIDS, behavior labeled delinquent), so special efforts can be devoted to this at risk population to prevent problems. Garvin, Leber, and Kalter (1991) provided an 8-week intervention program, including group discussions, activities, and role playing, for fourth- and fifth-graders of divorced parents (n = 53). Goals were to:

- Normalize common experiences.

- Clarify divorce-related issues and terms.

- Provide a supportive forum in which children could experience and rework potentially stressful aspects of postdivorce life.

- Develop coping strategies for dealing with difficult feelings and situations.

- Involve parents in the concerns of their children.

Children identified as at risk for adjustment problems (their scores suggested a clinical depression) showed especially significant gains.

Tertiary prevention refers to providing services after problems have occurred, for example, preventing them from becoming worse. Offering clients skills that can be used in a range of situations may prevent future problems. Preventative programs for children and adolescents may involve intervention at a number of levels including individual, family, school, and community (e.g., Jensen & Fraser, 2011). A public health model is preventative in thrust as illustrated by community programs designed to promote health, for example, safe-sex behaviors. A review by Merzel and D'Afflitti (2003) of research on community-based health promotion suggest limited effects.

Summary

A sound assessment will help you and your clients select effective plans or to discover that no promising options are available. The steps in choosing plans include posing well-formed questions regarding information needs, searching efficiently and effectively for related research, critically appraising what you find, drawing on your practice expertise to integrate diverse sources of information including client preferences and values and application obstacles, reviewing options, selecting a plan that is acceptable to involved parties, trying it out, and evaluating the results. You and your clients must decide whom to involve, what they will do, and what settings to use. You may have to arrange prompts and incentives to encourage valued behaviors. Mutual responsibilities should be clearly described. Success may require use of multiple helping roles at a variety of system levels (e.g., individual, community, service system, policy). You may have to broker, mediate, advocate, teach, and enable and, to do so, you may talk to clients, agree on tasks to be carried out in real-life settings, practice skills in role plays, and/or directly intervene in the natural environment. You will often have to work with, within, and among agencies and coordinate services provided by a number of agencies. As in other phases, your support and encouragement are vital helping components.

Criteria for evaluating plans include feasibility, probable effectiveness, efficiency, intrusiveness, and the likelihood of positive and negative side effects. The plan's acceptability to clients and significant others and the likelihood of generalization and durability of positive outcomes are important to consider. Compromises must often be made among what would be ideal, what is feasible, and what is acceptable to participants. Being informed about the relative effectiveness of different practices and policies as suggested by related research and the reasons they cannot be offered, such as lack of resources, will help you and your clients to make sound decisions and to avoid unfairly blaming yourself or your clients for limited options and success. This information should be drawn on to direct advocacy efforts to increase needed resources. Ongoing tracking of progress allows timely changes as needed. Clear descriptions of what was done and what happened will help you to discover obstacles and decide on next steps. Anticipating problems will make setbacks less likely. However, unanticipated obstacles often arise, and creativity, knowledge, and flexibility will be valuable in addressing them.

Reviewing Your Competencies

Reviewing Content Knowledge

1. You can pose well-structured questions regarding selection of practices, programs, and policies.

2. You can identify helpful databases for discovering practice- and policy-related research.

3. You can accurately appraise the evidentiary status of different kinds of research related to effectiveness and prevention questions.

4. You can accurately describe potential obstacles to applying research findings to particular clients in specific settings.

5. Given examples of desired outcomes for particular clients, you can accurately estimate gaps between your current knowledge and research findings available.

6. Describe criteria that should be considered when selecting plans.

7. Describe different intervention roles and the requisites for each.

8. Describe the advantages of involving significant others.

9. Distinguish between enactive and vicarious methods and discuss their relative effectiveness.

10. Describe steps you can take to increase the likelihood that clients complete agreed-on tasks.

11. Given examples of application problems, you can describe possible options for overcoming them.

12. Describe your responsibilities in implementing plans.

13. Describe clients' responsibilities in carrying out plans.

14. Identify characteristics of successful assignments.

15. Identify correct and incorrect use of specific practice methods used in your agency, based on videotaped or written descriptions.

16. Accurately critique the clarity and potential effectiveness of proposed plans drawing on related research findings and unique client characteristics and circumstances.

17. Identify ethical issues related to selecting and implementing plans.

18. Identify agency and public policies and related legislation that affect client options.

Reviewing What You Do

1. You focus on outcomes of concern to clients and significant others.

2. You pose well-formed questions related to decisions that must be made and search effectively and efficiently for related research findings.

3. You accurately appraise the quality of research studies you find.

4. You accurately estimate the relevance of what you find for particular clients.

5. You effectively integrate data from diverse sources.

6. You involve clients as informed participants in selecting plans and consider their values and preferences.

7. You select services that are acceptable to clients and are most likely to help clients attain hoped-for outcomes.

8. Plans selected are closely linked to assessment data.

9. Services involve minimal use of artificial procedures and are minimally intrusive.

10. Plans selected build on client assets and community resources.

11. Plans are tailored to individual characteristics and circumstances of clients and significant others (including cultural differences) as needed to maximize success.

12. You clearly describe plans in writing.

13. You give clients written descriptions of plans.

14. You take advantage of opportunities to rearrange the physical environment in useful ways.

15. Plans include description of clear intermediate steps.

16. You describe the rationale for recommended methods to clients, and check to see if they understand what you have said and agree with your rationale.

17. You seek clients' agreement to participate.

18. You involve significant others in plans.

19. You arrange collateral services as needed and effectively coordinate them.

20. You keep your commitments to clients and to staff.

21. You arrange prompts and incentives as necessary.

22. You implement plans with a high degree of fidelity.

23. Plans consider cultural differences in values and norms.

24. You anticipate and avoid obstacles when possible.

25. Assignments agreed on are relevant, feasible, and clearly described; research suggests that they will help clients to attain hoped-for outcomes.

26. You refer clients to programs that use effective methods and that carefully track progress.

27. You can teach another person how to pose well-structured questions related to information needs.

Reviewing Results

1. Valued outcomes are achieved.

2. Clients feel better when they leave your office than when they came in.

3. Referrals are effective; clients use and benefit from services provided.

4. Agreed-on tasks are completed.

5. Completion of assignments results in hoped-for outcomes as judged by both self-report and by objective data (e.g., observation in real life).

6. Probable success of plans is accurately predicted.

22

Evaluating Outcomes as Integral to Problem Solving

OVERVIEW   Guidelines for evaluating practices and policies are suggested in this chapter, as well as sources of error that result in incorrect estimates of outcome and incorrect assumptions about the contribution of services to outcome. Questions that arise and options for answering them are described, as well as steps to take when plans are successful and steps to take when they are not. Practical and ethical advantages of ongoing evaluation of outcomes are highlighted, including discovering how to enhance quality of services.

YOU WILL LEARN ABOUT

- The value of timely feedback
- Questions and decisions
- Options
- Practical and ethical advantages of sound evaluation
- Reasons given against careful evaluation
- Sources of error in making judgments about progress and related causes
- The value of visual feedback
- A closer look at options for reviewing progress
- Single-case designs
- Exploring whether intervention was responsible for outcomes
- Seeking answers to other questions
- Next steps when plans are successful
- When there is no progress
- What if problems get worse?
- Program and policy evaluation
- Obstacles to evaluation
- Helpful tools
- Evaluating your progress

The Value of Timely Feedback

Evaluating outcomes is essential for informed decision making. Policies, programs, and plans for individuals are hypotheses (guesses) to be tested against reality and corrected in the light of feedback. Evaluation methods selected reflect one's theory about problems and outcomes (e.g., see Birckmayer & Weiss, 2000). Creators of service programs have beliefs about problems they address including the problem, causes, and what methods may result in hoped-for outcomes. There is a marked lack of data regarding satisfaction with service on the part of some groups including children (e.g., Tilbury, Osmond, & Crawford, 2010). Policies directly affect our lives and thus are vital to evaluate (Oxman, Bjorndal, Beccara-Posada, Gibson, Angel, Block, et al., 2010).

Hoped-for outcomes may concern changes in behavior, status, overall functioning, attitudes, feelings, and/or environmental circumstances. Empowerment evaluation emphasizes expanding clients' options and influence (Fetterman & Wandersman, 2007); clients may acquire job skills, increase their income, acquire child care, obtain stable housing, and learn how to access services on their own. Housing may change from a crisis situation (being homeless) to a stable safe location. Relying on inaccurate measures or "off the cuff estimates" may result in unwise decisions, such as referring clients to agencies that use ineffective methods or continuing policies and programs that harm rather than help clients. Only if we discover whether there is a need for improvement can we change interventions in a timely manner. Anthony Flew (1985) contends that the sincerity of our interest in helping clients is reflected in the efforts we make to find out whether we do help them. Compassion for the troubles of others requires finding out if we did help. All but clients may benefit from sloppy evaluation; programs may continue to be funded because the evaluations prepared do not threaten the ongoing flow and growth of agency turf.

Questions and Decisions

Evaluation concerns discovering the outcomes of practices, programs, and policies. Do they help, harm, or make no difference? Consider the example in Exhibit 22.1. Evaluation research often starts with a policy question (e.g., what are policy issues, how can we improve programs, what is their impact (compared with what), how cost-effective is the program, and what resources are needed to implement it effectively?). Examples of valued outcomes include increased social support, more effective problem-solving skills, less crime in a neighborhood, less harassment at work, a decrease in punitive police surveillance and less need for restrictive services such as residential care. Measures used by agency administrators may include percentage of yearly goals attained, increase in staff morale, increase in funding, and more positive views of an agency by community members and

---

EXHIBIT 22.1

What Would You Do?

Jean works with seniors and their families. She helps family members of elderly relatives arrange respites from caregiving and helps them to alter behaviors that prevent frail elderly people from continuing to live with their relatives. There are many ways she and her clients could evaluate services. She could rely on her opinion: Do her clients seem to be better off? She could ask her clients what they think. She could ask family members to keep track of valued behaviors such as completing specific chores or arranging enjoyable activities. Should she use both objective and subjective measures? If both, what would you recommend?

---

funders. Measures on a community organization evaluation scale included the following:

- Community residents recognize the group as a route to social change.

- There is an agreed-on, clearly defined structure containing rules, operating procedures, and a known way for participants to hold one another accountable.

- Individual members have a greater sense of community.

- Group members have a sense of solidarity.

- A fund-raising plan has been designed.

- Success in recruiting and retaining indigenous leaders.

- Success in maintaining a steady funding level.

- Success in forming coalitions with other organizations. (Shields, 1992)

As in other helping phases, many decisions are involved such as deciding: (1) the purpose of evaluating outcomes, (2) what measures to use, (3) level of outcomes viewed as a success, (4) how often to gather data, (5) how to summarize data, and (6) when and how to share data and with whom. If a teacher tells you that a student's behavior has improved, will you be satisfied and leave it at that? Will you also ask the student? Should you go to the school and see for yourself or ask the teacher to collect data on the degree of progress? Do scales of level of functioning accurately reflect outcomes for a client? You and your clients must decide what to do if progress is less than hoped for or if things get worse. Here too practice- and policy-related research may offer a guide for answering questions such as: In residential settings for youth, what are the most valid measures of progress in enhancing quality of staff–youth interactions? The purpose of evaluating progress will suggest the kind of data that will be useful. Possible goals include the following:

- Get a rough estimate of progress.

- Get an ongoing, accurate estimate of progress so that plans can be made in a timely way based on accurate feedback.

- Be accountable to clients.

- Prevent harm.

- Motivate clients to continue participation.

- Provide data for supervisory review.

- Provide data for administrative review.

- Add to the knowledge base of social work.

- Explore the role of intervention in outcomes achieved.

- Enhance clients' understanding of themselves.

- Provide feedback to other service providers.

- Provide data to third-party payers (insurance companies).

Does a plan achieve hoped-for outcomes? Are complaints improving, getting worse, or staying the same? Do outcomes attained make a difference in the quality of clients' lives? Has a policy achieved what it was intended to achieve? Are service programs reaching clients? If so, to what degree? How can we increase the acceptability of effective plans? Are outcomes a result of services provided? Which kinds of service are most effective? Which method does a client like best? Other questions, such as "Was the intervention responsible for the change?" may sometimes be critical in making decisions and are important in the pursuit of additional knowledge. Exploring what method offered by whom, is most effective for what person with what problem, under which circumstances, requires a program of research investigation over time. Asking general questions, such as whether psychotherapy is effective or whether social work is effective, is like asking if medicine is effective. With some problems it is; with others it is not. The question "Where's the evidence?" applies to all of these questions (see Baer, 1988).

Options

All social workers evaluate their practice. They differ in how they evaluate it. Some use process measures such as the number of sessions attended and services offered. Some use outcome measures such as self-reports by clients and significant others, opinions of social workers, standardized self-report measures, and observation in role plays or in real life. Different choices have different opportunity costs (e.g., not discovering early on that services have harmful effects). "All genuine evaluations produce findings that are better than speculation" (Berk & Rossi, 1990, p. 34). Your aim should be to gather accurate, timely information to inform your decisions about services. The less precise your answers need to be to evaluate progress, the rougher your estimates can be.

EXHIBIT 22.2

Ten Ways to Fool Yourself and Your Clients About Degree of Progress

1. Focus on vague outcomes.

2. Rely on testimonials.

3. Rely on your intuition.

4. Select measures because they are easy to use, even though they are not related to hoped-for outcomes and are not sensitive to change.

5. Do not gather baseline data (discover the frequency of behaviors, thoughts, or feelings of concern to clients before service).

6. Assess progress only in artificial settings such as the office.

7. Under no circumstances, graph data.

8. Use only pre-post measures (do not track progress in an ongoing manner).

9. Use only post measures.

10. Do not gather follow-up data.

You can evaluate progress in a vague, haphazard manner relying on surrogate measures or endpoints or in a systematic way that allows you and your clients to make informed, timely changes in plans based on ongoing, accurate feedback or, in some variation in between. Surrogate measures are those that are used to stand for (but may not accurately represent) hoped-for outcomes. They are indirect measures alleged to predict a key outcome such as use of plaque in arteries to predict later stroke. Some evaluation methods are more likely than others to avoid biases that get in the way of accurately estimating progress and what was responsible for it (see Exhibit 22.2). You will often have a choice between feedback that can improve the soundness of decisions and feedback that prevents "debugging" (identifying and remedying errors) (Bransford & Stein, 1984). Careful evaluation requires clear description of hoped-for outcomes and plans and identification and monitoring of relevant, feasible, sensitive progress indicators. These should be:

Relevant: Meaningful to clients and significant others.
Specific: Clearly described.
Sensitive: Reflect changes that occur.
Feasible: Possible to obtain at reasonable cost in time and effort.
Unintrusive: Not interfere with service provision.
Valid: Measure what they are supposed to measure.
Reliable: Show consistency over different measurements in the absence of change.

Any time we claim that a plan, program, or policy was successful, we assume that we know what it was supposed to accomplish. If desired outcomes are vague, we neither know what we are trying to achieve or when we have done so. Evaluation should include clear descriptions of process (what was done), so that the integrity of services can be evaluated; accurate estimates of outcome, so that results can be known; and assessment of social validity (see later discussion). Clients have real-life problems such as lack of housing or medical care and being accused of child neglect. Inaccurate estimates of progress may result in poor decisions about what to do next. Unless you track progress in an ongoing way using valid measures, you may believe progress has been made when it has not or miss improvements when there has been some.

Indirect Measures

Indirect measures include verbal reports by clients and significant others about progress. This offers information about social validity: Do the outcomes attained make a difference to clients and significant others (Wolf, 1978)? Social validity is always important to explore, and indirect measures usually are easy to gather. David Burns (2004 gathers feedback from clients following each meeting regarding various characteristics of the helper and the session including its helpfulness. Clients complete a brief questionnaire in the waiting room. This allows comparison of client's and counselor's views and timely discussion of any client concerns at the very next meeting (see also Duncan et al., 2003). Social workers' opinions about progress is another kind of indirect measure. The problem is that they are not unbiased reporters.

Reports of clients are subject to the hello–goodbye effect (reporting conditions as worse than they really are at the beginning of contact and as better than they really are following intervention) (Hathaway, 1948). For example, Schnelle (1974) found that 37% of parents reported that their children's school attendance had improved when it had decreased. Measures of consumer satisfaction seem to encourage a "congratulatory" reaction. That is, most consumers of therapy report that they are satisfied with services, typically over 80% (e.g., Lebow, 1983; McNeil, Nicholas, Szechy, & Lach, 1998; Seligman, 1995). Global ratings of satisfaction do not offer information about what service components contributed to progress and quality of care. High client satisfaction ratings may be based on a helper's relationship skills; empathic helpers may be rated highly even though the methods they offer clients are not those most likely to help them attain hoped-for outcomes.

Process measures—also indirect measures—refer to how service is delivered. Examples are the number of sessions attended, methods used, and assignments completed. Process measures do not provide information about whether any changes occurred in real life (e.g., an increase in positive parenting behaviors at home). Ideally, both process (descriptions of what was done) and outcome (what happened) should be described. The former

provides a check of the quality of service. The latter provides information about results. The higher the correlation between process and outcome measures, the more you can rely on process measures as a guide to outcome.

Direct Measures

Direct measures assess change in real-life settings. Examples are the number of conversations initiated, daily rate of positive feedback to children, percentage of clients receiving food stamps, and percentage of desired outcomes attained by a neighborhood council. The importance of using both indirect and direct measures is highlighted by studies showing that parental attitude is more predictive of referral of a child to a clinic than is the child's rate of deviant behavior, which may not differ from that of his peers or siblings (Arnold, Levine, & Patterson, 1975). This has also been found in classroom settings. A lack of agreement between direct and indirect measures may indicate that problems of most concern to clients have not been addressed. Progress measures used may not be sensitive to change.

Assessment of Social Validity and Invalidity: Consumer and Extended Community Input

The purpose of social validity assessments is to evaluate the acceptability or viability of a program. Questions regarding social validity concern the following three areas: (1) are the goals of the procedures important and relevant to desired changes? (2) are the methods used acceptable to consumers and the community, or do they cost too much (e.g., in terms of effort, time, discomfort, ethics, etc.)? and (3) are the consumers satisfied with the outcome, including predicted changes, as well as unpredicted effects? (Wolf, 1978). Social validity data provide an important supplement to measuring clear, valid, reliable outcome measures (Carter, 2010). As Schwartz and Baer (1991) emphasize, the key purpose of such assessments is to anticipate the rejection of a program before that happens and for this reason should be obtained from all relevant consumers of a program. These include: (1) *direct consumers*, the main recipients of a program; (2) *indirect consumers*, those who purchase a program or are strongly affected by the changes pursued in the program but are not its recipients; (3) *members of the immediate community*, people who interact with direct and indirect consumers on a regular basis; and (4) *members of the extended community*, people who live in the same community but who do not directly know of or interact with the direct or indirect consumers. Consider a group home for juveniles. The juveniles would be the direct consumers; the referring agency an indirect consumer; the neighbors would be members of the immediate community; and readers of newspaper articles about the group home would be members of the extended community.

Only if the right questions are asked of the right people (e.g., the four consumer groups discussed above), at the right time, and the results are used to enhance the acceptability of programs, are social validity assessments useful. Information gathered should be used to improve the acceptability of services; otherwise, as Schwartz and Baer (1991) note, such assessments are in some sense fraudulent. This emphasizes the value of information about social *in*validity (e.g., complaints about specific aspects of a program), as well as social validity. The point is not to encourage false praise and fake positive reports, but to identify specific sources of trouble (which program aspects are liked and which ones are not liked) that can then be addressed. Too often consumer satisfaction ratings are used merely to obtain continued funding or to provide vague assurance that all is well when in fact there may be many complaints and effective programs may not be used. (See *Bureaucratic Propaganda* by Altheide & Johnson, 1980.) Complaints provide valuable information about how to improve services. Some successful businesses view unsolicited complaints as free gifts they can use to enhance services and increase profits. Your agency should have a clear, user-friendly system for gathering complaints and compliments and acting on the results. Clients could describe these on the agency website while in waiting rooms. Forms should be available in waiting rooms and staff should have access to summaries of related information.

Settling for Approximations, Being Creative

Concerns about cost, acceptability to clients, and feasibility will limit options. Clients or significant others may be unwilling to gather data, or you may not have time to carefully evaluate outcome. Still, you can do the best you can under given circumstances. Let us say you are facilitating a bereavement group. You and your clients could identify valued outcomes (e.g., a positive outlook toward the future), and participants could rate them on a scale ranging from 1 (not at all) to 5 (very much) at the beginning and end of each group meeting. The clients could keep a journal and review it for indicators of progress. You will have to decide whether it is ethical to proceed without ongoing data about degree of progress. Some reasonably accurate measure of progress is needed to make informed decisions about what to do next. Keep in mind that every decision has an *opportunity cost*; certain options are foregone as a result. An opportunity cost of not accurately assessing progress is not having the benefit of finding out what can be improved and taking steps to do so.

Practical and Ethical Advantages of Careful Evaluation

As always, we should consider our purpose. Why should we carefully evaluate the effects of practices, programs, and policies? Answers may differ depending on whose perspective we consider (e.g., clients, significant others, service providers, administrators, the public, politicians who make funding decisions).

Practical Advantages

Testing guesses about the effects of services has many advantages, whether working with individuals, families, groups, communities, or organizations: (1) both staff and clients receive ongoing feedback about degree of success; (2) plans can be changed in a timely manner depending on outcomes; (3) positive feedback increases clients' motivation; and (4) the relationship between services and outcomes can be explored. Evaluation helps you and your clients to make informed decisions about the next steps you should take and to avoid faulty decisions based on incorrect estimates of progress and related factors. Timely corrective feedback is essential in catching and correcting harmful unintended effects at an early point. Careful evaluation takes some of the guesswork out of practice. Also, helping clients often requires many intermediate steps. Recognizing small wins will help you and your clients to keep going (Weick, 1984).

Careful evaluation can help you decide when to introduce a plan, whether to continue it, and whether to combine it with other methods. For example, one of my students had her field placement in a hospital (Vance, 1992). She discovered that a young girl with beta thalassemia (an inherited chronic illness) was not doing well, even though she was following her prescribed treatment regimen. The student discovered this because she monitored both the girl's compliance and the results of her lab tests. The lack of expected match between compliance and the lab results led to the discovery that a treatment change recommended a year before had never been implemented, a discovery that may have saved this girl's life. If you and your clients do not know whether things are getting better or worse or staying the same, you do not have the information you need to plan next steps. You are "working in the dark."

The more rapid and continuous the feedback is, the more sensitive and valid the outcome measures are; and the more clearly outcomes are described, the more opportunities there are to make timely changes. Many social workers see clients over a number of sessions and so have many opportunities to alter decisions. Programs and policies may be in effect for months and years, providing many opportunities for corrective feedback. The ease of evaluation is related to the clarity of the outcomes pursued. Ideally, the same measures used to gather baseline data should be used to monitor progress. For example, Julie continued to monitor her worry-free time (see the case examples later in this chapter). The point is to select an evaluation method that offers sreasonably accurate ongoing feedback in a feasible way.

Ethical Advantages

Clients have a right to know whether they benefit from or are harmed by services. They have a right to know whether their effort, time, and (often) money are well spent. Preventing avoidable harm is an ethical obligation of professionals. This can only be done if outcomes are tracked on an ongoing basis using valid measures rather than uninformative surrogates; for example, harmful programs can be stopped. Court rulings highlight the role of evaluation in providing services in residential programs:

> The courts have identified regular evaluation of client progress, periodic reevaluation of treatment or educational plans, and removal from a course of treatment that worsens one's condition as clients' rights that require ongoing evaluation by the residential treatment program....It is only through evaluation that a program can be accountable, and only through accountability that it can continue to be legally safe, much less functional and effective. (Christian & Romanczyki, 1986, p. 145)

Decisions about continuing or ending programs should be based on clear outcome criteria (not on guesses), and all involved parties should help select service plans and outcome measures.

Reasons Given Against Careful Evaluation

Objections to obtaining corrective feedback often are related to misconceptions about careful evaluation. Given the potential benefits of corrective feedback concerning practice and policy decisions, such as stopping harmful practices at an early point and fully informing clients about the outcomes of service, if you subscribe to any of these views, you should reconsider them. The alternative to collecting data describing the outcome of services is basing decisions on "guesstimates" (uninformed guesses).

It Requires Selecting Trivial Outcomes or Measures

Some people believe that rigor requires rigor mortis, that evaluation requires selecting trivial or irrelevant outcomes and measures of them. Hundreds of reports in the professional literature demonstrate that outcomes can be assessed in a relevant, informative way. It is true that evaluating progress in a relevant, nonintrusive manner requires creativity, flexibility, knowledge, and skill. It also is true that there has been too much emphasis in the professional literature on being objective and rigorous and not enough emphasis on describing the relationship of these characteristics to accountability to clients and case planning. This has resulted in ritualistic practices such as using a measure simply because it is available, with little regard for whether it provides a meaningful estimate of outcome. If your purpose is to find out whether you are helping clients, outcome measures must be relevant, and clients and significant others should be involved in selecting them.

It Interferes with Offering Services

You may believe that evaluation interferes with offering services (e.g., clients do not like it, it interferes with the helping relationship). As with any other helping phase, evaluation can be implemented either well or poorly. The aim is to use evaluation to fulfill the ethical requirement of accountability to clients and also the practical goal of making timely, well-reasoned decisions. Keeping these purposes clearly in view will help you and your clients to select evaluation methods that contribute to, rather than detract from, helping. Evaluation does not require adhering to rigid arbitrary schedules. To the contrary, *practice concerns come first*. Flexibility is one of the advantages of the single-case designs described later in this chapter. Clients report that they like the feedback they receive from careful evaluation (Campbell, 1988). In a quality assurance review program that graphed the progress toward each goal for more than 2,000 psychiatric patients, clients reported that they appreciated the careful evaluation of progress (Bullmore, Joyce, Marks, & Connolly, 1992). Rather than interfering with services, evaluation facilitates this aim.

It Is Not Possible

Some people believe that careful evaluation is not possible because no one knows how to measure progress. Clients have real-life hoped-for outcomes: we can determine if we help them to achieve them. Some believe that evaluating real-life outcome is unnecessary because the quality of the helping relationship determines effectiveness (Penka & Kirk, 1991). Our ethical obligations to clients require that we find out if we are helping more than we are harming. In their survey of 296 social workers, Penka and Kirk (1991) found that many social workers believed that change often occurs too long after services have ended to measure it. Even if this is true, changes may occur earlier that predict later effects.

It Requires Use of Behavioral Methods

No matter what your theoretical preferences, hoped for outcomes can be clearly identified and progress monitored. Hundreds of studies illustrate that progress can be assessed within many different practice approaches.

It Requires a Lot of Extra Time

Identifying clear, relevant objectives is a key assessment task that may take time. However, identifying clear objectives is not solely for the purpose of evaluating progress. This key task serves many other functions such as understanding client concerns and selecting relevant outcomes and effective plans. Careful evaluation will save effort and time in the long run by allowing timely changes in ineffective methods and ending unnecessary services.

It Is the Same as Research

My students sometimes are told by their supervisors that they cannot keep track of progress because this is research and requires the approval of the agency's human subjects committee. This confusion between research and evaluation may occur because identifying clear objectives and progress indicators and tracking them on an ongoing basis is not a typical agency practice. Research and evaluation have different goals, although they may overlap. Progress is evaluated for both ethical and practical reasons. By providing timely feedback about gains and harms, evaluation offers guidelines to what to do next so that service is not continued beyond what is necessary, so that harmful methods can be removed, so that additional methods can be added as needed, and/or so that consultation can be sought in a timely manner. Thus, evaluation is integral to helping clients and avoiding harming them. Consider the example of the youth with beta thalassemia major described earlier. Only through careful monitoring of both outcomes and adherence to a medical regime was a medication error detected that could be corrected. The purpose of research is to yield new knowledge. Applied research has a dual goal—to discover knowledge and to help clients. The growth of knowledge requires methods that critically test theories. Although some evaluation methods involve such tests, many do not (see later discussion in this chapter). Evaluating practice does not necessarily add to knowledge about the effectiveness of specific interventions, nor do poorly designed research efforts (see chapter 11).

Sources of Error in Making Judgments About Progress and Related Causes

Biases that may lead us astray in estimating progress and what was responsible for it are shown in Exhibit 22.3. (Reviews of related research can be found in Gambrill, 2012b; Hastie & Dawes, 2001; and Plous, 1993.) If you are familiar with them, you have a greater chance of avoiding these sources of error and their unwanted effects, such as continuing harmful or ineffective plans or programs. Many of these biases also affect decisions in other helping phases (e.g., understanding problems). Ignoring feedback or relying on incomplete or irrelevant feedback may result in incorrect judgments. You may confuse correlation and cause or chance and cause. The vaguer the outcome measures are, the more likely that bias will creep in because there is less chance for corrective feedback.

Hindsight Bias

We have a tendency to say that we "knew it all along" when a certain outcome occurs, especially when it is consistent

---

EXHIBIT 22.3

Sources of Error in Estimating Progress and Identifying Related Factors

- Being swayed by hindsight bias.
- Being overconfident.
- Engaging in wishful thinking.
- Having an illusion of control.
- Overlooking the role of chance (coincidences).
- Overlooking confounding causes such as regression effect.
- Attributing success to your own efforts and failure to other factors.
- Attending only to successes and ignoring disconfirming data (confirmation bias).
- Relying on observed rather than relative frequency (see chapter 20).
- Overlooking the interaction between predictions and their consequences.
- Mistaking correlation for causation.
- Relying on weak criteria (e.g., testimonials).

---

with our preconceptions. In fact, we often cannot recall what we predicted before an outcome is known or misrecall in a biased direction. This encourages overestimates of predictability (e.g., overestimating the relationship between returning a child to the home of his biological parents and subsequent child abuse). Knowledge of an outcome encourages the view that it was inevitable, that we should have known what it would be, even though there was no way we could have known the outcome beforehand. We tend to assume a direct relationship between an outcome and certain causes when no evidence is offered for or against such an assumption. We can easily come up with explanations, so possible accounts are readily at hand. Hindsight bias often results in blaming people for what appear to be errors that could have been avoided. For example, you may unfairly blame or praise yourself for what were lucky guesses. Looking back, you may assume "I should have known" when in fact, there was no way you "could have known" (e.g., Hastie & Dawes, 2001).

Overconfidence

We tend to be overconfident in the accuracy of our judgments. This is common among experts, as well as among laypeople. Hindsight bias encourages overconfidence by inflating estimates of the relationship between certain causes and outcomes. This overconfidence may get in the way of accurately estimating the effects of a program.

Wishful Thinking

We tend to see what we want to see. Helpers and clients value positive outcomes. This "set" encourages biased estimates.

The Illusion of Control

Our need to feel in control of what happens to us (to hide uncertainty) and to make sense of our lives encourages biased perceptions of progress and false estimates of the strength of the relationship between variables (such as an intervention and an outcome).

Overlooking the Role of Chance

What you believe is a result of your intervention may have occurred by chance. We underestimate the role of chance and can easily come up with explanations (Hastie & Dawes, 2001). Underestimating the role of chance and coincidences is one result of our interest in making sense of the world.

Overlooking Confounding Causes

What you think is a result of intervention may be the result of a confounding factor such as maturation or history (see Exhibit 11.3). Positive outcomes may be due to the act of intervention rather than the intervention itself (i.e., a placebo effect) (Beneditti, 2009). Negative, as well as positive, placebo effects may occur. The former have a negative impact on outcome and/or result in negative side effects. These may be related to subtle signs of inattention or a raised eyebrow. One or more of the following reactive effects may contribute to the placebo effect:

- *Hello–goodbye effect.* Clients present themselves as worse than they are when they seek help and as better than they are when service has ended. This leads to overestimating progress (Hathaway, 1948).

- *Hawthorne effect.* Improvements may result from being the focus of attention. Going to a well-known clinic or being seen by a famous therapist may result in positive outcomes.

- *Rosenthal effect.* We tend to give observers what we think they want—to please people we like or respect.

- *Observer bias.* The observer's expectations may result in biased data.

- *Social desirability effect.* We tend to offer accounts viewed as appropriate. For example, clients may underreport drinking.

Regression

Extreme values tend to become less extreme on repeated assessment. If you do unusually well on a test, you are likely to do less well the next time around. Conversely, if you do very poorly, you are likely to do better the next time. These are called regression effects. There is a regression (a return) toward the mean (your average performance level). Overlooking these effects can lead to faulty judgments. A supervisor may say, "Joe did unusually well the first time he took our employee evaluation test but did not do well the second time. I don't think he wants the promotion."

Attributions for Success and Failure

We tend to attribute success to our skills and failure to chance. Use of vague or irrelevant feedback obscures the true relationship (or lack thereof) between our judgments and outcomes.

Confirmation Biases

Partiality in the use of evidence is a common source of bias. We look at only part of the picture. We tend to focus on data that support our assumptions and may even recall data that were not present that support our views (Nickerson, 1998). We tend to ignore and not search for disconfirming data. Feedback may be ignored, especially if it contradicts hoped-for outcomes. Trying to recall events is an active process in which we often reconstruct accounts (i.e., revise memories) (see Brainerd & Reyna, 2005; Loftus & Ketchum, 1994). This reconstruction may involve a selective focus (confirmatory bias) that encourages overconfidence in judgments.

Relying on Observed Rather Than Relative Frequency

We tend to focus on our "hits" and overlook our "misses." To accurately estimate your track record (or anyone else's), you must examine both "hits" and "misses," as well as what would have happened without intervention (see chapter 20). This is one reason why anecdotal experience may provide a misleading view; you may recall clients with whom you were successful and ignore those with whom you were not.

Overlooking the Interaction Between Predictions and Related Actions

The interactive nature between the actions we take as a result of the predictions we make may obscure the true relationship between the effects of our actions and outcomes. We tend to forget that actions taken as a result of predictions influence the outcomes. Consider the prediction that the banks will fail, followed by a "run on the banks" and their subsequent failure. If you believe you can help a group, you may extend greater effort, which may increase the probability of a positive outcome. If an applicant is accepted for a job, opportunities on the job may ensure future success. Those who are rejected do not have these opportunities. (See Rigney, 2010.)

Relying on Misleading Criteria

Relying on questionable criteria such as testimonials and case examples will give false estimates of "what works," as discussed in chapter 4.

The Value of Visual Feedback

A picture is worth a thousand words. Graphed data provide a valuable source of feedback (see Exhibits 22.4 and 22.5). Progress shown may enhance motivation to continue to pursue difficult goals. Only if a graph is effective in accurately communicating information is it useful. For example, a graph may illustrate the relationship between depression and frequency of pleasant events. Data should be clearly and accurately represented, and graphs should be readily accessible to clients and significant others. You and your clients will have to decide how to aggregate data (e.g., daily or weekly) and how many graphs to use to describe best what is happening. If many measures are plotted on one graph or if the graphs are sloppy, discovering trends will be difficult or impossible. Mrs. Ryan kept track of the number of social contacts she had each day and then combined daily figures into a weekly total (see Exhibit 22.5). A social contact was defined as a social exchange with someone other than a relative that lasted at least 10 minutes.

How to Construct Graphs

Some time measure (days or weeks) is represented along the horizontal axis and a response measure (number, rate, duration, or percentages) is noted on the vertical axis. Be sure to label your graphs so that what is recorded (the time periods involved, and the different phases, such as different service methods) is clear. You could note days on which a behavior could not occur by not connecting the data points on either side of this day (or week). If a student is monitoring a classroom behavior that can occur only on weekdays, he can plot only weekdays. If the behavior could have occurred but was not monitored, you could draw a dotted rather than a solid line between the days on either side. Include data gathered after intervention on the same graph that presents baseline information, so that degree of change can be readily seen. Different phases (e.g., baseline and intervention) can be indicated by dropping a vertical line between phases and by not connecting the data points between phases. (See Exhibit 22.4.) If a behavior can seldom occur, such as making a bed each morning, you can group the data collected daily by week in order to see trends more clearly. Take advantage of computer programs that allow you to convert data gathered into graphs.

Measures of duration, magnitude, or a behavior product, such as number of points earned, could be graphed. In *criterion-referenced graphs*, the desired level of performance (e.g., writing one letter each day) is noted on the graph by drawing a line from this value horizontally across the chart. Whether performance met, exceeded, or fell below the criterion level is noted for each day (or week). In a *cumulative graph*, the number of behaviors on any day is added to the number on previous days. The slope of the line between data points indicates the rate of change. The higher the slope, the higher the rate of behavior. A cumulative graph can only go up; it cannot go down because values are added to each other. Thus if you try to construct such a graph and the line between data points goes up and down, you have not succeeded. Bar graphs (or histograms) can be useful for summarizing data. A response measure is noted to the left, and one of a variety of measures may be indicated along the bottom, such as different people or groups.

Other Kinds of Visual Representations

Mark Mattaini (1993) provides many examples of different kinds of visual representations including changes in social contacts

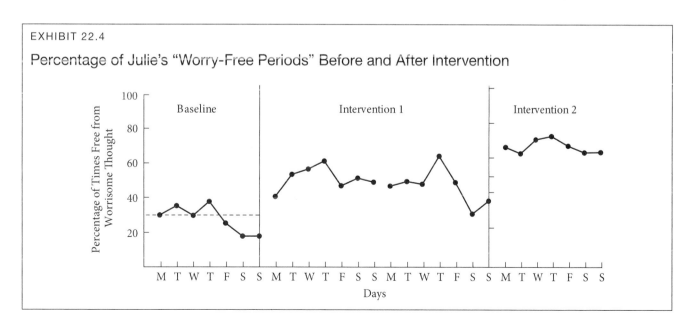

EXHIBIT 22.4

Percentage of Julie's "Worry-Free Periods" Before and After Intervention

EXHIBIT 22.5

Frequency of Mrs. Ryan's Social Contacts Before and After Intervention

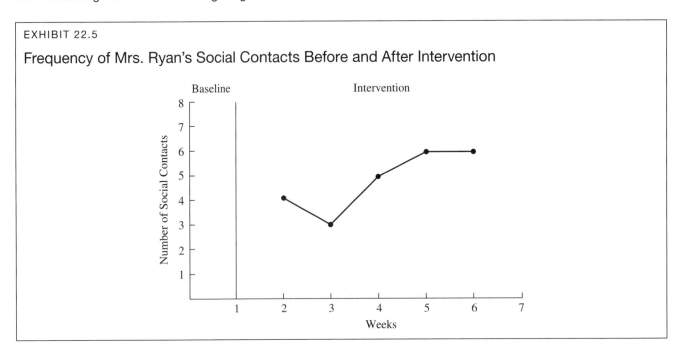

Visual Inspection and Statistical Analysis

Changes that are important to clients should be obvious from looking at the data. You can see how many data points during intervention overlap with those during baseline and examine trends in different phases. You can supplement visual inspection with statistical analysis to determine whether there have been statistically significant changes. You can find out whether the mean level of behavior during intervention falls above the mean level during baseline. Remember, however, that statistical significance is not necessarily correlated with clinical significance. That is, there may be no change of value to clients, even though statistical analysis shows a significant change. Ongoing review of data allows timely alterations in plans (unlike post hoc statistical analysis of effects). Those who favor statistical analysis point out that "eyeballing" may not reveal changes and so lead to abandoning promising procedures and that inconsistent decisions are made on the basis of visual inspection. This does not have to be an either/or decision; you can use both visual inspection and statistical analysis. A number of easy-to-use statistical tests, such as the celeration line, have been developed to analyze data from single-case studies (e.g., Bloom, Fischer, & Orme, 2009).

A Closer Look at Options for Reviewing Progress

The next section offers more detailed descriptions of how you and your clients could evaluate the outcomes of service. Clients may ask you to accept their self-reports in the interview about degree of progress and refuse to collect data regarding outcomes via self-monitoring or observation that may be needed to check accuracy and plan next steps (see chapter 17). In this case, you will have to ask: "Can we make informed decisions without this information?" If the answer is "No," then you will have to discuss this with your clients. Perhaps there are ways to collect needed data that you both can agree on. If you cannot reach an agreement, you may have to inform a client that you cannot proceed without this information. Keep in mind that we are talking about information needed to make informed decisions about what to do next (e.g., to continue a plan or to change a plan if it has negative effects). The alternative is to forge ahead without the necessary data, that is, to make uninformed decisions based on questionable grounds.

Goal Attainment Scaling

This involves identifying a series of objectives in terms of their desirability such as homework assignments completed in a week (Kiresuk, Smith, & Cardillo, 2009). You can use baseline levels as a reference point. The expected level is the one considered most likely. Outcomes that represent more and less than this are indicated above and below this level.

Task Completion

You can review the completion of tasks using the following scale suggested by Reid and Epstein (1977):

4. Complete. Tasks are fully accomplished (e.g., a job has been found, a homemaker secured). If the goal was to reduce quarreling, a rating of (4) could be given if hostile interchanges seldom occur, no longer present a problem, and clients see no need for further work.

3. Substantial. The task is largely accomplished, though further action may be needed.

2. Partial. Progress has been made, but considerable work remains to be done.

1. Minimal (or not at all). No progress has been made, or progress is insignificant or uncertain.

You can calculate the percentage of success for each task. Let us say that 10 tasks were agreed on. Complete success would be 10×4, or 40. A key question here concerns the relationship between task completion and achievement of valued outcomes.

Probes

This involves occasional assessment of an outcome. Probes provide a convenient alternative to ongoing tracking of progress. Mr. Colvine used probes to review the Lakelands' progress in improving their negotiation skills. He tape-recorded their discussions while they were trying to resolve a conflict during a baseline period lasting 10 minutes, as well as at the end of the fourth training session and at a follow-up meeting. A supervisor can randomly select cases from each staff member's caseload to review various indicators of service.

Social Comparison

A student's level of unacceptable classroom behavior can be compared with that of students who behave acceptably in class. Problems with using normative data include undesirable normative standards (e.g., low rates of positive teacher feedback) and difficulty identifying a normative group. What is normative is not necessarily desirable.

Critical Incidents Can Be Recorded

Events or exchanges of concern can be identified and noted in a diary. Suppose that women staff are concerned about emotional abuse. They could record related incidents and then group them by type, such as humiliation by a superior (e.g., checking and rechecking work beyond what is necessary), isolation (e.g., ignoring requests for meetings), and misuse of power (e.g., taking credit for your work, demanding loyalty when you make complaints) (NiCarthy, Gottlieb, & Coffman, 1993).

Reviewing Pre-Post Change

You can collect global client satisfaction ratings before and after service and compare them with client ratings of progress in particular areas. For example, Mrs. Lakeland emphasized the importance of the decline of Brian's nasty talk, whereas Brian related improvement mostly to a decrease in his parents' nagging. You can compare your ratings with those of your clients. You can supplement these measures with other measures. For example, you can review daily mood ratings in addition to scores on the Beck Depression Inventory before and after a 5-week group program. If possible, use objective measures of change to supplement subjective global ratings.

Although pre-post change can indicate degree of progress over time, it does not provide ongoing (day-to-day, week-to-week) feedback about progress. Ongoing evaluation allows timely changes in plans as needed. Also, because of rival hypotheses that may account for change, we cannot assume that intervention was responsible for outcomes observed (see Exhibit 22.3). Since there is no control group, we do not know if clients who did not receive service would have done as well or better. Regression effects are another problem (e.g., people who do very poorly at first tend to do better later, and people who do very well at first tend to perform more poorly later).

Single-Case Designs

Single-case designs are a kind of interrupted time-series design involving repeated measurement of some outcomes of interest over time. (See Barlow, Nock, & Hersen, 2008.) They range from B designs (tracking progress only during intervention, so there is no baseline) to designs that are complex and allow exploration of the role of intervention in relation to outcome (i.e., experimental single-case designs). They differ from case studies and anecdotal reports in carefully tracking clearly described outcomes of interest over time. Requirements for using single-case designs include: (1) clear description of measures, (2) different phases (such as baseline and intervention), and (3) repeated measurement of outcomes of interest in each phase. At least three data points should be included in each phase. If there are fewer than three, you will not be able to distinguish a trend and variability around a trend. Variability, level, and trend in behavior within each phase are evaluated in relation to variability, level, and trend in other phases.

Different single-case designs offer different information. Some provide information about whether change occurred but not whether intervention was responsible. There are too many rival explanations (see Exhibit 11.3). Single-case designs can be used to answer questions such as, "Is there progress?" For example, Julie wanted to increase time out from worry. (Her self-monitoring assignment is described in chapter 17.) A daily percentage was calculated of the number of 1-hour periods in which she was free of worry out of all the 1-hour periods she monitored each day. These percentages were then graphed (see Exhibit 22.4). There are many variations between anecdotal case reports characterized by unsystematic data collection and vague outcome measures and experimental single-case studies that differ in accuracy of feedback and threats to internal validity (rival assumptions about the role of intervention in relation to outcome). Ongoing tracking of progress allows timely changes in plans. This provides feedback that can correct inaccurate views of progress due to one or more of the biases discussed earlier. Some single-case designs offer information about the comparative effectiveness of different methods or the relative importance of components of a procedure that contains many components, such as parent training.

Pros and Cons

First, we should distinguish among different kinds of single-case designs. Key requisites of A-B (baseline followed by intervention) and B (intervention) designs, such as a clear description of objectives and ongoing tracking of progress using clear, relevant progress indicators, are also practical and ethical requirements for case management and accountability. Thus A-B or B designs should be used when possible because they provide information needed to make informed, timely decisions. Single-case designs attend to individual variations in outcomes of interest and related circumstances. They provide a way to respect the uniqueness of each client's particular characteristics, circumstances, and degree of progress. They can help you and your clients to test your hunches.

Baseline data (information about the frequency of behaviors of interest before intervention) can often be gathered and may be needed to clearly describe behaviors and circumstances and discover promising options. For example, assessment data regarding what happens right before and after behaviors of concern often are gathered along with data about the frequency of behaviors of interest (see chapter 17). This provides information about the functions of behaviors of interest and alternative positive behaviors that may be critical in planning interventions.

If baseline data are available, outcomes can be compared with these initial levels providing accurate estimates of progress, so that well-informed decisions about next steps can be made.

Opportunities may arise to use a more informative design (one that provides information about the role of intervention in outcome seen) with little extra effort or cost, either to you or to your clients. Selection of a design will be an evolving process depending on what information is needed to help clients, what is possible, and degree of progress. *Practice and ethical concerns come first.* This is the very reason for carefully evaluating outcome. Consider an occupational therapist's recommendation to use sensory integration therapy to decrease hitting on the part of a nonverbal 8-year-old boy with autism. Monitoring of effects showed that this was harmful. (See Exhibit 22.6.)

What is the downside? Gathering information needed to make timely, informed decisions takes time and effort and may require special training for both you and your clients. You may be tempted to rely on irrelevant standardized measures rather than on measures uniquely suited to your client. You will have to forgo relying on unexamined hunches, and you and your clients will have to candidly confront less than hoped-for success or harms that result from intervention.

Single-Case Compared to Group Designs

Single-case in contrast to group designs involve the careful study of the variability of behavior of individuals. Practice

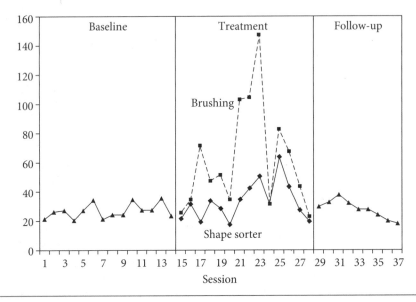

EXHIBIT 22.6

Hitting Episodes per Hour During Discrete Trial Training Sessions

Note: During the intervention phase, the child received sensory integration therapy (brushing and joint compression; broken line) or instruction in using a shape sorter (solid line) just prior to his discrete trial session. The follow-up phase was a return to the baseline condition in which neither sensory integration therapy nor shape sorter instruction was given prior to the daily session.

Source: S. Kay & S. Vyse, S. (2005). Helping parents separate the wheat from the chaff: Putting autism treatments to the test. In J. W. Jacobson, J. A. Muliek, R. M. Foxx (Eds.), *Controversial therapies for developmental disabilities: Fad, fashion, and science in professional practice* (p. 272). Hillsdale, NJ: Lawrence Erlbaum Associates. Reprinted with permission.

considerations "drive" what is done. For example, you and your clients may decide to try another plan if progress is minimal. In group designs, a prearranged protocol is often followed. Group means are compared. Lack of attention to individual differences in prearranged protocols may compromise success. Allowances may not be made for individual differences that, if attended to, would enhance success. (See discussion of practice guidelines in chapter 11.) In contrast, single-case designs are flexible. Experimental group designs require the random distribution of clients to different groups, which may be impossible, unethical, or unnecessary to discover the effects of services (see chapter 11). Even if there is no evidence that the usual agency practices are effective, staff may object to randomly placing some clients in groups offering the usual agency services and assigning others to a new method whose effectiveness may or may not have been tested.

Baselines

Baselines describe preintervention levels of behaviors of concern. Needed information about related circumstances is often gathered at the same time. Baselines can be used to estimate the frequency of behaviors in the future, if the client's life circumstances remain stable. A baseline allows you to estimate what the variability, trend (slope), and level of behavior would have been if an intervention had not been introduced. In variable baselines, there is no clear trend. Variability in a baseline may be a result of the influence of unrecognized extraneous variables such as fatigue or motivational changes. Ideally, to explore the role of an intervention in relation to outcome, the baseline should be stable or be changing in a direction opposite to that desired. Practice concerns come first. These will indicate whether it is feasible or ethical to gather baseline data. These will also indicate whether it is ethical not to do so (e.g., concerns are not clearly described so progress cannot be accurately assessed.).

How Long Should Baselines Be?

If possible, baselines should be continued until the pattern of behavior is fairly clear. If monitoring results in positive effects, it could be continued. Baseline data may reveal a higher than expected frequency of positive behaviors. If so, you and your clients can renegotiate the focus of service or review the adequacy of baseline measures. Perhaps they do not reflect the client's concerns. The severity of concerns may have been over-estimated.

When Should You Change Phases?

Examine the pattern, trend, and stability of data in earlier phases to decide when to shift phases (e.g., from one kind of program to another). If the data are unstable, you have several options: (1) seek the source of variability, (2) wait until a more stable pattern emerges, (3) try out different temporal units of analysis (e.g., weeks instead of days), or (4) go on anyway to the next phase.

If there is good progress and behaviors have stabilized at desired levels, you and your clients can implement plans for generalizing and maintaining gains, as described in chapter 23. The clearer the criteria for deciding when hoped-for outcomes have been reached, the easier it will be to decide what to do next. Also, keep in mind that unchanging data may be due to a number of variables that cancel out each other.

What If Change Occurs Slowly?

Change may occur slowly. Involving more community members in a neighborhood action group may require varied plans that take a year. Many skills may be needed to attain a desired outcome. Although single-case designs often trace changes that occur over a relatively short period, this is by no means required. Rather than plotting days along the time dimension, you could plot weeks, months, or even years. For example, you could track over months the percent of community residents involved in a neighborhood action group. You also could note on a graph the different steps taken to encourage resident participation. That is, you could use an annotated graph. You can make an estimate of when change might occur based on a practice theory.

A-B Designs

A-B designs require the repeated measurement of some behavior, thought, or feeling during baseline (the A phase) and also during intervention (the B phase). The B phase may consist of any type of intervention (e.g., Bradshaw, 2003). The data collected are examined to determine changes in stability, trend, or level over phases. It is assumed that the trend, level, or variability seen in the initial phase would continue if nothing were done. A sharp change in the level of behavior or a reversal of a trend offers more confidence that intervention may have been responsible than does a change of trend in a similar direction. A change in level refers to a discontinuity in graphed data at the point of phase change. A change in slope refers to a difference in trend across phases. (See Exhibit 22.6.) The A-B design offers information about whether a change occurred and describes its magnitude. It does not provide information as to whether the change was a result of service; there are too many rival hypotheses (see Exhibit 11.3).

An increase in desired behavior during baseline may be due to a positive surveillance effect (a change due to monitoring). Baseline data may reveal a decreasing trend. If the desired outcome is to decrease behavior, then here too there is a positive surveillance effect: monitoring behavior has decreased negative behaviors. If the trend is great enough, you may just continue monitoring. Remember, though, that the effects of self-monitoring are usually temporary (see chapter 17). An increasing trend in desired behavior during baseline—although good from a practice perspective—is not good for determining whether intervention was responsible for the change, since the behavior is already increasing. You also may find negative surveillance effects (behavior changes in an undesired way). For example, negative thoughts may increase if they are monitored. A-B designs are often feasible to use in everyday practice. If one procedure is not effective, others can be added.

B Designs and Their Variations

You may not have time to gather baseline data. However, even in "crisis" situations, you can still track progress. If intervention is successful, you will not need to introduce other procedures. If it is not, other plans may be selected. Earlier procedures may or may not be continued depending on progress. For example, social skills training (B) may be only partially successful in increasing social contacts. You and your clients may decide to add other procedures, such as relaxation training (C) and reevaluation of unrealistic expectations (D). Each new method may offer additional gains. One procedure may be ended when another is introduced if the first one had few or no effects.

Exploring Whether Intervention was Responsible for Outcomes

Sometimes it is important to find out not only whether the intervention is working but also whether it was responsible for change. For example, it may be important to rule out medical causes as illustrated in the classic study of Gardner (1967). The degree of confidence that can be assumed in relation to an observed change depends on a number of factors, including the length of time that baseline data were gathered, their stability, and whether multiple data sources indicate similar changes. A sharp change in slope or level when intervention is introduced offers greater confidence

than a gradual change does. You can use brief planned withdrawals of intervention as probes to find out whether behavior is maintained under real-life contingencies. Natural withdrawals as a result of vacations or illness are opportunities to see whether gains are maintained without special procedures. The changing-criterion design is useful when a goal is pursued in a series of steps and when changes in behavior can be expected fairly soon after each new criterion is introduced (e.g., Bigelow, Huynan, & Lutzker, 1993). A baseline is first taken, and then a criterion level is selected. The consequences for reaching or not reaching this level are usually arranged beforehand. If behavior changes, a new criterion is set.

Multiple Baseline Designs

You may have opportunities to use multiple baseline designs, in which you introduce the same intervention following baselines of different lengths. In multiple baselines across behaviors, a baseline is taken for different behaviors, and intervention is applied to one at a time while continuing to track all behaviors (see Exhibits 22.7 and 22.8). Behaviors may involve different behaviors by the same person in the same situation or the same behavior by one person in different situations (e.g., sharing toys on the playground, at lunch, and during recess). In each case, the intervention is applied to one behavior at a time (while continuing to monitor all involved behaviors). If a change occurs in its frequency and no change takes place in the other behaviors, then the intervention is applied to the next behavior. As the number of behaviors increase that change in frequency only after intervention is introduced, confidence grows that change is related to intervention. If behaviors are influenced by similar factors (i.e., they are not independent), changes in other behaviors will occur when intervention is introduced.

EXHIBIT 22.7

A Multiple Baseline Across Behaviors Evaluating Assertion Training

A multiple-phase design across behaviors was used to evaluate assertion training with a 56-year-old carpenter who was hospitalized after an explosive argument with his supervisor at work (Foy, Eisler, & Pinkston, 1975). He reacted to what he considered "unreasonable demands from others" with verbal abuse and physical assaultiveness. His marriage had been described as full of strife, and he was physically abusive toward his wife. Baseline data were collected during seven work-related role plays that involved situations such as "you are blamed for making a mistake that is not your fault." Each scene was described first, and then the counselor (playing the role of supervisor) introduced the prompt; for example, "I am not sure that you deserve a raise" (p. 135).

A review of the client's behavior during role plays revealed the following concerns: hostile comments, compliance to unreasonable requests, irrelevant comments, and not requesting changes in behavior. These were addressed within a multiple baseline design. The effectiveness of different procedures was explored. The first procedure (modeling alone) was applied to all four behaviors at once. Modeling plus instructions was then introduced in a staggered fashion (see Exhibit 22.8).

The addition of instructions enhanced the effects of model presentation. Gains were maintained at a 6-week follow-up. The client reported that his relationship with his supervisor had improved. He used less verbal abuse and made more appropriate requests. As a result, his supervisor had made positive changes in the client's working conditions. The client also reported that his new skills had improved his relationship with his son.

EXHIBIT 22.8

Target Assertive Behaviors During the Four Phases

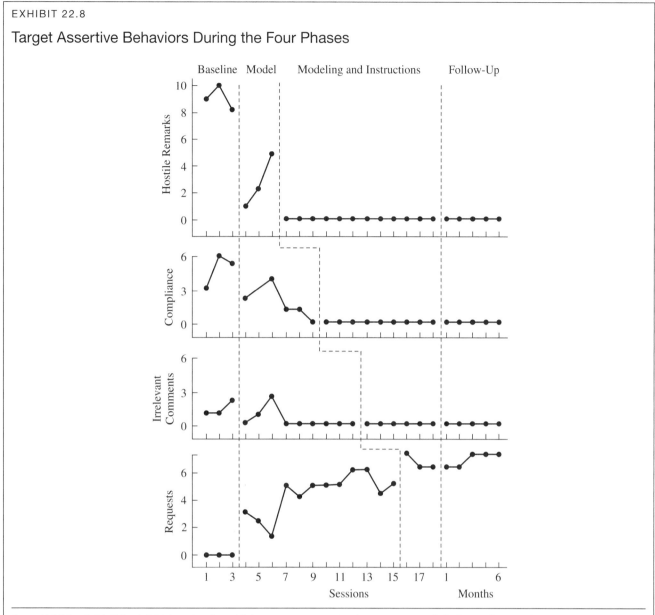

Source: D. W. Foy, R. M. Eisler, & S. Pinkson (1975). Modeled assertion in a case of explosive rages. *Journal of Behavior Therapy and Experimental Psychiatry, 6,* 136. Reprinted with permission.

Multiple baseline designs may also be carried out over different individuals. Multiple baseline designs across settings can be valuable in reviewing the quality of care that staff provide to residents. Schnelle and Traughber (1983) used a multiple baseline across different nursing homes to assess the effects of training in both homes. This offered information about the external validity of the training methods (the extent to which they can be used with success in different settings).

Seekins, Mathews, and Fawcett (1984) worked with the executive board of a low-income, self-help center to develop and implement a training procedure for chairing meetings. The role of the chairperson at board meetings provided an opportunity for poor people to achieve success in a leadership position. The role of chair rotated among the members. A review of the literature and discussions with people who conducted good meetings suggested 40 specific chairperson behaviors under categories such as opening and closing meetings, leading discussions, and solving problems. A combination of behavioral specifications, examples, rationales, study guides, practice, and feedback were used to teach these behaviors. A multiple baseline design allowed exploration of the effects of training on the observed behaviors of persons serving as chairperson. There were marked increases in desired activities—to near mastery levels. The percentage of agenda items on which closure was reached rose from an average of 30% to more than 85%. Multiple baseline design can also be used across different groups.

Cautions About Assumption of Effects

A number of factors—such as questionable reliability and validity of measures, variations in how measures are used, and short unstable baselines—may limit confidence in whether a procedure was responsible for a change. You may not be able to offer and withdraw plans at will. Conditions that covary with intervention may make it impossible to determine the role of intervention alone. External validity (the degree to which results can be generalized to other behaviors, people, or situations) may be compromised by use of a certain sequence of procedures (i.e., generalization may be limited to situations in which the same sequence is used).

The Role of Replication

You could explore whether effects can be replicated with other clients (intersubject replication). For example, many A-B designs with clients with similar desired outcomes can be gathered using similar interventions. You could use intrasubject replication. That is, you could replicate the effects of an intervention with one client by repeatedly introducing and removing a procedure. Let us say that your clients want to find out whether stress-management skills or programming of other activities is more effective in decreasing family arguments. You could help your clients acquire related skills and ask them to use them on alternate weekends. (See also Busse, Kratochwill, & Elliot, 1995.)

Seeking Answers to other Questions

You can explore whether one method is more effective than another by using experimental group designs or certain types of single-case designs. Practice constraints often rule out group designs, but you may have opportunities to use single-case designs to explore whether one method is more effective than another. In *simultaneous-treatment designs*, two or more interventions are simultaneously available. In a classic study by Browning and Stover (1971), observation of interaction in a residential center among a boy, the staff, and his peers revealed that three contingencies were in effect for bragging: positive attention, being ignored, and verbal admonishment. Three groups of two staff each simultaneously and successively used the three conditions for 3 weeks following a baseline period. This comparison showed that ignoring bragging was most effective.

You or your clients may want to know whether combining two or more methods improves outcome. You may want to explore whether relaxation training is a useful adjunct to social skills training. You could use both procedures at first and then withdraw relaxation training. If gains are maintained, then additional training may be unnecessary. You could use a periodic treatment design to explore the effects of interventions that take place during interviews, as separate from methods used between interviews. For example, Ms. Landis saw Julie once a week for 8 weeks. To explore the effects of these meetings separately from use of thought stopping during the week, Julie and Ms. Landis could examine the graph of worry-free periods to see if they increased right after their meetings. You could explore changes within sessions, for example, in anxiety, social skills, or group interaction.

If you are using a procedure with many components and suspect that one or more may not be necessary, you could omit some and assess the effects. Most procedures consist of many components. Consider parent training. This includes discrimination training (parents learn to identify specific behaviors), learning how to monitor behavior and detect contingencies, acquiring a new vocabulary to describe behaviors and related events, and enhancing effective use of instructions, positive reinforcement, extinction, and time-outs (e.g., Scott et al., 2010). You and your clients will also make decisions about service level (e.g., weekly or bi-weekly meetings). You could explore the effects of varying levels on outcome.

Next Steps When Plans Are Successful

If intervention is successful, gradually remove any parts of the program that are not part of the client's real-life environments. For example, in behavioral activation programs for depression, the scheduling of activities is gradually faded out as a client becomes more active and less depressed (Hopko et al., 2003). The point program designed for the Lakeland family was gradually faded out (see Exhibit 22.9). You could gradually withdraw your involvement in community programs as residents acquire needed skills. Group leaders should gradually phase out their involvement as group members assume leadership responsibilities.

Ongoing evaluation of outcomes will indicate whether gains are maintained at desired levels as intervention is phased out. Further planning may be needed to maintain desired outcomes and generalize valued behaviors to other contexts as described in chapter 23. Keep in mind that success does not necessarily indicate that services offered were responsible. Focusing on vague outcomes, not tracking progress using valid measures, and not taking a baseline will get in the way of determining degree of progress and exploring the role of intervention in contributing to outcome. Follow-up data will allow you and your clients to see if hoped-for outcomes are maintained. Gathering this provides an opportunity to support clients and to offer additional service as needed. Agency's policy will influence whether you can obtain follow-up data. For example, your agency may have a policy against continued contact with clients.

When There Is No Progress

Options when there is no improvement include waiting longer, adding or subtracting services, or changing goals. Services could

EXHIBIT 22.9

Case Examples

BRIAN AND HIS PARENTS

The point program was successful in increasing the number of chores that Brian completed, from a baseline of one per week to eight per week during the fourth week of the program. Teasing the dog decreased, and addressing Mrs. Lakeland in a polite fashion increased from zero to once a day during the fourth week. Brian's quiz grades increased from C- to B- in two of his courses over a 3-month period. Both he and his parents reported that they were pleased with these changes. Comparison of the baseline rates of praise and criticism of Brian by his parents with those during the fourth week of intervention indicated an increase in praise (from .23 per hour to .5 per hour for Mrs. Lakeland, and from .24 to .42 per hour for Mr. Lakeland) and a decrease in criticism (from 1.5 per hour during baseline to .13 for Mrs. Lakeland, and from .62 to .07 per hour for Mr. Lakeland). Brian gained access to reinforcers, such as fishing trips with his father.

Mr. Colvine used both direct and indirect measures to evaluate negotiation training. He asked the Lakelands whether they had noticed any change in how they resolved conflicts. In addition, Mr. and Mrs. Lakeland kept track of the percentage of conflicts successfully resolved. A review of tape-recorded exchanges between Brian and his parents (one at baseline and one during the fourth training session) indicated that the clients increased their frequency of complete communications (from zero to five) and also made gains on statement of issues (from two to six) and suggestions of options (from one to seven). Brian and his parents said that they had fewer arguments at home and that they were able to settle disagreements more easily. The percentage of conflicts successfully resolved at home increased from zero to 70%. All three measures indicated that positive changes had been made.

The Lakelands reported that they got along better, and neither Mr. nor Mrs. Lakeland indicated any interest in having Brian removed from their home. But they wondered how long these gains would last, since the family did "have its ups and downs." Mr. Colvine also spoke to Brian's older brother and his sister to get their view of how things were. They agreed that the household was calmer. Brian said that he no longer got sleepy at school since the dosage of his medication had been lowered and that he did not mind taking it now. He still had difficulty with some of his teachers and still found it irresistible at times to tease his sister. However, his parents now ignored this, and his sister also paid less attention to Brian. The school counselor, however, was not impressed with Brian's progress and made a gloomy forecast of what was to come.

MRS. RYAN AND THE GREENS

Mrs. Slater used graphs to review progress with her clients. Mrs. Ryan thought the graphs were wonderful: "What a good idea. I wish I had known about that long ago. I can see how I am doing, right on the wall of my own room." Mrs. Ryan increased the number of her social contacts from a baseline level of one per week to six per week at the end of the fifth week of intervention. She noted the enjoyment value of these in a diary that she kept, which also included brief descriptions of her new acquaintances. As Mrs. Slater predicted, based on her assessment of Mrs. Ryan's social skills, Mrs. Ryan soon made friends at the center and was receiving invitations from others. Indeed, during a visit with Mrs. Ryan to the center on the fifth week, Mrs. Slater saw four people greet Mrs. Ryan when she entered the building. Mrs. Ryan confessed that she had originally had a very inaccurate view of what went on at senior centers. She had thought that there would be dull people sitting around doing "dull things like working with beads."

Mrs. Ryan's letter writing increased from one letter per week to five per week, and by the fifth week she had started to receive more mail. She did not do too well with her daily walks. At first, they increased from a baseline of almost zero to once a day, but by the fifth week, they had fallen back to twice a week. Mr. and Mrs. Green had agreed on three chores that Mrs. Ryan could do: straighten up the living room each day in the late afternoon or evening, take the dishes out of the dishwasher each evening, and clean the washbasin in the bathroom twice a week. She had agreed to keep track of these chores so that she could see whether she did them more often, but she did not. She did report, however, that she "helped out more," and Mr. and Mrs. Green confirmed this. Mrs. Slater decided not to ask her to record questions about her grandchildren's activities and talking less about "old times" at dinner, but during their meetings she did ask Mrs. Ryan what her grandchildren were doing. Other family members reported that Mrs. Ryan now talked more about her social outings.

Both Mr. and Mrs. Green reported that their meeting with the social worker concerning Medicare and the book Mrs. Slater had suggested had been helpful. Mrs. Slater asked them if they could describe a couple of ways the book had been of value. They said that it helped them understand some of the changes that people go through when they are Mrs. Ryan's age, such as wondering why they are still alive, even feeling guilty, and worrying about who will take care of them if they become disabled. They seemed to be better able to put themselves into Mrs. Ryan's shoes. They also acknowledged that having more time to themselves

(continued)

EXHIBIT 22.9 (Continued)

was really up to them and did not have anything to do with Mrs. Ryan, that they had simply fallen into some bad habits of not planning evenings out. They had gone out twice in the past four weeks and had had a good time.

The outcomes shared by Mrs. Ryan and Mr. and Mrs. Green were learning to express their feelings more constructively and deciding where Mrs. Ryan would live. They were not interested in using behavior rehearsal to practice sharing their feelings in a more positive way, but they did read the book and had listened to the tape Mrs. Slater had lent them. The tape illustrated effective and ineffective ways to share feelings. Mrs. Slater helped them think about the last discussion they had had at home and to compare this with the tape. Mrs. Green chose reacting empathetically rather than defensively; Mrs. Ryan chose not blaming others; and Mr. Green chose paraphrasing statements (see chapter 15). Mrs. Green had thought up a strategy of counting to five before she said anything except "hmmm" following a statement by Mrs. Ryan. One important topic that came up during their meetings was that Mr. and Mrs. Green said they felt guilty about not spending more time with Mrs. Ryan. But Mrs. Ryan assured them that she liked having time to herself and did not expect more time with them. The Greens seemed to feel relieved after this discussion. Mrs. Ryan said that she did not have concerns "on her mind" to share with the Greens, but she did share her pleasure with her new social life.

What about deciding where Mrs. Ryan should live? At the last session, after they discussed their progress in other areas, Mrs. Slater reminded them of this question. After a moment's silence, Mrs. Green said, "I wouldn't think of having my mother living anywhere else unless she's unhappy living with us." Mr. Green agreed and noted that everyone seemed happier now. Mrs. Ryan also stated that she wanted to continue living "with her family."

JULIE

Julie's baseline data showed that she was free of worry on 28% of the occasions on which she checked this. Her thought stopping and self-instruction training was only partially successful. The percentage increased to 46% over a 2-week period. Ms. Landis suggested using a cue to remind Julie to use her new skills, asked her to practice these skills for 15 minutes each evening, and arranged an agreed-on reinforcer that Julie would receive if the percentage decreased by 20% or more. These additional procedures increased the percentage of worry-free periods to 61% at the end of the third week, where they remained.

Ms. Landis's assessment suggested that three factors seemed to be related to Julie's unplanned pregnancy: (1) Julie's lack of information about birth-control methods, (2) her lack of assertive skills, and (3) her low self-efficacy. Ms. Landis evaluated Julie's newly acquired information concerning birth control in a discussion. Julie discarded her belief in the rhythm method as an effective birth-control procedure and decided that she would like to be fitted for a diaphragm. She said that she had decided not to have intercourse but thought she should be prepared, just in case. Skill in refusing unwanted sexual overtures was evaluated in role plays. A comparison of Julie's behavior during assessment with her behavior during these role plays revealed that Julie now had different ways to respond to such pressure that were acceptable to her. Self-efficacy is assumed to be related to success experiences in everyday life, and the focus is on increasing such experiences. Change in self-efficacy was assessed by comparing Julie's expectations of doing very well (3), well (2), fair (1), or poorly (0) in three situations each day. The average daily rating increased from one during baseline to two during the fifth week. Julie reported that she "liked herself better." Ms. Landis reminded herself to update her knowledge related to decreasing unwanted teen pregnancies.

be ended or the client referred elsewhere. Incorrect use of plans can be identified early on by staying in contact with clients by telephone or email between meetings. The initial plan selected should be the one most likely to work, with the most comfort and acceptability to clients and significant others in the most efficient manner with the fewest negative and most positive side effects, given available resources and constraints. Considerable thought should have been devoted to choosing it, and you and your clients should not lightly discard it. Exhibit 22.10 suggests questions to ask before deciding that a plan was a flop. Setting realistic goals increases opportunities for success. Be sure to consider the typical success rate in attaining a given hoped-for outcome when evaluating progress. Social workers try to help clients achieve many kinds of goals. Opportunities for success are minimal for some.

Was the Plan Used?

Staff in other agencies to which you referred your clients may have been overburdened, resulting in limited or no services. Maybe a program or plan was not implemented. Be sure to check this before assuming that a plan was ineffective. If a plan was never tried, find out why.

Was Progress Monitored?

Clients may ask you to accept their "guesstimates" about progress. They may say, "I know what is happening without keeping track of changes." Actually, no one knows what is happening if progress is not monitored. Explore objections to suggested ways to assess progress and make changes as necessary. Keep in mind

EXHIBIT 22.10

Questions to Raise When There Is No Improvement

1. Was the intervention used most likely to be successful in achieving hoped-for outcomes?

2. Does your plan include requisites known to be related to success?

3. Was the intervention carried out as planned? How do you know?

4. Is the plan acceptable to clients and significant others? Do they believe it will be effective?

5. Does the plan address clients' concerns? Are outcomes pursued important to clients and significant others?

6. Have you overlooked related concerns?

7. Is there evidence that suggests that another plan would be successful?

8. Have you used specific, relevant, sensitive outcome measures?

9. Do participants have the required skills, resources, and time to carry out agreed-on tasks? How do you know?

10. Did you arrange needed prompts?

11. Are positive incentives sufficiently strong and frequent and given in appropriate contexts?

12. Are there competing contingencies such as negative reactions from significant others or loss of a financial benefit such as disability payments? Do clients fear negative consequences of change?

13. Should other mediators be involved? Who? How?

14. Have you allowed enough time for change to occur?

15. Are there problems in the helper–client relationship? (See chapter 14.)

16. Should you seek consultation?

17. Should you end service?

18. Should you refer the client elsewhere? If so, what criteria will you use to decide where to refer the client?

19. How will you maximize the likelihood of your client seeking help elsewhere?

that evaluation methods must be feasible, as well as meaningful to clients.

Are Measures Used Sensitive to Change?

Measures used may not be sensitive to change. Perhaps you selected a measure based on its availability rather than on its accuracy in reflecting change. Perhaps the units you and your clients use in collecting or graphing data (e.g., weeks rather than days) obscure change. Keep in mind that client satisfaction is usually quite high. However, are there objective changes in clients or their circumstances? (See discussion of self-report in chapter 17.) We need to be only as precise as we have to be to determine if hoped-for changes occurred.

> Our discussion will be adequate if it has as much clearness as the subject matter admits of, for precision is not to be sought for alike in all discussions, any more than in all the products of the crafts.... In the same spirit, therefore, should each type of statement be received, for it is the mark of an educated man to look for precision in each class of things just so far as the nature of the subject admits; it is evidently equally foolish to accept probable reasoning from a mathematician and to demand from a rhetorician scientific proofs. (Aristotle on Precision in Ethics, *Nicomachean Ethics*, 350 B.C.)

Was the Plan Used as Agreed?

Find out exactly how the plan was implemented. Perhaps the services offered differed from those originally decided on. Program fidelity is important to review.

Reviewing the Fidelity of Intervention

Intervention fidelity refers to the degree to which plans match those known to be effective. Review the requirements for procedures used to see if important components were included. Were interventions used that are most highly correlated with positive outcome such as exposure for anxiety (Chorpita, Becker, & Daleiden, 2007; Chorpita & Daleiden, 2009)? (See discussion of modular approach in chapter 21.) Find out whether tasks were carried out as agreed on in a consistent manner. What percentage of assignments was adequately completed? A review of records kept by clients may indicate that an intervention was not used at all or was not implemented appropriately. A plan that is not used will not be effective. The frequency of reinforcement and practice is related to degree of behavior change. If there is little practice, it should not be surprising if there is little progress. A user-friendly record-keeping procedure will help you and your clients to review fidelity and progress. (See chapter 17.)

Not following recommended guidelines is common. Strayhorn (1988) used the term "Dilution Effects (A Drop in the Bucket)" to refer to two ways in which progress may be compromised: (1) many skills are required to achieve outcomes but only some are addressed and (2) many influences affect whether skills can be attained and maintained but only some are considered. You may not have time to implement a plan properly and so offer an approximation. Effective use of a method may require 10 group meetings, but you may offer only four. A client may need five different skills to achieve a valued outcome (e.g., making more friends), but your program may provide training on only two. It is not surprising if there is little progress.

Progress may be limited if many environmental circumstances affect whether a client uses skills, and you address only some of them. Perhaps you do not have time to help a client decrease her social anxiety or to alter unrealistic expectations (e.g., "I have to please everyone") that hamper use of skills.

Explore possible reasons for not following agreed-on plans. Plans may deviate from what is optimal because of interfering beliefs, a lack of knowledge or skill on your part, a lack of required resources, or because clients and significant others do not carry out agreed-on plans, perhaps because of lack of reminders and incentives. Cultural differences requiring alterations in plans may be ignored. Effective use of a program may drift over time. You may believe that you know best how to implement a procedure, even though research shows that your method is not effective. Helpers who are well trained in a method are less likely to deviate from optimal practices. The more complex an intervention is, the greater the need for thorough training. Perhaps you have tried to do too much, with too few resources or too little knowledge about what is needed to help clients attain hoped-for outcomes. Trying to address too many outcomes may compromise service fidelity and decrease chances for success in areas of most concern to clients.

Other Points to Check

Perhaps your plan is not feasible. Perhaps you neglected to give clients practice in required skills. Perhaps outcomes focused on are of little interest to clients and significant others. Plans may be too complex or intrusive. Perhaps you dislike a client and so were not as warm and supportive as usual. You may have underestimated environmental obstacles, such as high-crime neighborhoods and health problems. If progress has been monitored and plans carried out as agreed and there is little or no change, check to see whether you arranged adequate cues and incentives. You may have to arrange prompts for valued behaviors. Ms. Landis suggested that Julie use a cue (a special bracelet or ring) to remind her to use self-instructions. Additional services may be required or other change agents may have to be involved (e.g., parents, neighbors). Perhaps you expected change to occur in too brief a time. Your review of possible reasons will indicate needed changes. You could add or subtract intervention components. If no other plans are feasible or other methods have also failed, seek consultation or refer clients elsewhere if other options are available. Also keep in mind that people have a right to participate on their own terms. Sarason and Lorentz (1979) suggest that "the individual's right to fail is something that professionals have extraordinary difficulty comprehending" (p. 116).

Dealing with Discrepancies

What if there are discrepancies between different measures? For example, during the first 2 weeks of intervention, Mr. and Mrs. Lakeland said that they did not feel very much was changing, even though review of data they collected showed that Brian had completed more chores and had engaged in other desired behaviors more often. It seemed that one fight during the week was enough to discourage Mr. and Mrs. Lakeland. The disrupting effect of emotional reactions on discrimination is an important reason for keeping an objective record of progress. If a discrepancy between measures persists, explore the reasons for this. Perhaps you are not addressing outcomes of most concern to clients. Perhaps progress measures are not sensitive to change.

What If There Is Deterioration?

If this occurs, explore possible reasons. Is it the result of intervention? Would this have happened anyway? For example, maybe a gang expanded its territory into a neighborhood, disrupting efforts to increase the residents' involvement in citizens' groups. Perhaps matters have to get worse before they get better. If you believe this, can you make a sound argument for this view (one that is consistent with what is known about behavior)? Perhaps the measures you and your clients are using are not valid. If it seems that the intervention is responsible for deterioration, it should be stopped unless research shows that things do get worse before they get better. You may have to circle back to assessment. The causes of many problems clients confront cannot be addressed by social workers such as poor quality schools for poor children. Without a contextual view, you may blame clients and/or yourself and become a contributor to problem mystification (see chapter 5).

Program and Policy Evaluation

Guidelines for program and policy evaluation are similar to those for evaluating progress with individuals, groups, families, or communities except that even more players are involved rendering the process prone to political and economic influences. Here, too, data regarding inputs and outcomes allow timely, informed decisions and the potential for clarity differs depending on methods used. For example, if goals are vague, careful evaluation is not possible. Here, too, we should ask, "Compared with what?" in relation to a program (e.g., no program, a different program, or a different intensity of the same program). Here too cost and benefits are of concern. Baer (2004) emphasizes that the evaluation must not threaten the survival and growth of the organization.

Significant others (stakeholders) must be considered (e.g., who will benefit and lose and in what ways from given methods of evaluation; what program components are liked and disliked by whom), as well as resources and validity of measures (Baer, 2004). (See earlier discussion of social validity.) Various groups within an organization may be differently affected by a given evaluation method (or plan for one)—rigorous versus Saturday-night special—including: (1) line staff, (2) supervisors, (3) middle-level management, and (4) top level management. Administrators may wish to continue to misrepresent outcomes related to their agency. Possible benefits of misrepresentation of service outcome to administrators include maintaining prestige and funding. Although some benefits may flow as well to staff lower in the organizational hierarchy, some of the costs may differentially fall on their shoulders. For example, line staff involved in a case in which a child in care dies due to a faulty monitoring policy may be sued.

Andrew Oxman and his colleagues (2010) suggest the following requisites for informed decision making about public programs.

- Adequate funding

- Development of capacity of both researchers to undertake evaluative research and to support policy makers' needs for research, and of policymakers' understanding and ability to use research appropriately

- Organisational structures or processes to lend support to systematic and transparent use of research evidence to inform decisions before starting new programmes

- Rigorous prospective impact evaluations of programmes, including:

  - Planning evaluations in advance

- Ensuring clear objectives that are aligned to the programmes' goals

- Measurement of important outcomes and processes

- Processes for prioritising which programmes are most in need of evaluation

- Effective methods for managing conflicts of interests

- Involvement of the public, including community organizations, unions, and professional associations

- International collaboration to ensure that knowledge and learning are shared, to reduce duplication of efforts and to develop capacity

- Avoidance of ineffective bureaucratic structures

- Monitoring and assessment of implementation and effects of related legislation. (p. 430)

The "logic model" approach examines implementation (inputs, components, objectives) and intended outcomes (outputs, linking constructs) (McDavid & Hawthorn (2006). (See Exhibit 22.11.) Goals, including hoped-for level of success,

---

EXHIBIT 22.11

Logic Model for Nova Scotia COMPASS Program

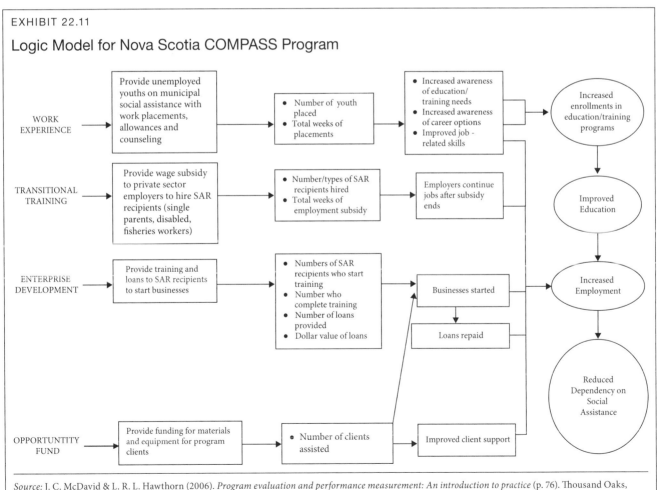

Source: J. C. McDavid & L. R. L. Hawthorn (2006). *Program evaluation and performance measurement: An introduction to practice* (p. 76). Thousand Oaks, CA: Sage. Reprinted with permission.

should be clearly described. Clear, sensitive, relevant measures should be used. Questions are:

- *Whom* is the information for, and who will use the findings?

- *What* kinds of information are needed?

- *How* is the information to be used? For what purposes?

- *When* is the information needed?

- *How* much will it cost to get?

- *What* resources are available to gather needed data (what evaluations are feasible)?

- *How* accurate are different data sources? What systematic errors may be present? (Berk & Rossi, 1990)

Answers to such questions may reveal conflicting goals and interests and different views about what to do. Both immediate and distant outcomes may be of interest. For example, mentoring at-risk youth by adult volunteers may be hypothesized to result in youth modeling the mentor's values and behaviors and to use leisure time constructively, which in turn is expected to decrease contact with anti-social peers and decrease delinquent behavior (distal outcomes). Program implementation and service integrity are important to review, especially if there is little progress or harmful effects are found. An accountability checklist for agencies is suggested in Exhibit 22.12.

Program evaluation, compared with evaluation of individuals, families, and groups, is more complex and may be more conflictual depending on the number of involved individuals and groups inside and outside the agency or organization. It may be impossible to please everyone. Equity and access are important to review. Questions of concern suggested by Berk and Rossi (1990) include the following:

1. Is the program reaching the appropriate beneficiaries?

2. Is the program being properly delivered?

3. Are funds being used appropriately?

4. Can effectiveness be clearly evaluated? What is the evaluability potential? Potential here is influenced by clarity of program goals and programs used, whether programs are uniformly delivered and whether requisite resources are available (p. 74).

5. Did the program work? How good is good enough? Unless the size of the program effect required is clearly [described], "evaluators are shooting at a moving target" (p. 76).

6. Was the program worth it? Answering this question requires comparing benefits and costs.

EXHIBIT 22.12

Accountability Checklist for Agencies and Institutions

- Goals are clearly described and agreed on.

- Intermediate steps required to attain goals are described.

- Both negative and positive outcomes of services are monitored and results shared with all involved parties including clients (e.g., on an agency website).

- Models of effective interventions are provided and available on an ongoing basis (e.g., on videotapes or smartphones).

- Accurate feedback regarding both process and outcome is available to clients, staff, and the public.

- Staff performance is regularly reviewed based on accurate agreed-on indicators.

- Competent performance is reinforced.

- Harmful and ineffective methods are discontinued.

- Procedures are in place to discover how all agency characteristics, including error rate and kind, affect service quality.

- Staff receive needed training and attain required competency levels as shown by a review of their knowledge and skills (e.g., with use of standardized clients).

- A system is in place that allows administrators to find out if something is going wrong.

- A high percentage of those in need of services receive it and a high percentage benefit.

- All staff receive feedback on their performance from both those above (e.g., administrators) and those below (e.g., supervisees) based on clear, agreed-on criteria (360 degree evaluation).

- Staff evaluate progress in an ongoing manner using relevant, sensitive progress indicators. These data are collected for administrative review and are shared with staff and clients.

- Significant others are involved in assessing progress.

- Indirect measures of change are compared with direct measures.

- Case records clearly describe methods used and outcomes achieved.

- Evaluation methods used enhance services and suggest opportunities for improving services.

Here, too, critical thinking values, knowledge, and skills are vital. Berk and Rossi suggest that "evaluation research should not be undertaken by persons who prefer to avoid controversy, or who have difficulty facing criticism. Often, moreover, the criticism is 'political' and not motivated by scientific concerns" (1990, p. 14).

Possible reasons for a program's failure include (1) excessive staff discretion in providing service, resulting in variations that decrease success; (2) minimal, watered-down programs (the dilution effect); (3) what works when used by well-trained, motivated staff does not when used by others; (4) what works for some clients does not work for others; and (5) clients refuse to participate. Perhaps programs were not implemented at all. Practices such as "creaming" (offering services only to clients who are most likely to benefit) will artificially inflate estimates of success. Costs, services, and outcomes provided can be reviewed over time (e.g., in a time series design) to get an overall view. Program outcomes may be compared with:

1. the outcomes of similar programs;

2. the outcomes of the same program the previous year;

3. the outcomes of model programs in the field;

4. the outcomes of programs known to have difficulty;

5. the stated goals of the program;

6. external standards of desirability as developed by the profession;

7. standards of minimum acceptability (e.g., basic licensing standards);

8. ideals of program performance.

The "compared with what" question is critical. Are you comparing a program with lack of a program, comparing two different programs, or exploring the effectiveness of different levels of a program (e.g., follow-up services for 6 months and 3 months)? "Success or failure is always relative to some bench mark" (Berk & Rossi, 1990, p. 76). Different components of services may differ in their effectiveness. For example, various components of case management for adults with developmental disabilities or those with diagnoses of severe mental illness may differ in their efficiency and effectiveness.

Ongoing Program Evaluation

Quality assurance systems should be in place to assess the efficiency, quality, and effectiveness of services provided and this information used to improve staff performance. Identifying areas for improvement is a key aspect of any sound management system. Lower than hoped-for standards of service provide opportunities for improvement. The periodic service review (PSR) described by Gary LaVigna and his colleagues contains four integrated elements:

1. *Performance standards* consisting of clear descriptions of desired procedures and outcomes, the sum total of which define the quality to which the agency aspires.

2. *Performance monitoring* refers to the methods by which the agency verifies whether or not it is carrying out the procedures intended and is achieving its desired outcomes. The results of such monitoring set the stage for supervisory and management feedback.

3. *Supervisory and management feedback* are provided based on the results of performance monitoring to improve and maintain quality of services. Specific feedback is offered based on graphed data.

4. *Staff training* is provided to ensure that staff can competently carry out the procedures required to achieve the desired outcomes of the agency. (1994, pp. 15–16)

A focus on *systems* (e.g., how a group home is operating rather than on individual staff performance) encourages cooperative involvement of all staff. Individual feedback should also be provided by each supervisor to each staff member. Clear guidelines should be described regarding who is responsible for carrying out expected tasks and how task completion will be verified. Fairness to staff is one advantage of identifying clear performance standards for all job categories. Staff know what is expected. The criteria should be realistic and may be based on average or best past performance. Staff at all levels should help set standards, monitor progress, and decide on objectives. Their acceptance of monitoring can be encouraged by focusing on standards met and acknowledging the effort and good work this represents. Dimensions of service quality include accessibility, friendliness, clarity of communication, staff competency, quality control (high quality services over all service components), courtesy, timeliness of services, and usefulness of referrals. Routine coaching and provision of feedback are vital to maintenance of desired staff behavior.

Clear performance standards provide a guide for the design of training programs. Competency-based criterion-referenced training should be provided as needed. This refers to training based on what is known about how to achieve valued outcomes (what competencies are required) and which includes specific criteria that can be used to determine whether desired knowledge and skill levels have been achieved. Reviewing samples of relevant staff behaviors make quality assurance programs workable (for descriptions of organizational requirements for evidence-based services, see Gray, 2001a; see also chapter 27. For further discussion of program evaluation, see Berk and Rossi, 1999; Patton, 1987, 2008 ; Rossi, Lipsey, & Freeman, 2004; Scriven, 1991).

Obstacles to Evaluation

If we agree that ongoing tracking of outcomes is needed both for practical and ethical reasons, we should explore what stands in the way. Reasons given by social workers include not knowing methods well enough to use them, no encouragement from agencies, and insufficient time (Penka & Kirk, 1991).

Overlooking Ethical and Practical Benefits

Staff may not appreciate the importance of clearly describing outcomes and tracking them in order to improve plans, or the ethical concerns raised by pursuing vague outcomes and relying on vague outcome measures such as not detecting unintended negative effects. Pursuit of vague outcomes gives helpers wide discretion to explore areas that are of little interest to clients.

It Is Scary and Threatening

A clear description of outcomes and services increases the visibility of what was done with what result. People can see what you are up to. Vague goals and "guesstimates" about outcomes make it easy to assume that you are helping clients when you may not be. Embarrassing and threatening questions are avoided, such as "Do agency services help clients?" Evaluation can be especially threatening if you have received punishing feedback. Feared negative consequences that may result from a poor showing (e.g., a decrease in funding) may discourage accurate evaluation of outcomes (Altheide & Johnson, 1980). Recognizing the ethical and practical benefits of evaluation for helping clients and avoiding harming them and viewing less than hoped-for success as an opportunity for improvement, will encourage you to seek rather than avoid data regarding outcome.

Management Policies and Practices Do Not Encourage It

Clients may be shifted from one service provider to another, with little time to coordinate their efforts. Prompts and incentives that encourage evaluation may not be available. The administrators' first interest may be in maintaining funding, not in candidly reviewing the outcomes of programs. Authority rather than critical inquiry may be relied on in making decisions. It is up to management to encourage a culture that views evaluation as an essential part of helping clients—a culture that values truth over ignorance and prejudice.

Lack of Creativity, Skill, and Knowledge

You may not know how to identify clear hoped-for outcomes or valid, feasible outcome measures and arrange for their ongoing tracking. It takes creativity to come up with easy-to-use valid progress measures (e.g., Favell, Realon, & Sutton, 1996). Consult practice-related research to get ideas. This describes many innovative ways to evaluate outcome. For example, high-risk mothers used a cardsort to evaluate 32 program services (Pharis & Levin, 1991). Items rated high in importance included "Helped you learn more about how children develop and what they need to grow up healthy and happy," "Helped you have more confidence in yourself," "Helped you understand yourself better," and "Gave you a person to talk to who really cared about you." You may have to develop your skills in posing well-formed questions regarding selection of valid, sensitive progress indicators. (See chapter 10.)

Trying to Do Too Much

You may select outcome measures that are relevant but not feasible. Progress measures do not have to be "perfect" and rarely can be. Ask: "Is there an easy yet valid way we can assess outcome?" Be only as precise as you need to be. Stay focused on what is needed for case planning—making informed decisions about next steps. The "so what?" question is always important (e.g., "How will I use this information?"). Lack of resources may limit options. Keep track of obstacles to evaluating outcome (e.g., excessive caseloads, fragmented service delivery systems) to discover possibilities for reducing them. (See description of the Philosophy of Practice in chapter 1.)

Competing Beliefs, Values, and Styles

Staff may believe that setting clear goals and determining degree of progress interferes with creating a collaborative working relationship with clients. Ethical obligations to clients include a commitment to involve them as informed participants. Evaluation may be viewed as unnecessary rather than integral to problem solving. Only if hoped-for outcomes are clear can you search effectively for related research about how to attain them. (See chapters 9 and 10.) Staff may rely on poor substitutes such as appeals to tradition (what has been done in the past) or testimonials. They may rely on intuition to test guesses about outcome. Intuition is essential for coming up with good ideas about what may be true or false and for discovering ways to test them, but it cannot critically test assumptions (see chapter 4). Even when behaviors occur in public places, staff may object to collecting data that could improve services. For example, I suggested to a student in a research course that she base her project on staff behavior during hospital rounds in which she participated. She could keep a critical incident record of staff behavior that encouraged helpful patient reactions, as well as staff behavior that seemed to discourage such reactions. Her supervisor refused to allow her to collect this information because it might make staff members uncomfortable. The supervisor ignored the potential benefits to clients and opportunities for staff to improve their skills.

Take Advantage of Helpful Tools

You can make evaluation easier by taking advantage of helpful tools such as mobile phones and standardized, user-friendly, valid measures (e.g., Jordan & Franklin, 2010; Bloom, Fischer, & Orme, 2009). You could use the contextual analysis form in Exhibit 7.2 to see if it makes a difference in outcomes. Mark Mattaini (1989) reported that students who used ecomapping paid more attention to higher-level systems than did students who did not use this. Computer programs can be used to graph and summarize data. Over the past decade increased attention has been paid to evaluating quality of life. Guidelines suggested by Guyatt and Rennie (2002) for using articles about Health Related Quality of Life (HRQL) include the following:

Are the Results Valid?
- Have the investigators measured aspects of clients' lives that clients consider important?

- Did the HRQL instruments work in the intended way?

- Have important aspects of HRQL been omitted?

- If there are trade-offs between quality and quantity of life, or if an economic evaluation has been performed, have the most appropriate measures been used?

What Are the Results?
- How can we interpret the magnitude of the effect on HRQL?

How Can I Apply the Results to Client Care?
- Will the information from the study help clients make informed decisions about services?

- Did the study design simulate clinical practice? (p. 311)

Survey instruments have been developed to assess the quality of care in nursing homes. For example, average number of deficiencies can be plotted over years over nursing homes (e.g., Lowe, Lucas, Castle, Robinson, & Crystal, 2003). Edward Bullmore and his colleagues (1992) designed a computerized quality assurance program that allows entry of up to four goals for each client, with four objectives for each. Both helpers and clients rate problem severity, goal difficulty, and present level of social functioning. Problem severity and goal difficulty may not be related. That is, a problem may be severe but reaching related goals may be easy, or a problem may be only moderately severe but attaining related goals may be difficult. Clients and helpers also rate clients' present mood and quality of life (work, home, and social). The data are graphed for review.

Realistic Evaluation and Practice Research

Developers of "realistic evaluation" (see Kazi, 2003; Pawson & Tilley, 1997) argue that this form of evaluation aids in the understanding of contextual factors that influence outcomes, as well as aspects of intervention that make it effective. In a critique, Farrington (2003) sums up related arguments as follows:

1. Past evaluation research has failed because of its focus on what works;

2. Instead, researchers should investigate context-mechanism-outcome configurations;

3. These configurations should be studied using qualitative, narrative, ethnographic research focusing on people's choices; and

4. The purpose of evaluation projects is to test theories. (p. 63)

Farrington notes that procedures such as those described in the Campbell Collaboration tradition already emphasize "the need to study moderators and mediators and to test theories and evaluation research" (p. 66). He does not agree that the best method of investigating relationships between context, mechanisms, and outcomes is in qualitative, narrative, or ethnographic research. He argues that these methods are useful in generating hypotheses, but experimental or quasi-experimental research is needed to test causal hypotheses. Practitioners and administrators have access to different kinds of data that may be of value. The term "practice research" is used to refer to data collected by line staff, supervisors, and/or administrators that can inform social work practice and policy. There are many opportunities to gather such information, for example, percentage of clients with certain kinds of presenting concerns or percentage of clients reporting attainment of valued goals. Feedback from every client regarding degree of success is a key aspect of applied behavior analysis.

Evaluating Your Progress

One of the advantages of being a professional is continuing to enhance your skills over your career. Self-directed learning skills are needed to make the most of this advantage. Questions here are

- What gaps exist between my current values, knowledge, and skills, and what I need to help my clients?

- How can I discover these gaps?

- What exactly would I do differently if I had these values, knowledge, and skills?

- What criteria would most accurately provide feedback as to whether I now have and use this knowledge?

- How can I generalize new skills and knowledge to all situations in which they would be of value?

- What tools and training programs would be most effective in helping me close these gaps?

It takes courage and a commitment to client welfare to candidly review the match between your values, knowledge, and skills and what is needed to help clients and avoid harm. This review will help you to spot learning opportunities. You are more likely to continue to enhance your professional knowledge and skills if you are open to new ideas and select effective training programs. So, evaluation is not just for clients, it is for you, too. It also is for supervisors and administrators so that they can be informed about the quality of services provided by their staff and use this information to improve services. In what areas do staff do well? In what areas do they not do so well? This information is needed to select continuing education programs.

Summary

The proof of the pudding concerning the effects of practices, programs, and policies is whether or not hoped-for outcomes result. The history of the helping professions clearly shows that caring (a good heart) is not enough to protect clients from ineffective or harmful "service." Even a benevolent fox may have difficulty fulfilling his guard duties. No one really knows if a program is harming or helping clients or making no difference at all unless the outcomes are carefully explored. The more vague the assessment of progress, the greater the opportunities for the unrecognized play of biases that may harm clients. Our preferences influence what we see and do unless we have strategies for avoiding related biases. Key questions include (1) What information do my clients and I need to make informed decisions about what to do next? (2) What data would provide accurate, timely estimates of progress at the least cost in time, effort, and money? and (3) How can we increase the acceptability of effective methods?

Accountability is a requirement of ethical practice. Clients have a right to know whether services help or harm or are irrelevant. Does parent training decrease the frequency of child abuse? Do staff members in an agency acquire and use more effective conflict resolution skills? To answer these questions, hoped-for outcomes must be clearly described, and relevant, feasible, sensitive outcome measures must be identified and monitored. Careful evaluation serves an important planning function. Ongoing review of progress allows timely changes in plans based on degree of success. It will help you and your clients avoid common sources of error such as overconfidence and hindsight bias that result in inaccurate estimates of progress and the role of services. Feedback about positive outcomes provides an incentive to continue the hard work often needed for success. Direct measures such as observation allow you and your clients to see whether changes did occur. Both subjective and objective feedback about progress are important. Myths about evaluation include the belief that it requires selection of trivial outcomes and that it interferes with the helping relationship.

A lack of resources including time may limit opportunities for careful evaluation. You and your clients will often have to choose an approximation. Focusing on helping clients will contribute to making well-reasoned decisions. Clear descriptions of services offer valuable information to review if plans are not successful (intervention fidelity can be assessed). You can use your skills in evaluating progress with clients to assess and upgrade your own skills.

Reviewing Your Competencies

Reviewing Content Knowledge

1. Describe the relationship between evaluation and case planning.

2. Discuss the ethical and practical problems of not evaluating progress.

3. Describe criteria that can be used to evaluate progress and critique each.

4. Describe and give examples of biases that may result in incorrect estimates of progress.

5. Describe biases that may result in an incorrect assumption that services were responsible for outcomes.

6. Describe what is meant by the term "social validity" and give examples of ways to assess this. Describe the purpose of assessing social validity and identify groups that should be involved.

7. Discuss the relationship between clarity of objectives and evaluation of outcome.

8. Accurately critique different kinds of evaluation methods.

9. Describe the requisites for single-case designs and describe how they differ from pre-post designs.

10. Give examples of multiple baseline designs.

11. Describe questions to raise when services offered are not successful.

12. Describe confounding factors in different types of single-case and group designs related to the assumption that outcomes resulted from services offered. Draw on material in chapter 11 as needed.

13. Describe reasons for using both subjective and objective measures of progress.

14. Discuss the importance of clearly describing the level of progress hoped for in program evaluation.

15. Identify and critique different criteria against which a program could be evaluated.

16. Describe the characteristics of a well-designed quality assurance program.

17. Describe the role of management practices in influencing services provided by line staff.

18. Describe how goals may differ in evaluation and research.

19. Identify political, social, and economic obstacles to careful evaluation and suggest steps to overcome them.

20. Accurately describe your knowledge and skill levels related to specific practice methods and identify relevant, feasible, sensitive progress measures to evaluate improvement in these competencies.

Reviewing What You Do

1. When possible, you evaluate progress in an ongoing manner using valid, unintrusive measures, and write clear, accurate summaries of outcomes in case records. Criteria: objectives and progress indicators are clear and relevant (e.g., meaningful to clients); accurate graphed summaries of data are available.

2. You identify valid measures of progress in specific situations and design appropriate visual representations.

3. You draw effectively on practice-related research to evaluate the quality of services and outcomes attained.

4. You can accurately plot data on a graph.

5. You can accurately and concisely summarize graphed data and make sound recommendations about next steps.

6. Given an example of graphed data, you can determine the average value within different phases (e.g., baseline, intervention) and draw correct inferences about the effects of service.

7. Given examples of claims about progress and/or the role of intervention in attaining outcomes, you can accurately identify alternative hypotheses and fallacies in reasoning.

8. You use both direct (e.g., observation) and indirect (self-report) measures to evaluate progress when feasible.

9. You involve significant others, as well as clients, in selecting progress measures.

10. You clearly describe to clients the reasons for evaluating progress (e.g., as determined by review of audiotaped interviews).

11. You carefully review your clients' progress in each interview.

12. You ask helpful questions and take appropriate steps when there is no progress.

13. Given examples, you accurately identify sources of bias that result in incorrect estimates of progress.

14. You refer clients to agencies in which staff use valid progress measures and assess social validity.

15. You make effective use of probes to determine the need for continued service.

16. You gather baseline data when possible.

17. You assume increasing responsibility for identifying specific personal learning goals, for selecting accurate ways to assess your current performance levels, and for arranging effective training opportunities.

18. You help a fellow student to clearly describe a learning goal and a way to monitor progress.

19. You design sound program evaluations.

20. You gather accurate data regarding specific liked and disliked aspects of service programs based on review of client compliments and complaints and use this information to increase service acceptability and effectiveness.

Reviewing Results

1. You make timely changes in plans based on evaluation of progress.

2. Acceptability of practices and programs to clients increases.

3. You avoid influence by propagandistic claims about the effectiveness of intervention.

23

Planning for Endings

OVERVIEW   Both planned and unplanned endings are discussed in this chapter. Reasons for unplanned endings are described, as well as components of planned endings and steps you can take to increase the probability that positive outcomes occur in real-life contexts and are maintained.

YOU WILL LEARN ABOUT

- How to plan for endings

- Contributors to unplanned endings

- The importance of planning for generalization and maintenance

- Encouraging generalization and maintenance

- Ethical issues

Only some endings will be planned (objectives are met and arrangements are made to maintain positive outcomes) or appropriate referrals are made. You will also have unplanned endings in which clients may not return even though agreed-on goals have not been met. However, not all dropouts are failures. Some clients may benefit from a single meeting (Littrell, Malia, & Vanderwood, 1995; Perkins, 2006; Talmon, 1990). Others may require continued support over a long period. How you end with your clients will depend on whether you have developed a therapeutic alliance, provided information about problems and possible solutions, helped the client to reconceptualize concerns in a more hopeful fashion in which the client takes credit for change (nurture a sense of personal agency) developed a supportive environment, and ensured that clients have effective coping skills including those used in relapse prevention.

Clients differ in the challenges they face and present to others including social workers. Clients with a history of abuse and neglect (victimization) may suffer from post traumatic stress. A high percentage of people diagnosed as having severe mental illness have such a history (e.g., Springer, Sheridan, Kao, & Carnes, 2007) (see also Riggs, 2010). Helping skills and interventions of value here, in addition to those described, may include appropriate medications, forging community ties with others who can provide support, addressing basic needs including safety, helping clients to regulate symptoms, guiding the client in finding meaning in pain and transforming it, addressing the impact of trauma and troubling behavior on significant others, and addressing issues of possible revictimization (Meichenbaum, 2009).

How to Plan for Endings

It should be obvious to you, as well as to your clients, when you will hold your last meeting: agreed-on outcomes have been achieved and plans to maintain gains are in place (see Exhibit 23.1). Or you may have been able to offer only an approximation to what is needed, perhaps because of lack of resources, and next steps must be decided on, such as a referral. (See Bickman, 1996.) You may have to plan for transitions from one environment to another (e.g., see Bigby & Socwk, 2000; McDonnell & Hardman, 2010). Planning for endings should begin during initial interviews. Endings will be planned to the extent to which you and your client: (1) clearly describe outcomes to focus on and criteria to evaluate progress and levels of progress hoped for; (2) clearly describe expectations and responsibilities; (3) monitor progress; and (4) plan for generalization and maintenance of gains. It does little good to develop needed skills if these are not used in (do not generalize to) real-life situations of concern to clients.

Preparing for endings will avoid negative emotional reactions such as anger, frustration, or guilt that may result from unfocused work. Even if you are not successful in helping clients attain valued outcomes, if you have used evidence-informed methods to pursue clear relevant objectives, and high quality relationship skills or have done what can be done in an impossible job, you have given your best. Review your beliefs and feelings about endings to make sure they encourage planned endings. You may have difficulty ending because you assume more responsibility for the well-being of clients than is realistic (or good for clients) or try to solve unsolvable problems. Keep in mind that clients make decisions about their degree and kind of participation. They, as well as you, are responsible for choices made.

Limiting service to a set number of interviews is common under managed care and may motivate clients to become involved at an early point. Many clients prefer brief compared to long-term service and most clients attain most benefit during the first few sessions (see Lambert & Ogles, 2004). You can remind clients of time limits by occasional statements such as "Well, we have 3 more meetings." Unnecessarily extending meetings may have negative effects, for example, increased dependency. Strupp and Hadley (1985) argue that one of the causes of negative outcome in psychotherapy is failing to be aware of and to discourage excessive dependency. Contacts may stop when an involuntary arrangement such as probation or parole ends. If you have not been of help, both you and your client will probably feel relieved when the last meeting arrives.

If you have been of help, ending interviews provide an opportunity to celebrate successes, to support clients for their contributions, and to help clients plan how to maintain gains. If success has been limited, "small wins" can be noted, work that remains to be accomplished discussed, and helpful next steps decided on (perhaps a referral). Contact may end because of budget cuts. For example, the state mental health department of Massachusetts laid off 25 percent of its case managers for the mentally ill during 2009–2011 "severing important relationships for thousands of people with serious mental illness and transferring them to younger, lower-paid workers in the private sector" (Sontag, 2011a, p. A24). Here again, as in child welfare, the younger, most inexperienced staff may be assigned to the most challenging clients. Such rearrangement may result in harm to staff as seen in the murder of a young social worker by a patient in June 2011. (Examples of planning for endings can be seen in Exhibits 23.2 to 23.4.)

EXHIBIT 23.1

Checklist for Planned Endings

1. Desired outcomes are clearly described.

2. Clear, agreed-on criteria for evaluating progress are identified.

3. Expectations of clients are clearly described.

4. Responsibilities of helpers are clearly described, including what can be offered and what cannot.

5. A specific number of meetings is agreed on in the first interview.

6. Progress is evaluated on an ongoing basis.

7. Arrangements are made for generalization and maintenance.

8. Feelings about ending are discussed.

9. Gains made are noted and supported.

10. Clients' contributions are described and supported.

11. Helpful next steps (e.g., referrals, follow-up meetings) are planned.

Contributors to Unplanned Endings

Clients will usually not continue contact if they receive little or nothing of value, or feel misunderstood, ignored, patronized, or "put down"—unless they have to do so. Unplanned endings are more likely under the following circumstances:

1. The purpose of meetings is not clearly identified.

2. Expectations are not clearly described.

3. Progress is not monitored.

EXHIBIT 23.2

Examples of Planning for Endings

In all three of the examples that follow, the social workers paid careful attention to significant others and focused on behaviors that would continue to be reinforced after services ended. Artificial reinforcers and schedules were removed and procedures were selected that clients could apply themselves, thus decreasing dependence on the social worker. The rationales for plans were explained, conditions that might present future obstacles identified, and coping skills developed to use in such situations. Clients were given written descriptions of plans to take home with them.

CASE EXAMPLE 1: BRIAN AND HIS PARENTS

Mr. Colvine helped Brian and his parents to develop more positive ways of talking to each other in the office. He asked his clients to practice the skills they had learned twice each week as one effort to generalize use of effective problem-solving skills to the home. Specific topics to be discussed were agreed on to make sure these could be handled with their new skills. He used prompts to encourage clients to identify issues and gradually faded them out as clients acquired skill. Knowing that Mr. Colvine would ask them about their practice sessions served as a reminder to practice new skills at home.

Brian now received a weekly allowance of up to 10 dollars, contingent on carrying out specific chores and obtaining certain grades. Three extra bonus dollars were offered for "a good week." This was defined as completing all scheduled chores, doing an extra "thoughtful deed" for a family member, or getting a very good grade on a test or assignment, or as a final grade. Examples of thoughtful deeds included taking the dog out for a walk even though this was not his job, and helping his mother unload the groceries. All artificial reinforcers were removed before the last session. Brian had joined a woodworking class at the local recreation center and had made two acquaintances through this class. Mr. Colvine helped his clients to identify situations that were likely to lead to backsliding, such as fatigue on the part of the parents, and to identify methods they could use to counter downward trends and maintain positive gains, such as occasionally monitoring praise given to Brian. Mrs. Lakeland said that this helped her to remember to focus on "the good" rather than "the bad."

Mr. Colvine gradually faded out contacts with his clients from once a week to one in-person contact every other week and biweekly telephone contact, to one in-person contact every three weeks and biweekly phone contacts, and then to once-a-month phone contacts. Booster sessions were scheduled every 3 months for a year. Brian and his parents reported that they looked forward to these meetings because they provided an opportunity to review successes, as well as to discuss concerns that had been raised. They reported that having written copies of steps to follow when discussing differences helped them to remember what to do. Brain made no physical threats against his parents over the 1-year follow-up period. His grades hovered at about a B average, and his school counselor still waited for what he believed would be the inevitable backsliding. The family still had its ups and downs and its arguments, as most families do. The difference was that now family members had more control over them.

CASE EXAMPLE 2: JULIE

Arranging prompts (reminders) for new behaviors in the natural environment was an important aspect of Ms. Landis's work with Julie. Special cues were arranged to remind Julie to use her new skills when she started to worry. Ms. Landis did not fade her contacts with Julie but let it be known that her door was open in case Julie wanted to consult her after the last planned session. The last session was used to review progress and to offer positive feedback to Julie for her contributions. Julie said that she felt more "sure of herself" and that she thought she would be able to refuse unwanted overtures. Ms. Landis reminded her to review the tape of various ways to refuse unwanted requests if she became uncertain in the future. She reminded Julie to consult her copy of instructions for decreasing worrisome thoughts and increasing self-confidence if she found herself slipping. She and Julie agreed to speak together within 3 months.

At a 6-month follow-up Julie reported that she was enjoying school more and things were "going OK" with her boyfriend. She was not sure she wanted to confine her social activities to "only him." She did feel sad at times about the abortion, but if this lasted too long, she reminded herself about the commitment-enhancing methods she had learned from Ms. Landis. She believed that she had made the right decision and said she would not put herself in this position again. She was not using any birth control procedures except "not doing it."

CASE EXAMPLE 3: MRS. RYAN AND THE GREENS

Mrs. Slater made arrangements to get in touch with Mrs. Ryan and the Greens within 6 months and extended an open-door policy to them. When she spoke to the clients she learned that Mrs. Ryan had a mild heart attack 3 months after the last session but that she was recovering well and was gradually resuming visits to the senior center. The Greens had been very helpful during

(continued)

EXHIBIT 23.2 (Continued)

her recovery. Mrs. Ryan's letter writing had decreased during her illness but was now picking up again. The Greens had decided that they liked getting out of the house occasionally. Little seemed to have changed in discussions at the dinner table except that family members seemed more tolerant of each other.

THE FUTURE

What does the future hold for these clients? Base-rate data could be consulted to gain some idea. Ms. Landis knew that there was a good probability that Julie might get pregnant again. Is there anything else Ms. Landis could do other than having an open-door policy and sharing information with Julie about the possible consequences of certain courses of action or inaction?

There is a high probability that Mrs. Ryan will have another heart attack within the next few years. Her greatest fear was that she would linger in a debilitated condition at great financial and psychological expense both to herself and to her significant others. Could this be avoided? What steps can she take to prevent this, such as completing a "living will"? Mrs. Slater provided information about legal rights and suggested sources of information to her clients. She also provided information about financial resources. Although the Greens were still worried about finances if Mrs. Ryan became chronically ill, her age and fragility increased their sense of closeness to and warmth for her. This was indeed a family in transition—the children were getting older and Mrs. Ryan's health was not good.

The Lakeland family was also a family in transition. One son was in college and would probably be off on his own in a couple of years. Brian would enter high school soon. Given the lack of aggressive behavior in Brian's early history and the absence of aggressive behavior over the past year, there was a good chance that troublesome behaviors of this kind would not recur if reinforcement for positive behaviors was maintained.

4. Outcomes focused on are not important to clients or do not complement their values.

5. A time frame is not agreed on.

6. Plans suggested and/or the rationale for them are not acceptable to clients and/or significant others.

7. There are problems in the helping relationship, such as mistrust.

Unplanned endings may occur because clients move or become ill. Some clients will return, not because they have benefited from meetings with you but because they still hope to do so. Or they may have received some benefit, but not as much as hoped for. Clients may feel angry or frustrated if there is no progress. If you have not helped clients to identify specific valued outcomes and steps to achieve them, you may feel guilty or frustrated and are in an embarrassing spot—so embarrassing that you may choose not to recognize it. If you have not followed a process that permits planned endings, you may start to feel uncomfortable with clients and even start to dislike them. Use your feelings as a cue to explore related reasons. You will not be able to help all your clients. Overestimating the potential for success may result in frustration, as well as a tendency to overlook limited progress. Candid appraisal of degree of progress will help you and your clients to take appropriate next steps.

EXHIBIT 23.3

Ending Sessions of a Group

"During the final phase, the emphasis was placed on reviewing the skills that had been taught and planning for dealing with stress after the group ended. In session nine, Lydia [the facilitator] suggested some extra group tasks that would help members think of how they could maintain the skills they had learned during the previous 8 weeks." She noted that without planning for maintenance, the benefits of training may dwindle. Each group member discussed the principles of transfer and maintenance. Lydia suggested that they use the principles to develop a personal maintenance plan that would be the focus of the last session. Everyone agreed to try it out. During the 10th session group members reviewed each other's plan. Jim planned to read some books on assertiveness and stress management....Ellen was going to...keep a diary of stress situations and how she handled them and to continue walking 2 miles a day, and Susan would accompany her. Susan had joined a church group in which she hoped to use the assertive techniques she learned in the group. Janet was going to join a yoga class to improve her relaxation. A booster session was planned in 3 months. "They could discuss how they had used their stress management skills, refresh any skills that had been forgotten, and do problem solving."

Source: Adapted from S. D. Rose (1989). *Working with adults in groups* (pp. 325–326). San Francisco: Jossey-Bass.

EXHIBIT 23.4

Planning the Last Group Session

SESSION SIX: REVIEW, LOOKING AHEAD, AND ENDING

I. Objectives

To support and consolidate what has been learned.

To identify and support suggestions for building and maintaining support networks and maintaining hope.

To discuss feelings about ending.

To discuss issues related to future contact. To briefly address issues not covered.

To evaluate the group experience.

II. Preparation

Review information on group dynamics with special focus on endings. Gather information about other support services.

Review follow-up forms from previous sessions to identify specific incomplete areas of discussion and information not distributed.

Be prepared for the following content and group process:

Session is seen as last chance to "get it all out."

Members may pressure others to maintain contact.

Feelings of abandonment.

Fear of endings.

Select role plays for review (e.g., "Meeting each other in person"; "Continuing contact"). An example is:

Your telephone support group has ended and you want to find another type of group in your area. You are unsure who may provide this information and are concerned about telling people what kind of group you are looking for. How can you get the information you want? Who will you ask? What will you ask?

III. Suggested Activities

"Check-in" (brief reports from members about how they have been since last session). Ask group members to summarize what has been covered in previous sessions and give input as necessary. Ask if there is any subject they want to discuss briefly.

Review strategies for getting help and available resources.

Raise the issue of ending and how everyone is feeling about this.

If group members want to continue contact, discuss a way to do this (e.g., exchange phone numbers and addresses). Do this carefully so no one feels pressured to maintain contact.

IV. Ending the Session

Ask for feedback about group members' experience in the group.

Source: M. Galinsky, K. Rounds, A. Montague, & E. Butowsky (1993). *Leading a telephone support group for persons with HIV disease* (pp. 44–46). Chapel Hill, NC: School of Social Work, University of North Carolina at Chapel Hill. Reprinted with permission.

The Importance of Planning for Generalization and Maintenance

Arranging for generalization and maintenance of positive outcomes is an important part of planned endings. Lack of generalization is a common problem. "Generalization involves the occurrence of valued behaviors under different, nontraining conditions (i.e., across subjects, settings, people, behaviors, and/or time) without the scheduling of the same events in those conditions as had been scheduled in the training conditions" (Stokes & Baer, 1977, p. 350). It may occur across behaviors (response generalization), time (maintenance), or across individuals or situations (stimulus generalization). Behaviors that are similar in form to those focused on are likely candidates for generalization, although if diverse behaviors serve the same function (they are in the same operant), a change may occur in very different behaviors. Preventing a downward drift in positive outcomes often requires careful planning. A concern for the durability of positive outcomes should be a consideration when selecting assessment and intervention methods. Whenever intervention does not take place in real-life settings, a program should be designed to arrange for the generalization of desired behaviors to real-life environments. Different procedures may be needed to encourage generalization or transfer of changes than to maintain changes. Not arranging for the maintenance of positive outcomes may be related to a belief that methods used and outcomes attained will inoculate clients against the effects of environmental contingencies. Lack of generalization may be due to a train and hope approach—providing training and hoping that new ways of responding will occur in real-life situations. This approach is not likely to be effective.

If an outcome is valued (such as receiving positive feedback from others, one aim may be to increase the range of situations in which this occurs. This could be accomplished by decreasing obstacles (e.g., fatigue), broadening the stimulus control (see chapter 25), and/or reminding significant others to reinforce valued behaviors. If new ways of acting may result in changes in how others react, prepare clients for this. If a client wants other people to be more responsive, learns new social behaviors that result in more friendly overtures, and does not know how to handle them, finds them anxiety provoking, or wonders if he deserves them, he is not likely to continue using his new skills. "Probes" for generalization can offer information about whether changes of behavior in one situation result in changes of behavior in other situations or other behaviors in the same context. They are most effective when they do not occur too frequently and are nonreactive.

Maintenance programs will be required whenever reinforcement for new behaviors will not be naturally provided in real-life settings or when reinforcement may decrease over time. Lack of maintenance of valued outcomes is a major problem. Often, there is a drift toward less frequent use of positive contingencies and more frequent use of punishment. Poor housing, insufficient income, high crime rates, and poor health may increase stress, which, in turn, may compromise use of effective parenting skills. If we are under emotional stress, it is harder to make discriminations (e.g., identify positive behaviors to support). Positive behaviors may be ignored and parents may fall back into the reinforcement trap (reinforcing undesired behavior because this is followed by some immediate peace at the cost of increasing unwanted behavior in the future).

Encouraging Generalization and Maintenance

You cannot count on generalization. Instead, careful planning is required. You may, for example, ask clients to carry out assignments in real life to encourage generalization and maintenance. Stokes and Osnes (1989) describe three general principles of programming for generalization: (1) take advantage of natural communities of reinforcement; (2) train diversely; and (3) incorporate functional mediators (e.g., self-instructions) (see Exhibit 23.5). Maintenance can be enhanced by changing the frequency or magnitude of reinforcement, the locus of reinforcement, or the form of reinforcement. Decisions will have to be made about what components of plans should be continued. Maintenance may require changing cultures (see Mattaini & McGuire, 2006, as well as chapter 27).

EXHIBIT 23.5

Guidelines for Encouraging Generalization and Maintenance

1. Focus on behaviors that will be reinforced in real-life settings.

2. Train to a proficiency level that makes behaviors of value functional (i.e., they occur in real-life settings and valued outcomes follow).

3. Prompt and reinforce behaviors; involve significant others.

4. Recruit natural communities of reinforcement and teach clients how to do so.

5. Use varied stimuli and responses (train loosely).

6. Make learning situations similar to real-life circumstances. When possible, train in real-life settings in which skills will be used and train in other settings as necessary.

7. Choose methods that clients can make use of on their own.

8. Remove artificial cues, reinforcers, and schedules.

9. Encourage beliefs about the causes of problems that contribute to persistence.

10. Identify high-risk situations for relapse and help clients to acquire coping skills to prevent and handle them.

11. Give clients written descriptions of plans.

12. Arrange follow-up contacts.

13. Arrange needed supports on an ongoing basis.

14. Use similar contingencies.

15. Offer opportunities for overlearning.

16. Reinforce unprompted generalizations.

Focus on Relevant Behaviors

New behaviors created in one context may generalize to others, but whether they are maintained (continued over time) will depend on whether they are reinforced in these other contexts. Honoring the *relevance-of-behavior rule* (teaching behaviors that will continue to be reinforced after helping efforts end) provides the greatest assurance of maintenance (Ayllon & Azrin, 1968). If there is little possibility that new ways of responding will be supported in real life, think twice about progressing on to intervention. The purpose of a task analysis is to identify behaviors needed to attain a certain outcome (see chapter 18). Satisfying the relevance-of-behavior rule may require creating new reinforcers. For example, social approval from adults may not function as a reinforcer for some children. Given that this is involved in the socialization of children, a program may be designed to establish this consequence as a reinforcer by pairing social approval with events that are reinforcing. New activities may acquire reinforcing functions. If learning new skills is reinforced, learning itself may become rewarding. Tracking use of new behaviors (e.g., coping skills), as well as progress, will indicate the relationship between the new behaviors and valued outcomes. A review of daily mood ratings and daily number of pleasant activities (both plotted on one graph) may show a relationship between mood and frequency of pleasant events.

Prompt and Reinforce Valued Behaviors; Involve Significant Others

Arrange for prompts and reinforcement of valued behaviors as needed. The rationale for involving significant others is their continuing influence on clients. Whenever possible, make arrangements to ensure that new behaviors on their part will continue to be supported. One way to do this is to follow the relevance-of-behavior rule (see preceding discussion). You could include significant others in group or family meetings. The purpose of many community organization programs is to enhance the effectiveness of residents' skills in seeking valued outcomes. Changes in the behavior of a significant other (such as a parent, teacher, or supervisor) that result in desired changes in a client's behavior may create a chain reaction in which, due to positive changes, the mediator reacts to the client in a more positive way, which results in further positive changes on the part of the client. In such cases, maintenance is likely. At other times, additional support will have to be arranged, for example, from other family members. Mrs. Slater included Mrs. Ryan in her work with Mr. and Mrs. Green and also spoke to Mrs. Ryan's grandchildren who lived with her. Mr. Colvine saw Brian and his parents together and involved all three in case planning. He also spoke to Brian's older brother.

Peer-mediated interventions have been successful in establishing, maintaining, and generalizing behaviors (e.g., Broussard & Northup, 1997). Involvement of peers has many advantages. They are readily available and provide a natural resource (e.g., see Webel et al., 2010). Variations of peer-mediated interventions include involving a child as a peer counselor to one or more classmates. For example, rather than receiving points for his improved performance, the child could award points to classmates when they offer desired behaviors. Or peers could be recruited to prompt and reinforce his behavior. You could help clients learn how to prompt and reinforce their own behaviors. (See later section on choosing methods that clients can make use of on their own.) Parents may be involved in training other parents (Neef, 1995). (See also DuPaul, George, Ervin, Hook, & McGoey, 1998.)

Recruit Natural Communities of Reinforcement

Take advantage of natural reinforcing communities in which clients can learn to "recruit" reinforcement for valued behaviors (Stokes, Fowler, & Baer, 1978). In the community reinforcement approach to problem drinking developed by Azrin (1976), people with similar concerns are brought together within a constructional approach to change (see also Meyers & Miller, 2001). The Internet provides opportunities to create linked groups of individuals with similar interests (e.g., see Finn & Steele, 2010). Community resources such as recreation centers may be available that will help clients maintain and increase valued skills and opportunities for reinforcement. Mrs. Slater introduced Mrs. Ryan to the local senior center, and her social skills were amply supported in this setting. Peers are a valued source of reinforcement in the neighborhood, school, or playground as described earlier. There is a rich literature describing the recruitment of peer reinforcement as described earlier (see also Tessaro et al., 2000).

Use Varied Stimuli and Responses

You can encourage generalization by including multiple trainers and models (so that new behaviors will not be influenced by one person only); multiple settings (so that behaviors will not be limited to one setting); and multiple types and sources of reinforcement (so behaviors will not be influenced only by one kind of reinforcement). Consider the following example by Stokes and Osnes (1989).

Steven [was] a mildly retarded autistic boy with Tourette syndrome. He engaged in frequent aggression, destruction, and self-abuse. These problems precluded continuation of placement in a school for deaf and blind individuals. Assessment of the functional environment revealed likely contingencies of coercion and escape. Intervention involved differential reinforcement of behaviors other than self-abuse or self-stimulation. Reinforcing consequences included praise, talk, affectionate touch, edibles, and activities such as listening to music. Self-abuse was followed by loss of access to a preferred ongoing activity. The program also included extinction contingencies for demands and threats and physical guidance following noncompliance, so that Steven could not escape from demands....

Multiple settings and trainers were involved as training progressed. Variations in appropriate responding were considered acceptable, and more children were added to the responsibility of the staff member working with Steven so that more distractions/stimuli were provided under more natural situations. The intrusiveness of the program was faded as quickly as possible, and behaviors of adaptive value (e.g., self-help) were taught.

Steven's teachers and parents came to the residential facility and were taught by the staff to implement Steven's program in a manner consistent with the specialized treatment. After Steven's transfer back to the school for deaf and blind persons, the program staff initially implemented the program in that setting along with the teachers. As the teachers demonstrated mastery of the program, school visits were decreased, systematically fading residential program involvement based on the teachers' mastery and continuation of the programming. Steven's improvements maintained well under these conditions, to the extent that he was later described as a model student (pp. 13–14).

Let us say you have been asked to help community residents acquire "canvassing skills" to encourage resident participation in local community groups. Training should include a variety of different kinds of reactions they may encounter. If the goal is for a child to follow instructions from both parents, both parents should be involved in training. Mr. Colvine encouraged his clients to practice negotiation skills when discussing conflicts. Julie rehearsed refusing different kinds of requests in different situations. Offer a variety of examples of behaviors of interest during training (e.g., different ways to refuse unwanted requests). This provides clients with different response options. Training loosely (including varied training conditions) decreases the likelihood that real-life variations interfere with generalization and maintenance.

Make Learning Conditions Similar to Real-Life Conditions

If possible, intervention should be carried out in real-life settings and should involve significant others who influence behaviors of concern. For example, when training was given in a one-to-one training session, skills acquired by autistic children did not generalize to a group setting, even when groups as small as two children with one teacher were used (Koegel & Rincover, 1974). A gradual increase in group size together with "thinning" reinforcement schedule did improve performance in a classroom of eight children with one teacher. This was important because the aim was to find out whether autistic children could be integrated into a regular classroom.

Choose Methods That Clients Can Make Use of on Their Own

Gains are more likely to be maintained if clients learn skills they can use on their own. Institutionalized girls labeled delinquent were taught how to increase positive feedback from staff members who rarely reinforced appropriate behaviors (Seymour & Stokes, 1976). Clients can learn self-instructions that function as cues for desired behaviors. Cognitive-behavioral programs focus on helping clients acquire valuable skills such as problem-solving skills (e.g., see Bond & Dryden, 2004; Steele, Elkin, & Roberts, 2008; Weisz, 2010). For example, children who are impulsive or easy to anger or to become discouraged might learn to say "Uh-oh, made a mistake. Next time I'll think ahead" or "This is tough, but I'll keep practicing." (See Hall, Jones, & Claxton, 2008; Fraser, Nash, Galinsky, & Darwin, 2000.) (See also chapters 24 and 25.)

Self-reinforcement may be used to maintain gains. This involves observation of behavior, evaluation of behavior based on some criteria, and feedback indicating whether performance meets criteria selected. Examples of self-reinforcing consequences used by children with disabilities include points recorded on a counter, tokens, marks such as on a piece of paper, and self-praise. The former three consequences could be traded for backup reinforcers such as money, free time, food, or special privileges. (See also Baumeister & Vohs, 2004.)

Occasional self-monitoring may help to maintain positive changes. For example, if a client believes that her rate of positive self-statements is decreasing, she could keep track of their frequency for a few days. If positive statements have decreased, procedures could be temporarily reintroduced, such as text-message reminders to replace negative self-statements with positive ones. Periodic tracking of pleasing and displeasing events can be used to catch and reverse the beginning stages of a downward trend in positives. Self-monitoring can remind clients about the relationship between behaviors such as exercising and valued outcomes such as maintaining a certain weight or increasing a positive mood. Clients can be given e-mail reminders to monitor behavior. Self-management training in which clients learn how to alter their behavior has been successful with a range of clients (see, for example, Mather & Goldstein, 2005; Smith & Sugai, 2000; Wolfe & Mash, 2008; Yeung et al., 2009). Helping clients to acquire problem-solving skills may encourage maintenance (see chapter 24). For example, teachers may learn to gather data as a first step when confronted with annoying behavior on the part of a child. An employee may learn to ask her supervisor to clarify vague criticisms before responding. You can increase the probability of generalization by overlearning (providing additional practice after mastery of a skill), and by clearly describing the rationale for use of skills.

Remove Artificial Cues/Reinforcers/Schedules

Gradually remove artificial components of plans unless they are needed on an ongoing basis to support behavior. Your praise and attention should become less important as natural reinforcers become more important. If artificial reinforcers, such as points or tokens, have been used, fade them out and arrange for natural reinforcers such as social approval to reinforce behavior (see Boerke & Reitman, 2011). Or you could increase the value of self-reinforcement. The point is to return to real-life schedules. Most behavior in real life is maintained on intermittent schedules of reinforcement (reinforcement is not offered after every response) (see chapter 7). If "artificial" schedules of reinforcement have been used (such as continuous reinforcement—every response is reinforced), these should be changed to resemble those in real life. Reinforcement can be gradually thinned. Higher performance criteria can be required for a given number of points, or fewer and fewer points can be given as natural reinforcers take effect.

Tracking progress on an ongoing basis will let you know whether you are "thinning" a schedule too rapidly. Training that involves failure, as well as success, increases durability of change. Dweck (1975) found that children who only had success experiences on math problems showed deterioration in performance when confronted with failure, whereas children who had failure, as well as success, and who received attribution training in which they were encouraged to try harder following a failure (a message that this resulted from too little effort rather than lack of skill) maintained or improved their performance following failure (see also Elliott & Dweck, 2005). Persistence of behavior can be enhanced by increasing the delay between behavior and its consequences. Gradually fading contacts may contribute to maintaining gains. You and your clients could change meetings from twice a week to once a week, then to biweekly contact and then to monthly meetings or telephone contact. This pattern of contact may be useful in discovering problems that arise in maintaining positive outcomes. Managed care regulations will limit your options.

Develop Helpful Attributions

How we attribute the outcomes of our behavior influences its durability. We are more likely to continue to use skills if we see the connection between them and outcomes we value. If we believe that success is a result of our efforts, we will persist longer when confronted with adversity. You can explore clients' understanding of the rationale for methods suggested by asking them to describe this. Mr. Colvine helped Brian and his parents to learn three behaviors of value in discussing conflicts (see chapter 21). To check on clients' understanding and the clarity of his explanation, he asked each family member to describe skills focused on in their own words, the situations in which each was of value, and the rationale for using each skill. Focus on changes that are compatible with clients' beliefs. If we succeed in new endeavors, but feel like impostors, we are less likely to continue new ways of acting. Developing helpful attributions sets the stage for use of valuable skills. Studies of successful programs designed to help people stop smoking suggest that earlier steps lay the groundwork for later ones. (See chapter 14.)

Offer Relapse Training

Another way to maintain gains is to help clients and significant others to identify situations that may result in relapse (loss of gains) and to develop constructive reactions to "slips." Maintenance programs may only forestall rather than prevent relapse. The persistence of effects will depend on the stability of environmental conditions (do contingencies continue to support desired behaviors?) and the client's skills in catching and countering downward drifts and developing new skills that will be required in novel situations. The term "relapse training" is used to refer to helping clients acquire skills for catching and reversing downward trends in valued outcomes. Clients learn to view these as slips requiring corrective actions rather than as signs of failure or hopelessness of ever succeeding (Marlatt & Donovan, 2008). High-probability situations for drinking are described as decision points in terms of whether to drink or not, and clients acquire coping skills to handle such situations. For example, they may weigh the ultimate aversive consequences of drinking against the immediate positive effects and learn how to resist pressure from others to drink. Relapse training has been and is a part of many programs (e.g., Bowen, Chawla, & Marlatt, 2011; Marlatt, Larimer, & Witkiewitz, 2010; Richards & Perri, 2012).

Discussing problems that might arise in maintaining progress forewarns clients that setbacks will occur and that they are not a sign of failure. This discussion sets the stage for learning how to deal constructively with setbacks. The likelihood of dips in positive moods following cognitive behavioral intervention for depression is high. Clients are forewarned of this. Stuart (1980) offered couples "what-if" exercises as part of a maintenance program. These involved situations that commonly arose but may not have been discussed. Some of these exercises were used as probes during final sessions to evaluate skills and to offer practice opportunities to enhance them. Clients were required to gradually assume more responsibility for discussing situations on their own.

Give Clients Descriptions of Methods Used

Written, text-messages, or audiotaped descriptions of methods used and related skills can serve as useful reminders. Clients can review them as an aid to maintaining gains. Check steps consist of questions to ask before, during, and after each task to increase the likelihood of success. Stuart (1980) gave each couple a written summary of plans. This included a description of the nature of presenting concerns, a reformulation of initial requests as a set of positive change goals, and a summary of assignments used. Clients were asked to review this whenever they felt uneasy about their relationship, as well as during a monthly review of success in maintaining valued outcomes. Giving clients copies of plans together with check steps for each part of the plan has been recommended for some time (Anthony, Cohen, & Farkas, 1990).

Plan Follow-Up Contacts and Arrange Ongoing Services as Needed

Follow-up sessions offer information about the effectiveness of services, as well as opportunities to catch downward drifts at an early stage. Anticipation of follow-up meetings may remind clients to use new skills. Periodic telephone calls or e-mails can be used to support new skills. Decisions must be made about what data to gather at follow-up, how to collect it, and who to involve. Booster sessions refer to periodic meetings following more frequent contact to support useful skills and troubleshoot. The sheer persistence of a behavior or thought such as a high frequency of negative self-statements over many years may make it necessary to periodically reintroduce special programs to maintain changes (e.g., see Tolan, Gorman-Smith, Henry, & Schoeny, 2009). A contextual analysis will suggest the likelihood of maintenance of valued behaviors. Without supporting contingencies, there is no reason to expect lasting change. The futility of expecting short-term solutions to problems that require long-term efforts suggests the value of additional periodic contact.

There may be a continuing need for supportive services (e.g., see McNaughton & Beukelman, 2010). Patients with severe mental illness may need help over the rest of their lives. Volunteers may be recruited to provide ongoing services. Children could participate in enriching day-care programs to make up for lack of parenting skills in encouraging children's cognitive development. Prosthetic devices such as railings in bathrooms and easy-to-use devices that allow people to signal for help may allow clients to remain in their homes. Ongoing support groups could be arranged. Maintaining participation in social action efforts may require ongoing support. Hoped-for changes may be in the distant future. Only by valuing and recognizing intermediate small steps may needed efforts continue. Planning for transitions is often a weak link in service programs (e.g., see Bigby & Socwk, 2000; Collins, 2001).

Ethical Issues

Whenever clients need help with real-life problems, generalization and maintenance are key concerns. We have an ethical obligation, to plan for generalization (Stokes & Osnes, 1989). This suggests an ethical mandate to inform clients about the likelihood of generalization and maintenance. To do this, you will have to be informed about the probability of durable change given specific circumstances and have content knowledge and related skills needed to plan effectively for generalization and maintenance. If you work in an agency in which little or no attention is given to generalization and maintenance, you should raise this as a concern. You could start by sharing research findings showing the lack of generalization and maintenance of valued outcomes.

Summary

Some endings will be planned. Others will not. Final meetings should allow time to discuss feelings about ending, to review progress, to celebrate successes, and to plan next steps. Planned endings are more likely if you focus on specific outcomes that clients value and track progress on an ongoing basis. Planned endings require arranging for the generalization and maintenance of positive outcomes and support for the clients' contributions to progress. You can encourage generalization by making training conditions as similar as possible to those in the natural environment, arranging practice in a variety of settings and with a variety of trainers, explaining the rationale for methods used, and arranging cues and reinforcers to encourage generalization. To maintain valued outcomes, you can involve significant others, encourage behaviors that will continue to be supported in real life, develop helpful attributions, arrange community supports, remove artificial procedural components, and select methods that give clients personal control (they are self-mediated). You can identify situations in which slips may occur and help clients acquire skills for preventing and handling them. Some clients will require ongoing services. What is needed will depend on the unique characteristics of each client and his or her circumstances.

Reviewing Your Competencies

Reviewing Content Knowledge

1. Describe characteristics of planned endings.

2. Identify reasons for unplanned endings.

3. Define the terms *generalization* and *maintenance* and give examples.

4. Given specific examples, you can identify feasible effective ways to enhance generalization.

5. Given specific examples, you can identify feasible effective ways to increase the durability of valued outcomes.

6. Describe attributions that enhance the durability of positive outcomes.

7. Describe what is meant by relapse training and give examples of what this involves.

8. Discuss the ethical obligations of helpers regarding generalization and maintenance.

Reviewing What You Do

1. Observation of your ending interviews demonstrates that important components of planned endings are included such as evidence-informed plans for maintaining valued outcomes.

2. You plan for generalization of change.

3. You plan for the maintenance of change both in early and later phases.

4. You provide training in relapse prevention as needed.

Reviewing Results

1. Generalization of positive outcomes occurs.

2. Desired outcomes are maintained.

3. Clients use relapse prevention skills with success.

Part 9

Intervention Options

24

Empowering Clients: Providing Information and Skill Building

OVERVIEW   Clients can expand their options by acquiring information and enhancing their skills, for example, learning how to manage anger reactions and to effectively advocate for needed services. Acquiring new social skills contributes to attaining many valued outcomes. Guidelines for achieving these goals are described in this chapter. Reframing problems as solvable by acquiring knowledge and skills, rather than as due to unchangeable personality traits, will encourage positive expectations and help clients and significant others to view each other in more positive ways. This focuses on identifying and increasing client strengths rather than on their lacks. Options for developing new behaviors include shaping, prompting, and fading, and social skills training. An overview of cognitive and cognitive-behavioral methods is also included. Seek guided learning opportunities to become adept in using methods with a track record of success.

YOU WILL LEARN ABOUT

- Providing information
- Enhancing options by developing new skills
- Shaping
- Model presentation
- Social skills training
- Enhancing self-management skills
- Helping clients change their cognitive ecology
- Problem-solving training
- Enhancing skills in managing emotions
- Mixed and multisystem programs

Providing Information

Providing information is a key role of social workers. This is often needed to increase access to services and to help clients to make informed decisions (e.g., see Gottlieb, 2003; Goulding, 2004). It is key in developing new views of concerns that help clients attain hoped-for goals (see later discussion of insight). It is a key aspect of empowering clients—to help clients gain greater influence over their environments (Schwartz & Woloshin, 2011). And it is an important component of psychoeducational interventions. Clients may benefit from learning how to obtain needed services or about norms describing typical patterns of behavior in different developmental phases (see Exhibit 24.1). Sources of information include relatives, friends, and acquaintances; specialized web sites on the Internet and consumer groups.

Questions often asked by clients in health settings include the following:

- Is this a problem? What is causing it?

- How does my experience compare with that of other people?

- Is there anything I can do myself to address my concerns and prevent it in the future?

EXHIBIT 24.1

Information of Potential Benefit to Clients

- How to obtain needed services.

- What to do if unfairly denied a service.

- How to locate certain kinds of self-help and support groups.

- Adverse effects of medications (e.g., see http://www. criticalthinkrx.org; www.pharmedout.org).

- How to obtain certain kinds of information.

- Relationships between personal troubles and social, political, and economic conditions (e.g., social policies).

- Options for increasing community/neighborhood resources.

- About developmental norms and others who share concerns.

- Common reactions during life transitions.

- Costs and benefits of certain patterns of behavior (e.g., drug use).

- Alternative options for attaining valued goals.

- How they influence others and how to make helpful changes.

- How others influence them and how to alter related patterns.

- Steps they can take to alter their neighborhood environments.

- Should I get a test? Are there alternatives? What is the purpose of the test?

- What are my options?

- What are the risks and benefits of different options?

- What will happen if I do nothing?

- How can I tell if my health care provider is telling me what I need to know to make an informed decision?

- What will it cost?

- Where can I get more information about my concerns and options? (See Jansson, 2011.)

Communicating accurate information to clients about the risks and benefits of different options is a challenge as described in chapter 20. Group work with clients often has a dual role of providing information and support (see Exhibit 24.2). Guidelines for offering information are suggested in Exhibit 24.3. Steps suggested by Gray (2001a) for providing information to clients include: (1) finding available research evidence using effective search techniques, (2) appraising that evidence to identify the best evidence available, and (3) determining whether the best evidence available is relevant to the individual client. This involves determining the likelihood the client will benefit, the magnitude of any benefit, and the probability of adverse effects and their magnitude (pp. 341–342).

Information should be offered to clients in a form that they find useful and that is individually tailored for each client, for example, how likely is it that a particular client will benefit from a service. Identifying helpful information and providing this in a manner that enhances its use is an important skill. Information is more likely to be acted on if it is provided in a clear manner and the rationale for its use explained. Check clients' understanding of material. Anticipate and if possible remove obstacles to using information. For example, clients may need certain skills to make use of new information. Write down important points and give a copy to clients.

Information can be provided verbally, in written form, via interactive computer programs, a website, by videotape, smartphone, and/or audiotape. It may be provided by a self-help group such as the Hearing Voices Network (http://www.hearing-voices. org). An MSW student at USC and former Marine Corps officer Kristen Kavanaugh co-founded the Military Acceptance Project, a web site providing information and resources concerning the repeal of "Don't Ask, Don't Tell." This also serves a social support role (*Newsbytes*, USC, June 26, 2011). The Internet provides opportunities to create virtual "communities" for social networking in order to pursue shared goals. Written handouts or text-messages can be used to supplement discussions during interviews as in programs designed to help parents acquire effective skills for communicating with professionals (Kohr, Parrish, Neef, Driessen, & Hallinan, 1988). Wandersman, Andrews, Riddle, and Fawcett (1983) used bibliographic approaches to

EXHIBIT 24.2

Coping With the Medical Care System and Social Service Agencies

1. *Acquire information about treatments*: Clients can request appointments with their physician to explain their treatment in more detail. They can take a list of questions to their appointments and ask doctors to write down important information. They can meet with a nurse or hospital social worker to discuss their concerns, consult relevant web sites, or read on their own about the various options. They can talk to each other or other individuals who are HIV positive. They can call the National AIDS Hotline (1-800-342-2437). In seeking and providing information, it is important that group members keep in mind that illness progression and reactions to treatment vary among individuals.

2. *Become informed about patients' rights*: Group members can learn about their rights as patients by:

    Sharing information with each other and with the group leader.
    Finding out who the patient advocacy persons and social workers are at their hospital or clinic and talking to them.
    Calling, e-mailing, or writing AIDS advocacy groups.

3. *Acquire effective assertion skills*: Group members may find it difficult to request services or speak up when they feel they are not treated properly. They could practice valuable skills in role plays.

4. *Increase support*: Family members and friends can help group members cope with the medical and social care systems by providing emotional support, assisting with red tape, being advocates, and visiting group members when they are in the hospital. Group members can increase support by educating significant others about HIV, and how to interact with medical social service personnel.

5. *Other options*:

    Going to appointments with a supportive person who takes notes.
    Asking for a number to call if a problem arises.

Source: Adapted from M. Galinsky, K. Rounds, A. Montague, & E. Butowsky (1993). *Leading a telephone support group for persons with HIV disease* (pp. 24–25). Chapel Hill, NC: School of Social Work, University of North Carolina. Reprinted with permission.

establish neighborhood block organizations. As they note, providing knowledge about how behavior is influenced by the environment can help clients to create, select, and transcend their environments. Programs may be offered to newly arrived migrants and refugees to help them to succeed in their new environments. Providing information is a key part of client and cause advocacy. Sources including the Internet, governmental agencies, policy institutes, the media, and agency newsletters (for further discussion, see chapter 27). Obstacles to effective diffusion of material include staff who fail to distribute leaflets to promote informed choice in maternity care (O'Cathain, Walters, Nicholl, Thomas, & Kirkham, 2002).

Clients may believe that they have little influence over what they learn, perhaps because of nonrewarding and punishing experiences at home and school. Pessimistic beliefs highlight the importance of careful selection of material so that efforts are successful and clients can enhance the quality of their lives.

Recommendations for preparing informational material such as brochures and computerized decision aids for clients suggested by Coulter, Entwistle, and Gilbert (1999) include the following:

The process:

1. Involve [clients] throughout the process.

2. Involve a wide range of clinical experts.

3. Be specific about the purpose of the information and the target audience.

4. Consider the information needs of minority groups.

5. Review the research evidence and use systematic reviews wherever possible.

6. Plan how the materials can be used within a wider program promoting shared decision making.

7. Consider cost and feasibility of distribution and updating when choosing media.

8. Develop a strategy for distribution.

9. Evaluate the materials and their use.

10. Make arrangements for periodic review and updating.

11. Publicize the availability of materials.

The content:

1. Use [client's] questions as the starting point.

2. Ensure that common concerns and misconceptions are addressed.

3. Refer to all relevant intervention options.

EXHIBIT 24.3

Guidelines for Giving Information

- Be selective. The fewer the instructions given, the greater the recall.

- Organize material. We have greater recall of information presented in the first third of an exchange and of the first instruction given.

- Prepare the client in advance for what you are about to say (e.g., "First, I am going to describe _____, then I will describe _____").

- Be specific, clear, detailed, and simple in giving instructions. Use short words and sentences. Use down-to-earth, non-technical language. Give concrete illustrations.

- Attend to cultural differences (e.g., in manner of presenting information, meaning of concepts).

- Give small amounts of information at each visit. Do not overload clients with details. Individually pace and tailor content given.

- Different clients need different kinds of information at different points. Check for receptivity and understanding.

- Involve clients and significant others in planning.

- Do not oversell programs.

- Describe the rationale for suggested plans (e.g., how they relate to goals clients value), the specific behaviors involved, and the possible consequences of following or not following recommendations.

- Tie to personal experience.

- Explore whether the information is compatible with the client's beliefs about the problem and what should be done about it. Review the client's view of agreed-on methods at the time they are initiated, as well as at later points.

- Help clients develop strategies to recall material (e.g., summaries and outlines).

- Supplement verbal descriptions with audiovisual material and visual graphic aids (diagrams, charts, audiotapes, videotapes, films, brochures). Be sure that clients can comprehend written material.

- Emphasize the importance of following agreed-on plans.

- Check comprehension. Ask questions and request feedback. Encourage clients to raise questions and take notes or write summaries.

- Ask the clients to describe the information given in their own words.

- Be sure that clients have the skills required to follow recommendations.

- Individualize instructions and give feedback and praise for efforts.

- Build up the client's self-confidence that he or she can be successful in using information.

- Help clients diminish or remove barriers caused by the procedures themselves.

- Supplement education with other methods (e.g., planned phone calls to troubleshoot).

Source: Adapted from D. Meichenbaum & D. C. Turk (1987). *Facilitating treatment adherence* (pp. 131–132). New York: Plenum.

4. Include accurate information about benefits and risks.

5. Include quantitative information where possible.

6. Include checklists and questions to ask.

7. Include sources of further information.

8. Use non-alarmist, non-patronizing language in active rather than passive voice…

9. Include good illustrations.

10. Be explicit about authorship and sponsorship.

11. Include reference to sources used.

12. Include the publication date. (p. 320)

Providing sources of accurate information will counter incorrect or incomplete information presented by individuals and groups with vested interests in persuading clients to use certain methods.

Self-Help Books and Client Manuals

The term *bibliotherapy* is a fancy way to describe asking clients to read material. Self-help materials have been developed related to a wide range of outcomes (see Norcross et al., 2003). Review material beforehand to make sure that it informs (rather than misinforms) and that content will not "turn off" readers because it is sexist, homophobic, racist, or classist. Ask: "Is there any evidence that this self-help book will help my client?" Evidence-informed selection of material increases the likelihood that what is read helps rather than harms clients. Be sure to consider required reading level and preferred language so content matches clients' skills. Self-help material is available for a number of cognitive-behavioral programs (see, for example, Burns, 2006; Craske & Barlow, 2007).

The Internet and Computer-Based Education and Decision-Aids

Many clients now access information from the Internet. Hundreds of support groups use the Internet to network and to provide information and support (see Anthony, Nagel, & Goss, 2010). You can help clients learn how to critically appraise content on the Internet, for example: Are original references given? Who funds the source? Are there signs of pseudoscience or quackery? (See chapters 4 and 11.) The term *health informatic services* includes Internet sites, teleservice (e-mail consultations or counseling), and software (such as interpretation of tests). Your skills in locating and critically appraising information on the web will determine how much help you can provide to clients. Clients may set up their own self-help web sites with or without collaboration of professionals.

Computer-based education has many advantages, such as allowing us to ask questions that we are particularly interested in. People differ in the kinds of questions and information that may be relevant. Computer-based education can be tailored to different reading levels. Thousands of web sites are available related to thousands of different concerns and interests. Computer programs can be used to simulate real-life situations by asking clients to respond to vignettes related to client concerns. Decision aids have been developed to help clients make decisions (O'Connor et al., 2009). Such aids are of particular value when there are multiple options, uncertainty regarding outcomes, and when people differ in how they value different benefits and harms. Web-based tools can be used to organize people with a similar interest as described in chapter 27.

Insight as Information: Reframing Concerns

A first step to changing behaviors, thoughts, or feelings may be helping clients to understand how their behavior is influenced by their environments and how they in turn influence their environments (see chapter 25). A contextual approach highlights economic, political, and social influences on personal and social problems. (See chapter 12.) Concerns are reframed as challenges to be overcome by acquiring new skills. Troubling behaviors are understood in relation to their functions—even suicide, e.g., to escape from unbearable loneliness rather than as a mental illness. Gilbert's (1989) work suggests that battered women may benefit from understanding their reactions within an evolutionary perspective in which defeat states (e.g., helplessness) are typical ways of avoiding further aggression. The kind of insight emphasized differs in different practice approaches, and different people may value different kinds. In *Psychoanalytic Terms and Concepts* (1990), Moore and Fine define *insight* as "the capacity or act of apprehending the nature of a situation or one's own problems" (p. 99).

Within a psychoanalytic perspective, insight is assumed to have two components: affective and cognitive. Helping clients reconceptualize their concerns in a more helpful way—one that gives direction for steps to take to alter difficult circumstances and encourages belief in self-efficacy—is a key skill. This lays the groundwork for taking action to pursue hoped-for outcomes. Such reconceptualizations help clients to transform pain into meaning that encourages taking steps to improve life. Dialectical behavior theory (DBT) and acceptance and commitment approaches encourage clients to accept life as it is, not as it is supposed to be, as well as the need to change despite and because of this reality (e.g., see Hayes, Follette, & Linehan, 2004; Linehan, 1993, 1995; Miller, Rathus, & Linehan, 2007). Insight including reframing is neither a necessary nor sufficient condition for change. For example, if clients do not have the skills required to act in effective ways, insight and reframing will not alter behavior in real-life settings.

Information, Advocacy, and Consciousness Raising

Helping clients to understand the relationship between personal troubles and political, social, and economic factors has been a key emphasis of sociologists and others critical of the biomedicalization of life (e.g., see Illich, 1976; Rapley, Moncrieff, & Dillon, 2011; Szasz, 2001; Cohen & Timimi, 2008). Paulo Freire (1973) argues that "oppression comes from within the individual as well as from without: and hence that felt needs must be…questioned as to their causes if people are to be freed from blind adherence to their own world views as well as to the world views of others which they have uncritically internalized" (p. 89). In his critical pedagogy the role of the teacher is to help others to penetrate false consciousness—to help others to understand how "dominant social and economic groups impose values and methods that legitimize their own power and policies of control" (Brookfield, 1995, p. 208). Skinner (1953, 1971) advocated wide distribution of knowledge about the principles of behavior so that we understand how our behavior is influenced by our environments and can be more effective in resisting unwanted influence and seeking valued change.

Information is a resource. Embarrassing information is closely guarded by organizations and governmental agencies, and punishing consequences may be heaped on whistle-blowers. Scientists have been threatened with lawsuits if they publish research findings judged by "Big Pharma" to be negative. Professionals have been sued for raising questions about dubious claims (e.g., Sweet, 2011). The suppression of information is one of the major ways in which politicians and the media wield influence (e.g., see Bagdikian, 2004; Gambrill, 2012a), as well as also discussion of propaganda in chapter 4. Providing information about problems/causes and possible solutions is common in social action efforts as described in chapter 27. The Internet provides new opportunities to involve people in mutually valued efforts, for example, to share information and to advocate for services and to plan protests (Hick & McNutt, 2002). Consider the success of MoveOn.org (http://front.moveon.org/). Simply informing citizens about a problem may mobilize them to participate in advocacy efforts. Relevant information may be found in a variety of sources including governmental web sites (see chapter 11).

> Information is the key to effective advocacy. It comes in many forms. Some pieces of information are numbers—the answers to questions like: How many children live here? How many are in school? How much money is available? But data include much more than numbers. Answers to questions like: What kind of services are there for children with physical disabilities? Where can you find them? Who's in charge of them? Are they any good? Do parents know about them? involve valuable facts that go beyond numbers. You'll need to know officials' names, addresses, phone numbers and responsibilities. You'll want to know who your allies are and who is likely to oppose what you want. You'll need to know about relevant rules, laws, guidelines, policies, and regulations. You'll want to see budgets, program activity reports, statements of priorities and plans, and evaluations of programs affecting individuals you're concerned with.
>
> Gathering information will enable you to reveal officials' evasions, question their assumptions, and, if necessary, counter their figures. (Shur & Smith, 1980, pp. 1–3)

This statement is as true today as it was over 30 years ago. You can help clients learn how to critically evaluate information distributed by social service agencies. As noted earlier, such material may be more propagandistic than accurate (for example, inflate claims and hide disliked alternative views) (Altheide & Johnson, 1980). There are hundreds of consumer groups many of which are concerned with a specific problem, such as caring for someone who has Alzheimer's disease. *Health Consumer News* is a newsletter published by the Health Consumer Alliance. Examples of National Consumer Organizations include:

Center for Science in the Public Interest: <http://www.cspinet.org>

Coalition Against Insurance Fraud: <http://www.insurancefraud.org>

Consumer Action: <http://www.consumer-action.org>

National Consumers League: <http://www.nclnet.org>

National Community Reinvestment Coalition: <http://www.ncrc.org>

National Consumer Law Center: <http://www.consumerlaw.org>

Public Citizen, Inc.: <http://www.citizen.org>

Hearing Loss Association of America: <http://www.hearingloss.org>

Community Education

Broad-based community involvement is emphasized in community education. If residents are to work together to attain valued outcomes, they must have access to helpful information (see Tett, 2010). What concerns are shared? What are related contingencies at different system levels? What stakeholders are involved? A needs assessment may be carried out to identify shared interests (see chapter 27). David Mathews (1990) suggests that an effective community has the following characteristics:

1. It educates itself as a whole, in all of its subdivisions and groups, about the *whole* of its interests.

2. It has more than just facts; it knows what the facts mean in the lives of the people in the community and helps people to think and use those facts effectively.

3. It talks through issues to develop shared knowledge.

4. It knows the difference between mass opinion and "public judgments."

5. It makes a distinction between government officials and public leaders.

Larry Decker (1992) highlights the importance of community education as a process. He suggests four components:

1. Provision of diverse educational services to meet the varied learning needs of residents of all ages;

2. Development of interagency cooperation and public–private partnerships to reduce duplication of efforts and improve overall effectiveness of the delivery of human services;

3. Encouragement of improvement efforts that make the community more attractive to both current and prospective residents and businesses; and

4. Involvement of residents in community problem solving and decision making. (p. 263)

Community schools provide a key resource in facilitating education. Such schools reflect "the fact that people's learning needs are both full-time and lifelong. In contrast to the traditional school, a community school serves all ages and functions 12 to 18 hours a day, 7 days a week, 12 months a year" (p. 265). (See also chapter 27.)

Enhancing Options by Developing New Skills

Clients and significant others may benefit from enriching their skills including self-care, social, vocational, and/or recreational skills. Skills focused on may include work-related skills, respite care skills, skills for parents with children with disabilities, leisure skills, integration skills for students with disabilities, and skills for managing various kinds of illnesses as in behavioral medicine. Neighbors may acquire positive methods to request changes in annoying behaviors. Community residents may learn how to form coalitions to seek change. Participants on community boards may learn how to influence group process. Aggressive children may learn how to make and keep friends. A supervisor may enhance her skills in providing positive feedback to staff. Skills of value to clients include dealing with stress, planning skills, and social skills such as starting conversations and asking for help. Skill training is a component of psychiatric rehabilitation programs with mixed results (Tungpunkom, Maayan, & Soares-Weiser, 2012). Interventions may be delivered over the Internet (Finn & Schoech, 2008; L'Abate & Kaiser, 2011).

Most procedures designed to develop new skills, such as social skills training, consist of a number of components including shaping, chaining, prompting and fading, model presentation, and rehearsal. (See, for example, Lecroy, 2008; Steele et al., 2008.) Creating a distraction-free environment will increase the effectiveness of training sessions as will assessment of each client's entry-level competencies and a task analysis in which clear objectives and intermediate steps are described (see chapter 24). In this way you "start where the client is" and have a planned agenda that includes positive feedback for each step. "Access behaviors" should be identified and encouraged. This term refers to behaviors that increase access to reinforcing environments and provide opportunities for additional skill acquisition (Hawkins, 1986). (See also discussions of behavioral cusps, Rosales & Baer, 1997.) If you are responsible for helping clients to acquire new skills, you will need competencies in developing new behaviors. If you are in a case manager role, you can also use this knowledge to assess programs provided by other agencies.

Shaping

Shaping involves the differential reinforcement of successive approximations to a desired behavior. Successive approximations are variations of behavior that increasingly resemble the final behavior desired. Shaping takes advantage of the variability of behavior, selecting variations that are closest to desired behavior and reinforcing them, while ignoring others. We are all involved in shaping behavior (and are being shaped by others). Helping clients to acquire positive shaping methods is a common goal. Skilled negotiators and mediators are skilled shapers. Shaping can be used when instructions and model presentation cannot be relied on alone. It is often used to develop self-care, social, recreational, academic, and vocational skills of both children and adults with developmental disabilities.

Positive and Punitive Approaches

There are both positive and negative ways to shape behavior. Skilled athletic coaches are expert shapers, as are effective drama coaches. Skill in using positive methods to shape behavior will be one of your most valuable repertoires. Positive compared to negative methods are more effective and more pleasant for all involved parties. They make learning enjoyable (even fun) and are less likely to create resistance and negative feelings. Reliance on positive methods requires identification of suitable positive reinforcers. People often rely on aversive methods (yelling, threatening, or removing privileges) because they lack positive shaping skills. Preferences for positive rather than negative influence are related to our values, as well as our skills. Caring and respect for others encourage use of positive methods that make people's day brighter rather than dimmer. The discussion of evolutionary influences in chapter 7 illustrates the difference between societies in which status and order is maintained through fear and intimidation and those in which they are maintained through positive consequences, such as caregiving and signals of reassurance. We live in a society in which fear and intimidation are rife (Furedi, 2006). Many people learn neither positive skills for influencing their environment nor values that encourage their use (Sidman, 1989).

What Is Involved

Two procedures are used in shaping: positive reinforcement for successive approximations to a desired behavior and operant extinction for other behaviors. In the latter, reinforcement is withheld; behavior occurs but is not reinforced. Shaping relies on the use of positive feedback and builds on current repertoires (starts where the client is). The concept of successive approximations is a key one. Shaping involves the following steps:

1. Select the target behavior.

2. Identify the behavior the client currently performs that most closely resembles desired behaviors.

3. Select effective reinforcers to use to reinforce desired behaviors including successive approximations.

4. Reinforce successive approximations to desired behaviors each time they occur.

5. Reinforce target behaviors each time they occur.

6. Do not reinforce other behavior.

7. Reinforce desired behaviors until they occur frequently and move to an intermittent schedule of reinforcement when the target behavior occurs often.

Establishing a conditioned reinforcer allows you to immediately reinforce approximations. You could pair a clicker with a reinforcer such as food or tokens or points established as a reinforcer (clicker training). When an approximation occurs, the conditioned reinforcer (e.g., clicker) can be immediately presented as a signal that reinforcement will follow. You can use prompts (verbal instructions, gestures, physical guidance, or environmental changes) to encourage closer approximations. Prompts are gradually removed so behavior will occur without reminders. Additional reinforcement may be provided for closer approximations. Select reinforcers that can be delivered immediately and are nondistracting and nonsatiating (they do not quickly lose their reinforcing potential). Skill is required in deciding when to reinforce only a closer approximation, in recovering from backsliding toward more distant approximations, and in withholding reinforcement for behaviors that do not approximate desired outcomes (see Exhibit 24.4). *Don't Shoot the Dog: The New Art of Teaching and Training* (1999) by Karen Pryor provides a sound, clear, entertaining description of shaping.

If You Are Not Successful

Indicators of poor shaping skills include lack of success in altering behavior in desired ways, attempts to escape from the situation, and negative emotional reactions (e.g., anger and anxiety). Common errors include:

- Vague descriptions of entering repertoires, desired outcomes, and intermediate steps so it is difficult to decide what to reinforce and what not to.

- Selecting performance requirements that are too difficult.

- Giving too much or too little reinforcement for approximations.

EXHIBIT 24.4

Skills Involved in Shaping

- Obtain the person's attention.
- Determine the operant level (the closest approximation).
- Demonstrate the desired behavior.
- Start with the correct step (reinforcing the closest approximation).
- Proceed to the next step appropriately.
- Return to an earlier step when necessary.
- Ignore undesired behavior.
- Prepare the context correctly (providing needed props and removing distraction).
- Train for one task at a time.

Rewarding

- Find an effective reinforcer.
- Give the reinforcer right after the approximation.
- Pair verbal reinforcement with material reinforcers.
- Offer verbal or physical reinforcers, such as a hug reinforcement enthusiastically.
- Pair physical reinforcement with the material reinforcer (e.g., hugging a child and offering him a bite of food).
- Use praise to establish chains of behavior (so material reinforcement can be faded out).
- Alter the reinforcer as necessary (for example, if satiation occurs).
- Withhold reinforcement correctly.

Communicating

- Get acquainted before training.
- Give the correct emphasis to key words when providing instructions.
- Use valuable verbal instructions.
- Use the person's name before the instruction.
- Use gestures that supplement verbal cues.
- Use physical prompts effectively.
- Fade prompts and gestures as soon as possible.
- Show patience, interacting in a respectful manner.

Source: Adapted from J. M. Gardner, D. J. Brust, & L. S. Watson (1970). A scale to measure proficiency in applying behavior modification techniques to the mentally retarded. *American Journal of Mental Deficiency, 74*, 633–636.

If an approximation is reinforced too often, variability of behavior will decrease and closer approximations will occur less often. Remember, shaping takes advantage of the natural variability of behavior. So the more often one variation is reinforced, the fewer variations are likely to occur. If an approximation is not reinforced often enough, behavior may drift back to a more distant one. If you are not successful, review Exhibit 24.4, as well as discussions of positive reinforcement and operant extinction in chapter 25.

Verbal instructions and manual guidance may be needed, or they may have been included when no longer necessary, preventing the person from independently carrying out a chain of behavior. Distractions such as other people in the learning environment may impede progress. Perhaps you reinforced an awkward way of performing an approximation that makes next steps difficult. You may have to reinforce an earlier approximation, increase verbal prompts, use physical guidance, or reduce requirements. Satiation or fatigue may intensify as work progresses. If so, reinforce a successfully performed response and end the training session.

Chaining and Shaping

Shaping and chaining are closely related. Behaviors that are shaped often involve a chain of behaviors. The term *behavior chain* refers to a sequence of responses in which specific cues signal behavior in a sequence that ends with a reinforcer. One useful feature of chaining is the possibility of breaking down any component behavior into a more detailed set of behaviors. This allows you to tailor training to the unique skill levels and progress of each client. A task analysis may be needed to identify the specific behaviors and their sequence that are involved in a chain. This is often required in working with children and adults with developmental disabilities (e.g., ordering food in a fast food restaurant). Nine behaviors are included in the sequence described below for teaching a child how to put on a pair of slacks.

1. Taking the slacks from the dresser drawer.

2. Holding the slacks upright with the front facing away from the individual.

3. Putting one leg in the slacks.

4. Putting the other leg in the slacks.

5. Pulling the slacks to the knees.

6. Pulling the slacks to the thighs.

7. Pulling the slacks all the way up.

8. Doing up the button or snap.

9. Doing up the zipper.

Process task analysis involves the design of strategies for teaching content (e.g., certain concepts such as "besides," "on-top"). Examples include *matching to sample* (presenting an object and asking the learner to select from a group of objects the one that matches) and *oddity* (the learner selects from a group of objects the one that does not belong). Skill in designing and conducting such training is important for teachers of individuals with developmental disabilities. Some chains of behavior such as shoe tying are more easily established by starting from the end of the chain. In *backward chaining,* the last part of the task is taught first, then the next to last, and so on. In *forward chaining,* the first part of a task is taught first, then the next, and so on. In total task presentation, the entire task is presented and reviewed. Feedback (to let the learner know what is wanted and if he is achieving it) may be offered before, during, and/or after practice. This may be verbal (e.g., praise), nonverbal (a symbol, for example, a smiling face), or consist of direct guidance. The term *criterion* refers to a predetermined point at which it is decided that learning has taken place (e.g., repeated observation of the behavior under the conditions in which it is expected to occur).

Without an understanding of chaining, you may skip necessary steps resulting in lack of progress and/or backsliding, not reinforce each step along the way, or steps may be "out of order" making learning difficult. Chaining and shaping are additional ways in which individual differences are considered. We each have a different entering repertoire in relation to a skill. Without knowledge about each client's unique repertoire and the steps required to achieve an outcome, frustration and failure may result rather than success and pleasure in accomplishment. Chains of behavior are easier to interrupt in the early parts of the chain that are furthest removed from the final reinforcer. Some chains of behavior are more difficult to disrupt than are others. For example, couples who are dissatisfied with their relationships have a more difficult time stopping dysfunctional conversations about their communication problems than do satisfied couples.

Prompting and Fading

Prompting and fading can be used to provide additional guidance or cues for valued behaviors. Prompting refers to use of a cue (a prompt) to signal someone to carry out a certain behavior. Prompts are discriminative stimuli (cues) that are not part of the natural environment. They may be verbal, gestural, or physical. Fading involves the gradual removal of a prompt. This "is used to foster independence by reducing or eliminating the control that the prompter (instructor) and prompts have had over the student's behavior" (Foxx, 1982, p. 83). You could, for example, decrease the number of words in an instruction or reduce the size of gestures. Prompting and fading can be used to prevent backsliding of valued behaviors that may result in an intrusive intervention such as institutionalization.

Model Presentation

Model presentation is used in many ways in everyday practice. You may model helpful problem-solving steps to your clients. Important social skills can be presented on smartphones for review (see also Darden-Brunson, Green, & Goldstein, 2008). Model presentation was used to demonstrate effective communication skills to Brian and his parents (see chapter 21). Mrs. Slater loaned an audiotape to Mrs. Ryan and the Greens illustrating effective and ineffective ways to share feelings. She also modeled useful skills in the office and gave her clients written descriptions. Ms. Landis used model presentation with Julie to enhance her skills in resisting unwanted sexual overtures. Group leaders model behaviors that group members may benefit from learning. Supervisors and managers should model communication methods they would like their staff to use. Components involved in the effective use of modeling include:

- Clear description of specific behaviors to be altered.

- Presentation of a model.

- Observation of the model.

- Practice of modeled behaviors.

- Corrective feedback.

- Repeat as needed.

Modeling will be more effective if attention is drawn to particular behaviors that are valued. For example, you could point out the effect of empathic comments on decreasing anger. A mediator may model requests for solutions and suggestions of compromises. Modeling of valued behaviors is an integral part of social skills training. Strayhorn (1994) encouraged parents to read stories to their children that presented models of valued behaviors and to avoid modeling negative behaviors. In his competency-based program for young children and their parents, he explained the importance of parents' modeling valued behaviors and of omitting models of violence, sarcasm, and hostility. He encouraged parents to "raise their consciousness about the degree of violence in entertainment. A useful exercise is counting the violent acts in even G-rated Disney classics, and pondering the consequences of injury and death if those acts were carried out in real life. A slapstick blow on the head could result in a concussion and permanent seizure disorder" (p. 59). He encouraged parents

> not to present the boycott of violent entertainment as the withdrawal of a good thing that should be a privilege and a pleasure for everyone. The parent takes some time to explain that violence is a big problem in our society, that violent entertainment promotes this problem, and that the family is trying to boycott violent entertainment out of a spirit of not wanting to "vote" for the continuation of a major cause of such a bad problem. In other words, the parent attempts to convert the child to a social activist stance rather than to attribute to the child a high vulnerability to violent behavior. (p. 60)

He also encouraged parents to use plays, songs, and dances that model valued attitudes, feelings, thoughts, and actions. Additional guidelines for making effective use of models are described in the next section.

Social Skills Training

Social skills training is designed to enhance effective social behavior. It is used to "empower" people by increasing their influence over their environments including dealing with service providers (e.g., see Kopelowicz, Liberman, & Zarate, 2006; Steele et al., 2008). It is widely used with children and adults, including those with developmental disabilities (e.g., Goldstein, Kaczmarek, & English, 2002; Lösel & Beelmann, 2003; McGinnis, 2011; Sailor et al., 2009; Springer & Rubin, 2009; Weisz, 2010). Training may be carried out with individuals or in groups. Groups provide a number of advantages (see chapter 26). Programs have been developed to enhance the quality of care provided to residents in institutional settings (Risley & Favell, 1979), to enhance friendship skills of both adults and children, to enhance social skills of clients diagnosed with schizophrenia (Bellack, Mueser, Gingerich, & Agresta, 2004), to increase skills of family members (e.g., Lochman, 2000), and to decrease risky sexual behaviors (Johnson, Hedges, & Diaz, 2004).

The main goal of social skills training may be to prevent problems, for example, by decreasing risk factors and increasing protective factors related to antisocial behavior (see Rapp-Paglicci, Dulmus, & Wodarski, 2004). You can help clients to acquire relationship skills they can use to enrich their social networks. Examples of relevant behaviors include offering positive feedback to others (empathy and listening), expressing feelings, personal disclosure, requesting behavior changes, negotiating, and refusing requests (see chapters 15 and 16). (See, for example, the work of John Gottman and his colleagues.) Natural contexts provide many opportunities to enhance valued skills. Broadly speaking, parent training programs and programs designed to enhance communication among family members can be viewed in part as social skills training because they involve social behaviors (e.g., see Barth et al., 2008; Lutzker & Bigelow, 2002; Webster-Stratton, 2009). Assertion training is a form of social skills training (e.g., see Gambrill, 1995).

Assessment Comes First

Social skills training should be preceded by a contextual assessment. Helpers sometimes jump into training too soon without clear descriptions of client goals and how to attain them. Only through a careful assessment can you determine if a lack of social skills is an issue. Cultural differences in what is viewed as appropriate must be considered. Clients may have skills but not use them. Research related to children alleged to have ADHD (attention-deficit/hyperactivity disorder) suggests that these children may have social skills but not use them (Hinshaw, 1995).

Identify Situations of Concern

Exactly what situations are involved, who is involved, and where do relevant exchanges occur? What are the client's goals? Social behavior is situationally specific in terms of what is effective. A behavior that is effective in achieving a given outcome in one situation may not be successful in another. This highlights the importance of clearly describing situations of concern.

Clearly Describe Behaviors Required for Success

What behaviors are required for success? The behaviors that make up an effective reaction differ in different situations. Definitions of socially effective behavior differ in the extent to which personal outcomes (effects on oneself), as well as social outcomes (effects on others), are considered. Most definitions emphasize providing reinforcing consequences in a way that is socially acceptable and does not harm others. How can you find out what behaviors are required to achieve certain outcomes in a situation? Let us say a client does poorly in job interviews. What do people do who succeed? What is success? Practice-related literature may offer guidelines about what is effective.

Situations of concern, as well as effective response options, have been identified for many groups including psychiatric patients, adolescents, the elderly, and individuals with different kinds of physical disabilities. Task analyses of behaviors of interest may be available. These provide an empirically based training guide. Willner et al. (1977) asked youth residing in a halfway house to rate specific staff behaviors on a scale ranging from A to F. Examples of highly rated behavior included joking and doing what was promised. Disliked behavior included criticism and not following through on promises. Degree of success in real life will offer feedback about whether relevant skills have been identified and were used and with what consequences. Be cautious about using your experience as a guide. It may be limited or unusual. You could ask clients to observe people in similar roles who are effective and to note the situation, what was done (including both verbal and nonverbal behaviors), and what happened. Normative criteria may be used as a criterion (what most people do in a situation). A concern here is that the norm may not reflect what is desirable. For example, school teachers may give low rates of praise and high rates of criticism. You would not want to encourage this pattern.

Clearly Describe Entering Repertoires

This step requires identifying what skills clients already possess. The gap between current and required skills can then be accurately assessed. Role plays are valuable for this purpose as described in chapter 17.

Identify Possible Obstacles

What obstacles (e.g., negative thoughts or feelings) interfere with success? Does anxiety or anger get in the way? If so, is it related to negative self-statements or unrealistic expectations (I should always get my way)? Be sure to find out how clients feel about altering their behavior in specific situations. Unique socialization patterns may get in the way of changing behavior in positive directions. Beliefs such as "I must please everyone" that pose obstacles to acting in new ways may have to be identified and reevaluated. (See chapter 19.) Clients may have inappropriate goals (those that cannot be met or are met at a high cost such as social rejection). For example, children who have difficulty making friends may value dominance over cooperation. Poor choice of goals may result in poor choice of social behaviors (those that result in punishing rather than positive consequences). Aggressive compared to nonaggressive boys differ in their social-cognitive processes (e.g., Cook & Cook, 2009; Lochman & Dodge, 1994).

Steps Involved in Training

An explain-demonstrate-practice-feedback model is used in which explanations are first offered about why certain skills are of value and situations in which they can be used are identified (see Exhibit 24.5). Training should be individually tailored to each client's unique entry-level skills and obstacles that may interfere with acquiring and using skills. Repeated practice and feedback are key in developing mastery and enhancing comfort with new skills. Practice is usually preceded by model presentation of effective responses and identification of specific behaviors (both verbal and nonverbal) to be increased, decreased, or varied. Overt behavior includes both verbal (what is said) and nonverbal (smiles, facial expression, eye contact) components. Other skills include rewardingness (offering friendly reactions such as smiling and positive verbal statements), self-presentation, and empathy (ability to take the role of others).

Model Presentation

Observational learning via model presentation is an important component of social skill training. Models can be presented in many different ways including written scripts, audiotape, videotape, on smartphones, film, or live. One advantage of written and smartphone descriptions is that they can be referred to as needed. The more extensive the lack of skills, the more likely model presentation, rehearsal, feedback, and instructions will be needed to develop skills. In other cases, practice or instructions alone may be sufficient to achieve desired outcomes. Computer-based programs offer opportunities for repeated model presentations of how to handle specific situations. Virtual reality sites allow practice opportunities. Model presentation has been used for decades in parent training. For example, videotaped presentations of problem situations and demonstrations of parents successfully handling them were shown to parents who abused their children as one part of a program to enhance positive parenting skills (Denicola & Sandler, 1980). Videotaped modeling is a key part of Webster-Stratton's Incredible Years Parent Training Program (see her web site, http://www.incredibleyears.com) as

---

EXHIBIT 24.5

Steps Involved in Social Skills Training

ASSESSMENT

_____ Describe specific social situations of concern.

_____ Identify specific goals in each. Review for appropriateness.

_____ Identify behaviors required in each situation to attain goals sought.

_____ Review clients entering repertoire (what they can now do).

_____ Identify additional skills needed, as well as when to use them to good effect.

_____ Identify obstacles to using skills (e.g., anxiety, unrealistic expectations).

_____ Encourage positive expectations.

SOCIAL SKILLS TRAINING

_____ Model effective alternatives.

_____ Engage clients in practice (behavioral rehearsal).

_____ Prompt and cue participants as needed during role plays.

_____ Provide constructive feedback following each role play (e.g., identify and encourage improvements in relevant verbal and nonverbal skills in small, attainable increments).

_____ Repeat model presentation, practice, and feedback as necessary (until skill levels required for success are met).

_____ Discourage behavior that gets in the way (e.g., joking in groups). For example, you could ignore it.

_____ Address obstacles to success (e.g., interfering thoughts and feelings).

_____ Help clients to identify relevant homework assignments and seek their commitment to carry these out.

_____ Review results of homework assignment.

_____ Provide additional training as necessary.

_____ Help clients develop self-management skills that contribute to maintaining valued skills (e.g., periodically keep track of particular skills and outcomes).

---

well as programs designed to increase skills of children and adults with developmental disabilities.

Coach clients to observe effective models in real-life contexts to learn new behaviors and to increase knowledge about when certain behaviors can be used with success. Their observations can be discussed, noting effective reactions, as well as other situations in which specific behaviors could be of value. Draw attention to important behaviors for example, you could coach a client to notice the model's eye contact and body orientation. Model helpful self-statements during role plays if negative thoughts interfere with success. They can first be spoken out loud by the client when imitating the model's behavior and then, by instruction, moved to a covert level.

If an attempt to use model presentation fails, check to determine whether the requisites for use of the procedure have been satisfied. Specific behaviors may have to be individually established before they can be combined in a complex chain of behavior; you may have to break steps down into smaller units. Perhaps the client did not attend carefully to the modeled behavior. You may have to prompt attention and/or offer incentives to encourage imitation. When working with children or adults with severe behavior deficits, a first step is to teach them to imitate behaviors. You could use physical guidance to encourage desired behaviors. Modeling effects can be enhanced if observers have an opportunity to practice the observed behavior and if they are asked to identify relevant behaviors and to describe rules for using them.

Behavior Rehearsal (Role Playing)

Behavioral rehearsal involves the practice of behaviors. For example, a client who has difficulty during job interviews can practice effective ways of acting after watching a model. Direct skill practice with a parent's own child is a key predictor of success in parenting programs (Kaminski et al., 2008). Analogue situations include those in which clients interact with significant others in an artificial environment such as the office, as well as situations in which clients participate in role plays with someone other than a real-life significant other (e.g., a social worker). Role playing offers a safe environment to practice new behaviors, given that tasks and criteria for success are clearly defined, and constructive feedback is used that is tailored to each person's unique skill levels.

Participation in role plays may change attitudes. Brian and his parents were more willing to listen to what each other had to say after negotiation training. Mrs. Lakeland reported that she could now see how they would all have to work together to make things better at home and that it was not all Brian's fault. Role reversal in which a client assumes the role of a significant other may increase awareness of what it is like to be in someone else's shoes. Be sure to clearly describe situations used in role plays, as well as how they relate to client concerns. You can encourage participation in role plays by:

- Asking clients to read from a prepared script.
- Decreasing the length of role plays.
- Clarifying the purpose of role plays.
- Identifying clear, achievable criteria for success.
- Reinforcing participation.
- Pointing out that initial discomfort is usual.
- Selecting easier situations.
- Coaching and prompting clients during role plays.

Coaching and Prompting

Take advantage of coaching and prompting to encourage desired behaviors. You could give clients control over prompts. Let us say you are working with a teenager who wants to learn new ways to maintain conversations. You could ask him to start off by himself and to draw written prompts from a box suggesting topics only as necessary. You can decrease a client's anxiety by modeling behaviors to be practiced, offering reassurance, and clearly describing procedures to be used. You could ask for volunteers if you are using a group. A group provides a valuable context for role playing because many models and varied sources of feedback are available. You could give clients a list of written prompts related to specific verbal and nonverbal behaviors. You could use hand signals to coach clients during role plays. Fade out prompts and guidance as skills increase. Keep a training record to track progress. You could list behaviors of interest to the left and leave room along the top for successive role plays. You and your clients can assess progress by evaluating skills at the beginning and end of each session.

Programming Change

Identify initial skill levels and build on them in a step-by-step manner that complements degree of mastery. You and your clients should decide on specific goals for each training session. Only one or two behaviors may be focused on during a session. Or initial skill levels may allow practice of all required behaviors. Use the data collected during assessment from role plays or observation in real-life contexts to describe available skills. Repeat model presentation, rehearsal, prompts, and feedback as needed until desired skill and comfort levels are demonstrated. Be sure to identify clear criteria to determine when a skill has been mastered. Including difficult situations that may arise in role plays will help clients practice how to handle them in real-life. Distractions and provocations by people playing the role of clients were built into scenes in which child welfare

workers role played interviews with clients (Greene, Kessler, & Daniels, 1996). A "parent" would interact inappropriately with "her children" (yell, ridicule, threaten, or make inappropriate physical contact) or the client would tell the social worker, "These AA meetings you're making me go to are stupid." Emphasize coping rather than mastery.

Provide Constructive Feedback

Be sure to provide constructive feedback after each role play. First, note specific positive aspects of the performance, then give specific suggestions for improvement. Be sure to give praise for improvement in relation to each client's unique baseline repertoire rather than in comparison with other people. Note and praise improvements, even small ones. Avoid critical comments such as "You can do better," or "That wasn't too good." *Specific* feedback based on clearly defined criteria will help clients to identify what to do to enhance their effectiveness. Also, using constructive feedback offers a model for participants to follow. Enthusiasm will encourage positive feelings and participation.

You can encourage involvement of all group members by using a structured format in which specific behaviors related to a goal are written down in a checklist format and each group member rates each role play guided by the criteria on the checklist. They could rate each behavior as needing work, improved, or good. Examples of nonverbal behavior may include eye contact, posture, and facial expression. Content may include relevance to situation. Paralinguistic components may include voice loudness, tone, and fluency. A recording sheet used in training parents how to use "planned ignoring" included the following entries (Hall & Hall, 1980, p. 25): (1) look away from child; (2) move away from child (at least 3 feet); (3) impassive face; (4) ignore all requests; (5) if necessary, leave room.

Homework Assignments

Select homework assignments that offer clients real-life practice opportunities after criterion level skill and comfort levels have been achieved in role plays. Encourage behaviors that will result in positive outcomes for both clients and significant others and that have a high probability of success at a low cost in discomfort. You could write down important components on cards and give a copy to clients that they can review as necessary (e.g., prior to employment interviews) or program these on smartphones. You could arrange periodic reminders on cell phones. Remind clients that new ways of acting may not immediately alter the behavior of others in desired directions. Change may be slow, and new reactions may initially create negative feelings and consequences. For example, attempts to initiate conversations may be ignored. Job interviewers may be rude. If such reactions may occur, help clients to develop coping skills for handling them before they try out new behaviors in real life. A contextual understanding of the situations involved will help you to prepare clients for or avoid negative outcomes. When possible, involve significant others in role plays. Behaviors in real-life settings may not be an exact replica of those rehearsed. Encourage clients to combine new knowledge and skills with their own unique effective styles.

If You Are Not Successful

There are many ways a training program can go wrong. You may go too fast or too slow. The more behaviors that must be learned, the more complex they are, the greater the needed training competencies on your part. Needed prompts and coaching may be missing. Homework assignments may be too few or too difficult. A common mistake is spending too much time talking about what to do and not enough time on modeling, practice, and feedback. Homework assignments may be too difficult or there may be few opportunities to practice new skills. Valued behaviors may be punished in real-life settings and/or not reinforced. If progress is disappointing, check out these possibilities (see also chapter 22). Helping clients to enhance their skills requires many skills on your part.

Particular kinds of information are needed. Developing new skills often requires a task analysis in which behaviors needed to attain valued goals are identified, including immediate steps. Entering repertoires (what clients can already do) must be discovered and an "agenda" for change planned. Without finding out what clients can now do and what they cannot, you may skip necessary steps or move too slowly. Conducting skills training in a group requires preparation and planning to maximize effectiveness. Special arrangements may be needed to encourage generalization as described in chapter 23. Shooting from the hip in skill training is not a good idea; you may set clients up for failure and overlook opportunities to help them.

Enhancing Self-Management Skills

Self-management skills are used to pursue desired outcomes, including pain control (Ebert & Kerns, 2011), anger management (Taylor & Novaco, 2005), and stress reduction (Moore & Penk, 2011). Essentially, we manage our behavior in the here and now to achieve desired goals such as making more friends or getting our work done. (See Baumeister & Vohs, 2004.) Self-management training has been used to pursue a wide variety of goals with a wide variety of clients including decreasing stereotypic behavior of students with autism (Koegel & Koegel, 1990; Williams & Williams, 2010), and decreasing drinking in adults (Sobell & Sobell, 1993). It has been used for over 40 years to decrease impulsive behavior of children and adults (Meichenbaum & Goodman, 1971). (See also Koegel, Frea, & Surratt, 1994.)

A variety of skills including self-management skills for regulating emotions are encouraged in dialectical therapy (Linehan, 1993; Miller, Rathus, & Linehan, 2007). Self-management skills are involved in helping students study and helping people to maintain and enhance good health by eating a more nutritious diet, maintaining an exercise regimen, and stopping smoking. Steps include: (1) identifying a goal; (2) identifying the steps needed to attain the goal; (3) designing a plan to monitor related behaviors in a consistent way; and (4) arranging consequences that will maintain related behaviors. (See also Miltenberger & Gross, 2011; Christensen, & Antoni, 2008.)

We may rearrange cues and consequences related to behavior of interest and acquire skills such as relaxation that offer us greater influence over our environments (see Watson & Tharp, 2007). Self-management skills have been discussed at many points in this book including chapter 23 under the section on choosing methods that clients can make use of on their own. Self-instruction training is a kind of self-management training. We learn to prompt and reinforce valued behaviors (see later discussions of problem-solving training and programs designed to help clients to manage their emotions). Enhancing self-reinforcement skills is valuable when support will not be offered in real life. Clients could increase positive self-statements, as well as access to specific reinforcers contingent on desired behaviors. Positive self-statements should reward accomplishment, be specific, and be acceptable to clients. Prompts provided on mobile phones may be needed to remind clients of important steps (e.g., questions such as "Is my goal clear?"). Clients may be dubious about the potential success of self-managed efforts because of past failures related to false hopes (Polivy & Herman, 2002).

Helping Clients Change Their Cognitive Ecology

What clients say to themselves (their self-statements) may contribute to problems. For example, how youth interpret the social behavior of others influences their reactions (see Dodge, 2006). Albert Ellis, Aaron Beck, and Donald Meichenbaum have taken a leading role in highlighting the role of thoughts in problem-related feelings and behaviors. Clients may have dysfunctional rules about how to act or what consequences to expect in certain situations. A client may believe that if she does not get what she wants in a situation "It is a disaster." Changing cognitive ecology may involve changing equivalence relations either among stimuli or functions. You may, for example, help a client no longer equate being rejected and viewing oneself as a failure. Changing what people say to themselves may involve decreasing excessive rule governance (e.g., "I must please everyone") or increasing rule governance (e.g., following through with choices we have made).

People who have angry outbursts may relive imagined slights and exaggerate their importance. What we say to ourselves is influenced by our learning histories. The term *cognitive restructuring* refers to methods that focus on changing what people say to themselves. *Reframing* can be used to alter views of problems.

This refers to encouraging a different way of viewing events/behaviors (Hayes et al., 2004; Watzlawick, Weakland, & Fisch, 1974). For example, you may encourage a client to view a disliked characteristic as an asset. *Thought stopping* is designed to decrease the frequency of persistent thoughts. This consists of helping clients to identify thoughts to be decreased and increased and arranging practice in stopping negative thoughts via self-instructions (e.g., saying "stop" covertly or overtly). This is combined with helping clients to focus on constructive thoughts or tasks. (See also Dattilio & Freeman, 2010.)

Cognitive-behavioral methods have become increasingly popular over the past years (e.g., Gallagher-Thompson, Steffan, & Thompson, 2007; Kendall, 2012; O'Donohue & Fisher, 2008; Mayer et al., 2009; Otis, 2007; Ronen & Freeman, 2007; Segal et al., 2001). They are used to address a wide range of concerns, including depression, aggression, pain, substance abuse, and anger. Such methods attend to both overt and covert behaviors. Clients learn to identify negative thoughts and related cognitive distortions related to problems and to replace them with positive self-statements (e.g., Brewin, 2006; Burns, 1999). Cognitive-restructuring may require identifying schemas and related beliefs underlying negative self-statements such as "I am worthless." Without this, change efforts may be of little value because core beliefs remain untouched. Schemas are broad pervasive themes about one's self and one's relationship with others developed during childhood and elaborated throughout one's lifetime (http://www.schematherapy.org). (See Young, Klosko, & Weishaar, 2003.) Increasing mindfulness has received more attention as has acceptance and commitment therapy (Hayes, Follette, & Linehan, 2004). Identification of common elements in varied manuals concerning a given problem makes your task easier in terms of selecting key procedures (e.g., see Chorpita et al., 2007; Barth, Lee, Lindsey, Collins, Strieder, Chorpita, Becker, & Sparks, 2011).

Problem-Solving Training

Effective problem-solving skills are valuable at all levels of intervention (individual, group, family, organization, community, legislative bodies) (e.g., Fraser, Nash, Galinsky, & Darwin, 2000; McMurran & McGuire, 2005; D'Zurilla & Nezu, 2007). Clients are encouraged to clearly identify desired outcomes, alternative ways to achieve them, and the consequences of each (see examples in earlier chapters). (See Exhibit 13.2.) Community residents may be unsuccessful in attaining valued goals because they do not clearly describe concerns and related hoped-for outcomes. Paulo Freire (1973) used a mix of organizing and educational approaches to enhance group solidarity and the effectiveness of social action organizations via a problem-solving process (for further discussion of community-level interventions, see chapter 27). Community living for clients with developmental disabilities may require solving a variety of problems (see Foxx &

Bittell, 1989), as well as providing support as in Independent Living Centers.

Only through legal action may clients obtain access to greater choice of living arrangements and access to needed support. For example, a Consent degree in *Ligas v. Hamos*, June 15, 2011, in Chicago expands community living options for people with developmental disabilities. Those who now live in large private, state-supported facilities can move to smaller community-based settings with the necessary support. An additional 3,000 people with such disabilities living at home will be provided community-based care (http://accessliving.org).

Programs designed to help children and adolescents to acquire effective social problem-solving skills, most of which have a self-management component involving self-instructions, have been available for many years (see Elias & Tobias, 1996; LeCroy, 2008). A social problem-solving curriculum used with learning disabled and low-achieving youth labeled delinquent, designed by Larson and Gerber (1987), involved three lessons in verbal self-instruction. These encouraged youth to covertly (via thoughts) cue themselves to stop and think before responding to situations in which impulsive reactions might result in negative consequences. Nine lessons in social metacognitive awareness guided youth in what to consider when facing a social problem. They learned how to identify salient "self" and "other" variables and how to evaluate the usefulness of information about these variables to assess problem difficulty and identify response requirements.

During 10 lessons in social metacognitive influence skills, participants learned a seven-step problem-solving strategy for using social information: (1) clearly describe the problem; (2) propose solutions; (3) decide on the best one; (4) be ready with a backup alternative; (5) anticipate obstacles and plan step-by-step procedures to carry out chosen options; (6) carry out the plan; and (7) review results. Both trainer and youth read lessons aloud. Each lesson plan was organized around cartoon-like posters to encourage focus and attention. Problem situations were presented daily and youths practiced applying new skills. Group activities included: (1) sharing experiences in applying skills; (2) reading lesson plans aloud; (3) discussing questions presented; (4) practicing steps and problem-solving methods; (5) modeling specific skills; and (6) assigning "homework" tasks to practice a skill. To maximize generalization, trainers illustrated the usefulness of each skill, focused on problems similar to those in real life, reminded youths to use skills, gave homework assignments, and involved youth as active participants.

Using the phrase "choices and consequences" highlights individual responsibility in making choices and considering consequences. In acceptance and commitment counseling, clients are encouraged to accept responsibility for their choices and to accept and get beyond things they cannot change (e.g., see Hayes, Follette, & Linehan, 2004). Examples include events that occurred in the past (e.g., our past behaviors and behaviors of others over which we have no control), events that really do not matter, and our emotional reactions to everyday events. For example, rather than saying "I am too anxious to approach that person to start a conversation even though I want to," you might say, "I want to approach that person to start a conversation *and* I feel anxious approaching him." In the second example we acknowledge our feelings but act anyway. When we focus on getting rid of an unpleasant feeling such as anxiety or depression, this may only make matters worse (we may feel more depressed) and it gets in the way of acting in spite of our feelings. Clients may benefit from learning how to carry out mini cost-benefit analyses as a guide to how to act. You could help clients to prepare prompts noting specific behaviors they could engage in at times of stress, for example, pet the cat, take a walk, or text a friend.

Enhancing Skills in Managing Emotions

Feelings can be altered by changing related overt and covert (i.e., thoughts) behaviors. Increasing exercise has been found to decrease depression and anxiety (Parker, Hetrick, Jorm, Yung, McGorry, MacKinnon, et al., 2011). Programs have been developed to help clients with anger, panic attacks, anxiety in social situations, pain, and posttraumatic stress reactions. Here too interventions may be computer delivered (e.g., see Titov, Andrews, & Sachdev, 2010). Such a format may be of particular value in rural areas (for further detail concerning social work in rural areas see Ginsberg, 2011; Pugh & Cheers, 2010). Recording of feelings via smartphones can help clients to detect how specific environmental events affect their emotions. they could record notes regarding these experiences in real-time. Interpersonal therapy for depression focuses on the interpersonal relationships of clients including related emotions. An anger control training example is shown in Exhibit 24.6.

The concept of emotional intelligence has received a great deal of attention over the past years. This refers to awareness and managing of feelings, empathy, impulse control, perspective taking, and settling disputes. It includes perceiving, accurately appraising, and expressing emotions; accessing and/or generating feelings when they facilitate thought; understanding emotion and emotional knowledge; and regulating emotions in ways that promote emotional and intellectual growth (see Goleman, 2010). You may help a client to understand how their emotional reactions are related to their past developmental history. (See, for example, Graham-Bermann & Levendosky, 2011.) Skill in managing emotions may be valuable in resisting pressures to abuse substances and to be assaultive. Education and problem solving are components of cognitive-behavioral programs designed to help clients manage their emotions by, for example, increasing effective problem solving in volatile interpersonal situations. Clients learn how feelings and thoughts influence their behavior and how their behavior influences what they think and feel. These programs may help to "inoculate" us against unpleasant

---

EXHIBIT 24.6

An Anger Control Training Example

		Definition	Example
Step 1:	Identify triggers	External events and internal self-statements that provoke anger and aggression	Being close to a particular coworker or having one's space suddenly invaded
Step 2:	Identify cues	Individual physical events such as clenched fists, raised hand, flushed face, particular vocal sounds, and so forth, that let someone know he or she is angry	Becoming red in the face and starting to vocalize loudly
Step 3:	Using reminders	Self-statements such as "Calm down" or "Relax" or nonhostile explanations of others' behaviors	Saying to oneself, "Take a break," or "Talk quietly" (using a trained sign, symbol, or vocalization)
Step 4:	Using reducers	Techniques designed to lower the level of anger, such as deep breathing, counting backward, imagining a peaceful scene, or thinking about the long-term consequences of one's behavior	Walk to a designated quiet area in the room and listen to music using headphones and a portable tape deck Taking out a wallet and looking at pictures of 3–4 favorite scenes or activities that took place that week
Step 5:	Using self-education	Reflecting on how well the situation was handled	Being told by a staff person that he or she did very well and later, saying to self, "Good job"

Source: L. H. Meyer & I. M. Evans (1989). *Nonaversive intervention for behavior problems* (p. 138). Baltimore: Paul H. Brookes. Reprinted with permission.

and dysfunctional levels of emotions (e.g., anxiety or anger). Skills focused on in school-based programs designed to increase social competence included the following

- Identifying and labeling feelings.
- Expressing feelings.
- Assessing the intensity of feelings.
- Managing feelings.
- Delaying feelings.
- Controlling impulses.
- Reducing stress.
- Knowing the difference between feelings and actions.

Related cognitive skills included: (1) self-talk; (2) interpreting social cues; (3) problem solving and decision making (e.g., to control impulses, set goals, identify alternative actions, and anticipate consequences); (4) understanding the perspective of others; (5) understanding norms (what is and what is not acceptable behavior); and (6) self-awareness (e.g., identifying unrealistic expectations). Behavioral skills include both nonverbal and verbal behaviors, such as making clear requests, responding effectively to criticism, resisting negative influences, listening to others, and helping others.

In stress management training, clients learn to identify feelings and thoughts associated with emotional reactions such as anxiety and anger and to use them as cues for constructive thoughts and actions (Moore & Penk, 2011). The relationship between thoughts, feelings, and behavior is emphasized. For example, stress experienced in unexpected traffic delays could be avoided by allowing more time to complete journeys and by having interesting activities available (e.g., listening to "books-on-tape"). Clients are encouraged to view emotions as reactions they can influence rather than as feelings that are out of their control. They are encouraged to identify low levels of unpleasant arousal so they can use mood-altering skills at an early point to prevent escalation. Stress-producing situations are broken down into four stages (preparing for the stressor, controlling a stressor, coping with feelings of being overwhelmed, and reinforcing self-statements), and constructive self-statements are developed for each stage (Meichenbaum, 1977). (See Exhibit 24.7.)

Viewing situations from the other person's perspective and focusing on common goals will help clients maintain constructive levels of arousal. Goals such as "telling him off" are not likely to result in positive outcomes. Research on anger has shown that such goals encourage negative feelings and counterattacks and are not likely to be achieved (Averill, 1982; Potegal, Stemmler, & Spielberger, 2010). Clients may benefit from acquiring relaxation skills that help them handle stressful situations (e.g., see Burish, Snyder, & Jenkins, 1991; Suls, Davidson, & Kaplan, 2010). Relaxation training is a part of systematic desensitization

---

EXHIBIT 24.7

Examples of Coping Self-Statements Used in Stress Inoculation Training

Preparing for a stressor
What is it I have to do?
I can develop a plan to deal with it.
No negative self-statements; just think rationally.
Don't worry, worry won't help.
Maybe what I think is anxiety is eagerness.

Confronting and handling a stressor
Just "psych" myself up—I can meet this challenge.
One step at a time; I can handle the situation.
Think about what I want to do.
Anxiety is a reminder to use my coping skills.
This tenseness can be an ally; a cue to cope.
Relax. Take a deep breath.

Coping with the feeling of being overwhelmed
When fear comes, just pause.
Focus on the present; what's my goal?
Don't try to eliminate fear, just keep it manageable.
Even if fear increases, it's no big deal.

Reinforcing self-statements
It worked; I did it.
It wasn't as bad as I expected.
It's getting easier each time.

Source: Adapted from D. Meichenbaum (1977). Cognitive behavior modification: An integrative approach. New York: Plenum.

---

methods for reducing anxiety (Wolpe, 1990). (For descriptions of relaxation methods, see Bernstein, Borkovec, Hazlett-Stevens, 2000; Lehrer, Woolfolk, & Sime, 2007.)

Forming a Stimulus Hierarchy

Exposure to feared situations is the key ingredient in overcoming fear reactions (Barlow, 2002; Foa et al., 2007; Richard & Lauterbach, 2007). A list of anxiety (or anger) provoking situations is first created. A hierarchy can be arranged in terms of degree of anxiety or anger related to each situation. Exposure may start with situations that create only a small amount of discomfort and, as anxiety or anger decrease, more difficult ones are introduced. In vivo systematic desensitization was used to decrease anxiety of an 18-year-old adolescent to men (Meyer & Evans, 1989). She avoided male staff members in her new group home and had a tantrum whenever they approached her. She also refused to see professionals, such as an optometrist, who were men. Although her foster mother suspected that her fear resulted from sexual abuse, the cause was unknown. Examples from the hierarchy of situations developed to provide opportunities for direct experiences with men include the following:

1. On outings into the community, such as to a fast food restaurant, staff will try to select a table near a group of men. Donna can sit in the middle of her own group.

2. On similar occasions it will again be arranged to be near men, and Donna will sit on the outside.

3. When the opportunity arises to interact with a male in an official role (e.g., delivery person, store assistant), Donna is to make eye contact and smile.

4. Staff will try to select stores, banks, and so forth, that have male service personnel; Donna has to approach a man, with one of her friends, and ask for something.

5. Male staff in the home will sit on the other side of the room from her and talk to other female clients, not Donna. (p. 141)

Care was taken to protect her from realistic dangers. Donna learned not to talk to male strangers unless other people were around or unless they had some official role and received counseling in the dangers of sexual abuse.

Mixed and Multisystem Programs

A contextual assessment will often indicate that a multicomponent program is needed. Consider children diagnosed with ADHD (attention-deficit/hyperactivity disorder). Programs may include both self-management training (e.g., in self-monitoring) and anger management training in a group setting. Helping people who are depressed often involves multiple kinds of intervention. This may include changing environmental stressors, as well as what people say to themselves, and what they do (i.e., behavior activation). Changing social interactions may be required. Clients often have multiple concerns (e.g., see Jeffrey et al., 2004). Programs designed to reduce risk behaviors related to AIDS usually comprise a variety of methods including education, assertion training, self-management training, and enhancing social support. The community reinforcement approach (CRA) that Azrin and his colleagues developed to decrease alcohol abuse (Azrin, 1976; Meyers & Miller, 2001) includes attention to family relationships, helping clients to find jobs, establishing a nondrinking social network, and developing recreational opportunities. A buddy system was developed and a social club arranged that provided social opportunities without drinking alcohol. In addition the program included drink refusal training, training in controlling urges to drink, and an anti-abuse program. A key feature of the CRA is altering clients' social networks to create a nondrinking culture. Multicomponent programs have also been used to decrease drug abuse (see, for example, Springer & Rubin, 2009).

Ecobehavioral programs with families involve multisystem interventions (Lutzker & Bigelow, 2002) as do wraparound programs directed toward children in foster care (Chamberlain, Fisher, & Moore, 2002). (See also Lipsey et al., 2010; Webster-Stratton, 2009; Wilson & Lipsey, 2005.) Helping clients to obtain jobs often requires attending to both individual and environmental characteristics (Azrin, Philip, Thienes-Hontos, & Besalel, 1980; Mowbray, Collins, Bellamy, Mcgivern, Bybee, & Szilvagyi, 2005). The same applies to working with youth who belong to gangs (see resources at http://www.ojp.usdoj.gov/programs/yvp_gangs.htm). Dan Olweus (2007) developed and evaluated a multilevel program for decreasing bullying at school. Intervention is conducted at the community, school, class, and individual levels (see also Jensen, Dieterich, Brisson, Bender, & Powell, 2010; Jimerson et al., 2010; Swearer et al., 2009; Venberg & Biggs, 2010). Multisystemic therapy consists of a number of components. (For a systematic review of this model, see Littell, Popa, & Forsythe, 2005.) Decreasing school violence and enhancing the quality of educational experiences may require school-wide interventions including using cultural traditions to encourage nonviolent peace making (Astor, Benbenishty, & Estrada, 2009; Sailor et al., 2009).

Summary

Helping clients may require increasing their knowledge and skills. Giving people more options for influencing their environment is key to empowerment. Providing information can help clients to identify promising options and to reframe problems in constructive ways. Information is a key resource in advocacy efforts to mobilize community members and to suggest strategies to seek valued outcomes. Options for helping clients to acquire new skills include shaping, modeling, and social skills training. If your job involves helping clients to learn new skills, you should develop expert skill-building competencies. A variety of cognitive-behavioral methods are available to help clients to alter thoughts, emotions, and behaviors.

Reviewing Your Competencies

Reviewing Content Knowledge

1. You can describe key skills involved in shaping.

2. You can describe components of social skills training.

3. You can describe why careful assessment is a prerequisite to successful skills training.

4. You can accurately describe guidelines for giving information.

5. Given examples of social skills training, you can describe how to improve the likelihood of success.

6. Given examples of shaping, you can accurately describe how to enhance success.

7. You can describe how to maximize the effectiveness of model presentation.

8. You can accurately describe the characteristics of constructive feedback.

9. You can describe intervention options for helping clients change their cognitive ecology and emotional reactions.

Reviewing What You Do

1. You can teach someone how to use shaping.

2. Review of your interviews shows that you take advantage of opportunities to offer clients valuable information and do so in a way that maximizes the likelihood that the client will use it successfully.

3. You can shape a behavior of your instructor, peer, or significant other.

4. Review of skills training programs you use show that you effectively implement component methods.

5. You help clients identify obstacles that get in the way of using effective skills.

6. You can use cognitive-behavioral methods to alter one of your own behaviors.

7. You can design a multi-intervention program for specific concerns drawing on related research..

Reviewing Results

1. You help a group of parents acquire accurate knowledge about child development.

2. You help citizens gather and disseminate information that exposes a serious community problem.

3. You help a client to acquire self-care skills.

4. You help teenagers learn effective skills for refusing invitations to drink.

5. You help a teacher communicate more effectively with her students.

6. You help a parent acquire positive parenting skills.

7. You help a depressed single parent learn more effective problem-solving skills.

8. You help residential staff control their anger when confronted with annoying behaviors on the part of residents.

9. You help a client control angry outbursts.

10. You help a client with chronic pain to maximize "time-outs" from thinking about the pain.

11. You help community members to participate effectively at local board meetings.

25

Helping Clients Learn Positive Behavior Change Skills

OVERVIEW   This chapter describes positive methods for helping clients to enhance the quality of their lives. Disliked situations may occur because of a lack of positive behavior change skills. Options for altering what happens before behavior are described, as well as options for rearranging consequences. Clients may be parents, students, teachers, community residents, members of support groups, staff in residential settings, or administrators. A contextual assessment will indicate whether it is possible to alter contingencies, if so how, at what levels (e.g., individual, family, group, community, organization, or service system), and in what settings within each level.

YOU WILL LEARN ABOUT

- The value of positive behavior change skills
- Myths and misconceptions about contingency management
- Increasing behavior
- Positive reinforcement
- Negative reinforcement
- Decreasing behavior
- Differential reinforcement
- Extinction
- Response cost
- Punishment: the least desirable alternative
- Positive alternatives to the use of punishment
- Rearranging antecedents

The Value of Positive Behavior Change Skills

Helping clients involves altering behavior (see Exhibit 25.1). If you are a community organizer trying to encourage people

Examples of Behaviors Related to Different Intervention Levels

Political/Legislative	• Vote yes on legislation that increases in-home support services. • Write letters to legislators to encourage them to fund community-based service centers. • Register to vote. • Attend hearings regarding proposed policies/programs. • Distribute a fact-sheet about a problem/situation (e.g., health care).
Service System	• Arrange regular exchange of information with staff in all agencies concerned with specific individuals and families. • Design a common face-sheet to be used by interlinked agencies. • Design an information management system compatible across agencies. • Select and pursue one legislative goal of mutual interest.
Organization	• Reinforce staff for desired behaviors. • Clarify goals. • Establish an ombudsman service for clients/staff. • Arrange for the participation of all staff in decisions that concern them.
Community	• Attend and participate in parent–teacher meetings. • Raise issues of concern at city council meetings. • Form a neighborhood block organization.
Group	• Suggest solutions to problems. • Offer to help others. • Reinforce other group members for valued behaviors. • Clarify desired outcomes of group.
Family	• Share mutually enjoyable activities. • Care for an elderly relative. • Provide proper nutrition to children. • Use positive parenting skills.
Individual	• Positive self-statements. • Request services (e.g., food stamps, medical help, tutoring for children). • Initiate conversations. • Participate in neighborhood groups.

both to register to vote and to vote, these are behaviors. People have to do something. For example, they have to go to the polls on election day and vote. A focus on changing the behavior of individuals is often confused with a psychological focus. There is a confusion between means (methods) and outcomes (goals). This confusion may result in discounting individually focused methods that result in valued changes at other levels (e.g., in groups, schools, communities, organizations, or legislation). The question is: What is the purpose of altering the behavior of individuals? At what system level(s) are changes in behavior directed toward? (See Exhibit 25.2.) The relationship skills described elsewhere in this book, such as active listening, empathy, and warmth—as well as consultation skills, such as arranging practice opportunities and providing corrective feedback are valuable complements to knowledge and skills required to help clients and significant others rearrange contingencies.

Knowledge and skill in rearranging contingencies (relationships between behavior and the environment) are valuable at all levels of intervention. The principles of behavior described in chapter 7 offer guidelines for altering behavior through rearranging environmental circumstances. A contingency is the complete description of a specific operant. It includes a clear description of the behaviors that result in certain consequences (the operant class), as well as related antecedents and setting events (situations in which certain consequences influence related behaviors). Positive reinforcement and many forms of stimulus control (rearranging antecedents) rely on positive methods, removing the need for negative methods, such as criticizing, removing privileges, and blaming (e.g., see McDonnell, 2010). Their use may also prevent extreme actions such as severing relationships with family members or pets because of lack of knowledge of or interest in learning positive behavior change skills (see, for example, the article "The Problem of Unwanted Pets," Irvine, 2003). Most child maltreatment occurs in a context of trying to alter behavior. Once clients acquire valuable skills, they can help other clients learn these skills (e.g., Neef, 1995). Behavioral parenting programs are effective in altering parenting attitudes and behavior which, in turn, improve behavior of their children (e.g., Tully, 2009).

Myths and Misconceptions About Contingency Management

Misconceptions and misinformation about the rearrangement of contingencies that may get in the way of drawing on valuable methods are discussed next.

Altering Contingencies Dehumanizes People

For both practical and ethical reasons, goals pursued should be selected by clients and significant others, and a collaborative working relationship should be established that emphasizes

EXHIBIT 25.2

Examples of Focus and Outcomes

Focus	In Order To	Which Will
• Increase job-related social skills.	• Maintain employment.	• Maintain or enhance independence.
• Encourage community members to register to vote and to vote.	• Influence which politicians are elected.	• Increase likelihood of passing certain legislation.
• Form self-help groups of parents who care for an elderly relative.	• Provide respite, validation, information, and problem-solving assistance.	• Prevent institutionalization; enhance positive family relationships.
• Help clients acquire employment skills.	• Get a job.	• Enhance or maintain independence and self-esteem, support family.
• Help community residents form a social action group.	• Acquire funds to establish a shelter for battered women.	• Provide services to abused women and their children.

client involvement in making decisions. A contextual assessment in which relevant environmental contingencies are explored decreases the likelihood of "victim blaming"—viewing victims as the cause of personal and social problems. Helping clients acquire positive behavior change skills will increase their influence over their environments in ways that maximize positive consequences.

Contingencies Are All-Powerful

Often it is not an easy matter to change someone's behavior without his or her awareness. If we do not want our behavior altered, it is unlikely that others can do so unless they have access to influential contingencies. Other limiting factors include unique biological boundaries.

Underlying Causes Are Not Addressed

In contrast to the belief that contingencies are all-powerful is the belief that they have little or no influence and, that if we focus on them, we ignore underlying causes such as feelings and thoughts. Behavior, feelings, and thoughts are all influenced by environmental contingencies. Thousands of studies both in laboratory and applied settings have demonstrated the effects of consequences on behavior, thoughts, and feelings (see references in chapter 7). This does not imply radical environmentalism (the belief that our behavior is determined by environmental events); many other influences come into play (see chapter 12). And, any approach, including contingency analysis, can be carried out in a superficial manner in which important contingencies are ignored. A contextual analysis of both self-presented and environmental contingencies is required to clearly describe concerns and identify promising options. (See chapter 12.) Such an analysis accompanied by related plans minimize the likelihood of unwanted negative effects due to an incomplete assessment.

Thoughts and Feelings Are Not Considered

Thoughts and feelings provide clues about contingencies (e.g., our experiences with certain individuals), and cognitive-behavioral programs include a focus on altering them (e.g., increasing positive self-statements as described in chapter 24). Thoughts are integrally involved in "rule-governed" behavior (verbal description of contingencies that may or may not reflect those in real life). However, focusing solely on thoughts and feelings (as in "He hit her because he was angry") provides *incomplete* accounts. For example, we do not know the antecedents to "anger" nor the consequences of related behaviors such as hitting that may maintain them.

Individual Differences Are Ignored

Attention to individual differences is a hallmark of contingency analysis. Individuals, families, groups, organizations, and communities differ in their reinforcer and punisher profiles (what is valued and what is disliked) and related contingencies. Only if the unique value of different consequences to different individuals, groups, organizations, or communities is understood can successful programs be implemented. For a classic example of the failure of economic development programs due to lack of attention to cultural differences, see Kunkel (1970). Each individual has a unique learning history molded by his or her culture, as well as by genetic and physiological differences. Individual learning histories create unique "meanings" of events for each individual, group, organization, or community (Biehl, Good, & Kleinman, 2007). Cultures differ in their reinforcer profile.

The Helper–Client Relationship Is Unimportant

Warmth, respect, and empathy contribute to mutual understanding and a collaborative working relationship (see chapter 15).

However, the relationship is not viewed as the only or even key source of change. And, there is an effort to clearly identify specific relationship behaviors that contribute to valued outcomes. Candid recognition of the social influence effects in the helping process decreases the likelihood that they will be used (knowingly or not) in unethical and ineffective ways. Ignoring such influences does not make them go away. Rather it allows their use in an unsystematic or undercover way. It has been argued that nondirective counseling in which objectives remain vague and progress is not monitored is the most controlling of all approaches because sources of influence are unrecognized (see, for example, Jurjevich, 1974).

People Learn How to Manipulate Each Other

Manipulation refers to influencing others in an unfair or fraudulent way for one's own profit (*Webster's New World Collegiate Dictionary*, 1988). Helping clients attain specific outcomes they value is hardly manipulative. As the old saying goes, "We cannot not communicate." There may be situations when an ethical argument could be made for showing some individuals how to change the behavior of others without the awareness of the latter. For example, residents in institutional settings could learn how to gain more positive feedback from staff reluctant to provide this. In a classic study, students aged 12 to 15 were taught how to increase their teachers' positive statements and to decrease their negative statements (Graubard, Rosenberg, & Miller, 1971). If residents or students have no other way to alter the behavior of significant others (e.g., staff or teachers), isn't it unethical to withhold such knowledge from them? Helping clients to acquire effective behavior change skills increases their influence over their environments (a large part of which may be provided by other people), but it does not teach them to manipulate this environment in an insidious or unfair way. So, too, with social skills training in which clients acquire more effective relationship skills that offer benefits both to themselves and to others (see chapter 24) (see also Catania, 2011).

Control Is Imposed Where None Exists

This incorrect belief overlooks sources of influence already present. People have been trying to change other people's behavior throughout the centuries. Many people either do not possess or do not use positive change skills and rely instead on negative methods such as criticism, nagging, hitting. Much unhappiness and misery results. Problems are often aggravated by use of punitive methods. Not only may this be ineffective, it creates bad feelings, as well as counteraggression as described in chapter 7. Both punishing and nonreinforcing environments contribute to burnout among helpers and are related to problems such as depression and anxiety (e.g., Trower, Gilbert, & Sherling, 1990).

It is true that preexisting contingencies may not be "planned." This does not mean that they are without influence. Viewing people as totally free contributes to misplaced blame on families

and individuals for problems such as poverty; political and economic causes are overlooked. Denying the influence of environmental contingencies no more negates their effects than would the law of gravity be suspended if we did not believe it. However, denial of such influence does permit those in privileged positions to blame poverty, discrimination, and oppression on those who experience them.

Contingencies That Already Exist Are More Natural

It is sometimes said that the contingencies that already exist are "more natural," meaning that no one has arranged them to attain given ends and that they do more good than harm. Actually, many contingencies are deliberately arranged by, for example, governmental agencies. The public relations and advertising industries are in business to influence our behavior and to make a profit in doing so. (See discussion of human service propaganda in chapter 4.) Ethical problems cannot be avoided by refusing to recognize influence and its implications (Skinner, 1953). The question is: "Who benefits and who loses from ignorance about influential contingencies?" If knowledge about and skill in altering real-life contingencies provide freedom from unwanted influences, isn't this a benefit rather than a harm?

I'm Already Doing It

One way to discount something new is to say: "I already know that"; "I already do it." We rearrange contingencies every day. This does not mean that we do so in a systematic way in pursuit of specific outcomes. It is the systematicness and completeness with which contingencies are analyzed and altered in relation to specific objectives and the ongoing monitoring of progress that are key to success. Consider the poor track record of following New Year's resolutions. Occasional unevaluated use of positive incentives to change vaguely defined or even well-defined behaviors is not likely to be successful. Or success will be less than would be possible. (See Watson & Tharp, 2007, for a helpful guide to self-change.) Malott (1994) suggests that we often resort to unconscious motivational explanations to understand why we and others do not follow through with actions that correspond with our values because of limited understanding of the causes of poor self-management.

Extrinsic Reinforcers Undermine Intrinsic Ones

Some people argue that using external reinforcement to alter behavior (for example, to increase study behavior) undermines the intrinsic reinforcing value of behaviors. Phillip Hineline (1995) argues that this is a destructive half-truth. It is true that using contrived reinforcers may reflect the user's rather than the client's values and that we must be vigilant that this is not the case. It is also true that it is of little value to rely on reinforcers that will not maintain behavior after the trainer leaves. The destructive half-truth is arguing that contingent consequences should not be used or are of no value in educational and helping contexts. Reiss (2005) illustrates the murkiness of the term "intrinsic motivation," the related value judgments, and the oversimplification of dividing all motivation into two categories (intrinsic and extrinsic) and critiques-related research. Research in many areas illustrates the key role of reinforcement in learning and maintaining behavior.

External reinforcers should not be introduced when intrinsic ones are present unless the latter result in injury to self or others. Contrived reinforcers should only be used when natural consequences are not feasible. And new repertoires "should be made functional by bringing them into contact with reinforcing consequences that are natural to the situation" (Hineline, 1995, p. 1). Avoid incentives that are not already part of the natural environment when possible. If it is necessary to introduce artificial reinforcers such as tokens or points, plan their removal so that behavior is maintained by real-life contingencies (see also Eisenberg & Cameron, 1996; Sansone & Harackiewicz, 2000; and Schunk & Zimmerman, 2008 for detailed discussion).

Rearranging Contingencies Takes Little Skill

There are a relatively small number of key concepts related to rearranging contingencies; however, their application in real life is often complex (see, for example, Exhibit 7.2). Unless you understand the complexities of rearranging contingencies, they may seem simpleminded. You might say everyone knows that consequences affect behavior. Rearranging contingencies in a way that maximizes the likelihood of attaining outcomes clients value requires knowledge and skill. Knowledge and accompanying procedural skills are needed to translate client concerns into observable behaviors, to discover maintaining conditions, and to select and implement effective plans.

Contingency Management Is Only Useful at the Individual Level

Understanding and rearranging contingencies are key aspects of work at all system levels including community organization, policy planning, and pursuit of legislative changes. Many examples have already been given in this book. This is required to discover misapplied and unapplied contingencies related to situations of concern (see for example Crone et al., 2010; Sailor et al., 2009). Arranging management systems in service agencies that ensure high-quality services is of concern not only to professionals, but to clients as well. Quality performance can be encouraged by identifying clear standards of performance, arranging needed training and feedback, and involving all staff in setting standards and selecting feedback methods. Contingency analysis is also useful at the cultural level to explore how environmental circumstances at different levels (individual, family, group, organization, community, policy, and related legislation) influence behaviors of interest.

Increasing Behavior

Some problems involve behaviors that do not occur often enough. Behavioral activation is a key method used to decrease depression (Martell, Dimidjian, Herman-Dunn, & Lewinsohn, 2010). A supervisor may seldom provide positive feedback to her staff. A parent may seldom praise her children. A legislator may seldom vote for proposals to increase accessibility of health care for all residents. You may seldom offer yourself positive feedback for behaviors you value. Options for increasing behavior include rearranging consequences, antecedents, and setting events (see Exhibit 25.3).

Positive Reinforcement

The term *positive reinforcement* refers to a procedure in which an event (a reinforcer) is presented following a behavior and there is an increase in the future likelihood of that behavior. Positive reinforcement provides a way to increase behavior that is already occurring. It also plays a key role in developing new behaviors (see chapter 25).

Making Effective Use of Positive Reinforcement

Requisites for effective use of positive reinforcement include:

- Identify an observable, countable behavior.

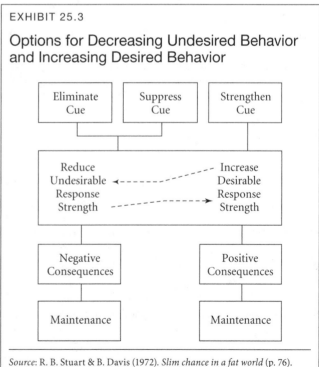

EXHIBIT 25.3

Options for Decreasing Undesired Behavior and Increasing Desired Behavior

Source: R. B. Stuart & B. Davis (1972). *Slim chance in a fat world* (p. 76). Champaign/Urbana, IL: Research Press. Reprinted with permission.

- Select an event that will function as a reinforcer (see chapter 19).

- Arrange for the behavior to occur.

- Make sure the reinforcer follows the behavior immediately.

- Use an appropriate criterion for reinforcement (e.g., it is achievable).

- Reinforce often.

- Reinforce immediately.

- Reinforce behavior across multiple behaviors, settings, and time.

Reinforcers are relative. They are known not by their physical characteristics but by their function (their effects on behavior). Many programs fail because the relativity of reinforcers is ignored. We each have a unique history of reinforcement. This refers to the frequency, schedule, intensity, and/or duration with which particular behaviors have been reinforced in particular situations. Because of different learning histories, an event that functions as a reinforcer for one person may not for another. On the other hand, because of similar learning histories in a given society, the same reinforcer may have identical functions for many people. An event that functions as a reinforcer in one situation may not do so in another. Significant others, such as parents, partners, or teachers, often assume that what is reinforcing for them is reinforcing for others. This may not be so. Such events could, however, be developed as reinforcers. For example, teacher approval could be established as a reinforcer by pairing it with consequences that already function as a reinforcer. Some reinforcers are substitutable (they may satisfy the same or similar needs). Others are not. Different reinforcement patterns in different cultures create different reinforcer profiles. Considering the relativity of reinforcers is part of what it means to be culturally sensitive. Whenever possible, use "natural" rather than artificial reinforcers, and reinforce behaviors that will continue to be supported in real-life environments. Positive reinforcement is often combined with operant extinction of undesired behaviors (see later discussion of differential reinforcement).

Variables That Influence the Effectiveness of Reinforcement

Timing, schedule, amount, and frequency influence the effectiveness of reinforcement (see chapter 7). An ideal reinforcer:

1. Can be presented immediately following behavior with little trouble to the person providing it.

2. Can be presented in a consistently effective form (critical dimensions of the reinforcer can be kept constant).

3. Does not lose effectiveness through satiation.

4. Is a strong influence on behavior.

5. Delivery can be accurately recorded.

Reinforcement should encourage task completion rather than time spent on a task. Increasing time spent on a task such as cleaning or studying may not result in an increase in task completion. (Guidelines for discovering reinforcers are described in chapter 19.) Deprivation of a reinforcer increases the likelihood of all behaviors that may result in its acquisition (see discussion of establishing operations in chapter 7). If children are deprived of social contacts, they are more likely to engage in behaviors that result in such contacts. If they are "satiated," there will be a cessation of responding. Satiation involves providing a reinforcer in such quantity and frequency that it no longer functions as a reinforcer. This is one way to decrease behavior. It is usually not used because of the practical limitations of providing large quantities of a reinforcer, the temporary nature of satiation effects with reinforcers such as food, the negative effects of providing large quantities of some reinforcers such as food, and the gradualness of change. Both reinforcer exposure (observing another person using a reinforcer) and reinforcer sampling (providing a reinforcer noncontingently) may increase the effectiveness of a reinforcer.

Frequency refers to how often a behavior is reinforced. Many people make the mistake of waiting for a low-frequency behavior to occur rather than reinforcing approximations (see discussion of shaping in chapter 24). Selecting small steps to reinforce makes frequent reinforcement possible. The more often a behavior is reinforced, the more rapidly it will be established.

Timing is important. A reinforcer should follow desired behaviors immediately. If it does not, it may follow some other behavior and increase this instead of the one of interest. Errors in timing are one of the main reasons people are not successful in using reinforcement. For example, reinforcement may be provided too long after the behavior of interest. As Karen Pryor points out, "The dog sits, but by the time the owner says 'good dog' the dog is standing again" (1984, p. 27). Delays between a behavior and later consequences can be "bridged" in older children and adults by reminders about the contingency (e.g., if I study for this test I will get a good grade). If a mother tells her child that, because he broke a plate, his father will spank him when he comes home, this interim may be filled with anticipated unpleasant events ("thinking about the punishment to come") if such threats have been followed up in the past. If a child is very young, no connection may be made between later punishment and earlier behaviors. Tokens or points may be used to "bridge" delays in access to backup reinforcers (e.g., see Donohue & Azrin, 2002).

We may also offer reinforcers too soon. Karen Pryor suggests that saying "That's the way to go, you almost got it right" may reinforce trying rather than successful performance and encourage saying "I can't." Considering the long-term (e.g., ultimate aversive consequences), as well as the short-term consequences of behavior can be difficult, as illustrated by the many people who continue to smoke even though they are aware of the health risks.

Amount of reinforcement influences the effects of reinforcement. Too much may result in satiation, too little in no change in behavior. How big a reinforcer should you use? "The answer is as small as you can get a way with" (Pryor, 1984, p. 30). This decreases waiting time because of distractions by the reinforcer (e.g., playing with a toy, eating food). Richard Malott (1994) argues that we often fail in our efforts to alter our own behavior or that of others because related contingencies have inconsequential effects. Consider seat belt use and teeth flossing. He argues that the immediate consequences of these behaviors are inconsequential (e.g., a slight reduction in fear of injury, less chance of losing one's teeth in 20 years) and so of little or no influence. Only if we arrange circumstances to heighten consequences are such behaviors likely to occur on a regular basis.

Schedule refers to the particular pattern that describes the relationship between behavior and its consequences. Schedules influence the rate of behavior, the maintenance of behavior, and resistance to extinction (how difficult it is to decrease a behavior) (see chapter 7). Continuous reinforcement schedules provide for the fastest acquisition of behavior and for the most rapid decrease of behavior when reinforcement is no longer provided. Maintenance of behavior in real-life settings usually requires shifting to an intermittent schedule after behavior stabilizes at a desired level. Transition from a low variable-ratio schedule in which small outputs are sometimes reinforced, to a large fixed-ratio schedule requiring considerable output of behavior may disrupt behavior. This may account in part for lower output when a person is shifted from a job where tasks are reinforced on a variable schedule to one where behavior is reinforced only after a set high number of behaviors. Thus, lack of interest in initiating an activity may be due to too thin a schedule of reinforcement. Fixed-ratio strain is a unique property of high-ratio schedules; we may be disinclined to work if too much behavior is required for reinforcement.

A special history is needed to develop behavior maintained on large fixed- or variable-ratio schedules. Many small and intermediate schedules must first be used. Expected behaviors may not occur because this process of approximating larger ratios has not been completed. Without an understanding of the role of schedules, lack of success may be mistakenly blamed on individual characteristics of clients (he is lazy). Occasional reinforcement may maintain behavior. Parents who try to decrease behavior by no longer reinforcing it often do this only part of the time. They provide periodic reinforcement, which will establish behavior that is difficult to decrease.

Other Factors

Quality of a reinforcer refers to its reinforcing potential relative to other reinforcers. The higher the quality, the more reinforcing potential it may have. For example, you may like certain kinds of ice cream better than others. Novelty also influences the effectiveness of reinforcers. The more varied, the more reinforcing they may be, perhaps because satiation is less likely. Karen Pryor (1984) recommends occasional use of "jackpots" (giving a much bigger reward than the usual—the reinforcer comes as a surprise). Describing contingencies may increase the effects of new reinforcement patterns; however, it is not essential. Relationships between behavior and consequences can be highlighted by describing the contingency before, as well as when it occurs.

If You Are Not Successful

Lack of success may be due to misapplied and unapplied contingencies including an overly narrow focus on one system level. For example, you may work with a child to alter her behavior and ignore problem-related contingencies in her family. You may involve supervisors in an agency but overlook contingencies administrators provide to supervisors. Contingencies altered may result in small, inconsequential effects. Use the form in Exhibit 21.1 to review your focus in relation to what seems to be needed. If your efforts to use positive reinforcement are not successful, review the following possibilities and take appropriate action:

- The consequence used as a reinforcer does not fill this function, perhaps because there is no establishing condition (see chapter 7). It may be too small to make a difference or of poor quality. The consequence selected may not be a reinforcer for this individual.

- Behavior is not reinforced often enough. An easier approximation may have to be selected.

- The reinforcer can be obtained via other behaviors.

- The reinforcer is delayed too long.

- The reinforcer is not presented consistently following the behavior (perhaps because relevant behaviors are not clearly described).

- Competing behaviors receive richer schedules of reinforcement.

- Satiation occurs because of lack of variation of reinforcers.

- A behavior seldom occurs so there is little opportunity to reinforce it.

- Punishment and/or response cost is mixed with positive reinforcement.

- Insufficient time has been allowed for change.

- Prompting may be required (see later section on rearranging antecedents).

Advantages and Disadvantages

Positive reinforcement "feels good." We like people who offer us positive consequences and are likely to continue behaviors that are maintained by positive reinforcement in the absence of external surveillance (e.g., threats and nagging). Unlike punishment, positive reinforcement does not encourage escape and avoidance. Quite the opposite. It encourages approach. One disadvantage of positive reinforcement is its "seductiveness." We are less likely to "rebel" against it (exert counter control) because it "feels good." Advertisers and politicians take advantage of this fact. This was one of Skinner's (1971) major points in *Beyond Freedom and Dignity* (perhaps his most misunderstood book).

Another disadvantage is that people may become dependent on a narrow range of positive reinforcers and those who provide them. For example, clients may become overly dependent on their therapists. You can avoid this by using a variety of reinforcers, involving significant others, and encouraging self-reliance. A third disadvantage is that it usually takes a while for positive reinforcement to change behavior in contrast with punishment, which may have an immediate (though temporary) effect. This is one reason people often rely on aversive means of influence. A fourth challenge is that it often takes more effort and creativity to identify consequences that will function as positive reinforcers without unwanted side effects than to identify negative ones.

Myths and Misunderstandings About Positive Reinforcement

Some people object to the use of positive reinforcement on the grounds that this is bribery. In *Webster's New World Collegiate Dictionary* (1988), a *bribe* is defined as "anything, especially money, given or promised to induce a person to do something illegal or wrong." Thus, the use of positive reinforcement to increase desired behaviors cannot accurately be considered bribery. People are often willing to punish undesired behavior but unwilling to offer positive incentives contingent on desired behaviors. (See also earlier section on myths and misconceptions.)

Negative Reinforcement

Behavior can be increased by delaying, preventing, or removing unwanted consequences contingent on behavior. Like the definition of positive reinforcement, the definition of negative reinforcement also includes two parts: (1) *description of a procedure* (the removal of an event contingent on a behavior); and (2) *a behavioral effect* (a subsequent increase in the future probability of the behavior). As with positive reinforcers, the classification of an event as a negative reinforcer depends on its effects on behavior. In both positive and negative reinforcement, behaviors are followed by a change in the environment. In the former,

something is presented. In the latter, something is removed. Both procedures *increase* the future probability of behavior and both involve contingencies (relationships between behavior and the environment). Negative, as well as positive, reinforcement plays a key role in the development and maintenance of behaviors.

Making Effective Use of Negative Reinforcement

Requisites for using negative reinforcement are similar to those for using positive reinforcement except that a negative consequence is removed, delayed, or prevented following a behavior. Because it is often the form of escape or avoidance behavior that is problematic (not the function), desirable alternatives should be reinforced. For example, a wife may complain of being sick (when she is not) because this is followed by attention from a neglectful partner (Layng, 2009). The same parameters that influence the effectiveness of positive reinforcement influence the effectiveness of negative reinforcement (immediacy, amount, schedule, and frequency). If negative reinforcement is not effective, it may be because one of the requisites for effective use of punishment is not satisfied (see later discussion of punishment).

Advantages and Disadvantages

Both negative and positive reinforcement increase behavior. Many self-managed contingencies are maintained by negative reinforcement (e.g., studying removes guilt and worry). The close relationship between punishment and negative reinforcement (aversive events must be presented or threatened if they are to be removed) is a disadvantage of relying on negative reinforcement. However, punishment is a daily part of real-life environments. Donald Baer (1984) points out that "many of our most useful skills, like walking or driving a car, are skills that get us to positive reinforcers, but that were learned and are maintained under severe, consistent punishment for almost any small errors. Yet we do not consider that our interactions with the surface of the planet or with our automobiles are problems in need of intervention, despite the pervasively aversive nature of the contingencies surrounding them" (p. 557). Contingencies, including punishment and negative reinforcement, provide us with information (e.g., clues about how we could alter our behavior to increase positive outcomes and to decrease negative ones). Malott (1994) suggests that we should make greater use of negative reinforcement to attain outcomes we value (e.g., learning, wearing seat belts, exercising).

Myths and Misunderstandings

Negative reinforcement is often confused with punishment. Although punishment and negative reinforcement both involve aversive events, they differ in their effects (one increases behavior and may be associated with positive emotional reactions such as relief; the other decreases behavior and is associated with negative emotional reactions such as fear and anxiety). Many highly adaptive behaviors are maintained by negative reinforcement (e.g., turning the wheel of a car to avoid an accident, wearing protective gloves to decrease risk of HIV infection among nurses).

Decreasing Behavior

Many problems involve unwanted behaviors, behaviors that occur too often, at the wrong time, or in the wrong form. There are many options for decreasing behavior. Some are more effective with less hassle and negative effects than are others. Levels of intrusiveness suggested by O'Heare (2009) include the following:

- Level 1: Rearranging antecedents.

- Level 2: Shaping and response prevention.

- Level 3: Differential positive reinforcement (positive reinforcement of low rates of behavior (DRL), or of other behavior(s) (DRO), or of incompatible behavior (DRI), or of alternative behavior(s) (DRA) and extinction of undesired behavior.

- Level 4: Positive reinforcement of desired behavior and response cost for undesired one.

- Level 5: Graded differential negative reinforcement of desired behavior and extinction of undesired behavior.

- Level 6: Positive reinforcement for desired behavior and punishment of undesired behavior.

Attending to and rearranging antecedents should be a part of all levels.

Differential Reinforcement

Differential reinforcement of alternative behavior (DRA) is widely used to decrease undesired behavior and to increase desired behavior. Reinforcement is withheld following behaviors to be decreased (operant extinction) and presented following desired behaviors (positive reinforcement). Behavior surfeits (behaviors that occur too often and create problems such as hitting) are often related to behavior deficits (lack of desired behaviors such as sharing toys). In differential reinforcement of other behaviors (DRO), reinforcement is offered if a certain time passes in which a behavior does not occur. A child may receive a reinforcer if he is not accused of stealing for an entire day. Reinforcement can be offered contingent on a specific low rate of behavior (DRL). For example, a student may receive points if he talks out of turn only once every hour. In differential reinforcement of

incompatible behaviors (DRI) a behavior incompatible with one to be decreased is reinforced. Techniques designed to decrease anxiety, such as desensitization and stress-management training, involve increasing alternative behaviors such as calming self-instructions.

Extinction

In operant extinction, the consequences that usually follow a behavior no longer occur.

Making Effective Use of Extinction

Only if reinforcers are consistently withheld will extinction be effective. If they are not or if the reinforcer maintaining a behavior cannot be identified, the behavior will be occasionally reinforced, which will maintain the behavior. Extinction should be combined with the positive reinforcement of desired behaviors. This will avoid the initial increase in undesired behavior, increase a specific other desirable behavior, and avoid negative emotional effects that accompany extinction. Questions suggested when considering the use of extinction include the following (Alberto & Troutman, 1990, p. 264):

1. Can the behavior be tolerated temporarily?

2. Can an increase in the behavior be tolerated?

3. Is the behavior likely to occur?

4. Are the reinforcers known?

5. Can reinforcement be withheld?

6. Have alternative behaviors been identified that can be reinforced?

If it is not possible to withhold reinforcement following a behavior, other procedures must be used. You can only be certain that the reinforcers have been identified after they are no longer provided and a subsequent decrease in behavior occurs.

Advantages and Disadvantages of Extinction

Extinction is not as aversive as some other means of decreasing behavior such as punishment. It may be easy to implement and effective provided that all involved parties are consistent in withholding reinforcement. Disadvantages of extinction when used alone include an initial increase in the intensity, severity, and frequency of the behavior being extinguished that may be aversive to others. Even when extinction is combined with positive reinforcement of desired behaviors (which it should be), it may take a few days to see a change in behavior. There may be periods of "spontaneous recovery" of the behavior. Occasional reinforcement may undo an extinction procedure. Also, keep in mind that no specific desired responses may be increased. In fact, other undesirable behaviors may occur because of negative emotional reactions. Aggressive reactions may occur, as well as negative emotional effects. Withholding reinforcement elicits aggressive attack behavior in a range of species. Feelings of discouragement, failure, and helplessness and depression may accompany extinction. Social anxiety may be due not only to punishing consequences, but to a lack of positive reinforcement in social situations (i.e., nonreward). Being ignored in social situations is not emotionally neutral for most people. It is unpleasant.

If You Are Not Successful

You may not be successful because reinforcement was not consistently withheld. Resistance to extinction is influenced by the reinforcement schedule that has maintained a behavior (see discussion of schedules of reinforcement in chapter 7). It is also influenced by the amount, number, and quality of reinforcers, number of previous extinction trials, and effort required to engage in a behavior.

Myths and Misconceptions

Successful use of extinction requires withholding reinforcement for all instances of a behavior. Occasional, sporadic withholding of reinforcement will not be effective. Extinction creates negative emotional reactions. And, as noted above, extinction does not increase any other particular behavior.

Response Cost

In response cost a positive reinforcer is removed, contingent on a behavior. This is often combined with positive reinforcement of desired behaviors. Response cost may be used as a part of token or point programs. Tokens or points could be deducted contingent on certain behaviors (or their lack). Removal of tangible items such as access to TV is often difficult and involves attention that might reinforce inappropriate behavior.

Making Effective Use of Response Cost

Select an observable, countable behavior, as well as a positive reinforcer to be removed, and arrange the consistent removal of this event following the behavior. Be sure to combine response cost with positive reinforcement of desired behaviors. Arrange the precise cost beforehand (e.g., how many days will use of a car be lost?). The loss should match the severity of the behavior, be consistently and immediately applied, and the contingency should be verbally described. Time out involves response cost (see later discussion).

If You Are Not Successful

Perhaps the consequence removed is not a reinforcer. Not enough reinforcement may be offered for alternative behaviors (see also discussion of punishment).

Advantages and Disadvantages

Advantages of response cost include ease of combining it with other methods (e.g., positive reinforcement of desired behaviors) and rapid effects on behavior. Disadvantages are similar to those of punishment (e.g., increased aggression, avoidance of the response cost enforcer and contexts in which positive consequences are removed, and focus on negative behaviors).

Myths and Misunderstandings

Response cost decreases behavior. It does not necessarily increase any other behavior despite beliefs and hopes that "He should know what to do." And it creates negative emotional reactions.

Punishment: The Least Desirable Alternative

Punishment is a procedure in which an aversive event is presented following a behavior and there is a subsequent decrease in that behavior (see also chapter 7). Behaviors maintained on "thin schedules" of reinforcement are especially likely to be disrupted by punishment. Aversive events differ in their intensity, ranging from a mild verbal rebuke to a slap in the face. Aversive events, like positive ones, are relative. That is, what functions as aversive events varies from person to person and from time to time for the same person, depending on each person's unique history and current situation. Some argue that it is never necessary to use aversive methods. They argue that other procedures are available for decreasing behavior including differential reinforcement of other behavior or positive reinforcement combined with time out (Sailor & Carr, 1994). Others argue that there is no way to avoid the use of punishment if we want to enhance freedom, which requires individual responsibility, which, in turn, requires sharing the costs and pain that result from behavior (Birnbrauer, 1990, 1994). They argue that to insist that socialization or self-management can occur without any use of punishment (e.g., verbal reprimands) is simply wrong. With some behaviors, such as head banging, it may not be possible to withhold reinforcement for the behavior, and so operant extinction cannot be used.

The frequency of a behavior may be so high that it interferes with desired behavior, and so these cannot be reinforced. Punishment may be necessary to reduce this high frequency so that positive behaviors can be reinforced. Positive consequences are not always successful in altering behavior in desired directions. In certain instances, for example, with severe self-destructive behavior, it may be more humane to use punishment combined with positive reinforcement than to combine the latter with planned ignoring because the former is more rapidly effective. Carr and his colleagues (1990) believe that the question "Should aversives be used?" is the wrong question. They believe that the right question is "What does a functional assessment indicate is necessary to accomplish valued outcomes with minimal use of aversives and maximum reliance on positive methods?"

Birnbrauer (1990) suggests that the "solution is to institute and maintain contingencies that maximize positives and minimize negatives for each member of the group" (p. 232). Thus, both the individual and the group must be considered in relation to costs and benefits. Because the effects of offensive behavior are usually positive for the offender and only negative to others, "planning priorities should be placed upon instituting and maintaining contingencies of reinforcement, both positive and negative, so that (a) the need for punishment is diminished, (b) the unsystematic use of aversives is diminished, and (c) aversives are employed only in contexts that maximize effectiveness in the shortest period of time" (p. 233) (see also Sailor & Carr, 1994).

Making Effective Use of Punishment

Requisites for the effective use of punishment include:

- Identify specific behaviors.

- Withhold positive reinforcement for these behaviors.

- Select an event that will function as a punishing consequence that elicits as little aggression as possible.

- Arrange the consistent presentation of this immediately following the behavior.

- Reinforce desired alternatives.

If punishment is used, it should be combined with reinforcement for desired behaviors (e.g., alternate ways to gain desired consequences). Criticism can be decreased by identifying and reinforcing desired behaviors. Unwanted escape from the contingency must be prevented and, if possible, every instance of behavior to be decreased should be followed by the punishing event. Make sure that the punishing event is not associated with positive reinforcement; otherwise, it may serve as a cue that valued consequences will follow and undesired behaviors may increase; they become cues that reinforcement will follow. It is more effective to punish early rather than later components in a chain of behavior. Early components are more easily disrupted, and reinforcement of undesired behaviors that may occur if the behavior chain is completed is avoided. Remove cues and reinforcers for undesired behavior; otherwise, the effects of punishment will be diluted by continued reinforcement. In everyday

life, many undesired behaviors are followed by both reinforcement and punishment. As long as the amount of reinforcement exceeds the amount of punishment, the behavior will continue, especially if no alternative source of reinforcement is provided. You can bring behavior under the influence of verbal cues such as "No" or "Stop that" by pairing such statements with punishment. Behavior can then be influenced by the verbal cue alone. Providing reasons why certain actions should be avoided or taken may be helpful.

Variables That Influence the Effectiveness of Punishment

The same variables that influence the effectiveness of reinforcement influence the effectiveness of punishment, including the immediacy with which a negative event follows behavior, the intensity of this event, the schedule of punishment, and the proportion of responses punished (Lerman & Toole, 2011). Punishment is more effective if initially introduced at an intense level than if it is introduced at moderate or mild levels. If punishment is mild, habituation to the punishing event may occur, resulting in a decrease in the effect of the aversive consequence. That is, stronger levels of punishment may be required to achieve the same behavioral effect. Continuous, in contrast to intermittent, punishment is more effective.

If undesired behaviors are still being reinforced, the effects of punishment will be influenced by the schedule of reinforcement in effect. For example, tantrums may be reinforced by attention delivered on a variable-ratio schedule. This will decrease the effects of punishment. However, if an alternative way is provided to obtain a reinforcer, punishment can be very effective in decreasing unwanted behavior and increasing desired behaviors. Deprivation decreases the effects of punishment. If a person is deprived of a reinforcer, such as social approval, punishment of behaviors that result in this reinforcer will not be as effective. Punishment will be ineffective if escape from the contingency is possible. If a mother tells her son that because he was late for dinner he will receive no dinner that evening, and if he can go out and have dinner with a friend, her words may have little impact.

If You Are Not Successful

Check the following possibilities and rearrange plans as needed:

- The consequence used is not aversive.

- The behavior is being positively reinforced.

- There are no alternative routes to obtain positive reinforcers.

- Escape is possible.

- One of the other requisites for the effective use of punishment has not been satisfied.

Disadvantages of Reliance on Punishment

Avoid use of punishment when possible. The many disadvantages of punishment are described in chapter 7. Punishment only teaches what not to do and leaves the development of desirable behaviors to chance. It does not eliminate reinforcement for undesired behavior. Aversive consequences, especially moderate or high-level ones, should only be used under extreme circumstances (e.g., behaviors that pose a great danger to self or others) and only when positive and less aversive methods have not been effective. Some legislation such as the Hughes Bill (1993) requires that staff must demonstrate that positive methods were appropriately used and were not successful before aversive methods can be used. Guidelines suggested by Alberto and Troutman (1990) include the following:

1. Demonstrated and documented failure of alternative nonaversive methods to alter behavior. (This is required in legislation, the Hughes Bill, 1993).

2. Informed written consent of the client and significant others (e.g., legal guardians) through due process procedures and assurance of their right to withdraw their consent at any time.

3. A decision to use an aversive procedure made by a designated body of qualified professionals.

4. A prearranged timetable to review the effectiveness of the method and to ensure its discontinuance as soon as possible.

5. Periodic observation to ensure consistent and reliable use of the method.

6. Documentation of the effectiveness of the method, as well as evidence of increased accessibility to instruction.

7. Use of the method only by designated staff member(s) who have had prior instruction in its use, have reviewed published studies in its use, and who are familiar with procedure-specific guidelines and possible negative effects.

8. Arranging positive reinforcement of incompatible behavior whenever possible. (pp. 276–278)

Myths and Misconceptions

Many people rely on punishment because they believe it is effective. Although it may be temporarily effective, no other particular desired alternative is encouraged, which may be the main goal of the "punisher." Punishment teaches what not to do, not what to do.

Why Do So Many People Rely on Punishment?

Use of punishment is encouraged by its immediate effects, lack of knowledge and skill in positive behavior change methods, and a low tolerance for undesirable behavior. For example, staff in a residential center may neither know about nor be skilled in using positive contingencies. They may know about them but not have the skills required to implement them effectively. Use of positive methods requires creativity to discover or create positive reinforcers. It usually does not take much thought to identify what can be taken away from a client or what can be presented that will be unpleasant. Staff may be concerned that their physical safety and/or that of others cannot be assured unless aversive methods are used. Research suggests that in most cases, safety can be maximized via use of positive methods (e.g., see LaVigna et al., 1994). Crittenden (1998) suggests that parents who abuse their children may do so because of fears that their children are not safe; their fears create anger reactions "aimed at keeping children from doing dangerous things such as… running into the street" (p. 17). She notes that there are more dangers in poor neighborhoods to protect children against. Thus, she suggests that some abuse is "motivated" (not necessarily consciously) to protect children from harm.

Overcorrection

This method can be used to decrease inappropriate behaviors and to provide practice of desired alternatives (e.g., Cole, Montgomery, Wilson, & Milan, 2000). It involves the use of aversive events. In restitutional overcorrection, the person is required to correct the results of his behavior by restoring the situation to an improved state compared to that which existed before the behavior. For example, a youth who spits on the floor may be required to wash the entire floor. Positive-practice overcorrection involves the practice of correct behaviors. A youth who throws trash around could practice placing trash in wastebaskets. (See other sources for more detailed descriptions, Martin & Pear, 2010.)

Time-Out

In time-out an individual is removed to a less reinforcing environment for a *brief* period contingent on undesired behavior or lack of a desired behavior (e.g., Turner & Watson, 1999). A person is removed from one environment (the "time-in" environment) to another that is less reinforcing (the time-out environment), contingent on a behavior (or its lack). This procedure is often used with young children and can be very effective especially when combined with positive reinforcement of desired behaviors. Time-out contingencies involve a variety of components, including: (1) response cost (removal of positive reinforcers, the "time-in" environment); (2) negative reinforcement (time-out is ended only after inappropriate behavior has ended); (3) punishment (isolation itself may be unpleasant); and (4) positive reinforcement (valued behaviors are reinforced following the end of time-out). Time-out should be combined with positive reinforcement of desired behavior and time-out duration should be brief, about 5 to 15 minutes. Time-out will not be effective if undesired behavior is reinforced during time-out.

Effective use of time-out requires specialized knowledge and training. You must identify specific behavior(s), select a time-out area that does not contain positive reinforcers, and arrange for the removal of the person to this area contingent on specific behavior(s) (or their lack). Time will be needed to train significant others how to use time-out correctly, and arrangements should be made to monitor its use and provide corrective feedback as necessary. Questions to review include the following:

1. Have I overlooked use of more positive procedures, such as differential reinforcement?

2. Have I considered both nonseclusionary and seclusionary time-out methods?

3. Can time-out be used with minimal client resistance? Can significant others handle possible resistance?

4. Have the rules for desired behavior and the results of undesired behavior been clearly explained and understood?

5. Have the rules for behavior while in time-out been clearly explained and understood?

6. Have regulations concerning use of time-out been reviewed and followed?

7. Will desired behavior be reinforced in conjunction with the use of time-out? (Alberto & Troutman, 1990, p. 275)

Common errors in attempting to use time-out include providing reinforcing attention and physical contact on the way to time-out. In such cases, time-out may function as a positive reinforcer. Time-out may function as a positive reinforcer if the time-in environment is not positive. Other possibilities you should consider if time-out is not effective include the following: the time-out area is reinforcing; time-out is not consistently enforced; time-out periods are too long (e.g., the longer the fewer opportunities for reinforcement of appropriate behaviors in the time-in settings); or time-out may not be immediately implemented following undesired behavior. Positive alternatives may not be reinforced. Time-out periods may be ended even though inappropriate behavior is occurring.

Positive Alternatives to the Use of Punishment

There are a variety of alternates to the use of punishment that focus on increasing desired behaviors and avoid the negative effects of punishment (e.g., see Matson, 2009; Repp & Horner, 1999; Sarafino, 2012; Sturmey, 2007).

Reinforcing Desired Behaviors

Reinforcing desired behaviors is a positive alternative to punishment (see prior discussion of differential reinforcement). Quality assurance programs emphasize use of positive consequences and involve all staff in discovering opportunities to improve services (Daniels, 2000; LaVigna et al., 1994). You can discover alternatives to punishment by identifying the cues and consequences related to behaviors of interest as suggested in Exhibit 25.4. Undesired behaviors may have an escape function maintained by negative reinforcement. For example, if unrealistic work standards are imposed on staff, they may find ways to show these are being met (when they are not) to avoid loss of pay or other positive consequences.

A key assessment goal is to discover the functions of behaviors of concern. The goal of *functional communication training* is to teach people language that allows them to convey messages in a manner that results in desired consequences (e.g., Carr & Levin, 2000). The basic idea is that valued behaviors will increase when they are functional (when they result in valued consequences). These methods are designed to increase motivation to communicate in effective ways. You can enhance motivation to engage in desired behaviors by making sure that behaviors: (1) have utility for those involved; (2) are acquired in the context in which they will be used; (3) are age appropriate for participants; and (4) are generalizable to other situations. Objectives pursued should have *functional relevance* for clients. They should make a difference in real life.

You can replace disruptive behaviors maintained by attention by developing desired alternatives to obtain these consequences, for example, helping students with severe disabilities initiate and maintain conversations with nondisabled peers. Teaching children how to prompt feedback by asking "How is my work?" will increase teacher attention. Young adults with severe disabilities in integrated work settings learned how to recruit feedback for their performance (Mank & Horner, 1987). They learned how to monitor a target behavior, to evaluate their performance in relation to a specific criteria, and then to request feedback from supervisors. Improved work rate was related to self-recruited feedback. This kind of program increases the influence people have over the quality of their environments. Pictures can be used to help people who cannot speak clearly (or at all) to communicate more effectively with others. For example, pictures of various food items could be placed on a chart and clients can point to desired items when ordering food in fast-food restaurants.

Other Positive Options

Incidental teaching takes advantage of naturally occurring training opportunities. For example, to encourage requests you could place a desired item out of reach and wait for the student to request it. Natural reinforcers are used, and functionally significant behaviors are increased without use of prompts.

EXHIBIT 25.4

Source of Motivation, Possible Communicative Messages, and Related Interventions

Motivational Source	Possible Communicative Message(s)	Teach Replacement Response	Functionally Related Alt-R Procedures	Change Antecedents
I. *Positive reinforcement* Attention maintains behavior.	"Pay Attention to me." "Play with me." "Help me."	Teach a variety of ways to request attention (e.g., tap on arm, greeting sign, "Play," "Help").	Use attention to reinforce already occurring alternative behaviors. Direct instructions + social reinforcement of new alternative behaviors.	Alter environment to provide noncontingent attention.
Material reinforcers (e.g., food, objects)	"I want _____."	Teach manual sign for desired consequence.	Use desired materials to reinforce already occurring alternative behaviors. Direct instruction + social reinforcement of new, alternative responses.	Alter environment to provide noncontingent access to material reinforcers (stimulus satiation).
II. *Negative reinforcement* Ending an aversive stimulus or situation.	"I don't want to do this anymore." "Stop!" "No." "I don't understand."	Teach manual/gestural sign to end activity—to escape.	Reinforce alternative escape behaviors.	Alter context to decrease/eliminate aversiveness; simplify tasks; increase value of other tasks; alter instructional demands.
III. *Extinction frustration* Previously available reinforcers are no longer available.	"Help me." "Why can't I have...?" "You used to give me _____," "I want it now."	Teach communication skills to obtain desired reinforcers; and/or to enlist aid to obtain them.	Reinstate previously available reinforcers contingent on alternative responses.	Alter environment to provide previously available reinforcers; alter instructions, provide richer reinforcement schedule.
IV. *Arousal induction* Behavior provides sensory stimulation that is intrinsically reinforcing.	"I'm bored." "I'm not getting the input I want."	Teach how to obtain sensory input, e.g., request for sensory activity.	Provide reinforcing sensory input through alternative activities. Direct instruction + reinforcement of alternative behaviors.	Alter environment to provide more stimulation.

(continued)

EXHIBIT 25.4 (Continued)

Motivational Source	Possible Communicative Message(s)	Teach Replacement Response	Functionally Related Alt-R Procedures	Change Antecedents
V. *Arousal reduction* Behavior is maintained by termination of aversive overstimulation (e.g., it "blocks out" excess sensory input).	"I'm anxious/excited/over-whelmed." "Help me."	Teach alternative means for expressing distress/enlisting aid.	Provide and reinforce alternative means of removing the aversive over-stimulation; vigorous exercise. Relaxation Response	Alter environment to decrease stimulation and demands.
VI. *Respondent conditioning* Behavior originated from a traumatic event (e.g., loud noise, pain) that triggers the behavior. Behavior is then maintained by positive or negative reinforcement.	"I'm afraid." "This is a bad habit that I can't control." "I want _____. to stop." "Help."	Teach how to express distress or enlist assistance.	Reinforce gradual tolerance of trigger stimulus; systematic desensitization. Direct instruction + reinforcement of alternative responses to trigger stimulus.	Alter environment to preclude trigger stimulus.
VII. *Physiological Behavior* is the product of a physiological process.	"I hurt." "I'm tired."	Teach communicative means to express distress.	Not applicable.	Not applicable.

Source: Adapted from A. M. Donnellan, P. L. Mirenda, R. A. Mesaros, & L. L. Fassbender (1984). Analyzing the communicative functions of aberrant behavior. *Journal of the Association for Persons with Severe Handicaps, 9,* 207, 206–207. Reprinted with permission.

(See http://www.lovaas.com). Time delay methods are designed to decrease errors and thus increase success experiences and to allow clients to decide when to continue a task. For example, significant others may wait a few seconds before prompting desired behavior. Relaxation and exercise provide nonaversive methods to alter behavior. For example, relaxation training resulted in a decrease in hyperventilation and seizures in a profoundly disabled epileptic child (Kiesel, Lutzker, & Campbell, 1989). Exercise has been found to decrease aggressive and hyperactive behaviors of adults with severe disabilities (McGimsey & Favell, 1988). (See also Ströhle, 2009.) Giving clients small, frequent requests that can be easily followed can be used to increase request following. Positively reinforced pre-task requests ease transitions from less demanding and more reinforcing settings (recess) to more demanding and less reinforcing ones (academic work).

Rearranging Antecedents

Another way to alter behavior is to rearrange antecedents (Smith, 2011). This is known as stimulus control. Cues for desired behaviors are enhanced and cues for undesired ones muted or removed. Removing a discriminative stimulus (S^D) for a behavior or presenting an S^Δ (stimulus delta) will decrease associated behaviors. A problem in stimulus control exists whenever instructions (including self-instructions) are given and hoped-for behavior does not occur. Teachers often label children "disobedient" who do not follow their instructions. Perhaps the children do not understand or do not have the knowledge or skills to comply with the instructions. Perhaps behavior has not been brought under the influence of particular cues. Teachers may have "too many" rules. "There's no point in surrounding ourselves with unnecessary rules and regulations that only breed resistance" (Pryor, 1984).

Stimulus control is a key aspect of any skilled activity (e.g., playing in an orchestra, dancing). Most of our behavior consists of *discriminated operants* (behaviors that occur only in certain situations, those in which they are reinforced). Antecedent events acquire influence over our behavior through their association with reinforcing consequences. For example, we ask certain kinds of questions ("How do you feel?" "How are you?") only in certain situations. We are more likely to engage in particular behaviors in situations in which they have been reinforced in the past and less likely to perform them in situations in which they have been punished or not reinforced. Characteristics of situations unrelated to whether or not behavior is reinforced but that are usually present may also influence behavior if they change radically. Trying to "problem solve" when this is not possible because of fatigue or competing goals, such as completing work, is a waste of time. A specific future time to think about a topic could be selected (unless a crisis is at hand). Goldiamond (1965) suggested setting up a "sulking stool" where a client could go and sit when he brooded. The purpose was to decrease negative thoughts about his partner by narrowing the range of situations in which they occurred. Ms. Landis used stimulus control to help Julie remember to use thought stopping to decrease worrisome thoughts (see chapter 25). (For discussion of thought stopping, see Bakker, 2009.)

You may rearrange the physical environment to encourage desired patterns of behavior. For example, placing chairs around tables (rather than against walls) increased talking among residents (Peterson, Knapp, Rosen, & Pither, 1977). Stimulus control is often used in behavioral medicine. You could, for example, help a client to associate a specific cue (e.g., yellow gown) with painful but necessary procedures (such as changing burn dressings), decreasing anxiety reactions in other contexts (when the yellow gown is not worn) (Shorkey & Taylor, 1973). Home safety for children can be enhanced by altering physical conditions at home (Barone, Greene, & Lutzker, 1986) (see also Miltenberger & Gross, 2011). You can encourage desired behaviors by removing cues for competing behaviors. For example, to increase studying you could remove cues for writing letters, texting, or daydreaming. You in effect "purify" the context by allowing only desired behaviors to occur in that setting. You remove cues for undesired reactions and enhance cues for desired ones. Altering the meaning (the cueing function) of feelings and environmental events (making these cues for constructive thoughts, feelings, or actions rather than for dysfunctional ones) is the goal of cognitive-behavioral methods such as anxiety and anger management training.

Making Effective Use of Rearranging Antecedents

"To establish stimulus control, you shape a behavior and then in effect shape the offering of this behavior during or right after some particular stimulus. This stimulus then becomes the cue, a signal, for the behavior" (Pryor, 1984, p. 85). Behavior is reinforced in the presence of the cue that will influence the behavior and not reinforced in its absence. As Pryor (1984) emphasizes, the discipline required to achieve stimulus control via positive means (many people rely on coercion) is on the part of the trainer or coach. In errorless discrimination learning or fading, a discrimination is established without the occurrence of errors and with minimal disruption of behavior by starting out with large differences between two or more stimuli that are easily distinguishable and then gradually making these more similar. This method is useful when people have intense negative reactions when they make errors. Fading, compared to extinction and punishment, does not result in escape behavior.

Factors That Influence the Effectiveness of Rearranging Antecedents

Reinforcement history will influence the degree to which a cue affects the frequency of a behavior. Other influences include the number and intensity of competing cues for other behaviors and the particular schedules of reinforcement in effect for each. The "learner" must "recognize" the signal and be capable of carrying out hoped-for behaviors. Options for rearranging cues differ in different settings.

Advantages and Disadvantages

As Karen Pryor notes in *Don't Shoot the Dog* (1984), stimulus control yields "cooperation without coercion." This captures its main advantage.

> People who have a disciplined understanding of stimulus control avoid giving needless instructions, unreasonable or incomprehensible commands, or orders that can't be obeyed. They try not to make requests they're not prepared to follow through on; you always know exactly what they expect. They don't fly off the handle at a poor response. They don't nag, scold, whine, coerce, beg, or threaten to get their way, because they don't need to. And when you ask them to do something, if they say yes, they do it. When you get a whole family, or household, or corporation working on the basis of real stimulus control—when all the people keep their agreements, say what they need, and do what they say—it is perfectly amazing how much gets done, how few orders ever need to be given, and how fast the trust builds up. Good stimulus control is nothing more than true communication—honest, fair communication. (pp. 105–106)

Disadvantages of altering behavior via rearrangement of antecedents include prelearning dips and related temper tantrums. Prelearning dips refer to a discouraging decrease in hoped-for behaviors during learning. They can be frustrating for both teachers and learners. Karen Pryor calls this reaction a temper tantrum and suggests that this phase is related to attending to the signal (cue) that interferes with responding.

If You Are Not Successful

Lack of success may be due to relying on cues that are difficult to distinguish and/or to unsystematic use of reinforcement with the result that behavior does not come under the influence of particular cues. Lack of patience is an obstacle. Bringing behavior under new stimulus control takes time. You may have to circle back to assessment (e.g., see Watson & Steege, 2003).

Summary

Helping clients acquire positive behavior change skills is a common goal. This often entails helping clients to shift from use of punishment (e.g., criticism, hitting, removing privileges) to use of positive methods (e.g., praise for accomplishments, asking for what one wants). Clients learn that intent is not necessarily related to outcome. For example, a supervisor may intend to help a student by her critical feedback; however, if this feedback

decreases desired behaviors, it is punishing, not reinforcing. There are many positive shortcuts for altering behavior including rearranging antecedents (changing what happens before behaviors of interest). Options for rearranging contingencies will vary in different circumstances. Guided instruction may be needed to maximize success. Parents and teachers often benefit from acquiring such skills, so avoiding the negative effects of reliance on punishment. Acquiring positive ways to alter behavior will help clients to be more effective in acquiring needed services from professionals and others.

Reviewing Your Competencies

Reviewing Content Knowledge

1. Describe the requisites for use of positive reinforcement.

2. Describe the advantages of using positive reinforcement.

3. Describe common errors in attempting to use positive reinforcement.

4. Describe parameters that influence the effectiveness of reinforcement.

5. Distinguish between negative and positive reinforcement and give examples of each.

6. Describe two lost-cost methods that can be used to increase behaviors.

7. Describe procedures that can be used to decrease behaviors and give an example of each.

8. Describe the disadvantages of using punishment.

9. Give two examples from your own experience of rearranging antecedents to alter behavior.

10. Describe situations in which it would be appropriate to use artificial reinforcers, such as tokens or points (see chapter 21).

11. Describe the different emotional effects of positive and negative contingencies.

Reviewing What You Do

1. You effectively use positive reinforcement to increase behavior.

2. You effectively rearrange antecedents to alter behavior.

3. You can show another person how to use positive reinforcement to attain a valued outcome.

4. You can show another person how to rearrange antecedents to achieve a desired outcome.

5. Reinforcement plans are carried out with a high degree of fidelity.

6. Methods you select have the best chance of success, given available resources.

Reviewing Results

1. Positive outcomes are achieved.

   - You help parents learn positive behavior change (or maintenance) methods.

   - You help staff in a residential setting shift from reliance on punishment to reliance on positive methods that support accomplishments and increase independence of residents.

   - You help community members to increase opportunities for positive informal exchanges.

   - You help participants of a support group to increase behaviors they want to see more of and decrease behaviors they want to see less often.

   - You help administrators to provide more positive feedback to staff for valued behaviors.

   - You help caregivers to increase use of positive methods to maintain self-care skills of their elderly relatives.

2. Clients acquire positive skills for altering the behavior of others.

3. Clients acquire positive skills for altering their own behavior.

4. Clients understand the difference between intent and outcome.

5. Clients decrease use of punishment.

26

Working with Groups and Families

OVERVIEW   This chapter provides additional guidelines for working with families and groups. Many examples throughout this book involve families. The guidelines in previous chapters are relevant to families and groups, as well as to individuals, organizations, and communities including critical thinking skills. The relationship skills described in chapters 15 and 16 are of value in group settings, including case conferences, team meetings, and meetings with community residents.

YOU WILL LEARN ABOUT

- What is a family?

- Assessing families

- Intervention options

- Working with groups

- Making decisions in groups

- Self-help and mutual help groups

What Is a Family?

This is a controversial question that has implications for the way resources are distributed. For example, same-sex (or cohabiting heterosexual) couples living in long-term relationships may not be entitled to employer-provided medical coverage for their partner. Families may be defined by biological relatedness and/or living arrangements. Kinds of families include stepfamilies, nuclear families, extended families, gay-lesbian families, single-parent families, families without children, families with grown children, and bicultural families (e.g., see Congress & Gonzales, 2005; Wright et al., 2012). Many children grow up in blended families because of divorce and remarriage. Families caring for children with disabilities confront unique challenges (e.g., McCart, Wolf, Sweeney, Markey, and Markey, 2009) as do families caring for individuals labeled as "schizophrenic" (e.g., Pharoah, Rathbone, Mari, & Steiner, 2004). Immigrants and refugees also confront unique problems (Chang-Muy & Congress,

2009; Chuang & Moreno, 2011). Families serve a variety of functions for society and the individual, including raising children, regulating sexual relations, socializing family members into social roles valued by society or by a particular cultural group, economic maintenance, and household management. Functions of families have changed over time.

Assessing Families

Each person has a family history, which may be more or less positive or negative. It is always unique. Families are influenced by the community and society in which they live. Feminist critics argue that family theories do not recognize historic, social, economic, and political influences on the family that encourage and maintain subordination of women to men in access to resources. They argue that we live in a patriarchal social order that encourages oppressive gender-typed family roles and results in blaming women for problems such as battering, rape, and incest. This societal and historic level of understanding is important in a contextual view. Acceptance of oppressive gender-based roles may pose a significant obstacle to changing interaction patterns including domestic violence and child abuse (Renzetti, Edleson, & Bergan, 2011). A contextual approach to families suggests the questions in Exhibit 26.1. Both family structure (e.g., who is in the family), and process (how often they see each other) and function (e.g., who reinforces whom for what) may relate to problems. All these characteristics may be influenced by cultural differences (e.g., see Furman & Negi, 2010; Singh et al., 2010). Exhibit 26.2 describes goals that are often of interest in work with families.

Whom you decide to see gives messages to clients about who is involved in a problem. Both assessment needs and feasibility will influence decisions (e.g., are all family members willing to participate?). Seeing all family members together provides valuable opportunities to observe interaction styles. How do family members relate to each other? What does each person hope to gain? What changes would they like? (See interview in chapter 13). It may be important to see children separately, as well as with their parents to allow opportunities for them to talk without other family members present. Meetings with families, as with meetings with individuals, provide opportunities to model helpful behaviors such as attentive listening and to identify and to support family strengths, including caring about each other. Here too as with individuals, roles should be clarified (yours and theirs) and confidentiality issues discussed.

Family Stresses

Families involved in the public social welfare system often experience environmental stressors such as lack of money, poor-quality housing, lack of health care, and lack of day care for children. These stresses may create other problems such as substance abuse. Divorce and separation may create a spiraling series of negative effects that persist over time (Patterson & Forgatch, 1990). Families may have unique caregiving burdens requiring special support. Stress may be created by a youth taking an unconventional life path (Ryan, Russell, Huebner, Diaz, & Sanchez, 2010). Couples and families with alternative lifestyles confront unique challenges (e.g., see Cahill & Tobias, 2006; Hunter, 2012). Policies regarding families alter opportunities (Bogenschneider, 2006).

Living Situation

What is the family's living space like? How much space is available? How is space used? What effect does the living space have on family relationships? Are there health hazards such as exposed wires (see Tertinger, Greene, & Lutzker, 1984)? What is the neighborhood like? How does this neighborhood affect family life?

Composition and Extended Networks

Who lives in this family? Is there an extended family network and, if so, what role(s) does it play in this family? Kinship care for children has expanded over the past decade.

Power

Families differ in who can influence whom to do what. Questions here include the following:

- Who makes what decisions in the family?
- Whose preferences are usually followed?
- Who does most of the talking?
- Who speaks for others?
- Who controls whom by covert means (e.g., complaints)?
- Are positive or negative consequences usually relied on?
- Who provides what kinds of help in the family (e.g., shopping, cooking, cleaning, money)?

Cultural norms and values influence power structure. Power balances may shift over the life cycle of families and in response to changes such as illness, unemployment, or relocation. For example, a woman who usually stays home may be the only one able to get a job when a family moves to a new location. This may change the family power structure. Power is not always obvious. Family members may control each other through illness or depression. For example, family members may remove pressures on wives who complain of depression. Complaints may be negatively reinforced (demands are removed following complaints). Family members may be satisfied or unhappy with current power structures. Power structures may be stable or unstable. Families with antisocial children have coercive interaction styles in which family members rely on punishment and negative reinforcement to gain desired outcomes (Reid, Patterson, & Snyder, 2002).

EXHIBIT 26.1

Questions to Ask About Families

A. LIVING ENVIRONMENT

- How much space is available?
- Are safe play spaces available for children?
- Are neighbors available for aid?
- Are there physical hazards in the home (e.g., exposed wires)?
- How safe is the neighborhood?
- Is transportation easily accessible?
- Are contexts available for informal exchanges?

B. COMPOSITION AND EXTENDED NETWORKS

- What is the family composition?
- Who else lives in the family?
- Is there an extended family?
- What stage of the life cycle is this family in?
- What subsystems exist in this family (coalitions/alliances)?
- What cultural differences should be considered?
- Who spends time with whom in this family?
- How much contact do family members have with the outside world? Are family boundaries too rigid or too permeable?

C. FAMILY STRESSES

- What caregiving responsibilities do family members have?
- Are economic resources sufficient?
- What external strains does the family experience?
- Have typical family supports been removed (refugees and immigrants)?
- Has this family had to deal with any recent stresses such as illness or unemployment?
- Are one or more family members depressed?
- Are there generational differences in acculturation?
- Do cultural differences contribute to stresses?
- Are caregiving burdens unusually heavy?
- What outside support does this family have?

D. FAMILY STRENGTHS/RESOURCES

- What are strengths of this family?
- Do family members like each other?
- Can relatives help out in times of need?
- Is there enough money to cover basic needs?
- What unique strengths do particular cultures offer?
- What positive events do family members share?
- Who helps whom with what and in what ways?

E. COMMUNICATION STYLES AND INTERACTION PATTERNS

- What are preferred communication styles?
- Who reinforces whom for what in what context?
- Is the interaction style reciprocal or coercive?
- What is the level of violence in this home?
- How effective are family members' conflict resolution and problem-solving skills?
- How effective are parenting skills?
- What cultural differences should be considered?
- What is the level of intimacy in this family? Who is attached to whom? Are attachments positive or conflicted? Who shares what information with whom?
- Who is responsible for what in this family? What are family roles?

F. RULES, BELIEFS, AND VALUES

- What are the rules in this family?
- What cultural norms and values are important in the family?
- What role does religion play in this family?

G. POWER

- Who makes decisions about what in this family?
- Who can influence whom to do what?
- How does culture affect power distribution?

Decision Making

Who makes what decisions in a family about disciplining children, handling finances, dealing with relatives, distributing household chores, and so on? Decision making is related to power. Dissatisfaction with how decisions are made may be a concern. Some family members may feel that they are excluded from the decision-making process. Decision-making patterns may be related to presenting problems such as an "unmanageable child"; parents may argue about how to discipline children.

Common Goals in Family/Couple Counseling

- Enhance problem-solving/conflict resolution skills. Help clients to communicate more effectively, to:

    Clearly describe problems/desired outcomes.

    Avoid blame and critical comments.

    Listen without interrupting others.

    Paraphrase what others say.

    Validate concerns/interests of other family members.

    Suggest options.

    Suggest and accept compromises.

    Neutralize escalating negative exchanges.

    Reinforce each other for valued behaviors.

    Avoid unnecessary confrontations.

- Alter misconceptions and distorted views of significant others.
- Alter family alignments.
- Help family members acquire needed material resources.
- Help family members cope with caregiving responsibilities.
- Help families deal with transitions.
- Enhance positive parenting skills.
- Enhance positive behavior change skills:

    Decrease punishment.

    Decrease reliance on negative reinforcement.

    Increase positive reinforcement for valued behaviors.

    Help family members understand cultural differences among family members of different generations.

Caregiving Skills

Families often have caregiving responsibilities for children. Are these responsibilities fulfilled? Are parenting skills adequate? Examples include monitoring, involvement, discipline, problem solving, and positive reinforcement (Reid, Patterson, & Snyder, 2002). Family members may also care for elderly or sick relatives. Is the quality of care satisfactory? What supports are needed such as respite care?

Rules, Beliefs, and Values

Families have rules about who can do what to whom and what may or may not be discussed by whom in what context. They have rules about how family members should act with people outside the family. Rules are often implicit rather than explicit. They may be helpful or harmful in relation to responsibilities of family members such as raising children. They may conflict with rules followed by other community residents. Families differ in the flexibility of rules and in sanctions imposed for rule violation. Cultural differences between family members may create clashes between children and parents, or between partners from different cultural backgrounds.

Communication Styles

Families differ in their preferred modes of communication and in their problem-solving and conflict resolution skills (Segrin & Flora, 2011). They differ in what they argue about. They differ in what they talk about. Examples of problematic communication styles are illustrated in Exhibit 18.6. Problems may involve "receiver" skills (listening, validating) and/or "sender" skills (owning feelings, communicating approval) (Vangelisti, 2004). Enhancing problem-solving and conflict management skills of family members is a common goal. Family members may be occupied with defending their positions rather than listening to others and validating their concerns. Helping clients to listen to each other and to recognize other points of view is a common goal (see case example in chapter 21). Encouraging more positive interaction styles will require talking about how family members communicate with each other (meta communication).

Patterns of Interaction and Affection

Do family members like each other? They may not. The family is the most common site of violence of all kinds (e.g., Helander, 2008). What subsystems exist in the family? Minuchin (1974) emphasized the importance of attending to particular coalitions and alliances that may be based on interest, gender, generation, or responsibilities (such as meal preparation). He highlights the importance of clear, well-defined boundaries between spouse, parental, and sibling subsystems that allow family members to carry out required functions but yet are flexible enough to permit resource exchange among subsystems. Family rules (which are influenced by cultural norms and values) influence the boundaries between subsystems.

The concept of "enmeshment" is a key one in structural family therapy. This refers to excessive closeness in which family members think and feel alike; there is little opportunity for independent functioning, and what happens to one family member immediately affects others. In enmeshed families, one subsystem (for example, a mother and son) may form a coalition against another family member (a father). Or a mother may act as a sister (rather than a parent) to a daughter. Identifying and managing alliances (including those between yourself and family member(s)) is important so that dysfunctional ones are not encouraged. Enmeshed families can be contrasted with "disengaged" families in which family members have little emotional involvement with one another. Triangulation is a concept used in family therapy. This refers to a dysfunctional relationship among three people. For example, a third person may be involved in a relationship to act as an ally or distraction when one person feels powerless, pressured, or distressed.

What is the level of trust in the family? Who trusts (and distrusts) whom in relation to what? Do family members support each other, or do they do their best to tear each other down and compromise each other's self-esteem? Do family members help each other to enhance their skills and positive experiences? Or do they hinder growth and enjoyment? Do they support dysfunctional behavior of one or more family members? For example, does a spouse contribute to her partner's alcohol abuse? Who reinforces whom for what? Do family members control each other mainly by punishment and negative reinforcement? Or do they rely on positive feedback for encouraging valued reactions? Family members may rely on punishment as a way to maintain dominance. Status hierarchies are a significant aspect of our evolutionary heritage (Gilbert, 1989, 1992).

Connection with Outside World

How connected is the family to the outside world? Many families in which abuse/neglect occur are isolated. Isolation decreases opportunities for social support and corrective feedback.

Family Life Stage

Families progress through developmental stages. Both predictable (retirement) and unpredictable life events (illness) influence families (see Conger et al., 2004; Miller, 2010; Solinger et al., 2010). Stepfamilies are common (Allan, Crow, & Hawker, 2011). Relationships change over time (see, for example, Erera, 2002); early experiences influence later ones (Kananen et al., 2010; Riggs, 2010; Zhang et al., 2010). A given event may have a different effect in different life stages. For example, severe illness of a new mother will have a different effect than illness when a child is older. Stages of family development include:

- Unattached young adult.

- New couple.

- Family with young children.

- Family with adolescents.

- Family with grown children.

- Family much later in life.

Cultural norms and values influence behavior in each stage. Dysfunctional myths about different stages may create problems.

Family Strengths

What are family assets? These may include emotional (caring about each other), material (a comfortable home or stable source of income), or interactional (positive conflict-management skills) strengths. Families, like individuals, are made up of more than their problems.

Shared Beliefs

Families differ in their shared beliefs about life and the world. Some families believe that most people are benevolent (try to do the right thing). Other families believe that people are basically out for themselves and will try to do you in, given a chance. These beliefs and related contingencies influence both behavior and emotions. For example, they may influence relationships with neighbors and service providers. They may function as self-fulfilling prophecies. Here, too, unique cultural experiences influence what we think, feel, and do. Some groups tend to be fatalistic—to believe in luck or God's will. Norms for interacting with authority figures will influence how family members interact with service providers. Family members may believe that they should know what other family members want without being told. Clients may not be aware of unrealistic expectations that create and maintain problems.

Family Roles

The term *role* refers to the behaviors expected of a person in a certain position, such as a parent, sibling, or employer. Families differ in how roles are distributed among family members, in how satisfied family members are with this arrangement, and in how open family members are to changing roles. Role distribution may facilitate or hinder attainment of valued goals. Family members may have distorted views about their responsibilities. A mother may expect to meet all the needs of her family. Cultural norms and values influence how roles are distributed, how easy it is to alter them, and how clearly roles are defined. Families differ in degree of outside support (or interference) for preferred role allocations. Changes in a family such as illness of a family member or need to care for an elderly relative may create burdens. Family roles change over the life of a family. Stepparenting usually requires a rearrangement of family roles. Kinship care for children is now common.

Expression of Feelings

Families, like individuals, differ in the range and intensity of feelings expressed. Positive emotions such as happiness may prevail in families in which behavior is maintained mainly by the exchange of positive reinforcers. Negative emotions such as anger, anxiety, and sadness may prevail in families in which there is little interaction or in which family members rely on punishment and negative reinforcement. Cultural norms and values influence what emotions can be expressed when and to whom. They influence whether feelings are expressed indirectly (e.g., by doing a chore for another family member to show liking and appreciation) or directly (by verbally expressing caring).

Family Goals

Families differ in the goals they have and whether these are shared. Examples of family goals include increasing material comfort, moving closer to relatives, or keeping the yard looking good to impress the neighbors. Goals may be implicit or explicit and functional or dysfunctional in their effects. For example, a parent's interest in keeping the house immaculate may interfere with a teenager's wish to have friends visit.

Initial Sessions

Initial sessions provide an opportunity to clarify roles and responsibilities and describe norms for meetings such as sharing feelings. Clarifying hopes and hesitations is important. What reservations do clients have? As in work with individuals, initial sessions provide an opportunity to establish rapport with clients and offer support. Here too, the quality of the alliance is important. (See chapter 15.) Family therapists differ in their views about establishing alliances with subgroups in a family.

Intervention Options

Options include working with the partners of uncooperative substance-abusing partners (Thomas & Ager, 1993; Thomas, Yoshioka, & Ager, 1996), with couples (e.g., see publications of John Gottman), with all family members (Corcoran, 2003; Dishion & Kavanagh, 2005); and with extended families. (Examples of working with families are given in earlier chapters.) (See also Lebow, 2005; Forgatch & Patterson, 2010; Webster-Stratton & Reid, 2010). Here, too, the roles of broker, mediator, enabler, educator, and/or advocate may be required. There is extensive literature describing how to increase positive parenting skills (e.g., see Barth, Landsverk, Chamberlain, Reid, Rolls, Hurlburt, et al., 2005; Forgatch & Patterson, 2010; Webster-Stratton & Reid, 2010). There is a rich literature describing assessment, intervention, and evaluation methods with couples (e.g., Bigner & Wetchler, 2012; Jacobson & Gottman, 1995; Gurman, 2008; Wetchler, 2011). Distressed compared to nondistressed couples engage in a higher frequency of negative statements. Enhancing positive communication skills is a key focus in many approaches. Clients become aware of how they communicate with each another, explore what kind of relationships they would like, and develop more effective ways of communicating. Structural approaches emphasize alliances within families, boundary disputes, and patterns of communication.

Instructions for encouraging "feeling talk" offered by Gottman, Notarius, Gonso, and Markman (1976) include the following: The speaker must: (1) get in touch with what he is feeling; (2) put the feelings into words; (3) edit the words so they can be heard by the listener; and (4) the listener must hear and validate what is said.

- *Use "I" statements.* Statements that begin with "you" sound like an accusation and may create defensiveness. Those that begin with "it," "we," "others," or "some people" avoid personal responsibility.

- *Use statements rather than questions.* Questions are often an indirect way of making a point or an accusation. If questions are required, asking "how" is preferable to asking "why." The former is less accusatory.

- *Be present oriented.* Saying "I feel angry when…" is better than saying "It used tblo upset me when…" which may leave the listener unsure of how things stand now. (See also Gottman & Silver, 1999.)

Feeling talk is not a license for total candor. Few relationships could withstand the effects of total honesty. Simply prefacing nasty remarks with "I feel…" does not remove the destructive potential of uncensored communication.

Sue and Sue (1990) suggest that both the communication and structural approaches to family therapy are appropriate in working with minority groups because they highlight the importance of the family as a unit and focus on the resolution of concrete issues. Behavioral family therapies share these emphases (Fisher & Chamberlain, 2000). (See Exhibit 26.3.) Szapocznik and his colleagues (1988) developed a systems approach to working with Latino families in which adolescents are suspected of or were observed using drugs. Patterns of family interaction that interfere with change are restructured to encourage participation of family members (see also Leidy, Guerra, & Toro, 2010; Robbins et al., 2009).

Preventative efforts focus on identifying and supporting protective factors for vulnerable families including enhancing social networks, attending to the context in which families live, including community characteristics and related policies, facilitating professionals and natural helpers to work together, and attending to interactions among different system levels that affect families (e.g., see Stagner & Lansing, 2009).

Working with Groups

Helping clients requires participation in many different kinds of groups (see Gitterman & Salmon, 2009). A group can be defined as three or more individuals who meet together to address a shared task or problem or enjoy a shared interest. Social group work is a traditional part of social work practice. (See, for example, Garvin, Gutierrez, & Galinsky, 2006; Rose, 1989; Toseland, 1990; Toseland & Rivas, 2012.) Cognitive-behavior therapy is often carried out in groups (Bieling, McCabe, & Antony, 2006; White 2000).

Recommended Culturally Sensitive Practice Guidelines

1. Discuss client–helper differences if this will facilitate the development of trust.

2. Allow clients to define "family." Do not assume that only people living in the household are family members. Allowing the family to define the unit increases the likelihood that significant others will be involved. Some home visits may occur in the homes of extended family members.

3. Evaluate level of acculturation. Explore whether problems are related to intergenerational conflict. If appropriate, help family members to understand the role of intergenerational differences and the realities and stressors each generation confronts.

4. Enhance opportunities for clients to influence the quality of their environments. Form a collaborative set.

5. Make referrals to resources and services within the community before exploring alternatives. Clients are more likely to use familiar services and agencies. Local services offer the advantage of continued availability after service ends.

6. Collect information about the client's community. Read about and get to know the communities and neighborhoods in which your clients live. What businesses are there? Who are the community leaders? What resources are available? Participate in community social change efforts.

7. Continue to add to your knowledge about different cultures. Advocate for recruitment of diverse staff and useful training opportunities.

Source: Adapted from V. G. Hodges (1991). Providing culturally sensitive intensive family preservation services to ethnic families. In E. M. Tracy, D. A. Haapala, J. Kinney, and P. J. Pecora (Eds.),. *Intensive family preservation services: An instructional sourcebook* (pp. 110–111). Cleveland, Ohio: Mandel School of Applied Social Science, Case Western Reserve University.

Different Kinds of Groups

Social work practice involves many kinds of task groups, those formed to achieve a shared goal. Some are designed to help clients, some to meet agency needs, and some to help community members pursue desired goals (e.g., see Greif & Ephross, 2011). Committees are an inescapable aspect of organizations. Some groups are time-limited and deal with a particular task (e.g., a task force created to decide how to decrease teenage pregnancy). Other groups meet on a regular basis to attend to certain functions such as coordinating work between intake and other staff. Case conferences and multidisciplinary team meetings may be held regularly. Increasing attention is being given to enhancing the effectiveness of such teams (e.g., see Levy, 2007). Creation of a multidisciplinary team increases the likelihood of considering the pros and cons of different approaches and thus of informed consent on the part of clients and their significant others. Head and his colleagues (2011) recommend that this approach be implemented in all areas to enhance the likelihood of making evidence-informed decisions.

Community organization may involve creating coalitions and social action groups. Many different kinds of interventions are provided in a group setting, including parent training and harm reduction programs. Aims may include education, skill building, and providing support and companionship (Hopps & Pinderhughes, 1999). Groups include support groups (e.g., for clients who have just lost a parent), education groups (e.g., to help clients learn how to manage their blood pressure), therapy groups (e.g., help clients learn how to manager their anger), self-development groups (e.g., help clients to become more aware of their communication styles), and socialization groups (e.g., help clients to enhance their skills in making and keeping friends). Here, too, cultural differences should be considered. Social workers often facilitate self-help groups.

Advantages of Group Settings

Groups have many advantages:

- They provide varied models of how to handle certain situations/roles.

- They provide a sense of community.

- They offer opportunities to normalize and validate concerns.

- They provide opportunities to learn new skills.

- They provide an opportunity for catharsis, confession, and criticism.

- They provide opportunities to meet new people.

- They provide "partners" for carrying out assignments outside the group.

- They provide sources of support.

- They save time and expense.

- They may be less threatening for some people compared to individual exchanges.

- They provide diverse opportunities for role plays.

The advantages of group settings provide a guide for making decisions when to consider using a group. Interventions designed to enhance parenting skills are often given in group settings (e.g., Scott, O'Connor, Futh, Matias, Price, & Doolan, 2010; McDaniel, Braiden, Onyekwelu, Murphy, & Regan, 2011). (See also Potter-Efron, 2005.) Decisions required when using groups include the following:

- What is the purpose of the group?

- What criteria should be used to decide who to include in the group?

- What rules (if any) should be agreed on?

- How often should the group meet?

- Should more people be allowed to join the group anytime?

- How will time be structured? Exactly what will be done in the group?

- Will there be a group leader? If so, how active will he or she be? Will there be one or two?

- Will participants have assignments outside the group?

- How will success be evaluated?

- What activities (if any) will be used for what purpose?

Goals may be shared or diverse. For example, all members may share the goal of finding a job or enhancing problem-solving skills. Each person may apply skills learned to his or her own unique situation. The goals of the group will provide guidelines about group size and composition.

Group Structure and Process

Components of group structure include: (1) patterns of attraction and rejection among group members; (2) communication (who talks to whom about what); (3) roles (a status with certain associated behaviors such as leader); (4) division of labor (how tasks are allocated); and (5) power (patterns of influence) (Garvin et al., 2006). Cultural differences may influence patterns of interaction. Roles evolve over time as the group continues. Questions to consider, depending on goals, include the following:

- Who speaks for whom?

- Who influences whom?

- Who feels close to whom?

- Who dislikes whom?

- How do group members feel about the "leader"?

- Who assumes what kind of role(s) (e.g., placater, jokester, naysayer).

- Who offers whom positive support?

- Who offers whom punishing consequences?

Perhaps the most well-known system for describing behavior in groups is SYMLOG (System of Multiple Level of Observation of Groups) (Bales, 2002). Categories include positive reactions, attempted answers, questions, and negative reactions. Graphic representations can be useful in describing group process (Mattaini, 1993). Groups differ in how power is shared and who has power (who can influence whom to do what and/or who has access to valued resources outside the group). People differ in the roles they prefer and/or are assigned. Some enjoy the role of maintaining a constructive group process. They may encourage others to participate, diffuse rising tensions, suggest compromises, and emphasize common interests. Roles may be functional or dysfunctional. Helpful roles include:

- Educator

- Compromiser

- Encourager

- Seeker of information

- Questioner of dubious assertions

- Validator

- Attentive listener

- Diffuser of tension

Dysfunctional roles include:

- Ridiculer

- Dominator

- Complainer

- Scapegoat

- Attention seeker

Methods used should build on client assets (individual skill levels) in a step-by-step manner that provides opportunities for practice, feedback, and coaching (see discussion of skills training in chapter 24). This will require description of each person's current skill levels, as well as skills required to attain outcomes that clients value.

Groups, like individuals, communities, or organizations, develop a culture with unique norms, values, and rules. Examples of helpful and unhelpful behaviors can be seen in Exhibit 26.4. Group process is influenced by the particular activities introduced. One of the group leader's responsibilities is to structure group process in a way that helps group members achieve goals they value. Effective group workers are knowledgeable and skilled in selecting activities that contribute to valued outcomes.

EXHIBIT 26.4

Example of Helpful and Dysfunctional Behaviors in Groups

Helpful	Dysfunctional
• Offering useful suggestions.	• Interrupting.
• Validating other people's comments.	• Belittling, sarcastic remarks.
• Active listening.	• Blaming, attacking, name-calling.
• Sharing experiences.	• Excessively loud talking.
• Maintaining focus.	• Barely audible speech.
• Participating in group tasks.	• Distracting mannerisms, noises.
• Owning feelings ("I" feel…).	• Excessive joking.
• Considering other people's views and preferences.	• Making fun of others.
• Asking others for their opinions.	• Giving advice prematurely and excessively.
• Encouraging others to participate.	• Sidetracking to irrelevant topics.
• Supporting other people's assets.	• Punishing valuable behaviors.
• Using humor effectively.	• Disregarding agreed-on norms.
• Following group norms.	• Encouraging groupthink by discouraging consideration of other points of view.
• Responding positively to feedback.	• Unwillingness to accept responsibility for actions.
• Identifying clear progress indicators.	• Repeating certain experiences over and over.
• Participating in discussions.	• Unwillingness to share feelings.
• Accurately perceiving and translating social signals.	• Telling others what they should think, feel, do.
• Cooperating with others.	• Talking only to the group leader.
• Helping to maintain focus.	• Being a "natterer" (only complain).

These may be games or plays. What is appropriate will depend on the age of the participants and their goals. Conflict is common in groups due to different interests, values, and preferred styles of communication. Process variables will influence what conflicts occur, how they are handled, and who suggest ideas.

Group norms should be established to maximize effectiveness (see Exhibit 26.5). They may concern agreements about confidentiality, turn-taking, expectations about attendance, and being polite. Norms should be clarified regarding what can be discussed and what cannot be. Can clients see each other outside of the group?

Group Phases

Groups move through different phases. Here, too, as when working with individuals and families, there are beginnings, middles, and endings. The pregroup phase includes planning before a group meets. Goals in the beginning phase include negotiating the purpose of the group, dealing with ambivalence about participation, beginning to develop a group structure, starting to form relationships among participants, establishing norms, and deciding on plans. Obtaining resources may also be part of this phase. Tasks in initial meetings include the following:

- Describe the purpose of the group.
- Discuss confidentiality.
- Describe group format.
- Explain content to be covered.
- Describe your role.
- Acknowledge awkwardness/anxiety/ambivalence.
- Build group cohesiveness and encourage relaxation (e.g., use an "ice breaker" such as asking people to introduce themselves to each other).

A final phase includes planning for maintenance and ending. Exhibit 26.6 provides an example of objectives, preparation, role plays, suggested activities, and guidelines for ending a group

EXHIBIT 26.5

Developing Group Norms

GL: So it's not like we want to come up with a lot of rules, but you know, having some idea about how we as a group want to handle certain things is good because it helps create an environment in which we all feel safe to talk. So, for example, something I think we should talk about and well, is always important in support groups, is confidentiality. People in the group should know that anything they say here is going to stay right here with us. It's real easy to want to share stuff with your wife or a good friend but you know, even if you don't use the person's name, well, they might piece things together and decide they know the person. So, does that make sense, I mean, do we all agree that that's a good norm to have?

B: Well, yeah, I feel more comfortable knowing that we all agree to that.

C: Yeah, me too. I mean you just don't know who knows who, so yeah, that suits me.

GL: Another idea that I wanted to present has to do with the way our conversations are handled. Because we're on the phone I can't see your faces to tell if someone is quiet because they're sad, or they are just getting a lot out of listening that day. But because of this, sometimes I'll ask like, "A, do you have anything you want to add?" You can either answer or just say "I pass." That's fine if you just want to pass.

(laughter)

GL: (CONTINUES): So, if that's OK I'll move on.

(All respond affirmatively).

Source: M. Galinsky, K. Rounds, A. Montague, & E. Butowsky (1993). *Leading a telephone support group for persons with HIV disease* (pp. 58–59). Chapel Hill, NC: School of Social Work, University of North Carolina. Reprinted with permission.

session. Web-based activities and contacts provide opportunities for between session participation.

Roles Social Workers Play in Groups

Roles of value when working on other levels (e.g., individual and community) are also of value when working with groups. These include broker, enabler, mediator, educator, and facilitator. You may, as a broker, refer group members to helpful resources. As a mediator, you may help group members resolve problems and handle conflicts. As an educator, you may enhance participants' conflict resolution skills and inform them about constructive approaches to problems. As a broker you may direct clients to useful resources. As a facilitator, you may encourage the participation of all members, remind the group of its agenda, and review what has been accomplished. Groups differ in the extent to which leadership is shared. One of the purposes of a group may be to transfer leadership skills to group members. Roles and tasks of the group leader can be seen in Exhibit 26.7. Preparation is a key leader responsibility. Group leadership skills include:

- Planning agendas/setting goals.
- Encouraging participation.
- Regulating participation.
- Handling hostile participants.
- Handling reluctant participants.
- Handling monopolizers.
- Handling apathy.
- Offering positive feedback.

- Anticipating obstacles.
- Identifying common interests.
- Avoiding premature closure on an option.
- Effective pacing.
- Summarizing skills.

Common Mistakes

Planning for effective group requires careful thought and preparation. Lack of preparation is a key obstacle. Trying "to wing it" will dilute effects that can be achieved and may result in harm (participants who could benefit leave the group and become more discouraged). What are the goals of this group? How would group members know they were met? Vagueness of goals is a common error that leads to drift. It is important to be familiar with activities that can be introduced to encourage helpful behaviors and discourage those that get in the way of attaining valued goals. Skill training in groups requires many competencies (see chapter 24). Facilitating groups requires skills such as regulating turn taking. Is the group drifting away from a focus on agreed-on goals? Is there a problem in group composition, for example, too great a difference in intensity of emotions (e.g., in a partner loss group)? Perhaps you did not screen potential clients carefully enough. This may require individual meetings (or telephone conversations) with clients prior to a decision to allow a person to join a group. Is the group meeting site readily available? Is parking easy? Can clients contact you between meetings? How many absences will be allowed? All these questions illustrate the importance of careful planning including agreement on group norms. Consider what could be offered by someone who is well trained compared to what you could offer.

EXHIBIT 26.6

Preparing for a Group Session

Session 4: Coping with feelings and beliefs related to being HIV positive

The purpose of this session is to provide members with a safe environment where they can openly discuss personal issues, including sexuality and sexual behavior. By the end of Session 4 group members will have begun to identify and explore uncomfortable feelings related to their illness; shared their experiences and ways of coping with changes in sexual behavior; identified new and helpful ways of coping with these changes; and reinforced and expanded knowledge of safer sex practices.

These subjects may prove somewhat difficult for both group members and the group leader to discuss. They are left until Session 4 so that group members' level of confidence and trust in one another will be high, facilitating an open discussion.

Objectives

- To help members recognize troubling feelings and beliefs related to having HIV disease.
- To help members understand that these feelings are common.
- To learn ways of coping with troubling feelings and beliefs.
- To share experiences in coping with changes in sexual behavior.
- To gain information about safer sex practices.
- To encourage and reinforce the practice of safer sex.

Preparation

- It may be helpful for you to review some of the salient feelings and beliefs that each group member has expressed in previous sessions.
- You may want to review some of the literature to increase your understanding of AIDS prevention and your knowledge of safer sex practices. You may also need to explore your own feelings and prepare for an open discussion of sensitive issues and materials. It is important that you are familiar with your state laws regarding an individual's responsibility to disclose his or her HIV status. You should consider your feelings and concerns regarding personal and professional ethics regarding disclosure issues.

    This session is primarily focused on HIV transmission as it relates to sexual activity. However, if group members are participating in or are associated with injection drug use, you may want to review literature on ways to minimize the risk of transmission by needles.

- The following is a list of potentially difficult content and group process issues that may arise during this session:
  Extreme mood swings of members.
  Severe depression of members.
  Members may feel upset hearing about others' troubling feelings.
  Suicidal thoughts and how to handle them.
  Misunderstandings about HIV transmission.
  Different levels of interest in sex and different levels of sexual activity.
  Concerns about how to tell a partner or potential partner about diagnosis.
  Member may reveal that s/he is practicing unsafe sex.
  Member may reveal that s/he has been unable to tell partner(s) about diagnosis.
  Members may be of different sexual orientations and experience discomfort because of this Reluctance to discuss sexual behavior.
  Legal and ethical obligations to tell others about HIV diagnosis.

Role Plays
Feelings and Beliefs

- Lately you have been feeling depressed. You lack motivation, and even though you're still fairly healthy and mobile, you don't enjoy your favorite activities anymore. You've been trying to conceal your feelings but you've decided it may be good to talk to a friend.
- Have group members think about some of the strong, troubling feelings they have had, when they have them, and who they were with when they had them. Ask if they would like to role play these types of situations to see if there are ways of handling the situation that make them feel better.

(continued)

EXHIBIT 26.6 (Continued)

Changes in Sexual Behavior

- You found out this week that you are HIV positive. You have been dating a man for a few weeks and recently the two of you have become sexually involved. The two of you have been practicing safer sex and have been honest about your personal histories and concerns about contracting AIDS. Tonight is the first time you have seen him since your diagnosis.
- You were diagnosed HIV positive about six months ago, but, until you met Jane last week, you thought you would never have sex again. Both of you are very attracted to each other, and you feel you must tell her about your diagnosis now because sex seems inevitable. She has just arrived at your house.
- Since learning your diagnosis, you have been very careful to practice safer sex through the use of condoms. You have been seeing a man for several weeks and you decide to sleep together for the first time. When you pull out a condom, he says to you "I never use those things. I hate the way they feel. Let's just do it natural."

Suggested Activities

- "Check in" with each group member by asking for brief reports on the previous week.
- Before beginning the discussion, ask members if there are any topics/subjects they would like to add to this week's session.
- To begin the discussion have members name any feelings they have had related to having HIV disease.
- Encourage a discussion of how the members handle these feelings. Group members may be able to make suggestions to one another on methods of coping with different feelings related to having HIV disease.
- Certain troubling feelings may relate directly to changes in sexual behavior. Examples are: frustration, guilt, and depression. To make the transition from talking about feelings and beliefs to changes in sexual behavior, you might ask members if they have experienced any troubling feelings because of changes in sexual behavior. Ask members if they would be willing to share any of these changes in sexual behavior and related feelings with the group. It may be helpful to use vignettes to initiate the discussion. The vignettes will allow group members to talk about changes in sexual behavior in the third person until they feel comfortable enough to bring up their own issues.
- Ask members to share ways they cope with changes in sexual behavior and sexual frustrations. You may need to offer suggestions for coping with these changes. Strategies for coping with troubling feelings and changes in sexuality include: learning safe ways to express sexuality such as massage, masturbation, fantasy, caresses, and hand holding. Other techniques for feeling better include refocusing, reframing, spending time on enjoyable activities and meditation, positive thinking tapes, and similar activities. Stress and anxiety can be lowered by getting involved in non-HIV related activities, getting out of the house when able to walk, exercising or just sitting and enjoying a favorite spot, watching movies, reading, meditating, and learning relaxation techniques.
- A discussion of safer sex practices and prevention is important, particularly for individuals who may have been given information but never had the chance to ask specific questions. Begin this discussion by asking what preventive measures members are taking. It is likely that this subject will follow naturally from the discussion on changes in sexual behavior.
- The discussion will include information giving, as well as facilitation of mutual support and encouragement among members. The amount of information you need to give will vary depending on group members' knowledge.
- Initiate a discussion about informing sexual partners if the members do not bring it up. Group members will need to explore their fears about telling others and to understand that it is normal to have these fears. You can help frame disclosure in terms of taking control of the situation. Group members may want to rehearse potential disclosure scenes from their own lives.

Ending the Session

- Summarize some of the main themes of the discussion emphasizing ways of coping with troubling feelings and changes in sexual behavior. Support members' beliefs that they can cope with these feelings and situations.
- Remind group members that any pending issues can be brought up again next week and that the next session will be about issues surrounding living with a life-threatening illness, as well as practical matters related to insurance, legal assistance, and wills.

Source: M. Galinsky, K. Rounds, A. Montague, & E. Butowsky (1993). *Leading a telephone support group for persons with HIV disease* (pp. 32–37). Chapel Hill, NC: School of Social Work, University of North Carolina. Reprinted with permission.

EXHIBIT 26.7

Roles and Tasks of the Group Leader

ENCOURAGE MUTUAL HELP AND SUPPORT

Ask open-ended questions.

Aim for balanced participation.

Make connections between what group members say; find common threads.

Turn questions and comments directed toward you back to the group, when possible.

Respect clients' abilities to offer each other support while intervening to build the group process.

Encourage clients to raise issues they want to discuss.

MAINTAIN FOCUS

Keep group members from drifting off-track.

Bring discussion back to the "here and now," "so how does this affect us personally, now?"

Remind participants at the start of each session about the topics for that session, and at the end of each session about topics for the next one.

EDUCATE/GIVE INFORMATION

Try not to take on the burden of being the only one who provides information. Clients may have the latest information about some questions.

Encourage members to teach each other new skills.

Encourage accurate information. Do reality testing when you hear inaccurate information, for example, around how AIDS is transmitted.

Call in "experts" when appropriate.

MODEL USEFUL BEHAVIOR

Model acceptance, support, encouragement, and expression of feelings.

Recognize the strengths and achievements you see in group members.

Break tasks into component behaviors and model them (e.g., how to ask for help).

ENHANCE SELF-EFFICACY

Support clients' beliefs that they take actions that will help them live with their illness.

Provide opportunities to practice new behaviors (e.g., discuss one's illness with a family member).

Source: Adapted from M. Galinsky, K. Rounds. A. Montague, & E. Butowsky (1993). *Leading a telephone support group for persons with HIV disease* (pp. 11–12). Chapel Hill, NC: School of Social Work, University of North Carolina. Reprinted with permission.

If this gap is large, consider whether you should take on related tasks.

Making Decisions in Groups

Decisions are often made in groups. Community residents may discuss shared concerns and decide which one(s) to focus on. Decisions that influence clients are made in multidisciplinary case conferences and staff meetings. The process used to make decisions will influence their soundness. Guidelines for encouraging effective discussion include the following:

- Avoid getting sidetracked on minor issues.

- Encourage brevity.

- Encourage members to listen attentively to each speaker.

- Combine wise control of time and size of problem.

- Sum up often and keep members informed where they are in a discussion.

- Secure equal sharing of responsibility.

- Provide facilitating physical conditions. (Edwards, 1938)

Groups differ in their preferred decision-making style. Some are authoritarian. The opinion of one or a few individuals wins the day rather than the most well-reasoned argument. An intuitive style may be used in which feelings are emphasized. The opinion of alleged experts who are brought in may weigh heavily (see Eden & Ackerman, 2010).

Group Process Variables That Interfere With Sound Decision Making

Observation of case conferences shows that decisions may be made, not through careful consideration of evidence, but on the basis of influence by pitches and/or denunciations on the part of influential group members (Dingwall, Eekelaar, & Murray, 1983). In his classic article "Why I do not attend case conferences," Meehl (1973) identified characteristics of case conferences and group meetings that decrease the quality of decisions such as rewarding everything, "gold and garbage" alike. That is, no matter what anybody says, it is regarded as profound and informative. "The prestigious thing to do is to contribute ideas to the conference...whether or not the quality of evidence available is adequate to support the view offered" (Meehl, 1973, p. 235). Participants may be reluctant to criticize other views (even though they may be uninformative or inaccurate) because of the "buddy-buddy syndrome" (not criticizing friends). The value of high-quality data is often disregarded. The tendency to be impressed by plausible-sounding, but uninformative explanations is encouraged by not asking questions such as: "What evidence is there for this view?" or "How does this help us understand and know what to do about this problem?"

Trivial statements that are uninformative because they are true of all people may be made (Kadushin, 1963). This is called the Barnum effect. Examples are "She has intrapsychic conflicts" or "He has problems with object relations" or "There is a contingency management problem here." Unreliability of and lack of validity of measures may be overlooked, resulting in dubious conclusions. Another obstacle is the belief that hardheaded means hard-hearted. Regard for rigorous examination of a topic may be viewed as cold, unemotional, and unfeeling, whereas a disregard for vagueness, non sequiturs, and tolerance of fallacies may be considered a mark of caring and compassion. Participants may use different standards to review the quality of disliked arguments than to review their own argument. A polarization of attitudes, beliefs, values, and judgments may occur that impedes sound decisions and judgments. Other sources of errors that may get in the way of arriving at reasoned judgments are described in chapter 8. Use the culture of thoughtfulness scale in Gambrill and Gibbs (2009) to review your work environments including case conferences and team meetings.

Groupthink "refers to deterioration of mental efficiency, reality testing, and moral judgments that result from in-group pressures" (Janis, 1982, p. 9). Causes of groupthink include isolation of a group, cohesiveness, biased leadership, and high stress. Indicators of groupthink include:

- An illusion of invulnerability that results in overoptimistic and excessive risk taking.

- Belief in the group's inherent morality.

- Pressure applied to any group member who disagrees with the majority view.

- Collective efforts to rationalize or discount warnings.

- A shared illusion of unanimity.

- Self-appointed "mind guards" who protect the group from information that might challenge the group's complacency.

- Self-censorship of deviation from what seems to be the group's consensus.

- Stereotypical views of adversaries as too evil to make negotiating worthwhile, or too stupid or weak to pose a serious threat. (Janis, 1982)

Methods that Janis suggests to discourage groupthink include the following:

1. The leader should assign the role of critical evaluation to each member. Every member should be encouraged to air objections and doubts and to look for new sources of information.

2. The leader should not state his or her own judgments or preferences at the outset.

3. Several independent policy planning groups should be established, each with a different leader.

4. The group should divide into subgroups and meet separately and then later come together to work out differences.

5. Members should discuss deliberations of the group with qualified outsiders.

6. Qualified outsiders should be invited in for group deliberations.

7. One member of the group should be assigned the role of devil's advocate. (Assigning just one devil's advocate in a group may not be effective because of the strong tendencies of groups to persuade a lone dissenter (see, for example, the classic study by Asch, 1956).

8. After the group has reached an agreement, another meeting should be held in which every member is encouraged to express any doubts and to rethink the issue.

Enhancing Your Effectiveness in Team Meetings and Case Conferences

There are many steps you can take to improve the quality of team meetings and case conferences (Tropman, 2003). One is to prepare for meetings. If you want to introduce an idea at a case conference, prepare beforehand by rehearsing what you will say and by reviewing your argument and related evidence. Anticipate and be prepared to respond to disagreements and counter proposals. Effective skills in entering conversations and expressing opinions will be valuable (see chapter 16). Present your ideas clearly in a way that links your view to a shared goal. Do not take things personally. If you do, your emotional reactions will get in the way of constructive participation. Focus on service goals—helping clients.

Be sure to reinforce others for valuable contributions. Valuing truth over winning will help you to contribute to a culture of inquiry. Distinguish between strong opinions and bias (see chapter 5) so that you do not mistakenly assume that a person with a strong opinion is not open to considering different points of view. Guidelines emphasized by Fisher and Ury (1991) include focusing on the problem not the people, focusing on interests not positions, using objective criteria, and seeking options that benefit all parties. (See also Salas, Rosen, & DiazGranados, 2010.)

Knowledge about group process and structure will help you to anticipate and avoid problems. If possible, know whom you are dealing with (be familiar with the goals and preferred interaction styles of participants). Although it may not be possible to change styles that compromise the quality of decision making, they can be muted in a number of ways (e.g., by agreeing on group norms, focusing on the problem not the person, and reinforcing alternative positive behaviors). Agreeing on an agenda increases the likelihood that important topics will be addressed. If people get off the track, remind participants of agenda items. Helpful norms include: (1) not interrupting other people; (2) not hogging the floor; (3) holding speakers responsible for accompanying assertions with a description of related reasons and evidence; and (4) avoiding personal attacks. (See also code of conduct for discussing controversial issues in chapter 5.) Being familiar with propaganda strategies such as distorting arguments, dragging in a red herring, and appealing to self-interest or fear, and developing effective skills to counter them will contribute to thoughtful discussions.

Focusing on service goals will help you to keep emotion in bounds even with people who are skilled in aggravating others. Intellectual empathy will encourage listening to and understanding other points of view (see Exhibit 5.3). Many problems are complex requiring input from different kinds of professionals including a physician, a pharmacist, a nurse, a social worker, a financial counselor, or a dietician. In addition values and preferences of clients and their significant others must be considered.

Self-Help and Mutual Help Groups

Self-help groups are based on the assumption that people with similar problems can help one another (Gitterman & Shulman, 2005). There is an extensive literature describing involving users of mental health services in providing services to other users (e.g., Simpson & House, 2002). A self-help group can be defined as a small group of individuals who meet together voluntarily for mutual aid in the accomplishment of a specific purpose (Katz, 1993). Examples include the following:

- Depressives Anonymous
- Neurotics Anonymous
- Narcotics Anonymous
- Adoptees' Liberty Movement Association (for adopted children seeking their natural parents)
- Parents Anonymous (for parents who abuse their children)
- Overeaters Anonymous
- Gamblers Anonymous
- Hearing Voices Network

Mutual help programs offer the best of all worlds in that both givers and recipients may benefit (e.g., Exhibit 26.8). Self-help groups serve many functions. Benefits include support,

---

EXHIBIT 26.8

Examples of People Helping Other People

Foster grandparent	Low-income individuals aged 60 and older work with children (e.g., in hospital pediatric wards, institutions for people alleged to be mentally and emotionally disturbed, correctional facilities, homes for dependent and neglected children, public school classrooms for exceptional children, day-care centers, and private homes). (see http://www.seniorcorps.gov)
Senior Companion	People 60 and older provide services to adults with special needs, especially older individuals. They work in private homes, as well as hospitals, nursing homes, and senior centers.
Big Brothers and Big Sisters	Adults are matched with children or teenagers to provide support/recreation/models/validation to these children.

---

information, insight, acquiring coping skills, validation, sense of community, and normalization. They provide affiliation with people who are similar in some way and who are sympathetic to concerns shared by all members.

> Bringing people together who share the same problems, feelings, and experiences overcomes the tendency to ostracize one's self. The negative value placed on the uniqueness of one's situation is reduced when the individual discovers that others have been there. Probably the most common reaction of relief that is reported in mutual assistance groups and probably in all group therapy is the sense that "I am not the only one. I am not crazy. I am not alone!" The unique personal, previously defined as deviant and isolating, become social. Under some conditions, the discovery that the problem is social and not personal can be a stimulus for members of the group to undertake social and political action to change social conditions that come to be defined as oppressive or to encourage the larger society to devote resources to the group's central interest. (Levine, 1988, p. 171)

Unique characteristics of self-help groups that make them an attractive alternative (and perhaps a better one) to professional services include the following (see, for example, Katz, 1993):

- Ease of communication because members are peers.
- Opportunities for socialization.

- Individual differences can be eased by group discussion and confrontation.

- More natural contexts compared to professional relationships or institutional settings.

- Status is defined in terms of group goals and needs; each person's status in the group is relatively clear.

- Opportunities for learning from others.

- Multiple sources of support.

- Normalization of concerns and experiences.

- Avoidance of one-down status inherent in professional contact.

- Inexpensive.

- Opportunities to help others, increasing self-esteem.

Levine, Perkins, and Perkins (2005) describe five types of self-help groups. In one, members have some characteristics that may result in social isolation, stigmatization, scorn, pity, or social rejection (some characteristic that disqualifies them as "normal" and results in discrimination that limits opportunities). Examples include people labeled as mentally ill, ex-convicts, gamblers, people who are gay or lesbian, the elderly, and overweight people. Some groups accept society's definition of a behavior or characteristic as wrong and seek to decrease associated behaviors while emphasizing the worthwhileness of participants. The aim of other groups is to change public attitudes about a problem/characteristic; society's definition of a "problem" is rejected. Examples include civil rights organizations and gay rights groups.

In a second type, those who are related to individuals with a stigmatizing characteristic are involved such as parents of antisocial children and Al-Anon for partners of substance abusers. A third kind of self-help group is comprised of individuals who tend to be socially isolated, not because of a particular characteristic but perhaps because of lack of public resources. Examples include widows' groups, parents without partners, and parents of children with cancer. Ethnicity, religion, or race are the basis for a fourth kind of self-help group. Such groups may provide education, recreational opportunities, and cultural preservation. Pursuit and preservation of specific interests such as opposition to school busing is the basis of a fifth kind of quasi-political group. Other purposes may be to limit taxation, to preserve the character of a neighborhood, and to develop a community. Any one group may have a mix of purposes.

Increasing skills in gaining support is a focus of many self-help groups. For example, one of six group sessions provided to clients with HIV is devoted to helping participants to enhance social support (Galinsky et al., 1993). A group formed in Raleigh, North Carolina, in a poor African American neighborhood met once a month for both social and service aims (Korte, 1983). This group identified neighbors in need of services and assumed responsibility for offering assistance. Recipients of services could offer one of many services the club valued. Support groups for caregivers are widely used. Social support and mutual aid groups can be used as a preventative strategy for people in transition from one life stage to another (e.g., prospective parents, people about to retire, those at risk due to loss of a significant other because of death, divorce, or separation). Personal growth groups are another kind of self-help group. The aim of some groups is to provide support and to help members resolve a problem (e.g., Alcoholics Anonymous). Internet support groups are available for varied concerns. Be familiar with different kinds of groups available in your community so you can suggest relevant ones. Take advantage of newsletters, daily newspapers, and information on the Internet to stay informed about options (e.g., see National Mental Health Consumers' Self-Help Clearinghouse, http://mhselfhelp.org).

The Limits and Potentials of Self-Help

Do self-help groups help people? Do they have harmful effects? As with any method, claims of effectiveness should rest on critical tests. Some writers believe that professionals are the least likely to succeed or be interested in creating self-help resources because of vested interests in maintaining an elite status and tendencies to focus on client deficiencies. They argue that these characteristics conflict with those of successful resource exchanges (e.g., the assumption that everyone has something to offer and that everyone has equal rights in decision making; Sarason & Lorentz, 1979). Be sure that programs developed support rather than undermine the competencies of indigenous helpers by creating dependencies on professionals. Support groups led by peers have been found to be as effective as groups led by professionals (Toseland, 1990).

Self-help, like any form of intervention, has limits on what can be achieved. For example, in *Complaints and Disorders: The Sexual Policies of Sickness* (1973), Ehrenreich and English point out that "Self help is not an alternative to confronting the medical system with the demands for reform of existing institutions" (p. 85). They also note that the problems that confront women differ in different economic classes and emphasize the importance of recognizing these differences in self-help efforts.

Summary

Working with families and groups is an integral aspect of social work. The diversity of families calls for knowledge about different kinds of families and how these differences may influence problems and options. Families include those that are blended (including stepparents), single parent, gay/lesbian, and nuclear.

Group work is a traditional aspect of social work practice. Knowledge about group process, composition, structure, and development, as well as skills in using this knowledge to facilitate group goals, will help you to work effectively with groups of clients and colleagues. Valuable skills include offering helpful models, planning agendas, reinforcing constructive behaviors, regulating group process, involving participants in helpful activities, identifying common interests, and transferring leadership skills to group members. Encouraging a culture of thoughtfulness will be valuable in avoiding "groupthink" that may result in poor decisions. Advantages of group settings include opportunities to enhance a sense of community, validation, and normalization of concerns and opportunities to learn new coping skills from a variety of individuals. Support groups and self-help groups provide valuable options.

Reviewing Your Competencies

Reviewing Content Knowledge

1. Describe how family composition has changed over the past years.

2. Describe some cultural differences regarding families.

3. Identify major dimensions that can be of value in understanding families.

4. Discuss the influence of economic resources on family life.

5. Describe different kinds of groups in which social workers participate.

6. Describe different group phases and important tasks in each.

7. Identify factors you should consider in composing groups.

8. Identify problems that may arise in group process and suggest helpful remedies for them.

9. Describe preparations that should be made for each group session and why they are important.

10. Describe indicators of groupthink.

11. Describe what can be done to discourage groupthink.

12. Identify major indicators of a culture of thoughtfulness.

Reviewing What You Do

1. You accurately describe power relations in families and groups.

2. Observation of your work with families shows that you model and support valuable behaviors.

3. Observation of your behaviors in groups shows that you are well prepared and exercise good leadership.

4. You accurately spot and counter weak appeals in case conferences.

5. You raise important questions in case conferences and introduce valuable points of view.

6. You accurately identify problems in group process and suggest valuable remedies based on practice-related literature.

Reviewing Results

1. Family members acquire effective problem-solving skills.

2. Family members report that they are happier.

3. Intergenerational differences at home work to strengthen family cohesiveness.

4. Groups attain goals they value.

5. Sound decisions are made at group conferences.

27

Organizations and Communities

OVERVIEW   This chapter provides an overview of social work practice with organizations and communities. Helping clients may require intervention at the organizational and community levels. Skill in identifying and rearranging contingencies related to behaviors of interest at these levels will help you to discover options.

YOU WILL LEARN ABOUT

- Advocacy: The many levels and forms

- Understanding and changing organizations and service systems

- The evidence-informed organization

- Obstacles to organizational change

- Working at the neighborhood and community levels

- Community development

- Social planning and program development

- Community-based social action

- Influencing legislation

- Economic and social development

Advocacy: The Many Levels and Forms

Helping clients often requires advocating for clients. Here is a description from the Scottish government:

Advocacy is about promoting people's rights and helping them maintain control over their own lives. Advocacy can promote social inclusion and raises awareness of the obstacles faced by excluded and isolated individuals. Advocacy involves supporting and empowering people to speak for themselves, speaking on behalf of people who are unable to speak for themselves, helping people to explore the range of options open to them and clarifying a particular course of action. It can enable people who are marginalized, such as drug users, to express their views, to be heard and to have a say in crucial decisions that affect their lives. (Retrieved on December 24, 2011, from http://www.scotland.gov.uk, p. 1)

Case advocacy includes educating clients about their rights, referring them to agencies that provide high quality services, and serving as a broker to gain needed services. Cause advocacy includes seeking legislative and policy change that enhance the quality of clients' lives. This may include seeking changes in administrative policies such as increasing client input in decisions about services. The code of practice for advocates described by the Scottish government includes the right to raise any issue on behalf of the service user and the obligation to undertake needed training. Advocacy includes self-advocacy in which clients speak up on their own behalf. Other forms of advocacy include citizen advocacy where someone else speaks up on behalf of the service user and/or helps them to speak up, peer advocacy in which service users who have experienced similar problems (such as getting the "brush off" from gatekeepers of a service) may help others, professional advocacy in which an expert such as a lawyer is hired to speak on behalf of someone else, and collective advocacy where a group of people advocate for change. Often both case and cause advocacy will be needed to help clients.

Understanding and Changing Organizations and Service Systems

Most social work practice takes place in an organizational context. Many people spend part of their lives in an institutional setting. It is estimated that one-third of elderly people will spend some time in a nursing home. Our prisons and jails are overflowing. Residential settings for youth are thriving businesses. Quality of services is influenced by the contingency systems both within and external to agencies and institutions. For example, funding patterns may compromise quality of services (Meinhold & Mulick, 1990). Skill in being a good bureaucrat (negotiating the stresses, opportunities, and constraints in organizational life) will help to prevent burnout and maximize service quality (Gibelman & Furman, 2008; Pruger, 1973; Weinbach & Taylor, 2011). Organizational diagnostician and reformer are two of the ten roles highlighted as important by Weissman, Epstein, and Savage (1983). Skill in consensus building is valuable. You may help staff to:

- Clarify agency mission and related goals.

- Clarify client concerns, as well as related factors.

- Prioritize goals; clarify values.

- Identify key stakeholders.

- Identify the conditions required to accomplish hoped-for outcomes; what has to be in place?

- Estimate the likelihood of attaining goals given current assets.

- Help staff to identify relevant research findings of value in achieving hoped-for outcomes.

- Enhance the accuracy and timeliness of evaluating service quality and outcome(s).

- Arrange a more effective distribution of roles (e.g., innovator, facilitator, broker, mentor, director)

- Create and maintain a culture and climate in which critical appraisal and learning flourishes (see chapter 5).

- Create and implement a user-friendly client feedback system and use this to enhance service quality and inform clients and potential service users.

- Enhance positive communication.

- Acquire more funding; e.g., prepare successful grants.

- Create effective information retrieval and storage systems, for example, to acquire access to practice- and policy-related databases.

- Help staff to increase the percentage of evidence-informed decisions.

- Create new resources.

- Identify sources of error and view errors as an opportunity to learn how to improve services.

- Translate legal regulations and/or directives from a board of directors into evidence-informed policies and practices.

- Identify feasible strategies to decrease obstacles to fulfilling agency mission (e.g., in communication styles and channels, authority structure, use of information technology, personnel policies).

- Create policies and practices that involve clients as informed participants.

- Identify and decrease obstacles to evidence-informed practices and policies.

- Describe clear performance standards.

- Create timely, positive feedback systems to maintain high quality performance.

- Adapt constructively to decreasing resources.

You may help an agency to decide where to focus, for example, on policy (e.g., eligibility requirements), programs or practices (how services are offered), and/or personnel (e.g., hire bilingual staff, involve volunteers). Logic modeling can be used to identify the problem/need, the goals and related objectives, inputs (resources) needed, methods used (activities to put resources into use), and both short- and long-term results (e.g., Alter & Egan, 1997).

Like individuals, families, groups, and neighborhoods, agencies are influenced by their external environment, including other organizations, funding sources, and vested interests of political and client groups. Access to service may be limited by agency policies and procedures including outdated technologies, lack of coordination among agencies, and limited access to needed resources. Agencies differ in their responsiveness to cultural differences (e.g., Chow & Austin, 2008). Goal displacement may limit services. This occurs when an agency's means become its ends. For example, an agency may use process measures such as number of client interviews to evaluate outcomes. Knowledge about how organizations and service systems function, as well as external constraints (e.g., funding patterns), will be useful in discovering options and obstacles (e.g., Hasenfeld, 2009; Ivancevich, Matteson, & Konopaske, 2011; Netting, Kettner, McMurtry, & Thomas, 2012; Robbins & Judge, 2012; Patti, 2009). A contextual assessment including a description of organizational culture and climate will be valuable in identifying options for improving services. Consider the following questions when thinking about options. These questions emphasize gaps between current practices and what is needed to maximize opportunities to help clients.

- What physical characteristics of agencies influence service delivery?

- Who has power over whom? What information do different stakeholders wield?

- What are influential communication channels? What ones are unused?

- What criteria are used to select intervention methods? What criteria should be used?

- What contingencies support valued behaviors and outcomes? What could be used?

- What contingencies hinder achieving valued outcomes?

- How are clients involved? How should they be involved?

- What obstacles exist (e.g., limited time, skill, or other resources, negative attitudes, funding sources, competition for clients)? How can they be minimized?

- What resources are available? How can they be increased?

- What format(s) are used in supervision and continuing education? What formats should be used?

- What feedback systems are used to facilitate learning? What should be used?

You could visually describe the interrelationships among staff to explore how they influence services (e.g., draw a series of circles, write in the names of particular staff or note staff level in each, and use arrows of different colors to note who interacts with whom and the nature of the exchange—basically positive, negative, or neutral; Tichy & Sherman, 1993). Both formal and informal communication links could be noted. Exhibit 27.1 provides a guide for describing organizations.

EXHIBIT 27.1

A Brief Framework for Describing Human Service Organizations

Focus	Tasks
A. The agency's task environment	• Identify funding sources, as well as sources of noncash revenues. • Describe clients and client sources. • Identify other constituents.
B. Agency/environment relations	• Describe relationships with clients, resource sources, and competitors.
C. The organization	• Describe corporate authority and mission including goals of the agency. • Describe programs and services. • Describe organizational structure. • Describe administrative, management, and leadership styles. • Describe the organization's culture. • Describe technology used (e.g., equipment, computer use, records management). • Describe personnel policies and procedures. • Describe how the organization deals with community relations. • Describe methods of financial management and accountability. • Describe facilities.

Source: Adapted from F. E. Netting, P. M. Kettner, & S. L. McMurtry (1993). *Social work macro practice* (p. 160). New York: Longman.

Organization Culture and Climate

Organizations develop cultures and climates (Glisson, 2000; Glisson, Landsverk, Schoenwald, Kelleher, Hoagwood, Mayberg, et al., 2008; see also Glossary at the end of the chapter). Certain values are preferred, and certain norms and rules are followed. Components of culture include history, contingencies in effect, patterns of communication, symbols, decision-making styles, rituals and routines, philosophy, myths, and stories. Valuable communication styles described by Klauss and Bass (1982) include (p. 47): (1) careful transmitter (chooses words carefully); (2) open and two-way (considers other points of view, follows up conversations with feedback); (3) frank (levels with others); (4) careful listener (attends to what the speaker is saying, lets others finish speaking before commenting); and (5) informal (relaxed, natural). Examples of organizational culture include perceiving that leadership cares about ethics/values as much as the bottom line, feeling safe to deliver "bad news," and feeling treated fairly. Cultures differ in whether there is pressure to compromise values. Is ethical behavior rewarded? Is there acceptance and appreciation for diversity? Are employees treated fairly? Are they involved in decisions that affect the quality of their work life? Does the organization have an employee, community, or self-interest focus? (e,g,. see <http://www.ethics.org>)

Credibility dimensions include trustworthiness (just, kind), informative (well informed on issues concerning areas of responsibility), and dynamic (energetic). You may help an agency improve the quality of interactions between clients and agency staff. Examples of negative encounters with social insurance officers reported by 5,801 clients on long-term sick leave in Sweden included not believing what they said, regarding them as stupid, rejecting their suggestions, treating them with disrespect, not listening to them, and being too impersonal (Upmark, Hagberg, & Alexanderson, 2009). You can review your communication style by completing Exhibit 27.2. (See also culture of thoughtfulness scale in Gambrill and Gibbs, 2009.) Indicators of a well-functioning client-centered organization are suggested in Exhibit 27.3. Some agencies go out of their way to avoid the seven "sins of service" including apathy, the brush-off, coldness, condescension, robotism, the rule book, and the run around (Albrecht, 1990).

Although status (ranking) is important in all organizations, the criteria on which it is based differ in different organizations, for example, longevity of service, charisma, expertise, provision of positive incentives, and/or coercive power. Contingencies may or may not support behaviors that benefit clients and bring out the best in staff (Daniels, 2000). Valued behaviors may be punished or ignored and undesired behaviors reinforced. Bureaucratic propaganda may obscure policies and practices (Altheide & Johnson, 1980). Organizations differ in the clarity with which their philosophy, mission, goals, and related objectives are described and the extent to which all staff are involved in making decisions. The clearer the description of goals, related objectives, and hoped-for success levels, the easier it will be to evaluate the extent to which desired outcomes are attained and to detect negative and positive side effects. Style, philosophy, and

---

EXHIBIT 27.2

How Proactive and Positive Are You?

Complete the items below and review your answers to discover opportunities to be proactive and offer positive feedback. Add other items you think are important.

1. I offer positive feedback to colleagues for behaviors that contribute to effective services.	0	1	2	3	4
2. I describe specific changes needed to enhance service quality and involve my colleagues in seeking changes.	0	1	2	3	4
3. I validate helpful points my colleagues make.	0	1	2	3	4
4. I seek feedback to enhance my skills and knowledge.	0	1	2	3	4
5. When I have a complaint, I discuss it with the person involved rather than talk about it behind his or her back.	0	1	2	3	4
6. I arrange opportunities to discuss practice/policy issues/topics with colleagues.	0	1	2	3	4
7. I send e-mail congratulations to others regarding professional or personal events/accomplishments.	0	1	2	3	4
8. I come prepared for team meetings and case conferences.	0	1	2	3	4

Key: 0 (not at all); 1 (a little); 2 (a fair amount); 3 (a great deal); 4 (best that could be).

EXHIBIT 27.3

Indicators of a Well-Designed Client-Centered Organization

1. All staff are involved in deciding on agency philosophy, mission, and related objectives.

2. Performance standards are clearly described for each staff position. Criteria used as a guide to competence are based on practice and policy research findings.

3. Quality of performance is monitored for all staff positions based on agreed-on evidence-informed criteria.

4. Feedback is provided to all staff, including administrators, at agreed-on intervals based on monitoring of agreed-on relevant indicators.

5. There is an emphasis on how well the agency or specific units within it are doing, as well as on how well individual staff are meeting agreed-on standards. This encourages a sense of teamwork, a sharing of responsibility.

6. Training is provided as needed and is criterion referenced and competency-based (i.e., knowledge and skills to be acquired are clearly described and are related to outcomes pursued and are assessed via clear, relevant written, performance, and outcome reviews).

7. Less-than-hoped-for success and errors are used as opportunities for improvement. Staff are open about problems/mistakes/shortcomings and seek remedies for avoiding them in the future. They feel free to point out difficulties because they expect problems to be addressed and are optimistic that they can be solved.

8. Staff are encouraged to identify and advocate for improvements in practices and policies. Practices and policies are improved based on systematic feedback regarding outcomes and related research findings. Staff think problems through and make changes to improve services. They consider both long-term and short-term consequences of procedures and policies.

9. It is OK to challenge the boss. Nonconformity is tolerated. Staff are not preoccupied with status, territory, or second-guessing higher management.

10. Assignment of responsibilities is based on knowledge, skills, interests, work load, and timing rather than organizational level.

11. Input from all staff levels is sought and valued. Staff are encouraged to critically examine suggestions. Staff work together to address frustrations and crises. They support and offer constructive feedback for other people's ideas.

12. Personal needs of staff and their interrelationships are addressed.

13. Staff request help/seek advice when needed.

14. Structures are in place that support client participation in decision making and minimize power differences such as a client advisory board.

15. Differences of opinion are viewed as important to problem solving, decision making, troubleshooting, and growth; critical discussion and testing is valued as a way to arrive at sound decisions.

16. Staff help each other to enhance their skills. On-the-job learning is a routine part of work. Resources are shared.

17. Staff value and care about one another. Individuals do not feel isolated.

18. People trust each other. There is a sense of freedom and mutual responsibility.

19. Leadership is flexible, changing as needed in style and person.

20. Organization structure, procedures, and policies are designed to help staff provide high quality services. They are changed as needed. There is a sense of order coupled with innovation.

21. The organization provides tools needed for staff to make effective use of external research findings.

22. Staff take reasonable risks when this would improve service.

23. Red tape is minimized.

24. Yearly reviews of outcomes achieved are held in light of agency philosophy, mission, and related objectives and external research findings and changes made as necessary.

25. Clients have access to the evidentiary status of agency-provided services on a user-friendly agency web site.

26. Clients and other community members are involved in program assessment.

27. Barriers to effective service delivery are identified and addressed including language and cultural differences.

Source: See, for example, D. Hardina (2005). Ten characteristics of empowerment-oriented social service organizations. *Administration in Social Work*, 29: 23–42. G. W. LaVigna et al. (1994). *The periodic service review*. Baltimore: Paul H. Brookes. R. W. Weinbach & L. M. Taylor (2011). *The social worker as manager*. Upper Saddle, NJ: Harlow & Pearson Education. R. J. Patti (2009). *The Handbook of Human Services Management*. Los Angeles, CA: Sage.

competencies promoted as part of agency culture at Spectrum, an agency providing services to children, families, and schools, include the following (Keyworth, 1990):

Style	Philosophy	Competencies
Open, honest	Social action	Behavior
Humor	Integration	analysis
Assertiveness	Nonaversive	Education (of
Independence	Data-guided	self/clients)
Flexibility	Outcome oriented	Communication
Hard-working	Vision	Problem solving
Ability to accept	Responsibility	Consultation
feedback	for learning	Writing skills
Teamwork	Behavioral	Computer
Passion	Scientific	literacy
Integrity		Evaluation
Pragmatic		

Organizations differ in the extent to which they engage in strategic planning within their own agency and together with other agencies. They differ in the extent to which they value and empower clients, as well as staff (see Reid et al., 2011). Advantages of planning include the following (e.g., see Quinn et al., 2007):

- Provides a sense of identity.

- Helps staff see what they are doing in a wider context (e.g., consider remote, as well as current, contingencies).

- Decisions are made in light of the future.

- Requires discussion of mission, aims, goals, and resource allocation.

- Creates a network of information.

- Forces the system to take stock of all resources, both internal and external.

- Encourages and gives direction to long-term studies that contribute to sound decisions.

- Provides a forum for critical discussion.

- Provides options for alternative directions. Alternative paths become clearer.

Organizations differ in terms of their attentiveness to cultural and other differences that influence the effectiveness of services. For example: Are outreach activities and preventive programs designed to meet the needs of culturally diverse populations? Are any populations ignored? If so, why? Other characteristics of agencies regarding sensitivity to diversity include the following (Cultural Competence Self-Assessment Instrument, undated):

- Outreach activities and preventive services are designed to meet the needs of culturally diverse populations.

- Interventions use culturally diverse natural helping networks.

- Staff consider the impact of acculturation, assimilation, and historical perspectives on the cultural or ethnic group.

- Outreach services are provided in culturally diverse communities and neighborhoods, on reservations, or at other locations familiar to its clients.

- Bilingual services are provided when needed.

- In making placement decisions, the agency considers the unique identities of clients.

- Staff understand child-rearing customs, family functioning, and adult development from the cultural perspective of clients.

Decision-Making Styles

Supervisors make decisions about how to monitor the quality of practice of their supervisees, how to encourage valued behaviors, how to respond to unsatisfactory behavior or outcomes, and what steps to take to advocate for supervisees when agency policies and practices hinder effective services. Administrative decisions include those related to hiring staff, purchasing services, selecting training programs, monitoring quality of services, what kind of work culture to encourage, and how to monitor the extent to which it is implemented and contributes to services. Organizations differ in how decisions are made and in how conflicts, uncertainty, and less-than-hoped-for success are handled. They differ in their leadership style (e.g., consensus based, nonparticipatory) (e.g., see Rainey, Ronquillo, & Avellaneda, 2010). They differ in the extent to which staff seek clear, accurate information about outcomes and use this information to improve services and in the extent to which they encourage a learning culture in which critical discussion is valued and feedback sought (see chapters 5 and 22).

A learning-focused culture will increase the likelihood of sound decisions; it will discourage groupthink (see chapter 26) and rule by cliques. Different styles of decision making include an *incremental model* in which decisions are made in small steps; policy is changed a little at a time. In a *rational model*, decision makers describe problems and hoped-for outcomes, search for alternative solutions, and select the most promising one. Challenges here include lack of information about alternatives and their likely outcomes requiring a "satisfying model." (See chapter 8.)

Working in Teams

Social workers often work as part of an interdisciplinary team. A physician, social worker, physical therapist, occupational therapist, and nurse may all contribute to serving frail elderly clients. Social workers and nurses work closely together in hospice work. Considerable attention is now being devoted to creation of effective multidisciplinary teams. Skills required of team leaders include motivating staff, resolving conflicts, setting up information networks and disseminating information, making decisions, allocating resources, developing positive working relationships, and facilitating team meetings. The involvement of different professionals with different helping approaches, and perhaps interests, highlights the potential for misunderstandings and conflict. Shared goals and values will contribute to success, including a culture in which everyone participates, agreed-on tasks are clear, differences of opinion are viewed as learning opportunities, and there is an interest in understanding other points of view (people listen to each other). Suggestions for encouraging effective group meetings include:

- Avoid getting sidetracked on minor issues.

- Encourage brevity.

- Invite all members to listen attentively to each speaker and to participate.

- Match time allotted to importance of topic.

- Sum up often to keep members informed where they are in the discussion.

- Arrange facilitating physical conditions. (Edwards, 1938)

Dimensions suggested by Resnick (1982) to evaluate team effectiveness include the following: (1) degree of mutual trust; (2) degree of mutual support; (3) communication (e.g., guarded to open); (4) team objectives (not understood to clear); (5) handling conflict (deny, avoid, confront); (6) use of member resources; (7) control methods (imposed to self-influence); and (8) organizational environment (e.g., pressure to conform). Good will, as well as relationship skills and mutual respect, will be valuable in negotiating differences and distributing responsibilities. (See also Head, Bogers, Serruys, Takkenberg, & Kapetein, 2011; Zwarenstein, Goldman, & Reeves, 2009.)

Technology Relied on and Criteria Used to Select It

Agencies differ in the service methods they use and the criteria they use to select them (e.g., scientific, tradition) (see Exhibit 4.6). They differ in the extent to which they draw on research findings to select policies, programs, and practices that have a track record of success and in the extent to which criteria used to select methods are candidly discussed and the degree to which service outcomes are reviewed. Related decisions influence the quality of services clients receive. Your agency may rely on methods that focus on helping clients to change their behaviors, thoughts, or feelings; people processing techniques (e.g., giving people labels that increase access to certain services); and/or methods that focus on changing the environments in which people live. Technologies used may contribute to or detract from

helping clients. For example, unhelpful time-consuming recording requirements may detract from face-to-face contact with clients. Computer programs may not be user-friendly. Electronic decision support systems may be available but not used.

Client Involvement

Agencies differ in the extent to which and how they involve clients. (See Exhibit 27.3.) They may be service-oriented (distribute welfare benefits), as well as empowerment-oriented (help clients to acquire skills and support needed to avoid reliance on welfare). (See later section on social change and community organizing.) Agencies differ in the extent to which they involve clients as informed participants and include them on their boards.

Administrative Tasks

Management tasks include budgeting, coordinating activities, resolving conflicts, encouraging compliance with expected standards, and coordinating agency needs and goals and external requirements from regulatory or funding sources including provision of data concerning outcomes (Hasenfeld, 2009; Patti, 2009). (See also discussion of quality assurance programs in chapter 22.) Providing effective staff training is a key administrative role. Administrators are responsible for ensuring trainers' expertise. Maintenance roles include harmonizer (solving disagreements and reducing tension), consensus tester (checking whether a group is nearing a decision), encourager (being friendly and warm), and compromiser (e.g., changing a position when called for) (Resnick, 1982). Administrators also serve a reality tester role (to see if a suggestion would work). Administrators rely on different power bases. Some form valuable alliances and encourage reciprocity via positive social exchanges. Others rely on coercive power. Some have a consensual style of management—they involve staff in decisions. Others have an authoritarian style—they make decisions with little staff input. Administrators can encourage an effective working environment by:

- Modeling and promoting tolerance for diversity, conflict, expression of grievances, and constructive approaches to conflict resolution.

- Encouraging and facilitating unit or program interdependency and team approaches to tasks that cut across programs and professions.

- Minimizing the "height" of the organizational hierarchy ("flat" hierarchies tend to promote communication and improve staff morale).

- Delegating authority and responsibility to all levels of the hierarchy, particularly in areas that directly affect job performance.

- Providing opportunities and rewards for participating, planning, and decision making.

- Establishing effective formal channels for sharing information across all levels and programs.

- Clarifying and promoting understanding of organizational goals, ethics, and ideology.

- Clarifying staff roles and responsibilities.

- Encouraging diffusion of innovations (Greenhalgh et al., 2004)

Administrators have a responsibility to design and implement procedures that provide accurate feedback to all staff (including themselves) that are acceptable to involved parties and to monitor the extent to which services provided help clients to achieve goals they value. The NASW Code of Ethics calls on social workers to draw on external research findings and to keep up-to-date with them. This requirement places responsibilities on all staff. Administrators choose among methods that differ in the opportunities they provide to make transparent the quality of services offered to clients and therefore to enhance quality. Elements of quality assurance suggested by Maxwell (1984) to describe and measure quality of care include the following:

- *Relevance*: the service is required by the individual or population.

- *Accessibility*: time, distance, and structural access are within accepted norms.

- *Effectiveness*: the service achieves hoped-for benefits for the client or population.

- *Acceptability*: reasonable expectations of the clients and community are met.

- *Efficiency*: resources are well used.

- *Equity*: there is a fair share for all the community.

Characteristics of health care quality suggested by the Institute of Medicine (2001) include safety (clients should not be harmed), effectiveness (integration of the best research evidence with clinical expertise and client values avoiding underuse of effective care, as well as overuse of ineffective services), efficiency, timeliness, client-centered (includes qualities of compassion, empathy, and responsiveness to the needs, values, and expressed preferences of the individual client), and equity (services should not vary in quality because of personal characteristics such as gender, ethnicity, geographic location, and sexual orientation). How does your field work agency match up to these characteristics?

Audit, Benchmarks, and Evaluation

Audit is a quality control process. Performance is assessed in relation to predetermined standards or criteria. This term originated in the financial area. Audit can be defined as the systematic, critical appraisal of the quality of services, including procedures used for assessment and intervention, use of resources, and resulting outcomes for clients. Steps include: (1) clear description of the aim(s) of audit; (2) identification of clear standards; (3) assessment of quality; (4) identification of needed changes; and (5) selection of strategies to achieve changes (Kogan et al., 1995, pp. 101–102). Audits differ in attention to outcomes. Like any other procedure, performance review can be carried out in a dysfunctional or helpful manner. In *Technology as Magic* (2002), Stivers argues that a change in a management technique such as a new audit method is often viewed as the very indicator of success in the absence of any data that it enhances quality of services or is accurate. Many authors have described this kind of goal displacement (e.g., Power, 1997; Munro, 2011).

Benchmarking is used by an organization to evaluate their success in relation to what are viewed as "best practices" or standards. This is common in child welfare, for example, how many children are moved out of foster care in a certain amount of time. Both audit and benchmarking are descriptive processes. Neither may accurately describe outcomes of service. Benchmarks used may not be correlated with outcomes such as quality of life (Bartholet, 2009). Evaluation is concerned with the social and economic impact of processes used. Do they work? For whom? (See discussion of program evaluation in chapter 22.)

Efficiency, quality, and effectiveness of service may all be compromised by inadequate monitoring of staff performance and lack of an incentive system that supports valued behaviors. Operative goals reflected in staff activities and their outcomes may differ from those officially described, to the detriment of clients as suggested by Altheide and Johnson (1980) in *Bureaucratic Propaganda*. Client feedback may not be solicited or, if solicited, ignored. Process measures such as number of client interviews may be used to evaluate services that do not provide information about outcomes. Information of value includes kinds of people served, how many, their needs, extent to which their needs are met, and who are missed. Key questions include: "Do we reach those we hope to help and to what effect? What is the cost of our services? Are we wasting money? Effective audit procedures should enhance quality of service in part by planning how to prevent problems before they happen. Sampling of relevant staff behaviors (or products such as case records) make audits workable. Decisions include: (1) how many cases to review to get an accurate estimate of fidelity of services and outcomes; (2) how many different kinds of cases to review; (3) how to select cases; and (4) what adjustments to make regarding variations in problems addressed, for example, in difficulty. Increasing attention has been given to involving users of services in reviews. A *feed-up* procedure should be in place that allows line and supervisory staff to give administrators suggestions for improvement. (See also later section on evidence-based performances and outcome review.)

The Evidence-Informed Organization

Organizations differ in the extent to which they minimize the gap between available knowledge and what is used. In many there is a large gap between practices and policies offered and their evidentiary status. This may range from offering services that do more harm than good, to organizations that have a small gap between available knowledge and that which is used on all levels—line staff, supervisory, and administrative. An evidence-informed organization is one in which staff at all levels "are able to find—appraise, and use knowledge from research evidence" (p. 249). (See Exhibit 27.4.) Ineffective or harmful services are discontinued and effective services started or continued. Drawing on practice- and policy-related research findings in making life-affecting decisions is a hallmark of evidence-informed practice (Greenhalgh & MacFarlane, 1997; Lavis et al., 2008). Another hallmark is transparency of what is done to what effect.

Gray (2001a) characterizes the evidence-based organization as having "an obsession with finding, appraising, and using research-based knowledge as evidence in decision making" (p. 250). Such an organization helps social workers and their clients to deal "with inadequate information in ways that can help to identify really important uncertainties, uncertainties that are often reflected in dramatic variations in clinical practice and which cry out for coordinated efforts to improve knowledge" (Chalmers, 2004, p. 475). Although quality of services is emphasized in the social work literature, research suggests a wide range including outright quackery (Pignotti & Thyer, 2009; Thyer & Pignotti, in press). Court challenges to child welfare practice illustrate lack of quality (Eamon & Kopels, 2004; Gainsborough, 2010). (See also web sites such as National Center for Youth Law, http://www.youthlaw.org.)

Confronting Scarce Resources and Considering Populations, as Well as Individuals

No matter what the system of social services, there will never be enough resources to satisfy everyone's wants or needs (Eddy, 1994a). Distribution of scarce resources is a key ethical concern. Who will get what kind of services and when? Decisions that must be made include:

- How much of which services to buy, for whom and from whom.

- The best role for the public in making different decisions and methods for involving them.

- How to collaborate with other involved professionals in deciding and implementing priorities.

- How to collaborate with providers in changing contracts, agreeing on practice guidelines, audit methods, and outcome measures. (Øvretveit, 1995, p. 106)

Standard 3.07(a) of NASW Code of Ethics states that "social work administrators should advocate within and outside their agencies for adequate resources to meet clients' needs." Standard 3.07(b) calls on administrators to "advocate for resource allocation procedures that are open and fair. When not all clients' needs can be met, an allocation procedure should be developed that is nondiscriminatory and is based on appropriate and consistently applied principles."

Restriction (rationing) of services goes on in every agency, although this may be neither recognized nor discussed. Criteria used to restrict services may be implicit for a number of reasons including being too painful for staff to acknowledge that some clients suffer as a result of lack of resources to meet clear needs. Øvretveit (1995) defines rationing as "restricting supply by explicit or implicit means where demand exceeds supply, and where market mechanisms do not relate supply to demand in an acceptable way" (p. 104). Implicit rationing may be by:

- price

- queuing/waiting

- prioritization of need

- debarring rules

- restrictions on direct access

- according to likelihood of benefit

- personal opinion of provider

- restricting time on one case

- failure to publicize

- deterrent low standard of service

- deterrence, deflection, dilution, and delay. (p. 102)

Prioritizing can be defined as "deciding who goes first, or the relative proportion of resources allocated to a client, client group, population or service" (Øvretveit, 1995, p. 104). *Prioriphobia* refers to "the inability to set and carry through priorities due to an awareness of the suffering which will be caused by denying care and a refusal to value one person's life or quality of life more highly than another" (p. 105). Justifications for not purchasing, withholding, or constraining services include:

- Diverts resources from other services (benefit-opportunity cost).

- Some needs/conditions are less life-threatening or painful than others.

- Unproven need, or capacity to benefit.

- Service ineffective, or untested, or benefits low for high cost.

- Little public support for public finance for this purpose.

EXHIBIT 27.4

Strategies for Creating and Sustaining an Evidence-Informed Organizational Culture

I. Team or unit level

- Develop and disseminate an in-house newsletter to highlight relevant research.
- Form and support monthly journal clubs to discuss relevant research and to encourage knowledge sharing.
- Include research on the agendas of supervisory, unit, and departmental meetings.
- Involve students in agency field placements in searching for, summarizing, and sharing research related to practice and policy decisions.
- Create a library of relevant research articles, reports, and books.
- Help staff to use existing databases (e.g., Cochrane and Campbell Databases).

II. Department or agency level

- Develop an organizational culture that encourages use of relevant research findings in making decisions at all levels of the organization including an orientation program to inform staff about EBP.
- Identify and mobilize champions of EBP.
- Senior and middle management model EBP.
- Provide needed resources (e.g., internet access, training, library materials).
- Establish a committee responsible for implementing EBP.
- Support the design and use of service evaluations.
- Create a climate of continuous learning and improvement—a learning organization.
- Promote evidence-informed training and decision making.
- Develop a system of e-mail alerts of recent, relevant articles.
- Supervisors encourage EBP.
- Create in-service training in EBP and lobby for similar content in local educational programs.
- Arrange protected reading time for staff to review research related to life-affecting decisions staff and clients make.

III. University/institute/agency partnerships for research development and dissemination

- Provide clear user-friendly descriptions of research findings related to key questions.
- Conduct research relevant to the service mission of the organization.
- Develop research and evaluation partnerships between agencies and universities/institutes.
- Use multiple methods of dissemination.
- Build dissemination efforts into all research projects.
- Gather questions of concern to clients and practitioners to identify topics for search/research.

IV. Implications for senior management

- Create and circulate a policy statement clearly describing EBP including:
  - Ethical obligations to client.
  - Discovering promising practices.
  - Making decisions.
  - Purchasing services.
- Design an orientation program to inform staff about EBP and design an organizational culture that encourages EBP.
- Identify an advocate of EBP to guide organizational change needed and to serve as the agency's information officer (knowledge manager).
- Identify a university/institute partner to work together to:
  - Identify questions of concern to clients/staff.
  - Prepare CATS (critically appraised topics).
  - Design strategies to incorporate new knowledge into ongoing practice and to evaluate the outcomes.
  - Coordinate agency efforts to promote EBP through the agency's information officer.

Source: Adapted from Center for Evidence-based Social Services (2004). Becoming an evidence-based organization: Applying, adapting, and acting on evidence—Module 4. *The evidence guide: Using research and evaluation in social care and allied professions*. Exeter, UK: University of Exeter.

- Avoidable by more responsible individual behavior.

- Individuals have alternatives to public service (private insurance, wealth). (p. 102)

Steps that may be involved in restricting services include the following:

1. *Needs-exclusion or restriction from publicly funded services.* Some needs may be excluded because no effective services are available. Needs and services excluded should be reviewed and include public and staff views, and continued attention should be given to criteria used to justify exclusion.

2. *Service exclusion or restriction, with poor cost-effectiveness.* The second step involves "reviewing which services are known to have no benefits or to have low cost-effectiveness. This involves assessing the added value of different [services] and considering the effect of [intervening or not intervening]. It also involves recognizing that there may be exceptions, and developing ways of authorizing providers to use certain [services in certain cases]."

3. *Provider exclusion with poor outcome performance.* This involves selecting the best provider using criteria such as good outcome performance, low cost, and public preference. Relevant information must be gathered and discussion with providers held (p. 121).

Failure to openly acknowledge restrictions imposed by service providers means that clients cannot be included in making decisions. Criteria used to distribute scarce resources should be clearly described so they can be reviewed from both ethical and practical points of view. A candid recognition that resources are scarce and an open exploration of related implications (not all people will get what they want) requires consideration of populations, as well as individuals. That is, administrators and policy makers should consider what populations they are required to or could provide what services to, with what likely effect, based on related external evidence, and what populations they now provide what kind of services to with what effect. Considerations include the following:

- *Efficacy* of an intervention in a controlled setting. Is there research evidence that the intervention can produce a desired result?

- *Effectiveness*: Do external research findings show evidence that the intervention produces the desired result in most everyday settings?

- *Provider outcome performance*: For services found to be effective, what outcomes do potential or current providers achieve, compared to other providers?

- *Provider costs*: What is the cost-outcome ratio for different providers?

- *Acceptability* to providers and to clients.

- *Use and take up* is also affected by accessibility.

- *Need and capacity to benefit* involves selecting the right clients. (Øvretveit, 1995, p. 107)

Information about needs will always be partial and subject to dispute. Still, administrators should try to identify as accurately as possible the incidence and severity of need in setting priorities and purchasing services. (See other sources describing now to carry out a needs assessment). Ethical decisions require an awareness of and consideration of the limitations of descriptive data regarding needs, a commitment to enhance the accuracy of the picture, and an accurate estimate of the likelihood that certain services can meet client needs based on sound arguments or related research findings. "Defining need in terms of capacity to benefit from services does make needs assessment more manageable, but, by definition, may not measure needs for which there are [no effective services]" (p. 108). Only by thinking about populations, as well as individuals, are we likely to make ethical decisions about the distribution of scarce resources.

Evidence-Informed Management Skills

Characteristics of an evidence-based chief administrator suggested by Gray (2001a) include modeling searching for evidence, appraising evidence, storing important evidence in a way that allows it to be easily retrieved, and using evidence to make decisions. Such administrators encourage evidence-informed audit and purchasing and take responsibility for providing tools and training needed by staff to offer clients evidence-based practices. They help those accountable to the chief administrator to develop evidence-informed management skills (p. 251). Each organization has a unique work climate and culture; certain behaviors are welcomed, others are ignored, and some are punished. Administrators have a responsibility to create a work environment in which behaviors that contribute to positive outcomes for clients are maximized and behaviors that diminish such outcomes are minimized. Standard 3.07(d) of the NASW Code of Ethics states that:

Social work administrators should take reasonable steps to ensure that the working environment for which they are responsible is consistent with and encourages compliance with the NASW Code of Ethics. Social work administrators should take reasonable steps to eliminate any conditions in their organizations that violate, interfere with, or discourage compliance with the Code.

Valued behaviors that contribute to ethical conduct should be clearly identified and contingencies to support them arranged.

Many of these behaviors are described in this book, such as selecting assessment measures shown to be accurate, choosing service methods that maximize the likelihood of attaining valued outcomes, and agreeing on clear performance standards that contribute to helping clients. In addition, behaviors that detract from such outcomes should be identified and steps taken to minimize them.

Cultivating a Culture of Thoughtfulness

Knowledge can grow only in an open environment in which clients and staff are free to raise questions (express criticism) about current practices and policies and their outcomes. (See Culture of Thoughtfulness Scale in Gambrill & Gibbs, 2009.) Criticism provides vital information that may help to minimize avoidable mistakes. The Code of Ethics for Child Welfare Professionals (1996) calls on administrators to:

- Provide a working environment that permits frank discussion and criticism of agency operations and with an administrative means for dissent, assurance of due process, and safeguards against reprisal.

- Enhance organizational capacity for open communication, creativity, efficiency, and dedication.

- Maintain truthfulness and honesty and not compromise them for advancement, recognition, or personal gain. (p. 15)

Evidence-Informed Selection of Practices and Policies

In an evidence-informed organization, practices and policies are selected based on their track record of success in helping clients to attain valued outcomes. Practices and policies that have been found to harm clients or to be ineffective are not used. Evidence concerning effectiveness alone does not imply that a practice or policy should be adopted; there are many other considerations such as preferences of clients and needs of different populations; adoption of an intervention should depend on whether the benefit is sufficiently large relative to the risks and costs (Sheldon, Guyatt, & Haines, 1998). (See also discussion of "What is Evidence?" in chapter 9.) Staff may use ineffective or harmful practices for many reasons, including clients' preferences, a need to do something, or rituals (Doust & Del Mar, 2004). Most practices and policies have never been subject to critical testing; we do not know if they help or not.

Evidence-Informed Purchase of Services

State agencies contract out services to other agencies. This kind of "outsourcing" has increased dramatically over the past years as has attention to performance-based contracting (e.g., see Taylor & Shaver, 2010). For example, child welfare staff contract out services to other providers. Each agency uses certain criteria to purchase services from other agencies. Criteria differ in the extent to which they maximize high-quality services. Critical appraisal encourages questions such as: What evidence is there that an agency helps clients? (See Exhibit 27.5). Does the agency help clients like those I will send? What percentage of clients referred achieve hoped-for outcomes? Evidence-informed purchasing refers to purchasing of services on the basis of their evidentiary status—they have been found via critical appraisal to maximize the likelihood of achieving hoped-for outcomes for the least cost in resources. Cost-effectiveness issues should be considered when purchasing services. Øvretveit (1995) argues that if purchasers are not able to justify their decisions, then they are "acting unethically in directly or indirectly causing avoidable suffering" (p. 99).

For each service purchased, we should ask: Is anything known about its effectiveness? If so, what? Do we know if a service: (1) does more good than harm; (2) does more harm than good; (3) is of unknown effect—not in research setting or in poor-quality research; (4) is of unknown effect, but in a good quality research program (Gray, 2001a)? For each service provider, we should examine the gap between what is provided to referred clients, and what could be provided based on best current evidence.

Clear agreements should be drawn up with agencies from which services are purchased describing services to be provided and their evidentiary status, as well as how quality of services and outcomes will be evaluated and when data will be shared. Those who purchase services have an obligation to monitor the quality of services provided. Guidelines suggested regarding when we should act on the evidence, either as a purchaser of services or as an individual practitioner at the direct-line level, include the following:

1. It is necessary to prioritize, since not all research findings should or can be implemented.

2. "The decision whether to implement research evidence depends on the quality of the research, the degree of uncertainty of the findings, relevance to the clinical setting, whether the benefits to the [client] outweigh any adverse effects, and whether the overall benefits justify the costs when competing priorities and available resources are taken into account." (p. 139)

3. Systematic as opposed to authoritarian reviews that show consistent results usually provide more reliable research evidence. (Sheldon, Guyatt, & Haines, 1998)

Policies that Øvretveit (1995) proposes to enhance quality of services purchased include the following:

1. Require audit.

2. Require that audit be conducted according to established guidelines.

3. Require providers to use outcome data.

4. Require providers to take part in established national/regional audit.

5. Require that audit uses systems that allow comparisons.

6. Specify which outcome data are to be collected.

7. Require the provider to share outcome information with purchaser.

8. Specify outcomes standards in contract.

9. Educate staff and clients about the effectiveness of different services and what to ask providers about outcome, and/or publicize outcome data from providers. (p. 163) (Based on Pollit, 1990)

"The aim is to allocate resources equitably, and in ways in which resources can do the most good for the least cost, and to ensure that providers do the same, where it is appropriate to prescribe provider actions" (Øvretveit, 1995, p. 121).

Effective coordination of services is vital when multiple services are required to attain hoped-for outcomes. Many helpers are case managers who coordinate services provided to an individual or family. Without careful planning and coordination, plans may overlap, contradict each other, consume more time than is needed, and not be evidence-informed. Administrators, together with supervisory and line staff, should develop effective methods for maximizing effective service coordination including written purchase of service agreements (see Gambrill & Shlonsky, 2001) and agree on clear distribution of responsibilities for reviewing services provided by staff in other agencies. Clear criteria should be identified for minimally acceptable coordination and viable, effective audit and evaluation procedures should be in place for monitoring the quality of service coordination. (See chapter 22.)

Tools Are Available That Maximize Knowledge Flow

The evidence-informed organization is deeply involved with maximizing knowledge flow. Consider Gray's (1998) suggestion

of hiring knowledge officers whose role it is to maximize knowledge flow within the organization, from within to without, and from without the organization to within. Questions that arise include: What evidence is needed? When it is needed and in what situations and in what form? And how can we get it when we need it? (Gray, 2001a). Attention to application problems such as ready access to research findings related to life-affecting decisions is reflected in the philosophy of evidence-based practice described by its originators (see chapter 9). Does an agency provide resources such as high-speed computers with access to relevant databases to its practitioners? Gray describes an evidence-based knowledge-rich learning organization as one in which:

1. The creation and use of knowledge is valued and the availability of knowledge is assured.

2. There is a commitment to knowledge management to ensure that systems and skills for finding, appraising, and using evidence are developed and supported.

3. Both tacit and explicit knowledge are readily available when and where needed. (p. 248)

He suggests that each organization have an evidence center such as a library with the following:

1. Access to the World Wide Web;

2. Subscriptions to the most relevant data sources, such as [the Cochrane and Campbell Libraries];

3. A limited number of appropriate books and journals;

4. Arrangements in place for obtaining documents or copies thereof, such as reprints of articles;

5. Someone who can manage these resources and promote their use, such as a librarian. (p. 253)

User-friendly web sites describing the evidentiary status of services are one way to maximize knowledge flow.

Evidence-Informed Selection of Training Content and Formats

Criteria used to select programs differ in the likelihood that they contribute to helping clients. Training programs may be selected based on entertainment value or popularity. Relying on such criteria does not maximize the likelihood that those offered are most likely to enhance the quality of services provided to clients. User-friendly performance review systems can be used to identify training needs. (See chapter 22.) A Cochrane review of the effectiveness of continuing education meetings and workshops reported greater effects of mixed interactive and didactic methods (Forsetlund, Bjørndal, Rashidian, Jamtvedt, O'Brien, Wolf, et al., 2009). Participants' ratings of training programs

---

EXHIBIT 27.5

Reviewing the Evidentiary Status of Agency Services Including Those Purchased

Indicate what percentage of services fall into each of the following categories.

———1. Services that have been critically tested and been found to help clients.

———2. Services of unknown effectiveness.

———3. Services that have been critically tested and found to be harmful.

or testimonials may not be associated with on-the-job changes in performance and are therefore not a sound guide to whether or not a program results in improved quality of services. Administrators have a responsibility to arrange for training that maintains all staff at minimally acceptable competency levels in relation to practice-related knowledge and skills required to attain valued outcomes. Standard 3.08 of the NASW Code of Ethics states that:

> Social work administrators and supervisors should take reasonable steps to provide or arrange for continuing education and staff development for all staff for whom they are responsible. Continuing education and staff development should address current knowledge and emerging developments related to social work practice and ethics. (p. 181)

Without providing effective training as needed in posing questions, searching efficiently and effectively for related research findings, critically appraising what is found, and using clinical expertise to integrate information from diverse sources, including clients' values and expectations, an organization cannot be evidence-informed. Thus, effective professional education and training programs are a central ongoing concern (e.g., see Koh, Khoo, Wong, & Koh, 2008). Are educational formats used most likely to help participants to acquire helpful skills? Here, too, we can compare the gap between criteria used to select programs and what criteria would maximize quality of services to clients. Training should be tailored as needed to the unique entering repertoires of each staff member. One social worker may benefit from guidance in the use of accurate assessment methods. Another may benefit from enhancing skills in integrating data collected. Gaps between content provided in professional education programs and what is needed on the job suggests the value of effective on-site training.

Maximizing Opportunities for Corrective Feedback: Creating Self-Learning Organizations

Learning organizations are characterized by ongoing improvement in the quality of decisions made, as well as the development of new knowledge, including new ways of using and managing knowledge developed by others. An increased emphasis on accountability to clients, advances in information technology (e.g., computer processing of data), and decreasing resources all point to the value of self-learning organizations—those that seek and use corrective feedback from multiple sources about how they can improve services and constructively adapt to changing circumstances including loss of usual funding (see Argyris & Schön, 1996; Easterby-Smith & Lyles, 2011). A cultural change will often be needed to create a self-learning organization; the idea is for the entire organization to focus on learning (Gray, 2001a, p. 245). Gray refers to Senge's five "disciplines" in becoming a learning organization:

1. *Personal mastery*: continually clarifying and deepening personal vision and objectivity.

2. *Making mental models*: creating a mental model of what the organization is, what it stands for, and how it works.

3. *Building shared visions*.

4. *Team learning*: ensuring that the collective intelligence of a team is greater than the sum of the individual intelligence.

5. *Systems thinking*: putting individual elements together into a coordinated set of activities with a common set of objectives.

Gray (2001a) suggests that knowledge in an organization can be increased by transforming tacit knowledge into explicit knowledge (see discussion of tacit and explicit knowledge in chapter 4). The notion of a learning organization suggests an active pursuit of the flow of knowledge from all relevant sources and developing knowledge rather than a passive stance which characterizes many social service organizations. For example, do agencies take advantage of opportunities to learn how to improve services from a review of factors related to adverse events (Rzepnicki et al., 2012)? Avoidable harms are an ongoing concern (Gambrill, 2012a). There are wide variations in practices and policies and a high rate of avoidable errors (Longtin, Sax, Leape, Sheridan, Donaldson, & Pettit, 2010). Options here include effective audit systems, shifting from a blaming culture to a learning culture, in which reporting of errors is encouraged as an opportunity to improve services, and implementation of user-friendly effective complaint and compliment retrieval systems.

Evidence-Based Performance and Outcome Review

A well-designed system that provides corrective feedback will encourage evidence-informed decisions. Program implementation and service integrity are important to review, especially if there is little progress or harmful effects are found (see chapter 22). Possible reasons for a program's failure include:

1. Excessive staff discretion in providing service, resulting in variations that decrease success.

2. Minimal, watered-down programs (the dilution effect).

3. What works when used by well-trained, motivated staff does not when used by others.

4. What works for some clients does not work for others.

5. Clients refuse to participate.

6. Staff are rude, cold, or apathetic in their interactions with clients.

Perhaps programs were not implemented at all. Practices such as "creaming" (offering services only to clients who are most likely to benefit) will artificially inflate estimates of success (Berk & Rossi, 1999). Services offered can be compared with those research suggests are best to achieve hoped-for outcomes. To what degree are agency practices and policies evidence-informed? This comparison will identify opportunities to change practices and policies in promising directions. We can compare what practitioners do against what is suggested as best. As Sheldon, Guyatt, and Haines (1998) note: "Policy makers should insure that policies on treatment reflect and are consistent with research evidence, and that the incentive structure within the health system promotes cost-effective practice. They must also insure that there is an adequate infrastructure for monitoring changes and practice and for producing, gathering, summarizing, and disseminating evidence" (p. 139). (See also Oxman et al., 2010.) A variety of factors should be considered in reviewing the effectiveness of applying evidence:

Setting priorities

- National policies and guidelines.
- Priorities of the local agencies.
- Local client needs due to factors such as level of deprivation, age of population.
- Less obvious issues, for example, practitioner–client relationships.

Practice resources

- Level of teamwork.
- Computer systems.
- Availability of evidence.
- Existing quality assurance systems.
- Staff with time and skill to take on a particular role, for example, data collection, appraisal of guidelines.
- Information about significant events.

Local resources

- A local library.
- Expertise in graduate programs or university departments.
- Training for staff in audit or monitoring methods.
- Local peer review groups. (Baker & Grol, 1998, p. 85)

Audit may be a valuable tool or a meaningless waste of time in that it does nothing to improve services. Indeed, it may be a distraction occupying time better spent in face-to-face contact with clients (Munro, 2011; Power, 1997). It is thus important that audit systems be carefully designed to make sure they contribute to, rather than detract from, helping clients. Research concerning the helping process shows that process variables such as warmth and empathy affect outcome. (See chapter 15.) Related publications describe easy to use process and outcome measures at the individual helper level that can be collated and used to provide feedback at the unit and agency level. Thus, data of value in providing high quality services to clients at the individual level can also be used at the administrative level to review process and outcome. And, identification of poor performance or ethical misconduct is of little value unless effective remedies are in place.

Supervisors are responsible for taking what steps are possible to alter conditions that contribute to poor performance or misconduct on the part of their supervisees. The Code of Ethics for Child Welfare Professionals (1996) calls on supervisors to "consult with supervisees and help with remedial action if they have knowledge of the supervisees' impairment due to personal problems, mental health problems, or substance abuse" (p. 14) and "provide necessary training and guidance when supervisees' personal or cultural differences could result in biased or discriminatory professional intervention with a particular individual or groups" (p. 14). Power imbalance issues may include abuse of authority (exploiting supervisees) and sexual activities with supervisees. Possible contributors include work pressure/workload and poor supervisor–supervisee relationships. Staff may be under pressure to "cut corners" and to violate rules to get their work done. Ineffective methods of addressing diversity issues may compromise service (e.g., Stockdale & Crosby, 2004). It may be necessary to blow the whistle on practices and policies that have harmful consequences. You should be familiar with your agency's policies on whistle-blowing, as well as related information outside of your agency.

Learning from Errors

All professionals make mistakes. Many are unavoidable; they could not have been prevented by the most skilled of the skilled. Others are avoidable by better training, more effective audit procedures, or appropriate incentive systems. Eileen Munro (1996) reviewed 45 inquiries in Britain concerning mishaps in child welfare services. She came to the conclusion that confirmation biases (seeking information only to support one's preferred view) were a key factor in such errors. In his detailed review of 20 case studies of child abuse, Howitt (1992) highlighted the role of what he referred to as "ratcheting" (once choosing a view, continuing on in one direction without looking back and reconsidering a decision). We tend to judge the quality of a process by its outcome. For example, those told that there is a poor outcome, evaluate a decision or action more negatively. This is referred to as outcome bias.

In general, we react, after the fact, as if the knowledge we now possess was available to the operators then. This oversimplifies or trivializes the situation confronting the practitioners, and masks the processes affecting practitioner behavior before-the-fact. As a result, hindsight and outcome bias blocks our ability to see the deeper story of systematic factors that predictably shape human performance. (Woods & Cook, 1999, p. 147)

Staff willingness to identify mistakes is influenced by agency culture. If reporting mistakes is punished, few will do it. On the other hand, if agency policy clearly recognizes that mistakes will be made and that they are vital for learning how to do better in the future, and staff are encouraged to discuss them with their supervisors at an early point, they are less likely to result in further negative effects and provide an opportunity to learn how to avoid them in the future, if it is an avoidable mistake. Given that it may be possible to prevent and minimize some mistakes by identifying and planning how to decrease them, it is vital that administrators have in place a method to do so. A clear policy and procedure in relation to mistakes should be formed and implemented in conjunction with input from supervisory and line staff and from clients—one that is learning rather than blame directed.

Woods and Cook (1999) note that "factors that reduce error tolerance or block error detection and recovery degrades system performance" (p. 144). There is extensive research regarding error and failure—how it occurs, when it occurs, why it occurs, and what could be done about it in the areas of health, aviation, nuclear energy, and environmental concerns, such as chemical spills. Related research shows that errors typically involve systemic causes, including, poor training programs (Reason, 2001). There is little of this kind of research in social work, psychiatry, and psychology. A number of factors increase the likelihood of errors (e.g., see Longtin et al., 2010). Work demand is related to error—the relationship between demands made and resources available (Feltovich, Ford, & Hoffman, 1997). Errors may occur because of incorrect views of client concerns or lack of needed information. Cues may be misinterpreted or ignored. Situations may not be recognized as ones that require change in a course of action. Risk (threat or danger) levels may be misassessed. (See discussion of the importance of situation awareness in chapter 8.) We may misjudge the time we have. Goals may conflict (safety versus productivity, mission completion or social factors). Consequences may not be anticipated or evaluated (Woods & Cook, 1999).

In discussing errors, we should consider the extent to which employees control their work life. Complete control occurs if there is no accountability on the part of anyone but the worker. This undercontrolled situation can be contrasted with an over-controlled situation. Singer (1978) suggests that incompetence, callousness, and planned error are three factors that explain organizational error behavior. Examples of organizational incompetence include:

1. The lack of any means of checking whether key tasks are carried out.

2. Not checking the quality of communication with clients.

3. Lack of steps for arranging feedback on all important decisions so that staff can learn from this feedback how to improve performance in the future.

4. Not doing a cost-benefit analysis.

5. Not using procedures that have been shown to be effective.

6. Continuing to use procedures that have been shown to be ineffective.

7. Using procedures that have been found to harm clients.

Singer (1978) argues that errors of callousness occur in "cases where errors are revealed but produce no willingness to take action" (p. 31). "When key people within organizations or institutions are made aware of a problem, persistent or exceptional, and do not take steps to correct it or to rectify injustices, we have errors of callousness" (p. 31).

Learning from Clients

Clients are actively involved in many ways in evidence-informed organizations (Gambrill, 2006). Their preferences and expectations are actively solicited and attended to in planning services. User-friendly complaint and compliment systems are in place and information collected is acted on. Client feedback, as well as feedback from their significant others, is a key part of applied behavior analysis. (For further discussion, see Coulter, 2002; Coulter & Collins, 2011; Edwards & Elwyn, 2001.)

Evidence-Informed Management of Innovations

In an evidence-informed organization, questions such as the following are posed, and answers pursued: How good is the evidence used to justify investment in a new procedure. What criteria should be used to select these? How should they be introduced? (See, e.g., Bogenschneider & Corbett, 2010.) Gray (2001a) proposes establishment of a committee concerned with innovations that would be guided by the following:

- *Starting right*—those innovations that do more good than harm, and which are *affordable*, are introduced at a defined standard of quality.

- *Starting stopping*—those innovations that do more harm than good but have already entered the service are no longer offered.

- *Stopping starting*—those innovations that do more harm than good are not introduced.

- *Promoting trials*—innovations of unknown effect are investigated during trials.

- *Slowing starting*—those innovations that require training and infrastructure are introduced in a planned way. (p. 273)

Gray suggests that "part of the management of innovation is to identify interventions that do more good than harm at affordable cost and drive them into the service quickly and effectively, starting right. It is no longer acceptable to allow important innovations to drift into practice in a piecemeal fashion" (p. 275).

Eddy (1994a) offers the following criteria for funding a particular service:

- There is sufficient evidence to draw a conclusion about the intervention's effects on outcome.

- The evidence shows that the intervention can be expected to produce its intended effects on outcome.

- The intervention's expected beneficial effect outweighs its expected harmful effect.

- The intervention is the most cost-effective method available to achieve hoped-for outcomes. (p. 279)

Interventions designed to promote behavior change among health professionals vary in their effectiveness (Robertson & Jochelson, 2006). These include individual, organizational, national, and multifaceted levels. Reviews report that educational materials are generally viewed as ineffective in influencing clinician behavior; such efforts are more effective if combined with other interventions. Large-scale educational didactic meetings are generally ineffective. Educational outreach efforts may be effective if combined with social marketing techniques. The effectiveness of audit is influenced by who provides the feedback, its timeliness, quality, relevance, buy-in by clinicians, and whether it is active or passive. (See Robertson & Jochelson, 2006). Improving services may require greater costs. Providing a parent-training program that maximizes the likelihood of achieving hoped-for outcomes may be costly. We can use money spent on ineffective programs to offer effective programs. In considering whether or not to implement innovations, Gray (2001a) suggests three kinds: (1) ridiculously cheap, should be implemented immediately; (2) cost unreasonable; and (3) reasonable cost that offers good value for money.

Obstacles to Organizational Change

There are formidable barriers to encouraging use of evidence-based practices and policies. These include characteristics of the practice environment such as financial disincentives, organizational constraints, practitioner characteristics (lack of courage)

and client values and expectations (Oxman & Flottorp, 1998). Prevailing opinion may be an obstacle—influence by standards of practice, opinion leaders, and professional education. Yet a third source suggested by Oxman and Flottorp concerns knowledge and attitudes including uncertainty, feelings of incompetency regarding new practices, need to act, and information overload. Some people are absorbed in their own lives and care little about the effect of services on clients. This applies to quacks and hucksters. Propagandists of others are often self-propagandists (believe their own propaganda). Such individuals may believe that they are in the profession to help clients when a description of their activities and its consequences reveals that they do not help clients. Certainly the history of psychiatry reflects such a possibility.

The topic of self-deception is closely related to identifying avoidable errors and planning how to minimize them. We all deceive ourselves in a variety of ways. (See literature on self-deception.) We exaggerate our contributions to positive outcomes and minimize our responsibility for negative ones. If we deceive ourselves about the consequences of our actions, we are unlikely to acquire the feedback needed to change our behavior in order to identify and minimize avoidable mistakes. (See discussion of self-deception in chapter 28.)

Environmental obstacles include funding patterns, vested interests in current power networks and related contingencies, limited resources, and preferred ideologies. There may be conflicts between professional values and agency practices. Personal obstacles include a belief that change is not possible, a view of conflict as inappropriate, a patronizing attitude toward clients, and a high need for social approval. Feared losses as a result of proposed changes may contribute to resistance. Another factor is inertia. Bringing harmful or questionable services to staff's attention or services found to be effective but not used would require changes in agency practice. It would require effort and may lead to stressful interpersonal exchanges that we may rather avoid. People may disagree over goals or simply not like each other. Strained personal relationships or friendships between staff and management may get in the way. Staff may not express their concerns because they are afraid of losing their job, offending friends or have been criticized by supervisors for doing so. They may lack effective behavior change skills (see chapters 16 and 25). Decisions will have to be made about how to handle disagreements among staff who advocate for change and administrators who oppose it. There may be a reluctance to "bear witness" (see chapter 28).

Staff may underestimate options for altering harmful or ineffective practices and policies or be reluctant to discuss known problems (Block, 2011). A search for ideal solutions may breed dissatisfaction and get in the way of making small but valuable improvements. We may expect "too much too soon" and so forgo opportunities to support successive approximations. Seeking approximations to valued goals may pose less of a threat to those who fear changes. Valuing and recognizing them will help staff to persist in long-term change efforts. A belief that administrators do not care about clients may interfere with collaborative pursuit of common goals. What appears to be noncaring on the part of administrators may reflect pressures they experience. Perhaps the timing of a proposed change is not good. Perhaps staff have just gone through many changes.

The organizational culture and climate (e.g., beliefs, norms, values, contingencies) influence options for change. Identify facilitating and constraining factors to review options. Other factors include preferred criteria for selecting practices and policies, the competencies of and relationships among staff, legal, and administrative factors, and information and communication channels. Staff may prefer selecting practices and policies based on tradition rather than on evidentiary grounds; opinions may be treated as facts. Preferred styles of communication and problem solving may be an obstacle. Feminist writers note that women prefer win-win rather than win-lose approaches; they prefer collaborative styles in which interpersonal relationships are valued in and of themselves, not merely as a means to an end. Valuing critical discussion as a route to improving services will encourage a work climate in which clashing points of view are welcomed. New roles in public services suggested by Raven (1984) include critic, muckraker, whistle-blower, organizational invader, prophet, and visionary (p. 79).

Views of errors and mistakes may pose an obstacle. Social organizations have a great deal to gain in the short term by the view that errors are caused by particular individuals in an organization. Such agencies reflect a "blame culture." Consider, for example, how tragic events such as deaths of children in foster care are often handled—by blaming an individual. This has prevented a systemic look at the culture and climate of the organization to identify related factors (e.g., Gambrill & Shlonsky, 2001; Munro, 2011). We know from the study of error in other areas that the causes are typically systemic. In most cases we cannot understand them by looking solely at an individual. In view of this considerable literature, we must ask why fields such as child welfare have not been more responsive. Thus, a key reason errors and mistakes continue to occur is that no one takes any steps to: (1) identify them; (2) bring them to people's attention; and (3) take action to minimize avoidable errors. This is a quite different approach compared to ignoring error, blaming clients or staff, blaming the system but taking no steps to change it, trivializing the consequences of error, or covering up errors and their consequences. Clients will benefit from shifting from a blame-oriented culture to a learning-based one.

The Importance of Political "Savvy"

Political knowledge and skills are of value in understanding and dealing with constraints. Conflict is inevitable in all spheres of life including organizations. It is how conflicts are viewed and handled that is critical to outcome. (See discussion of the value of culture clashes in chapter 5.) Forming a coalition of interested parties is often a useful step to take (Otis, 2004; Schneider & Lester, 2001). A group of individuals seeking change will have more clout than an individual. Learn to recognize political ploys

used to avoid change, such as denying that a proposed change merits serious consideration and mobilizing biased others to exclude consideration of opposing viewpoints.

The denial of conflict is one of the more underhanded uses of power (Bachrach & Baratz, 1971). Other ploys include stonewalling (e.g., assurances of change unaccompanied by any effort to bring them about or flat-out refusal to consider changes) and stalling (forming endless committees). Be prepared to handle what Austin (1988) calls "intimidation rituals" used to "cool out" troublemakers such as discounting, isolation, defamation (attacking the individual's character), and/or dismissal. Familiarity with the political decision-making process is valuable in understanding policy decisions and how to influence them (Rocha, 2007). This highlights the role of different values such as equity, liberty, equality, and rights and various means of persuasion including "facts," numbers, and symbols.

Involving Clients

Limited options for changing agencies and service systems may require helping residents/clients to alter agency practices and staff behavior. It may require both case and cause advocacy. For a classic example, see Seymour & Stokes, 1976. Willner and his colleagues described how to run an effective halfway house for delinquent youth in which self-government is encouraged and residents evaluate staff (see, for example, Willner et al., 1977). Resident rights groups should be created in all residential settings to work with staff to enhance service quality and to protect client rights. Clients may be involved in identifying, documenting, and exposing avoidable inequities and discrimination.

Working at the Neighborhood and Community Levels

Helping clients will often require working on multiple system levels including the neighborhood, community, and service system (DeFilippis & Saegert, 2008; Gutierrez et al., 2005; Hardina, 2002). (See also discussion of preventative and integrated systems in chapter 21.) Social workers have little control over political and economic factors related to many problems clients confront such as homelessness, lack of medical care, poor housing, low-quality education, and unemployment. Health problems such as poor water and nutrition result in millions of avoidable illnesses each year. Health disparities are widely acknowledged but often ignored in terms of taking active steps to minimize them (e.g., see Edwards & Ruggiero, 2011; Marmot, 2011; Zarocostas, 2007). This does not mean that social workers can have no influence over these conditions. They can write to legislators in support of proposed bills, form coalitions of like-minded people to lobby for a change, empower clients to be their own advocates, and seek changes in policies, procedures, and programs. A contextual-constructional approach to solving problems is as useful here as it is when working with individuals and families (e.g., see chapters 12 and 13). Social workers can help clients to organize to confront the many forms of oppression and discrimination in society including state crime (Chambliss, Michalowkski, & Kramer, 2010) exploitation (e.g., child labor), marginalization, violence, and lack of power. Enhancing social justice is a key value in social work. Only by creating social movements and alliances may the less powerful be able to overcome the common tactic of "divide and conquer." (See discussion of Webster's views in chapter 6.)

Neighborhood types described by Warren & Warren (1977) vary from anomic neighborhoods in which there is an absence of a shared value system to integral neighborhoods in which there is a high potential for problem solving. Fisher (1994) describes three approaches to neighborhood organizing: social welfare, political activism, and neighborhood maintenance. In the first, social workers help residents increase access to services via means such as coalition building and lobbying. The term "community" is a complex one, especially in this age of globalization (see Pyles, 2009). A *community* can be defined as that combination of social units and systems that perform the major social functions that meet residents' local needs. Important functions include support, social control, socialization, social participation, and production, distribution, and consumption related to food, shelter, transportation, medical care, sanitation, and recreation.

Rothman (2001) suggests three models of community organization. Community development stresses self-help and enhancing community capacity via a range of participatory actions on the part of many individuals and groups. A social planning model emphasizes problem solving regarding community concerns via public policies and programs. Social action emphasizes the redistribution of power and increasing access to resources for marginalized groups. Social action has the goal of shifting power relationships and resources. Models differ on dimensions such as: (1) assumptions about community structure and problem definitions; (2) basic change strategy; (3) change tactics and techniques; (4) key practitioner roles; (5) medium of change; (6) orientation toward power structures; (7) boundary definition of the community–client system; (8) assumptions about interests of community groups; (9) view of client population; and (10) conception of client roles (see Rothman, Erlich, & Tropman, 2008). Some emphasize consensus. In others, disagreement and conflict are expected and may even be encouraged (e.g., Hardcastle, Powers, & Wenocur, 2004; Kahn, 2003; Netting, Kettner, McMurtry, & Thomas, 2012). Many initiatives are a blend of all three models. Pyles (2009) suggests a progressive community organizing spectrum ranging from transformational to utilitarian (p. 62). Progressive organizing frameworks attend to race, class, and gender disparities (engage in cultural critiques), frame issues in the language of those most affected, and have a preference for consensus-oriented decision making (Pyles, 2009, p. 72). The satisfactions of helping community residents can be rich. "I don't think anything equals the feeling you get in seeing people take real control of their lives, which grass-roots organizing allows for," says Irma Rodrigues, social worker and past associate director of the multiservice Forest Hills Community House in New York City (Hiratsuka, 1990).

Skills in networking and coalition building may be needed to help clients attain resources. Change efforts at the local level may be directed toward city or county officials, planning commissioners, school boards, law enforcement agencies, local court systems, and/or community organizations. Fawcett, Mathews, and Fletcher (1980) suggest that the following service characteristics enhance neighborhood and community influence:

- Inexpensive
- Effective
- Decentralized
- Flexible
- Sustainable
- Simple
- Compatible with existing customs, beliefs, and values

Vested interests in maintaining the status quo, as well as funding needs and patterns, may limit options. The complex nature of interventions involved in community-based change efforts poses a challenge for evaluation of outcomes. One approach has been to gain participants' input regarding desired changes in a community to identify early, intermediate, and desired outcomes together with related benchmarks. These are then tracked. (See discussions of "theory of change evaluation," Connell, Kubisch, Schorr, & Weiss, 1995.) Randomized controlled trials have been carried out. For example, Moving to Opportunity (MTO) was a randomized experiment carried out in five cities to explore whether public housing outcomes could be enhanced by enabling residents to relocate to a low-poverty census tract (see Orr, Feins, Jacob, Beechcroft, Sanbonmatsu, Katz, et al., 2003).

Community Development

Community development emphasizes self-help and voluntary cooperation to achieve valued goals. Key helping roles include enabler, coordinator, and supporter of problem-solving skills. Citizens are viewed as participants in a shared problem-solving process. A collection of community groups may seek help. Identifying shared concerns may be a first step. Involving community members in all steps along the way will help to mobilize residents and ensure that their preferences are considered. Goals, such as preserving neighborhoods, removing tax assessments, increasing safety, and decreasing crime, have been pursued through neighborhood block organizations (Chavis &

Wandersman, 1990; Fisher, 1994; Prestby, Wandersman, Florin, Rich, & Chavis, 1990).

To empower residents we should give them more than a "feeling" that they are empowered. We should help them to increase the influence they have over decisions that affect the quality of their lives drawing on literature in social work, as well as other fields such as community psychology. Examples include teaching community board members to speak effectively at board meetings (Briscoe, Hoffman, & Bailey, 1975), helping people decide on agendas (Seekins & Fawcett, 1987), enhancing advocacy skills of people with physical disabilities (Balcazar et al., 1994; Balcazar, Seekins, Fawcett, & Hopkins, 1990; Fawcett et al., 1994), involving community residents in identifying community needs (Schriner & Fawcett, 1988), enhancing leadership skills (Seekins, Mathews, & Fawcett, 1984), helping community members to disseminate information to funding sources resulting in additional money for valued services (Seekins & Fawcett, 1987), lowering utility rates (Seekins, Maynard-Moody, & Fawcett, 1987), and extending community control of new methods through study circles (Fawcett, Seekins, Whang, Muiu, & Suarez de Balcazar, 1984). For a review of collaborative partnerships for improving community health, see Roussos and Fawcett 2000; Chaskin et al., 2009.

Minkler views empowerment as operating on two levels in community organization. First, people may gain increased social support and sense of control, which may enhance personal confidence, coping capacity, and certain benefits (e.g., access to health care). Second, a community may become more effective in participating in shared efforts to gain valued outcomes (e.g., see Minkler, 2005; Minkler & Wallerstein, 2008). Self-directed change and resources are seen as important in their own right. Clients are integrally involved in evaluation (see Exhibit 27.6). Paulo Freire (1973) emphasized involving community members in developing their own programs for learning and changing oppressive conditions. Potential for empowering clients will be influenced by: (1) knowledge of problems and possible solutions; (2) skill in presenting issues, leading groups, and using related strategies; (3) degree of influence over consequences for key actors in the system; and (4) environmental and structural variables such as access to agendas of meetings of elected officials. Social movements create alliance of individuals in many locations to promote change and equal rights (Annetts, Law, McNeish, & Mooney, 2009). (See also description of client organizations in other sources.) Community development approaches differ in terms of the extent to which they focus on asset development—help residents to take advantage of local assets, for example, by identifying them and organizing them to pursue shared goals. The traditional development model emphasizes help from outside the community. Pyles (2009) suggests that the asset approach shifts the focus from taking back power emphasized by Alinsky (1971) to helping residents recognize their own power. (See also Green & Haines, 2011.)

Understanding Communities and Neighborhoods

Just as it may be impossible to understand an individual's environment and how he or she influences it and in turn is influenced by it without seeing for yourself, it may be impossible to understand a neighborhood or community and how residents influence it and are influenced by it without observing this yourself and gaining views of residents (Astor, Meyer, & Pitner, 1999; Welsh, 2000). The fields of community psychology (Moritsugu, Wong, & Duffy, 2010), environmental psychology (Bell, Greene, Fisher, & Baum, 2006; Bechtel & Churchman, 2006), and community organization (see previous citations) provide a rich source of

---

EXHIBIT 27.6

Differences Between Conventional Evaluation and Participatory Evaluation

	Conventional evaluation	Participatory evaluation
Who	External experts.	Community, project staff, expert as facilitator.
What	Predetermined indicators of success, primarily cost and health outcomes or gains.	People identify their own indicators of success, which may include health outcomes and gains.
How	Focus on "scientific objectivity" distancing evaluators from other participants, uniform, complex procedures; delayed, limited access to results.	Self-evaluation; simple methods adapted to local culture; open, immediate sharing of results through local involvement in evaluation processes.
When	Usually completion; sometimes also midterm.	Merging of monitoring and evaluation; hence, frequent small-scale evaluations.
Why	Accountability, usually summative, to determine if funding continues.	To empower local people to initiate, control, and take corrective action.

Source: Adapted from PROWWESS/United Nations Development Program, 1990. Minkler & Wallerstein (2008), p. 203.

information about neighborhoods and communities, including how to accurately describe and understand them. Guidelines for assessing communities are suggested in Exhibit 27.7.

Advances in technology such as geographic information systems permitt more informed measurements of important community characteristics such as distance from services or jobs. Spatial data analysis programs for understanding geographical distribution of problems may be available but not used (e.g., Freisthler, Lery, Grunewald, & Chow, 2006). This may reveal inequities in use of urban space (Burton et al., 2011;

EXHIBIT 27.7

Framework for Assessing Communities

A. COMMUNITY BOUNDARIES AND DEMOGRAPHIC CHARACTERISTICS

- What are the geographical boundaries of relevance?
- Describe groups that live in the community and their demographic profiles (e.g., economic, gender, age, ability, racial, and ethnic).
- Identify neighborhoods in the community and describe how people in each influence each other (if they do).
- Describe housing and ratio of industrial to residential areas.
- To what extent do jurisdictional boundaries of health and human service programs match that of the community?

B. DOMINANT VALUES

- What cultural values, traditions, or beliefs are important to different community groups?
- Which ones are generally shared?
- What value and style conflicts exist?

C. PROFILE OF RESOURCES/NEEDS

- Describe existing community agencies and volunteer groups that provide services. What services do they provide to which residents?
- What are the primary sources of funding for services?
- Are there strong indigenous leaders within the community?
- What stores are available/needed?
- What police protection is available/needed?
- What transportation services are available/needed?
- What health services are available/needed?
- What recreational resources are available/needed?
- What is the quality of schools?

D. PROFILE OF PROBLEMS

- Describe problems that affect residents (including frequency and variety, percentage of residents affected by each).
- Are some subgroups affected more than others?
- What contingencies influence each problem of concern?
- What kind of information is available concerning social problems, how accurate is it, and how is it used in the community?
- Who collects the data, and is this an ongoing process?
- What are options to better track problems and their frequency?
- Are there barriers that interfere with residents becoming integrated into the community?
- What forms of discrimination are common?

E. SERVICE DELIVERY

- How is resource distribution influenced by neighborhood and community characteristics?
- How is resource distribution influenced by extracommunity characteristics?
- What potential exists to organize residents to advocate for changes they value?
- What service programs are needed?
- What barriers exist to organizing residents to advocate for changes they value?

Source: Adapted from F. E. Netting, P. M. Kettner, & S. L. McMurty (1993). *Social work macro practice* (pp. 91–92). New York: Longman.

Sutton & Kemp, 2011). Increased attention has been given to enhancing the social capital of disadvantaged residents (e.g., see Baron, Field, & Schuller, 2002). Efforts to develop quality of life indicators suggest a wide range including standard of living, housing, economic development, health, safety, the built and natural environments, social connectedness, civil and political rights, knowledge and skills available for effective participation in society and the people themselves and how they are changing (Jamieson, 2004).

Conducting needs assessment is an important practice skill. Questions include: What are the needs in a community? Who should be involved in identifying them? What criteria should be used to identify them? You could: (1) compare what exists with an expert's standard; (2) ask residents what they want (i.e., perceived need); (3) determine service use (expressed need); or (4) determine the gap between those who use a service and similar others who do not. Each method has advantages and disadvantages in relation to accuracy (Bradshaw, 1972; Rossi, Lipsey, & Freeman, 2007). Counting the number of people who need a given kind of service may be useful in planning services. Some efforts involve community residents at all stages of data collection. For example, Sarri and Sarri (1992) involved youth in low-income neighborhoods in Detroit in gathering data about community needs.

Schriner and Fawcett (1988) developed a community concern report method that involved all residents in completing a survey about community needs. Involving residents is consistent with the philosophy and tradition of empowerment. It emphasizes influence by citizens in contrast to control by experts (Rappaport, 1987). First, items were identified that related core human values to the basic functions of community: (1) freedom; (2) general welfare; (3) dignity or self-esteem; (4) justice; and (5) security or survival. These values were placed in relationship with 18 community functions and institutions including local government, citizen participation, community services, education, and employment opportunities. For example, the value of security was related to the community function of entertainment and recreation in the survey item "Community parks and recreation areas are safe."

The value of dignity or self-esteem was related to the function of local government in the item "The individual is treated with respect by local government officials." Items were added, modified, or deleted based on a search of the community development literature and extensive interviews with approximately 25 community leaders, city government officials, and other residents commonly recognized as experts in one or another aspect of community functioning (pp. 307–308). Community representatives developed a 30-item survey based on items identified. This survey was then given to all community residents. For each item, respondents indicated how important it was and how satisfied they were. Strengths identified included the following:

1. Good fire protection (90% satisfied; 97% important).

2. Availability of ambulance service (85% satisfied; 97% important).

3. Far East Lawrence Improvement Association involvement in community improvement (83% satisfied; 96% important).

4. Overall quality of the neighborhood (78% satisfied; 96% important).

5. Safety of community (70% satisfied; 95% important).

6. Availability of recreational facilities for children (66% satisfied; 84% important).

Problems identified included the following:

1. Availability of an affordable grocery store (22% satisfied; 85% important).

2. Well-managed bus or transit system (27% satisfied; 88% important).

3. Adequate dog control in the neighborhood (29% satisfied; 88% important).

4. New homes on lots of adequate size (36% satisfied; 84% important).

5. Enforcement of speeding and muffler regulations (38% satisfied; 88% important).

6. People care for the appearance of their homes (62% satisfied; 94% important).

This information provided the basis for informed selection of objectives.

Organizing and Sharing Information

After you collect information about community needs, a next step is to organize and disseminate it. Education about community needs can be empowering, as eloquently argued by Paulo Freire (1973) in his concept of "education for critical consciousness." This will require listening to others, understanding issues, and critical discussion. Be sure to consider your audience. Some will be allies. Others include the uninvolved and ambivalent and active opponents. Questions suggested by Richan (2006) include the following:

1. Are you dealing with one audience or several? If the latter, are some more important to reach than others?

2. What concerns are uppermost in members' minds? It is these concerns you want to tap into right at the beginning.

3. What do members know about the topic, and what do they presume in advance? What they know is what you build upon to further understanding. What they presume may be a barrier to further learning.

4. How do they feel about the subject? If the subject involves a particular risk population, are members of the

audience positively disposed toward that population? If a government program, is the audience inclined to favor such a role of government? Richan notes that research is particularly important here because of your own tendency to stereotype audience reactions.

5. How do they feel about you or people like you? You have an identity: age, sex, race, ethnicity, class, religion, education, and occupation, even height and weight. It will influence how your message is received.

6. How do you feel about people like them? Honest answers only.

You could prepare a problem/policy analysis that describes problems and related factors, identifies assumptions, clarifies terms and concepts, and isolates key issues that need to be resolved.

1. A clear description of the problem and related hoped-for outcomes and affected groups.

2. A description of different views of the concern based on related research.

3. A description of public and private programs concerned with the problem and their track record of success in addressing the concern.

4. Possible options for attaining hoped-for outcomes based on best available research.

5. Estimated costs and impacts of current programs and of other options.

6. Objectives that might be met by action designed to achieve valued outcomes.

7. Criteria that might be used to track progress.

8. Description of obstacles.

9. A description of additional study and analysis needed and an estimate of the cost and duration.

Media Outreach

Distributing information via Internet web sites, twitter, texting, blogs, newspapers, television, and radio are other ways to bring problems and possible remedies to the attention of a wider audience—to educate and to encourage action among concerned people. (See also later section on social action).

Enhancing Social Support

Enriching social support systems may be needed to help clients to attain and maintain hoped-for outcomes (e.g., see Koegel, Koegel, & Dunlap, 2004). Take advantage of natural support systems (see chapter 19). New social media technologies provide new opportunities to create support networks. We can draw on past research to discover promising uses of these new resources. Chat rooms provide an Internet source of support. Fawcett and his colleagues (1976) developed a low-cost community education system to increase self-help and mutual assistance skills among residents in low-income communities (see also Mathews & Fawcett, 1977). Skill areas included: how to handle legal aid referrals and how to handle emergency medical requests. They designed learning units and trained low-income residents who worked at a neighborhood service center to administer standardized learning units to their peers. This program was effective in training low-income community residents to serve as proctors for a community education system. Use of social support development groups has a long history. For example, Gottlieb and Todd (1979) provided information about social support, developed network maps of relationships, and discussed social support issues. D'Augelli (1989) developed a helping community for lesbians and gay men. (See also Points of Contact: LGBT Advocacy and Support Agencies, 2007.) (For other sources, see Brown & Wituk, 2010; Gitterman & Shulman, 2005; Minkler & Wallerstein, 2008).

Residents may be reluctant to participate in groups designed to enhance social support. Meredith Minkler (1985, 1992) used an innovative indirect approach to increasing social support and developing collective problem-solving groups. Elderly residents of single-room occupancy hotels were offered blood pressure screenings, coffee, and refreshments in the hotel lobby. The interactions that occurred around the check station resulted in forming an informal discussion group. Seven additional groups were created in other inner-city hotels. Environmental approaches to prevention and habilitation, such as building networks via shared activities and restructuring social settings, are often ignored. Rural indigenous helpers including ministers, housewives, hairdressers, merchants, teachers, and local service workers were involved in the Community Helpers Project (D'Augelli, Vallance, Danish, Young, & Gerdes, 1981) in which participants acquired: (1) helping skills (e.g., nonverbal attending); (2) life development skills (e.g., decision making); and (3) crisis resolution skills (e.g., assessing precipitating factors and developing a problem-solving strategy). Following training, pairs of trainers co-lead small group sessions for local residents. Guidelines for exploring opportunities to enhance positive social exchanges are suggested in Exhibit 27.8. (See also texts on rural social work.)

Neighbors may provide resources and support. The advantages of help from neighbors over professional help are their concrete, practical, experience-based, commonsense-oriented, spontaneous, and caring aspects (Bulmer, 1986, p. 43). Care must be taken to augment these aspects of help among neighbors, not train them out. Encouraging positive links with neighbors and enhancing social skills for meeting people and making friends may decrease social isolation that is associated with child maltreatment. You could help neighborhood residents to design a proactive neighboring program in which behaviors are encouraged that may prevent future problems.

Neighboring potential is related to unique characteristics of each neighborhood (who lives there, the physical arrangements, stores (e.g., their variety), the daily hassles and crises that affect social interactions, and political and economic factors related to these events). Programs designed to increase helpful neighboring behaviors should be based on a contextual assessment. This may include identification of behaviors neighbors value and the circumstances in which residents can offer them with positive results, as well as identification of behaviors and events that annoy neighbors and interfere with well-being. This provides information about the actual and potential social relationships among individuals in a neighborhood. Obstacles to a proactive stance toward neighboring include ambivalence about offering, asking for, and receiving help; misunderstanding of different cultures; and limited resources. The greater the diversity of the community, the more difficult it may be to discover common interests and norms that transcend differences. Care must be taken not to overburden already stressed families. Accurate understanding of the experience of clients is vital.

Limits to Community Development

Limits to community development include need for changes at higher levels. Unless residents have links with people outside their neighborhood and community and unless these individuals have links to influential city and national political groups, little

may be gained as illustrated by Jane Jacobs (1992). Communities may be so impoverished that residents have no cushion of time or energy to devote to improving community conditions. Profit-making concerns of corporations often assume precedence over local community interests resulting in environmental injustices such as locating polluting facilities in or near poor communities (Pellow & Bruile, 2007). Corporate headquarters are now often located far away, perhaps even in another country. Administrative staff may be moved in and out of communities, decreasing opportunities for businesspeople to take an ongoing leadership role in addressing community problems.

Professional involvement in volunteer programs may have negative effects (Wolf, 1985). Policy makers could view increased helping among neighbors as an excuse to make cuts in statutory service programs. A focus on self-help and social support may encourage "blaming the victim." Residents themselves may be active participants in their own oppression requiring a consciousness raising intervention to solve problems (Freire, 1973). Indeed retrenchment of social services provided by state and federal government is often rationalized as returning help for others to the community where "it belongs" (e.g., see Handler & Hasenfeld, 2007). Funds available will limit options. Use the contingency diagrams in Exhibits 7.2 and 7.4 to explore options (see also Exhibit 27.8).

EXHIBIT 27.8

Describing the Ecology of Social Opportunities

A. *Settings that provide opportunities for positive social exchanges*

1. Their nature, variety, and rate of availability.

2. Kinds of individual who participate including available models.

3. Positive social consequences available, their schedule, and the probability of maximizing positive outcomes given needed skills.

4. Negative social consequences likely and their schedule given high/moderate/low skill levels (e.g., lack of positive outcomes, aversive outcomes).

5. Knowledge and skills required to obtain valued social outcomes in each setting.

6. How often each can be sampled with positive effects and considering competing activities (e.g., work, sleep, child care).

7. Current obstacles to taking advantage of opportunities.

   a. interfering responses such as social anxiety, aggression

   b. lack of social skills

   c. lack of self-management skills

   d. lack of transportation, money

   e. competing contingencies (work, child care)

   f. cultural norms/taboos

   g. competing cultural contingencies (to make money rather than provide social opportunities for citizens)

B. *Settings that could be created* (same questions as above).

C. *Obstacles to both A and B that could be removed and plan for doing so* (e.g., lack of skills, social anxiety, lack of correct information)

Social Planning and Program Development

Social workers plan and evaluate programs and analyze policies. Weissman, Epstein, and Savage (1987) view program developer as one of ten key social work roles. New programs may be developed to meet unmet needs or to overcome bureaucratic obstacles. Considerable attention has been given to evaluating supported employment programs (e.g., Heffernan & Pilkington, 2011; Mueser et al., 2004). Developmental planning programs related to a certain problem/population may be pursued over many years as in Jack Rothman's (1991) work with runaway youth and the research of Edwin Thomas and his colleagues with partners of substance abusers (e.g., see, Thomas & Ager, 1993). Unlike the community development model in which clients are involved as active participants in all stages, here they are viewed as consumers or recipients of services. Key helper roles include fact gatherer, analyst, and implementer. Planning phases include analysis, design of programs, implementation, and evaluation. Program development steps include the following:

1. Describe the problem and translate it into what clients need.

2. Marshal support for program development.

3. Allocate responsibilities to a board or advisory council.

4. Describe the purpose (or overall goal) of the program.

5. Identify clear subgoals or objectives.

6. Carry out a feasibility study.

7. Seek needed financial resources.

8. Describe how the program will provide services.

9. Get the program going.

10. Plan how services will be effectively provided on an ongoing basis (Hasenfeld, 1987).

Criteria to consider when reviewing options include cost, employee requirements, facilitating and competing contingencies, needed facilities and equipment, and anticipated support of goals by other agencies and the community (Clauss-Ehlers & Weist, 2004).

Community-Based Social Action

Mondros and Wilson (1994) describe three models of social action organizations—groups formed to gain power: (1) grassroots; (2) lobbying; and (3) mobilizing. (See also Alinsky, 1971.) Community-based social action programs usually address specific issues and populations such as providing services to rape victims, the homeless, or runaway youths (Sen, 2003). Clients are viewed as coparticipants. Kinds of groups that engage in social action include the following:

- Pressure groups that seek to advance a particular legislative issue.

- Citizen participation groups designed to influence policies and actions.

- Citizen action groups (e.g., welfare rights groups).

- Community groups that want to improve local or personal conditions.

- Social movements (groups that seek relatively large-scale changes).

- Improvement associations (e.g., League of Women Voters, Sierra Club). (Zander, 1990)

Questions of concern include:

- What do we think should be changed? How?

- How should we organize ourselves? Who will do what?

- Who should we approach for help?

- How shall we try to convince these people to develop this innovation?

- What methods should we use? Why?

- How can we maximize the likelihood of success?

- How can we get ready to take action and keep up our morale? (Zander, 1990, p. 2)

Agencies, professionals, and/or community members may acquire expertise in specific issues and form coalitions with other organizations and agencies that share concerns. They may participate in both local and national voter registration drives and endorse and support candidates viewed as sympathetic to their interests. Consider the success of moveon.org. An example of successful social action can be seen in Exhibit 27.9.

Social action includes a consciousness-raising goal (increasing awareness of problems, related factors, and what could be done to alter or prevent them). In *Pedagogy of the Oppressed*, Freire (1996) emphasized the role of expanding awareness of oppression via problem-posing education:

A deepened consciousness of their situation leads men to apprehend that situation as an historical reality susceptible of transformation. Resignation gives way to the drive for transformation and inquiry, over which men feel themselves in control. If men, as historical beings necessarily engaged with other men in a movement of inquiry, did not control that movement, it would be (and is) a violation of men's humanity. Any situation in which some men prevent others

---

EXHIBIT 27.9

Public Efforts Make a Difference: DES

BACKGROUND

DES (diethylstilbestrol) was hailed as a great achievement offering enormous practical value in preventing miscarriages, facilitating growth in cattle, treating problems of menopause, acne, gonorrhea in children, and certain types of cancer. Early on, research raised concerns about carcinogenic effects of DES. Early results showed "the first known human occurrences of transplacental carcinogenesis—the development of cancer in offspring due to exposure in utero to a substance that crossed the mother's placenta." The following quote illustrates the role of social action groups in informing people about the dangers of DES.

The origins of DES Action go back to 1974, when Pat Cody and a few other women in Berkeley, California, dismayed at the continuing lack of information and resources for DES victims, decided that something had to be done. They formed a group to work on the problem and developed an informational pamphlet. This pamphlet circulated widely through informal networks and as the information spread, so did concern and commitment. By 1978, at least five other DES groups had formed around the country. They agreed to establish a national network, with a common name and common objectives. Their motto: "Don't Mourn, Organize!!!"

This motto could hardly have been more apt. By 1987, there were over sixty DES Action groups around the country and throughout the world. Their activities have been manifold, ranging from public and professional education, to the development of technical resources such as audiovisual materials and physician referral lists. Two national DES newsletters provide current information on medical, legal, and legislative developments. Largely as a result of lobbying by DES groups, more than fourteen states have considered or passed bills or resolutions dealing with DES, and at least three (New York, California, Illinois) also appropriated funds. One of the most effective laws was New York's, passed in 1978, which set up special DES-screening centers around the state and a DES registry for research and follow-up. An intensive media campaign mandated by the N.Y. legislation almost doubled public awareness of DES in the state.

DES advocates have been active nationally as well, testifying at various congressional hearings. DES Action lobbyists were instrumental in getting HEW to form federal task forces on DES in 1978, and again in 1985. Letters from local DES Action groups helped convince Congress to declare a "National DES Awareness Week" in 1985. The efforts of DES Action may also have helped sensitize judges to the special legal problems of DES victims. Starting with the *Sindell* decision in California [Dutton, chapter 8], a number of courts have allowed DES daughters to sue major DES manufacturers without having to identify the specific brand that caused the injury—in effect, shifting the burden of proof from the victim to the manufacturer. In California, several industry-sponsored attempts to overturn the *Sindell* ruling were defeated, and press coverage gave credit for these defeats to "DES victims," in particular the opposition of DES Action. In New York, six years of lobbying by DES Action finally led, in 1986, to the passage of a law adopting a three year "discovery rule" for filing DES lawsuits, thereby removing an important obstacle to recovery by DES victims.

A crucial factor in DES Action's success has been the intense commitment of the women involved, many of whom have been personally affected by DES. The consequences of DES exposure are frightening and potentially lethal. Ties to the women's health movement helped transform these personal fears into political action. Women's health activists, all too familiar with being marginal to mainstream medicine, financially threatening to the drug industry, and low priority for the federal government, have schooled DES advocates in the tactics of self-help through collective action, sharing resources and contacts. DES Action has also benefited greatly from the involvement of compassionate physicians. But it has been DES Action's ties to its local constituents that are its greatest source of strength. This community base has kept the organization publicly accountable while allowing it to flourish entirely outside any formal structure of government, academia, or industry. With this base, DES Action has shown growing numbers of women how to take political as well as personal control of their medical destinies.

Source: D. B. Dutton (1988). *Worse than the disease: Pitfalls of medical progress* (pp. 339–340). New York: Cambridge University Press. Reprinted with permission.

---

from engaging in the process of inquiry is one of violence. The means used are not important; to alienate men from their own decision-making is to change them into objects. (p. 57)

Alinsky (1971) viewed low-income communities as disenfranchised in comparison to those "with money and power." He emphasized enhancing the problem-solving skills and resources of a community, including fostering indigenous leadership.

Encouraging discomfort with the "status quo" was one method used to encourage participation. (See also Freire, 1973.) Nancy Amidei (1982) suggests the value of "truth squads." As she suggests, misinformation that goes unchallenged often becomes accepted.

Wild charges appear in newspapers, small and large, and are repeated by ill-informed people on radio talk shows. These charges get the stamp of truth when television news programs and newspapers present information inaccurately or in ways that reflect public prejudices...

We can do something to solve this problem.... [This] will require a conscious effort to set the record straight whenever misinformation about social programs or those who depend on them appears; it means joining with others to form "truth squads" of people who view winning a better understanding of social programs as part of their civic or professional responsibility.... Concerned people, armed with good information, need to divide up the media in their states and communities, and use information at their command to present a more accurate picture of public benefits and those who use them. (p. 38)

Transformative approaches focus on challenging practices that contribute to oppression; they engage in cultural critique including race, class, and gender analysis. Educational approaches may also be used in addition to a "Freirian problem-posing process, for example to help residents engage in dialogue about shared problems and their causes to generate potential action plans" (Minkler, 2005, p. 275). You may have to lobby, persuade, bargain, teach, inform, advise, and analyze formal and informal power structures (Ezell, 2005; Schneider & Lester, 2001). See, for example, the description of a grassroots campaign which lobbied successfully for a local ordinance protecting GLBT (gay/lesbian/bisexual/transgender) rights in Louisville (Grise-Owens, Vessels, & Owens, 2004). Mobilizing voters, forming coalitions, and gaining access to the media to educate or expose problems may be required. You will have to decide whether to rely on politicians and/or to create independent advocacy groups. Contingency analysis skills will help you to describe the "power ecology" in settings of interest (see chapters 7 and 25). Achieving change will often require involving many people at varied system levels. Schneider and Lester (2001) provide detailed guidelines for advocacy efforts, both client and cause. (See also Jansson, 2011.) Perils of community organizing suggested by Pyles (2009) include anger, fear, despair, and joy. Co-optation is a constant concern. Compatibility of interests between clients and professionals cannot be assumed.

Coalitions are of value not only in community work, but in seeking change in your own agency as well. Characteristics that weaken coalitions include elitism, hidden agendas, and processes that waste time. Characteristics that strengthen them include reminding members of the benefits of seeking shared goals. Resources needed include: (1) money; (2) energy; (3) facilities; (4) political legitimacy; (5) expertise and knowledge; and (6) political mobilization. Decision-making skills are also needed. Intermediate steps may include raising issues in a community and getting an issue on the formal agendas of policy-setting groups. You will have to decide whether to focus on a single issue such as voter registration or to pursue broader consciousness-raising efforts. Clearly describing goals and objectives and concentrating on those of greatest concern will focus efforts.

Influencing Legislation

Helping clients may require changing legislation. Legislators may have to be contacted and their support obtained. Changing legislation may require years of focused work involving different groups and individuals including civic, political, business, community, and religious leaders as illustrated by successful efforts to decrease discrimination and increase social justice for lesbian, gay, bisexual, and transgender individuals (e.g., Otis, 2004). Understanding the legislative process will help you to seek change in an effective manner. You can increase your impact by mobilizing concerned others. Involve interest groups that share your goals. Writing skills include drafting legislation and amendments, summarizing bills, and documenting need. You may establish web sites, prepare editorials for newspapers, letters of support/opposition, legislative reports, or press releases. Speaking skills include testifying at special hearings, in committees, and speaking to civic groups, as well as during informal exchanges. Draw on skills of individuals in local American Civil Liberty Union Associations. Developments in technology facilitate access to information. Types of useful Internet sites suggested by Rocha (2007) include resources for policy practice activities; sites for locating legislators at the national, state, and local levels; and policy analysis and watchdog organizations. (See also L'Abate & Kaiser, 2011.)

Economic and Social Development

Economic development is concerned with increasing access to gainful employment opportunities including self-employment (see, for example, Midgley & Conley, 2010). Social development goals (helping people to work collaboratively together) are often pursued at the same time (e.g., Chaskin, Brown, Venkatesh, & Vidal, 2009). Methods used include human capital development such as asset accumulation and investment, employment creation, and micro-enterprise in poor areas (Sherraden, McBride, & Beverly, 2010; Sherraden & Sherraden, 2007). Housing inequities are vital to consider (e.g., see Braubach, Jacobs, & Ormandy, 2011; Schwartz, 2010). Work is in nonstate organizations and local communities. Social development initiatives have changed over the years as societies have changed (e.g., toward industrialization) and are always in danger of being co-opted by those with power. There is a rich literature describing economic development projects in countries around the world, as well as in the United States. Some programs eliminate middlemen as in microlending programs (e.g., giving sewing machines to residents so they do not have to pay rent for them). (See also discussion of micro-insurance, Midgley, 2011.) Success will require expertise in identifying and developing employment-related skills and opportunities. We can draw on literature describing how to create and maintain jobs for people with various kinds of disabilities. Supported education is a route to employment for adults with psychiatric disabilities (Mowbray et al., 2005). Many core social work skills such as helping people to work collaboratively together to achieve mutually valued outcomes are needed for success.

Inattention to cultural differences may result in programs that are ineffective or harmful (e.g., Echanove & Srivastava, 2011; Kunkel, 1970). Moving Western technologies into non-Western countries may do more harm than good because of lack of attention to unique values (Biehl, Good, & Kleinman, 2007; Hook & Eagle, 2002). Gray (2010) argues that the transformative potential of social development designed to address inequalities, deprivation, and social exclusion is being co-opted by process of professionalization and neoliberal politics into mainstream social work. She argues that in this process it is losing its transformative, critical edge, and changing into a neoliberal, social investment approach that removes the responsibility of the government for the welfare of its residents. Reducing corruption that diverts aid from its intended use is a priority (e.g., see Transparency International). Meblum, Moene, and Torvik (2006) describe those who siphon off money for aid as parasites. Reducing avoidable miseries such as torture and famine may require addressing state crime (Chambliss, et al., 2010).

International Enterprises: Exposing and Minimizing Avoidable Suffering

International social work is a growing area (Negi & Furman, 2010; Tice & Long, 2009). (See also International Federation of Social Workers.) Different approaches to international social work include institutional, communitarian, and statist. Weisskopf (2011) suggests that today's globalization differs from past ones in many ways including the spread of information, for example via the Internet, and greater international competition. We are daily exposed to avoidable suffering of others both at home and in distant lands. Newspaper editorials bring attention to young children sold into prostitution by their parents (e.g., Kristoff, 2011a, 2011b). Migration and the constant wars in many countries contribute to basic needs for food and water, shelter, freedom from violence, and basic medical care (e.g., see Bhugra, Craig, & Bhui, 2010). Lack of access to basic needs, including being free of harm created by work (coal dust) and from tainted water occur in the United States, as well as other countries (e.g., see Sarnoff's (2009) discussion of Appalachia. The refugee problem continues to swell as do the effects of population growth. We live in an unequal world rife with various forms of discrimination and oppression that create avoidable suffering (e.g., see Agier, 2011; Centeno & Newman, 2010.)

Amnesty International has long had an interest in exposing and decreasing human rights violations. The European Union emphasizes human rights. The philosophy of practice described in chapter 1 emphasizes the importance of identifying, documenting, exposing, and advocating to minimize avoidable suffering. We should not depend on journalists to do this. Organizations like Amnesty International and MindFreedom

are international in scope. Here, too, technology has a vital role to play (e.g., see Ashford & Hall, 2011; Dartnell, 2006; Murphy, 2009).

Summary

Acquiring needed services for clients may require rearranging agency practices, programs, and policies. Knowledge about how organizations function, as well as effective communication skills, will be useful in seeking valued outcomes. Offering clients high quality services will require evidence-informed organizations that maximize knowledge flow at all levels including user-friendly ways to identify client complaints and use of this information to enhance service quality. Other requirements include informative, acceptable audit systems that provide information about the effectiveness of services offered and errors that occur and related causes, and selection of continuing education programs that contribute to helping clients. In an evidence-informed organization raising questions about the effectiveness of services is encouraged, as is use of evidentiary criteria for purchasing services.

Community efforts include both cooperative development efforts and conflictual social action. Here, too, as with individuals, education can be vital—helping residents to learn more about their concerns—their prevalence, causes, and potential remedies. Here, too, political skills and knowledge will be valuable in identifying competing interests of different actors and options. Contingency analysis skills will help you and your clients to identify leverage points at different system levels. Too seldom are jobs available to pay social workers to engage in the kind of community organization and social and economic development efforts needed to enhance clients' assets and independence. Local conditions are affected by global events and there has been increasing interest in international social work and learning from successful programs in developing countries. Advances in technology, such as smartphones and Internet access, provide powerful tools for those with little to seek more. It is a new world in this sense.

Reviewing Your Competencies

Reviewing Content Knowledge

1. You can describe agency characteristics that influence the quality of services clients receive and make feasible evidence-informed suggestions for changing them in positive directions.

2. You can accurately describe your agency culture.

3. You can describe causes and indicators of groupthink and suggest effective remedies for avoiding it.

4. You can describe different kinds of administrative decision-making styles and their advantages and disadvantages.

5. You can give examples of the influence of external funding sources and political interests on services agencies offer.

6. You can describe the philosophy and preferred technologies of your agency and implications for clients.

7. You can identify characteristics of teams that contribute to and detract from effective decision making.

8. You can accurately describe gaps between services offered by an agency and what should be used to achieve its goals.

9. You can draw an accurate diagram of the organizational structure of your agency.

10. You can draw an accurate diagram describing formal and informal communication channels in your agency.

11. You can draw an accurate diagram describing the relationships of your agency with other agencies and community groups that provide services to clients.

12. You can accurately describe both obstacles and facilitating factors related to proposed innovations in agency practices or programs or in a community.

13. You can accurately describe neighborhood and community characteristics that influence residents' quality of life.

14. You can identify organizations and individuals outside a community who can help to attain outcomes residents value.

15. You can describe valuable characteristics of coalitions.

16. You can describe the skills required of community organizers.

17. You can accurately describe community characteristics such as social, cultural, and economic capital that influence a community's success in collaborative efforts to seek shared goals.

18. You can accurately identify gaps in service systems that should be remedied and suggest evidence-informed ways to decrease them.

19. You can accurately describe contingencies related to problems such as lack of health care and sex trafficking of children including global influences.

20. You can identify useful web sites and other Internet resources that facilitate advocating for clients.

21. You can identify different kinds of advocacy.

Reviewing What You Do

1. You identify and implement helpful changes in group meetings that enhance their quality.

2. You prepare concise reports describing the effects of agency policies, programs, or practices and make sound, feasible recommendations based on your analysis.

3. You facilitate group discussions effectively (e.g., prompt behaviors that encourage critical discussion).

4. You prepare contingency diagrams describing factors that influence concerns of community residents.

5. You carry out accurate needs assessment of a community.

6. You prepare a feasible budget for an agency program.

7. You identify ways to provide more positive feedback to staff for valued behaviors.

8. You make effective presentations at community meetings (e.g., people listen to your presentation and consider your points of view/facts in making decisions).

9. You identify community residents who are most likely to be of help in pursuing desired changes.

10. You use an effective problem-solving process to resolve organizational and/or community conflicts.

11. You help others to use effective problem-solving processes to address concerns.

12. You accurately identify gaps between tools needed to facilitate evidence-informed practice and policies and what is used in your agency and suggest feasible ways to attain these.

13. You take advantage of on-line tools to facilitate valuable organizational, service system, and community changes.

14. You accurately identify gaps between current agency audit systems and what kind of audit is needed for evidence-based practice and policy and take steps to decrease gaps.

Reviewing Results

1. Improved relationships between staff and administrators.

2. Obstacles to effective service provision decrease.

3. Creation of clear staff performance standards and an efficient, accurate 360 degree feedback system for tracking and evaluating performance.

4. An agency shifts from an authoritarian decision-making style to a participatory, transparent, evidence-informed one.

5. A community successfully lobbies politicians for additional resources.

6. Community residents form a neighborhood block association.

7. Interagency linkages improve resulting in increased and earlier client access to services.

8. Community residents gain access to public school facilities for community meetings.

9. Minority group members participate more effectively at board meetings.

10. Community residents identify and prioritize needs.

11. Community members become effective fundraisers to pursue goals they value.

12. Clients become more proficient in using on-line tools for gaining resources.

13. Different ethnic groups work more collaboratively together to achieve shared goals.

14. Communities enhance their social and economic capital.

15. You accurately describe agency policy regarding mistakes and errors and design and implement an acceptable, effective method to identify errors and use them as opportunities to improve services.

16. Clients are involved as informed participants in decisions made, for example, via a client advisory group and client access to information regarding agency services (including their track record of success) on computers in waiting rooms.

Glossary

Advocacy: "The exclusive and mutual representation of a client(s) or a cause in a forum, attempting to systematically influence decision making in an unjust or unresponsive service system" (Schneider & Lester, 2001, p. 65).

Autocratic model: Reliance on power, authority, and obedience.

Boundary spanners: People with communication links both with people in their neighborhood (or agency or department), as well as with people outside (e.g., with people in other units and in the wider community).

Bureaucracy: Large, complex administrative systems operating with impersonal detachment from people.

Charisma: Leaders who have a great influence on their followers by force of their personal characteristics.

Clique: A group of people who are linked often by friendship.

Coalition: Temporary alliances among people to pursue a shared aim.

Coercive power: Based on fear and reliance on response cost, punishment, and negative reinforcement.

Cohesiveness: The extent to which people stick together, rely on each other, and desire to be a member of a group.

Collegial model: Reliance on teamwork to build employee responsibility.

Community empowerment: "Process of increasing control by groups over consequences that are important to their members and to others in the broader community" (Fawcett et al., 1984, p. 146) (e.g., forming a tenants' rights organization in a public housing project to obtain improvements in housing conditions).

Conflict: Disagreement over what goals to pursue and/or how to pursue them.

Conformity: Following what others do without independent thinking.

Consensus: Agreement on the part of most people of a group.

Consultive management: A management focus in which employees are encouraged to contribute ideas before decisions are made.

Credibility gap: Difference between what a person says and what he does.

Cultural distance: Degree of difference between two contingency systems.

Expert power: Influence based on a person's knowledge of and skills related to certain tasks/problems.

Grievance system: An established procedure for discussing complaints.

Informal organization: The pattern of social relationships that arise spontaneously as people associate with one another in an organization.

Legitimate power: Based on the authority of one individual to influence another (e.g., as given within an agreed-on social structure). Those in position to use legitimate power may also use coercive and/or reward power.

Management by objectives (MBO): A system in which managers and staff agree on clear employee objectives, as well as on the criteria used to assess accomplishment.

Mediator: An outside person who helps parties in a dispute to come to an agreement.

Mentor: Someone who serves as a role model to others (e.g., to give advice and model valuable behaviors).

Morale: Level of job satisfaction.

Neighborhood: People who live near each other and share certain common spaces.

Network: Linkage among a defined set of people. Networks differ in degree of connectedness and reciprocity.

Nominal group technique: A method to arrive at a group decision.

Normative (legitimate) power: Based on the belief in the right of others to control our behaviors.

Ombudsperson: An individual who mediates conflicts among people.

Organization: Roberts and Hunt (1991) define this as "A social invention for accomplishing tasks or goals" (p. 9).

Organizational climate: The atmosphere in an organization (e.g., happy/stressed, connected/isolated). Climate is influenced by organizational culture.

Organizational culture: Assumptions, beliefs, and values shared among members; kinds and patterns of contingencies in effect.

Organizational politics: Actions taken by staff to acquire and use power and other resources to attain desired outcomes.

Overmanning: A setting that has more people in it than it can accommodate.

Performance standards: Description of expected levels of knowledge, skills, and outcomes.

Position: A person's place in the social system.

Power: Influence over others.

Referent power: Influence based on admiration/respect.

Reward power: Influence based on positive reinforcement.

Role: A set of behaviors expected of an occupant of a position (e.g., supervisor).

Role ambiguity: Vague expectations concerning expected behaviors in a given position.

Role conflict: This may refer to competition among roles or differences in opinion about how a role is to be fulfilled.

Role models: Leaders who serve as examples for their followers.

Role perceptions: How people think they are supposed to act in their own roles and others should act in their roles.

Sanctions: Rewards and penalties that a group uses to persuade persons to conform to its norms.

Satisficing: Arriving at a solution that is acceptable but probably not optimal.

Sociogram: A diagram representing feelings among people in a group (e.g., who likes or dislikes whom).

Status: Rank or prestige accorded an individual (this may be achieved or ascribed).

Undermanning: Insufficient people to carry out essential program and maintenance tasks.

Utilitarian power: Power as a result of control over contingencies.

Values: Our view of the desirability of certain goals (psychological, social, or economic).

Source: Some items based on K. H. Roberts & D. M. Hunt (1991). *Organizational behavior* (p. 41). Boston: PWS-Kent. See also Newstrom (2011).

Part 10
The Long Run

Maintaining Skills and Staying Happy in Your Work

OVERVIEW   This chapter describes steps you can take to continue to enjoy your work and maintain effective skills. Viewing uncertainty and setbacks as learning opportunities will help you to continue to learn. Paying attention to the context of practice (e.g., the agency in which you work, your profession, and the society in which you and your clients live), you help you to avoid blaming either clients or yourself for limited options and to identify promising directions. You can avoid self-handicapping strategies, involve clients as informed participants, seek further educational opportunities to enhance your knowledge and skills, and help clients become effective advocates by taking advantage of the Internet via handheld computers and social media.

YOU WILL LEARN ABOUT

- Develop constructive skills for handling uncertainty

- Increase self-awareness

- Recognize the limits of the help that can be provided

- Pay attention to context

- Develop positive alternatives to dysfunctional reactions

- Be an activist

- Preventing burnout/job stress

- Learning as a journey

Some options for enjoying your work will benefit clients. Others will not, such as relying on questionable criteria to evaluate service outcomes and to select practices and policies and complaining without doing anything to alter disliked situations. Your philosophy of practice will influence your job satisfaction, as well as the services you provide (see chapter 1). The suggestions in this chapter should help you to increase your effectiveness and to maintain an identity as a social worker who advocates for clients. Many suggestions, such as questioning beliefs and responding to setbacks as learning opportunities, involve problem solving and critical thinking skills emphasized throughout this book.

Develop Constructive Skills for Handling Uncertainty

Your decisions will be made in the face of uncertainty about their likely effects. As one social worker said: "And how do we know we're right? That's the frightening bit—have I made the right decision? This is one of the things that tires you out" (Fineman, 1985, p. 70).

> In this job you never know whether you've done anything right—especially with kids. How can you decide that the decision you've made (albeit with other people) is the right one? You don't know until that child is grown up. The choices are more clear cut with the elderly—you can see the results when you put in a home help for an old person, or move an old person from a grotty house to a decent one. But with children and teenagers you just don't know. Maybe some initial improvement, and then it will go back. (Fineman, 1985, p. 70)

Only so much information can be gathered due to time constraints. Plans must be selected even though you and your clients have little information about their likely effectiveness. "Practitioners are asked to solve problems everyday that philosophers have argued about for the last two thousand years and will probably debate for the next two thousand. Inevitably, arbitrary lines have to be drawn and hard cases decided" (Dingwall, Eekelaar, & Murray, 1983, p. 244). Uncertainty breeds a temptation to deny it, perhaps fearing that recognizing it would stifle needed action. For example, child welfare workers may put off making decisions because of the risks associated with different options; they may ignore the consequences of not making timely decisions.

Use uncertainty as a cue to see if you can decrease it. For example, consult related research literature. Use a contextual assessment framework to understand client characteristics, circumstances, and options. Log on to the UK Database of Uncertainties about the Effects of Treatments (DUETS) occasionally to remind yourself about the uncertainties involved in helping clients. Track progress so that you and your clients can make timely decisions based on what you discover. Estimate your degree of confidence in your predictions. Making clear estimates and comparing them with results offers more precise feedback than vague estimates such as "I think it will be effective" and so may improve the accuracy of future predictions.

Increase Self-Awareness

There is a rich literature on self-deception that you can draw on to increase self-awareness. "Although our goal in belief formation is usually to believe the truth (or to have appropriate confidence), sometimes it would seem better to believe what is false" (Baron,

2000). Self-deception serves many goals. For example, deceiving yourself that you are doing well with your clients (when you are not) may serve a goal of feeling good and saving time and effort. We may convince ourselves that a claim is true despite evidence against it. The concept of self-deception suggests that we have two selves: the deceiver and the person deceived (Baron, 2000)

> If we want to believe that smoking is harmless, for example, we can make ourselves believe this by seeking evidence in favor of our belief and ignoring evidence against it. We must be sure to not take fully into account the fact that we have done these things, for, if we do, we will see that the evidence we use was as good as useless, "cooked" to order. It might as well have been made up. (pp. 63–64)

Such biased search can become a matter of habit so that we do not know that we behave this way. This suggests that self-deception "is almost necessary a part of poor thinking" (p. 64). The key task is to recognize poor thinking. White (1971) raises the question: "To what extent, if at all, is self-deception itself 'morally questionable'?" (p. 34). He suggests that the answer relates to what efforts a person has made to minimize self-deception. "A person can be fairly blamed if he makes little or no effort to recognize and counteract it." This seems to be a good guideline in relation to professionals. That is, if we assert that the services used in our agency are evidence-informed when research shows that this is not the case, and, when confronted with this information, we make no effort to look into the situation, White suggests that this is not being morally responsible. (See also discussion of callousness in chapter 27.) This view is compatible with professional codes of ethics—the requirement to draw on practice-related research and to be competent. However, competence is defined as matching standards of practice in a community; such standards may do little to protect clients from receipt of ineffective or harmful methods.

Recognize the Limits of the Help That Can Be Provided

You will not be able to help all the people you see. No one may be able to help clients attain some outcomes such as housing in a particular neighborhood. Policies, laws, or lack of resources may limit options. Literature, art, and music throughout the ages show that life is often not an easy place. Life brings suffering, as well as happiness. Young children die, the elderly linger on in physical discomfort, lovers leave and friends abandon us. People lose jobs through no fault of their own. Karl Popper has argued that trying to make people happy is not only futile, but results in imposing allegedly better policies on citizens, even if against their will.

Social workers cannot solve the world's problems. Yet often they promise to do so (e.g., remove poverty). The pursuit of utopian goals distracts us from working in many small ways to minimize avoidable suffering and may encourage a drift into dysfunctional reactions (see later discussion). You can do no more than give your best. Giving your best includes making informed decisions (e.g., using effective methods), helping clients use and expand their own resources, and taking whatever steps possible to improve service systems. Some of your efforts to redress inequities may not benefit today's clients but may help others in the future.

Pay Attention to Context

Professional practice is influenced by the context in which it occurs (e.g., see Charlton, 2010; Gambrill, 2012a). Taking occasional time-outs to reflect on the context of practice will help you to keep the larger picture in mind and resist the wearing down effect of difficult work environments and scarce resources. This contextual view will remind you to attend to the interrelationship between personal troubles such as ill health and environmental circumstance such as inadequate housing. (See, for example, Bakalar, 2011; Braubach, Jacobs, & Ormandy, 2011; Cushon et al., 2011; Preedy & Watson, 2010). Understanding the helping professions (how they develop, constraints on them) may encourage you to work toward changes in your professional organization that will improve services. Contingency analysis skills will help you to explore who benefits or loses from given policies, laws, programs, and practices. (See chapters 7, 12, and 25.) Ignoring political and economic influences may result in offering clients ineffective methods and inappropriately blaming yourself or your clients for lack of success and not taking steps to make changes that improve services.

Keeping the "big picture" in view will remind you that change can occur, and that it often takes effort and time. Consider Ignas Semmelweiss who around 1840 discovered that the death rate of mothers from childbed fever could be decreased from 25% to 2% if surgeons washed their hands before delivering babies (Sinclair, 1909). Not until the end of that century did the medical profession act on his recommendations. Women won the vote in the United States only in 1920. Slavery was declared illegal in the United States only in 1865. Only recently did the Equal Employment Opportunity Commission declare that employers cannot refuse to hire people with disabilities because of concerns about their effect on health insurance costs. We prepare the way, well or poorly, for the next generation of clients and social workers.

Develop Positive Alternatives to Dysfunctional Reactions

Work in many agencies requires learning how to deal constructively with difficult situations (see Exhibit 28.1). Often, there is a discrepancy between what is needed and what can be offered. Money may not be available for in-home services, requiring elderly clients to enter residential care. Many social workers who work in public agencies feel frustrated. Literature both current and past reflects such feelings.

> Nobody in the headquarters sees the pressure here; nobody wants to see it! They just don't seem to understand that we can't keep piling on more cases for social workers—they'll stop functioning. (Fineman, 1985, p. 74)

> It's so frustrating. At times I've taken action in the best interests of a client which has been blocked by bureaucratic action—or I've been making demands on the wrong budget at the wrong time. I give up in these circumstances. (Fineman, 1985, p. 73)

EXHIBIT 28.1

Options for Coping with Difficult Situations

Self-Handicapping Strategies	Constructive Strategies
• Become fatalistic. Complain without taking action together with others to pursue goals that help clients.	• Seek positive alternatives. Identify desired changes and how they could be attained, and take steps in that direction.
• Blame others/Blame yourself.	• Same as above.
• Do your job in a "routinized" uncaring manner.	• Recognize you are burned out and take constructive actions.
• Congratulate yourself on services offered even though few are provided or no one knows what is accomplished.	• Accurately evaluate progress and share findings with all stakeholders including clients.
• Claim you do not make decisions.	• Recognize the decisions you make, identify factors that limit options, and meet with others to see how these could be altered.
• Struggle on by yourself.	• Involve others in seeking outcomes that help clients; form coalitions.

When our skills and resources do not match the challenges we confront, we seek reasons. We may assume that what is must be (become fatalistic that nothing can be done to improve conditions). We may overestimate what we can achieve or have achieved. We may focus on concerns that are not of key importance to clients (e.g., recommend that a client participate in counseling even though this will not address problem-related environmental circumstances). We may overlook harming done in the name of helping. We may deny that we make decisions. We may accept excuses that help us to live with limitations, but do not help clients attain hoped-for outcomes. We may fall into quackery (see Exhibit 28.2).

Reasons given by social workers for limited success such as lack of resources and high caseloads often do reflect reality. Objectives may be difficult or impossible to attain. Excuses, like any other behavior, serve different functions, which at first may not be obvious. Even when resources are cut, reactions may be constructive or dysfunctional. Positive strategies include expanding volunteer services, seeking innovative models others have used to handle cuts and maintain service quality, exploring how resources could be shared, involving other interested parties in problem solving and lobbying to regain resources. So, when you offer an excuse ask: "Does this work for or against me and my clients?" "Does this increase or decrease the probability of providing needed services

and enjoying my work?" To the extent to which excuses relieve you from assuming undue responsibility for the welfare of your clients and encourage reasonable risk taking, they are helpful. They are self-handicapping if they reduce options for achieving goals (if they get in the way of recognizing obstacles that could be removed). They are dysfunctional when they interfere with offering effective services and avoiding harm and making changes that could enhance success and work satisfaction.

Be an Activist

An understanding of the big picture coupled with a genuine concern for the hardships clients confront will encourage advocacy to decrease these hardships. An activist stance can be taken at the agency level, as well as at other levels. Nattering (defined here as complaining with no intention to do anything about the situation) will not result in change. Simply complaining that "caseloads are too high" may forestall lobbying efforts to lower caseload size. A constructive way to handle discrepancies between services needed and those available is to provide whatever help you can to clients while taking steps to decrease mismatches (e.g., talk to other staff, bring them to the attention of administrators

---

EXHIBIT 28.2

Why Professionals Become Quacks

Quackery refers to promoting services known to be ineffective, or which are untested, for a profit. Given that social workers get paid for what they do whether they work in public agencies or are in private practice, they profit from their work. Why is it that some professionals start to act like quacks? In *Dubious Dentistry* (1990), William Jarvis suggests a number of reasons.

POSSIBLE REASONS

- *Boredom.* Daily work can become humdrum. Pseudoscientific ideas can be exciting.
- *Low self-esteem.* Social work is not the most highly regarded profession. Dissatisfaction with a limited scope of practice may encourage pursuit of grandiose goals and unwarranted claims of effectiveness.
- *Reality shock.* Social workers regularly see very troubling situations. This requires learning how to handle these. Some helpers are simply not up to it.
- *Belief encroachment.* Science is limited in dealing with problems that are possible to solve. This constraint may become burdensome and aims embraced such as helping people with religious questions.
- *The profit motive.* Quackery can be lucrative.
- *The Prophet motive.* Some clients experience uncertainty, doubt, and fear about the meaning and purpose of life. Others confront seemingly hopeless situations. The Prophet role offers awesome power. Egomania is commonly found among quacks. They enjoy the adulation and discipleship their pretense of superiority evokes. By promoting themselves they project superiority to their colleagues and to their professional community.
- *Psychopathic traits.* Glibness and superficial charm, grandiose sense of self-worth, lying, conning/manipulative behavior, lack of guilt, proneness to boredom, and lack of empathy.
- *The conversion phenomenon.* Some professionals who become quacks have experienced difficulties such as a practice failure, midlife crisis, divorce, or life-threatening illnesses.

Source: Based on William Jarvis (1990). *Dubious dentistry.* Loma Linda, CA: Loma Linda University.

and legislators, form a coalition of interested parties to pursue change, use social media to organize a protest). Social action may include conducting a needs assessment to document situations that require attention, writing to legislators advocating passage of a bill, exposing abuses in residential settings, volunteering time to help elect socially conscious representatives, participating in public hearings, or organizing a group to seek a specific change. Understanding how bills are developed, introduced, and guided through passage will help to demystify the legislative process. Both students and faculty can lobby for greater attention to be given to community organization and social development courses in schools of social work. You can push for course content about discriminatory practices based on sexual orientation, race, gender, ethnicity, age, ability, and class.

Be on the look out for opportunities to add to practice-related research of value to clients. Effective practice and sound research require many overlapping attitudes, skills, and knowledge. Data from individual clients can be collected in a series of AB designs related to a desired outcome, such as how to help clients find employment (see chapter 22). Take advantage of computers and smart phones to ease the burden of case recording, evaluating progress, and locating and storing helpful practice-related research findings.

Be a Life-Long Learner

If you want to maintain effective skills and upgrade your competencies, assume responsibility for this yourself. Arrange prompts and incentives that encourage valuable skills (see chapter 25). Take advantage of theory and research concerning how to maintain and enhance professional competencies. Seek support for knowledge, skills, and outcomes that contribute to success from colleagues and supervisors including routine coaching and feedback. If this is not possible in your agency, locate other professionals who share your values and goals and form a support/consultation group. Set up a journal club (Swift, 2004). You could meet monthly to share successes, seek options for handling setbacks, and discover new ways to help clients. Seek out systematic reviews of service effectiveness and rely on rigorous criteria to review claims (see chapter 11). Focus on constructing repertroies that contribute to well-being drawing on varied sources of information (e.g., Kamerman, Phipps, & Ben-Arieh, 2010).

You may become discouraged because you do not set clear goals or monitor progress. Evaluating outcomes in an ongoing manner will allow you and your clients to recognize and celebrate "small wins." Keep in mind that negative outcomes may not reflect poor decisions. Take advantage of visual representations of problems, options, and data (e.g., Venn diagrams, graphed data describing progress). If competencies drift downward, use your contingency analysis skills to find out how you can reverse this trend (see chapters 7 and 25). What prompts and consequences support valued skills? Are such skills punished? Are competing behaviors reinforced? How can you rearrange your environment to increase positive feedback for skills that

contribute to helping clients? Can prompts be arranged? Are necessary tools available? Critical thinking skills will help you to get out of loops and avoid "dead end accounts" that do not offer intervention knowledge.

Respond to setbacks as learning opportunities. We learn from our mistakes, as well as our successes. We learn by acting ("risking") and responding to the resulting feedback. This offers opportunities to discover what we understand and what we do not, what we can do and what we cannot, and what is effective and what is not. Experts have effective troubleshooting skills. You may not have time to correct a mistake at the time you make it. Review and rethinking may have to come later. At other times you can correct an error immediately. If you ask a confusing question, you could say, "Let me start again…" and restate the question. Take advantage of effective interpersonal skills to avoid social predicaments, encourage client participation, obtain needed resources, and negotiate differences of opinion.

Preventing Burnout/Job Stress

The term *burnout* refers to feelings of stress, boredom, depression, depersonalization, or fatigue related to work, as well as a sense of helplessness and hopelessness, among people who work with others (Maslach & Leiter, 2008; Schaufeli, Maslach, & Merek, 1993). There is a loss of concern for clients. Turnover rates are high in certain areas such as child welfare. Some social workers lose sight of why they chose social work as a career, such as wanting to help clients improve the quality of their lives. Depersonalization refers to a lack of feeling or callous or negative reactions toward clients; clients are treated in a detached, mechanical manner. Job stress and burnout contribute to poor quality services for clients and high job turnover. "Compassion fatigue" has received increasing attention.

Causes of burnout include personal, organizational, and social factors. Personal causes involve not getting enough sleep, ineffective planning and goal-setting skills, unrealistic expectations, and lack of assertion. Inflexibility and intolerance of ambiguity contribute to stress. Just as positive emotions encourage generosity toward others and contribute to effective problem solving, negative emotions have the opposite effect. (See chapter 8.) You may be overinvolved or underinvolved with your clients (Larson, 1993). Organizational factors related to burnout include unsupportive peer and supervisory relationships, high caseloads, limited supportive help, vague expectations, lack of positive feedback, and conflicting role demands. Societal factors include individual competitiveness and shrinking resources. Social workers usually work with clients who are distressed, perhaps due to injustice and even cruelty. To continue to care requires effective handling of what some have called the "vicarious trauma" that results from empathizing with people who are hurting.

You can take steps to prevent burnout even if you work in an agency that encourages it (e.g., form a support group to pursue valued changes). Viewing mistakes as learning opportunities, recognizing the limits of help you can provide, accepting the uncertain nature of decisions, and using methods that contribute to success will help. Burnout is less likely if you pursue clear, agreed-on objectives and evaluate progress. Use stress and dissatisfaction as cues to identify related causes. Perhaps you take your work home with you. Perhaps you have lost sight of the decisions you do make on the job and feel unnecessarily helpless. You may accept unreasonable assignments because you have difficulty refusing requests and take on excessive responsibility for your clients. (See chapter 16.) You may have to enhance your time management skills. You may blame yourself for limited resources rather than recognizing the role of social, political, and economic patterns.

Caring, Courage, and Critical Thinking: A Formidable Threesome

Placing clients' interests front and center will give you the courage and the reason to act on their behalf. Focusing on helping clients will also help to bring along others in a joint quest to do the right thing. What is best for clients? This question provides a light to find courage to raise important questions. Your critical thinking skills will provide a guide for questions to raise, such as "Is there any evidence that x helps clients?" "Are we overlooking some well-argued alternative?" "How can we just send this client to a psychiatrist for medication when she would benefit from counseling as well?" You may have to cultivate courage to raise questions that should be asked to discover options. (See chapter 5.). It takes courage, as well as empathy, to truly see others' miseries in the absence of immediate options to relieve them. Focusing on clients rather than on yourself or other staff will make it easier to raise these questions. Cultivating your curiosity should encourage you to raise important questions. Berlyne (1960) suggested that curiosity was a basic drive. This threesome—caring, courage, and critical thinking—will help you to avoid being bamboozled and in turn missing opportunities to help clients.

Learning as a Journey

Becoming a skilled social worker is like a journey with many potential sidetracks and pitfalls—a kind of social work dungeons and dragons. In spite of good intentions, many potential paths lie ahead besides your destination—to enjoy your work and offer high quality services to clients, a professional who not only believes that she helps clients, but really does. As with all journeys there will be detours and setbacks. One of the aims of this book is to encourage you to view mistakes and setbacks as inevitable and as learning opportunities. Setbacks and detours are quite different from dead ends. Dead ends refer to getting permanently sidetracked at a destination that you do not like

and did not plan on (although you may kid yourself that this is what you really wanted). For example, you may offer service in a routinized uncaring manner, blame clients for lack of success, or continue to rely on a practice framework that does not provide intervention knowledge. Propaganda in the helping professions abounds, as does a justification approach to knowledge (see chapter 4). Maintaining social bonds will be more important to many than discovering how to help clients and avoid harm. Authorities may punish those who raise probing questions. Courage and self-awareness and a focus on helping clients will provide sound guides.

Summary

The quality of becoming rather than of being characterizes a professional. This requires a commitment to enhance and maintain values, knowledge, and skills that maximize the likelihood of helping clients and avoiding harm. Responding to mistakes as learning opportunities and recognizing the limits of your ability to help as well as the uncertainty involved in everyday practice will help you to avoid the dissatisfaction and negative emotional reactions reflected in burnout. Avoiding self-handicapping excuses will also serve this end. Understanding how agencies and professional organizations function, as well as social, political, and economic causes of problems, will help you to identify constraints and options. Other steps you can take to maintain high quality service include evaluating your work with clients, selecting practice knowledge and skills based on what has been found to be effective, and focusing on clear outcomes that clients value. Developing a guiding philosophy of practice and reviewing this in times of stress and discouragement will help you to focus on valued goals. If you develop the skills discussed in this chapter, you will not allow your vision of the potential of practice to be limited by what "is."

Reviewing Your Competencies

Reviewing Content Knowledge

1. Identify steps you can take to decrease the uncertainty involved in your work.

2. Describe factors related to burnout and what you can do to avoid them.

3. Identify specific changes that could be made in your agency to increase your work satisfaction and the quality of service.

4. Identify self-handicapped excuses and suggest constructive alternatives.

5. Describe steps you can take to enhance and maintain valuable skills.

Reviewing What You Do

1. You welcome opportunities to examine the accuracy of your beliefs as shown in discussions with colleagues and clients (e.g., you seek constructive criticism).

2. Given an example of a setting in which staff experience burnout, you collect useful data and offer helpful recommendations.

3. You can help a colleague design methods to maintain valued skills.

Reviewing Results

1. You rate yourself high on work satisfaction and personal efficacy. This rating corresponds to actual help offered to clients as shown by relevant data from clients.

2. Clients, supervisors, and administrators give you high competency ratings.

3. Your practice skills increase as assessed by a review of methods used and goals attained which clients value.

4. Clients become more effective advocates for themselves and others.

References

Abbott, A. (1988). *The system of professions: An essay on the division of expert labor.* Chicago: University of Chicago Press.

Abbott, A. A. (2010). *Alcohol, tobacco and other drugs: Challenging myths, assessing theories, individualizing interventions* (2nd ed.). Washington, DC: National Association of Social Workers.

Abramovitz, M. (1988). *Regulating the lives of women: Social welfare policy from colonial times to the present.* Boston: South End Press.

Abramson, L. Y., Seligman, M. E. P., & Teasdale, J. D. (1978). Learned helplessness in humans: Critique and reformulation. *Journal of Abnormal Psychology, 87,* 49–74.

Ackerman, M. J. (2010). *Essentials of forensic psychological assessment.* Hoboken, NJ: John Wiley & Sons.

Adams, J. L. (1986). *Conceptual blockbusting: A guide to better ideas* (3rd ed.). Reading, MA: Addison-Wesley Publishing Co.

Addis, M. E., & Krasnow, A. D. (2000). A national survey of practicing psychologists' attitudes towards psychotherapy treatment manuals. *Journal of Consulting and Clinical Psychology, 68,* 331–339.

Agens, J. E. (2010). Chemical and physical restraint use with the older person. *BJMP,* March 3(1). Retrieved December 15, 2011.

Agier, M. (2011). *Managing the undesireables: Refugee camps and humanitarian government.* Malden, MA: Polity.

Aguilera, A. (2012). There's an App for that information technology applications for cognitive behavioral practitioners. *The Behavior Therapist, 35,* 645–673.

Alberti, R. E., & Emmons, M. L. (2008). *Your perfect right: Assertiveness and equality in your life and relationships* (9th ed.). Atascadero, CA: Impact.

Alberto, P. A., & Troutman, A. C. (1990). *Applied behavior analysis for teachers.* Columbus: Merrill (5th ed., 1999; 6th ed., 2002). (See also 8th ed., 2008.)

Albrecht, K. (1990). *Service within: Solving the middle management leadership crisis.* Homewood, IL: Business One Irwin.

Alderson, P., & Roberts, I. (2000). Should journals publish systematic reviews that find no evidence to guide practice? Examples from injury research. *BMJ, 32,* 376–377.

Alessi, G. (1988). Diagnosis diagnosed: A systemic reaction. *Professional School Psychology, 32,* 145–151.

Alexander, M. (2010). *The new Jim Crow laws: Mass incarceration in the age of colorblindness.* New York: New Press.

Alinsky, S. (1971). *Rules for radicals: A practical primer for realistic radicals.* New York: Random House.

Allan, G., Crow, G., & Hawker, S. (2011). *Stepfamilies*. New York: Palgrave.

Allan, J., Pease, B., & Briskman, L. (Eds.). (2010). *Critical social work*. Crows Next, N.S.W., Australia: Allen & Unwin.

Allday, E. (2011). Support for ambiguously gendered kids. *San Francisco Chronicle*, May 7, A1, A6.

Alter, C., & Egan, M. (1997). Logic modeling: A tool for teaching critical thinking in social work practice. *Journal of Social Work Education, 33*(1), 85–102.

Altheide, D. L. (2002). *Creating fear: News and the construction of crises*. New York: Aldine de Gruyter.

Altheide, D. L., & Johnson, J. M. (1980). *Bureaucratic propaganda*. Boston: Allyn & Bacon.

Altman, D. G. (2002). Poor-quality medical research: What can journals do? *Journal of the American Medical Association, 287*, 2765–2767.

American Psychiatric Association (2000). *Diagnostic and statistical manual of mental disorders* (4th ed.). Washington, DC: American Psychiatric Association.

Amidei, N. (1982). How to be an advocate in bad times. *Public Welfare, 40*(3), 37–42.

Anderson, J. A., McIntyre, J. S., Rotto, K. I., & Robertson, D. C. (2002). Developing and maintaining collaboration in systems of care for children and youths with emotional and behavioral disabilities and their families. *American Journal of Orthopsychiatry, 72*(4), 514–525.

Andronis, P. T., Layng, T. V., & Johnson, K. (1997). Workshop on systemic, non-linear, constructional approaches to behavior change. International conference of applied behavior analysis. Chicago, IL, May 1997.

Angell, M. (2004). *The truth about drug companies: How they deceive us and what to do about it*. New York: Random House.

Angell, M. (2009). Drug companies & doctors: A story of corruption. *New York Review of Books*, August 10, 1/15.

Angold, A. (2002). Diagnostic interviews with parents and children. In M. Rutter & E. Taylor (Eds.), *Child and adolescent psychiatry* (4th ed., pp. 32–51). Malden, MA: Blackwell.

Annetts, J., Law, A., McNeish, W., & Mooney, G. (2009). *Understanding social welfare movements*. Bristol: Policy Press.

Anthony, K., Nagel, D. M., & Goss, S. (Eds.) (2010). *The use of technology in mental health: applications, ethics and practice*. Springfield, IL: Charles C. Thomas.

Anthony, W. A., Cohen, M. R., & Farkas, J. R. (1990). *Psychiatric rehabilitation*. Boston Center for Psychiatric Rehabilitation, Boston University.

Antman, E. M., Lau, J., Kupelnick, B., Mosteller, F., & Chalmers, T. C. (1992). A comparison of results of meta-analyses of randomized controlled trials and recommendations of clinical experts: Treatments for myocardial infarction. *Journal of the American Medical Association, 268*(2), 240–248.

Antonuccio, D. O., Burns, D. D., & Danton, W. G. (2002). Antidepressants: A triumph of marketing over science. *Prevention & Treatment*, 5 (article 25) posted July 15, pp. 1–17.

Antony, M. M., & Stein, M. B. (2009). *Oxford handbook of anxiety and related disorders*. New York: Oxford University Press.

Appelbaum, P. S. (2007). Assessment of a patient's competence to consent to treatment. *New England Journal of Medicine, 357*, 1834–1840.

Arendt, H. (1958). *The human condition*. Chicago: University of Chicago Press.

Argyris, C., & Schön, D. A. (1996). *Organizational learning II: Theory, method, and practice*. Reading, MA: Addison Wesley.

Arkowitz, H., et al. (2008). *Motivational interviewing in the treatment of psychological problems*. New York: Guilford.

Arkowitz, H., Westra, H. A., Miller, W. R., & Rollnick, S. (Eds.) (2008). *Motivational interviewing in the treatment of psychological problems*. New York: Guilford.

Armstrong, J. C. (1980). Unintelligible management research and academic prestige. *Interfaces, 10*, 80–86.

Arnoult, L. H., & Anderson, C. A. (1988). Identifying and reducing causal reasoning biases in clinical practice. In D. C. Turk & P. Salovey (Eds.), *Reasoning, inference and judgment in clinical psychology* (pp. 209–232). New York: Free Press.

Arnold, J. E., Levine, A. G., & Patterson, G. R. (1975). Changes in sibling behavior following family intervention. *Journal of Consulting and Clinical Psychology, 43*, 683–688.

Aronson, J. K. (2003). Anecdotes as evidence: We need guidelines for reporting anecdotes of suspected adverse drug reactions. Editorial. *British Medical Journal, 326*, 1346.

Asch, S. E. (1956). Studies of independence and conformity: Minority of one against a unanimous majority. *Psychological Monographs, 70*(9), Whole No. 416.

Ashford, N. A., & Hall, R. P. (2011). *Technology, globalization, and sustainable development: Transforming the industrial state*. New Haven, CT: Yale University Press.

Asimov, I. (1989). The relativity of wrong. *The Skeptical Inquirer, 14*, 35–44.

Astor, R., Van Acker, R., & Guerra, N. G. (2010). How can we improve social safety research? Special Issue. *Educational Researcher, 39*, 69–78.

Astor, R. A., Benbenishty, R., & Estrada, J. N. (2009). School violence and theoretically atypical schools: The principal's centrality in orchestrating safe schools. *American Educational Research Journal* 423–461.

Astor, R. A., Meyer, H. A., & Pitner, R. O. (1999). Mapping school violence with students, teachers, and administrators. In L. Davis (Ed.), *Working with African American Males: A practice guide* (pp. 129–144). Thousand Oaks, CA: Sage.

Austin, C. (1992). Have we oversold case management as a "quick fix" for our long-term care system? *Journal of Case Management, 7*, 61–65.

Austin, M. J. (1988). Managing up: Relationship building between middle management and top management. *Administration in Social Work, 12*, 29–46.

Averill, J. (1982). *Anger and aggression: Implications for theories of emotion*. New York: Springer-Verlag.

Azar, S. T., Lauretti, A. F., & Loding, B. V. (1998). The evaluation of parental fitness in termination of parental rights cases: A functional-contextual perspective. *Clinical Child and Family Psychology Review, 1*, 77–100.

Axelrod, S., Spreat, S., Berry, B., & Moyer, L. (1993). A decision-making model for selecting the optimal treatment procedure. In R. Van Houten & S. Axelrod (Eds.), *Behavior analysis and treatment* (pp. 183–202). New York: Plenum Press.

Ayllon, T., & Azrin, N. H. (1968). *The token economy: A motivational system for therapy and rehabilitation*. New York: Appleton-Century-Crofts.

Azrin, N. H. (1976). Improvements in the community-reinforcement approach to alcoholism. *Behavior Research and Therapy, 14*, 339–348.

Azrin, N. H., & Holz, W. C. (1966). Punishment. In W. K. Honig (Ed.), *Operant behavior: Areas of research and application* (pp. 380–347). New York: Appleton-Century-Crofts.

Azin, N. H., Philip, R. A., Thienes-Hontos, P., & Besalel, V. A. (1980). Comparative evaluation of the job club program with welfare recipients. *Journal of Vocational Behavior, 16,* 133–145.

Bachrach, P., & Baratz, M. S. (1971). *Power and poverty: Theory and practice.* London: Oxford University Press.

Bacon, F. ([1620] 1985). *The Essays* (Appendix 4: Idols of the mind). In J. Pitcher (Ed.). New York: Penguin Books.

Baer, D. M. (1982). Applied behavior analysis. In G. T. Wilson & C. M. Franks (Eds.), *Contemporary behavior therapy: Conceptual and empirical foundations* (pp. 277–309). New York: Guilford.

Baer, D. M. (1984). Future directions? Or, is it useful to ask, "Where did we go wrong?" before we go? In R. F. Dangel & R. A. Polster (Eds.), *Parent training: Foundations of research and practice* (pp. 547–557). New York: Guilford.

Baer, D. M. (1987). Weak contingencies, strong contingencies, and many behaviors to change. *Journal of Applied Behavior Analysis, 20,* 335–337.

Baer, D. M. (1988). If you know why you're changing a behavior, you'll know when you've changed it enough. *Behavior Assessment, 10,* 219–223.

Baer, D. M. (2004). Program evaluation: Arduous, impossible, and political. In H. E. Briggs & T. L. Rzepnicki (Eds.), *Using evidence in social work practice: Behavior perspectives* (pp. 310–322). Chicago: Lyceum Press.

Baer, D. M., Wolf, M. M., & Risley, T. R. (1968). Some current dimensions of applied behavior analysis. *Journal of Applied Behavior Analysis, 1,* 91–97.

Baer, D. M., Wolf, M. M., & Risley, T. R. (1987). Some still current dimensions of applied behavior analysis. *Journal of Applied Behavior Analysis, 20,* 311–327.

Bagdikian, B. H. (2004). *The new media monopoly* (Rev.ed.). Boston: Beacon Press.

Bakalar, N. (2011). Researchers link deaths to social ills. *New York Times,* July 5, D5.

Bakeman, R., & Gottman, J. M. (2010). *Observing interaction: An introduction to sequential analysis.* New York: Cambridge University Press.

Baker, P. J., Anderson, L. E., & Dorn, D. S. (1993). *Social problems: A critical thinking approach* (2nd ed.). Belmont, CA: Wadsworth.

Bakker, G. M. (2009). In defence of thought stopping. *Clinical Psychologist, 13,* 59–68.

Balcazar, F. E., Mathews, R. M., Francisco, V. T., Fawcett, S. B., et al. (1994). The empowerment process in four advocacy organizations of people with disabilities. *Rehabilitation Psychology, 39,* 189–203.

Balcazar, F. E., Seekins, T., Fawcett, S. B., & Hopkins, B. L. (1990). Empowering people with physical disabilities through advocacy skills training. *American Journal of Community Psychology, 18*(2), 281–296.

Bales, R. F. (2002). *Social interaction systems: theory and measurement.* New Brunswick, NJ: Transaction Press.

Baltes, M. M. (1988). The etiology and maintenance of dependency in the elderly: Three phases of operant research. *Behavior Therapy, 19,* 301–319.

Bandura, A. (1986). *Social foundations of thought and action.* Englewood Cliffs, NJ: Prentice Hall.

Bandura, A. (1999). Moral disengagement in the perpetration of inhumanities. *Personality and Social Psychology Review, 3,* 193–209.

Bandura, A., Blanchard, E. B., & Ritter, B. (1969). Relative efficacy of desensitization and modeling approaches for inducing behavioral, affective, and attitudinal changes. *Journal of Personality and Social Psychology, 13,* 173–199.

Barber, J., Shlonsky, A., Black, T., Goodman, D., & Trocmé, N. (2008). Reliability and predictive validity of a risk assessment tool. *J. of Public Child Welfare, 2,* 173–195.

Barker, R. L. (2003). *The social work dictionary* (5th ed.). Washington, DC: NASW Press. (See also 1987 Ed.)

Barkley, R. A., Cook, E. H., Diamond, A., Zametkin, A., Thapar, A., Teeter, A., et al. (2002). International Consensus Statement on ADHD. *Clinical Child and Family Psychology Review, 5,* 89–111.

Barlow, D. H. (2002). *Anxiety and its disorders: The nature and treatment of anxiety and panic.* New York: Guilford.

Barlow, D. H., & Craske, M. G. (2007). *Mastery of your anxiety and panic: A workbook* (4th ed.). New York: Oxford University Press.

Barlow, D. H., Nock, K., & Hersen, M. (2009). *Single case experimental designs: Strategies for studying behavior change* (3rd ed.). Boston: Pearson Allyn & Bacon.

Barnett, R., & Rivers, C. (2004). *Same differences: How gender myths are hurting our relationships, our children, and our jobs.* New York: Basic Books.

Baron, J. (1985). *Rationality and intelligence.* New York: Cambridge University Press.

Baron, J. (1994). *Thinking and deciding.* New York: Cambridge University Press.

Baron, J. (2000). *Thinking and deciding* (3rd ed.). New York: Cambridge University Press.

Baron, J. B., & Sternberg, R. J. (1993). *Teaching thinking skills: Theory and practice.* New York: Freeman.

Baron, S., Field, J., & Schuller, T. (Eds.). (2002). *Social capital: Critical perspectives on community and bowling alone.* New York: Oxford University Press.

Barone, V. J., Greene, B. F., & Lutzker, J. L. (1986). Home safety with families being treated for child abuse and neglect. *Behavior Modification, 10,* 93–114.

Barrera, M., Sandler, I. N., & Ramsey, T. B. (1981). Preliminary development of a scale of social support: Studies on college students. *American Journal of Community Psychology, 9,* 435–447.

Barrett, S., Jarvis, W. T., Kroger, M., & London, W. H. (2002). *Consumer health: A guide to intelligent decisions* (7th ed.). New York: McGraw-Hill.

Barth, R. P., Landsverk, J., Chamberlain, P., Reid, J. B., Rolls, J. A., & Hurlburt, M. S., et al. (2005). Parent-training programs in child welfare services: Planning for a more evidence-based approach to serving biological parents. *Research on Social Work Practice, 15,* 353–371.

Barth, R. P., Lee, B. R., Lindsey, M. A, Collins, K. S., Strieder, F., Chorpita, B. F., Becker, K. D., & Sparks, J. A. (2011). Evidence-based practice at a crossroads: The timely emergence of common elements and common factors. *Research on Social Work Practice, 22,* 108–119.

Bartholet, E. (2009). The racial disproportionality movement in child welfare: False facts and dangerous directions. *Arizona Law Review, 51,* 871–932.

Bartley, W. W., III (1984). *The retreat to commitment* (2nd ed.). LaSalle, IL: Open Court.

Batson, C. D., Jones, C. H., & Cochrane, P. J. (1979). Attributional bias in counselor's diagnosis: The effects of resources on perception of need. *Journal of Applied Social Psychology, 9,* 377–393.

Batson, C. D., O'Quin, K., & Psych, V. (1982). An attribution theory analysis of trained helpers inferences about clients needs. In T. A. Wills (Ed.), *Basic processes in helping relationship* (pp. 59–80). New York: Academic Press.

Batten, D. (2011). *Gayle Encyclopedia of American Law.* Detroit, MI: Gale.

Batty, D. (2009). Timeline: Baby P case. *Guardian*, October 7.

Bauer, H. H. (2001). *Fatal attractions: The troubles with science.* New York: Paraview Press.

Bauer, H. H. (2004). Science in the 21st century: Knowledge monopolies and research cartels. *Journal of Scientific Exploration, 18,* 643–660.

Bauer, H. H. (2007). *The origin, persistence and failings of the HIV/AIDS theory.* Jefferson, NC: McFarland.

Baumeister, R. F., Campbell, J. D., Krueger, J. I., & Vohs, K. D. (2003). Does high self-esteem cause better performance, interpersonal success, happiness, or healthier lifestyles? *Psychological Science in the Public Interest, 4*(1), 1–44.

Baumeister, R. F., & Vohs, K. D. (Eds.). (2004). *Handbook of self-regulation: Research, theory, and applications* (pp. 392–407). New York: Guilford.

Bechtel, R. B., & Churchman, A. (Eds.). (2006). *Handbook of environmental psychology.* New York: John Wiley & Sons.

Beck, J. S., (2011). *Cognitive behavior therapy: Basics and beyond.* New York: Guilford.

Becker, H. S. (1996). The epistemology of qualitative research. In R. Jessor, A. Colby, & R. A. Shweder (Eds.), *Ethnography and human development: Context and meaning in social inquiry* (pp. 53–71). Chicago: University of Chicago Press.

Beckett, C. (2003). *Child protection: An introduction.* Thousand Oaks, CA: Sage.

Bell, P. A., Greene, T. C., Fisher, J. D., & Baum, A. (Eds.). (2006). *Environmental Psychology.* (5th ed.). Mahwah, NJ: Erlbaum.

Bellack, A. S., Mueser, K. T., Gingerich, S., & Agresta, J. (2004). *Social skills training for schizophrenia* (2nd ed.). New York: Guilford.

Benedetti, F. (2009). *Placebo effects: Understanding the mechanisms in health and disease.* New York: Oxford University Press.

Bensley, D. A. (1998). *Critical thinking in psychology: A unified skills approach.* Pacific Grove, CA: Brooks/Cole.

Bensman, H. (1967). *Dollars and sense: Ideology, ethics, and the meaning of work in profit and nonprofit organizations.* New York: Macmillan.

Bergan, J. R., & Kratochwill, T. R. (1990). *Behavioral consultation and therapy.* New York: Plenum.

Bergeron, L. R., & Gray, B. (2003). Ethical dilemmas of reporting suspecting elder abuse. *Social Work, 48,* 96–105.

Bergman, K., Sarkar, P., Glover, V., & O'Connor, T. G. (2008). Quality of child-parent attachment moderates the impact of antenatal stress on child fearfulness. *J Child Psychol Psychiatry, 49,* 1089–1098.

Berk, R. A., & Rossi, P. H. (1990). *Thinking about program evaluation.* Newbury Park, CA: Sage.

Berk, R. A., & Rossi, P. H. (1999). *Thinking about program evaluation* (2nd ed.). Newbury Park, CA: Sage.

Berlyne, D. E. (1960). *Conflict, arousal, and curiosity.* New York: McGraw-Hill.

Berner, E. S., & Graber, M. L. (2008). Overconfidence as a cause of diagnostic error in medicine. *Am. J. of Med, 121* (5 Suppl), S2–S23.

Bernstein, D. A., Borkovec, T. D., & Hazlett-Stevens, H. (2000). *New directions in progressive relaxation training: A guidebook for helping professionals.* Westport, CT: Praeger.

Besharov, D. J. (1985). *The vulnerable social worker: Liability for serving children and families.* Silver Spring, MD: National Association of Social Workers.

Best, J. (2004). *More dammed lies and statistics: How numbers confuse public issues.* Berkeley: University of California Press.

Beyth-Marom, R., Fischhoff, B., & Quadrel, M. J. (1991). Teaching decision making to adolescents: A critical review. In J. Baron & R. V. Brown (Eds.), *Teaching decision making to adolescents* (pp. 19–59). Hillsdale, NJ: Lawrence Erlbaum.

Bhugra, D., Craig. T. K. J., & Bhui, K. (2010). *Mental health of refugees and asylum seekers.* Oxford, UK: Oxford University Press.

Bickman, L. (1996). A continuum of care: More is not always better. *American Psychologist, 51,* 689–701.

Biehl, J., Good, B., & Kleinman, A. (Eds.). (2007). *Subjectivity: Ethnographic investigations.* Berkeley: University of California Press.

Bieling, P. J., McCabe, R. E., & Antony, M. M. (2006). *Cognitive-behavioral therapy in groups.* New York: Guildford.

Bigby, C., & Socwk, M. (2000). *Moving on without parents: Planning transitions and sources of support for middle-aged and older adults with intellectual disability.* Baltimore: Brooks Cole.

Bigelow, K. M., Huynen, K. B., & Lutzker, J. R. (1993). Using a changing criterion design to teach fire escape to a child with developmental disabilities. *Journal of Developmental and Physical Disabilities, 5,* 121–128.

Biglan, A. (1995). *Changing cultural practices: A contextualist framework for intervention research.* Reno, NV: Context Press.

Biglan, A., Flay, B. R., Embry, D. D., & Sandler, I. N. (2012). The critical role of nurturing environments for promoting human well-being. *American Psychologist, 67,* 257–271.

Biglan, A., Lewin, L., & Hops, H. (1990). A contextual approach to the problem of aversive practices in families. In G. R. Patterson (Ed.), *Depression and aggression in family interaction* (pp. 103–129). Hillsdale, NJ: Lawrence Erlbaum and Associates.

Bigner, J. J., & Wetchler, J. L. (2012). *Handbook of LGBT: Alternative couples and family therapy.* London: Routledge.

Bikchandani, S., Hirshleifer, D., & Welch, I. (1998). Learning from the behavior of others: Conformity, fads, and informational cascades. *Journal of Economic Perspectives, 12,* 151–170.

Birckmayer, J. D., & Weiss, C. H. (2000). Theory-based evaluation in practice. What do we learn? *Evaluation Review, 24,* 407–431.

Birnbrauer, J. S. (1990). Responsibility and quality of life. In A. C. Repp & N. N. Singh (Eds.), *Perspectives on the use of non-aversive and aversive interventions for persons with developmental disabilities* (pp. 231–236). Sycamore, IL: Sycamore Press.

Birnbrauer, J. S. (1994). Should only positive methods be used by professionals who work with children and adolescents? No. In M. A. Mason & E. Gambrill (Eds.), *Debating children's lives: Current controversies on children and adolescents* (pp. 237–242). Newbury Park, CA: Sage.

Bisson, J. I. (2003). Single-session early psychological interventions following traumatic events. *Clin. Psych Rev, 23,* 481–499.

Black, A. D., Car, J., Pagliari, C., Anandan, C., Cresswell, K., Bakun, T. et al. (2011). The impact of ehealth on the quality and safety of health care: A systematic review. *PLoS Med, 8*:e1000387.

Black, N. (1994). Experimental and observational methods of evaluation. (Letter) *British Medical Journal, 309,* 540.

Blenkner, M., Bloom, M., & Nielsen, M. (1971). A research and demonstration project of protective services. *Social Casework, 52,* 483–499.

Block, P. (2011). *Flawless consulting: A guide to getting your expertise used.* San Diego, CA: Pfeiffer (ebook).

Bloom, M., Fischer, J., & Orme, J. G. (2009). *Evaluating practice: Guidelines for the accountable professional* (2nd ed.). Englewood Cliffs, NJ: Prentice Hall.

Blow, C. M. (2010). America's most vulnerable. *New York Times*, December 11, A19.

Blow, C. M. (2011a). America: Exploding pipe dream. *New York Times*, October 29, A17.

Blow, C. M. (2011b). Drug bust. *New York Times*, June 11, A19.

Blow, C. M. (2011c). Empire at the end of a decadence. *New York Times*, February 18.

Boal, K. & Meckler, M. (2010). Decision errors of the 4th, 5th, 6th kind. In P. C. Nutt & D. C. Wilson (Eds.), *Handbook of decision making* (pp. 327–348). Hoboken, NJ: John Wiley & Sons.

Boerke, K. W. & Reitman, D. (Eds.). (2011). Token economies. In W. W. Fisher, C. C. Piazza, & H. S. Roane, (Eds.), *Handbook of applied behavior analysis* (pp. 370–382). New York: Guilford.

Bogenschneider, K. (2006). *Family policy matters: How policymaking affects families and what professionals can do.* Mahwah, NJ: Erlbaum.

Bogenschneider, K., & Corbett, T. (2010). *Evidence-based policy making: Insights from policy minded researchers and research minded policy-makers.* New York: Taylor & Frances.

Bond, F. W., & Dryden, W. (Eds.). (2004). *Handbook of brief cognitive behavior therapy.* New York: John Wiley & Sons.

Bonnie, R. J., & Wallace, R. B. (Eds.). (2003). *Elder Mistreatment: Abuse, neglect, and exploitation in an aging America.* Washington, DC: National Academies Press.

Bossuyt, P. M., Reitsma, J. B., Bruns, D. E., Gatsonis, C. A., Glasziou, P. P., Irwig, L. M., Ligmer, J. G., Moher, D., Rennie, D., & de Vet, H. C. (2003). Towards complete and accurate reporting of studies of diagnostic accuracy: The STARD initiative. *BMJ, 326,* 41–44.

Bourgois, P., Lettiere, M., & Quesada, J. (2003). Social misery and the sanctions of substance abuse: Confronting HIV risk among homeless heroin addicts in San Francisco. In J. D. Orcutt & D. R. Rudy (Eds.), *Drugs, Alcohol, and Social Problems* (pp. 257–278). New York: Oxford University Press. Originally published in *Social Problems* (1997), *44,* 155–173.

Bowen, S., Chawla, S., & Marlatt, G. A. (2011). *Mindfulness-based relapse prevention for addictive behaviors: A clinicians' guide.* New York: Guilford.

Bowles, S., Durlauf, S. N., & Hoff, K. (Eds.). (2006). *Poverty traps.* New York: Russell Sage Foundation.

Boyer, R. O., & Morais, H. H. (1994). *Labor's untold story* (3rd ed.). Pittsburgh, PA: United Electrical, Radio and Machine Workers of America. (Originally published in 1974.)

Boyle, M. (2002). *Schizophrenia: A scientific delusion?* (2nd ed.). London: Routledge.

Bracken, P. J., & Thomas, P. (2005). *Postpsychiatry.* New York: Oxford University Press.

Braddock, C. H., Edwards, K. A., Hasenberg, N. M., Laidley, T. L., & Levinson, W. (1999). Informed decision making in outpatient practice. Time to get back to basics. *Journal of the American Medical Association, 282(24),* 2313–2320.

Bradshaw, J. (1972). The concept of social need. *New Society, 30,* 640–643.

Bradshaw, W. (2003). Use of single-system research to evaluate the effectiveness of cognitive-behavioral treatment of schizophrenia. *British Journal of Social Work, 33,* 885–899.

Brainerd, C. J., & Reyna, V. F. (2005). *The science of false memory.* New York: Oxford University Press.

Bransford, J. D., & Stein, B. S. (1984). *The IDEAL problem solver: A guide for improving thinking, learning, and creativity.* New York: W. H. Freeman.

Braubach, M., Jacobs, D. E., & Ormandy, D. (Eds.). (2011). Environmental burden of disease associated with inadequate housing. Available online PDF [237p.] at: http://bit.ly/mEllw4

Braun, M., Scholz, U., Hornung, R., & Martin, M. (2010). The burden of spousal caregiving: A preliminary psychometric evaluation of the German version of the Zarit burden inventory. *Aging Mental Health, 14,* 159–167.

Breggin, P. R. (1991). *Toxic psychiatry.* New York: St. Martin's Press.

Breggin, P. R. (1997). *Brain-disabling treatments in psychiatry: Drugs, electroshock, and the psychopharmaceutical complex* (2nd ed.). New York: Springer.

Brewin, C. R. (2006). Understanding cognitive behavior therapy: A retrieval competition account. *Behavior Research and Therapy, 44,* 765–784.

Brickman, P., Rabinowitz, V. C., Karuza, J., Jr., Coates, D., Cohn, E., & Kidder, L. (1982). Models of helping and coping. *American Psychologist, 37,* 368–384.

Briscoe, R. V., Hoffman, D. B., & Bailey, J. S. (1975). Behavioral community psychology: Training a community board to problem solve. *Journal of Applied Behavior Analysis, 8,* 157–168.

Broadhurst, K., Wastell, D., White, S., Hall, C., Peckover, S., Thompson, K., et al. (2010). Performing "initial assessment": Identifying the latent conditions for error at the front door of local authority children's services. *British Journal of Social Work, 40,* 362–370

Brody, H. (2007). *Hooked: Ethics, the medical profession and the pharmaceutical industry.* New York: Rowman & Littlefield.

Bronfenbrenner, U. (1979). *The ecology of human development: Experiments by nature and design.* Cambridge, MA: Harvard University Press.

Brookfield, S. (1995). *Becoming a critically reflective teacher.* San Francisco: Jossey-Bass.

Brookfield, S. D. (1987). *Developing critical thinkers: Challenging adults to explore alternative ways of thinking and acting.* San Francisco: Jossey-Bass.

Brounstein, P. J., Emshoff, J. G., Hill, G. A., & Stoil, M. J. (1997). Assessment of methodological practices in the evaluation of alcohol and other drug (AOD) abuse prevention. *Journal of Health and Social Policy, 9,* 1–19.

Browning, R. M., & Stover, D. O. (1971). *Behavior modification in child treatment: An experimental and clinical approach.* Chicago: Aldine.

Broussard, C., & Northup, J. (1997). The use of functional analysis to develop peer interventions for disruptive classroom behavior. *School Psychology Quarterly, 12,* 65–76.

Brown, G. W., & Harris, T. (1978). *Social origins of depression: A study of psychiatric disorders in women.* New York: Free Press.

Brown, L. D., & Witak, S. (Eds.). (2010). *Mental health self-help: Consumer and family initiatives.* New York: Springer.

Budd, K. (2005). Assessing parenting capacity in a child welfare context. *Children and Youth Services Review, 27,* 429–444.

Budd, K. S., Poindexter, L. M., Feliz, E. D., & Naik-Polan, A. T. (2001). Clinical assessment of parents in child protection cases: An empirical analysis. *Law and Human Behavior, 25,* 93–108.

Bullmore, E., Joyce, H., Marks, I. M., & Connolly, J. (1992). A computerized quality assurance system (QAS) on a general psychiatric ward: Towards efficient clinical audit. *Journal of Mental Health, 1,* 257–263.

Bulmer, M. (1986). *Neighbors: The work of Phillip Abram.* Cambridge, UK: Cambridge University Press.

Bunge, M. (1984). What is pseudoscience? *Skeptical Inquirer, 9*(1), 36–47.

Bunge, M. (2003). The pseudoscience concept, dispensable in professional practice, is required to evaluate research projects: A reply to Richard J. McNally. *Scientific Review of Mental Health Practice, 2,* 111–114.

Burish, T. J., Snyder, S. L., & Jenkins, R. A. (1991). Preparing patients for cancer chemotherapy: Effects of coping preparation and relaxation interventions. *Journal of Consulting and Psychology, 59,* 518–525.

Burnham, J. C. (1987). *How superstition won and science lost: Popularizing science and health in the United States.* New Brunswick, NJ: Rutgers University Press.

Burns, B. J., & Hoagwood, K. (2002). *Community treatment for youth: Evidence-based interventions for severe emotional and behavioral disorders.* New York: Oxford University Press.

Burns, D. D. (1990). *Feeling good: The new mood therapy.* New York: Morrow.

Burns, D. D. (1999). *Feeling good: The new mood therapy* (2nd ed.). New York: Avon.

Burns, D. D. (1999). *The feeling good handbook.* New York: Plume.

Burns, D. (2004). Workshop on fast, effective treatment for personality disorders. Concord, California, October. 22 and 23.

Burns, D. (2006). *When panic attacks: The new drug free anxiety therapy that can change your life.* New York: Broadway Books.

Burton, L. M., Kemp, S. P., Leung, M., Matthews, S., & Takeuchi, D. T. (Eds.) (2011). *Communities, neighborhoods, and health: Expanding the boundaries of place.* New York: Springer Publishing.

Buss, D. M. (2011). *Evolutionary psychology: The new science of the mind.* New York: Prentice Hall.

Busse, R. T., Kratochwill, T. R., & Elliott, S. N. (1995). Meta-analysis for single-case consultation outcomes: Applications to research and practice. *Journal of School Psychology, 33,* 269–285.

Butzlaff, R. L., & Hooley, J. M. (1998). Expressed emotions and psychiatric relapse: A meta-analysis. *Archives of General Psychiatry, 55*(6), 547–552.

Bynum, W. F., Browne, E. J., & Porter, R. (Eds.). (1985). *Dictionary of the history of science.* Princeton, NJ: Princeton University Press.

Cahill, S., & Tobias, S. (2006). *Policy issues affecting lesbian, gay, bisexual and transgender families.* Ann Arbor, MI: University of Michigan Press.

Calton, T., Ferriter, M., Huband, N., & Spandler, H. (2008). A systematic review of the Soteria paradigm for the treatment of people diagnosed with schizophrenia. *Schizophrenia Bulletin, 34,* 181–192.

Campbell, D. T. (1969). Reforms as experiments. *American Psychologist, 24,* 409–429.

Campbell, D. T. (1996). Can we overcome worldview incommensurability/relativity in trying to understand the other? In R. Jessor, A. Colby, & R. A. Shweder (Eds.), *Ethnography and human development: Context and meaning in social inquiry* (pp. 153–172). Chicago: University of Chicago Press.

Campbell, D. T., & Stanley, J. C. (1963). *Experimental and quasi-experimental design for research.* Chicago: Rand McNally.

Campbell, J. A. (1988). Client acceptance of single-system evaluation procedures. *Social Work Research and Abstracts, 24,* 21–22.

Canda, E. R., & Furman, L. D. (2010). *Spiritual diversity in social work practice: The heart of helping* (2nd ed.). New York: Oxford University Press.

Caplow, T. (1994). *Perverse incentives: The neglect of social technology in the public sector.* Westport, CT: Praeger.

Carey, B. (2011). Study ties suicide rate in workforce to economy. *New York Times*, April 14.

Carey, W. (2003). Is attention deficit hyperactivity disorder a valid disorder? https//f.about.com/z/js/ spr07sm.htm 5/17/03.

Carlson, M. J., & England, R. (Eds.) (2011). *Social class and changing families in an unequal America.* Stanford, CA: Stanford University Press.

Carpenter, K. J. (1986). *The history of scurvy and vitamin C.* New York: Cambridge University Press.

Carr, E. G., Levin, L., McConnachie, G., Carlson, J. I., Kemp, D. C., & Smith, C. E. (1994). *Communication-based intervention for problem behavior: A user's guide for producing positive change.* Baltimore, MD: Paul H. Brookes.

Carr, E. G., et al. (2000). *Communication-based intervention for problem behavior: A user's guide for producing positive change.* Baltimore, MD: Paul H. Brookes.

Carr, E. G., Robinson, S., & Palumbo, L. W. (1990). The wrong issue: Aversive versus nonaversive treatment. The right issue: functional versus nonfunctional treatment. In A. C. Repp & N. N. Singh (Eds.), *Perspectives on the use of nonaversive and aversive interventions for persons with developmental disabilities* (pp. 361–379). Sycamore, IL: Sycamore Press.

Carroll, D. W. (2001). Using ignorance questions to promote thinking skills. *Teaching of Psychology, 28,* 98–100.

Carter, S. L. (2010). *The social validity manual: A guide to subjective evaluation of behavior interventions in applied behavior analysis.* San Diego, CA: Academic Press.

Cash, W. M., & Evans, I. M. (1975). Training preschool children to modify their retarded siblings' behavior. *Journal of Behavior Therapy and Experimental Psychiatry, 6,* 13–16.

Cassidy, J., & Shaver, P. R. (Eds.). (2008). *Handbook of attachment: Theory, research, and clinical* applications(2nd ed.). New York: Guilford.

Catania, A. C. (2011). Basic operant contingencies. Main effects and side effects. In Fisher, et al. (Eds.), *Handbook of applied behavior analysis* (pp. 34– 54). New York: Guilford.

Cavanaugh, M. M. & Gelles, R. J. (2012). *Intimate violence and abuse in families* (4th ed.). New York: Oxford.

Cawelti, J. G. (1965). *Apostles of the self-made man.* Chicago: University of Chicago Press.

Ceci, S. J., & Bruck, M. (1993). Suggestibility of the child witness: A historical review and synthesis. *Psychological Bulletin, 113*(3), 403–439.

Ceci, S. J., & Bruck, M. (1995). *Jeopardy in the courtroom: A scientific analysis of children's testimony.* Washington, DC: American Psychological Association.

Ceci, S. J., Crotteau-Huffman, M., Smith, E., & Loftus, E. W. (1994). Repeatedly thinking about non-events. *Consciousness and Cognition, 3,* 388–407.

Ceci, S. J., Gilstrap, L., & Fitneva, S. A. (2002). Children's testimony. In M. Rutter & E. Taylor (Eds.), *Child and adolescent psychiatry* (4th ed.) (pp. 117–27). Malden, MA: Blackwell.

Cecile, M., & Born, M. (2009). Intervention in juvenile delinquency: Danger of iatrogenic effects? *Children and Youth Services Review, 31,* 1217–1221.

Cemlyn, S. (2008). Human rights practice: Possibilities and pitfalls for developing emancipatory social work. *Ethics and Social Welfare, 2,* 222–242.

Centeno, M. A. & Newman, K. S. (Eds.) (2010). *Discrimination in an unequal world.* New York: Oxford University Press.

CDC Health Disparities and Inequalities Report—United States (2011). Centers for Disease Control and Prevention: Morbidity and Mortality Weekly Report. Supplement/Vol. 60, Jan. 14, 2011. U.S. Department of Health and Human Services, Centers for Disease Control and Prevention.

Chalmers, I. (1983). Scientific inquiry and authoritarianism in perinatal care and education. *Birth, 10,* 151–166.

Chalmers, I. (1990). Underreporting research limitations is scientific misconduct. *Journal of the American Medical Association, 263(10),* 1405–1408.

Chalmers, I. (2003). Trying to do more good than harm in policy and practice: The role of rigorous, transparent, up-to-date evaluations. [reprinted from] *The ANNALS of the American Academy of Political and Social Science, 589,* 22–40.

Chalmers, I. (2004). Well informed uncertainties about the effects of treatments. *BMJ, 328,* 475–476.

Chalmers, I. (2007). Addressing uncertainties about the effects of treatments offered to NHS patients: Whose responsibility? *Journal of the Royal Society of Medicine, 100,* 440.

Chamberlain, P. (2003). *Treating chronic juvenile offenders: Advances made through the Oregon multidimensional treatment foster care model.* Washington DC: American Psychological Association.

Chamberlain, P., & Baldwin, D. V. (1988). Client resistance to parent training: Its therapeutic management. In T. R. Kratochwill (Ed.), *Advances in school psychology* (Vol. 6 of a series) (pp. 131–171). Hillsdale, NJ: Lawrence Erlbaum.

Chamberlain, P., Fisher, P. A., & Moore, K. (2002). Multidimensional treatment foster care: Applications of the OSLC intervention model to high-risk youth and their families. In J. B. Reid, G. R. Patterson, & J. Snyder (Eds.), *Antisocial behavior in children and adolescents* (pp. 203–218). Washington, DC: American Psychological Association.

Chamberlain, P., & Patterson, G. R. (1995). Discipline in child compliance in parenting. In M. H. Bornstein (Ed.), *Handbook of parenting,* Vol. 4: *Applied and practical parenting* (pp. 205–225). Mahwah, NJ: Laurence Erlbaum.

Chambliss, W. J., Michalowski, R., & Kramer, R. C. (Eds.) (2010). *State crime in the global age.* Cullompton, Devon, UK: Willan Publishing.

Chang-Muy, F. & Congress, E. P. (Eds.) (2009). *Social work with immigrants and refugees: Legal issues, clinical skills and advocacy.* New York: Springer.

Chapman, L. J., & Chapman, J. P. (1969). Illusory correlation as an obstacle to the use of valid psychodiagnostic signs. *Journal of Abnormal Psychology, 74,* 271–280.

Charlton, B. G. (2009). Replacing education with psychometrics: How learning about IQ almost completely changed my mind about education. *Medical Hypotheses,* July 11.

Charlton, B. G. (2010), The cancer of bureaucracy. *Medical Hypotheses, 74,* 961–965.

Chaskin, R. J., Brown, P., Venkatesh, S., & Vidal, A. (2009). *Building community capacity.* New Brunswick, NJ: Aldine Transaction.

Chavis, D., & Wandersman, A. (1990). Sense of community in the urban environment: A catalyst for participation and community development. *American Journal of Community Psychology, 18,* 55–82.

Chorpita, B. F., Becker, K. D., & Daleiden, E. L. (2007). Understanding the common elements of evidence based practice: Misconceptions and clinical examples. *J. Am. Acad. Child & Adolescent Psychiatry, 46,* 647–652.

Chorpita, B. F. & Daleiden, E. L. (2009). Mapping evidence-based treatments for children and adolescents: Application of the distillation and matching model to 615 treatments from 322 randomized controlled trials. *J. of Consul & Clin Psych, 77,* 566–579.

Chow, J., & Austin, M. (2008). The culturally responsive social service agency: The application of an evolving definition to a case study. *Administration in Social Work, 32*(4), 39–64.

Christensen, A. J., & Antoni, M. H. (2008). *Chronic physical disorders: Behavioral medicine's perspective.* Oxford, UK: Blackwell.

Christensen, A., & Jacobson, N. S. (1994). Who (or what) can do psychotherapy: The status of and challenge of nonprofessional therapies. *Psychological Science, 5,* 8–14.

Christian, W. P., & Romanczyki, R. G. (1986). Evaluation. In F. J. Fucco & W. P. Christian (Eds.), *Behavior analysis and therapy in residential programs* (pp. 145–193). New York: Van Nostrand.

Chuang, S. S. & Moreno, R. P. (2011). *Immigrant children: Change, adaptation, and cultural transformation.* Lanham, MD: Lexington Books.

Chun, K. M., Organista, P. B., & Marin, G. (Eds.). (2009). *Acculturation: advances in theory, measurement, and applied research.* Washington, DC: American Psychological Association (ebook).

Church, A. T., Katigbak, M. S., Reyes, J. A., Salanga, M. G., Miramontes, L. A., & Adams, N. B. (2008). Prediction and cross-situational consistency of daily behavior across cultures: Testing trait and cultural psychology perspectives. *J. Res. Pers, 42,* 1199–1215.

Cialdini, R. B. (1984). *Influence: The new psychology of modern persuasion.* New York: Quill.

Cialdini, R. B. (2001*). Influence: Science and practice* (4th ed.). Boston: Allyn & Bacon.

Cialdini, R. B. (2008). *Influence: Science and practice* (5th ed.). Boston: Pearson Education.

Cicchitti, D. & Cohen, D. J. (Eds.) (2006). *Developmental psychopathology* (2nd ed.). New York: John Wiley & Sons.

Cipani, E., & Shock, K. M. (2011). *Functional behavioral assessment, diagnosis, and treatment: a complete system for education and mental health settings* (2nd ed.). New York: Springer.

Clark, D. A. (2007). *Cognitive-behavioral therapy for OCD.* New York: Guilford.

Clarke, A. E., Mamo, L., Fosket, J. R., Fishman, J. R., & Shim, J. K. (Eds.) (2010). *Biomedicalization: Technoscience, health, and illness in the U.S.* Durham, NC: Duke University Press.

Clauss-Ehlers, C. S., & Weist, M. D. (Eds.) (2004). *Community planning to foster resilience in children.* New York: Kluwer Academic.

Cloward, R. A., & Epstein, I. (1965). Private social welfare's disengagement from the poor: The case of family adjustment agencies. In M. N. Zald (Ed.), *Social welfare institutions: a sociological reader* (pp. 623–644). New York: John Wiley & Sons.

Cochrane, A. L. (1999). *Effectiveness & efficiency: Random reflections on health services.* Cambridge. England: The Royal Society of Medicine Press, and The Nuffield Trust, Cambridge University Press.

Code of Ethics for Child Welfare Professionals. (1996). Illinois Department of Children and Family Services. Chicago, IL.

Coghill, D. (2001) A naive use of evidence. Letter to the editor. *BMJ,* November 26.

Cohen, C. I., & Timimi, S. (Eds.) (2008). *Liberatory psychiatry. Philosophy, politics, and mental health.* New York: Cambridge University Press.

Cohen, D., & Jacobs, D. (1998). A model consent form for psychiatric drug treatment. *International Journal of Risk & Safety in Medicine, 11*, 161–164.

Cohen, C. I. & Timimi, S. (Eds.) (2008). *Liberatory psychiatry: Philosophy, politics and mental health.* Cambridge, MA: Cambridge University Press.

Cohen, J. (1977). *Statistical power analysis for the behavioral sciences.* New York: Academic Press.

Cohen, S., Gordon, L. U., & Gottlieb, B. H. (2000). *Social support measurement and intervention: A guide for health and social scientists.* New York: Oxford University Press.

Cohen-Mansfield, J., Creedon, M. A., Malone, T., Parpura-Gill, A., Dakheel-Ali, M., Heasly (2006). Dressing of cognitively impaired nursing home residents: description and analysis. *The Gerontologist, 46*, 89–96.

Cohn, J. (2011). The two year window: The new science of babies and brains—and how it could revolutionize the fight against poverty. *The New Republic*, No. 9. (Downloaded Nov. 20, 2011.)

Cole, G. A., Montgomery, R. W., Wilson, K. M., & Milan, M. A. (2000). Parametric analysis of overcorrection duration effects: Is longer really better than shorter? *Behavior Modification, 24*(3), 359–378.

Collins, M. E. (2001). Transition to adulthood for vulnerable youths: A review of research and implications for policy. *Social Service Review, 75*(2), 271–291.

Collins, R. (1988). Lessons in compassion for student doctors. *Sunday Times*, Aug. 7, A7.

Conger, R. D., Lorenz, F. O., & Wickrama, K. A. S. (Eds.). (2004). *Continuity and change in family relations: Theory, methods and empirical findings.* Mahwah, NJ: Erlbaum.

Congress, E. P. & Gonzales, M. (Eds.) (2005). *Multicultural perspectives in working with families* (2nd ed.). New York: Springer.

Connell, J. P., Kubisch, A., C., Schorr, L. B., & Weiss, C. H. (1995). *New approaches to evaluating community initiatives.* Volume 1: *Concepts, methods, and context.* Washington, D.C.: Aspen Institute.

Conrad, P. (2007). *The medicalization of society: On the transformation of human conditions into treatable disorders.* Baltimore: Johns Hopkins University Press.

Conrad, P., & Potter, D. (2000). From hyperactive children to ADHD adults: Observations on the expansion of medical categories. *Social Problems, 47*, 559–582.

Conrad, P., & Schneider, J. W. (1992). *Deviance and medicalization: From badness to sickness.* Philadelphia: Temple University Press.

Cook, J. L. & Cook, G. (2009). *Child development: Principles and perspectives* (2nd ed.). Pearson:

Cook, T. D., & Campbell, D. T. (1979). *Quasi-experimentation: Design and analysis issues for field settings.* Boston: Houghton-Mifflin.

Cooper, J. O., Heron, T. E., & Heward, W. L. (1987). *Applied behavior analysis.* Columbus, OH: Merrill.

Corcoran, J. (2003). *Clinical applications of evidence-based family interventions.* New York: Oxford University Press.

Corcoran, K., & Fischer, J. (2009). *Measures for clinical practice: A sourcebook* (4th ed.), Vol. 1: *Couples, families, and children.* Vol. 2: *Adults.* New York: Free Press.

Coren, E., & Fischer, M. (2006). *The conduct of systematic research reviews for SCIE knowledge and reviews.* London: Social Care Institute for Excellence.

Cormier, W. H., Nurius, P. & Osborn, C. J. (2009). *Interviewing strategies for helpers: Fundamental skills and cognitive behavioral interventions* (4th ed.). Monterey, CA: Brooks/Cole.

Cornish, J. A. E., Schreier, B. A., Nadkarni, L. I., Metzger, L. H., & Rodolfa, E. R. (2010). *Handbook of multicultural counseling competencies.* Hoboken, NJ: John Wiley & Sons. ebook 17c.

Cosgrove, L. (2010). Diagnosing conflict-of-interest disorders. *Academe Online.* 96(6).

Cosgrove, L., Bursztajn, H. J., Krimsky, S., Anaya, M., & Walker, J. (2009). Conflicts of interest and disclosure in the American Psychiatric Association's clinical practice guidelines. *Psychotherapy and Psychosomatics, 78*, 228–232.

Costello, J. C. (2003). "Wayward and noncompliant" people with mental disabilities: What advocates of involuntary outpatient commitment can learn from the juvenile court experience with status offense jurisdiction. *Psychology, Public Policy, and Law, 9*, 233–257.

Cottle, M. (1999). Selling shyness. *New Republic*, August 2, 24–29.

Coulter, A. (2002). *The autonomous patient: Ending paternalism in medical care.* London: Nuffield Trust.

Coulter, (2006). *Assessing the quality of information to support people in making decisions about their health and health care.* Oxford: The Picker Institute, Europe.

Coulter, A. & Collins, A. (2011). *Making shared decision-making a reality: No decision about me without me.* London: King's Fund.

Coulter, A., Entwistle, V., & Gilbert, D. (1999). Sharing decisions with patients: Is the information good enough? *BMJ, 318*, 318–322.

Council on Social Work Education (2008). *Educational policy and accreditation standards.* 1725 Duke St., Suite 4500, Alexandria, VA.

Cowger, C. (1994). Assessing client strengths: Clinical assessment for client empowerment. *Social Work, 39*, 262–268.

Craighead, W. E., Mercatoris, M., & Bellack B. (1974). A brief report on mentally retarded residents as behavioral observers. *Journal of Applied Behavior Analysis, 7*, 333–340.

Craske, M. G., & Barlow, D. H. (2006). *Mastery of your anxiety & worry: Workbook.* New York: Oxford University Press.

Cresswell, J. (2011). Even funds that lagged paid richly. *New York Times*, March 31.

Crittenden, P. M. (1998). Dangerous behavior and dangerous contexts: A 35-year perspective on research on the developmental effects of child physical abuse. In P. K. Trickett & C. J. Schellenbach (Eds.), *Violence against children in the family and the community* (pp. 11–38). Washington, DC: American Psychological Association.

Cronch, L. E., Viljoen, J. L., & Hansen, D. J. (2006). Forensic interviewing in child sexual abuse cases: Current techniques and future directions. *Aggression and Violent Behavior, 11*, 195–207.

Crone, D. A., & Horner, R. H. (2003). *Building positive behavior support systems in schools: Functional behavioral assessment.* New York: Guilford.

Crone, D. A., Hawken, L. S., & Horner, R. H. (2010). *Responding to problem behavior in schools: The behavior education program* (2nd ed.). New York: Guilford.

Cultural Competence self-assessment instrument. (2002). Washington, D.C.: Child Welfare League of America.

Cummings, N. A. (1977). Prolonged (ideal) versus short-term (realistic) psychotherapy. *Professional Psychology, 2*, 491–501.

Cushon, J. A., Vu, L. T. H., Janzen, B. L., & Muhajarine, N. (2011). Neighborhood poverty impacts children's physical health and well-being over time: Evidence from the Early Development Instrument. *Early Education & Development, 22*, 183–205.

Cutler, B. L. (Ed.) (2009). *Expert testimony on the psychology of eye witness identification.* New York: Oxford University Press.

Damer, T. E. (1995). *Attacking faulty reasoning: A practical guide to fallacy free arguments* (3rd ed.). Belmont, CA: Wadsworth. (Also see 6th ed., 2009.)

Daniels, A. C. (2000). *Bringing out the best in people: How to apply the astonishing power of positive reinforcement.* New York: McGraw Hill.

Darden-Brunson, F., Green, A., & Goldstein, H. (2008). Video-based instruction for children with autism. In Luiselli, et al., *Effective practices with children with autism: Educational and support interventions that work* (pp. 241–268). New York: Oxford University Press.

Dartnell, M. (2006). *Insurgency online: Web activism and global conflict.* Toronto: University of Toronto Press.

Dattilio, F. M., & Freeman, A. (2010). *Cognitive-behavioral strategies in crisis intervention* (3rd ed.) New York Guilford.

D'Augelli, A. R. (1989). The development of a helping community for lesbians and gay men: A case study in community psychology. *Journal of Community Psychology, 17,* 18–29.

D'Augelli, A. R., Vallance, T. R., Danish, S. J., Young, C. E., & Gerdes, J. L. (1981). The community helpers' project: A description of a prevention strategy for rural communities. *Journal of Prevention, 1,* 209–224.

Davey, B., & Seale, C. (Eds.). (2002). *Experiencing and explaining disease.* (3rd ed). Philadelphia: Open University Press.

Davies, P. (2004). *Is evidence-based government possible?* Jerry Lee lecture, 4th Annual Campbell Collaboration Colloquium, Washington D.C., February 19, 2004.

Dawes, R. M. (1988). *Rational choice in an uncertain world.* Orlando: Harcourt, Brace Jovanovich.

Dawes, R. M. (1993). Prediction of the future versus an understanding of the past: A basic asymmetry. *American Journal of Psychology, 106,* 1–24.

Dawes, R. M. (1994a). *House of cards: Psychology and psychotherapy built on myth.* New York: Free Press.

Dawes, R. M. (1994b). On the necessity of examining all four cells in a 2 x 2 table. *Making better decisions, 1*(2), 2–4. Pacific Grove, CA: Brooks/Cole.

Day, W. (1983). On the difference between radical and methodological behaviorism. *Behaviorism, 11,* 89–102.

de Anda, D. (1984). Bicultural socialization: Factors affecting the minority experience. *Social Work, 29*(3), 101–107.

Deacon, J. R., & Konarski, E. A., Jr. (1987). Correspondence training: An example of rule-governed behavior? *Journal of Applied Behavior Analysis, 20,* 391–400.

Decker, L. E. (1992). Thinking and acting from a broad perspective: Community education. In C. Collins & J. N. Mangieri (Eds.), *Teaching thinking: An agenda for the twenty-first century* (pp. 257–268). Hillsdale, NJ: Erlbaum.

Deenadayalan, J., Grimmer-Somers, K., Prior, M., & Kumar, S. (2008). How to run an effective journal club: A systematic review. *J. Eval. Clin Prac, 14,* 898–911.

DeFilippis, J., & Saegert, S. (Eds.) (2008). *The community development reader.* New York: Routledge.

Demott, B. (1990). *The imperial middle: Why Americans can't think straight about class.* New York: William Morrow.

Denicola, J., & Sandler, J. (1980). Training abusive parents in cognitive-behavioral techniques. *Behavior Therapy, 11,* 263–270.

DePanfilis, D. (2003a). Review of IAIU investigations of suspected child abuse and neglect. In *DYFS out-of-home care settings in New Jersey.* Final Report. Baltimore: School of Social Work, University of Maryland.

DePanfilis, D., & Salus, M. K. (2003). *Child protective services: A guide for caseworkers.* Washington, DC: U.S.

DeParle, J., Gebeloff, R., & Tavernise, S. (2011). Meet the near poor: Older, married, suburban and struggling. *New York Times,* Nov. 9, A1/13.

Department of Health and Human Services, Administration for Children and Families. Children's Bureau, Office on Child Abuse and Neglect.

Depp, C. A., Mausbach, B., Granholm, E., Cardenas, V., Ben-Zeev, D., Patterson, T. L., et al. (2010). Mobile interventions for severe mental illness: design and preliminary data from three approaches. *J Nerv Ment Dis, 198,* 715–721.

Dewey, J. (1933). *How we think: A restatement of the relation of reflective thinking to the education process.* Boston: Heath.

Deyo, & S. D. Ramsey (Eds.), *Evidence-based clinical practice: Concepts and Approaches* (pp. 83–93). Boston: Butterworth Heinemann.

Dickson, D. T. (1998). *Confidentiality and privacy in social work: A guide to the law for practitioners and students.* New York: Free Press.

Diener, E., & Seligman, M. E. P. (2004). Beyond money: Toward an economy of well-being. *Psychological Science in the Public Interest, 5*(1), 1–31.

Diller, L. H. (2006). *The last normal child: Essays on the intersection of kids, culture and psychiatric drugs.* Westport, CT: Praeger.

Dinges, N. G., Atlis, M. M., & Ragan, S. L. (2000). Assessment of depression among American Indians and Alaska Natives. In R. H. Dana (Ed.), *Handbook of cross-cultural and multicultural personality assessment* (pp. 623–646). Mahwah, NJ: Erlbaum.

Dingwall, R., Eekelaar, J., & Murray, T. (1983). *The protection of children.* Oxford, England: Basil Blackwell.

DiNitto, D. M. (2000). *Social welfare: Politics and public policy* (7th ed.). Upper Saddle River, NJ: Harlow Pearson. (See also 2010 Ed.)

Discriminatory laws and practices and acts of violence against individuals based on their sexual orientation and gender identity. United Nations High Commission for Human Rights. Dec. 2011.

Dishion, T. J., & Granic, I., (2004). Naturalistic observation of relationship processes. In S. N. Haynes & E. M. Heiby (Eds.), *Comprehensive handbook of psychological assessment,* vol. 3, (pp. 143–161). New York: Wiley.

Dishion, T. J., & Kavanagh, K. (2005). *Intervening in adolescent problem behavior: A family centered approach.* New York: Guilford.

Dishion, T. J., Patterson, G. R., & Kavanaugh, K. A. (1992). An experimental test of the coercion model: Linking theory, measurement, and intervention. In J. McCord & R. E. Tremblay (Eds.), *Preventing antisocial behavior: Interventions from birth through adolescence* (pp. 253–282). New York: Guilford.

Dodge, K. A. (2006). Translational science in action: hostile attributional style and the development of aggressive behavior problems. *Developmental Psychopathology, 18,* 791–814.

Dodge, K. A., Dishion, T. J., & Lansford, J. E. (2006). *Deviant peer influences in programs for youth: Problems and solutions.* New York: Guilford.

Domenighetti, G., Grilli, R., & Liberati, A (1998). Promoting consumers' demand for evidence based medicine. *International Journal of Technology Assessment in Health Care, 14*(11), 97–105.

Domhoff, G. W. (2007). *Who rules America? Challenges to corporate and class dominance* (6th ed.). (See also *Wealth, income and power.* www2.ussc.edu/whorulesamerica (2011).

Domjan, M. (1983). Biological constraints on instrumental and classical conditioning: Implications for general process theory.

In G. H. Bower (Ed.), *The psychology of learning and motivation* (pp. 215–277). New York: Academic.

Donnellan, A. M., Mirenda, P. L., Mesaros, R. A., & Fassbender, L. L. (1984). Analyzing the communicative functions of aberrant behavior. *Journal of the Association for Persons With Severe Handicaps, 9,* 201–212.

Double, D. B. (2006). *Critical psychiatry: The limits of medicine.* New York: Palgrave Macmillan.

Douglass, F. (1950). West India Emancipation speech delivered at Canandaigua, New York, August 4, 1857. In P. S. Foner, (Ed.), *The Life and Writings of Frederick Douglas* (Vol. 2, p. 437). New York: International Publishers.

Doust, J., & Del Mar, C. (2004). Why do doctors use treatments that do not work? For many reasons–including their inability to stand idle and do nothing. *BMJ, 328,* 474–475.

Downer, J. T., Booren, L. M., Lima, O. K., Luckner, A. E., & Pianta, R. C. (2010). The individualized classroom assessment scoring system (inCLASS): Preliminary reliability and validity of a system for observing preschoolers' competence in classroom interactions. *Early Childhood Research Quarterly, 25,* 1–16.

Dreyfus, H. L., & Dreyfus, S. E. (1986). *Mind over machine: The power of human intuition and expertise in the era of the computer.* New York: Free Press.

Drummond, A. E., Parker, C. J., Gladman, J. R., & Logan, P. A. (2001). Development and validation of the Nottingham Leisure Questionnaire (NLQ). *Clinical Rehabilitation, 15,* 647–656.

Drury, S. S. (1984). *Assertive supervision: Building involved teamwork.* Champaign, IL: Research Press.

Drury, S. S., et al. (2011). Telomere length and early severe social deprivation: linking early adversity and cellular aging. *Molecular Psychiatry, 17,* 719–727.

Drwecki, B. B., Moore, C. F., Ward, S. E, & Prkachin, K. M. (2011). Reducing racial disparities in pain treatment: The role of empathy and perspective-taking. *Pain, 152,* 1001–1006.

Dubois, V. (2010). *The bureaucrat and the poor: Encounters in French welfare offices.* Burlington, VT: Ashgate.

Dudley, R. E., & Over, D. E. (2003). People with delusions jump to conclusions. *Clinical Psychology and Psychotherapy, 10,* 263–274.

Dugger, C. W. (1992). As mother killed her son, protectors observed privacy. *New York Times.* February 10, A1/16.

Duncan, B. L., Miller, S. D., Sparks, J. A., & Claud, D. A., Reynolds, L. R., Brown, J. & Johnson, L. D. (2003). The session rating scale: Preliminary psychometric properties of a "working" alliance measure. *Journal of Brief Therapy, 3,* 3–12.

Duncan, B. L., Miller, S. D., Wampold, B. E., & Hubble, M. A. (2010). *The heart and soul of change: Delivering What works in therapy* (2nd ed.). Washington, D.C.P: American Psychological Association.

Dunlap, G., Koegel, L. K., & Koegel, R. L. (2004). *Positive behavioral support: Including people with difficult behavior in the community.* Baltimore, MD: Paul H. Brookes.

Dunning, D., Heath, C., & Suls, J. M. (2004). Flawed self-assessment: Implications for health, education, and the work place. *Psychological Science and the Public Interest, 5,* 69–106.

DuPaul, G, J., Ervin, R. A., Hook, C. L., & McGoey, K. E. (1998). Peer tutoring for children with attention-deficit hyperactivity disorder: Effects on classroom behavior and academic performance. *Journal of Applied Behavior Analysis, 31,* 579–592.

Dutton, D. B. (1988). *Worse than the disease: Pitfalls of medical progress* (pp. 339–340). New York: Cambridge University Press.

Dweck, C. S. (1975). The role of expectations and attributions in the alteration of learned helplessness. *Journal of Personality and Social Psychology, 31,* 674–685.

Dwyer, J. (2011). Side effects of arrests for marijuana. *New York Times,* June 17, A27.

D'Zurilla, T. J., & Nezu, A. M. (2007). *Problem-solving therapy: A positive approach to clinical intervention.* New York: Springer.

Eamon, M. K., & Kopels, S. (2004). 'For reasons of poverty': Court challenges to child welfare practices and mandated programs. *Children and Youth Services Review, 26,* 821–836.

Easterby-Smith, & Lyles, M. A. (2011). *The Blackwell handbook of organizational learning and knowledge management* (2nd ed.). Hobokan, NJ: John Wiley & Sons.

Ebbersold, S. (2011). *Inclusion of students with disabilities in tertiary education and employment.* Paris: Organization for Economic Co-operation and Development.

Ebert, M. H., & Kerns, R. D. (2011). *Behavioral and pharmacologic pain management.* New York: Cambridge University Press.

Echanove, M. & Srivastava, R. (2011). Hands off our houses. *New York Times,* May 31.

Eddy, D. M. (1990). Comparing benefits and harms: The balance sheet. *Journal of the American Medical Association, 263,* 3077, 3081, 3084.

Eddy, D. M. (1993). Three battles to watch in the 1990s. *Journal of the American Medical Association, 270,* 520–526.

Eddy, D. M. (1994a). Principles for making difficult decisions in difficult times. *Journal of the American Medical Association, 271,* 1792–1798.

Eddy, D. M. (1994b). Rationing resources while improving quality. *Journal of the American Medical Association, 272,* 817–824.

Eden, C. & Ackerman, F. (2010). Decision making in groups. In P. C. Nutt & D. C. Wilson (Eds.), *Handbook of behavior modification* (pp. 231–271). New York: Wiley.

Edwards, A., & Elwyn, G. (2001). *Evidence-based patient choice: Inevitable or impossible?* New York: Oxford University Press.

Edwards, A., Elwyn, G., & Mulley, A. (2002). Explaining risks: Turning numerical data into meaningful pictures. *BMJ, 324,* 827–830.

Edwards, N., & Ruggiero, E. (2011). Exploring which context matters in the study of health inequities and their mitigation. *Scandinavian Journal of Public Health, 39,* 43–49.

Edwards, V. (1938). *Group leader's guide to propaganda analysis.* New York: Institute for Propaganda Analysis.

Egan, G. (1975). *The skilled helper: A model for systematic helping and interpersonal relating.* Pacific Grove, CA: Brooks/Cole.

Egan, G. (1982). *The skilled helper: Model, skills, and methods for effective helping* (2nd ed.). Pacific Grove, CA: Brooks/Cole.

Egan, G. (1994). *The skilled helper* (5th ed.). Pacific Grove, CA: Brooks/Cole.

Ehrenreich, B. (1990). *Fear of falling: The inner life of the middle class.* New York: First Harper Perennial Ed.

Ehrenreich, B., & English, D. (1973). *Complaints and disorders: The sexual politics of sickness.* Glass Mountain Pamphlet #2. New York: Feminist Press.

Ehrenreich, J. H. (1985). *The altruistic imagination: A history of social work and social policy in the United States.* Ithaca, NY: Cornell University Press.

Einsaren, S., et al (2010). *Bullying and emotional abuse in the workplace: International perspectives in research and practice* (2nd ed.). New York: Taylor & Francis.

Eisenberg, R., & Cameron, J. (1996). Detrimental effects of reward: Reality or myth? *American Psychologist, 51,* 1153–1166.

Ekman, P. (1992). An argument for basic emotions. *Cognition and Emotion, 6,* 169–200.

Ekman, P. (1994). All emotions are basic. In P. Ekman & R. J. Davidson (Eds.), *The nature of emotion: Fundamental questions* (pp. 15–19). New York: Oxford University Press.

Ekman, P., & Davidson R. J. (Eds.). (1994). *The nature of emotion: Fundamental questions.* New York: Oxford University Press.

Elliott, A. J. & Dweck, C. S. (2005). *The handbook of competence and motivation.* New York: Guilford.

Elliott, R., Bohart, A. C., Watson, J. C., & Greenberg, L. S. (2011). Empathy. In J. C. Norcross (Ed.), *Psychotherapy relationships that work: Evidence-based responsiveness* (2nd ed.*)* (pp. 132–152). New York: Oxford University Press.

Ellis, A. (1996). *Better, deeper, and more enduring brief therapy: The rational-emotive behavior therapy approach.* New York: Brunner/Mazel.

Ellis, A., & Yeager, R. J. (1989). *Why some therapies don't work.* Buffalo, NY: Prometheus Books.

Ellul, J. (1965). *Propaganda: The formation of men's attitudes.* New York: Vintage.

Elmore, J. G., & Boyko, E. J. (2000). Assessing accuracy of diagnostic and screening tests. In J. P. Geyman, R. A. Deyo, and S. D. Ramsey (Eds.) *Evidence-based clinical practice:concepts and approaches* (pp. 83–93). Boston: Butterworth Heineman.

Elstein, A. S., Shulman, L. S., Sprafka, S. A., et al. (1978). *Medical problem solving: An analysis of clinical reasoning.* Cambridge, MA: Harvard University Press.

Elwyn, G., Edwards, A., Wensing, M., Hood, K., Atwell C., & Grol, R. (2003). Shared decision making: Developing an OPTION scale for measuring patient involvement. *Quality and Safety in Health Care, 12,* 93–99.

Ely, J. W., Osheroff, J. A., Ebell, M. H., Chambliss, M. L., Vinson, D. C., Stevermer, J. J., & Pifer, E. A. (2002). Obstacles to answering doctors' questions about patient care with evidence: Qualitative study. *BMJ, 324,* 710–718.

Engel, S. M. (1994). *With good reason: An introduction to informal fallacies* (5th ed.). New York: St. Martin's Press. (See also 6th ed.)

Ennis, R. H. (1987). A taxonomy of critical thinking dispositions and abilities. In J. B. Baron & R. J. Sternberg (Eds.), *Teaching thinking skills: Theory and practice* (pp. 9–26). New York: W. H. Freeman.

Ensalaco, M., & Majka, L. C. (2005). *Children's human rights: Programs and challenges for children worldwide.* Lanham, MD: Rowman & Littlefield.

Entwistle, N. (1987). A model of the teaching-learning process. In J. T. Richardson, M. W. Eysenck, & D. W. Piper (Eds.), *Student learning: Research in education and cognitive psychology* (pp. 13–28). Milton Keynes, U.K.: Society for Research into Higher Education and Open University Press.

Entwistle, V. A., Sheldon, T. A., Sowden, A. J., & Watt, I. A. (1998). Evidence-informed patient choice. *International Journal of Technology Assessment in Health Care, 14,* 212–215.

Epling, W. F., & Pierce, W. D. (1988). Applied behavior analysis: New directions from the laboratory. In G. Davey & C. Cullen (Eds.), *Human operant conditioning and behavior modification* (pp. 43–58). New York: John Wiley.

Erera, P. I. (2002). *Family diversity: Continuity and change in the contemporary family.* Thousand Oaks, CA: Sage.

Erickson, J. (2011). Air pollution near Michigan schools linked to poorer student health, academic performance. *Michigan Today,* April 2011.

Everson, M. D., & Boat, B. W. (1994). Putting the anatomical doll controversy in perspective: An examination of the major uses and criticisms of the dolls in child sexual abuse evaluations. *Child Abuse and Neglect, 18,* 113–129.

Evertson, C. M., & Green, J. L. (1986). Observation as inquiry and method. In M. C. Wittrock (Ed.), *Handbook of research on teaching* (3rd ed.) (pp. 162–213). New York: Macmillan.

Ezell, M. (2005). *Advocacy in the human services.* Belmont, CA: Brooks/Cole.

Fabry, P. L., & Reid, D. H. (1978). Teaching foster grandparents to train severely handicapped persons. *Journal of Applied Behavior Analysis, 11,* 111–123.

Faden, R., Beauchamp, T., & King, N. (1986). *A history and theory of informed consent.* New York: Oxford University Press.

Fairweather, G. W., & Fergus, E. O. (1993). *Empowering the mentally ill.* Austin, TX: G. W. Fair-weather Publishing.

Fairweather, G., Sanders, D., Cressler, D., & Maynard, H. (1969). *Community life for the mentally ill.* Chicago: Aldine.

Faller, K. C., Froming, M. L., & Lipovsky, J. (1991). The parent–child interview: Use in evaluating child allegations of sexual abuse by the parent. *American Journal of Orthopsychiatry, 61,* 552–557.

Faller, K. C. (2007). *Interviewing children about sexual abuse: Controversies and best practices.* New York: Oxford University Press.

Farber, B. A., & Doolin, E. M. (2011). Positive regard and affirmation. In J. C. Norcross (Ed.), *Psychotherapy and relationships that work: Evidence-based responsiveness* (2nd ed.) (pp. 168–186). New York: Oxford University Press.

Farmer, P. (2004). *Pathologies of power: Health, human rights and the new war on the poor.* Berkeley, CA: University of California Press.

Farmer, P. E., Nizeye, B., Stulac, S., & Keshavjee, S. (2006). Structural violence and clinical medicine. *PloS Med, 3:e499.*

Farrington, D. (2003). Methodological quality standards for evaluation research. *The ANNALS of the American Academy of Political and Social Science, 587,* 49–68.

Favell, J. E., & McGimsey, J. F. (1993). Defining an acceptable treatment environment. In R. Van Houten & S. Axelrod (Eds.), *Behavior analysis and treatment* (pp. 25–45). New York: Plenum.

Favell, J. E., Realon, R. E., & Sutton, K. A. (1996). Measuring and increasing the happiness of people with profound mental retardation and physical handicaps. *Behavioral Interventions, 11,* 47–58.

Fawcett, B. (2011). Post-modernism in social work. In V. E. Cree (Ed.), *Social work: A reader* (pp. 227–235). New York: Routledge.

Fawcett, S. B. (1991). Some values guiding community research and action. *Journal of Applied Behavior Analysis, 24,* 621–636.

Fawcett, S. B., Mathews, R. M., & Fletcher, R. K. (1980). Some promising directions for behavioral community technology. *Journal of Applied Behavior Analysis, 15,* 505–518.

Fawcett, S. B., Mathews, R. M., Fletcher, R. K., Morrow, R., & Stokes, T. F. (1976). Personalized instruction in the community: Teaching helping skills to low-income neighborhood residents. *Journal of Personalized Instruction, 1,* 86–90.

Fawcett, S. B., Seekins, T., Whang, P. L., Muiu, C., & Balcazar, Y. S. (1982). The concerns report method: Involving consumers in setting local improvement agendas. *Social Policy, 13,* 35 H.

Fawcett, S. B., Seekins, T., Whang, P. L., Muiu, C., & Suarez-Balcazar, Y. (1984). Creating and using social technologies for community empowerment. In J. Rappaport, C. Swift, & R. Hess (Eds.), *Studies in empowerment: Steps toward understanding and action* (pp. 145–171). New York: Haworth.

Fawcett, S. B., White, G. W., Balcazar, F. E., Suarez-Balcazar, Y., Mathews, R. M., Paine-Andrews, A., Seekins, T., & Smith, J. (1994). A contextual-behavioral model of empowerment: Case studies involving people with physical disabilities. *American Journal of Community Psychology, 22*(4), 471–496.

Feinstein, A. R. (1967). *Judgement*. Baltimore: Williams & Williams.

Feltovich, P. J., Ford, K. M., & Hoffman, R. R. (1997). *Expertise in context*. Cambridge, MA: MIT Press.

Ferster, C. B. (1972). The experimental analysis of clinical phenomenon. *Psychological Record, 22*, 1–16.

Ferster, C. B., Culbertson, S., & Boren, M. C. P. (1975). *Behavior Principles* (2nd ed.). Englewood Cliffs, NJ: Prentice Hall.

Feser, E. (1998). Hayek on social justice: Reply to Lukes and Johnston. *Critical Review, 11*, 581–606.

Fetterman, D., & Wandersman, A. (2007). Empowerment evaluation: Yesterday, today & tomorrow. *American J. of Evaluation, 28*, 179–198.

Feynman, R. (1969). What is science? *The Physics Teacher, 17*(6).

Feynman, R. (1989). *What do you care what other people think?* New York: Bantam.

Feynman, R. L. (1997). *Surely you're joking Mr. Feynman!* New York: W. W. Norton.

Feynman, R. (2007). *What do you care what other people think? Further adventures of a curious character*, London: Penguin.

Field, J. (2003). *Social capital*. New York: Routledge.

Finch, A. E., Lambert, M. J., & Brown, J. S. (2000). Attacking anxiety: A naturalistic study of a multimedia self-help program. *Journal of Clinical Psychology, 56*, 1–11.

Fineberg, S. A. (1949). *Punishment without crime: What you can do about prejudice*. Garden City, NY: Doubleday.

Fineman, S. (1985). *Social work stress and intervention*. Aldershot, England: Gower.

Finkielkraut, A. (1995). *The defeat of the mind*. New York: Columbia University Press.

Finn, J. & Schoech, D. (2008). Introduction to special issue on Internet-delivered therapeutic interventions in human services: Methods, issues, and evaluation. *Journal of Technology in Human Services, 46*(2–4).

Finn, J. & Steele, T. (2010). Online self-help/mutual aid groups in mental health practice. In L. D. Brown & S. Wituk (Eds.), *Mental health self-help: Consumer and family initiatives* (pp. 87–105). New York: Springer.

Fiore, S. M., Rosen, M. A., & Salas, E. (2011). Uncertainty management and macrocognition in teams. In K. L. Mosler & U. M. Fisher (Eds.), *Informed by knowledge: Expert performance in complex situations* (pp. 247–260). New York: Psychology Press.

Fisher, J. D., Rytting, M., & Heslin, R. (1976). Hands touching hands. *Sociometry, 39*, 416–421.

Fisher, P. A., & Chamberlain, P. (2000). Multidimensional treatment foster care: A program for intensive parenting, family support, and skill building. *Journal of Emotional and Behavioral Disorders, 8*(3), 155–164.

Fisher, R. (1994*). Let the people decide: Neighborhood organizing in America*. New York: Twayne Publishers.

Fisher, R., & Ury, W. (1991). *Getting to yes: Negotiating agreement without giving in* (2nd ed.). New York: Penguin.

Fisher, W. W., Piazza, C. C., & Roane, H. S. (2011). *Handbook of Applied Behavior Analysis*. New York: Guilford.

Flannelly, L. T., & Flannelly, K. J. (2000). Reducing people's judgment bias about their level of knowledge. *Psychological Record, 50*, 587–600.

Flew, A. (1985). *Thinking about social thinking*. Oxford, England: Blackwell.

Flexner, A. (1915). Is social work a profession? Proceedings of the National Conference of Charities and Corrections (pp. 577–590). Chicago: Hildmann.

Foa, E., Hembree, E. & Rothbaum, B. O. (2007). *Prolonged exposure therapy for PTSD: Emotional processing of traumatic experiences: therapist guide*. New York: Oxford University Press.

Fogler, H. S., & LeBlanc, S. E. (2008). *Strategies for creative problem solving* (2nd ed.). Upper Saddle River, NJ: Prentice Hall.

Folkman, S., & Lazarus, R. S. (1980). An analysis of coping in a middle-aged community sample. *Journal of Health and Social Behavior, 21*, 219–239.

Follette, W. C.& Hayes, S. C. (2000). Contemporary behavior therapy. In C. R. Snyder & R. E. Ingram (Eds.), *Handbook of psychological change: Psychotherapy processes and practices for the 21st century* (pp. 381–408). New York: John Wiley & Sons.

Forehand, R. L., & MacMahon, R. J. (1981). *Helping the noncompliant child: A clinician's guide to parent training* New York: Guilford.

Foner, P. S. (Ed.). (1950). *The life and writings of Frederick Douglas* (vol. 2). New York: International.

Forgatch, M. S., & Patterson, G. R. (2010). Parent-management training. Oregon model: An intervention for anti-social behavior in children and adolescents. In J. R. Weisz & A. E. Kazdin (Eds.), *Evidence-based psychotherapies for children and adolescents* (2nd Ed.) (pp. 179–193). New York: Guilford.

Forsetlund, L., Bjorndal, A., Rashidian, A., Jamtvedt, G., O'Brien, M. A., Wolf, F., et al. (2009). Continuing education meetings and workshops: Effects on professional practice and health care outcomes. *Cochrane Review*. Issue 3.

Foster, W. S. (1978). Adjunctive behavior: An under reported phenomenon in applied behavior analysis? *Journal of Applied Behavior Analysis, 11*, 545–546.

Foucault, M. (1973). *The birth of the clinic: An archeology of medical perception*. New York: Pantheon.

Foucault, M. (1979). On governmentality. *Ideology and Consciousness, 5*, 5–22.

Fox, R. C., & Swazey, J. P. (1974). *The courage to fail*. Chicago, IL: University of Chicago Press.

Foxx, R. M. (1982). *Increasing behaviors of severely retarded and autistic children*. Champaign, IL: Research Press.

Foxx, R. M., & Bittel, R. G. (1989). *Thinking it through: Teaching a problem-solving strategy for community living*. Champaign, IL: Research Press.

Foy, D. W., Eisler, R. M., & Pinkston, S. (1975). Modeled assertion in a case of explosive rages. *Journal of Behavior Therapy and Experimental Psychiatry, 6*, 135–137.

Frances, A. (2006). The first draft of DSM-V: If accepted, will fan the flames of false positive diagnoses. *BMJ, 340*, c1168.

Frances, A. (2010). Normality is an endangered species: Psychiatric fads and overdiagnosis. *Psychiatric Times*, July 6.

Frank, J. D. (1961). *Persuasion and healing: A comparative study of psychotherapy*. Baltimore, MD: Johns Hopkins University Press.

Frank, J. D. (1976). Restoration of morale and behavior change. In A. Burton (Ed.), *What makes behavior change possible*. New York: Brunner/Mazel.

Frank, J. D., & Frank, J. B. (1991). *Persuasion and healing: A comparative study of psychotherapy* (3rd ed.). Baltimore: John Hopkins University Press.

Frankl, V. E. (1967). *Psychotherapy and Existentialism: Selected papers on logotherapy.* New York: Simon & Schuster.

Frankl, V. E. (1984). *Man's search for meaning: An introduction to logotherapy.* New York: Simon & Schuster.

Fraser, M. W., Nash, J. K., Galinsky, M. J., & Darwin, K. E. (2000). *Making choices: Social problem-solving skills for children.* Washington, DC: NASW Press.

Frazer, J. G. (1925). *The golden bough: A study in magic and religion.* London: Macmillan.

Freedman, B. J., Donahoe, C. P., Rosenthal, L., Schlundt, D. G., & McFall, R. M. (1978). A social-behavioral analysis of skill deficits in delinquent and nondelinquent adolescent boys. *Journal of Consulting and Clinical Psychology, 46,* 1448–1462.

Freidson, E. (1973). Professions and the occupational principle. In E. Freidson (Ed.), *The professions and their prospects* (pp. 19–38). Beverly Hills, CA: Sage.

Freidson, E. (1986). *Professional powers: A study of the institutionalization of formal knowledge.* Chicago: University of Chicago Press.

Freire, P. (1973). *Education for critical consciousness.* New York: Continuum.

Freire, P. (1996). *Pedagogy of the oppressed* (2nd ed.). Harmondsworth: Penguin.

Freisthler, B., Lery, B., Gruenewald, P., & Chow, J. (2006). Methods and challenges of analyzing spatial data for social work problems: The case of examining child maltreatment geographically. *Social Work Research, 30*(4), 198–210.

French, J. R. P., Jr., & Raven, B. (1959). The bases of social power. In D. Cartwright (Ed.), *Studies in social power.* Ann Arbor: University of Michigan, Institute for Social Research.

Freud, A. (1967). *The ego and the mechanisms of defense* (rev. ed.). New York: International Universities Press.

Friedman, R. M., & Drews, D. A. (2005). Evidence-based practices, systems of care and individualized care. Department of Child and Family Studies. University of South Florida.

Fromm, E. (1963). *Escape from freedom.* New York: Holt, Rinehart & Winston.

Furedi, F. (2006). *Culture of fear revisited.* New York: Continuum.

Furman, R. & Negi, N. (2010). *Social work practice with Latinos: Key issues and everyday theories.* Chicago, IL: Lyceum.

Gahagan, J. (1984). *Social interaction and its management.* London: Methuen.

Gainsborough, J. F. (2010). *Scandalous politics: Child welfare policy in the United States.* Washington, D.C.: Georgetown University Press.

Gaissmaier, W. & Gigerenzer, G. (2011). When misinformed patients try to make informed health decisions. In G. Gigerenzer, & J. A. M. Gray (Eds.), *Better doctors, better patients, better decisions: Envisioning health care 2010* (pp. 29–43). Cambridge, MA: MIT Press.

Galinsky, M., Rounds, K., Montague, A., & Butowsky, E. (1993). *Leading a telephone support group for persons with HIV disease.* Chapel Hill, NC: School of Social Work, University of North Carolina.

Gallagher-Thompson, D., Steffan, A. & Thompson, L. W. (2007). *Handbook of behavioral and cognitive therapies with older adults.* New York: Springer.

Galper, J. H. (1975). *The politics of social services.* Englewood Cliffs, NJ: Prentice Hall.

Gambrill, E. D. (1995). Assertion skills training. In W. O'Donohue & L. Krasner (Eds.), *Handbook of psychological skills training: Clinical techniques and applications* (pp. 81–118). Boston: Allyn and Bacon.

Gambrill, E. D. (1997). Social work education: Possible futures. In M. Reisch & E. Gambrill (Eds.), *Social work in the 21st century* (pp. 317–327). Thousand Oaks, CA: Pine Forge Press.

Gambrill, E. D. (1999). Evidence-based practice: An alternative to authority-based practice. *Families in Society: Journal of Contemporary Human Services, 80*(4), 341–350.

Gambrill, E. (2001). Social work: An authority-based profession. *Research on Social Work Practice, 11,* 166–175.

Gambrill, E. (2006). Evidence-based-practice: Choices ahead. *Research on Social Work Practice, 16,* 338–357.

Gambrill E. (2008). Informed consent. In M. C. Calder (Ed.). *The carrot or the stick? Toward effective practice with involuntary clients in safeguarding children* (pp. 37–55). Lyme Regis, UK: Russell House.

Gambrill, E. (Ed.) (2009). *Social work ethics.* International Library of essays in public and professional ethics. Burlington, VT: Ashgate.

Gambrill, E. (2011). Evidence-based practice and the ethics of discretion. *Journal of Social Work, 11,* 26–48.

Gambrill, E. (2012a). *Propaganda in the helping professions.* New York: Oxford University Press.

Gambrill, E. D. (2012b). *Critical thinking in clinical practice: Improving the accuracy of judgments and decisions* (3rd ed.). Hobokan, NJ: John Wiley & Sons.

Gambrill, E. D., & Gibbs, L. (2002). Making practice decisions: Is what's good for the goose good for the gander? *Ethical Human Sciences & Services, 4*(1), 31–46.

Gambrill, E. & Gibbs, L. (2009). *Critical thinking for helping professionals: A skills-based workbook* (3rd ed.). New York: Oxford University Press.

Gambrill, E. & Reiman, A. (2011). A propaganda index for reviewing manuscripts and articles: An exploratory study. *PloS One, 6,* e19516.

Gambrill, E. D., & Richey, C. A. (1975). An assertion inventory for use in assessment and research. *Behavior Therapy, 6,* 547–549.

Gambrill, E. D., & Richey, C. A. (1988). *Taking charge of your social life* (4th printing). Berkeley: Behavioral Options.

Gambrill, E., & Shlonsky, A. (2001). The need for comprehensive risk management systems in child welfare. *Children and Youth Services Review, 23,* 79–107.

Gambrill, E. D., Thomas, E. J., & Carter, R. D. (1971). Procedure for socio-behavioral practice in open settings. *Social Work, 16,* 51–62.

Gamwell, L., & Tomes, N. (1995). *Madness in America: Cultural and medical perceptions of mental illness before 1914.* Binghamton University Art Museum: Cornell University Press.

Garb, H. N. (1997). Race bias, social class bias, and gender bias in clinical judgment. *Clinical Psychology: Science and Practice, 4*(2), 99–120.

Garb, H. N., & Boyle, T. A. (2003). Understanding why some clinicians use pseudoscientific methods: Findings from research on clinical judgment. In S. O. Lilienfeld, S. J. Lynn, and J. M. Lohr (Eds.), *Science and pseudoscience in clinical psychology* (pp. 17–38). New York: Guilford.

Garbarino, J. (1992). *Children and families in the social environment* (2nd ed.). New York: Aldine de Gruyter.

Gardner, J. E. (1967). Behavior therapy treatment approach to a psychogenic seizure case. *Journal of Consulting Psychology, 31,* 209–212.

Gardner, J. M., Brust, D. J., & Watson, L. S. (1970). A scale to measure proficiency in applying behavior modification techniques to the mentally retarded. *American Journal of Mental Deficiency, 74,* 633–636.

Garfield, S. I. (1994). Research on client variables in psychotherapy. In S. I. Garfield & A. E. Bergin (Eds.), *Handbook of psychology and behavior change* (4th ed.) (pp. 190–228). New York: John Wiley & Sons.

Garland, D. F. (1916). The municipality and public welfare. *Proceedings of the National Conference of Charities and Corrections* (pp. 316–316). 43rd session. Indianapolis, IN. May. Chicago: Hildman Printing Co.

Garvin, C. D., Gutierrez, L. M., & Galinsky, M. J. (Eds.) (2006). *Handbook of social work with groups.* New York: Guilford.

Garvin, V., Leber, D., & Kalter, N. (1991). Children of divorce: Predictors of change following preventive intervention. *American Journal of Orthopsychiatry, 61,* 438–447.

Gatrell, A. C. & Elliot, S. J. (2009). *Geographies of health: An introduction* (2nd ed.). Mauldon, MA: Wiley-Blackwell.

Gawande, A. (2010). *The checklist manifesto: How to get things right.* New York: Metropolitan Books.

Gazzaniga, M. W. Reuter-Lorenz, P. A., et al. (2010). *The cognitive neuroscience of mind: A tribute to Michael S. Gazzaniga.* Cambridge, Mass: MIT Press.

Gelles, R. J. (1982). Applying research on family violence to clinical practice. *Journal of Marriage and the Family, 44,* 9–20.

Gellner, E. (1992). *Postmodernism, reason, and religion.* New York: Routledge.

George, V., & Wilding, P. (1984). *The impact of social policy.* London: Routledge & Kegan Paul.

Gibbs, L. E. (1991). *Scientific reasoning for social workers: Bridging the gap between research and practice.* New York: Macmillan.

Gibbs, L. E. (2003). *Evidence-based practice for the helping professions.* Pacific Grove, CA: Brooks/Cole.

Gibbs, L., & Gambrill, E. (2002). Evidence-based practice: Counterarguments to objections. *Research on Social Work Practice, 12,* 452–476.

Gibelman, M. & Furman, R. (2008). *Navigating human service organizations.* Chicago, IL: Lyceum.

Gigerenzer, G. (2002). *Calculated risks: How to know when numbers deceive you.* New York: Simon & Schuster.

Gigerenzer, G. (2005). Fast and frugal heuristics: The tools of bounded rationality. In D. J. Koehler & N. Harvey (Eds.), *The Blackwell handbook of judgment and decision making* (pp. 62–88). Oxford, England: Blackwell Publishing.

Gigerenzer, G. (2007). *Gut feelings: The intelligence of the unconscious.* New York: Viking.

Gigerenzer, G. & Brighton, H. (2011). Homo heuristicus: Why biased minds make better inferences. In G. Gigerenzer, R. Hertwig, & T. Pachur (Eds.), *Heuristics: The foundations of adaptive behavior* (pp. 2–27). New York: Oxford University Press.

Gigerenzer, G., & Gray, J. A. M. (Eds.) (2011). *Better doctors, better patients, better decisions: Envisioning health care 2020.* Cambridge, MA: MIT Press.

Gigerenzer, G., Hertwig, R., & Pachur, T. (Eds.) (2011). *Heuristics: The foundations of adaptive behavior.* New York: Oxford University Press.

Gilbert, N. (2008). *A mother's work: How feminism, the market, and policy shape family life.* New Haven, CT: Yale University Press.

Gilbert, P. (1989). *Human nature and suffering.* New York: Guilford.

Gilbert, P. (1992). *Depression: The evolution of powerlessness.* New York: Guilford.

Gilbert, P. (1993). Defense and safety: Their function in social behaviour and psychopathology. *British Journal of Clinical Psychology, 32,* 131–153.

Gilbert, P. (1994). Male violence: Toward an integration. In J. Archer (Ed.), *Male violence.* London, U.K.: Routledge.

Gilbert, R., & Logan, S. (2000). Assessing diagnostic and screening tests. In V. A. Moyer (Editor-in-chief), E. J. Elliot (Senior assoc. ed.), R. L. Davis, R. Gilbert, T. Klassen, S. Logan, C. Mellis, & K. Williams (Associate eds.), *Evidence based pediatrics and child health* (pp. 24–36). London: BMJ Books.

Gilligan, C. (1982). *In a different voice.* Cambridge, MA: Harvard University Press.

Ginsberg, L. (2011). *Social work in rural communities* (5th ed.). Alexandria, VA: CSWE.

Gitterman, A., & Salmon, R. (2009). *Encyclopedia of social work with groups.* New York: Routledge.

Gitterman, A., & Shulman, L. (Eds.). (2005). *Mutual aid groups, vulnerable and resilient populations, and the life cycle.* New York: Columbia University Press.

Glasziou, P., Del Mar, C., & Salisbury, J. (2003). *Evidence-based medicine workbook.* London: BMJ Books.

Glasziou, P., Vandenbroucke, J., Chalmers, I. (2004). Assessing the quality of research. *BMJ, 328,* 39–41.

Glenn, S. S. (1991). Contingencies and meta-contingencies: Relations among behavioral, cultural and biological evolution. In P. A. Lamal (Ed.), *Behavioral analysis of societies and cultural practices* (pp. 39–73). New York: Hemisphere.

Glisson, C. (2000). Organizational climate and culture. In R. J. Patti (Ed.), *The handbook of social welfare management* (pp. 395–423). Thousand Oaks, CA: Sage.

Glisson, C., Landsverk, J., Schoenwald, S. K., Kelleher, K., Hoagwood, K. E., Mayberg, S., et al. (2008). Assessing the organizational social context (OSC) of mental health services for implementation research and practice. *Administration and Policy in Mental Health and Mental Health Services Research, 35,* 98–113.

Glockner, A. & Witteman, C. (2010). Beyond dual process models: A categorization of processes underlying intuitive judgement and decision making. *Thinking & Research, 16,* 1–25.

Glosoff, H. L., Herlihy, B., & Spence, E. B. (2000). Privileged communication in the counselor–client relationship. *Journal of Counseling and Development, 78,* 454–462.

Goldenberg, I. I. (1978). *Oppression and social intervention: The human condition and the problem of change.* Chicago: Nelson Hall.

Goldfried, M. R. (2011). Generating research questions from clinical experience: Therapists' experiences in using CBT for panic disorder. *The Behavior Therapist, 34,* 57–62.

Goldiamond, I. (1965). Self-control procedures in personal behavior problems. *Psychological Reports, 17,* 851–868.

Goldiamond, I. (1974). Toward a constructional approach to social problems: Ethical and constitutional issues raised by applied behavior analysis. *Behaviorism, 2,* 1–84.

Goldiamond, I. (1978). The professional as double-agent. *Journal of Applied Behavior Analysis, 11,* 178–184.

Goldiamond, I. (1984). Training parent trainers and ethicists in nonlinear analysis of behavior. In R. F. Dangel & R. A. Polster

(Eds.), *Parent training: Foundations of research and practice* (pp. 504–546). New York: Guilford.

Goldstein, A. P. (1980). Relationship enhancement methods. In F. H. Kanfer and A. P. Goldstein (Eds.), *Helping people change: A textbook of methods* (pp. 18–57). Elmsford, NY: Pergamon.

Goldstein, H., Kaczmarek, L. A., & English, K. M. (Eds.). (2002). *Promoting social communication: children with developmental disabilities from birth to adolescence.* Baltimore, MD: Paul H. Brookes.

Goldstein, R. S., & Baer, D. M. (1976). R.S.V.P.: A procedure to increase the personal mail and number of correspondents for nursing home residents. *Behavior Therapy, 7,* 348–354.

Goleman, D. (2010). *Emotional intelligence: Why it can matter more than I. Q.* London: Bloomsburg.

Gomory, T. (1999). Programs of assertive community treatment (PACT): A critical review. *Ethical Human Sciences and Services, 1*(2), 147–163.

Gondolf, E. W., & Fisher, E. R. (1988). *Battered women as survivors: An alternative to treating learned helplessness.* Lexington, MA: Lexington Books.

Goode, E. (2011). Many in U.S. are arrested by age 23 study finds. *New York Times,* December 19.

Goode, E., & Schwartz, J. (2011). Police lineups start to face fact: Eyes can lie. *New York Times,* August 28.

Goode, W. J. (1960). Encroachment, charlatanism, and the emerging professions: Psychology, sociology, and medicine. *American Sociological Review, 25,* 902–914.

Goode, W. J. (1978). *The celebration of heroes: Prestige as a social control system.* Berkeley: University of California Press.

Goodwin, D. L., & Coates, T. J. (1976). The teacher–pupil interaction scale. *Journal of Applied Behavior Analysis, 9,* 114.

Gorenstein, E. E. (1992). *The science of mental illness.* New York: Academic Press.

Gorman, D. M. (1998). The irrelevance of evidence in the development of school-based drug prevention policy, 1986–1996. *Evaluation Review, 22,* 118–146.

Gorman, D. M., & Huber (2009). The social construction of evidence-based drug prevention programs: A reanalysis of data from the Drug Abuse Resistance Education (DARE) Program. *Evaluation Review, 33,* 396–414.

Gottlieb, B. H. (1978). The development and application of a classification scheme of informal helping behaviors. *Canadian Journal of Behavioral Science, 10,* 105–115.

Gottlieb, B. H., & Todd, D. M. (1979). Characterizing and promoting social support in natural settings. In R. F. Munoz, L. R. Snowden, J. G. Kelly & Associates (Eds.), *Social and psychological research in community settings* (pp. 183–242). San Francisco: Jossey-Bass.

Gottlieb, N. (1978). Helpful hints for responding to sexist put-downs. Unpublished manuscript. School of Social Work University of Washington, Seattle, WA.

Gottlieb, S. (2003). One in three doctors don't tell patients about services they can't have. *BMJ, 327,* 123.

Gottman, J. M., & Silver, N. (1999). *The seven principles for making marriage work.* New York: Three Rivers Press.

Gottman, J., Notarius, C., Gonzo, J., & Markman, H. (1976). *A couples guide to communication.* Champaign, IL: Research Press.

Gøtzsche, P. C., Liberati, A., Torri, V., & Rossetti, L. (1996). Beware of surrogate endpoints. *International Journal of Technology Assessment in Health Care, 12,* 238–246.

Gøtzsche, P. C. & Jørgensen, K. J. (2011). The breast screening program and misinforming the public. *J. R. Soc. Med., 104,* 361–369.

Gould, S. J. (1995). Ladders and cones: Constraining evolution by canonical icons. In R. B. Silvers (Ed.), *Hidden histories of science.* New York: New York Review Books.

Goulding, R. (2004). One in twelve older people are prescribed the wrong drug. *Archives of Internal Medicine, 164,* 305–312.

Graham-Bermann, S. A., & Levendosky, A. A. (Eds.) (2011). *How intimate partner violence affects children.* Washington, D.C.: American Psychological Association.

Graubard, P. S., Rosenberg, H., & Miller, M. B. (1971). Student applications of behavior modification to teachers and environments or ecological approaches to social deviancy. In E. A. Ramp and B. L. Hopkins (Eds.), *A new direction for education: Behavior analysis,* (Vol. 1.) (pp. 81–101). Lawrence University of Kansas, Department of Human Development.

Gray, J. (1987). *The psychology of fear and stress* (2nd ed.). Cambridge, U.K.: Cambridge University Press.

Gray, J. A. M. (1997). *Evidence-based health care: How to make health policy and management decisions.* New York: Churchill Livingstone.

Gray, J. A. M. (1998). Where is the chief knowledge officer? *BMJ, 317,* 832.

Gray, J. A. M. (2001a). *Evidence-based health care: How to make health policy and management decisions* (2nd ed.). New York. Churchill Livingstone.

Gray, J. A. M. (2001b). Evidence-based medicine for professionals. In A. Edwards & G. Elwyn (Eds.), *Evidence-based patient choice: Inevitable or impossible?* (pp. 19–33). New York: Oxford University Press.

Gray, M. (2010). Social development and the status quo: Professionalization and Third Way co-optation. *International Journal of Social Welfare, 19,* 463–470.

Gray, M. Coates, J., & Yellow Bird, M. (2008). *Indigenous social work around the world: Toward Culturally relevant education and practice.* Burlington, VT: Ashgate.

Gray, W. D. (1991). *Thinking critically about New Age ideas.* Belmont, CA: Wadsworth.

Gray-Little, B., & Kaplan, D. (2000). Race and ethnicity in psychotherapy research. In C. R. Snyder & R. E. Ingram (Eds.), *Handbook of psychological change* (pp. 591–613). New York: John Wiley & Sons.

Green, C. W., Reid, D. H., White, L. K., Halford, R. C., Brittain, D. P., & Gardner, S. M. (1988). Identifying reinforcers for persons with profound handicaps: Staff opinion versus systematic assessment of preferences. *Journal of Applied Behavioral Analysis, 21,* 31–43.

Green, G. P., & Haines, A. (2011). *Asset building & community development* (3rd ed.). Thousand Oaks, CA: Sage Publications, Inc.

Green, K. D., Forehand, R., & McMahon, R. J. (1979). Parental manipulation of compliance and noncompliance in normal and deviant children. *Behavior Modification, 3,* 245–266.

Greene, B. F., Kessler, M. L., & Daniels, M. E. (1996). Issues in child welfare: Competency training for family preservation and reunification service personnel. Unpublished manuscript. Carbondale, IL: Southern Illinois University, Psychology Department.

Greenhalgh, T. (2010). *How to read a paper: The basis of evidence-based medicine* (3rd ed.). London: BMJ Press.

Greenhalgh, T., & Hurwitz, B. (1998). *Narrative based medicine: Dialogue and discourse in clinical practice.* London: BMJ Press.

Greenhalgh, T., & MacFarlane, F. (1997). Towards a competency grid for evidence-based practice. *Journal of Evaluation in Clinical Practice, 3*(2), 161–165.

Greenhalgh, T., Robert, G., Macfarlane, F., Bate, P., & Kyriakidou, O. (2004). Diffusion of innovations in service organizations: systematic review and recommendations. *The Milbank Quarterly, 82*, 581–629.

Greenhalgh, T., & Smyth, R. L. (2002). Lessons from this correspondence. *BMJ*, 1/10 Rapid Responses.

Greenwald, G. (2009). *Drug decriminalization in Portugal: Lessons for creating fair and successful drug policies.* Cato Institute.

Greenwald, A. G., Poelman, T. A., Uhlmann, E., & Banaji, M. R. (2009). Understanding and using the Implicit Association Test: III. Meta-analysis of predictive validity. *Journal of Personality and Social Psychology, 97*, 17–41.

Greer, R. D. (2007). *Designing teaching strategies: An applied behavior analysis systems approach.* New York: Elsevier.

Greif, J. L., & Ephross, P. H. (2011). *Group work with populations at risk* (3rd ed.). New York: Oxford University Press.

Griffin, W. V., Montsinger, J. L., & Carter, N. A. (1995). *Resource guide on personal safety for administrators and other personnel.* Durham, NC: Brendan Associates and IRL.

Grilli, R., Magrini, N., Penna, A., Mura, G., & Liberati, A. (2000). Practice guidelines developed by specialty societies: The need for a critical appraisal. *Lancet, 355*, 103–106.

Grise-Owens, E., Vessels, J., & Owens, L. W. (2004). Building coalitions and changing communities. Organizing for change: One city's journey toward justice. *Journal of Gay & Lesbian Social Services, 16(3/4)*, 1–15.

Gross, J. J. (2007). *Handbook of emotion regulation.* New York: Guilford.

Gross, P. R., & Levitt, N. (1994). *Higher superstition: The academic left and its quarrels with science.* Baltimore: Johns Hopkins University Press.

Grove, W. M., & Meehl, P. E. (1996). Comparative efficiency of informal (subjective, impressionistic) and formal (mechanical, algorithmic) prediction procedures: The clinical-statistical controversy). *Psychology, Public Policy & Law, 2*, 293–323.

Guevara, J. P., & Stein, M. T. (2001). Evidence based management of attention deficit hyperactivity disorder. *BMJ, 323*, 1232–1235.

Gummer, B. (1997). Is the Code of Ethics as applicable to agency executives as it is to direct service practitioners? NO. In E. Gambrill & R. Pruger (Eds.), *Controversial issues in social work ethics, values and obligations* (pp. 143–148). Boston: Allyn & Bacon.

Gurman, A. S. (2008). *Clinical handbook of couple therapy.* New York: Guilford.

Gusfield, J. R. (2003). Constructing the ownership of social problems: Fun and profit in the welfare state. In J, D. Orcutt & D. R. Rudy (Eds.), *Drugs, alcohol, and social problems* (pp. 7–18). New York: Rowman & Littlefield Publishers.

Gutierrez, L. M. (1990). Working with women of color: An empowerment perspective. *Social Work, 35*, 149–153.

Gutierrez, L., Lewis, E. A., & Nagda, B. (2005). Multicultural community practice strategies and inter group empowerment. In M. Weil (Ed.), *The handbook of community practice* (pp. 341–359). Thousand Oaks, CA: Sage.

Guyatt, G., & Rennie, D. (2002). *Users' guide to the medical literature: A manual for evidence-based clinical practice.* The Evidence-Based Medicine Working Group JAMA & Archives. American Medical Association.

Guyatt, C. Rennie, D., Meade, M. O., & Cook, D. J. (2008). *User's guide to the medical literature: A manual for evidence-based clinical practice* (2nd ed.). The Evidence-Based Medicine Working Group. JAMA & Archives. Chicago, IL: American Medical Association.

Haase, R. F., & Tepper, D. T., Jr. (1972). Nonverbal components of empathic communication. *Journal of Counseling Psychology, 19*, 417–424.

Hakim, D. (2011). A disabled boy's death, and a system in disarray. *New York Times.* June 5.

Haley, J. (1969). The art of being a failure as a therapist. *American Journal of Orthopsychiatry, 39*, 691–695.

Halfpenny, P. (1982). *Positivism and sociology.* London: George Allen & Unwin.

Hall, A. S. (1974). *The point of entry: A study of client reception in the social services.* London: Allen & Unwin.

Hall, J. D., Jones, C. H., & Claxton, A. F. (2008). Evaluation of the Stop & Think Social Skills Program with kindergarten students. *J of Applied Social Psychology, 24*, 265–283.

Hall, R. V., & Hall, M. C. (1980). *How to use planned ignoring.* Lawrence, KS: H. H. Enterprises.

Halpern, D. F. (2003). *Thought & knowledge: An introduction to critical thinking* (4th ed.). Mahwah, NJ: Lawrence Erlbaum.

Halpern, J. (2001). *From detached concern to empathy: Humanizing medical practice.* New York: Oxford University Press.

Halpert, S. C. (2002). Suicidal behavior among gay male youth. *Journal of Gay & Lesbian Psychotherapy, 6(3)*, 53–79.

Hamilton, C. (2008). *Cognition and sex differences.* New York: Palgrave Macmillan.

Hammond, K. R. (1996). *Human judgment and social policy: Irreducible uncertainty, inevitable error, and unavoidable injustice.* New York: Oxford.

Handler, J. F. (1973). *The coercive social worker: British lessons for American social services.* Chicago: Rand McNally College Publications.

Handler, J. F., & Hasenfeld, Y. (1991). *The moral construction of poverty: Welfare reform in America.* Newbury Park, CA: Sage.

Handler, J. F., & Hasenfeld, Y. (2007). *Blame welfare, ignore poverty and inequality.* New York: Cambridge University Press.

Hanley, B., Truesdale, A., King, A., Elbourne, D., & Chalmers, I. (2001). Involving consumers in designing, conducting, and interpreting randomised controlled trials: Questionnaire survey. *BMJ, 322*, 519–523.

Hardcastle, D. A., Powers, P. R., & Wenocur, S. (2004). *Community practice: Theories and skills for social workers* (2nd ed.). New York: Oxford University Press.

Hardin, R. (1990). The artificial duties of contemporary professionals. *Social Service Review, 64*, 528–541.

Hardina, D. (2002). *Analytical skills for community organization practice.* New York: Columbia University Press.

Hardina, D. (2005). Ten characteristics of empowerment-oriented social service organizations. *Administration in Social Work, 23*, 23–42.

Hargie, O. (Ed.) (2006). *Handbook of communication skills* (3rd ed.). New York: Routledge.

Harmon, T. M., Nelson, R. O., & Hayes, S. C. (1980). Self-monitoring of mood versus activity by depressed clients. *Journal of Consulting and Clinical Psychology, 48*, 30–38.

Harris, G. (2004). F.D.A. panel urges stronger warning on anitdepressants. *New York Times*, September 15, A1/19.

Harris, G. (2011). Antipsychotic drugs called hazardous for the elderly. *New York Times.* May 9.

Hart, B., & Risley, T. R. (1995). *Meaningful differences in the everyday experience of young American children.* Baltimore, MD: Paul H. Brookes.

Hartocollis, A. (2011). For whistle-blower in medicaid suit, finding guidance in parents and Capra. *New York Times*, November 1, A22.

Hartman, D. P., Barrios, B. A., & Wood, D. D. (2004). Principles of behavioral observation. In S. N. Haynes & E. M. Heiby (Eds.), *Comprehensive handbook of psychological assessment.* Vol. 3 (pp. 108–127). New York: Wiley.

Hasenfeld, Y. (1987a). Power in social work practice. *Social Service Review, 61,* 469–483.

Hasenfeld, Y. (1987b). Program development. In F. M. Cox, J. L. Erlich, J. Rothman, & J. E. Tropman (Eds.), *Strategies of community organization: Macro practice* (4th ed.). Itasca, IL: F. E. Peacock.

Hasenfeld, Y. (2000). Organizational forms as moral practices: The case of welfare departments. *Social Services Review, 74,* 329–351.

Hasenfeld, Y. (2009). *Human services as complex organizations.* Thousand Oaks, CA: Sage.

Hastie, R., & Dawes, R. (2001). *Rational choice in an uncertain world: The psychology of judgment and decision making.* Thousand Oaks, CA: Sage.

Hathaway, S. R. (1948). Some considerations relative to nondirective counseling as therapy. *Journal of Clinical Psychology, 4,* 226–231.

Hawkins, R. P. (1986). Selection of target behaviors. In R. O. Nelson & S. C. Hayes (Eds.), *Conceptual foundations of behavioral assessment* (pp. 331–385). New York: Guilford.

Hawkins, R. P., Peterson, R. F., Schweid, E., & Bijou, S. W. (1966). Behavior therapy in the home: Amelioration of problem parent–child relations with the parent in a therapeutic role. *Journal of Experimental Child Psychology, 4,* 99–107.

Hawthorne, L. (1975). Games supervisors play. *Social Work, 20,* 179–183.

Hayek, F. A. (1976). *Law, legislation and liberty,* Vol. 2: *The mirage of social justice.* Chicago: University of Chicago Press.

Hayes, J. A. Gelso, C. J., & Hummel, A. M. (2011). Managing Countertransference. In J. C. Norcross (Ed.), *Psychotherapy relationships that work: Evidence-based responsiveness* (pp. 239–258). New York: Oxford University Press.

Hayes, S. C., Barnes-Holmes, D., & Roche, B. (2001). *Relational frame theory: A post-Skinnerian account of human language and cognition.* New York: Kluwer Academic/Plenum.

Hayes, S. C., Follette, V. M., & Linehan, M. M. (Eds.). (2004). *Mindfulness and acceptance: Expanding the cognitive-behavioral tradition.* New York: Guilford.

Hayes, S. C., Strosahl, K. D., & Wilson, K. G. (2012). *Acceptance and commitment therapy* (2nd ed.). New York: Guilford.

Haynes, R. B., Devereaux, P. J., & Guyatt, G. H. (2002). Clinical expertise in the era of evidence-based medicine and patient choice. (Editorial) *ACP Journal Club, 136:* A11, 1–7.

Haynes, R. B., Ackloo, E., Sahota, N., McDonald, H. P., & Yao, X. (2008). Interventions for enhancing medication adherence. *Cochrane Database Syst Rev, 16*(2:CD000011.

Haynes, S. N. (1992). *Models of causality and psychopathology: Toward dynamic, synthetic and nonlinear models of behavior disorders.* New York: Macmillan.

Hays, D. G., & Erford, B. T. (Eds.) (2010). *Developing multicultural competence: A systems approach.* Columbus, OH: Pearson Merrill Prentice Hall.

Head, S. J., Bogers, A. J. C, Serruys, P. W., Takkenberg, J. J. M., & Kapetein, A. P. (2011). A crucial factor in shared decision making: The team approach. *The Lancet, 377,* 1836.

Health Disparities and Inequalities Report. (2011). Center for Disease Control, United States.

Healy, D. (2004). *Let them eat Prozac: The unhealthy relationship between the pharmaceutical industry and depression.* New York: New York University Press.

Healy, L. M. & Link, R. J. (2012). *Handbook of international social work: Human rights, development, and the global profession.* New York: Oxford University Press.

Heffernan, J. & Pilkington, P. (2011). Supported employment for persons with mental illness: Systematic review of the effectiveness of individual placement and support in the UK. *J Ment Health, 20,* 368–380.

Helander, E. (2008). *Children and violence: The world of the defenseless.* New York: Palgrave Macmillan.

Henrich, J., Heine, S. J., & Norenzayan, A. (2010). The weirdest people in the world? *Behavioral and Brain Sciences, 3,* 61–83.

Henry, M. (1990) One drug-using mother's story. *Youth Law News, 11,* 19.

Herbert, B. (2011). Separate and unequal. Editorial. *New York Times,* March 22, A23.

Herbert, M., & Harper-Dorton, K. (2002). *Working with children, adolescents and their families* (3rd ed.). Cambridge, MA: Blackwell Publishing Co.

Herbst, A., Ulfelder, H., & Poskanzer, D. (1971). Adenocarcinoma of the vagina: Association of maternal stilbestrol therapy with tumor appearance in young women. *New England Journal of Medicine, 284,* 878–881.

Herek, G. M., Janis, I. L., & Huth, P. (1989). Quality of U.S. decision making during the Cuban missile crisis: Major errors in Welsh's reassessment. *Journal of Conflict Resolution, 33,* 446–459.

Heritage, J. & Clayman, S. (2010). *Talk in action: Interventions, identities and institutions.* Malden, MA: Wiley-Blackwell.

Hertel, S. & Libal, K. (2011). *Human rights in the United States: Beyond exceptionalism.* New York: Cambridge University Press.

Herzberg, D. (2009). *Happy pills in America: From Miltown to Prozac.* Baltimore: John Hopkins University Press.

Heyman, G. M. (2009). *Addiction: A disorder of choice.* Cambridge, MA: Harvard University Press.

Heyman, R. E., & Slep, A. M. S. (2004). Analogue behavioral observation. In S. N. Haynes & E. M. Heiby (Eds.), *Comprehensive handbook of psychological assessment,* Vol. 3, (pp. 162–180). New York: Wiley.

Hick, S. F., & McNutt, J. G. (Eds.). (2002). *Advocacy, activism, and the Internet: Community organization and social policy.* Chicago , IL: Lyceum Books, Inc.

Hickey, S. & Mitlin, D. (2009). *Rights-based approaches to development: Exploring the potential and pitfalls.* Bloomfield, CT: Kumarian Press.

Higgins, J. P. T. & Greene, S. (Eds.) (2008). *Cochrane handbook for systematic reviews of interventions.* Chichester, West Sussex, England: John Wiley & Sons. Ltd. (See also computer file version 5.1.01 updated March 2011.)

Hilgartner, S., & Bosk, C. L. (1988). The rise and fall of social problems: A public arenas model. *American Journal of Sociology, 94,* 53–78.

Hill, C. E., & Knox, S. (2002). Self-disclosure. In J. C. Norcross (Ed.), *Psychotherapy relationships that work: Therapists' contributions and responsiveness to patients* (pp. 255–265). New York: Oxford University Press.

Hill, C. E., & O'Grady, K. E. (1985). List of therapist intentions illustrated in a case study and with therapists of varying theoretical orientations. *Journal of Counseling Psychology, 32,* 3–22.

Hill, P. C., Pargament, K. I., Hood, R. W., Jr., Mc-Cullough, M. E., Swyers, J. P., Larson, D. B., & Zinnbauer, B. J. (2000). Conceptualizing religion and spirituality: Points of commonality, points of departure. *Journal for the Theory of Social Behavior, 30,* 51–77.

Hilton, N. Z., Harris, G. T., & Rice, M. E. (2006). Sixty-six years of research on the clinical versus actuarial prediction of violence. *The Counseling Psychologist, 34,* 400–409.

Hineline, P. N. (1995). President's column: External reinforcers, entrance reinforcers and awards. *Division 25, Recorder, 30*(2), Summer, 1–2.

Hinshaw, S. P. (1995). Enhancing social competence: Integrating self-management strategies with behavioral procedures for children with ADHD. In E. D. Hibbs, & P. S. Jensen (Eds.), *Psychological treatment for child and adolescent disorders: Empirically based strategies for clinical practice* (pp. 285–309). Washington, D. C.: American Psychological Association.

Hiratsuka, J. (1990). Social work "step child" awaits resurgence. Community organizing: Assembling power. *NASW News, 35,* p. 3 (Sept.).

Hirdes, J. P., Poss, J. W., Curtin-Telegdi, N. (2008). The method for assigning priority levels (MAPLe): a new decision support system for allocating home care resources. *BMC Med, 6,* 9 doi: 10.1186/1741.

Hobbs, C. J., & Wynne, J. M. (1989). Sexual abuse of English boys and girls: The importance of anal examination. *Child Abuse and Neglect, 13,* 195–210.

Hobbs, N. (1975). *The futures of children.* San Francisco: Jossey-Bass.

Hochschild, A. R. (2003). *Commercialization of intimate life: Notes from home and work.* Berkeley: University of California Press.

Hodge, D. R. (2001). Spiritual assessment: A review of major qualitative methods and new framework for assessing spirituality. *Social Work, 46*(3), 203–214.

Hodges, V. G. (1991). Providing culturally sensitive intensive family preservation services to ethnic minority families. In E. M. Tracy, D. A. Haapala, J. Kinney, & P. J. Pecora (Eds.), *Intensive family preservation services: An instructional sourcebook* (pp. 95–116). Cleveland, OH: Case Western Reserve University Mandel School of Applied Social Sciences.

Hofer, B. K., & Pintrich, P. R. (Eds.). (2002). *Personal epistemology: The psychology of beliefs about knowledge and knowing.* Mahwah, NJ: Erlbaum.

Hoffman, S. & Podarski, A. (2009). E-health hazards: Provider liability and electronic health record systems. *Berkeley Technology Law Journal, 24,* 1523–1581.

Hogarth, R. M. (2001). *Educating intuition.* Chicago: University of Chicago Press.

Holland, J. H., Holyoak, K. J., Nisbett, R. E., & Thagard, P. R. (1986). *Induction: Processes of inference, learning and discovery.* Cambridge, MA: MIT Press.

Hollon, S. D., & Kendall, P. C. (1980). Cognitive self-statements in depression: Development of an automatic thoughts questionnaire. *Cognitive Therapy and Research, 4,* 109–143.

Holmbeck, G. N., Greenley, R. N., & Franks, E. A. (2003). Developmental issues and considerations in research and practice. In A. E. Kazdin, J. R. Weisz (Eds.), *Evidence-based psychotherapies for children and adolescents.* New York: Guilford.

Holtzworth-Munroe, A., & Hutchinson, G. (1993). Attributing negative intent to wife behavior: The attributions of maritally violent versus nonviolent men. *Journal of Abnormal Psychology, 102,* 206–211.

Homel, R., & Burns, A. (1989). Environmental quality and the well being of children. *Social Indicators Research, 21,* 133–158.

Hook, D., & Eagle, G. (Eds.) (2002). *Psychopathology and social prejudice.* Cape Town, South Africa: University of Cape Town Press.

Hopko, D. R., Lejuez, C. W., LePage, J. P., Hopko, S. D., & McNeil, D. W. (2003). A brief behavioral activation treatment for depression. *Behavior Modification, 27,* 458–469.

Hops, H., Davis, B., & Longoria, N. (1995). Methodological issues in direct observation: Illustrations with the Living in Familiar Environments (LIFE) coding system. *Journal of Clinical Child Psychology, 24*(2), 193–203.

Hopps, J. G., & Pinderhughes, E. (1999). *Group work with overwhelmed clients: How the power of groups can help people transform their lives.* New York: Free Press.

Horner, R. H., Meyer, L. H., & Fredericks, H. D. (1986). *Education of learners with severe handicaps: Exemplary service strategies* (pp. 161–187). Baltimore, MD: Paul H. Brookes.

Horvath, A. O., Del Re, A. C., Flückiger, C., & Symonds, D. (2001). Alliance in individual therapy. In J. C. Norcross (Ed.), *Psychotherapy relationships that work: Evidence-based responsiveness* (2nd ed.) (pp. 25–69). New York: Oxford University Press.

Houston, T. K., Cooper, L. A., & Ford, D. F. (2002). Internet support groups for depression: a 1-year prospective cohort study. *Am. J. Psychiatry, 159,* 2062–2068.

Houts, A. C. (2002). Discovery, invention, and the expansion of the modern diagnostic and statistical manuals of mental disorders. In L. E. Beutler & M. L. Malik (Eds.), *Rethinking the DSM: A psychological perspective* (pp. 17–65). Washington, DC: American Psychological Association.

Howitt, D. (1992). *Child abuse errors: When good intentions go wrong.* New York: Harvester Wheatsheaf.

Huck, S. W., & Sandler, H. M. (1979). *Rival hypotheses: Alternative interpretations of data based conclusions.* New York: Harper & Row.

Hudson, D. L. (2007). *Prisoner's rights.* New York: Chelsea House.

Hughes, B. (1993). See Positive Behavioral Intervention Regulations.

Hughes, C. E. & Stevens, A. (2010). What can we learn from the Portuguese decriminalization of illicit drugs? *British Journal of Criminology, 50,* 999–1022.

Hunsley, J. & Mash, E. J. (Eds.) (2008*). The science and art of clinical assessment.* New York: Oxford University Press.

Hunsley, J., Lee, C. M., & Wood, J. M. (2003). Controversial and questionable assessment techniques. In S. O. Lilienfeld, S. J. Lynn, & J. M. Lohr (Eds.), *Science and pseudoscience in clinical psychology* (pp. 39–76). New York: Guilford.

Hunter, S. (2012). *Lesbian and gay couples: lives, issues and practices.* Chicago: Lyceum.

Hutchinson, A. M., Milke, D. L., Maisey, S., Johnson, C., Squires, J. E., Teare, G., & Estabrooks, C. A. (2010). The resident assessment instrument-minimum data set 2.0 quality indicators: Aa systematic review. *BMC health Services Research, 10,* 166.

Huxley, A. (2005). *Brave new world and brave new world revisited.* New York: Harper Perennial.

Hyde, C. A. (2003). More harm than good? Multicultural initiatives in human service agencies. *Social Thought, 22,* 23–40.

Illich, I. (1976). *Limits to medicine: Medical nemesis, the expropriation of health.* London: M. Boyars.

Illich, I., et al. (1978). *Disabling professions.* New York: M. Boyars.

Illouz, E. (2008). *Saving the modern soul: Therapy, emotions, and the culture of self-help.* Berkeley: University of California Press.

Imel, Z. E., Wampold, B. E., Miller, S. D., & Fleming, R. R. (2008). Distinctions without a difference: Direct comparisons of psychotherapies for alcohol use disorders. *Psychology of Addictive Behaviors, 22,* 533–543.

In court: Duty to warn vs. confidentiality. (1990). *NASW News, 35,* 16.

Ioannidis, J. P. A. (2005). Why most published research findings are false. *PloS Med* 2(8):e124.

Irvine, L. (2003). The problem of unwanted pets: A case study in how institutions "think" about clients' needs. *Social Problems, 50*(4), 550–566.

Ivancevich, J. M., Matteson, M. T., & Konopaske, R. (2011). *Organizational behavior and management.* Boston: McGraw-Hill/ Irwin.

Jaarsma, T. (2005). Inter-professional team approach to patients with heart failure. *Heart, 91,* 832–838.

Jacobs, J. (1992). *The death and life of great American cities.* New York: Vintage.

Jacobson, J. W., Foxx, R. M., & Mulick, J. A. (Eds.) (2005). *Controversial therapies for developmental disabilities: Fad, fashion and science in professional practice.* Mahwah, NJ: Lawrence Erlbaum.

Jacobson, J. W., Mulick, J. A., & Rojahn, J. (2007). *Handbook of intellectual and developmental disabilities.* New York: Springer.

Jacobson, J. W., Mulick, J. A., & Schwartz, A. A. (1995). A history of facilitated communication: Science, pseudoscience, and antiscience working group on facilitated communication. *American Psychologist, 50,* 750–765.

Jacobson, N. S., & Gottman, J. M. (2007). *When men batter women.* New York: Simon & Schuster.

Jadad, A. R. & Enkin, M. W. (2007). *Randomized controlled trials. Questions, answers and musings* (2nd ed.). Malden, MA: Blackwell Publishing.

James, R. K. (2008). *Crisis intervention strategies* (2nd ed.). Belmont, CA: Thomson/Brooks Cole.

Jamieson, K. (2004). A collaborative approach to developing and using quality of life indicators in New Zealand's largest cities. In M. J. Sirgy, D. Rahtz, & Dong-jin, L. (Eds.), *Community quality of life indicators. Best cases* (pp. 75–109). Dordrecht, Netherlands: Kluwer Academic Publishers

Janis, I. L. (1982). *Group think: Psychological studies of policy decisions and fiascos* (2nd ed.). Boston: Houghton Mifflin.

Janis, I. L., & Mann, L. (1977). *Decision making: A psychological analysis of conflict, choice and commitment.* New York: Free Press.

Janoff-Bulman, R. (1979). Characterological versus behavioral self-blame: Inquiries into depression and rape. *Journal of Personality and Social Psychology, 37,* 1798–1809.

Jansson, B. S. (2011). *Improving healthcare through advocacy. A guide for the health and helping professions.* New York: Wiley.

Jarvis, W. T. (1990). *Dubious dentistry: A dental continuing education course.* Loma Linda University School of Dentistry, Loma Linda, CA 92350.

Jaspers, M. W. M., Smeulers, M., Vermeulen, H., & Peute, L. W. (2011). Effects of clinical decision-support systems on practitioner performance and patient outcomes: A synthesis of high-quality systematic review findings. *J. Am. Med. Inform Assoc, 18,* 327–334.

Jeffery, D. P., Ley, A., McLaren, S., & Siegfried, N. (2004). Psychosocial treatment programmes for people with both severe mental illness and substance misuse (Cochrane Review). In *Cochrane Library,* Issue 3. Chichester, UK: John Wiley & Sons, Ltd.

Jennings, D. L., Amabile, T. M., & Ross, L. (1982). Informal covariations assessment: Data-based versus theory-based judgements. In D. Kaheman, P. Slovic, & A. Tversky (Eds.), *Judgment under uncertainty: Heuristics and biases* (pp. 211–230). New York: Cambridge University Press.

Jensen, D. D. (1989). Pathologies of science, precognition, and modern psychophysics. *The Skeptical Inquirer, 13,* 147–160.

Jensen, J. M. & Fraser, M. W. (2006). *Social policy for children and families: A risk and resilience perspective.* Thousand Oaks, CA: Sage.

Jensen, J. M. & Fraser, M. W. (2011). *Social policy for children and families: A risk and resilience perspective* (2nd ed.). Thousand Oaks, CA: Sage.

Jenson, J. M., Dieterich, W. A., Brisson, D., Bender, K. A., & Powell, A. (2011). Preventing childhood bullying: Findings and lessons from the Denver public schools trial. *Research on Social Work Practice, 20,* 509–517.

Jessor, R., Colby, A., & Shweder, R. A. (Eds.). (1996). *Ethnography and human development: Context and meaning in social inquiry.* Chicago: University of Chicago Press.

Jimerson, S. R., Swearer, S. M., & Espelage, D. (2010). *Handbook of bullying in schools: An international perspective.* New York: Routledge.

Johnson, M. S., & Bailey, J. S. (1977). The modification of leisure behavior in a half-way house for retarded women. *Journal of Applied Behavior Analysis, 10,* 273–282.

Johnson, S. M., & White, G. (1971). Self-observation as an agent of behavioral change, *Behavior Therapy, 2,* 488–97.

Johnson, W. L. (2011). The validity and utility of the California Family Risk Assessment under practice conditions in the field: A prospective study. *Child Abuse & Neglect, 35,* 18–28,

Johnson, W. D., Hedges, L. V., & Diaz, R. M. (2004). Interventions to modify sexual risk behaviors for preventing HIV infection in men who have sex with men. (Cochrane Review). In *Cochrane Library,* Issue 3. Chichester, England: John Wiley & Sons, Ltd.

Johnston, D. (1997). Hayek's attack on social justice. *Critical Review, 11,* 81–100.

Johnston, L., Titov, N., Andrews, G., Spence, J., & Dear, B. F. (2011). A randomized controlled trial of a transdiagnostic Internet delivered treatment for anxiety disorders. *PLoS One, 6*(11), e28.

Jones, J. M. (1986). Racism: A cultural analysis of the problem. In S. Gaertner & J. Davidio (Eds.), *Prejudice, discrimination, and racism.* New York: Academic Press.

Jordan, C., & Franklin, C. (2010). *Clinical assessment for social workers: Quantitative and qualitative methods* (3rd ed.). Chicago: Lyceum.

Jordan-Young, R. M. (2010). *Brain storm: The flaws in the science of sex differences.* Boston, MA. Harvard University Press.

Jørgensen, K. J., & Gøtzsche, P. C. (2004). Presentation on websites of possible benefits and harms from screening for breast cancer: Cross sectional study. *British Medical Journal, 328,* 148–155.

Judson, H. F. (2004). *The great betrayal: Fraud in science.* New York: Harcourt.

Jurjevich, R. M. (1974). *The hoax of Freudism: A study of brainwashing the American professionals and laymen.* Philadelphia: Dorrance.

Kadushin, A. (1963). Diagnosis and evaluation for (almost) all occasions. *Social Work, 8,* 12–19.

Kadushin, A. (1968). Games people play in supervision. *Social Work, 13,* 23–32.

Kadushin, A., & Harkness, D. (2002). *Supervision in social work* (4th ed.). New York: Columbia University Press.

Kadushin, A., & Kadushin, G. (1997). *The social work interview: A guide for human service professionals* (4th ed.). New York: Columbia University Press.

Kadushin, A., & Martin, J. A. (1981). *Child abuse: An interactional event.* New York: Columbia University Press.

Kagle, J. D. (2008). *Social work records* (3rd ed.). Long Grove, IL: Waveland Press.

Kahane, H. (1995). *Logic and contemporary rhetoric: The use of reason in everyday life* (7th ed.). Belmont, CA: Wadsworth.

Kahn, S. (2003). *Organizing: A guide for grassroots leaders.* Silver Spring, MD: NASW Press.

Kahneman, D. (2011). *Thinking fast and slow.* New York: Farrar, Straus and Giroux.

Kamerman, S. B., Phipps, S., Ben-Arieh, A. (Eds.) (2010). *From child welfare to child well-being: An international perspective on knowledge in the service of policy making.* New York: Springer.

Kaminski, J. W., Valle, L. A., Filene, J. H., & Boyle, C. (2008). A meta-analytic review of components associated with parent training program effectiveness. *Journal of Abnormal Child Psychology, 36,* 567.

Kananen, L., et al. (2010). Childhood adversities are associated with shorter telomere length at adult age both in individuals with an anxiety disorder and controls, *PloS ONE* 5: e10826, 2010.

Kane, R. A., & Kane, R. L. (1981). *Assessing the elderly: A practical guide to measurement.* Lexington, MA: Lexington Books.

Kanfer, F. H. (1970). Self-monitoring and clinical applications: Methodological limitations. *Journal of Consulting and Clinical Psychology, 35,* 148–152.

Kanfer, F. H., & Phillips, J. S. (1969). A survey of current behavior therapies and a proposal for classification. In C. M. Franks (Ed.). *Behavior therapy: Appraisal and status* (pp. 445–475). New York: McGraw-Hill.

Kanner, A. D., Coyne, J. C., Schaefer, C., & Lazarus, R. S. (1981). Comparison of two modes of stress measurement: Minor daily hassles and uplifts versus major life events. *Journal of Behavioral Medicine, 4,* 1–40.

Kanter, J. W., Cautilli, J. D., Busch, A. M., & Baruch, D. E. (2005). Toward a comprehensive functional analysis of depressive behavior: Five environmental factors and a possible sixth and seventh. *The Behavior Analyst Today, 6,* 65–81.

Kantrowitz, L. & Ballou, M. (1992). A feminist critique of cognitive-behavioral theory. In M. Ballou & L. Brown (Eds.), *Theories of personality and psychopathology* (pp. 70–79). New York: Guilford.

Karger, H. J., & Stoesz, D. (2009). *American social welfare policy: A pluralist approach* (6th ed.). Boston: Allyn & Bacon.

Karls, J. M., & Wandrei, K. E. (Eds.). (1994). *Person-in-environment system: The PIE classification system for social functioning problems.* Annapolis Junction, MD: NASW Press.

Karlsson, H. (2011). How psychotherapy changes the brain: Understanding the mechanisms. *Psychiatric Times, 28* (August 11).

Karsh, B-T., Weinger, M. B., Abbott, P. A., & Wears, R. I. (2010). Health information technology: Fallacies and sober realities. *JAMA, 17,* 617–623.

Kassirer, J. P. (1994). Incorporating patient preferences into medical decisions. *New England Journal of Medicine, 330,* 1895–1896.

Kassirer, J. P. (2005). *On the take: How medicine's complicity with big business can endanger your health.* New York: Oxford University Press.

Katz, A. H. (1993). *Self-help in America: A social movement perspective.* New York: Twayne.

Katz, J. (2002). *The silent world of doctor and patient.* Baltimore: Johns Hopkins University Press.

Katz, M. B. (1989). *The undeserving poor: From the war on poverty to the war on welfare.* New York: Pantheon.

Katz, M. B. (1996). *In the shadow of the poorhouse: A social history of welfare in America* (Rev ed.). New York: Basic Books.

Katz, S. H. (1995). *Is race a legitimate concept for science? AAPA Revised Statement on Race: A brief analysis and commentary.* Philadelphia: University of Pennsylvania.

Kaufman, J. C., & Sternberg, R. J. (2010). *The Cambridge handbook of creativity.* Cambridge, NY: Cambridge University Press.

Kay, S., & Vyse, S. (2005). Helping parents separate the wheat from the chaff: Putting autism treatments to the test. In J. W. Jacobson, R. M. Foxx, & J. A. Mulick (Eds.), *Controversial therapies for developmental disabilities: Fad, fashion, and science in professional practice* (pp. 265–277). Mahwah, NJ: Lawrence Erlbaum.

Kazdin, A. E., French, N. H., & Sherick, R. B. (1981). Acceptability of alternative treatments for children: Evaluations by inpatient children, parents, and staff. *Journal of Consulting and Clinical Psychology, 49,* 900–907.

Kazi, M. A. (2003). *Realist evaluation in practice: Health and social work.* Thousand Oaks, CA: Sage.

Kelly, M., Noell, G., & Reitman, D. (2002). *Practitioner's guide to empirically based measures of school behavior.* AABT clinical assessment series. New York: Kluwer.

Kendall, P. C. (Ed.). (2012). *Child and adolescent therapy: Cognitive-behavioral procedures* (2nd ed.). New York: Guilford.

Kennedy, N. J., & Sanborn, J. S. (1992). Disclosure of tardive dyskinesia: Effect of written policy on risk disclosure. *Pharmacology Bulletin, 28*(1), 93–100.

Kerig, P. K., & Baucom, D. H. (Eds.). (2004). *Couple observational coding systems.* Mahwah, NJ: Erlbaum.

Kerig, P. K., & Lindahl, K. M. (Eds.). (2004). *Family observational coding systems: Resources for systemic research.* Mahwah, NJ: Erlbaum.

Kerr, P. (1992a). Centers for head injury accused of earning millions for neglect. *New York Times.* February 16, A1. Profits from trauma: A special report.

Kerr, P. (1992b). Mental hospital chains accused of much cheating on insurance. *New York Times,* November 24, p. 1, 28.

Keyworth, R. (1990). Performance pay—An evolving system at Spectrum Center. *Performance Management Magazine, 8,* 6–10.

Kiesel, K. B., Lutzker, J. R., & Campbell, R. V. (1989). Behavioral relaxation training to reduce hyperventilation and seizures in a profoundly retarded epileptic child. *Journal of the Multihandicapped Person, 2,* 179–190.

Kifer, R. E., Lewis, M. A., Green, D. R., & Phillips, E. L. (1974). Training pre-delinquent youths and their parents to negotiate conflict situations. *Journal of Applied Behavior Analysis, 7,* 357–364.

King, L. S. (1981). *Medical thinking: A historical preface.* Princeton, NJ: Princeton University Press.

King, P. M., & Kitchener, K. S. (2002). The reflective judgment model: Twenty years of research on epistemic cognition. In B. K. Hofer & P. R. Pintrich (Eds.), *Personal epistemology: The psychology of beliefs about knowledge and knowing* (pp. 37–61). Mahwah, NJ: Erlbaum.

Kinney, J., Haapala, D., & Booth, C. (1991). *Keeping families together: The Homebuilders model.* New York: Aldine de Gruyter.

Kiresuk, T. J., Smith, A., & Cardillo, J. E. (Eds.). (2009). *Goal attainment scaling: Applications, theory and measurement.* New York: Psychology Press.

Kirk, S. A. (2010). Science and politics in the evolution of the DSM. Seabury Lecture. University of California, Berkeley, April.

Kirk, S. A., & Kutchins, H. (1988). Deliberate misdiagnosis in mental health practice. *Social Service Review, 62,* 225–237.

Kirk, S. A., & Kutchins, H. (1992a). *The selling of DSM: The rhetoric of science in psychiatry.* New York: Aldine de Gruyter.

Kirk, S. A., & Kutchins, H. (1992b). Five arguments for using DSM-III-R and why they are wrong. In E. Gambrill & R. Pruger (Eds.), *Controversial issues in social work* (pp. 146–154). Boston, MA: Allyn & Bacon.

Kirsh, I. (2010). *The emperor's new drugs: Exploding the antidepressant myth.* New York: Basic Books.

Kirschenbaum, D. S., & Karoly, P. (1977). When self-regulation fails: Tests of some preliminary hypotheses. *Journal of Consulting and Clinical Psychology, 45,* 1116–1125.

Kissane, R. J. (2003).What's need got to do with it? Barriers to use of nonprofit social services. *Journal of Sociology & Social Welfare, 30,* 127–149.

Klauss, R., & Bass, B. M. (1982). *Interpersonal communication in organizations.* San Diego: Academic.

Klein, G. (1998). *Sources of power: How people make decisions.* Cambridge, MA: MIT Press.

Kleinfield, N. R. & Secret, M. (2011). A bleak life, cut short at 4, harrowing from the start. *New York Times,* May 9, A1, 19.

Kleinman, A. & Fitz-Henry, E. (2007). The experimental basis of subjectivity: How individuals change in the context of societal transformation. In J. Biehl, B. Good, & A. Kleinman (Eds.), *Subjectivity: Ethnographic investigation* (pp. 52–65). Berkeley: University of California Press.

Kling, J. R., Liebman, J. B., & Katz, L. F. (2001). "Bullets don't got no name": Consequences of fear in the Ghetto. JCPR working paper 225/4/16/2001. www.jcpr.org

Kling, J. R., Liebman, J. B., & Katz, L. F. (2007). Experimental analysis and neighborhood effects, *75,* 83–119.

Knapp, M. L., & Hall, J. A. (2010). *Nonverbal communication in human interaction* (7th ed.). Boston, MA: Wadsworth/Cengage Learning.

Know Your Rights: Sexual Harassment at Work. Equal Rights Advocates. www.equalrights.org Retrieved 12/11/11.

Kocieniewski, D. (2011). G. E.'s strategies let it avoid taxes altogether. *New York Times,* March 24.

Koegel, L. K., Koegel, R. L., & Dunlap, G. (2004). *Positive behavioral support: Including people with difficult behavior in the community.* Baltimore, MD: Paul H. Brookes.

Koegel, R. L., & Rincover, A. (1974). Treatment of psychotic children in a classroom environment: I. Learning in a large group. *Journal of Applied Behavior Analysis, 7,* 45–49.

Koegel, R. L., Frea, W. D., & Surratt, A. V. (1994). Self-management of problematic social behavior. In E. Schopler & G. B. Mesibov (Eds.), *Behavioral issues and autism: Current issues in autism* (pp. 81–97). New York: Plenum Press.

Kogan, M., Redfern, S. J., Kober, A., et al. (1995). *Making use of medical audit: A guide to practice in the health professions.* Philadelphia: Open University Press.

Koh, G. C-H., Khoo, H. E., Wong, M. L. & Koh, D. (2008). The effects of problem-based learning during medical school on physician competency: A systematic review. *Canadian Medical Association Journal, 178,* 34–41.

Kohatsu, E. L., Concepcion, W. R., & Perez, P. (2010). Incorporating levels of acculturation in counseling practice. In J. G. Ponterratto, J. M. Casas, L. A. Suzuki, & C. M. Alexander, *Handbook of multicultural counseling* (3nd ed.) (pp. 343–356). Thousand Oaks, CA: Sage.

Kohlberg, L., & Lickona, T. (1986). *The stages of ethical development: From childhood through old age.* New York: Harper.

Kohr, M. A., Parrish, J. M., Neef, N. A., Driessen, J. R., & Hallinan, P. C. (1988). Communication skills training for parents: Experimental and social validation. *Journal of Applied Behavior Analysis, 21,* 21–30.

Kolata, G. (1998). Fourth-grader challenges alternative therapy. *New York Times.* April 11, A1.

Kolden, G. C., Klein, M. H., Wang, C. C., & Austin, S. B. (2011). Congruence/genuineness. In J. C. Norcross (Ed.), *Psychotherapy relationships that work: Evidence-based responsiveness* (2nd ed.) (pp. 187–202). New York: Oxford University Press.

Kondro, W., & Sibbald, B. (2004). Drug company experts advised staff to withhold data about SSRI use in children. *Canadian Medical Association, 170*(5), 783.

Koocher, G. P., Goodman, G. S., White, C. S., Friedrich, W. N., Sivan, A. B., & Reynolds, C. R. (1995). Psychological science and the use of anatomically detailed dolls in child sexual abuse assessments. *Psychological Bulletin, 118,* 199–222.

Kopelowicz, A., Liberman, R. P., & Zarete, R. (2006). Recent advances in social skills training for schizophrenia. *Schizophrenia Bulletin, 32*(Suppl. 1), S12–S23.

Korfmacher, J., Green, B., Staerkel, F., Peterson, C., Cook, G., Roggman, L., et al. (2008). Parent involvement in early childhood home visiting. *Child Youth Care Forum, 37,* 171–196.

Korotitsch, W. J., & Nelson-Gray, R. O. (1999). An overview of self-monitoring research in assessment and treatment. *Psychological Assessment, 11,* 415–425.

Korte, C. (1983). Help-seeking in the city: Personal and organizational sources of help. In A. Nadler, J. D. Fisher, & B. M. DePaulo (Eds.), *New directions in helping.* Vol. III, *Applied perspectives on help seeking and receiving* (pp. 255–271). New York: Academic Press.

Kottler, J. A., & Blau, D. S. (1989). *The imperfect therapist: Learning from failure in therapeutic practice.* San Francisco: Jossey-Bass.

Kowalski, R. M. (Ed.) (2001). *Behaving badly: Aversive behaviors in interpersonal relationships.* Washington, DC: American Psychological Association.

Kozloff, M. A. (1979). *A program for families of children with learning and behavior problems.* New York: John Wiley.

Kozol, J. (1990). *The night is dark and I am far from home.* New York: Simon & Schuster (Rev. ed.).

Krimsky, S. (2003). *Science in the private interest: Has the lore of profits corrupted biomedical research?* Lanham, MD: Rowman and Littlefield.

Kristof, N. D. (2011a). Raiding a brothel in India. *New York Times,* May 26, A27.

Kristof, N. D. (2011b). She's 10 and may be sold to a brothel. *New York Times,* June 2, A23.

Kruglanski, A. W., & Gigerenzer, G. (2011). Intuitive and deliberative judgements are based on common principles. *Psychological Review, 118,* 97–109.

Krugman, P. (2011). We are the 99.9%. *New York Times,* November 25, A29.

Kuhn, T. S. ([1962] 1970). *The structure of scientific revolutions* (2nd ed.). Chicago: University of Chicago Press.

Kuhn, T. S. (1996). Logic of discovery or psychology of research? In I. Lakatos & A. Musgrave (Eds.), *Criticism and the growth of knowledge* (pp. 1–23). Cambridge, MA: Cambridge University Press.

Kung, W. W. (2003). Chinese Americans' help seeking for emotional distress. *Social Service Review, 77*(1), 110–115.

Kunkel, J. (1970). *Society and economic growth: A behavioral perspective of social change.* New York: Oxford University Press.

Kuno, E., & Rothbard, A. B. (2002). Racial disparities in antipsychotic prescription patterns for patients with schizophrenia. *American Journal of Psychiatry,159,* 567–572.

Kunst, H., Groot, D., Latthe, P. M., Latthe, M., & Khan, K. S. (2002). Accuracy of information on apparently credible websites: Survey of five common health topics. *BMJ, 324,* 581–582.

Kupersmidt, J. B. & Dodge, K. A. (2004). *Children's peer relations: From development to intervention.* Washington, D.C.: American Psychological Association.

Kutchins, H., & Kirk, S. A. (1997). *Making us crazy: DSM: The psychiatric bible and the creation of mental disorders.* New York: Free Press.

L'Abate, L. & Kaiser, D. (2011). *Handbook of technology in psychology, psychiatry, and neurology: Theory, research and practice.* Hauppauge, NY: Nova Sci Pub.

LaCasse, J. R., & Gomory, T. (2003). Is graduate social work education promoting a critical approach to mental health practice? *Journal of Social Work Education, 39,* 383–408.

Lambert, M. J. (2004a). Introduction and historical overview. In M. J. Lambert (Ed.), *Bergin & Garfield's handbook of psychotherapy and behavior change* (5th ed.) (pp. 3–15). New York: John Wiley & Sons.

Lambert, M. J. (Ed.). (2004b). *Bergin & Garfield's handbook of psychotherapy and behavior change*(5th ed.). New York: John Wiley & Sons.

Lambert, M. J. (2006). Are differential treatment effects inflated? *Clinical Psychology: Science and Practice, 6,* 127–130.

Lambert, M. J., & Barley, D. E. (2002). Research summary on the therapeutic relationship and psychotherapy outcome. In J. C. Norcross (Ed.), *Psychotherapy relationships that work: Therapists' contributions and responsiveness to patients* (pp. 17–32). New York: Oxford.

Lambert, M. J., & Ogles, B. M. (2004). The efficacy and effectiveness of psychotherapy. In M. J. Lambert (Ed.), *Bergin and Garfield's handbook of psychotherapy and behavior change* (5th ed.) (pp. 139–193). New York: Wiley.

Lambert, M. J., & Shimokawa, K. (2011). Collecting client feedback. *Psychotherapy, 48,* 72–79.

Lane, C. (2007). *Shyness: How normal behavior became a sickness.* New Haven, CT: Yale University Press.

Lane, H. L. (1992). *Mask of benevolence: Disabling the deaf community.* New York: Knopf.

Lane, K. L., Menzies, M., Bruhn, A. L., & Crnobori, M. (2011*). Managing challenging behaviors in schools: Research-based strategies that work.* New York: Guilford.

Langer, E., & Rodin, J. (1976). The effects of choice and enhanced personal responsibility: A field experiment in an institutional setting. *Journal of Personality and Social Psychology, 34,* 191–198.

Larrick, R. P. (2005). Debiasing. In D. J. Koehler & N. Harvey (Eds.), *Blackwell handbook of judgement and decision making* (pp. 316–337). Malden, MA: Blackwell.

Larson, D. G. (1993). *The helpers' journey: Working with people facing grief, loss, and life-threatening illness.* Champaign, IL: Research Press.

Larson, K. A., & Gerber, M. M. (1987). Effects of metacognitive training for enhancing alert behavior in learning disabled and low achieving delinquents. *Exceptional Children, 54,* 201–211.

Larson, M. S. (1977). *The rise of professionalism: A sociological analysis.* Berkeley: University of California Press.

Last, J. M. (2001). *A dictionary of epidemiology* (2nd ed.). New York: Oxford University Press.

Lauffer, A. (2011). *Understanding your social agency* (3rd ed.). Thousand Oaks, CA: Sage.

LaVigna, G. W., Willis, T. J., Schaull, J. F., Abedi, M., & Sweitzer, M. (1994). *The periodic service review: Total quality assurance system for human services in education.* Baltimore, MD: Paul H. Brookes.

Lavis, J. N., Moynihan, R., Oxman, A. D., & Paulsen, E. J. (2008). Evidence-informed health policy 4—Case descriptions of organizations that support the use of research evidence. *Implementation Science, 3,* 56 doi: 10.1186/1748–5908-3–56.

Lavis, J. N., Oxman, A. D., Moynihan, R., & Paulsen, E. J. (2008). Evidence-informed health policy 1-Synthesis of findings from a multi-method study of organizations that support the use of research evidence. *Implementation Science,* 3, p. 53. Retrieved November 2, 2011. http://www.implementationscience.com

Lavond, D. G., & Steinmetz, J. E. (2003). *Handbook of classical conditioning.* New York: Kluwer Academic.

Lawrie, S. M., McIntosh, A. M., & Rao; S. (2000). *Critical appraisal for psychiatry.* New York: Churchill Livingstone.

Layng, T. V. J. (2009). The search for effective clinical behavior analysis: the nonlinear thinking of Israel Goldiamond. *Behavior Analyst, 32,* 163–184.

Layng, T. V. J., & Andronis, P. T. (1984). Toward a functional analysis of delusional speech and hallucinatory behavior. *Behavior Analyst, 7,* 139–156.

Lazarus, R. S. (1982). The costs and benefits of denial. In S. Breznitz (Ed.), *The denial of stress.* New York: International Universities Press.

Leary, M. R. (1995). *Self-presentation, impression management and interpersonal behavior.* Madison, WI: Brown & Benchmark.

Leavitt, S., & McGowan, B. (1991). Transferring the principles of intensive family preservation services to different fields of practice. In E. M. Tracy, D. A. Haapala, J. Kinney, & P. J. Pecora (Eds.), *Intensive family preservation services: An instructional sourcebook* (pp. 51–69). Cleveland: Case Western Reserve University, Mandel School of Applied Social Sciences.

Lebow, J. (1983). Research assessing consumer satisfaction with mental health treatment: A review of findings. *Evaluation and Program Planning, 6,* 211–236.

Lebow, J. (2005). *Handbook of clinical family therapy.* Hobokan, NJ: Wiley & Sons.

Lecroy, C. W. (2008). *Handbook of evidence-based treatment manuals for children and adolescents* (2nd ed.). New York: Oxford University Press.

Leever, M., DeCiani, G., Mulaney, E., & Hasslinger, H., in conjunction with E. Gambrill (2002). *Ethical child welfare practice.* Washington, DC: CWLA Press.

Lehrer, P. M., Woolfolk, R. L., & Sime, W. E. (2007). *Principles and practice of stress management* (3rd ed.). New York: Guilford.

Leiby, J. (1978). *A history of social welfare and social work in the United States.* New York: Columbia University Press.

Leichtman, M. D., & Ceci, S. J. (1995). The effects of stereotypes and suggestions on preschoolers' reports. *Developmental Psychology, 31,* 568–578.

Leidy, M., Guerra, N. G., & Toro, R. (2010). Family-based interventions to prevent youth violence among Latinos: A review and synthesis of the literature. *Hispanic Journal of Behavioral Sciences, 32,* 5–36.

Leitenberg, H., Agras, W. S., Thompson, L. E., & Wright, D. E. (1968). Feedback in behavior modification: An experimental analysis in two phobic cases. *Journal of Applied Behavior Analysis, 1,* 131–137.

Lemert, E. (1967). *Human deviance, social problems and social control.* Englewood Cliffs, NJ: Prentice Hall.

Lenrow, P., & Cowden, P. (1980). Human services, professionals, and the paradox of institutional reform. *American Journal of Community Psychology, 8,* 463–484.

Lenzer, J. (2004). Bush plans to screen whole U.S. population for mental illness. *BMJ, 328,* 1458.

Leo, J., & Cohen, D. (2003). Broken brains or flawed studies? A critical review of ADHD Neuroimaging research. *Journal of Mind and Behavior, 24,* 29–56.

Lerman, H. (1992). The limits of phenomenology: A feminist critique of humanist personalities. In M. Ballou & L. Brown (Eds.), *Theories of personality and psychopathology* (pp. 8–19). New York: Guilford.

Lerman, D. C., & Toole, L. M. (2011). Developing function-based punishment procedures for problem behavior. In W. W. Fisher, C. C. Piazza, & H. S. Roane (Eds.), *Handbook of applied behavior analysis* (pp. 348–359). New York: Guilford.

Lerner, M. (1980). *The belief in a just world: A fundamental delusion.* New York: Plenum.

Leslie, J. L.& Millenson, J. R. (1996). *Principles of behavioral analysis.* Amsterdam, Netherlands: Harwood Academics.

Lester, B. M., Tronick, E., Nestler, E., Abel, T., Kosofsky, B., Kuzawa, C., et al. (2011). Behavioral epigenetics. *Annals of the New York Academy of Sciences, 1226*(1), 14–33.

Leventhal, A. M., & Martell, C. R. (2006). *The myth of depression as disease: Limitations and alternatives to drug treatment.* Westport, Ct: Praeger.

Levine, M. (1988). An analysis of mutual assistance. *American Journal of Community Psychology, 16,* 167–188.

Levine, M., & Perkins, D. O., & Perkins, D. V. (2005). *Principles of community psychology: Perspectives and applications* (3rd ed.). New York: Oxford University Press.

Levinson, D. R. (2011). *Medicare atypical antipsychotic drug claims for elderly nursing home residents.* Department of Health and Human Services. Officer of Inspector General, May, OEI-07–08-00150.

Levy, C. J. (2002a). Ingredients of a failing system: a lack of state money, a group without a voice. *New York Times,* April 28.

Levy, C. J. (2002b). Voiceless, defenseless and a source of cash. *New York Times,* April 30.

Levy, C. J. (2002c). Where hope dies. Here, life is squalor and chaos. *New York Times,* April 29, A1.

Levy, C. J. & Luo, M. (2005). New York Medicaid fraud may reach into billions. *New York Times,* July 18.

Levy D. (2007). *Group dynamics for teams* (2nd ed.). Thousand, CA: Sage.

Levy, K. N., Ellison, W. D., Scott, L. N., & Bernecker, S. L. (2011). Attachment style. In J. C. Norcross (Ed.), *Psychotherapy relationships that work: Evidence-based responsiveness* (2nd ed.) (pp. 377–401). New York: Oxford University Press.

Lewin, J. (1990). Neglect at nursing home: In a first, suits are won. *New York Times,* July 12, A-1/14.

Lewis, M., & Haviland-Jones, J. M., & Barrett, L. F. (Eds.) (2011). *Handbook of emotions.* New York: Guilford.

Lewontin, R. C. (1991). *Biology as ideology: The doctrine of DNA.* New York: Harper Collins.

Lewontin, R. C. (1994). *Inside and outside: Gene, environment, and organism.* Worcester, MA: Clark University Press.

Lewontin, R. C. (1995). Genes, environment and organisms. In R. B. Silvers (Ed.), *Hidden histories of science* (pp. 115–139). New York: New York Review Book.

Lewontin, R. C. (2009). Where are the genes? Retrieved October 1, 2011 from http://www. Council for responsiblegenetics.org

Liberati, A., Altman, D. G., Tetzlaff, J., Mulrow, C., Gøtzsche, P. C., Ioannidis, J. P. A., Clarke, M., Devereaux, P. J., Kleijnen, J., & Moher, D. (2009). The PRISMA statement for reporting systematic reviews and meta-analyses of studies that evaluate health care interventions: Explanation and elaboration. *PloS Med, 6,* e1000100.

Lilienfeld, S. O., Lynn, S. J., & Lohr, J. M. (2003). *Science and pseudoscience in clinical psychology.* New York: Guilford.

Lilienfeld, S., Ammirati, R., & Landfield, K. (2009). Giving debiasing away: Can psychological research on correcting cognitive errors promote human welfare? *Perspectives on Psychological Science, 4,* 390–398.

Lilienfeld, S. O., Wood, J. M., & Garb, H. N. (2000). The scientific status of projective techniques. *Psychological Science in the Public Interest, 1,* 27–66.

Lincoln, K. D. & Chae, D. H. (2011). Emotional support, negative interaction and major depressive disorder among African Americans and Caribbean Blacks: Findings from the National Survey of American life. *Soc Psychiatry Psychiatr Epidemiol,* doi: 10.1007/s00127–011-0347-y

Lindsey, D. (1994). *The welfare of children.* New York: Oxford University Press. (See also 2004 ed.)

Lindsley, O. R. (1964). Geriatric behavioral prosthetics. In R. Kastenbaum (Ed.), *New thoughts on old age* (pp. 41–60). New York: Springer-Verlag.

Linehan, M. M. (1993). *Cognitive-behavioral treatment of borderline personality disorder.* New York: Guilford.

Linehan, M. M. (1995). *Understanding borderline personality disorder The dialectical approach.* New York: Guilford.

Lipinski, D. P., Black, J. L., & Nelson, R. O., et al. (1975). Influence of motivational variables on the reactivity and reliability of self-recording. *Journal of Consulting and Clinical Psychology, 43,* 637–646.

Lipka, O. & Siegel, L. S. (2010). Early identification and intervention to prevent reading difficulties. In D. Aram & O. Korat (Eds.), *Literacy development and enhancement across orthographies and cultures* (Vol. 2) (pp. 205–219). New York: Springer.

Lipman, M. (2003). *Thinking in education.* New York: Cambridge University Press.

Lipsey, M. W., Howell, J. C., Kelly, M. R., Chapman, E., & Carver, D. (2010). *Improving the effectiveness of juvenile justice programs: a new perspective on evidence-based programs.* Center for Juvenile Justice Reform. December.

Lipsky, M. (2010). *Street-level bureaucracy: Dilemmas of the individual in public services.* New York: Russell Sage.

Liptak, A. (2011a). No crime, but an arrest and two strip-searches. *New York Times National,* March 8, A15.

Liptak, A. (2011b). 34 years later supreme court will revisit eyewitness IDs. *New York Times,* August 22.

Lister, M., & Gardner, D. (2006). Engaging hard to engage clients: A Q methodological study involving clinical psychologists. *Psychology and Psychotherapy: Theory, research and practice, 79,* 419–443.

Littell, J. H. (2008). Evidence-based or biased? The quality of published reviews of evidence-based practices. *Children and Youth Services Review, 30,* 1299–1317.

Littell, J. H., Alexander, L. B., & Reynolds, W. W. (2001). Client participation: Central and under investigated elements of intervention. *Social Service Review, 75*(1), 1–29.

Littell, J. H., Corcoran, J., & Pillai, V. (2008). *Systematic reviews and meta-analysis.* New York: Oxford University Press.

Littell, J. H., & Girvin, H. (2002). Stages of change: A critique. *Behavior Modification, 26,* 223–273.

Littell, J., Popa, M., & Forsythe, B. (2005). *Multisystemic therapy for social, emotional, and behavioral problems in youth aged 10–17.* Cochrane Library, 4, Chichester, UK: Wiley.

Littrell, J. M., Malia, J. A., & Vanderwood, M. (1995). Single-session brief counseling in high schools. *Journal of Counseling & Development, 73,* 341.

Liu, W. M. (2011*). Social class and classism in the helping professions: Research, theory and practice.* Thousand Oaks, CA: Sage.

Lo, B., & Field, M. J. (Eds.) (2009). *Conflict of interests in medical research, education and practice.* Institute of Medicine. Washington, DC: National Academy Press.

Lochman, J. E. (2000). Parent and family skills training in targeted prevention programs for at-risk youth. *Journal of Primary Prevention, 21,* 253–263.

Lochman, J. E., & Dodge, K. A. (1994). Social-cognitive processes of severely violent, moderately aggressive, and nonaggressive boys. *Journal of Consulting and Clinical Psychology, 62,* 366–374.

Lock, M. (1993). *Encounters with aging: Mythologies of menopause in Japan and North America.* Berkeley: University of California Press.

Lock, M. (1998). Menopause: Lessons from anthropology. *Psychosomatic Medicine, 60,* 410–419.

Locke, E. A., & Latham, G. P. (2002). Building a practically useful theory of goal setting and task motivation: A 35-year odyssey. *American Psychologist, 57,* 705–717.

Lösel, F., & Beelmann, A. (2003). Effects of child skills training in preventing antisocial behavior: A systematic review of randomized evaluations. *The ANNALS of the American Academy of Political and Social Science, 587,* 84–109.

Loeske, D. R. (1999). *Thinking about social problems: An introduction to constructionist perspectives.* New York: Aldine de Gruyter.

Lofland, J., & Lofland, L. H. (2003). *Analyzing social settings: A guide to qualitative observation and analysis* (3rd ed.). Belmont, CA: Wadsworth.

Loftus, E. F. (1979). *Eyewitness testimony.* Cambridge, MA: Harvard University Press.

Loftus, E. F. (2004). Memories of things unseen. *Current Directions in Psychological Science, 17,* 145–147.

Loftus, E. F., & Guyer, M. J. (2002). Who abused Jane Doe? The hazards of the single case history, Part 1. *Skeptical Inquirer, 26*(3), 22–32.

Loftus, E. F. & Ketcham, K. (1994). *The myth of repressed memory: False memories and allegations of abuse.* New York: St. Martin's Press.

Logsdon, R. G., & Teri, L. (1997). The Pleasant Events Schedule-AD: Psychometric properties and relationship to depression and cognition in Alzheimer's disease patients. *Gerontologist, 37,* 40–45.

Longtin, Y., Sax, H., Leape, L. L., Sheridan, S. E., Donaldson, L., & Pittet, D. (2010). Patient participation: Current knowledge and applicability to patient safety. *Mayo Clinic Proceedings, 85,* 53–62.

Lopez, M. L., & Cooper, L. (2010). Social support measures review. Final report. National Center for Latino Child and Family Research. First 5. Champions For Our children. Los Angeles, CA.

Lopez, S. J., & Snyder, C. R. (2003). *Positive psychological assessment: A handbook of models and measures.* Washington, D. C.: American Psychological Association.

Lord, C., Ross, L., & Lepper, M. R. (1979). Biased assimilation and attitude polarization: The effects of prior theories on subsequently considered evidence. *Journal of Personality and Social Psychology, 37,* 2089–2109.

Losel, F., & Beelmann, A. (2003). Effects of child skills training in preventing antisocial behavior: A systematic review of randomized evaluations. In *The ANNALS of the American Academy of Political and Social Science, 587,* 84–109.

Lowe, T. J., Lucas, J. A., Castle, N. G., Robinson, J. P., & Crystal, S. (2003). Consumer satisfaction in long-term care: State initiatives in nursing homes and assisted living facilities. *The Gerontologist, 43*(6), 883–896.

Luborsky, L., Diguer, L., Seligman, D. A., Rosenthal, R., Krause, E. D., Johnson, S., Halperin, G., Bishop, M., Berman, J. S., & Schweizer, E. (1999). The researcher's own therapy allegiances: A "wildcard" in comparisons of treatment efficacy. *Clinical Psychology: Science and Practice, 6*(1), 95–106.

Luborsky, L. B., Barrett, M. S. (2006). What else materially influences what is represented and published as evidence? In J. C. Norcross, L. E. Beutler, & R. F. Levant (Eds.), *Evidence-based practices in mental health: Debates and dialogues on fundamental questions* (pp. 257–267). Washington, D.C.: American Psychological Association.

Luepker, E. T. (2012). *Record keeping in psychotherapy and counseling: Protecting confidentiality and the professional relationship* (2nd ed.). New York: Routledge.

Luiselli, J. K. (2008). Antecedent (preventive) intervention. In J. K. Luiselli, et al., *Effective practices with children with autism* (p. 393–412). New York: Oxford University Press.

Luiselli, J. K., Russo, D. C., Christian, W. P., & Wilczynski, S. M. (2008). *Effective practices with children with autism: educational and support interventions that work.* New York: Oxford University Press.

Lukes, S. (1997). Social justice: The Hayekian Challenge. *Critical Review, 11,* 65–80.

Lum, D. (2004). *Social work practice & people of color: A process-stage approach.* Belmont, CA: Brooks/Cole/Thomson.

Luo, F., Florence, C. S., Quispe-Agnoli, M., Ouyang, L., & Crosby, A. E. (2011). Impact of business cycles on US suicide rates 1928–2007. *American Journal of Public Health.*

Lutzker, J. R., & Bigelow, K. M. (2002). *Reducing child maltreatment: A guidebook for parent services.* New York: Guilford.

Luyben, P. D. (2009). *Applied behavior analysis: Understanding and changing behavior in the community.* Philadelphia, PA: Taylor & Frances.

Lynch, E. W. & Hanson, M. J. (1992). *Developing cross-cultural competence: A guide for working with young children and their families.* Baltimore, MD: Paul H. Brooks.

Lynch, E. W., & Hanson, M. J. (2011). *Developing cross-cultural competence: A guide for working with children and their families* (4th ed.). Baltimore, MD: Paul H. Brookes.

MacBrayer, E. K., Milich, R., & Hundley, M. (2003). Attributional biases in aggressive children and their mothers. *Journal of Abnormal Psychology, 112,* 698–708.

MacCoun, R. (1998). Biases in the interpretation and use of research results. *Annual Review of Psychology, 49,* 259–287.

MacCoun, R. J., & Reuter, P. (2001). *Drug war heresies: Learning from other vices, times, & places.* New York: Cambridge University Press.

MacGorge, E. L., Graves, A. R., Feng, B., Gillihan, S. J., & Burleson, B. R. (2004). The myth of gender cultures: Similarities outweigh differences in men's and women's provision of and responses to supportive communication. *Sex Roles, 50,* 143–175.

MacLean, E. (1981). *Between the lines: How to detect bias and propaganda in the news and everyday life.* Montreal, Canada: Black Rose Books.

Maclure, M. (1985). Popperian refutation in epidemiology. *American Journal of Epidemiology, 121*(3), 343–350.

MacPhillamy, D. J., & Lewinsohn, P. M. (1982). The pleasant events schedule: Studies on reliability, validity, and scale intercorrelation. *Journal of Consulting and Clinical Psychology, 50,* 363–380.

Madden, G. J. (2013). *APA handbook of behavior analysis.* Washington, D.C.: American Psychological Association.

Madden, R. G. (2003). *Essential law for social workers.* New York: Columbia University Press.

Magee, J. (1985). *Philosophy in the real world.* LaSalle, IL: Open Court.

Mager, R. F. (1972). *Goal analysis.* Belmont, CA: Fearon.

Mager, R. F., & Pipe, P. (1970). *Analyzing performance problems.* Belmont, CA: Fearon.

Mai, X, Ge, Y., Tao, L., Tang, H., Liu, C., et al. (2011). Eyes are windows to the Chinese soul: Evidence from the detection of real and fake smiles. *PloS One, 6,* e19903.

Maletzky, B. M. (1974). Behavior recording as treatment: A brief note. *Behavior Therapy, 5,* 107–111.

Mallon, G. R. (2009). *Social work practice with transgender and gender variant youth.* New York: Routledge.

Malott, R. W. (1994). *Rule-governed behavior, self-management, and performance management.* Kalamazoo, MI: Western Michigan University, Department of Psychology.

Mallott, R. W. (2008). *Principles of behavior.* Upper Saddle River, NJ: Pearson Prentice Hall.

Maluccio, A. N. (1979). *Learning from clients.* New York: Free Press.

Mank, D. M., & Horner, R. H. (1987). Self-recruited feedback: A cost-effective procedure for maintaining behavior. *Research in Developmental Disabilities, 8,* 91–112.

Margolin, L. (1997). *Under the cover of kindness: The invention of social work.* Charlottesville: University of Virginia Press.

Marlatt, G. A. & Donovan, D. M. (2008). *Relapse prevention: Maintenance strategies in the treatment of addictive disorders.* New York: Guilford.

Marlatt, G. A., Larimer, M. E., & Witkiewitz, K. (Eds.) (2012). *Harm reduction: Pragmatic strategies for managing high-risk behaviors* (2nd ed.). New York: Guilford.

Marmot, M. (2011). Social determinants and the health of indigenous Australians. *The Medical Journal of Australia, 194*(10), 512–513.

Marmot, M. G., & Wilkinson, R. G. (2006). *Social determinations of health.* New York: Oxford University Press.

Marris, P. (1996). *The politics of uncertainty: Attachment in private public life.* New York: Routledge.

Martell, C. R., Dimidjian, S., Herman-Dunn, R., & Lewinsohn, P. M. (2010). *Behavioral activiation for depression: A clinician's guide.* New York: Guilford.

Martin, G., & Pear, J. (1988). *Behavior modification: What it is and how to do it* (3rd ed.). Englewood Cliffs, NJ: Prentice Hall.

Martin, G. & Pear, J. (2010). *Behavior modification: What it is and how to do it.* Boston: Pearson.

Martin, K. A. (1998). Becoming a gendered body: Practices of pre-schools. *American Sociological Review, 63*(4), 494–511.

Martin, R. (1975). *Legal challenges to behavior modification: Trends in schools, corrections, and mental health.* Champaign, IL: Research Press.

Martin, K. S., Rogers, D. L., Cook, J. T., & Joseph, Q. M. (2004). Social capital is associated with decreased risk of hunger. *Social Science & Medicine, 58,* 2645–2654.

Maslach, C. & Leiter, M. P. (2008). *The truth about burnout: How organizations cause personal stress and what to do about it.* Hobokan, NJ: John Wiley & Sons (ebook).

Maslach, C., Schaufeli, W., et al. (2001). Job burnout. *Annual Review of Psychology, 52,* 397–422.

Masson, J. M. (1984). *The assault on truth: Freud's suppression of the seduction theory.* New York: Farrar, Straus & Giroux.

Mather, N., & Goldstein, S. (2005). *Learning disabilities and challenging behaviors: a guide to intervention and classroom management.* Baltimore, MD: Paul H. Brookes.

Mathews, D. (1990). Effective communities are different. In L. Decker & Associates (Eds.), *Community education: Building learning communities* (pp. 1–11). Alexandria, VA: National Community Education Association.

Mathews, R. M., & Fawcett, S. B. (1977). Community applications of instructional technology: Training low-income proctors. *Journal of Applied Behavior Analysis, 10,* 747–784.

Matson, J. L. (2009). *Applied behavior analysis for children with autism spectrum disorder.* New York: Springer (ebook).

Matson, J. L., Andrasik, F., & Matson, M. L. (2009). *Assessing childhood psychopathology and developmental disabilities.* New York: Springer (ebook).

Matsumoto, D. R. (2010). *APA handbook of intercultural communication.* Washington, D.C: American Psychological Association.

Mattaini, M. A. (1989). Eco-mapping in family assessing: Preliminary empirical support. Unpublished manuscript. School of Social Work, Columbia University (described in Mattaini, 1993, p. 250).

Mattaini, M. A. (1993). *More than a thousand words: Graphics for clinical practice.* Washington, DC: NASW Press.

Mattaini, M. A. (2002). Understanding and reducing collective violence. *Behavior and Social Issues, 12,* 90–108.

Mattaini, M. & McGuire, M. S. (2006). Behavioral strategies for constructing nonviolent cultures for youth. *Behavior Modification, 30,* 184–224.

Matthies, D., (1996). *Precision questioning,* Stanford University Center for Teaching and Learning. Mindworks, 5/11/96.

Maxwell, R. (1984). Quality assessment in health care. *BMJ, 288,* 1470.

Maybery, D. J., Jones-Ellis, J., Neale, J., & Arentz, A. (2006). The Positive Event Scale: Measuring uplift frequency and intensity in an adult sample. *Social Indicators Research, 78,* 61–83.

Maybery, D. J., Neale, J., Arentz, A., & Jones-Ellis, J. (2007). The Negative Event Scale: Measuring frequency and intensity of adult hassles. *Anxiety, Stress and Coping, 20,* 163–176.

Mayer, J. E., & Timms, N. (1970). *The client speaks: Working class impressions of casework.* New York: Atherton Press.

Mayer, M. J., VanAcker, R., Lochman, J. E., & Gresham, F. M. (Eds.) (2009). *Cognitive-behavioral interventions for emotional and behavioral disorders: school-based practice.* New York: Guilford.

Maxwell, R. J. (1984). Quality assessment in health. *BMJ, 288,* 1470–1472.

McCagg, E. B. (1879). The charities of Chicago. In F. B. Sanborn (Ed.), *Proceedings of the sixth annual conference of charities,* Chicago, June (pp. 145–152). Boston: Williams & Co.

McCann, J. T., Shindler, K. L., & Hammond, T. R. (2003). The science and pseudoscience of expert testimony. In S. O. Lilienfeld., S. J. Lynn, & J. M. Lohr (Eds.), *Science and Pseudoscience in clinical psychology* (pp. 77–108). New York: Guilford.

McCart, A., Wolf, N., Sweeney, H. M., Markey, U., & Markey, D. J. (2009). Families facing extraordinary challenges in urban communities: Systemic level applications of positive behavioral support. In W. Sailor G. Dunlap, & R. Horner (Eds.). *Handbook of positive behavior support* (pp. 257–278). New York: Springer.

McClannahan, L. E., & Risely, T. R. (1973). A store for nursing home residents. *Nursing Homes, 7,* 26–31.

McClannahan, L. E., & Risley, T. R. (1975). Design of living environments for nursing home residents: Increasing participation in recreational activities. *Journal of Applied Behavior Analysis, 8,* 261–268.

McCloskey, M. (1983). Intuitive physics. *Scientific American, 248,* 122–130.

McCord, J. (1978). A thirty-year follow-up of treatment effects. *American Psychologist, 33,* 284–289.

McCord, J. (2003). Cures that harm: Unanticipated outcomes of crime prevention programs. *The ANNALS of the American Academy of Political and Social Science, 587,* 16–30.

McCoy, R. (2000). *Quack! Tales of medical fraud from the museum of questionable medical devices.* Santa Monica, CA: Santa Monica Press.

McCulloch, Rev. (1879). Associated charities, 1880. In R. B. Sanborn (Ed.), *Proceedings of the annual conference of charities.* Chicago, June 1879. Boston: Williams & Co.

McDaniel, P. A. (2003). *Shrinking Violets and Caspar Milquetoasts.* New York: New York University Press.

McDaniel, B., Braiden, H. J., Onyekwelu, J., Murphy, M. & Regan, H. (2011). Investigating the effectiveness of the incredible years basic parenting programme for foster carers in Northern Ireland. *Child Care in Practice, 17,* 55–67.

McDavid, J. C., & Hawthorn, L. R. L. (2006). *Progress evaluation and performance measurement: An introduction to practice.* Thousand Oaks, CA: Sage.

McDermott, C. J. (1989). Empowering the elderly nursing home resident: The resident rights campaign. *Social Work, 34,* 155–157.

McDonnell, A. A. (2010). *Managing aggressive behavior in care settings: understanding and applying low arousal approaches.* Malden, MA: Wiley-Blackwell.

McDonnell, J. & Hardman, M. L. (2010). *Successful transition programs: Pathways for students with intellectual and developmental disabilities.* Thousand Oaks, CA: Sage.

McDowell, B. (2000). *Ethics and excuses: The crisis of professional responsibility.* Westport, CT: Quorum Books.

McDowell, J. J. (1988). Matching theory in natural human environments. *Behavior Analyst, 11,* 95–109.

McFall, R. M. (1970). The effects of self-monitoring on normal smoking behavior. *Journal of Consulting and Clinical Psychology, 35,* 135–142.

McGimsey, J. F., & Favell, J. E. (1988). The effects of increased physical exercise on disruptive behavior in retarded persons. *Journal of Autism and Developmental Disorders, 18,* 167–179.

McGimsey, J. F., Greene, B. F., & Lutzker, J. R. (1995). Competence in aspects of behavioral treatment and consultation: Implications for service delivery and graduate training. *Journal of Applied Behavior Analysis, 28,* 301–315.

McGinnis, E. (2011). *Skill streaming the adolescent: A guide for teaching prosocial skills* (3rd ed.). Champaign, IL: Research Press.

McInnis, K. (1991). Ethnic sensitive work with Hmong refugee children. *Child Welfare, 70*(5), 571–580.

McKibbon, A., Eady, A., & Marks, S. (1999). *PDQ evidence-based principles and practice.* Hamilton, U.K.: B. C. Decker.

McMahon, R., & Forehand, R. L. (2003). *Helping the noncompliant child: Family based treatment for oppositional children* (2nd ed.). New York: Guilford.

McMurran, M. & McGuire, J. (2005). *Social problem solving and offending: Evidence, evaluation and evolution.* Hobokan, NJ: Wiley.

McNaughton, D. B. & Beukelman, D. R. (2010). *Transition strategies for adolescents and young adults who use AAC.* Baltimore, MD: Paul H. Brook.

McNeill, T., Nicholas, D., Szechy, K., & Lach, L. (1998). Perceived outcome of social intervention: Beyond consumer satisfaction. *Social Work in Health Care, 26*(3), 1–18.

Meany, M. (2010). Epigenetics and the biological definition of gene environmental interactions. *Child Development, 81,* 41–79. *Journal of Neuroscience, 30,* 13130–13137.

Meblum, H., Moene, K., & Torvik, R. (2006). Parasites. In S. Bowles, S. N. Durlauf, & K. R. Hoff (Eds.), *Poverty traps* (pp. 79–94). New York: Russell Sage.

Medical Ethics (1990). Should medicine turn the other cheek? *Lancet, 336,* 846–847.

Meehl, P. E. (1973). Why I do not attend case conferences. *Psycho diagnostic Papers.* Minneapolis: University of Minnesota Press.

Meichenbaum, D. (1971). Examination of model characteristics in reducing avoidance behavior. *Journal of Personality and Social Psychology, 17,* 298–307.

Meichenbaum, D. (1977). *Cognitive behavior modification: An integrative approach.* New York: Plenum.

Meichenbaum, D. (2009). Core tasks of psychotherapy: What do "expert" therapists do? Downloaded from Internet, 12/2/11.

Meichenbaum, D., & Turk, D. C. (1987). *Facilitating treatment adherence: A practitioner's handbook.* New York: Plenum.

Meichenbaum, D. H., & Goodman, J. (1971). Training impulsive children to talk to themselves: A means for developing self-control. *Journal of Abnormal Psychology, 77,* 115–126.

Meinhold, P., & Mulick, J. A. (1990). Counter-habilitative contingencies for mentally retarded people: Ecological and regulatory influences. *Mental Retardation, 28,* 67–73.

Mercer, J. R. (1973). *Labeling the mentally retarded.* Berkeley: University of California Press.

Merelman, R. M. (1975). Social stratification and political socialization in mature industrial societies. *Comparative Education Review, 19*(1), 13–30.

Merry, S. N. et al. (2012). The effectiveness of SPARX, a computerized self help intervention for adolescents seeking help for depression: randomized controlled-non-inferiority trial. *BMJ, 344,* e2598.

Merton, R. K. (1949). Discrimination and the American creed. In R. M. MacIver (Ed.), *Discrimination and national welfare* (pp. 77–145). New York: Harper.

Merzel, C., & D'Afflitti, J. (2003). Reconsidering community-based health promotion: Promise, performance, and potential. *American Journal of Public Health, 93,* 557–574.

Mesquita, B., (2001). Culture and emotion: Different approaches to the question. In T. J. Mayne & G. A. Bonanno (Eds.), *Emotions: Current issues and future directions* (pp. 214–250). New York: Guilford.

Messing, J. T. (2011). The social control of family violence. *Journal of Women and Social Work, 26*(2), 154–168.

Meyer, L. H., & Evans, I. N. (1989). *Nonaversive intervention for behavior problems: A manual for home and community*. Baltimore, MD: Paul H. Brookes.

Meyers, R. J., & Miller, W. R. (Eds.) (2001). *A community reinforcement approach to addiction treatment*. Cambridge, New York: Cambridge University Press.

Michael, J. L. (2004). *Concepts and principles of behavior analysis*. Kalamazoo, MI: Western Michigan University and International Association for Society for Behavior Analysis.

Michael, M., Boyce, W. T., & Wilcox, A. J. (1984). *Biomedical bestiary: An epidemiological guide to flaws and fallacies in the medical literature*. Boston: Little, Brown.

Midgley, J. (2011). From mutual aid to microinsurance: Strengthening grassroots social security in the developing world. *Social Development Issues, 33*, 1–12.

Midgley, J., & Conley, A. (2010). *Social work and social development*. New York: Oxford University Press.

Mill, J. S. (1911). A system of logic. Book 3: Of induction. Chapter 5: Of the law of universal causation, pp. 211–242.

Miller, A. L., Rathus, J. H., & Linehan, M. M. (2007). *Dialectical behavior therapy with suicidal adolescents*. New York: Guilford.

Miller, D. (1994). *Critical rationalism: A restatement and defense*. Chicago: Open Court.

Miller, S. D., Duncan, B. L., Brown, J., Sorrell, R., & Chalk, M. B. (2006). Using formal client feedback to improve retention and outcome: Making ongoing, real-time assessment feasible. *Journal of Brief Therapy, 5*, 5–22.

Miller, T. W. (2010). *Handbook of stressful transitions across the lifespan*. New York: Springer.

Miller, W. R., Meyers, R. J., Hiller-Sturmhofel, S. (2005). The community reinforcement approach. *Alcohol Research and Health*, (pp. 116–120). pubs.niaaa.nih.gov. Retrieved 12/20/2011.

Mills, C. W. (1959). *The sociological imagination*. New York: Oxford University Press.

Miltenberger, R. G. (2008). *Behavior modification: Principles and procedures* (4th ed.). Belmont, CA: Wadsworth/Thomson Learning.

Miltenberger, R. G., & Gross, A. C. (2011). Teaching safety skills to children. In Fisher, et al. (Eds.), *Handbook of applied behavior analysis* (pp. 417–432). New York: Guilford.

Mindel, C. H. & Habenstein, R. W. (Eds.) (1981). Ethnic families in America: Patterns and variations (2nd ed.). New York: Elsevier (see also 5th ed. 2012).

Minkler, M. (1985). Building supportive ties and sense of community among the inner-city elderly: The Tenderloin Senior Outreach Project. *Health Education Quarterly, 12*, 303–314.

Minkler, M. (1992). Community organizing among the elderly poor in the United States: A case study. *International Journal of Health Services, 22*, 303–316.

Minkler, M. (Ed.). (2005). *Community organizing and community building for health*. New Brunswick, NJ: Rutgers University Press.

Minkler, M. & Wallerstein, N. (Eds.) (2008*). Community-based participatory research for health: From process to outcomes* (2nd ed.). San Francisco: Jossey-Bass.

Minuchin, S. (1974). *Families and family therapy*. Cambridge, MA: Harvard University Press.

Mirowsky, J., & Ross, C. E. (1989). *Social causes of psychological distress*. New York: Aldine de Gruyer.

Mirowsky, J., & Ross, C. E. (2003). *Social causes of psychological distress* (2nd ed.). New York: Aldine de Gruyter.

Miser, W. F. (1999). Critical appraisal of the literature. *Journal of the American Board of Family Practice, 12*, 315–333.

Miser, W. F. (2000). Applying a meta-analysis to daily clinical practice. In J. P. Geyman, R. A. Deyo, & S. D. Ramsey (Eds.), *Evidence-based clinical practice: Concepts and approaches* (pp. 57–64). Boston, MA: Butterworth & Heinemann.

Miser, W. F. (2000). Critical appraisal of the literature: How to assess an article and still enjoy life. In J. P. Geyman, R. A. Deyo, & S. D. Ramsey (Eds.), *Evidence-based clinical practice: Concepts and approaches* (pp. 41–56). Boston: Butterworth-Heinemann.

Mitchell, C. W. (2009). *Effective techniques for dealing with highly resistant clients* (2nd ed.). Johnson City, TN: C. W. Mitchell.

Mohnen, S. M., Groenewegen, P. P., Volker, B., & Flap, H. (2011). Neighborhood social capital and individual health. *Social Science & Medicine, 72*, 660–667.

Moncrieff, J. (2007). Are antidepressants as effective as claimed? No, they are not effective at all. *Canadian Journal of Psychiatry, 52*, 96–97.

Moncrieff, J. (2008a). Neoliberism and biopsychiatry: A marriage of convenience. In C. I. Cohen & S. Timimi (Eds.), *Liberatory psychiatry: Philosophy, politics, and mental health* (pp. 235–255). New York: Cambridge University Press.

Moncrieff, J. (2008b). *The myth of the chemical cure: A critique of psychiatric drug treatment*. Palgrave Macmillan.

Mondros, J. B., & Wilson, S. M. (1994). *Organizing for power and empowerment*. New York: Columbia.

Mooney, H. (2011). Three out of 12 hospitals fail to meet essential standards in care for older people finds watchdog. *BMJ, 342*:d3346.

Moore, B. E., & Fine, B. D. (Eds.). (1990). *Psychoanalytic terms and concepts*. New Haven and London: American Psychoanalytic Association and Yale University Press.

Moore, B. & Penk, W. (2011). *Treating PTSD in military personnel: A clinical handbook*. New York: Guilford.

Moos, R. H., & Lemke, S. (1994). *Group residences for older adults: Physical features, policies, and social climate*. New York: Oxford University Press.

Moritsugu, J., Wong, F. Y., & Dulfy, K. G. (2010). *Community psychology*. Boston, MA: Allyn & Bacon.

Morris, R. (1986). *Rethinking social welfare: Why care for the stranger?* White Plains, NY: Longman.

Morris, G. H., & Chenail, R. J. (Eds.) (1995). *The talk of the clinic: Explorations in the analysis of medical and therapeutic discourse*. Hillsdale, NJ: Lawrence Erlbaum.

Mosher, L. R. (2004). Non-hospital, non-drug interventions with first episode psychosis. In J. Reed, L. R. Mosher, & R. Bentall (Eds.), *Models of madness: Psychological, social and biological approaches to schizophrenia* (pp. 349–364). Hove, UK: Brunner-Routledge.

Mowbray, C. T., Collins, M. E., Bellamy, C. D., Megivern, D. A., Bybee, D., & Szilvagyi, S. (2005). Supported education for adults with psychiatric disabilities: An innovation for social work and psychosocial rehabilitation practice. *Social Work, 50*, 7–20.

Moynihan, R. & Cassels, A. (2005). *Selling sickness: How the world's biggest pharmaceutical companies are turning us all into patients*. New York: Nation Books.

Moynihan, R., Heath, I., & Henry, D. (2002). Selling sickness: The pharmaceutical industry and disease mongering. *BMJ, 324,* 886–891.

Moynihan, R. & Mintzes, B. (2010). *Sex, lies and pharmaceuticals: How drug companies plan to profit from female sexual dysfunction.* Vancouver, Canada: Greystone Books.

Mueser, K. T., Bond, G. R., Drake, R. E., & Resnick, S. G. (1998). Models of community care for severe mental illness: A review of research on case management. *Schizophrenia Bulletin, 24,* 37–74.

Mueser, K. T., Clark, R. E., Haines, M., Drake, R. E., McHugo, G. J., Bond, G. R., Essock, S. M., Becker, D. R., Wolfe, R., & Swain, K. (2004). The Hartford study of supported employment for persons with severe mental illnesses. *Journal of Consulting and Clinical Psychology, 72,* 479–490.

Munakata, T. (1989). The socio-cultural significance of the diagnostic label "Neurasthenia" in Japan's mental health care system. *Culture, Medicine, and Psychiatry, 13,* 203–213.

Munro, E. (1996). Avoidable and unavoidable mistakes in child protection work. *British Journal of Social Work, 26,* 793–808.

Munro, E. (2004). A simpler way to understand the results of risk assessment instruments. *Children and youth services Review, 26,* 873–883.

Munro, E. (2010). Learning to reduce risk in child protection. *Br. J. Soc Work, 40,* 1135–1151.

Munro, E. (2011). *Munro review of child protection: Final report.* London: Department for Education. May.

Munz, P. (1985). *Our knowledge of the growth of knowledge: Popper or Wittgenstein?* London: Routledge & Kegan Paul.

Munz, P. (1992). What's postmodern, anyway? *Philosophy and Literature, 16,* 333–353.

Murphy, T. (2009). *New technology and human rights.* New York: Oxford University Press.

Murray, C. (1984). *Losing ground: American social policy, 1950–1990.* New York: Basic Books.

Myers, J. E. B. (Ed.) (2011). *The APSAC handbook on child maltreatment* (3rd ed.). Los Angeles, CA: Sage.

Naar-king, S., Ellis, D. A., & Frey, M. A. (2008). *Assessing children's well being: A handbook of measures.* New York: Psychology Press.

Naftulin, D. H., Ware, J. E., & Donnelly, F. A. (1973). The Doctor Fox lecture: A paradigm of educational seduction. *Journal of Medical Education, 48,* 630–635.

Nagourney, A. (2011). "Homeless veterans sue over neglected campus." *New York Times,* June 9, A15.

Najavits, L. M., & Strupp, H. H. (1994). Differences in the effectiveness of psycho-dynamic therapists: A process-outcome study. *Psychotherapy, 31,* 114–123.

National Association for Community Mediators. www.nafcm.org

National Association of Social Workers. (2001). *Standards for cultural competence in social work practice.* Washington, DC: Author.

National Association of Social Workers (2005) (4th ed.). *Procedures for professional review.*

National Association of Social Workers (2008). *Code of ethics.* Silver Spring, MD: NASW.

National Science Foundation (2006). Surveys of public understanding of science and technology: 1979–2006. Retrieved 8/22/2011 from http://www.ropercenter.uconn.edu

Nee, C. (1993). Car theft: The offender's perspective. *Home Office Research and Statistics Department, Research Findings, 3,* Feb. Home Office, 50 Queen Anne's Gate, London, SW 1H 9AT, Information Department, Research and Planning Unit.

Neef, N. A. (1995). Pyramidal parent training by peers. *Journal of Applied Behavior Analysis, 28,* 333–337.

Neef, N. A., Parrish, J. M., Egel, A. L., & Sloan, M. E. (1986). Training respite care providers for families with handicapped children: Experimental analysis and validation of an instructional package. *Journal of Applied Behavior Analysis, 19,* 105–124.

Negi, N., & Furman, R. (Eds.) (2010). *Transnational social work practice.* New York: Columbia University Press.

Neifert, J. (1995). Field work report. Unpublished paper, University of California at Berkeley.

Nelson, T. D. (Ed.) (2009*). Handbook of prejudice, stereotyping, and discrimination.* New York: Psychology Press.

Nelson-Jones, R. (2005). *Practical counseling & helping skills: Text and activities for the lifeskill counseling.* Thousand Oaks, CA: Sage.

Netting, F. E., Kettner, P. M., & McMurtry, S. L. (1993). *Social work macro-practice.* New York: Longman.

Netting, F. E., Kettner, P. M., McMurtry, S. L., & Thomas (2012). *Social work macro-practice.* New York: Longman.

Nettler, G. (1970). *Explanations.* New York: McGraw Hill.

Nettleton, S., & Bunton, R. (1995). In R. Bunton, S. Nettleton, & R. Burrows (Eds.), *The sociology of health promotion: Critical analyses of consumption, lifestyle and risk.* London and New York: Routledge.

New Freedom in Mental Health Commission (2004). New Freedom Initiative, http://www.whitehouse.gov/infocus/newfreedom/toc-2004.html.

Newstrom, J. W. (2011). *Organizational behavior: Human behavior at work* (13th ed.). Boston: McGraw-Hill/Irwin.

Newton, S. J., Horner, R. H., Algozzine, R. F., Todd, A. W., & Algozzine, K. M. (2009). Using a problem-solving model to enhance data-based decision making in schools. In W. Sailor et al (Eds.), *Handbook of positive behavioral support* (pp. 551–580). New York: Springer.

Nicarthy, G., Gottlieb, N., & Coffman, S. (1993). *You don't have to take it!: A woman's guide to confronting emotional abuse at work.* Seattle, WA: Seal Press.

Nichols, M. P., with Schwartz, R. C. (2009) *Family therapy: Concepts and methods* (9th ed.). Boston: Allyn & Bacon.

Nichols, D. S., Padilla, J., & Gomez-Magueo, E. L. (2000). Issues in the cross-cultural adaptation and use of the MMPI-2. In J. H. Dana (Ed.), *Handbook of cross-cultural and multicultural personality assessment* (pp. 247–266). Mahwah, NJ: Lawrence Erlbaum.

Nickerson, R. S. (1986). *Reflections on reasoning.* Hillsdale, NJ: Lawrence Erlbaum.

Nickerson, R. S. (1988–89). On improving thinking through instruction. In E. Z. Rothkopf (Ed.), *Review of research in education* (pp. 3–57). Washington, DC: American Educational Research Association.

Nickerson, R. S. (1998). Confirmation bias: A ubiquitous phenomena in many guises. *Review of General Psychology, 2,* 175–220.

Nisbett, R. E. (2003). *The geography of thought: How Asians and Westerners think differently. and why.* New York: Free Press.

Nisbett, R. E., Aronson, J., Blair, C., Dickens, W., Flynn, J., Halpern, D. F., & Turkheimer, E. (2012). Intelligence: New findings and theoretical developments. *American Psychologist, 67,* 130–159.

Nisbett, R., & Ross, L. (1980). *Human inference: Strategies and shortcomings of social judgement.* Englewood Cliffs, NJ: Prentice Hall.

Nock, M. (2009). *Understanding nonsuicidal self-injury: Origins, assessment, and treatment.* Washington, D.C.: American Psychological Association.

Nolen-Hoeksema, S. & Watkins, E. R. (2011). A heuristic for developing transdiagnostic models in psychopathology: Explaining multifinality and divergent trajectories. Perspectives on *Psychological Science, 6*, 589–609.

Norcross, J. C. (2002). Empirically supported therapy relationships. In J. C. Norcross (Ed.), *Psychotherapy relationships that work: Therapists' contributions and responsiveness to patients* (pp. 3–16). New York: Oxford University Press.

Norcross, J. C. (Ed.). (2011). *Psychotherapy relationships that work: Evidence-based* responsiveness (2nd ed.). New York: Oxford University Press.

Norcross, J. C., et al (2003). *Authoritative guide to self-help resources in mental health.* New York: Guilford.

Norcross, J. C., Beutler, L. E., & Levant, R. F. (Eds.) (2006). *Evidence-based practices in mental health: Debate and dialogue on the fundamental questions.* Washington, DC: American Psychological Association.

Norcross, J. C., Krebs, P. M., & Prochaska, J. O. (2011). Stages of change. In J. C. Norcross (Ed.), *Psychotherapy relationships that work: Evidence-based responsiveness* (2nd ed.) (pp. 279–300). New York: Oxford University Press.

Novaco, R. W., Swanson, R. D., Gonzales, O. L., Gahm, G. A., & Reger, M. D. (2012). Anger and postcombat mental health: Validation of a brief anger measure with U.S. soldiers postdeployed from Iraq and Afghanistan. *Psychological Assessment.* (Epub ahead of print).

Novak, M., & Guest, C. (1989). Application of a multidimensional caregiver burden inventory. *Gerontologist, 29,* 798–803.

Nutt, P. C. & Wilson, D. C. (Eds.) (2010). *Handbook of decision making.* Chichester, West Sussex, England: John Wiley & Sons.

Oakes, M. (1986). *Statistical inference: a commentary for the social and behavioral sciences.* Chichester: John Wiley & Sons.

Oakley, A. (1976). *Women's work: The housewife, past and present.* New York: Vintage.

O'Cathain, A., Walters, S. J., Nicholl, J. P., Thomas, K. J., & Kirkham, M. (2002). Use of evidence based leaflets to promote informed choice in maternity care: Randomized controlled trial in everyday practice. *BMJ, 324,* 643–647.

O'Connor, A. M., Bennett, C. L., Stacey, D, Barry, M., Col, N. F., Eden, K. B., et al. (2009). Decision aids for people facing health treatment or screening decisions. *Cochrane Database of Systematic Reviews,* Issue 3. Art. No.: CD001431.

O'Connor, A. M., Wennberg, J. E., Legare, F., Llewellyn-Thomas, H. A., Moulton, B. W., Sepucha, K. R., Sodano, A. G., & King, J. S. (2007). Toward the 'tipping point': Decision aids and informed patient choice. *Health Affairs, 26,* 716–725.

O'Connor, A. M. (2001). Using patient decision aids to promote evidence-based decision making. *EMP Notebook, 6,* July–August.

O'Donohue, W. T. & Fisher, J. E. (Eds.). (2008). *Cognitive behavior therapy: Applying empirically supported techniques in your practice.* Hoboken, NJ: John Wiley & Sons.

O'Donohue, W. T., & Levensky, E. R. (Eds.) (2006). *Promoting treatment adherence: A practical handbook for health care providers.* Thousand Oaks, CA: Sage.

O'Donohue, W., Fisher, J. E., Plaud, J. J. (1989). What is a good treatment decision? The client's perspective. *Professional Psychology: Research and Practice, 20,* 404–407.

Ofshe, R., & Watters, E. (1994). *Making monsters: False memories, psychotherapy, and sexual hysteria.* New York: Charles Scribner's.

O'Heare, J. (2009). The least intrusive effective behavior intervention (LIEBI) algorithm and levels of intrusiveness table: A proposed best practice model. *Journal of Applied companion Animal Behavior, 3,* 7–25.

Ohman, A. (1993). Fear and anxiety as emotional phenomena: Clinical phenomenology, evolutionary perspectives, and information-processing mechanisms. In M. Lewis & J. M. Haviland (Eds.), *Handbook of emotions* (pp. 511–534). New York: Guilford.

Ollendick, T. H., & King, N. J. (2006). Empirically supportive treatments typically produce outcomes superior to non-empirically supported treatment therapies. In J. C. Norcross, L. E. Beutler, & R. E. Levant (Eds.), *Evidence-based practices in mental health: Debate and dialogue on the fundamental questions* (pp. 308–328). Washington, D.C.: American Psychological Association.

Olsson, A. (2012). Observational fear learning. In N. M. Seel (Ed.), *Encyclopedia of the sciences of learning.* New York: Springer.

Olweus, D. (1993). *Bullying at school: What we know and what we can do.* Oxford: Blackwell Press.

Olweus, D. (2007). *Olweus bullying prevention program: School wide guide.* Center City, MN: Hazelden.

O'Neill, R. E., Horner, R. H., Albin, R. W., Storey, K., & Sprague, J. R. (1990). *Functional analysis of problem behavior: A practical assessment guide.* Sycamore, IL: Sycamore Press.

Opotow, S., & Weiss, L. (2000). Denial and the process of moral exclusion in environmental conflict. *Journal of Social Issues, 56,* 475–490.

Orr, L., Feins, J. D., Jacob, R., Beechcroft, E., Sanbonmatsu, L., Katz, L. F., Liebman, J. B., & Kling, J. R. (2003). *Moving to opportunity for fair housing demonstration program: Interim impacts evaluation.* Washington, DC: U.S. Department of Housing and Urban Development.

Ortiz de Montellano, B. (1992). Magic melanin: Spreading scientific illiteracy among minorities: Part II. *Skeptical Inquirer, 16,* 162–166.

Orwell, G. (1958). Politics and the English language. In S. Orwell & I. Angus (Eds.), *The collected essays, journalism and letters of George Orwell: Vol. 4. In front of your nose, 1945–1950* (pp. 127–140). London: Secker & Warburg.

Otis, J. D. (2007). *Managing chronic pain: A cognitive-behavioral therapy approach.* New York: Oxford University Press.

Otis, M. D. (2004). Building coalitions and changing communities. One community's path to greater social justice: Building on earlier successes. *Journal of Gay & Lesbian Social Services, 16(3/4),* 17–33.

Øvretveit, J. (1995). *Purchasing for health: A multi-disciplinary introduction to the theory and practice of health purchasing.* Philadelphia: Open University Press.

Owen, J., & Imel, Z. (2010). Rating scales in psychotherapy practice. In L. Baer & M. A. Blais (Eds.), *Handbook of clinical rating scales and assessment in psychiatry and mental health* (pp. 257–270). New York: Humana Press.

Oxman, A. D., Bjorndal, A., Becerra-Posada, F., Gibson, M., Block, M. A. G., Haines, A., et al. (2010). A framework for mandatory impact evaluation to ensure well informed public policy decisions. *The Lancet, 375,* 427–431.

Oxman, A. D., Cook, D. J., & Guyatt, G. M. For the evidence-based medicine working group. (1994). Users' guide to the medical literature. V1: How to use an overview. *Journal of the American Medical Association, 272,* 1367–1371.

Oxman, A. D., Davis, D., Haynes, R. B., & Thomson, M. A. (1995). No magic bullets: a systematic review of 102 trials of interventions to help health professionals deliver services more effectively and efficiently. *Canadian Medical Association Journal, 153,* 1423–1443.

Oxman, A. D., & Flottorp, S. (1998). An overview of strategies to promote implementation of evidence based health care. In C. Silagy & A. Haines (Eds.), *Evidence based practice in primary care.* London: BMJ Books.

Oxman, A. D., & Guyatt, G. H. (1993). The science of reviewing research. In K. S. Warren & F. Mosteller (Eds.), *Doing more good than harm: The evaluation of health care interventions* (pp. 125–133). New York: New York Academy of Sciences.

Paling, J. (2006). *Helping patients understand risks: 7 simple strategies for successful communication.* Gainesville, FL: Risk Communication Institute.

Pargament, K. I., Koenig, H. G., & Perez, L. M. (2000). The many methods of religious coping: Development and initial validation of the RCOPE. *Journal of Clinical Psychology, 56*(4), 519–543.

Parker, A. G., Hetrick, S. E., Jorm, A. F., Yung, A. R., McGorry, P. D., Mackinnon, A., et al. (2011). The effectiveness of simple psychological and exercise interventions for high prevalence mental health problems in young people: A factorial randomised controlled trial. *Trials, 12,* 76.

Patai, D., & Koertge, N. (2003). *Professing feminism: Education and indoctrination in women's studies* (new ed.). Lanham, MD: Lexington Books.

Patterson, C. J., & Wainright, J. (2011). Adolescents with same sex parents: Findings from the National Longitudinal Study of Adolescent Health. In D. Brodzinsky & A. Pertman (Eds.), *Adoptions by lesbians and gay men: A new dimension in family diversity* (pp. 85–111). New York: Oxford University Press.

Patterson, G. R. (2002). The early development of coercive family process. In J. B. Reid, G. R. Patterson, & J. Snyder (Eds.), *Antisocial behavior in children and adolescents: A developmental analysis and model for intervention* (pp. 25–44). Washington, DC: American Psychological Association.

Patterson, G. R., & Chamberlain, P. (1994). A functional analysis of resistance during parent training therapy. *Clinical Psychology: Science and Practice, 1,* 53–70.

Patterson, G. R., & Forgatch, M. S. (1985). Therapist behavior as a determinant for client noncompliance: A paradox for the behavior modifier. *Journal of Consulting and Clinical Psychology, 53,* 846–851.

Patterson, G. R., & Forgatch, M. S. (1990). Initiation and maintenance of process disrupting single-mother families. In G. R. Patterson (Ed.), *Depression and aggression in family interaction* (pp. 209–245). Hillsdale, NJ: Erlbaum.

Patterson, G. R. & Forgatch, M. S. (2005). *Parents and adolescents living together.* Champaign, IL: Research Press.

Patterson, G. R., & Forgatch, M. S. (2005). Initiation and maintenance of process disrupting single-mother families. In G. R. Patterson (ed.), *Depression and aggression in family interaction* (pp. 209–245). Hillsdale, N.J.: Lawrence Erlbaum.

Patterson, G. R., & Reid, J. B. (1970). Reciprocity and coercion: Two facets of social systems. In C. Neuringer & J. L. Michael (Eds.), *Behavior modification in clinical psychology.* New York: Appleton-Century-Crafts.

Patti, R. J. (2009). *The handbook of human services management.* Los Angeles, CA: Sage.

Patton, M. Q. (2008). *Utilization-focused evaluation: The new century text* (4th ed.) Los Angeles, CA: Sage.

Patton, M. Q. (1987). *Creative evaluation* (2nd ed.). Newbury Park, CA: Sage.

Paul, G. L., Licht, M. H., Mariotto, M. J., Power, C. T., & Engel, K. L. (1987a). *The staff-resident interaction chronograph: Observational assessment instrumentation for service and research.* Champaign, IL: Research Press.

Paul, G. L., Licht, M. H., Mariotto, M. J., Power, C. T., & Engel, K. L. (1987b). *The time-sample behavioral checklist: Observational assessment instrumentation for service and research.* Champaign, IL: Research Press.

Paul, R. (1992). *Critical thinking: What every person needs to survive in a rapidly changing world* (2nd ed.). Foundation for Critical Thinking. http://www.criticalthinking.org.

Paul, R. (1993). *Critical thinking: What every person needs to survive in a rapidly changing world* (3rd ed.). Foundation for Critical Thinking. http://www.criticalthinking.org.

Paul, R. W. & Elder, L. (2012). *Critical thinking: Tools for taking charge of your learning and your life* (3rd Ed.). Boston, MA: Pearson Education.

Pavlov, I. P. (1927). *Conditioned reflexes* (G. V. Anrip, Trans.). New York: Liveright.

Pawson, R., & Tilley, N. (1997). *Realistic evaluation.* London: Sage.

Pawson, R., Boaz, A., Grayson, L., Long, A., & Barnes, C. (2003). *Types and quality of knowledge in social care.* London: Social Care Institute for Excellence.

Payne, M. (2009). *Modern social work theory* (4th ed.). Chicago: Lyceum.

Peale, N. V. (1952). *The power of positive thinking.* New York: Prentice Hall.

Pear, R. (2004). US finds fault in all 50 states' child welfare programs, and penalties may follow. *New York Times,* April 26, A27.

Pear, R. (2011). "U.S. panel suggests research into causes and prevalence of health issues facing gays," *New York Times,* April 1, A16.

Pedersen, P. B., Lonner, W. J., Draguns, J. G., & Trimble, J. E. (Eds.). (2007). *Counseling across cultures.* Thousand Oaks, CA: Sage.

Peele, S. (1999). *Diseasing of America: How we allowed recovery zealots and the treatment industry to convince us we are out of control.* San Francisco: Jossey-Bass.

Pellow, D. N., & Brulle, R, J. (2007). Poisoning the planet: The struggle for environmental justice. *Contexts, 6,* 37–41.

Pelton, L. H. (1989). *For reasons of poverty: A critical analysis of the public child welfare system in the U.S.* New York: Praeger.

Pelton, L. H. (2008). Informing child welfare: The promise and limits of empirical research. In D. Lindsey & A. Shlonsky (Eds.), *Child welfare research: Advances for practice and policy* (pp. 25–48). New York: Oxford University Press.

Penka, C., & Kirk, S. (1991). Practitioner involvement in clinical evaluation. *Social Work, 36,* 513–518.

Pennsylvania Human Relations Commission. (2007). *Points of contact: LGBT advocacy and support groups.* Harrisburg, PA: Pennsylvania Human Relations Commission.

Penston, J. (2010). *Stats.con: How we've been fooled by statistics-based research in medicine.* UK: London Press.

Pepper, C. (1984). *Quackery: A $10 billion scandal.* Subcommittee on health and long-term care of the Select Committee on Aging. U.S. House of Representatives. No. 98–435. U.S. Government Printing House.

Pepper, S. (1981). Problems in the quantification of frequency expressions. In D. W. Fiske (Ed.), *New directions for methodology of social and behavioral science. No. 9. Problems with Language Imprecision* (pp. 25–41). San Francisco: Jossey-Bass.

Perkins, D. (1992). *Smart schools: From training memories to educating minds.* New York: Free Press.

Perkins, D. (1995). *Outsmarting IQ: The emerging science of learnable intelligence.* New York: Free Press.

Perkins, R. (2006). The effectiveness of one session of therapy using a single-session therapy approach for children and adolescents with mental health problems. *Psychology and Psychotherapy: Theory, Research & Practice, 79,* 215–227.

Perkinson, H. (1993). *Teachers without goals, students without purposes.* New York: McGraw-Hill.

Perlman, H. H. (1957). *Social casework: A problem-solving process.* Chicago: University of Chicago Press.

Perlman, H. H. (1976). Believing and doing: Values in social work education. *Social Casework, 57,* 381–390.

Perlman, H. H. (1979). *Relationship: The heart of helping.* Chicago: University of Chicago Press.

Peterson, C., Maier, S. F., & Seligman, M. E. P. (1993). *Learned helplessness: A theory for the age of personal control.* New York: Oxford University Press.

Peterson, C., Semmel, A., von Baeyer, C., Abramson, L. Y., & Seligman, M. E. P. (1982). The attributional style questionnaire. *Cognitive Therapy and Research, 6,* 287–299.

Peterson, D. R. (1987). The role of assessment in professional psychology. In D. R. Peterson & D. B. Fishman (Eds.), *Assessment for decisions* (pp. 5–43). New Brunswick, NJ: Rutgers University Press.

Peterson, R. F., Knapp, T. J., Rosen, J. C., & Pither, B. F. (1977). The effects of furniture arrangement on the behavior of geriatric patients. *Behavior Therapy, 8,* 464–467.

Petr, C. (Ed.) (2008). *Multidimensional evidence-based practice: Synthesizing knowledge, research, and values.* New York: Routledge.

Petrocelli, W., & Repa, B. K. (1992). *Sexual harassment on the job.* Berkeley: Nolo Press.

Petrosino, A., Turpin-Petrosino, C., & Buehler, J. (2003). Scared Straight and other juvenile awareness programs for preventing juvenile delinquency: A systematic review of the randomized experimental evidence. *ANNALS of the American Academy of Political and Social Science, 589,* 41–62.

Pewsner, D., Battaglia, M., Minder, C., Marx, A., Bucher, H. C., & Egger, M. (2004). Ruling a diagnosis in or out with "SpPIn" and "SnNOut": A note of caution. *BMJ, 329,* 209–213.

Pharis, M. E., & Levin, V. S. (1991). "A person to talk to who really cared": High-risk mothers' evaluations of services in an intensive intervention research program. *Child Welfare, 70,* 307–320.

Pharoah, R. M., Rathbone, J., Mari, J. J., & Streiner, D. (2004). Family intervention for schizophrenia (Cochrane Review). In *Cochrane Library,* Issue 3. Chichester, UK: John Wiley & Sons, Ltd.

Phillips, D. C. (1987). *Philosophy, science and social inquiry: Contemporary methodological controversies in social science and related applied fields of research.* New York: Pergamon Press.

Phillips, D. C. (1990). Postpositivistic science: Myths and realities. In E. G. Guba (Ed.), *The paradigm dialog.* Thousand Oakes, CA: Sage.

Phillips, D. C. (1992). *The social scientist's bestiary: A guide to fabled threats to, and defenses of, naturalistic social studies.* New York: Pergamon.

Phillips, D. C. (2000). *The expanded social scientist's bestiary.* Lanham, MD: Rowman & Littlefield Publishers.

Phillips, J. K., Klein, G., & Sieck, W. R. (2005). Expertise in judgment and decision making: A case for training intuitive decision skills. In D. J. Koehler & N. Harvey (Eds.), *Blackwell handbook of judgment and decision making* (pp. 297–315). Malden, MA: Blackwell.

Pignotti, M. & Thyer, B. A. (2009). The use of novel unsupported and empirically supported therapies by licensed clinical social workers. *Social Work Research, 33,* 5–17.

Pincus, A., & Minahan, A. (1973). *Social work practice: Model and method.* Itasca, IL: Peacock Publishers.

Pinkston, E. M., & Linsk, N. L. (1984). *Care of the elderly: A family approach.* New York: Pergamon.

Piven, F. F., & Cloward, R. A. (Eds.). (1993). *Regulating the poor: The functions of public welfare* (2nd ed.). New York: Vintage.

Plato ([1954] 1993). *The last days of Socrates.* (H. Tredennick & H. Tarrant, trans.) New York: Penguin.

Plomin, R. (2011). Commentary: Why are children in the same family so different? Non-shared environment three decades later. *In. J. Epidemiology, 40,* 582–591.

Plous, S. (1993). *The psychology of judgement and decision making.* New York: McGraw-Hill.

Polivy, J. & Herman, C. P. (2002). If at first you don't succeed: False hopes of self-change. *American Psychologist, 57,* 677–689.

Pollitt, C. (1990). Doing business in the temple. *Public Administration, 68,* 435–452.

Polowy, C., Morgan, S., Khan, A., & Gorenberg, C. (2011). *Client confidentiality and privileged communications.* Washington, DC: NASW Press.

Pommer, D. A., & Streedbeck, D. (1974). Motivating staff performance in an operant learning program for children. *Journal of Applied Behavior Analysis, 7,* 217–221.

Ponce, N. A., Cochran, S. D., Pizer, J. C., et al. (2010). The effects of unequal access to health insurance for same-sex couples in California. *Health Affairs, 29,* 1–10.

Ponterotto, J. G., Casas, J. M., Suzuki, L. A., & Alexander, A. M. (2010). *Handbook of multicultural counseling* (3rd ed.). Thousand Oaks, CA: Sage.

Popper, K. R. (1961). *The poverty of historicism.* New York: Harper & Row.

Popper, K. R. ([1963] 1972). *Conjectures and refutations: The growth of scientific knowledge* (4th ed.). London: Routledge & Kegan Paul.

Popper, K. R. (1992). *In search of a better world: Lectures and essays from thirty years.* London: Routledge & Kegan Paul.

Popper, K. R. (1994). *The myth of the framework: In defense of science and rationality.* M. A. Notturno, Ed. New York: Routledge.

Popper, K. (1998). *The world of Parmenides: Essays on the pre-Socratic enlightenment.* New York: Routledge.

Popple, P. R., & Leighninger, L. (2002). *Social work, social welfare, and American society* (2nd ed.). Boston: Allyn & Bacon.

Portes, A. (1998). Social capital: Its origins and applications in modern sociology. *Annual Review of Sociology, 24*(1), 1–24.

Positive Behavioral Intervention Regulations. California Department of Education, July 1993. 721 Capitol Mall, P.O. Box 944272, Sacramento, CA 94244–2720.

Potegal, M., Stemmler, G., & Spielberger, C. D. (Eds.) (2010). *International handbook of anger: Biological, psychological and social processes.* New York: Springer.

Potter-Efron, R. T. (2005). *Handbook of anger management: group, individual, couple and family approaches.* Binghamton, NY: Haworth.

Pottick, K. L., Wakefield, J. C., Kirk, S. A., & Tian, X. (2003). Influence of social workers' characteristics on the perception of mental disorder in youths. *Social Service Review, 77,* 431–454.

Power, M. (1997). *The audit society: rituals of verification.* New York: Oxford University Press.

Praderas, K., & MacDonald, M. L. (1986). Telephone conversational skills training with socially isolated, impaired nursing home residents. *Journal of Applied Behavior Analysis, 19,* 337–348.

Prain, M., McVilly, K., Ramcharan, P., Cufrie, S., & Reece, J. (2010). Observing the behaviour and interactions of adults with congenital deafblindness living in community residences. *Journal of Intellectual & Developmental Disability, 35,* 82–91.

Pratkanis, A. R. (2007). *The science of social influence: Advances and future progress.* New York: Psychology Press.

Preedy, V. R., & Watson, R. R. (2010*). Handbook of disease burdens and quality of life.* New York: Springer.

Premack, D. (1965). Reinforcement theory. In D. Levine (Ed.), *Nebraska Symposium on Motivation* (pp. 23–180). Lincoln: University of Nebraska Press.

Prestby, J., Wandersman, A., Florin, P., Rich, R., & Chavis, D. (1990). Benefits, costs, incentive management and participation in voluntary organizations: A means to understanding and promoting empowerment. *American Journal of Community Psychology, 18,* 117–150.

Prilleltensky, I., Prilleltensky, O., & Voorhees, C. (2008). Psychopolitical validity in the helping professions: applications to research, interventions, case conceptualization, and therapy. In C. I. Cohen & S. Timimi (Eds.), *Liberatory psychiatry: Philosophy, politics and mental health* (pp. 105–130). New York: Cambridge University Press.

Prinz, R. J., Sanders, M. R., Shapiro, C. J., Whitaker, D. J., & Lutzker, J. R. (2009). Population-based prevention of child maltreatment: The U. S. triple p system population trial. *Prev Sci, 10,* 1–12.

Proctor, R. N. & Schlebinger, L. (Eds.) (2008). *Agnotology: The making and unmaking of ignorance.* Palo Alto, CA: Stanford University Press.

Professional therapy never includes sex. (2009). California Department of Consumer Affairs.

Pronin, E., Puccio, C., & Ross, L. (2002). Understanding misunderstanding: Social, psychological perspectives. In T. Gilovich, D. Griffin, & D. Kahneman (Eds.), *Heuristics and biases: The psychology of intuitive judgment* (pp. 636–665). New York: Cambridge University Press.

Prounis, C. (2004). The art of advertorial. *Pharmaceutical Executive,* May 1.

Pruger, R. (1973). The good bureaucrat. *Social Work, 18,* 26–32.

Pryor, K. (1984). *Don't shoot the dog.* New York: Bantam Books.

Pryor, K. (1999). *Don't shoot the dog: The new art of teaching and training.* (Rev. ed.)

Ptacek, J. (2010). *Restorative justice and violence against women.* New York: Oxford University Press.

Pullman, M. D., Kerbs, J., Koroloff, N., Vech-White, E., Gayler, R., & Sieler, D. (2006). Juvenile offenders with mental health needs: Reducing recidivism using wraparound. *Crime and Delinquency, 52,* 375–397.

Pugh, R. & Cheers, B. (2010). *Rural social work: an interdisciplinary perspective.* Bristol,U.K.: Policy Press.

Putnam, R. D. (2000). *Bowling alone: The collapse and revival of American community.* New York: Simon & Schuster.

Pyles, L. (2009). *Progressive community organizing: A critical approach for a globalizing world.* New York: Routledge.

Quinn, R. E., et al. (2007). *Becoming a master manager: A competing values approach* (4th ed.). New York: John Wiley & Sons.

Quinsey, V. L., Harris, G. T., Rice, M. E., & Cormier, C. A. (2006). *Violent offenders: Appraising and managing risk* (2nd ed.). Washington, DC: American Psychological Association.

Rachlin, H. (1980). *Behaviorism in everyday life.* Englewood Cliffs, NJ: Prentice Hall.

Rachlin, H. (1989). *Judgment, decision, and choice: A cognitive/behavioral synthesis.* New York: W. H. Freeman.

Raffaelli, M., & Ontai, L. L. (2004). Gender socialization in Latino/a families: results from two retrospective studies. *Sex Roles: A Journal of Research, 50,* 287–299.

Rainey, H. G., Ronquillo, J. C., & Avellaneda, C. N. (2010). Decision making in public organizations (pp. 349–378). In P. C. Nutt & D. C. Wilson (Eds.), *Handbook of decision making.* Chichester, West Sussex, England: John Wiley & sons.

Rampton, S., & Stauber, J. (2001). *Trust us, we're experts! How industry manipulates science and gambles with your future.* New York: Penguin.

Ramos, K. D., Schafer, S., & Tracz, S. M. (2003). Validation of the Fresno test of competence in evidence based medicine. *BMJ, 326,* 319–321.

Rank, H. (1984). *The peptalk: How to analyze political language.* Park Forest, IL: Counter-Propaganda Press.

Rapley, M., Moncrieff, J., & Dillon, J. (Eds.) (2011). *De-medicalizing misery: Psychiatry, psychology, and the human condition.* Houndmills, Basingstoke, Hampshire England: Palgrave Macmillan.

Rappaport, J. (1987). Terms of empowerment/exemplars of prevention: Toward a theory for community psychology. *Journal of Community Psychology, 15,* 121–148.

Raven, J. (1984). *Competence in modern society: Its identification, development and release.* London: H. K. Lewis & Co.

Ravitch, D. (2003). *The language police: How pressure groups restrict what students learn.* New York: Alfred A. Knopf.

Reamer, F. G. (1993). *Ethical dilemmas in social services* (2nd ed.). New York: Columbia University Press.

Reamer, F. G. (2003a). *Tangled relationships: Managing boundary issues in the human services.* New York: Columbia University Press.

Reamer, F. G. (2003b). *Social work malpractice and liability: Strategies for prevention* (2nd ed.). New York: Columbia University Press.

Reamer, F. G. (2006). *Ethical standards in social work: A review of the NASW code of ethics* (2nd ed.). Washington, D.C.: NASW Press.

Reamer, F. G. (2006). *Social work values and. ethics.* New York: Columbia University Press.

Reason, J. (1997). *Managing the risks of organizational accidents.* Aldershot: Ashgate.

Reason, J. (2001). Understanding adverse events: The human factor. In C. Vincent (Ed.), *Clinical risk management: Enhancing patient safety* (2nd ed.) (pp. 9–30) London: BMJ Books.

Regehr, C. & Kanani, K. (2006). *Essential law for social work practice in Canada.* New York: Oxford University Press.

Reichert, E. (Ed.) (2007). *Challenges in human rights: A social work perspective.* New York: Columbia University Press.

Reid, D. H., O'Kane, N. P., & Macurik, K. M. (2011). Staff training and management. In Fisher, et al (Eds.), *Handbook of applied behavior analysis* (pp. 281–294). New York: Guilford.

Reid, J. B. (1978). *A social learning approach to family interaction.* Vol. 2. *A manual for coding family interactions.* Eugene, OR: Castalia.

Reid, J. B. & Eddy, J. M. (1997). The prevention of anti-social behavior: Some considerations in the search for effective interventions. In D. M. Stoff, J. Breiling, & J. D. Maser (Eds.), *A handbook of anti-social behavior* (pp. 343–35). New York: Wiley.

Reid, J. B., Patterson, G. R., & Snyder, J. (Eds.). (2002). *Antisocial behavior in children and adolescents: A developmental analysis and the Oregon model for intervention.* Washington, DC: American Psychological Association.

Reid, W. J., & Epstein, L. (1977). *Task centered casework.* New York: Columbia University Press.

Reiman, J. (2004). *The rich get richer and the poor get prison* (7th ed.). Boston: Allyn and Bacon.

Reiss, S. (2005). Extrinsic and intrinsic motivation at 30: Unresolved scientific issues. *The Behavior Analyst, 28,* 1–4.

Renstrom, L., Andersson, B., & Marton, F. (1990). Students' conceptions of matter. *Journal of Educational Psychology, 82,* 555–569.

Renzetti, C. M., Edleson, J. L., & Bergan, R. K. (2011). *Sourcebook on violence against women* (2nd ed.). Thousand Oaks, CA: Sage.

Repp, A. C. & Horner, R. H. (1999). *Functional analysis of problem behavior: From effective assessment to effective support.* Belmont, CA: Wadsworth.

Rescorla, R. A. (1998). Pavlovian conditioning: It's not what you think it is. *American* environment three decades later. *Int. J. Epidemiology, 46,* 582–592.*Psychologist, 43,* 151–160.

Resnick, H. B. (1982). Facilitating productive staff meetings. In I. M. Austin & W. E. Hershey (Eds.). *Handbook of mental health administration* (pp. 196–197). San Francisco: Jossey-Bass.

Reuter-Lorenz, P. A., Baynes, K., Mangun, G. R., & Phelps, E. A. (2010). *The cognitive neuroscience of mind: a tribute to Michael S. Gazzaniga.* Cambridge, MA: MIT Press.

Rhoads, S. E. (2004). *Taking sex differences seriously.* San Francisco, CA: Encounter Books.

Richan, W. C. (2006). *Lobbying for social change* (3rd ed.). New York: Hayworth.

Richard, D. C. & Lauterbach, D. (2007). *Handbook of exposure therapies.* Boston, MA: Elsevier.

Richards, P. S., & Bergin, A. E. (1997). *A spiritual strategy for counseling and psychotherapy.* Washington, D.C.: American Psychological Association.

Richards, S. S., & Perri, M. G. (2010). *Relapse prevention for depression.* Washington, D.C.: American Psychological Association.

Richmond, M. E. (1917). *Social diagnosis.* New York: Russell Sage Foundation.

Richmond, V. P., McCroskey, J. C., & Hickson, M. (2008). *Nonverbal behavior in interpersonal relations.* Boston, MA: Pearson/Allyn & Bacon.

Riggs, S. A. (2010). Childhood emotional abuse and the attachment system cross the life cycle: What theory and research tell us. *Journal of Aggression, Maltreatment, and Trauma, 19,* 5–51.

Rigney, D. (2010). *The Matthew effect: How advantage begets further advantage.* New York: Columbia University Press.

Riley, M. W. (1988). On the significance of age in sociology. In M. W. Riley (Ed.), *Social structures & human lives* (pp. 24–25). Newbury Park, CA: Sage.

Risley, T. R., & Favell, J. (1979). Constructing a living environment in an institution. In L. A. Hammerlynck (Ed.), *Behavioral systems for the developmentally disabled,* II. *Institutional, clinic, and community environments* (pp. 3–24). New York: Brunner/Mazel.

Risley, T. R. & Twardosz, S. (1976). The preschool as a setting for behavior intervention. In H. Leitenberg (Ed.), *Handbook of behavior modification and behavior therapy* (pp. 453–474). Englewood Cliffs, NJ: Prentice-Hall.

Robbins, M. S., Szapocznik, J., Horigian, V. E., Feaster, D. J., Puccinelli, M., & Jacobs, P. (2009). Brief strategic family therapy for adolescent drug abusers: A multi-site effectiveness study. *Contemporary Clinical Trials, 30,* 269–278.

Robbins, S. P., & Judge, T. (2012). *Organizational behavior* (15th ed.). Upper Saddle River, NJ: Prentice Hall.

Roberts, A. R. (2005). *Crisis intervention handbook: Assessment, treatment, and research* (2nd ed.). New York: Oxford University Press.

Roberts, A. R., & Yeager, K. R. (2009). *Pocket guide to crisis intervention.* New York: Oxford University Press.

Roberts, K. H., & Hunt, D. M. (1991). *Organizational behavior.* Boston: PWS-Kent Publishing Co.

Roberts, I., Kramer, M. S., & Suissa, S. (1996). Does home visiting prevent childhood injury? A systematic review of randomized controlled trials. *BMJ, 312,* 29–33.

Robertson, R., & Jochelson, K. (2006). *Interventions that change clinician behaviour: Mapping the literature.* London, U.K.: The National Institute for Health and Clinical Excellence (NICE).

Robinson, D. N. (1974). Harm, offense, and nuisance: Some first steps in the establishment of an ethics of treatment. *American Psychologist, 29,* 233–238.

Rocha, C. J. (2007). *Essentials of social work policy practice.* Hoboken, NJ: John Wiley & Sons.

Rodin, J., & Langer, E. J. (1977). Long-term effects of a control relevant intervention with the institutionalized aged. *Journal of Personality and Social Psychology, 35,* 897–902.

Rodriguez, N., Myers, H. F., Mira, C. B., Flores, T., & Garcia-Hernandez, L. (2002). Development of the multidimensional acculturative stress inventory for adults of Mexican origin. *Psychological Assessment, 14*(4), 451–461.

Roediger, H. L., & Bergman, E. T. (1998).The controversy over recovered memories. *Psychology, Public Policy, & Law, 4*(4), 1091–1109.

Rogers, C. R. (1957). The necessary and sufficient conditions of therapeutic personality change. *Journal of Social Issues, 21,* 95–103.

Rogers, C. R., & Skinner, B. E (1956). Some issues concerning the control of human behavior. *Science, 124,* 1057–1066.

Rogers, R. (2008). *Clinical assessment of malingering and deception* (3rd ed.). New York: Guilford.

Rogowski, S. (2010). *Social work. The rise and fall of a profession?* Bristol, England: The Policy Press.

Ronen, T. & Freeman, A. (2007). *Cognitive behavior therapy in clinical social work practice.* New York: Springer.

Rook, K. S. (1984). The negative side of social interaction: Impact on psychological well being. *Journal of Personality and Social Psychology, 46,* 1097–1108.

Rook, K. S. (1990). Social relationships as a source of companionship: Implications for older adults' psychological well-being. In B. R. Sarason, I. G. Sarason, & G. R. Pierce (Eds.), *Social support: An interactional view* (pp. 219–250). New York: Wiley.

Rosales-Ruiz, J., & Baer, D. M. (1997). Behavioral cusps: A developmental and pragmatic concept for behavior analysis. *Journal of Applied Behavior Analysis, 30,* 533–544.

Rose, N. (1999). *Powers of freedom: Reframing political thought.* New York: Cambridge University Press.

Rose, D., Fleischmann, P., Wykes, T., Leese, M., & Bindman, J. (2003). Patients' perspectives on electro-convulsive therapy: Systematic review. *BMJ, 326,* 1363–1367.

Rose, S. C., Bisson, J., Churchill, R., & Wessely, S. (2002). Psychological debriefing for preventing post traumatic stress disorder (PTSD) (Cochrane Review). In *Cochrane Library,* Issue 2. Chichester: Wiley.

Rose, S. D. (1989). *Working with adults in groups: A cognitive behavioral approach.* San Francisco: Jossey-Bass.

Rosen, A. (1994). Knowledge use in direct practice. *Social Service Review, 68,* 561–577.

Rosen, A., & Proctor, E. K. (Eds.). (2003). *Developing practice guidelines for social work interventions: Issues, methods and research agenda.* New York: Columbia University Press.

Rosen, A., Proctor, E. K., Morrow-Howell, N., & Staudt, M. (1995). Rationales for practice decisions: Variations in knowledge use by decision task and social work service. *Research on Social Work Practice, 15*(4), 501–523.

Rosenau, P. M. (1992). *Post-modernism and the social sciences: Insights, inroads, and intrusion.* Princeton: Princeton University Press.

Rosenbaum, P. R. (2002). *Observational studies (Springer series in statistics)* (2nd ed.) New York: Springer-Verlag.

Rosenhan, D. (1973). On being sane in insane places. *Science, 179,* 250–258.

Rosenthal, R. (1994). On being one's own study: Experimenter effects in behavioral research—30 years later. In W. R. Shadish & S. Fuller (Eds.), *The social psychology of science* (pp. 214–229). New York: Guilford.

Rosenthal, R. (2001). *Workshop on meta-analysis.* Berkeley: University of California.

Rosenthal, R., & Jacobson, L. (2003). *Pygmalion in the classroom: Teacher expectation and pupils' intellectual development.* Carmarthen: Crown House.

Rosenthal, T. (1994). Science and ethics in conducting, analyzing, and reporting psychological research. *Psychological Science, 5*(3), 127–134.

Rossi, P. H., Lipsey, M. W., & Freeman, H. E. (2004). *Evaluation: A systematic approach* (7th ed.). Thousand Oaks, CA: Sage.

Rothman, J. (1980). *Social R & D: Research & development in the human services.* Englewood Cliffs, NJ: Prentice Hall.

Rothman, J. (1991). *Runaway and homeless youth: Strengthening services for families and children.* New York: Longman.

Rothman, J. (2001). *Approaches to community intervention.* In J. Rothman, J. Erlich, & J. E. Tropman (Eds.), *Strategies in community organization: Macro practice.* Pacific Grove, CA: Wadsworth.

Rothman, J., Erlich, J., & Tropman, J. E. (2008). *Strategies of community intervention: Macro practice* (7th ed.). Peosta, IA: Eddie Bowers Pub.

Rothman, J., & Thomas, E. J. (Eds.). (1994). *Intervention research: Design and development for behavior service.* New York: Hayworth.

Rotter, J. B. (1966). Generalized expectancies for internal versus external control of reinforcement. *Psychological Monographs, 80*(609), 1–28.

Roussos, S. T., & Fawcett, S. B. (2000). A review of collaborative partnerships as a strategy for improving community health. *Annual Review of Public Health, 21,* 369–402.

Roysircar-Sodowsky, G., & Maestas, M. V. (2000). Acculturation, ethnic identity, and acculturative stress: Evidence and measurement. In R. H. Dana (Ed.), *Handbook of cross-cultural and multicultural personality assessment* (pp. 131–171). Mahwah, NJ: Erlbaum.

Rubin, A., & Parrish, D. (2007). Problematic phrases in the conclusions of published outcome studies: Implications for evidence-based practice. *Research on Social Work Practice, 17,* 592–602.

Rubin, K. H., Bukowski, W. M., & Laursen, B. P. (2009). *Handbook of peer interactions, relationships, and groups.* New York: Guilford.

Ruggiero, V. R. (1988). *Teaching thinking across the curriculum.* New York: Harper and Row. (See also 3rd ed., 1991).

Rutter, M., & Taylor, E. (2002). Clinical assessment and diagnostic formulation. In M. Rutter & E. Taylor (Eds.), *Child and adolescent psychiatry* (4th ed.) (pp. 18–31). Malden, MA: Blackwell.

Rutter, M. & Taylor, E. (Eds.) (2010). *Child and adolescent psychiatry* (5th ed.). Malden, MA: Blackwell.

Rutter, M., & Yule, W. (2002). Applied scientific thinking in clinical assessment. In M. Rutter & E. Taylor (Eds.), *Child and adolescent psychiatry* (4th ed.) (pp. 103–126). Malden, MA: Blackwell.

Ryan, C., Russell, S. T., Huebner, D., Diaz, R., & Sanchez, J. (2010). Family acceptance in adolescence and the health of LGBT young adults. *Journal of Child and Adolescent Psychiatric Nursing, 23,* 205–213.

Ryan, W. (1976). *Blaming the victim.* New York: Vantage.

Rzepnicki, T. L., & Johnson, P. R. (2005). Examining decision errors in child protection: A new application of root cause analysis. *Children and Youth Services Review, 27,* 393–408.

Rzepnicki, T. L., Johnson, P. R., Kane, D. Q., Moncher, D., Coconato, L., & Shulman, B. (2012). Learning from data: the beginning of error reduction in Illinois child welfare. In T. L. Rzepnicki, S. G. McCracken, & H. E. Briggs (Eds.), *From task-centered social work to evidence-based and integrative practice* (pp. 156–178). Chicago, IL: Lyceum.

Saarikallio, S. (2011). Music as emotional self-regulation throughout adulthood. *Psychology of Music, 39,* 307–327.

Sackett, D. L. (1979). Bias in analytic research. *Journal of Chronic Disease, 32,* 51–63.

Sackett, D. L., Richardson, W. S., Rosenberg, W., & Haynes, R. B. (1997). *Evidence-based medicine: How to practice and teach EBM.* New York: Churchill Livingstone.

Sackett, D. L., Straus, S. E., Richardson, W. S., Rosenberg, W., & Haynes, R. E. (2000). *Evidence-based medicine: How to practice and teach EBM* (2nd ed.). New York: Churchill Livingstone.

Safran, J. D., Muran, J. C., & Eubanks-Carter, C. (2011). Repairing alliance ruptures. In J. C. Norcross (Ed.), *Psychotherapy relationships that work: Evidence-based responsiveness* (2nd ed.) (pp. 224–238). New York: Oxford University Press.

Sagan, C. (1987). The burden of skepticism. *Skeptical Inquirer, 12,* 38–74.

Sagan, C. (1990). Why we need to understand science. *Skeptical Inquirer, 14,* 263–269.

Sailor, W., & Carr, E. G. (1994). Should only positive methods be used by professionals who work with children and adolescents? Yes. In M. A. Mason & E. Gambrill (Eds.), *Debating children's lives: Current controversies on children and adolescents* (pp. 225–227). Newbury Park, CA: Sage.

Sailor, W., Dunlap, G., Sugai, G., & Horner, R. (Eds.) (2009). *Handbook of positive behavior support.* New York: Springer.

Salas, E., & Klein, G. (Eds.). (2001). *Linking expertise and naturalistic decision making.* Mahwah, NJ: Erlbaum.

Salas, E., Rosen, M. A., & DiazGranados, D. (2010). Expertise-based intuition and decision making in organizations. *Journal of Management, 36,* 941–973.

Saleebey, D. (2001). The diagnostic strengths manual? *Social Work, 46*(2), 183–187.

Saleebey, D. (2013). *The strengths perspective in social work practice.* Boston: Ayllon & Bacon.

Sally Clark (2003). Sally Clark freed after appeal court quashes her convictions. *News British Medical Journal, 326,* 304.

Sansone, C., Harackiewicz, J. M. (Eds.). (2000). *Intrinsic and extrinsic motivation: The search for optimal motivation and performance.* San Diego: Academic Press.

Santrock, J. W. (2003). *Life-span development* (9th ed.). Boston, MA: MacGraw-Hill.

Sarason, B. R., Sarason, I. G., & Pierce, G. R. (Eds.). (1990). *Social support: An interactional view.* New York: John Wiley.

Sarason, S. B., & Lorentz, E. (1979). *The challenge of the resource exchange network: From concept to action.* San Francisco: Jossey-Bass.

Sarafino, E. P. (2012). *Applied behavior analysis: Principles and procedures for modifying behavior.* Hobokan, NJ: John Wiley & Sons.

Sarnoff, S. K. (2001). *Sanctified snake oil: The effects of junk science on public policy.* Westport, CT: Praeger.

Sarnoff, S. K. (2009). An Appalachian example: Issues of social and economic justice. In C. J. Tice & D. D. Long (Eds.), *International social work policy and practice: practical issues and perspectives* (pp. 161–183). Hobokan, NJ: John Wiley & Sons.

Sarri, R., & Finn, J. (1992). Child welfare policy and practice: Rethinking the history of our uncertainties. *Children and Youth Services Review, 14,* 219–236.

Sarri, R. C., & Sarri, C. M. (1992). Organizational and community change through participatory action research. *Advances in Social Work, 16,* 99–122.

Savarese, M., & Weber, C. M. (1993). Case management for persons who are homeless. *Journal of Case Management, 2,* 3–8.

The Scandal of Social Work Education. National Association of Scholars. 9/11/2007.

Schaufeli, W. B., Maslach, C., & Marek, T. (Eds.). (1993). *Professional burnout: Recent developments in theory and research.* Washington, DC: Taylor & Francis.

Scheff, T. J. (1984). *Labeling madness* (2nd ed.). Englewood Cliffs, NJ: Prentice Hall.

Schemo, D. J. (2007). Report accounts horrors of youth boot camps. *New York Times,* Oct. 11.

Schensul, J. J. (1993). Approaches to case management in Puerto Rican communities. *Journal of Case Management, 2,* 18–25.

Scheper-Hughes, N. (1992). *Death without weeping: The violence of everyday life in Brazil.* Berkeley: University of California Press.

Scheper-Hughes, N., & Lovell, A. M. (Eds.). (1987). *Psychiatry inside out: Selected writings of Franco Basaglia.* New York: Columbia.

Schlenker, B. R. (2003). Self-presentation. In M. R. Leary & J. P. Tangney (Eds.), *Handbook of self and identity* (pp. 492–518). New York: Guilford.

Schnaitter, R. (1986). Behavior as a function of inner states and outer circumstances. In T. Thompson & M. D. Zeiler (Eds.), *Analysis and integration of behavioral units* (pp. 247–274). Hillsdale, NJ: Erlbaum.

Schneider, W. H. (1965). *Danger: Men talking.* New York: Random House.

Schneider, R. L. & Lester, L. (2001*). Social work advocacy: A new framework for action.* Belmont, CA: Brookes/Cole.

Schnelle, J. F. (1974). A brief report on invalidity of parent evaluations of behavior change. *Journal of Applied Behavior Analysis, 7,* 341–343.

Schnelle, J. F., & Traughber, B. (1983). A behavioral assessment system applicable to geriatric nursing facility residents. *Behavioral Assessment, 5,* 231–243.

Schön, D. (1990). *Educating the reflective practitioner,* (new ed.) San Francisco: Jossey-Bass.

Schraagen, J. M., Militello, L. G., Ormerod, T., & Lipshitz, R. (2008). *Naturalistic decision making and macrocognition.* Burlington, VT: Ashgate.

Schrader, C., & Levine, M. (1994). *PTR: Prevent, teach, reinforce* (2nd ed.). 454 Gallinas, San Rafael, CA 94903: Behavioral Counseling and Research Center. 415–499–8455.

Schriner, K. F., & Fawcett, S. B. (1988). Development and validation of a community concerns report method. *Journal of Community Psychology, 16,* 306–316.

Schroeder, S., Oster-Granite, M. L., & Thompson, T. (2002). *Self-injurious behavior: gene-brain-behavior relationships.* Washington, D. C.: American Psychological Association.

Schultz, R. (1976). Effects of control and predictability on the physical and psychological well-being of the institutionalized aged. *Journal of Personality and Social Psychology, 33,* 563–573.

Schulz, K. F., Altman, D. G., Moher, D. for the CONSORT Group. (2010). CONSORT 2010 statement: Updated guidelines for reporting parallel group randomised trials. *BMJ, 340,* 698–702.

Schunk, D. H. & Zimmerman, B. J. (2008). *Motivation and self-regulated learning: theory, research and applications.* Mahwah, NJ: Lawrence Erlbaum.

Schwartz, A. (2010). *Housing policy in the United States.* New York: Routledge.

Schwartz, A., & Goldiamond, I. (1975). *Social casework: A behavioral approach.* New York: Columbia University Press.

Schwartz, L. M. & Woloshin, S. (2011). The drug facts box: Making informed decisions about prescription drugs possible. In G. Gigerenzer & J. A. M. Gray (Eds.) (2011*). Better doctors, better patients, better decisions* (pp. 233–242). Cambridge, MA: MIT Press.

Schwartz, I. M. (1989). *(In)justice for juveniles: Rethinking the best interests of the child.* Lexington, MA: Lexington.

Schwartz, I. S., & Baer, D. M. (1991). Social validity assessments: Is current practice state of the art? *Journal of Applied Behavior Analysis, 24,* 189–204.

Schweingruber, D., & McPhail, C. (1999). A method for systematically observing and recording collective action. *Sociological Methods & Research, 27,* 451–498.

Scott, S., Knapp, M., Henderson, J., & Maughan, B. (2001). Financial cost of social exclusion: Follow-up study of anti-social children into adulthood. *BMJ, 323,* 191–194.

Scott, S., O'Connor, T. G., Futh, A., Matias, C., Price, J., & Doolan, M. (2010). Impact of a parenting program in a high-risk, multi-ethnic community: The PALS trial. *Journal of Child Psychology and Psychiatry, 51,* 1331–1341.

Scriven, M. (1976). *Reasoning.* New York: McGraw-Hill.

Scriven, M. (1991). *Evaluation thesaurus* (4th ed.). Newbury Park, CA: Sage.

Scull, A. (2005). *Madhouse: A tragic tale of megalomania and modern medicine.* New Haven: Yale University Press.

Seech, Z. (1993). *Open minds and everyday reasoning.* Belmont, CA: Wadsworth.

Seekins, T., & Fawcett, S. F. (1987). Effects of a poverty-clients' agenda on resource allocations by community decision makers. *American Journal of Community Psychology, 15,* 305–320.

Seekins, T., Mathews, R. N., & Fawcett, S. B. (1984). Enhancing leadership skills for community self-help organizations through behavioral instruction. *Journal of Community Psychology, 12,* 155–163.

Seekins, T., Maynard-Moody, S., & Fawcett, S. B. (1987). Understanding the policy process: Preventing and coping with community problems. In L. A. Jason, R. E. Hess, R. D. Felner, & J. N. Moritsugu (Eds.), *Prevention: Toward a multidisciplinary approach, Vol. 5, Issue 2* (pp. 65–89). New York: Haworth Press.

Segal, D. L., & Hersen, M. (Eds.) (2010). *Diagnostic interviewing* (4th ed.). New York: Springer.

Segal, Z. V., Williams, J. M., & Teasdale, J. D. (2001). *Mindfulness-based cognitive therapy for depression: A new approach to preventing relapse.* New York: Guilford.

Segrin, C., & Flora, J. (2011). *Family communication.* New York: Routledge.

Seligman, M. E. P. (1975). *Helplessness: On depression, development and death.* San Francisco: W. H. Freeman & Co. Pub.

Seligman, M. E. P. (1995). The effectiveness of psychotherapy: The *Consumer Reports* study. *American Psychologist, 12,* 965–974.

Sen, A. (2009). *The idea of justice.* Cambridge, MA: Belknap Press of Harvard University.

Sen, R. (2003*). Stir it up: Lessons in community organizing and advocacy.* San Francisco: Jossey-Bass.

Senge, P. M. (1990). *The fifth discipline: The art & practice of the learning organization.* New York: Currency, Doubleday.

Seymour, F. W., & Stokes, T. F. (1976). Self-recording in training girls to increase work and evoke staff praise in an institution for offenders. *Journal of Applied Behavior Analysis, 9,* 41–54.

Shadish, W. R., Cook, T. D., & Campbell, D. T. (2002). *Experimental and quasi-experimental designs for generalized causal inference.* Boston: Houghton-Mifflin.

Shadish, W. R., Navarro, A. M., Matt, G. E., & Phillips, G. (2000). The effects of psychological therapies under clinical representative conditions: A meta-analysis. *Psychological Bulletin, 126,* 512–529.

Shaffer, V. A., & Hulsey, L. (2009). Are patient decision aids effective? Insight from revisiting the debate between correspondence and coherence theories of judgment. *Judgment and Decision Making, 4,* 141–146.

Sharpe, V. A., & Faden, A. I. (1998). *Medical harm: Historical, conceptual, and ethical dimensions of iatrogenic illness.* New York: Cambridge University Press.

Sheldon, B., & Chilvers, R. (2000). *Evidence-based social care: A study of prospects and problems.* Lyme Regis: Russell House Publishing.

Sheldon, T. A., Guyatt, G. H., & Haines, A. (1998). Getting research findings into practice: When to act on the evidence. *BMJ, 317,* 139–142.

Shepard, M., & Campbell, J. (1992). The abusive behavior inventory: A measure of psychological and physical abuse. *Journal of Interpersonal Violence, 7*(3), 291–305.

Sherraden, M. & Sherraden, M. S. (2007). Credit markets for the poor. *Social Service Review, 81,* 191–193.

Sherraden, M. S., McBride, A. M., & Beverly, S. G. (2010). *Striving to save: Creating policies for financial security of low-income families.* Ann Arbor, MI: University of Michigan Press.

Shields, J. J. (1992). Evaluating community organization projects: The development of an empirically based measure. *Social Work Research and Abstracts, 28,* 15–20.

Shonkoff, J. P., & Garner, A. S. (2012). The lifelong effects of early childhood adversity and toxic stress. *Pediatrics, 129,* e232–e246.

Shorkey, C. T., & Taylor, J. E. (1973). Management of maladaptive behavior of a severely burned child. *Child Welfare, 52,* 543–547.

Shotton, A. (1990). State appellate courts move toward definitions of "reasonable efforts." *Youth Law News, 11*(3), 1–6.

Shuman, A. L., & Shapiro, J. P. (2002). The effects of preparing parents for child psychotherapy on accuracy of expectations and treatment attendance. *Community Mental Health Journal, 38*(1), 3–16.

Shulman, L. (1977). *A study of the helping process.* Vancouver, Canada: Social Work Department, University of British Columbia Press.

Shulman, L. (2006). *The skills of helping individuals, families, groups, and communities.* Itasca, IL: F. E. Peacock.

Shulman, L. (1991). *Interactional social work practice: Toward an empirical theory.* Itasca, IL: F. E. Peacock.

Shur, J. L. & Smith, P. V. (1980). *Where do you look? Whom do you ask? How do you know? Information Resources for Child Advocates.* Children's Defense Fund.

The Sicily Statement on Evidence-based Practice (2005). *BMC Medical Education, 5*(1).

Sidman, M. (1989). *Coercion and its fallout.* Boston: Authors Cooperative.

Sidman, M. (1994). *Equivalence relations and behavior: A research story.* Boston: Authors Cooperative.

Sievert, A. L., Cuvo, A. J., & Davis, P. K. (1988). Training self-advocacy skills to adults with mild handicaps. *Journal of Applied Behavior Analysis, 21,* 299–309.

Sikkema, K. J., Kelly, J. A., Winett, R. A., et al. (2000). Outcomes of a randomized community-level HIV prevention intervention for women living in 18 low-income housing developments. *American Journal of Public Health, 90,* 57–63.

Silver, A. (2011). A legal assault on animal-abuse whistle-blowers. *New York Times,* June 14.

Silverman, K. (1986). *Benjamin Franklin: The autobiography and other writings.* New York: Penguin.

Silverman, W. A. (1980). *Retrolental fibroplasia: A modern parable.* New York: Grune & Stratton.

Silversides, A. (2004). Schizophrenia linked to urban living. *Canadian Medical Association Journal, 170,* 456.

Simon, B. L. (1994). *The empowerment tradition in American social work: A history.* New York: Columbia University Press.

Simon, H. (1982). *Models of bounded rationality.* Cambridge, MA: MIT Press.

Simpson, E. L., & House, A. O. (2002). Involving users in the delivery and evaluation of mental health services: systematic review. *BMJ, 325,* 1265–1270.

Sinclair, W. J. (1909). *Semmelweis, his life and his doctrine: A chapter in the history of medicine.* Manchester, England: University Press.

Singer, B. D. (1978). Assessing social errors. *Journal of Social Policy, 9*(2), 27–34.

Singh, S. P., Harley, K., & Suhail, K. (2011). Cultural specificity of emotional overinvolvement: A systematic review. *Schizophrenia Bulletin.* Published online 12/20/11.

Slater, L. K. & Finck, K. R. (2012). *Social work practice and the law.* New York: Springer.

Skinner, B. F. (1953). *Science and human behavior.* New York: Macmillan.

Skinner, B. F. (1956). A debate with Carl Rogers. *Science, 124,* 1057–1066.

Skinner, B. F. (1969). *Contingencies of reinforcement: A theoretical analysis.* New York: Appleton-Century-Crofts.

Skinner, B. F. (1971). *Beyond freedom and dignity.* New York: Knopf.

Skinner, B. F. (1974). *About behaviorism.* New York: Knopf.

Skinner, B. F. (1981). Selection by consequences. *Science, 213,* 501–504.

Skinner, B. F. (1987). *Upon further reflection.* Englewood Cliffs, NJ: Prentice Hall.

Skrabanek, P., & McCormick, J. (1998). *Follies and fallacies in medicine* (3rd ed.). Whithorn, Scotland: Tarragon Press.

Slovic, P., Fischhoff, B., & Lichtenstein, S. (1982). Facts versus fears: Understanding perceived risk. In D. Kahneman, P. Slovic, & A. Tversky (Eds.), *Judgment under uncertainty: Heuristics and biases* (pp. 463–489). Cambridge, England: Cambridge University Press.

Smedley, B. D., Stith, A. Y., & Nelson, A. R. (Eds.). (2003). *Unequal treatment: Confronting racial and ethnic disparities in health care.* Washington, DC: Institute of Medicine; National Academies Press. http://www.nap.edu.

Smith, B. W., & Sugai, G. (2000). A self-management functional assessment-based behavior support plan for a middle school student with EDD. *J. of Positive Behavior Interventions, 2,* 208–217.

Smith, E. J. (1981). Cultural and historical perspectives in counseling blacks. In D. W. Sue (Ed.), *Counseling the culturally different: Theory and practice* (pp. 141–185). New York: John Wiley.

Smith, G. C. S. & Pell, J. P. (2003). Parachute use to prevent death and major trauma related to gravitational challenge: a systematic review of randomized controlled trials. *BMJ, 327,* 7429.

Smith, R. G. (2011). Developing antecedent interventions for problem behavior. In Fisher et al (Eds.), *Handbook of applied behavior analysis* (pp. 297–316). New York: Guilford.

Snyder, M., & Swann, W. B. (1978). Behavioral confirmation in social interaction: From social perception to social reality. *Journal of Experimental Social Psychology, 14,* 148–162.

Soares, H. P., Daniels, S., Kumar, A., Clarke, M., Scott, C., Swann, S., & Djulbegovic, B. (2004). Bad reporting does not mean bad methods for randomized trials: Observational study of randomized controlled trials performed by the Radiation Therapy Oncology Group. *BMJ, 328,* 22–24.

Sobell, M. B., & Sobell, L. C. (1993). *Problem drinkers: Guided self-change treatment.* New York: Guilford.

Social justice in the OECD: How do the member states compare? Governance indicators 2011. www.bertelsmann-stiftung

Solinger, R., et al. (2010). *Interrupted lives: experiences of incarcerated women in the United States.* Berkeley: University of California Press.

Sontag, D. (2011a). A schizophrenic, a slain worker, troubling questions. *New York Times,* June 16, A1/24.

Sontag, D. (2011b). Teenager's path and a killing put spotlight on mental care. *New York Times,* Aug. 3, P1/17.

Spade, J. Z. & Valentine, C. G. (2011). *The kaleidoscope of gender.* Los Angeles, CA: Pine Forge Press.

Specht, H. & Courtney, M. (1994). *Unfaithful angels: How social work has abandoned its mission.* New York: Free Press.

Springer, D. W. & Rubin, A. (2009). *Substance abuse treatment for youth and adults: Clinician's guide to evidence-based practice.* Hobokan, NJ: John Wiley & Sons.

Springer, K. W., Sheridan, J., Kuo, D., & Carnes, M. (2007). Long-term physical and mental health consequences of childhood physical abuse: Results of large population based sample of men and women. *Child Abuse & Neglect, 31,* 517–530.

Stacey, J., & Biblarz, T. J. (2001). (How) does the sexual orientation of parents matter? *American Sociological Review, 66,* 159–183.

Stagner, M. W., & Lansing, S. J. (2009). Progress toward a prevention perspective. *Preventing Child Maltreatment,* 19(2), Princeton-Brookings, The Future of Children.

Stanovich, K. E. (1992). *How to think straight about psychology* (3rd ed.). New York: Harper Collins. (See also 7th ed. [2004], Boston: Allyn & Bacon.)

Starcevic, V. (2002). Opportunistic rediscovery of mental disorders by the pharmaceutical industry. *Psychotherapy and Psychosomatics, 71,* 305–310.

Steege, M. W., & Watson, T. S. (2009). *Conducting school-based functional behavioral assessments: A practitioner's guide* (2nd ed.). New York: Guilford.

Steele, R. G., et al (Eds.) (2008). *Handbook of evidence-based therapies for children and adolescents.* New York: Springer.

Steele, R. G., Elkin, T. D., & Roberts, M. C. (Eds.) (2008). *Handbook of evidence-based therapies for children and adolescents: Bridging science and practice.* New York: Springer.

Stefanek, M. E., Ollendick, T. H., Baldock, W. P., Francis, G., & Yaeger, N. J. (1987). Self-statements in aggressive, withdrawn and popular children. *Cognitive Research and Therapy, 11,* 229–239.

Stein, T. J. (2004). *The role of law in social work practice and administration.* New York: Columbia University Press.

Stein, T. J., Gambrill, E. D., & Wiltse, K. T. (1978). *Children in foster homes: Achieving continuity of care.* New York: Praeger Special Studies.

Sternberg, R. J. (1986). *Intelligence applied: Understanding and increasing your intellectual skills.* San Diego: Harcourt Brace Jovanovich.

Sternberg, R. J. (1987). Teaching intelligence: The application of cognitive psychology to the improvement of intellectual skills. In J. D. Baron and R. J. Sternberg (Eds.), *Teaching thinking skills: Theory and practice* (pp. 182–218). New York: W. H. Freeman.

Sternberg, R. J., & Lubart, T. I. (1995). *Defying the crowd: Cultivating creativity in a culture of conformity.* New York: Free Press.

Sterne, J. A., Eger, M., & Smith, G. D. (2001). Investigating and dealing with publication and other biases. In M. Egger, G. D. Smith, & D. G. Altman (Eds.), *Systematic reviews in healthcare: Metaanalysis in context* (2nd ed.) (pp. 189–208). London: BMJ Books.

Stets, J. E. & Turner, J. H. (2006). *Handbook of the sociology of emotions.* New York: Springer.

Steurer, J., Fischer, J. E., Bachmann, L. M., Koller, M., & ter Riet, G. (2002). Communicating accuracy of tests to general practitioners: A controlled study. *BMJ, 324,* 824–826.

Stewart-Williams, S. & Podd, J. (2004). The placebo effect: Dissolving the expectancy versus conditioning debate. *Psychological Bulletin, 130,* 324–826.

Stivers, R. (2001). *Technology as magic: The triumph of the irrational.* New York: Continuum.

Stockdale, M. S., & Crosby, F. J. (Eds.). (2004). *The psychology and management of workplace diversity.* Malden, MA: Blackwell Publishing.

Stoesz, D. (1997). The end of social work. In M. Reisch & E. Gambrill (Eds.), *Social work in the 21st century.* Thousand Oaks, CA: Pine Forge Press.

Stoesz, D., Karger, H. J., & Carrilio, T. (2010). *A dream deferred: How social work education lost its way and what can be done.* New Brunswick, NJ: Transaction.

Stokes, T. F., & Baer, D. M. (1977). An implicit technology of generalization. *Journal of Applied Behavior Analysis, 10,* 349–367.

Stokes, T. F., Fowler, S. A., & Baer, D. M. (1978). Training preschool children to recruit natural communities of reinforcement. *Journal of Applied Behavior Analysis, 11,* 285–303.

Stokes, T. F. & Osnes, P. G. (1989). An operant pursuit of generalization. *Behavior Therapy, 20,* 337–355.

Stone, A. A., Turkkan, J. S., Bachrach, C. A., Jobe, J. B., Kurtzman, H. S., & Cain, V. S. (Eds.). (2000). *The science of self-report: Implications for research and practice.* Mahwah, NJ: Erlbaum.

Stone, G. C. (1979). Patient compliance and the role of the expert. *Journal of Social Issues, 35,* 34–59.

Straus, S. E., & McAlister, D. C. (2000). Evidence-based medicine: A commentary on common criticisms. *Canadian Medical Journal, 163*(7), 837–841.

Straus, S., Richardson, W. S., Glasziou, P, & Haynes, R. B. (2005). *Evidence-based medicine: How to practice and teach EBM* (3rd ed.). New York: Churchill Livingstone.

Strayhorn, J. M. (1977). *Talking it out: A guide to effective communication and problem solving.* Champaign, IL: Research Press.

Strayhorn, J. M. (1988). *The competent child: An approach to psychotherapy and preventive mental health.* New York: Guilford.

Strayhorn, M. J. (1994). Psychological competence-based therapy for young children and their parents. In C. W. LeCroy (Ed.), *Handbook of child and adolescent treatment manuals* (pp. 41–91). New York: Lexington Books.

Strean, H. S. (Ed.) (1994). *The use of humor in psychotherapy.* Northvale, NJ: Jason Aronson.

Ströhle, A. (2009). Physical activity, exercise, depression and anxiety disorders. *J. Neual. Transm, 116,* 777–784.

Strohman, R. C. (2003). Genetic determination as a failing paradigm in biology and medicine: Implications for health and wellness. *Journal of Social Work Education, 39,* 169–191.

Strom-Gottfried, K. (2003). Understanding adjudication: Origins, targets, and outcomes of ethics complaints. *Social Work, 48,* 85–95.

Stone, G. C. (1979). Patient compliance and the role of the expert. *Journal of Social Issues, 35,* 34–59.

Stroul, B., & Friedman, R. (1986). A system of care for children and youth with severe emotional disturbances. Washington, D.C.: Georgetown University Child Development Center. Na. Tech. Assis. Ctr for Children's Mental Health.

Strupp, H. (1976). The nature of the therapeutic influence and its basic ingredients. In A. Burton (Ed.), *What makes behavior change possible?* (pp. 96–112). New York: Brunner/Mazel.

Strupp, H. H., & Anderson, T. (1997). On the limitations of therapy manuals. *Clinical Psychology: Science and Practice, 4,* 76–82.

Strupp, H. H., & Hadley, S. W. (1979). Specific versus nonspecific factors in psychotherapy: A controlled study of outcome. *Archives of General Psychiatry, 36,* 1125–1136.

Strupp, H. H., & Hadley, S. W. (1985). Negative effects and their determinants. In D. T. Mays & C. M. Franks (Eds.), *Negative outcome in psychotherapy and what to do about it* (pp. 20–55). New York: Springer.

Stuart, R. B. (1980). *Helping couples change: A social learning approach to marital therapy.* New York: Guilford.

Stuart, R. B. & Davis, B. (1972). *Slim chance in a fat world: Behavioral control of obesity.* Champaign, IL: Research Press.

Sturmey, P. (2007). *Functional analysis in clinical treatment.* Boston, MA: Academic Press.

Sue, D. W., & Sue, D. (1990). *Counseling the culturally different: Theory and practice.* New York: Wiley-Interscience.

Sue, D. W., & Sue, D. (2003). *Counseling the culturally diverse: Theory and practice* (4th ed.). New York: John Wiley-Interscience.

Sue, D. W., & Sue, D. (2008). *Counseling the culturally diverse: Theory and practice* (5th ed.). New York: John Wiley-Interscience.

Suicide Risk and Prevention for Lesbian, Gay, Bisexual and Transgender Youth. Suicide Prevention Resource Center. (2009). Newton, MA: Education Development Center, Inc. Available from www.sprc.org

Suls, J. M., Davidson, K. W., & Kaplan, R. M. (2010). *Handbook of health psychology and behavioral medicine.* New York: Guilford.

Summerfield, D. (2001). The invention of post-traumatic stress disorder and the social usefulness of a psychiatric category. *BMJ, 322,* 95–98.

Summers, C. H. (1996). Pathological social science: Carol Gilligan and the incredible shrinking girl. In P. H. Gross, N. Levitt,& M. W. Lewis (Eds.), *The flight from science and reason* (pp. 369–381). New York: New York Academy of Sciences.

Sundel, M., & Sundel, S. S. (2005). *Behavior change in the human services: Behavioral and cognitive principles and applications* (5th ed.). Thousand Oaks, CA: Sage.

Sutton, S. E., & Kemp, S. P. (Eds.) (2011). *The paradox of urban space: Inequity and transformation in urban communities.* New York: Palgrave Macmillan.

Suzuki, L. A. & Ponterotto, J. G. & Miller, P. J. (2008). *Handbook of multicultural assessment: Clinical, psychological and educational applications* (3rd ed.). San Francisco, CA: Jossey-Bass.

Swartz, R. J., & Perkins, D. N. (1990). *Teaching thinking: Issues and approaches.* Pacific Grove, CA: Critical Thinking Press and Software, P.O. Box 448, 93950, 408–375–2455.

Sweet, M. (2011). Doctor who complained to regulator about weight loss product is sued for libel. *BMJ, 342:*d3728.

Swearer, S. M., Limber, S. P., & Alley, R. (2009). Developing and implementing an effective anti-bullying policy. In S. M. Swearer, D. L. Espelage, & S. A. Napolitano (Eds.), *Bullying: Prevention and intervention* (pp. 39–52). New York: Guilford.

Swift, G. (2004). How to make journal clubs interesting. *Ad in Psychia Treatment, 10,* 67–72.

Swift, J. K. & Callahan, J. L. (2009). The impact of client treatment preferences on outcome: A meta analysis. *J. of Clin Psych, 65,* 368–381.

Swift, J. K., & Callahan, J. L. (2010). A comparison of client preferences for intervention: empirical support versus common therapy variables *Journal of Clinical Psychology, 66,* 1217–1231.

Sykes, C. J. (1993). *A nation of victims: The decay of the American character.* New York: St. Martin's Press.

Symon, J. F. G., & Boettcher, M. A. (2008). Family support and participation. In Luiselli, et al., *Effective practices for children with autism* (pp. 455–490). New York: Oxford University Press.

Szasz, T. S. (1961). *The myth of mental illness.* New York: Hoeber-Harper.

Szasz, T. S. (1970). *The manufacture of madness: A comparative study of the inquisition and the mental health movement.* New York: Harper and Row.

Szasz, T. S. (1987). *Insanity: The idea and its consequences.* New York: John Wiley & Sons.

Szasz, T. S. (1994). *Cruel compassion: Psychiatric control of society's unwanted.* New York: John Wiley.

Szasz, T. S. (2001). *Pharmacracy: Medicine and politics in America.* Westport, CT: Praeger.

Szasz, T. S. (2002). *Liberation by oppression: a comparative study of slavery and psychiatry.* New Brunswick, NJ: Transaction Press.

Tallent, N. (1993). *Psychological report writing* (4th ed.). Englewood Cliffs, NJ: Prentice Hall.

Talmon, M. (1990). *Single-session therapy: Maximizing the effect of the first (and often only) therapeutic encounter.* San Francisco: Jossey-Bass.

Tanne, J. H. (2010). U.S. drug companies paid $15 bn in fines for criminal and civil violations over the last five years. *BMJ, 341* c7360.

Tanne, J. H, (2011). U.S. Health Department recovers $4 bn through antifraud action. *BMJ, 342:*d615.

Tapper, T., & Salter, B. (1978). *Education and the political order.* New York: Macmillan.

Task Force on Psychological Intervention Guidelines (1995). *Template for developing guidelines: Interventions for mental disorders and psychological aspects of physical disorders.* Washington, DC: American Psychological Association.

Tavare, A. (2012). Scientific misconduct is worryingly prevalent in the UK, shows *BMJ* survey. *BMJ, 334:e377.*

Tavernise, S. & Gebeloff, R. (2011). New way to tally poor recaste views of poverty. *New York Times,* November 7.

Tavris, C. (1992). *The mismeasure of women.* New York: Simon & Schuster.

Taylor, E. (2004). ADHD is best understood as a cultural construct. *British Journal of Psychiatry, 184,* 8–9.

Taylor, E., & Rutter, M. (2002). Classification. Conceptual issues and substantive findings. In M. Rutter & E. Taylor (Eds.), *Child and adolescent psychiatry* (4th ed.) (pp. 3–17). Malden, MA: Blackwell.

Taylor, J. L. & Novaco, R. W. (2005). *Anger treatment for people with developmental disabilities: A theory, evidence and manual based approach.* Hobokan, NJ: John Wiley & Sons.

Taylor, K., & Shaver, M. (2010). Performance-based contracting: Aligning incentives with outcomes to produce results. In M. F. Testa & J. Portner (Eds.), *Fostering accountability: Using evidence to guide and improve child welfare policy* (pp. 291–327). New York: Oxford University Press.

Taylor, S. E., & Brown, J. D. (1988). Illusion and well being: A social psychological perspective on mental health. *Psychological Bulletin, 103,* 193–210.

Tertinger, D. A., Greene, B. F., & Lutzker, J. R. (1984). Home safety: Development and validation of one component of an ecobehavioral treatment program for abused and neglected children. *Journal of Applied Behavior Analysis, 17,* 159–174.

Tesh, S. N. (1988). *Hidden arguments of political ideology and disease prevention policy.* New Brunswick, NJ: Rutgers University Press.

Tessaro, I. A., Taylor, S., Belton, L., Campbell, M. K., Benedict, S., Kelsey, K., & DeVellis, B. (2000). Adaption of natural (lay) helpers model of change for worksite health promotion. *Health Ed. Res, 15,* 603–614.

Tetlock, P. E. (2005). *Expert political judgement: How good is it? How can we know?* Princeton, NJ: Princeton University Press.

Tett, L. (2010). *Community education: learning and development.* Edinborough: Dunedin Academic Press.

Tharp, R. G., & Wetzel, R. J. (1969). *Behavior modification in the natural environment.* New York: Academic Press.

The Future of Children. (2011). *Immigrant children.* Princeton-Brookings.

Thomas, E. J., & Ager, R. D. (1993). Unilateral family therapy with spouses of uncooperative alcohol abusers. In T. O'Farrell (Ed.), *Treating alcohol problems: Marital and family interventions* (pp. 3–33). New York: Guilford.

Thomas, E. J., Walter, C. L., & O'Flaherty, K. (1974). A verbal problem checklist for use in assessing family verbal behavior. *Behavior Therapy, 35,* 235–246.

Thomas, E. J., Yoshioka, M., & Ager, R. D. (1996). Spouse enabling of alcohol abuse: Conception, assessment, and modification. *Journal of Substance Abuse, 8,* 61–80.

Thompson, J. B. (1987). Language and ideology. *Sociological Review, 35,* 517–536.

Thompson, N. (2011). *Crisis intervention.* Lyme Regis, Dorset: Russell House.

Thornley, B., & Adams, C. (1998). Content and quality of 2000 controlled trials in schizophrenia over 50 *years. BMJ, 317,* 1181–1184.

Thouless, R. H. (1974). *Straight and crooked thinking: Thirty-eight dishonest tricks of debate.* London: Pan Books.

Thyer, B. A. (2005). The misfortunes of behavioral social work: Misprized, misread, and misconstrued. In S. A. Kirk (Ed.), *Mental health in the social environment: Critical perspectives* (pp. 330–343). New York: Columbia University Press.

Thyer, B. A. & Pignotti, M. (2010). Science and pseudoscience in developmental disabilities: Guidelines for social workers. *Journal of Social Work in Disability & Rehabilitation, 9,* 110–129.

Thyer, B. A. & Pignotti, M. (in press). *Pseudoscience in social work.* New York: Oxford University Press.

Thyer, B. A., & Wodarski, J. S. (1990). Social learning theory: Toward a comprehensive conceptual framework for social work education. *Social Service Review, 64,* 144–152.

Thyer, B. A., Wodarski, J. S., Myers, L. L., & Harrison, D. F. (Eds.) (2010). *Cultural diversity and social work practice* (3rd ed.). Springfield, IL: Charles C. Thomas.

Tice, K. W. (1998). *Tales of wayward girls and immoral women: Case records and the professionalization of social work.* Urbana, IL: University of Illinois Press.

Tice, C. J. & Long, D. D. (Eds.) (2009). *International social work policy and practice: Practical insights and perspectives.* Hoboken, NJ: John Wiley & Sons.

Tichy, N. M., & Sherman, S. (1993). *Handbook for revolutionaries.* New York: Doubleday.

Tilbury, C., Osmond, J., & Crawford, M. (2010). Measuring client satisfaction with child welfare services. *Journal of Public Child Welfare, 4,* 77–90.

Timimi, S. (2002). *Pathological child psychiatry and medicalization of childhood.* London: Brunner-Routledge.

Timimi, S. (2008). Children's mental health and the global market: An ecological analysis. In C. I. Cohen & S. Tamimi (Eds.), *Liberatory psychology: Philosophy, politics, and mental health* (pp. 163–180). New York: Cambridge University Press.

Timimi, S. & Leo, J. (2009). *Rethinking ADHD: from brain to culture.* New York: Palgrave Macmillan.

Timimi, S., & Taylor, E. (2004). ADHD is best understood as a cultural construct. *British Journal of Psychiatry, 184,* 8–9.

Titov, N., Andrews, G., & Sachdev, P. (2010). Computer-delivered cognitive behavioral therapy: Effective and getting ready for dissemination. *Med Reports, 2,* 49 (doi: 10.3410/M2–49) July.

Todd, J. T., & Morris, E. K. (1983). Misconception and miseducation: Presentations of radical behaviorism in psychology textbooks. *Behavior Analyst, 96,* 153–160.

Tolan, P. H., Gorman-Smith, D., Henry, D., & Schoeny, M. (2009). The benefits of booster interventions: Evidence from a family-focused prevention program. *Prevention Science, 10,* 287–297.

Tompkins, M. A. (2004). *Using homework in psychotherapy: Strategies, guidelines and forms.* New York: Guilford.

Torgrimson, B. N., & Minson, C. T. (2005). Sex and gender: What's the difference? *J of Applied Physiology, 99,* 785–787.

Toseland, R. W., & Rivas, R. F. (2012). *An introduction to group work practice* (5th ed.). Boston, MA: Allyn & Bacon.

Tracy, E. M., & Whittaker, J. K. (1993). The social network map: Assessing social support in clinical practice. In J. B. Rauch (Ed.), *Assessment: A sourcebook for social work practice* (pp. 295–300). Milwaukee, WI: Families International, Inc.

Tracey, E. M., Haapala, D. A., Kinney, J., & Pecora, P. J. (Eds.). (1991) *Intensive Family Preservation Services: An instructional Sourcebook.* Cleveland Ohio: Mandel School of Applied Social Sciences. Case Western Reserve University.

Transparency International. www.transparency.org

Trattner, W. I. (1999). *From poor law to welfare state: A history of social welfare in America* (6th ed.). New York: Free Press.

Tropman, J. E. (2003). *Making meetings work: Achieving high quality group decisions* (2nd ed.). Thousand Oaks, CA: Sage.

Trower, P., Bryant, B., & Argyle, M. (1978). *Social skills and mental health*. London: Methuen.

Trower, P., Gilbert, P., & Sherling, G. (1990). Social anxiety, evolution, and self presentation. In H. Leitenberg (Ed.), *Handbook of social and evaluation anxiety* (pp. 11–45). New York: Plenum.

Truax, C. (1966). Reinforcement and nonreinforcement in Rogerian psychotherapy. *Journal of Abnormal Psychology, 71,* 1–9.

Truzzi, M. (1976). Sherlock Holmes: Applied social psychologist. In W. B. Sanders (Ed.), *The sociologist as detective: An introduction to research methods* (2nd ed.). New York: Praeger.

Tuchman, B. W. (1985). *The march of folly: From Troy to Vietnam.* New York: Ballantine.

Tuffs, A. (2004). Only 6% of drug advertising material is supported by evidence. *BMJ, 328,* 485.

Tufte, E. R. (2006). *Beautiful evidence.* Cheshire, CT: Graphics Press.

Tully, L. (2009). What makes parenting programs effective? An overview of recent research. *Research to Practice Notes.* Ashfield NSW: Centre for Parenting and Research NSW Department of Community Services. researchtopractice@community.nsw.gov.au

Tulving, E. & Craik, F. (Eds.) (2000). *The Oxford handbook of memory.* Oxford: Oxford University Press.

Tungpunkom, P., Maayan, N., & Soares-Weiser, K. (2012). Life skills programmes for chronic mental illnesses. *Cochrane Database of Systematic Reviews,* January 18,1:CD000381.

Turk, D. & Melzack, R. (2011). *Handbook of pain assessment.* New York: Guilford.

Turner, H. S., & Watson, T. S. (1999). Consultant's guide for the use of time-out in the preschool and elementary classroom. *Psychology in the Schools, 36*(2), 135–148.

Turner, J. S. (2002). *Families in America: A reference handbook.* Santa Barbara, CA: ABC/Clio.

Turner, E. H., Matthews, A. M., Linardatos, E., Tell, R. A., & Rosenthal, R. (2008). Selected publication of antidepressants trails and its influence on apparent efficacy. *N. Engl. J. Med, 358,* 252–260.

Tversky, A., & Kahneman, D. (1973). Availability: A heuristic for judging frequency and probability. *Cognitive Psychology, 5,* 207–232.

Tversky, A., & Kahneman, D. (1974). Judgment under uncertainty: Heuristics and biases. *Science, 185,* 1124–1131.

Tweed, R. G., & Lehman, D. R. (2002). Learning considered within a cultural context: Confucian and Socratic approaches. *American Psychologist, 57,* 89–99.

Tyrka, A. R., Price, L. H., Kao, H. T, Porton, B, Marsella, S. A., & Carpenter, L. L. (2010). Childhood maltreatment and telomere shortening: Preliminary support for an effect of early stress on cellular aging. *Biological Psychiatry, 67,* 531–535.

Tyron, W. W. (1996). Observing contingencies: Taxonomy and methods. *Clinical Psychology Review, 16,* 215–230.

Ueda, K. (1974). Sixteen ways to avoid saying "No" in Japan. In J. C. Condon & M. Saito (Eds.), *International encounters with Japan: Communication—contact and conflict* (pp. 184–192). Tokyo: Simul.

Unamuno, M. (1972). *The tragic sense of life in men and nations.* Princeton, NJ: Princeton University Press.

United Nations. (1948). *Universal Declaration of Human Rights* (1948). National General Assembly. Paris. Dec. 12.

Upmark, M., Hagberg, J. & Alexanderson, K. (2009). Negative encounters with social insurance officers—experiences of women and men on long-term sick leave. *International Journal of Social Welfare.* Published online: November 23, 2009.

Urbina, S. (2004). *Essentials of psychological testing.* Hobokan, NJ: John Wiley & Sons.

U'ren, R. (1997). Psychiatry and capitalism. *Journal of Mind and Behavior, 18,* 1–12. Downloaded Nov. 4, 2011.

U'ren, R. (2011). *Social perspective: the missing element in mental health practice.* Toronto CA: University of Toronto Press.

U.S. Department of Health and Human Services (1999). Mental Health: A Report of the surgeon general. Rockville, MD: U.S. Department of Health and Human Services Substance Abuse and Mental Health Service Administration, Center for Mental Health Services, National Institutes of Health, National Institute of Mental Health.

Valenstein, E. S. (1986). *Great and desperate cures: The rise and decline of psychosurgery and other radical treatments for mental illness.* New York: Perseus Books.

VanBiervliet, A., Spangler, P. F., & Marshall, A. M. (1981). An ecobehavioral examination of a simple strategy for increasing mealtime language in residential facilities. *Journal of Applied Behavior Analysis, 14,* 295–305.

Vance, L. (1992). *Treatment of a child with thalassemia.* Unpublished manuscript, School of Social Welfare, University of California at Berkeley.

van den Pol, R. A., Iwata, B. A., Ivancic, M. T., Page, T. J., Neef, N. A., & Whitley, F. P. (1981). Teaching the handicapped to eat in public places: Acquisition, generalization, and maintenance of restaurant skills. *Journal of Applied Behavior Analysis, 14,* 61–69.

Vangelisti, A. L. (2004). *Handbook of family communication.* Mahwah, NJ: Erlbaum.

VanHouten, R., Axelrod, S., Bailey, J. S., Favell, J. E., Foxx, R. M., Iwata, B. A., & Lovaas, O. I. (1988). The right to effective behavioral treatment. *Journal of Applied Behavior Analysis, 21,* 381–384.

Venberg, E. M. & Biggs, B. K. (Eds.) (2010). *Preventing and treating bullying and victimization.* New York: Oxford University Press.

Volpe, R. J., DiPerna, J. C., Hintze, J. M., & Shapiro, E. S. (2005). Observing Students in Classroom Settings: A Review of Seven Coding Schemes. *School Psychology Review, 34,* 454–474.

Vos, M. S., Putter, H., van Houwelingen, H. C., & de Haes, H. C. (2011). Denial and social and emotional outcomes in lung cancer patients: The protective effect of denial. *Lung Cancer, 72,* 119–124.

Vrij, A., Granhag, P. A., & Porter, S. (2010). Pitfalls and opportunities in nonverbal and verbal lie detection *Psychological Science in the Public Interest, 11,* 89–121.

Vul, E., Harris, C., Winkielman, P., & Pashler, H. (2009). Puzzling high correlations in fMRI studies of emotion, personality and social cognition. *Perspectives on Psychological Science, 4,* 274–290.

Wacquant, L. (2009). *Punishing the poor: The neoliberal government of social insecurity.* Durham, NC: Duke University Press.

Wahler, R. G. (1980). The insular mother: Her problems in parent child treatment. *Journal of Applied Behavior Analysis, 13,* 207–219.

Wahler, R. G., & Fox, J. J. (1981). Setting events in applied behavior analysis: To ward a conceptual and methodological expansion. *Journal of Applied Behavior Analysis, 14,* 327–338.

Waitzkin, H. (1991). *The politics of medical encounters: How patients and doctors deal with social problems.* New Haven: Yale University Press.

Wakefield, J. C. (1992). Why psychotherapeutic social work don't get no re-Specht. *Social Service Review, 66,* 141–151. (See also reply by Specht, pp. 152–159.)

Wakefield, J. C. (1998). Foucauldian fallacies: An essay review of Leslie Margolin's *Under the cover of kindness. Social Service Review, 72,* 545–587.

Walker, S. (2011). *Sense and nonsense about crime, drugs and communities* (7th ed.). Belmont, CA: Wadsworth.

Walton, D. (1997). *Appeal to expert opinion.* University Park, PA: Pennsylvania State University Press.

Walton (2008). *Informal logic: A pragmatic approach* (2nd ed.). New York: Cambridge University Press.

Wampold, B. E. (2001). *The great psychotherapy debate: Models, methods, and findings.* Mahwah, NJ: Erlbaum.

Wampold, B. E. (2006). Not a scintilla of evidence to support empirically supported treatments as more effective than other treatments. In J. C. Norcross, L. E. Beutler, & R. F. Levant (Eds.), *Evidence-based practices in mental health: Debate and dialogue on the fundamental questions* (pp. 299–308). Washington, D.C.: American Psychological Association.

Wampold, B. E. (2006). The psychotherapist. In J. C. Norcross, L. E. Beutler, & R. F. Levant (Eds.), *Evidence-based practices in mental health: Debate and dialogue on the fundamental issues* (pp. 200–208). Washington, D.C.: American Psychological Association.

Wampold, B. E. (2010). The research evidence for the common factors models: A historically situated perspective. In B. M. Duncan, S. D. Miller, M. A. Hubble, & B. E. Wampold (Eds.), *The heart and soul of therapy* (pp. 49–82). Washington, D. C.: Psychological Association.

Wandersman, A., Andrews, A., Riddle, D., & Fawcett, C. (1983). Environmental psychology and prevention. In R. Felner, L. Jason, J. M oritsugu, & S. Farber (Eds.), *Preventive psychology: Theory, research and practice* (pp. 104–127). Elmsford, NY: Pergamon.

Warren, R. B., & Warren, D. I. (1977). *The neighborhood organizer's handbook.* Notre Dame, IN: University of Notre Dame Press.

Wasserman, J., Flannery, M. A., & Clair, J. M. (2007). Rasing the ivory tower: the production of knowledge and distrust of medicine among African Americans. *J. of Med Ethics, 33,* 177–180.

Watson, T. S., & Steege, M. W. (2003). *Conducting school-based functional behavioral assessments: a practitioner's guide.* New York: Guilford.

Watson, D. L., & Tharp, R. G. (2007). *Self-directed behavior: Self-modification for personal adjustment: a practitioner's guide* (9th ed.). Monterey, CA: Thomson/Wadsworth.

Watzlawick, P., Beavin, J. H., & Jackson, D. D. (1967). *Pragmatics of human communication—A study of interactional patterns, pathologies, and paradoxes.* New York: W. W. Norton & Co., Inc.

Watzlawick, P., Weakland, J. H., & Fisch, R. (1974). *Change: Principles of problem formation and problem resolution.* New York: W. W. Norton & Co., Inc.

Webel, A. R., Okonsky, J., Trumpeta, J., & Hazemer, W. L. (2010). A systematic review of the effectiveness of peer-based intervention in health-related behaviors in adults. *Am. J. Public Health, 100,* 247–253.

Webster, Y. O. (1992). *The racialization of America.* New York: St. Martin's Press.

Webster, Y. O. (1997). *Against the multicultural agenda: A critical thinking alternative.* Westport, CT: Praeger.

Webster-Stratton, C. (2009). Affirming diversity: Multi-cultural collaboration to deliver the Incredible Years Parent Program. *Inter J. of Child Health and Human Development, 2,* 17–32.

Webster-Stratton, C., & Reid, M. J. (2010). Incredible years parents, teachers, and children training series: A multifaceted treatment approach for young children with conduct disorder. In J. R. Weisz & A. E. Kazdin (Eds.), *Evidence-based psychotherapies for children and adolescents* (pp. 194–210). New York: Guilford.

Webster's New World Collegiate Dictionary. (1988). Third College Ed. New York: Webster's New World.

Webster's New World Dictionary. (1988). Third College Edition. New York: Webster's New World.

Wegwarth, O. & Gigerenzer, G. (2011). Statistical illiteracy in doctors. In G. Gigerenzer & J. A. M. Gray (Eds.) (2011*). Better doctors, better patients, better decisions* (pp. 137–151). Cambridge, MA: MIT Press.

Weick, K. E. (1984). Small wins: Redefining the scale of social problems. *American Psychologist, 39,* 40–49.

Weinbach, R. W., & Taylor, L. M. (2011). *The social worker as manager: A practical guide to success.* Upper Saddle River, NJ: Harlow: Pearson Ed.

Weiner, S. J., LaPorte, M., Abrams, R. I., Moswin, A., & Warnecke, R. (2004). Rationing access to care to the medically uninsured: The role of bureaucratic front-line discretion at large healthcare institutions. *Medical Care, 42,* 306–312.

Weisburd, D., Lum., C. M., & Yang, S. M. (2003). When can we conclude that treatments or programs "Don't Work"? *Annals of the American Academy of Political and Social Science, 587,* 31–48.

Weiser, B. (2011). In New Jersey, rules are changed on witness IDs. *New York Times,* August 24.

Weisskopf, T. E. (2011). Reflection on globalization, discrimination and affirmative action. Eleventh M. N. Srinivas Memorial Lecture. May 15.

Weissman, H. H., Epstein, I. E., & Savage, A. (1983). *Agency-based social work: Neglected aspects of clinical practice* (pp. 74–75). Philadelphia, PA: Temple University Press.

Weisz, J. (2010). *Evidence-based psychotherapies for children and adolescents* (2nd ed.). New York: Guilford.

Weisz, J., Suwanlert, S., Chaiyasit, W., & Walter, B. R. (1987). Over and under controlled referral problems among children and adolescents from Thailand and the United States: The *Wat* and *Wai* of cultural differences. *Journal of Consulting and Clinical Psychology, 55,* 719–726.

Weisz, J. R., Jensen-Doss, A., & Hawley, K. M. (2006). Evidence-based youth psychotherapies versus usual clinical care. *American Psychologist, 61,* 671–689.

Welch, G. (2004). *Should I be tested for cancer? May be not and here's why.* Berkeley: University of California Press.

Welsh, W. N. (2000). The effects of school climate on school disorder. *Annals of the American Academy of Political and Social Science, 567,* 88–108.

Welch, H. G., Schwartz, L. M., & Woloshin, S. (2011). *Overdiagnosed: making people sick in the pursuit of health.* Boston: Beacon Press.

Wennberg, J. E. (2002). Unwarranted variations in healthcare delivery: Implications for academic medical centres. *BMJ, 325,* 961–964.

Wensing, M., & Elwyn, G. (2003). Methods for incorporating patients' views in health care. *BMJ, 326,* 877–879.

Westermeyer, J. (1987). Cultural factors in clinical assessment. *Journal of Consulting and Clinical Psychology, 55,* 471–478.

Weston, A. (1992). *A rule book for arguments* (2nd ed.). Indianapolis: Hackett Publishing Co.

Wetchler, J. L. (2011). *Handbook of clinical issues in couple therapy.* New York: Routledge.

Whitaker, R. (2010). *Anatomy of an epidemic: magic bullets, psychiatric drugs and the astonishing rise of mental illness in America.* New York: Crown.

White, A. D. ([c.1896] 1993). *A history of the warfare of science with theology in Christendom.* Vols. I and II. New York: Prometheus.

White, J. (2000). *Treating anxiety and stress: A group psychoeducational approach using brief CBT.* Hobokan, NJ: John Wiley & Sons.

White, R. K. (1971). Propaganda: Morally questionable and morally unquestionable techniques. In R. D. Lambert (Ed.), & A. W. Heston (Assistant Ed.). *The ANNALS of the American Academy of Political and Social Science.* Philadelphia, PA: American Academy of Political and Social Science.

Wilbern, Y. (1984). Types and levels of public morality. *Public Administration Review, 44,* 102–108.

Wilkes, M. S., & Hoffman, J. R. (2001). An innovative approach to educating medical students about pharmaceutical promotion. *Academic Medicine, 76,* 1271–1277.

Wilkinson, I. (2005). *Suffering: A sociological introduction.* Malden, MA: Polity.

Wilkinson, R. G., & Pickett, K. (2009). *The spirit level: Why greater equality makes society stronger.* New York: Bloomsbury Press.

Williams, B. F. & Williams, R. L. (2010). *Effective programs for treating autism spectrum disorder: Applied behavioral analysis models.* London: Routledge.

Willner, A. G., Braukmann, C. J., Kirigin, K. A.,Fixen, D. L., Phillips, E. L., & Wolf, M. M. (1977). The training and validation of youth-preferred social behaviors of childcare personnel. *Journal of Applied Behavior Analysis, 10,* 219–230.

Wills, T. A. (1978). Perceptions of clients by professional helpers. *Psychological Bulletin, 85,* 968–1000.

Wills, T. A. (1982). Nonspecific factors in helping relationships. In T. A. Wills (Ed.), *Basic processes in helping relationships* (pp. 381–404). New York: Academic Press.

Wilson, J. A. (2001). Pseudoscientific beliefs among college students. *Reports of the National Center for Science Education, 21,* 9–36.

Wilson, J. S. & Lipsey, M. W. (2005). *The effectiveness of school-based violence prevention programs for reducing disruptive and aggressive behavior.* Revised report for the National Institute of Justice School Violence Prevention Research Planning Meeting. May.

Witkiewitz, K., & Marlott, G. A. (Eds.) (2007). *Therapist's guide to evidence-based relapse prevention.* New York: Elsevier.

Witte, C. L., Witte, M. H., & Kerwin, A. (1994). Suspended judgment: Ignorance and the process of learning and discovery in medicine. *Controlled clinical trials, 15,* 1–4.

Witteman, C. (2003). Psychotherapy treatment decisions. Supported by SelectCare. In F. J. Maarse, A. E. Akkerman, A. N. Brand, & L. J. M. Mulder (Eds.), *Clinical assessment, computerized methods, and instrumentation* (pp. 144–154). Exton, PA: Swets & Zeitlinger.

Wolfe, D. A., & Mash, E. J. (Eds.) (2008). *Behavioral and emotional disorders in adolescents: nature, assessment and treatment.* New York: Guilford.

Wolf, J. H. (1985). Professionalizing volunteer work in a black neighborhood. *Social Service Review, 59,* 423–434.

Wolf, M. M. (1978). Social validity: The case for subjective measurement or how applied behavior analysis is finding its heart. *Journal of Applied Behavior Analysis, 11,* 203–214.

Woloshin, S., Schwartz, L. M., & Welch, H. G. (2008). *Knowing your chances: Understanding health statistics.* Berkeley: University of California Press.

Wolpe, J. (1986). Individualization: The categorical imperative of behavior therapy practice. *Journal of Behavior Therapy and Experimental Psychiatry, 17,* 145–154.

Wolpe, J. (Ed.) (1990). *The practice of behavior therapy.* Elmsford, NY: Pergamon.

Woltmann, E. M., Wilkniss, S. M., Teachout, A., McHugo, G. J., & Drake, R. E. (2011). Trial of an electronic decision support system to facilitate shared decision making in community mental health. *Psychiatric Services, 62,* 54–60.

Woods, D. D., & Cook, R. I. (1999). Perspectives on human error: Hindsight biases and local rationality. In F. T. Durso, R. S. Nickerson, R. W. Schvaneveldt, S. T. Dumais, D. S. Lindsay, & M. T. Chi. (Eds.), *Handbook of applied cognition* (pp. 141–171). New York: John Wiley.

Woodward, K. L. (2004). A political sacrament. *New York Times,* May 28, Sect. A, Column 2, p. 21.

Worthman, C. M., Plotsky, P. M., Schechter, D. S., & Cummings, C. A. (Eds.) (2010). *Formative experiences: The interaction of caregiving, culture and developmental psychobiology.* New York: Cambridge University Press.

Wright, R. H., Mindel, C. H., Van Tran, T., & Habenstein, R. W. (2012). *Ethnic families in America: Patterns and variations.* Boston: Pearson.

Wronka, J. (2012). Overview of human rights: The UN conventions and machinery. In L. M. Healy & R. J. Link (Eds.), *Handbook of international social work: Human rights, development, and the global profession* (pp. 439–446). New York: Oxford University Press.

Wyatt, W. J. (1990). Radical behaviorism misrepresented: A response to Mahoney. *American Psychologist, 45,* 1181–1184.

Yeh, M., & Weisz, J. R. (2001). Why are we here at the clinic? Parent–child (dis)agreement on referral problems at outpatient treatment entry. *Journal of Consulting and Clinical Psychology, 69,* 1018–1025.

Yeung, A., Feldman, G, & Fava, M. (2009). *Self-management of depression: A manual for mental health and primary care professionals.* Cambridge: Cambridge University Press.

Young, D. S. (2008). Social work practice in the justice system. In D. M. DiNitto & C. A. McNeece (Eds.), *Social work: Issues and opportunities in a challenging profession* (3rd ed.) (pp. 311–332). Chicago, IL: Lyceum Books.

Young, J. E., Klosko, J. S., & Weishaar, M. E. (2003). *Schema therapy: A practitioner's guide.* New York: Guilford.

Young, J. H. (1992). *American health quackery.* Princeton: Princeton University Press.

Young, K. R., & West, R. P., Howard, V. F., & Whitney, R. (1986). Acquisition, fluency training, generalization, and maintenance of dressing skills of two developmentally disabled children. *Education and Treatment of Children, 9,* 16–29.

Zander, A. (1990). *Effective social action by community groups.* San Francisco, CA: Jossey-Bass.

Zarocostas, J. (2007). Community care could prevent deaths of thousands of severely malnourished children. *BMJ, 334,* 1239 (16 June).

Zegiob, L., Arnold, S., & Forehand, R. (1975). An examination of observer effects in parent–child interactions. *Child Development, 46,* 509–512.

Zhang, W., Gu, D., & Hayward, M. (2010). Childhood nutritional deprivation and cognitive impairment among older Chinese people. *Social Science & Medicine, 71,* 941–949.

Zola, I. K. (1972). Medicine as an institution of social control. *Sociological Review, 20,* 487–504. Reprinted in P. Conrad (Ed.), (2009), *The sociology of health and illness: Critical perspectives* (8th ed.) (pp. 470–480). New York: Worth Publishing.

Zsambok, C. E., & Klein, G. (Eds.). (1997). *Naturalistic decision making.* Mahwah, NJ: Erlbaum.

Zucchi, J. (1992). *The little slaves of the harp: Italian child street musicians in nineteenth century Paris, London and New York.* London: McGill-Queen's University Press.

Zwarenstein, M., Goldman, J., & Reeves, S. (2009). Interpersonal collaboration: Effects of practice-based interventions on professional practice and health care outcomes. *Cochrane Database of Systematic Reviews,* Issue 3.

Index

Italicized page numbers refer to exhibits.

A-B designs, 501–2
absolute risk, 456
  compared to relative risk, 241
abstraction, 139
  different levels of, 139
abuse
  and challenging social situations, 370
  and child, 54, 110, 311–12, *327*, 394,
    428, *455*
  and elder, 50, 72, 120, *137*
  and emotional, on job, 362–63, 376–77
  and false allegations, 178
  and homophobia, 133
  and maltreatment, 310–11
  and questions, 241, 252, 389
  and sexual, 390–91, 428
  and substance, 174–77, *207*, *319*, 434, 437
Abusive Behavior Inventory, *396*
Academy of Certified Social Workers
  (ACSW), 12
acceptability (of plans), 476, 478, 590, 593
accessibility, 590
accountability, 51, *510*, 514
acculturation, 31, 39, 276
accuracy, 239–41
  and observer, 420
  and self-monitoring, 405
  and test, 455–56
action, *325*
activism, 620–21
adaptation, 124–25, 136
addiction, 104
ADHD (attention deficit hyperactive
  disorder)
  and controversy, 123
  and developmental model, *130*
  and diagnosis, 101, 104, 256, *257*, 260,
    485, 546
  and explanation, 127
ad hominem appeals, *75*, 76
adjunctive behaviors, 155
administrative tasks, 589–90

Adoptees' Liberty Movement
  Association, 580
advanced accurate empathy, 344
advanced economy, 4
advice giving, 346
advocacy, 472–73, 583–84, 612
  and activism, 620–21
  and decisions and options, 470
  and enhancing strengths of clients,
    17–18, 28, 34, 531, 533–34
  and ethical and legal issues regarding,
    55, 58, 63, 192
  and information organization/
    interpretation, 426, 440
  and knowledge, 76
  and organizations and communities,
    600, 602, 605, 609
  and posing questions, 208, 211
  and problem definition, 122, 124
  and problem solving, 135, 168, 170
  and service plans, 478–79
advocate, 469, 472–73
African Americans, 32, 132, 133, *253*, 254,
  309, 356, 358, 427, 430, 448, 581
age, 375, 376
agencies. *See also* clients
  and accountability checklist, *510*
  and characteristics, 422
  and client participation, *320*
  and comparative model of family
    support agency, *481*
  and contextual assessment, 251,
    252–53, 272
  and decision making, 180
  and ethical behavior, 47–49, 52–56,
    62–64
  and evaluating outcomes, 293–94
  and evidence-based practice, 100, 197
  and framework for human service, 585
  and helping clients, *472*
  and knowledge, 75, 84, 89, 100
  and organizational culture, *592*

agencies (*cont.*)
   and posing questions, 208, 211
   and problem-solving, 118, 122
   and procedural guidelines, 296, 297
   and resources and obstacles
      review of, 243
   and route to, 22–25
   and service and surveillance systems,
      427–29
   and services and criteria, *30*
   and social policy, 28, *29*
   and social service, *531*
   and social welfare, 118
   and technologies and criteria, 28–30
   and U.S. federal, 218
agenda, 303, 335
aggression, 104, 148, 149–50
aggressive behavior, 364, *365*
AIDS, 7, 229, *531*, 546
air pollution, 274
Alcohol, Tobacco and Other Drugs
      (NASW), 143
Alcoholics Anonymous, 581
allegiance effects, 225, 343
alliance, positive, 343
   rupture, 343
Alliance for Human Research Protection,
      47, 55, 84
alternative accounts, 453
Alzheimer's disease, 49, 454–55, 480, 534
American Child Liberties Union, 55
American Civil Liberty Union
      Associations, 609
American Medical Association
      (AMA), 85
American Psychiatric Association, 120,
      122, 178, 209
American Psychological Association,
      212, 242, 390
Amnesty International, 55, 610
analytic thinking, 78, 108
analytical studies, 222
anatomically correct dolls, 390–91
anchoring, 175
anecdotal observations, *411*
anger, *380*, 448–49
anger management, 196, *366*, *544*, 546
Anglo-Americans, 356
antecedent event, 267
antecedents, behavioral, 150–52
   and contextual assessment, 267–68
   and establishing operations, 152
   and models, 152
   and necessary and facilitating, 152
   and observation, 418
   and occasions for behavior, 151–52
   and respondent and operant behavior
      interaction, 154–57
   and rearranging, 563–64
anticipatory empathy, 334–35
antiscience, 83, 92, 143

antisocial behavior, developmental
      model, *130*
antisocial personality disorder, 127
anxiety, *380*
   and behavioral principles, 153–57
   and challenging social situations,
      285, 297
   and contextual assessment, 253, 256,
      258–60, 267
   and critical thinking, 96, 100, 111
   and posing questions, 208, 212
   and problem definition, 123
   and problem solving, 117–20,
      122, 179
   and propaganda, 84–85, 180
applicability, 139
applicants, 24–25
applied behavioral analysis, 131
approximations, 493
arbitrary, 145
argumentation ad populum, 185
arguments, 101–2
argumentum ad hominem, 185
arousal induction, *561*
arousal reduction, *562*
artificial cues, 523–24
Asian American, 31
Asian culture, 356
Asian immigrants, 309
assertion training, *502*, *503*
assertive behavior, 364, *365*, *380*
assessment, 421. *See also* contextual
      assessment
   and case examples, *445–47*
   and common errors, 255
   and communities, *603*, 604
   and compared to diagnosis, 451–52
   and content knowledge, 249
   and critical appraisal of, 250
   and data, 387–92
   and decisions, 250
   and families, 567–71
   and frameworks, 386
   and ideals and actualities, 458–59
   and incomplete, *253*, 255, *443*
   and intervention and, 465–67
   and making of value to clients, 266
   and questionable methods, 390–91
   and questions, 281
   and relation to intervention, 465
   and reliability and validity, 391–92
   and role playing, *413*
   and social skills training, 538–39, *540*
   and social validity and invalidity,
      492–93
assessment questions, *203*, 204, 252
assignments, 473, *474*
   self monitoring, 401
assimilation, 39
Association for Behavior Analysis, *60*
associative thinking, 175

attention, 272, *273*, 328, 359, 451, 453,
      483, 619
attention-deficit disorder, 451
attentive listening, 346
attitudes, critical thinking, 96–97
attributional biases, *435*
attributional style questionnaire, *396*
attributions, 434–35, 496, 524
attrition, 228
attrition bias, 225
audit, 590, 597
authority
   appeal to, 56, 185
   and critical thinking, 45, 95, 97, 105
   and ethics, 47
   and evidence-based practice, 188–89
   and handling of, 335
   and knowledge, 70, 74–75, 86
   and posing questions, 205, 211
   and problem solving, 121, 126
authority-based practice, 86, 188–89, 193
autism, 181
autocratic model, 612
Automatic Thoughts Questionnaire,
      391, *396*, 435
availability (heuristic), 174
available alternative behaviors, *265*
avoidance behavior, 148, 161
aware, 182

backward chaining, 537
backward conditioning, 156
Bandolier, 216
Barnum effect, 579
baseline, 301, *305*
baselines, *500*, 501
baserate, 453
base rate probability, 398
Beck Depression Inventory, 70, 250, 499
begging the question, 103, 104
behavior, 268, 418. *See also* positive
      behavior change skills
   and baseline data, 301
   and bulimia, *269*
   and client participation, 324
   and compatibility, 448
   and consequences, 267
   and contingencies, 144–47, 300
   and cost-benefit analyses, *265*
   and encouraging ethical, 62–64
   and encouraging helpful views and,
      351–53
   and escape-motivated, *417*
   and evolutionary influences, 157–60
   and focus on relevant, 521–22
   and form and function, 268–70
   and increasing and decreasing, 552, 556
   and ineffective social, *379*
   and influencing real-life, 474
   and monitoring others, *400*
   and motivation vs., 270

and occurrence of problem-related, 402–4
and positive, *481*
and positive alternative, 300
and requesting changes, 372–75
behavioral analysis, 265
and interventions, 158–60
and nonlinear, 265
and systemic, 265
and topical, 265
behavior changes, requesting, 372
behavioral explanations, 129, 131–32
behavioral principles, 141–42
and behavioral explanations, 129, 131–33
and contingencies, 144–47
and controversies, 123–25
and emotion, 154
and evolutionary influences, 157–60
and genetic explanations, 126–27
and knowledge on contingencies, 142–44
and motivation, 153–54
and radical behaviorism, 131–32
and reinforcement, 147–50
and respondent behavior, 156–57
and role of antecedents, 150–52
and social learning theory, 132
and variables influencing operant learning, 154–56
and verbal influences, 152–53
behavioral rehearsal, 540–41
behavioral treatment, *60*
behavior chain, 537
belief encroachment, *620*
beliefs, 434–35, 437, 512, *568*, 570
and clients', 25–27
and critical appraisal of research, 242
and critical thinking, 95–111
and ethics, 56–59, 64
and evidence-based practice, 86, 95–111
and helpers', 27–28
and knowledge, 70, 72, 73, 76, 77
and philosophy of practice, 14–15
and posing questions, 224
and problem solving, 126, 135
and relativism, 83–84
benchmarks, 590
beneficence, 43–44
benefits, communicating information, 456–57
best evidence, 212
best practice, 212
Beyond Freedom and Dignity (Skinner), 555
biases, 35, 39, 111, 173–75, 178, *435*
and abstracting, 225
and attribution, 434–35, 496, 524
and attrition, 225
and confounders, 225
and framing, 225
and hindsight, 495, 514
and retrievability, 235
and sample, 453

and selection, 229, 231–32, 235, 457
and submission, 225
and validity, 225–26
bibliotherapy, 533
Big Brothers, 431, *580*
Big Pharma, 270, 534
Big Sisters, 431, *580*
biological psychiatry, 127, 254
biomedical explanations, 127–28
biomedical factors, 274–75
biomedical industrial complex, 58–59, 270, 426
biomedicalization, 122
biomedicalization of deviance, *121*, 122–23
biopsychosocial approach, 264, 266
bipolar, 331
blame, 302
blinding, 230
bogus claims
and critical appraisal of research, 228
and critical thinking, 103, 106
and ethical obligations, 194
and knowledge, 72, 80, 83, 84, 111
Boolean searching, 206, *207*
boredom, *620*
boundary spanners, 612
Bowling Alone (Putnam), 430
brain disease, *128*
bribery, 433
Brief Anger Measure, *396*
British Medical Journal, 169
brochures, informational, 531–33
broker, 469, 471
Buddhism, 31, 108, 309
buddy-buddy syndrome, 103, 578
bulimia, *269*
bullying, 106, 228, *273*, 293, 376, 421, 479, 546
bureaucracy, 612
bureaucratic ideology, 57
Bureaucratic Propaganda (Altheide and Johnson), 493, 590
burnout, 621–22

Cambridge-Somerville Youth Study, 231
Campbell Collaboration, 208, 216, 513
capitalistic ideology, 57–58
capitalist society, 133–34
Caribbean Blacks, 430
case conferences, 579–80
case control studies, 232–33
case examples, 69–77
case formulation, 248
case management, 29
case records, 406, 460–61
ethical issues, 51
case series studies, 233
causality, *447*
causal model, *447*
causal variables, 448
causes, 236

and clues to, 447
and compatibility with resources, 448
and confusing form and function, 449
and confusion with correlation, 449
and confusion with effects, 448
and discrimination and oppression, 125
and explanations, 448
and guidelines for discovery, 449
and interrelated, 447–48
and necessary and sufficient, 447
and organizing and interpreting information, 444, 447–54
and presumed, *466*
and questions about, 237
and sources of error, 450
and thinking about, 444
censorship
and critical thinking, 136
and evidence-based practice, 179, 193, 197, 221
and intervention, 579
and knowledge, 84, 100, 103
Center for Media Education (CME), 85
Center for Science in the Public Interest, 534
Centre for Evidence-Based Child Health, 208
Centre for Evidence-Based Mental Health, 208, 216
Centre for Evidence-Based Nursing, 208
chaining and shaping, 537
chains of behavior, 146
challenging social situations, 362–82
and assertive, passive, and aggressive behavior, 364, *365*
and creating and responding to, 363–64
and feedback, 370–72
and handling abuse on job, 376–77
and interpersonal problem solving, 364–67
and listening more, 377–78
and obstacles, 378–79
and raising questions and disagreeing, 367–70, *366*
and refusing requests, 372
and requesting behavior changes, 372–75
and responding to criticism, 370–72
and responding to put-downs, 375–76
and safety, 379–81
and speaking more, 377, *378*
chance, 448
overlooking role of, 495
charisma, 612
charitable, 89
Charity Organization Societies (COSs), 8, 10
checklists and rating scales, 396
child abuse, 311–12, 394, 428
child antisocial behavior, *130*
childhood depression, *468*

children
    and abuse, 54, 311–12, *327*, 394, 428, *455*
    and interviewing, 394–95
    and suggestibility, *393*
Chinese Americans, 356
choices and consequences, 543
Citizen's Commission on Human Rights
        International, 47, 209
Civil Rights Act, 376
claims
    and critical appraisal of research,
        225, 228
    and critical thinking, 94–95, 98, 101–2
    and evidence-based practice, 45–47, 180,
        181, 183, 192–93, 196–97
    and knowledge, 59, 69, 72–73, 74
    malpractice, 54–55
    and philosophy of practice, 14
    and posing questions, 204, 206, 209
    and problem definition, 123
    and problem solving, 166, 168, 175, 179
clan, *432*
clarity, 354, 357, 371
class, 309
classifications, 256–61
class theories, problems, 132–33
client manuals, 533
client participation, 317–37
    and anticipating hesitations, 323–24
    and checklist, *322*
    and credibility, 330–31
    and critical thinking, 318, *319*
    and ethics, 336
    and factors influencing, 318–21
    and formal feedback, 331–32
    and helpfulness, *320*, 323, 331
    and labels and labeling, 319, 331, *332*
    and labels and blame, 331, *332*
    and organizational policies, 332
    and outcome focus, 323
    and positive expectations, 329–30
    and preparing for interviews, 333–36
    and process of change and
        intervention, *326*
    and relationship skills, 326–29
    and reminders and incentives, 332–33
    and social psychological
        persuasion, 336
    and stages of change and intervention,
        324, *325*
    and steps encouraging, 321–23
    and tailoring differences, 324–25
clients, 24–25, 439. *See also* helper-client
        exchanges
    and advocacy, 583–84
    and beliefs, expectations, and goals,
        25–27
    and biomedical factors, 274–75
    and characteristics and circumstances,
        187
    and collaborative relationship, 295–97

    and concerns and outcomes, 285,
        288–89, 293
    and contextual assessment, 250, *251*,
        253–56
    and cultural diversity, 30–33
    and decision making, 211, 212
    and describing problems and contexts,
        297, 299–301
    and difficult social situations, 363–64
    and emotions and feelings, 275–76
    and empowering, 460
    and enhancing client strengths, 479
    and errors, *450*
    and evidence-based practice, 192
    and expectations, *26*
    and honesty, 296–97
    and hoped-for-outcomes, 262
    and illegal behavior of professionals,
        55–56
    and interviews and exchanges, 284–85
    and involvement, 589
    and learning from, 598
    and legislation, 609
    and making assessment of value, 261
    and mandated, 297
    and mentally ill, 49
    and offering support, 474–75
    and participation, 336–37
    and planning for endings, 516–25
    and plan selection, 475–82
    and positive behavior change skills,
        548–65
    and preferences and actions, 187
    and priorities, 294–95
    and problems and causes, 301–2
    and referrals, 293–94
    and refusing requests, 372
    and repertoires, 263–64
    and research findings, 210–11
    and reviewing assessment measures, *398*
    rights to effective behavior treatment, *60*
    and self-monitoring, 400–405
    and self-report, 392–95
    and service agencies, *472*
    and strengths, 300
    and support, 301
    and talking to, 473
    and thoughts, 275
    and trust and rapport, 295–96
    and understanding, and
        circumstances, *273*
    and untested method, 212
    and values of, 187
    and working with mandated, 307
clients, empowering, 529–46
    and changing cognitive ecology, 542–43
    and developing new skills, 535
    and as informed participants, 485
    and managing emotions, 544–46
    and mixed and multisystem programs,
        545–46

    and model presentation, 537–38
    and problem-solving training, 543–44
    and providing information, 529–35
    and self-management skills, 542
    and shaping, 535–37
    and social skills training, 538–42
client strengths, enhancing
    and changing cognitive ecology, 542–43
    and developing new behaviors, 535–37,
        540–41
    and managing emotions, 544–46
    and mixed and multisystem
        programs, 546
    and model presentation, 537–38
    and problem solving, 543–44
    and providing information, 529–35
    and self-management skills, 542
    and shaping, 535–57
    and social skills training, 538–42
client uniformity myth, 475
climate, organization, 586, 588
Clinical Evidence, 216
clinical expertise, 187
clique, 612
coaching, 541
coalition, 612
Coalition Against Institutionalized Child
        Abuse, 55
Coalition Against Insurance Fraud, 534
Cochrane and Campbell Databases, 89,
        188–89, 207–8, 210
Cochrane Collaboration, 190, 192,
        207–8, 234
Cochrane Consumer Network, 209
Cochrane Schizophrenia Group, 222
Code of Ethics
    and administration, 590
    and allocating resources, 484–85
    and knowledge, 83, 108
    and NASW, 8, 9, 15, 16, 19, 42–43, 48–53,
        55, 65, 191
    and sexual harassment, 376
    and social justice, 44, 58
coercion, avoidance of, 47–48
coercive power, 612
    being honest about, 223
cognition, 275
cognitive-behavioral methods, 543
cognitive biases
    and behavioral principles, 154
    and critical thinking, 99, 105, 107
    and posing questions, 213
    and problem solving, 165, 179, 183
cognitive distortions, *436*
cognitive ecology, 275, 542–39
cognitive explanations, 129, 131–33
cognitive restructuring, 542–43
cohesiveness, 612
cohort differences, 147
cohort effects, 136
cohort studies, 232

coincidences, underestimating, 448
collaborative process, 261, 295–97
collegial model, 612
common factors, 344
communication, 104, 377, *561–62*
  and families, 569
  and information about risks and
    benefits, 456–57
  and problems, *414*
  and providing information to clients,
    529–35
  and relationship skills, 326–29
  and role playing, *412*
  and structuring exchanges, 349–51
  and training, 560
communities
  and development, 601–6
  and enhancing social support, 605–6
  and framework for assessing, *603*
  and limits to development, 606
  and media outreach, 605
  and natural reinforcing, 522
  and neighborhood, 422, 426, 429–30,
    600–601
  and organizing and sharing
    information, 604–5
  and social action, 607–9
  and social planning and
    development, 607
  and social support, 605–6
community education, 534–35
community empowerment, 612
Community Networks Strategies, 430
community reinforcement approach
  (CRA), 546
comparative model, family support
  agency, *481*
comparison group, 227
compassion, 460
compensatory model, 27
competence
  and ethics and legal issues regarding,
    42, 51
  and evidence-based practice, 195
  and information gathering, 329, 387
  and interpersonal helping skills, 434–35
  in posing questions, 202, 211
*Complaints and Disorders: The Sexual
  Policies of Sickness* (Ehrenreich and
  English), 581
complex schedules, 155–56
compliance, 318
compromise, 375
computer-based education, 533
concreteness, 354
concurrent schedules, 156
concurrent validity, 391
conditioned reinforcers, 147
conditioned stimuli, 156
conduct disorder, *130*
confidence intervals, 234

confidentiality, 50–51, 323–24, 427–28
confirmation biases, 178, 451, 496
confirmatory bias, 453
conflict, 370, 612
conformity, 612
confounders, 225, *226*
confounding causes, 496
confounding factors, 448
confrontation, 346, 352–53
confusion, 107, 449
congruence, 345–46
consciousness raising, *326*, 533–34
consensus, 612
consequences, 267, *306*, 366, *380*, *418*
consistency, 154, 346
CONSORT, 109, 210, 222, 227, 230
construction, 124–25
constructional questionnaire, *282*, 434
construction of repertoires, 263–64, 304
constructive feedback, 541
constructive skills, 618
construct validity, 234, 391
consultive management, 612
consumer action, 534
contemplation, 324, *325*
content knowledge, *72*, 170, *249*
content validity, 391
contextual assessment, 126, 247–79, 459
  and antecedents, importance of,
    267–68, *266*
  and assessment, 54, 261
  and biomedical factors, 274–75
  and characteristics, 247–52, *251*, 261–68
  and client participation, 336–37
  and constructional, 263
  and contingencies are of interest, 266
  and cost-benefit analysis, 265
  and critical appraisal, 248–50
  and critical thinking, 98–100
  and cultural differences, 276
  and decisions, 250–52
  and developmental considerations,
    276–77
  and diagnosis, 54
  and distinctions, 268–70
  and emotions and feelings, 275–76
  and ethics, 277
  and form versus function, 268
  and global influences, 270
  and influences, 270–77
  and labels, 256–61
  and motivation, 276
  and personal and social problems,
    133–39
  and physical environment, 272, 274
  and problem-solving guide, 283
  and questions, 252–53
  and religion and spirituality, 276
  and resources and obstacles, 425–27
  and selecting goals, 303
  and social policies and legislation, 270–72

  and social supports, 272
  and sources of influence, 270–77
  and tasks and resources, 274
  and thoughts, 275
  and understanding clients, *273*
  and what is at stake, 253–56
  and when not possible, 495
contingencies, 144, *145*, 161, 266–68,
    428, *446*
  and arranging supporting, 483
  and behavior, 144–47, 300
  and consequences, different kinds, 267
  and cultures, 147
  and diagram, *151*
  and lack of success, 554
  and management, 161
  and myths and misconceptions, 549–52
  and narrative recording, 402
  and performance-management
    model, *146*
  and table, *452*
continuance, *145*
continuous schedule of reinforcement, 155
contrary-to-fact hypothesis, 451
contrast effect, 336
control, 551
controversies
  and construction or adaptation, 124–25
  and critical appraisal, 242
  and evidence, 198–99
  and inside and outside, 124
  and level of focus, 123–24
  and problem definition, 123–25
  and psychiatric labels, 258–60
  and social work, 10–11
  and social workers, 12–13
conversation, 377
conversion phenomenon, *620*
COPES questions, 202, *203*
corporate freeloaders, *138*
corporate welfare, 4
correlations, 449
  illusionary, *452*
corruption, helping professions, 84–85
cost-benefit analyses, *265*, 366
  and client participation, 318
  and questions, *203*, 204
Council on Social Work Education,
  7, 14, 106
counseling, families, *569*
counterattacks, *145*
counter conditioning, 157, *326*
countertransference effects, 327, 343
courage, 17, 106–7
covariations, 452
creaming, 511, 597
creativity, 169–70, 512
credibility, enhancing, 111, 330–31
credibility gap, 612
criminal justice, 486
criminology, 230

crisis situations, 313
criteria, questionable knowledge, 74–79
criterion, 537
criterion-referenced graphs, 497
critical, 213
critical appraisal, 219
    and bias, 225–26
    and causes, 236
    and contextual assessment, 248–50
    and controversial issues, 242
    and data, 387–92
    and diagnosis and screening, 239–41
    and effectiveness and prevention, 229–33
    and evidence, levels of, 229
    and experiences, 238–39
    and knowledge, 243
    and myths hindering, 222–25
    and observational data, 418–20
    and obstacles, 243
    and practice guidelines, 242
    and prevalence and incidence, 237
    and prognosis, risk and protective
        factors, 241
    and questions, 226–29
    and research, 209–10
    and self-report data, 392–94
    and skepticism, need for, 222
    and standardized measures, 396–97
    and systematic reviews and meta-
        analyses, 233–36
Critical Appraisal Skills Program (CASP),
    209, 223
critical attitude, 87–88, 96–97
critical discussion, 92
critical incidents, 499
critical periods, 447
critical rationalism, 80
critical reflection, 108
critical thinking, 114
    and benefits of, 98–105, 99
    and characteristics, 95
    and claims and arguments, 101–2
    and client participation, 318, 319
    and communication, 104
    and costs and benefits, 105–9
    and courage, 106–7
    and creating environments, 100–101
    and ethical dilemmas, 44–45, 46
    and evidence-based practice, 96
    and evidence-informed practice, 45–47
    and examples of, skills, 98
    and hallmarks of, 94–96
    and ignorance, 100
    and informal fallacies, 103
    and intellectual traits, 97
    and labels, 256–61
    and plans, 475–82
    and prevalence of uncritical, 105–6
    and propaganda, pseudoscience and
        quackery, 103–4
    and resource allocation, 108

    and self-awareness, 101
    and taxonomy of Socratic questions, 113
    and theories, 138–39
criticism
    and essence of science, 80
    and essential for learning, 105
    and responding to, 370–72, 368
cross-cultural counseling, 33–37
crossover, 145
cross-sectional studies, 233
cultural adaptation, 31
cultural change, 31
cultural determinism, 126
cultural differences
    and cultural blocks, 178
    and importance of considering, 479
cultural distance, 612
cultural diversity
    and clients, 30–33
    and cross-cultural counseling, 33–37
    and health care, 479–80
    and Hmong, 432
    and overlooking, 433
    and paying attention to, 359
    and problem solving, 366, 369
culturally sensitive practice, 309–10, 572
cultural pluralism, 39
cultural relativism, 31
culture, 39, 276, 309
    and contingencies, 147
    and evidence-informed
        organizational, 592
    and organization, 586, 588
    and thoughtfulness, 594
culture of thoughtfulness, 579, 594
cumulative graph, 497
cynicism, 92

DARE programs, 188
data analyses, 228
Database of Uncertainties about the Effects
        of Treatment (DUETS), 49, 169, 618
data collection, guidelines for
        collecting, 387
    critically appraising, 387
dead-end accounts, 449
Death and Life of Great American Cities,
        The (Jacobs), 422
decision-aids, 533
decision rule, 176
decisions and decision making. See also
        evidence-based practice (EBP)
    and approaches focusing on bias, 133
    and clients, 211–12
    and contextual assessment, 250–52
    and decisions and options, 167, 168,
        169, 470
    and during initial interviews, 293
    and evaluating outcomes, 490–91
    and families, 568
    and fast and frugal heuristics, 176–78

    and groups, 578–80
    and helping clients make, 165–85
    and information gathering, 385–87
    and intervention, 568–69, 586–88
    and learning through mistakes, 177–78
    and making final, 481–82
    and models for ethical, 62
    and organizations, 586–88
    and plan selection, 473–78
    and problem solving, 166–69
    and program and policy evaluation,
        508–11
    and research, 169–73
    and responsibility, 63
    and self-monitoring, 401
    and service plans, 490–91
    and setting priorities, 294
    and styles, 170, 173, 182, 588
    and using tests, 454–58
deficiency model, 426
deficits, motivational vs. behavioral, 270
delinquency, 230–31, 258
demand characteristics, 388
Department of Veterans Affairs, 427
depression, 85, 127, 128, 196, 241, 411,
        448–49, 451, 468
Depressives Anonymous, 580
deprivation, 440
DES Action, 608
description questions, 203, 204, 252
descriptions, 415, 416
descriptive analysis, 266
descriptive validity, 226, 234
desire to be (and appear) consistent, 336
detection bias, 225
deterioration, 508
development, 129
developmental characteristics, 276
developmental explanations, 129
developmental model, 130
developmental norms, 276–77
deviance, 120–23
diagnosis, 239–41, 256, 257, 260–61, 451–52
    and accuracy, 239
    and assessment, 256
    and screening, 239
Diagnostic and Statistical Manual of
        Mental Disorders (DSM), 28
    and contextual assessment, 258
    and critical appraisal of research, 239
    and problem solving, 122, 178
dialectical behavior theory (DBT), 533
diethylstilbestrol (DES), 608
differential reinforcement, 556
dignity of person, 42, 49–50
dilemmas, false, 454
direct measures, 492
disability, 376
disagreement, 367–70
disclosure, self-, 353–54
discrepancies, 407, 508

discretion, professional, 59
discriminated operants, 152, 563
discrimination, 34–35, 36, 37, 39, 125, 152, 162, 376–77
discriminative stimulus, 152, 162
discriminative stimulus functions, *160*
disruptive behavior, *268*
distance, 404
disturbing behaviors, *265*
domestic violence, 310–11
Don't Ask, Don't Tell, 530
Don't Shoot the Dog: The New Art of Teaching and Training (Pryor), 536, 564
doubt, *380*
dramatic relief, *326*
drapetomania, 259
drop-out rates, 228
double agent, 48
drug use, *184*, 250, *321*
drug war, 119
drunkard, 331
Dubious Dentistry (Jarvis), *620*
duration measure, 404, 418, 497
Dysfunctional Attitudes Scale, 435
dysfunctional behaviors, *574*
dysfunctional reactions, 619–20
dysfunctional roles, 573
dyslexia, 183–4
dysthymia, 127

eclecticism, 92
ecobehavioral programs, 546
ecological, 133
ecological validity, 232
ecology, *134*, 162, *606*
economic development, 609–10
economics
    and evidence-based practice, 191
    and problem framing, 118–20
education
    and beliefs about learning and, 86–90
    and community, 534–35
    and computer based, 533
    and schooling compared to indoctrination, *87*
educational environments, 86
Educational Policy and Accreditation Standards, 7, 14, 19–21, 69, 77, 94
effectiveness, 242, 593
Effectiveness & Efficiency (Cochrane), 460
effectiveness questions, *203*, 204
effect sizes, 289
efficacy, 242, 593
efficiency, 590
either-oring fallacies, 103, 185, 254–55, 260
elderly clients, *398*
eliciting stimulus, 157, 162
emotional abuse, job, 376–77
emotional appeals, *75*, 76, 103
emotional intelligence, 436, 544

emotions, 275–76
    and behavior, 154
    and lack of skills, 270
    and skills in managing, 544–46
empathy, 17
    and challenging social situations, 373
    and critical thinking, 95, 97, 105
    and cultural differences, 34, 36, 37
    in engaging client participation, 323, 334–35
    and interpersonal helping skills, 344–45, 467, 473, 483
empiricism, 92
empowering clients, 460
    and developing new skills, 535–47
    and providing information, 529–35
empowerment, 47–48, 460
    and advocate, 472–73
    and communities, 602
    and evaluation, 490
Empowerment Tradition in American Social Work, The (Simon), 125
empty nest syndrome, 129
enabler, 469, 473
enactive methods, 473
endings, 350
endings, planning for, 516–25
    and ethics, 525
    and examples, *518–19*
    and generalization and maintenance, 520–25
    and groups, 519
    and structuring exchanges, 350–51
    and unplanned, 517, 519
engagement
    and contextual assessment, 249, 267
    and interpersonal helping skills, 353
    and problem solving, 283
    and social workers, 20
enmeshment, 569–70
entertainment value, *75*, 76
environments
    and contextual view, 133–39
    and critical thinking, 100–101
    and observation, 405–6
    and task, 180
epigenetics, 127
epistemology, 93
equilibrium time, *447*
equity, 590
equivalence class, 153, 162
errors
    and avoiding, 183–84
    and client concerns, *450*
    and contextual assessment, 255
    and deciding on plan, *476*
    and decision making, 176–77, 195
    and due to relying on similarity, 183–84
    and empathy, 345
    and estimating progress, *495*
    and evaluating progress, 495

    and gathering assessment data, *389*
    and integrating information, 213
    and interpreting tests, 398
    and judgments about progress, 495–97
    and learning from, 597–98
    and listening, 346–47
    and observation, *410*, *419*
    and posing questions, 205, 348
    and problem solving, *171–72*
    and random, 388
    and research, 209
    and resulting in incomplete accounts, 450
    and searching, 208
    and social work practice, 310
    and value of, 499
escape-motivated behavior, *417*
establishing operations, 152, 162
establishment of repertoires, 263–64
ethical decisions, model, 62
ethical dilemmas, 44–45, *46*
ethical obligations, honoring, 193–95
ethical principles, 42
ethics, 41–65
    and allocating scare resources, 484
    and case records, 51–52
    and client participation, 336
    and competence, 51
    and confidentiality, 50–51
    and contextual assessment, 277
    and critical thinking and evidence-informed practice, 45–47
    and encouraging behavior, 62–64
    and endings, 525
    and ethical principles, 42
    and evaluation, 493–94
    and evidentiary issues, 145
    and failing to act, *46*
    and guidelines, *379*
    and ideals vs. realities, 64
    and ideology, 56–59
    and information gathering, 407
    and informed consent, 48–49
    and obstacles, 61–62, 148
    and patient bill of rights, *61*
    and policy and planning, 52–53
    and selecting plans, 484–85
    and selection of outcomes, 459–60
    and self-determination and empowerment, 47–48
    and sexual conduct, 52
    and values and obligations, 42–45
ethnic identity, 39
ethnicity, 17, 19, 39
    and challenging social situations, 375
    and classifications of, 17, 19, 31–33
    and contextual assessment, 259
    and culturally sensitive practice, 309
    and engaging client participation, 324, 330
    and ethics, 44, 52

ethnicity (*cont.*)
  and multiculturalism, 33, 274
  and problem definition, 123, 132–33
ethnocentrism, 39
ethnographic research, 238–39
Ethnography and Human Development
    (Jessor, Colby and Shweder), 238
evaluating skills, 214, 219
evaluation
  and conventional and participatory, *602*
  and different opinions about, 106
  and direct and indirect measures, 492
  and feedback, 490
  and helpful tools, 513
  and interventions, 502–4
  and next steps, 504, *505–6*
  and no improvement, 504, 506–8
  and obstacles, 512, 512
  and options, 491–93, 498–99
  and organizations and services, 590
  and outcomes, 214, 489–515
  and practical and ethical advantages,
    493–94
  and program and policy, 508–11
  and progress, 498–99, 513–14
  and questions and decisions, 490–91
  and reasons given against, 494–95
  and seeking answers to questions, 504
  and single-case decisions, 499–502
  and sources of error, 495–97
  and value of visual feedback, 497–98
evidence, 92, 106, *198*, 229
  and controversies about, 198
  and different opinions about, 106
evidence-based, 83
evidence-based diagnosis, 260
evidence-based practice (EBP), 186–90,
    219. *See also* critical thinking
  and alternative to authority-based
    practice, 188–89
  and application challenges, 202
  and assessment, 249–50
  and attention, 108
  and benefits of critical thinking, 98–105
  and contributions, *194, 195*
  and controversies, 198–99
  and critical thinking, 96
  and ethical obligations, 195
  and evaluating skills, 214
  and evaluating what happens, 213
  and hallmarks and philosophy implica-
    tions, 193–97
  and haphazard review, *193*
  and kinds of questions, 189
  and knowledge, 86
  and knowledge dissemination, 191–92
  and knowledge flow, 196–97
  and misrepresentations, 197–98
  and objections, 197–98
  and obstacles to, 198
  and organizational culture, *592*

  and origins, 190–93
  and philosophies, 189
  and process of, 189
  and questions, 189
  and questions of motivation, 214
  and styles, 189–90
  and systematic review, 192, *193*
  and systemic approach, 196
  and updated model, *187*
  and values, skills and knowledge, 96–98
evidence-based report, *257*
evidence-informed assessment, 262–63
evidence-informed organization, 591–99
  and corrective feedback, 596–98
  and creating and sustaining, *592*
  and knowledge flow, 595
  and management of innovations, 598–99
  and purchase of services, 594–95
  and resources and populations, 591, *593*
  and selection of practices and
    policies, 594
  and training content and formats,
    595–96
evocative effect, 152
evolutionary influence, behavior, 157–60
exchange, 284–85, 341
expectations, positive, 329–30
experience. *See also* intuition
  and critical appraisal of research, 237–39
  and critical thinking, 105
  and evidence-based practice, 185, 187,
    190, 192, 199
  and knowledge, *75*, 77–78
  and posing questions, 213, 215
  and problem definition, 120, 123
  and problem solving, 175–77
expert power, 612
experts and expertise, 11
  and clinical, 187
  and critical appraisal of research, 128,
    223–23
  and critical thinking, 170
  and disagreement about research, 211
  and ethics, 53–55
  and evidence-based practice, 190, 198
  and information gathering, 391, 531,
    578, 604
  and knowledge, 70, 71, 75, 78
  and posing questions, 205, 211
  and problem definition, 123
  and problem solving, 122, 133, 166,
    169, 495
expert testimony, 391
expert witness, 54
explanations
  and behavioral, 129–32
  and biomedical, 127–28
  and cognitive, 129
  and developmental, 129
  and genetic, 126–27
external validity, 226, 234, 504

extinction, 150, 162, 556–57, *561*
extrinsic reinforcers, 551–52
eyeballing, 498
eyewitness accounts, 391

face validity, 391
facial expression, 357–58
facilitation, 335
facts, 111
fading, 537
failures, 178, *181*
fallacies
  of composition, 184
  of division, 184
  and ecological, 231
  of false cause, 448
  of false dilemma, 104
  and informal, 103
  of labeling, 184
  and single cause, 453
  of stereotyping, 174
false cause, 184
False Claims Act, 56
false dilemmas, 454
false knowledge, 70, *72*, 86, 92
false negative rate, *456*
false negatives, 397
false positive rate, 399, *456*
false positives, 397
falsification approach to knowledge, 92
families, 566–67. *See also* groups
  and assessment, 567–71
  and beliefs, *568*, 570
  and caregiving skills, 569
  and communication styles, 569
  and counseling, *569*
  and decision making, 568
  and feelings, 570–71
  and goals, 571
  and intervention options, 571
  and life stage, 570
  and patterns of interaction and affection,
    569–70
  and power, 567, *568*
  and roles, 570
  and strengths, 570
  and stresses, 567, *568*
family systems, *481*
fast and frugal heuristics, 176–78
faulty inferences, 184–85
fear, *380*, 433
feasibility, 392, 479
Federal Trade Commission, 85
feedback
  and analyzing, 405, 586
  and challenging social situations, 373–74
  and client participation, 331–32
  and constructive, 541
  and evaluating outcomes,
    490, 497–98, 511
  and interpersonal helping skills, 356

as a learning opportunity, 370
and opportunities for corrective, 596–98
and personalizing, 374
and responding to criticism, 370–72
and value of timely, 490
and visual, 497
feed-up procedure, 590
feelings, 275–76, 301, 550
expression of, 570–71
female sexual dysfunction, 127
five-step approach, 305–6
fixed-ratio schedule, 155
flexibility, 354, 366–67, 454, 454
flow chart
and performance problems, *471*
and problem-solving, *173*
focusing, clients' attention, 349–50, 451
focus levels
and controversial issues, 123–24
and outcomes, *550*
Follies and Fallacies in Medicine
(Skrabanek and McCormick), 258
follow-up services, 524–25
Food and Drug Administration (FDA), 85
form and function, confusion of, 449
forward chaining, 537
foster care, 294
fraud, helping professions, 84–85
freeloaders, corporate, *138*
frequency, 154, 387, 403, 496, 553
functional analysis, 266
functional objectives, 460
functional relevance, 560
function test, 410
fundamental attribution error, 405, 410,
448, 449
fuzzy thinking, 177

Gamblers Anonymous, 580
gaps
and evidence and use, 91
and needs and resources, 297
gay rights movement, 119
gays and lesbians, 173–74, 426
gaze, 358
gender differences, 13, 17, 32
and challenging social situations,
25, 375, 376
and contextual assessment, 251, 254, 426,
460, 567, 590, 601, 603
and engaging clients, 472
and interpersonal helping skills, 35–37
and multiculturalism, 33
and problem definition, 119, 125, 132–33
and social justice, 44
generalization, planning for, 520–25
generalized reinforcers, 148
genetic determinism, 126
genetic explanations, 126–27
genocide, 39
genograms, 249

genotype, 127
genuineness, 345–46
geographic mapping systems, 429
gestures, 358
global influences, 270
global perspective, 14
goal attainment scaling, 498
goals, 303–5, 355, 356, 366, 405
gold standard, *457*, 459
good intentions, *75*, 76
Graduate Record Examination
(GRE), 236
graphs, 497–98, 513
grievance system, 612
group designs, 500–501
group interaction, 158–60
groups, 571–78
and advantages of settings, 572–73
and common mistakes, 575, 578
and data describing, 414
and decision making, 578–80
and helpful and dysfunctional behaviors,
573, *574*
and mutual help, 580–81
and norms, *575*
and phases, 574–75
and preparing for session, *576–77*
and reassurance and threat, 158
and roles and tasks of leader, *578*
and self-help, 580–81
and social worker role planning, 575
and structure and process, 573–74
and team meetings and case conferences,
579–80
groupthink, 579
guided imagery, 395
guilt, *380*
gullibility, 55, 96, 104

hallucinations, 265
haphazard reviews, *193*
harm
avoidance of, 43, 59–60, 73
and contextual assessment, 249, 253,
255, 259
and critical appraisal of research,
222, 230, 233, 234
and critical thinking, 98, 99
and ethics, 43–44, 56, 62
and evidence-based practice, 191
and knowledge, 73, *74*, 84–85, 104, *105*
and posing questions, *203*, 204
and screening, 399–400
and service plans, 490, 494, 495, 500, 512
hasty generalization, 184
hasty thinking, 177
Hawthorne effect, 496
health care, 479–80, *531*
Health Consumer Alliance, 534
Health Consumer News, 534
health informatic services, 533

Health Insurance Portability and
Accountability Act (HIPAA), 50
Health Letter, 85
health maintenance organizations
(HMOs), 53
Health Related Quality of Life (HRQL), 513
Hearing Loss Association of America, 534
Hearing Voices Network, 530, 531, 580
hello-goodbye effect, 496
helper-client exchanges, 22–39, 70, 266
and avoiding harming, 73
and barriers and remedies for cross-
cultural helping, *34*
and changing cognitive ecology, 542–43
and client participation, *320*, 323, 331
and clients' beliefs, expectations, and
goals, 25–27
and effective social behavior, 355–56
and helpers' beliefs, expectations, and
goals, 27–28
and help-seeking before professionals,
23–24
and hesitations, 324
and malpractice, 54–55
and organizing and interpreting data,
442–43
and profession, influence of, 28–30
and punctuating, 350–51
and relationship skills, 326–29, 342–44,
550–51
and requesting behavior changes, 372–75
and social influence process, 25–27
and structuring exchanges, 349–51
and working with groups, 571–78
helpful tools, 513
helping, 341–61
and advocacy, 583–84
as an art, 187
and asking helpful questions, 348–49
and attentive listening, 346–47
and beliefs about, 437
and challenges, 354–55
and clarity/concreteness, 354
and congruence, 345–46
and empathy, 344–45
and encouraging views and behaviors,
351–53
and history, past, 264
and nonverbal behavior, 357–59
and recognizing limits of, 618–19
and relationship skills, 354
and respect and positive regard, 347–48
and self-disclosure, 353–54
and social behavior, 355–56
and social influence process, 25–27,
342–44
and structuring exchanges, 349–51
and verbal behavior, 356–57
and working in groups, 571–78
hermeneutics, 92
heroin use, 250, *321*

hesitation, client participation, 323–24
heuristics, 173, 176–78
    fast and frugal, 176
Higher Than Hope (Mandela), 106
hindsight bias, 495
historical perspective, 13, 90–91, *122*
HIV positive, *576–77*
Hmong, *432*
homework assignments, 541–42
homosexuality, 119, 122, 175, 180, 460
honesty
    and critical thinking, 96, 98
    and intervention, 571, 594
    and evidence-based practice, 189
    and gathering information, 391
    and interpersonal helping skills, 343
    and posing questions, 211
    and procedural guidelines, 49, 296–95
hoped-for outcomes, 490
hostile, 331
*House of Cards: Psychology and
    Psychotherapy Built on Myth*
    (Dawes), 12
How Superstition Won and Science Lost
    (Burnham), 83
How to Read a Paper, 222
human relationships, *42*
human rights, 44
humor, 354
hunting gap, 208
hyperactive, 258
hypothesis, *418*

ideals and actualities, 458–59
ideology, ethics and, 56–59
    and bureaucratic, 57
    and optimistic, 57
    and pessimistic, 57
    and professional, 57
    and socialist, 57–58
ignorance, 454
    and behavioral principles, 512, 551
    and critical thinking, 45, 97, 105
    and ethics, 51, 56, 64
    and evidence-based principles, 192–97
    and information organization/
        interpretation, 454
    and knowledge, 70, 83, 86, 90, 96,
        100, 179
    and posing questions, 213, 214
    and problem solving, 139, 143, 179, 185
illusion of control, 496
illusory correlations, 452
immediacy, 346
implementation, plans and programs,
    482–84
Implicit Association Test, 348
Improving Healthcare Through Advocacy
    (Jannson), 440
incidence questions, 237
incidental teaching, 560

incomplete accounts, 449, *450*
incomplete assessment, *253, 255, 443*
incremental model, 588
Indian Child Welfare Act, 31
indirect measures, 492
individualized assessment, 262
individualized education program (IEP),
    53, 305
individual racism, 39
individual responsibility, 125
Individuals with Disabilities Act
    (IDEA), 53
indoctrination, education, *87*
inert knowledge, 70, *72*
inferences
    and contextual assessment, 262–63
    and critical thinking, 37, 98, 102, 109
    and information organization/
        interpretation, 396, 406, 407, 410, 411,
        415–16, 458
    and knowledge, 77, 78
    and posing questions, 213
    and faulty, 184–85
    and problem solving, 139, 174, 515
informal fallacies, 103
informal organization, 612
information, 533–34
    and brochures, 527–29
    and empowering clients, 529–35
    and guidelines for giving, *532*
    and integrating different sources, 210–13
    and organizing and sharing, 604–5
    and potential benefit to clients, *530*
    and problem-related, 436
information based on observation, 409–24,
    410, 411
    and critical appraisal, 418–20
    and natural environment, 414–18
    and obstacles, 423
    and physical environment, 420–22
    and role play, 411–14
    and task analysis, 422–23
    and value, 409–11
information gathering, 385–408
    and asking clients to collect data,
        400–405
    and case records, 406
    and critical appraisal of data, 387–92
    and data by professionals, 406–7
    and decisions and options, 385–87
    and discrepancies, 407
    and errors, *389*
    and ethics, 407
    and guidelines, *387*
    and observation, 405–6
    and physical examination, 406
    and physiological measures, 406
    and problems related to, 43, 436
    and questionable assessment methods,
        390–91
    and self-monitoring, 400–405

    and self-reports, 392–95
    and standardized measures,
        395–400, *396*
    and storage, 407
information, organization and
    interpretation, 442–62
    and case examples, 445–47
    and causes, 444, 447–54
    and difficulty with, 443–44
    and ethics, 459–60
    and ideals and actualities, 458–59
    and problem framings, 444
    and record keeping, 460–62
    and using tests in decision making,
        454–58
information about resources and obstacles,
    424–41
    and advocacy, 440
    and contextual thinking, 425–27
    and neighborhood and community,
        429–30
    and personal, 434–40
    and service and surveillance systems,
        427–29
    and significant others, 431–34
    and social networks and social support
        systems, 430–31
informed consent, 11
    and contextual assessment, 268, 277
    and critical thinking, 98
    and engaging client participation,
        318, 485
    and ethics, 48–49, 62, 440
    and evidence-based practice, 189, 190,
        191, 194–95, 197–98
    and philosophy of practice, 18
    and posing questions, 212
innate capacity, 124–25
innovations, management of, 495, 598–99
innumeracy, 453
insight, 533
institutional poverty traps, 426
institutions, accountability checklist, *510*
instrumental questions, 348
integrating information, 210–13
    common errors, 205
integrity, *42*
intellectual traits, *97*
intelligence, 436
intentions, *75, 76*
interactional view of deviance, 121
intermediate behaviors, 303
intermittent schedule, 155
internal validity, 225, 234
international enterprises, 610
International Federation of Social Workers,
    142, 266
International Rescue Committee, *472*
Internet, 85, 190, 192, 208, 530, 533,
    595, 605
interpersonal helping skills, 341–61

and asking helpful questions, 348–49
and attentive listening, 346–47
and challenges, 354–55
and concreteness, 354
and effective social behavior, 355–56
and empathy, 344–45
and encouraging helpful views and
    behaviors, 351–53
and helping as social influence process,
    342–44
and improving skills, 355
and nonverbal behavior, 357–59
and respect, 347–48
and self-disclosure, 353–54
and structuring exchanges, 349–51
and verbal behavior, 356–57
and warmth and genuineness
    (congruence), 345–46
interpersonal problem solving, 364–67
interpersonal skills, 437
interpretations, 347, 353, 398–95. See
    also information, organizing and
    interpreting
interrelated causes, 447–48
interruptions, 377
interval recording, 416–17
interval schedules, 155
intervention, 228, 268, 451. See also positive
    behavior change skills
    and assessment, 465–67, 463
    and B designs, 501, 502
    and behaviors related to, levels, 549
    and client participation, 320, 325, 326
    and decisions involved in selecting,
        469–71
    and fidelity of, 507–8
    and helper-client connection, 344
    and lack of skill and knowledge, 432–33
    and motivation, communication and,
        561–62
    and next steps, 504, 505–6
    and options, 571
    and outcomes, 502–4
    and restrictive plan, 480
    and roles, 469, 469
    and visual representation, 497, 498
intervention outcomes, 263
intervention rationale, 269
interviews
    and checklist for, 314–15
    and children, 394–95
    and client participation, 333–36
    and initial, 228, 286, 298–99
    and introductory statements, 289
    and preparing for, 334
    and punctuating exchanges, 350–51
    and social work practice, 284–85,
        286–88, 298–99
    and structured, 349–47, 392
introductory statements, 289
intuition, 75, 78–79, 169–70, 180, 224, 458

Japanese Americans, 356
job stress, 621–22
jog memory, 180
judgments
    and critical thinking, 104, 107–8, 111
    and engaging clients, 175, 184, 323, 398
    and evidence-based practice, 94
jumping to conclusions, 213, 318
justification approach to knowledge, 92
juvenile delinquency, 135–36

knowledge, 69–72, 92, 454, 512
    and assessing values, and skills, 87–88
    and beliefs about, 109–11
    and burden of, 90
    and content, in assessment, 249
    and critical rationalism, 80
    and critical thinking, 96–98
    and data assessment, 387–92
    and developmental explanations, 129
    and difference between science and
        pseudoscience, 83
    and dissemination, 191
    and domain specific, 454
    and evaluating claims, 72–73
    and evidence-based practice, 191–92,
        196–97
    and evidentiary possibilities, 81
    and exploring beliefs about, 71
    and falsification approach to, 92
    and flow, 196
    and historical perspective, 90–91
    and ignorance as a kind of, 454
    and inert, 70
    and lack of skill and, 432–33
    and legal regulations and resources,
        53–54
    and misrepresenting, 142–44
    and misunderstandings and
        misrepresentations, 79–80
    and patterns and regularities, 81
    and performance, 70
    and political savvy, 600
    and problem solving, 178–79
    and propaganda, fraud and corruption,
        84–85
    and quackery, 84
    and questionable criteria, 74–79
    and refutable and testable statements,
        80–81
    and relativism, 83–84
    and research methods used, 242
    and reviewing and updating
        background, 334
    and science and scientific criteria,
        79–83
    and scientific objectivity, 82
    and situational requirements and
        options, 355–56
    and tools maximizing, flow, 595
    and verificationist vs. refutationist, 82

and websites, 110
knowledge monopolies, 91

labeling and labels, 299–300, 302
    and client participation, 319, 331, 332
    and minimizing negative, 331
    and naming rather than explaining, 451
    and problem/outcome profile,
        290–91, 292
    and psychiatric labels, 258
    and thinking critically about, 256–61
language, 453–54
    and misleading use, 105
    and problem definition, 123
language of thoughtfulness, 104
latency, 387
latency of causal effects, 447
lateral classism, 309
Latino, 32, 358
lawsuits, malpractice, 54–55
learning
    and becoming a lifelong learner, 535
    and beliefs about, and education, 86–90
    and cultivating skills, 88
    and evaluation and feedback as a
        journey, 213–14, 370
    and journey, 622
    and life-long learner, 621
    and mistakes, errors and lack of
        success, 108
    and paradigms, 88
    and problem solving, 108
    and role of mistakes, 86
    and supervision, 89–90
legal issues
    agency policies and planning, 52–53
    and clients, 55–56
    and confidentiality, 50–51
    and ideology, 56–59
    and knowledge of liability, 54–55
    and knowledge of regulations and
        resources, 53–54
    and self-determination, 47–48
    and sexual conduct, 52
legislation, influencing 427–25, 609
legitimate power, 612
LGBT (lesbian, gay, transgender and
    bisexual), 144
liability, 54
liberation, 273
licensing, 55
LIFE coding system, 412
Ligas v. Hamos, 543
likelihood ratio, 240, 398–99
Limits to Medicine (Illich), 122
listening, 327, 346, 354, 371, 377–78
literature, 223
logically consistent, 139
logical positivism, 93
logic model, 509
loneliness, 131

loose associations, *455*
Losing Ground (Murray), 11
loudness, 357

McMartin Preschool trial, 390
magic, 27, 80, 84, *122*, 215
magic bullet, 350
magnitude, 154
maintenance, planning for, *325*, 520–25
malpractice, liability, 54–55
maltreated children, 202, 485
maltreatment, social work practice, 310–11
management
    and by objectives, 612
    and evidence-informed, skills, 593–94
    and organizational culture, *592*
managerialism, 272
mandated clients, 307
manipulation, 551
manner of presentation, 78
March of Folly, The (Tuchman), 13
marginality, 39
marker variables, 129
matching law, 156, 162
maxims, 109–10
measures, 227–28
    and screening, 399
    and standardized, 395–98
media outreach, 605
mediating variable, *447*
mediator, 469, 471, 612
medical care system, *531*
medicalization of defiance, 259
medical or disease model, 27
Medicare, 427, 480
medication, 85, 90, 91, 100
meeting, 341
memory, as reconstruction, 180
memory work, 395
mental disorders, 258–60
mental illness, 10
    and contextual assessment, 256
    and critical appraisal of research, 208
    and critical thinking, 100, *104*
    and ethics and legal issues regarding,
      47, 49, 58–59
    and knowledge, 78, 85
    and problem definition, 123, 127
    and problem solving, 118–20, *120*
mentor, 612
Meritor Sav. Bank v. Vinson, 376
meshing skills, 351
meta-analyses, 233–36
metacognitive, 181, 182
Military Acceptance Project, 530
Mindfreedom, 47, 55, 610
Minnesota Multiphasic Personality
    Inventory (MMPI), 396
minority group, 39
misconceptions, 107, 549–52, 557, 559
misleading criteria, 497

Mismeasure of Women, The (Tavris),
    106, 132, 259
misrepresentations
    and behavioral principles, 131–32
    and critical thinking, 100
    and evidence-based practice, 197–98
    and fraud, 85
    and knowledge, 79–80, 142–44
mistakes, 177–78. *See also* errors
mistreated children, 202
misunderstandings, 555–56
mixed and multisystem programs, 546
model presentation, 152, 537–34, 539–40
monitoring, 400–405
monopolizers, 377
morale, 612
Morales v. Turman, 53
motivation, *561–62*
    and behavioral principles, 153–54
    and blocks, 74
    and contextual assessment, 251, 254,
      270, 276
    and posing questions, 205, 214–15
    and problem solving, 179
    and self-monitoring, 392, 405
MoveOn.org, 534
Moving to Opportunity (MTO), 601
multiculturalism, 33
Multidimensional Acculturative Stress
    Inventory, *396*
multiple baseline designs, 502–3
multisystem programs, 546
mutual defensiveness, 158
mutual dependence, 158
mutual help groups, 580–81
Myth of the Framework, The (Popper), 105
myths, 222–25, 549–52, 555–56, 557, 559

naming rather than explaining, 451
Narcotics Anonymous, 580
narrative recording, 402
narrow thinking, 177
National Association of Black Social
    Workers (NABSW), 12
National Association of Puerto Rican
    Social Service Providers
    (NAPRSSP), 12
National Association of Social Workers
    (NASW), 12, 106, 261, 390
    Code of Ethics, 8, 9, 15, 16, 17, *42*, 48,
      108, 136, 191, 591, 593
    ethics cases, 52
    Standards for Cultural Competence in
      Social Work Practice, 33–37
National Center on Child Abuse and
    Neglect, 394
National Coalition Against Censorship, 84
National Community Reinvestment
    Coalition, 534
National Consumer Organizations, 534
National Consumers League, 534

National Council Against Health Fraud, 85
National DES Awareness Week, *608*
National Health Service (NHS), 208
National Indian Social Worker Association
    (NISWA), 12
National Senior Citizens Law Center, 55
Native Americans, 31, 309
natural environment, observation, 414–18
natural frequencies, estimating risk,
    457–58
natural reinforcing communities, 522
necessary and facilitating, 152
need-resource gaps, *297*
negative predictive value (NPV), 240, *457*
negative reinforcement, 148–49, 162,
    555–56, *561*
negative reinforcer, 148, 162
neglected children, 202
negligence, 54–55
negotiation process, 306–7
neighborhoods, 422, 426, 429–30, 600–601,
    602–4, 605–6, 612
networks, families, 567, *568*, 612
neurasthemic, 261
Neurotics Anonymous, 580
New Deal, Roosevelt, 9
New Freedom in Mental Health
    Commission, 241
nominal group technique, 613
noncontingent reinforcement, 162
nondefensiveness, 346
nonjustificationist epistemology, 93
nonlinear approach, 300
non-malfeasance, 43–44
nonprofit organizations, *4*
nonspecific factors, 344, 467
nonverbal behavior, 357–59, 363
nonverbal harassment, 377
nonvoluntary clients, 517. *See also*
    mandated clients
normative power, 613
norms, 392, *575*
Nova Scotia COMPASS Program, *509*
number needed to harm (NNH), 204, 211,
    233, 457, 481
number needed to treat (NNT), 211, 233,
    457, 482
numbers, knowledge, 75
nursing home, 421–22, *429*

objectives, 303–5, *304*, 306–7, *305*
    selection of 303–6
objective tests, 396
objectivity, 82
observation, 263, 263, 409–20
    and critically appraising, 418
    and guidelines for, 475
    and interval recording, 416–17
    and natural environment, 414–18
    and role playing, 411–14
    and sequential recording, 416

and sources of error, 419
and time sampling, 417
and value, 409–11, *410*
observational learning, 152
observational studies, 231–33
observer accuracy, 420
observer bias, 496
observer drift, 420
obsessive compulsive disorder (OCD), 85
obstacles. *See also* information, about
     resources and obstacles
  and critical appraisal, 243
  and ethics, 61–62
  and evaluation, 512
  and evidence-based practice, 198
  and identifying possible, 539
  and integrating research, 213
  and observation, 423
  and organizational change, 599–600
  and physical assets and, 437–38
  and planning guide, *306*
  and posing questions, 205
  and research, 210
  and searching, 208–9
  and significant others, 431–34
  and social situations, 378–79
  and social support, 431
odds ratio, 234–35
ombudsperson, 613
one-shot recording, 403
operant, 144, 162
operant aggression, 149–50
operant behavior, 162
operant learning, 154–56, 157, 162
opinions, 106, 111
opportunity cost, 493
oppositional defiant disorder, *130*
oppression, 34–35, 36, 39, 124, 125, *273*
optimistic ideologies, 57
options
  and decisions, *470*
  and evaluation outcomes, 491–93
  and information gathering, 387
organizational climate, 613
organizational culture, 613
organizational politics, 613
Organization for Economic Cooperation
     and Development (OECD), 11
organizations, 613. *See also* agencies
  and administrative tasks, 589–90
  and audit, benchmarks and
     evaluation, 590
  and client involvement, 589
  and confronting scarce resources, 591
  and cultural and climate, 586–89, 594
  and decision-making styles, 588
  and evidence-informed, 591–99, *592*
  and framework for describing, *585*
  and management of innovations, 598
  and obstacles to change, 599–600
  and public and nonprivate, 580–81

and technology relied on, 589
and understanding and changing,
     584–90
and well-designed client-centered, *587*
outcome resistance, 318
outcomes
  and client participation, 323
  and ethical issues in selection of, 459–60
  and fear of loss of valued, 433
  and focus, *550*
  and goals and objectives, 303–5
  and intervention, *263*, 371, 502–4
  and overview of desired, 285
  and planning guide, *306*
  and problem/outcome profile,
     290–91, *292*
  and social work practice, 285, 288–89,
     293, 302–7
overconfidence, 495
overcontrolled behavior, 309
overcontrolled syndrome, 309
overcorrection, 559
Overeaters Anonymous, 580
overgeneralizations, 453
overinterpretation, 178
overmanning, 613
oversimplification, 452

pace, 357
pacing, 351
panic disorder, 85
paper-and-pencil analogs, 396, 412
paradigm, 93
Paradox of Urban Space, The (Sutton and
     Kemp), 422
paralanguage, 357
parameter, *447*
paranoid, 258
paraphrases of content, 344
Parents Anonymous, 580
parent-training program, *289*
parroting, 346
parroting problem, 170
parsimony, 82, 139
participation. *See* client participation
passive behavior, 364, *365*
pathological approaches, 265
  and appeal of, 142
patient bill of rights, *61*
Patient Protection and Affordable Care Act
     of 2010, 440
patient uniformity myth, 257, 262
patronizing, 347
Paxil fraud, 85
Pedagogy of the Oppressed (Freire), 607
pediatric bipolar disorder, 11
peer review, 60, 91, 192, 225, 228, 391, 597
perception, 275, 356
performance and outcome review, 596
performance bias, 225
performance, checklist for analyzing, 307

performance knowledge, 70, *72*
performance-management model, *146*
performance monitoring, 511
performance problems, *471*
performance standards, 511, 613
periodic service review (PSR), 511
persistence, 366–67, 375
personal blocks, 180–81
personality disorder, 319
personalizing feedback, 374
person-environment fit, 255–56
Person-In-Environment (PIE), 261
Persuasion and Healing (Frank), 343
persuasion strategies, 336
perverse incentives, 144
pessimistic ideologies, 57
phenomenology, 93
philosophy of practice, 14–18
  and evidence-based practice, 46–47, 189
phoniness, 345
physical appearance, 359
physical assets and obstacles, 437
physical environment, 272, 274, 420–22
  and observation of, 420–22
physical examination, 406
physical harassment, 377
physiological behavior, *562*
physiological measures, 406
PICO questions, 202, *203*
pitch, 357
placebo effect, 329
planner, 469, 473
planning and program development, 607
planning guide, *306*
plans, 356
  and checklist for reviewing, *477*
  and decisions, 469–74
  and decisions involved in selecting, 467
  and describing, 476
  and ethics in selecting, 484–85
  and ideals and actualities, 458
  and implementation, 482–84
  and planning for endings, 516–25
  and questionable criteria for
     selecting, 485
  and restrictions of, 480
  and thinking critically about, 475–82
play of chance, 448
Pleasant Events Schedule, *396*, 440
policies, service and surveillance, 427–29
policy decisions, ethics, 52–53
politics
  and knowledge and skills, 600
  and problem framing, 118–20
popularity, knowledge, 75
posing well formed questions, 202–5
  and obstacles to, 205
position, 613
positive behavior change methods, 548–65
  and decreasing behavior, *552*, 556
  and differential reinforcement, 556

positive behavior change methods (*cont.*)
  and extinction, 556–57
  and increasing behavior, 552
  and myths and misconceptions, 549–52
  and positive alternatives to punishment, 560–63
  and positive reinforcement, 552–55
  and rearranging antecedents, 563–64
  and value of, 548–49
positive expectations, encouraging, 329–27
positive feedback, 373, 375, *586*
positive predictive value (PPV), 240, *457*
positive regard, 347–44
positive reinforcement, 147–48, 162, 552–55, *561*
positive reinforcer, 147, 162, 433
positivism, 93
positivistic view, 120
postmodernism, 83–84, 93
postpositivism, 93
posttest odds, 240
posttest probability, 240
posttraumatic stress disorder (PTSD), 85, 190
posture and position, 358
potential refutability, 138
poverty, 4–9, 11, 42, 100, 137, *271*
power
  and agency influences, 25
  and behavioral principles, 136, 142, 157
  and contextual assessment, *273*
  and critical thinking, 98–99, 106, 108
  and ethics, 19–21, 44, 56, 59, 63
  and evidence-based practice, 191, 192
  and intervention, 567, *568*, 601, 612
  and problem definition, 118, 119, 121
practice, 109, 242, 248, *418*
practice guidelines, 242, 468, 484
practice research, 513
practicing skills, 316, 316. *See also* behavioral rehearsal
practicing, service roles, 473–74
prebaseline, 301
preconceptions, 174
precontemplation, 324, *325*
prediction questions, *203*, 204
predictions
  and critical appraisal of research, 239, 241
  and critical thinking, 99
  and evaluating outcomes, 496
  and knowledge, 73, 74, 78, 81, 90
  and posing questions, 204
  and problem solving, 139, 169, 177
predictive accuracy, 455, *456*
predictive validity, 391
predictive value of negative test, *456*
predictive value of positive test, *456*
preferences, 86, 111, 169, 187–89, 194
pregnancy, 376
prejudice, 39–40

prejudices, 35
Premack Principle, 162
premenstrual dysphoric disorder (PMDD), 85
preparation, 324, *325*
pre/post change, 499
pretend understanding, 346–47
pretest odds, 240
pretest probability, 240
prevalence, 240
prevalence questions, 237
prevalence rate, *456*
prevention
  and problems, 485–86
  and questions, *203*, 204
primary-level accurate empathy, 344
primary prevention, 485
primary reinforcers, 147
principle of approximation to truth, 16
principle of charity, 89
principle of fallibility, 16
principle of liking, 336
principle of rational discussion, 16
principle of social proof, 336
prioriphobia, 591
priorities, 294–95
prioritizing, 591
PRISMA, 210, 222
privileged communication, 50–51
probabilistic nature of prediction, *447*
probabilities, 453
probes, 348, 499
problem
  and behavioral analysis, *158, 159, 160*
  and clear description of, 297
  and contextual assessment, 254
  and description and context, 297, 299–301
  and deviance as a, 120–23
  and flowchart for analyzing performance, *471*
  and organizing and interpreting data, 443–44
  and prospects, 254
  and views, concepts, causes, *121*, 301–2
problem-based learning, 89, 178, 187, 189, 243
problem crusaders, 119
problem definition, 120
  and community, 601, 603
  and competing, 139, 153
  and discrimination and oppression, 125
  and individual responsibility, 125
  and language of, 123
  and ongoing controversies, 123–25
  and proposed causes, *120*
problem framing
  and choosing among, 444
  and consequences, 119–20
  and critical phase, 170
  and political conflicts over values, 119

  and politics and economics of, 118–20
  and professionals, 117–18
  and questions, 444
problem/outcome profile, *290–91, 292, 293*
problem solvers, 181–82
problem solving, 108
  and advantages of practice model, 165–66
  and barriers, 178–81
  and confirmation biases, 178
  and contextual assessment, 254–55
  and creativity and intuition, 169–70
  and decision making, 166
  and flow chart, *173*
  and guides, 50, 281
  and ignorance and propaganda, 179
  and information processing factors, 179–80
  and interpersonal, 364–67
  and limited knowledge, 178–79
  and memory, 180
  and outcome profile, *290–92*
  and personal blocks, 180–81
  and phases and tasks, 170, *171–72, 283*
  and relationship to decision making, 166–69
  and research, 169–73
  and strength enhancing, 254
  and styles and skills, 434
  and task environment, 180
  and training, 543–44
  and uncertainty, 169
problem solving, evaluating outcomes, 489–515
  and deterioration, 508
  and evaluation tools, 509–10, 513
  and feedback, 490
  and interventions, 502–4
  and next steps, 504, *505–6*
  and no improvement, 504, 506–8
  and obstacles, 512
  and options, 491–93
  and practical and ethical advantages, 493–94
  and program and policy evaluation, 508–11
  and progress evaluation, 513–14
  and questions and decisions, 490–91
  and reasons given against, 494–95
  and reviewing progress, options for, 498–99
  and single-case designs, 499–502
  and sources of error, 495–97
  and value of visual feedback, 497–98
problem-solving guide, 281–84, *283*
procedural fidelity, 51
procedural guidelines
  and assessing risks, 311–12
  and collaborative working relationship, 295–97
  and crises, 312

and culturally sensitive practice, 309–10
and encouraging helpful views, 301–2
and initial interviews and exchanges,
   284–86
and outcomes, 302–7
and possible services, 297
and priorities, 294–95
and problem-solving guides, 281–84
and profile of problems and desired
   outcomes, 292, 301–2
and progress indicators, 309
and reporting maltreatment, 310–11
and review of practice skills, 316
and service agreements, 307–9
procedural knowledge, 170
process of change, *326*
process resistance, 318
professional data, 406–7
professional organizations, ethics, 53
professions and professionals, 11–13
   and clients and illegal behavior by, 55–56
   and data provided by, 406–7
   and evidence-based practice,
      191, 192, *195*
   and help-seeking before, *23–24*
   and ideologies, 57
   and influence of, 28–30
   and limits on discretion of, 59–61
   and previous contacts with, 25
   and problem framers, 117–18
   and propaganda, fraud, and corruption,
      84–85
   and quackery, *620*
   and role in society, 12
   as social reformers, 12, 64
   and social work as, 11–13
profit motive, *620*
prognosis
   and contextual assessment, 252–53,
      260–61, *261*
   and critical appraisal of research,
      224, 241
   and evidence-based practice, 189
   and posing questions, 204, 206, 216
program evaluation, 508–11
programming change, 541
progress indicators, 309
Progressive Era ideology, 58
Project Censored, 118
*Project Censored, Censored: The News That
   Didn't Make the News and Why*, 105–6
projective drawings, 390
projective tests, 396
promotive factors, *135–36*
prompts and prompting, 288, 329, 335–36,
   417, 537, 541
propaganda, 103–4, 111, 179, 622
   and helping professions, 84–85
   and hypnotic effect of words, *100*
   and ideology as, 56–57
Prophet motive, *620*

protective factors, *135–36*, 241, 260–61,
   261, 277
proximity, 358
pseudoexplanations, 256
pseudoscience, *103–4*
   and contextual assessment, 253
   and critical thinking, 99, 103–4, 105
   and evidence-based practice, 194, 196
   and knowledge, 79, 81, 83, 84, 91, 93
   and multiculturalism, 33
psychiatric intervention, 253
psychiatric labels and narratives
   and contextual assessment, 248–50,
      258–60, 278
   and critical appraisal of research, 239–41
   and problem definition, 120
Psychoanalytic Terms and Concepts (Moore
   and Fine), 533
psychoanalytic theory, 126
psychobabble, 453–54
psychological debriefing, 206
psychological distress, 8
psychopathic traits, *620*
psychotherapy, 58
publication biases, 225, 235
publication gap, 208
Public Citizen, 55, 534
Public Citizens Research Group, 85
public organizations, *4*
Puerto Rican families, 479
Punishing the Poor (Wacquant), 10, 274
punishment
   and alternatives to, 560–64
   and behavioral principles, 147, 149–50
   and positive behavior change skills,
      557–64
   and problem definition, 119, 122, 132
punishment acceleration, *145*
purchase of services, 594
put-downs, 375–76

quackery, 84, 93, 103–4, *620*
qualitative research, 225, 237–38, 252
quality, 154, 196, 552
   and observational data, *420*
   and research, 213
   and services, 594–95
quality assurance, 511
quality control, 590
quality filters, 206–7, 213
quality gap, 208
quality of life, *271*, 274
questionable criteria, relying on, 181, 485
question begging, 103, 104
questionnaires, 395–96
questions, 109–10, 189
   about diagnosis and screening, 239–41
   and asking helpful, 348–49
   and bias, 225–26
   and causes, 236–37
   and constructional questionnaire, *282*

and contextual assessment, 252–53
and critically appraising research,
   209–10
and different kinds, 202, 252
and effectiveness and prevention, 229–33
and evaluating outcomes, 490–91
and evidence-based practice, 201–2
and experiences, 237–39
and families, *568*
and health settings, 530
and information gathering, 386
and motivation, 214–15
and no improvement, *507*
and observing physical environment,
   420–21
and posing well-formed, 202–5, 220
and practice guidelines, 242
and prevalence and incidence, 237–38
and problem framing, 444
and problem solving, *171–72*
and prognosis, risk and protective
   factors, 241, 252–53
and raising, 367–66
and requesting behavior change, 372–75
and research, 226–29
and resources and obstacles, 426
and searching for research findings,
   206–9
and search planning worksheet, *207*
and self-evaluation, 219
and social work practice, *281*
and taxonomy of Socratic, 113
and types of studies, *224*

race, 25, 27, 40
   and challenging social situations,
      375, 376
   and client participation, 460, 472,
      581, 601
   and contextual assessment, 259
   and ethics, 44, 52
   and multiculturalism, 33
   and problem definition, 123, 132–33
racial, ethnic, and class theories, 132–33
racialization, 37
racial problem, 136
racial theory of social relations, 40, 132–33
racism, 356
radical behaviorism, 131–32
radical environmentalism, 126
randomized controlled trials, 222, 229–31
rapport, 295–96, 343
ratcheting, 176
rate of behavior, 403
rationality, 93
rational model, 588
rationing, 591
ratio schedules, 155
reactive effects, 404–5, 420
realistic evaluation, 513
reality shock, *620*

real-life behavior, 474, 523
real-life observations, 409–11, 414–18, *416*
reasoning, 111
recency effects, 175, 185, 419
reciprocity rule, 336
recognition primed decision-making
    (RPD), 170
recording, interval, 416–17
recording behavior, 402–4
recording data, 423
record keeping/sharing, 28
    and ethics and legal issues regarding,
       50, 51–52
    and information gathering, 460–62
    and information organization/
       interpretation, 533
    and observation, 423
records. *See* case records
records, value of, 460–62
    and multiculturalism, 33
redundancy, 454
referent power, 613
referrals, 293–94
reflection, 94, 108–9
reflections of feelings, 344
reflective, 182
reframing, 533, 542
refusing requests, 372
refutationist, approach to knowledge, *82*
regression, 496
reinforcement, 147–49, *326*, 522
    and behavior, 147–50
    and differential, 556
    and noncontingent, 162
    and schedules of, 155–56
reinforcer profile, 438
reinforcers, 147–48, 152, 274, 438–40,
    523–24, 536, 551–52
reinforcer sampling, 439
reinforcing event, 267
reinforcing stimulus functions, *159*
relapse training, 524
relationship skills, 437
    and client participation, *320*, 326–29
    and helping, 326–29, *342*, 338–44, 354,
       550–51
    and nonverbal behavior, 357–59
    and positive alliance, 339
    as related to positive alliance, 331
    and troubleshooting, *359*
    and verbal behavior, 356–57
relative risk, 456
    compared to absolute risk, 241
relativism, 83–84, 93
relevance, 392, 590
relevance gap, 208
relevance-of-behavior rule, 305, 310, 521
relevant research, 212
reliability, 227–28, 391–92, 420
religion, 276
relying on similarity, 183–84

remedies, 210
repertoires, 263–64, 274, 274, *306*, 539,
    539, 552
replication, 504
requesting behavior changes, 372–75
research cartels, 91
research findings
    about behavior and environment, 141–82
    and behavioral principles, 141–44
    and critical appraisal, 128, 209–10, 222
    and ethics and legal issues, 43–44,
       45–47, 51, 54, 57, 59, 64
    and evidence-based practice, 86, 94, 98,
       104–6
    and integration with other information,
       210–13
    and knowledge, 69–70, *71, 72, 73, 74,*
       78–79, 96, 98, 106, 242
    and posing questions, 206–9, 210–14,
       226–28
    and problem solving, 122, 127, 131
    and searching for, 206–9
    and use of quality filters, 206–7, 213
research literature, *223*
resemblance, influence by, 175
residential environments, 421–22
resilience, 15, 126, 260, 272–74, 300, 446
resistance, 318, 319, 321
resisters, 24–25
resource allocation, 108, 484–85
resources, 429. *See also* information, about
       resources and obstacles
    and contextual assessment, 247–50,
       254–55, 261, 268
    and critical thinking, 99, 100, 108, 109
    and ethics, 42, 44, 48, 53–54, 56, 63
    and evidence-based practice, 86, 189,
       191, 194, 197–98
    and guidelines for reviewing, 426
    and information as, 533–34
    and neighborhoods and communities,
       429, 471
    and personal, 434
    and posing questions, 202, 204, 208, 210,
       213–14, 220
    and problem solving, 119, 120, 136,
       165–73, 179
    as related to services and surveillance
       services, 427–29
    and service plans, 451, 454, 494
    and social networks and support
       systems, 430
respect, clients, 347–48
    and critical thinking, 97, 99
    and cultural differences, 17, 31
    and ethics, 42–43, 49–50
    and evidence-based practice, *195*
    and interpersonal helping skills, *365*, 369
    and problem definition, 139–40
respondent behaviors, 156–57, 162
respondent conditioning, *562*

respondent extinction, 157, 162
respondent learning, 156–57, 162
responding with cliché, 346
response cost, 150, 162, 557
response functions, *158*
response generalization, 152
responsibility, *63*, 125, 371
restriction of services, 591, 593
restrictive plans, 480
retrospective accuracy, 455, *456*
reward power, 613
Rich Get Richer and the Poor Get Prison,
    The, 32
risk assessment, 389
risk estimation, natural frequencies,
    457–58
    and relative and absolute, 456
risks, 241–42, 260–61, *261*, 277
    and contextual assessment, 311–12
    and critical appraisal of research, 209–10
    and ethics and legal issues regarding,
       46–49, 54
    and evidence-based practice, 187, 191,
       195, 197
    and information organization/
       interpretation, 456–58
    and posing questions, *203*, 204, 252–53
    and problem definition, 119, 126, 129,
       135–36
    and propaganda, 379
    and risks and benefits, 456
Ritalin, 247
role, 356, *466*, 613
    of family, 570
    of service, 473–74
role ambiguity, 613
role conflict, 613
role models, 613
role of chance, 496
role of replication, 504
role perceptions, 613
role plays
    and advantages and disadvantages,
       412, 413
    and assessing communication styles, *412*
    and assessment, *413, 415*
    and behavioral rehearsal, 540
    and critically appraising, 414
    and use in group session, *576–77*
    and guidelines for, 416
    and simulating real-life, 411–14
    and social skills training, 540–41
    and sources of error, 415
Roosevelt, F. D., New Deal, 9
Rorschach Ink Blot Test, 249, 390, 396
Rosenthal effect, 496
rule-governed behavior, 153, 162
rules, 355, *568*, 569

safety, social situations, 379–81
sample approach, 263

sample bias, 453
sample size, 227
sanctions, 613
satisficing, 613
scarcity principle, 336
Scared Straight programs, 196
schedule, 554
schedule of reinforcement, 154–56, 162
schedule of self-monitoring, 405
schedules of reinforcement, 523–24
schizophrenia, *128*, 274
schizophrenic, 49, 259
school attendance, *267*
schooling, education, *87*
school-wide behavior systems, *481*
science, 93
   and antiscience, 143
   and behavioral principles, 131
   and critical thinking, 80, 108
   and evidence-based practice, 99, 108,
      183, 189
   and knowledge, 79–83, 91
   and misconceptions and
      misrepresentations about, *79–80*
   and problem solving, 122, 131, 139
   and role of criticism in, 82
   vs. pseudoscience, 33, 59, 83, 84,
      103–4, 194
scientific objectivity, 82, 93
scientism, 93
screening, 239, 241, *457*
screening measures, 399–400
search rule, 176
search methods
   and common errors, 253
   and evidence-based practice, 96, 189,
      192, 195
   and obstacles and remedies, 255
   and posing questions, 204, 205, 225, 233
   and use of quality filters, 206–7, 213
secondary prevention, 486
secondary reinforcers, 147
segregation, 40
selection bias, 225, 231–32, 453
self-anchored scales, 404
self-awareness, 16–17, 101, 618
self-correction, 80, 182
self-critical attitude, 16
self-determination, values, 47–48
self-disclosure, 346, 353–54
self-efficacy, 162, 435, 473
self-esteem, 174, *620*
self-evaluation questions, 219
self-fulfilling prophecy, 178, 453
self-handicapping, 434
self-harm, 311–12
self-help books, 533
self-help groups, 580–81
self-image, *380*
self-knowledge, *72*, 98
self-labels, 435

self-learning organizations, 596–98
self-liberation, *326*
self-management skills, 436–37, 542
self-monitoring, *401*, 498, 523
   and accuracy, 405
   and data collection, 400–405
   and reactive effects, 404–5
self-reevaluation, *326*
self-reinforcement, 523
self-report, information gathering, 392–95
self-statements, 435–36, *545*
Selling of DSM, The (Kirk and Kutchins), 259
sensitivity, 329, 392, 455, *456*, 507
sensitivity analysis, 232
sequential recording, 416
service, *42*, 43–44
service agencies, *472*
service agreement, 307–9, *308*, 594–95
service and surveillance systems, 427–29
service focus, *466*
service ideologies, 57
service roles, 473–74
service systems
   and administrative tasks, 589–90
   and audit, benchmarks and
      evaluation, 590
   and client-entered organization, *587*
   and client involvement, 589
   and decision-making styles, 588
   and evidence-informed purchase of,
      594–95
   and framework, *585*
   and organization culture and climate,
      586, 588
   and social work practice, 293–94
   and technology, 589
   and understanding and changing,
      584–90
   and working in teams, 588–89
setting event, 268
sexual abuse, 54, 76, 110, 178, 310, 390–91,
      394, 399, 428, 453
sexual conduct, 52
sexual harassment, 376–77
sexual identity, 32
sexual orientation, 32–33, 309, 375, 376
shaping, 535–37
side effects, plans, 480–81
sidetracks, 375
sign approach, 263
significant others, 439, 535
   and resources and obstacles, 431–34
   and valued behaviors, 522
silence, 328, 351, 357, 375
similarity, relying on, 183–84
simplifying strategies, 173
simultaneous-treatment designs, 504
Sindell decision, *608*
single-case designs, 499–502
single-cause fallacy, 452
situational awareness, 451

skepticism, 82, *83*, 89, 93, 222
skill development, 535
skills. *See also* positive behavior change
     methods
   and constructive, 618
   and evidence-informed management,
      593–94
   and maintaining, 617–23
   and political savvy, 600
   and self-management, 436–37, 542
   and shaping, *536*
   and social, training, 538–42
social action, community-based, 607–9
social anxiety, 127
social anxiety disorder, 256, 258
social capital, 429–30
Social Care Institute for Excellence
     (SCIE), 86
Social Casework: A Behavioral Approach
     (Schwartz and Goldiamond), 100
social control, 9–10, 162
social cues, 356
social desirability effect, 388, 394, 496
social development, 609–10
Social Development Issues, 14
Social Diagnosis (Richmond), 8
social influence process, helping, 25–27,
     342–44
social issues, *137*
socialization, 162
social justice, 11, *42*, 44, 58
social learning theory (SLT), 132
social networks and support systems,
     272, 430–27, 605–6
social planning and program
     development, 607
social policies, 270–72
social problems, 118, 119, 132–33, *137*
social psychological persuasion
     strategies, 336
social reform, 8–9
social reformer, professional as, 64
Social Scientist's Bestiary, The (Phillips), 79
social skills, *363. See also* challenging social
     situations
   and assessment, 538–39
   and homework assignments, 541–42
   and model presentation, 539–40
   and training, 538–42
   and when not successful, 542
social skills training, 538–42
Social Support Inventory, *396*
social networks and support systems,
     272, 430–31, 605–6
social traps, 356
social validity assessments, 492–93
social welfare, 3–5, 8–11
social work, 610
   and advantages and disadvantages, 7
   and controversial issues, 10–11
   and examples of, at work, 5–7

social work (*cont.*)
  and functions of, 8–11
  and global perspective, 14
  and goals of, *5*
  and historical perspective, 13
  and introduction, 3–18
  and person-environment fit, 255–56
  and philosophy of practice, 14–18
  as a profession, 11–13
  and safety, 379–81
  and social welfare, 3–5
Social Work, 367
social workers
  and advocacy, 472–73
  and consultants, 261
  and providing information, 529–35
  and role playing, 575
  and service and surveillance systems,
    427–29
  and social planning and program
    development, 607
  and working in teams, 588–89
Social Workers Across Nations (SWAN), 14
social work practice
  and collaboration, 295–97
  and concerns and outcomes, 285,
    288–89, 293
  and constructional questionnaire, *282*
  and crisis situations, 312
  and cultural sensitivity, 309–10
  and errors, 310
  and five-step approach, 305–6
  and helping clients, *296*
  and interviews, *286–88, 298–99*
  and interviews and exchanges, 284–85
  and introductory statements, *289*
  and maltreatment reporting, 310–11
  and needs-resources gaps, *297*
  and objectives, *304, 307*
  and outcomes, 302–7
  and planning guide, *306*
  and practice skills, 316
  and priorities, 294–95
  and problem/outcome profile,
    290–91, 292
  and problems and causes, 301–2
  and problems and context, 297, 299–301
  and problem-solving guide, 281–84, *283*
  and progress indicators, 309
  and risk of self-harm, suicide and abuse,
    311–12
  and service agreement, 307–9, *308*
  and service provision, 293–94
  and support, 301
Society and Economic Growth (Kunkel), 143
socioeconomic status, 32, 120
sociogram, 613
Socratic questions, 113
sources of information, 387
specificity, 240, 455, *456*
speculative thinking, 451

speech disturbances, 357
spirituality, 276
sponsorship, 227
spontaneity, 345
sprawling thinking, 177
Staff-Resident Interaction
    Chronograph, 421
staff training, program, 511
standardized measures, 395–400
  and checklist for reviewing, *397*
  and critical appraisal, 396–97
  and interpreting tests, 398–99
  and limitations, 397–98
  and screening, 399–400
  and varieties of, 395–96
standards, 19
  and ethics, 33–34, 42–43, 51
  and evidence-based practice, 97, 189, 191
  and knowledge, 77, 85, 87
  and posing questions, 207, 210
STARD, 210
statistical analysis, 498
statistical conclusion validity, 234
statistical significance, 228
status, 613
status offender, 259
stereotypes, 35
stimulus, 152
  and control, *326, 468,* 563
  and discrimination, 152
  and equivalence, 157
  and establishing, 152
  and generalization, 152
  and hierarchy, 545–46
stopping rule, 176
storage, information, 407
strategic, 182
straw person arguments, 103
strength-based practices, 254, 264, 273
strength enhancing, 254–55, 479
stress, 206, 567, *568,* 621–22
stress-management skills, 437
stress management training, 545
structuring exchanges, 354
study design, 227
substance abuse
  and evidence-based practice, 100, 105
  and knowledge, 81
  and posing questions, 207
  and problems definition, 124, 130, 159
success, factors influencing, 467–69
sufficient cause, *447*
suggestibility, 393
suicide, 311–12
summaries, 350
sunk cost error, 105
superstitious conditioning, 149, 198
supervision, 89–90
support, offering, 301, 354, 474–75
surveys, 236, 238–39
survived rigorous tests, 139

sweeping generalization, 103
SYMLOG (System of Multiple Level of
    Observation of Groups), 573
symptoms, 198, 257, 260, *261,* 274, 406
systematic review, 192, *193,* 206
systematic reviews, 233–36
systemic approach, evidence-based
    practice, 196
systemic behavior analysis, *265*

tacit, 182
tailoring, 324–25
Talk of the Clinic (Morris and Chenail), 284
*Tarasoff v. Regents of the University of
    California,* 50
target behaviors, *265*
task analysis, 303, 422–23
task completion, 498–99
task environment, 180
teacher, 469, 473
team meetings, 579–80
teams, 588–89, *592*
technology, 28, 589
Technology as Magic (Stivers), 590
telephone use, 328–29
temporal precedence, *447*
tentativeness, 346
tertiary prevention, 486
testifying in court, 54
testimonials, *75,* 77, 185
testing inferences, 262–63
test sensitivity, 455, *456*
test specificity, 455, *456*
Thematic Apperception test, 390
theories
  and critical thinking, 111, 138–39
  and ethics, 56–57, 62
  and evidence-based practice, 96, 98, 101,
    104, 108
  and knowledge, 72, 73, 79, 80–82
  and problems definition, 125–29, 132–33
  and problem solving, 120, 123
theory ladenness, 93
therapist relationship, 50–51, 342, 484, 496,
    500, 555
therapy, validity screen, *230*
thoughtfulness, 594
thoughts, 275, 550
thought stopping, 543
time limits, 309
time-out, 559–60
Time-Sample Behavioral Checklist, 421
time samples, 403–4, 417
timing, 154, 369, 371, 373, 405, 553
tone, 357
tools, helpful, 513
topical nonlinear analyses, *265*
touch, 358–59
touching, 52
tradition, relying on, 75
training

and evidence-informed, 595–96
  and problem solving, 543–44
  and social skills, 538–42
transference effects, 326
transgender, 426
transitions, 276–77, 350
translation, 139, 356
transparency, 195
treatment manuals, 484
tree diagram, *455*
triangulation, 570
triggers, 183
true negative rate, *456*
true positive rate, *456*
trust, 295–96, 570
truth, 93
  and cultural differences, 37
  and critical thinking, 45, 96, 97, 104,
    105, 111
  and evidence-based practice, 99, 101,
    107, 189
  and knowledge, 70, 79, 80–82, 90
  and philosophy of practice, 16
truth squads, 608, 609

uncertainty, 37, 618
uncritical documentation, 179
uncritical thinking, 105–6
undercontrolled syndrome, 309
undermanning, 613
Under the Cover of Kindness (Margolin), 99
United Kingdom, 428
University of Washington Parenting
    Clinic, 416
unmanageable, 256
unmotivated, 331

unplanned endings, 517, 519
untested method, 212
U.S. federal agencies, 218
U.S. Health Department, 86
utilitarian power, 613
utility, 392

vague terms, 299–300, 394
validity, 225–26, 227–28, *230*, *237*, 263,
    391–92
values, 41–65
  and case records, 51–52
  and clients' options, 55–56
  and confidentiality, 50–51
  and critical thinking, 45–47, 96–98
  and ethics, 42–45, 52–53
  and evidence-informed practice, 45–47
  and families, *568*, 569
  and ideology, 56–59
  and informed consent, 48–49
  and issues of competence, 51
  and knowledge and skills, 53–54, 87–88
  and liability, 54–55
  and listening, *327*
  and observation, 409–11, *410*, 422–23
  and posing questions, 210, 212, 214
  and positive behavior change skills, 558–59
  and record keeping, 460–62
  and respect for dignity and worth of
    people, 49–50
  and self-determination and
    empowerment, 47–48
  and sexual conduct, 52
  and translation and integration skills, 139
variations in service effects, 190
variations in services offered, 190

Venn diagram, *184*
verbal harassment, 376
verbal put-downs, 375–76
verificationist approach to knowledge, *82*
vertical validity, 263
Vietnam, *472*
violence, family, 569
visual feedback, 497–98
visual representations, 497–98
vividness, 175
voice qualities, 357
vulnerability, *447*

warmth, 345–46
war on drugs, 254
websites, *110*, 216–17
welfare, 4
well-being, *273*
What Manner of Man (King), 87
whistle-blowers, 55–56
Whitree v. New York State, 52
Widowhood in an American City
    (Lopata), 606
wishful thinking, 496
Woozle Effect, 83
worth of person, *42*, 49–50
written schedules, 440
Wyatt v. Stickney, 53

YMCA, 430
You Don't Have to Take It (Nicarthy), 372
youth gangs, contingency diagram, *151*
Youth Law News, 53

zaps, 375
zero time bias, 225